THE COMPLETE PERSONALIZED PROMISE BIBLE

EVERY PROMISE IN THE BIBLE FROM GENESIS TO REVELATION, WRITTEN JUST FOR YOU

by
James R. Riddle

Harrison House
Tulsa, OK

09 08 07 06 05   12 11 10 9 8 7 6 5 4

The Complete Personalized Promise Bible: Every Promise in the Bible
From Genesis to Revelation, Written Just for You
ISBN 1-57794-537-9 (Formerly ISBN 55306-07608)
Copyright © 2000, 2004 by James R. Riddle
6930 Gateway East
El Paso, Texas 79915

Published by Harrison House, Inc.
P.O. Box 35035
Tulsa, Oklahoma 74153

DEDICATION

I dedicate this book to Laura M. Riddle. It was her idea that I share it with the Body of Christ. I originally intended to use it for my own personal meditation, but she would not allow me to keep it to myself. She saw the power in it and continually encouraged me to develop it until it became the book that you now hold in your hands. If it weren't for her, it may never have been published. Laura was my wife for eleven years before going to be with the Lord on June 23, 1999.

A SPECIAL NOTE OF APPRECIATION

I would also like to thank my family (Jinny, Chris, Jerome, Jermaine, and Caleb) for always supporting me and being the best family in the whole world. I have never known a more generous bunch of Jesus lovers! Surely I am the proudest dad in the whole world!

ACKNOWLEDGMENTS

I want to thank my pastors Charles and Rochelle Neiman for teaching me the Word and guiding me in the affairs of this life. The two of you are a gift and a treasure to me. I will forever praise our Father for allowing me to be under your leadership.

CONTENTS

PREFACE

When Jim Riddle told me he was going to write *The Complete Personalized Promise Bible*, I wasn't sure what to expect. Needless to say, I was taken back when I saw the finished product. *The Complete Personalized Promise Bible* can and will change your life.

Jim has been an active member of our church for years. He is not a casual Christian. He is involved in the advancement of God's kingdom. His desire is to see the Word of God produce fruit in your life. That is the purpose behind *The Complete Personalized Promise Bible*.

I pray you will use this book as it was intended to be used. Read it, and say what God says about your life. Remember, the Bible is the Lord's personal Word to you!

Charles Nieman, Pastor
Abundant Living Faith Center
El Paso, Texas

INTRODUCTION

It is the application of God's Word in our lives that causes the reality of the truth and principles of the Bible to have an effect on our daily living. To Christians, God's Word is the cornerstone of all that we believe. God's Word is His letter to all of us; it is His letter to *you*.

Hundreds of promises that God has given to every believer concerning every aspect of our lives are written within its pages. But until the truth that is expressed with ink on paper gets into our hearts and is applied to our lives, it is void of power. For instance, the promise of salvation given to us in John 3:16 is just words on paper until we believe it and receive it and pray the prayer of acceptance. Only then does it become a reality in our lives.

The author has identified all the promises in the Bible from Genesis to Revelation and, in this book, provided each original Scripture verse and an expanded thought concerning the truth found in each particular Scripture. We encourage you to use this book as a guide in helping you become aware of all the promises that are found in God's Word and how to apply to your life the truth they contain.

The personalized, expanded thought that the author has written under each Bible promise could be used as a devotion or a meditation; it could also be used as a prayer. You might want to declare it over your life by speaking it aloud as a positive affirmation of that promise for your life.

We pray that the Lord will use this promise Bible companion to help you experience the fullness of all that He has promised to you. We believe that the truth and power of the Scriptures will become more alive in your heart and that your life will be dramatically impacted by the application of these truths.

—Harrison House Publishers

HOW TO USE THIS BOOK

This book is based on a principle of success found throughout the Scriptures concerning meditation in the Word. Joshua 1:8 reads:

> This Book of the Law shall not depart from your mouth, but you shall meditate in it day and night, that you may observe to do according to all that is written in it. For then you will make your way prosperous, and then you will have good success.

The definition of the word *meditate* in this passage is "to speak to one's self in a low tone of voice." Therefore, according this verse, if we want to be successful as Christians, we need to speak God's Word to ourselves day and night. To meditate in the Word is to personalize it, make it an integral part of who we are and how we live. The verse also says that we are not to let the Word depart from our mouths. Vacation from the Word is not an option. It has to have first place in all of our daily living. We cannot ever let it *depart from our mouths* because of distractions or the cares of this life.

Notice the importance that God has placed on the *spoken* word. It is easy to understand why when we know just how powerful our words truly are. James tells us our tongue is the very rudder of our lives (James 3:2,4). Proverbs 18:20-21 reads:

> A man's stomach shall be filled with the fruit of his mouth; From the produce of his lips shall he be filled.

> Life and death are in the power of the tongue, And those who love it shall eat its fruit.

When we begin to understand the awesome power in our words, we will not be so quick to speak. We see how the seed of our words will bring us the things of life or the things of death. If this is true of our own personal words, how much more powerful is it when we speak the Word of God into our lives? Are you catching a glimpse of the power in this principle of meditation in the Word?

Let's take this a little further. Here is a quick, cursory study of just how powerful the Word of God is to us:

- God has placed His Word even higher than His name (Psalm 138:2).
- God and His Word are one and the same (John 1:1).
- God holds all things together by His Word (Hebrews 1:3).
- We are born again through the Word (1 Peter 1:23).

- We become partakers of the divine nature through the Word (2 Peter 1:4).
- Our lives are cleansed through the Word (Ephesians 5:26).
- The Word is a sure guide to us in any and every situation (Psalm 119:105,133).
- The Word brings goodness and happiness to our lives (Proverbs 16:20).
- We receive our healing through the Word (Psalm 107:20; Proverbs 4:20-22).
- The Word supplies us with strength for daily living (Psalm 119:28,50,107).
- The Word brings wealth and riches into our lives (Psalm 112:1-3).
- We overcome demon forces through the Word (Matthew 4:1-11; Ephesians 6:17; 1 John 2:14).
- Our food is cleansed and sanctified through the Word (1 Timothy 4:4,5).
- Angels minister to us through the Word (Psalm 103:20).
- We will be judged by the Word (John 12:48).
- Through the Word our children are blessed (Psalm 112:2).
- Our covenant with God is based upon the Word (Psalm 105:8; Deuteronomy 28:1-14).
- We become disciples of Jesus through the Word (John 8:31).
- Only through the Word can we walk in God's perfect will for our lives (Psalm 119:9).
- By the Word we become members of Jesus' family (Luke 18:21).
- Through the Word we gain victory over sin (Psalm 119:11).
- We are saved and delivered through the Word (Romans 10:8-10).
- All of our prayers are answered through the Word (John 15:7).
- God watches over His Word and promises to perform it in our lives (Jeremiah 1:12; Lamentations 2:17).
- The Word has within it the power of fulfillment (Isaiah 55:11).
- The Word is spirit. It is made alive by the very Spirit of God (John 6:63; Haggai 2:5; Hebrews 4:12).
- We are commanded to be doers of the Word and not just hearers only (James 1:22).
- It is the Word that shows us who we are and what we have in Christ (James 1:23-25).
- The Word is a seed that we can sow into our lives in order to live the way that God wants us to live (Mark 4:14-20; 2 Timothy 2:9-15).
- We become one with God through the Word (John 17:17-21).

- The Lord becomes our partner in life through the Word (Mark 16:20).
- Faith comes only by the Word (Romans 10:17).
- Our faith is only effective through the Word (John 5:24; Hebrews 11:1-6).
- The Word is only profitable to us when we speak it in the spirit of faith (Hebrews 4:2; 2 Corinthians 4:13).
- God used His Word as a carrier of His faith in order to create the world and He has called us to live the same way (Hebrews 11:1-6; Romans 4:13-22).

In all of this we can see that nothing in our Christian walk is as important as engrafting the Word into our lives.

In my own personal life I have a simple mission statement: "Be the person God created you to be." I know that the only way I can be the person I am created to be is to speak God's Word into my life until it becomes such a part of me that in all that I do it has precedence. There is no other way to be the Christian we are called to be. There is no other way to walk in our rights and privileges as children of God.

Some may argue that it is arrogance to assume that all of the promises of the Bible are given to them personally. This is false humility. It is actually arrogant to contradict what God has said. It's like saying that our ways and manner of thinking are higher than His ways and manner of thinking. In 2 Corinthians 1:20 He declares that ALL of His promises are given to those who are in Christ. It is implied that if we ask according to His promise, the answer is a resounding YES and AMEN (call it done)! Oh reader, if I only had the space to teach you how much God loves you and wants you to have every promise of His Word!

The treasure that you hold in your hands is a reflection of God's heart. It is His precious Word made personal. Everything that the Bible says about who you are, what you have, and how you are supposed to act as a child of God is here personalized so you can speak it into your life. Every book of the Bible is covered. No part of what God has for you is left out.

You will notice that each *Declaration of Faith* is fully cross-referenced. Each of these references are added so the reader can understand how the verse harmonizes with the overall message of the Bible. For instance, we may read Genesis 13:2 and see how Abraham was rich in livestock and gold, but not see how that applies to us. Therefore, the cross-references of Galatians 3:6-14, etc., are added so we can see that we are to be blessed in the same ways that Abraham was blessed. These cross-references are extremely powerful in establishing key concepts of the Word into our lives. The Bible says, in the mouth of two or three credible witnesses let every word be established (Deut. 19:15). Therefore, each personalized text is complete with at least two establishing cross-references.

Before you get started I want to remind you again that this book is not to be read, it is to be said. Don't let the words remain on the page. Speak them in the spirit of faith knowing that you are speaking God's will for your life. This is our covenant. It is the very blueprint of all that we are and all that we have in Christ Jesus. With every Word, we have an image of the Christian God desires for us to be. We should make it our daily meditation and let the devil know that his foothold in our world has come to an end!

CHAPTER ONE

GENESIS

The promises found in the book of Genesis mark the beginning of our Lord's relationship with us. We are created in His image and likeness for the purpose of intimate and meaningful fellowship. We serve the great Father God. His nature is a Father's nature. His deepest desire is to have a close relationship with His kids.

When Adam lost that relationship, God immediately set out to restore it. He watched until He found a man with whom He could cut a covenant in order to start a righteous lineage that would usher in the birth of a messiah who would save all of mankind and restore them to the Father-child relationship that was lost. The man He found was Abraham.

Nearly all of the promises found in the book of Genesis, or the entire Bible for that matter, stem from that covenant that God cut with Abraham. As Christians, we are to be blessed with the blessing of Abraham. Therefore, every blessing we see that Abraham enjoyed is a blessing that we should enjoy as well.

All of the promises of the book of Genesis are promises that will establish you in a proper pattern of living for your relationship with God. As you speak these promises into your life, know that you are speaking God's will for you in order to establish closeness and intimacy between you and your Father.

GENESIS 1:26-28 KJV

And God said, Let us make man in our image, after our likeness: and let them have dominion over the fish of the sea, and over the fowl of the air, and over the cattle, and over all the earth, and over every creeping thing that creepeth upon the earth. So God created man in his own image, in the image of God created he him; male and female created he them. And God blessed them, and God said unto them, Be fruitful, and multiply, and replenish the earth, and subdue it: and have dominion over the fish of the sea, and over the fowl of the air, and over every living thing that moveth upon the earth.

─── *DECLARATION OF FAITH* ───

I am created in the image and likeness of almighty God. I have been given authority (complete rule and dominion) over the fish of the sea, the birds of the air, the beasts of the field and every creeping thing on the earth. I am a representation of God's authority and likeness, and have been given rulership of this planet. He has blessed me and commanded me to take dominion over it and subdue it for His glory.

(Romans 8:29,30; 2 Corinthians 5:16-21; Psalm 8:4-8; Luke 9:1; Matthew 28:18-20)

Genesis 6:8,9 KJV

But Noah found grace in the eyes of the Lord. These are the generations of Noah: Noah was a just man and perfect in his generations, and Noah walked with God.

─── *DECLARATION OF FAITH* ───

I have abundant favor with God. I am a just and righteous man/woman and I walk in continual fellowship with Him.

(Psalm 5:12; Proverbs 12:2; 2 Corinthians 5:21; 1 John 1:3-9)

Genesis 6:22; 7:5 NIV

Noah did everything just as God commanded him.
And Noah did all that the Lord commanded him.

─── *DECLARATION OF FAITH* ───

I do all that the Lord commands me to do.

(John 15:10-12; Deuteronomy 28:1)

Genesis 8:22 NKJV

"While the earth remains, seedtime and harvest, cold and heat, winter and summer, and day and night shall not cease."

─── *DECLARATION OF FAITH* ───

While the earth remains, I can absolutely count on seedtime and harvest, cold and heat, summer and winter, and day and night.
These fixed and certain laws remain in the earth. Therefore, I know beyond a shadow of doubt that I will reap what I have sown.

When I sow my seed, I can count on a harvest.

(2 Corinthians 9:6-10; Galatians 6:7,8; Matthew 13:24-32; Mark 4:2-20)

GENESIS 9:1-3 AMP

And God pronounced a blessing upon Noah and his sons and said to them, Be fruitful and multiply and fill the earth. And the fear of you and the dread and terror of you shall be upon every beast of the land, every bird of the air, all that creeps upon the ground, and upon all the fish of the sea; they are delivered into your hand. Every moving thing that lives shall be food for you; and as I gave you the green vegetables and plants, I give you everything.

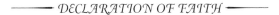

God has abundantly blessed me with good things of every kind.
God created me to live and walk in dominion.
The Lord has provided to me all of the resources in the earth. All things are His, and He has made me a steward of His riches in this earth.

(Luke 10:18-20; John 10:10; Deuteronomy 28:1-14; 33:12-16; Psalm 24:1-6; 50:7-15,23)

GENESIS 12:1-3 KJV

Now the Lord had said unto Abram, Get thee out of thy country, and from thy kindred, and from thy father's house, unto a land that I will shew thee: And I will make of thee a great nation, and I will bless thee, and make thy name great; and thou shalt be a blessing: And I will bless them that bless thee, and curse him that curseth thee: and in thee shall all families of the earth be blessed.

——— DECLARATION OF FAITH ———

I have been called by God to fulfill the destiny that He has for my life. He has made me great and has blessed me with an abundance of all good things. All of my needs and desires are fully met in Him.
If I honor God He has promised to promote me to a position of prominence.
I am blessed and I am a blessing. In this awesome prosperity that I enjoy from my heavenly Father, I have plenty for myself, with an abundance left over so that I can be a blessing to others.
God blesses those who bless me and curses those who curse me.
He brings me to the place of abundant favors and confers on me happiness and prosperity.

(Jeremiah 29:11; Hebrews 12:1-3; 2 Corinthians 9:8,9; Exodus 23:20-22; Psalm 23)

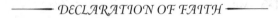

GENESIS 12:16 NKJV

He treated Abram well for her sake. He had sheep, oxen, male donkeys, male and female servants, female donkeys, and camels.

———— *DECLARATION OF FAITH* ————

I walk in the power of God's favor. I am treated well by the authorities and, through Jesus, I gain an abundance of possessions.

(Genesis 39:2-5; 41:41-43; Daniel 1:9; 2:46-49; 2 Peter 1:3; Philippians 4:19)

GENESIS 13:2 KJV

And Abram was very rich in cattle, in silver, and in gold.

———— *DECLARATION OF FAITH* ————

I am blessed just like Abraham because I serve the same God. My God is my Provider and He is in lack of nothing. He is a God of abundance who rejoices in my prosperity. In Him, I have an abundance in all things.

(Genesis 30:43; 1 Corinthians 2:9; 2 Corinthians 6:10; 8:9; Deuteronomy 8:8-18; Psalm 35:27; Galatians 3:6-14)

GENESIS 14:23 NIV

That I will accept nothing belonging to you, not even a thread or the thong of a sandal, so that you will never be able to say, 'I made Abram rich.'

———— *DECLARATION OF FAITH* ————

It is God, and none other, that has made me rich.

(Deuteronomy 8:8-18; 1 Corinthians 2:9; 2 Kings 5:15,16; 2 Corinthians 8:9)

GENESIS 15:1 AMP

After these things, the word of the Lord came to Abram in a vision, saying, Fear not, Abram, I am your Shield, your abundant compensation, and your reward shall be exceedingly great.

———— *DECLARATION OF FAITH* ————

I am afraid of nothing! God, the Creator of the universe, is my Shield. He grants me abundance to the extreme. My reward, in Him, is exceedingly great.

(2 Timothy 1:7; Joshua 1:5-9; Psalm 3:3; 5:12; Deuteronomy 28:1-14; 2 John 8)

GENESIS 15:6 AMP

And he [Abram] believed in (trusted in, relied on, remained steadfast to) the Lord, and He counted it to him as righteousness (right standing with God).

DECLARATION OF FAITH

I believe in God. I have steadfast confidence in His complete integrity. Because of this, He has given me the right to stand fearlessly in His presence.

(2 Timothy 1:7,12; Psalm 18:30; Isaiah 55:11; Hebrews 4:16)

GENESIS 15:11 NKJV

And when the vultures came down on the carcasses, Abram drove them away.

DECLARATION OF FAITH

I have a covenant with God. When [demon forces] come to defile that covenant, I forcefully drive them away. The terms of my covenant with God shall stand, and I will not allow the devil to rob me of its benefits.

(Hebrews 12:22-24; 13:20,21; Genesis 9:9; Luke 9:1; 10:19; Mark 4:15; Psalm 103:1-5)

GENESIS 15:15 KJV

And thou shalt go to thy fathers in peace; thou shalt be buried in a good old age.

DECLARATION OF FAITH

I will live a full and abundant life. I spend my days in peace and will leave this earth at a ripe old age.

(Psalm 91:16; Isaiah 46:4; John 10:10; 2 Peter 3:9-12)

GENESIS 17:1,2 AMP

When Abram was ninety-nine years old, the Lord appeared to him and said, I am the Almighty God; walk and live habitually before Me and be perfect (blameless, wholehearted, complete). And I will make My covenant (solemn pledge) between Me and you and will multiply you exceedingly.

DECLARATION OF FAITH

I live my life blamelessly before God. I give Him my whole heart and He makes me complete. He has sworn to me on His oath, our covenant of love, to increase me in His prosperity and multiply me in His abundance.

(Jude 24; Hebrews 10:14; Psalm 1:1-3; 2 Corinthians 9:6-11; Deuteronomy 8:18; 28:1-14)

GENESIS 17:6-9 KJV

And I will make thee exceeding fruitful, and I will make nations of thee, and kings shall come out of thee. And I will establish my covenant between me and thee and thy seed after thee in their generations for an everlasting covenant, to be a God unto thee, and to thy seed after thee. And I will give unto thee, and to thy seed after thee, the land wherein thou art a stranger, all the land of Canaan, for an everlasting possession; and I will be their God. And God said unto Abraham, Thou shalt keep my covenant therefore, thou, and thy seed after thee in their generations.

——— *DECLARATION OF FAITH* ———

God has firmly established His covenant with me. He makes both me and my children to be great in the earth. He gives us the land where we are strangers. He is our God and we will keep our covenant with Him.

(Hebrews 10:16,17; Psalm 103:17; Deuteronomy 6:4-12)

GENESIS 18:27 NKJV

Then Abraham answered and said, "Indeed now, I who *am but* dust and ashes have taken it upon myself to speak to the Lord."

——— *DECLARATION OF FAITH* ———

I am bold to stand before God and speak to Him on behalf of those in need.

(Hebrews 4:16; Ezekiel 22:30; Ephesians 6:18-20; Job 22:27-30)

GENESIS 22:17,18 KJV

That in blessing I will bless thee, and in multiplying I will multiply thy seed as the stars of the heaven, and as the sand which is upon the sea shore; and thy seed shall possess the gate of his enemies; and in thy seed shall all the nations of the earth be blessed; because thou hast obeyed my voice.

——— *DECLARATION OF FAITH* ———

With the blessing of Abraham, my Father blesses me. With the multiplying of Abraham, my Father multiplies me. Everything that Abraham received by faith, I can receive by faith!

Through Abraham's Seed [Jesus] I possess the gates of my enemies. In Him, I have received happiness, peace, prosperity and good things of every kind.

(Galatians 3:6-14; Psalm 18; 2 Corinthians 1:19-22; 2 Peter 1:3)

GENESIS 24:35 NIV

The Lord has blessed my master abundantly, and he has become wealthy. He has given him sheep and cattle, silver and gold, menservants and maidservants, and camels and donkeys.

——— *DECLARATION OF FAITH* ———

The Lord has blessed me with His abundance. He has placed upon me the mark of heavenly nobility and has granted me the ability to produce a surplus in my life.

(Deuteronomy 8:6-18; 28:1-14; Genesis 12:1-3; 13:2; Malachi 3:10-12; 2 Corinthians 8:9; 9:8)

GENESIS 26:12-14 KJV

Then Isaac sowed in that land, and received in the same year an hundredfold: and the Lord blessed him. And the man waxed great, and went forward, and grew until he became very great: For he had possession of flocks, and possession of herds, and great store of servants: and the Philistines envied him.

——— *DECLARATION OF FAITH* ———

The Lord has blessed me with abundance.

His favor finds a home in me.

He receives the seed that I have sown and blesses it so that it will bring forth the maximum yield.

He has taken hold of me in His powerful arm and promoted me. In Him, I find wealth and position. I have been separated from the world. He has placed within me special and unique supernatural qualities. My supply is great with His blessing in my life.

(Romans 4:17; Philippians 4:19; 2 Corinthians 9:6-11; Mark 4:13-20; Deuteronomy 8:6-18; Daniel 1:20)

GENESIS 27:27-29 KJV

And he came near, and kissed him: and he smelled the smell of his raiment, and blessed him, and said, See, the smell of my son is as the smell of a field which the Lord hath blessed: Therefore God give thee of the dew of heaven, and the fatness of the earth, and plenty of corn and wine: Let people serve thee, and nations bow down to thee: be lord over thy brethren, and let thy mother's sons bow down to thee: cursed be every one that curseth thee, and blessed be he that blesseth thee.

———— *DECLARATION OF FAITH* ————

The Lord is ever with me to bless me. He gives me abundance in every area of my life. Those who curse me, curse only themselves, and those who bless me are blessed with God's own endowment of abundance.

(Deuteronomy 28:1-14; 33:27-29; Psalm 46:1; 54:4; Genesis 12:1-3; 39:5)

GENESIS 28:13-15 KJV

And, behold, the Lord stood above it, and said, I am the Lord God of Abraham thy father, and the God of Isaac: the land whereon thou liest, to thee will I give it, and to thy seed; And thy seed shall be as the dust of the earth, and thou shalt spread abroad to the west, and to the east, and to the north, and to the south: and in thee and in thy seed shall all the families of the earth be blessed. And, behold, I am with thee, and will keep thee in all places whither thou goest, and will bring thee again into this land; for I will not leave thee, until I have done that which I have spoken to thee of.

———— *DECLARATION OF FAITH* ————

My heavenly Father, the God of Abraham, Isaac and Jacob, is with me at all times. He is ever mindful of our covenant and sees to it that its blessings are ful-filled in my life. He is always with me and watches over me wherever I go. I have His Word that no matter what may take place in my life, He will provide for me and sustain me through it.

(Hebrews 13:5,6; Deuteronomy 28:1-14; Nehemiah 1:5,6; Isaiah 43:1-13; 46:4)

GENESIS 28:18-22 KJV

And Jacob rose up early in the morning, and took the stone that he had put for his pillows, and set it up for a pillar, and poured oil upon the top of it. And he called the name of that place Bethel: but the name of that city was called Luz at the first. And Jacob vowed a vow, saying, If God will be with me, and will keep me in this way that I go, and will give me bread to eat, and raiment to put on, So that I come again to my father's house in peace; then shall the Lord be my God: And this stone, which I have set for a pillar, shall be God's house: and of all that thou shalt give me I will surely give the tenth unto thee.

———— *DECLARATION OF FAITH* ————

Jesus has become my Rock. He is with me wherever I go and provides for my every need. He keeps me in safety at all times. He continually watches over me, giving me food to eat and clothes to wear. Therefore, I will not fail to pay Him the tithe of all of my continual, God-given increase.

(1 Corinthians 10:3,4; Philippians 4:11-19; Psalm 5:11,12; 23; Matthew 6:25-33; Malachi 3:8-12)

GENESIS 30:29,30 NIV

Jacob said to him, "You know how I have worked for you and how your livestock has fared under my care. The little you had before I came has increased greatly, and the Lord has blessed you wherever I have been. But now, when may I do something for my own household?"

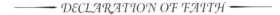

Those whom I serve (employers, pastors, family, etc.) are blessed because of me. Their possessions increase and multiply because of the anointing on my life. The Lord showers them with favor and blessings for my sake.

(Ephesians 6:5,6; Titus 2:9,10; Genesis 39:2-5)

GENESIS 30:43 NKJV

Thus the man became exceedingly prosperous, and had large flocks, female and male servants, and camels and donkeys.

I enjoy a continual increase of good things in my life. The Lord blesses me and makes my name great. In Him, I have become rich.

(Genesis 12:2; 13:2; 2 Corinthians 8:9; 9:10; Revelation 2:9; 3:18)

GENESIS 32:9-11 KJV

And Jacob said, O God of my father Abraham, and God of my father Isaac, the Lord which saidst unto me, Return unto thy country, and to thy kindred, and I will deal well with thee: I am not worthy of the least of all the mercies, and of all the truth, which thou hast shewed unto thy servant; for with my staff I passed over this Jordan; and now I am become two bands. Deliver me, I pray thee, from the hand of my brother, from the hand of Esau: for I fear him, lest he will come and smite me, and the mother with the children.

——— *DECLARATION OF FAITH* ———

My Father has set His heart on doing nothing but good by me. He repeatedly displays His faithfulness and loving kindness toward me, and continually increases me in His abundance. He protects me in all of my ways and sees to it that my enemies cannot prosper over me.

(Psalm 25:8-10; 84:11; 115:12,13; 136; Romans 2:4; 3 John 11; Nahum 1:7; Isaiah 43:10-13; 54:17)

GENESIS 32:12 AMP

And You said, I will surely do you good and make your descendants as the sand of the sea, which cannot be numbered for multitude.

——— *DECLARATION OF FAITH* ———

God has determined to do nothing but good towards me and to bless my children after me.

(Psalm 25:8-10; 84:11; 103:17; 115:12,13; 136; Romans 2:4; 3 John 11)

GENESIS 32:24-28 KJV

And Jacob was left alone; and there wrestled a man with him until the breaking of the day. And when he saw that he prevailed not against him, he touched the hollow of his thigh; and the hollow of Jacob's thigh was out of joint, as he wrestled with him. And he said, Let me go, for the day breaketh. And he said, I will not let thee go, except thou bless me. And he said unto him, What is thy name? And he said, Jacob. And he said, Thy name shall be called no more Jacob, but Israel: for as a prince hast thou power with God and with men, and hast prevailed.

——— *DECLARATION OF FAITH* ———

I am a scrapper when it comes to the things of God. I refuse to give in until I have received all that God desires for me to have.

(Matthew 11:12; 12:29; 2 Timothy 2:1-6; Joshua 1:5-9; 2 Corinthians 10:4)

GENESIS 35:5 NIV

Then they set out, and the terror of God fell upon the towns all around them so that no one pursued them.

Satan, demons, and all the forces of darkness are fearful of covenant believers and none of them dares to pursue me.

(Deuteronomy 2:25; Luke 10:19; Ephesians 6:10-18; Exodus 23:22; James 4:7)

GENESIS 39:2-5 KJV

And the Lord was with Joseph, and he was a prosperous man; and he was in the house of his master the Egyptian. And his master saw that the Lord was with him, and that the Lord made all that he did to prosper in his hand. And Joseph found grace in his sight, and he served him: and he made him overseer over his house, and all that he had put into his hand. And it came to pass from the time that he had made him overseer in his house, and over all that he had, that the Lord blessed the Egyptian's house for Joseph's sake; and the blessing of the Lord was upon all that he had in the house, and in the field.

————— DECLARATION OF FAITH —————

The Lord is always with me to make me prosperous and very successful.

Those who have been appointed as my supervisors can clearly see that the Lord is with me. They see how He makes everything that I set my hand to do to thrive and prosper.

He grants me abundant favor with those in authority over me. They look upon me as one who is called to lead and the Lord blesses them for my sake. For my sake, all that they have is blessed.

(Genesis 30:29,30; Deuteronomy 8:6-18; 28:1-14; Daniel 1:20; Acts 7:9,10)

GENESIS 39:20-23 KJV

And Joseph's master took him, and put him into the prison, a place where the king's prisoners were bound: and he was there in the prison. But the Lord was with Joseph, and shewed him mercy, and gave him favour in the sight of the keeper of the prison. And the keeper of the prison committed to Joseph's hand all the prisoners that were in the prison; and whatsoever they did there, he was the doer of it. The keeper of the prison looked not to any thing that was under his hand; because the Lord was with him, and that which he did, the Lord made it to prosper.

————— DECLARATION OF FAITH —————

No matter what the circumstances may be in my life, I prosper, for the Lord is with me to show me mercy, loving-kindness, and an abundance of favor with all of those I come in contact with. I have favor with my employers, my pastors, my teachers and my administrators. They see that I am called to be a leader and the Lord makes everything that I am put in charge of to prosper.

(Psalm 1:1-3; 5:11,12; 23; Genesis 12:1-3; 30:29,30; 39:2-5; Deuteronomy 28:1-14)

GENESIS 41:38 NKJV

And Pharaoh said to his servants, "Can we find *such a one* as this, a man in whom *is* the Spirit of God?"

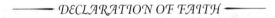
DECLARATION OF FAITH

I have the Spirit of the Living God dwelling within me. To this, rulers, leaders and people in positions of authority in the world take notice.

(1 Corinthians 3:16; Acts 2:4; Ephesians 5:18; Romans 8:9; Daniel 1:17,20; 2:22,23)

GENESIS 45:8 NIV

"So then, it was not you who sent me here, but God. He made me father to Pharaoh, lord of his entire household and ruler of all Egypt."

DECLARATION OF FAITH

God is the One in charge of my life. No one can rule over me or exercise authority over my life in any way unless He has ordained it.

God sends me where He will and places me in positions of authority as He sees fit.

(1 Peter 2:13-20; Romans 13:1-7; Deuteronomy 28:13; Isaiah 22:20-23)

GENESIS 48:15,16 NKJV

And he blessed Joseph, and said:

"God, before whom my fathers Abraham and Isaac walked,

The God who has fed me all my life long to this day,

The Angel who has redeemed me from all evil,

Bless the lads;

Let my name be named upon them,

And the name of my fathers Abraham and Isaac;

And let them grow into a multitude in the midst of the earth."

The Lord has been the Shepherd of my life from the day I was born until now, and He will continue to be my Shepherd throughout all of eternity.

He continually sends His angel to deliver me from all harm.

He blesses me, makes my name great and increases me upon the earth in a shower of His abundance.

(Psalm 23; 34:7; 91:11; Genesis 12:1-3; Deuteronomy 16:14-17; Malachi 3:10)

GENESIS 49:22-26 KJV

Joseph is a fruitful bough, even a fruitful bough by a well; whose branches run over the wall: The archers have sorely grieved him, and shot at him, and hated him: But his bow abode in strength, and the arms of his hands were made strong by the hands of the mighty God of Jacob; (from thence is the shepherd, the stone of Israel:) Even by the God of thy father, who shall help thee; and by the Almighty, who shall bless thee with blessings of heaven above, blessings of the deep that lieth under, blessings of the breasts, and of the womb: The blessings of thy father have prevailed above the blessings of my progenitors unto the utmost bound of the everlasting hills: they shall be on the head of Joseph, and on the crown of the head of him that was separate from his brethren.

I am a fruitful branch of the Vine. My branches scale walls and cover them.

I remain steady in the midst of adversity. My strong arms remain at ready, for the hand of my Lord—my Shepherd, my Rock—helps me.

The Almighty blesses me with blessings that come down from heaven, blessings that come up from the earth. My Father's blessings are greater than all and His bounty mocks the bounty of kings.

(James 1:2-4; John 15:1-8; 1 Corinthians 15:58; Genesis 28:11-22; Zechariah 8:12; Psalm 24:1-6)

CHAPTER TWO

EXODUS

In accordance with our covenant, we are given promises of deliverance from life's difficulties. The book of Exodus provides us with several of these promises. When Israel found themselves as slaves in Egypt, the Word says that the Lord remembered His covenant that He made with Abraham and set out to deliver the house of Israel from bondage.

These same promises are applicable to us today. When we find ourselves in situations where we need deliverance, the Lord is there to provide it for us. As you pray these promises, know that you are praying God's will for your freedom and prosperity.

EXODUS 2:24 NKJV

So God heard their groaning, and God remembered His covenant with Abraham, with Isaac, and with Jacob.

——— *DECLARATION OF FAITH* ———

My Father earnestly remembers the covenant He has made with me. It activates His complete attention and He is quick to honor it.

(Deuteronomy 7:12; 8:6-18; 28:1-14; Leviticus 26:9; Nehemiah 1:5; Psalm 89:1-4; Hebrews 8:6; 10:15-17)

EXODUS 3:21,22 AMP

And I will give this people favor and respect in the sight of the Egyptians; and it shall be that when you go, you shall not go empty-handed. But every woman shall [insistently] solicit of her neighbor and of her that may be residing at her house jewels and articles of silver and gold, and garments, which you shall put on your sons and daughters; and you shall strip the Egyptians [of belongings due to you].

The Lord gives me favor in the sight of my enemies. God will give me abundance where I once had lack, prosperity where I once had poverty. The enemy will be forced to give back to me all he has stolen and much, much more.

(Ephesians 6:12; Genesis 39:5; Numbers 31; Psalm 5:11,12; Proverbs 19:14;
2 Chronicles 20:15-24)

EXODUS 6:4-6 NIV

I also established my covenant with them to give them the land of Canaan, where they lived as aliens. Moreover, I have heard the groaning of the Israelites, whom the Egyptians are enslaving, and I have remembered my covenant.

The Lord has established His covenant with me. He has delivered me out of the hands of my enemies. He has lifted me out from the burdens of the oppressor and has freed me from the yoke of bondage. The Lord has rescued me with a mighty, outstretched arm.

My heavenly Father springs to action at the call of my prayer and delivers me with powerful acts of judgment.

(Hebrews 8:6; Deuteronomy 7:12; 8:6-18; 28:1-14; Psalm 18:1-19; 71:4; Colossians 1:13;
Isaiah 61:1-3; Job 5:15)

EXODUS 11:2,3 KJV

Speak now in the ears of the people, and let every man borrow of his neighbour, and every woman of her neighbour, jewels of silver, and jewels of gold. And the Lord gave the people favour in the sight of the Egyptians. Moreover the man Moses was very great in the land of Egypt, in the sight of Pharaoh's servants, and in the sight of the people.

I have favor in the sight of my enemies. They may not like it, or even understand why, but their wealth has become my provision. I am held in high esteem (in their sight) and they will be required to give back to me what is rightfully mine.

(Ephesians 6:12; Exodus 3:21,22; Proverbs 13:22; 16:7; Luke 10:19; Acts 19:15)

Exodus 12:12,13 AMP

For I will pass through the land of Egypt this night and will smite all the first-born in the land of Egypt, both man and beast; and against all the gods of Egypt I will execute judgment [proving their helplessness]. I am the Lord. The blood shall be for a token or sign to you upon [the doorposts of] the houses where you are, [that] when I see the blood, I will pass over you, and no plague shall be upon you to destroy you when I smite the land of Egypt.

———— DECLARATION OF FAITH ————

When the world is judged, I am not harmed. No plague can come upon me to destroy me, for I am covered with the blood of the Lamb!

(John 5:24; Psalm 91; 1 Peter 1:18,19; Exodus 15:26; 1 Corinthians 5:7)

Exodus 12:23 AMP

For the Lord will pass through to slay the Egyptians; and when He sees the blood upon the lintel and the two side posts, the Lord will pass over the door and will not allow the destroyer to come into your houses to slay you.

———— DECLARATION OF FAITH ————

When the destroyer comes to put plagues on the world, the Lord will not allow him to come into my house.

A hedge and a shield of protection have been built around my family and the destroyer cannot touch us.

The blood of the Lamb is upon my household. Therefore, I remain safe.

(1 John 5:18; Job 1:10; 1 Corinthians 5:7; Isaiah 53:4-7; Psalm 91:10)

Exodus 13:9 NKJV

"It shall be as a sign to you on your hand and as a memorial between your eyes, that the Lord's law may be in your mouth; for with a strong hand the Lord has brought you out of Egypt."

———— DECLARATION OF FAITH ————

My Passover [Jesus] is as a sign to me upon my hand and as a memorial before my eyes, so that the Word of the Lord is continually being spoken out of my mouth; for with a mighty hand He has delivered me out of the land of bondage.

(1 Corinthians 5:7; 11:23-26; 2 Corinthians 4:13; Romans 10:8; Colossians 1:13)

EXODUS 14:13-15 KJV

And Moses said unto the people, Fear ye not, stand still, and see the salvation of the Lord, which he will shew to you to day: for the Egyptians whom ye have seen to day, ye shall see them again no more for ever. The Lord shall fight for you, and ye shall hold your peace. And the Lord said unto Moses, Wherefore criest thou unto me? speak unto the children of Israel, that they go forward.

——— *DECLARATION OF FAITH* ———

I fear nothing! I stand firm and confident under God's powerful hand. He works for me to produce a mighty salvation. I am still and at peace for I know that God, my heavenly Father, the Creator of the universe, loves me and fights on my behalf. Therefore, I will not allow fear to hold me back, but will go forward and conquer!

(Joshua 1:5-9; 2 Timothy 1:7; Romans 8:31-39; 2 Chronicles 20:15-24; Deuteronomy 1:30)

EXODUS 15:25,26 AMP

And he cried to the Lord, and the Lord showed him a tree which he cast into the waters, and the waters were made sweet. There [the Lord] made for them a statute and an ordinance, and there He proved them, saying, If you will diligently hearken to the voice of the Lord your God and will do what is right in His sight, and will listen to and obey His commandments and keep all His statutes, I will put none of the diseases upon you which I brought upon the Egyptians, for I am the Lord Who heals you.

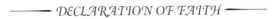

——— *DECLARATION OF FAITH* ———

I have a covenant with God. I diligently listen, giving my complete attention to His Word, and I do what is right in His sight. My ear is open to His voice and I am prepared to follow His commands.

I have His Word that no disease can come upon me which is brought upon the world; for my God is Jehovah Rapha, the God who heals me. He is the Lord of my health.

(Hebrews 8:6; 10:16,17; Deuteronomy 28:1; Isaiah 30:21; 53:5; Psalm 103:1-5)

EXODUS 17:15 NKJV

And Moses built an altar and called its name, The LORD IS MY BANNER.

DECLARATION OF FAITH

The Lord is Jehovah Nissi: the Lord my Banner. He is my standard and my rallying point in battle.

(Isaiah 11:10-12; 18:3; Exodus 14:14; Song of Solomon 2:4)

Exodus 19:4 NIV

'You yourselves have seen what I did to Egypt, and how I carried you on eagles' wings and brought you to myself. Now if you obey me fully and keep my covenant, then out of all nations you will be my treasured possession. Although the whole earth is mine.

DECLARATION OF FAITH

The Lord has delivered me from my enemies. He bore me on eagles' wings and brought me unto Himself. I have been reconciled unto almighty God!

(2 Corinthians 5:16-21; 1 John 3:8; Isaiah 40:31; Colossians 1:13)

Exodus 22:27 KJV

For that is his covering only, it is his raiment for his skin: wherein shall he sleep? and it shall come to pass, when he crieth unto me, that I will hear; for I am gracious.

DECLARATION OF FAITH

The Lord is gracious and merciful to me. He is not good to me just some of the time—He is good to me all of the time!

(Psalm 25:8-15; 34:8-10; 69:16; 73:1; 84:4-12; 86:5; 103:1-5,8,10-14; 119:65-68)

Exodus 22:28 NKJV

"You shall not revile God, nor curse a ruler of your people."

DECLARATION OF FAITH

I place in high esteem the rulers that the Lord has appointed over me. I give them respect and honor them as the Lord would have me do.

(Romans 13:1-7; 1 Peter 2:13-16; Acts 23:5; Ephesians 6:5-8)

EXODUS **23:2** NIV

"Do not follow the crowd in doing wrong. When you give testimony in a lawsuit, do not pervert justice by siding with the crowd."

DECLARATION OF FAITH

I do not follow the worldly crowd to do what is evil in the Lord's sight. I remain separate from those things that are acceptable to men, but abominable to God.

(Romans 8:5-29; 12:1,2; Galatians 5:22-25; 2 Corinthians 6:14)

EXODUS **23:19** NIV

"Bring the best of the firstfruits of your soil to the house of the Lord your God. Do not cook a young goat in its mother's milk."

DECLARATION OF FAITH

I bring the firstfruits of all of my increase and pay it in the house of God. My tithe is holy and I will be faithful in paying it.

(Malachi 3:6-12; Numbers 18:26; Deuteronomy 14:22-29; Proverbs 3:9,10)

EXODUS **23:20-23** KJV

Behold, I send an Angel before thee, to keep thee in the way, and to bring thee into the place which I have prepared. Beware of him, and obey his voice, provoke him not; for he will not pardon your transgressions: for my name is in him. But if thou shalt indeed obey his voice, and do all that I speak; then I will be an enemy unto thine enemies, and an adversary unto thine adversaries. For mine Angel shall go before thee, and bring thee in unto the Amorites, and the Hittites, and the Perizzites, and the Canaanites, the Hivites, and the Jebusites: and I will cut them off.

DECLARATION OF FAITH

The Lord sends His angel before me to protect and guard me on my way and to bring me to the place that He has prepared for me. Therefore, the Lord shows Himself to be an enemy to my enemies and will distress those who try to distress me, for His angel goes before me to do His will.

(Psalm 34:11; 91:11; 103:20; Hebrews 1:13,14; Genesis 12:1-3; Numbers 24:9)

EXODUS 23:25,26 KJV

And ye shall serve the Lord your God, and he shall bless thy bread, and thy water; and I will take sickness away from the midst of thee. There shall nothing cast their young, nor be barren, in thy land: the number of thy days I will fulfil.

———— *DECLARATION OF FAITH* ————

I serve the Lord my God and He blesses my bread and water.
He has taken sickness from my spirit and I am healed in my body.
My children shall live a long, full and abundant life.
(Young Women: "I am not barren, nor do I miscarry my babies.")
The Lord fulfills the number of my days on the earth.
He sends His terror before me and throws all of my enemies into confusion.
They turn from me and run utterly terrified.

(Deuteronomy 2:25; 1 Timothy 4:4,5; Ephesians 6:1-3; Psalm 91:16; 103:1-5; Isaiah 46:4; James 4:7; Luke 9:42; 10:19)

EXODUS 30:12 NKJV

"When you take the census of the children of Israel for their number, then every man shall give a ransom for himself to the Lord, when you number them, that there may be no plague among them when you number them."

———— *DECLARATION OF FAITH* ————

I have been numbered with the children of God. Therefore, no plague is allowed to come upon me.

(1 John 3:2; Psalm 91:10; 103:1-5; Romans 8:14-17; Isaiah 53:5)

EXODUS 33:13,14 NIV

"If you are pleased with me, teach me your ways so I may know you and continue to find favor with you. Remember that this nation is your people." The Lord replied, "My Presence will go with you, and I will give you rest."

———— *DECLARATION OF FAITH* ————

My heavenly Father is pleased with me. I have found favor in His sight so that I may know Him intimately as well as perceive and understand all that He has for me.
His presence is always with me.
He Himself dwells within me and I am at peace.

(1 John 5:20; Ephesians 2:14; Psalm 18:19; 1 Corinthians 2:10-16; 3:16; John 14:17)

EXODUS 34:26 NKJV

"The first of the firstfruits of your land you shall bring to the house of the Lord your God. You shall not boil a young goat in its mother's milk."

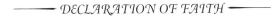

DECLARATION OF FAITH

I pay the firstfruits of all of my increase in the house of God. I will not dishonor Him by holding back my tithe.

(Deuteronomy 14:22-29; Malachi 3:6-12; Proverbs 3:9,10)

EXODUS 35:5 KJV

Take ye from among you an offering unto the Lord: whosoever is of a willing heart, let him bring it, an offering of the Lord; gold, and silver, and brass.

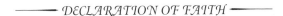

DECLARATION OF FAITH

I am free (unrestrained) and unselfish in my giving. I bring all of my offerings before the Lord with a willing and generous heart.

(Luke 6:38; 1 Corinthians 9:9-12; 2 Corinthians 8:3-9; 9:6-15)

EXODUS 35:21 NIV

And everyone who was willing and whose heart moved him came and brought an offering to the Lord for the work on the Tent of Meeting, for all its service, and for the sacred garments.

DECLARATION OF FAITH

I stir up my spirit to a joyful willingness to give to the work of the Lord. When I give, it is with a spirit of happiness and elation.

(1 Corinthians 9:9-12; 2 Corinthians 8:1-9:15; Ephesians 3:16)

EXODUS 35:29 NKJV

The children of Israel brought a freewill offering to the Lord, all the men and women whose hearts were willing to bring *material* for all kinds of work which the Lord, by the hand of Moses, had commanded to be done.

DECLARATION OF FAITH

My spirit man makes me willing to give to the work of God freely and unrestrained.

(1 Corinthians 9:9-12; 2 Corinthians 8:1-9; 15; Ephesians 3:16)

Exodus 35:34,35 KJV

And he hath put in his heart that he may teach, *both* he, and Aholiab, the son of Ahisamach, of the tribe of Dan. Them hath he filled with wisdom of heart, to work all manner of work, of the engraver, and of the cunning workman, and of the embroiderer, in blue, and in purple, in scarlet, and in fine linen, and of the weaver, *even* of them that do any work, and of those that devise cunning work.

——— *DECLARATION OF FAITH* ———

God has given me supernatural ability to teach. He has filled me will all wisdom and ability to do what He has called me to do. *[And He has called me to do great things in the earth.]*

(Daniel 1:17,20; 1 Corinthians 1:30; 2:10-16; 2 Timothy 2:7; Philippians 1:6; 2:13)

Exodus 36:2 NKJV

Then Moses called Bezalel and Aholiab, and every gifted artisan in whose heart the Lord had put wisdom, everyone whose heart was stirred, to come and do the work.

——— *DECLARATION OF FAITH* ———

As God's child, I am very wise and well able to do what He has called me to do. He has placed in me a mind of wisdom and supernatural ability. Therefore, I stir up my spirit to this end and fulfill my calling in this earth.

(Daniel 1:17,20; 1 Corinthians 1:30; 2:10-16; Philippians 1:6; 2:13; Ephesians 3:16; 2 Timothy 1:6; 2:7)

CHAPTER THREE

LEVITICUS

Often, we Christians breathe a heavy sigh when it comes to the reading of the book of Leviticus. We see little purpose in knowing a law that no longer rules us. However, the book of Leviticus has something that is essential for us all to understand. It shows us the provision of access into the Holy of Holies. It shows us a type of the fellowship that we are to enjoy with our heavenly Father. Because of what Jesus did for us, we now have the privilege of entering the Holy of Holies of heaven any time we want. We can now come boldly before the throne of grace to obtain mercy and grace to help us in our time of need.

The promises found in the book of Leviticus will surely bring you joy unspeakable. You will find promises for the power you need to fulfill your calling, the provision you need to advance God's kingdom, and unfailing protection for you and your family.

LEVITICUS 5:1 NIV

If a person sins because he does not speak up when he hears a public charge to testify regarding something he has seen or learned about, he will be held responsible.

———— DECLARATION OF FAITH ————

I stand up for what is right and testify against what I know to be wrong. I do not stand idly by and allow evil to run rampant around me. I continually stand against it, not allowing it to enter my presence without a fight.

(Job 1:1; Psalm 1:1; Proverbs 8:13; Nehemiah 5:1-11; Ephesians 6:10-18)

LEVITICUS 10:8,9 KJV

And the Lord spake unto Aaron, saying, Do not drink wine nor strong drink, thou, nor thy sons with thee, when ye go into the tabernacle of the congregation, lest ye die: *it shall be* a statute for ever throughout your generations.

——— *DECLARATION OF FAITH* ———

I am not given to wine, strong drink, or other alcoholic beverages.
I have wisdom to make the distinction between what is holy and what is not.

(Proverbs 20:1; 23:31; Ephesians 5:18; 1 Corinthians 1:30; 1 John 5:19-21)

LEVITICUS 11:44,45 AMP

For I am the Lord your God; so consecrate yourselves and be holy, for I am holy; neither defile yourselves with any manner of thing that multiplies in large numbers or swarms. For I am the Lord Who brought you up out of the land of Egypt to be your God; therefore you shall be holy, for I am holy.

——— *DECLARATION OF FAITH* ———

The Lord is my God, my Father and my example. I set myself apart from the world as one of His holy children. I consecrate myself to be holy, because my Father is holy.

(Ephesians 5:1,2; Romans 12:1,2; Matthew 5:48; 1 Peter 1:13-16; Revelation 22:11,14)

LEVITICUS 14:52,53 NIV

"He shall purify the house with the bird's blood, the fresh water, the live bird, the cedar wood, the hyssop and the scarlet yarn. Then he is to release the live bird in the open fields outside the town. In this way he will make atonement for the house, and it will be clean."

——— *DECLARATION OF FAITH* ———

My house is cleansed and set apart by the Blood. Jesus has made atonement for my house and it is clean and clear of all demonic activity.

(1 John 1:7; 5:18; Job 1:10; 1 Corinthians 5:7; Luke 10:18-20; Exodus 12:13)

LEVITICUS 22:32 NKJV

"You shall not profane My holy name, but I will be hallowed among the children of Israel. I *am* the Lord who sanctifies you."

——— *DECLARATION OF FAITH* ———

It is the Lord who consecrates me and makes me holy. I will never profane His holy name.

(Hebrews 10:14; 1 Corinthians 1:30; Exodus 20:7; Leviticus 18:21)

LEVITICUS 24:2,4 KJV

Command the children of Israel, that they bring unto thee pure oil olive beaten for the light, to cause the lamps to burn continually. He shall order the lamps upon the pure candlestick before the Lord continually.

——— *DECLARATION OF FAITH* ———

I shall keep the anointing of the Holy Spirit burning within me continually. I am as a lamp of pure gold. The oil of the Spirit is ever full within me and my light shall never go out.

(Ephesians 5:18; Matthew 5:14-16; 25:1-13; 1 Peter 2:12)

LEVITICUS 26:5 NIV

Your threshing will continue until grape harvest and the grape harvest will continue until planting, and you will eat all the food you want and live in safety in your land.

——— *DECLARATION OF FAITH* ———

I thresh the fruit of my harvest from the time of gathering through to the time of planting. I never go without. I live my life blessed with God's abundance. In Jesus, I have all that I desire and dwell in safety in the land.

(2 Corinthians 9:6-11; Psalm 112:1-9; Philippians 4:19; Deuteronomy 28:1-14)

LEVITICUS 26:6 NKJV

I will give peace in the land, and you shall lie down, and none will make *you* afraid; I will rid the land of evil beasts, and the sword will not go through your land.

——— *DECLARATION OF FAITH* ———

The peace of God has filled my life.
I fear nothing.
I lie down in peace. Nothing, absolutely nothing, can fill me with dread and no enemy can make me afraid.

(Genesis 13:2; 15:11; Joshua 1:5-9; 2 Timothy 1:7; Luke 10:19; Isaiah 43:1-13)

LEVITICUS 26:7,8 KJV

And ye shall chase your enemies, and they shall fall before you by the sword. And five of you shall chase an hundred, and an hundred of you shall put ten thousand to flight: and your enemies shall fall before you by the sword.

———— *DECLARATION OF FAITH* ————

I chase down my enemies and they fall before me. I am on the offensive in the army of God. It is not in my nature to maintain a defensive posture. I am an attacker and I go forward with my brothers and sisters in Christ to conquer in the name of Jesus. Five of us chase a hundred and a hundred of us put ten thousand to flight.

(Joshua 2:24; 8:1; Matthew 28:18-20; 1 Timothy 6:12; Romans 8:37; Deuteronomy 32:30)

LEVITICUS 26:9-13 KJV

For I will have respect unto you, and make you fruitful, and multiply you, and establish my covenant with you. And ye shall eat old store, and bring forth the old because of the new. And I will set my tabernacle among you: and my soul shall not abhor you. And I will walk among you, and will be your God, and ye shall be my people. I *am* the Lord your God, which brought you forth out of the land of Egypt, that ye should not be their bondmen; and I have broken the bands of your yoke, and made you go upright.

———— *DECLARATION OF FAITH* ————

The Lord looks upon me with favor.
He causes everything that I do to be fruitful and prosperous.
He multiplies me in all good things and in every good way.
He sets me apart unto Himself, establishing and ratifying His covenant with me.
I am living in the fullness of His abundance.
My increase is continual, so that I must regularly clear out the old to make room for the new.
The Lord has set His dwelling place within me and has given me His Word that He will never leave me nor forsake me. His Spirit is ever with me and is indeed within me. He walks with me and His presence surrounds me. He is my closest companion in this earth.
The Lord is my God and Father, and I am His son/daughter.
He has broken the bars of the yoke of slavery that were once on my shoulders. He dashed them to pieces and declared that I am free! He has enabled me to walk with my head held high, free of all bondage.
He has made me His own son/daughter and an heir to His kingdom.

(Psalm 5:11,12; Genesis 13:2; 39:2-5; Deuteronomy 8:6-18; 28:1-14; Hebrews 8:6; 13:5,6; 1 Corinthians 3:16; John 10:10; Romans 8:14-17; Galatians 4:4-6; 5:1)

LEVITICUS 27:30 NKJV

'And all the tithe of the land, *whether* of the seed of the land or of the fruit of the tree, *is* the Lord's. It *is* holy to the Lord.'

——— *DECLARATION OF FAITH* ———

I honor the Lord with the tithe of all of my increase. It is the Lord's and it is holy to Him. I pay it without reservation.

(Malachi 3:6-12; Deuteronomy 14:22-29; Nehemiah 10:37,38; Proverbs 3:9,10)

CHAPTER FOUR

NUMBERS

The book of Numbers should be a book that records the time of the taking of the promised land. However, the children of Israel, because of a lack of faith in God's Word, ended up wandering the wilderness until a generation of faith would arise. God had no choice but to clean house. He had to put things in order. He had to wait until His covenant children would take Him at His Word and go forward to do His will.

In our day, a generation of faith has risen and we have a promised land to take. The devil has run rampant in our schools, neighborhoods and cities long enough. The book of Numbers has within it promises that will build within us the overcoming spirits of true children of the living God. It is time for us to put things in order and know who we are. If God be for us, who can be against us? What odds are insurmountable when we have a loving heavenly Father who is tipping the scales in our favor?

As you pray these precious promises, know that the God who is in you is greater than all. Stand fast in the face of fear and every circumstance. Know of a certainty that you are not a grasshopper! You are a conqueror!

NUMBERS 6:24-27 KJV

The Lord bless thee, and keep thee: The Lord make his face shine upon thee, and be gracious unto thee: The Lord lift up his countenance upon thee, and give thee peace. And they shall put my name upon the children of Israel; and I will bless them.

—— DECLARATION OF FAITH ——

The Lord has conferred upon me every blessing that heaven has to offer.

His eyes are trained upon me and He relentlessly watches over me to ensure my safety.

He is my ever-present Helper who supports me in all that I do.

His face shines upon me to enlighten my way and show me mercy, kindness and an abundance of favor.

In Jesus, He has given me His permanent stamp of approval and has granted me continuous peace.

I bear His name as His own child and He blesses me with all good things.

(Psalm 5:11,12; 23; 84:11; Proverbs 3:3,4; Nehemiah 1:5,6; Ephesians 1:3-14; 2:14)

NUMBERS 10:9 NKJV

"When you go to war in your land against the enemy who oppresses you, then you shall sound an alarm with the trumpets, and you will be remembered before the Lord your God, and you will be saved from your enemies."

——— *DECLARATION OF FAITH* ———

When the enemy comes and the oppressor takes his stand against me, I am not afraid. I need only to sound the war trumpet in the heavenlies, crying out in faith to my heavenly Father, and He will rout them and see to it that I have the victory.

(Joshua 1:5-9; Psalm 18:1-19; 1 Corinthians 4:13; 5:7; 15:57; 1 John 5:4)

NUMBERS 11:23 AMP

The Lord said to Moses, Has the Lord's hand (His ability and power) become short (thwarted and inadequate)? You shall see now whether My word shall come to pass for you or not.

——— *DECLARATION OF FAITH* ———

The Lord's hand is not shortened and His ability ever remains the same. His Word to me is accomplished and I will see the results with my own eyes.

(Hebrews 13:8; Isaiah 50:2; 55:11; 59:1; Numbers 23:19; 2 Corinthians 1:20)

NUMBERS 12:7,8 NIV

But this is not true of my servant Moses; he is faithful in all my house. With him I speak face to face, clearly and not in riddles; he sees the form of the Lord. Why then were you not afraid to speak against my servant Moses?"

——— *DECLARATION OF FAITH* ———

I am faithful and trusted in the family of God.

My heavenly Father speaks with me directly and clearly, and I have a full understanding of His Word.

(Psalm 15:1-4; 1 Corinthians 2:10-16; 4:2; 2 Timothy 2:7; Hebrews 1:1,2; Ephesians 1:9; Colossians 1:9; Matthew 13:11,15,16)

NUMBERS 13:30-33 KJV

And Caleb stilled the people before Moses, and said, Let us go up at once, and possess it; for we are well able to overcome it. But the men that went up with him said, We be not able to go up against the people; for they *are* stronger than we. And they brought up an evil report of the land which they had searched unto the children of Israel, saying, The land, through which we have gone to search it, *is* a land that eateth up the inhabitants thereof; and all the people that we saw in it *are* men of a great stature. And there we saw the giants, the sons of Anak, *which come* of the giants: and we were in our own sight as grasshoppers, and so we were in their sight.

——— DECLARATION OF FAITH ———

I am well able to take the land that the Lord has called me to take.

The greater One is within me, and outside of Him, there are none who are stronger than I.

I eat giants for breakfast. Those formidable enemies that the devil has arrayed against me are nothing but pesky bugs. Though the inhabitants of the land be mighty in the eyes of the world, they pose no problem for me. I am a covenant-bearing child of the living God! I am not a grasshopper! I am a conqueror!

(Romans 8:37; 1 John 4:4; 1 Samuel 17:1-51; Mark 9:23; Numbers 14:8)

NUMBERS 14:8,9 NIV

"If the Lord is pleased with us, he will lead us into that land, a land flowing with milk and honey, and will give it to us. Only do not rebel against the Lord. And do not be afraid of the people of the land, because we will swallow them up. Their protection is gone, but the Lord is with us. Do not be afraid of them."

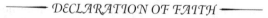

——— DECLARATION OF FAITH ———

My Father delights in me.

He has brought me into a spacious and fertile land and has bid me to claim it as my own. I will not rebel against His wishes, nor will I fear those who are now its inhabitants. They are bread for me. They have no defense that can stand against the Lord. He has removed all protection from them and has bid me to take the land. Therefore, I will take it. The Lord is with me and I am well able.

I have no fear of the giants in the land!

(Psalm 18:19; 23; 1 Samuel 17:1-51; Joshua 15:13-15; Romans 8:31; Mark 9:23)

NUMBERS 14:24 NKJV

"But My servant Caleb, because he has a different spirit in him and has followed Me fully, I will bring into the land where he went, and his descendants shall inherit it."

——— DECLARATION OF FAITH ———

I have a spirit different from that of the world.
I am loyal to the Lord and follow Him wholeheartedly.
I shall possess the land for His glory.

(2 Corinthians 5:17; 6:14; Deuteronomy 6:4-12; 28:1-14; Numbers 14:8)

NUMBERS 21:34 AMP

But the Lord said to Moses, Do not fear him, for I have delivered him and all his people and his land into your hand; and you shall do to him as you did to Sihon king of the Amorites, who dwelt at Heshbon.

——— DECLARATION OF FAITH ———

I have no fear of my enemies, for the Lord has delivered every one of them into my hands.

(Joshua 1:5-9; Ephesians 1:17-23; 6:12; Luke 10:19; Deuteronomy 3:2)

NUMBERS 22:12 NKJV

And God said to Balaam, "You shall not go with them; you shall not curse the people, for they *are* blessed."

——— DECLARATION OF FAITH ———

The Lord has set His face against all those who would curse me, for He has declared that I am to be blessed.

(Genesis 12:1-3; 22:17; Exodus 23:22; Numbers 23:20; Ephesians 1:3)

NUMBERS 23:19 KJV

God *is* not a man, that he should lie; neither the son of man, that he should repent: hath he said, and shall he not do *it?* or hath he spoken, and shall he not make it good?

―――― *DECLARATION OF FAITH* ――――

My Father is not a man that He would lie to me. He does not shrink back from any of His promises. What He has said, He does. What He has spoken comes to pass in my life.

(Isaiah 55:11; 2 Corinthians 1:20; Psalm 119:89,90,138-140,160-162; Mark 11:22-25)

NUMBERS 23:20-22 NIV

I have received a command to bless; he has blessed, and I cannot change it. "No misfortune is seen in Jacob, no misery observed in Israel. The Lord their God is with them; the shout of the King is among them. God brought them out of Egypt; they have the strength of a wild ox."

―――― *DECLARATION OF FAITH* ――――

Men are commanded to bless me and not curse me.
No evil or misfortune may befall me, for my Father is ever with me.
The shout of my King is with me as well. He has brought me from the place of bondage and has empowered me to fulfill my calling.

(Genesis 12:1-3; 22:17; Numbers 22:12; Psalm 18:1; 91:10; 1 John 5:18; Colossians 1:13,27-29)

NUMBERS 23:23,24 NKJV

"For *there is* no sorcery against Jacob,
Nor any divination against Israel.
It now must be said of Jacob
And of Israel, 'Oh, what God has done!'
Look, a people rises like a lioness,
And lifts itself up like a lion;
It shall not lie down until it devours the prey,
And drinks the blood of the slain."

―――― *DECLARATION OF FAITH* ――――

There is no spell that can work against me. No sorcery or divination can have any power over me.
When the enemy attacks, I rise up as a lioness and lift myself up as a lion.

(Psalm 91:10; 1 John 5:18; Colossians 1:13; Ephesians 6:10; Deuteronomy 33:20,21)

NUMBERS 24:5-9 KJV

How goodly are thy tents, O Jacob, *and* thy tabernacles, O Israel! As the valleys are they spread forth, as gardens by the river's side, as the trees of lign aloes which the Lord hath planted, *and* as cedar trees beside the waters. He shall pour the water out of his buckets, and his seed *shall be* in many waters, and his king shall be higher than Agag, and his kingdom shall be exalted. God brought him forth out of Egypt; he hath as it were the strength of an unicorn: he shall eat up the nations his enemies, and shall break their bones, and pierce *them* through with his arrows. He couched, he lay down as a lion, and as a great lion: who shall stir him up? Blessed *is* he that blesseth thee, and cursed *is* he that curseth thee.

DECLARATION OF FAITH

I am like a garden beside a flowing river—like an aloe planted by the Lord.
It is God's will that I live in an attractive dwelling.
Water flows freely from me to nourish the seed that I have sown.
I have my own sources of riches and plenty—an endless provision from my heavenly Father.
My children dwell within the flood of His abundance.
My Father has delivered me from the hand of bondage and has given me strength as of a wild ox. I am poised and prepared to conquer life's difficulties. I am as a couched lion that no enemy dares to arouse. I crush all of my enemies beneath my feet. Those who bless me shall themselves be blessed—those who curse me curse only themselves.

(Psalm 1:1-3; 103:17; 112:1-3; John 7:38,39; Deuteronomy 8:6-18; 2 Corinthians 9:6-15; Philippians 4:19; Proverbs 13:22; Genesis 12:1-3; 39:1-5; Romans 16:20)

NUMBERS 25:12,13 NKJV

"Therefore say, 'Behold, I give to him My covenant of peace; and it shall be to him and his descendants after him a covenant of an everlasting priesthood, because he was zealous for his God, and made atonement for the children of Israel.'"

DECLARATION OF FAITH

I have a covenant of peace with my heavenly Father—a priestly covenant, secure and dependable.
God Himself has made me a priest in His royal priesthood, for I am jealous for Him and intolerant of evil.

(Isaiah 54:10; Hebrews 8:6; 10:15-17; Ephesians 2:14; 1 Peter 2:9; Leviticus 5:1)

CHAPTER FIVE

DEUTERONOMY

Deuteronomy is like Leviticus expressed in a cloud of God's love. So much of your Father's heart comes out in this book. The provisions of our covenant are carefully detailed so that you can know of a certainty exactly what you are supposed to have as God's covenant child. When you read Deuteronomy in the light of your redemption, it takes on a different face. We know that we are redeemed from the curse of the law, therefore we can take as a promise that none of the curses are allowed to remain upon us!

Central to all of the promises in the book of Deuteronomy is the fact that God wants fellowship with His children. As you pray these promises, see yourself where God wants you to be: resting between His shoulders.

✣

DEUTERONOMY 1:11 AMP

May the Lord, the God of your fathers, make you a thousand times as many as you are and bless you as He has promised you!

—— *DECLARATION OF FAITH* ——

My heavenly Father, the God of my forefathers, increases me and blesses me with His abundance just as He has promised. His Word reigns true in my life.

(Genesis 13:2; 14:22,23; Psalm 103:17; Deuteronomy 8:18; 28:1-14; Isaiah 55:11)

DEUTERONOMY 1:17 NIV

Do not show partiality in judging; hear both small and great alike. Do not be afraid of any man, for judgment belongs to God. Bring me any case too hard for you, and I will hear it.

—— *DECLARATION OF FAITH* ——

I, like my Father, do not show partiality, nor do I fear any man. I judge all men by the same standard and my ear is opened to both the small and the great.

(Romans 2:11; Ephesians 5:1,2; Hebrews 13:6; James 2:1-13)

DEUTERONOMY 1:21 NKJV

'Look, the Lord your God has set the land before you; go up *and possess it,* as the Lord God of your fathers has spoken to you; do not fear or be discouraged.'

———— *DECLARATION OF FAITH* ————

The Lord has set the land before me. I am not afraid. I will go forth and possess it, for He has made me well able.

(Joshua 1:5-9; 23:9-11; Romans 8:31; Numbers 14:8; Philippians 4:13)

DEUTERONOMY 2:7 AMP

For the Lord your God has blessed you in all the work of your hand. He knows your walking through this great wilderness. These forty years the Lord your God has been with you; you have lacked nothing.

———— *DECLARATION OF FAITH* ————

The Lord my God blesses all of the work of my hands.

My walk in this earth is as if I am walking through a great wilderness. The world system is so contrary to my new nature that I am like a stranger in a strange land. But this is not a fearful thing for me, for my Father blesses me abundantly in the land and I lack no good thing.

(Deuteronomy 28:12; Hebrews 11:13-16; 13:5,6; 1 John 2:15; Psalm 34:10)

DEUTERONOMY 2:25 KJV

This day will I begin to put the dread of thee and the fear of thee upon the nations that are under the whole heaven, who shall hear report of thee, and shall tremble, and be in anguish because of thee.

———— *DECLARATION OF FAITH* ————

This day my Father has put the fear and dread of me on all of my enemies. They shall hear His report of me and be in great anguish, for the Lord is on my side.

(James 4:7; 1 John 4:4; Romans 8:31; Luke 10:19; Exodus 23:22,27)

DEUTERONOMY 3:22 NIV

"Do not be afraid of them; the Lord your God himself will fight for you."

DECLARATION OF FAITH

I have absolutely no fear of my enemies, for it is the Lord who goes before me. He is the first to confront the enemy on my behalf. He fights for me, routs them, and grants me the victory.

(Joshua 1:5-9; Exodus 14:13,14; Romans 8:31,37; 1 Corinthians 15:57; Psalm 2)

DEUTERONOMY 4:9 NKJV

"Only take heed to yourself, and diligently keep yourself, lest you forget the things your eyes have seen, and lest they depart from your heart all the days of your life. And teach them to your children and your grandchildren."

DECLARATION OF FAITH

I attend and give my complete attention to all that the Lord has done for me. I do not let it slip from my mind. I keep these things in the midst of my heart all the days of my life. I will teach them to my children and my grandchildren as long as I have breath within me.

(Deuteronomy 6:4-12; 8:19; 29:2-8; Genesis 18:9; Psalm 103:18; 119:11)

DEUTERONOMY 4:29 AMP

But if from there you will seek (inquire for and require as necessity) the Lord your God, you will find Him if you [truly] seek Him with all your heart [and mind] and soul and life.

DECLARATION OF FAITH

I set my face like flint to seek my Father with all of my heart. With every fiber of my being I cling to Him, thirsting for His fellowship, for I know that it is His good pleasure to make Himself known to me. When I seek Him, I find Him, if I seek Him with all of my heart.

(Deuteronomy 6:4,5; 1 John 5:20; 1 Corinthians 2:12; Matthew 6:33; 7:7)

DEUTERONOMY 4:39,40 KJV

Know therefore this day, and consider *it* in thine heart, that the Lord he *is* God in heaven above, and upon the earth beneath: *there is* none else. Thou shalt keep therefore his statutes, and his commandments, which I command thee this day, that it may go well with thee, and with thy children after thee, and that thou mayest prolong *thy* days upon the earth, which the Lord thy God giveth thee, for ever.

——— *DECLARATION OF FAITH* ———

I know, understand, and give my complete attention to the fact that my heavenly Father is the one true God in heaven above and on earth beneath. There is no other.

He is my Father, my Lord, my Master, my Teacher and my Example.

I obey all of His commands, for by them it goes well with me and with my children after me.

He has engrafted His Word into my heart so that I may prolong my days in a full and abundant life in the land that He has given me as an inheritance for all of eternity.

(Isaiah 43:10,11; 44:6; 45:5,6; 46:4,9; Psalm 91:16; 103:17; Ephesians 5:1,2)

DEUTERONOMY 5:33 NIV

Walk in all the way that the Lord your God has commanded you, so that you may live and prosper and prolong your days in the land that you will possess.

——— *DECLARATION OF FAITH* ———

I walk in all of the ways of God. He is my Mentor and the example by which I live.

I obey His every command.

His Word is life to me and I will obey it so that it may go well with me and that I may live long in the land that He has given me.

(Ephesians 5:1,2; Deuteronomy 28:1; John 15:10-17; Psalm 119:66-68; Isaiah 46:4)

DEUTERONOMY 6:2 NKJV

"That you may fear the Lord your God, to keep all His statutes and His commandments which I command you, you and your son and your grandson, all the days of your life, and that your days may be prolonged."

——— *DECLARATION OF FAITH* ———

I put my complete trust in the Lord my God. I, my children and my grandchildren, keep all of His statutes and it goes well with us. Our inheritance, in Him, is a long, satisfying and abundant life full of the blessings of the Lord.

(Proverbs 3:5,6; Psalm 91:16; 103:17; Isaiah 46:4; Acts 16:31,32; Romans 8:14-17)

DEUTERONOMY 6:5-13 KJV

And thou shalt love the Lord thy God with all thine heart, and with all thy soul, and with all thy might. And these words, which I command thee this day, shall be in thine heart: And thou shalt teach them diligently unto thy children, and shalt talk of them when thou sittest in thine house, and when thou walkest by the way, and when thou liest down, and when thou risest up. And thou shalt bind them for a sign upon thine hand, and they shall be as frontlets between thine eyes. And thou shalt write them upon the posts of thy house, and on thy gates. And it shall be, when the Lord thy God shall have brought thee into the land which he sware unto thy fathers, to Abraham, to Isaac, and to Jacob, to give thee great and goodly cities, which thou buildedst not, And houses full of all good *things*, which thou filledst not, and wells digged, which thou diggedst not, vineyards and olive trees, which thou plantedst not; when thou shalt have eaten and be full; *Then* beware lest thou forget the Lord, which brought thee forth out of the land of Egypt, from the house of bondage. Thou shalt fear the Lord thy God, and serve him, and shalt swear by his name.

―――― *DECLARATION OF FAITH* ――――

I love my heavenly Father with all of my mind, all of my spirit and all of my physical strength.

His Word is implanted and deeply rooted in my mind and in my heart.

I whet and sharpen the Word within me that it may pierce through to my mind and my spirit.

I impress the statutes of my God diligently upon the minds of my children. I talk of them when I sit in my house, when I walk by the wayside, when I lie down and when I rise up. I bind them as a sign on my hand and as an ornament before my eyes. I write them on the door posts of my house and upon my gates.

By these statutes I receive an abundance of blessings.

By the promise of the Lord, I am brought into a prosperous dwelling. Through Him, my home is supplied with an abundance of good things.

All that I have has been given to me by His grace.

It is the Lord who prospers me and gives me an inheritance of things that I did not provide.

I will not forget what He has done for me.

(Deuteronomy 4:29; 8:6-18; Ephesians 3:17; Mark 4:13-20; Psalm 112:1-3; Romans 5:1,2,17; 8:14-17; Philippians 4:19)

DEUTERONOMY 6:18,19 AMP

And you shall do what is right and good in the sight of the Lord, that it may go well with you and that you may go in and possess the good land which the Lord swore to give to your fathers, to cast out all your enemies from before you, as the Lord has promised.

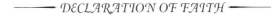

——— *DECLARATION OF FAITH* ———

I do what is right according to my calling as a child of God and it goes well with me in all that I do.

I thrust my enemies from the land that God has given me and take possession of that which He has promised me.

(Psalm 128; Numbers 21:34; Joshua 15:14; Mark 3:27; 2 Corinthians 1:20)

DEUTERONOMY 6:24,25 KJV

And the Lord commanded us to do all these statutes, to fear the Lord our God, for our good always, that he might preserve us alive, as *it is* at this day. And it shall be our righteousness, if we observe to do all these commandments before the Lord our God, as he hath commanded us.

——— *DECLARATION OF FAITH* ———

I obey the Word of my God so that I may always prosper and be kept alive. By His statutes I live a full and abundant life.

In Jesus, I stand in my Father's presence perfected in righteousness.

(Psalm 91:16; Isaiah 46:4; John 10:10; 2 Corinthians 5:21; Hebrews 10:14)

DEUTERONOMY 7:14,15 AMP

You shall be blessed above all peoples; there shall not be male or female barren among you, or among your cattle. And the Lord will take away from you all sickness, and none of the evil diseases of Egypt which you knew will He put upon you, but will lay them upon all who hate you.

——— *DECLARATION OF FAITH* ———

I am blessed above all worldly people.

There is no one, nor is there anything, barren in my house.

Everyone in my house is blessed. We live in God's favor and abound in His prosperity.

There is no sickness allowed near my dwelling. The Lord has taken all sickness from me. He does not permit any of the diseases of the world to come upon my household. Instead, they are laid upon my enemies.

(Deuteronomy 28:1-14; Psalm 103:1-5,17; Proverbs 13:22; Exodus 15:26; 23:22)

DEUTERONOMY 7:21-23 KJV

Thou shalt not be affrighted at them: for the Lord thy God *is* among you, a mighty God and terrible. And the Lord thy God will put out those nations before thee by little and little: thou mayest not consume them at once, lest the beasts of the field increase upon thee. But the Lord thy God shall deliver them unto thee, and shall destroy them with a mighty destruction, until they be destroyed.

—— *DECLARATION OF FAITH* ——

I have no fear of my enemies, for my Father is a great and awesome God. Little by little He routs them, bringing them to confusion and panic before me until they fall with a great destruction.

(Ephesians 6:12; Joshua 1:5-9; Isaiah 28:10-13; Exodus 23:20-30; Matthew 13:31,32; 2 Chronicles 20:15-24; Psalm 2)

DEUTERONOMY 8:3-5 NIV

He humbled you, causing you to hunger and then feeding you with manna, which neither you nor your fathers had known, to teach you that man does not live on bread alone but on every word that comes from the mouth of the Lord. Your clothes did not wear out and your feet did not swell during these forty years. Know then in your heart that as a man disciplines his son, so the Lord your God disciplines you.

—— *DECLARATION OF FAITH* ——

My life is not sustained by food alone, but by every Word that proceeds from the mouth of my Father.

I set His Word continually before me, for it is life to me.

My clothes do not wear out and my feet do not swell.

As a father loves, disciplines and deeply cares for his child, so does the Lord love, discipline and deeply care for me.

(Matthew 4:4; Isaiah 46:4; Psalm 103:13; 119:93,105-107; Hebrews 12:4-13)

DEUTERONOMY 8:11-18 KJV

Beware that thou forget not the Lord thy God, in not keeping his command-ments, and his judgments, and his statutes, which I command thee this day: Lest *when* thou hast eaten and art full, and hast built goodly houses, and dwelt *therein;* And *when* thy herds and thy flocks multiply, and thy silver and thy gold is multiplied, and all that thou hast is multiplied; Then thine heart be lifted up, and thou forget the Lord thy God, which brought thee forth out of the land of Egypt, from the house of bondage; Who led thee through that great and terri-ble wilderness, *wherein were* fiery serpents, and scorpions, and drought, where *there was* no water; who brought thee forth water out of the rock of flint; Who fed thee in the wilderness with manna, which thy fathers knew not, that he might humble thee, and that he might prove thee, to do thee good at thy latter end; And thou say in thine heart, My power and the might of *mine* hand hath gotten me this wealth. But thou shalt remember the Lord thy God: for *it is* he that giveth thee power to get wealth, that he may establish his covenant which he sware unto thy fathers, as *it is* this day.

———— DECLARATION OF FAITH ————

I am careful to keep my Father in my mind at all times. I am resolved to be God-inside minded. When I build magnificent dwellings to live in, I remember Him. As my silver and gold multiplies, I recognize Him. As all that I have increases, I give Him credit. As I dwell in the realm of abundance that He has provided for me, I praise Him.

I always take notice of my Provider and recognize that it is He who has brought me out of bondage. He has led me through the wilderness, trampling down the fiery serpents and scorpions along the way.

He has brought me water from the rock and fed me with the manna of heaven. All that He does for me, or to me, is for good. He is good to His children. He is good to me.

I know that it is not my own power that has brought me into the land of abundance. It is God who has given me power and supernatural ability to create wealth in order that He may establish His covenant with me.

I am a wealth creator. Day and night I am given unfailing ideas for the pro-duction of wealth in my life.

God expects me to take part in His gracious provision. He wants me to have material things. It is the way I'm supposed to live.

I will never forget Him or take Him for granted. I will never fail to recognize how my wealth has been achieved.

To God be the glory!

(1 John 4:4; Deuteronomy 6:5-13; 28:1-14; Genesis 13:2; 1 Timothy 6:17; Luke 10:19; Nahum 1:7; Galatians 4:5,6; John 10:10; Psalm 34:8-10; 35:27; 91:9-13; 112:1-9; 1 Corinthians 3:16; 10:4)

DEUTERONOMY 9:3 NKJV

"Therefore understand today that the Lord your God *is* He who goes over before you *as* a consuming fire. He will destroy them and bring them down before you; so you shall drive them out and destroy them quickly, as the Lord has said to you."

———— *DECLARATION OF FAITH* ————

I understand that it is God who drives out my enemies from my midst. He goes before me as a devouring fire, destroying, dispossessing and bringing them to nothing in my presence.

(Ephesians 6:12; Romans 16:20; Exodus 14:14; 23:20-30; Colossians 1:29; Psalm 18:1-19)

DEUTERONOMY 10:14 NIV

To the Lord your God belong the heavens, even the highest heavens, the earth and everything in it.

———— *DECLARATION OF FAITH* ————

All of the heavens, and the heaven of heavens, are the Lord's.
The earth and everything in it is His.
I am His heir.

(Psalm 24:1; 50:10-12; Exodus 19:5; 1 Corinthians 10:26; Nehemiah 9:6; Romans 8:17)

DEUTERONOMY 11:18-28 KJV

Therefore shall ye lay up these my words in your heart and in your soul, and bind them for a sign upon your hand, that they may be as frontlets between your eyes. And ye shall teach them your children, speaking of them when thou sittest in thine house, and when thou walkest by the way, when thou liest down, and when thou risest up. And thou shalt write them upon the door posts of thine house, and upon thy gates: That your days may be multiplied, and the days of your children, in the land which the Lord sware unto your fathers to give them, as the days of heaven upon the earth. For if ye shall diligently keep all these commandments which I command you, to do them, to love the Lord your God, to walk in all his ways, and to cleave unto him; Then will the Lord drive out all these nations from before you, and ye shall possess greater nations and mightier than yourselves. Every place whereon the soles of your feet shall tread shall be yours: from the wilderness and Lebanon, from the river, the river Euphrates, even unto the uttermost sea shall your coast be. There shall no man be able to stand before you: *for* the Lord your God shall lay the fear of you and the dread of you upon all the land that ye shall tread upon, as he hath said unto you. Behold, I set before you this day a blessing and a curse; A blessing, if ye obey the commandments of the Lord your God, which I command you this day: And a curse, if ye will not obey the commandments of the Lord your God, but turn aside out of the way which I command you this day, to go after other gods, which ye have not known.

─────── *DECLARATION OF FAITH* ───────

I give my whole heart, soul and mind in submission to the Word of God. I meditate upon it in its entirety. I bind all of His statutes as if they were a sign upon my hand and an ornament before my eyes. I write them on the doorposts of my houses and upon my gates.

By the Word of my Father the days of my children are multiplied.

I love Him and walk in all of His ways.

I am resolved to attach myself to Him in love.

He is my example and is ever with me.

He drives out my enemies from before me and dispossesses them.

Every place that the sole of my foot treads is mine. I hereby claim it for the kingdom of God.

There is not a soul in all of creation who has the ability to triumph over me.

He sets before me the choice of living under His blessing, or living under the curse. The choice is mine. I can be blessed if I choose to believe in and adhere to His Word and the statutes therein, or I can be cursed if I choose to reject them.

I choose the blessing!

(Deuteronomy 2:25; 6:4-13; Joshua 1:8; 2:9-11; 24:15; Ephesians 6:1-3; Exodus 14:14; 23:20-30; Romans 8:31; James 4:7)

DEUTERONOMY 13:4,5 AMP

You shall walk after the Lord your God and [reverently] fear Him, and keep His commandments and obey His voice, and you shall serve Him and cling to Him.

But that prophet or that dreamer of dreams shall be put to death, because he has talked rebellion and turning away from the Lord your God, Who brought you out of the land of Egypt and redeemed you out of the house of bondage; that man has tried to draw you aside from the way in which the Lord your God commanded you to walk. So shall you put the evil away from your midst.

───── *DECLARATION OF FAITH* ─────

I walk in the ways of my heavenly Father.

I keep His Word and heed His voice.

I serve Him and cling to Him with all of my heart.

I refuse to listen to those who rebel against the Word and try to keep me from His presence.

My Father has redeemed me from the hand of bondage and has placed me in the land of abundance. I will not listen to or associate myself with those who would try to convince me otherwise.

(John 10:7-18; Galatians 5:1; 2 Peter 2; 2 Corinthians 8:9,14; 9:8; Genesis 13:2; Romans 16:17-19; Colossians 2:8)

DEUTERONOMY 14:22-29 KJV

Thou shalt truly tithe all the increase of thy seed, that the field bringeth forth year by year. And thou shalt eat before the Lord thy God, in the place which he shall choose to place his name there, the tithe of thy corn, of thy wine, and of thine oil, and the firstlings of thy herds and of thy flocks; that thou mayest learn to fear the Lord thy God always. And if the way be too long for thee, so that thou art not able to carry it; *or* if the place be too far from thee, which the Lord thy God shall choose to set his name there, when the Lord thy God hath blessed thee: Then shalt thou turn *it* into money, and bind up the money in thine hand, and shalt go unto the place which the Lord thy God shall choose: And thou shalt bestow that money for whatsoever thy soul lusteth after, for oxen, or for sheep, or for wine, or for strong drink, or for whatsoever thy soul desireth: and thou shalt eat there before the Lord thy God, and thou shalt rejoice, thou, and thine household, And the Levite that *is* within thy gates; thou shalt not forsake him; for he hath no part nor inheritance with thee. At the end of three years thou shalt bring forth all the tithe of thine increase the same year, and shalt lay *it* up within thy gates: And the Levite, (because he hath no part nor inheritance with thee,) and the stranger, and the fatherless, and the widow, which *are* within thy gates, shall come, and shall eat and be satisfied; that the Lord thy God may bless thee in all the work of thine hand which thou doest.

——— *DECLARATION OF FAITH* ———

I am faithful to pay a tithe on all of my God-given increase. It is holy to the Lord and I will not rob Him of it.

It is my tithes and offerings that provide for the work of the Gospel.

As I provide for the Gospel, God provides for me. When I tithe, I have His promise that He will prosper all of the work of my hands. It is a declaration that my finances are under the rulership and guardianship of almighty God!

(Malachi 3:6-12; Nehemiah 10:37-39; Deuteronomy 28:12; Proverbs 3:9,10)

DEUTERONOMY 15:4-6 AMP

But there will be no poor among you, for the Lord will surely bless you in the land which the Lord your God gives you for an inheritance to possess, If only you carefully listen to the voice of the Lord your God, to do watchfully all these commandments which I command you this day. When the Lord your God blesses you as He promised you, then you shall lend to many nations, but you shall not borrow; and you shall rule over many nations, but they shall not rule over you.

——— *DECLARATION OF FAITH* ———

There is no one who is poor in the family of God. I am not, nor will I ever be, poor. My Father has blessed me and has given me an inheritance to possess now in this life. It is an ever-present provision for me that I can draw upon in time of need.

I am careful to keep all of my Father's statutes and He blesses me just as He has promised. I lend to many and borrow from none.

I will not be the slave of a lender. I am not called to be in bondage, but to lead. My Father has ordained that I be the head, and not the tail, above only and not beneath.

(Revelation 2:9; 2 Corinthians 8:9; Psalm 37:25; Philippians 4:19; Deuteronomy 28:12-14; Proverbs 22:7)

DEUTERONOMY 15:10,11 AMP

You shall give to him freely without begrudging it; because of this the Lord will bless you in all your work and in all you undertake. For the poor will never cease out of the land; therefore I command you, You shall open wide your hands to your brother, to your needy, and to your poor in your land.

I give to the poor in the land freely and without reservation. Because of this, my Father blesses all of my work. Everything that I set my hand to do prospers and all of my enterprises are brought to unfailing success. It is my Father's great pleasure to grant me an abundance of good things and I willingly share my bounty with the poor in the land.

(2 Corinthians 8:2-5; 9:5-8; Genesis 39:1-5; Psalm 41:1-3; 84:11; Luke 12:32; Proverbs 19:17)

Deuteronomy 16:15 NKJV

"Seven days you shall keep a sacred feast to the Lord your God in the place which the Lord chooses, because the Lord your God will bless you in all your produce and in all the work of your hands, so that you surely rejoice."

—— *DECLARATION OF FAITH* ——

It is God's will for me to enjoy the prosperity and provision that He has provided for me through Jesus. He causes me to produce good things in abundance and continually blesses everything that I set my hand to do.

(3 John 2; Deuteronomy 8:18; 28:12; 2 Corinthians 9:8; Psalm 35:27)

Deuteronomy 18:14 NIV

The nations you will dispossess listen to those who practice sorcery or divination. But as for you, the Lord your God has not permitted you to do so.

—— *DECLARATION OF FAITH* ——

I do not give my ear to sorcery and divination. All of the psychics and soothsayers in the earth today have no part in my life. I do not listen to them or support what they do in any way.

(Jeremiah 27:8-11; Malachi 3:5; Micah 5:12; Leviticus 19:26,31)

Deuteronomy 20:3,4 KJV

And shall say unto them, Hear, O Israel, ye approach this day unto battle against your enemies: let not your hearts faint, fear not, and do not tremble, neither be ye terrified because of them; For the Lord your God *is* he that goeth with you, to fight for you against your enemies, to save you.

I rush into battle against my enemies. I will not allow them to trespass on my Father's land. I boldly take the offensive, for I know the One in whom I believe and I am fully aware of His capabilities within me.

It is the Lord who goes before me. He is the first to confront the enemy on my behalf. I have nothing to fear. I refuse to give in to terror, trembling, or panic. The Lord fights for me and I stand in His victory!

(Exodus 14:13-15; Luke 10:19; Mark 3:27; 2 Timothy 1:12; Joshua 1:5-9; 1 Corinthians 15:57)

DEUTERONOMY 26:12-15 AMP

When you have finished paying all the tithe of your produce the third year, which is the year of tithing, and have given it to the Levite, the stranger and the sojourner, the fatherless, and to the widow, that they may eat within your towns and be filled, Then you shall say before the Lord your God, I have brought the hallowed things (the tithe) out of my house and moreover have given them to the Levite, to the stranger and the sojourner, to the fatherless, and to the widow, according to all Your commandments which You have commanded me; I have not transgressed any of Your commandments, neither have I forgotten them. I have not eaten of the tithe in my mourning [making the tithe unclean], nor have I handled any of it when I was unclean, nor given any of it to the dead. I have hearkened to the voice of the Lord my God; I have done according to all that You have commanded me. Look down from Your holy habitation, from heaven, and bless Your people Israel and the land which You have given us as You swore to our fathers, a land flowing with milk and honey.

—————— *DECLARATION OF FAITH* ——————

I pay all of the tithe—the first and best part of all of my increase. I say before the Lord, "I have brought the tithe of my increase into the house of God. I have not forgotten this holy ordinance. I have not transgressed this sacred command. I make this a top priority in my life. Therefore, I call upon You, Father, to look down from Your throne and bless me according to Your oath. Bless me with Your abundant provision in the land which You have given me."

(Malachi 3:6-12; Nehemiah 10:37-39; Deuteronomy 14:22-29; Proverbs 3:9,10)

DEUTERONOMY 28:1-14 KJV

And it shall come to pass, if thou shalt hearken diligently unto the voice of the Lord thy God, to observe *and* to do all his commandments which I command thee this day, that the Lord thy God will set thee on high above all nations of the earth: And all these blessings shall come on thee, and overtake thee, if thou shalt hearken unto the voice of the Lord thy God. Blessed *shalt* thou *be* in the city, and blessed *shalt* thou *be* in the field. Blessed *shall be* the fruit of thy body, and the fruit of thy ground, and the fruit of thy cattle, the increase of thy kine, and the flocks of thy sheep. Blessed *shall be* thy basket and thy store. Blessed *shalt* thou *be* when thou comest in, and blessed *shalt* thou *be* when thou goest out. The Lord shall cause thine enemies that rise up against thee to be smitten before thy face: they shall come out against thee one way, and flee before thee seven ways. The Lord shall command the blessing upon thee in thy storehouses, and in all that thou settest thine hand unto; and he shall bless thee in the land which the Lord thy God giveth thee. The Lord shall establish thee an holy people unto himself, as he hath sworn unto thee, if thou shalt keep the commandments of the Lord thy God, and walk in his ways. And all people of the earth shall see that thou art called by the name of the Lord; and they shall be afraid of thee. And the Lord shall make thee plenteous in goods, in the fruit of thy body, and in the fruit of thy cattle, and in the fruit of thy ground, in the land which the Lord sware unto thy fathers to give thee. The Lord shall open unto thee his good treasure, the heaven to give the rain unto thy land in his season, and to bless all the work of thine hand: and thou shalt lend unto many nations, and thou shalt not borrow. And the Lord shall make thee the head, and not the tail; and thou shalt be above only, and thou shalt not be beneath; if that thou hearken unto the commandments of the Lord thy God, which I command thee this day, to observe and to do *them:* And thou shalt not go aside from any of the words which I command thee this day, *to* the right hand, or *to* the left, to go after other gods to serve them.

——— DECLARATION OF FAITH ———

I heed the voice of the Lord my God. I keep all of His statutes and forever hold His Word dear to my heart, for by the Word of the Lord I am set high above all worldly people.

All of these blessings come upon me and overtake me.

I am blessed (given divine favor, good fortune, happiness, prosperity, and good things of every kind) in the city, and I am blessed (given divine favor, good fortune, happiness, prosperity, and good things of every kind) in the country.

Blessed are my children, my animals and my garden.

Blessed are the increase of my cattle and the offspring of my flocks.

Blessed are my produce and my gatherings.

I am blessed when I come in and blessed when I go out.

The Lord causes my enemies who rise up against me to be defeated before my face. They rise up against me in one direction, but flee from me in seven directions.

The Lord commands blessings on all of my treasuries and on everything that I set my hand to do. He gives me abundant prosperity in the land, which He has given me.

My heavenly Father establishes me before the world as a holy person that He has set apart unto Himself. He makes His declaration that I am His and under His guardianship. This is His promise to me if I hold fast to His Word and walk in His ways.

All of the people of the world clearly see that I am called by the name of the Lord. They recognize that I am in His family. I am His son/daughter and heir, and His blessings are evident in my life. This fact sparks terror in the hearts of my enemies.

The Lord gives me a tremendous surplus of prosperity for my home and family. The fruit of my body, the young of my cattle and the produce of my ground are blessed with His abundance.

My Lord gives rain to my land precisely when I need it. He has opened to me His heavenly treasury. With perfect timing He rains it down upon me and blesses all the work of my hands.

He has made me a lender and not a borrower. I shall lend to many and borrow from none.

I am the head and not the tail, above only and not beneath. I am destined to take the lead in any enterprise I undertake. My Father has placed me at the top and never at the bottom, for I keep His Word and I am careful to adhere to His statutes.

I do not reject any of my Father's requirements. I do not steer away from them even a little to the right or to the left. I set them firm in my heart and place my complete trust in them regardless of what my eyes may see or what other gods may offer.

The righteous requirement of the Law is fulfilled in me. I do not live my life in habitual sin, but in holiness before the Lord.

I have been made the very righteousness of God in Christ Jesus.

My trust is firmly planted in Him.

(Genesis 12:1-3; 13:2; 39:2-5; Leviticus 26:9; Ephesians 2:6; 6:12; 2 Corinthians 5:21; Deuteronomy 2:25; 8:18; 11:25; Psalm 1:1-3; 5:11,12; 112:1-3; Philippians 4:17-19; Isaiah 43:1,2; John 15:7; Romans 8:4; Malachi 3:10; 1 John 3:9; Proverbs 3:5,6)

DEUTERONOMY 28:15-68 KJV

But it shall come to pass, if thou wilt not hearken unto the voice of the Lord thy God, to observe to do all his commandments and his statutes which I command thee this day; that all these curses shall come upon thee, and overtake thee: Cursed *shalt* thou *be* in the city, and cursed *shalt* thou *be* in the field. Cursed *shall be* thy basket and thy store. Cursed *shall be* the fruit of thy body, and the fruit of thy land, the increase of thy kine, and the flocks of thy sheep. Cursed *shalt* thou *be* when thou comest in, and cursed *shalt* thou *be* when thou goest out. The Lord shall send upon thee cursing, vexation, and rebuke, in all that thou settest thine hand unto for to do, until thou be destroyed, and until thou perish quickly; because of the wickedness of thy doings, whereby thou hast forsaken me. The Lord shall make the pestilence cleave unto thee, until he have consumed thee from off the land, whither thou goest to possess it. The Lord shall smite thee with a consumption, and with a fever, and with an inflammation, and with an extreme burning, and with the sword, and with blasting, and with mildew; and they shall pursue thee until thou perish. And thy heaven that *is* over thy head shall be brass, and the earth that is under thee *shall be* iron. The Lord shall make the rain of thy land powder and dust: from heaven shall it come down upon thee, until thou be destroyed. The Lord shall cause thee to be smitten before thine enemies: thou shalt go out one way against them, and flee seven ways before them: and shalt be removed into all the kingdoms of the earth. And thy carcase shall be meat unto all fowls of the air, and unto the beasts of the earth, and no man shall fray *them* away. The Lord will smite thee with the botch of Egypt, and with the emerods, and with the scab, and with the itch, whereof thou canst not be healed. The Lord shall smite thee with madness, and blindness, and astonishment of heart: And thou shalt grope at noonday, as the blind gropeth in darkness, and thou shalt not prosper in thy ways: and thou shalt be only oppressed and spoiled evermore, and no man shall save *thee.* Thou shalt betroth a wife, and another man shall lie with her: thou shalt build an house, and thou shalt not dwell therein: thou shalt plant a vineyard, and shalt not gather the grapes thereof. Thine ox *shall be* slain before thine eyes, and thou shalt not eat thereof: thine ass *shall be* violently taken away from before thy face, and shall not be restored to thee: thy sheep *shall be* given unto thine enemies, and thou shalt have none to rescue *them.* Thy sons and thy daughters *shall be* given unto another people, and thine eyes shall look, and fail *with longing* for them all the day long: and *there shall be* no might in thine hand. The fruit of thy land, and all thy labours, shall a nation which thou knowest not eat up; and thou shalt be only oppressed and crushed alway: So that thou shalt be mad for the sight of thine eyes which thou shalt see. The Lord shall smite thee in the knees, and in the legs, with a sore botch that cannot be healed, from the sole of thy foot unto the top of thy head. The Lord shall bring thee, and thy king which thou shalt set over thee, unto a nation which neither thou nor thy fathers have known; and there shalt thou serve other gods, wood and stone. And thou shalt become an astonishment, a proverb, and a byword, among all nations whither the Lord shall lead thee. Thou shalt carry much seed out into the field, and shalt gather *but* little in; for the locust shall consume it. Thou shalt plant vineyards, and dress *them,* but shalt neither drink *of* the wine, nor gather *the grapes;* for the worms shall eat them. Thou shalt have olive trees throughout all thy coasts, but thou shalt not anoint *thyself* with the oil; for thine olive shall cast *his fruit.* Thou shalt beget sons and daughters, but thou shalt not enjoy them; for they shall go into captivity. All thy trees and fruit of thy land shall the locust consume. The stranger that *is* within thee shall get up above thee very high; and thou shalt come down very low. He shall lend to thee, and thou shalt not lend to him: he shall be the head, and thou shalt be the tail. Moreover all these curses shall come upon thee, and shall pursue thee, and overtake thee, till thou be destroyed; because thou hearkenedst not unto the voice of the Lord thy God, to keep his commandments and his statutes which he commanded thee: And they shall be upon thee for a sign and for a wonder, and upon thy seed for ever. Because thou servedst not the Lord thy God with joyfulness, and with gladness of heart, for the abundance of all *things;* Therefore shalt thou serve thine enemies which the Lord shall send against thee, in hunger, and in thirst, and in nakedness, and in want of all *things:* and he shall put a yoke of iron upon thy neck, until he have destroyed thee. The Lord shall bring a nation against thee from far, from the end of the earth, *as swift* as the eagle flieth; a nation whose tongue thou shalt not understand; A nation of fierce countenance, which shall not regard the person of the old, nor shew favour to the young: And he shall eat the fruit of thy cattle, and the fruit of thy land, until thou be destroyed: which *also* shall not leave thee *either* corn, wine, or oil, *or* the increase of thy kine, or flocks of thy sheep, until he have destroyed thee. And he shall besiege thee in all thy gates, until thy high and fenced walls come down, wherein thou trustedst, throughout all thy land: and he shall besiege thee in all thy gates throughout all thy land, which the Lord thy God hath given thee. And thou shalt eat the fruit of thine own body, the flesh of thy sons and of thy daughters, which the Lord thy God hath given thee, in the siege, and in the straitness, wherewith thine enemies shall distress thee: *So that* the man *that is* tender among you, and very delicate, his eye shall be evil toward his brother, and toward the wife of his bosom, and toward the remnant of his children which he shall leave: So that he will not give to any of them of the flesh of his children whom he shall eat: because he hath nothing left him in the siege, and in the straitness, wherewith thine enemies shall distress thee in all thy gates. The tender and delicate woman among you, which would not adventure to set the sole of her foot upon the ground for delicateness and tenderness, her eye shall be evil toward the husband of her bosom, and toward her son, and toward her daughter, And toward her young one that cometh out from between her feet, and toward her children which she shall bear: for she shall eat them for want of all *things* secretly in the siege and straitness, wherewith thine enemy shall distress thee in thy gates. If thou wilt not observe to do all the words of this law that are written in this book, that thou mayest fear this glorious and fearful name, THE LORD THY GOD; Then the Lord will make thy plagues wonderful, and the plagues of thy seed, *even* great plagues, and of long continuance, and sore sicknesses, and of long continuance. Moreover he will bring upon thee all the diseases of Egypt, which thou wast afraid of; and they shall cleave unto thee. Also every sickness, and every plague, which *is* not written in the book of this law, them will the Lord bring upon thee, until thou be destroyed. And ye shall be left few in number, whereas ye were as the stars of heaven for multitude; because thou wouldest not obey the voice of the Lord thy God. And it shall come to pass, *that* as the Lord rejoiced over you to do you good, and to multiply you; so the Lord will rejoice over you to destroy you, and to bring you to nought; and ye shall be plucked from off the land whither thou goest to possess it. And the Lord shall scatter thee among all people, from the one end of the earth even unto the other; and there thou shalt serve other gods, which neither thou nor thy fathers have known, *even* wood and stone. And among these nations shalt thou find no ease, neither shall the sole of thy foot have rest: but the Lord shall give thee there a trembling heart, and failing of eyes, and sorrow of mind: And thy life shall hang in doubt before thee; and thou shalt fear day and night, and shalt have none assurance of thy life: In the morning thou shalt say, Would God it were even! and at even thou shalt say, Would God it were morning! for the fear of thine heart wherewith thou shalt fear, and for the sight of thine eyes which thou shalt see. And the Lord shall bring thee into Egypt again with ships, by the way whereof I spake unto thee, Thou shalt see it no more again: and there ye shall be sold unto your enemies for bondmen and bondwomen, and no man shall buy *you.*

DECLARATION OF FAITH

(The curse of the law, or, the curses of the covenant.)

I am redeemed from the curse of the law (Galatians 3:13). I do not have to tolerate the curses of the covenant, for I am in Jesus and am firmly established in His righteousness (Galatians 3:16). I will not allow any of the curses of the law to come upon me and overtake me.

I am redeemed from confusion and rebuke in the enterprises I undertake.

I am redeemed from destruction and shall not perish before my time. I am blessed to live a long, full and satisfying life (Psalm 91:16).

I am redeemed from all pestilence which brings agonizing death.

I am redeemed from tuberculosis, cancer and the progressive wasting of the body.

I am redeemed from fever.

I am redeemed from inflammation.

I am redeemed from the effects of draught.

I am redeemed from blight and decay.

I am redeemed from mildew.

I am redeemed from the sun scorching my garden.

I am redeemed from the ground choking my roots.

I am redeemed from powdery soil and dust.

I am redeemed from being defeated by my enemies.

I am redeemed from the fear of my enemies.

I am redeemed from boils.

I am redeemed from tumors.

I am redeemed from malignant diseases, which cause a discharge.

I am redeemed from scurvy (bleeding gums and livid skin patches).

I am redeemed from scabies, hives, rashes and all skin diseases, which cause an itch.

I am redeemed from madness (insanity). I have a sound mind and keep a clear head in every situation.

I am redeemed from blindness.

I am redeemed from confusion and the unsettling of the mind.

I am redeemed from indecision for lack of direction.

I am redeemed from being robbed.

I am redeemed from others sleeping with my spouse.

I am redeemed from others taking (stealing, or confiscating) from me what I have built for myself.

I am redeemed from others gathering and taking (stealing, or confiscating) my harvest from me. I have sown my seed and I will reap an abundant harvest.

I am redeemed from my animals being taken from me.

I am redeemed from my transportation being repossessed.

I am redeemed from my belongings being taken from me and given to my enemies.

I am redeemed from my sons and daughters being taken from me and given to another people. My hands are given power to prevent this.

I am redeemed from strangers consuming the fruit of my labor.

I am redeemed from being oppressed and crushed continually.

I am redeemed from being driven crazy by the things that I see.

I am redeemed from both leprosy and elephantiasis.

I am redeemed from infirmities of the knees and the legs.

I am redeemed from permanent runny sores that cannot be healed.

I am redeemed from being brought into slavery and forced to serve other gods.

I am redeemed from being jeered at for lack of blessing in my life.

I am redeemed from the worm eating the produce of my vine.

I am redeemed from sowing much seed, but gathering little harvest because the locusts [demons] have devoured it. All evil forces are bound and rebuked by the Lord! They cannot consume, steal, or restrain my harvest in any way! (Malachi 3:11.)

I am redeemed from having much, but not having the oil of anointing. My wealth is covered by the burden-removing, yoke-destroying power of God. Therefore, the abundance of my possessions cannot bring me anxiety in any shape or form.

I am redeemed from having my sons and daughters go into captivity.

I am redeemed from having locusts possess all of my trees, the fruit of my ground and the products of my labor [my paycheck].

I am redeemed from having a stranger to the covenant, and promises mount up higher and higher above me, while I go down lower and lower.

I am redeemed from having to borrow, which would make me the tail and not the head.

I am redeemed from having curses pursue me, come upon me and overtake me until I am destroyed.

I am redeemed from being a sign and a warning to other people of what it is like to be cursed because I chose to reject the abundance of God's blessings.

I am redeemed from having to serve my enemies.

I am redeemed from hunger and thirst.

I am redeemed from lack of clothing and being in want of all good things.

I am redeemed from having a yoke of iron around my neck until I am destroyed.

I am redeemed from being overcome by ruthless people.

I am redeemed from being besieged by a ruthless and powerful enemy.

I am redeemed from such severe famine that my only food would be my own sons and daughters.

I am redeemed from the strife that is caused by having all of my belongings taken from me.

I am redeemed from every sickness and plague that has a long duration.

I am redeemed from every disease that is brought upon the world.

I am redeemed from known sicknesses and unknown sicknesses.

I am redeemed from every sickness that has ever been or ever will be.

I am redeemed from being evicted from my land.

I am redeemed from myself and my loved ones being scattered and sent into slavery.

I am redeemed from having no rest from my labors.

I am redeemed from exhaustion in my heart [literally], my eyes, my mind, and my spirit.

I am redeemed from having my life hang in doubt so that I do not know what the future holds for me.

I am redeemed from being worried and having no assurance of what will take place in my life.

I am redeemed from hating life because of anxiety and dread due to the curses of the covenant.

I am redeemed from being sold again into slavery and hated so much that people see me as not even being worthy of bondage.

I AM REDEEMED FROM ALL OF THIS! None of it may come upon my life! I am in Christ Jesus and He has set me free!

(Hebrews 9:11,12; Isaiah 40:2; 52:13-53:12; John 8:32-36; 10:10; Exodus 15:26; Deuteronomy 7:15; Psalm 103)

DEUTERONOMY 29:9 NKJV

"Therefore keep the words of this covenant, and do them, that you may prosper in all that you do."

——— DECLARATION OF FAITH ———

I remain in God's Word and adhere to the statutes of His covenant, for by them I deal wisely in the affairs of this life and prosper in all that I set my hand to do.

(John 15:7; Joshua 1:8; Psalm 1:1-3; 119:97-101; 105-107; Deuteronomy 28:12)

DEUTERONOMY 30:9,10 AMP

And the Lord your God will make you abundantly prosperous in every work of your hand, in the fruit of your body, of your cattle, of your land, for good; for the Lord will again delight in prospering you, as He took delight in your fathers,

If you obey the voice of the Lord your God, to keep His commandments and His statutes which are written in this Book of the Law, and if you turn to the Lord your God with all your [mind and] heart and with all your being.

——— DECLARATION OF FAITH ———

My Father takes great pleasure in the abundance of my prosperity.

He prospers my children, my land, and my cattle.

He sets me apart from the rest of the world and blesses me with an abundance of good things. I have been singled out by God Himself to be a recipient of His blessings and His goodness.

I will keep the statutes of His covenant with all of my heart, all of my soul and everything that is within me.

(Psalm 35:27; 103:17; Romans 8:28-30; Ephesians 1:3-14; Deuteronomy 6:4-12)

DEUTERONOMY 30:14-16 KJV

But the word *is* very nigh unto thee, in thy mouth, and in thy heart, that thou mayest do it. See, I have set before thee this day life and good, and death and evil; In that I command thee this day to love the Lord thy God, to walk in his ways, and to keep his commandments and his statutes and his judgments, that thou mayest live and multiply: and the Lord thy God shall bless thee in the land whither thou goest to possess it.

─── *DECLARATION OF FAITH* ───

The Word of faith is in my mouth continually. I keep it near to me—in my mouth, in my mind, and in my spirit—so that I may do and have what I say.

The Lord has set before me life and good things, but also death and evil things. The choice is mine. I choose to adhere to the statutes of His covenant. I walk in all of His ways so that I may live His abundant life and multiply in this earth.

Because I have chosen life, my Father is very pleased to bless me with His divine favor, good fortune, happiness, prosperity and good things of every kind.

(Romans 10:8-10; Deuteronomy 11:26,27; Joshua 24:15; Psalm 35:27; 112:1-3)

DEUTERONOMY 31:6 NKJV

"Be strong and of good courage, do not fear nor be afraid of them; for the Lord your God, He *is* the One who goes with you. He will not leave you nor forsake you."

─── *DECLARATION OF FAITH* ───

My Father is with me in everything that I do. I remain strong and full of courage at all times. I am not shaken by what I see in my enemies. God is on my side and He will not fail me. I have His Word that He will never leave me nor forsake me.

(Hebrews 13:5-8; Joshua 1:5-9; 10:25; 2 Kings 6:15-17; 1 Chronicles 22:13)

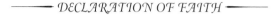

DEUTERONOMY 31:8 NKJV

"And the Lord, He is the one who goes before you. He will be with you, He will not leave you nor forsake you; do not fear nor be dismayed."

——— *DECLARATION OF FAITH* ———

It is the Lord God who goes with me wherever I may go. He marches before me and is the first to confront the enemy on my behalf.

God Himself has taken up residence within my spirit. He holds me close to His heart and gives me His Word that He will not fail me.

I will not give in to cowardice or flinching. My spirit remains steadfast and unbroken. I will not allow myself to become depressed, dismayed, or unnerved.

I continually trust in My God and I stand in His victory.

(Exodus 13:21,22; Isaiah 43:1-13; 1 John 4:4; Hebrews 13:5-8; Joshua 1:5-9; 1 Peter 5:5-7)

DEUTERONOMY 32:1-4 KJV

Give ear, O ye heavens, and I will speak; and hear, O earth, the words of my mouth. My doctrine shall drop as the rain, my speech shall distil as the dew, as the small rain upon the tender herb, and as the showers upon the grass: Because I will publish the name of the Lord: ascribe ye greatness unto our God. *He is* the Rock, his work *is* perfect: for all his ways *are* judgment: a God of truth and without iniquity, just and right *is* he.

——— *DECLARATION OF FAITH* ———

I boldly take my stand, believing and speaking the words of faith. Heaven and earth take notice of the words of my mouth. They drop as a gentle rain upon tender grass and as the showers upon the herb.

I proclaim above all things the name and presence of the Lord my God. I concede and ascribe to His greatness. He is my Rock of Bethel. His work is perfect and all of His ways are just. He is faithful in all that He does and performs all of His promises without breach or deviation. His Word to me stands true forever.

(2 Corinthians 4:13; Romans 10:8; Isaiah 55:11; Genesis 28:10-22; Psalm 103:20; 107:20; 119:89-93, 160-165)

DEUTERONOMY 32:10-13 AMP

He found him in a desert land, in the howling void of the wilderness; He kept circling around him, He scanned him [penetratingly], He kept him as the pupil of His eye. As an eagle that stirs up her nest, that flutters over her young, He spread abroad His wings and He took them, He bore them on His pinions. So the Lord alone led him; there was no foreign god with Him. He made Israel ride on the high places of the earth, and he ate the increase of the field; and He made him suck honey out of the rock and oil out of the flinty rock.

———— *DECLARATION OF FAITH* ————

My heavenly Father found me in a desert place and pulled me from a barren wilderness. He encompassed me and drew me unto Himself so that I may find refuge in His arms. He keeps watch over me with an unfailing devotion and guards me as the apple of His eye. As an eagle stirs up her nest and hovers over her young, He spreads His wings about me and bears me up in His pinions.

The Lord alone is my direction. He leads me and guides me in my way.

He makes me to ride upon the high places of the earth.

He bids me to eat from His abundance. He gives me honey from the rock and oil from the flinty crag.

He is my Lord and my Savior. He continually watches over me so that I may enjoy the fullness of every good thing that life has to offer.

(Isaiah 43:19-21; Psalm 17:8; 27:11; 34:10; 91:1-4; 103:1-5; Genesis 28:10-22; 2 Peter 1:3)

DEUTERONOMY 33:12-16 KJV

And of Benjamin he said, The beloved of the Lord shall dwell in safety by him; *and the Lord* shall cover him all the day long, and he shall dwell between his shoulders. And of Joseph he said, Blessed of the Lord *be* his land, for the precious things of heaven, for the dew, and for the deep that coucheth beneath, And for the precious fruits *brought forth* by the sun, and for the precious things put forth by the moon, And for the chief things of the ancient mountains, and for the precious things of the lasting hills, And for the precious things of the earth and fulness thereof, and *for* the good will of him that dwelt in the bush: let *the blessing* come upon the head of Joseph, and upon the top of the head of him *that was* separated from his brethren.

———— *DECLARATION OF FAITH* ————

My Father loves me. He lifts me up in His tender embrace all the day long and I find my dwelling place between His shoulders.

I am kept in perfect safety in Him.

He blesses me with precious gifts from heaven and from the deep that couches beneath. He gives me all of the precious gifts that are under the sun and the finest that the months can yield. He furnishes me with the choicest products of the mountains and with the precious things from the everlasting hills. He gives me the best of all that the earth has to offer and grants me abundant favor in His presence.

All of these blessings rain down upon me in their abundance.

(Psalm 24:1; 84:11; 103:13; Mark 9:36,37; 10:16; Isaiah 43:1-13; Deuteronomy 10:14; 33:27-29)

DEUTERONOMY 33:20,21 AMP

And of Gad he said: Blessed is He Who enlarges Gad! Gad lurks like a lioness, and tears the arm, yes, the crown of the head. He selected the best land for himself, for there was the leader's portion reserved; yet he came with the chiefs of the nation, and the righteous will of the Lord he performed, and His ordinances with Israel.

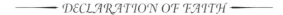

DECLARATION OF FAITH

Blessed is the person who blesses me! Blessed are they that enlarge my borders and promote me! An abundance of blessings be upon them!

I live in the land like a lion. I do not permit the enemy's presence. The Lord has set aside His best for me. A leader's portion has become my inheritance.

I will continually carry out the Lord's righteous will in my life.

(Genesis 12:1-3; 39:1-5; Ephesians 6:12; Numbers 23:24; Romans 8:17; Psalm 84:11)

DEUTERONOMY 33:27-29 KJV

The eternal God *is thy* refuge, and underneath *are* the everlasting arms: and he shall thrust out the enemy from before thee; and shall say, Destroy *them.* Israel then shall dwell in safety alone: the fountain of Jacob *shall be* upon a land of corn and wine; also his heavens shall drop down dew. Happy *art* thou, O Israel: who *is* like unto thee, O people saved by the Lord, the shield of thy help, and who *is* the sword of thy excellency! and thine enemies shall be found liars unto thee; and thou shalt tread upon their high places.

DECLARATION OF FAITH

My Father, the eternal God, is my refuge and my habitation.

His everlasting arms hold me as a loving Father holds His child.

He has driven the enemy from before me. He has charged me with destroying the strongholds of the enemy in this earth. I dwell in safety under my Father's protection and live in the land of abundance where He drops His dew down upon me from the heavens.

I am happy! Blessings are mine! The Lord is my Shield and the Sword that exalts me!

My enemy comes before me cringing in submission and obedience, and I tread upon his high places!

In all of this, I give glory to the Lord Most High!

(Psalm 3:3; 5:11,12; 28:7; 91; Joshua 2:9-11; Deuteronomy 2:25; 11:25; 33:12-16; Exodus 14:13-15; Ephesians 2:6; 1 Peter 5:7; Mark 3:27; Luke 10:19)

CHAPTER SIX

JOSHUA

The book of Joshua records the acts of a generation of faith. These are the promises given to those who are willing to do what God has called them to do. You will notice that each of these promises are of faith and victory over the enemy. We no longer need to be afraid of what Satan may do in our lives. If we will only resist him, he will flee from us in stark terror. See these promises as promises of resistance. Believe them, speak them and know that the greater One dwells within you to perform them.

As you pray these promises, know that God is speaking to you personally. He is with you at all times and in every situation. If you meditate on these promises and have no fear of the circumstances, you are destined to succeed. You have His Word on it!

JOSHUA 1:5-9 KJV

There shall not any man be able to stand before thee all the days of thy life: as I was with Moses, *so* I will be with thee: I will not fail thee, nor forsake thee. Be strong and of a good courage: for unto this people shalt thou divide for an inheritance the land, which I sware unto their fathers to give them. Only be thou strong and very courageous, that thou mayest observe to do according to all the law, which Moses my servant commanded thee: turn not from it *to* the right hand or *to* the left, that thou mayest prosper whithersoever thou goest. This book of the law shall not depart out of thy mouth; but thou shalt meditate therein day and night, that thou mayest observe to do according to all that is written therein: for then thou shalt make thy way prosperous, and then thou shalt have good success. Have not I commanded thee? Be strong and of a good courage; be not afraid, neither be thou dismayed: for the Lord thy God *is* with thee whithersoever thou goest.

——— DECLARATION OF FAITH ———

Through all the days of my life, not one of my enemies will be able to stand against me.

My Father is with me. Even more so, He has taken up residence inside of me.

Therefore, I will be strong and courageous. I have complete confidence in His ability to give me the victory. I encounter danger and difficulties with firmness and without fear. I am bold, brave, and resolute. I fulfill my calling in a spirit of valor and determination that overcomes any obstacle that the enemy would put in my path.

I do not turn from God's Word. I make it the cornerstone of my life so that I may prosper in all that I do.

I speak the Word continually. I meditate upon it day and night so that I may do all that is written therein. By this, I make my way prosperous, have good success, and deal wisely in all of the affairs of my life.

I do not shrink back from God's Word. I am faithful, strong, vigorous, bold, and very courageous! Fear has no place in my life, for the Lord is with me wherever I go!

(Romans 8:31-37; Ephesians 3:16-19; Hebrew 6:12; Deuteronomy 31:6,7; Psalm 1:1-3; Isaiah 41:10)

JOSHUA 2:24 NKJV

And they said to Joshua, "Truly the Lord has delivered all the land into our hands, for indeed all the inhabitants of the country are fainthearted because of us."

——— *DECLARATION OF FAITH* ———

The Lord has delivered my inheritance into my hands. I will go forth and possess it, for the Lord has made me well able.

All of my enemies melt in fear because of me. There is not an enemy in existence that can keep me from claiming what is rightfully mine!

(Psalm 37:9,22; Exodus 23:31; James 4:7; Leviticus 26:8; Deuteronomy 2:25; 32:30)

JOSHUA 8:1 NIV

Then the Lord said to Joshua, "Do not be afraid; do not be discouraged. Take the whole army with you, and go up and attack Ai. For I have delivered into your hands the king of Ai, his people, his city and his land."

——— *DECLARATION OF FAITH* ———

I have no fear and I am not dismayed.

I gather together with the church and we arise in pursuit of the enemy. Our Father has delivered him into our hands. We go forth and conquer all of his people, the city, and the land he has taken control of.

We do not permit the presence of the enemy in our midst.

(Deuteronomy 1:21; 31:6-8; Joshua 1:5-9; Ephesians 6:12; Hebrews 10:25; Luke 10:19)

JOSHUA 8:24-26 KJV

And it came to pass, when Israel had made an end of slaying all the inhabitants of Ai in the field, in the wilderness wherein they chased them, and when they were all fallen on the edge of the sword, until they were consumed, that all the Israelites returned unto Ai, and smote it with the edge of the sword. And *so* it was, *that* all that fell that day, both of men and women, *were* twelve thousand, *even* all the men of Ai. For Joshua drew not his hand back, wherewith he stretched out the spear, until he had utterly destroyed all the inhabitants of Ai.

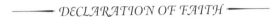

DECLARATION OF FAITH

I will not allow any of Satan's snares of sin to enter my life, I will stand against them, I will not relent, I will fight them as my enemies, I will give no place to the devil. I will give no place to sin. I will live a life of righteousness. I will not be slack in living a life of honor before my God.

(Hebrews 1:13; Joshua 6:20,21; 1 Samuel 15:2,3; 2 Corinthians 10:3-6; Ephesians 6:10)

JOSHUA 10:24,25 AMP

When they brought out those kings to Joshua, [he] called for all the Israelites and told the commanders of the men of war who went with him, Come, put your feet on the necks of these kings. And they came and put their feet on the [kings'] necks. Joshua said to them, Fear not nor be dismayed; be strong and of good courage. For thus shall the Lord do to all your enemies against whom you fight.

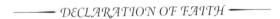

DECLARATION OF FAITH

I am strong in the Lord and in the power of His might! I am a man/woman of violent faith! I shall never yield to Satan and his allies! I continually slam the enemy to the ground and place my heel upon his neck!

(Ephesians 6:10-17; Matthew 11:12; Colossians 1:27-29; Psalm 107:40; Isaiah 26:5,6)

JOSHUA 10:42 NKJV

All these kings and their land Joshua took at one time, because the Lord God of Israel fought for Israel.

——— DECLARATION OF FAITH ———

I, with my brothers and sisters in Christ, conquer every spiritual kingdom in this earth one by one, starting with the ruler of my city.

(Ephesians 6:12; Luke 10:19; Matthew 28:18-20; 2 Corinthians 10:3-6; Joshua 10:14)

JOSHUA 14:7-13 KJV

Forty years old *was* I when Moses the servant of the Lord sent me from Kadeshbarnea to espy out the land; and I brought him word again as *it was* in mine heart. Nevertheless my brethren that went up with me made the heart of the people melt: but I wholly followed the Lord my God. And Moses sware on that day, saying, Surely the land whereon thy feet have trodden shall be thine inheritance, and thy children's for ever, because thou hast wholly followed the Lord my God. And now, behold, the Lord hath kept me alive, as he said, these forty and five years, even since the Lord spake this word unto Moses, while *the children of* Israel wandered in the wilderness: and now, lo, I *am* this day fourscore and five years old. As yet I *am as* strong this day as *I was* in the day that Moses sent me: as my strength *was* then, even so *is* my strength now, for war, both to go out, and to come in. Now therefore give me this mountain, whereof the Lord spake in that day; for thou heardest in that day how the Anakims *were* there, and *that* the cities *were* great *and* fenced: if so be the Lord *will be* with me, then I shall be able to drive them out, as the Lord said. And Joshua blessed him, and gave unto Caleb the son of Jephunneh Hebron for an inheritance.

——— DECLARATION OF FAITH ———

I am a man/woman with a good report.

I follow the Lord my God wholeheartedly.

Every place that the sole of my foot treads has become my inheritance. I claim it for the kingdom of God! It is an inheritance for my children and I for all of eternity! In this land, Jesus will reign supreme!

The Lord keeps me in strength and full of vigor all the days of my life.

I keep myself prepared for war. I am ever ready to do battle in the name of the Lord!

I maintain a spirit of strength and courage at all times.

The Lord is ever with me and I conquer the giants of the land.

I am bold to declare that I am to be blessed. In Jesus' name, I lay claim to my inheritance!

(Genesis 12:1-3; Joshua 1:5-9; Numbers 14:6-9; Deuteronomy 34:7; Isaiah 46:4; Ephesians 6:10-18; Romans 8:37; Galatians 4:5,6)

JOSHUA 18:3 AMP

Joshua asked the Israelites, How long will you be slack to go in and possess the land which the Lord, the God of your fathers, has given you?

———— *DECLARATION OF FAITH* ————

I am not slow or sluggish in claiming my inheritance. I go forth into battle in the power and might of almighty God and with unquestionable valor. With God on my side, I shall possess what is rightfully mine!

(Judges 18:9; Ephesians 6:10; 2 Corinthians 10:3-6; Romans 8:31; Proverbs 6:6)

JOSHUA 21:44,45 NIV

The Lord gave them rest on every side, just as he had sworn to their forefathers. Not one of their enemies withstood them; the Lord handed all their enemies over to them. Not one of all the Lord's good promises to the house of Israel failed; every one was fulfilled.

———— *DECLARATION OF FAITH* ————

Not one of my enemies has the power to withstand me. The Lord has delivered them all into my hands and has given me freedom from fatigue, troubles, and disturbances on all sides.

(Romans 8:31; Joshua 1:5-9; Deuteronomy 7:23,24; 1 Kings 8:56; Colossians 1:13; 2:13-15)

JOSHUA 22:3 NKJV

"You have not left your brethren these many days, up to this day, but have kept the charge of the commandment of the Lord your God."

———— *DECLARATION OF FAITH* ————

I do not desert my brothers and sisters in the Lord.
I am true to my calling and my place in the family.

(Hebrews 10:25; Numbers 32:33; 2 Thessalonians 1:11; Romans 11:29)

JOSHUA 22:8 AMP

And he said to them, Return with much riches to your tents and with very much livestock, with silver, gold, bronze, iron, and very much clothing. Divide the spoil of your enemies with your brethren.

——— *DECLARATION OF FAITH* ———

I spoil the enemy and take back what is rightfully mine. I return from battle with great wealth and riches; with an abundance of livestock and a plentiful supply of silver, gold, bronze, iron, and fine clothing. I return with an abundance of riches and divide the spoils with the Church.

(Numbers 31:27; 1 Samuel 30:24; Exodus 12:36; Joel 2:25,26; 2 Corinthians 6:10; 8:9)

JOSHUA 23:3 NIV

You yourselves have seen everything the Lord your God has done to all these nations for your sake; it was the Lord your God who fought for you.

——— *DECLARATION OF FAITH* ———

I give God all of the glory for the defeat of my enemies. It is He who has fought for me and has bid me to walk in His victory.

(Psalm 44:3; Exodus 14:14; Deuteronomy 1:30; 1 Corinthians 15:57)

JOSHUA 23:7-14 KJV

That ye come not among these nations, these that remain among you; neither make mention of the name of their gods, nor cause to swear *by them,* neither serve them, nor bow yourselves unto them: But cleave unto the Lord your God, as ye have done unto this day. For the Lord hath driven out from before you great nations and strong: but *as for* you, no man hath been able to stand before you unto this day. One man of you shall chase a thousand: for the Lord your God, he *it is* that fighteth for you, as he hath promised you. Take good heed therefore unto yourselves, that ye love the Lord your God. Else if ye do in any wise go back, and cleave unto the remnant of these nations, *even* these that remain among you, and shall make marriages with them, and go in unto them, and they to you: Know for a certainty that the Lord your God will no more drive out *any of* these nations from before you; but they shall be snares and traps unto you, and scourges in your sides, and thorns in your eyes, until ye perish from off this good land which the Lord your God hath given you. And, behold, this day I *am* going the way of all the earth: and ye know in all your hearts and in all your souls, that not one thing hath failed of all the good things which the Lord your God spake concerning you; all are come to pass unto you, *and* not one thing hath failed thereof.

———— *DECLARATION OF FAITH* ————

I do not mix with, combine with, or adopt as a companion (close friend) any unbeliever. I know that bad conduct corrupts good character. I am an example to the world, not a companion of the world.

I am a born-again child of the living God. I embrace my heavenly Father and cling to Him continually.

He has driven the enemy out from before me and has made it so that no one has the ability to withstand me. He fights for me in all of my battles just as He promised me on His solemn oath. A thousand of my enemies flee before me in a single battle.

I do not mix with unbelievers. I will not allow their doubt and unbelief to become a trap and a snare for me, nor will I allow their influence to rob me of my healing, peace and prosperity. I know that the abominations they place before my eyes will only cause me to stumble in my walk with God.

I am careful to set my love upon my Father with a pure and sincere heart. I commit myself wholly to Him and He fulfills His every promise to me.

(2 Corinthians 1:20; 6:14; Psalm 16:4; John 1:12; Joshua 1:5; Deuteronomy 32:30)

JOSHUA 24:11,12 NKJV

'Then you went over the Jordan and came to Jericho. And the men of Jericho fought against you—*also* the Amorites, the Perizzites, the Canaanites, the Hittites, the Girgashites, the Hivites, and the Jebusites. But I delivered them into your hand.'

———— *DECLARATION OF FAITH* ————

The Lord scatters the enemy before me. He sends His terror into their hearts and they panic in my presence.

(Psalm 2; 18:1-19; 44:3; Exodus 23:28; Luke 10:19; James 4:7; Deuteronomy 2:25; 32:30)

JOSHUA 24:15-18 KJV

And if it seem evil unto you to serve the Lord, choose you this day whom ye will serve; whether the gods which your fathers served that *were* on the other side of the flood, or the gods of the Amorites, in whose land ye dwell: but as for me and my house, we will serve the Lord. And the people answered and said, God forbid that we should forsake the Lord, to serve other gods; For the Lord our God, he *it is* that brought us up and our fathers out of the land of Egypt, from the house of bondage, and which did those great signs in our sight, and preserved us in all the way wherein we went, and among all the people through whom we passed: And the Lord drave out from before us all the people, even the Amorites which dwelt in the land: *therefore* will we also serve the Lord; for he *is* our God.

——— *DECLARATION OF FAITH* ———

As for me and my house, we will serve the Lord.

Far be it from me to forsake my Father who paid such an awesome price to recreate me in this way.

He brought me out of the land of slavery and from the house of bondage.

He has done great signs and wonders on my behalf and I will not forget it.

(1 Kings 18:21; Psalm 116:16; Exodus 23:24,25; Acts 4:23-31; Colossians 1:13; Luke 4:18)

CHAPTER SEVEN

JUDGES

The book of Judges contains promises of restoration and power to do the work God has called you to do. Even when we fail and it seems that we have ruined our chances for greatness, God is always there to restore. He never leaves you and never forsakes you. He always thinks of you within the boundaries of His mercy and grace. Just ask any backslider who has returned to the Lord. He will restore you and set you right back on the path of success!

These are promises of grace and power. No matter who you are or what you have done, God loves you and wants you to walk in His victory. As you pray these promises, remember that God sees the end from the beginning. He doesn't look at you through the veil of your sin; He looks at you through the triumph of Jesus' victory.

JUDGES 2:18 AMP

When the Lord raised them up judges, then He was with the judge and delivered them out of the hands of their enemies all the days of the judge; for the Lord was moved to relent because of their groanings by reason of those who oppressed and vexed them.

— DECLARATION OF FAITH —

My Father loves me and does not tolerate oppression against me. He is with me in all that I do and delivers me from the hands of my enemies.

(Psalm 18:1-19; Hebrews 13:5,6; Exodus 14:13,14; Joshua 1:5-9)

JUDGES 5:9 NKJV

My heart *is* with the rulers of Israel who offered themselves willingly with the people. Bless the Lord!

——— *DECLARATION OF FAITH* ———

I offer myself up as a servant to the family of God.
I bless the Lord and He holds me dear to His heart.

(Romans 12:1,2; Philippians 2:4; Psalm 103:1-18; Galatians 5:13)

JUDGES 5:31 NIV

"So may all your enemies perish, O Lord! But may they who love you be like the sun when it rises in its strength." Then the land had peace forty years.

——— *DECLARATION OF FAITH* ———

I am like the sun when it rises in its strength. All of my enemies perish before me and I live my life in peace and security.

(Psalm 37:6; 89:36,37; 2 Samuel 23:4; Ephesians 2:14)

JUDGES 6:12-14 KJV

And the angel of the Lord appeared unto him, and said unto him, The Lord *is* with thee, thou mighty man of valour. And Gideon said unto him, Oh my Lord, if the Lord be with us, why then is all this befallen us? and where *be* all his miracles which our fathers told us of, saying, Did not the Lord bring us up from Egypt? but now the Lord hath forsaken us, and delivered us into the hands of the Midianites. And the Lord looked upon him, and said, Go in this thy might, and thou shalt save Israel from the hand of the Midianites: have not I sent thee?

——— *DECLARATION OF FAITH* ———

I am a warrior in the army of God. I am intrepid—full of courage and valor—and the Lord is with me in everything that I do.

I do not allow circumstances to direct my faith. I go forward fearlessly in the will and power of almighty God.

It is my Father, the God of the entire universe, that has sent me to do His work. He has ordained me in my calling. He has anointed (empowered) me and I am well able to do what He has called me to do.

(Ephesians 6:10-18; Joshua 1:5-9; Isaiah 41:10; Philippians 2:12,13; Romans 11:29; 1 John 2:27)

JUDGES 6:23,24 NKJV

Then the Lord said to him, "Peace *be* with you; do not fear, you shall not die." So Gideon built an altar there to the Lord, and called it The LORD IS PEACE. To this day it *is* still in Ophrah of the Abiezrites.

——— *DECLARATION OF FAITH* ———

The Lord is Jehovah-Shalom to me. He is my peace. Therefore, I fear nothing. I will live out my days on this earth in a full and abundant life. I shall not die before my time.

(Ephesians 2:14; 2 Timothy 1:7; John 10:10; Psalm 91:16; Isaiah 46:4)

JUDGES 11:24 NKJV

'Will you not possess whatever Chemosh your god gives you to possess? So whatever the Lord our God takes possession of before us, we will possess.'

——— *DECLARATION OF FAITH* ———

The Lord has restored me to my rightful inheritance. What He has given, I will possess, for I am well able to possess it.

(Numbers 21:29; Ephesians 6:12; 1 Kings 11:7; Deuteronomy 9:4,5; Colossians 2:15)

JUDGES 15:14-16 KJV

And when he came unto Lehi, the Philistines shouted against him: and the Spirit of the Lord came mightily upon him, and the cords that *were* upon his arms became as flax that was burnt with fire, and his bands loosed from off his hands. And he found a new jawbone of an ass, and put forth his hand, and took it, and slew a thousand men therewith. And Samson said, With the jawbone of an ass, heaps upon heaps, with the jaw of an ass have I slain a thousand men.

——— *DECLARATION OF FAITH* ———

The Spirit of the Lord is inside of me. I function in all of His power and authority through Jesus' name. All of His strength and ability are within me at this very moment. I can easily break the bonds of my enemies and put them to flight. Even a thousand of them pose no problem for me.

(Joshua 23:10; 1 John 2:27; Philippians 2:12,13; Deuteronomy 32:30; Ephesians 6:10-18)

CHAPTER EIGHT

RUTH

These are words of consecration and commitment. Ruth left her old life and began anew with the children of God. The promises found in the book of Ruth give us hope that no matter who we are or what we have done, God is always ready to embrace us with love. He does not look for reasons to reject us. If we will but turn and give our lives to Him, He will receive us and give us our place in His family.

As you pray these promises, consecrate yourself to your heavenly Father. Make the commitment that He is your God and Father, and that you belong among His people.

RUTH 1:16 NKJV
But Ruth said:
"Entreat me not to leave you,
Or to turn back from following after you;
For wherever you go, I will go;
And wherever you lodge, I will lodge;
Your people *shall be* my people,
And your God, my God."

—— DECLARATION OF FAITH ——

I will not turn back to my old ways of living. I take my place in the family of God. They are my people and my dwelling is in their midst.

(2 Kings 2:2-6; Romans 8:12-17,29; 2 Corinthians 6:14)

RUTH 2:12 NIV

"May the Lord repay you for what you have done. May you be richly rewarded by the Lord, the God of Israel, under whose wings you have come to take refuge."

————— DECLARATION OF FAITH —————

I have taken refuge under my Father's wing and He has given me a full reward. Though I was not a part His family, He has adopted me, recreated me so that I am actually born again as His own son/daughter, and has given me all of the rights and privileges of an heir to His kingdom. He has comforted me and given me abundant favor in His sight.

(1 Samuel 24:19; Psalm 17:8; 36:7; 58:11; 91:1-4; Galatians 4:4-6; Romans 8:14-17; 2 Corinthians 1:3,4; 5:17)

CHAPTER NINE

1 SAMUEL

First Samuel is the story of the beginnings of the monarchy of Israel. The key figures in the book are King Saul and King David. Saul allowed pride and selfishness to enter his life and it led him to destruction. However, David was said to be a man after God's own heart. David didn't see God as distant and hard to reach. To the contrary, He saw Him as ever-present and ever-willing to help. David understood that God longed for fellowship. He understood that God's law was there for the purpose of guiding us to a fulfilling and joyful life, and not as a means of bondage. He understood that the law was for man, not man for the law. David's life shows us how God empowers and protects those who love Him. It shows us that God sees us differently from the way others see us. When others may see you as weak and without talent, God sees you as strong and well able to do what you are called to do.

As you pray these promises, know that, even though circumstances don't seem to be in your favor, they truly are. Time will expose your true calling and God's blessings upon you will be evident to all. Know that you are a favored one of God. He has set you apart and anointed you as His ambassador. You are a part of the royal line. You are a child of the King!

---

1 SAMUEL 1:17,18 NKJV
Then Eli answered and said, "Go in peace, and the God of Israel grant your petition which you have asked of Him." And she said, "Let your maidservant find favor in your sight." So the woman went her way and ate, and her face was no longer sad.

———— DECLARATION OF FAITH ————

I have chosen to be filled with joy. The Lord has given me His favor and peace, and has granted all of my petitions. Therefore, I will live in the fullness of His joy in my life.

(John 16:24; Psalm 20:3-5; Nehemiah 8:10; Romans 5:13; 14:17; 1 John 5:14,15)

1 SAMUEL 2:3,4 NIV

"Do not keep talking so proudly or let your mouth speak such arrogance, for the Lord is a God who knows, and by him deeds are weighed. The bows of the warriors are broken, but those who stumbled are armed with strength."

——— *DECLARATION OF FAITH* ———

I refuse to let arrogance go forth from my mouth. It is the Lord who works in me and not my own power.

He knows me thoroughly and weighs my actions.

He has lifted me from the place where I had fallen and has girded me with the strength to do His work.

(Psalm 94:4; 37:15; 46:9; Philippians 2:12,13; Ephesians 1:17-23; Jude 24)

1 SAMUEL 2:8-10 KJV

He raiseth up the poor out of the dust, *and* lifteth up the beggar from the dunghill, to set *them* among princes, and to make them inherit the throne of glory: for the pillars of the earth *are* the Lord's, and he hath set the world upon them. He will keep the feet of his saints, and the wicked shall be silent in darkness; for by strength shall no man prevail. The adversaries of the Lord shall be broken to pieces; out of heaven shall he thunder upon them: the Lord shall judge the ends of the earth; and he shall give strength unto his king, and exalt the horn of his anointed.

——— *DECLARATION OF FAITH* ———

My Father has raised me from the dust (the place where I am easily driven by the wind).

He has delivered me from the dunghill (the place of deep and filthy poverty). He has separated me from the beggarly elements of life and has seated me with kings and nobles.

He has made me righteous in the earth.

He guards all of my ways and gives me strength to do His will.

My Father thunders from heaven and my adversaries are defeated.

He gives me strength to walk in His victory and continually intensifies His burden-removing, yoke-destroying power within me.

(Ephesians 4:14; 2 Corinthians 8:9; Romans 5:17; Psalm 18:1-19; 1 John 2:27; 5:18)

1 SAMUEL 3:19 AMP

Samuel grew; the Lord was with him and let none of his words fall to the ground.

──────── *DECLARATION OF FAITH* ────────

The Lord is with me in everything that I do. He lets none of the words that I speak in faith, fall short of their intended purpose.

(Hebrews 13:5,6; Mark 11:22-25; Proverbs 18:20,21; Isaiah 55:11; 2 Corinthians 4:13)

1 SAMUEL 3:21 NIV

The Lord continued to appear at Shiloh, and there he revealed himself to Samuel through his word.

──────── *DECLARATION OF FAITH* ────────

The Lord reveals Himself to me through His Word. He sets it before me as an open display of Himself and through it I have intimate knowledge of Him as my Father.

(Hebrews 1:1,2; Daniel 2:22-29; Psalm 119:34-38; 97-101; 130; 1 John 5:20)

1 SAMUEL 9:6 NKJV

And he said to him, "Look now, *there is* in this city a man of God, and *he is* an honorable man; all that he says surely comes to pass. So let us go there; perhaps he can show us the way that we should go."

──────── *DECLARATION OF FAITH* ────────

I am a child of God held in high honor.

Everything that I say [in faith based upon His covenant promises] comes to pass.

I am set in this earth to be a guide to those who lack discernment and to those who cannot see the Light of life.

(Psalm 91:15; Mark 11:22-25; Proverbs 18:20,21; Job 29:21-25; 2 Corinthians 5:18-20)

1 SAMUEL 10:6 NIV

The Spirit of the Lord will come upon you in power, and you will prophesy with them; and you will be changed into a different person.

──────── *DECLARATION OF FAITH* ────────

The Spirit of the Lord is within me. I am not as I once was. I am a child of the living God! He dwells within my spirit. He is actually inside of me at this very moment. I am a son/daughter in the royal family! I have been born from above! I have been given the ambassadorship of heaven!

(Philippians 2:12,13; John 1:12; 3:3-8; 2 Corinthians 5:17-21; Ephesians 1:17-23)

1 SAMUEL 11:6 KJV

And the Spirit of God came upon Saul when he heard those tidings, and his anger was kindled greatly.

I do not tolerate an evil report. I stir up the fire of holy anger within me against all of the works of the devil. I will not permit him to operate in my circle of influence. The Spirit of the Lord prospers and thrives within me. By His Spirit and by the authority of His Word I come against and bring to naught all the plans, purposes, and strategies the enemy has arrayed against me.

(Numbers 13:30-33; 14:6-9; Luke 10:19; Mark 3:23-27; 1 John 3:8; Deuteronomy 33:27)

1 SAMUEL 12:22-24 KJV

For the Lord will not forsake his people for his great name's sake: because it hath pleased the Lord to make you his people. Moreover as for me, God forbid that I should sin against the Lord in ceasing to pray for you: but I will teach you the good and the right way: Only fear the Lord, and serve him in truth with all your heart: for consider how great *things* he hath done for you.

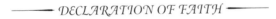

God has promised me that He will never leave me nor forsake me.

It pleases Him and gives Him great joy to call me His child.

He has placed me in His family. I now have a multitude of brothers and sisters of every race and nation. Far be it from me to ever cease to pray for them. They are my family. We are of the same blood.

The Lord directs and imparts His knowledge to me continually. He leads me in a plain path that is good and right.

I will honor and serve Him with all of my heart.

I will never forget the good things He has done for me.

(Hebrews 13:5,6; Isaiah 5:12; 43:21; Deuteronomy 7:6-11; 10:21; 31:6; Colossians 1:19-22)

1 Samuel 14:6 AMP

And Jonathan said to his young armor-bearer, Come, and let us go over to the garrison of these uncircumcised; it may be that the Lord will work for us. For there is nothing to prevent the Lord from saving by many or by few.

——— *DECLARATION OF FAITH* ———

I have absolutely no fear of the enemy. He may rise up against me with a garrison of soldiers, but the victory will be mine. It makes no difference to the Lord whether He demonstrates His victory through many or through few. I am His child; therefore, I am never alone. No matter what the testimony of the circumstances is showing, I have the victory!

(Matthew 19:26; 28:20; 2 Chronicles 14:11; Romans 8:31,37; Zechariah 4:6)

——— *DECLARATION OF FAITH* ———

1 Samuel 16:13 NKJV

Then Samuel took the horn of oil and anointed him in the midst of his brothers; and the Spirit of the Lord came upon David from that day forward. So Samuel arose and went to Ramah.

——— *DECLARATION OF FAITH* ———

I am anointed. God Himself has empowered me to be victorious in every situation I may face. His Spirit is within me in burden-removing, yoke-destroying power. From this day forward, regardless of what I see, feel, or even think, I recognize that this power is within me and I will act upon it in accordance with God's will.

(1 John 2:20,27; Ephesians 1:17-23; Philippians 2:12,13; Colossians 1:27)

1 Samuel 16:18 NIV

One of the servants answered, "I have seen a son of Jesse of Bethlehem who knows how to play the harp. He is a brave man and a warrior. He speaks well and is a fine-looking man. And the Lord is with him."

——— *DECLARATION OF FAITH* ———

The very Spirit of God has taken up residence within me. He has empowered me to be skillful in everything that I set my hand to do. He gives me extraordinary ability to perform the duties of my profession. In a spirit of excellence, He causes me to stand out from the rest of the world.

He has made me brave, courageous, and valiant. I am intrepid in danger.

He has given me power to express myself clearly and appropriately in influential and impressive speech. I am an engaging and attractive personality, for the Lord dwells in my heart and manifests His character both in and through me.

(Ephesians 5:18; Daniel 1:17,20; Genesis 39:2-5; Joshua 1:5-9; Acts 6:10; 1 John 3:24)

1 SAMUEL 17:45-48 KJV

Then said David to the Philistine, Thou comest to me with a sword, and with a spear, and with a shield: but I come to thee in the name of the Lord of hosts, the God of the armies of Israel, whom thou hast defied. This day will the Lord deliver thee into mine hand; and I will smite thee, and take thine head from thee; and I will give the carcases of the host of the Philistines this day unto the fowls of the air, and to the wild beasts of the earth; that all the earth may know that there is a God in Israel. And all this assembly shall know that the Lord saveth not with sword and spear: for the battle is the Lord's, and he will give you into our hands. And it came to pass, when the Philistine arose, and came and drew nigh to meet David, that David hasted, and ran toward the army to meet the Philistine.

——— *DECLARATION OF FAITH* ———

I have no fear of the giants in the land! They may come against me with their weapons of destruction, but I come against them in the name of the Lord of Hosts! I have the great and mighty army of heaven on my side and my captain is King of Kings and Lord of Lords! No great and powerful individual who defies the truth of God's Word can stand against me. This very day the Lord has delivered the giant into my hands. I will smite him down and cut his head off!

I run quickly and with purpose into the battle, for it is the Lord who fights for me!

(Deuteronomy 33:27-29; Exodus 14:14; Psalm 124:8; 2 Corinthians 10:3-6; Romans 8:31; Isaiah 52:10)

1 SAMUEL 18:14 AMP

David acted wisely in all his ways and succeeded, and the Lord was with him.

——— *DECLARATION OF FAITH* ———

I act wisely in all of my ways and succeed in all of my endeavors, for the Lord my God is with me to prosper everything that I set my hand to do.

(Joshua 6:27; Psalm 1:1-3; Deuteronomy 28:12,13; Proverbs 14:24; Genesis 39:2-5)

1 Samuel 20:14,15 NKJV

"And you shall not only show me the kindness of the Lord while I still live, that I may not die; but you shall not cut off your kindness from my house forever, no, not when the Lord has cut off every one of the enemies of David from the face of the earth."

——— DECLARATION OF FAITH ———

My Father is kind and loving towards me. He gives me a long, full, and abundant life on this earth and prevents death from taking me before my appointed time.

He does not cut off His kindness from my family from this day to eternity.

He has cut off every enemy from our midst and has stripped death of its power in our lives. We shall live and not die!

(Isaiah 46:4; Psalm 91:15,16; 103:13,17; 119:37; Deuteronomy 7:9; Job 5:26; 1 Corinthians 15:51-57)

1 Samuel 30:6 NKJV

Now David was greatly distressed, for the people spoke of stoning him, because the soul of all the people was grieved, every man for his sons and his daughters. But David strengthened himself in the Lord his God.

——— DECLARATION OF FAITH ———

When turmoil comes in like a flood, I will encourage myself in the Lord. I look to God and His Word for my confidence.

When others fail me and forsake me, God takes His stand on my behalf. Together, we overcome any and every problem that I may face.

(Isaiah 25:4; 59:19; Habakkuk 3:17-19; 2 Timothy 1:6; Acts 4:23-31)

CHAPTER TEN

2 SAMUEL

Second Samuel records more of the promises given in the life of David. Take note that David understood that he was in a covenant relationship with God. This brought him great joy and satisfaction in life. We too need to know that we are in a covenant relationship with God. His promises are presently for us and He is more than willing to fulfill them in our lives. This fact should spark such joy in our hearts that our praise becomes much like David's. He loved the Lord with all of his heart and worshiped Him with all of his might and with a sincerity that captured the heart of heaven.

As you pray these prayers, remember who you once were and how far God has taken you. Take account of His blessings upon you and forever be grateful for the wondrous things He has done in your life.

✠

2 SAMUEL 5:20 AMP

And David came to Baal-perazim, and he smote them there, and said, The Lord has broken through my enemies before me, like the bursting out of great waters. So he called the name of that place Baal-perazim [Lord of breaking through].

——— DECLARATION OF FAITH ———

The Lord routs my enemies like the breaking through of great waters—like the bursting of a dam which floods and overpowers everything in its path.

I storm through every obstacle that the enemy has devised for my destruction, for my Father is the God of my breakthrough.

(Psalm 18:1-19; Isaiah 28:21; Joel 2:1-11; 2 Corinthians 10:3-6)

2 SAMUEL 6:14 NIV

David, wearing a linen ephod, danced before the Lord with all his might.

—— DECLARATION OF FAITH ——

I give to my Lord a whole, sincere, and enthusiastic heart of praise. I loose myself from the bonds of dignity and praise Him with all of my might. I give Him my all and hold nothing back.

(Psalm 30:11; 42:1,2; 103:1; 149:3; 150; Deuteronomy 6:5; Acts 4:19)

2 SAMUEL 6:21,22 KJV

And David said unto Michal, *It was* before the Lord, which chose me before thy father, and before all his house, to appoint me ruler over the people of the Lord, over Israel: therefore will I play before the Lord. And I will yet be more vile than thus, and will be base in mine own sight: and of the maidservants which thou hast spoken of, of them shall I be had in honour.

—— DECLARATION OF FAITH ——

I will have fun, with a pure heart of enjoyment, in the presence of my Father. He has made me a child in His family. I am of royal blood!

I could care less what the world thinks! Let them think I am crazy! Let them think I'm undignified! My Father is worthy and I will exalt His name regardless of what others think.

(Psalm 103:1; 150; John 1:12; 2 Corinthians 5:17; Acts 4:19,20; 2 Samuel 6:14)

2 SAMUEL 8:6 NKJV

Then David put garrisons in Syria of Damascus; and the Syrians became David's servants, *and* brought tribute. The Lord preserved David wherever he went.

—— DECLARATION OF FAITH ——

The Lord preserves and protects me. He keeps me safe from harm and destruction. He is with me always and gives me victory wherever I go.

(Psalm 23; 91; Romans 8:37; 2 Corinthians 2:14; Deuteronomy 32:38)

2 SAMUEL 8:14 NIV

He put garrisons throughout Edom, and all the Edomites became subject to David. The Lord gave David victory wherever he went.

God has put garrisons at my command and gives me victory in all of my endeavors.

He preserves my life and keeps me from all harm.

(Matthew 26:53; Hebrews 1:14; 2 Corinthians 2:14; Psalm 91; Genesis 27:29,37-40)

2 SAMUEL 14:17 NKJV

"Your maidservant said, 'The word of my lord the king will now be comforting; for as the angel of God, so *is* my lord the king in discerning good and evil. And may the Lord your God be with you.'"

—— DECLARATION OF FAITH ——

My God is with me in all that I do. He has given me a mind of discernment like that of an angel.

The words that I speak give me peace and security on all sides.

(Proverbs 18:20,21; 1 John 5:20; 2 Timothy 2:7; Daniel 1:17,20; 2:22,23; 1 Kings 3:9)

2 SAMUEL 22:2-4 KJV

And he said, The Lord *is* my rock, and my fortress, and my deliverer; The God of my rock; in him will I trust: he *is* my shield, and the horn of my salvation, my high tower, and my refuge, my saviour; thou savest me from violence. I will call on the Lord, *who is* worthy to be praised: so shall I be saved from mine enemies.

—— DECLARATION OF FAITH ——

The Lord is my immovable fortress, my Rock of salvation and my deliverer from all of life's troubles. He is the source of my strength and my capacity to withstand the force of the enemy without breaking or yielding. In Him, I take my refuge. He is my stronghold and my guardian so that the thief cannot plunder me.

(Deuteronomy 32:4; Hebrews 2:13; Proverbs 18:10; Psalm 9:9; 46:1,7,11; John 10:10)

2 SAMUEL 22:5-25 KJV

When the waves of death compassed me, the floods of ungodly men made me afraid; The sorrows of hell compassed me about; the snares of death prevented me; In my distress I called upon the Lord, and cried to my God: and he did hear my voice out of his temple, and my cry *did enter* into his ears. Then the earth shook and trembled; the foundations of heaven moved and shook, because he was wroth. There went up a smoke out of his nostrils, and fire out of his mouth devoured: coals were kindled by it. He bowed the heavens also, and came down; and darkness *was* under his feet. And he rode upon a cherub, and did fly: and he was seen upon the wings of the wind. And he made darkness pavilions round about him, dark waters, *and* thick clouds of the skies. Through the brightness before him were coals of fire kindled. The Lord thundered from heaven, and the most High uttered his voice. And he sent out arrows, and scattered them; lightning, and discomfited them. And the channels of the sea appeared, the foundations of the world were discovered, at the rebuking of the Lord, at the blast of the breath of his nostrils. He sent from above, he took me; he drew me out of many waters; He delivered me from my strong enemy, *and* from them that hated me: for they were too strong for me. They prevented me in the day of my calamity: but the Lord was my stay. He brought me forth also into a large place: he delivered me, because he delighted in me. The Lord rewarded me according to my righteousness: according to the cleanness of my hands hath he recompensed me. For I have kept the ways of the Lord, and have not wickedly departed from my God. For all his judgments *were* before me: and *as for* his statutes, I did not depart from them. I was also upright before him, and have kept myself from mine iniquity. Therefore the Lord hath recompensed me according to my righteousness; according to my cleanness in his eye sight.

DECLARATION OF FAITH

I will not forget that I was once overwhelmed by the waves of death and terrified by the torrents of destruction. I remember when hell had me in its grasp. I was trapped—without hope and without God in the world.

But, in my distress, I called out to God for mercy. I laid my soul bare before Him and cried out for forgiveness.

My cry for help came before Him and He heard me.

He stood to His feet and shouted in defiance of the enemy. He made His proclamation that the enemy cannot have me.

My Lord shouted from heaven in a voice like the thunder. He sent His arrows and scattered the enemy. He sent His brightness and confounded them. He broke my bonds and set me free!

The forces of darkness came upon me in the day of my calamity and overtook me. They had me in their grasp, but God was my stay.

He stood up and fought for me. He took my troubles as His own and made intercession for me. He defeated all of my enemies and gave me His victory and His strength.

He brought me up into a prosperous place.

He delivered me because He loves me. He delights in me as the apple of His eye. He has rewarded me according to my righteousness—a righteousness He has given to me as a free gift. He has compensated me and has given me an abundance of benefits. For this, I am forever grateful.

I will walk in the ways of my Father. I now live according to God's way of living and thinking. I imitate His actions like a true disciple. I am firmly resolved to never turn aside from His statutes and His ordinances. I set my face like flint to live my life like a child of the Most High God.

(Psalm 16:8; 18:1-24; 31:8; 63:8; 104:3; 111:5; 119:3; 144:7; Ephesians 1:4; 2:1-14; Isaiah 10:20; 64:1; Deuteronomy 28:1; 32:23; Exodus 14:14)

2 SAMUEL 22:29-41 KJV

For thou *art* my lamp, O Lord: and the Lord will lighten my darkness. For by thee I have run through a troop: by my God have I leaped over a wall. *As for* God, his way *is* perfect; the word of the Lord *is* tried: he *is* a buckler to all them that trust in him. For who *is* God, save the Lord? and who *is* a rock, save our God? God *is* my strength *and* power: and he maketh my way perfect. He maketh my feet like hinds' *feet:* and setteth me upon my high places. He teacheth my hands to war; so that a bow of steel is broken by mine arms. Thou hast also given me the shield of thy salvation: and thy gentleness hath made me great. Thou hast enlarged my steps under me; so that my feet did not slip. I have pursued mine enemies, and destroyed them; and turned not again until I had consumed them. And I have consumed them, and wounded them, that they could not arise: yea, they are fallen under my feet. For thou hast girded me with strength to battle: them that rose up against me hast thou subdued under me. Thou hast also given me the necks of mine enemies, that I might destroy them that hate me.

——— DECLARATION OF FAITH ———

My Lord lights my way before me. He gives me His clear instruction to keep me firmly on the path of righteousness.

By Him, I claim victory over the enemy. I run through a garrison and leap over their fortified walls.

God's Word is ever before me. It is tested, tried and true. I put my complete trust in Him.

He is my Shield and my Refuge! He is my Rock and my Fortress!

He supervises my way before me and enlightens my understanding of His plan for my life.

He has set me free from all hindrances.

He makes my feet like that of a deer—firm and able—swift and graceful.

He has made me secure and capable. I maintain a steadfast resistance against the attacks of the enemy.

He has set me on the heights (as His top priority) and has established me with steadfast assurance and a boldness that cannot be shaken.

He trains my hands to do battle so that my arms can bend a bow of bronze. He has given me the shield of His salvation.

By His grace, He came down to my level that I may be lifted up to His level. He has enlarged my steps under me to keep me from falling.

His greatness is within me and by His strength I destroy the enemy. I refuse to turn back until they are consumed. I keep them at bay and they shall not arise!

My Lord has girded me with strength for the battle. I see nothing but the backs of my enemies as they turn tail and run from me utterly terrified!

(Ephesians 2:6; 6:12; Psalm 5:11,12; 12:6; 18:32; 27:1; 44:5; 119:105; Joel 2:1-11; Matthew 5:48; Hebrews 13:21; Isaiah 33:16; Proverbs 4:12; Malachi 4:3; 1 John 4:4; James 4:7; Romans 8:29-32)

2 SAMUEL 22:48-51 NKJV

"*It is* God who avenges me,
And subdues the peoples under me;
He delivers me from my enemies.
You also lift me up above those who rise against me;
You have delivered me from the violent man.
Therefore I will give thanks to You, O Lord, among the Gentiles,
And sing praises to Your name.
He is the tower of salvation to His king,
And shows mercy to His anointed,
To David and his descendants forevermore."

─────── *DECLARATION OF FAITH* ───────

It is God who executes vengeance on my behalf. He has brought down my enemies and placed them under my feet. He lifts me up above those who rise against me and delivers me from every violent attack. For this, I give credit where credit is due.

I thank my Father God for all that He has made me to be. I lift Him up, exalt and magnify His holy name. He is my strong tower of salvation and my great deliverance.

He is kind and loving to me at all times and has anointed me with His burden-removing, yoke-destroying power from this day unto eternity.

(Psalm 89:20; 144:2,10; Romans 15:9; Ephesians 1:17-23; 2:10; 1 John 2:27)

2 SAMUEL 23:2-5 NIV

"The Spirit of the Lord spoke through me; his word was on my tongue. The God of Israel spoke, the Rock of Israel said to me: 'When one rules over men in righteousness, when he rules in the fear of God, he is like the light of morning at sunrise on a cloudless morning, like the brightness after rain that brings the grass from the earth.' Is not my house right with God? Has he not made with me an everlasting covenant, arranged and secured in every part? Will he not bring to fruition my salvation and grant me my every desire?"

———— *DECLARATION OF FAITH* ————

The Spirit of the Lord dwells within me and His Word, in all of its power, is continually on my lips.

I have been established in this earth with supernatural power and authority. I rule in righteousness and in reverence for my God. He has made me like the light of the morning at sunrise on a cloudless day—like the brightness after the rain that brings grass from the earth. This is how my house (my family) stands before God. We are safe, secure and well established. This is a firm and fixed ordinance of His everlasting covenant with me.

His covenant with me stands sure so that all things in my life are ordered aright. He is my ever-present help and grants my every desire. All praise be to His holy name!

(John 14:16,17; 1 Corinthians 3:16; Joshua 1:8; Psalm 8:6; 89:29,36; Genesis 17:7)

CHAPTER ELEVEN

1 KINGS

First Kings begins with the passing of David and the emergence of the reign of Solomon. Any study of Solomon is replete with references to his unequaled wisdom. The mistake we sometimes make, however, is to think that he was just a special case and that such wisdom is beyond our attaining. This simply is not true. Solomon gained wisdom because he asked for wisdom. Have you asked for wisdom? Do you believe that you have received that wisdom? Then you have that wisdom!

Take note that with the wisdom God gave Solomon came health, financial prosperity and an abundance of blessings. As you pray these promises, know that you are no less than any of the characters in the book of 1 Kings. Solomon, Elijah and the rest were just men. God does not think of any of them as being any greater or less than you are. Therefore, if you have a need, ask according to these promises and you can rest assured that you will have their blessings in your life.

1 Kings 2:2,3 NKJV

"I go the way of all the earth; be strong, therefore, and prove yourself a man. And keep the charge of the Lord your God: to walk in His ways, to keep His statutes, His commandments, His judgments, and His testimonies, as it is written in the Law of Moses, that you may prosper in all that you do and wherever you turn."

——— DECLARATION OF FAITH ———

I am girded with the strength of almighty God. I walk in the power of His might and show myself to be His son/daughter. I walk in all of His ways and keep all of His statutes. His precepts and testimonies are forever on my lips.

I am a child of discernment, sound judgment, and discretion. I am enlightened with supernatural ability to learn. God's ways are opened to me and I am bold, shrewd, and wise in all of the ways of life.

In all that I set my hand to do, I am found to be successful and prosperous.

(Deuteronomy 28:12; 29:9; 31:7; Joshua 1:7,8; 1 Chronicles 22:12,13; Daniel 1:17,20)

1 KINGS 3:5 NIV

At Gibeon the Lord appeared to Solomon during the night in a dream, and God said, "Ask for whatever you want me to give you."

————— *DECLARATION OF FAITH* —————

My Father has given me the high privilege of asking what I will of Him. He welcomes me before His throne and entertains my every prayer.

(John 14:13,14; 15:7; 16:23,24; Hebrews 4:16; 1 John 5:14,15)

1 KINGS 3:9-14 KJV

Give therefore thy servant an understanding heart to judge thy people, that I may discern between good and bad: for who is able to judge this thy so great a people? And the speech pleased the Lord, that Solomon had asked this thing. And God said unto him, Because thou hast asked this thing, and hast not asked for thyself long life; neither hast asked riches for thyself, nor hast asked the life of thine enemies; but hast asked for thyself understanding to discern judgment; Behold, I have done according to thy words: lo, I have given thee a wise and an understanding heart; so that there was none like thee before thee, neither after thee shall any arise like unto thee. And I have also given thee that which thou hast not asked, both riches, and honour: so that there shall not be any among the kings like unto thee all thy days. And if thou wilt walk in my ways, to keep my statutes and my commandments, as thy father David did walk, then I will lengthen thy days.

————— *DECLARATION OF FAITH* —————

As God's child, I have a mind of the deepest understanding.

My spirit is perceptive and I have a hearing heart that is discerning between what is right and what is wrong. I clearly discern between the voice of my Father and the voice of the devil.

I seek my Father's kingdom and He is pleased with my prayer life.

I do not set my eyes upon riches to lust after them.

I seek the kingdom of God and His righteousness.

I am focused on attaining a discerning heart of wisdom.

I have been given supernatural ability to obtain and deal rightly with knowledge.

I do not have to worry about riches and protection. God surrounds me with these. I walk in the ways of my Father and do what is right in His sight. He lengthens my days on this earth and grants me the desires of my heart.

(Daniel 1:17,20; 1 John 5:20; 1 Corinthians 1:30; 2:10-16; Matthew 6:19-33; John 10:2-10; 1 Timothy 6:9)

1 KINGS 4:32-34 NKJV

He spoke three thousand proverbs, and his songs were one thousand and five. Also he spoke of trees, from the cedar tree of Lebanon even to the hyssop that springs out of the wall; he spoke also of animals, of birds, of creeping things, and of fish. And men of all nations, from all the kings of the earth who had heard of his wisdom, came to hear the wisdom of Solomon.

——— *DECLARATION OF FAITH* ———

I am creative and innovative.

I do not need to mimic what others have done, but have the creative ability within me to come up with new things to bless the world with.

I have a thorough understanding of my surroundings and I am an innovator and inventor of what is unknown in the earth.

My Father has given me tremendous insight into the workings of all of His creation.

(Daniel 1:17,20; 2:22,23; Ecclesiastes 12:9; 1 Corinthians 1:30; 2:6-16; 2 Corinthians 5:17-21)

1 KINGS 5:12 NIV

The Lord gave Solomon wisdom, just as he had promised him. There were peaceful relations between Hiram and Solomon, and the two of them made a treaty.

——— *DECLARATION OF FAITH* ———

The Lord has given me wisdom, common sense, and extensive knowledge, and I have peace on every side.

(Daniel 1:17,20; 2:22,23; 1 Corinthians 1:30; 2:6-16; Psalm 29:11)

1 KINGS 8:15 NKJV

And he said: "Blessed *be* the Lord God of Israel, who spoke with His mouth to my father David, and with His hand has fulfilled *it,* saying."

——— *DECLARATION OF FAITH* ———

My Father speaks with me face to face and fulfills all of His promises to me.

(2 Samuel 2:12,13; 2 Corinthians 1:20; 1 John 1:3)

1 KINGS 8:23 AMP

And he said, O Lord, the God of Israel, there is no God like You in heaven above or on earth beneath, keeping covenant and showing mercy and loving-kindness to Your servants who walk before You with all their heart.

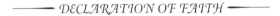

——— *DECLARATION OF FAITH* ———

I walk before the Lord with reverence and commitment. He makes His covenant with me to stand firm so that He may show me His loving kindness and tender mercies all the days of my life. His covenant with me is always for good and never for evil.

(Genesis 12:1-3; Deuteronomy 7:9; Nehemiah 1:5; Daniel 9:4; Hebrews 8:6; 10:16,17)

1 KINGS 8:56 KJV

Blessed *be* the Lord, that hath given rest unto his people Israel, according to all that he promised: there hath not failed one word of all his good promise, which he promised by the hand of Moses his servant.

——— *DECLARATION OF FAITH* ———

The Lord has given me rest.

All of His promises to me are manifested in my life. None of His promises fail me. Not one word that my Father has spoken to me fails to come to pass.

(Deuteronomy 12:10; Hebrews 3; 2 Corinthians 1:20; Isaiah 55:11)

1 KINGS 17:24 NIV

Then the woman said to Elijah, "Now I know that you are a man of God and that the word of the Lord from your mouth is the truth."

——— *DECLARATION OF FAITH* ———

I am a child of the living God and every word of His on my lips is truth—it is the true reality of my life.

(John 1:12; Psalm 119:30; Romans 8:14-17; 10:6-11; Mark 11:22-25; Joshua 1:8)

1 KINGS 18:21 NKJV

And Elijah came to all the people, and said, "How long will you falter between two opinions? If the Lord is God, follow Him; but if Baal, follow him." But the people answered him not a word.

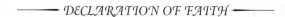

——— *DECLARATION OF FAITH* ———

I am fixed and steadfast in my faith. I do not waiver between opposing opinions. My heavenly Father is God. There is no other.

I turn my back on the forces of darkness and follow my God with all of my heart.

(2 Kings 17:41; Mark 11:22-25; Matthew 6:24; Joshua 24:15; James 1:6-8)

1 KINGS 22:5 AMP

But Jehoshaphat said to the king of Israel, Inquire first, I pray you, for the word of the Lord today.

——— *DECLARATION OF FAITH* ———

I do not go hastily into battle. My hands will not go to war until I have consulted my Father on the issue.

(Ephesians 6:12; Hebrews 4:16; 2 Kings 3:11; Isaiah 52:12; 1 Peter 5:5-7)

CHAPTER TWELVE

2 KINGS

Second Kings records the end of the life of Elijah (on earth), and the life of his successor, Elisha. The rest of the book records excerpts from the lives of various kings of Israel and Judah. Some of these kings were evil and some were good, but throughout their reigns, God's promises remained true.

The promises that stand out in the book of 2 Kings deal almost invariably with how God protects His children and grants them favor in all that they do. As you pray these promises, know that your Father stands with you as a sentinel in your life. He is your perpetual deliverer from all harm.

2 KINGS 5:10-14 KJV

And Elisha sent a messenger unto him, saying, Go and wash in Jordan seven times, and thy flesh shall come again to thee, and thou shalt be clean. But Naaman was wroth, and went away, and said, Behold, I thought, He will surely come out to me, and stand, and call on the name of the Lord his God, and strike his hand over the place, and recover the leper. *Are* not Abana and Pharpar, rivers of Damascus, better than all the waters of Israel? may I not wash in them, and be clean? So he turned and went away in a rage. And his servants came near, and spake unto him, and said, My father, *if* the prophet had bid thee *do some* great thing, wouldest thou not have done *it?* how much rather then, when he saith to thee, Wash, and be clean? Then went he down, and dipped himself seven times in Jordan, according to the saying of the man of God: and his flesh came again like unto the flesh of a little child, and he was clean.

— DECLARATION OF FAITH —

I am not offended by the requirements of the Lord and His prophets. Whatever the Lord requires of me, I am obedient to perform. Therefore, I arise cleansed of my infirmities. Sickness and disease cannot cling to me, for I have done what the Lord requires and He has declared that I am healed.

(2 Chronicles 20:20; Deuteronomy 28:1; John 14:15; Isaiah 53:4,5; Psalm 103:1-5; Exodus 15:26; James 5:14-16)

2 Kings 6:5,6 NKJV

But as one was cutting down a tree, the iron *ax head* fell into the water; and he cried out and said, "Alas, master! For it was borrowed." So the man of God said, "Where did it fall?" And he showed him the place. So he cut off a stick, and threw *it* in there; and he made the iron float.

DECLARATION OF FAITH

I do not show fear in adverse circumstances. In whatever state I am in, I know that God is on my side and will provide the miracle that I need to see me through.

(Joshua 1:5-9; Deuteronomy 28:12; Hebrews 13:5,6; Romans 8:31; Philippians 4:11-19; 1 Peter 5:5-7)

2 Kings 6:12 NIV

"None of us, my lord the king," said one of his officers, "but Elisha, the prophet who is in Israel, tells the king of Israel the very words you speak in your bedroom."

DECLARATION OF FAITH

The Lord makes known to me all that I need to know to do His will. He even tells me the deepest secrets of kings so that I may mount a defense for my family, my church, my city, my country, and myself.

(1 John 5:20; Daniel 2:22,23; 1 Corinthians 2:10-16; Isaiah 30:21; John 16:13)

2 Kings 6:13-18 KJV

And he said, Go and spy where he *is*, that I may send and fetch him. And it was told him, saying, Behold, *he is* in Dothan. Therefore sent he thither horses, and chariots, and a great host: and they came by night, and compassed the city about. And when the servant of the man of God was risen early, and gone forth, behold, an host compassed the city both with horses and chariots. And his servant said unto him, Alas, my master! how shall we do? And he answered, Fear not: for they that *be* with us are more than they that *be* with them. And Elisha prayed, and said, Lord, I pray thee, open his eyes, that he may see. And the Lord opened the eyes of the young man; and he saw: and, behold, the mountain was full of horses and chariots of fire round about Elisha. And when they came down to him, Elisha prayed unto the Lord, and said, Smite this people, I pray thee, with blindness. And he smote them with blindness according to the word of Elisha.

──── DECLARATION OF FAITH ────

I am not afraid when the enemy comes in like a flood. Though they come in by night and surround me with a great army, I am not stirred to terror. When others panic and cry out in fear, I remain steadfast.

I know the One in whom I have put my trust. I also know that there are more that be on my side than any army the enemy can muster.

I do not trust in what I see, for I know that what I do not see is where the real power is.

The Lord's angels have surrounded me to do battle on my behalf. Therefore, I cannot be shaken and I will not be afraid!

(Isaiah 59:19; Joshua 1:5-9; Exodus 14:13,14; 2 Chronicles 32:7; Psalm 55:18; 103:20; Matthew 26:53; 2 Corinthians 5:7; Hebrews 1:14; 2 Timothy 1:7)

2 KINGS 10:10 AMP

Know now that nothing which the Lord spoke concerning the house of Ahab shall be unfulfilled or ineffective; for the Lord has done what He said through His servant Elijah.

──── DECLARATION OF FAITH ────

Not one Word of the Lord spoken from my mouth goes unfulfilled.

(Isaiah 55:11; Proverbs 18:20,21; Mark 11:22-25; Romans 10:6-11)

2 KINGS 10:27 NKJV

Then they broke down the *sacred* pillar of Baal, and tore down the temple of Baal and made it a refuse dump to this day.

──── DECLARATION OF FAITH ────

I tear down, cast out and destroy everything in my life that brings glory to the devil.

(2 Corinthians 10:3-6; Matthew 5:29; 2 Chronicles 33:9-16; 2 Kings 10:15-30)

2 KINGS 13:4 NIV

Then Jehoahaz sought the Lord's favor, and the Lord listened to him, for he saw how severely the king of Aram was oppressing Israel.

─── *DECLARATION OF FAITH* ───

When I call out to my Father, His ear is opened to my prayers. He sees all of the circumstances in my life and is ever prepared to move on my behalf.

(Exodus 3:7-9; 1 Peter 5:5-7; John 15:16; 16:27; Hebrews 4:16)

2 KINGS 13:23 AMP

But the Lord was gracious to them and had compassion on them and turned toward them because of His covenant with Abraham, Isaac, and Jacob, and would not destroy them or cast them from His presence yet.

─── *DECLARATION OF FAITH* ───

My Father is always gracious and compassionate toward me. His actions toward me are always for good and never for evil. He has given me abundant favor in this earth and I have His Word that He will never cast me from His presence.

(Psalm 5:11,12; 103:8-18; Genesis 13:16,17; 17:2-7; John 10:28,29)

2 KINGS 18:3-8 KJV

And he did *that which was* right in the sight of the Lord, according to all that David his father did. He removed the high places, and brake the images, and cut down the groves, and brake in pieces the brasen serpent that Moses had made: for unto those days the children of Israel did burn incense to it: and he called it Nehushtan. He trusted in the Lord God of Israel; so that after him was none like him among all the kings of Judah, nor *any* that were before him. For he clave to the Lord, *and* departed not from following him, but kept his commandments, which the Lord commanded Moses. And the Lord was with him; *and* he prospered whithersoever he went forth: and he rebelled against the king of Assyria, and served him not. He smote the Philistines, *even* unto Gaza, and the borders thereof, from the tower of the watchmen to the fenced city.

─── *DECLARATION OF FAITH* ───

I do what is right in the sight of my God. All things that bring glory to the devil are cast away from my sight.

I put my complete confidence in my heavenly Father. I embrace Him with all of my heart. I cling to Him and follow Him without fail.

My heavenly Father is the God of my prosperity. By Him, I prosper in everything that I set my hand to do.

I refuse to serve the enemy! The enemy is smitten before my face and I arise as his conqueror in Jesus' name!

(Deuteronomy 28:1,12; Matthew 5:29; 2 Corinthians 10:3-6; Proverbs 3:5,6; Psalm 112:1-3; Romans 8:37)

2 KINGS 18:29-36 KJV

Thus saith the king, Let not Hezekiah deceive you: for he shall not be able to deliver you out of his hand: Neither let Hezekiah make you trust in the Lord, saying, The Lord will surely deliver us, and this city shall not be delivered into the hand of the king of Assyria. Hearken not to Hezekiah: for thus saith the king of Assyria, Make *an agreement* with me by a present, and come out to me, and *then* eat ye every man of his own vine, and every one of his fig tree, and drink ye every one the waters of his cistern: Until I come and take you away to a land like your own land, a land of corn and wine, a land of bread and vineyards, a land of oil olive and of honey, that ye may live, and not die: and hearken not unto Hezekiah, when he persuadeth you, saying, The Lord will deliver us. Hath any of the gods of the nations delivered at all his land out of the hand of the king of Assyria? Where *are* the gods of Hamath, and of Arpad? where *are* the gods of Sepharvaim, Hena, and Ivah? have they delivered Samaria out of mine hand? Who *are* they among all the gods of the countries, that have delivered their country out of mine hand, that the Lord should deliver Jerusalem out of mine hand? But the people held their peace, and answered him not a word: for the king's commandment was, saying, Answer him not.

———— DECLARATION OF FAITH ————

I am faithful and loyal to my heavenly Father. I am not moved by the threats, or even the wonderful offers, of the enemy.

Though sin has its pleasures for a season, I know the price that it demands. Therefore, I will not give in to it. My Lord has delivered me from sin. It has absolutely no power over my life.

The unrighteous pose no real danger for me. My heavenly Father has already delivered me from their hand. I am under His shield of protection and only blessings are allowed to cling to me. Almighty God Himself has taken His stand with me. With Him as my faithful ally, the threats of the unrighteous become increasingly ludicrous.

(Ecclesiastes 12:13; Hebrews 11:25; 1 John 3:8; Colossians 1:13; Psalm 2; 5:11,12; Genesis 12:1-3; Romans 8:31; Exodus 14:13,14)

2 KINGS 19:6,7 NKJV

And Isaiah said to them, "Thus you shall say to your master, 'Thus says the Lord: "Do not be afraid of the words which you have heard, with which the servants of the king of Assyria have blasphemed Me. Surely I will send a spirit upon him, and he shall hear a rumor and return to his own land; and I will cause him to fall by the sword in his own land."'"

─── *DECLARATION OF FAITH* ───

I have no fear of the words of the enemy and his underlings. My Father has delivered me with a sure and certain deliverance. When the enemy comes against me, he will fall by a sword from his own kingdom.

(Colossians 1:13; John 10:28,29; Psalm 2; 112:1-7; 2 Kings 19:35-37; 2 Chronicles 20:14-24)

2 KINGS 19:19 NIV

"Now, O Lord our God, deliver us from his hand, so that all kingdoms on earth may know that you alone, O Lord, are God."

─── *DECLARATION OF FAITH* ───

There is but one God in heaven above and on earth beneath, and He is my Father. He has delivered me from the hand of the enemy so that all may know that He alone is God and there is no power greater than He.

(Deuteronomy 6:4: Isaiah 43:10; Colossians 1:13; Psalm 83)

2 KINGS 19:21-35 KJV

This *is* the word that the Lord hath spoken concerning him; The virgin the daughter of Zion hath despised thee, *and* laughed thee to scorn; the daughter of Jerusalem hath shaken her head at thee. Whom hast thou reproached and blasphemed? and against whom hast thou exalted *thy* voice, and lifted up thine eyes on high? *even* against the Holy *One* of Israel. By thy messengers thou hast reproached the Lord, and hast said, With the multitude of my chariots I am come up to the height of the mountains, to the sides of Lebanon, and will cut down the tall cedar trees thereof, *and* the choice fir trees thereof: and I will enter into the lodgings of his borders, *and into* the forest of his Carmel. I have digged and drunk strange waters, and with the sole of my feet have I dried up all the rivers of besieged places. Hast thou not heard long ago *how* I have done it, *and* of ancient times that I have formed it? now have I brought it to pass, that thou shouldest be to lay waste fenced cities *into* ruinous heaps. Therefore their inhabitants were of small power, they were dismayed and confounded; they were *as* the grass of the field, and *as* the green herb, *as* the grass on the housetops, and *as corn* blasted before it be grown up. But I know thy abode, and thy going out, and thy coming in, and thy rage against me. Because thy rage against me and thy tumult is come up into mine ears, therefore I will put my hook in thy nose, and my bridle in thy lips, and I will turn thee back by the way by which thou camest. And this *shall be* a sign unto thee, Ye shall eat this year such things as grow of themselves, and in the second year that which springeth of the same; and in the third year sow ye, and reap, and plant vineyards, and eat the fruits thereof. And the remnant that is escaped of the house of Judah shall yet again take root downward, and bear fruit upward. For out of Jerusalem shall go forth a remnant, and they that escape out of mount Zion: the zeal of the Lord *of hosts* shall do this. Therefore thus saith the Lord concerning the king of Assyria, He shall not come into this city, nor shoot an arrow there, nor come before it with shield, nor cast a bank against it. By the way that he came, by the same shall he return, and shall not come into this city, saith the Lord. For I will defend this city, to save it, for mine own sake, and for my servant David's sake. And it came to pass that night, that the angel of the Lord went out, and smote in the camp of the Assyrians an hundred fourscore and five thousand: and when they arose early in the morning, behold, they were all dead corpses.

———— *DECLARATION OF FAITH* ————

I laugh at those who mock and revile me because of my lifestyle in the Kingdom, for it is not me that they have insulted, but the Lord Himself.

As for me, I shall eat the fat of the land. I take root downward and bear fruit upward.

My Father defends me from all attacks. He sends His angel before me to rout the enemy so that I may live in peace.

(Psalm 2; 20:7,8; 91:11,12; 139:1-3; Matthew 5:10-12; Romans 13:1; Job 41:2; Isaiah 31:5; Hebrews 1:14; Exodus 23:20-23)

2 KINGS 20:2-5 NIV

Hezekiah turned his face to the wall and prayed to the Lord, "Remember, O Lord, how I have walked before you faithfully and with wholehearted devotion and have done what is good in your eyes." And Hezekiah wept bitterly. Before Isaiah had left the middle court, the word of the Lord came to him: "Go back and tell Hezekiah, the leader of my people, 'This is what the Lord, the God of your father David, says: I have heard your prayer and seen your tears; I will heal you. On the third day from now you will go up to the temple of the Lord.'"

——— *DECLARATION OF FAITH* ———

I refuse to lay claim to an evil report. Any and every report that contradicts the Word of my God I consider to be false and misleading.

I know the power of God that is at work within me. He is faithful and what He has spoken will come to pass in my life.

Therefore, when the evil report comes, I set my face to the wall. I do not look upon, nor listen to, that which is contrary to the Word. I will accept nothing less than what God has promised.

I lay claim to my inheritance as God's son/daughter. Peace, joy, healing, and prosperity belong to me. I need only to remind my Father of these things and He changes the bad report to good.

(Philippians 4:6-9; Ephesians 1:3,11,17-23; Isaiah 43:26; 55:11; Psalm 56:1-11; Numbers 14:5-9)

2 KINGS 22:18-20 NKJV

"But as for the king of Judah, who sent you to inquire of the Lord, in this manner you shall speak to him, 'Thus says the Lord God of Israel: "*Concerning* the words which you have heard—because your heart was tender, and you humbled yourself before the Lord when you heard what I spoke against this place and against its inhabitants, that they would become a desolation and a curse, and you tore your clothes and wept before Me, I also have heard *you*," says the Lord. "Surely, therefore, I will gather you to your fathers, and you shall be gathered to your grave in peace; and your eyes shall not see all the calamity which I will bring on this place."'" So they brought back word to the king.

——— *DECLARATION OF FAITH* ———

I do not have to endure the present judgment on the world. When an evil report arises, I turn to my Father and lay claim to His promises. Because of this, He hedges me in with His protection. I will live out my days on this earth in a full and abundant life free of disaster and destruction.

(Galatians 3:13; 2 Corinthians 1:20; Job 1:10; Psalm 91; John 10:10; Isaiah 46:4)

CHAPTER THIRTEEN

1 CHRONICLES

The Chronicles are generally thought of as just history books. They "chronicle" the lives of David, Solomon, and many other kings and prophets mainly from the lineage of the tribe of Judah. Some have said that 1 Chronicles contains some of the most boring reading in the entire Bible. Yet, within these chapters comes such promises as the prayer of Jabez, and promises of protection and of God's anointing of creativity and inventiveness in your life. But, above all, you will find promises of God's desire for you to be His own child.

In receiving salvation, you are set apart from the rest of the world. You become a part of the lineage of the tribe of Judah. You are adopted into the family and Jesus becomes your elder brother. The Father's name becomes your family name and you become an heir to His kingdom.

As you pray these prayers, know that you are God's own child. Focus on how much you are loved. You are truly the apple of His eye and He loves you with all of His heart.

---

1 CHRONICLES 4:9,10 NIV

Jabez was more honorable than his brothers. His mother had named him Jabez, saying, "I gave birth to him in pain." Jabez cried out to the God of Israel, "Oh, that you would bless me and enlarge my territory! Let your hand be with me, and keep me from harm so that I will be free from pain." And God granted his request.

—— *DECLARATION OF FAITH* ——

I refuse to listen to false and disparaging reports that are contrary to what God says that I am. I am now a born-again child of the living God. I am bold to ask my Father for the deepest desires of my heart and I lay claim to all that He has given me.

God's hand is ever with me and His fellowship sustains me. When I enter His throne room I remain completely honest and without pretentiousness. Because of this, He gives me a place of high honor in His presence and pours out an unfailing endowment of abundance into my life. He enlarges my borders and shields me from all evil. Under my Father's tender care, I live a life free of worry and misery.

(Philippians 3:13,14; 4:8; Hebrews 4:16; Galatians 3:13; 4:5; 1 John 5:18; Psalm 103:1-18)

1 CHRONICLES 5:20 NKJV

And they were helped against them, and the Hagrites were delivered into their hand, and all who *were* with them, for they cried out to God in the battle. He heeded their prayer, because they put their trust in Him.

DECLARATION OF FAITH

My God is a shield to me in times of war. I arise as the victor in every battle because I cling to Him and put my complete trust in Him.

(Psalm 3:3; 5:11,12; 23; Romans 8:37; Genesis 15:1)

1 CHRONICLES 5:22 AMP

For a great number fell mortally wounded, because the battle was God's. And [these Israelites] dwelt in their territory until the captivity [by Assyria more than five centuries later].

DECLARATION OF FAITH

I am not moved by what I see. Vast numbers and overwhelming odds cannot nullify God's promises. The battle is His and I will always have the victory.

(2 Corinthians 2:14; 5:7; Hebrews 11:1; Joshua 23:10; Isaiah 55:11; 2 Kings 6:15-17)

1 CHRONICLES 10:13,14 KJV

So Saul died for his transgression which he committed against the Lord, *even* against the word of the Lord, which he kept not, and also for asking *counsel* of *one that had* a familiar spirit, to enquire *of it;* And enquired not of the Lord: therefore he slew him, and turned the kingdom unto David the son of Jesse.

DECLARATION OF FAITH

I am obedient to the Word of God. I do not consult psychics, mediums, and spiritists for guidance. The dead do not guide me. I am guided by the true and living God! I set this forth as a covenant commitment and I will not forget it.

(Deuteronomy 28:1; Leviticus 19:31; Jeremiah 27:9,10; Romans 8:14; John 16:13)

1 Chronicles 11:9 NIV

And David became more and more powerful, because the Lord Almighty was with him.

——— *DECLARATION OF FAITH* ———

My Father is with me and causes me to increase continually.

(2 Corinthians 9:6-11; 1 Samuel 16:18; Psalm 1:1-3; Deuteronomy 28:1-14)

1 Chronicles 12:32 NKJV

Of the sons of Issachar who had understanding of the times, to know what Israel ought to do, their chiefs were two hundred; and all their brethren were at their command.

——— *DECLARATION OF FAITH* ———

I am a child of understanding. I have unwavering ability to understand the workings of God and I know what I am called to do.

(1 John 2:20,27; 5:20; Daniel 1:17,20; 2:22,23; Luke 24:45; 1 Corinthians 2:6-16; Romans 11:29)

1 Chronicles 13:8 AMP

And David and all Israel merrily celebrated before God with all their might, with songs and lyres and harps and tambourines and cymbals and trumpets.

——— *DECLARATION OF FAITH* ———

I rise above all things that would hinder me from praising my God with a whole heart. I cast off all restraint and praise Him with all of my might in a spirit of celebration!

(2 Samuel 6:5,14; 2 Chronicles 20:19-22; Psalm 42; 150)

1 Chronicles 13:14 KJV

And the ark of God remained with the family of Obededom in his house three months. And the Lord blessed the house of Obededom, and all that he had.

——— *DECLARATION OF FAITH* ———

God's presence is ever with me to bless me. All that I have is blessed with His abundance.

(Genesis 12:1-3; 13:2; 14:22,23; 17:6,7; 28:18-22; 39:2-5; Galatians 3:9; Ephesians 1:3)

1 CHRONICLES 14:11 NKJV

So they went up to Baal Perazim, and David defeated them there. Then David said, "God has broken through my enemies by my hand like a breakthrough of water." Therefore they called the name of that place Baal Perazim.

——— DECLARATION OF FAITH ———

I serve the God of the breakthrough! By my own hand, He has broken through the strongholds of my enemies like the bursting forth of many waters! By His power within me, I swarm over the enemy like a flood and conquer them like a storm!

(1 John 4:1-4; Romans 8:37; Isaiah 35:3-10; Joel 2:25,26; Ephesians 6:10; Genesis 49:8)

1 CHRONICLES 14:17 NIV

So David's fame spread throughout every land, and the Lord made all the nations fear him.

——— DECLARATION OF FAITH ———

I am recognized in the kingdom of the enemy. At the sound of my name, they are terrified.

(Acts 19:15; Luke 10:19; James 4:7; Deuteronomy 2:25)

1 CHRONICLES 15:22 AMP

Chenaniah, leader of the Levites in singing, was put in charge of carrying the ark and lifting up song. He instructed about these matters because he was skilled and able.

——— DECLARATION OF FAITH ———

I am skilled in what God has called me to do. He has anointed me with great expertise on the job and in the work of the kingdom. In all matters that I am faced with, I am competent and well able to perform extraordinarily well.

(Daniel 1:17,20; 2:22,23; Ecclesiastes 3:22; Genesis 39:2-5; 1 John 2:20; Philippians 2:12,13; 1 Corinthians 2:6-16)

1 CHRONICLES 16:8-11 KJV

Give thanks unto the Lord, call upon his name, make known his deeds among the people. Sing unto him, sing psalms unto him, talk ye of all his wondrous works. Glory ye in his holy name: let the heart of them rejoice that seek the Lord. Seek the Lord and his strength, seek his face continually.

─────── *DECLARATION OF FAITH* ───────

I am grateful for what my Father has done for me.

I will continually call on His name and make His works known among the people.

I am devout and diligent in my worship. I will sing His praises continually.

I meditate on and speak of His works without ceasing.

My heart rejoices in His presence!

I am constant in my effort to seek Him in all of His strength. I embrace Him in love and put my whole heart into continually recognizing His presence within me.

(Psalm 105:1-15; Deuteronomy 4:9,10,29,40; Matthew 6:33; Romans 8:9)

1 CHRONICLES 16:14-17 NIV

He is the Lord our God; his judgments are in all the earth. He remembers his covenant forever, the word he commanded, for a thousand generations, the covenant he made with Abraham, the oath he swore to Isaac. He confirmed it to Jacob as a decree, to Israel as an everlasting covenant.

─────── *DECLARATION OF FAITH* ───────

My Father is the God of all the earth. His statutes and laws are in continual operation. I will work them and abide by them in steadfast commitment.

I am ever mindful of His covenant with me. He has commanded His promises to me and has established them in my life. His covenant with me has been confirmed, ratified, made definite, settled, secured, proven, and verified! It is mine forever!

(Genesis 12:1-3; 17:2; 28:10-15; 35:11,12; Deuteronomy 28:1-14; Hebrews 8; 10:16)

1 CHRONICLES 16:21-24 KJV

He suffered no man to do them wrong: yea, he reproved kings for their sakes, *Saying*, Touch not mine anointed, and do my prophets no harm. Sing unto the Lord, all the earth; shew forth from day to day his salvation. Declare his glory among the heathen; his marvellous works among all nations.

─────── *DECLARATION OF FAITH* ───────

My Father allows no one to do me wrong and get away with it. He rebukes even kings for my sake saying, "Do not touch my anointed one!"

I will sing to the Lord of His great salvation! I will declare among the people His marvelous works!

(Isaiah 54:17; Genesis 12:3,17; 1 John 2:27; Numbers 24:9; Psalm 105:1-15)

1 CHRONICLES 16:34 AMP

O give thanks to the Lord, for He is good; for His mercy and loving-kindness endure forever!

──────── DECLARATION OF FAITH ────────

My Father is good to me. His mercy and loving-kindness toward me endure forever!

(Ezra 3:11; Psalm 103:1-18; Hebrews 13:5,6,8; Genesis 50:20; Nahum 1:7)

1 CHRONICLES 17:8-10 NKJV

"And I have been with you wherever you have gone, and have cut off all your enemies from before you, and have made you a name like the name of the great men who *are* on the earth. "Moreover I will appoint a place for My people Israel, and will plant them, that they may dwell in a place of their own and move no more; nor shall the sons of wickedness oppress them anymore, as previously, "since the time that I commanded judges *to be* over My people Israel. Also I will subdue all your enemies. Furthermore I tell you that the Lord will build you a house."

──────── DECLARATION OF FAITH ────────

God is with me in everything that I do. He has cut off all of my enemies from before me. He has appointed a place for me in this world and has firmly established me.

The children of wickedness have no power over me. He has subdued my enemies beneath my feet and has established my house forever.

(Romans 8:31; John 14:16,17; Genesis 12:1-3; 24:40; Deuteronomy 29:9)

1 CHRONICLES 17:23 AMP

Therefore now, Lord, let the word which You have spoken concerning Your servant and his house be established forever, and do as You have said.

——— *DECLARATION OF FAITH* ———

The Word of the Lord concerning me has been established for all of eternity. Therefore, I can count on it being accomplished in my life.

(Isaiah 55:11; Proverbs 21:30; Psalm 119:89-93; 114-116; 2 Corinthians 1:20)

1 CHRONICLES 17:25-27 KJV

For thou, O my God, hast told thy servant that thou wilt build him an house: therefore thy servant hath found *in his heart* to pray before thee. And now, Lord, thou art God, and hast promised this goodness unto thy servant: Now therefore let it please thee to bless the house of thy servant, that it may be before thee for ever: for thou blessest, O Lord, and *it shall be* blessed for ever.

——— *DECLARATION OF FAITH* ———

I have confidence in my heavenly Father. He is on my side and I have no reason to fear. I have His Word that He will build my house in safety. My family—all of my posterity—is blessed. I rejoice in God's blessings upon my family, for I have this confidence: what the Lord blesses is blessed forever!

(Joshua 1:5-9; Romans 8:31; 1 Peter 5:5-7; Psalm 4:8; 103:17; Ephesians 1:3,13,14)

1 CHRONICLES 18:6 AMP

Then David put garrisons in Syria, [whose capital was] Damascus; the Syrians became David's servants and brought tribute. Thus the Lord preserved and gave victory to David wherever he went.

——— *DECLARATION OF FAITH* ———

Garrisons of angels fight for me against all of the attacks of the enemy and God gives me victory wherever I go.

(Hebrews 1:14: Matthew 26:53; Exodus 23:20-23; 2 Corinthians 2:14; 1 Corinthians 15:57)

1 CHRONICLES 18:13 AMP

He put garrisons in Edom, and all the Edomites became David's servants. Thus the Lord preserved and gave victory to David wherever he went.

——— *DECLARATION OF FAITH* ———

When I fight, the victory is sure! My Father preserves me in safety and gives me victory in whatever situation I find myself in!

(Matthew 26:53; 28:18-20; 2 Corinthians 2:14; Proverbs 18:10; Psalm 91; 1 Corinthians 15:57)

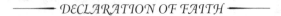

1 CHRONICLES 19:13 AMP

Be of good courage and let us behave ourselves courageously for our people and for the cities of our God; and may the Lord do what is good in His sight.

——— *DECLARATION OF FAITH* ———

I am strong and very courageous! My actions are not birthed in fear, but in courage. I am a bold and fearless child of the living God! I stand up courageously for my people! Through me, the Lord does what is good and right in this earth!

(Joshua 1:5-9; 2 Timothy 1:7; Philippians 2:12,13; 1 John 4:1-4)

1 CHRONICLES 21:24 AMP

And King David said to Ornan, No, but I will pay the full price. I will not take what is yours for the Lord, nor offer burnt offerings which cost me nothing.

——— *DECLARATION OF FAITH* ———

I honor the Lord with the fruits of my increase. I will not bring an offering to Him that has cost me nothing.

(Malachi 3:6-12; Proverbs 3:9,10; Deuteronomy 14:22-29)

1 CHRONICLES 22:9 NKJV

'Behold, a son shall be born to you, who shall be a man of rest; and I will give him rest from all his enemies all around. His name shall be Solomon, for I will give peace and quietness to Israel in his days.'

——— *DECLARATION OF FAITH* ———

I am a child of peace. My Father has given me rest even in the presence of my enemies.

(Matthew 5:9; 1 Corinthians 7:15; Hebrews 4; Psalm 23:4,5)

1 CHRONICLES 22:12,13 KJV

Only the Lord give thee wisdom and understanding, and give thee charge concerning Israel, that thou mayest keep the law of the Lord thy God. Then shalt thou prosper, if thou takest heed to fulfil the statutes and judgments which the Lord charged Moses with concerning Israel: be strong, and of good courage; dread not, nor be dismayed.

——— *DECLARATION OF FAITH* ———

I am a child of wisdom and understanding. I have been anointed with an abundance of wisdom so that I may be greatly successful in my calling.

Everything that I set my hand to do prospers and is brought to unfailing success.

I refuse to give in to fear and doubt. I am not dismayed. I am strong and of good courage, for the Lord is always with me to shield me and give me the victory.

(1 Corinthians 1:30: 2:6-16; 15:57; Daniel 1:17,20; Deuteronomy 28:12; Genesis 39:2-5; James 1:5-8; Joshua 1:5-9)

1 CHRONICLES 28:6 AMP

And He said to me, Solomon your son shall build My house and My courts, for I have chosen him to be My son, and I will be his father.

——— *DECLARATION OF FAITH* ———

God is my Father. He chose me to be His own child. I will not forget this great honor.

(Romans 8:29; John 6:37-39; 2 Thessalonians 2:13; Ephesians 1:4,5)

1 CHRONICLES 28:9 AMP

And you, Solomon my son, know the God of your father [have personal knowledge of Him, be acquainted with, and understand Him; appreciate, heed, and cherish Him] and serve Him with a blameless heart and a willing mind. For the Lord searches all hearts and minds and understands all the wanderings of the thoughts. If you seek Him [inquiring for and of Him and requiring Him as your first and vital necessity] you will find Him; but if you forsake Him, He will cast you off forever!

——— *DECLARATION OF FAITH* ———

I know my great Father God and I appreciate Him. I have personal and intimate knowledge of Him. I understand Him and hear Him. I serve Him with all of my heart and with a willing mind. He is the first and most vital necessity in my life. I am His forever.

(1 John 1:3; 4:7-21; 5:20; John 17:3; Jeremiah 9:23,24; Deuteronomy 8:3)

1 CHRONICLES 28:19,20 NIV

"All this," David said, "I have in writing from the hand of the Lord upon me, and he gave me understanding in all the details of the plan." David also said to

Solomon his son, "Be strong and courageous, and do the work. Do not be afraid or discouraged, for the Lord God, my God, is with you. He will not fail you or forsake you until all the work for the service of the temple of the Lord is finished."

———— *DECLARATION OF FAITH* ————

My Father gives me understanding in all that He has called me to do. I am well able to accomplish every task that is set before me. I have no reason to fear or be dismayed. I am strong and very courageous. I will not forget that my Father God is with me in everything that I do. He will not fail me. He sees to it that I have all that I need and stays with me as an ever-present help until all of the work is finished.

(1 Corinthians 2:6-16; 1 John 5:20; Daniel 1:17,20; Joshua 1:5-9; Hebrews 13:5,6)

1 CHRONICLES 29:5-9 KJV

The gold for *things* of gold, and the silver for *things* of silver, and for all manner of work *to be made* by the hands of artificers. And who *then* is willing to consecrate his service this day unto the Lord? Then the chief of the fathers and princes of the tribes of Israel, and the captains of thousands and of hundreds, with the rulers of the king's work, offered willingly, And gave for the service of the house of God of gold five thousand talents and ten thousand drams, and of silver ten thousand talents, and of brass eighteen thousand talents, and one hundred thousand talents of iron. And they with whom *precious* stones were found gave *them* to the treasure of the house of the Lord, by the hand of Jehiel the Gershonite. Then the people rejoiced, for that they offered willingly, because with perfect heart they offered willingly to the Lord: and David the king also rejoiced with great joy.

———— *DECLARATION OF FAITH* ————

I give offerings to the Lord freely—an abundance of riches—with a willing heart. I consecrate myself to giving as one consecrates himself to the priesthood. For me, it is a lifelong commitment and a joy. I am a happy and hilarious giver!

(2 Corinthians 8:2-5,12; 9:1,2,5-11; Exodus 35:21-35; Luke 12:33,34)

1 CHRONICLES 29:11-13 NIV

"Yours, O Lord, is the greatness and the power and the glory and the majesty and the splendor, for everything in heaven and earth is yours. Yours, O Lord, is the kingdom; you are exalted as head over all. Wealth and honor come from you; you are the ruler of all things. In your hands are strength and power to exalt and give strength to all. Now, our God, we give you thanks, and praise your glorious name."

———— *DECLARATION OF FAITH* ————

I am a child of the kingdom where my Father reigns supreme. His is the greatness, the power, the glory, the victory, and the majesty in my life. All of the heavens and the earth are His and He is exalted as head over all. He is my Father! It is He who grants me riches and honor—who makes me strong and causes me to become great.

God's name is my family name. I am His heir.

(Galatians 4:5,6; 1 Timothy 1:17; Ephesians 1:17-23; Genesis 12:1-3; Romans 8:32)

1 CHRONICLES 29:14-18 KJV

But who *am* I, and what *is* my people, that we should be able to offer so willingly after this sort? for all things *come* of thee, and of thine own have we given thee. For we *are* strangers before thee, and sojourners, as *were* all our fathers: our days on the earth *are* as a shadow, and *there is* none abiding. O Lord our God, all this store that we have prepared to build thee an house for thine holy name *cometh* of thine hand, and *is* all thine own. I know also, my God, that thou triest the heart, and hast pleasure in uprightness. As for me, in the uprightness of mine heart I have willingly offered all these things: and now have I seen with joy thy people, which are present here, to offer willingly unto thee. O Lord God of Abraham, Isaac, and of Israel, our fathers, keep this for ever in the imagination of the thoughts of the heart of thy people, and prepare their heart unto thee.

———— *DECLARATION OF FAITH* ————

I know that all that I have comes from the Lord. All that I can give was His to begin with. Therefore, all of my strength and ability to give offerings comes from Him alone. I am humbled by the realization that I am a steward, not a proprietor.

Therefore, all of my boasting is in Him! All of my joy is in Him! I do not give grudgingly, but cheerfully. I consider it an honor and a privilege to be able to give for the support of the kingdom. My giving is a declaration that God alone is in charge of my prosperity.

My purpose in life is to live the kingdom way — in God's way of being and doing things. He is the director of my thoughts and purposes. He establishes my heart as loyal toward Him and gives me every ability to walk in the power of His anointing.

(Malachi 3:6-12; Romans 14:17; 2 Corinthians 9:5; Matthew 6:33; Psalm 112)

1 CHRONICLES 29:28 NKJV

So he died in a good old age, full of days and riches and honor; and Solomon his son reigned in his place.

DECLARATION OF FAITH

I live out my life in satisfaction with a full number of days and will die at a ripe old age with riches and honor as an inheritance for my posterity.

(Isaiah 46:4; Psalm 91:16; 112; 119:37; Job 5:26; 29:18; Proverbs 13:22)

CHAPTER FOURTEEN

2 CHRONICLES

Second Chronicles records an account of the fall of the dynasty of David to the Babylonian exile. We learn from 2 Chronicles the importance of believing in God's Word and applying it to our lives. Without the Lord, our lives are meaningless and we will invariably find ourselves in bondage and depression.

The promises found in 2 Chronicles tell of the forgiveness and mercy that God grants us no matter how great our sin may be. No matter what we have done, our Father still loves us. He gives us His Word that if we will return to Him, He will be an enemy to our enemies and hedge us about with the shield of His protection.

As you pray these promises, examine yourself and take account of your weakness and know that when you are weak, your Father is strong.

2 CHRONICLES 1:1 AMP

Solomon son of David was strengthened in his kingdom, and the Lord his God was with him and made him exceedingly great.

——— *DECLARATION OF FAITH* ———

God stands with me as my partner in the kingdom. Everything that is done in my life, we do together. He is here with me at this very moment to strengthen me.

(Romans 3:31; Genesis 12:1-3; 39:2-5; Philippians 2:12,13; 1 John 4:1-4)

2 CHRONICLES 1:7-12 KJV

In that night did God appear unto Solomon, and said unto him, Ask what I shall give thee. And Solomon said unto God, Thou hast shewed great mercy unto David my father, and hast made me to reign in his stead. Now, O Lord God, let thy promise unto David my father be established: for thou hast made me king over a people like the dust of the earth in multitude. Give me now wisdom and knowledge, that I may go out and come in before this people: for who can judge this thy people, *that is so* great? And God said to Solomon, Because this was in thine heart, and thou hast not asked riches, wealth, or honour, nor the life of thine enemies, neither yet hast asked long life; but hast asked wisdom and knowledge for thyself, that thou mayest judge my people, over whom I have made thee king: Wisdom and knowledge *is* granted unto thee; and I will give thee riches, and wealth, and honour, such as none of the kings have had that *have* been before thee, neither shall there any after thee have the like.

——— DECLARATION OF FAITH ———

My Father is always ready to grant my requests.

He has given me His Word, with its many promises, that I may know His will.

He is always loving towards me and ever-ready to show me His kindness and mercy.

I am His own child and He loves me with all of His heart.

I am bold to make my requests known to Him.

Chiefly, I seek His kingdom that I may be wise in my dominion of it. Because of this, He has given me an anointed mind with tremendous ability to retain knowledge. He has given me His wisdom so that I may deal justly and righteously in all circumstances.

As a natural branch of His wisdom, He has given me supernatural ability to create and obtain wealth. It is my heavenly Father's great joy to give me an abundance of riches, possessions, honor, and glory.

He places the lives of my enemies under my power.

He is pleased to bless me continually so that I may live a long, full and abundant life.

(John 10:10; 14:13,14; 15:7; 1 Corinthians 1:30; 2:6-16; 2 Corinthians 1:20; 1 John 2:27; 5:14,15,20; Psalm 91:16; 112:1-9; 103:1-18; Hebrews 4:16; Matthew 6:33; Daniel 1:17,20: 2:22,23; Deuteronomy 8:18; Luke 10:19; Genesis 22:17; Job 29:18)

2 CHRONICLES 1:15 NIV

The king made silver and gold as common in Jerusalem as stones, and cedar as plentiful as sycamore-fig trees in the foothills.

——— DECLARATION OF FAITH ———

I am in the royal family and an heir to its riches! I am a child of the King!

(Psalm 112:1-3; Deuteronomy 8:18; Genesis 12:1-3; 13:2; Galatians 4:5; 2 Corinthians 8:9; 9:5-11; Matthew 6:25-33; Romans 8:17)

2 CHRONICLES 5:13,14 NKJV

Indeed it came to pass, when the trumpeters and singers were as one, to make one sound to be heard in praising and thanking the Lord, and when they lifted up their voice with the trumpets and cymbals and instruments of music, and praised the Lord, *saying: "For He is* good, For His mercy *endures* forever," that the house, the house of the Lord, was filled with a cloud, so that the priests could not continue ministering because of the cloud; for the glory of the Lord filled the house of God.

My Father inhabits my praises to Him.

I am intimately familiar with His goodness, mercy, and loving-kindness. He is not good to me just some of the time—He is good to me all of the time!

I am the temple (the house) of His Spirit. His love dwells within me! His glory fills this house!

(Psalm 22:3; 136; 1 Corinthians 3:16; 6:19; Galatians 4:6; Romans 5:5; 8:9,29)

2 CHRONICLES 6:20,21 NIV

May your eyes be open toward this temple day and night, this place of which you said you would put your Name there. May you hear the prayer your servant prays toward this place. Hear the supplications of your servant and of your people Israel when they pray toward this place. Hear from heaven, your dwelling place; and when you hear, forgive.

God's eyes are upon me day and night. He is relentless in His care and concern for me.

He has placed His name upon me and His presence is ever with me.

He listens to me and answers my every prayer.

He has forgiven all of my sins and claimed me as His very own.

(Psalm 23; Nehemiah 1:5,6; Job 36:7; Hebrews 4:16; 10:15-17; 13:5,6; Ephesians 1:4)

2 CHRONICLES 6:27 AMP

Then hear from heaven and forgive the sin of Your servants, [all of] Your people Israel, when You have taught them the good way in which they should walk. And send rain upon Your land which You have given to Your people for an inheritance.

God is pleased to forgive my every sin. He teaches me the way of goodness and rains His blessings down upon me so that I can live my life in prosperity and abundance.

(Psalm 103:1-18; 119:33-38; Deuteronomy 8:6-18; 28:1-14; Hebrews 10:15-17)

2 CHRONICLES 6:29-31 KJV

Then what prayer *or* what supplication soever shall be made of any man, or of all thy people Israel, when every one shall know his own sore and his own grief, and shall spread forth his hands in this house: Then hear thou from heaven thy dwelling place, and forgive, and render unto every man according unto all his ways, whose heart thou knowest; (for thou only knowest the hearts of the children of men:) That they may fear thee, to walk in thy ways, so long as they live in the land which thou gavest unto our fathers.

—————— *DECLARATION OF FAITH* ——————

All of my supplications, the prayers that I pray with a sense of need, are important in God's sight. From His throne in heaven He hears every one. And yet, I realize that He responds to each person according to their ways and not their needs.

Therefore, I make my ways the ways of God. My supplications are answered because I respond to His promises in the spirit of faith. I believe them with all of my heart and declare their reality in my life regardless of the circumstances. This is His way of receiving and I make it my own.

(Hebrews 4:16; 11:1,6; 1 John 5:14,15; Ephesians 6:18; Matthew 6:33; 21:19-22; Mark 11:22-25; 2 Corinthians 4:13)

2 CHRONICLES 6:39 NIV

Then from heaven, your dwelling place, hear their prayer and their pleas, and uphold their cause. And forgive your people, who have sinned against you.

—————— *DECLARATION OF FAITH* ——————

My Father has forgiven all of my sins.
He maintains my cause and answers my every prayer.

(Hebrews 4:16; 10:15-17; Psalm 18:1-19; John 14:13,14; 15:7; 1 John 5:14,15)

2 CHRONICLES 7:14-16 AMP

If My people, who are called by My name, shall humble themselves, pray, seek, crave, and require of necessity My face and turn from their wicked ways, then will I hear from heaven, forgive their sin, and heal their land. Now My eyes will be open and My ears attentive to prayer offered in this place. For I have chosen and sanctified (set apart for holy use) this house, that My Name may be here forever, and My eyes and My heart will be here perpetually.

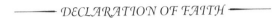

DECLARATION OF FAITH

The land that I dwell on is subject to my dominion.

When I humble myself and seek the face of my Father, He hears from heaven and brings healing to the land.

His ears are ever opened to my prayers and His eye never leaves me.

He has chosen me and set me apart as an ambassador of the kingdom.

He has placed His name upon me and His eyes and heart are with me both now and forevermore.

(Psalm 8:6; Ephesians 1:22; James 4:10; 1 John 5:14,15; 2 Corinthians 5:17-21; Genesis 12:1-3)

2 CHRONICLES 9:22,23 AMP

King Solomon surpassed all the kings of the earth in riches and wisdom. And all the kings of the earth sought the presence of Solomon to hear his wisdom which God had put into his mind.

DECLARATION OF FAITH

As an heir of the kingdom of God, I have the promise of riches and wisdom.

People notice the wisdom that God has placed in my mind and they seek my presence for understanding.

(Philippians 4:19; Daniel 1:17,20; 2:22,23; 1 Corinthians 1:30; 2:12)

2 CHRONICLES 12:7 NKJV

Now when the Lord saw that they humbled themselves, the word of the Lord came to Shemaiah, saying, "They have humbled themselves; *therefore* I will not destroy them, but I will grant them some deliverance. My wrath shall not be poured out on Jerusalem by the hand of Shishak."

―――― *DECLARATION OF FAITH* ――――

I have humbled myself and given my life to God. Therefore, He has vowed that He will not destroy me. His plans for me are for good things and never evil. He grants me deliverance from my enemies and His wrath shall never be poured out upon me.

(1 Peter 5:5-7; Ephesians 2:8-15; Jeremiah 29:11; Colossians 1:13; John 5:24)

2 Chronicles 13:7 KJV

And there are gathered unto him vain men, the children of Belial, and have strengthened themselves against Rehoboam the son of Solomon, when Rehoboam was young and tenderhearted, and could not withstand them.

―――― *DECLARATION OF FAITH* ――――

I do not follow the counsel of the ungodly. I am decisive in all that I do and I am well able to resist them when they try to turn me from the ways of God.

(Psalm 1:1-3; Proverbs 4:14; 2 Corinthians 6:14; James 4:7)

2 Chronicles 13:12 NIV

"God is with us; he is our leader. His priests with their trumpets will sound the battle cry against you. Men of Israel, do not fight against the Lord, the God of your fathers, for you will not succeed."

―――― *DECLARATION OF FAITH* ――――

My Father goes before me to shield me in all of my endeavors. His army is ever-present with me to sound the alarm in the event of danger. Therefore, no weapon, plan, strategic maneuver, nor instrument of destruction that is set against me can prosper. Those who stand against me are standing against the very Lord of the universe, for it is He who leads me into battle. I cannot be defeated.

(Isaiah 54:17; Psalm 2; Romans 8:31,37; Exodus 14:13,14; Hebrews 10:25)

2 Chronicles 13:15 AMP

Then the men of Judah gave a shout; and as they shouted, God smote Jeroboam and all Israel before Abijah and Judah.

DECLARATION OF FAITH

At the sound of my voice (my battle cry) my Father routs all of my enemies. It is He who fights for me and He gives me the spoils of victory.

(Psalm 2; 18:1-19; Exodus 14:13,14; 1 Corinthians 15:57; Deuteronomy 1:30; 8:6-18)

2 CHRONICLES 13:18 NIV

The men of Israel were subdued on that occasion, and the men of Judah were victorious because they relied on the Lord, the God of their fathers.

DECLARATION OF FAITH

My trust is in God alone. Therefore, the victory is mine.

(Proverbs 3:5,6; 1 Corinthians 15:57; 2 Corinthians 2:14; Romans 8:37)

2 CHRONICLES 14:6,7 AMP

And he built fortified cities in Judah, for the land had rest. He had no war in those years, for the Lord gave him peace. Therefore he said to Judah, Let us build these cities and surround them with walls, towers, gates, and bars. The land is still ours, because we sought the Lord our God; we have sought Him [yearning for Him with all our desire] and He has given us rest and peace on every side. So they built and prospered.

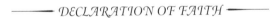

DECLARATION OF FAITH

The Lord grants me His peace in every circumstance.
I have put my complete faith and trust in Him.
I seek Him, longing for His presence with all of the passion that is within me.
He has given me rest in the comfort of His mighty arms.
I will work and build wondrous dwellings for His glory and enjoy the splendor of His prosperity.

(1 Peter 5:5-7; Proverbs 3:5,6; Psalm 35:27; Deuteronomy 4:29; 8:6-18; 33:12)

2 CHRONICLES 14:11-13 KJV

And Asa cried unto the Lord his God, and said, Lord, *it is* nothing with thee to help, whether with many, or with them that have no power: help us, O Lord our God; for we rest on thee, and in thy name we go against this multitude. O Lord, thou *art* our God; let not man prevail against thee. So the Lord smote the Ethiopians before Asa, and before Judah; and the Ethiopians fled. And Asa and the people that *were* with him pursued them unto Gerar: and the Ethiopians were overthrown, that they could not recover themselves; for they were destroyed before the Lord, and before his host; and they carried away very much spoil.

The Lord is my strong tower against the mighty. When a powerful enemy rises against me and the odds seem overwhelming, I need only to call upon the Lord, my Father. He is my shelter and a mighty warrior who takes His stand in my defense. He cannot be defeated. He routs all of my enemies [Satan and his allies] before me and bids me to plunder them of their riches.

(Proverbs 18:10; Psalm 18:1-19; Genesis 15:1; Exodus 14:13,14; Romans 8:31,37)

2 Chronicles 15:2 NKJV

And he went out to meet Asa, and said to him: "Hear me, Asa, and all Judah and Benjamin. The Lord *is* with you while you are with Him. If you seek Him, He will be found by you; but if you forsake Him, He will forsake you."

My Father is with me as long as I desire to be with Him. I seek Him with all of my heart. I crave His presence in my life as my soul's first necessity. He alone can bring me fulfillment in this life.

(James 4:8; Deuteronomy 4:29; Matthew 7:7; Proverbs 3:5,6; Psalm 91:16)

2 Chronicles 15:6-8 KJV

And nation was destroyed of nation, and city of city: for God did vex them with all adversity. Be ye strong therefore, and let not your hands be weak: for your work shall be rewarded. And when Asa heard these words, and the prophecy of Oded the prophet, he took courage, and put away the abominable idols out of all the land of Judah and Benjamin, and out of the cities which he had taken from mount Ephraim, and renewed the altar of the Lord, that *was* before the porch of the Lord.

I am strong in the Lord and in the power of His might. I will not let my hands be weak or sluggish, for I know that my hard work shall be rewarded.

I am strong and very courageous against evil. I cast it from my midst, dashing it to pieces in a wave of destruction.

I take special care and consideration for the things of God and the building up of His Church.

(Ephesians 1:17-23; 6:10; Psalm 2; 18:1-19; Proverbs 6:6; Malachi 3:6-12)

2 CHRONICLES 15:12,13 AMP

And they entered into a covenant to seek the Lord, the God of their fathers, and to yearn for Him with all their heart's desire and with all their soul; And that whoever would not seek the Lord, the God of Israel, should be put to death, whether young or old, man or woman.

——— *DECLARATION OF FAITH* ———

I take my oath before the Lord this day to seek Him with all of my heart—to cling to Him with all that is within me. I set it forth as a covenant contract, for the Lord has promised that if I seek Him with all of my heart, I shall find Him, and if I draw near to Him, He will draw near to me. In this, I find cause to shout, sing, and praise His holy name!

(Deuteronomy 4:29; Psalm 42:1; James 4:8; Nehemiah 10:29; Proverbs 3:5,6)

2 CHRONICLES 16:7 AMP

At that time Hanani the seer came to Asa king of Judah and said to him, Because you relied on the king of Syria and not on the Lord your God, the army of the king of Syria has escaped you.

——— *DECLARATION OF FAITH* ———

The Lord is my provision. I do not put my trust and reliance on others in order to obtain what the Lord Himself has promised to provide.

(Philippians 4:19; Matthew 6:19-33; Isaiah 31:1; Genesis 22:14)

2 CHRONICLES 17:6 AMP

His heart was cheered and his courage was high in the ways of the Lord; moreover, he took away the high places and the Asherim out of Judah.

——— *DECLARATION OF FAITH* ———

My heart is filled with courage and joy in the ways of God.
I do not tolerate the devil's presence in my life. His ways bring fear, sorrow, pain, and destruction.

I follow the ways of the Lord and cast the devil, and everything that he stands for, away from my presence!

(Psalm 1:1-3; 2 Timothy 1:7; James 4:7; Mark 16:17; Luke 9:1; 10:17-19)

2 CHRONICLES 18:4 NIV

But Jehoshaphat also said to the king of Israel, "First seek the counsel of the Lord."

————— *DECLARATION OF FAITH* —————

My first thought in every circumstance is to seek a Word from the Lord.

(Matthew 6:33; 1 Samuel 23:2-9; 2 Samuel 2:1; Psalm 119:105)

2 CHRONICLES 19:9 AMP

The king charged them, Do this in the fear of the Lord, faithfully, with integrity and a blameless heart.

————— *DECLARATION OF FAITH* —————

I fulfill my calling faithfully, with integrity and an undivided heart.

(2 Samuel 23:3; 2 Peter 1:10; Romans 11:29; Philippians 3:14)

2 CHRONICLES 20:6-12 KJV

And said, O Lord God of our fathers, *art* not thou God in heaven? and rulest *not* thou over all the kingdoms of the heathen? and in thine hand *is there not* power and might, so that none is able to withstand thee? *Art* not thou our God, *who* didst drive out the inhabitants of this land before thy people Israel, and gavest it to the seed of Abraham thy friend for ever? And they dwelt therein, and have built thee a sanctuary therein for thy name, saying, If, *when* evil cometh upon us, *as* the sword, judgment, or pestilence, or famine, we stand before this house, and in thy presence, (for thy name *is* in this house,) and cry unto thee in our affliction, then thou wilt hear and help. And now, behold, the children of Ammon and Moab and mount Seir, whom thou wouldest not let Israel invade, when they came out of the land of Egypt, but they turned from them, and destroyed them not; Behold, *I say, how* they reward us, to come to cast us out of thy possession, which thou hast given us to inherit. O our God, wilt thou not judge them? for we have no might against this great company that cometh against us; neither know we what to do: but our eyes are upon thee.

——— *DECLARATION OF FAITH* ———

When the enemy comes in great numbers to spark fear and dread in the hearts of men, I will stand my ground. The greater One dwells within me with His awesome power and might. He has drawn me close to Himself and has made me His companion and friend. With Him on my side, no one can stand against me. Therefore, I will keep my eyes fixed upon my Redeemer and I will not be afraid.

(2 Timothy 1:7; 2 Kings 6:15-17; Joshua 1:5-9: 1 John 4:1-4; Romans 8:31)

2 CHRONICLES 20:15-26 KJV

And he said, Hearken ye, all Judah, and ye inhabitants of Jerusalem, and thou king Jehoshaphat, Thus saith the Lord unto you, Be not afraid nor dismayed by reason of this great multitude; for the battle *is* not yours, but God's. To morrow go ye down against them: behold, they come up by the cliff of Ziz; and ye shall find them at the end of the brook, before the wilderness of Jeruel. Ye shall not *need* to fight in this *battle:* set yourselves, stand ye *still,* and see the salvation of the Lord with you, O Judah and Jerusalem: fear not, nor be dismayed; to morrow go out against them: for the Lord *will be* with you. And Jehoshaphat bowed his head with *his* face to the ground: and all Judah and the inhabitants of Jerusalem fell before the Lord, worshipping the Lord. And the Levites, of the children of the Kohathites, and of the children of the Korhites, stood up to praise the Lord God of Israel with a loud voice on high. And they rose early in the morning, and went forth into the wilderness of Tekoa: and as they went forth, Jehoshaphat stood and said, Hear me, O Judah, and ye inhabitants of Jerusalem; Believe in the Lord your God, so shall ye be established; believe his prophets, so shall ye prosper. And when he had consulted with the people, he appointed singers unto the Lord, and that should praise the beauty of holiness, as they went out before the army, and to say, Praise the Lord; for his mercy *endureth* for ever. And when they began to sing and to praise, the Lord set ambushments against the children of Ammon, Moab, and mount Seir, which were come against Judah; and they were smitten. For the children of Ammon and Moab stood up against the inhabitants of mount Seir, utterly to slay and destroy *them:* and when they had made an end of the inhabitants of Seir, every one helped to destroy another. And when Judah came toward the watch tower in the wilderness, they looked unto the multitude, and, behold, they *were* dead bodies fallen to the earth, and none escaped. And when Jehoshaphat and his people came to take away the spoil of them, they found among them in abundance both riches with the dead bodies, and precious jewels, which they stripped off for themselves, more than they could carry away: and they were three days in gathering of the spoil, it was so much. And on the fourth day they assembled themselves in the valley of Berachah; for there they blessed the Lord: therefore the name of the same place was called, The valley of Berachah, unto this day.

——— *DECLARATION OF FAITH* ———

I have set my face like flint to be true to the Lord. I hold fast to His promises and trust in the security of our covenant. Therefore, I remain confident that when the enemy attacks me with a great horde of allies bent on my destruction, the Lord shall stand to His feet and make His proclamation, "This battle is Mine!"

Whom shall I fear? Who can defeat my Father in heaven? He is the Lord of Hosts! I shall not be afraid! I shall take my position and stand my ground!

I listen for my Father's commands. I take heed to the voice of His prophets and I prosper in the midst of the turmoil. I praise His name for the victory even in the heat of the battle. I give Him glory, for His mercy and loving-kindness endure forever!

I shall see the enemy fall in a great destruction, for the battle belongs to the Lord! Despite the battles that I must endure, my Father showers me with an endless supply of blessings.

(Deuteronomy 1:29,30; 20:14; 1 Samuel 14:20; 17:47; Exodus 3:22; 14:13,14; Numbers 14:9; Isaiah 7:9; Judges 7:22; 2 Corinthians 1:20; Romans 8:31; Psalm 91; 136; Luke 10:17-19; Genesis 12:1-3)

2 CHRONICLES 20:27-30 AMP

Then they returned, every man of Judah and Jerusalem, Jehoshaphat leading them, to Jerusalem with joy, for the Lord had made them to rejoice over their enemies. They came to Jerusalem with harps, lyres, and trumpets to the house of the Lord. And the fear of God came upon all the kingdoms of those countries when they heard that the Lord had fought against the enemies of Israel. So the realm of Jehoshaphat was quiet, for his God gave him rest round about.

——— *DECLARATION OF FAITH* ———

The Lord gives me cause to rejoice at the defeat of my enemies. I will gather with His people regularly and lift His holy name high in shouts of praise. My Father has given me His peace and I have rest on every side.

(Ephesians 6:12; Nehemiah 12:43; 2 Chronicles 14:14; 1 Kings 22:41-43; James 4:7; Hebrews 4)

2 CHRONICLES 26:5 NKJV

He sought God in the days of Zechariah, who had understanding in the visions of God; and as long as he sought the Lord, God made him prosper.

I stand on the Lord's promise that as long as I seek Him, He will give me success in all that I do.

(Matthew 6:33; Deuteronomy 28:1-14; Genesis 39:2-5; 2 Chronicles 20:20)

2 CHRONICLES 26:15,16 AMP

In Jerusalem he made machines invented by skillful men to be on the towers and the [corner] bulwarks, with which to shoot arrows and great stones. And his fame spread far, for he was marvelously helped till he was strong. But when [King Uzziah] was strong, he became proud to his destruction; and he trespassed against the Lord his God, for he went into the temple of the Lord to burn incense on the altar of incense.

I have been given a mind of creativity for designing and building. In all that I do, I am greatly helped by the Lord.

I will not forget what He has done for me and will remain faithful to Him all the days of my life.

(1 Corinthians 1:30; 2:6-16; Daniel 1:17,20; Philippians 2:12,13; Psalm 103:1-5)

2 CHRONICLES 27:6 NKJV

So Jotham became mighty, because he prepared his ways before the Lord his God.

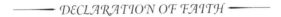

I am a person of dynamic energy and indomitable strength because I walk steadfastly before the Lord.

(Isaiah 40:29-31; 41:10; 1 Peter 3:1-6; Nehemiah 6:9; Ephesians 6:10)

2 CHRONICLES 30:6-9 KJV

So the posts went with the letters from the king and his princes throughout all Israel and Judah, and according to the commandment of the king, saying, Ye children of Israel, turn again unto the Lord God of Abraham, Isaac, and Israel, and he will return to the remnant of you, that are escaped out of the hand of the kings of Assyria. And be not ye like your fathers, and like your brethren, which trespassed against the Lord God of their fathers, *who* therefore gave them up to desolation, as ye see. Now be ye not stiffnecked, as your fathers *were, but* yield yourselves unto the Lord, and enter into his sanctuary, which he hath sanctified for ever: and serve the Lord your God, that the fierceness of his wrath may turn away from you. For if ye turn again unto the Lord, your brethren and your children *shall find* compassion before them that lead them captive, so that they shall come again into this land: for the Lord your God *is* gracious and merciful, and will not turn away *his* face from you, if ye return unto him.

──────── *DECLARATION OF FAITH* ────────

I commit myself wholly to my heavenly Father. I am submitted to Him and shall serve Him all the days of my life.

He is gracious and compassionate towards me. His love for me is incessant. His commitment to me is everlasting.

(Deuteronomy 4:29; 28:1; James 4:7; Psalm 103:1-18; Hebrews 10:15-17; John 3:16)

2 CHRONICLES 30:18-20 AMP

For a multitude of the people, many from Ephraim, Manasseh, Issachar, and Zebulun, had not cleansed themselves, yet they ate the Passover otherwise than Moses directed. For Hezekiah had prayed for them, saying, May the good Lord pardon everyone who sets his heart to seek and yearn for God—the Lord, the God of his fathers—even though not complying with the purification regulations of the sanctuary. And the Lord hearkened to Hezekiah and healed the people.

──────── *DECLARATION OF FAITH* ────────

Though I have sinned horribly in His sight, my Father has forgiven me. I sought Him with all of my heart and He heard my cry for mercy. Though I was unclean, He pardoned me. Though I was undeserving, He placed His loving hands upon me and healed me.

(Psalm 18:1-19; 103:1-12; 2 Chronicles 19:3; Romans 3:21-26; Ephesians 2:1-10)

2 CHRONICLES 30:27 NIV

The priests and the Levites stood to bless the people, and God heard them, for their prayer reached heaven, his holy dwelling place.

———— *DECLARATION OF FAITH* ————

God's ear is opened to all of my prayers. They reach His very throne in heaven and He answers every one.

(Hebrews 4:16; 1 John 5:15,16; John 14:13,14; 15:7; Psalm 91:15; Isaiah 43:1,2)

2 CHRONICLES 31:10 NKJV

And Azariah the chief priest, from the house of Zadok, answered him and said, "Since *the people* began to bring the offerings into the house of the Lord, we have had enough to eat and have plenty left, for the Lord has blessed His people; and what is left *is* this great abundance."

———— *DECLARATION OF FAITH* ————

Because I freely give my offerings in the Church, I have enough to eat and plenty to spare.

The Lord has blessed me with a tremendous blessing and has granted me an excessive bounty.

(2 Corinthians 9:6-11; Malachi 3:10,11; Proverbs 3:9,10; Exodus 36:2-7)

2 CHRONICLES 31:20,21 AMP

Hezekiah did this throughout all Judah, and he did what was good, right, and faithful before the Lord his God. And every work that he began in the service of the house of God, in keeping with the law and the commandments to seek his God [inquiring of and yearning for Him], he did with all his heart, and he prospered.

———— *DECLARATION OF FAITH* ————

I choose to do what is good, right, and faithful before the Lord. In everything that I do, in my service to the church and obedience to God's ways, I work wholeheartedly, seeking the advancement of His kingdom. And so, I prosper.

(Joshua 1:8; Matthew 6:33; 2 Kings 20:3; Psalm 1:1-3; Colossians 3:17)

2 CHRONICLES 32:7,8 AMP

Be strong and courageous. Be not afraid or dismayed before the king of Assyria and all the horde that is with him, for there is Another with us greater than [all those] with him. With him is an arm of flesh, but with us is the Lord our God to help us and to fight our battles. And the people relied on the words of Hezekiah king of Judah.

———— DECLARATION OF FAITH ————

I am strong and very courageous. I am not afraid of the vast army arrayed against me. I know the One in whom I have believed. The greater One is within me and nothing shall by any means harm me.

God's power is vastly more superior, more intense, more extreme and stronger than anything the enemy can muster. And His power has taken up residence within me. The very Lord of Hosts dwells within my spirit!

The enemy has been stripped of his power. His weapons are useless against me. Therefore, I refuse to be afraid!

(Joshua 1:5-9; 2 Kings 6:15-17; Isaiah 41:10; 43:1-13; 1 John 4:4; Ephesians 1:17-23; 6:10-18; Colossians 2:15; 2 Corinthians 10:3-6)

2 CHRONICLES 32:10-22 KJV

Thus saith Sennacherib king of Assyria, Whereon do ye trust, that ye abide in the siege in Jerusalem? Doth not Hezekiah persuade you to give over yourselves to die by famine and by thirst, saying, The Lord our God shall deliver us out of the hand of the king of Assyria? Hath not the same Hezekiah taken away his high places and his altars, and commanded Judah and Jerusalem, saying, Ye shall worship before one altar, and burn incense upon it? Know ye not what I and my fathers have done unto all the people of *other* lands? were the gods of the nations of those lands any ways able to deliver their lands out of mine hand? Who *was there* among all the gods of those nations that my fathers utterly destroyed, that could deliver his people out of mine hand, that your God should be able to deliver you out of mine hand? Now therefore let not Hezekiah deceive you, nor persuade you on this manner, neither yet believe him: for no god of any nation or kingdom was able to deliver his people out of mine hand, and out of the hand of my fathers: how much less shall your God deliver you out of mine hand? And his servants spake yet *more* against the Lord God, and against his servant Hezekiah. He wrote also letters to rail on the Lord God of Israel, and to speak against him, saying, As the gods of the nations of *other* lands have not delivered their people out of mine hand, so shall not the God of Hezekiah deliver his people out of mine hand. Then they cried with a loud voice in the Jews' speech unto the people of Jerusalem that *were* on the wall, to affright them, and to trouble them; that they might take the city. And they spake against the God of Jerusalem, as against the gods of the people of the earth, *which were* the work of the hands of man. And for this *cause* Hezekiah the king, and the prophet Isaiah the son of Amoz, prayed and cried to heaven. And the Lord sent an angel, which cut off all the mighty men of valour, and the leaders and captains in the camp of the king of Assyria. So he returned with shame of face to his own land. And when he was come into the house of his god, they that came forth of his own bowels slew him there with the sword. Thus the Lord saved Hezekiah and the inhabitants of Jerusalem from the hand of Sennacherib the king of Assyria, and from the hand of all other, and guided them on every side.

——— DECLARATION OF FAITH ———

I completely reject and regard as worthless the evil report of the enemy. I refuse to give ear to the bragging reports of victories in his campaigns. I refuse to allow what I see to guide my faith. I do not look to what is seen, but to what is unseen. Regardless of the testimony of the circumstances, I have the victory!

My strength and victory comes from the King of Kings and Lord of Lords! He hears my every prayer and sends His angel before me to annihilate the enemy. Those who rise against me shall flee from me in disgrace.

(Isaiah 10:12; Numbers 13:30-14:9; 2 Corinthians 5:7; Hebrews 11:1; 1 John 5:4; Exodus 23:20-30; Deuteronomy 28:7)

2 CHRONICLES 32:27-30 AMP

And Hezekiah had very great wealth and honor, and he made for himself treasuries for silver, gold, precious stones, spices, shields, and all kinds of attractive vessels, Storehouses also for the increase of grain, vintage fruits, and oil, and stalls for all kinds of cattle, and sheepfolds. Moreover, he provided for himself cities and flocks and herds in abundance, for God had given him very great possessions. This same Hezekiah also closed the upper springs of Gihon and directed the waters down to the west side of the City of David. And Hezekiah prospered in all his works.

——— DECLARATION OF FAITH ———

In Christ, I have been granted a position of high honor and have been given great riches. As I draw upon His provision, my dwellings are well supplied. It is God's will that my home be arrayed in the finest that heaven has to offer.

I am a builder in life and I continually increase. Everything that I set my hand to do prospers.

(Ephesians 1:3; 2:6; Philippians 4:17-19; 2 Corinthians 6:10; 8:9; Psalm 112:1-3; Genesis 13:2; 39:2-5; Galatians 3:9-14; Deuteronomy 8:6-18; 28:1-14)

2 CHRONICLES 33:12,13 AMP

When he was in affliction, he besought the Lord his God and humbled himself greatly before the God of his fathers. He prayed to Him, and God, entreated by him, heard his supplication and brought him again to Jerusalem to his kingdom. Then Manasseh knew that the Lord is God.

─────── *DECLARATION OF FAITH* ───────

When distressing days arrive, I remain humble before God and continually seek His favor.

Despite my shortcomings, God loves me and is ever-ready to forgive me and give ear to my prayers. Even if I fall, I will draw near to Him, for I have His promise that He will run to me, embrace me in His arms, and restore me to my rightful place in His kingdom.

(1 Peter 5:5-7; 1 John 1:9; James 4:8; 2 Chronicles 7:14; Psalm 51; Luke 15:11-32)

2 CHRONICLES 34:2 AMP

He did right in the sight of the Lord and walked in the ways of David his father [forefather] and turned aside neither to the right hand nor to the left.

─────── *DECLARATION OF FAITH* ───────

I choose to do what is right in the Lord's sight. I will not deviate from His ways, even a little to the right or to the left. I walk on the straight and narrow path of His will.

(Joshua 24:15; Deuteronomy 28:14; James 4:15; Psalm 27:11)

2 CHRONICLES 34:33 NKJV

Thus Josiah removed all the abominations from all the country that *belonged* to the children of Israel, and made all who were present in Israel diligently serve the Lord their God. All his days they did not depart from following the Lord God of their fathers.

─────── *DECLARATION OF FAITH* ───────

As long as I live, I will follow the Lord my God. I remove from my life everything that is detestable in His sight and live before Him in purity and holiness in accordance with His will.

(Deuteronomy 10:12; Matthew 5:29; 1 Peter 1:15,16; Jeremiah 3:10)

CHAPTER FIFTEEN

EZRA

Ezra records the events of the first and second wave of the return of the children of Israel from Babylonian captivity. Ezra needed favor and delivering power and God granted them.

The promises in the book of Ezra detail the provision that God gives in order to restore us to our rightful place in His family. Never think of yourself as being any less than a child of the King. Your Father is greater than all and will provide anything and everything that you need in order to live a peaceful and godly life.

As you are praying these promises, know that the Lord has provided your deliverance in every area of your life. He does not desire for you to be in bondage in any way. You are to be free in Jesus!

EZRA 3:10,11 KJV

And when the builders laid the foundation of the temple of the Lord, they set the priests in their apparel with trumpets, and the Levites the sons of Asaph with cymbals, to praise the Lord, after the ordinance of David king of Israel. And they sang together by course in praising and giving thanks unto the Lord; because *he is* good, for his mercy *endureth* for ever toward Israel. And all the people shouted with a great shout, when they praised the Lord, because the foundation of the house of the Lord was laid.

─── DECLARATION OF FAITH ───

The Lord is my foundation. His is the immovable base on which I rest and is the surety that I will stand. He is not good to me only some of the time, He is good to me all of the time. His love for me endures forever. I will praise Him with great shouts of joy all the days of my life.

(1 Corinthians 3:10,11; Ephesians 2:20; Psalm 136; 150; Hebrews 7:22)

EZRA 5:5 NKJV

But the eye of their God was upon the elders of the Jews, so that they could not make them cease till a report could go to Darius. Then a written answer was returned concerning this matter.

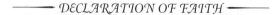

—— DECLARATION OF FAITH ——

The eyes of the Lord are always watching over me. His power and presence are with me to overcome any obstacle I may face.

(2 Chronicles 16:9; Psalm 33:18; Nehemiah 1:5,6; 2 Corinthians 2:14)

EZRA 6:3,4 NIV

In the first year of King Cyrus, the king issued a decree concerning the temple of God in Jerusalem: Let the temple be rebuilt as a place to present sacrifices, and let its foundations be laid. It is to be ninety feet high and ninety feet wide, with three courses of large stones and one of timbers. The costs are to be paid by the royal treasury.

—— DECLARATION OF FAITH ——

I am the temple of the Holy Spirit—the very dwelling place of God in this earth. The royal treasury of heaven provides all that I need to care for this holy temple.

(1 Corinthians 3:16; Philippians 4:19; Matthew 6:19-33; 2 Chronicles 32:27-30)

EZRA 6:7-14 KJV

Let the work of this house of God alone; let the governor of the Jews and the elders of the Jews build this house of God in his place. Moreover I make a decree what ye shall do to the elders of these Jews for the building of this house of God: that of the king's goods, *even* of the tribute beyond the river, forthwith expenses be given unto these men, that they be not hindered. And that which they have need of, both young bullocks, and rams, and lambs, for the burnt offerings of the God of heaven, wheat, salt, wine, and oil, according to the appointment of the priests which *are* at Jerusalem, let it be given them day by day without fail: That they may offer sacrifices of sweet savours unto the God of heaven, and pray for the life of the king, and of his sons. Also I have made a decree, that whosoever shall alter this word, let timber be pulled down from his house, and being set up, let him be hanged thereon; and let his house be made a dunghill for this. And the God that hath caused his name to dwell there destroy all kings and people, that shall put to their hand to alter *and* to destroy this house of God which *is* at Jerusalem. I Darius have made a decree; let it be done with speed. Then

Tatnai, governor on this side the river, Shetharboznai, and their companions, according to that which Darius the king had sent, so they did speedily. And the elders of the Jews builded, and they prospered through the prophesying of Haggai the prophet and Zechariah the son of Iddo. And they builded, and finished *it,* according to the commandment of the God of Israel, and according to the commandment of Cyrus, and Darius, and Artaxerxes king of Persia.

──── *DECLARATION OF FAITH* ────

My heavenly Father cares for me continually. His abundant provision is with me in every enterprise I undertake. His royal treasury provides all that I need to do His will in this earth. Whatever I need is given to me daily and without fail. Therefore, I cannot be hindered or stopped.

I offer myself as a living sacrifice before the Lord and continually pray for His leaders and children.

I am under constant protection as God's covenant partner. I am a member of the household of God. He has placed His name upon me and will overthrow any enemy who attempts to destroy me. This is the King's decree and His army carries it out with diligence.

I continually build and prosper under the direction of His prophets.

(Luke 11:3; Matthew 6:10,11; Romans 12:1; Psalm 23; 91; Galatians 4:4-6; 2 Chronicles 20:20; Daniel 3:29)

EZRA 7:6 AMP

This Ezra went up from Babylon. He was a skilled scribe in the five books of Moses, which the Lord, the God of Israel, had given. And the king granted him all he asked, for the hand of the Lord his God was upon him.

──── *DECLARATION OF FAITH* ────

God has brought me out from an evil place and has regenerated my spirit so that I may do His will. He has given me an able mind with all the ability that I need to teach His ways to others. I have a mind to know His will and purposes in this earth.

My heavenly Father grants my every request and His hand is upon me to prosper all that I set my hand to do.

(Titus 3:5; Daniel 1:17,20; 1 Corinthians 1:30; 2:6-16; 1 John 5:14,15; Genesis 39:2-5)

Ezra 7:9,10 NKJV

On the first *day* of the first month he began *his* journey from Babylon, and on the first *day* of the fifth month he came to Jerusalem, according to the good hand of his God upon him. For Ezra had prepared his heart to seek the Law of the Lord, and to do *it,* and to teach statutes and ordinances in Israel.

———— *DECLARATION OF FAITH* ————
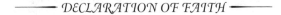

I am committed to study and show myself approved unto the Lord. I will learn and observe His ways of kingdom-living and teach them to others through both my word and my example.

The Lord's hand of favor is upon me everywhere I go and in everything that I do.

(2 Timothy 2:15; Nehemiah 2:18; Matthew 6:33; Deuteronomy 4:9,10; 28:12; Genesis 39:2-5)

Ezra 7:27,28 NIV

Praise be to the Lord, the God of our fathers, who has put it into the king's heart to bring honor to the house of the Lord in Jerusalem in this way and who has extended his good favor to me before the king and his advisers and all the king's powerful officials. Because the hand of the Lord my God was on me, I took courage and gathered leading men from Israel to go up with me.

———— *DECLARATION OF FAITH* ————

I take courage to do all that the Lord has commanded. He has given me favor with the rulers of this world and with their officials. He has set me in a position of high honor among them. Therefore, I am bold to take my place in His army and go forward to do His work.

(Joshua 1:5-9; Psalm 5:11,12; 91:15,16; Genesis 39:2-5; Ephesians 2:6)

Ezra 8:18 NKJV

Then, by the good hand of our God upon us, they brought us a man of under-standing, of the sons of Mahli the son of Levi, the son of Israel, namely Sherebiah, with his sons and brothers, eighteen men.

———— *DECLARATION OF FAITH* ————

God's hand of favor is upon me in all of my endeavors in life. Everything that I set my hand to do is brought to unfailing success.

(Psalm 1:1-3; 5:11,12; Joshua 1:5-9; Deuteronomy 28:1-14; Genesis 39:2-5)

EZRA 8:21-23 KJV

Then I proclaimed a fast there, at the river of Ahava, that we might afflict our-selves before our God, to seek of him a right way for us, and for our little ones, and for all our substance. For I was ashamed to require of the king a band of sol-diers and horsemen to help us against the enemy in the way: because we had spoken unto the king, saying, The hand of our God *is* upon all them for good that seek him; but his power and his wrath *is* against all them that forsake him. So we fasted and besought our God for this: and he was intreated of us.

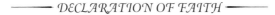

DECLARATION OF FAITH

I look to God alone as my safeguard from trouble. He protects my family and me in all circumstances and in every situation. My children dwell in safety within His powerful arms. He takes special care to guard all of those who are with me and sees to it that the enemy does not plunder us.

The Lord answers my every prayer. His gracious hand is upon me because I look to Him alone as my shield.

(Ezra 7:6; Psalm 5:11,12; 23; 33:18,19; Genesis 15:1; Romans 8:28; Malachi 3:11)

EZRA 8:31 NIV

On the twelfth day of the first month we set out from the Ahava Canal to go to Jerusalem. The hand of our God was on us, and he protected us from enemies and bandits along the way.

DECLARATION OF FAITH

The hand of the Lord is upon me to protect me from powerful enemies and bandits.

(Psalm 18:1-19; Malachi 3:11; Genesis 15:1; Deuteronomy 32:38; Ezra 8:22)

CHAPTER SIXTEEN

NEHEMIAH

Nehemiah records the events of the last wave of the return of the children of Israel from Babylonian captivity. Some have referred to the book of Nehemiah as the book of building. In many cases this is true, but there is an underlying theme in the book that is applicable to your own personal walk with God. All of us have areas in our lives that need rebuilding. Some of us need to rebuild relationships. Others need to rebuild due to bankruptcy or other financial crises. Some need to rebuild their self-esteem or to bounce back from health problems. Whatever the case, the promises in the book of Nehemiah are applicable.

As you pray these prayers, remember your anointing. God has anointed all of us for success in this life. He has promised us favor and blessings. He will surely prosper all that we set our hands to do. Whatever area of your life that needs rebuilding, these promises will see you through.

╬

NEHEMIAH 1:5,6 NIV

Then I said: "O Lord, God of heaven, the great and awesome God, who keeps his covenant of love with those who love him and obey his commands, let your ear be attentive and your eyes open to hear the prayer your servant is praying before you day and night for your servants, the people of Israel. I confess the sins we Israelites, including myself and my father's house, have committed against you."

———— *DECLARATION OF FAITH* ————

The Lord is a great and awesome God who keeps His covenant of love with me as a commitment commanding His utmost attention. His ears are ever-attentive to the sound of my voice and His eyes watch over me without fail. He is pleased to hear my prayers and is quick to respond to my faith.

I love my Father with all of my heart and will keep His commandments all the days of my life.

(Deuteronomy 7:9; John 14:15; 16:26,27; Exodus 34:6,7; 2 Chronicles 6:40; Job 36:7)

NEHEMIAH 1:10,11 KJV

Now these *are* thy servants and thy people, whom thou hast redeemed by thy great power, and by thy strong hand. O Lord, I beseech thee, let now thine ear be attentive to the prayer of thy servant, and to the prayer of thy servants, who desire to fear thy name: and prosper, I pray thee, thy servant this day, and grant him mercy in the sight of this man. For I was the king's cupbearer.

─── *DECLARATION OF FAITH* ───

The Lord has redeemed me from destruction by His great strength and powerful right arm. His ear is attentive to my prayers, for I delight in revering His name. By Him, I have success today and find favor with those I come in contact with.

(Isaiah 43:1; Hebrews 9:12; John 14:13,14; Joshua 1:8; Proverbs 3:3,4)

NEHEMIAH 2:8 NKJV

"And a letter to Asaph the keeper of the king's forest, that he must give me timber to make beams for the gates of the citadel which *pertains* to the temple, for the city wall, and for the house that I will occupy." And the king granted *them* to me according to the good hand of my God upon me."

─── *DECLARATION OF FAITH* ───

The Lord has placed His blessing of favor upon me. It is a shield to me in times of trouble.

(Psalm 5:11,12; Proverbs 11:27; Ezra 5:5; Exodus 12:36)

NEHEMIAH 2:20 AMP

I answered them, The God of heaven will prosper us; therefore we His servants will arise and build, but you have no portion or right or memorial in Jerusalem.

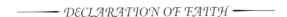

─── *DECLARATION OF FAITH* ───

My Father grants me success in all that I set my hand to do. He bids me to lay claim to my rightful inheritance in this earth.

(Genesis 39:2-5; Deuteronomy 28:12; Joshua 1:8; Galatians 4:5,6; Romans 8:17)

NEHEMIAH 4:4 NIV

Hear us, O our God, for we are despised. Turn their insults back on their own heads. Give them over as plunder in a land of captivity.

———— *DECLARATION OF FAITH* ————

The Lord shows Himself to be an enemy to my enemies.

(Exodus 23:22; Genesis 12:1-3; 2 Chronicles 20:15-24; Psalm 79:12; Deuteronomy 2:25)

Nehemiah 4:8,9 AMP

And they all plotted together to come and fight against Jerusalem, to injure and cause confusion and failure in it. But because of them we made our prayer to our God and set a watch against them day and night.

———— *DECLARATION OF FAITH* ————

When the enemy plots against me to stir up trouble in my life, I will turn my faith toward heaven and post a guard day and night to meet his threat.

(Matthew 26:40,41; Ephesians 6:10,11; 2 Corinthians 2:11; Numbers 14:9)

Nehemiah 4:14-18 KJV

And I looked, and rose up, and said unto the nobles, and to the rulers, and to the rest of the people, Be not ye afraid of them: remember the Lord, *which is* great and terrible, and fight for your brethren, your sons, and your daughters, your wives, and your houses. And it came to pass, when our enemies heard that it was known unto us, and God had brought their counsel to nought, that we returned all of us to the wall, every one unto his work. And it came to pass from that time forth, *that* the half of my servants wrought in the work, and the other half of them held both the spears, the shields, and the bows, and the habergeons; and the rulers *were* behind all the house of Judah. They which builded on the wall, and they that bare burdens, with those that laded, *every one* with one of his hands wrought in the work, and with the other *hand* held a weapon. For the builders, every one had his sword girded by his side, and *so* builded. And he that sounded the trumpet *was* by me.

———— *DECLARATION OF FAITH* ————

I am not afraid of the enemy when he comes against me. The greater One resides in my heart and I am well able to defend my wife, children, brothers and sisters, and home. I am ever-ready to stand against the attacks of the enemy. I am perpetually clothed in full armor. I do my work with sword in hand. My God is a great and awesome God and He fights both with me and for me. He frustrates and sets to confusion all of the enemy's plans. Therefore, my victory is made certain.

(Joshua 1:5-9; 1 John 4:1-4; Ephesians 6:10-18; Exodus 14:13,14; 2 Chronicles 20:15-24; 2 Samuel 10:12)

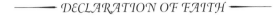

NEHEMIAH 5:19 NKJV

Remember me, my God, for good, *according to* all that I have done for this people.

——— *DECLARATION OF FAITH* ———

My heavenly Father remembers me with favor and none of my work for Him is done in vain.

(Colossians 3:17; 1 Corinthians 15:58; Hebrews 6:10; Philippians 2:16)

NEHEMIAH 6:9-16 KJV

For they all made us afraid, saying, Their hands shall be weakened from the work, that it be not done. Now therefore, *O God,* strengthen my hands. Afterward I came unto the house of Shemaiah the son of Delaiah the son of Mehetabeel, who *was* shut up; and he said, Let us meet together in the house of God, within the temple, and let us shut the doors of the temple: for they will come to slay thee; yea, in the night will they come to slay thee. And I said, Should such a man as I flee? and who *is there,* that, *being* as I *am,* would go into the temple to save his life? I will not go in. And, lo, I perceived that God had not sent him; but that he pronounced this prophecy against me: for Tobiah and Sanballat had hired him. Therefore *was* he hired, that I should be afraid, and do so, and sin, and *that* they might have *matter* for an evil report, that they might reproach me. My God, think thou upon Tobiah and Sanballat according to these their works, and on the prophetess Noadiah, and the rest of the prophets, that would have put me in fear. So the wall was finished in the twenty and fifth *day* of *the month* Elul, in fifty and two days. And it came to pass, that when all our enemies heard *thereof,* and all the heathen that *were* about us saw *these things,* they were much cast down in their own eyes: for they perceived that this work was wrought of our God.

——— *DECLARATION OF FAITH* ———

When the enemy tries to frighten me and begins to mock me saying that I do not have the power to complete the work I've been given to do, God strengthens my hands.

I have no cause to retreat from the advances of the enemy. I am a born-again child of the living God! I am made in God's own image and likeness. Should one such as I run away from the attacks of an impotent foe? I will not! There is not an enemy in existence who can intimidate me.

The enemy knows that God is on my side. When he knows that I know this, he will lose all of his self-confidence and flee from me in stark terror. For this reason, I will stand my ground and complete the work that I have been called to do.

(Psalm 126; Luke 14:28; Joshua 1:5-9; Genesis 1:26,27; John 1:12; Colossians 2:15; James 4:7; 2 Corinthians 10:3-6)

NEHEMIAH 8:9-12 NIV

Then Nehemiah the governor, Ezra the priest and scribe, and the Levites who were instructing the people said to them all, "This day is sacred to the Lord your God. Do not mourn or weep." For all the people had been weeping as they listened to the words of the Law. Nehemiah said, "Go and enjoy choice food and sweet drinks, and send some to those who have nothing prepared. This day is sacred to our Lord. Do not grieve, for the joy of the Lord is your strength." The Levites calmed all the people, saying, "Be still, for this is a sacred day. Do not grieve." Then all the people went away to eat and drink, to send portions of food and to celebrate with great joy, because they now understood the words that had been made known to them.

─── *DECLARATION OF FAITH* ───

This day is sacred to the Lord my God. I will rejoice and be glad in it.

The joy of the Lord is my strength. It is both a shield and a weapon to me. It is a power force that withstands every attack of the enemy.

I have no cause for grief, for the Lord has given me revelation knowledge of His Word so that I may have victory in every circumstance. For this cause I celebrate with joy unspeakable and full of glory!

(Numbers 29:1; Philippians 4:4; 1 John 5:20; 1 Corinthians 2:12; 2 Timothy 2:7)

NEHEMIAH 9:6-8 NKJV

You alone are the Lord;
You have made heaven,
The heaven of heavens, with all their host,
The earth and everything on it,
The seas and all that is in them,
And You preserve them all.
The host of heaven worships You.
"You *are* the Lord God,
Who chose Abram,
And brought him out of Ur of the Chaldeans,
And gave him the name Abraham;
You found his heart faithful before You,
And made a covenant with him
To give the land of the Canaanites,
The Hittites, the Amorites,
the Perizzites, the Jebusites,
And the Girgashites—

To give *it* to his descendants.
You have performed Your words,
For You *are* righteous.

———— *DECLARATION OF FAITH* ————

I serve a great and awesome God. He is creator of all things. He has given life to all that has life. And He has chosen to cut the covenant with me! He picked me to be His own son/daughter. He has recreated me and made my heart to be faithful. Because of this, all of His promises to me are fulfilled.

(Psalm 36:6; Genesis 11:31; 12:1-3; Galatians 3:7-18; Hebrews 10:14-17; Ephesians 1:4; 2 Corinthians 1:20; 5:17,21; 1 John 3:1,2)

NEHEMIAH 9:15 AMP

You gave them bread from heaven for their hunger and brought water for them out of the rock for their thirst; and You told them to go in and possess the land You had sworn to give them.

———— *DECLARATION OF FAITH* ————

When I am hungry, my Father gives me bread from heaven. When I am thirsty, He gives me water from the rock.

(John 6:31; 1 Corinthians 10:4; Numbers 20:8; Genesis 28:13-22)

NEHEMIAH 9:17-21 KJV

And refused to obey, neither were mindful of thy wonders that thou didst among them; but hardened their necks, and in their rebellion appointed a captain to return to their bondage: but thou *art* a God ready to pardon, gracious and merciful, slow to anger, and of great kindness, and forsookest them not. Yea, when they had made them a molten calf, and said, This is thy God that brought thee up out of Egypt, and had wrought great provocations; Yet thou in thy manifold mercies forsookest them not in the wilderness: the pillar of the cloud departed not from them by day, to lead them in the way; neither the pillar of fire by night, to shew them light, and the way wherein they should go. Thou gavest also thy good spirit to instruct them, and withheldest not thy manna from their mouth, and gavest them water for their thirst. Yea, forty years didst thou sustain them in the wilderness, *so that* they lacked nothing; their clothes waxed not old, and their feet swelled not.

My heavenly Father is forgiving and compassionate towards me. He grants me His unmerited favor as a free gift. His patience and love towards me have no end. He has given me His Word that He will never leave me nor forsake me.

Even when my faith has failed, He has remained faithful to me. He has never withheld His manna from my mouth and has always given me water for my thirst.

He has given me the Holy Spirit to instruct me in all of my ways.

He sustains me in every situation so that I lack no good thing. My clothes are not worn and ragged and my feet never swell from my journey in the life that He has called me to live.

(Psalm 103:1-18; Hebrews 13:5,6; John 16:13; Psalm 34:10; 106:45; Joel 2:13)

NEHEMIAH 9:25 AMP

And they captured fortified cities and a rich land and took possession of houses full of all good things, cisterns hewn out, vineyards, olive orchards, and fruit trees in abundance. So they ate and were filled and became fat and delighted themselves in Your great goodness.

────── DECLARATION OF FAITH ──────

I rally behind my great Commander and take captive fortified cities and fertile lands. I take possession of houses filled with good things of all kinds.

I live my life enjoying God's abundance.

I eat to the full and am well nourished.

I revel in God's great goodness!

(Deuteronomy 6:11; Joshua 24:13-15; John 10:10; Hosea 3:5; 2 Corinthians 9:8)

NEHEMIAH 9:27,28 AMP

Therefore You delivered them into the hand of their enemies, who distressed them. In the time of their suffering when they cried to You, You heard them from heaven, and according to Your abundant mercy You gave them deliverers, who saved them from their enemies. But after they had rest, they did evil again before You; therefore You left them in the hand of their enemies, so that they had dominion over them. Yet when they turned and cried to You, You heard them from heaven, and many times You delivered them according to Your mercies.

——— *DECLARATION OF FAITH* ———

My heavenly Father has tremendous compassion for me. He sends deliverers to rescue me when the enemy rises to oppress me. He hears me every time I call out to Him and He delivers me time after time.

(Psalm 91; 103:1-18; 106:41-43; Judges 2:14-18; Luke 4:18; Romans 15:30,31)

NEHEMIAH 9:30-32 AMP

Yet You bore with them many years more and reproved and warned them by Your Spirit through Your prophets; still they would not listen. Therefore You gave them into the power of the peoples of the lands. Yet in Your great mercies You did not utterly consume them or forsake them, for You are a gracious and merciful God. Now therefore, our God, the great, mighty, and terrible God, Who keeps covenant and mercy and loving-kindness, let not all the trouble and hardship seem little to You—the hardship that has come upon us, our kings, our princes, our priests, our prophets, our fathers, and on all Your people, since the time of the kings of Assyria to this day.

——— *DECLARATION OF FAITH* ———

God has been patient with me my whole life. He has always been with me to do me good. I cannot count the times when His hand has been evident in my life. He admonishes me by His Spirit through His prophets, but His mercy for me has never failed. He has always been there for me regardless of the circumstances or the things that I have done.

My heavenly Father is a great and awesome God and is my covenant partner in this life. Nothing that I ask of Him is trifling in His eyes.

(Hebrews 13:5,6; 1 Peter 1:11; Exodus 34:6,7; John 14:13,14)

NEHEMIAH 9:38 NIV

"In view of all this, we are making a binding agreement, putting it in writing, and our leaders, our Levites and our priests are affixing their seals to it."

——— *DECLARATION OF FAITH* ———

In view of all of this, I make my binding covenant agreement with God and affix my signature to it:

My Covenant Agreement with God:

I will keep the ways and statutes of my heavenly Father.

(Nehemiah 10:29)

I will pay all of my tithes to the treasury of the Church.

(Nehemiah 10:35-38)

I will not neglect the needs of the Church.

(Nehemiah 10:39)

My covenant prayer requests:

_____

_____

_____

_____

_____

_____

_____

_____

Signed _____

(2 Kings 23:3; 2 Chronicles 29:10; Ezra 10:3; Deuteronomy 26:1,2; Malachi 3:6-12; Hebrews 8:6; 10:25; 2 Corinthians 9:6-11)

NEHEMIAH 12:43 NKJV

Also that day they offered great sacrifices, and rejoiced, for God had made them rejoice with great joy; the women and the children also rejoiced, so that the joy of Jerusalem was heard afar off.

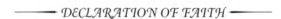

DECLARATION OF FAITH

I declare this day to be a day of rejoicing. God has done great things for me and today I will offer for Him the sacrifice of joyful praise.

(Philippians 4:4; Psalm 90:14; Joel 2:21; Romans 10:15)

NEHEMIAH 13:10-14 KJV

And I perceived that the portions of the Levites had not been given *them:* for the Levites and the singers, that did the work, were fled every one to his field. Then contended I with the rulers, and said, Why is the house of God forsaken? And I gathered them together, and set them in their place. Then brought all Judah the tithe of the corn and the new wine and the oil unto the treasuries. And I made treasurers over the treasuries, Shelemiah the priest, and Zadok the scribe, and of the Levites, Pedaiah: and next to them *was* Hanan the son of Zaccur, the son of Mattaniah: for they were counted faithful, and their office *was* to distribute unto their brethren. Remember me, O my God, concerning this, and wipe not out my good deeds that I have done for the house of my God, and for the offices thereof.

DECLARATION OF FAITH

I will not neglect the needs of the house of God. I pay all of my tithes into His storehouse. This is honorable before the Lord and He does not forget my faithfulness to His church and its services.

(Malachi 3:6-12; 2 Corinthians 9:6-11; Hebrews 6:10; 10:25; Proverbs 3:9,10)

NEHEMIAH 13:31 NKJV

And *to bringing* the wood offering and the firstfruits at appointed times. Remember me, O my God, for good!

DECLARATION OF FAITH

The Lord always remembers me with favor.

(Psalm 5:11,12; Proverbs 3:3,4; 12:2; Romans 14:18)

CHAPTER SEVENTEEN

ESTHER

Esther is often referred to as the book that doesn't mention God. Well, God doesn't have to be mentioned for us to know that He is there. Esther is an awesome example of how God places us in specific circumstances at specific times in order to fulfill a specific calling. All of us are called to a specific purpose and no one on earth can fulfill that purpose as well as we can. We are God's ideal choice to do what we are called to do.

As you pray the promises of the book of Esther, know that you have a specific purpose in this life that only you can fulfill. You are not where you are by accident. You have a purpose to fulfill and you are the best that God has to fulfill it!

ESTHER 3:2 NKJV
And all the king's servants who were within the king's gate bowed and paid homage to Haman, for so the king had commanded concerning him. But Mordecai would not bow or pay homage.

DECLARATION OF FAITH

I will not respect or give honor to those in the world who are morally degenerate.

(Psalm 15:4; 2 Corinthians 6:14; Leviticus 5:1)

ESTHER 4:14 NIV
"For if you remain silent at this time, relief and deliverance for the Jews will arise from another place, but you and your father's family will perish. And who knows but that you have come to royal position for such a time as this?"

DECLARATION OF FAITH

God chose me for a specific purpose. In His infinite wisdom, He has placed me in His kingdom for such a time as this. I am His ideal choice to carry out what He has called me to do. He has given me a mission to fulfill and I intend to fulfill it. I am the best that He has to fulfill my calling. I will not dishonor Him by forcing Him to find another to do my work for me.

(Romans 8:28; 2 Timothy 1:9; 1Timothy 4:14; Acts 9:15; Ephesians 3:7,8)

ESTHER 5:9-6:11 KJV

Then went Haman forth that day joyful and with a glad heart: but when Haman saw Mordecai in the king's gate, that he stood not up, nor moved for him, he was full of indignation against Mordecai. Nevertheless Haman refrained himself: and when he came home, he sent and called for his friends, and Zeresh his wife. And Haman told them of the glory of his riches, and the multitude of his children, and all *the things* wherein the king had promoted him, and how he had advanced him above the princes and servants of the king. Haman said moreover, Yea, Esther the queen did let no man come in with the king unto the banquet that she had prepared but myself; and to morrow am I invited unto her also with the king. Yet all this availeth me nothing, so long as I see Mordecai the Jew sitting at the king's gate. Then said Zeresh his wife and all his friends unto him, Let a gallows be made of fifty cubits high, and to morrow speak thou unto the king that Mordecai may be hanged thereon: then go thou in merrily with the king unto the banquet. And the thing pleased Haman; and he caused the gallows to be made. On that night could not the king sleep, and he commanded to bring the book of records of the chronicles; and they were read before the king. And it was found written, that Mordecai had told of Bigthana and Teresh, two of the king's chamberlains, the keepers of the door, who sought to lay hand on the king Ahasuerus. And the king said, What honour and dignity hath been done to Mordecai for this? Then said the king's servants that ministered unto him, There is nothing done for him. And the king said, Who *is* in the court? Now Haman was come into the outward court of the king's house, to speak unto the king to hang Mordecai on the gallows that he had prepared for him. And the king's servants said unto him, Behold, Haman standeth in the court. And the king said, Let him come in. So Haman came in. And the king said unto him, What shall be done unto the man whom the king delighteth to honour? Now Haman thought in his heart, To whom would the king delight to do honour more than to myself? And Haman answered the king, For the man whom the king delighteth to honour, Let the royal apparel be brought which the king *useth* to wear, and the horse that the king rideth upon, and the crown royal which is set upon his head: And let this apparel and horse be delivered to the hand of one of the king's most noble princes, that they may array the man *withal* whom the king delighteth to honour, and bring him on horseback through the street of the city, and proclaim before him, Thus shall it be done to the man whom the king delighteth to honour. Then the king said to Haman, Make haste, *and* take the apparel and the horse, as thou hast said, and do even so to Mordecai the Jew, that sitteth at the king's gate: let nothing fail of all that thou hast spoken. Then took Haman the apparel and the horse, and arrayed Mordecai, and brought him on horseback through the street of the city, and proclaimed before him, Thus shall it be done unto the man whom the king delighteth to honour.

——— *DECLARATION OF FAITH* ———

When the enemy plots against me to do me great harm due to my allegiance to God's will and standards, God takes His stand in my defense. My Father thwarts all of the enemy's attacks. Every plan that the enemy uses is turned back on his own head and he shall be brought to nothing.

As for me, the Lord turns the tide and the enemy's plans end up working for my good. No matter what weapons are used against me, I will emerge victorious. The Lord will raise me to a position of high honor because I revere His name.

(Psalm 2; 7:16; 91:15; 1 Samuel 25:39; 1 Kings 2:44; Nehemiah 4:4; Esther 9:25; Ephesians 2:6)

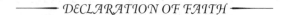

ESTHER 8:1,2 AMP

On that day King Ahasuerus gave the house of Haman, the Jews' enemy, to Queen Esther. And Mordecai came before the king, for Esther had told what he was to her. And the king took off his [signet] ring, which he had taken from Haman, and gave it to Mordecai. And Esther set Mordecai over the house of Haman.

——— *DECLARATION OF FAITH* ———

When the enemy plots my destruction, he is simply sowing the seeds of his own downfall.

(Psalm 2; 79:12; Genesis 15:14; Exodus 12:36; Matthew 5:10-12; Proverbs 13:22)

ESTHER 9:4 NKJV

For Mordecai *was* great in the king's palace, and his fame spread throughout all the provinces; for this man Mordecai became increasingly prominent.

——— *DECLARATION OF FAITH* ———

I humble myself to obey God's statutes. Because of this, I can fully expect Him to raise me to a prominent position. As His beloved child, I gain a reputation of honor and respect.

(1 Peter 5:5-7; Ephesians 2:6-10; Psalm 91:15; Genesis 12:1-3; Deuteronomy 28:13)

ESTHER 9:25 NIV

But when the plot came to the king's attention, he issued written orders that the evil scheme Haman had devised against the Jews should come back onto his own head, and that he and his sons should be hanged on the gallows.

——— *DECLARATION OF FAITH* ———

All of the evil schemes that the enemy brings against me are turned back on his own head. He shall fall by the very plans that he designed for my destruction.

(Psalm 2; 7:16; 79:12; 140:9; 1 Samuel 25:39; 1 Kings 2:44; Nehemiah 4:4)

CHAPTER EIGHTEEN

JOB

Some of you are in for a very pleasant surprise. The book of Job is seldom thought of as a book full of wonderful promises. However, in the midst of Job's sorrow, we find that God constantly reminded him of the blessings that belonged to him all along. This book is a testimony to God's faithfulness on our behalf. If we will focus on Him and believe in Him in spite of the circumstances, He will grant us His protection, favor and abundant provision.

As you pray these promises, make a commitment that no matter what happens in your life, you will never turn from your faith in God's Word. If you have not already settled that issue in your heart, settle it now.

JOB 1:1 KJV

There was a man in the land of Uz, whose name was Job; and that man was perfect and upright, and one that feared God, and eschewed evil.

— DECLARATION OF FAITH —

I choose to live a blameless and upright life before the Lord.
I trust in my God and shun all evil.

(Joshua 24:15; Deuteronomy 28:1; Genesis 17:1; Proverbs 16:6; 1 Peter 1:15,16)

JOB 1:8 NIV

Then the Lord said to Satan, "Have you considered my servant Job? There is no one on earth like him; he is blameless and upright, a man who fears God and shuns evil."

— DECLARATION OF FAITH —

My heavenly Father is very proud of me. I am special to Him and He holds me dear to His heart. I am unique among all of His creation. There is none like me in all of the earth.

It pleases Him greatly that I have chosen to trust Him, shun evil, and live blamelessly and upright before Him all the days of my life.

(Isaiah 42:1; Ephesians 1:3-6; Psalm 18:19; 103:13; Isaiah 62:4; Colossians 1:19)

JOB 1:10 NKJV

"Have You not made a hedge around him, around his household, and around all that he has on every side? You have blessed the work of his hands, and his possessions have increased in the land. But now, stretch out Your hand and touch all that he has, and he will surely curse You to Your face!"

——— *DECLARATION OF FAITH* ———

God has placed a hedge of protection around my family, myself and everything that I have, and the enemy cannot penetrate through it no matter how hard he tries.

The Lord blesses all of the work of my hands, making me prosperous and very wealthy.

(Psalm 5:11,12; 34:7; 112:1-3; Job 3:23; 1 John 5:18; Deuteronomy 8:18; 28:12)

JOB 1:22 AMP

In all this Job sinned not nor charged God foolishly.

——— *DECLARATION OF FAITH* ———

No matter what happens in my life—no matter what obstacles, difficulties, or heartaches I endure—I will not blame God or charge Him with wrongdoing. His heart is set on doing nothing but good by me. I will not turn from this truth.

(James 1:13; Psalm 39:1; Romans 9:20; Genesis 28:3-15; 32:12; 50:20; Deuteronomy 6:24)

JOB 2:3 AMP

And the Lord said to Satan, Have you considered My servant Job, that there is none like him on the earth, a blameless and upright man, one who [reverently] fears God and abstains from and shuns all evil [because it is wrong]? And still he holds fast his integrity, although you moved Me against him to destroy him without cause.

——— *DECLARATION OF FAITH* ———

I maintain my integrity in adverse circumstances. I continue to walk blamelessly and upright before my heavenly Father no matter what I am facing. I trust

Him and shun evil all the days of my life. I am firmly resolved to be a son/daughter that my Father can be proud of.

(Job 27:5,6; Daniel 3:8-25; 6:10-23; 1 Corinthians 1:8; Proverbs 16:6)

JOB 4:3,4 NIV

Think how you have instructed many, how you have strengthened feeble hands. Your words have supported those who stumbled; you have strengthened faltering knees.

——— *DECLARATION OF FAITH* ———

I am a man/woman of understanding. My words are pure and powerful. They instruct many in the ways of life. They strengthen the feeble and give support to those who have stumbled. They give power to those with weak hands and faltering knees.

(Daniel 1:17,20; 1 Corinthians 2:12; John 6:63; Proverbs 18:20,21; 2 Corinthians 5:18-20; Isaiah 35:3)

JOB 5:17-23 KJV

Behold, happy is the man whom God correcteth: therefore despise not thou the chastening of the Almighty: For he maketh sore, and bindeth up: he woundeth, and his hands make whole. He shall deliver thee in six troubles: yea, in seven there shall no evil touch thee. In famine he shall redeem thee from death: and in war from the power of the sword. Thou shalt be hid from the scourge of the tongue: neither shalt thou be afraid of destruction when it cometh. At destruction and famine thou shalt laugh: neither shalt thou be afraid of the beasts of the earth. For thou shalt be in league with the stones of the field: and the beasts of the field shall be at peace with thee. And thou shalt know that thy tabernacle *shall be* in peace; and thou shalt visit thy habitation, and shalt not sin.

——— *DECLARATION OF FAITH* ———

I do not despise the discipline of the Lord. His firm hand of correction is welcome in my life. It may wound me for a time, but God will heal my hurts.

From six calamities He will rescue me; in seven no harm will come to me. In time of famine, He will ransom me from death, and in battle, He will shield me from the sword. I am continually protected from the lash of the tongue and I have no fear when destruction is headed my way. I laugh at famine and destruction. I am stouthearted and have no fear of the beasts in the earth. I know Satan's position and I'm not of afraid of him or his allies.

(Hebrews 12:3-11; Psalm 33:19,20; 37:19; 91; Isaiah 54:17; Hosea 2:18)

JOB 5:26 NKJV

You shall come to the grave at a full age, as a sheaf of grain ripens in its season.

——— DECLARATION OF FAITH ———

I will live my life to the fullest and go to the grave at a ripe old age, full of vigor and strength unabated, like a sheave gathered in season.

(Isaiah 46:4, Psalm 91:16; Deuteronomy 34:7; John 10:10)

JOB 8:5-7 AMP

If you will seek God diligently and make your supplication to the Almighty, then, if you are pure and upright, surely He will bestir Himself for you and make your righteous dwelling prosperous again. And though your beginning was small, yet your latter end would greatly increase.

——— DECLARATION OF FAITH ———

I live a pure and upright life before my heavenly Father. I continually look to Him as my sole provider. I call to Him and He comes to my rescue. He restores me to my rightful place in this earth. Though my beginnings be humble, my latter end will be a powerful testimony of God's prosperity and success.

(Romans 12:1; Philippians 4:19; Genesis 22:14; Psalm 18:1-19; Job 42:12)

JOB 8:21,22 AMP

He will yet fill your mouth with laughter [Job] and your lips with joyful shouting. Those who hate you will be clothed with shame, and the tents of the wicked shall be no more.

——— DECLARATION OF FAITH ———

My Father fills my mouth with laughter and my lips with shouts of joy.
My enemies shall all be clothed in shame and the dwellings of the wicked shall be overthrown.

(Psalm 35:26; 109:29; 126:2,3; Leviticus 26:7,8; Number 16:26-32)

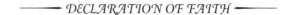

JOB 9:32-35 KJV

For *he is* not a man, as I *am, that* I should answer him, *and* we should come together in judgment. Neither is there any daysman betwixt us, *that* might lay his hand upon us both. Let him take his rod away from me, and let not his fear terrify me: *Then* would I speak, and not fear him; but *it is* not so with me.

———— *DECLARATION OF FAITH* ————

Through Jesus, God's rod has been removed from me. I can now speak with the Lord face-to-face, free of shame and all sense of inadequacy. Cause to fear has been removed from me and His awesome power no longer frightens me.

(John 3:13-18,36; Hebrews 4:16; 2 Timothy 1:7; 1 John 1:3; 4:17,18; Exodus 33:11)

JOB 11:13-15 AMP

If you set your heart aright and stretch out your hands to [God], if you put sin out of your hand and far away from you and let not evil dwell in your tents;

Then can you lift up your face to Him without stain [of sin, and unashamed]; yes, you shall be steadfast and secure; you shall not fear.

———— *DECLARATION OF FAITH* ————

My heart is devoted to the Lord. Sin has no place in my life and I shall allow no evil to dwell in my household.

I am proud to be a Christian. I lift up my face without shame and stand firm in the face of fear.

(Hebrews 12:1; Psalm 3:3; 101; Romans 1:16; Isaiah 41:10)

JOB 11:19 NKJV

You would also lie down, and no one would make *you* afraid; *Yes,* many would court your favor.

———— *DECLARATION OF FAITH* ————

I remain safe and secure in the hands of my heavenly Father. I go to sleep at night with no one to make me afraid.

Many shall see God's blessings on my life and court my favor.

(Psalm 4:8; 23; Deuteronomy 28:10; Ephesians 1:3; John 10:28,29; Job 29:7-25)

JOB 16:19-21 KJV

Also now, behold, my witness *is* in heaven, and my record *is* on high. My friends scorn me: *but* mine eye poureth out *tears* unto God. O that one might plead for a man with God, as a man *pleadeth* for his neighbour!

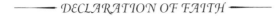

— DECLARATION OF FAITH —

At this very moment my Advocate stands in intercession for me. He is my friend and my Savior. He pleads for me as a man pleads for his best friend.

(Hebrews 7:25; 1 John 2:1,2; Exodus 33:11; John 15:14,15; James 2:23)

JOB 17:8,9 NIV

Upright men are appalled at this; the innocent are aroused against the ungodly. Nevertheless, the righteous will hold to their ways, and those with clean hands will grow stronger.

— DECLARATION OF FAITH —

I arouse myself to stand against the ungodliness of the world. I will keep my ways pure and grow in the Lord's power and might.

(Leviticus 5:1; Romans 12:1; Ephesians 6:10; Psalm 24:4)

JOB 22:21,22 NKJV

"Now acquaint yourself with Him, and be at peace; Thereby good will come to you. Receive, please, instruction from His mouth, and lay up His words in your heart.

— DECLARATION OF FAITH —

I am freely submitted to God to walk in all of His ways. There is peace between us and by His divine enabling He brings me to the place of abundant prosperity. I accept all of His instructions and lay up His words in the treasury of my heart.

(1 Peter 5:5-7; John 10:10; Psalm 119:11-16; Deuteronomy 28:1-14; Romans 5:1)

JOB 22:27-30 AMP

You will make your prayer to Him, and He will hear you, and you will pay your vows. You shall also decide and decree a thing, and it shall be established for you; and the light [of God's favor] shall shine upon your ways. When they make [you] low, you will say, [There is] a lifting up; and the humble person He lifts up and saves. He will even deliver the one [for whom you intercede] who is not innocent; yes, he will be delivered through the cleanness of your hands.

──────── *DECLARATION OF FAITH* ────────

My heavenly Father hears my every prayer and I am faithful to pay all of my vows to Him. What I decide on is firmly established and His light shines on all of my ways.

When I humble myself under His mighty hand, He exalts me in due time.

He delights in me as His own son/daughter and anoints me to do His will in the earth.

(1 John 5:14,15; James 4:3; 5:14-16; Psalm 50:14,15; Ezekiel 22:30; Galatians 4:4-7)

JOB 23:10-12 NIV

But he knows the way that I take; when he has tested me, I will come forth as gold. My feet have closely followed his steps; I have kept to his way without turning aside. I have not departed from the commands of his lips; I have treasured the words of his mouth more than my daily bread.

──────── *DECLARATION OF FAITH* ────────

My Father knows all of my ways and the choices that I make.

When He has tested me, I shall come forth as gold.

I am cleansed by the blood of Jesus.

I am refined in the fires of heaven.

My feet closely follow the paths that the Lord has set before me and I will keep His ways without fail. I shall not depart from the commands of my Master. I treasure His words within me even more than my daily bread.

(Psalm 1:6; 119:9,105; 139:1-4; James 1:12; Hebrews 9:14; Matthew 3:11)

JOB 28:28 NKJV

"And to man He said, 'Behold, the fear of the Lord, that *is* wisdom, and to depart from evil *is* understanding.'"

──────── *DECLARATION OF FAITH* ────────

I am a wise man/woman who reveres the Lord. I demonstrate my understanding by my rejection of evil things.

(Deuteronomy 4:6; 1 Corinthians 1:30; Proverbs 14:16; 22:3; James 1:5-8)

JOB 29:4-25 KJV

As I was in the days of my youth, when the secret of God *was* upon my tabernacle; When the Almighty *was* yet with me, *when* my children *were* about me; When I washed my steps with butter, and the rock poured me out rivers of oil; When I went out to the gate through the city, *when* I prepared my seat in the street! The young men saw me, and hid themselves: and the aged arose, *and* stood up. The princes refrained talking, and laid *their* hand on their mouth. The nobles held their peace, and their tongue cleaved to the roof of their mouth. When the ear heard *me*, then it blessed me; and when the eye saw *me*, it gave witness to me: Because I delivered the poor that cried, and the fatherless, and *him that had* none to help him. The blessing of him that was ready to perish came upon me: and I caused the widow's heart to sing for joy. I put on righteousness, and it clothed me: my judgment *was* as a robe and a diadem. I was eyes to the blind, and feet *was* I to the lame. I *was* a father to the poor: and the cause *which* I knew not I searched out. And I brake the jaws of the wicked, and plucked the spoil out of his teeth. Then I said, I shall die in my nest, and I shall multiply *my* days as the sand. My root *was* spread out by the waters, and the dew lay all night upon my branch. My glory *was* fresh in me, and my bow was renewed in my hand. Unto me *men* gave ear, and waited, and kept silence at my counsel. After my words they spake not again; and my speech dropped upon them. And they waited for me as for the rain; and they opened their mouth wide *as* for the latter rain. *If* I laughed on them, they believed *it* not; and the light of my countenance they cast not down. I chose out their way, and sat chief, and dwelt as a king in the army, as one *that* comforteth the mourners.

––––––– *DECLARATION OF FAITH* –––––––

The Lord is my intimate friend. His companionship is a blessing to my household. He holds His lamp before me to light my way in the darkness.

The Almighty is ever with me and my children dwell in safety at my side. Everything that I do succeeds and nothing is too difficult for me to accomplish. When I enter the city and sit with my friends in the public square, people greet me with respect. I am honored by everyone in town because of my Father's favor.

When I speak, people listen and hang on my every word.

People who know me speak well of me and my reputation goes before me to make my Father proud.

I am known for helping people in distress and for standing up for those who are in need.

My presence makes the widow's heart sing. She is overjoyed at all of my visits. All of my dealings with people are for good and I am known as a fair and generous man/woman.

I am eyes to the blind and feet to the lame—a father/mother to the orphan and a champion to victims of abuse.

I live a life deeply-rooted and well-watered.

My soul is covered in God's glory.

Men and women listen when I speak and afterwards ponder the words that God has given me. When I smile at them, their faces light up and their troubles take flight. I am a leader among them and set the pace by which they live.

I am the very image of my Father in heaven.

(John 15:14,15; James 2:23; Psalm 72:4; 90:16; 91:15; 103:17; 115:13,14; 119:105; Deuteronomy 28:9-13; Matthew 17:20; 1 Kings 4:34; 1 Corinthians 1:30; Acts 6:10; Proverbs 3:3,4; 29:7; James 1:27; Isaiah 61:1-3; Genesis 1:26,27; 12:1-3)

JOB 31:1-4 AMP

I dictated a covenant (an agreement) to my eyes; how then could I look [lustfully] upon a girl? For what portion should I have from God above [if I were lewd], and what heritage from the Almighty on high? Does not calamity [justly] befall the unrighteous, and disaster the workers of iniquity? Does not [God] see my ways and count all my steps?

———— DECLARATION OF FAITH ————

All of my sexual desires are for my spouse alone. I have made a covenant with my eyes not to look lustfully upon the nakedness of different women/men. I will not allow the sexual advertisement and pornography in society to enter my life space. So far as it is within my power, I will shield my eyes from it. I will not allow my heritage to be jeopardized by foolishness, nor will I follow the ways of the wicked. It is the Lord who guides my every step, giving me strength to overcome and keeping me from falling.

(Genesis 2:22-25; Matthew 5:28; Philippians 4:8; Proverbs 5; Psalm 1:1; 1 Corinthians 10:13; Jude 24)

JOB 31:24-28 KJV

If I have made gold my hope, or have said to the fine gold, *Thou art* my confidence; If I rejoiced because my wealth *was* great, and because mine hand had gotten much; If I beheld the sun when it shined, or the moon walking *in* brightness; And my heart hath been secretly enticed, or my mouth hath kissed my hand: This also *were* an iniquity *to be punished by* the judge: for I should have denied the God *that is* above.

——— *DECLARATION OF FAITH* ———

I do not put my trust in gold as my security, nor do I rejoice over the great riches that I have been given, or the fortune that I have gained by what I have set my hand to do. My heart cannot be secretly enticed to pay homage to any provider but one: The Lord my God! My faith and trust are in Him and Him alone!

(Matthew 6:19-33; 1 Timothy 6:17; Mark 10:17-25; Psalm 62:10; Deuteronomy 8:18)

JOB 32:8 NKJV

But *there is* a spirit in man, And the breath of the Almighty gives him understanding.

——— *DECLARATION OF FAITH* ———

It is my spirit man that gives me understanding. It is the breath of God within me that makes me wise.

(1 Corinthians 1:30; 2:10-16; 2 Timothy 2:7; Daniel 1:17,20; 2:21-23)

JOB 33:3,4 AMP

My words shall express the uprightness of my heart, and my lips shall speak what they know with utter sincerity. [It is] the Spirit of God that made me [which has stirred me up], and the breath of the Almighty that gives me life [which inspires me].

——— *DECLARATION OF FAITH* ———

The Spirit of God has made me and the breath of the Almighty has given me life. My words are pure within me and come forth from an upright heart.

(Genesis 2:7; Job 32:8; Titus 3:5; John 3:3-8; 1 Peter 3:10-12; Proverbs 10:20; 15:2-4)

JOB 33:23-30 KJV

If there be a messenger with him, an interpreter, one among a thousand, to shew unto man his uprightness: Then he is gracious unto him, and saith, Deliver him from going down to the pit: I have found a ransom. His flesh shall be fresher than a child's: he shall return to the days of his youth: He shall pray unto God, and he will be favourable unto him: and he shall see his face with joy: for he will render unto man his righteousness. He looketh upon men, and *if any* say, I have sinned, and perverted *that which was* right, and it profited me not; He will deliver his soul from going into the pit, and his life shall see the light. Lo, all these *things* worketh God oftentimes with man, To bring back his soul from the pit, to be enlightened with the light of the living.

── DECLARATION OF FAITH ──

God sends His angel before me. He declares to the enemy that I am ransomed and he shields me against death's advances. My flesh is then renewed like a child's and the strength of my youth is restored.

I set my prayer before the Lord and I am given favor. I see His face and shout for joy! I have been restored to a state of righteousness in His presence. I will declare my redemption to the world and tell everyone of the wonderful things He has done in my life. He has illuminated my path before me and has granted me a destiny of greatness.

(Hebrews 1:14; 4:16; Exodus 23:20; Hosea 13:14; Psalm 91:11,12; 103:1-5; 2 Corinthians 5:21; Matthew 28:18-20)

JOB 36:7-11 KJV

He withdraweth not his eyes from the righteous: but with kings *are they* on the throne; yea, he doth establish them for ever, and they are exalted. And if *they be* bound in fetters, *and* be holden in cords of affliction; Then he sheweth them their work, and their transgressions that they have exceeded. He openeth also their ear to discipline, and commandeth that they return from iniquity. If they obey and serve *him,* they shall spend their days in prosperity, and their years in pleasures.

── DECLARATION OF FAITH ──

The Lord's eyes never leave me. He keeps watch over all that I do and is my ever-present help to ensure my success.

He corrects and disciplines me when I waiver and makes sure that I know what I have done wrong. He then sets me back on the path of His prosperity and sees to it that I spend my days in peace and contentment.

(Nehemiah 1:5,6; Psalm 33:18; 34:15; 46:1; 91:15,16; Hebrews 12:1-16; 13:5,6; Joel 2:25,26)

JOB 36:15,16 AMP

He delivers the afflicted in their affliction and opens their ears [to His voice] in adversity. Indeed, God would have allured you out of the mouth of distress into a broad place where there is no situation of perplexity or privation; and that which would be set on your table would be full of fatness.

——— *DECLARATION OF FAITH* ———

My Father coaxes me away from life's troubles. He speaks to me in the midst of them, drawing me out into a spacious place, free of restrictions, and bids me to eat at the table of His blessings.

(Isaiah 30:21; 1 John 1:3-7; Psalm 18:19; 23:5; 36:8; 112:1-3; 118:5)

JOB 38:36 NKJV

Who has put wisdom in the mind? Or who has given understanding to the heart?

——— *DECLARATION OF FAITH* ———

The Lord has endowed my heart with wisdom and has given me a mind of tremendous understanding.

(1 Corinthians 1:30; 2:10-16; Daniel 1:17,20; 2:22,23; 2 Timothy 2:7)

JOB 42:10,12 AMP

And the Lord turned the captivity of Job and restored his fortunes, when he prayed for his friends; also the Lord gave Job twice as much as he had before. And the Lord blessed the latter days of Job more than his beginning; for he had 14,000 sheep, 6,000 camels, 1,000 yoke of oxen, and 1,000 female donkeys.

——— *DECLARATION OF FAITH* ———

My Father lifts me up from the thief's attacks and brings forth my prosperity. He restores double what the enemy has taken and sets me on the path of ever-increasing abundance so that the latter part of my life is much greater than the former.

(John 10:10; Colossians 1:13; Deuteronomy 8:18; James 5:11; Exodus 22:4,7,9; Zechariah 9:11-13; Joel 2:25,26)

CHAPTER NINETEEN

PSALMS

The book of Psalms has more authors than any other book in the Bible. Most of the Psalms, however, can be attributed to King David. As David was both king and prophet, much of what he wrote is prophetic in nature. You will also notice that one of the most recurring themes is God's protection of His children. If you are in a situation were you are under attack from either worldly or spiritual forces, the Psalms provides the promises that will see you through them.

It is important to notice that the Psalms present promises of protection in the form of praise. Remember how Jehoshaphat set the musicians before the army and God routed the enemy. The Psalms themselves declare that praise stills the enemy and quiets the avenger. The benefits of living under God's protection are peace, divine provision and fullness of joy. All of these attributes can be found in the promises of the book of Psalms.

Begin your personalized prayers of the Psalms with an attitude of thankfulness and praise. Give God the glory right now and recognize all that He has done in your life.

PSALM 1:1-3 NKJV
Blessed *is* the man
Who walks not in the counsel of the ungodly,
Nor stands in the path of sinners,
Nor sits in the seat of the scornful;
But his delight *is* in the law of the LORD,
And in His law he meditates day and night.
He shall be like a tree
Planted by the rivers of water,
That brings forth its fruit in its season,
Whose leaf also shall not wither;
And whatever he does shall prosper.

—— *DECLARATION OF FAITH* ——

I move forward in life in happiness and peace.

I follow the ways of the Word and I am blessed in all that I do.

I do not follow the advice nor the pattern of living of those who spurn the guidance of my heavenly Father.

I withdraw myself from the sinful activities that the world accepts.

I refuse to take sides with fools and mockers who scoff at morality.

My delight, gratification, and satisfaction are in the Word of the living God. In it I meditate—speaking it to myself day and night—engrafting and rooting it deeply into my spirit. By this, my way is made prosperous and I achieve tremendous success.

I am like a tree that is planted beside fresh water springs. I bear the best of fruit in my life.

Everything about me exudes life and everything that I set my hand to do prospers.

(Proverbs 4:14; Jeremiah 15:17; Joshua 1:8; Psalm 119:14-16,23,24; Genesis 39:2-5)

PSALM 2:1-9 KJV

Why do the heathen rage, and the people imagine a vain thing? The kings of the earth set themselves, and the rulers take counsel together, against the Lord, and against his anointed, *saying*, Let us break their bands asunder, and cast away their cords from us. He that sitteth in the heavens shall laugh: the Lord shall have them in derision. Then shall he speak unto them in his wrath, and vex them in his sore displeasure. Yet have I set my king upon my holy hill of Zion. I will declare the decree: the Lord hath said unto me, Thou art my Son; this day have I begotten thee. Ask of me, and I shall give *thee* the heathen *for* thine inheritance, and the uttermost parts of the earth *for* thy possession. Thou shalt break them with a rod of iron; thou shalt dash them in pieces like a potter's vessel.

—— *DECLARATION OF FAITH* ——

My Father laughs when my enemies conspire against me to break loose from the chains by which I have bound them. When they take their stand against me and plan my destruction, the Lord mocks them.

Then He rebukes them in His anger and terrifies them in the wake of His wrath. He makes His decree before them that Jesus is Lord and King over my life and that I am not to be harmed.

I have been reborn and recreated as the very brother/sister of Jesus. Every member of Satan's army is subject to my authority.

(Numbers 24:9; Mark 3:27; Psalm 18:1-19; 37:13; Acts 17:28; Deuteronomy 2:25; 11:25; John 3:3-8; Luke 10:19; Hebrews 2:11; James 4:7; Revelation 2:26,27)

Psalm 3:1-3 NKJV

Lord, how they have increased who trouble me!
Many *are* they who rise up against me.
Many *are* they who say of me,
"*There is* no help for him in God." Selah
But You, O Lord, *are* a shield for me,
My glory and the One who lifts up my head.

————— DECLARATION OF FAITH —————

When many rise against me to trouble me saying, "There is no help for
him/her in God," I will not throw down my faith. My heavenly Father is faithful.
He is my shield against all trouble and persecution. He lifts my head in honor
and covers me with His glory as a testimony to all of my enemies.

(Leviticus 26:13; Psalm 9:13; 27:6; Hebrews 10:35; Romans 1:16; 2 Timothy 3:12;
Romans 8:30-37)

Psalm 3:5-7 AMP

I lay down and slept; I wakened again, for the Lord sustains me. I will not be afraid
of ten thousands of people who have set themselves against me round about.

Arise, O Lord; save me, O my God! For You have struck all my enemies on the
cheek; You have broken the teeth of the ungodly.

————— DECLARATION OF FAITH —————

I stretch myself out to sleep in perfect peace, free of all anxiety.

When my rest is complete, I awake again and find the Lord at my side, keeping guard over my life. He is an ever-present sentinel who never fails to protect
me from the attacks of my enemies. I will not fear even tens of thousands drawn
up against me, for I am never alone. The Lord of Hosts is my companion and ally.
He strikes my enemies down in a fierce display of His power. His mighty fist shat-
ters their teeth.

So let the enemy bark all he wants. His bite is nothing to me.

(Leviticus 26:6; Psalm 4:8; 23:4; 27:3; 121; 127:2; Exodus 23:20-30; 1 John 4:1-4)

Psalm 4:3,4 NIV

Know that the Lord has set apart the godly for himself; the Lord will hear when
I call to him. In your anger do not sin; when you are on your beds, search your
hearts and be silent. Selah.

——— *DECLARATION OF FAITH* ———

The Lord has set me apart for Himself. He hears me when I call to Him and He is always ready to communicate with me.

When I burn with anger, I will not allow it to give birth to bitterness and sin. I direct my anger—it does not direct me.

When I lie down, I will listen for the voice of the Holy Spirit. I will search my heart and be silent.

(1 John 1:3; 5:14; 2 Timothy 2:19; Ephesians 4:26; Psalm 77:6)

PSALM 4:5-7 AMP

Offer just and right sacrifices; trust (lean on and be confident) in the Lord. Many say, Oh, that we might see some good! Lift up the light of Your countenance upon us, O Lord. You have put more joy and rejoicing in my heart than [they know] when their wheat and new wine have yielded abundantly.

——— *DECLARATION OF FAITH* ———

I continually offer the sacrifices of righteousness and forever put my trust in the Lord. When times are tough, I am tougher. When others see nothing good in their lives, I see everything good in mine. The Lord shines His face upon me and places gladness in my heart. My happiness increases in adversity even more than in times of increase, for I know the One in whom I believe and He has a double portion for me on the other side of the problem.

(Job 42:10; Hebrews 13:5,6; James 1:2-4; Romans 4:17,18; 2 Timothy 1:12)

PSALM 4:8 NKJV

I will both lie down in peace, and sleep;
For You alone, O Lord, make me dwell in safety.

——— *DECLARATION OF FAITH* ———

I will lie down and sleep in perfect peace—safe and secure in the arms of my heavenly Father.

(Psalm 3:5; Leviticus 25:18; Deuteronomy 12:10; 33:12; Ephesians 2:14)

PSALM 5:7-10 KJV

But as for me, I will come *into* thy house in the multitude of thy mercy: *and* in thy fear will I worship toward thy holy temple. Lead me, O Lord, in thy righteousness because of mine enemies; make thy way straight before my face. For *there is* no faithfulness in their mouth; their inward part *is* very wickedness; their throat *is* an open sepulchre; they flatter with their tongue. Destroy thou them, O God; let them fall by their own counsels; cast them out in the multitude of their transgressions; for they have rebelled against thee.

—— DECLARATION OF FAITH ——

Because of the multitude of my Father's mercies, I can come boldly into His presence. In deep reverence and respect I worship Him and send my praise before His throne.

My Father leads me in His righteousness because of my enemies and makes His way straight before me. He does not allow them to overtake me in any way. He pronounces them guilty before me and sentences them to fall by their own counsels. He casts them out of my presence for He has declared that when they come against me, they are coming against Him.

(Hebrews 4:16; Psalm 27:11; 1 Samuel 25:39; Deuteronomy 20:3,4; John 15:23,24)

PSALM 5:11,12 AMP

But let all those who take refuge and put their trust in You rejoice; let them ever sing and shout for joy, because You make a covering over them and defend them; let those also who love Your name be joyful in You and be in high spirits.

For You, Lord, will bless the [uncompromisingly] righteous [him who is upright and in right standing with You]; as with a shield You will surround him with goodwill (pleasure and favor).

—— DECLARATION OF FAITH ——

It is such a joy for me to be able to trust in the Lord. Knowing that His eyes never leave me and that He is always there to defend me fills my heart with elation! He has set me apart to bless me with His abundance and surrounds me with His favor as with a shield.

(Proverbs 3:3-6; Psalm 3:5,6; 11:4; 35:1; Nehemiah 1:5,6; 8:10; Genesis 12:1-3)

PSALM 6:8-10 NKJV

Depart from me, all you workers of iniquity; for the Lord has heard the voice of my weeping. The Lord has heard my supplication; the Lord will receive my prayer. Let all my enemies be ashamed and greatly troubled; let them turn back and be ashamed suddenly.

The Lord has heard my supplication and has risen in my defense. All of my enemies shall be defeated before my face. They have met with the fierce anger of my Father and run from me utterly terrified. Sudden disaster has come upon them and they shall not escape.

(Deuteronomy 2:25; 2 Chronicles 20:15-25; James 4:7)

PSALM 7:10 NKJV

My defense *is* of God, who saves the upright in heart.

My Father knows me thoroughly and weighs the thoughts and intents of my heart.

He is the very shield of my salvation. He is my defense in troubled times.

(1 Samuel 16:7; Hebrews 4:12; Psalm 35:1; Numbers 24:9; Genesis 15:1)

PSALM 7:13-16 KJV

He hath also prepared for him the instruments of death; he ordaineth his arrows against the persecutors. Behold, he travaileth with iniquity, and hath conceived mischief, and brought forth falsehood. He made a pit, and digged it, and is fallen into the ditch *which* he made. His mischief shall return upon his own head, and his violent dealing shall come down upon his own pate.

The wicked has conceived a strategy against me, but my Father has risen in my defense. He has sharpened His sword and His bow is bent and ready. His anger is kindled because of His love for me. The enemy must now face the Lord of the universe!

All that the enemy conceived against me has become his own undoing. His plan for my destruction has become the pit in which he shall fall. His trouble has returned to his own head and his violent dealings with me have become his own downfall.

The tide has now turned. I have the victory!

(Isaiah 41:10-13; 54:17; 2 Samuel 22; 2 Chronicles 20:15-25; 1 John 5:4)

PSALM 8:2 AMP

Out of the mouths of babes and unweaned infants You have established strength because of Your foes, that You might silence the enemy and the avenger.

——— *DECLARATION OF FAITH* ———

When trouble comes, and the odds seem overwhelming, I will sing praises to my Father. This is my strength and the weapon with which I silence the enemy and quiet the avenger.

(2 Chronicles 20:15-24; Psalm 111:1-10; 1 Samuel 16:14-23; Acts 16:22-26)

PSALM 8:4-6 NIV

What is man that you are mindful of him, the son of man that you care for him? You made him a little lower than the heavenly beings and crowned him with glory and honor. You made him ruler over the works of your hands; you put everything under his feet:

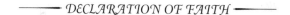

——— *DECLARATION OF FAITH* ———

God is ever-mindful of me and cares for me with unwavering diligence.
He has created me to be just short of divine (Elohim; God; heavenly beings) and has crowned me with glory and honor.

(Hebrews 2:6-8; Genesis 1:26-28; 1 Corinthians 15:27; Ephesians 1:17-23; 2:6-10)

PSALM 9:1-5 KJV

I will praise *thee,* O Lord, with my whole heart; I will shew forth all thy marvellous works. I will be glad and rejoice in thee: I will sing praise to thy name, O thou most High. When mine enemies are turned back, they shall fall and perish at thy presence. For thou hast maintained my right and my cause; thou satest in the throne judging right. Thou hast rebuked the heathen, thou hast destroyed the wicked, thou hast put out their name for ever and ever.

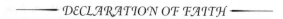

——— *DECLARATION OF FAITH* ———

The Lord inhabits my praises to Him. When I praise Him with my whole heart and rejoice in His presence, it produces a shield that stops the enemy in his tracks.
It is God who rises in my defense. My enemies fall and perish at His presence.

The Lord my God has maintained my cause. All of my enemies turn back from me and flee in terror.

(James 4:7; Psalm 8:2; 22:3; Exodus 23:27-30)

PSALM 9:9,10 AMP

The Lord also will be a refuge and a high tower for the oppressed, a refuge and a stronghold in times of trouble (high cost, destitution, and desperation).

And they who know Your name [who have experience and acquaintance with Your mercy] will lean on and confidently put their trust in You, for You, Lord, have not forsaken those who seek (inquire of and for) You [on the authority of God's Word and the right of their necessity].

DECLARATION OF FAITH

I seek the Lord with all of my heart. He is my refuge and stronghold in times of trouble. He is my trusted Friend who will never leave me nor forsake me.

(Deuteronomy 4:29; 2 Chronicles 15:4; Psalm 91:1,2; Hebrews 13:5,6)

PSALM 10:17,18 AMP

O Lord, You have heard the desire and the longing of the humble and oppressed; You will prepare and strengthen and direct their hearts, You will cause Your ear to hear, to do justice to the fatherless and the oppressed, so that man, who is of the earth, may not terrify them any more.

DECLARATION OF FAITH

The Lord has prepared my heart for His fellowship. His ear is attentive to the sound of my voice and He has prepared Himself to guide me in my way. Those who oppress me shall now meet His justice. He has risen in my defense so the oppressor can oppress me no more.

(Exodus 14:13,14; Psalm 31:3,4; Isaiah 41:10-13)

PSALM 11:4 NKJV

The Lord *is* in His holy temple,
The Lord's throne *is* in heaven;
His eyes behold,
His eyelids test the sons of men.

——— *DECLARATION OF FAITH* ———

The Lord examines my ways from His throne of grace in heaven. He is the regulator of my life and nothing escapes His attention.

(Isaiah 66:1; Acts 7:49,50; Psalm 23; Proverbs 16:9; Hebrews 4:12,13)

PSALM 11:7 NKJV

For the Lord *is* righteous,
He loves righteousness;
His countenance beholds the upright.

——— *DECLARATION OF FAITH* ———

*I am a man/woman of inflexible honesty and moral rectitude.
I will see the face of my Father in heaven.*

(Psalm 26:1-12; 33:5; 45:7; 86:11; 119:30; Proverbs 3:3; 12:17; Revelation 22:4; Job 2:3)

PSALM 12:6,7 KJV

The words of the Lord *are* pure words: *as* silver tried in a furnace of earth, purified seven times. Thou shalt keep them, O Lord, thou shalt preserve them from this generation for ever.

——— *DECLARATION OF FAITH* ———

God's Word to me is flawless. It is like silver refined in a furnace. He will not turn from His promise to protect me. From this day unto eternity, my heavenly Father will keep me safe from the plans, purposes, and pursuits of the wicked.

(2 Samuel 22:31; Psalm 18:30; 119:140; Proverbs 30:5; Exodus 23:20-23; 2 Corinthians 1:20)

PSALM 14:5,6 NKJV

There they are in great fear, for God is with the generation of the righteous. You shame the counsel of the poor, but the Lord is his refuge.

——— *DECLARATION OF FAITH* ———

I have chosen to do what is right in this earth and be the best man/woman that I can possibly be. For this reason, God has taken His stand at my side. He strengthens and protects me against all evil. This unnerves the wicked and they are filled with terror in my presence.

(Psalm 89:21-23; Hebrews 13:5,6; Deuteronomy 2:25; 11:25; 28:1,7,10; Joshua 2:9-11)

PSALM 15:2-5 KJV

He that walketh uprightly, and worketh righteousness, and speaketh the truth in his heart. *He that* backbiteth not with his tongue, nor doeth evil to his neighbour, nor taketh up a reproach against his neighbour. In whose eyes a vile person is contemned; but he honoureth them that fear the Lord. *He that* sweareth to *his own* hurt, and changeth not. *He that* putteth not out his money to usury, nor taketh reward against the innocent. He that doeth these *things* shall never be moved.

——— *DECLARATION OF FAITH* ———

I choose to live my life blamelessly and do what is right in the sight of God.

I speak the truth from my heart. No false tale or malicious report can be found on my tongue.

I do my neighbor no wrong. I make it a point to be attentive to the ways and needs of my fellowman.

I despise the ways of the world and give due honor to the children of God.

I keep my every promise, even when it hurts.

I lend money to my people, not expecting anything extra in return, and I do not accept bribes against the innocent.

I am steadfast in my commitment to the statutes of the Lord and I shall never be shaken.

(Joshua 24:15; Deuteronomy 28:1; 1 Peter 1:15,16; Proverbs 8:7; Romans 13:9,10; Ephesians 4:25; Esther 3:2; 2 Peter 1:10)

PSALM 16:2 AMP

I say to the Lord, You are my Lord; I have no good beside or beyond You.

——— *DECLARATION OF FAITH* ———

Without God, all that I am and all that I have is worthless.

(Philippians 3:8,9; Job 35:7; Isaiah 64:6; Romans 10:3)

PSALM 16:5-11 KJV

The Lord *is* the portion of mine inheritance and of my cup: thou maintainest my lot. The lines are fallen unto me in pleasant *places;* yea, I have a goodly heritage. I will bless the Lord, who hath given me counsel: my reins also instruct me in the night seasons. I have set the Lord always before me: because *he is* at my right hand, I shall not be moved. Therefore my heart is glad, and my glory rejoiceth: my flesh also shall rest in hope. For thou wilt not leave my soul in hell;

neither wilt thou suffer thine Holy One to see corruption. Thou wilt shew me the path of life: in thy presence *is* fulness of joy; at thy right hand *there are* pleasures for evermore.

——— *DECLARATION OF FAITH* ———

My heavenly Father has assigned me my share of His inheritance and my cup overflows continually. He has set my boundaries in a spacious and pleasant land, and has given me a delightful endowment.

I praise the Lord for His counsel. Even at night, my spirit guides me in His way. With Him at my right hand, I shall stand strong in every circumstance.

What a joy it is to be a child of God! My heart leaps within me and my tongue rejoices in His praise! I am raised with Jesus and shall never be abandoned to hell. He has made known to me the path of life and fills me with joy in His presence. At His right hand, I shall have abundant pleasures for all of eternity.

(Romans 6:3-5; 8:14-17; Ephesians 1:3,4; 2:6; 6:10; Psalm 23:5; 139:24; Acts 2:22-39; John 16:13)

PSALM 17:3-14 KJV

Thou hast proved mine heart; thou hast visited *me* in the night; thou hast tried me, *and* shalt find nothing; I am purposed *that* my mouth shall not transgress. Concerning the works of men, by the word of thy lips I have kept *me from* the paths of the destroyer. Hold up my goings in thy paths, *that* my footsteps slip not. I have called upon thee, for thou wilt hear me, O God: incline thine ear unto me, *and hear* my speech. Shew thy marvellous lovingkindness, O thou that savest by thy right hand them which put their trust *in thee* from those that rise up *against them.* Keep me as the apple of the eye, hide me under the shadow of thy wings, From the wicked that oppress me, *from* my deadly enemies, *who* compass me about. They are inclosed in their own fat: with their mouth they speak proudly. They have now compassed us in our steps: they have set their eyes bowing down to the earth; Like as a lion *that* is greedy of his prey, and as it were a young lion lurking in secret places. Arise, O Lord, disappoint him, cast him down: deliver my soul from the wicked, *which is* thy sword: From men *which are* thy hand, O Lord, from men of the world, *which have* their portion in *this* life, and whose belly thou fillest with thy hid *treasure:* they are full of children, and leave the rest of their *substance* to their babes.

——— *DECLARATION OF FAITH* ———

Though I am examined from the inside out and even surprised in the middle of the night, I shall not be caught in sinful speech. I am determined that the words of my mouth will be pure and in perfect agreement with the Word of God.

By the Word of God I keep my life safe from the paths of the destroyer. My feet do not slip and my ways remain upright.

I am held secure in the arms of my Father. When I call to Him, He hears me and rescues me from all oppression. He keeps me as the apple of His eye and hides me in the shadow of His wings.

When my enemies surround me and plot my ruin, God intervenes on my behalf. He draws His sword and clears the way before me. He takes the attack personally and delivers me with mighty acts of judgment.

The Lord cherishes me and holds me dear to His heart. He stills my hunger and supplies me with an abundance of provisions. My children live copiously with an unlimited supply of good things and I store up great wealth as an inheritance for each of them.

(Psalm 35:28; 103:13; 1 Peter 3:10; Proverbs 18:20,21; Mark 11:23,24; Matthew 12:37; Exodus 14:13,14; Deuteronomy 28:1-14; 33:12; Proverbs 13:22; 18:20,21; Philippians 4:19)

PSALM 18:3-19 KJV

I will call upon the Lord, *who is worthy* to be praised: so shall I be saved from mine enemies. The sorrows of death compassed me, and the floods of ungodly men made me afraid. The sorrows of hell compassed me about: the snares of death prevented me. In my distress I called upon the Lord, and cried unto my God: he heard my voice out of his temple, and my cry came before him, *even* into his ears. Then the earth shook and trembled; the foundations also of the hills moved and were shaken, because he was wroth. There went up a smoke out of his nostrils, and fire out of his mouth devoured: coals were kindled by it. He bowed the heavens also, and came down: and darkness *was* under his feet. And he rode upon a cherub, and did fly: yea, he did fly upon the wings of the wind. He made darkness his secret place; his pavilion round about him *were* dark waters *and* thick clouds of the skies. At the brightness *that was* before him his thick clouds passed, hail *stones* and coals of fire. The Lord also thundered in the heavens, and the Highest gave his voice; hail *stones* and coals of fire. Yea, he sent out his arrows, and scattered them; and he shot out lightnings, and discomfited them. Then the channels of waters were seen, and the foundations of the world were discovered at thy rebuke, O Lord, at the blast of the breath of thy nostrils. He sent from above, he took me, he drew me out of many waters. He delivered me from my strong enemy, and from them which hated me: for they were too strong for me. They prevented me in the day of my calamity: but the Lord was my stay. He brought me forth also into a large place; he delivered me, because he delighted in me.

———— DECLARATION OF FAITH ————

I will trust in the Lord, who is worthy of my praise—so shall I be saved from my enemies.

When the chains of hell entangle me, and the torrents of destruction storm over me, I remain safe and secure. When the forces of evil wrap their cords around me and I am confronted with the deadly traps of the enemy, I will not cower.

The Lord hears my voice in the midst of the turmoil.

All of this comes at the sound of my voice. When I cry out His name, He hears from heaven and rescues me in an instant. He reaches down from on high and draws me out of many waters. With Him as my refuge and battle cry, no enemy is too strong for me and no attack can overwhelm me. They may confront me in a day of disaster, but the Lord is my support. He draws me out of the fray and places me in a spacious land. He rescues me because He delights in me.

(2 Samuel 22; Psalm 4:1; 31:8; 80:1; 99:1; 144:1,7; Hebrews 2:13; Genesis 12:1-3; Exodus 23:20-30; John 3:16,17; Colossians 1:13; 2:15; Joshua 10:10; Isaiah 42:1)

PSALM 18:20-24 NKJV

The Lord rewarded me according to my righteousness; according to the cleanness of my hands He has recompensed me. For I have kept the ways of the Lord, and have not wickedly departed from my God. For all His judgments were before me, and I did not put away His statutes from me. I was also blameless before Him, and I kept myself from my iniquity. Therefore the Lord has recompensed me according to my righteousness, according to the cleanness of my hands in His sight.

———— DECLARATION OF FAITH ————

The Lord shows His power in my life because of my unyielding commitment to do His will. I have kept His ways and have not turned from Him. His Word is ever before me and His statutes are engrafted in my heart. I have made the quality choice to be blameless before Him and live my life without sin. By the power of His Spirit, I have remained clean and I am showered with a great recompense of reward.

(Deuteronomy 28:1; Ephesians 5:1,18; 1 Samuel 24:19; Romans 12:1; Hebrews 11:6)

PSALM 18:28-36 KJV

For thou wilt light my candle: the Lord my God will enlighten my darkness. For by thee I have run through a troop; and by my God have I leaped over a wall. *As for* God, his way *is* perfect: the word of the Lord is tried: he *is* a buckler to all those that trust in him. For who *is* God save the Lord? or who *is* a rock save our God? *It is* God that girdeth me with strength, and maketh my way perfect. He maketh my feet like hinds' *feet,* and setteth me upon my high places. He teacheth my hands to war, so that a bow of steel is broken by mine arms. Thou hast also given me the shield of thy salvation: and thy right hand hath holden me up, and thy gentleness hath made me great. Thou hast enlarged my steps under me, that my feet did not slip.

DECLARATION OF FAITH

The Lord keeps the fire burning within me and turns all of my darkness into light. He goes before me in my advance against the armies of darkness. His Word flows through me, in all of its perfection, as my shield, sword and refuge of protection.

It is my own heavenly Father who arms me with this strength and makes my way flawless before Him. He makes my feet fast and graceful as a deer, and enables me to stand in even the hottest of battles.

He trains me in the art of spiritual warfare and enables me to do what the world thinks impossible.

He gives me His shield of victory as an everlasting possession and His right hand sustains me every second of my life.

Yes, the Lord, my heavenly Father, has broadened the path beneath my feet so that in me there is no shadow of turning.

(Matthew 5:14-16; 25:1-13; Exodus 23:20-23; Psalm 119:41-43,50,93,116; Habakkuk 3:19; Ephesians 1:17-23; 2:6; 6:10-18; Genesis 12:1-3; Colossians 1:27-29)

PSALM 18:37-40 NKJV

I have pursued my enemies and overtaken them; neither did I turn back again till they were destroyed. I have wounded them, so that they could not rise; they have fallen under my feet. For You have armed me with strength for the battle; You have subdued under me those who rose up against me. You have also given me the necks of my enemies, so that I destroyed those who hated me.

─────── *DECLARATION OF FAITH* ───────

I take an offensive strategy against the enemy, relentlessly pursuing him and continually overtaking him. He wishes that I were never born. I refuse to turn back until he is utterly destroyed.

It is my Father who arms me with strength and has made all of my enemies to bow at my feet. At the sight of me, they turn their backs and flee in terror.

(2 Corinthians 10:3-6; Joshua 2:9-11; 10:19; Mark 3:27; Psalm 91:13; Deuteronomy 2:25; 11:25; 28:7,10; Exodus 23:27)

PSALM 19:7-11 NKJV

The law of the Lord is perfect, converting the soul;

The testimony of the Lord is sure, making wise the simple;

The statutes of the Lord are right, rejoicing the heart;

The commandment of the Lord is pure, enlightening the eyes;

The fear of the Lord is clean, enduring forever;

The judgments of the Lord are true and righteous altogether.

More to be desired are they than gold, yea, than much fine gold; sweeter also than honey and the honeycomb. Moreover by them Your servant is warned, and in keeping them there is great reward.

─────── *DECLARATION OF FAITH* ───────

My wisdom comes from the Word of my Father. The perfection of His ways have revived my soul and given joy to my heart. The radiance of His commands is the light by which I see.

The Word is more precious to me than the purest of gold and sweeter to me than honey from the comb. By it, I am warned of all pending danger and in keeping the statutes therein, I store up the greatest of rewards.

(Psalm 119:72,98-100,130; 1 Corinthians 2:6-10; Proverbs 8:10,11,19)

PSALM 20:4 NKJV

May He grant you according to your heart's *desire,* and fulfill all your purpose.

─────── *DECLARATION OF FAITH* ───────

The Lord grants me all of the desires of my heart and causes all of my plans to succeed.

(Proverbs 5:21; 15:22; 16:3; Psalm 21:2; Joshua 1:8; John 14:13,14; 15:7)

PSALM 20:7,8 NKJV

Some trust in chariots, and some in horses; but we will remember the name of the Lord our God. They have bowed down and fallen; but we have risen and stand upright.

DECLARATION OF FAITH

I do not put my trust in the things of the world to provide my security and protection in life. My bank account is not my security and my house is not my shelter, nor do worldly weapons provide my protection. My trust is in the name of the Lord Most High. He is my shelter, my shield and my unfailing provision. All other things will be brought down and crushed, but in the power of His name, I rise up and stand steady as an immovable rock.

(Deuteronomy 20:1; Isaiah 30:1; Psalm 33:16,17; Proverbs 21:31; Philippians 4:19)

PSALM 21:1-12 KJV

The king shall joy in thy strength, O Lord; and in thy salvation how greatly shall he rejoice! Thou hast given him his heart's desire, and hast not withholden the request of his lips. Selah For thou preventest him with the blessings of goodness: thou settest a crown of pure gold on his head. He asked life of thee, *and* thou gavest *it* him, *even* length of days for ever and ever. His glory *is* great in thy salvation: honour and majesty hast thou laid upon him. For thou hast made him most blessed for ever: thou hast made him exceeding glad with thy countenance. For the king trusteth in the Lord, and through the mercy of the most High he shall not be moved. Thine hand shall find out all thine enemies: thy right hand shall find out those that hate thee. Thou shalt make them as a fiery oven in the time of thine anger: the Lord shall swallow them up in his wrath, and the fire shall devour them. Their fruit shalt thou destroy from the earth, and their seed from among the children of men. For they intended evil against thee: they imagined a mischievous device, *which* they are not able *to perform.* Therefore shalt thou make them turn their back, *when* thou shalt make ready *thine arrows* upon thy strings against the face of them.

DECLARATION OF FAITH

I rejoice in the strength of my Father, for He has given me my heart's desire. He who knows me better than I know myself has prepared the way for me and has given me an inheritance to perfectly suit my needs and personality. All of my requests are granted and my joy knows no bounds!

A crown of pure gold has been placed upon my head and abundance rains down on me like a satisfying spring rain.

I asked life of Him and He gave it to me. The length of my days is now eternal! Forever I will praise His name!

My glory abounds in His salvation. Honor and majesty have been placed upon me. I am now born again under the bloodline of the King!

My Father's glory surrounds me and His presence is within me.

I trust in Him and I am not afraid. Because of His mercy, I shall not be moved.

All who rise against me have chosen to battle against the Lord almighty! He will search them out and destroy them! They shall be as ashes beneath my feet! My Father's anger is kindled against them. He shall swallow them up in His wrath and a fire shall devour them! All of their cohorts will fall together with them. They shall be destroyed from the earth. They shall be no more.

My enemies have devised and plotted wicked schemes against me that they will be unable to perform. My Father has drawn His bow and has aimed it right in their faces! He makes them turn back and flee from me in stark terror!

Be exalted, Lord, in Your strength! I pay tribute to Your power! Destroy all of my enemies! As You have promised, make them as nothing before me!

(John 16:23,24; Psalm 79:12; Genesis 12:1-3; Exodus 23:27; James 4:7; Isaiah 41:10-13; Deuteronomy 32:30; Ephesians 6:10-18)

PSALM 23 KJV

The Lord *is* my shepherd; I shall not want. He maketh me to lie down in green pastures: he leadeth me beside the still waters. He restoreth my soul: he leadeth me in the paths of righteousness for his name's sake. Yea, though I walk through the valley of the shadow of death, I will fear no evil: for thou *art* with me; thy rod and thy staff they comfort me. Thou preparest a table before me in the presence of mine enemies: thou anointest my head with oil; my cup runneth over. Surely goodness and mercy shall follow me all the days of my life: and I will dwell in the house of the Lord for ever.

———— DECLARATION OF FAITH ————

The Lord is my Shepherd, a fierce guardian who watches over me with a relentless eye.

He fills all of my needs and desires so that I am in want of nothing.

He makes me to lie down in green pastures—a fertile land of abundance.

He leads me beside the still and quiet streams of life-giving water.

He restores my life to full vitality.

He guides me in the paths of righteousness for His name's sake alone and not by my own merits.

Even if I am walking in the midst of death's domain, I will fear no evil, for I know that the Lord is with me. The rod of His wrath and the staff of His power bring me comfort.

He prepares a table for me of the choicest portions of His bounty right in the presence of my enemies. They look on in humiliation as I feast upon His blessings.

He covers my head with His burden-removing, yoke-destroying power and my prosperity flows from me in a shower of abundance.

His love and His mercy cling to me all the days of my life and He calls me His own forevermore.

(John 10:7-14; Philippians 4:19; Ezekiel 34:14; Revelation 7:17; Psalm 5:8-12; 104:15; Isaiah 43:1,2; 2 Timothy 1:7; 1 John 2:27)

PSALM 25:3-5 NIV

No one whose hope is in you will ever be put to shame, but they will be put to shame who are treacherous without excuse. Show me your ways, O Lord, teach me your paths; guide me in your truth and teach me, for you are God my Savior, and my hope is in you all day long.

——— DECLARATION OF FAITH ———

I will never be put to shame for trusting in the Lord. He shows me His ways and teaches me His paths so that I have a full understanding of His will for my life. He guides me in His truth and reveals to me all that I need to know to reign as a king in this life. My hope is in Him every second, of every minute, of every hour, of every day.

(Romans 1:16; 5:17; 1 Corinthians 2:6-16; Exodus 33:13; Psalm 5:8-12; 86:11)

PSALM 25:9-15 KJV

The meek will he guide in judgment: and the meek will he teach his way. All the paths of the Lord *are* mercy and truth unto such as keep his covenant and his testimonies. For thy name's sake, O Lord, pardon mine iniquity; for it *is* great. What man *is* he that feareth the Lord? him shall he teach in the way *that* he shall choose. His soul shall dwell at ease; and his seed shall inherit the earth. The secret of the Lord *is* with them that fear him; and he will shew them his covenant. Mine eyes *are* ever toward the Lord; for he shall pluck my feet out of the net.

─────── *DECLARATION OF FAITH* ───────

I humble myself under God's mighty hand and He guides me in the ways of righteousness. He teaches me His ways so that I have an intimate understanding of His will.

I have a thorough understanding of His love and faithfulness toward me. He is not good to me only some of the time; He is good to me all of the time.

I am His covenant partner and a child who bears His name.

He has forgiven my every iniquity and washed away even the worst of my stains. He has chosen a path for me to walk in and guides me in it without fail.

His desire for me is prosperity—a life full of riches and an abundance of all good things.

He has declared that my descendants will inherit the land.

I will never take my eyes off of Him, for He is my only hope of freedom from the invisible snares of the devil.

(1 Peter 5:5-7; 1 Corinthians 2:6-16; Psalm 27:11; 69:35,36; 91:3; 103:1-5; 143:11; John 10:10; 15:15; Leviticus 26:9; Hebrews 8:6; 10:15-17; Genesis 50:20)

Psalm 26:4-7 NKJV

I have not sat with idolatrous mortals, nor will I go in with hypocrites. I have hated the assembly of evildoers, and will not sit with the wicked. I will wash my hands in innocence; so I will go about Your altar, O Lord, that I may proclaim with the voice of thanksgiving, and tell of all Your wondrous works.

─────── *DECLARATION OF FAITH* ───────

I do not associate myself with deceitful people, nor do I consort with hypocrites. I separate myself from cheaters and perverters of truth, and despise the presence of those who practice evil. I wash my hands in innocence of their actions and give my whole heart to the ways of righteousness.

I am a man/woman with a good report who proclaims aloud the praises of my God, telling everyone who will listen of His mercy and wonderful deeds.

(2 Corinthians 6:14; Psalm 1:1; 31:6; 139:21; Jeremiah 15:17; Ephesians 5:6,7)

Psalm 27:1-3 NKJV

The Lord is my light and my salvation; whom shall I fear? The Lord is the strength of my life; of whom shall I be afraid? When the wicked came against me to eat up my flesh, my enemies and foes, they stumbled and fell. Though an army may encamp against me, my heart shall not fear; though war may rise against me, in this I will be confident.

──── *DECLARATION OF FAITH* ────

The Lord is my light and my salvation—I shall fear no one. The very creator of the universe is the impenetrable fortress of safety in my life. For me to fear any enemy would be ludicrous.

When the enemy advances against me to devour my flesh, they will trip over their own devices and fall with a great destruction. Though a vast, innumerable army surrounds me, demanding my surrender, my heart will be still and I will not give in to terror. Even if they all attack at once and the odds appear over-whelming, I will still remain confident and full of courage for I know that my Father has taken His stand at my side. No matter what the odds may be, my victory is made certain and I will never give in to fear. I will never give in or give up.

(Psalm 18:28; 62:7; 84:11; Isaiah 12:2; 33:2; 60:19,20; Exodus 15:2; 2 Timothy 1:7)

PSALM 27:4 NKJV

One thing I have desired of the Lord, that will I seek: that I may dwell in the house of the Lord all the days of my life, to behold the beauty of the Lord, and to inquire in His temple.

──── *DECLARATION OF FAITH* ────

I am the Lord's own child and will dwell in His house forever. With my own eyes I shall see the splendor of His glory.

But for now, I shall look inwardly for His fellowship in this holy temple (the temple of my body).

(Galatians 4:5,6; Psalm 23:6; Revelation 22:4; 1 Corinthians 3:16; 1 John 1:3)

PSALM 27:5,6 NKJV

For in the time of trouble He shall hide me in His pavilion; In the secret place of His tabernacle He shall hide me; He shall set me high upon a rock. And now my head shall be lifted up above my enemies all around me; Therefore I will offer sacrifices of joy in His tabernacle; I will sing, yes, I will sing praises to the Lord.

──── *DECLARATION OF FAITH* ────

In the day of trouble, the Lord keeps me safe in His holy dwelling. He hides me in the shelter of His tabernacle and sets me high upon an immovable rock. He bids me to hold my head up high above the enemy who surrounds me, and to shout joyful praises despite what I see. I will offer Him the sacrifice of my praises in every situation—singing and making music to Him with all of my heart.

(Psalm 3:3; 31:30; 91:1,2; Ephesians 5:19; Leviticus 26:13; 2 Corinthians 5:7)

PSALM 27:10,11 KJV

When my father and my mother forsake me, then the Lord will take me up. Teach me thy way, O Lord, and lead me in a plain path, because of mine enemies.

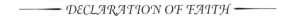

Even if my father and mother were to forsake me, the Lord would take me in. He loves me just the way that I am and receives me with great joy and gladness.

All of my oppressors present no problem for me, for the Lord is my Guide. He teaches me His ways and leads me on a clear path toward victory.

(Isaiah 49:15; Psalm 25:4; 86:11; 103:13; 119:33; Ephesians 2:8-9; 1 Corinthians 15:57)

PSALM 27:13,14 NKJV

I would have lost heart, unless I had believed that I would see the goodness of the Lord in the land of the living. Wait on the Lord; be of good courage, and He shall strengthen your heart; wait, I say, on the Lord!

I remain steadfast and confident in the fact that I will see the goodness of God in my life. I will be strong and take heart for I know that He is with me. I will wait for His manifestation of power. I will be patient and wait upon the Lord.

(Deuteronomy 6:24; Psalm 23:6; Ephesians 6:10; Isaiah 40:29-31)

PSALM 28:7 NKJV

The Lord is my strength and my shield; my heart trusted in Him, and I am helped; therefore my heart greatly rejoices, and with my song I will praise Him.

——— DECLARATION OF FAITH ———

The Lord is my ever-present helper. He is always there for me and brings me to victory no matter what situation or circumstance I find myself in. He is my strength and my shield, and I will trust in Him with a steadfast heart.

I leap for joy at the thought of Him. Joyful songs of thanksgiving spring from my heart in adoration of Him.

(Proverbs 3:5,6; Ephesians 5:19; Psalm 13:5; 18:2; 59:17; 112:7)

PSALM 29:11 AMP

The Lord will give [unyielding and impenetrable] strength to His people; the Lord will bless His people with peace.

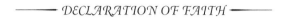

——— *DECLARATION OF FAITH* ———

The Lord gives me an abundance of strength and power for daily living and blesses me with His peace and security.

(Acts 1:8; Romans 14:17; Psalm 28:8; 68:35; Isaiah 40:29)

PSALM 30:2-7 NKJV

O Lord my God, I cried out to You, and You healed me. O Lord, You brought my soul up from the grave; You have kept me alive, that I should not go down to the pit. Sing praise to the Lord, you saints of His, and give thanks at the remembrance of His holy name. For His anger is but for a moment, His favor is for life; weeping may endure for a night, but joy comes in the morning. Now in my prosperity I said, "I shall never be moved." Lord, by Your favor You have made my mountain stand strong; You hid Your face, and I was troubled.

——— *DECLARATION OF FAITH* ———

When the enemy comes against my body, I will take my refuge in the Lord. When I call to Him, He heals me. He delivers me from the clutches of the grave and spares me from the consequences of hell and the curse.

I will sing His praises with a sincere and upright heart, for He has given me an intimate knowledge of His ways and His will.

His anger lasts only a moment, but His favor and abundance of blessings last a lifetime.

I may weep during the night, but He will raise me up with rejoicing in the morning.

The Lord loves me and favors me as His own son/daughter. He makes me to stand firm so that I will never be shaken. The stronghold that I have built is saturated with His anointing. I cannot be defeated or overrun.

(Psalm 97:12; 103:1-18; 2 Peter 2:24; Galatians 3:13; 1 Corinthians 2:6-16; Isaiah 26:20; 54:7)

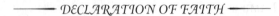

Psalm 31:3,4 NKJV

For You are my rock and my fortress; therefore, for Your name's sake, lead me and guide me. Pull me out of the net which they have secretly laid for me, for You are my strength.

─────── *DECLARATION OF FAITH* ───────

The Lord is my Rock and my fortress. He is the regulator of my ways. He faithfully leads me down His paths of righteousness and prosperity so that His name might be magnified in the earth.

He frees me from every trap that is set before me.

He is my refuge from the onslaughts of the enemy.

(1 Corinthians 10:4; John 16:13; Psalm 23:3; 25:11; 91:3; Exodus 23:20-30)

Psalm 31:7,8 NKJV

I will be glad and rejoice in Your mercy, for You have considered my trouble; You have known my soul in adversities, and have not shut me up into the hand of the enemy; You have set my feet in a wide place.

─────── *DECLARATION OF FAITH* ───────

My heart is filled with joy at the thought of God's love for me.

He saw me in my hour of affliction and understood the anguish of my soul. He refused to let the enemy take control of my life. Because of His deep love for me, He took up my case and came to my rescue.

My feet are now set in the spacious land of His prosperity where I can enjoy His blessings forevermore.

(Romans 8:38,39; Psalm 18:1-19; 1 John 2:1,2; John 10:27; Deuteronomy 32:30)

Psalm 31:12-24 KJV

I am forgotten as a dead man out of mind: I am like a broken vessel. For I have heard the slander of many: fear *was* on every side: while they took counsel together against me, they devised to take away my life. But I trusted in thee, O Lord: I said, Thou *art* my God. My times *are* in thy hand: deliver me from the hand of mine enemies, and from them that persecute me. Make thy face to shine upon thy servant: save me for thy mercies' sake. Let me not be ashamed, O Lord; for I have called upon thee: let the wicked be ashamed, *and* let them be silent in the grave. Let the lying lips be put to silence; which speak grievous things proudly and contemptuously against the righteous. *Oh* how great *is* thy goodness, which thou hast laid up for them that fear thee; *which* thou hast wrought for them that trust in thee before the sons of men! Thou shalt hide them in the secret of thy presence from the pride of man: thou shalt keep them secretly in a pavilion from the strife of tongues. Blessed *be* the Lord: for he hath shewed me his marvellous kindness in a strong city. For I said in my haste, I am cut off from before thine eyes: nevertheless thou heardest the voice of my supplications when I cried unto thee. O love the Lord, all ye his saints: *for* the Lord preserveth the faithful, and plentifully rewardeth the proud doer. Be of good courage, and he shall strengthen your heart, all ye that hope in the Lord.

──── *DECLARATION OF FAITH* ────

No matter what may happen in my life—even if my own sins have brought me to ruin and have made me a reproach among men, I will not lose faith, nor forget that I am a born-again son/daughter of the living God. I am one of God's redeemed ones and my rights are secured by the blood of Jesus!

When fear encompasses me on every side and my enemies come against me to destroy me, I will remember who I am and who I believe in. My trust is in God alone for my victory. I will not retaliate against them, but give place to the vengeance of my Father. All of my days are in His hands and He shall deliver me from my enemies and from those who persecute me.

He makes His face to shine upon me for His mercy's sake. For mercy's sake, He declares that I am perfect—free of all guilt. Therefore, the wicked who come against me shall be put to shame. They will be silent in their graves! Their proud and lying lips will be silenced and their harsh words against me shall be seen as insolent stupidity.

My Father hides me in His secret place from the plots of man. He shields me in His pavilion and nullifies the words of the wicked.

He has preserved me and strengthened my heart. Forever I will praise His name!

(Galatians 3:1-13; 2 Kings 6:14-18; Hebrews 10:14; Psalm 91:1,2)

PSALM 32:1,2 NIV

Blessed is he whose transgressions are forgiven, whose sins are covered. Blessed is the man whose sin the Lord does not count against him and in whose spirit is no deceit.

──── *DECLARATION OF FAITH* ────

I am blessed, for the Lord has forgiven all of my transgressions and has elimi-nated every sin that was set to my account.

I am blessed because my Father does not count any of my sins against me and has given me a spirit where deceit cannot be found.

(Psalm 103:10-12; Hebrews 10:14-17; Colossians 2:14; Romans 4:7,8; 2 Corinthians 5:17)

PSALM 32:7-10 NKJV

You are my hiding place; You shall preserve me from trouble; You shall surround me with songs of deliverance. Selah I will instruct you and teach you in the way you should go; I will guide you with My eye. Do not be like the horse or like the mule, which have no understanding, which must be harnessed with bit and bridle, else they will not come near you. Many sorrows shall be to the wicked; but he who trusts in the Lord, mercy shall surround him.

——— *DECLARATION OF FAITH* ———

God is my very hiding place against all harmful attacks. He shelters me in a hedge of protection. He preserves me from trouble and surrounds me with songs of deliverance.

It is the God of all the universe, my own heavenly Father, who counsels and watches over me with a relentless eye. He teaches me His ways and in His perfect instruction I am given specific knowledge of what I need to do in this life. I am not like a horse or a mule that needs to be led about by bridle and bit. I have a thorough understanding of God's will in my life. His unfailing love ever surrounds me and He sees to it that there is certainty in all that I do.

(1 Corinthians 1:30; 2:6-16; 1 John 1:3; John 16:13; Proverbs 16:20; 26:3)

PSALM 33:4 NKJV

For the word of the Lord is right, and all His work is done in truth.

——— *DECLARATION OF FAITH* ———

The Word of the Lord is faithful and true. I am confident and fully assured that I am who God says I am, and I can do what He says I can do.

(Mark 9:23; 11:22-25; Ephesians 2:10; 2 Corinthians 5:17; Galatians 4:5,6; Psalm 119:138,140; 1 Corinthians 2:12)

PSALM 33:11 NIV

But the plans of the Lord stand firm forever, the purposes of his heart through all generations.

————— *DECLARATION OF FAITH* —————

My Father's plans and purposes stand firm. They are settled in heaven for all of eternity. I am confident that every one of His promises will be accomplished in my life.

(2 Corinthians 1:20; Proverbs 19:21; Job 23:13; Psalm 119:89,90)

PSALM 33:18 NKJV

Behold, the eye of the Lord is on those who fear Him, on those who hope in His mercy.

————— *DECLARATION OF FAITH* —————

I am confident in my Father's unfailing love for me. His eye never leaves me and His purposes for me are always for good.

(1 Corinthians 13; 1 John 4:7,8; Job 36:7; 1 Peter 3:12; Nahum 1:7)

PSALM 34:4-10 KJV

I sought the Lord, and he heard me, and delivered me from all my fears. They looked unto him, and were lightened: and their faces were not ashamed. This poor man cried, and the Lord heard *him,* and saved him out of all his troubles. The angel of the Lord encampeth round about them that fear him, and delivereth them. O taste and see that the Lord *is* good: blessed *is* the man *that* trusteth in him. O fear the Lord, ye his saints: for *there is* no want to them that fear him. The young lions do lack, and suffer hunger: but they that seek the Lord shall not want any good *thing.*

————— *DECLARATION OF FAITH* —————

I seek the Lord with all of my heart and place His ways at the center of my thoughts.

He has become my refuge and deliverance from every fear.

He has made me to be radiant and to hold my head up high.

My confidence in Him is greatly rewarded and I am never put to shame. He hears my every prayer and delivers me out of every trouble.

His angel has been assigned to me to minister to all of my needs and give me provision and abundance in every circumstance. He encamps about me and fulfills God's purposes for me.

Experience has proven that the Lord is good. I take my refuge in Him and I am blessed. I have placed my steadfast confidence in Him and I lack no good thing in my life. Even the strongest in the world can become weak and hungry, but I am sustained and given great strength to persevere in every situation.

(Deuteronomy 4:29; 6:4; Joshua 1:8; Psalm 91; Hebrews 1:14; 4:16; Exodus 23:20-23)

PSALM 34:12-17 NKJV

Who is the man who desires life, and loves many days, that he may see good? Keep your tongue from evil, and your lips from speaking guile. Depart from evil and do good; seek peace and pursue it. The eyes of the Lord are on the righteous, and His ears are open to their cry. The face of the Lord is against those who do evil, to cut off the remembrance of them from the earth. The righteous cry out, and the Lord hears, and delivers them out of all their troubles.

———— *DECLARATION OF FAITH* ————

I love and enjoy the life that God has given me. All of my days are good ones, for I have chosen to live the God-kind of life. I have made my unyielding decision to keep my tongue from speaking evil things and to tell the truth in every situation. I have turned from the ways of the wicked and have focused my attention firmly on doing only that which is good.

I do not let peace escape from my life. I seek it like a relentless hunter and capture it as a precious prize.

The eyes of my Father never leave me and His ear is always opened to my prayers.

Though troubles come against me on a regular basis, the Lord delivers me out of every one!

(1 Peter 3:10-12; James 1:26; John 10:10; Romans 14:19; Isaiah 1:16,17; Amos 9:4; Psalm 145:19; 2 Timothy 3:12)

PSALM 34:18-22 NKJV

The Lord is near to those who have a broken heart, and saves such as have a contrite spirit. Many are the afflictions of the righteous, but the Lord delivers him out of them all. He guards all his bones; not one of them is broken. Evil shall slay the wicked, and those who hate the righteous shall be condemned. The Lord redeems the soul of His servants, and none of those who trust in Him shall be condemned.

———— *DECLARATION OF FAITH* ————

My Father comforts me when I am brokenhearted. When my spirit is crushed and I feel alone, He wraps His tender arms around me and embraces me in His love.

I am faced with troubles of many kinds, but the Lord delivers me out of every one.

I am identified with Jesus in every way. All that He did is set to my account. Therefore, I can count on my Father to protect me from all danger so that none of my bones can be broken.

Evil shall slay those who come against me and those who hate the righteousness I have chosen shall be desolate.

Through it all I stand unscathed. I am a redeemed and reborn son/daughter of the living God! There is absolutely no condemnation for me, for I have taken my refuge in the Lord.

(Acts 17:28; Psalm 51:17; 145:18; Proverbs 24:16; Genesis 12:1-3; 2 Timothy 3:12; Romans 8:1)

PSALM 35:1-8 KJV

Plead *my cause,* O Lord, with them that strive with me: fight against them that fight against me. Take hold of shield and buckler, and stand up for mine help. Draw out also the spear, and stop *the way* against them that persecute me: say unto my soul, I *am* thy salvation. Let them be confounded and put to shame that seek after my soul: let them be turned back and brought to confusion that devise my hurt. Let them be as chaff before the wind: and let the angel of the Lord chase *them.* Let their way be dark and slippery: and let the angel of the Lord persecute them. For without cause have they hid for me their net *in* a pit, *which* without cause they have digged for my soul. Let destruction come upon him at unawares; and let his net that he hath hid catch himself: into that very destruction let him fall.

—— *DECLARATION OF FAITH* ——

My Father contends with those who contend with me and fights against those who fight against me. He takes up His armor and shield, and rises to come to my aid. He shouts to the world that I am His and He is my salvation. If they want a piece of me, they're going to have to get through Him first!

By Him, all those who seek to destroy me are disgraced and put to shame. Those who plot my ruin shall turn from me in embarrassment. All of their plans are thwarted and set to confusion. Destruction shall come upon them suddenly. With the very net that they cast for me, they shall be trapped and not escape. They are like chaff in the wind as the angel of the Lord drives them away.

(Numbers 24:9; Exodus 23:20-30; Isaiah 29:5; Psalm 40:14,15; 73:18; 83:13)

PSALM 35:10-26 KJV

All my bones shall say, Lord, who *is* like unto thee, which deliverest the poor from him that is too strong for him, yea, the poor and the needy from him that spoileth him? False witnesses did rise up; they laid to my charge *things* that I knew not. They rewarded me evil for good to the spoiling of my soul. But as for me, when they were sick, my clothing *was* sackcloth: I humbled my soul with fasting; and my prayer returned into mine own bosom. I behaved myself as though *he had been* my friend or brother: I bowed down heavily, as one that mourneth *for his* mother. But in mine adversity they rejoiced, and gathered themselves together: *yea,* the abjects gathered themselves together against me, and I knew *it* not; they did tear *me,* and ceased not: With hypocritical mockers in feasts, they gnashed upon me with their teeth. Lord, how long wilt thou look on? rescue my soul from their destructions, my darling from the lions. I will give thee thanks in the great congregation: I will praise thee among much people. Let not them that are mine enemies wrongfully rejoice over me: *neither* let them wink with the eye that hate me without a cause. For they speak not peace: but they devise deceitful matters against *them that are* quiet in the land. Yea, they opened their mouth wide against me, *and* said, Aha, aha, our eye hath seen *it. This* thou hast seen, O Lord: keep not silence: O Lord, be not far from me. Stir up thyself, and awake to my judgment, even unto my cause, my God and my Lord. Judge me, O Lord my God, according to thy righteousness; and let them not rejoice over me. Let them not say in their hearts, Ah, so would we have it: let them not say, We have swallowed him up. Let them be ashamed and brought to confusion together that rejoice at mine hurt: let them be clothed with shame and dishonour that magnify *themselves* against me.

──────── *DECLARATION OF FAITH* ────────

God is on my side! Who can succeed against me?

My Father rescues me from destruction and the plans of evil people. He delivers me from those who are too strong for me. He takes up my case as His own and defends me as if He were defending Himself. Therefore, no one will plunder me and rob me of my goods.

When so-called friends become fierce witnesses and arise to do their best to catch me in my words, my Father exonerates me and stands as my advocate. My soul is sorrowful for such injustice, for I have prayed for them in their time of distress and looked out for them when they were in need. I prayed and fasted for them as if I myself were being afflicted. Yet they have repaid me with evil for my good.

In my adversity they have rejoiced. They conspired together behind my back and plotted my destruction. They tore at me and did not cease. Their words against me were hard and unjustified. But now the time of recompense has come.

My Father shall rescue me from their destructions! All praise be to His holy name! They shall not rejoice over me who have wrongly become my enemies. Their deceitfulness against me shall be brought to nothing! The eyes that they use to wink at each other in their plots against me shall be blinded. When they falsely accuse me and say, "Aha! We have seen it!" the Lord will not keep silent. He shall rise in my defense. They shall be ashamed and brought to confusion who rejoice at my pains. They shall see how much my Father loves me and will bow their heads in shame!

(Numbers 23:19-23; Genesis 12:1-3; Romans 8:31-39; Isaiah 41:10-13)

PSALM 35:27,28 NIV

May those who delight in my vindication shout for joy and gladness; may they always say, "The Lord be exalted, who delights in the well-being of his servant." My tongue will speak of your righteousness and of your praises all day long.

DECLARATION OF FAITH

The Lord is my mainstay. He delights in the abundance of my prosperity.

My tongue shall continually speak of His righteousness and sing His praises. May those who bear witness exalt His name forever.

(Isaiah 54:17; Jeremiah 29:11; Deuteronomy 6:7; Romans 12:15)

PSALM 36:7-9 NKJV

How precious is Your lovingkindness, O God! Therefore the children of men put their trust under the shadow of Your wings. They are abundantly satisfied with the fullness of Your house, and You give them drink from the river of Your pleasures. For with You is the fountain of life; in Your light we see light.

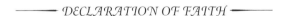
DECLARATION OF FAITH

I worship my Father for His unfailing love for me. I find sweet refuge in the shadow of His wings and I feast upon the abundance of His house. I have been granted a continuous flow of drink from His river of delights and He has reserved my portion of the fountain of life. He is the Light of my life and His way will always be made plain before me.

(Psalm 63:5; 91:1-4; 112:1-3; Isaiah 25:6; Jeremiah 31:12-14; Revelation 22:1)

PSALM 37:1-6 KJV

Fret not thyself because of evildoers, neither be thou envious against the workers of iniquity. For they shall soon be cut down like the grass, and wither as the green herb. Trust in the Lord, and do good; *so* shalt thou dwell in the land, and verily thou shalt be fed. Delight thyself also in the Lord; and he shall give thee the desires of thine heart. Commit thy way unto the Lord; trust also in him; and he shall bring *it* to pass. And he shall bring forth thy righteousness as the light, and thy judgment as the noonday.

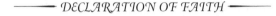

DECLARATION OF FAITH

I do not become stressed out over the actions of evil men, nor do I envy those who do wrong. They will all fade like the grass in winter, and like the green plants they will soon die away.

My purposes are set in the Lord to dwell in His spacious lands and enjoy the abundance of His pastures. I stand for what is good and right, and trust in Him with unfailing loyalty. He is my comfort and my delight, and He gives me all the desires of my heart. My way is committed to Him, to trust in Him in every circumstance. He will make my righteousness shine like the dawn and the justice of my cause will blaze like the noonday sun.

(1 Timothy 1:7; 1 Peter 5:5-7; Leviticus 5:1; Proverbs 3:5,6; 23:17; Psalm 90:5,6)

PSALM 37:9-11 NKJV

For evildoers shall be cut off; but those who wait on the Lord, they shall inherit the earth. For yet a little while and the wicked shall be no more; indeed, you will look carefully for his place, but it shall be no more. But the meek shall inherit the earth, and shall delight themselves in the abundance of peace.

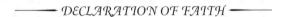

DECLARATION OF FAITH

Evil men will be brought down from their pedestals and I will inherit their land. I won't have to wait long to see this accomplished. I will inherit their land and enjoy God's peace in my lifetime.

(Proverbs 13:22; Psalm 37:35,36; 85:1-3; Hebrews 10:36; Isaiah 57:13; 60:21)

PSALM 37:18,19 NKJV

The Lord knows the days of the upright, and their inheritance shall be forever. They shall not be ashamed in the evil time, and in the days of famine they shall be satisfied.

——— DECLARATION OF FAITH ———

The Lord knows all of my days and is attentive to my needs and desires. My inheritance shall endure forever. Nothing, nor anyone, can take it from me. When disaster strikes, I remain calm, for I know that my provision comes from the Lord. In the hardest of times—through depression or famine—even then, I will enjoy His abundance. I never cease to have plenty in my life.

(Hebrews 9:15; Philippians 4:19; 2 Chronicles 31:10; Exodus 36:5; Malachi 3:10)

PSALM 37:21-26 KJV

The wicked borroweth, and payeth not again: but the righteous sheweth mercy, and giveth. For *such as be* blessed of him shall inherit the earth; and *they that be* cursed of him shall be cut off. The steps of a *good* man are ordered by the Lord: and he delighteth in his way. Though he fall, he shall not be utterly cast down: for the Lord upholdeth *him with* his hand. I have been young, and *now* am old; yet have I not seen the righteous forsaken, nor his seed begging bread. *He is* ever merciful, and lendeth; and his seed *is* blessed.

——— DECLARATION OF FAITH ———

I am not like the wicked who borrow and do not repay.

I give generously, with a happy and hilarious heart, and the Lord blesses me with His abundant provision. He has set aside a tremendous expanse of land as my inheritance.

My Father is overjoyed to spend His time with me. He rejoices as we walk this life together and He sees to it that all of my steps stand firm. Even if I stumble, I will not fall, for the Lord will catch me with His hand. He will never forsake me all the days of my life and my children shall never beg for a meal. I always have enough so that I may be generous and lend freely, and my children shall enjoy His abundance as well.

(2 Corinthians 8:2-5,12; 9:5-11; Philippians 4:10-20; Jude 24; Hebrews 13:5,6; 2 Chronicles 31:10; Psalm 40:2; 119:5; Proverbs 24:16; Deuteronomy 15:8)

PSALM 37:28 AMP

For the Lord delights in justice and forsakes not His saints; they are preserved forever, but the offspring of the wicked [in time] shall be cut off.

——— DECLARATION OF FAITH ———

The Lord loves me with unfailing passion and will never release me from His tender care. He has promised me on His oath that He will protect me forever.

(Psalm 103:13; John 6:37; 10:28,29; 16:27; 1 Peter 5:5-7; Hebrews 13:5,6)

PSALM 37:30-34 NKJV

The mouth of the righteous speaks wisdom, and his tongue talks of justice. The law of his God is in his heart; none of his steps shall slide. The wicked watches the righteous, and seeks to slay him. The Lord will not leave him in his hand, nor condemn him when he is judged. Wait on the Lord, and keep His way, and He shall exalt you to inherit the land; when the wicked are cut off, you shall see it.

——— DECLARATION OF FAITH ———

I am a man/woman of honor and integrity. My mouth speaks only the truth and wisdom flows from me like a fountain. God's Word is deeply rooted in my heart so that I will not stumble in my ways.

Though the wicked plot against me to take my very life, the Lord will not leave me in their power. I have no fear of their false accusations and unjust threats. When I am brought to trial I shall not be condemned, for the Lord, my righteous Advocate, has taken His stand at my side.

In His time, I shall be exalted to inherit the land, and when the wicked are cut off, I will be there to witness it.

(1 Corinthians 2:6-16; Psalm 2; 119:11; Isaiah 54:17; 1 Peter 5:5-7)

PSALM 37:37 NKJV

Mark the blameless man, and observe the upright; for the future of that man is peace.

——— DECLARATION OF FAITH ———

Because I have chosen to live my life blamelessly, the Lord has granted me a future full of prosperity and peace.

(Deuteronomy 28:1-14; Psalm 72:7; 112:1-10; Isaiah 2:4; Proverbs 13:22)

Psalm 37:39,40 nkjv

But the salvation of the righteous is from the Lord; He is their strength in the time of trouble. And the Lord shall help them and deliver them; He shall deliver them from the wicked, and save them, because they trust in Him.

———— DECLARATION OF FAITH ————

My salvation and deliverance come straight from the hand of God. He is my refuge and a secure stronghold in times of trouble. He sees to it that I have everything that I need and protects me from all danger. The wicked cannot overtake me, for I have taken my refuge in the Lord.

(Psalm 9:9; 22:4; 37:19; 91; Isaiah 31:5; Daniel 3:17; 6:23; 1 Chronicles 5:20)

Psalm 39:1 nkjv

I said, "I will guard my ways, lest I sin with my tongue; I will restrain my mouth with a muzzle, while the wicked are before me."

———— DECLARATION OF FAITH ————

When I am in the presence of the wicked I will keep my integrity. I will not be conformed to their ways and manner of speech. I place a muzzle over my mouth and my tongue refrains from all sin.

(2 Corinthians 6:14; Job 2:10; James 3:5-12; Psalm 34:13)

Psalm 39:4 nkjv

"Lord, make me to know my end, and what is the measure of my days, that I may know how frail I am."

———— DECLARATION OF FAITH ————

The Lord makes me to know my end and the length of my days I will spend on this earth. In this I will not be proud, but recognize how fragile my life truly is. I will never take for granted a single second of the life I am given.

(Psalm 21:4; Proverbs 3:1,2,13-17; James 4:13-16)

Psalm 40:1-4 kjv

I waited patiently for the Lord; and he inclined unto me, and heard my cry. He brought me up also out of an horrible pit, out of the miry clay, and set my feet upon a rock, *and* established my goings. And he hath put a new song in my mouth, *even* praise unto our God: many shall see *it,* and fear, and shall trust in the Lord. Blessed *is* that man that maketh the Lord his trust, and respecteth not the proud, nor such as turn aside to lies.

——— *DECLARATION OF FAITH* ———

I focus on the Lord alone for my unfailing provision. I wait patiently for His response to my prayers. I know His ear is inclined to me and He is ever faithful to answer me.

He delivers me from the horrible pit and pulls me out of the miry clay.

He has set my feet upon a rock and establishes my every step.

He has placed a new song in my mouth and His praises flood my lips.

Many will see what He has done and believe. My answered prayers are winning the souls of multitudes.

(1 John 5:14,15; Psalm 27:5,6)

PSALM 40:7,8 NKJV

Then I said, "Behold, I come; in the scroll of the book it is written of me. I delight to do Your will, O my God, and Your law is within my heart."

——— *DECLARATION OF FAITH* ———

My foremost desire is to do the will of my Father. His Word is engrafted in my spirit and I will accomplish His will for my life.

(John 4:32-34; 6:38; Matthew 26:39; Hebrews 10:7; 2 Corinthians 3:3)

PSALM 41:1-3 NKJV

Blessed is he who considers the poor; the Lord will deliver him in time of trouble. The Lord will preserve him and keep him alive, and he will be blessed on the earth; You will not deliver him to the will of his enemies. The Lord will strengthen him on his bed of illness; You will sustain him on his sickbed.

——— *DECLARATION OF FAITH* ———

The Lord delivers me out of every trouble and distressing situation. Because of this, I am a shield to those who lack the strength to stand against the devil's evil schemes.

He preserves my life from the attacks of the enemy and blesses me with His favor and abundance.

He sustains me when sickness comes to take me from His work. He restores me to my true, energetic and healthy self.

(Psalm 5:11,12; 27:12; 103:1-5; 112:1-3; Isaiah 40:29-31; James 5:14-16)

PSALM 42:5,8,11 NKJV

Why are you cast down, O my soul? And why are you disquieted within me? Hope in God, for I shall yet praise Him for the help of His countenance. The Lord will command His lovingkindness in the daytime, and in the night His song shall be with me—a prayer to the God of my life. Why are you cast down, O my soul? And why are you disquieted within me? Hope in God; for I shall yet praise Him, the help of my countenance and my God.

——— DECLARATION OF FAITH ———

I refuse to be depressed about any circumstance or situation I find myself in. I will never forget that my heavenly Father loves me with all of His heart and is caring for me every second of every day. He commands His lovingkindness in the daytime and at night His song remains with me. My Father never fails to be there for me. He is my Comforter who restores to me the joy of my salvation.

(Nehemiah 8:10; Psalm 51:12; Romans 14:17; Galatians 5:22; Philippians 4:4)

PSALM 43:1-5 KJV

Judge me, O God, and plead my cause against an ungodly nation: O deliver me from the deceitful and unjust man. For thou art the God of my strength: why dost thou cast me off? why go I mourning because of the oppression of the enemy? O send out thy light and thy truth: let them lead me; let them bring me unto thy holy hill, and to thy tabernacles. Then will I go unto the altar of God, unto God my exceeding joy: yea, upon the harp will I praise thee, O God my God. Why art thou cast down, O my soul? and why art thou disquieted within me? hope in God: for I shall yet praise him, *who is* the health of my countenance, and my God.

——— DECLARATION OF FAITH ———

My Father is always with me. He is my deliverer from deceitful and unjust men. He is the strength of my life and the surety of my victory. He will never cast me off or find reason to reject me. Therefore, when the enemy oppresses me, I will not allow it to bring me to ruin or cause my countenance to fall. The Lord sends out His light and His truth to guide my way. He leads me with joy into His holy place and bids me to feast upon His goodness. My hope springs eternal and I will forever praise His name!

(Hebrews 13:5,6; Psalm 18:2,3; 73:24-26; John 6:37)

Psalm 44:5-8 NKJV

Through You we will push down our enemies; through Your name we will trample those who rise up against us. For I will not trust in my bow, nor shall my sword save me. But You have saved us from our enemies, and have put to shame those who hated us. In God we boast all day long, and praise Your name forever. Selah

——— DECLARATION OF FAITH ———

With the strength of my heavenly Father I push back my enemies and through His name I trample over my foes. I have no need to trust in the weapons of this world to win my battles, because God has already fought the battle for me. The victory has already been won and all of my adversaries have been put to shame. Therefore, I will boast in His victory all the day long and praise His holy name forever.

(Psalm 34:2; 91:13; Luke 10:19; Joshua 2:9-11; Exodus 14:13,14; 1 Corinthians 15:57)

Psalm 45:1,2 NKJV

My heart is overflowing with a good theme; I recite my composition concerning the King; my tongue is the pen of a ready writer. You are fairer than the sons of men; grace is poured upon Your lips; therefore God has blessed You forever.

——— DECLARATION OF FAITH ———

My spirit is stirred and elated within me as I speak these words to my King. My tongue is as the pen of a ready writer to proclaim His praises today. He has made me to be the most excellent of men/women, and by His divine enabling, my lips carry His powerful anointing to the world.

His blessings upon me shall never end.

(2 Timothy 1:6; 2 Peter 1:13; Ephesians 1:3; Matthew 28:18-20; 2 Corinthians 5:17-21)

Psalm 45:7 NKJV

You love righteousness and hate wickedness; therefore God, Your God, has anointed You with the oil of gladness more than Your companions.

DECLARATION OF FAITH

Because I am a man/woman who loves righteousness and hates wickedness, the Lord has set me high above my peers and has anointed me with the oil of His joy. I have the God-given ability within me to rejoice in any given situation.

(Ephesians 2:6; Genesis 39:2-5; Romans 14:17; Psalm 2:2; 21:6; Hebrews 1:8,9)

PSALM 46:1-3 NKJV

God is our refuge and strength, a very present help in trouble. Therefore we will not fear, even though the earth be removed, and though the mountains be carried into the midst of the sea; though its waters roar and be troubled, though the mountains shake with its swelling. Selah

DECLARATION OF FAITH

God is my refuge and the power that sustains me. He is my ever-present help in time of need. Therefore, I refuse to be afraid. Even if the earth gives way and the mountains fall into the middle of the ocean, or if the seas swell and roar, causing the mountains to crumble to the ground, I will not be moved to fear or find cause to be terrified.

(Psalm 62:7; 91:1,2; 93:3,4; 145:18; 1 Timothy 1:7; Joshua 1:5-9; Deuteronomy 4:7)

PSALM 46:4,5 NKJV

There is a river whose streams shall make glad the city of God, the holy place of the tabernacle of the Most High. God is in the midst of her, she shall not be moved; God shall help her, just at the break of dawn.

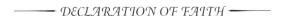

DECLARATION OF FAITH

There is a river that flows through me, bringing joy to my life. God is within me and I shall not be destroyed. The very God of the universe, my heavenly Father, is my ever-present help. He will never leave me nor forsake me.

(John 7:38,39; Romans 14:17; Hebrews 13:5,6)

PSALM 47:1-5 KJV

O clap your hands, all ye people; shout unto God with the voice of triumph. For the Lord most high *is* terrible; *he is* a great King over all the earth. He shall subdue the people under us, and the nations under our feet. He shall choose our inheritance for us, the excellency of Jacob whom he loved. Selah. God is gone up with a shout, the Lord with the sound of a trumpet.

─────── *DECLARATION OF FAITH* ───────

I will praise my Father with my whole heart and all that is within me. I will clap my hands and shout to Him with a voice of triumph! He is worthy of my praise and adoration. He is the great King over all the earth who subdues my enemies beneath my feet! He has specifically chosen my portion of His inheritance and I shall be with Him for all of eternity!

My Father ascends to encompass my shouts of praise. He is pleased to take His place in the midst of them.

(1 Corinthians 3:16; Psalm 68:24,25; 1 Chronicles 13:8; 2 Chronicles 20:15-24; 2 Samuel 6:14-22)

PSALM 48:14 NKJV

For this is God, our God forever and ever; He will be our guide even to death.

─────── *DECLARATION OF FAITH* ───────

God has made me His child forever. He will be my Guide to the very end.

(2 Corinthians 5:17; John 3:3-8; Galatians 4:5,6; Ephesians 1:4; 2:8-10; John 16:13)

PSALM 49:5-8 KJV

Wherefore should I fear in the days of evil, *when* the iniquity of my heels shall compass me about? They that trust in their wealth, and boast themselves in the multitude of their riches; None *of them* can by any means redeem his brother, nor give to God a ransom for him: (For the redemption of their soul *is* precious, and it ceaseth for ever:)

─────── *DECLARATION OF FAITH* ───────

I refuse to be afraid in days of adversity. When times are bad and the world is in turmoil, I remain confident. When iniquity surrounds me and snaps at my heels, I remain steadfast and stable. I do not trust in my wealth to provide my security. My hope is in God alone. He alone can give me certainty for the future. He alone is my redemption and shelter in this life.

(Joshua 1:5-9; Isaiah 41:10-13; Psalm 91; Galatians 3:1-14)

PSALM 49:15 AMP

But God will redeem me from the power of Sheol (the place of the dead); for He will receive me. Selah [pause, and calmly think of that]!

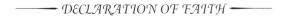

——— *DECLARATION OF FAITH* ———

My Father has redeemed me from the powers of hell. He has received me with a tender welcome and has taken me in as His very own.

(Isaiah 41:10; 43:1-3; Psalm 73:24; Hosea 13:4; Mark 16:6; Galatians 3:13)

PSALM 50:14,15 NIV

"Sacrifice thank offerings to God, fulfill your vows to the Most High, and call upon me in the day of trouble; I will deliver you, and you will honor me."

——— *DECLARATION OF FAITH* ———

I give my offerings with thanksgiving and fulfill all of my vows faithfully. By this, I bring honor to my Father and have the certainty that He will deliver me in the day of trouble.

(2 Corinthians 9:5-11; Proverbs 3:9,10; Numbers 30:2; Job 22:27)

PSALM 50:23 NKJV

"Whoever offers praise glorifies Me; and to him who orders his conduct aright I will show the salvation of God."

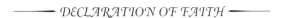

——— *DECLARATION OF FAITH* ———

I honor the Lord with my offerings of praise in sincere gratitude for all that He has done for me. I order my conduct aright so that He may be glorified through my life. By these, I prepare the way for Him to display even more of His delivering power both in and through me.

(Galatians 6:16; Proverbs 3:9,10; Deuteronomy 28:1-14; Psalm 1:1-3)

PSALM 51:1,2 NKJV

Have mercy upon me, O God, according to Your lovingkindness; according to the multitude of Your tender mercies, blot out my transgressions. Wash me thoroughly from my iniquity, and cleanse me from my sin.

———— *DECLARATION OF FAITH* ————

My Father has flooded me with His mercy. He loves me with all of His heart and has forgiven all of my sins. He has blotted out every transgression that I have, or ever will, commit. He has thoroughly stripped sin of its power in my life. I am now clean and perfect in His eyes.

(Isaiah 1:18; Colossians 2:8-14; Hebrews 10:14)

PSALM 51:6 NKJV

Behold, You desire truth in the inward parts, and in the hidden part You will make me to know wisdom.

———— *DECLARATION OF FAITH* ————

My Father's desire for me is to have a spirit of integrity and truth. It is through fellowship with my spirit that He teaches me His wisdom.

(Psalm 119:11,65-68,113-116; 1 Corinthians 2:6-16; 1 John 1:3; John 4:24; Job 32:8)

PSALM 51:10 KJV

Create in me a clean heart, O God; and renew a right spirit within me.

———— *DECLARATION OF FAITH* ————

My spirit has been recreated in purity and holiness. I can now walk steadily in the very righteousness of God.

(2 Corinthians 5:17; Ephesians 2:10; Ezekiel 18:31; John 3:3-8; Romans 6:3-10; 8:9)

PSALM 51:12 AMP

Restore to me the joy of Your salvation and uphold me with a willing spirit.

———— *DECLARATION OF FAITH* ————

This day, God has restored to me the joy of my salvation and I am sustained by a willing spirit.

(2 Corinthians 3:17; John 6:63; Nehemiah 8:10; Isaiah 46:4; Philippians 4:4)

PSALM 52:8,9 NKJV

But I am like a green olive tree in the house of God; I trust in the mercy of God forever and ever. I will praise You forever, because You have done it; and in the presence of Your saints I will wait on Your name, for it is good.

——— *DECLARATION OF FAITH* ———

I am like a green olive tree in the house of God. Everything that I do prospers and I never fail to bear good fruit.

I fully trust in God's mercy on my behalf. I know of a certainty that He loves me and has placed all of His wrath against me upon Jesus.

From this day to eternity I can count on receiving nothing but blessing from my great Father God. Forever will I praise His name!

(Psalm 1:1-3; John 5:24; 15:1,2; Colossians 2:8-14)

PSALM 54:4,5 NKJV

Behold, God is my helper; the Lord is with those who uphold my life.
He will repay my enemies for their evil. Cut them off in Your truth.

——— *DECLARATION OF FAITH* ———

I am in a fixed alliance with my great Father God. He sustains me in every situation and is a partner to those who stand with me.

All of the treachery that the enemy throws against me is recoiled back on his own head.

(Romans 8:31; Exodus 14:13,14; 23:20-30; Nehemiah 4:4; Esther 5:9-6:11; 9:25)

PSALM 55:12-19 KJV

For *it was* not an enemy *that* reproached me; then I could have borne *it*: neither *was it* he that hated me *that* did magnify *himself* against me; then I would have hid myself from him: But *it was* thou, a man mine equal, my guide, and mine acquaintance. We took sweet counsel together, *and* walked unto the house of God in company. Let death seize upon them, *and* let them go down quick into hell: for wickedness *is* in their dwellings, *and* among them. As for me, I will call upon God; and the Lord shall save me. Evening, and morning, and at noon, will I pray, and cry aloud: and he shall hear my voice. He hath delivered my soul in peace from the battle *that was* against me: for there were many with me. God shall hear, and afflict them, even he that abideth of old. Selah. Because they have no changes, therefore they fear not God.

——— *DECLARATION OF FAITH* ———

I do not plot against people who seek to harm me. No, instead I give place to the vengeance of my Father, for He has promised that those who reproach me shall come to ruin. Those who are one way in front of me and treacherous against me when my back is turned shall be exposed and destroyed. The one who calls himself a brother/sister and then backstabs me will be seized by death. They shall be given a chance to repent, but if they refuse, death will take them suddenly and they shall not escape.

As for me, I will call upon God and He will answer me. Morning, noon and night I will lift my voice to Him and He shall rise in my defense. He has redeemed my soul in peace from the battle that wages against me. No matter how many have attacked, God will afflict them all.

I pray, Lord, that they may change. I pray that they turn and fear you and repent of their wicked ways. But, if they refuse, may justice and righteousness reign!

(Acts 5:1-11; Isaiah 41:8-20; Exodus 23:20-30; Numbers 23:19-23; Psalm 91; Romans 12:9-21)

PSALM 55:22 NKJV

Cast your burden on the Lord,
And He shall sustain you;
He shall never permit the righteous to be moved.

——— *DECLARATION OF FAITH* ———

I cast all of my cares and anxieties upon the Lord and He faithfully supports me. He will never allow me to be overcome by my enemies or be shaken to the point of despair. In Him, I rest secure for all of eternity.

(1 Peter 5:5-7; Matthew 6:19-33; Jude 24; Psalm 91:11; Luke 12:22-31)

PSALM 56:3,4,10,11 NKJV

Whenever I am afraid, I will trust in You.
In God (I will praise His word), in God I have put my trust; I will not fear. What can flesh do to me?
In God (I will praise His word), in the Lord (I will praise His word),
In God I have put my trust; I will not be afraid. What can man do to me?

——— *DECLARATION OF FAITH* ———

When fear comes against me to make me tremble with anxiety, I stand firm against it. My trust is in the Lord of Hosts. He is the King of Kings and Lord of Lords, the almighty One, the El Shaddai who is more than enough to carry me. He is my Lord and my Savior—my faithful deliverer who takes His stand against all of my foes. He is faithful to me and has given me His Word that I shall not be harmed. Praise be to the Word He has given me!

So what is there to be afraid of? Who can stand against the awesome power of God? With me, fear has become a joke! It makes absolutely no sense whatsoever.

(2 Timothy 1:7; 1 Peter 5:5-7; Psalm 91; Romans 8:31-39; Hebrews 13:5,6)

PSALM 57:3-5 NKJV

He shall send from heaven and save me; He reproaches the one who would swallow me up. Selah. God shall send forth His mercy and His truth. My soul is among lions; I lie among the sons of men who are set on fire, whose teeth are spears and arrows, and their tongue a sharp sword. Be exalted, O God, above the heavens; let Your glory be above all the earth.

—— DECLARATION OF FAITH ——

The glory of my Father is revealed in me. Though I am in the midst of lions and I dwell among the raging beasts—though I must deal with men who have teeth like spears and arrows, and tongues that lash out like swords—God's glory will not be contained. From His throne on high, He sends me His ministers, a host of fierce warring angels, to deliver me from those who would trample me down and swallow me up. All who rise against me are routed without remedy, while I am taken aside to enjoy the benefits of God's mercy and loving-kindness.

(Romans 8:28; Matthew 26:53; Psalm 108:5; 144:5-7; Proverbs 30:14)

PSALM 58:10,11 NKJV

The righteous shall rejoice when he sees the vengeance; He shall wash his feet in the blood of the wicked, so that men will say, "Surely there is a reward for the righteous; surely He is God who judges in the earth."

—— DECLARATION OF FAITH ——

My Father rises as a warrior to defend me when the wicked come against me. His vengeance is fierce and absolute. I rejoice in His victory! When God moves on my behalf, men will admit that there is a reward for the righteous. They will admit that God is on my side!

(Romans 8:31; Genesis 15:1; Deuteronomy 2:25)

PSALM 59:1-13 KJV

Deliver me from mine enemies, O my God: defend me from them that rise up against me. Deliver me from the workers of iniquity, and save me from bloody men. For, lo, they lie in wait for my soul: the mighty are gathered against me; not *for* my transgression, nor *for* my sin, O Lord. They run and prepare themselves without *my* fault: awake to help me, and behold. Thou therefore, O Lord God of hosts, the God of Israel, awake to visit all the heathen: be not merciful to any wicked transgressors. Selah. They return at evening: they make a noise like a dog, and go round about the city. Behold, they belch out with their mouth: swords *are* in their lips: for who, *say they,* doth hear? But thou, O Lord, shalt laugh at them; thou shalt have all the heathen in derision. *Because of* his strength will I wait upon thee: for God *is* my defence. The God of my mercy shall prevent me: God shall let me see *my desire* upon mine enemies. Slay them not, lest my people forget: scatter them by thy power; and bring them down, O Lord our shield. *For* the sin of their mouth *and* the words of their lips let them even be taken in their pride: and for cursing and lying *which* they speak. Consume *them* in wrath, consume *them,* that they *may* not *be:* and let them know that God ruleth in Jacob unto the ends of the earth. Selah.

—————— *DECLARATION OF FAITH* ——————

When people rise against me without cause, I am not afraid. My heavenly Father has promised to defend me. He is always with me and has promised to destroy my enemies. No matter how mighty the enemy may be, I have the victory!

Those who speak harsh words against me shall be silenced. They plot against me in secret and think that no one hears. But God, my heavenly Father, hears all! He laughs at their plots against me and sets them in derision.

I will wait for my Father's instruction and do only that which He wants me to do. I will not forget that God alone is my strength and defense. I will wait upon His vengeance. My Father will come to meet me and He will show me His power as He routs my enemies. He will scatter them by His power and bring them to nothing. They will make no mistake about who has brought them down. They will know of a certainty that almighty God is on my side!

(Isaiah 41:8-20; Joshua 1:5-9; Deuteronomy 2:25; Exodus 14:13,14; Psalm 2; Genesis 15:1; 1 Samuel 17:45-47; Romans 8:31; 12:9-21)

PSALM 60:4 AMP

[But now] You have set up a banner for those who fear and worshipfully revere You [to which they may flee from the bow], a standard displayed because of the truth. Selah [pause, and calmly think of that]!

——— *DECLARATION OF FAITH* ———

The Lord has raised a banner in my name to be unfurled at the first sign of an enemy attack. Should the enemy dare to do so, the forces of heaven will rally under it in my defense.

(Song of Solomon 2:4; Psalm 20:5; 79:12; Isaiah 5:26; 11:12; 13:2; Matthew 26:53; Numbers 24:9)

PSALM 60:11,12 NKJV

Give us help from trouble,
For the help of man *is* useless.
Through God we will do valiantly,
For *it is* He *who* shall tread down our enemies.

——— *DECLARATION OF FAITH* ———

I do not look to others as my first source of strength in times of trouble. I understand the limitations of man. What can a doctor do against the incurable? What can a psychiatrist do against the oppression of a demon? No, I will rely on God as my first source of strength, for with Him, I am assured that I will do valiantly and have the victory over every adversary in every circumstance.

(Proverbs 3:5,6; Psalm 118:8; 146:3; Numbers 24:18; Joshua 1:5-9)

PSALM 61:1-6 KJV

Hear my cry, O God; attend unto my prayer. From the end of the earth will I cry unto thee, when my heart is overwhelmed: lead me to the rock *that* is higher than I. For thou hast been a shelter for me, *and* a strong tower from the enemy. I will abide in thy tabernacle for ever: I will trust in the covert of thy wings. Selah. For thou, O God, hast heard my vows: thou hast given *me* the heritage of those that fear thy name. Thou wilt prolong the king's life: *and* his years as many generations.

——— *DECLARATION OF FAITH* ———

My Father has tremendous concern for me. When my heart is overwhelmed, He leads me to the Rock that is higher than I. I will dwell in His house forever and trust in the shelter of His wings.

The Lord hears my vows and remembers our covenant. I have an inheritance that is immovable and enduring. He prolongs my life for His name's sake. My years cover many generations. He has prepared His mercy and truth to preserve me. I shall abide before my God forever more.

I will sing praises to God forever and daily will I perform my vows.

(Psalm 23; 50:14,15; 105:7,8; Deuteronomy 32:3,4; Proverbs 3:1-18)

PSALM 62:5-12 KJV

My soul, wait thou only upon God; for my expectation *is* from him. He only *is* my rock and my salvation: *he is* my defence; I shall not be moved. In God *is* my salvation and my glory: the rock of my strength, *and* my refuge, *is* in God. Trust in him at all times; *ye* people, pour out your heart before him: God *is* a refuge for us. Selah. Surely men of low degree *are* vanity, *and* men of high degree *are* a lie: to be laid in the balance, they *are* altogether *lighter* than vanity. Trust not in oppression, and become not vain in robbery: if riches increase, set not your heart *upon them.* God hath spoken once; twice have I heard this; that power *belongeth* unto God. Also unto thee, O Lord, *belongeth* mercy: for thou render-est to every man according to his work.

────── *DECLARATION OF FAITH* ──────

Rest for my soul can be found in God alone. I will wait in silent submission, and in great hope and earnest expectation of the wonders He will perform in my life. He alone is my Rock and my salvation. He is my deliverer who sets me in the place of highest honor.

I am an unshakable, immovable and ever-ready warrior in His army. My trust is in Him at all times and my heart is laid bare before Him crying out, "I am yours forever!"

I cannot be found forcing men to give to me what is rightfully mine, nor do I need to steal and cheat my way to prosperity. Even if I have gained such an abundance of earthly riches that I am the envy of the world, I will not set my heart on them. My heart belongs to my heavenly Father. He shows His love for me by the rewards that I have received, and by them I do rejoice, but my focus is on Him alone. He alone is the strength by which I live.

(Ephesians 2:6; Deuteronomy 8:6-18; Jeremiah 3:23; Isaiah 40:17; 1 Timothy 6:17)

PSALM 63:1-11 KJV

O God, thou *art* my God; early will I seek thee: my soul thirsteth for thee, my flesh longeth for thee in a dry and thirsty land, where no water is; To see thy power and thy glory, so *as* I have seen thee in the sanctuary. Because thy lov-ingkindness *is* better than life, my lips shall praise thee. Thus will I bless thee while I live: I will lift up my hands in thy name. My soul shall be satisfied as *with* marrow and fatness; and my mouth shall praise *thee* with joyful lips: When I remember thee upon my bed, *and* meditate on thee in the *night* watches. Because thou hast been my help, therefore in the shadow of thy wings will I rejoice. My soul followeth hard after thee: thy right hand upholdeth me. But those *that* seek my soul, to destroy *it,* shall go into the lower parts of the earth. They shall fall by the sword: they shall be a portion for foxes. But the king shall rejoice in God; every one that sweareth by him shall glory: but the mouth of them that speak lies shall be stopped.

──────── DECLARATION OF FAITH ────────

The Lord is my God. Early in the morning I will seek Him. My soul thirsts for Him. My flesh longs for Him in this dry and weary land where there is no water.

I seek my Father in His sanctuary for I long to see His power and glory. His loving-kindness toward me is better than life.

My lips shall praise Him. I will bless Him now, in this life. I will not put it off for another day. Now is the time. I will bless Him today. I will lift up my hands in His name. I will praise my great Father God for His mercy and kindness. My soul shall be satisfied as with marrow and fatness. Let joy flood my heart as I praise His holy name!

I will remember my Father on my bed at night. I meditate on Him in the night watches and consider the Word He has given me. He has been my never-failing help. I rejoice in the shadow of His wings.

My Father's right hand upholds me and He sees to it that I am not taken by the schemes of the wicked. My soul follows close behind Him as He leads me in this life. Those who seek to destroy me shall go into the lower parts of the earth. They shall fall by the sword. They have become a feast for the jackals.

But I shall rejoice in God. The Church and I shall glory and those who speak lies about me shall be silenced.

(Mark 1:35; Deuteronomy 4:29; Joshua 1:8; 24:15; Psalm 31:3,4; 91; 119:148)

PSALM 64:1-10 KJV

Hear my voice, O God, in my prayer: preserve my life from fear of the enemy. Hide me from the secret counsel of the wicked; from the insurrection of the workers of iniquity: Who whet their tongue like a sword, *and* bend *their bows to shoot* their arrows, *even* bitter words: That they may shoot in secret at the perfect: suddenly do they shoot at him, and fear not. They encourage themselves *in* an evil matter: they commune of laying snares privily; they say, Who shall see them? They search out iniquities; they accomplish a diligent search: both the inward *thought* of every one *of them,* and the heart, *is* deep. But God shall shoot at them *with* an arrow; suddenly shall they be wounded. So they shall make their own tongue to fall upon themselves: all that see them shall flee away. And all men shall fear, and shall declare the work of God; for they shall wisely consider of his doing. The righteous shall be glad in the Lord, and shall trust in him; and all the upright in heart shall glory.

DECLARATION OF FAITH

My Father hears my voice in my meditation. He preserves my life from fear of the enemy. With God on my side, no enemy can make me afraid or cause me to tremble and panic. The Lord hides me from the secret plots of the wicked. Those who speak evil things against me shall be brought to nothing. Those who scheme together against me and talk of laying secret snares to trap me, shall face the Lord.

When the enemy rises against me with curses of destruction, God arouses Himself on my behalf. He turns their own tongues against them and brings them to ruin. The very curses that they send to me are turned back on their own heads and all who see them will shake their heads in wonder of what possessed them to be so foolish. All who see what my Father does on my behalf will tremble with awe as they ponder over what has been done. They will openly proclaim that my God is the greatest and His works have no equal.

As for me, I will praise the Lord. My refuge is in Him and my joy will never end.

(Joshua 1:5-9; Genesis 12:1-3; Deuteronomy 2:25; Romans 8:31; 12:9-21; Nehemiah 4:4; Esther 5:9-6:11; 9:25; Psalm 31:11; 79:12)

PSALM 65:4,5 NIV

Blessed are those you choose and bring near to live in your courts! We are filled with the good things of your house, of your holy temple. You answer us with awesome deeds of righteousness, O God our Savior, the hope of all the ends of the earth and of the farthest seas.

DECLARATION OF FAITH

My Father has chosen me and adopted me as His own child. He has brought me near to Himself and has given me a place of honor in the courts of His palace. He fills me with all good things so that I am in need of nothing. All I have to do is ask and He freely gives me all that He has.

(Galatians 4:5,6; Ephesians 1:4; 2:6; James 4:8; John 14:13,14; 16:27; Romans 8:32)

PSALM 65:11 AMP

You crown the year with Your bounty and goodness, and the tracks of Your [chariot wheels] drip with fatness.

My year is crowned with the bounty of the Lord and all of my carts overflow with His abundance.

(Proverbs 3:9,10; 11:24; Malachi 3:10,11; John 10:10; 2 Corinthians 9:8)

PSALM 66:12 NKJV

You have caused men to ride over our heads; we went through fire and through water; but You brought us out to rich fulfillment.

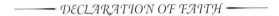

Though I have been through hardships by the dozens and have been weighed down by burden after burden; though men have ridden hard over my head and I have gone through the fire and the water, I will put the past behind me and look to the Lord. He has brought me into the spacious province of His abundance so that I may enjoy His kingdom living from this day unto eternity.

(Philippians 3:13,14; 2 Timothy 3:12; Isaiah 43:1,2; John 10:10; Matthew 6:19-33)

PSALM 66:18 NKJV

If I regard iniquity in my heart, the Lord will not hear.

——— DECLARATION OF FAITH ———

I will not hinder God's blessings in my life by cherishing sin in my heart.

(Psalm 119:11; Job 27:9; Isaiah 1:15-20; John 9:31; James 4:3)

PSALM 67:5-7 NKJV

Let the peoples praise You, O God; let all the peoples praise You. Then the earth shall yield her increase; God, our own God, shall bless us. God shall bless us, and all the ends of the earth shall fear Him.

——— DECLARATION OF FAITH ———

I will praise my Father in heaven for honoring His Word in my life, for then my land will yield its harvest and He will bless me with His abundant provision.

When I give Him the credit for what He is doing, He responds in a shower of His appreciation. It pleases Him greatly when I am expectant of the fulfillment of His promise. All who know me will gaze in awe and wonder at the blessings He rains into my life.

(Psalm 112:1-3; 119:34-38,162,169-173; Deuteronomy 28:1-14; Leviticus 26:4)

PSALM 68:5,6 NKJV

A father of the fatherless, a defender of widows, is God in His holy habitation. God sets the solitary in families; He brings out those who are bound into prosperity; but the rebellious dwell in a dry land.

──── *DECLARATION OF FAITH* ────

My God is a Father to the fatherless, a defender of the widow, and a companion to the lonely. He leads forth prisoners from their bondage with singing, and as His son/daughter, I do the same.

(Job 29:11-17; Psalm 10:14; 146:9; James 1:27; Acts 12:6-8; 16:22-26)

PSALM 68:7-10 KJV

O God, when thou wentest forth before thy people, when thou didst march through the wilderness; Selah: The earth shook, the heavens also dropped at the presence of God: *even* Sinai itself *was moved* at the presence of God, the God of Israel. Thou, O God, didst send a plentiful rain, whereby thou didst confirm thine inheritance, when it was weary. Thy congregation hath dwelt therein: thou, O God, hast prepared of thy goodness for the poor. The Lord gave the word: great was the company of those that published *it.*

──── *DECLARATION OF FAITH* ────

The Lord goes before me in an awesome display of His power. He gives me His abundant showers to refresh my inheritance. I am settled in it. From the treasury of His bounty, He provides me with a surplus of provisions for kingdom living.

(Exodus 23:20-30; Psalm 18:1-18; 74:19; Leviticus 26:4; Deuteronomy 11:11; 26:5)

PSALM 68:17-20 KJV

The chariots of God *are* twenty thousand, *even* thousands of angels: the Lord *is* among them, *as in* Sinai, in the holy *place.* Thou hast ascended on high, thou hast led captivity captive: thou hast received gifts for men; yea, *for* the rebellious also, that the Lord God might dwell *among them.* Blessed *be* the Lord, *who* daily loadeth us *with benefits, even* the God of our salvation. Selah. *He that is* our God *is* the God of salvation; and unto God the Lord *belong* the issues from death.

─────── *DECLARATION OF FAITH* ───────

The great army of the living God, is on my side. They have ascended from the great mountain of God to shield me on every side and to see to it that I am kept safe from the onslaughts of the enemy.

My heavenly Father takes up my every burden as His own. He bears them daily so that I may dwell in His presence in peace and comfort. He gives me a copious supply of daily provisions to fill all of my needs. He is my salvation from every trouble and my escape from the snares of death.

(2 Kings 6:15-17; Exodus 23:20-23; 1 Peter 5:5-7; Matthew 11:28-30; Deuteronomy 32:29; 33:2; Mark 16:19; Acts 1:8,9; Ephesians 4:8; Psalm 103:1-5; Romans 6:23)

PSALM 68:35 NKJV

O God, You are more awesome than Your holy places. The God of Israel is He who gives strength and power to His people. Blessed be God!

─────── *DECLARATION OF FAITH* ───────

My great and awesome Father God is dwelling within me at this very moment. He gives me strength and power to do His will and to live the life He has called me to. Praise be to His holy name!

(Psalm 76:12; 1 Corinthians 3:16; Philippians 2:12,13; Colossians 1:29)

PSALM 69:13 AMP

But as for me, my prayer is to You, O Lord. At an acceptable and opportune time, O God, in the multitude of Your mercy and the abundance of Your loving-kindness hear me, and in the truth and faithfulness of Your salvation answer me.

─────── *DECLARATION OF FAITH* ───────

I live in the time of God's favor. He loves me dearly and answers my every prayer with guaranteed salvation.

(Isaiah 61:1-3; Luke 4:17-19; John 14:13,14; 15:7; 16:23,24; 1 John 5:14,15)

PSALM 69:16-18 NKJV

Hear me, O Lord, for Your lovingkindness is good; turn to me according to the multitude of Your tender mercies. And do not hide Your face from Your servant, for I am in trouble; hear me speedily. Draw near to my soul, and redeem it; deliver me because of my enemies.

——— *DECLARATION OF FAITH* ———

My Father loves me with all of His heart and is quick to answer my every prayer. He extends me the everlasting hand of His mercy and never turns His face from me. He is quick to answer me in times of trouble and to rescue me from overwhelming circumstances. He sees and takes into consideration the scorn that I endure from men. He hears their mockery against me then takes His stand with me as both my defender and comforter.

(John 16:23-27; Hebrews 13:5,6; Psalm 2; 18:1-18; James 4:8; 2 Timothy 3:12)

PSALM 70:3 NKJV

Let them be turned back because of their shame, who say, "Aha, aha!"

——— *DECLARATION OF FAITH* ———

Those who seek reasons to accuse me are turned back from me in disgrace.

(Isaiah 54:17; Psalm 64:7-10; 79:12; Nehemiah 4:4; Esther 5:9-6:11; 9:25)

PSALM 71:3-5 NKJV

Be my strong refuge, to which I may resort continually; You have given the commandment to save me, for You are my rock and my fortress. Deliver me, O my God, out of the hand of the wicked, out of the hand of the unrighteous and cruel man. For You are my hope, O Lord God; You are my trust from my youth.

——— *DECLARATION OF FAITH* ———

My heavenly Father is always ready to receive me. He is a Rock where I can always go and find refuge. He surrounds me with His armaments as a defense against the attacks of the enemy and He gives the command to save me in times of trouble. He delivers me from the oppression of the cruel and the wicked. He is my one true hope and in Him alone do I put my unwavering trust.

(Hebrews 4:16; Exodus 23:20-23; Psalm 31:2,3; 44:4; Ephesians 6:10-18)

PSALM 71:10-16 KJV

For mine enemies speak against me; and they that lay wait for my soul take counsel together, Saying, God hath forsaken him: persecute and take him; for *there is* none to deliver *him.* O God, be not far from me: O my God, make haste for my help. Let them be confounded *and* consumed that are adversaries to my soul; let them be covered *with* reproach and dishonour that seek my hurt. But I will hope continually, and will yet praise thee more and more. My mouth shall shew forth thy righteousness *and* thy salvation all the day; for I know not the numbers *thereof.* I will go in the strength of the Lord God: I will make mention of thy righteousness, *even* of thine only.

──────── *DECLARATION OF FAITH* ────────

When hope seems lost and it seems that God has forsaken me, I will not lose faith. When my enemies take counsel together for my destruction, thinking that I am alone and without help, God rises in my defense. When they persecute me and plot my ruin, God makes haste to rescue me. He confounds and consumes every adversary of my soul. Those who seek to cause me pain shall receive injury back on themselves. But my hope shall remain. I will praise God continually, even in the midst of terror and destruction. I will speak forth His salvation regardless of the circumstances. I will go in the strength and power of almighty God! I will speak of His righteousness that secures my position in Him for eternity!

(Psalm 2; 16:8,9; Jeremiah 17:5-8; 1 Kings 2:44,45; Exodus 23:27; Ephesians 6:10; Romans 5:17)

PSALM 71:20,21 NIV

Though you have made me see troubles, many and bitter, you will restore my life again; from the depths of the earth you will again bring me up. You will increase my honor and comfort me once again.

──────── *DECLARATION OF FAITH* ────────

When troubles overwhelm me and it seems the weight of the world is on my shoulders, God shall quicken me once again. Though many distresses and misfortunes have rained upon me, I shall rise with the strength and power of heaven in my wake. God takes His stand with me in every circumstance. He increases my greatness and comforts me on every side.

(Psalm 34:6-8; Proverbs 24:16; Ephesians 6:10; Genesis 12:1-3; Exodus 14:13,14)

PSALM 72:1-19 KJV

Give the king thy judgments, O God, and thy righteousness unto the king's son. He shall judge thy people with righteousness, and thy poor with judgment. The mountains shall bring peace to the people, and the little hills, by righteousness. He shall judge the poor of the people, he shall save the children of the needy, and shall break in pieces the oppressor. They shall fear thee as long as the sun and moon endure, throughout all generations. He shall come down like rain upon the mown grass: as showers *that* water the earth. In his days shall the righteous flourish; and abundance of peace so long as the moon endureth. He shall have dominion also from sea to sea, and from the river unto the ends of the earth. They that dwell in the wilderness shall bow before him; and his enemies shall lick the dust. The kings of Tarshish and of the isles shall bring presents: the kings of Sheba and Seba shall offer gifts. Yea, all kings shall fall down before him: all nations shall serve him. For he shall deliver the needy when he crieth; the poor also, and *him* that hath no helper. He shall spare the poor and needy, and shall save the souls of the needy. He shall redeem their soul from deceit and violence: and precious shall their blood be in his sight. And he shall live, and to him shall be given of the gold of Sheba: prayer also shall be made for him continually; *and* daily shall he be praised. There shall be an handful of corn in the earth upon the top of the mountains; the fruit thereof shall shake like Lebanon: and *they* of the city shall flourish like grass of the earth. His name shall endure for ever: his name shall be continued as long as the sun: and *men* shall be blessed in him: all nations shall call him blessed. Blessed *be* the Lord God, the God of Israel, who only doeth wondrous things. And blessed *be* his glorious name for ever: and let the whole earth be filled *with* his glory; Amen, and Amen.

—— DECLARATION OF FAITH ——

I am well provisioned for kingdom living and God's justice reigns in my life. I am His own son/daughter and royal heir. He has clothed me in His righteousness and exalted me to the position of highest honor.

The mountains bring me His prosperity and the hills pour out to me the fruits of His righteousness.

I am a defender of the afflicted and a hero to needy children.

I am like the rain that falls on a mown field, and like a fresh spring rain, I water the earth.

I thrive at the height of success and good health, and my prosperity will abound until the moon is no more.

I am made to be a leader and an example in this earth. I am an epistle to the wayward and strength for the weak, for I am known as a deliverer of the needy and of those who cry out for help. I stand up for the afflicted one who has no one to turn to.

I take pity on the weak, lifting them from the snares of death. I rescue them from oppression, fraud and violence, for their blood is precious in my sight.

I am blessed with a long and satisfying life.

Gold is continually given to me in abundance and people go out of their way to bless and pray for me every day.

It is God who accomplishes these things in my life and I will render Him praise befitting of His marvelous deeds. May the whole earth be filled with His glory!

(Isaiah 2:4; 23:13; 49:23; 54:17; Romans 8:14-17; 2 Corinthians 5:17-21; Ephesians 2:6; Job 29:11-17; Mark 3:27; Luke 10:19; 3 John 2; Deuteronomy 8:6-18; 28:1-14; Genesis 12:1-3; 13:2; 39:2-5; Isaiah 46:4; Psalm 85:10; 89:36; 91:16)

PSALM 73:23-26 NKJV

Nevertheless I *am* continually with You;
You hold *me* by my right hand.
You will guide me with Your counsel,
And afterward receive me *to* glory.
Whom have I in heaven *but You?*
And *there is* none upon earth *that* I desire besides You.
My flesh and my heart fail;
But God *is* the strength of my heart and my portion forever.

──── DECLARATION OF FAITH ────

I am always with the Lord—He holds me by my right hand. He guides me continually with His counsel as I walk the many paths of this life, and He will stay with me until the day I am taken up to be with Him in glory. This earth has nothing that I desire outside of Him. Though flesh and heart fail, God is my strength and my portion forever.

(John 16:13; Psalm 16:5; 32:8; 48:14; 84:2; Isaiah 58:11; Philippians 3:8)

PSALM 74:19-23 NKJV

Oh, do not deliver the life of Your turtledove to the wild beast! Do not forget the life of Your poor forever. Have respect to the covenant; for the dark places of the earth are full of the haunts of cruelty. Oh, do not let the oppressed return ashamed! Let the poor and needy praise Your name. Arise, O God, plead Your own cause; remember how the foolish man reproaches You daily. Do not forget the voice of Your enemies; the tumult of those who rise up against You increases continually.

──── DECLARATION OF FAITH ────

When I am surrounded by the wicked and mocked in their presence, God remembers His covenant with me. He shall deliver me with a sure and certain salvation. I shall emerge with my head lifted high and my enemies shall all be put to shame.

(Deuteronomy 4:31; Proverbs 17:5; Psalm 3:3)

PSALM 77:1,2 NKJV

I cried out to God with my voice—

To God with my voice;

And He gave ear to me.

In the day of my trouble I sought the Lord;

My hand was stretched out in the night without ceasing;

My soul refused to be comforted.

——— *DECLARATION OF FAITH* ———

My Father always hears me when I cry out to Him. In the night hours I reach out to Him. My hands are extended to Him tirelessly and I am not satisfied until my answer has come.

(Luke 6:11,12; Deuteronomy 4:29-31)

PSALM 77:3-14 KJV

I remembered God, and was troubled: I complained, and my spirit was overwhelmed. Selah. Thou holdest mine eyes waking: I am so troubled that I cannot speak. I have considered the days of old, the years of ancient times. I call to remembrance my song in the night: I commune with mine own heart: and my spirit made diligent search. Will the Lord cast off for ever? and will he be favourable no more? Is his mercy clean gone for ever? doth *his* promise fail for evermore? Hath God forgotten to be gracious? hath he in anger shut up his tender mercies? Selah. And I said, This *is* my infirmity: *but I will remember* the years of the right hand of the most High. I will remember the works of the Lord: surely I will remember thy wonders of old. I will meditate also of all thy work, and talk of thy doings. Thy way, O God, *is* in the sanctuary: who *is so* great a God as *our* God? Thou *art* the God that doest wonders: thou hast declared thy strength among the people.

——— *DECLARATION OF FAITH* ———

When hope seems lost and I begin to feel that God is indifferent to my needs, I will remember all that He has done in my life. When I am so troubled that I cannot even find the words to speak, I will remember His intervention in days of old. I will meditate upon His great works. I will remember the great salvation that He wrought for me. My Father is the Lord Most High. There is none greater than He. He will not forget me or leave me comfortless. He will act on my behalf.

(Psalm 22:1-5; Deuteronomy 7:17,18; Joshua 1:8; 2 Timothy 2:8-10)

PSALM 78:4-7 NKJV

We will not hide them from their children, telling to the generation to come the praises of the Lord, and His strength and His wonderful works that He has done.

For He established a testimony in Jacob, and appointed a law in Israel, which He commanded our fathers, that they should make them known to their children;

That the generation to come might know them, the children who would be born, that they may arise and declare them to their children, that they may set their hope in God, and not forget the works of God, but keep His commandments.

———— DECLARATION OF FAITH ————

I will tell of God's wonderful deeds, how He has displayed His power in this earth, how He has decreed His statutes and established His laws, and how His Word is the stronghold of every generation. My children shall hear of it, as will the next generation yet to be born. They will stand by His statutes and put their trust in the one true God who has given them life.

(Romans 1:16; Deuteronomy 6:6-9; Proverbs 22:6; Isaiah 38:19; Exodus 13:8,14)

PSALM 78:52,53 NKJV

But He made His own people go forth like sheep, and guided them in the wilderness like a flock; And He led them on safely, so that they did not fear; but the sea overwhelmed their enemies.

———— DECLARATION OF FAITH ————

My Father guides me as a good shepherd guides his sheep. He leads me through the desert places and shelters me from every danger so that I may live my life without fear.

(John 10:7-16; Psalm 23; 77:20; 2 Timothy 1:7; Exodus 14:19,20)

PSALM 79:8-13 KJV

O remember not against us former iniquities: let thy tender mercies speedily prevent us: for we are brought very low. Help us, O God of our salvation, for the glory of thy name: and deliver us, and purge away our sins, for thy name's sake. Wherefore should the heathen say, Where *is* their God? let him be known among the heathen in our sight *by* the revenging of the blood of thy servants *which is* shed. Let the sighing of the prisoner come before thee; according to the greatness of thy power preserve thou those that are appointed to die; And render unto our neighbours sevenfold into their bosom their reproach, wherewith they have reproached thee, O Lord. So we thy people and sheep of thy pasture will give thee thanks for ever: we will shew forth thy praise to all generations.

——— *DECLARATION OF FAITH* ———

God does not hold my past against me. He eliminates from His memory the wrongs that I have committed and shows me His mercy and loving-kindness all the days of my life. He delivers me from the consequences of my sins for His name's sake. He sees the mockery of the heathen and declares that regardless of my past I am to be blessed.

The Lord sets me up as His covenant child and protects me against the onslaughts of those arrayed against me. Those who have chosen to be my enemies receive sevenfold what they have placed upon me.

As for me, I am a sheep in the Lord's pasture. He protects and provides for me without fail. I will praise His name throughout all generations. Forever I will praise His name!

(Psalm 18; 23; 103; John 10:1-10; Proverbs 6:30,31)

PSALM 81:13,14 NIV

"If my people would but listen to me, if Israel would follow my ways, how quickly would I subdue their enemies and turn my hand against their foes!"

——— *DECLARATION OF FAITH* ———

I choose to listen to what my Father has to say and I do whatever He wants me to do. Because I have made His ways my own, He quickly subdues my enemies under me and bids me to conquer them!

(John 10:7-16; Isaiah 48:18; Ephesians 5:1; Romans 8:37; Deuteronomy 28:1,7)

PSALM 81:16 NKJV

"He would have fed them also with the finest of wheat; And with honey from the rock I would have satisfied you."

My provision from God is the best that there is. He feeds me with the finest of wheat and satisfies me with fresh honey from the rock.

(Philippians 4:19; Deuteronomy 32:14; Job 29:6; Genesis 12:1-3; 13:2; Psalm 112:1-3)

PSALM 82:1,6 NKJV

God stands in the congregation of the mighty; He judges among the gods.

I said, "You are gods, and all of you are children of the Most High."

———— *DECLARATION OF FAITH* ————

I am created to be like a god in this earth — a very member of the great assembly. I am indeed a son/daughter of the Most High!

(Genesis 1:26-28; 2 Chronicles 19:6; Psalm 8:4-6; John 10:34; Romans 8:14-17; Ephesians 2:6-10)

PSALM 84:4-7 NKJV

Blessed are those who dwell in Your house; they will still be praising You. Selah. Blessed is the man whose strength is in You, whose heart is set on pilgrimage. As they pass through the Valley of Baca, they make it a spring; the rain also covers it with pools. They go from strength to strength; each one appears before God in Zion.

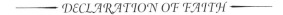

———— *DECLARATION OF FAITH* ————

I dwell in the very house of God and I am blessed in every way.

My praises continually soar into His presence.

Through Him, I have strength to do the task He has set before me. My heart is set on a pilgrimage to do His will.

As I pass through the valley of weeping, I make it a place of joy. In my presence, it becomes a place of fresh water springs and I shower blessings upon it like an autumn rain.

I press on from endeavor to endeavor and increase from strength to strength. I am a child of the Most High God and I appear regularly at His throne.

(Galatians 6:10; Ephesians 1:3; 2:19; Romans 11:29; Colossians 1:29; Proverbs 4:18; 2 Corinthians 3:18; Hebrews 4:16)

PSALM 84:11 AMP

For the Lord God is a Sun and Shield; the Lord bestows [present] grace and favor and [future] glory (honor, splendor, and heavenly bliss)! No good thing will He withhold from those who walk uprightly.

— DECLARATION OF FAITH —

My Father is my sun and my shield. He enlightens and enlivens me as I do His will, and He protects me from danger so that I remain secure.

He bestows on me His favor and honor, and I am held in high esteem by my peers.

No good thing will He withhold from me as I daily walk in His ways.

(Ezra 1:11-2:1; Psalm 23; 34:9,10; Proverbs 3:3,4; Ephesians 2:6; 1 Peter 5:5-7)

PSALM 85:1-3 KJV

Lord, thou hast been favourable unto thy land: thou hast brought back the captivity of Jacob. Thou hast forgiven the iniquity of thy people, thou hast covered all their sin. Selah. Thou hast taken away all thy wrath: thou hast turned *thyself* from the fierceness of thine anger.

— DECLARATION OF FAITH —

God has forgiven all of my sins and restored all of my fortunes. He has set aside His wrath and granted me His favor. All that the devil has stolen must now be returned to me, in Jesus' name!

(Hebrews 10:15-17; Joel 2:25; Jeremiah 27:22; Matthew 12:29; Mark 3:27; Proverbs 6:31)

PSALM 85:8,9 NKJV

I will hear what God the Lord will speak, for He will speak peace to His people and to His saints; but let them not turn back to folly. Surely His salvation is near to those who fear Him, that glory may dwell in our land.

— DECLARATION OF FAITH —

God has promised me peace in this life. His salvation is always near to me and His glory resides with me forevermore. I will not forfeit this right by returning to the folly of my old ways.

(Ephesians 2:14; Romans 14:17; 2 Corinthians 6:14; James 4:1-10; Isaiah 46:13)

PSALM 85:12,13 NKJV

Yes, the Lord will give what is good; and our land will yield its increase.
Righteousness will go before Him, and shall make His footsteps our pathway.

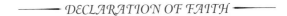
DECLARATION OF FAITH

The Lord never fails to give me an abundance of good things. His righteousness goes before me to prepare the way for my steps. My land shall indeed yield its harvest.

(Psalm 37:23; 84:11; 112:1-3; 2 Corinthians 9:5-11; James 1:17)

PSALM 86:5 NKJV

For You, Lord, *are* good, and ready to forgive, And abundant in mercy to all those who call upon You.

DECLARATION OF FAITH

God forgives me of all of my shortcomings. His love for me is boundless. I can expect nothing but good things from Him.

(1 John 1:9-2:2; Romans 8:38,39; Genesis 50:20; Deuteronomy 6:24; Nahum 1:7)

PSALM 86:11 NKJV

Teach me Your way, O Lord; I will walk in Your truth; unite my heart to fear Your name.

DECLARATION OF FAITH

The Lord leads me in His way and teaches me all of His precepts so that I may walk steadfastly in His Truth. In Him, I have an undivided heart that I may revere His holy name.

(John 16:13; Psalm 27:11; 143:8; 119:27,28,34-38,65-68,97-101,124,130-135,169-173)

PSALM 86:17 NKJV

Show me a sign for good, that those who hate me may see it and be ashamed, because You, Lord, have helped me and comforted me.

——— *DECLARATION OF FAITH* ———

My Father grants me clear signs of His goodness so that my enemies may see it and be put to shame. He comforts me in my way and lifts me up from life's many troubles.

(Mark 16:17-20; Acts 4:23-33; 1 Peter 5:5-7; Leviticus 26:13; 2 Corinthians 1:3,4)

PSALM 89:14-17 KJV

Justice and judgment *are* the habitation of thy throne: mercy and truth shall go before thy face. Blessed *is* the people that know the joyful sound: they shall walk, O Lord, in the light of thy countenance. In thy name shall they rejoice all the day: and in thy righteousness shall they be exalted. For thou *art* the glory of their strength: and in thy favour our horn shall be exalted.

——— *DECLARATION OF FAITH* ———

I walk in the light of the presence of almighty God. His love and faithfulness go before me. His righteousness and justice sustain me. I have learned to acclaim His mighty name in this earth. I rejoice in Him all the day long. I am lifted up and encompassed in His righteousness. He is my glory and strength, and by His favor, I am well established.

(1 John 1:3-7; Romans 8:38,39; Nehemiah 8:10; Psalm 75:10; 92:10; 132:17)

PSALM 89:28,29 NKJV

My mercy I will keep for him forever, and My covenant shall stand firm with him. His seed also I will make to endure forever, and his throne as the days of heaven.

——— *DECLARATION OF FAITH* ———

The Lord preserves and maintains His love for me forever. His covenant with me shall never fail. In Him, I am well established and my throne and lineage remain secure. I can absolutely count on Him to protect my children after me.

(Romans 8:38,39; Leviticus 26:9; Hebrews 8:6; Ephesians 2:6; Revelation 1:6)

PSALM 90:12 AMP

So teach us to number our days, that we may get us a heart of wisdom.

───── *DECLARATION OF FAITH* ─────

The Lord instructs me in my way. He teaches me to number my days, so that I may gain a heart of wisdom.

(Deuteronomy 32:29; Psalm 39:4; 119:27,28,34-38,65-68,97-101,124,130-135,169-173)

PSALM 90:17 NKJV

And let the beauty of the Lord our God be upon us, And establish the work of our hands for us; Yes, establish the work of our hands.

───── *DECLARATION OF FAITH* ─────

God's favor rests upon me. Everything that I set my hand to do prospers. He firmly establishes all of the work of my hands.

(Proverbs 3:3,4; Deuteronomy 28:12; Genesis 39:2-5; Psalm 27:4; Isaiah 26:12)

PSALM 91 KJV

He that dwelleth in the secret place of the most High shall abide under the shadow of the Almighty. I will say of the Lord, *He is* my refuge and my fortress: my God; in him will I trust. Surely he shall deliver thee from the snare of the fowler, *and* from the noisome pestilence. He shall cover thee with his feathers, and under his wings shalt thou trust: his truth *shall be thy* shield and buckler. Thou shalt not be afraid for the terror by night; *nor* for the arrow *that* flieth by day; *Nor* for the pestilence *that* walketh in darkness; *nor* for the destruction *that* wasteth at noonday. A thousand shall fall at thy side, and ten thousand at thy right hand; *but* it shall not come nigh thee. Only with thine eyes shalt thou behold and see the reward of the wicked. Because thou hast made the Lord, *which is* my refuge, *even* the most High, thy habitation; There shall no evil befall thee, neither shall any plague come nigh thy dwelling. For he shall give his angels charge over thee, to keep thee in all thy ways. They shall bear thee up in *their* hands, lest thou dash thy foot against a stone. Thou shalt tread upon the lion and adder: the young lion and the dragon shalt thou trample under feet. Because he hath set his love upon me, therefore will I deliver him: I will set him on high, because he hath known my name. He shall call upon me, and I will answer him: I *will be* with him in trouble; I will deliver him, and honour him. With long life will I satisfy him, and shew him my salvation.

———— *DECLARATION OF FAITH* ————

I dwell in the secret place of the Most High and rest, remaining steadfast and secure, under the shadow of the Almighty. He is my refuge and my fortress, my God and Father, and I trust Him with all of my heart.

He has given me a sure and certain deliverance from the traps of Satan and has freed me from all deadly pestilence.

He has covered me with His feathers and under His wings I have taken refuge. His faithfulness is my shield and my rampart.

I do not fear the terror of the night, nor the arrow that flies by day, nor the pestilence that stalks in the darkness, nor the plague that lays waste at noonday. A thousand may fall at my side, even ten thousand at my right hand, but it shall not come near me.

I will see with my own eyes the punishment of the wicked.

The Most High God, my heavenly Father, is my fortress and my habitation.

He has accepted me as His own. I am a son/daughter in His royal family.

Therefore, no evil may befall me and no plague, sickness, or disaster is allowed to come near my dwelling.

God has commanded the angels to set up camp around me as sentinels in my life. They guard me in all of my ways and keep me from all harm. They bear me up in their hands lest I dash my foot against a stone.

I tread upon the lion and the cobra. The young lion and the serpent, I trample under my feet. The devil's power over me has been completely stripped away. God has made a decree (a fixed law) concerning me saying, "I will rescue him/her from every calamity; I will protect him/her because he/she acknowledges my name. He/She will call upon Me and I will answer him/her. I will be with him/her in times of trouble. I will deliver him/her and set him/her in the place of highest honor. With long life I will satisfy him/her and show him/her My salvation."

(Psalm 9:10; 17:8; 27:5; 34:7; 37:34; 90:1; 112:7; 124:7; 142:5; Isaiah 25:4; 32:2; 43:1,2; 46:4; Proverbs 6:5; 12:21; Job 5:19; 2 Timothy 1:7; 1 John 5:18; Malachi 1:5; Matthew 4:6; 26:53; Hebrews 1:14; Exodus 23:20-23; 2 Kings 6:15-17; Luke 4:10,11; 10:19; Ephesians 2:6)

PSALM 92:4 NIV

For you make me glad by your deeds, O Lord; I sing for joy at the works of your hands.

──────── DECLARATION OF FAITH ────────

I rejoice at the deeds my Father has accomplished. His ways make me the happiest of men/women.

(Philippians 4:4; 1 Corinthians 10:26; Nehemiah 8:10; 9:6)

PSALM 92:12-15 NKJV

The righteous shall flourish like a palm tree, he shall grow like a cedar in Lebanon. Those who are planted in the house of the Lord shall flourish in the courts of our God. They shall still bear fruit in old age; they shall be fresh and flourishing, to declare that the Lord is upright; He is my rock, and there is no unrighteousness in Him.

──────── DECLARATION OF FAITH ────────

I flourish in this earth like the palm tree. Though the winds blow with hurricane force, I remain fixed, steadfast and secure.

I grow like the cedar of Lebanon. I am planted in the very house of almighty God.

Under His care, I thrive at the height of success and development. I continue to bear good fruit throughout my life and even in old age I remain fresh and green, with a shout of victory on my lips proclaiming, "The Lord is faithful and to be honored! He is my Rock and no wicked way can be found in Him!"

(Psalm 1:1-3; Matthew 7:24,25; Joshua 1:8; Jeremiah 29:11; 1 Corinthians 10:4)

PSALM 94:12-14 NKJV

Blessed *is* the man whom You instruct, O Lord, and teach out of Your law, that You may give him rest from the days of adversity, until the pit is dug for the wicked. For the Lord will not cast off His people, nor will He forsake His inheritance.

──────── DECLARATION OF FAITH ────────

I am blessed when my Father disciplines me and teaches me from His Word. His precepts bring joy, happiness, and all manner of prosperity into my life. By them, I find relief from the days of trouble.

I have God's Word that He will never leave me nor forsake me. I am a child of His inheritance both now and forevermore.

(Hebrews 12:5-12; Psalm 112:1-3; Hebrews 13:5,6; Romans 8:14-17)

PSALM 94:19 NKJV

In the multitude of my anxieties within me, Your comforts delight my soul.

——— *DECLARATION OF FAITH* ———

When fear and anxiety come against me, I find consolation in God. In Him, I find joy in every circumstance.

(1 Peter 5:5-7; 2 Timothy 1:7; Joshua 1:5-9; Philippians 4:4; Romans 14:17)

PSALM 97:10 NIV

Let those who love the Lord hate evil, for he guards the lives of his faithful ones and delivers them from the hand of the wicked.

——— *DECLARATION OF FAITH* ———

I love the Lord and hate evil. I am faithful to Him in all things and in every way. He is the Guardian of my life and my Deliverer from the hands of the wicked.

(Psalm 31:23; 34:14; Proverbs 2:8; 8:13; Amos 5:15; Romans 12:9; Daniel 3:28)

PSALM 99:4 NKJV

The King's strength also loves justice; You have established equity; You have executed justice and righteousness in Jacob.

——— *DECLARATION OF FAITH* ———

I will not forget that the Lord insists that I walk in honesty and integrity, that I love justice and live a virtuous life. He is holy and as His child, I am holy too.

(1 Peter 1:13-16; John 14:15)

PSALM 100 KJV

Make a joyful noise unto the Lord, all ye lands. Serve the Lord with gladness: come before his presence with singing. Know ye that the Lord he *is* God: *it is* he *that* hath made us, and not we ourselves; *we are* his people, and the sheep of his pasture. Enter into his gates with thanksgiving, *and* into his courts with praise: be thankful unto him, *and* bless his name. For the Lord *is* good; his mercy *is* everlasting; and his truth *endureth* to all generations.

─────── *DECLARATION OF FAITH* ───────

The joy of the Lord is my strength. I will make a joyful noise to Him with shouts of praise and thanksgiving. I will serve Him with gladness of heart. I am a happy man/woman.

I come before His presence with singing. I rejoice in His majesty. For the Lord, He is God. He has made me what I am. I am His child and a sheep in His pasture. I am ever-thankful for all He has done for me.

My Father does not keep account of what I've done wrong. He forgives me fully and never forsakes me. He is always good to me and His mercy toward me endures forever.

(Nehemiah 8:10; Psalm 32:11; 103:1-17; Philippians 4:4; Romans 9:20; John 10:1-10)

PSALM 101:2-8 KJV

I will behave myself wisely in a perfect way. O when wilt thou come unto me? I will walk within my house with a perfect heart. I will set no wicked thing before mine eyes: I hate the work of them that turn aside; *it* shall not cleave to me. A froward heart shall depart from me: I will not know a wicked *person*. Whoso privily slandereth his neighbour, him will I cut off: him that hath an high look and a proud heart will not I suffer. Mine eyes *shall be* upon the faithful of the land, that they may dwell with me: he that walketh in a perfect way, he shall serve me. He that worketh deceit shall not dwell within my house: he that telleth lies shall not tarry in my sight. I will early destroy all the wicked of the land; that I may cut off all wicked doers from the city of the Lord.

─────── *DECLARATION OF FAITH* ───────

I am careful to lead a blameless life. I walk in my house with a blameless heart fixed on doing nothing but good.

I refuse to allow my eyes to look upon that which is vile and abominable to my Father.

I hate the deeds of faithless men and will not let them cling to me in any way. I will not associate myself with men or women of a perverse heart. Their evil ways shall find no place in my life.

My eyes remain on the faithful in the land. Only the blameless and upright will minister unto me.

No one who practices deceit shall dwell in my house and no habitual liar shall stand in my presence.

(Romans 12:1; 2 Corinthians 4:13; 6:14; John 6:63; 1 Kings 11:4; Psalm 42:2,8; 75:10; 97:10; 119:115; Joshua 23:6; Mark 11:22-25; Proverbs 6:17)

PSALM 102:11,12 NKJV

My days *are* like a shadow that lengthens,
And I wither away like grass.
But You, O Lord, shall endure forever,
And the remembrance of Your name to all generations.

──── DECLARATION OF FAITH ────

I always keep in mind the measure of eternity. This life that I now live is but a fading shadow and like withering grass it will soon die away. It is but a grain of sand on eternity's beach. But my Father endures forever and He has placed eternity within my spirit. I will endure with Him forevermore.

(Ecclesiastes 3:11,12; Psalm 72:5-7)

PSALM 102:13-17 NKJV

You will arise and have mercy on Zion; for the time to favor her, yes, the set time, has come. For Your servants take pleasure in her stones, and show favor to her dust. So the nations shall fear the name of the Lord, and all the kings of the earth Your glory. For the Lord shall build up Zion; He shall appear in His glory. He shall regard the prayer of the destitute, and shall not despise their prayer.

──── DECLARATION OF FAITH ────

I am living in the time of God's favor. He is not up in heaven right now with a big stick looking to beat me every time that I do wrong. This is the day of His mercy and grace. He has placed all of His wrath upon Jesus. He has not reserved any for me. There is therefore now no condemnation for me because I am in Christ Jesus.

I can now take pleasure in all of the things of God. I revel in His goodness and mercy. The heathen shall see what God is doing in my life and they shall fear Him. Through me, the kings of the earth shall see the glory of His majesty!

The Lord shall build me up and manifest Himself through me in all of His splendor. He carefully considers my every prayer and together we walk in an intimate Father and son/daughter relationship here in this earth.

(Romans 3:21-26; 5:9,10; 8:1,2; Ephesians 3:20,21; 1 John 4:12-16)

PSALM 102:28 AMP

The children of Your servants shall dwell safely and continue, and their descendants shall be established before You.

All of my children shall dwell in the presence of the Lord. Even their descendants will be established before Him.

(Psalm 69:36; 72:4; 90:16; 103:17; 115:13,14; 1 Chronicles 17:23; Deuteronomy 7:9)

PSALM 103:1-18 KJV

Bless the Lord, O my soul: and all that is within me, *bless* his holy name. Bless the Lord, O my soul, and forget not all his benefits: Who forgiveth all thine iniquities; who healeth all thy diseases; Who redeemeth thy life from destruction; who crowneth thee with lovingkindness and tender mercies; Who satisfieth thy mouth with good *things; so that* thy youth is renewed like the eagle's. The Lord executeth righteousness and judgment for all that are oppressed. He made known his ways unto Moses, his acts unto the children of Israel. The Lord *is* merciful and gracious, slow to anger, and plenteous in mercy. He will not always chide: neither will he keep *his anger* for ever. He hath not dealt with us after our sins; nor rewarded us according to our iniquities. For as the heaven is high above the earth, *so* great is his mercy toward them that fear him. As far as the east is from the west, *so* far hath he removed our transgressions from us. Like as a father pitieth *his* children, *so* the Lord pitieth them that fear him. For he knoweth our frame; he remembereth that we *are* dust. *As for* man, his days *are* as grass: as a flower of the field, so he flourisheth. For the wind passeth over it, and it is gone; and the place thereof shall know it no more. But the mercy of the Lord *is* from everlasting to everlasting upon them that fear him, and his righteousness unto children's children; To such as keep his covenant, and to those that remember his commandments to do them.

———— DECLARATION OF FAITH ————

I stir up my inner man to praise the name of the Lord. My soul and all that is within me shall praise Him.

I will not forget all that God has done for me, all that He has for me, and all that He is doing in my life.

He has forgiven me of all of my sins and healed me of every possible disease.

He has redeemed my life from the pit and has crowned me with His love and compassion.

He satisfies my every desire with good things so that my youth is renewed within me, and that I may soar into this life like an eagle on the wing.

He works His justice on my behalf and has made me to be the righteousness of God in Christ Jesus forevermore.

He makes all of His ways known to me.

In any given moment, whatever the circumstance may be, I can expect His boundless favor and unconditional flood of compassion.

He is always reaching out to me with His love and His wrath has been removed from me for all time. All that He does to me is for my good, so that I may be a partaker of His holiness.

He does not punish me like my sins deserve or repay me according to the evil things that I have done. For as high as the heavens are above the earth, so great is His love for me. As far as the east is from the west, so far has He removed all of my sins from me. They will never be brought up again.

When I watch a loving father enjoying and delighting in his child, I see a shining example of the way my heavenly Father enjoys and delights in me. His compassion for me is beyond definition.

I have His Word that His love will never be taken from me, for He knows how I am formed. He knows my shortcomings and my limitations. He knows everything about me, and yet His love for me remains. As for common man, his days are like the grass and he flourishes like the flowers in the meadow. The wind blows over them and they are gone, and the memory of their beauty soon passes. But, from everlasting to everlasting God's love remains with me.

He extends His favor and His righteousness to my children and my grandchildren, as He does with all who keep His covenant of love and obey His precepts.

(Ephesians 3:16; Deuteronomy 7:9; 8:6-18; 2 Timothy 1:6; Galatians 3:13; Isaiah 40:7,31; 53:4,5; 54:17; Exodus 15:26; 34:6,7; Psalm 5:11,12; 2 Corinthians 5:21; Hebrews 10:16,17; 12:10; Ezra 9:13; Malachi 3:17; Romans 5:9; 8:38,39; Job 7:10)

PSALM 104:27,28 NKJV

These all wait for You, that You may give them their food in due season.
What You give them they gather in; You open Your hand, they are filled with good.

—— *DECLARATION OF FAITH* ——

I am calm and patient when waiting upon the Lord. I know that He answers my every prayer and will grant my petition in due season. His hand is open to me and my harvest overflows with good things.

(Hebrews 6:12; 1 John 5:14,15; Matthew 6:19-33)

PSALM 104:33,34 NIV

I will sing to the Lord all my life; I will sing praise to my God as long as I live.
May my meditation be pleasing to him, as I rejoice in the Lord.

——— DECLARATION OF FAITH ———

As long as I have breath within me, I will praise the Lord. I will sing to Him so long as I have my being.

I know that the Lord is good and merciful. My meditation in Him is never terrifying, but sweet and full of gladness.

(Psalm 33:3-5; 103:1-5; Joshua 1:8)

PSALM 105:8,14,15 NKJV

He remembers His covenant forever, the word which He commanded, for a thousand generations, He permitted no one to do them wrong; yes, He rebuked kings for their sakes, saying, "Do not touch My anointed ones, and do My prophets no harm."

——— DECLARATION OF FAITH ———

My Father earnestly remembers His covenant with me. It commands His utmost attention and He is quick to honor it. In my covenant I have His promise of protection from people who would do me wrong. When they act, God Himself stands up in my defense. He reproves even kings for my sake. I am His anointed and He does not tolerate those who would try to harm me.

(Genesis 17:7; Deuteronomy 28:1-14; 2 Chronicles 20:15)

PSALM 105:42-45 NKJV

For He remembered His holy promise,
And Abraham His servant.
He brought out His people with joy,
His chosen ones with gladness.
He gave them the lands of the Gentiles,
And they inherited the labor of the nations,
That they might observe His statutes
And keep His laws.
Praise the Lord!

——— DECLARATION OF FAITH ———

The Lord remembers His covenant with me to bring me forth in this life with rejoicing and to give me as an inheritance a land that others have toiled for. It is ordained that I shall reap the fruits of other people's labor as well as my own.

I too am equally diligent to remember my covenant with the Lord. I will keep His precepts and hold fast to His Word.

(Deuteronomy 4:1; 6:1-7; 28:1-14; Genesis 15:13,14; Joshua 11:16-23; Psalm 119:11)

PSALM 106:3-5 NKJV

Blessed are those who keep justice, and he who does righteousness at all times! Remember me, O Lord, with the favor You have toward Your people. Oh, visit me with Your salvation, that I may see the benefit of Your chosen ones, that I may rejoice in the gladness of Your nation, that I may glory with Your inheritance.

—— DECLARATION OF FAITH ——

I am a happy and prosperous man/woman and consistently do what is right. I make justice a top priority in my life.

My Father continually shows me His favor and assists me in doing His will so that I may enjoy the prosperity and success of His chosen ones.

I share in the joy of the church and join them in heartfelt praises to our God.

(Psalm 5:11,12; 112:1-3; Joshua 1:8; Genesis 18:19; Nehemiah 8:10; Galatians 6:9)

PSALM 106:6-10 KJV

We have sinned with our fathers, we have committed iniquity, we have done wickedly. Our fathers understood not thy wonders in Egypt; they remembered not the multitude of thy mercies; but provoked *him* at the sea, *even* at the Red sea. Nevertheless he saved them for his name's sake, that he might make his mighty power to be known. He rebuked the Red sea also, and it was dried up: so he led them through the depths, as through the wilderness. And he saved them from the hand of him that hated *them,* and redeemed them from the hand of the enemy.

—— DECLARATION OF FAITH ——

I am a child of God under His continuous protection. Even though I have failed and turned from Him, He has never turned from me. For His name's sake, He saves me and makes His mighty power known in my life. He saves me from the hand of those who hate me. I am redeemed from the hand of the enemy.

(Genesis 15:1; Psalm 103:2-4; Exodus 15:6-10)

Psalm 106:29-31 NKJV

Thus they provoked Him to anger with their deeds, and the plague broke out among them. Then Phinehas stood up and intervened, and so the plague was stopped. And that was accounted to him for righteousness to all generations forevermore.

DECLARATION OF FAITH

I have the power to stand in the gap for the wicked. When the devil comes in with his flood of turmoil and plagues, I take my stand against him. When I intervene, his plan is checked and can go no further.

(Job 22:27-30; Ezekiel 22:30; Numbers 25:7-13; Luke 10:19; Mark 3:27)

Psalm 106:44-46 NKJV

Nevertheless He regarded their affliction, when He heard their cry; And for their sake He remembered His covenant, and relented according to the multitude of His mercies. He also made them to be pitied by all those who carried them away captive.

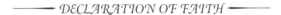

DECLARATION OF FAITH

When distress comes against me, God remembers our covenant. Out of His great love for me, He causes all who are appointed over me to grant me favor.

(Leviticus 26:9,41,42; Hebrews 8:6; 10:15-17; Genesis 39:2-5; Ezra 9:9)

Psalm 107:1,2 NKJV

Oh, give thanks to the Lord, for He is good! For His mercy endures forever. Let the redeemed of the Lord say so, whom He has redeemed from the hand of the enemy.

DECLARATION OF FAITH

I give thanks to my Father, for He is good to me and His mercy towards me endures forever. I am the redeemed of the Lord! I am redeemed from the hand of the enemy!

(1 Chronicles 16:34,35; Galatians 3:13)

Psalm 107:8,9 NIV

Let them give thanks to the Lord for his unfailing love and his wonderful deeds for men, for he satisfies the thirsty and fills the hungry with good things.

——— *DECLARATION OF FAITH* ———

I praise my Father for His goodness towards me. He is not good to me only some of the time, He is good to me all of the time! His wonderful works of kindness toward me have no end. He satisfies my longing soul! He fills my hungry soul with His favor and loving-kindness forevermore!

(Exodus 34:6,7; Psalm 5:11,12; 23)

Psalm 107:13,14 KJV

Then they cried unto the Lord in their trouble, *and* he saved them out of their distresses. He brought them out of darkness and the shadow of death, and brake their bands in sunder.

——— *DECLARATION OF FAITH* ———

In time of trouble I look to God as my source of strength. He saves me from my distresses and delivers me from every evil attack. He takes me by the hand and leads me out of the darkness and from the shadow of death. He breaks my bonds and sets me free!

(Exodus 13:14; Psalm 18:1,2; 23; Galatians 4:3-5)

Psalm 107:20,21 NKJV

He sent His word and healed them, and delivered them from their destructions. Oh, that men would give thanks to the Lord for His goodness, and for His wonderful works to the children of men!

——— *DECLARATION OF FAITH* ———

God has sent His Word into this earth to heal me and rescue me from death. His love for me never fails. He is always working to bring good things into my life and perform mighty deeds on my behalf.

(Matthew 8:8; 2 Kings 20:5; Isaiah 53:4,5; Psalm 30:2; Proverbs 3:3,4; Job 33:28-30)

Psalm 107:28-30 NKJV

Then they cry out to the Lord in their trouble, and He brings them out of their distresses. He calms the storm, so that its waves are still. Then they are glad because they are quiet; so He guides them to their desired haven.

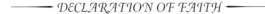
When troubles come my way, I call to God for assistance and He draws me from their grasp. In His great love for me, He stills the storms to a whisper and silences the raging waves of the sea. He restores my joy as praises fill my mouth. He then takes me by the hand and guides me to the realization of my dreams.

(1 Peter 5:5-7; Psalm 18:1-18; 51:12; 73:23; 89:9; Matthew 8:26)

PSALM 107:35-38 KJV

He turneth the wilderness into a standing water, and dry ground into water-springs. And there he maketh the hungry to dwell, that they may prepare a city for habitation; And sow the fields, and plant vineyards, which may yield fruits of increase. He blesseth them also, so that they are multiplied greatly; and suffereth not their cattle to decrease.

─────── *DECLARATION OF FAITH* ───────

God has brought me out of the wasteland and turned my desert places into pools of water. The parched ground that I once called my life is now a flowing spring.

He has called me to build and establish my city. Here, I will sow, plant and yield a fruitful harvest.

I am a blessed man/woman. All that I have, and all that I am, greatly increases.

(Psalm 114:8; Isaiah 41:17,18; Genesis 12:1-3; 17:16-20; 2 Corinthians 9:5-11; Deuteronomy 7:14)

PSALM 107:43 NIV

Whoever is wise, let him heed these things and consider the great love of the Lord.

─────── *DECLARATION OF FAITH* ───────

I am counted among the wise ones who observe and heed the Word of God.

I ponder, meditate on, and diligently consider the great love that God has for me. I will not let such a blessing escape from my mind.

(Psalm 64:9; Jeremiah 9:12; Hosea 14:9; Proverbs 1:5-7; Joshua 1:8)

PSALM 108:12,13 NKJV

Give us help from trouble,
For the help of man is useless.
Through God we will do valiantly,
For *it is* He *who* shall tread down our enemies.

——— *DECLARATION OF FAITH* ———

God is my strength and ever-present help against all of the attacks of the enemy. With Him, my victory is sealed and I will trample down every foe. The sign of my victory is the imprint of my heel upon the enemy's neck!

(Ephesians 6:10; 1 Corinthians 15:57; Luke 10:19; Psalm 60:12; Joshua 10:24)

PSALM 109:26-31 KJV

Help me, O Lord my God: O save me according to thy mercy: That they may know that this *is* thy hand; *that* thou, Lord, hast done it. Let them curse, but bless thou: when they arise, let them be ashamed; but let thy servant rejoice. Let mine adversaries be clothed with shame, and let them cover themselves with their own confusion, as with a mantle. I will greatly praise the Lord with my mouth; yea, I will praise him among the multitude. For he shall stand at the right hand of the poor, to save *him* from those that condemn his soul.

——— *DECLARATION OF FAITH* ———

The Lord is my mainstay in times of trouble. He rescues me in a tremendous display of His power because of the great love that He has for me.

The enemy knows of a certainty that God is on my side. When they curse, God blesses. When they attack, He humiliates them. They turn tail and run, wrapped in a garment of shame.

As for me, I am getting a big kick out of it. I am laughing, rejoicing and shouting praises in the name of the Lord! He is my Father and my God! I take my place among the mighty and enjoy His many blessings! My heavenly Father stands at my right hand to deliver me and has given me His Word that He will never ever leave me!

(Psalm 18:1-18; Romans 8:31; Genesis 12:3; 2 Samuel 6:11,12; Psalm 2; 35:4; Deuteronomy 28:7; Hebrews 10:25; 13:5,6; Isaiah 65:14)

PSALM 110:3 NKJV

Your people shall be volunteers in the day of Your power; in the beauties of holiness, from the womb of the morning, You have the dew of Your youth.

——— *DECLARATION OF FAITH* ———

I am a warrior in the army of almighty God. I am willing to fight and destroy the enemy on any battlefield. I spring forth as a conqueror clad in royal garments. The enemy shall see me as God sees me—arrayed in holy majesty—born again as from the womb of the dawn!

(Ephesians 6:10-18; 2 Corinthians 10:3-6; 2 Timothy 2:3,4; Romans 8:28-37)

PSALM 111:4,5 AMP

He has made His wonderful works to be remembered; the Lord is gracious, merciful, and full of loving compassion. He has given food and provision to those who reverently and worshipfully fear Him; He will remember His covenant forever and imprint it [on His mind].

———— DECLARATION OF FAITH ————

My Father works many miracles on my behalf. He causes me to remember the favor and compassion that He has shown me. His covenant with me stands immovable and His daily provision for me never fails.

(Mark 16:18-20; Psalm 103:13; Acts 4:23-31; Leviticus 26:9; Hebrews 8:6; Philippians 4:19; Matthew 6:19-33)

PSALM 111:7-10 NKJV

The works of His hands are verity and justice; all His precepts are sure. They stand fast forever and ever, and are done in truth and uprightness. He has sent redemption to His people; He has commanded His covenant forever: holy and awesome is His name. The fear of the Lord is the beginning of wisdom; a good understanding have all those who do His commandments. His praise endures forever.

———— DECLARATION OF FAITH ————

I am a child of sharp, clear and thorough understanding.

I follow God's precepts wholeheartedly. Because of this, He sees to it that all of His covenant promises are fulfilled in my life. His Word stands true and steadfast forever. He has provided my redemption and has decreed and established His covenant with me from this day unto eternity. Great and awesome is His name!

(Daniel 1:17,20; 1 Corinthians 2:6-16; Revelation 15:3; Galatians 3:13; Hebrews 8:6)

PSALM 112:1-9 KJV

Praise ye the Lord. Blessed *is* the man *that* feareth the Lord, *that* delighteth greatly in his commandments. His seed shall be mighty upon earth: the generation of the upright shall be blessed. Wealth and riches *shall be* in his house: and his righteousness endureth for ever. Unto the upright there ariseth light in the darkness: *he is* gracious, and full of compassion, and righteous. A good man sheweth favour, and lendeth: he will guide his affairs with discretion. Surely he shall not be moved for ever: the righteous shall be in everlasting remembrance. He shall not be afraid of evil tidings: his heart is fixed, trusting in the Lord. His heart *is* established, he shall not be afraid, until he see *his desire* upon his enemies. He hath dispersed, he hath given to the poor; his righteousness endureth for ever; his horn shall be exalted with honour.

DECLARATION OF FAITH

I give proper reverence to my heavenly Father and find great delight in His precepts.

I am blessed in all that I do.

Wealth and abundance of riches are in my house and my righteousness has no end.

I am gracious and compassionate, just like my Father.

Darkness turns to light in my presence. With me, there is no darkness at all.

Good things rain down upon me continually, for I have learned the blessings of generosity and give freely for the advancement of God's kingdom.

I am known as a just and righteous man/woman. I distribute gifts regularly to those in need and the resulting righteousness endures forever. When bad news comes, I am not shaken. When the spirit of fear comes against me, I face it with courage. I know the One in whom my trust is set and my victory in the end is absolutely certain.

(Deuteronomy 28:1-14; Psalm 1:1-3; 102:28; Proverbs 1:33; 3:16,24; 8:18; 10:7; Genesis 12:1-3; 13:2; Matthew 5:14-16; 6:19-33; Malachi 3:6-12; 2 Corinthians 9:5-11; 2 Timothy 1:7; Numbers 14:8; Hebrews 13:9; Isaiah 12:2)

PSALM 113:7-9 NKJV

He raises the poor out of the dust,
And lifts the needy out of the ash heap,
That He may seat *him* with princes—
With the princes of His people.
He grants the barren woman a home,
Like a joyful mother of children.
Praise the Lord!

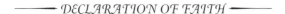

─── *DECLARATION OF FAITH* ───

God has lifted me out of the ash heap and has seated me with kings and princes. Where the devil brought me to destruction, God has raised me to the place of highest honor.

(For the women)

He establishes me in my house and makes me a happy mother of children. I am not barren in any way, but fruitful in all things.

(Ephesians 2:6; Revelation 1:5,6; Colossians 1:13; Psalm 72:12; Job 36:7; Deuteronomy 7:14; Isaiah 54:1)

PSALM 115:12-15 NKJV

The Lord has been mindful of us; He will bless us; He will bless the house of Israel; He will bless the house of Aaron. He will bless those who fear the Lord, both small and great. May the Lord give you increase more and more, you and your children. May you be blessed by the Lord, who made heaven and earth.

─── *DECLARATION OF FAITH* ───

I am always on God's mind. He is continually finding ways to bless me. My joy knows no bounds as He showers me with His wonderful gifts. He makes both me and my children to increase so that we have an abundance of all good things.

He has placed all of His creation into my hands so that I will never lack the things that I need. Everything that my Father has created in this earth is put here for my provision. There is more than enough for all of us to draw upon so that we can live a life of wealth and abundance.

(Psalm 128:1-4; Hebrews 6:10; Genesis 12:1-3; 13:2; 14:9; 2 Chronicles 31:10)

PSALM 116:5,6 NKJV

Gracious is the Lord, and righteous; yes, our God is merciful. The Lord preserves the simple; I was brought low, and He saved me.

─── *DECLARATION OF FAITH* ───

My Father's compassion for me has no limits. He protects me from every attack of the enemy. When I am in need, He sees to it that I am provided for.

(1 Corinthians 13; 1 John 4:7,8; 5:18; Hebrews 13:5,6; Philippians 4:19)

Psalm 116:13-16 NKJV

I will take up the cup of salvation, and call upon the name of the Lord.

I will pay my vows to the Lord now in the presence of all His people.

Precious in the sight of the Lord is the death of His saints.

———— *DECLARATION OF FAITH* ————

O Lord, truly I am Your servant; I am Your servant, the son of Your maidservant; You have loosed my bonds.

I will lift up the cup of my salvation for the Lord to fill with His good treasures.

I look to Him alone as my mainstay and fulfill all of my vows to Him faithfully. He looks to me with utter delight as I walk this earth and holds as precious the day when I finally leave here to enter His courts in heaven.

He has freed me from the chains of my old life. I am now His own son/daughter and I serve Him with all of my heart.

(Psalm 23:5; 72:14; 86:16; 119:125; 143:12; Colossians 1:13; Galatians 4:5,6; Revelation 14:13)

Psalm 118:5-17 KJV

I called upon the Lord in distress: the Lord answered me, *and set me* in a large place. The Lord *is* on my side; I will not fear: what can man do unto me? The Lord taketh my part with them that help me: therefore shall I see *my desire* upon them that hate me. *It is* better to trust in the Lord than to put confidence in man. *It is* better to trust in the Lord than to put confidence in princes. All nations compassed me about: but in the name of the Lord will I destroy them. They compassed me about; yea, they compassed me about: but in the name of the Lord I will destroy them. They compassed me about like bees; they are quenched as the fire of thorns: for in the name of the Lord I will destroy them. Thou hast thrust sore at me that I might fall: but the Lord helped me. The Lord *is* my strength and song, and is become my salvation. The voice of rejoicing and salvation *is* in the tabernacles of the righteous: the right hand of the Lord doeth valiantly. The right hand of the Lord is exalted: the right hand of the Lord doeth valiantly. I shall not die, but live, and declare the works of the Lord.

———— *DECLARATION OF FAITH* ————

When I was alone and without help, I cried out to God. I knew in my heart that only He could save me and deliver me from Satan's bondage. And faithful to His Word, He set me free. He dashed to pieces the chains that bound me and made me a prince/princess in His royal family.

He is now with me at all times and is totally devoted to my success in this life.

I have no fear when men try to destroy me, for I know that God is on my side. To be afraid would be utterly foolish — just as it is foolish to come against one of God's children.

I have the complete and unqualified certainty that victory is mine.

I would much rather take my refuge in the Lord than to trust in the ways of men. Even the princes of this earth are paupers compared to the ones who are in alliance with God.

All I need to do is lift up the name of Jesus in my defense and they are thwarted.

Even when I stumble in battle, the Lord lifts me up. He is always with me and He never stumbles. He is my strength, my song, and my continual salvation. Shouts of victory are constantly heard in my house, for the Lord is a mighty God and has done great things on my behalf!

(Ephesians 2:1-10; John 3:16,17; Colossians 1:13,14; Hebrews 13:5,6; 1 Corinthians 15:57; Romans 8:31; 12:9-21; 2 Timothy 1:7; 2:13; Genesis 12:3; 2 Chronicles 32:7; 2 Kings 6:15-17; Psalm 35:4; 54:4; 59:10; 88:17; 146:3)

PSALM 118:25-27 NKJV

Save now, I pray, O Lord; O Lord, I pray, send now prosperity. Blessed is he who comes in the name of the Lord! We have blessed you from the house of the Lord. God is the Lord, and He has given us light; bind the sacrifice with cords to the horns of the altar.

—— *DECLARATION OF FAITH* ——

My Father grants me success in all that I do. I am His own child, a bearer of His mighty name, and I enjoy all of the benefits of sonship. He has made the light of His favor shine upon me and has given me all of the rights of an heir to His kingdom.

(Galatians 4:5,6; Genesis 39:2-5; Deuteronomy 28:12; Psalm 5:11,12; Romans 8:14-17)

PSALM 119:1-8 KJV

ALEPH. Blessed *are* the undefiled in the way, who walk in the law of the Lord. Blessed *are* they that keep his testimonies, *and that* seek him with the whole heart. They also do no iniquity: they walk in his ways. Thou hast commanded *us* to keep thy precepts diligently. O that my ways were directed to keep thy statutes! Then shall I not be ashamed, when I have respect unto all thy commandments. I will praise thee with uprightness of heart, when I shall have learned thy righteous judgments. I will keep thy statutes: O forsake me not utterly.

I keep myself undefiled from the ways of the world and I am blessed in all that I do. My delight is in the Word. I keep God's testimonies and seek after Him with all of my heart. I refuse to allow sin to taint my life and rob me of God's blessings. My behavior is constant and unwavering. I have no reason to be ashamed, for I give utmost respect to the Lord's commandments. I walk in continual praise and adoration of my Father and He is with me in all that I do.

(Psalm 37:4,5; Deuteronomy 4:29; 28:1-14; Hebrews 12:14-17)

PSALM 119:9-24 KJV

BETH. Wherewithal shall a young man cleanse his way? by taking heed *thereto* according to thy word. With my whole heart have I sought thee: O let me not wander from thy commandments. Thy word have I hid in mine heart, that I might not sin against thee. Blessed *art* thou, O Lord: teach me thy statutes. With my lips have I declared all the judgments of thy mouth. I have rejoiced in the way of thy testimonies, as *much as* in all riches. I will meditate in thy precepts, and have respect unto thy ways. I will delight myself in thy statutes: I will not forget thy word. GIMEL. Deal bountifully with thy servant, *that* I may live, and keep thy word. Open thou mine eyes, that I may behold wondrous things out of thy law. I *am* a stranger in the earth: hide not thy commandments from me. My soul breaketh for the longing *that it hath* unto thy judgments at all times. Thou hast rebuked the proud *that are* cursed, which do err from thy commandments. Remove from me reproach and contempt; for I have kept thy testimonies. Princes also did sit *and* speak against me: *but* thy servant did meditate in thy statutes. Thy testimonies also *are* my delight *and* my counsellors.

I keep my way pure before the Lord and do those things that the Word commands.

I keep His precepts within my heart and refuse to stray from the ways of the Word.

The Lord teaches me all of the inner workings and practical relevancy of His Word.

My lips recount all of His laws as I meditate on them continually.

I rejoice in following His statutes as one rejoices in the discovery of a great treasure.

I daily give of my time to the Word, being careful not to neglect it.

In my meditation, God gives me revelation knowledge to expand my horizons and obtain a greater reward.

I know and understand that only good things are prepared for me and, through obedience to the Word, I will live a long, full and satisfying life.

Every minute of every day, His Word goes before me. I am totally consumed with desire for it, for in it, I live free of rebuke and the curse.

All scorn and contempt is removed from me (unable to cling to me) because I delight in the Word. Let the mockers and slanderers say what they may, I will not turn from meditating on and living by the precepts that God has established for me. They are my delight and sure counsel, and in them I am blessed in all that I do.

(Deuteronomy 28:1; Joshua 1:8; 1 Corinthians 2:6-16; Isaiah 46:4; 2 Chronicles 15:15; Luke 2:19; Psalm 1:1-3; 39:8; 116:7)

PSALM 119:27,28 NKJV

Make me understand the way of Your precepts; so shall I meditate on Your wonderful works. My soul melts from heaviness; strengthen me according to Your word.

—— *DECLARATION OF FAITH* ——

I am blessed with an intimate understanding of God's precepts. As I meditate on the Word, revelation knowledge is engrafted into my soul.

When I am weary and sorrow fills my heart, I turn to the Word, for in it I find strength and a zeal for persistence that spurs me on to victory.

(1 Corinthians 2:6-16; 1 John 5:20; 2 Timothy 2:7; Psalm 107:26)

PSALM 119:29-32 NKJV

Remove from me the way of lying, and grant me Your law graciously. I have chosen the way of truth; Your judgments I have laid before me. I cling to Your testimonies; O Lord, do not put me to shame! I will run the course of Your commandments, for You shall enlarge my heart.

—— *DECLARATION OF FAITH* ——

I will not defile myself with lies and deceit. I choose the way of truth. The Word of the Lord is my counsel and my delight. I run the way of God's commandments and He increases my understanding immeasurably.

(1 Peter 3:10-12; Psalm 1:1-3; Nehemiah 10:28,29)

PSALM 119:34-38 KJV

Give me understanding, and I shall keep thy law; yea, I shall observe it with *my* whole heart. Make me to go in the path of thy commandments; for therein do I delight. Incline my heart unto thy testimonies, and not to covetousness. Turn away mine eyes from beholding vanity; *and* quicken thou me in thy way. Stablish thy word unto thy servant, who *is devoted* to thy fear.

———— DECLARATION OF FAITH ————

My Father reveals to me the deepest meanings of His Word and I obey it with all of my heart.

His Word is a clear path set before me in the midst of a thorny jungle. It is a sure source of lasting pleasure in my life. My heart is fixed upon it and not toward selfish gain.

I turn my eyes away from the worthless ways of the world. I cast anything that does not bring honor to God far from my presence.

My life is established and preserved through the Word. Not one of God's promises fails to be fulfilled in me. I hold fast to them with all of my heart, for by this, I am revered and respected in the earth.

(1 Corinthians 2:6-16; 2 Corinthians 1:20; 1 John 5:20; Isaiah 33:15; 46:4; 55:11; Hebrews 13:5; Proverbs 23:5)

PSALM 119:41-43 NKJV

Let Your mercies come also to me, O Lord—Your salvation according to Your word. So shall I have an answer for him who reproaches me, for I trust in Your word. And take not the word of truth utterly out of my mouth, for I have hoped in Your ordinances.

———— DECLARATION OF FAITH ————

Though there are those who will taunt and make fun of me because of my trust in the Lord, I will not give in. I am convinced — completely sold out — on the fact that the promises of my God are true. His love for me will never fail and my deliverance is as sure as the devil's destruction. My Father's Word shall remain upon my lips regardless of the circumstances.

(Psalm 2; Isaiah 55:11; Romans 8:38,39; Joshua 1:8; Galatians 1:4)

PSALM 119:50 NIV

My comfort in my suffering is this: Your promise preserves my life.

My comfort in the midst of life's troubles is this: God has promised to deliver me out of every one of them!

(2 Timothy 4:18; 2 Peter 2:9; Job 6:10; Colossians 1:13; Romans 15:4)

PSALM 119:57-64 KJV

CHETH. *Thou art* my portion, O Lord: I have said that I would keep thy words. I intreated thy favour with *my* whole heart: be merciful unto me according to thy word. I thought on my ways, and turned my feet unto thy testimonies. I made haste, and delayed not to keep thy commandments. The bands of the wicked have robbed me: *but* I have not forgotten thy law. At midnight I will rise to give thanks unto thee because of thy righteous judgments. I *am* a companion of all *them* that fear thee, and of them that keep thy precepts. The earth, O Lord, is full of thy mercy: teach me thy statutes.

My covenant with almighty God has been sealed and ratified. I will obey His every command.

I seek His face with all of my heart, for He alone can provide what I need to fulfill my destiny.

His favor rests upon me and my path is made clear and certain. All of my ways are in keeping with His statutes.

When Satan comes against me to ensnare me in his wicked ways of bondage, I will look to the Word. Even if he comes in the middle of the night, I will rise and give God thanks, for His Word is true and in it I have my victory.

I am the friend and partner of all who hold fast to the Word with unwavering confidence. We are all knit together in the power of His love. I can be certain that in every circumstance God has someone who is standing with me.

(Leviticus 26:9; Hebrews 8:6; 10:25; Deuteronomy 4:29; 28:1; Psalm 5:11,12; 27:11; Acts 16:25; Matthew 4:1-11; Ezekiel 22:30)

PSALM 119:64-68 NKJV

The earth, O Lord, is full of Your mercy; teach me Your statutes. You have dealt well with Your servant, O Lord, according to Your word. Teach me good judgment and knowledge, for I believe Your commandments. Before I was afflicted I went astray, but now I keep Your word. You are good, and do good; teach me Your statutes.

————— *DECLARATION OF FAITH* —————

I am taught by the best. God, the very creator of heaven and earth, is my master instructor.

He delivered me from a life full of turmoil and has shown me the way to live in His peace.

His goodness to me is revealed in His Word. By it, I have learned to retain knowledge and good judgment. God is good and everything that He does for me is good.

With Him as my teacher, I am gaining extensive understanding of His ways and how I am to incorporate them into my life.

(Psalm 33:5; John 16:13; 2 Corinthians 5:17; Romans 14:17; Daniel 1:17,20; 2:22,23; Genesis 50:20; 1 Corinthians 2:6-16)

PSALM 119:74-81 KJV

They that fear thee will be glad when they see me; because I have hoped in thy word. I know, O Lord, that thy judgments *are* right, and *that* thou in faithfulness hast afflicted me. Let, I pray thee, thy merciful kindness be for my comfort, according to thy word unto thy servant. Let thy tender mercies come unto me, that I may live: for thy law *is* my delight. Let the proud be ashamed; for they dealt perversely with me without a cause: *but* I will meditate in thy precepts. Let those that fear thee turn unto me, and those that have known thy testimonies. Let my heart be sound in thy statutes; that I be not ashamed. CAPH. My soul fainteth for thy salvation: *but* I hope in thy word.

————— *DECLARATION OF FAITH* —————

The people of God recognize my commitment to the Word and they rejoice.

God's Word is the very discipline of my life, afflicting me when I need chastisement and comforting me even in the midst of my affliction.

God's unfailing love to me is revealed in His Word and His promises give me serenity in this life. The compassion of my heavenly Father that is revealed in His Word overwhelms me. I meditate upon His precepts and find tremendous delight in His righteous laws.

Those who come against me are put to shame, for I am a man/woman of the Word.

Those who understand it turn to me as a powerful ally because of my commitment to the precepts of my God.

(Psalm 1:1-3; 25:3; 34:2; 73:26; Hebrews 12:10; Joshua 1:8; Esther 5:9-6:11)

PSALM 119:89,90 NKJV

Forever, O Lord, Your word is settled in heaven. Your faithfulness endures to all generations; You established the earth, and it abides.

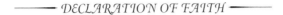

——— *DECLARATION OF FAITH* ———

I hold fast to the Word of God. It stands firm in the heavens and is faithful to all generations.

(Isaiah 40:8; 55:11; Psalm 89:2; Matthew 24:35; 1 Peter 1:25)

PSALM 119:93 AMP

I will never forget Your precepts, [how can I?] for it is by them You have quickened me (granted me life).

——— *DECLARATION OF FAITH* ———

I will never fail to remember the Word of God. By it, my health never fails and I shall live a long, happy and prosperous life.

(Deuteronomy 6:5-9; 8:6-18; Psalm 107:20; Isaiah 46:4; 53:5; 1 Peter 2:24)

PSALM 119:97-101 NKJV

Oh, how I love Your law!
It *is* my meditation all the day.
You, through Your commandments, make me wiser than my enemies;
For they *are* ever with me.
I have more understanding than all my teachers,
For Your testimonies *are* my meditation.
I understand more than the ancients,
Because I keep Your precepts.
I have restrained my feet from every evil way,
That I may keep Your word.

——— *DECLARATION OF FAITH* ———

I love God's Word with all of my heart. It is of supreme importance in my life.

I meditate upon it throughout the day and speak it continually so that the plans of my life are made right.

It makes me wiser than my enemies who never fail to grace me with their presence.

By it, I have more insight than even my teachers (who do not know the Word), for I have learned to speak it to myself so that it may be engrafted in my spirit.

I show that I have more understanding than many elders by my unyielding commitment to obey God's commands.

I am a wise man/woman who keeps his/her feet from every evil path.

In my life, the Word reigns supreme!

(Psalm 1:1-3; Joshua 1:8; Deuteronomy 4:6; Daniel 1:17,20; 2:22,23; 2 Timothy 3:15)

PSALM 119:105-107 NKJV

Your word is a lamp to my feet and a light to my path. I have sworn and confirmed that I will keep Your righteous judgments. I am afflicted very much; revive me, O Lord, according to Your word.

——— *DECLARATION OF FAITH* ———

God's Word is a lamp unto my feet and a light unto my path.

I have taken my oath, and confirmed it with deeds tried and true, that I will follow the precepts that my Father has laid out for me.

Therefore, I shall remain in good health and my vitality shall be preserved until I have lived a long, happy, and prosperous life.

(Proverbs 6:23; Nehemiah 10:29; 1 John 3:18; Isaiah 46:4; Psalm 107:20)

PSALM 119:111-116 KJV

Thy testimonies have I taken as an heritage for ever: for they *are* the rejoicing of my heart. I have inclined mine heart to perform thy statutes alway, *even unto* the end. SAMECH. I hate *vain* thoughts: but thy law do I love. Thou *art* my hiding place and my shield: I hope in thy word. Depart from me, ye evildoers: for I will keep the commandments of my God. Uphold me according unto thy word, that I may live: and let me not be ashamed of my hope.

——— *DECLARATION OF FAITH* ———

The Word is my heritage and the proclamation of my rights. It is the joy of my life and my heart is fixed on keeping it to the very end.

I refuse to mingle with, listen to, or debate with double-minded and faithless men. I will not allow their cancerous ways to pollute my life and draw me away from the joy and prosperity that my Father has provided.

I am focused on the Word. It is my shield and my refuge in times of trouble. By it, I am sustained in good health and will live a long and enjoyable life.

(Deuteronomy 33:4; 28:1; 2 Corinthians 6:14; James 1:5-8; Psalm 6:8; 25:2; 32:7; Matthew 7:23)

PSALM 119:130-133 NKJV

The entrance of Your words gives light; it gives understanding to the simple. I opened my mouth and panted, for I longed for Your commandments. Look upon me and be merciful to me, as Your custom is toward those who love Your name. Direct my steps by Your word, and let no iniquity have dominion over me.

———— *DECLARATION OF FAITH* ————

Revelation knowledge of God's Word gives me inveterate understanding of its life application. It sheds light on the way that is set before me.

I yearn for the Word as sustenance for my spirit man. Without it, the weakness of malnutrition reigns. Therefore, I shall feed on the Word all the days of my life. I shall remain strong, ever-abiding in God's mercy and always moving forward in the power of His name.

I let no sin rule over me. The Word of the living God directs my every step.

(1 Corinthians 2:6-16; Psalm 17:5; 19:13; 119:11,105; 2 Thessalonians 1:6; Romans 6:12)

PSALM 119:134,135 NKJV

Redeem me from the oppression of man, that I may keep Your precepts. Make Your face shine upon Your servant, and teach me Your statutes.

———— *DECLARATION OF FAITH* ————

I am redeemed from the oppression of evil men.

My master teacher instructs me in the ways of His Word and I have victory in every circumstance. His face continually shines upon me. I am His devoted pupil and I focus myself wholeheartedly on the lesson at hand.

(Galatians 3:13; John 16:13; 1 Corinthians 15:57; 2 Timothy 2:15)

PSALM 119:138-140 NKJV

Your testimonies, which You have commanded, are righteous and very faithful. My zeal has consumed me, because my enemies have forgotten Your words. Your word is very pure; therefore Your servant loves it.

———— *DECLARATION OF FAITH* ————

I know that every Word from God is fully trustworthy. Therefore, even though I may become weary in battle, I will not give in. The Word has been tested and tried time and again, and through it I have certain victory.

(Isaiah 55:11; Psalm 19:7-9; 69:9; John 2:17; 1 Corinthians 15:57)

PSALM 119:147-149 NKJV

I rise before the dawning of the morning, and cry for help; I hope in Your word. My eyes are awake through the night watches, that I may meditate on Your word. Hear my voice according to Your lovingkindness; O Lord, revive me according to Your justice.

DECLARATION OF FAITH

My hope is in the Word of the living God. I am focused and disciplined on keeping its precepts.

My prayers rise to heaven before the rising of the sun and my meditation continues through the watches of the night.

(Deuteronomy 28:1; Matthew 14:23-25; Luke 6:12; Psalm 5:3; 63:1,6)

PSALM 119:150-159 KJV

They draw nigh that follow after mischief: they are far from thy law. Thou *art* near, O Lord; and all thy commandments *are* truth. Concerning thy testimonies, I have known of old that thou hast founded them for ever. RESH. Consider mine affliction, and deliver me: for I do not forget thy law. Plead my cause, and deliver me: quicken me according to thy word. Salvation *is* far from the wicked: for they seek not thy statutes. Great *are* thy tender mercies, O Lord: quicken me according to thy judgments. Many *are* my persecutors and mine enemies; *yet* do I not decline from thy testimonies. I beheld the transgressors, and was grieved; because they kept not thy word. Consider how I love thy precepts: quicken me, O Lord, according to thy lovingkindness.

DECLARATION OF FAITH

My Father considers my afflictions and delivers me according to His Word. When I speak it, life and health flood into my body. I will not forget the power of the Word. God has given it to me to keep my life safe and provide healing and security for me in times of trouble. Great are my Father's mercies. The fullness of His blessings come to me through His Word.

(Deuteronomy 28:1-14; Psalm 107:20; John 6:63; Proverbs 18:20,21)

PSALM 119:160-162 NKJV

The entirety of Your word is truth, and every one of Your righteous judgments endures forever. Princes persecute me without a cause, but my heart stands in awe of Your word. I rejoice at Your word as one who finds great treasure.

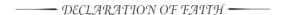

——— *DECLARATION OF FAITH* ———

I recognize that all of my Father's promises are eternally faithful. I tremble in knowing that they have been given to me on a personal level. When I find one, I rejoice as one who has found buried treasure and is made rich beyond his wildest dreams.

(Isaiah 45:23; 46:9-11; 55:11; 2 Corinthians 1:20; Matthew 24:35)

PSALM 119:165 NKJV

Great peace have those who love Your law, And nothing causes them to stumble. I am overwhelmed and enraptured by the peace that God has given me.

——— *DECLARATION OF FAITH* ———

Because I hold the Word in highest honor, nothing in this life can make me stumble.

(Ephesians 2:14; Romans 14:17; Jude 24; Proverbs 3:2; Isaiah 26:3; 32:17)

PSALM 119:169-173 NKJV

Let my cry come before You, O Lord; give me understanding according to Your word. Let my supplication come before You; deliver me according to Your word. My lips shall utter praise, for You teach me Your statutes. My tongue shall speak of Your word, for all Your commandments are righteousness. Let Your hand become my help, for I have chosen Your precepts.

——— *DECLARATION OF FAITH* ———

When I am in need, I do not look to the circumstance, but to the Word. My Father has given me tremendous understanding of its precepts, and in it, I find deliverance from all of the troubles of life.

God Himself is my master instructor who sees to it that I know all that I need to know to procure my victory. What a joy it is to be taught by the best! I will praise Him for His commands that bring my unfailing success. He is eager to teach me His ways so that I may stand against every attack of the enemy and enjoy the abundant life that He has provided for me.

I have made my choice. No matter what the circumstance, I will not turn from His Word.

(John 10:10; 16:13; Deuteronomy 11:26,27; Psalm 119:7,27,144; Joshua 24:22)

PSALM 120:1-7 KJV

In my distress I cried unto the Lord, and he heard me. Deliver my soul, O Lord, from lying lips, *and* from a deceitful tongue. What shall be given unto thee? or what shall be done unto thee, thou false tongue? Sharp arrows of the mighty, with coals of juniper. Woe is me, that I sojourn in Mesech, *that* I dwell in the tents of Kedar! My soul hath long dwelt with him that hateth peace. I *am for* peace: but when I speak, they *are* for war.

———— DECLARATION OF FAITH ————

My Father delivers me from my enemies who speak lies against me. He gives me the weapons of war and stands with me in the battle. Those who rise against me have no chance of victory. The Lord afflicts them with the sharpened arrows of the hero warrior and with the coals of Juniper. I am a man/woman of peace, but if they want to fight, the warrior within me will arise with the power of the Word and a deadly arsenal. I know of a certainty that the one who faces me faces the vengeance of my Father.

(Romans 12:17-21; Ephesians 6:10-18; Proverbs 18:20,21; Exodus 14:14; Romans 12:9-21)

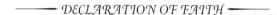

PSALM 121:2-8 KJV

My help *cometh* from the Lord, which made heaven and earth. He will not suffer thy foot to be moved: he that keepeth thee will not slumber. Behold, he that keepeth Israel shall neither slumber nor sleep. The Lord *is* thy keeper: the Lord *is* thy shade upon thy right hand. The sun shall not smite thee by day, nor the moon by night. The Lord shall preserve thee from all evil: he shall preserve thy soul. The Lord shall preserve thy going out and thy coming in from this time forth, and even for evermore.

———— DECLARATION OF FAITH ————

The world may turn to the psychiatrist, the psychic and the politician for help, but my help comes from the Creator of heaven and earth.

My destiny is fixed and I am resolved to attain it.

The One watching over me is tenacious. He never sleeps or even blinks an eye. He is the shade at my right hand so that nothing can even come close to harming me. I am shielded from all evil. My Father watches over my coming and my going, and everything in between, both now and forevermore!

(Genesis 15:1; 1 John 5:18; Psalm 16:8; 41:2; 124:8; 127:1; Proverbs 2:8; 3:6,23,26; 24:12; Isaiah 25:4; 27:3; 49:10; Deuteronomy 28:6)

PSALM 122:6-8 NKJV

Pray for the peace of Jerusalem: "May they prosper who love you. Peace be within your walls, prosperity within your palaces." For the sake of my brethren and companions, I will now say, "Peace be within you."

——— *DECLARATION OF FAITH* ———

God wants me to pray for the peace of Jerusalem. Therefore I will do so with all of my heart. I speak peace into that city and prosperity into her palaces. In this, my Father is well pleased and blesses me with His abundant provision.

I will not allow evil men to turn me from the abundance that God has provided for me. For the sake of the church, I will faithfully seek His prosperity.

(Psalm 35:27; 51:18; 2 Corinthians 4:13; Deuteronomy 28:1-14; Nehemiah 2:10; Malachi 3:6-12)

PSALM 124:1-8 KJV

If *it had not been* the Lord who was on our side, now may Israel say; If *it had not been* the Lord who was on our side, when men rose up against us: Then they had swallowed us up quick, when their wrath was kindled against us: Then the waters had overwhelmed us, the stream had gone over our soul: Then the proud waters had gone over our soul. Blessed *be* the Lord, who hath not given us *as* a prey to their teeth. Our soul is escaped as a bird out of the snare of the fowlers: the snare is broken, and we are escaped. Our help *is* in the name of the Lord, who made heaven and earth.

——— *DECLARATION OF FAITH* ———

God is on my side and He will not allow the enemy to have control over me. When the odds seem overwhelming and things begin to look grim, I still remain confident. I know that my Father will never leave me nor forsake me.

Therefore, no matter what happens, my victory in the end is deadly certain. The Lord never fails to fight for me. He will never let me be torn by the fangs of the enemy. All of the devil's traps are dashed to pieces and I escape like a bird out of every one.

I am not afraid to do my part in this fight. I stand in the face of the enemy with the courage and boldness of a lion. When I put up a steadfast resistance and speak the name of Jesus in the spirit of faith, the devil panics and desperately tries to get away from me.

(Romans 8:31; Psalm 2; 91:3; 121:2; Luke 10:19; James 4:7; Philippians 2:10; Joshua 1:5-9; Acts 16:16-18)

PSALM 125:2 NIV

As the mountains surround Jerusalem, so the Lord surrounds his people both now and forevermore.

——— *DECLARATION OF FAITH* ———

As the mountains surround Jerusalem, so the Lord surrounds me both now and forevermore.

(2 Kings 6:15-17; Hebrews 13:5,6; Psalm 5:11,12; 32:10; 91:1,2)

PSALM 126:4-6 NKJV

Bring back our captivity, O Lord, as the streams in the South. Those who sow in tears shall reap in joy. He who continually goes forth weeping, bearing seed for sowing, shall doubtless come again with rejoicing, bringing his sheaves with him.

——— *DECLARATION OF FAITH* ———

My Father restores my fortunes like the raging streams of the Negev.

I have sown my seed and shall reap an abundant harvest. Through hardship and turmoil I have gathered my seed and I have sown it in the midst of life's troubles. But oh my latter end! What I have sown in tears I will reap with joy! My harvest will be gathered in bundles so large they cannot be carried!

(Psalm 85:1-3; Joel 2:25; 2 Corinthians 9:5-11; Galatians 6:9; Job 42:12; Isaiah 61:3; Malachi 3:10,11)

PSALM 127:1-5 KJV

Except the Lord build the house, they labour in vain that build it: except the Lord keep the city, the watchman waketh *but* in vain. *It is* vain for you to rise up early, to sit up late, to eat the bread of sorrows: *for* so he giveth his beloved sleep. Lo, children *are* an heritage of the Lord: *and* the fruit of the womb *is his* reward. As arrows *are* in the hand of a mighty man; so *are* children of the youth. Happy *is* the man that hath his quiver full of them: they shall not be ashamed, but they shall speak with the enemies in the gate.

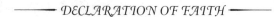

——— *DECLARATION OF FAITH* ———

God is the builder of my house.

He watches over all of my ways and sees to it that I am on the right track in my life.

I do not need to deprive myself of sleep in order to get Him to move on my behalf. I am a child loved by my Father and He grants me regular and restful sleep.

He rewards me with children for an inheritance. My kids are like arrows in the hand of a mighty warrior and my quiver is full of them. [Apply this to your family, and also to the souls you have won and are winning.]

(Psalm 52:8; 113:9; 121:3-5; 128:2,3; 144:12; Genesis 33:5; Joshua 24:3,4; Deuteronomy 7:13; 28:4; Proverbs 27:11)

PSALM 128:1-4 NKJV

Blessed is every one who fears the Lord, who walks in His ways. When you eat the labor of your hands, you shall be happy, and it shall be well with you. Your wife shall be like a fruitful vine in the very heart of your house, your children like olive plants all around your table. Behold, thus shall the man be blessed who fears the Lord.

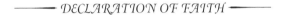

——— *DECLARATION OF FAITH* ———

I walk in the ways of almighty God as a good son/daughter and disciple. I mimic His ways. In every way possible, I live like God lives.

I eat the fruit of my labor and live my life in happiness, peace, divine favor and good fortune of every kind.

My wife/husband is fruitful and productive within my house, and my children are anointed and blessed at my table.

My life is a pleasure to live.

(Ephesians 5:1; John 10:10; Ecclesiastes 2:24; 3:22; Psalm 52:8; 144:12; 127:3-5; Proverbs 31:10-31; 1 Peter 3:10,11)

PSALM 129:4 NKJV

The Lord *is* righteous; He has cut in pieces the cords of the wicked.

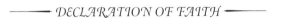

——— *DECLARATION OF FAITH* ———

God is faithful and dedicated to my success. He has set me free from the bonds of Satan so that I may work unfettered and produce an abundant harvest.

(Joshua 1:8; Colossians 1:13; John 10:10; 2 Corinthians 9:5-11; Galatians 3:13)

PSALM 130:7,8 NKJV

O Israel, hope in the Lord; for with the Lord there is mercy, and with Him is abundant redemption. And He shall redeem Israel from all his iniquities.

——— *DECLARATION OF FAITH* ———

I am redeemed from all of my sins. God's unfailing love saw its way to me and has erased everything that could hinder my success. I have a full redemption—not a partial redemption, but a full, ample, complete and abundant redemption that covers me in every area of my life!

(Galatians 3:13; Romans 5:17; 6:23; John 10:10; Isaiah 40:2; 43:1; 53:4-6; 61:1-3; Colossians 1:13,14; 2:11-14; Philippians 4:19)

PSALM 131:1-3 KJV

Lord, my heart is not haughty, nor mine eyes lofty: neither do I exercise myself in great matters, or in things too high for me. Surely I have behaved and quieted myself, as a child that is weaned of his mother: my soul *is* even as a weaned child. Let Israel hope in the Lord from henceforth and for ever.

——— *DECLARATION OF FAITH* ———

I am not a prideful and arrogant person. I do not think of myself as being above others. I live a humble life of love towards my fellow man.

I do not concern myself with matters beyond my capabilities, but give place to the power and presence of God in my life. Stress is not a factor in any of my dealings. I know that God is on my side and will not allow me to be overcome by the enemy. I am not like a child who gets upset and throws a tantrum. I am mature and well able to quiet myself in the midst of turmoil. My hope is in the Lord and I am at peace.

(Proverbs 6:16,17; Hebrews 13:5,6; Philippians 4:5-8)

PSALM 132:15,16 NKJV

I will abundantly bless her provision; I will satisfy her poor with bread. I will also clothe her priests with salvation, and her saints shall shout aloud for joy.

——— *DECLARATION OF FAITH* ———

I am blessed with abundant provisions. My resources have no limit and poverty can no longer hold me in its grasp.

I spring forth clothed in the salvation of almighty God and singing everlasting songs of joy!

(Psalm 112; Philippians 4:19; 2 Corinthians 8:9; 9:5-11; Deuteronomy 8:6-18)

PSALM 133:3 NIV

It is as if the dew of Hermon were falling on Mount Zion. For there the Lord bestows his blessing, even life forevermore.

─── *DECLARATION OF FAITH* ───

The Lord has commanded His blessings upon me. He has given me life everlasting and full of joy!

(Deuteronomy 28:8; John 3:16)

PSALM 136:1-4, 21-26 KJV

O give thanks unto the Lord; for *he is* good: for his mercy *endureth* for ever. O give thanks unto the God of gods: for his mercy *endureth* for ever. O give thanks to the Lord of lords: for his mercy *endureth* for ever. To him who alone doeth great wonders: for his mercy *endureth* for ever.

And gave their land for an heritage: for his mercy *endureth* for ever: *Even* an heritage unto Israel his servant: for his mercy *endureth* for ever. Who remembered us in our low estate: for his mercy *endureth* for ever: And hath redeemed us from our enemies: for his mercy *endureth* for ever. Who giveth food to all flesh: for his mercy *endureth* for ever. O give thanks unto the God of heaven: for his mercy endureth for ever.

─── *DECLARATION OF FAITH* ───

The Lord is good to me and His mercy towards me endures forever. All that He does to me is good. He shall never harm me nor bring destruction upon me. He has done a great work in me and will continue with it until He brings me into His courts with everlasting joy.

He has made me a child of His inheritance. I am an heir of God and a joint heir with Jesus Christ.

He remembers my low estate and never fails in His mercy towards me. He is patient with me and leads me on the path of His righteousness.

He redeems me from the hands of my enemies.

He nourishes me in every area of my life.

The Lord is so good to me and His mercy towards me endures forever.

(Psalm 103:13,14; 107:20,21; Philippians 1:6; Galatians 4:6,7; Exodus 23:20-30)

PSALM 138:2,3 NKJV

I will worship toward Your holy temple, and praise Your name for Your lovingkindness and Your truth; for You have magnified Your word above all Your name. In the day when I cried out, You answered me, and made me bold with strength in my soul.

——— DECLARATION OF FAITH ———

God has exalted His name and His Word above all things. They are the keys that open the door of certainty to all of my prayers. I am bold and stouthearted enough to enter into the very throne room of God and fully expect Him to fulfill His Word on my behalf.

(Isaiah 42:21; 55:11; John 14:13,14; 15:7; 16:23,24; Hebrews 4:16; Mark 11:22-25; 1 John 5:14,15)

PSALM 138:8 AMP

The Lord will perfect that which concerns me; Your mercy and loving-kindness, O Lord, endure forever—forsake not the works of Your own hands.

——— DECLARATION OF FAITH ———

No matter what has happened, the Lord will not abandon me. He is faithful and will fulfill His purpose for my life.

(Hebrews 13:5,6; 2 Timothy 2:13; Philippians 1:6; 2:12,13; Romans 8:28)

PSALM 139:5 NIV

You hem me in—behind and before; you have laid your hand upon me.

——— DECLARATION OF FAITH ———

The Spirit of my Father hems me in on all sides. His hand goes before me and guards my back as well. I live within His hedge of protection and the devil cannot get to me no matter how hard he tries.

(Job 1:10; 29:2-6; 1 John 5:18; John 10:28,29; Exodus 23:20-23; Psalm 23; 91)

PSALM 139:7-10 KJV

Whither shall I go from thy spirit? or whither shall I flee from thy presence? If I ascend up into heaven, thou *art* there: if I make my bed in hell, behold, thou *art there. If* I take the wings of the morning, *and* dwell in the uttermost parts of the sea; Even there shall thy hand lead me, and thy right hand shall hold me.

──── *DECLARATION OF FAITH* ────

My Father is with me wherever I go. No matter where I am or what I am doing, God is there for me. Whether I rise on the wings of the dawn or settle at the far side of the sea, God will be there to guide me—His right hand will hold me securely and His love will bolster my confidence in my success.

(Hebrews 13:5,6; Romans 8:14,31,37-39; John 10:28,29; 16:13; Joshua 1:8)

PSALM 139:14 NIV

I praise you because I am fearfully and wonderfully made; your works are wonderful, I know that full well.

──── *DECLARATION OF FAITH* ────

I am fearfully and wonderfully made, and God is very proud to call me His child. My thoughts of myself are pure and positive. I know that I am a very special and unique individual with a grand purpose and destiny in this life.

(Genesis 1:26,27; Job 1:8; Ephesians 1:4; Hebrews 2:10,11; Romans 8:28; Psalm 8:3-6)

PSALM 139:17 NKJV

How precious also are Your thoughts to me, O God! How great is the sum of them!

──── *DECLARATION OF FAITH* ────

I am always on my Father's mind. His thoughts of me are full of love and compassion. I am with Him at all times. He knows my every step and holds every one dear to His heart.

(Jeremiah 29:11; Psalm 37:23; 40:1,2)

PSALM 141:3,4 NKJV

Set a guard, O Lord, over my mouth; keep watch over the door of my lips. Do not incline my heart to any evil thing, to practice wicked works with men who work iniquity; and do not let me eat of their delicacies.

──── *DECLARATION OF FAITH* ────

God has set a guard over my mouth to respond to my spoken word. He has determined that I shall have the things that I say. Therefore, I will not let my heart be drawn into evil things. Words of doubt and unbelief shall be far from me. I refuse to consume the fruit of sin!

(Ecclesiastes 5:6,7; Psalm 103:20; Mark 11:22-25; 2 Corinthians 4:13; 6:14)

PSALM 141:10 NIV

Let the wicked fall into their own nets, while I pass by in safety.

——— *DECLARATION OF FAITH* ———

The wicked will fall into their own traps while I pass by them in safety.

(Psalm 35:8; 64:7-10; 79:12; 91; Nehemiah 4:4; Esther 5:9-6:11)

PSALM 142:5-7 KJV

I cried unto thee, O Lord: I said, Thou *art* my refuge *and* my portion in the land of the living. Attend unto my cry; for I am brought very low: deliver me from my persecutors; for they are stronger than I. Bring my soul out of prison, that I may praise thy name: the righteous shall compass me about; for thou shalt deal bountifully with me.

——— *DECLARATION OF FAITH* ———

The very Lord of Hosts is my refuge and my portion in the land of the living. He attends to my cries and rescues me from my persecutors. When my strength is not enough, His strength takes over. He takes up the battle as His own and delivers me from the prison that surrounds me. He lifts my head in freedom so that I may praise His name.

In my life, the righteous shall encompass me about and I shall continually enjoy the Lord's matchless bounty.

(Deuteronomy 33:27; Acts 12:3-10; Psalm 3)

PSALM 143:8 NIV

Let the morning bring me word of your unfailing love, for I have put my trust in you. Show me the way I should go, for to you I lift up my soul.

——— *DECLARATION OF FAITH* ———

The very morning brings me word of my Father's unfailing love for me. He never fails to be there for me. He makes certain that I understand the direction I must take.

(Romans 8:38,39; 1 Corinthians 13; 1 John 4:7,8; Psalm 5:8; 25:1; 46:5)

PSALM 143:10,11 NKJV

Teach me to do Your will, for You are my God; Your Spirit is good. Lead me in the land of uprightness. Revive me, O Lord, for Your name's sake! For Your righteousness' sake bring my soul out of trouble.

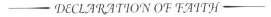

DECLARATION OF FAITH

God teaches me to do His will on the earth. His Spirit leads me on a level ground free of the bumps and potholes of confusion.

I am His own child and have taken the surname (family name) of God. For the sake of His name, He preserves my life and delivers me from trouble.

(1 Corinthians 2:6-16; John 16:13; Romans 8:14-17; Psalm 23; 91)

PSALM 144:1,2 NKJV

Blessed *be* the Lord my Rock,
Who trains my hands for war,
And my fingers for battle—
My lovingkindness and my fortress,
My high tower and my deliverer,
My shield and *the One* in whom I take refuge,
Who subdues my people under me.

DECLARATION OF FAITH

I am a soldier in the most powerful army in the universe.

The Rock of my salvation, the very captain of the hosts of heaven, is my own personal trainer. Under His instruction, I am learned in the art of spiritual warfare and my fingers are prepared to fight in an instant.

My trainer is the very Creator of the universe. I am alert to His instruction and He sees to it that I know what I am doing. He is my teacher, my guide, my fortress, my stronghold, my perpetual deliverer, and my shield in whom I take refuge as I subdue the enemy beneath my feet.

(2 Samuel 22:35; Ephesians 6:10-18; 2 Timothy 2:3,4; Psalm 18:34; Hebrews 2:10;
1 Corinthians 2:6-16; 2 Corinthians 10:3-6)

PSALM 144:12-15 KJV

That our sons *may be* as plants grown up in their youth; *that* our daughters *may be* as corner stones, polished *after* the similitude of a palace: *That* our garners *may be* full, affording all manner of store: *that* our sheep may bring forth thousands and ten thousands in our streets: *That* our oxen *may be* strong to labour;

THE COMPLETE PERSONALIZED PROMISE BIBLE

that there be no breaking in, nor going out; that *there be* no complaining in our streets. Happy *is that* people, that is in such a case: *yea,* happy *is that* people, whose God *is* the Lord.

——— *DECLARATION OF FAITH* ———

My sons are like plants tended by a master farmer. Their spiritual growth goes way beyond their years.

My daughters are like pillars carved to adorn a palace. They are like monuments beaming with the radiance of God's glory.

My storage places are filled to the brim with every kind of provision. All of my produce increases continually by thousands and tens of thousands.

My trucks bring in heavy loads filled with the bounty of my harvest.

I am under God's blanket of covering and there can be no breaching of my walls. I shall never go into captivity or cry out in distress in the streets.

My heavenly Father is the Lord of Hosts. Under His continual guidance and round-the-clock protection, I shall remain healthy, happy and prosperous all the days of my life.

(Proverbs 3:9,10; Psalm 1:1-3; 33:12; 91:1,2; 128:3; Isaiah 46:4; 61:1-3; Deuteronomy 4:39,40; 3 John 2)

PSALM 145:8,9 NKJV

The Lord is gracious and full of compassion, slow to anger and great in mercy. The Lord is good to all, and His tender mercies are over all His works.

——— *DECLARATION OF FAITH* ———

My Father shows His unyielding compassion for me by clothing me in His unmerited and gainful favor.

He is resonant in His love towards me, showing His patience and understanding every day of my life.

He is not easily angered and is always there to help me when I need Him. He will not turn away from me no matter what I have done. The second I turn to Him, He embraces me and brings me out of the devil's hold.

He longs to do good things for me. He is not only good to me some of the time, but He is good to me all of the time.

(Numbers 14:18; Nahum 1:7; Psalm 5:11,12; 103:8-13; 119:65; Romans 8:38,39; Hebrews 13:5,6; John 6:37; 1 John 1:7-9; Genesis 50:20)

PSALM 145:13-16 KJV

Thy kingdom *is* an everlasting kingdom, and thy dominion *endureth* throughout all generations. The Lord upholdeth all that fall, and raiseth up all *those that be* bowed down. The eyes of all wait upon thee; and thou givest them their meat in due season. Thou openest thine hand, and satisfiest the desire of every living thing.

DECLARATION OF FAITH

My Father loves me and is faithful to perform all of His promises to me.

When I fall, He upholds me in His arms.

When I am bowed down, He lifts me up and bids me to hold my head high and be proud of what He has made me to be.

He is always there to provide me with whatever I need. I am a vessel of His favor. His hand is always opened to satisfy my every desire.

(2 Corinthians 1:20; Jude 24; 2 Timothy 2:13; Psalm 3:3; 146:8; Philippians 4:19)

PSALM 145:18-20 NKJV

The Lord is near to all who call upon Him, to all who call upon Him in truth. He will fulfill the desire of those who fear Him; He also will hear their cry and save them. The Lord preserves all who love Him, but all the wicked He will destroy.

DECLARATION OF FAITH

My heart belongs to God and His to me. We bring great joy to each other in this life. He fulfills my every desire and is always there to take His stand at my side. His eyes never leave me, nor do mine leave Him. We two are dedicated to our covenant, and our love for each other will never run dry.

(John 4:24; 17:20-26; Deuteronomy 4:7; 6:5; Romans 8:31,38,39; Nehemiah 1:5,6; Hebrews 8:6; Psalm 31:23)

PSALM 146:7,8 NIV

He upholds the cause of the oppressed and gives food to the hungry. The Lord sets prisoners free, the Lord gives sight to the blind, the Lord lifts up those who are bowed down, the Lord loves the righteous.

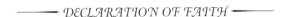

DECLARATION OF FAITH

The Lord has set me free from the chains of oppression.

He has given me all that I need.

He has healed my eyes and lifted my head.

I am His own special child and He loves me with all of His heart.

(Isaiah 61:1-3; Philippians 4:11-19; Psalm 3:3; Romans 8:14-17,38,39)

PSALM 147:11 NKJV

The Lord takes pleasure in those who fear Him, in those who hope in His mercy.

——— *DECLARATION OF FAITH* ———

I bring my Father great joy just because I'm me. I rest in His mercy.

(Titus 3:4,5; Ephesians 1:4,5; 2:1-10; John 17; Luke 12:32)

PSALM 147:15,18 KJV

He sendeth forth his commandment *upon* earth: his word runneth very swiftly. He giveth snow like wool: he scattereth the hoarfrost like ashes. He sendeth out his word, and melteth them: he causeth his wind to blow, *and* the waters flow.

——— *DECLARATION OF FAITH* ———

I am a wielder of the Word of God. It is my sword and a mighty weapon in my arsenal. When I hurl it into the battle, the enemy is routed.

(Ephesians 6:17; Hebrews 4:12; 2 Corinthians 10:3-6; Psalm 107:20; Job 37:10)

PSALM 147:19,20 NIV

He has revealed his word to Jacob, his laws and decrees to Israel. He has done this for no other nation; they do not know his laws. Praise the Lord.

——— *DECLARATION OF FAITH* ———

God favors me so highly that He has determined to reveal to me what the world can never truly know: His Word. He gives me special knowledge and keen insight into its deepest meanings.

(1 Corinthians 2:6-16; John 16:13; Matthew 13:11,15,16; 2 Timothy 2:7)

PSALM 149:4 AMP

For the Lord takes pleasure in His people; He will beautify the humble with salvation and adorn the wretched with victory.

───── DECLARATION OF FAITH ─────

The Lord delights in me and thoroughly enjoys my company. It is His great pleasure to crown me with His salvation.

(Luke 12:32; 1 John 1:3; Psalm 35:27; 132:16; Ephesians 1:4,5,9)

PSALM 150 KJV

Praise ye the Lord. Praise God in his sanctuary: praise him in the firmament of his power. Praise him for his mighty acts: praise him according to his excellent greatness. Praise him with the sound of the trumpet: praise him with the psaltery and harp. Praise him with the timbrel and dance: praise him with stringed instruments and organs. Praise him upon the loud cymbals: praise him upon the high sounding cymbals. Let every thing that hath breath praise the Lord. Praise ye the Lord.

───── DECLARATION OF FAITH ─────

I will praise the Lord in His sanctuary!
I will lift up, exalt and magnify His name toward the expanse of heaven!
I will praise Him for His mighty acts!
I will praise Him according to His excellent greatness!
I will praise Him with the sound of the trumpet and brass instruments!
I will praise Him with the harp and lyre!
I will praise Him with the tambourine and with dancing!
I will praise Him with stringed instruments, guitars and flutes!
I will praise Him with the drums and with loud clanging cymbals!
As long as I have breath within me, I will praise the Lord!

(Psalm 68:34; 145:5,6; Deuteronomy 3:24; 32:3; 1 Samuel 18:6; 2 Samuel 6:14; Ephesians 5:19; Colossians 3:16)

CHAPTER TWENTY

PROVERBS

Many of you have turned to Proverbs as the first book that you want to pray. Proverbs is another book written by several authors, the chief of which is King Solomon. The promises found in this book are very practical in nature. Some are just common-sense things that we need to be reminded of such as the consequences of adultery, lies and deceit. Others are more spiritual in nature, such as the giving of your firstfruits income and the receiving of favor. No matter which angle these promises come from, they are essential to apply to your daily walk with God.

As you pray these prayers, take note that wisdom is the principle thing in your life. From it stems every other blessing that God gives.

PROVERBS 1:8-10 KJV

My son, hear the instruction of thy father, and forsake not the law of thy mother: For they *shall be* an ornament of grace unto thy head, and chains about thy neck. My son, if sinners entice thee, consent thou not.

———— *DECLARATION OF FAITH* ————

I am a wise son/daughter. I listen carefully to my father's instructions and I do not forsake my mother's teaching. They are a garland to grace my head and an ornament to adorn my neck.

When sinners entice me to lead me away from the ways of righteousness, I will not give in to them.

(Proverbs 3:22; 4:1; Genesis 39:7-10; Ephesians 5:1-14; 2 Corinthians 6:14)

PROVERBS 1:23 NKJV

Turn at my rebuke;
Surely I will pour out my spirit on you;
I will make my words known to you.

———— *DECLARATION OF FAITH* ————

The Lord has poured out His Spirit upon me so that I may have a keen understanding of His Word.

(Psalm 119:17,18; Ephesians 1:17,18)

PROVERBS 1:33 NKJV

"But whoever listens to me will dwell safely, and will be secure, without fear of evil."

———— *DECLARATION OF FAITH* ————

I heed the ways of wisdom and live my life in safety. I am at peace—free from the fear that comes from an evil report.

(Numbers 14:8; Proverbs 3:24-26; Psalm 112:7)

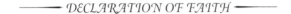

PROVERBS 2:3-8 KJV

Yea, if thou criest after knowledge, *and* liftest up thy voice for understanding; If thou seekest her as silver, and searchest for her as *for* hid treasures; Then shalt thou understand the fear of the Lord, and find the knowledge of God. For the Lord giveth wisdom: out of his mouth *cometh* knowledge and understanding. He layeth up sound wisdom for the righteous: *he is* a buckler to them that walk uprightly. He keepeth the paths of judgment, and preserveth the way of his saints.

———— *DECLARATION OF FAITH* ————

The search for wisdom is of prime importance in my life. For me, it is like searching for a great hidden treasure, for I know that when I find it, I will understand the fear of the Lord and gain personal and intimate knowledge of God. It is the Lord's good will to grant me wisdom, therefore I know that when I seek it out, He will make certain that I find it.

Through God's Word, I gain tremendous knowledge and understanding.

He holds victory in reserve for me and stands guard with me in every circumstance and endeavor that I undertake.

(1 Corinthians 1:30; 2:6-16; 15:57; Proverbs 3:14; James 1:5,6; 1 Kings 3:9-12)

PROVERBS 2:8-17 KJV

He keepeth the paths of judgment, and preserveth the way of his saints. Then shalt thou understand righteousness, and judgment, and equity; *yea*, every good path. When wisdom entereth into thine heart, and knowledge is pleasant unto thy soul; Discretion shall preserve thee, understanding shall keep thee: To deliver thee from the way of the evil *man*, from the man that speaketh froward things; Who leave the paths of uprightness, to walk in the ways of darkness; Who rejoice to do evil, *and* delight in the frowardness of the wicked; Whose ways *are* crooked, and *they* froward in their paths: To deliver thee from the strange woman, *even* from the stranger *which* flattereth with her words; Which forsaketh the guide of her youth, and forgetteth the covenant of her God.

The Lord guides me on a path of justice and preserves my way before me. I understand righteousness, justice, equity, and every good path. Wisdom finds its home in my heart and knowledge is pleasant to my soul. Discretion preserves me and understanding protects me. Through these I am delivered from those who are evil and who speak perverse things against me. I am delivered from those who leave the paths of uprightness to walk in the way of darkness. I am delivered from those who rejoice in evil and delight in the ways of the wicked. I am delivered from those whose ways are wicked and whose paths are perverted. I am delivered from the seductress who flatters with her words, who forsakes the Guide of her youth and forgets the covenant of her God. By wisdom and discretion, my life is kept safe.

(Psalm 25:19-21; Proverbs 11:4,5)

PROVERBS 2:20 NKJV

So you may walk in the way of goodness, and keep to the paths of righteousness.

——— *DECLARATION OF FAITH* ———

I walk in the ways of honorable men and women, and select my role models wisely.

(2 Corinthians 6:14; Proverbs 13:20; Ephesians 5:1-21)

PROVERBS 3:1-10 KJV

My son, forget not my law; but let thine heart keep my commandments: For length of days, and long life, and peace, shall they add to thee. Let not mercy and truth forsake thee: bind them about thy neck; write them upon the table of thine heart: So shalt thou find favour and good understanding in the sight of God and man. Trust in the Lord with all thine heart; and lean not unto thine own understanding. In all thy ways acknowledge him, and he shall direct thy paths. Be not wise in thine own eyes: fear the Lord, and depart from evil. It shall be health to thy navel, and marrow to thy bones. Honour the Lord with thy substance, and with the firstfruits of all thine increase: So shall thy barns be filled with plenty, and thy presses shall burst out with new wine.

DECLARATION OF FAITH

I do not forget the benefits of living wisely.

I understand the rules that I must follow in order to be a success in life and I submit to them willingly. Because of this, my life is prolonged by many years and my prosperity overflows like a geyser in a desert land.

I will never fail to let love and faithfulness fill me. I bind them about my neck and write them on the tablet of my heart. By them, favor prevails in my life and I obtain a good and honorable name in the sight of God and men.

I give my whole heart to trust in the Lord. I will not be the fool who balances his life on the brace of human understanding. I am God-inside minded at all times and never cease to acknowledge His presence to guide me in all that I do. He sees what I cannot see and knows what I do not know. With Him at the point, all of my paths are made straight. Therefore, I will never put my own wisdom before the Lord's.

I shun all evil and look to God for my provision. This brings health and vitality to my body and strength to all of my bones.

I would have nothing if it weren't for my heavenly Father. Therefore, I will honor Him with my wealth and the best part of all of my increase. I am a tither and a giver. Because of this, everything that I set my hand to do is blessed and brings forth an abundant harvest. My storage places are filled to overflowing and my vats brim over with new wine.

(Psalm 1:1-3; 37:3-5; 91:16; 103:1-5; Joshua 1:8; Deuteronomy 6:5-7; 28:1-14; Genesis 12:1-3; 39:2-5; Isaiah 46:4; Jeremiah 9:23,24; Romans 8:11; 12:16; John 16:13; 1 Corinthians 3:16; 10:26; Philippians 4:19; Malachi 3:6-12)

PROVERBS 3:12-18 AMP

For whom the Lord loves He corrects, even as a father corrects the son in whom he delights. Happy (blessed, fortunate, enviable) is the man who finds skillful and godly Wisdom, and the man who gets understanding [drawing it forth from God's Word and life's experiences], for the gaining of it is better than the gaining of silver, and the profit of it better than fine gold. Skillful and godly Wisdom is more precious than rubies; and nothing you can wish for is to be compared to her. Length of days is in her right hand, and in her left hand are riches and honor. Her ways are highways of pleasantness, and all her paths are peace. She is a tree of life to those who lay hold on her; and happy (blessed, fortunate, to be envied) is everyone who holds her fast.

——— *DECLARATION OF FAITH* ———

My Father instructs me according to His Word.

He enjoys my companionship and gives me the ability to function in every circumstance.

I am a happy and prosperous man/woman, full of wisdom and understanding.

I know the profits and returns of knowledge. I pursue her with a whole heart. It is a great joy to me when I find her. She is more precious to me than any treasure on the face of the earth. Long life is in her right hand and in her left are riches and honor. I have determined to embrace her like a lover. My union with her brings me happiness, prosperity, and health.

I shall enjoy the pleasantries of life, follow the paths of peace, and end my days an old, vibrant and happy man/woman.

(Psalm 119:34-38,65-68; 1 John 1:3; 2:27; 1 Corinthians 2:6-16; Job 28:13; Matthew 11:29; 13:44; 1 Timothy 4:8)

PROVERBS 3:21-26 KJV

My son, let not them depart from thine eyes: keep sound wisdom and discretion: So shall they be life unto thy soul, and grace to thy neck. Then shalt thou walk in thy way safely, and thy foot shall not stumble. When thou liest down, thou shalt not be afraid: yea, thou shalt lie down, and thy sleep shall be sweet. Be not afraid of sudden fear, neither of the desolation of the wicked, when it cometh. For the Lord shall be thy confidence, and shall keep thy foot from being taken.

——— *DECLARATION OF FAITH* ———

I keep sound wisdom and discretion. They are life unto my soul and grace unto my neck. I walk safely in this life and my foot does not stumble. When I lie down, I am not afraid. When I lie down, my sleep is sweet. I am not afraid of sudden terror or desolation from the wicked when it comes. For the Lord is my confidence. He shall preserve me in times of danger and keep my foot from being taken.

(Proverbs 1:8,9; Psalm 4:8; 119:116,117; Joshua 1:5-9)

PROVERBS 3:27,28 NKJV

Do not withhold good from those to whom it is due, when it is in the power of your hand to do *so*. Do not say to your neighbor, "Go, and come back, and tomorrow I will give *it*," when *you have* it with you.

———— *DECLARATION OF FAITH* ————

I give honor to whom honor is due. I do not hold back good things from those who have a right to them. When good things are placed within my power, I distribute them with justice and equity. I do not put off giving when the gift is within my hand.

(Romans 2:5-10; Luke 6:38; Psalm 84:11)

PROVERBS 3:29-35 KJV

Devise not evil against thy neighbour, seeing he dwelleth securely by thee. Strive not with a man without cause, if he have done thee no harm. Envy thou not the oppressor, and choose none of his ways. For the froward *is* abomination to the Lord: but his secret *is* with the righteous. The curse of the Lord *is* in the house of the wicked: but he blesseth the habitation of the just. Surely he scorneth the scorners: but he giveth grace unto the lowly. The wise shall inherit glory: but shame shall be the promotion of fools.

———— *DECLARATION OF FAITH* ————

I will never plot evil against my neighbor. Because of my anointing, he dwells securely beside me and we enjoy peace between us. I do not strive with others without a cause. I will not allow assumptions to move me against someone when they have done me no harm.

I do not envy an oppressor and I choose none of his ways. I know that the haughty and perverse are an abomination to the Lord. I will never turn to their ways.

I am the righteousness of God in Christ Jesus my Lord, and as His close and intimate friend, His secret is with me.

The curse of the Lord is on the house of the wicked, but my home is blessed. The Lord scorns the scorners, but He gives me His grace in abundance. Shame shall be the promotion of fools, but I shall inherit glory!

(Romans 12:17-21; Joshua 24:15; Deuteronomy 28)

PROVERBS 4:7-10 KJV

Wisdom is the principal thing; therefore get wisdom: and with all thy getting get understanding. Exalt her, and she shall promote thee: she shall bring thee to honour, when thou dost embrace her. She shall give to thine head an ornament of grace: a crown of glory shall she deliver to thee. Hear, O my son, and receive my sayings; and the years of thy life shall be many.

———— *DECLARATION OF FAITH* ————

Wisdom is the principle thing in my life. Therefore, I will get wisdom. And with all of my getting, I will get understanding. As I exalt wisdom in my life, she promotes me. When I embrace her, she brings me to honor. She places upon my head an ornament of grace. A crown of glory does she deliver to me. By wisdom, my days are prolonged upon the earth and I receive an abundance of everlasting rewards.

(Deuteronomy 4:5,6; 28:1-14; Isaiah 46:3,4)

PROVERBS 4:11,12 KJV

I have taught thee in the way of wisdom; I have led thee in right paths. When thou goest, thy steps shall not be straitened; and when thou runnest, thou shalt not stumble.

———— *DECLARATION OF FAITH* ————

The Lord teaches me the way of wisdom. He continually leads me in the right paths. Wherever I go, He makes my way straight and when I run, I never stumble.

(Nehemiah 9:19,20; Psalm 18:36; 27:11; Isaiah 40:28-31)

PROVERBS 4:18,20-22 KJV

But the path of the just is as the shining light, that shineth more and more unto the perfect day. My son, attend to my words; incline thine ear unto my sayings. Let them not depart from thine eyes; keep them in the midst of thine heart. For they are life unto those that find them, and health to all their flesh.

———— *DECLARATION OF FAITH* ————

The path the Lord has laid before me is as a shining light that shines more and more unto a perfect day.

I attend to the Words of the Lord and incline my ear to His sayings. I do not let them depart from my eyes, but keep them in the midst of my heart. For the Word is life to me and it brings health to all of my flesh.

(Psalm 107:20; 119:105; Deuteronomy 6:6-9)

PROVERBS 4:23-27 KJV

Keep thy heart with all diligence; for out of it are the issues of life. Put away from thee a froward mouth, and perverse lips put far from thee. Let thine eyes look right on, and let thine eyelids look straight before thee. Ponder the path of thy feet, and let all thy ways be established. Turn not to the right hand nor to the left: remove thy foot from evil.

––––––– *DECLARATION OF FAITH* –––––––

Above all else, I diligently guard my heart, for it is the wellspring of my life.

I do not speak perverse, obstinate, or wicked talk. Negative and corrupt language does not come out of my mouth.

My eyes look straight ahead. They are fixed on the prize set before me.

I achieve my goals without distraction or wavering. I deliberate and premeditate over every step that I take. I will only move forward in ways that are stable and well established.

I cannot be lured into the ways of Satan.

I follow the ways of the Lord.

(Psalm 1:1-3; 1 Corinthians 9:24; Proverbs 5:21; Ephesians 5:1-21; Deuteronomy 28:1; 2 Corinthians 2:11)

PROVERBS 5:3-11 KJV

For the lips of a strange woman drop *as* an honeycomb, and her mouth *is* smoother than oil: But her end is bitter as wormwood, sharp as a twoedged sword. Her feet go down to death; her steps take hold on hell. Lest thou shouldest ponder the path of life, her ways are moveable, *that* thou canst not know *them.* Hear me now therefore, O ye children, and depart not from the words of my mouth. Remove thy way far from her, and come not nigh the door of her house: Lest thou give thine honour unto others, and thy years unto the cruel: Lest strangers be filled with thy wealth; and thy labours *be* in the house of a stranger; And thou mourn at the last, when thy flesh and thy body are consumed.

I cannot be enticed by a seductress. I never forget that her ways are bitter as wormwood and sharp as a two-edged sword. I know that her feet will lead me to death and her steps take hold on hell. I know that her ways are unstable, therefore there is no need for me to try and understand her. I remove my way from her and will not go near her house. No, I will not forfeit my inheritance and give my honor to others. I will not sin with her and give my years unto the cruel. I know that to give in to her is to allow strangers to be filled with my wealth. I will not allow my labors to be in the house of a stranger. No, I will not be found mourning because I let my flesh and body be consumed by the seductress.

(Proverbs 7; Isaiah 1:4-8)

PROVERBS 5:18,19 KJV

Let thy fountain be blessed: and rejoice with the wife of thy youth. Let her be as the loving hind and pleasant roe; let her breasts satisfy thee at all times; and be thou ravished always with her love.

My heavenly Father blesses the fountain of my blood, life and wisdom.

I find great pleasure in my own spouse. She/He is at the center of all of my sensual desire and is the crowning joy of my life. There is no need for me to look to another for marital fulfillment. I am held captive by her/his love.

(Deuteronomy 24:5; Ecclesiastes 9:9; Malachi 2:14; Song of Solomon 2:9)

PROVERBS 6:2 NKJV

You are snared by the words of your mouth; You are taken by the words of your mouth.

I understand the power of my words. I will not be snared by the words of my mouth, nor will I allow them to place me in bondage.

(Proverbs 18:20,21; Matthew 12:36,37)

PROVERBS 6:6-11 KJV

Go to the ant, thou sluggard; consider her ways, and be wise: Which having no guide, overseer, or ruler, Provideth her meat in the summer, *and* gathereth her food in the harvest. How long wilt thou sleep, O sluggard? when wilt thou arise out of thy sleep? *Yet* a little sleep, a little slumber, a little folding of the hands to sleep: So shall thy poverty come as one that travelleth, and thy want as an armed man.

DECLARATION OF FAITH

I am wise in my undertakings. I consider the ways of the ant, who having no guide, overseer or ruler, provides her meat in the summer and gathers food in the harvest. I do not need to be ruled over or told what to do. I clearly see what needs to be done and I do it. I sow my seed and work hard for my harvest. I do not allow myself to be a lover of sleep, nor can I be found resting when there is no need for rest. By my hard work and diligence I repel poverty in my life.

(Proverbs 10:4-6; 19:15; 20:13; 2 Timothy 2:15)

PROVERBS 6:20-23 KJV

My son, keep thy father's commandment, and forsake not the law of thy mother: Bind them continually upon thine heart, and tie them about thy neck. When thou goest, it shall lead thee; when thou sleepest, it shall keep thee; and when thou awakest, it shall talk with thee. For the commandment is a lamp; and the law is light; and reproofs of instruction are the way of life:

DECLARATION OF FAITH

I keep the commands of righteousness that my father has taught me and I hold as dear the holy sayings of my mother. I bind them continually about my heart and hang them as a garland around my neck. They are a guide to me wherever I go and when I sleep they keep me safe. When I awake they speak with me and give me direction.

The commandment is my lamp and the law is a light to my way. Reproofs and instruction are a way of life to me.

(Proverbs 1:8,9; 3:11,12; 10:17; Psalm 119:105)

PROVERBS 6:30,31 KJV

Men do not despise a thief, if he steal to satisfy his soul when he is hungry; but if he be found, he shall restore sevenfold; he shall give all the substance of his house.

──────── *DECLARATION OF FAITH* ────────

Whatever Satan has stolen from me, he must restore to me sevenfold.

(Psalm 85:1-3; Joel 2:25; John 10:10)

PROVERBS 7:4,5 KJV

Say unto wisdom, Thou art my sister; and call understanding thy kinswoman:
That they may keep thee from the strange woman, from the stranger which flattereth with her words.

──────── *DECLARATION OF FAITH* ────────

*I say unto wisdom, "You are my sister." I call understanding my kinsmen and
counselor. They keep me from being deceived by the seductress and from strangers
who flatter me with their words.*

(Psalm 51:6; Proverbs 2:16)

PROVERBS 8:8,9 KJV

All the words of my mouth are in righteousness; *there is* nothing froward or perverse in them. They *are* all plain to him that understandeth, and right to them
that find knowledge.

──────── *DECLARATION OF FAITH* ────────

*Every word that comes out of my mouth is true and proper. Not one is
crooked or perverse. Those who discern the statutes of the Lord understand my
words and treasure their significance. They are faultless to those who understand
the knowledge of God.*

(Matthew 12:37; 1 Peter 3:10,11; 2 Corinthians 4:13; Hebrews 11:1)

PROVERBS 8:13,14 NKJV

The fear of the Lord *is* to hate evil; Pride and arrogance and the evil way and the
perverse mouth I hate. Counsel *is* mine, and sound wisdom; I *am* understanding, I have strength.

──────── *DECLARATION OF FAITH* ────────

*I hate pride, arrogance, and all evil. The evil behavior that the world delights
in, I find repulsive.*

I am a man/woman of prudent measures and sound judgment. God has given me an intimate relationship with knowledge and I have power like the world has never seen.

(2 Corinthians 6:14; Proverbs 3:7; 4:24; 16:6,17,18; Ephesians 1:17-23)

PROVERBS 8:18-21 KJV

Riches and honour *are* with me; *yea*, durable riches and righteousness. My fruit *is* better than gold, yea, than fine gold; and my revenue than choice silver. I lead in the way of righteousness, in the midst of the paths of judgment: That I may cause those that love me to inherit substance; and I will fill their treasures. I am wisdom's best friend and closest companion. Together we produce an abundance of riches, permanent wealth, and prosperity. The fruit that I produce is better than fine gold and my harvest surpasses the choicest treasures known to the world.

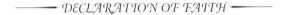

——— *DECLARATION OF FAITH* ———

I walk in the ways of righteousness and remain fixed on the paths of justice.

I have been anointed to become an affluent and wealthy man/woman. It is God's perfect will that all of my treasuries be full to the brim.

(Psalm 112:1-3; Proverbs 3:16,19; Genesis 13:2; 2 Corinthians 8:9; 9:5-11)

PROVERBS 8:35 NKJV

For whoever finds me finds life, and obtains favor from the Lord.

——— *DECLARATION OF FAITH* ———

My love for wisdom has brought me energy, spunk, vitality, and God's own favor. I will walk this life fully expecting God's blessings to come my way.

(Proverbs 3:3-6; John 17:3; Isaiah 61:1-3; Ephesians 1:3)

PROVERBS 9:6 NKJV

Forsake foolishness and live, and go in the way of understanding.

——— *DECLARATION OF FAITH* ———

I have put behind me those simple ways where I was easily enticed and seduced by the world, the flesh and the devil. I have left them behind and am now pressing forward in the ways of discernment, awareness, and understanding. My life is filled with joy, health, and abundant prosperity.

(2 Corinthians 6:14; Ephesians 5:1-21; Philippians 3:13,14; Romans 14:17; John 10:10)

PROVERBS 9:10-12 KJV

The fear of the Lord *is* the beginning of wisdom: and the knowledge of the holy *is* understanding. For by me thy days shall be multiplied, and the years of thy life shall be increased. If thou be wise, thou shalt be wise for thyself: but *if* thou scornest, thou alone shalt bear *it*.

——— *DECLARATION OF FAITH* ———

I know the Lord in whom I serve. I understand the immensity of His power and glory, and that without Him, I am of no great significance.

My respect for my heavenly Father is immeasurable. I tremble at the thought of His greatness and honor Him with every fiber of my being. What a joy it is to know that He is my own Father! I am not without Him—I am with Him! He loves me and does nothing but good things for me.

Through my understanding, He has added many years to my life and has given me an abundance of joy, health and prosperity to enjoy. My heavenly Father is a pleasure to serve!

(Ephesians 1:17-23; 2 Timothy 1:12; Isaiah 46:4; 1 John 3:1; 3 John 2)

PROVERBS 10:1 NKJV

A wise son makes a glad father, but a foolish son *is* the grief of his mother.

——— *DECLARATION OF FAITH* ———

I am a wise son/daughter who does those things that bring joy to my parents.

(Proverbs 15:10; 17:21; 19:13; 29:3,15; Ephesians 6:1-3)

PROVERBS 10:4 KJV

He becometh poor that dealeth with a slack hand: but the hand of the diligent maketh rich.

——— *DECLARATION OF FAITH* ———

My hands have been given skill over and above that of all worldly people, and I am clever and discerning in the art of obtaining wealth.

(Deuteronomy 8:18; Proverbs 12:24; 13:4; 21:5)

PROVERBS **10:6** AMP

Blessings are upon the head of the [uncompromisingly] righteous (the upright, in right standing with God) but the mouth of the wicked conceals violence.

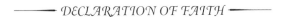
DECLARATION OF FAITH

God has placed a crown of His favor, peace, and permanent felicity upon my head.

(Psalm 5:11,12; 45:7; Philippians 4:1; 1 Thessalonians 2:19)

PROVERBS **10:8,9** KJV

The wise in heart will receive commandments: but a prating fool shall fall. He that walketh uprightly walketh surely: but he that perverteth his ways shall be known.

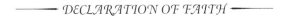
DECLARATION OF FAITH

I am wise in heart and both willingly and approvingly accept the commands of God. I am a man/woman of integrity whose walk is free of the pitfalls and decoys of evil schemes.

(Deuteronomy 28:1; Psalm 91:3; 119:16; 2 Corinthians 2:11; Ephesians 6:11)

PROVERBS **10:11** KJV

The mouth of a righteous man is a well of life: but violence covereth the mouth of the wicked.

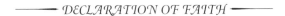
DECLARATION OF FAITH

The words of my mouth are a reservoir—a fountain—the very source that brings into being both who I am and what I have.

(Proverbs 18:20,21; Mark 11:22-25; Matthew 17:20; 2 Corinthians 4:13; Hebrews 11:1)

PROVERBS **10:13-15** KJV

In the lips of him that hath understanding wisdom is found: but a rod *is* for the back of him that is void of understanding. Wise *men* lay up knowledge: but the mouth of the foolish *is* near destruction. The rich man's wealth *is* his strong city: the destruction of the poor *is* their poverty.

——— *DECLARATION OF FAITH* ———

I am a man/woman of wise words who stores up knowledge as a precious commodity.

My wealth surrounds me like a fortified city.

(Psalm 112:1-3; 2 Timothy 2:15)

PROVERBS 10:19-21 NKJV

In the multitude of words sin is not lacking, but he who restrains his lips *is* wise. The tongue of the righteous *is* choice silver; the heart of the wicked *is worth* little. The lips of the righteous feed many, but fools die for lack of wisdom.

——— *DECLARATION OF FAITH* ———

I am careful with my words. Every word that I speak is carefully thought out. I am intimately familiar with the power of the spoken word. Therefore, I caution myself when I speak. I make sure that every word is in line with God's will and will produce a harvest of goodness in my life. My words are like choice silver. They nourish, sustain and supply the needs of many.

(Proverbs 18:20,21; Mark 11:22-25; James 1:19; 3:2-12; Matthew 12:35-37)

PROVERBS 10:22-24 KJV

The blessing of the Lord, it maketh rich, and he addeth no sorrow with it. It is as sport to a fool to do mischief: but a man of understanding hath wisdom. The fear of the wicked, it shall come upon him: but the desire of the righteous shall be granted.

——— *DECLARATION OF FAITH* ———

My Father has blessed me with an abundance of wealth and eternal riches free of all of the troubles that the wealthy of the world must endure.

I am a man/woman of understanding who finds great joy in the attainment of wisdom.

My first thought in all things is to seek my Father's counsel and He gives me all that I desire.

(Psalm 112:1-3; 145:19; Genesis 24:35; Daniel 1:17,20; John 16:13)

PROVERBS 10:27-32 KJV

The fear of the Lord prolongeth days: but the years of the wicked shall be short-ened. The hope of the righteous *shall be* gladness: but the expectation of the wicked shall perish. The way of the Lord *is* strength to the upright: but destruc-tion *shall be* to the workers of iniquity. The righteous shall never be removed: but the wicked shall not inhabit the earth. The mouth of the just bringeth forth wisdom: but the froward tongue shall be cut out. The lips of the righteous know what is acceptable: but the mouth of the wicked *speaketh* frowardness.

——— *DECLARATION OF FAITH* ———

I have added many years to my life because of my trust in the Lord. I humble myself under His mighty hand and give due reverence to His majesty. The hope that I have within me produces happiness and prosperity in my life. The way of the Lord is strength to me. I shall never be moved or caused to give up on my faith. I always stand strong in the Lord and in the power of His might. Wisdom comes forth from my mouth continually and I am always keenly aware of what is good and acceptable in the eyes of God.

(Isaiah 46:4; Ephesians 6:10; Nehemiah 8:10; Romans 12:1,2)

PROVERBS 11:1-6 KJV

A false balance *is* abomination to the Lord: but a just weight *is* his delight. *When* pride cometh, then cometh shame: but with the lowly *is* wisdom. The integrity of the upright shall guide them: but the perverseness of transgressors shall destroy them. Riches profit not in the day of wrath: but righteousness delivereth from death. The righteousness of the perfect shall direct his way: but the wicked shall fall by his own wickedness. The righteousness of the upright shall deliver them: but transgressors shall be taken in *their own* naughtiness.

——— *DECLARATION OF FAITH* ———

I am a fair and just man/woman and never allow myself to cheat others. When arrogant pride tries to enter my heart I stand strong against it. I always remain humble and aware of who I am. My integrity guides me and my trust is properly directed. My riches are but a tool. I know that they will not profit me in the day of wrath, but my righteousness will deliver me from death. Therefore, I let righteousness and purity direct me in my way. When trouble comes, righteousness shall deliver me.

(2 Corinthians 5:21; Romans 4; Colossians 2:18; 1 Peter 5:5-7)

PROVERBS 11:8,9 KJV

The righteous is delivered out of trouble, and the wicked cometh in his stead. An hypocrite with his mouth destroyeth his neighbour: but through knowledge shall the just be delivered.

──── *DECLARATION OF FAITH* ────

When the words of the unrighteous are used against me, my knowledge of God makes me too elusive to come to harm. I am rescued from every trap and evil plan that the devil uses to ensnare me. All of his assaults and raids against me are turned back on his own head.

(Exodus 23:27; 2 Corinthians 2:11; Ephesians 6:10-18; Genesis 12:3; Psalm 91:3; Esther 9:25)

PROVERBS 11:11 NKJV

By the blessing of the upright the city is exalted, but it is overthrown by the mouth of the wicked.

──── *DECLARATION OF FAITH* ────

I will not allow the words of my mouth to shower seeds of destruction on my city. I declare that my city is blessed, and by my blessing, it is exalted!

(Proverbs 14:34; 18:20,21; Genesis 12:1-3; Mark 11:22-25)

PROVERBS 11:14 KJV

Where no counsel is, the people fall: but in the multitude of counsellors there is safety.

──── *DECLARATION OF FAITH* ────

I am constant in seeking wise counsel in my life. I follow the path of those who have achieved victory so that my own victory is made certain.

(Proverbs 15:22; 1 Kings 12:1)

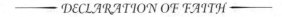

PROVERBS 11:18 KJV

The wicked worketh a deceitful work: but to him that soweth righteousness shall be a sure reward.

My wages are earned and my profits are justified. I gain an increasing repu-tation as a hardworking and fair man/woman.

I sow my seed in righteousness and my harvest is as sure as the Lord's return.

(Deuteronomy 28:12; 1 Thessalonians 4:11; 2 Corinthians 9:5-11)

PROVERBS 11:23-28 KJV

The desire of the righteous *is* only good: *but* the expectation of the wicked *is* wrath. There is that scattereth, and yet increaseth; and *there is* that withholdeth more than is meet, but *it tendeth* to poverty. The liberal soul shall be made fat: and he that watereth shall be watered also himself. He that withholdeth corn, the people shall curse him: but blessing *shall be* upon the head of him that sell-eth *it*. He that diligently seeketh good procureth favour: but he that seeketh mis-chief, it shall come unto him. He that trusteth in his riches shall fall: but the righteous shall flourish as a branch.

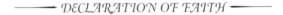

All of my desires are for good things.

I give freely, without restraint, and yet gain even more. My generosity causes a tremendous abundance of good things to pour forth into my life. When I refresh others, I also am refreshed. When my hand is ready to give and do good, my head is crowned with the blessings of God.

I seek what is good and find goodwill. By my actions, I show that my trust is not in riches, but in the prosperity that only God can provide. By Him, I have abundance and thrive like a green leaf.

(Malachi 3:10; 2 Corinthians 9:7,8; Psalm 1:1-3; 112:9; Job 31:24)

PROVERBS 11:30 NKJV

The fruit of the righteous *is* a tree of life, and he who wins souls *is* wise.

——— *DECLARATION OF FAITH* ———

I am a soul-winner! I am wise and discerning in the ways of righteousness and the fruit that I produce in my life is like a magnet, drawing the lost to Jesus.

(Daniel 12:3; 1 Corinthians 9:19-22)

PROVERBS 12:1,2 KJV

Whoso loveth instruction loveth knowledge: but he that hateth reproof is brutish. A good man obtaineth favour of the Lord: but a man of wicked devices will he condemn.

————— *DECLARATION OF FAITH* —————

I am a lover of discipline and knowledge, and have obtained the favor of the Lord.

(Proverbs 3:3,4; Daniel 1:17,20; Genesis 39:2-5)

PROVERBS 12:4 KJV

A virtuous woman is a crown to her husband: but she that maketh ashamed is as rottenness in his bones.

————— *DECLARATION OF FAITH* —————

(For those who are married)

My spouse is of a noble, virtuous and admirable character, and is the crowning joy of my life.

(Proverbs 31:23; 1 Corinthians 11:7; Ephesians 5:22-33)

PROVERBS 12:6,7 KJV

The words of the wicked are to lie in wait for blood: but the mouth of the upright shall deliver them. The wicked are overthrown, and are not: but the house of the righteous shall stand.

————— *DECLARATION OF FAITH* —————

The words of my mouth rescue me out of every trouble and my house stands firm and immovable against all attempts to destroy it.

(Mark 11:22-25; Proverbs 14:3; 18:20,21; Matthew 7:24,25)

PROVERBS 12:10 NKJV

A righteous *man* regards the life of his animal, but the tender mercies of the wicked *are* cruel.

I care for all of the needs of my animals. I do not neglect the creation that God has put me in charge of.

(Deuteronomy 25:4; Psalm 8:4-6)

PROVERBS 12:11 KJV

He that tilleth his land shall be satisfied with bread: but he that followeth vain persons is void of understanding.

———— *DECLARATION OF FAITH* ————

I do not chase after fantasies or "get rich quick" schemes that require no work on my behalf. It is the diligence of my hands that brings me abundant wealth. What I have, I have earned through hard work and keeping the precepts of the Lord my God.

(Proverbs 28:19; 20:13; Romans 12:11)

PROVERBS 12:14-16 KJV

A man shall be satisfied with good by the fruit of *his* mouth: and the recompence of a man's hands shall be rendered unto him. The way of a fool *is* right in his own eyes: but he that hearkeneth unto counsel *is* wise. A fool's wrath is presently known: but a prudent *man* covereth shame.

———— *DECLARATION OF FAITH* ————

I understand the laws of the spirit regarding the power of the tongue. By the fruit of my lips, my life is filled to overflowing with good things just as surely as the work of my hands rewards me.

I listen to sound advice and find good, honorable role models to help guide me in my prosperity.

Furthermore, it does not bother me when people have a problem with my pursuit of prosperity. Let them hurl their insults all they want, I will still choose to go forward in the ways of my Father.

(Proverbs 13:2; 18:20,21; Mark 11:22-25; 2 Corinthians 4:13; Psalm 35:27)

PROVERBS 12:18 KJV

There is that speaketh like the piercings of a sword: but the tongue of the wise is health.

───── *DECLARATION OF FAITH* ─────

I am a man/woman of understanding. I am wise in the methods of words.
My tongue brings healing from every direction and in every form.

(1 Corinthians 2:6-16; Proverbs 18:20,21; Mark 11:22-25)

PROVERBS 12:20 NKJV

Deceit is in the heart of those who devise evil, but counselors of peace have joy.

───── *DECLARATION OF FAITH* ─────

I am a promoter of peace who lives an ever-joyful and satisfying life.

(Matthew 5:9; Philippians 4:4; Nehemiah 8:10)

PROVERBS 12:24 KJV

The hand of the diligent shall bear rule: but the slothful shall be under tribute.

───── *DECLARATION OF FAITH* ─────

I am a hardworking, industrious, and creative man/woman.
I am destined for leadership.

(1 Thessalonians 4:11; Genesis 39:2-5; Deuteronomy 28:12,13)

PROVERBS 12:28 NKJV

In the way of righteousness *is* life, and in *its* pathway *there is* no death.

───── *DECLARATION OF FAITH* ─────

I am fixed on the path of righteousness and God's eternal life has become my
own. My life is filled with health, energy, vibrancy, wealth, power, prosperity, the
anointing, and an abundance of all good things.

(John 3:3,16; 10:10; 2 Corinthians 5:17; 8:9; 2 Peter 2:24; Romans 8:32)

PROVERBS 13:2-4 KJV

A man shall eat good by the fruit of *his* mouth: but the soul of the transgressors *shall eat* violence. He that keepeth his mouth keepeth his life: *but* he that openeth wide his lips shall have destruction. The soul of the sluggard desireth, and *hath* nothing: but the soul of the diligent shall be made fat.

By the words of my mouth, I obtain and enjoy all good things. I am careful not to speak those things that would strip me of my blessings. My words produce health, joy, love, peace, prosperity and power in my life. My mouth is stubborn and inflexible. My words are good ones, and coupled with my diligence and hard work, all of my desires are fully satisfied.

(Mark 11:22-25; Proverbs 18:20,21; Deuteronomy 28:12)

PROVERBS 13:11 KJV

Wealth gotten by vanity shall be diminished: but he that gathereth by labour shall increase.

——— DECLARATION OF FAITH ———

I do not seek after "get rich quick" schemes or money gained illegally or dishonestly. My wealth comes to me little by little through hard work and the application of the principles laid out for me in the Word. By these, I make my wealth grow until all of my storage places overflow and every "get rich quick" scheme becomes the laughing stock of my household.

(Proverbs 10:2; 20:21; Psalm 112:1-3; Malachi 3:10)

PROVERBS 13:14 KJV

The law of the wise is a fountain of life, to depart from the snares of death.

——— DECLARATION OF FAITH ———

My teaching is a life-producing blessing to all who heed it. Those who practice my instruction are freed from the snares of death.

(Psalm 91:3; Isaiah 61:1-3; Proverbs 6:22; 2 Samuel 22:6)

PROVERBS 13:15 KJV

Good understanding giveth favour: but the way of transgressors is hard.

——— DECLARATION OF FAITH ———

I am a child of understanding and have won the continuous favor of my heavenly Father.

(1 Corinthians 2:6-16; 1 John 5:20; Proverbs 3:3,4)

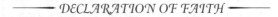

PROVERBS 13:18 NKJV

Poverty and shame *will come* to him who disdains correction, but he who regards a rebuke will be honored.

———— DECLARATION OF FAITH ————

I am wise enough to listen to counsel and instruction. I do not disdain correction, but embrace it thankfully so that I may stay on the path of the abundant life. By this, I obtain a place of honor among my peers.

(John 16:13; Proverbs 15:5,22,31,32)

PROVERBS 13:20 KJV

He that walketh with wise men shall be wise: but a companion of fools shall be destroyed.

———— DECLARATION OF FAITH ————

I choose my friends wisely. I am a companion of the wise, not of fools.
I have proven the path of wisdom and my insight is watered for continuous growth.

(2 Corinthians 6:14; Ephesians 5:1-14; 1 Corinthians 5:9)

PROVERBS 13:21,22 KJV

Evil pursueth sinners: but to the righteous good shall be repaid. A good *man* leaveth an inheritance to his children's children: and the wealth of the sinner *is* laid up for the just.

———— DECLARATION OF FAITH ————

I walk in my integrity as an honorable son/daughter of my heavenly Father and my reward in this life is exceedingly great.
I am wise in the ways of prosperity. Both my children and my grandchildren shall be blessed with a tremendous inheritance.
I am not shaken when the wicked prosper.

(Romans 5:17; Ephesians 5:1,2; Deuteronomy 8:18; Job 27:16,17; Ecclesiastes 2:26)

PROVERBS 13:24 KJV

He that spareth his rod hateth his son: but he that loveth him chasteneth him betimes.

——— DECLARATION OF FAITH ———

I will not show hatred to my children by refraining from the use of the rod. I show my love by disciplining them just as harshly as they need so that they will stay on the path of righteousness and live with me forever in heaven.

(Proverbs 19:18; 22:15; Ephesians 6:4)

PROVERBS 14:3 NKJV

In the mouth of a fool *is* a rod of pride, but the lips of the wise will preserve them.

——— DECLARATION OF FAITH ———

The words of my mouth are a shield of protection in my life.

(Mark 11:22-25; Proverbs 18:20,21)

PROVERBS 14:6 KJV

A scorner seeketh wisdom, and findeth it not: but knowledge is easy unto him that understandeth.

——— DECLARATION OF FAITH ———

I am a child of deep insight. To me, knowledge comes as easily as breathing.

(Daniel 1:17,20; 2:22,23; Ephesians 1:17-23; 1 Corinthians 2:6-16)

PROVERBS 14:11 KJV

The house of the wicked shall be overthrown: but the tabernacle of the upright shall flourish.

——— DECLARATION OF FAITH ———

My home is stable and secure. Its foundation is immovable.

(Psalm 112; Matthew 7:24,25; 1 Corinthians 3:11)

PROVERBS 14:18 KJV

The simple inherit folly: but the prudent are crowned with knowledge.

——— DECLARATION OF FAITH ———

I am a discerning child of God crowned with a supernatural ability to obtain and retain knowledge.

(Daniel 1:17,20; 2:22,23; 1 Corinthians 1:30; 2:6-16; 1 John 5:20)

PROVERBS 14:21-24 KJV

He that despiseth his neighbour sinneth: but he that hath mercy on the poor, happy *is* he. Do they not err that devise evil? but mercy and truth *shall be* to them that devise good. In all labour there is profit: but the talk of the lips *tendeth* only to penury. The crown of the wise *is* their riches: *but* the foolishness of fools *is* folly.

———— *DECLARATION OF FAITH* ————

I show myself to be concerned and compassionate toward the needy.

All of the plans that I pursue are for the good of my fellow man as well as myself.

I work hard to bring forth profit in my life. I understand the joy of diligence and the reward of persistence.

Wisdom, love, faithfulness and perseverance are engrafted into my spirit.

I wear abundance of wealth as a crown of blessing from God Himself.

(Psalm 112:1-3,9; Deuteronomy 28:12; Proverbs 19:17)

PROVERBS 14:26 NKJV

In the fear of the Lord *there is* strong confidence, and His children will have a place of refuge.

———— *DECLARATION OF FAITH* ————

My fortress is secure. For my children, it is a place of refuge.

(Psalm 112; Matthew 7:24,25; 1 Corinthians 3:11; Deuteronomy 6:5-7)

PROVERBS 14:29,30 KJV

He that is slow to wrath is of great understanding: but he that is hasty of spirit exalteth folly. A sound heart is the life of the flesh: but envy the rottenness of the bones.

———— *DECLARATION OF FAITH* ————

I am a patient and self-controlled man/woman with a deep understanding of the ways of life.

My spirit is at peace within me and it gives health and vitality to my body.

(Galatians 5:22,23; Romans 8:11; 14:17; Proverbs 16:32; James 1:19)

PROVERBS 14:31 KJV

He that oppresseth the poor reproacheth his Maker: but he that honoureth him hath mercy on the poor.

DECLARATION OF FAITH

I am kind and generous to those who are in need, thereby giving great honor to my heavenly Father.

(2 Corinthians 8:3-5; James 2:2-6; Romans 2:11)

PROVERBS 15:1 KJV

A soft answer turneth away wrath: but grievous words stir up anger.

DECLARATION OF FAITH

I provide a gentle answer in every dispute so that I may chase the spirit of strife from my presence.

(Proverbs 25:15; 1 Samuel 25:10)

PROVERBS 15:4 NKJV

A wholesome tongue *is* a tree of life, but perverseness in it breaks the spirit.

DECLARATION OF FAITH

My words bring healing to all who are touched by them. They are a tree of life, with limbs branching out and roots spreading within, forming an impregnable fortress of God's glory in this earth.

(Proverbs 18:20,21; Mark 11:22-25; Psalm 107:20)

PROVERBS 15:6 KJV

In the house of the righteous is much treasure: but in the revenues of the wicked is trouble.

DECLARATION OF FAITH

My house contains an abundance of godly treasures. It is a storehouse of all good things.

(Psalm 112:1-3; Romans 8:32; Malachi 3:10)

PROVERBS 15:15 KJV

All the days of the afflicted are evil: but he that is of a merry heart hath a continual feast.

——— *DECLARATION OF FAITH* ———

I am joyful always. For me, life is a continual feast — a perpetual party!

(Philippians 4:4; 1 Peter 3:10,11; Proverbs 17:22)

PROVERBS 15:21,22 KJV

Folly *is* joy to *him that is* destitute of wisdom: but a man of understanding walketh uprightly. Without counsel purposes are disappointed: but in the multitude of counsellors they are established.

——— *DECLARATION OF FAITH* ———

I am a man/woman of great understanding and I keep a straight course in my life. I am a team player with many wise and godly coaches to advise and encourage me. Their advice, in perfect alignment with God's Word, absolutely guarantees my success in this life.

(Ephesians 5:1-15; Proverbs 11:14; Joshua 1:8)

PROVERBS 15:28 NKJV

The heart of the righteous studies how to answer, but the mouth of the wicked pours forth evil.

——— *DECLARATION OF FAITH* ———

I am not quick with an answer. I weigh each of my words carefully and speak only those things that bring glory to God.

(1 Peter 3:15; Titus 11:2-15)

PROVERBS 15:30 KJV

The light of the eyes rejoiceth the heart: and a good report maketh the bones fat.

——— *DECLARATION OF FAITH* ———

I am a man/woman of many smiles and a cheerful countenance. I am known to bring a good report. When I speak, health and vitality flow into the bones of those who hear.

(Philippians 4:4; Nehemiah 8:10; Numbers 14:8; Psalm 107:20)

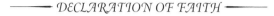
PROVERBS 15:31,32 KJV

The ear that heareth the reproof of life abideth among the wise. He that refuseth instruction despiseth his own soul: but he that heareth reproof getteth understanding.

——— *DECLARATION OF FAITH* ———

I remain teachable at all times and listen carefully to a life-giving rebuke. I am humble enough to accept, admit to, and take responsibility for all of my mistakes. This ensures my welcome among the wise and demonstrates my unlimited understanding of the way that is set before me.

(Proverbs 9:8; 27:5; Romans 12:1,2)

PROVERBS 15:33 NKJV

The fear of the Lord *is* the instruction of wisdom, and before honor *is* humility.

——— *DECLARATION OF FAITH* ———

My deep and committed respect for my heavenly Father places my wisdom on open display for all to see. When I humble myself in the presence of His majesty, He lifts me to the place of highest honor.

(Romans 1:16; 1 Peter 5:5-7; Ephesians 2:6; Proverbs 1:7; 18:12)

PROVERBS 16:3 KJV

Commit thy works unto the Lord, and thy thoughts shall be established.

——— *DECLARATION OF FAITH* ———

I commit my way to the Lord. Everything that I do is covered and saturated with His anointing, and all of my plans are destined to succeed.

(James 4:7; 1 John 2:27; Psalm 37:5; 1 Peter 5:5-7; Proverbs 3:6)

PROVERBS 16:7 NKJV

When a man's ways please the Lord, He makes even his enemies to be at peace with him.

——— *DECLARATION OF FAITH* ———

I choose to live in ways that are pleasing to the Lord, and He makes even my enemies to be at peace with me.

(Ephesians 5:1-15; Deuteronomy 28:1; 1 Kings 2:33)

PROVERBS 16:9 KJV

A man's heart deviseth his way: but the Lord directeth his steps.

——— *DECLARATION OF FAITH* ———

In my heart I determine the direction that I will take, making plans and set-ting all of my goals in accordance with the will of God. When my dream is made plain and I am focused on my destiny, the Lord directs my every step to fulfill it.

(Romans 12:2; 1 John 5:20; Proverbs 19:21; 20:24)

PROVERBS 16:16-19 KJV

How much better *is it* to get wisdom than gold! and to get understanding rather to be chosen than silver! The highway of the upright *is* to depart from evil: he that keepeth his way preserveth his soul. Pride *goeth* before destruction, and an haughty spirit before a fall. Better *it is to be* of an humble spirit with the lowly, than to divide the spoil with the proud.

——— *DECLARATION OF FAITH* ———

With me, wisdom is so much better than gold. I cherish understanding infi-nitely more than fine silver. Riches are fleeting, but wisdom always remains.

My path in this life is completely separate from evil things. I keep my way pure and in so doing I preserve my soul. I do not allow arrogance to enter my heart and cause me to fall. No, my spirit always remains humble and in true sub-mission to God. I would much rather hang out with the homeless, than divide riches with the proud and arrogant.

(2 Chronicles 1:7-12; Proverbs 2:6-8; 1 Corinthians 1:18-31)

PROVERBS 16:20 KJV

He that handleth a matter wisely shall find good: and whoso trusteth in the Lord, happy is he.

——— *DECLARATION OF FAITH* ———

I consider the instruction of wise counsel and do those things that bring glory to my heavenly Father.

I trust in God with all of my heart and give my full attention to His precepts. By this, I prosper in all that I do and obtain a full treasury of joy, power, prosper-ity and all good things.

(Proverbs 3:5,6; 15:22; Ephesians 5:1-15; Deuteronomy 28:1-14; Psalm 34:8)

PROVERBS 16:24 NKJV

Pleasant words *are like* a honeycomb, sweetness to the soul and health to the bones.

——— *DECLARATION OF FAITH* ———

My words are pleasant words. They are as a honeycomb, sweet to the mind and healing to the bones.

(Proverbs 15:1,4,30; 18:20,21; Psalm 107:20)

PROVERBS 17:5 KJV

Whoso mocketh the poor reproacheth his Maker: and he that is glad at calamities shall not be unpunished.

——— *DECLARATION OF FAITH* ———

I never mock the poor. They are made in the image and likeness of God and are not deserving of mockery. I never enjoy watching others suffer. When suffering comes, the compassion within me rises to bring healing to the situation.

(James 3:8-10; Matthew 9:36-38; 14:14)

PROVERBS 17:9 KJV

He that covereth a transgression seeketh love; but he that repeateth a matter separateth very friends.

——— *DECLARATION OF FAITH* ———

When someone does wrong and sins, I am compassionate towards them. I do not expose them in a spirit of division. I cover them, guard them and do whatever I can to guide them back to the path of righteousness.

(Galatians 6:1,2; Proverbs 10:12; 1 Corinthians 13:5-7)

PROVERBS 17:22 NKJV

A merry heart does good, *like* medicine, but a broken spirit dries the bones.

——— *DECLARATION OF FAITH* ———

I have a cheerful, happy and positively joyful heart, which sends its healing power to every fiber of my being!

(Philippians 4:4; Nehemiah 8:10; Proverbs 12:25; Romans 8:11)

PROVERBS 17:27 KJV

He that hath knowledge spareth his words: *and* a man of understanding is of an excellent spirit.

——— *DECLARATION OF FAITH* ———

I understand the tremendous power of my words and I weigh each one carefully so that when I speak, their power will bring glory to my heavenly Father.

I am an even-tempered man/woman, self-controlled and balanced in all of the ways of life.

(Proverbs 18:20,21; Mark 11:22-25; Proverbs 10:19; James 1:19; 3:2-13)

PROVERBS 18:4 KJV

The words of a man's mouth are as deep waters, and the wellspring of wisdom as a flowing brook.

——— *DECLARATION OF FAITH* ———

The words of my mouth are as deep waters and the wellspring of my wisdom is as a flowing brook.

(Proverbs 16:22; 18:20,21;Matthew 12:36,37)

PROVERBS 18:10 NKJV

The name of the Lord *is* a strong tower;
The righteous run to it and are safe.

——— *DECLARATION OF FAITH* ———

The name of the Lord is my strong tower. I run to it and am kept safe in times of trouble.

(Philippians 2:10; 2 Samuel 22:2,3,33; Psalm 18:2)

PROVERBS 18:14 NKJV

The spirit of a man will sustain him in sickness, but who can bear a broken spirit?

——— *DECLARATION OF FAITH* ———

My spirit is powerful and full of joy. It sustains me when sickness wages war against my body.

(Ephesians 3:16; Romans 8:11; Nehemiah 8:10)

PROVERBS 18:15,16 KJV

The heart of the prudent getteth knowledge; and the ear of the wise seeketh knowledge. A man's gift maketh room for him, and bringeth him before great men.

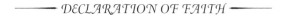

——— *DECLARATION OF FAITH* ———

My heart is diligent in obtaining knowledge and my ears are alert and perceptive when it comes.

I am clever and wise in my giving. I choose the right place and the right time to give and thereby I am given access to the great men and women in the earth.

(Matthew 13:9; Proverbs 2:10; 22:29; Ecclesiastes 11:1,2)

PROVERBS 18:20,21 NIV

From the fruit of his mouth a man's stomach is filled; with the harvest from his lips he is satisfied. The tongue has the power of life and death, and those who love it will eat its fruit.

——— *DECLARATION OF FAITH* ———

My words produce the fruit that fills my stomach, and my lips produce the harvest by which I am satisfied. The elements of life and death yield themselves to the power of my tongue. My words are seeds of life and prosperity to the kingdom of God, but death and destruction to the kingdom of the enemy. I sow my words wisely and reap a harvest that makes my Father proud.

(Proverbs 12:14; 13:2; Mark 11:22-25; Galatians 6:7-9)

PROVERBS 18:22 NKJV

He who finds a wife finds a good *thing,*
And obtains favor from the Lord.

——— *DECLARATION OF FAITH* ———

(To those who are married)

My husband/wife is a blessing to me. He/She is faithful and good, and brings tremendous joy to my life. Through him/her, I receive a special blessing of favor from the Lord.

(Genesis 2:18; Proverbs 12:4; 19:14)

PROVERBS 19:2 NIV

It is not good to have zeal without knowledge, nor to be hasty and miss the way.

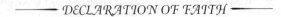

I will not proceed with a heart of passion and zeal without seeking first the knowledge and counsel of the Holy Spirit. I refuse to be hasty and miss all of the great things that He has for me.

(John 16:13; Psalm 31:22; 116:11)

PROVERBS 19:8 AMP

He who gains Wisdom loves his own life; he who keeps understanding shall prosper and find good.

I seek wisdom and godly living and thereby show the importance I place upon my soul. Because I keep sound wisdom and understanding, I will find good in my life.

(Psalm 119:129; Proverbs 2:10; 3:21-24)

PROVERBS 19:11 KJV

The discretion of a man deferreth his anger; and *it is* his glory to pass over a transgression.

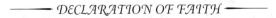

My wisdom makes me a patient man/woman. It is to my glory to overlook an offense.

(Galatians 5:22,23; 6:1,2; James 1:19; Ephesians 4:32)

PROVERBS 19:14 NKJV

Houses and riches are an inheritance from fathers, but a prudent wife is from the Lord.

——— DECLARATION OF FAITH ———

God has given me a prudent wife/husband and my posterity shall enjoy an abundance of riches for their inheritance.

(Proverbs 13:22; 18:22)

PROVERBS 19:17 AMP

He who has pity on the poor lends to the Lord, and that which he has given He will repay to him.

DECLARATION OF FAITH

My kindness and generosity to the poor is like lending to the Lord. He will repay everything that I have given, while adding His own compound interest as my reward.

(Deuteronomy 15:7,8; Ecclesiastes 11:1; Matthew 10:42; 2 Corinthians 9:6-9)

PROVERBS 19:18 NIV

Discipline your son, for in that there is hope; do not be a willing party to his death.

DECLARATION OF FAITH

I render my children consistent and godly discipline. By this, I give them hope and ensure them a stable future. I refuse to be a party to their destruction, either by restraining from the rod, or by giving it too harshly and without good reason.

(Proverbs 13:24; 22:6; Ephesians 6:4)

PROVERBS 19:21 NIV

Many are the plans in a man's heart, but it is the Lord's purpose that prevails.

DECLARATION OF FAITH

I keep my plans in perfect line with God's will. In this, I am guaranteed success.

(Romans 12:2; Psalm 33:10,11; Hebrews 6:17; James 4:13-17)

PROVERBS 19:23 KJV

The fear of the Lord *tendeth* to life: and *he that hath it* shall abide satisfied; he shall not be visited with evil.

DECLARATION OF FAITH

My heart is fixed in a trembling, worshipful reverence for my heavenly Father. In Him, I have cause to be content and I am like an immovable rock in times of trouble.

(Proverbs 14:27; 1 Timothy 4:8; Hebrews 13:5,6)

PROVERBS 20:1 NIV

Wine is a mocker and beer a brawler; whoever is led astray by them is not wise.

——— *DECLARATION OF FAITH* ———

I am known to be a wise man/woman. I cannot be led astray by the deception found in drinking alcoholic beverages. I will never allow them to rule or reign in my life in any way.

(Ephesians 5:17,18; 1 Corinthians 2:6-16; Proverbs 23:29-35; Isaiah 28:7; Hosea 4:11)

PROVERBS 20:3 NKJV

It is honorable for a man to stop striving, since any fool can start a quarrel.

——— *DECLARATION OF FAITH* ———

I will not afford myself the uncertain satisfaction of strife. I cast it far from my life and show myself to be a man/woman of honor.

(Proverbs 17:14; 1 Thessalonians 4:11)

PROVERBS 20:7 AMP

The righteous man walks in his integrity; blessed (happy, fortunate, enviable) are his children after him.

——— *DECLARATION OF FAITH* ———

I walk blamelessly in the ways of my heavenly Father and my children enjoy the bounty of my reward.

(Ephesians 5:1; 2 Corinthians 1:12; Psalm 37:25,26)

PROVERBS 20:13 NIV

Do not love sleep or you will grow poor; stay awake and you will have food to spare.

——— *DECLARATION OF FAITH* ———

I refuse to allow my flesh to lead me on the path of poverty by loving to sleep. I sleep only as long as it takes to refresh my body, then I awake and focus on prospering another day.

(Proverbs 6:6-11; Psalm 119:147,148; Joshua 1:8)

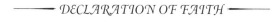

PROVERBS 20:18 KJV

Every purpose is established by counsel: and with good advice make war.

──── *DECLARATION OF FAITH* ────

I will not make any major plans without the security of godly counsel. Before I wage war, I seek the guidance that will ensure my victory.

(1 Samuel 23:2-9; 2 Chronicles 17:1-4; Proverbs 24:6; Luke 14:31)

PROVERBS 20:22 NKJV

Do not say, "I will recompense evil";
Wait for the Lord, and He will save you.

──── *DECLARATION OF FAITH* ────

I am not quick to seek revenge when I am wronged. The Lord is a lot better at it than I am. I will wait for His intervention on my behalf, for I know that He will right every wrong done to me.

(Deuteronomy 32:35; Proverbs 17:13; 24:29; Romans 12:17-19; 2 Samuel 16:12)

PROVERBS 20:25 AMP

It is a snare to a man to utter a vow [of consecration] rashly and [not until] afterward inquire [whether he can fulfill it].

──── *DECLARATION OF FAITH* ────

I am not quick to commit myself to anything. I think through my every vow carefully, for when my word is given, I intend to keep it.

(Proverbs 14:29; 20:21; 21:5; 25:8; 29:20; Isaiah 55:11)

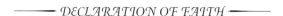

PROVERBS 21:5 NIV

The plans of the diligent lead to profit as surely as haste leads to poverty.

──── *DECLARATION OF FAITH* ────

My plans in life are carefully laid out before me. I have considered them from every angle, making certain that they are in line with the precepts of God, and my diligence to fulfill them absolutely ensures an abundance of profits for my storehouses.

(Proverbs 10:4; 15:22; Joshua 1:8; Psalm 1:1-3; 112:1-3)

PROVERBS 21:6 NKJV

Getting treasures by a lying tongue *is* the fleeting fantasy of those who seek death.

——— *DECLARATION OF FAITH* ———

I maintain my integrity in all of my business dealings. I do not use lies and deceit to gain my treasures. Such foolishness is a vanity tossed to and fro of them that seek death and I will not be a part of it.

(Proverbs 8:7-21; 13:11; Revelation 18:19)

PROVERBS 21:12 KJV

The righteous *man* wisely considereth the house of the wicked: *but God* overthroweth the wicked for *their* wickedness.

——— *DECLARATION OF FAITH* ———

I consider the dwelling of the wicked and understand the folly of their ways. I know that one day they shall be overthrown; therefore, I cannot be seduced to follow them on their path of destruction.

(Exodus 23:1,2; Psalm 7:9-16)

PROVERBS 21:20 NIV

In the house of the wise are stores of choice food and oil, but a foolish man devours all he has.

——— *DECLARATION OF FAITH* ———

I am a wise man/woman whose house is filled with an abundance of provisions. I do not eat my seed or spend all that I earn. I am wise to set aside what is the Lord's, give generously for the advancement of His kingdom, and invest a substantial amount for myself and those in my circle of influence.

(Psalm 112:1-3; Malachi 3:6-12; Proverbs 8:21)

PROVERBS 21:21 NKJV

He who follows righteousness and mercy finds life, righteousness and honor.

——— *DECLARATION OF FAITH* ———

I pursue love and righteousness with all of my heart, for in them I find life and vitality, wealth and prosperity.

(Proverbs 15:9; Matthew 5:6; Romans 2:7; 14:17; 1 Corinthians 15:58; Job 29:4-11)

PROVERBS 21:23 AMP

He who guards his mouth and his tongue keeps himself from troubles.

—— *DECLARATION OF FAITH* ——

I am careful not to speak negative things that bring calamity into my life.

(Proverbs 18:20,21; Mark 11:22-25; Matthew 12:37)

PROVERBS 21:26 AMP

He covets greedily all the day long, but the [uncompromisingly] righteous gives and does not withhold.

—— *DECLARATION OF FAITH* ——

I give without sparing and my life is satisfied with all good things.

(2 Corinthians 9:5-11; Romans 8:32; Proverbs 22:9; Ephesians 4:28)

PROVERBS 21:31 NIV

The horse is made ready for the day of battle, but victory rests with the Lord.

—— *DECLARATION OF FAITH* ——

I prepare myself for battle knowing full well that my victory is made certain in the Lord.

(Ephesians 6:10-18; 1 Corinthians 15:57; Psalm 3:8)

PROVERBS 22:1 KJV

A *good* name *is* rather to be chosen than great riches, *and* loving favour rather than silver and gold.

—— *DECLARATION OF FAITH* ——

My name is more important to me than all of the riches of the world.

(Genesis 12:1-3; Proverbs 3:3,4; 10:7; Ecclesiastes 7:1)

PROVERBS 22:4 NKJV

By humility *and* the fear of the Lord *are* riches and honor and life.

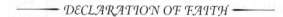

I humble myself with a deep and solemn trust in my heavenly Father and He brings me wealth, honor and a good life in return.

(1 Peter 5:5-7; James 4:6-10; John 10:10; Psalm 112:1-3)

PROVERBS 22:6 NIV

Train a child in the way he should go, and when he is old he will not turn from it.

──── DECLARATION OF FAITH ────

I consistently train my children in the ways of righteousness. I hold them to the ways of the Lord, so that when they move out on their own, they will be stout against temptation and have the tools to live a blessed and prosperous life.

(Ephesians 6:4; 2 Timothy 3:15; Deuteronomy 6:5-7)

PROVERBS 22:9 NKJV

He who has a generous eye will be blessed,
For he gives of his bread to the poor.

──── DECLARATION OF FAITH ────

I am a generous man/woman who shares his/her abundance with those in need. By this, I receive blessings from every direction.

(2 Corinthians 9:5-11; Proverbs 19:17; Ecclesiastes 11:1,2)

PROVERBS 22:15 NIV

Folly is bound up in the heart of a child, but the rod of discipline will drive it far from him.

──── DECLARATION OF FAITH ────

It is my duty to keep my children on the path of righteousness. When foolishness is bound up in the heart of my child, I drive it far from him/her with the rod of correction.

(Proverbs 13:4; 23:13,14; 22:6; Ephesians 6:4)

PROVERBS 22:24,25 KJV

Make no friendship with an angry man; and with a furious man thou shalt not go: Lest thou learn his ways, and get a snare to thy soul.

——— DECLARATION OF FAITH ———

I will not be a companion of an angry person. A person who cannot control their temper is not worthy of my friendship. I will not allow the foolishness of rage to enter my life space and become a snare for my soul.

(Genesis 49:5-7; Psalm 55:9-13; Proverbs 13:20)

PROVERBS 22:29 AMP

Do you see a man diligent and skillful in his business? He will stand before kings; he will not stand before obscure men.

——— DECLARATION OF FAITH ———

I am diligent in my business. I am a hard worker who constantly finds ways to make things better. In my diligence I have earned the right to stand in the presence of kings. Mediocre men will find no peer in me.

(Proverbs 10:4; 12:24; 30:28; Psalm 119:146)

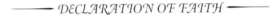

PROVERBS 23:4 NIV

Do not wear yourself out to get rich; have the wisdom to show restraint.

——— DECLARATION OF FAITH ———

I do not wear myself out trying to get rich. I am already God's heir; therefore, I will walk in wisdom and show restraint.

(Romans 8:17,32; 12:16; Proverbs 28:20; Matthew 6:19)

PROVERBS 23:6-8 KJV

Eat thou not the bread of *him that hath* an evil eye, neither desire thou his dainty meats: For as he thinketh in his heart, so *is* he: Eat and drink, saith he to thee; but his heart *is* not with thee. The morsel *which* thou hast eaten shalt thou vomit up, and lose thy sweet words.

——— DECLARATION OF FAITH ———

I will not make a role model of one who has an evil eye. Just because they have made themselves rich and live in luxury does not make them worthy to imitate. I understand the selfish heart of evil. They may bid me to join in with them, but their heart is not with me. For profit, they would turn on me. Their friendship is but a lie.

(Proverbs 13:20; 28:7; Psalm 119:63; Micah 7:2-7)

PROVERBS 23:9 NIV

Do not speak to a fool, for he will scorn the wisdom of your words.

——— *DECLARATION OF FAITH* ———

I do not offer the wisdom of the Lord to a fool. I understand that fools are foolish and they despise wisdom and correction.

(Proverbs 12:1; Matthew 7:6)

PROVERBS 23:13,14 NKJV

Do not withhold correction from a child,
For *if* you beat him with a rod, he will not die.
You shall beat him with a rod,
And deliver his soul from hell.

——— *DECLARATION OF FAITH* ———

I do not withhold discipline from my child. I can see the big picture and I know what is at stake. I will not allow the devil to influence my kids and take them to hell. They're coming to heaven with me.

(Proverbs 13:24; 19:18; 22:6,15; Ephesians 6:4)

PROVERBS 23:17 NKJV

Do not let your heart envy sinners,
But *be zealous* for the fear of the Lord all the day.

——— *DECLARATION OF FAITH* ———

I do not envy sinners, nor do their ways have any appeal to me. I thoroughly understand the folly of fools and will not allow myself to be influenced by them. It is my zeal, my zest, and my joy to follow the ways of the Lord.

(2 Corinthians 6:14; Ephesians 5:1-14; Psalm 37:1; Proverbs 24:1,19)

PROVERBS 23:20,21 KJV

Be not among winebibbers; among riotous eaters of flesh: For the drunkard and the glutton shall come to poverty: and drowsiness shall clothe *a man* with rags.

DECLARATION OF FAITH

I am not a companion of drinkers or gluttons. I am a sober and temperate man/woman. I will not be influenced by the destructive ways of those who choose to live outside of the will of God.

(Ephesians 5:1-18; 1 Corinthians 2:6-16; Proverbs 23:29-35; Isaiah 28:7; Hosea 4:11)

PROVERBS 24:3,4 AMP

Through skillful and godly Wisdom is a house (a life, a home, a family) built, and by understanding it is established [on a sound and good foundation],
And by knowledge shall its chambers [of every area] be filled with all precious and pleasant riches.

DECLARATION OF FAITH

The foundations of my household are carefully planned and well established. Through extensive knowledge it is built and all of its rooms are filled with rare and costly treasures.

(Matthew 7:24,25; Psalm 112:1-3; Deuteronomy 8:6-18)

PROVERBS 24:5,6 NIV

A wise man has great power, and a man of knowledge increases strength; for waging war you need guidance, and for victory many advisers.

DECLARATION OF FAITH

I am a man/woman of extraordinary miracle-working power who is full of wisdom and ever-increasing in strength.

I embrace the counsel of many wise and godly advisors to guide me in battle and ensure my victory.

(Acts 6:5-8; Ephesians 1:17-23; 6:10; Proverbs 15:22; Luke 14:31)

PROVERBS 24:10 AMP

If you faint in the day of adversity, your strength is small.

I do not falter in times of trouble. At all times, I remain steady, trusting in the Lord.

(Deuteronomy 20:8; Hebrews 12:3; Galatians 6:9)

PROVERBS 24:14 NKJV

So *shall* the knowledge of wisdom *be* to your soul;
If you have found *it,* there is a prospect,
And your hope will not be cut off.

────── *DECLARATION OF FAITH* ──────

Wisdom is sweet to my soul. When I find it, I have gained hope for the future, and my hope will not be cut off.

(Psalm 19:10; 37:37; 58:11; Proverbs 23:18)

PROVERBS 24:16 AMP

For a righteous man falls seven times and rises again, but the wicked are overthrown by calamity.

────── *DECLARATION OF FAITH* ──────

I am stubborn as a mule against temptation and sin. No matter how many times I fall, I get right back up and fight again.

(1 Corinthians 10:13; 2 Corinthians 4:5-11; Psalm 34:19; 1 John 2:1,2)

PROVERBS 25:5-7 KJV

Take away the wicked *from* before the king, and his throne shall be established in righteousness. Put not forth thyself in the presence of the king, and stand not in the place of great *men:* For better *it is* that it be said unto thee, Come up hither; than that thou shouldest be put lower in the presence of the prince whom thine eyes have seen.

────── *DECLARATION OF FAITH* ──────

I do not associate myself with unbelievers and those whose ways are not fixed in the Lord, nor do I exalt myself in God's presence and claim some lofty position among His mighty princes. My exaltation comes from God alone. I am nothing more and nothing less than He has made me to be. I will do my part in this life,

working hard to advance His kingdom, and humbly accept any position that He
chooses to give me.

(1 Peter 5:5-7; 2 Corinthians 6:14; Ephesians 2:6-10; 5:1-18)

PROVERBS 25:15 NIV

Through patience a ruler can be persuaded, and a gentle tongue can break a bone.

———— *DECLARATION OF FAITH* ————

I am in perfect control of my emotions and have the ability to persuade
rulers with patience and calm, gentle answers.

(Ephesians 5:22,23; Proverbs 15:1; 2 Timothy 1:7)

PROVERBS 25:21,22 KJV

If thine enemy be hungry, give him bread to eat; and if he be thirsty, give him
water to drink: For thou shalt heap coals of fire upon his head, and the Lord
shall reward thee.

———— *DECLARATION OF FAITH* ————

I do not lash out against those who make themselves to be my enemies. To
the contrary, if they are hungry, I give them food. If they are thirsty, I give them
something to drink. This is a burning source of frustration for them and con-
founds their every act and plan against me.

When all is said and done, I have a great reward coming from the Lord for
my persistent patience and perfect self-control.

(Exodus 23:4,5; Matthew 5:4; 6:4-6; Romans 12:20)

PROVERBS 25:26 AMP

Like a muddied fountain and a polluted spring is a righteous man who yields,
falls down, and compromises his integrity before the wicked.

———— *DECLARATION OF FAITH* ————

I stand my ground against the wicked no matter what the cost.

(Ephesians 6:12,13; Leviticus 5:1; Exodus 14:13,14; Acts 6:8-15; 7:54-60)

Proverbs 25:27 NKJV

It is not good to eat much honey;
So to seek one's own glory *is not* glory.

───── *DECLARATION OF FAITH* ─────

I do not seek to exalt myself or promote my own honor, nor do I revel in the riches that I have gained. I know that too much honey makes the stomach sour. Therefore, I will maintain discretion in all areas of my life, always remembering that God alone is my source of provision.

(1 Peter 5:5-7; Deuteronomy 8:6-18; Proverbs 27:2; Luke 14:11)

Proverbs 27:1,2 KJV

Boast not thyself of to morrow; for thou knowest not what a day may bring forth. Let another man praise thee, and not thine own mouth; a stranger, and not thine own lips.

───── *DECLARATION OF FAITH* ─────

I do not brag about what I am or what I am going to do, and I remain flexible to change. If there is any praise for the things that I do, it will come from others and not my own lips.

(James 4:6,13-17; Luke 12:19-21; Proverbs 25:27; 2 Corinthians 10:12,18; 12:11)

Proverbs 27:12 NIV

The prudent see danger and take refuge, but the simple keep going and suffer for it.

───── *DECLARATION OF FAITH* ─────

I am always alert and discerning of danger. When it comes my way, I shield myself against it.

(Ephesians 5:16; 6:12,13; 2 Corinthians 2:11; 10:3-6)

Proverbs 27:17 AMP

Iron sharpens iron; so a man sharpens the countenance of his friend [to show rage or worthy purpose].

———— *DECLARATION OF FAITH* ————

As iron sharpens iron, so do I sharpen my companions and they sharpen me.

(Proverbs 11:14; 13:20; 15:22)

PROVERBS 27:18 NIV

He who tends a fig tree will eat its fruit, and he who looks after his master will be honored.

———— *DECLARATION OF FAITH* ————

I understand that the keeper of the fig tree has earned the right to eat the fruit thereof. I do not hesitate to take in provision from the things I have built and worked on and I do not despise others when they do so. I know that the laborer is worthy of his reward.

When others despise my pastors or employers for reaping opulent wages, I guard them with wisdom and protect them with my words. In this, I have earned great honor among them.

(Luke 10:7; 1 Timothy 5:18; Genesis 39:2-5)

PROVERBS 27:23,24 KJV

Be thou diligent to know the state of thy flocks, *and* look well to thy herds. For riches *are* not for ever: and doth the crown *endure* to every generation?

———— *DECLARATION OF FAITH* ————

I am diligent to know the exact state of my financial affairs. I keep a careful accounting and know where every penny goes. I know every element of my business so that I can guard against those things that would rob me of my substance.

(Luke 14:28-31; 1 Chronicles 28:1; Malachi 3:6-12)

PROVERBS 28:1 NKJV

The wicked flee when no one pursues,
But the righteous are bold as a lion.

———— *DECLARATION OF FAITH* ————

Worry cannot gain a foothold in my life. I maintain my focus upon my Lord and remain strong at all times. I never forget who dwells within me. I am the righteousness of God in Christ Jesus and have the courage and boldness of a lion!

(Matthew 6:19-33; Joshua 1:5-9; 1 John 4:4; 2 Corinthians 5:21; Philippians 4:4-8)

PROVERBS 28:5 AMP

Evil men do not understand justice, but they who crave and seek the Lord understand it fully.

———— *DECLARATION OF FAITH* ————

I understand justice. I seek my Father and have been given the capacity to understand all things.

(Matthew 13:14; John 13:7; 1 Corinthians 13:2)

PROVERBS 28:6 NIV

Better a poor man whose walk is blameless than a rich man whose ways are perverse.

———— *DECLARATION OF FAITH* ————

I would rather be poor and walk in honesty and integrity, than be filthy rich and have a perverse and deceitful heart.

(Psalm 119:118,119; Proverbs 16:19; 20:17)

PROVERBS 28:8 AMP

He who by charging excessive interest and who by unjust efforts to get gain increases his material possession gathers it for him [to spend] who is kind and generous to the poor.

———— *DECLARATION OF FAITH* ————

Those who gain wealth dishonestly and unfairly are merely gathering it all together to place it into my bank account. My Father knows my heart. I am blessed to be a blessing. I will take the wealth of the ungodly and be a blessing to those in need.

(Proverbs 13:22; Genesis 12:1-3)

PROVERBS 28:9 KJV

He that turneth away his ear from hearing the law, even his prayer *shall be* abomination.

─── *DECLARATION OF FAITH* ───

I will not turn a deaf ear to the Law, thereby making my prayers detestable. I consider the Law to be precious and I joyfully fulfill its righteous requirement in my life.

(Psalm 66:18; 109:7; Proverbs 15:8; Mark 11:25; Romans 8:4; Hebrews 10:15-17)

PROVERBS 28:10 NIV

He who leads the upright along an evil path will fall into his own trap, but the blameless will receive a good inheritance.

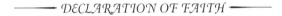

─── *DECLARATION OF FAITH* ───

I lead God's people on the path of righteousness and my inheritance is filled with good and wonderful things.

(Romans 8:32; Hebrews 6:12; 1 Peter 3:9; Daniel 12:3)

PROVERBS 28:13 NIV

He who conceals his sins does not prosper, but whoever confesses and renounces them finds mercy.

─── *DECLARATION OF FAITH* ───

I do not prohibit the flow of prosperity in my life by harboring unconfessed sin. It is my continuous prayer that the Holy Spirit reveal to me anything in my life that does not glorify Him and I am reliable to renounce and turn away from all sin no matter how menial it may seem.

(Psalm 32:3-5; 1 John 1:8-10; James 4:1-10)

PROVERBS 28:19,20 KJV

He that tilleth his land shall have plenty of bread: but he that followeth after vain *persons* shall have poverty enough. A faithful man shall abound with blessings: but he that maketh haste to be rich shall not be innocent.

─── *DECLARATION OF FAITH* ───

I am a faithful and industrious man/woman, and God blesses and prospers all that I set my hand to do.

Unlike the one who chases after riches to gain them at any cost, I remain focused upon the Lord, doing those things that are good and proper in His sight.

By this, I have made my prosperity certain, for I know that God alone has provided all that I have. He alone is my source of supply and He has promised to bless me abundantly.

(Matthew 6:33; Deuteronomy 28:8; Proverbs 10:22; John 10:10)

PROVERBS 28:21 NKJV

To show partiality *is* not good,
Because for a piece of bread a man will transgress.

──── *DECLARATION OF FAITH* ────

I am not a brown-noser. I am not a respecter of persons who shows partiality to people simply because they have great wealth or great looks. I keep my heart pure and always remember that all men are created in the image and likeness of God.

(James 2:1-9; Psalm 40:4; Romans 2:11)

PROVERBS 28:22 AMP

He who has an evil and covetous eye hastens to be rich and knows not that want will come upon him.

──── *DECLARATION OF FAITH* ────

I do not focus on a greedy pursuit of riches. I refuse to have an evil eye that searches for ways to get rich in spite of the moral consequences. I know that such a person leads a life of destruction and will one day lose everything.

(Proverbs 13:11,22; Job 15:20-29)

PROVERBS 28:25-27 KJV

He that is of a proud heart stirreth up strife: but he that putteth his trust in the Lord shall be made fat. He that trusteth in his own heart is a fool: but whoso walketh wisely, he shall be delivered. He that giveth unto the poor shall not lack: but he that hideth his eyes shall have many a curse.

──── *DECLARATION OF FAITH* ────

I trust in the Lord with all of my heart and my prosperity is as certain as seedtime and harvest.

I walk in wisdom and am kept safe.

I give to the poor and lack no good thing in my life.

(Genesis 8:22; Proverbs 3:5,6; 19:17; 22:9; 29:25; Deuteronomy 15:7)

PROVERBS 29:7,8 NIV

The righteous care about justice for the poor, but the wicked have no such concern.

Mockers stir up a city, but wise men turn away anger.

——— *DECLARATION OF FAITH* ———

I am a righteous man/woman and I consider the cause of the poor.

(Deuteronomy 15:11; Proverbs 14:31; Leviticus 19:15)

PROVERBS 29:11 NKJV

A fool vents all his feelings,
But a wise *man* holds them back.

——— *DECLARATION OF FAITH* ———

I have complete control over my emotions. I direct my anger—it does not direct me.

(Galatians 5:22,23; 2 Timothy 1:7; Ephesians 4:26)

PROVERBS 29:15 AMP

The rod and reproof give wisdom, but a child left undisciplined brings his mother to shame.

——— *DECLARATION OF FAITH* ———

I impart wisdom to my children with a rod of correction. I will not allow foolishness to gain the ascendancy in their lives and see them become a disgrace to their mother.

(Proverbs 13:24; 19:18; 22:15; 23:13,14; Ephesians 6:4)

PROVERBS 29:17 NIV

Discipline your son, and he will give you peace; he will bring delight to your soul.

——— *DECLARATION OF FAITH* ———

I am consistent in disciplining my children and they bring peace, comfort, and joy to my soul.

(Proverbs 13:24; 19:18; 22:15; 23:13,14; Ephesians 6:4)

PROVERBS 29:18 KJV

Where *there is* no vision, the people perish: but he that keepeth the law, happy *is* he.

——— *DECLARATION OF FAITH* ———

I clearly understand what I am called to do in the kingdom. I have a vision—a revelation of His redemption as it applies to my life.

I am obedient to the Word.

I am fixed in the covenant and happy, fortunate and enviable in all of my ways.

(Habakkuk 2:2; 1 Samuel 3:1; Amos 8:11,12; Proverbs 8:32; John 13:17)

PROVERBS 29:23 NKJV

A man's pride will bring him low,
But the humble in spirit will retain honor.

——— *DECLARATION OF FAITH* ———

I am a humble man/woman. I do not exalt myself to a position of honor. That is God's business.

(1 Peter 5:5-7; Proverbs 15:33; 18:12; 25:5-7; James 4:6-10; Ephesians 2:6)

PROVERBS 29:25 NIV

Fear of man will prove to be a snare, but whoever trusts in the Lord is kept safe.

——— *DECLARATION OF FAITH* ———

I do not allow fear to become a snare in my life. My complete and impenetrable trust is in my heavenly Father.

(2 Timothy 1:7; Genesis 12:12; 20:2; Luke 12:4; Joshua 1:5-9; John 12:42,43)

PROVERBS 30:5,6 KJV

Every word of God *is* pure: he *is* a shield unto them that put their trust in him. Add thou not unto his words, lest he reprove thee, and thou be found a liar.

———— *DECLARATION OF FAITH* ————

I know that the Word of my Father is flawless. He is a shield and a refuge to me in times of trouble. I need not, and I will not, add to the Word that He has given me. He has said it, and that settles it.

(Psalm 18:30; 84:11; 119:89,140; Deuteronomy 4:2; Revelation 22:18)

PROVERBS 30:8 NIV

Keep falsehood and lies far from me; give me neither poverty nor riches, but give me only my daily bread.

———— *DECLARATION OF FAITH* ————

I keep falsehood and lies far from me. I am not overly anxious for poverty, or riches. My focus is always on the Lord. He will provide my daily bread — the portion of my inheritance as a child of the King. Therefore, I will remain content in whatever state I find myself in.

(Matthew 6:11,19-33; 1 Peter 3:10,11; 1 Timothy 6:9; Hebrews 13:5,6; Philippians 4:9-13)

PROVERBS 31:4,5 NKJV

It is not for kings, O Lemuel,
It is not for kings to drink wine,
Nor for princes intoxicating drink;
Lest they drink and forget the law,
And pervert the justice of all the afflicted.

———— *DECLARATION OF FAITH* ————

As a prince/princess in the royal house of God, I am not given to wine, nor do I crave beer. I remain sober and alert so that I will not forget the precepts of the Word.

(Romans 8:14-17; 1 John 3:1,2; Ecclesiastes 10:17; Ephesians 5:18; Proverbs 20:1)

PROVERBS 31:8 AMP

Open your mouth for the dumb [those unable to speak for themselves], for the rights of all who are left desolate and defenseless.

──── *DECLARATION OF FAITH* ────

I am a voice to those who cannot speak for themselves. In me, the destitute find a warrior advocate who will fight on their behalf.

(Job 29:12-17; Ezekiel 22:30; Psalm 58; 82:3,4; 106:29-31)

PROVERBS 31:10-31 KJV

Who can find a virtuous woman? for her price *is* far above rubies. The heart of her husband doth safely trust in her, so that he shall have no need of spoil. She will do him good and not evil all the days of her life. She seeketh wool, and flax, and worketh willingly with her hands. She is like the merchants' ships; she bringeth her food from afar. She riseth also while it is yet night, and giveth meat to her household, and a portion to her maidens. She considereth a field, and buyeth it: with the fruit of her hands she planteth a vineyard. She girdeth her loins with strength, and strengtheneth her arms. She perceiveth that her merchandise *is* good: her candle goeth not out by night. She layeth her hands to the spindle, and her hands hold the distaff. She stretcheth out her hand to the poor; yea, she reacheth forth her hands to the needy. She is not afraid of the snow for her household: for all her household *are* clothed with scarlet. She maketh herself coverings of tapestry; her clothing *is* silk and purple. Her husband is known in the gates, when he sitteth among the elders of the land. She maketh fine linen, and selleth *it;* and delivereth girdles unto the merchant. Strength and honour *are* her clothing; and she shall rejoice in time to come. She openeth her mouth with wisdom; and in her tongue *is* the law of kindness. She looketh well to the ways of her household, and eateth not the bread of idleness. Her children arise up, and call her blessed; her husband *also,* and he praiseth her. Many daughters have done virtuously, but thou excellest them all. Favour *is* deceitful, and beauty *is* vain: *but* a woman *that* feareth the Lord, she shall be praised. Give her of the fruit of her hands; and let her own works praise her in the gates.

──── *DECLARATION OF FAITH* ────

(The confession of a noblewoman—a manifestation of a true daughter of God.)
I am a wife of noble character who is worth far more than rubies to my husband.
My husband has reason to put his complete confidence in me.
I bring him good things all the days of my life and I shall never treat him badly.
As far as I'm concerned, he shall lack nothing of true value and enduring worth.

I am eager to work with my hands and God blesses what I set my hand to do.

I am like a merchant ship bringing in priceless commodities for my family.

I get up while it is still dark to ensure that my family and my servants are well provided for.

I consider my investments wisely. I invest and reinvest until my earnings become like a fruitful vine in a fertile vineyard.

I set about my work vigorously and my arms are strong to complete every task. All of my trading and the work that I have done are profitable, and my lamp does not go out in fearful and troublesome times.

I am diligent and industrious, ever ready to create what is needed for my own life and that of others.

My arms are filled and opened to the poor. Whatever they need, in spirit, soul, or body, I am ready and able to provide.

I have no fear of the blizzard, for my family is clothed warmly and well provided for.

I provide warm and beautiful coverings for my bed and am clothed with the finest that the world can offer.

My husband is respected on account of me. He takes his seat among the rulers of the land.

I am a buyer and a seller, and I gain a tremendous profit from my endeavors.

I am clothed with dignity and strength.

I laugh at the troublesome days to come.

My mouth is full of wisdom and faithful instruction is on my tongue.

I am a faithful guardian over the affairs of my household and will not allow myself to be lazy.

My husband and children arise and call me blessed.

My husband praises me for the blessings that I bring into his life.

The women of the world may do noble things, but I surpass them all. I am a daughter of the living God and I show myself worthy of respect. I earn a tremendous award for my diligence and my name is one to be honored.

(Ruth 3:11; Proverbs 12:4; 19:14; 20:13; Romans 12:11; Luke 12:42; Genesis 12:1-3; Deuteronomy 8:6-18; 28:12; Ephesians 4:28; 5:22-24; Philippians 4:19; 1 Corinthians 2:6-16)

CHAPTER TWENTY-ONE

ECCLESIASTES

Vanity of vanities, everything is vanity! Well, Solomon, without Jesus you are absolutely correct!

At first reading, the book of Ecclesiastes can sound very depressing. It is full of irony from beginning to end. However, when you understand that Solomon is writing about life without God, it becomes very enlightening.

The promises of the book of Ecclesiastes, like Proverbs, are very practical in nature. They are promises that cover the laws of life that God has placed in the earth. These laws are unfailing and we can apply them on a daily basis. They show us the purpose of life and how it is to be lived. God promises us a life of enjoyment, but it is up to us to do what it takes to live that way.

As you pray the prayers of Ecclesiastes, keep in mind that without God, everything is truly pointless and empty. He is the only way to your personal fulfillment.

ECCLESIASTES 2:24-26 NIV

A man can do nothing better than to eat and drink and find satisfaction in his work. This too, I see, is from the hand of God, for without him, who can eat or find enjoyment? To the man who pleases him, God gives wisdom, knowledge and happiness, but to the sinner he gives the task of gathering and storing up wealth to hand it over to the one who pleases God. This too is meaningless, a chasing after the wind.

—— DECLARATION OF FAITH ——

I reap the benefits of my labor and find great satisfaction in my work.

I take the time to enjoy the blessings of prosperity that God has provided for me.

God has given me wisdom, knowledge, and happiness. In Him, I have a clever and resourceful mind.

(Ecclesiastes 3:12,13,22; 5:10,18-20; 8:15; 9:9; 1 Corinthians 1:30; 2:6-16; Proverbs 13:22)

ECCLESIASTES 3:1-8 KJV

To every *thing there is* a season, and a time to every purpose under the heaven:
A time to be born, and a time to die; a time to plant, and a time to pluck up *that
which is* planted; A time to kill, and a time to heal; a time to break down, and a
time to build up; A time to weep, and a time to laugh; a time to mourn, and a
time to dance; A time to cast away stones, and a time to gather stones together;
a time to embrace, and a time to refrain from embracing; A time to get, and a
time to lose; a time to keep, and a time to cast away; A time to rend, and a time
to sew; a time to keep silence, and a time to speak; A time to love, and a time to
hate; a time of war, and a time of peace.

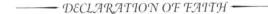

DECLARATION OF FAITH

I am wise and discerning in the ways of life.

I understand the time of birth and the time of death.

I know when to plant my seed and when to uproot.

I know when to tear down and when to build.

I know when to weep and when to laugh.

I know when to mourn and when to dance.

I know when to scatter stones and when to gather them together.

I know when to embrace and when to abstain from embracing.

I know when to search and when searching is futile.

I know when to keep things and when to throw things away.

I know when to tear things apart and when to mend them.

I know when to be silent and when to speak.

I know when to love and when to hate.

I know when to wage war and when to make peace.

*Through the knowledge and wisdom that God has given me, all of my
actions have their perfect timing.*

(Ecclesiastes 3:17; 8:6; Hebrews 9:27; Romans 12:9-21; 1 Corinthians 1:30; 2:6-15)

ECCLESIASTES 3:12,13 AMP

I know that there is nothing better for them than to be glad and to get and do
good as long as they live; And also that every man should eat and drink and
enjoy the good of all his labor—it is the gift of God.

I do good and remain happy all the days of my life. I find great satisfaction in the work of my hands and continually enjoy the benefits of the prosperity that God has provided for me.

(Ecclesiastes 2:24-26; 3:22; 5:18-20; 8:15; 9:9; 1 Timothy 6:17; Philippians 4:4,13,19)

ECCLESIASTES 3:22 NKJV

So I perceived that nothing *is* better than that a man should rejoice in his own works, for that *is* his heritage. For who can bring him to see what will happen after him?

——— *DECLARATION OF FAITH* ———

What I do for a living brings me great joy and satisfaction. It is my God-given right to obtain employment that I enjoy doing.

(Ecclesiastes 2:24-26; 3:12,13; 5:18-20; 8:15; 9:9; 1 Thessalonians 4:11)

ECCLESIASTES 4:9-12 KJV

Two are better than one; because they have a good reward for their labour. For if they fall, the one will lift up his fellow: but woe to him *that is* alone when he falleth; for *he hath* not another to help him up. Again, if two lie together, then they have heat: but how can one be warm *alone?* And if one prevail against him, two shall withstand him; and a threefold cord is not quickly broken.

——— *DECLARATION OF FAITH* ———

I am wise to seek godly companionship in the things that I do. I understand that two can bring in a better harvest than one, for if one of us falls, the other can lift him (or her) up. Furthermore, if one of us is overpowered, the other can step in and lend a hand so that we can withstand every foe.

I am not an island in my walk with God. I am a companion of God's children and together, with God entwined in us and through us, we will be victorious in every situation.

(Proverbs 15:22; Ephesians 5:1-18; Hebrews 10:25; Deuteronomy 32:30)

ECCLESIASTES 5:1-3 AMP

Keep your foot [give your mind to what you are doing] when you go [as Jacob to sacred Bethel] to the house of God. For to draw near to hear and obey is better than to give the sacrifice of fools [carelessly, irreverently] too ignorant to know that they are doing evil. Be not rash with your mouth, and let not your heart be hasty to utter a word before God. For God is in heaven, and you are on earth; therefore let your words be few. For a dream comes with much business and painful effort, and a fool's voice with many words.

──── *DECLARATION OF FAITH* ────

When I go into the house of worship, I carefully consider my purpose. I am a man/woman drawing near to God to hear and learn from His Word so that I may do what His precepts demand. I am not like the fool who goes in to offer an empty sacrifice and never lets the Word have the ascendancy in his life. I am steady and fixed in my obedience.

My words are precious and power-filled. I present each one before my heavenly Father with a specific purpose and intent. I do not multiply my words, as does the fool. I carefully consider them, planting each one as a seed toward the fulfillment of my dreams.

(James 1:21-25; 4:6-10; Hosea 6:6; Proverbs 10:19; 18:20,21; 20:25)

ECCLESIASTES 5:10 NKJV

He who loves silver will not be satisfied with silver; Nor he who loves abundance, with increase. This also is vanity.

──── *DECLARATION OF FAITH* ────

I am content with what I have in the Lord. I do not love and serve money—I love and serve my heavenly Father. All that I have is His gift to me so that I may have joy, satisfaction and fulfillment in this life.

(Matthew 6:24-33; Hebrews 13:5,6; 1 Corinthians 10:26; 1 Timothy 6:17)

ECCLESIASTES 5:18-20 NIV

Then I realized that it is good and proper for a man to eat and drink, and to find satisfaction in his toilsome labor under the sun during the few days of life God has given him—for this is his lot. Moreover, when God gives any man wealth and possessions, and enables him to enjoy them, to accept his lot and be happy in his work—this is a gift of God. He seldom reflects on the days of his life, because God keeps him occupied with gladness of heart.

——— *DECLARATION OF FAITH* ———

As a child of God, it is my right to have tremendous satisfaction on the job, and to be able to thoroughly enjoy the fruit of my labor. God has given me great wealth and many possessions, and He enables me to enjoy them.

I lay claim to my right to have a job that brings me happiness and fulfill-ment. This is God's gift to me and I receive it with thanksgiving.

I do not waste time worrying about riches or other things—I am too occu-pied with my heavenly Father and the gladness that He brings me.

(Deuteronomy 8:18; Proverbs 21:20,21; Matthew 6:24-33; Hebrews 13:5,6; Ecclesiastes 2:24-26; 3:12,13,22; 8:15; 9:9)

ECCLESIASTES 7:12 AMP

For wisdom is a defense even as money is a defense, but the excellency of knowl-edge is that wisdom shields and preserves the life of him who has it.

——— *DECLARATION OF FAITH* ———

I am sheltered by my wisdom as well as the wealth that God has provided for me. I store up an abundance of knowledge and my wisdom preserves my life.

(1 Corinthians 1:30; 2:6-16; Ecclesiastes 9:18; Proverbs 3:18)

ECCLESIASTES 7:16-18 KJV

Be not righteous over much; neither make thyself over wise: why shouldest thou destroy thyself? Be not over much wicked, neither be thou foolish: why shouldest thou die before thy time? It is good that thou shouldest take hold of this; yea, also from this withdraw not thine hand: for he that feareth God shall come forth of them all.

——— *DECLARATION OF FAITH* ———

I avoid all extremes in my life. I am not over-righteous, thereby making myself overbearing and annoying; nor am I over-wise, thereby making myself haughty and unteachable. I maintain a well-balanced walk with God.

I reject wickedness and foolishness so that I will live a full and abundant life.

(Proverbs 25:16; Philippians 3:6; Romans 12:3; Psalm 55:23; Ecclesiastes 3:14; 5:7; 8:12,13)

ECCLESIASTES 8:1 NKJV

Who *is* like a wise *man?* And who knows the interpretation of a thing? A man's wisdom makes his face shine, And the sternness of his face is changed.

——— *DECLARATION OF FAITH* ———

Wisdom brightens my face and turns my stern countenance into a welcoming radiance.

(Proverbs 4:8,9; Acts 6:15; Deuteronomy 28:50; Psalm 3:3)

ECCLESIASTES 8:15 AMP

Then I commended enjoyment, because a man has no better thing under the sun [without God] than to eat and to drink and to be joyful, for that will remain with him in his toil through the days of his life which God gives him under the sun.

——— *DECLARATION OF FAITH* ———

My life is given to me by God for my enjoyment. I will eat, drink and be happy in His presence. Joy accompanies me in my work all the days of my life. I show my appreciation by receiving and enjoying all that God has given me.

(Ecclesiastes 2:24-26; 3:12,13,22; 5:18-20; 9:9; Philippians 4:4,13,19; 1 Timothy 6:17)

ECCLESIASTES 9:7-10 AMP

Go your way, eat your bread with joy, and drink your wine with a cheerful heart [if you are righteous, wise, and in the hands of God], for God has already accepted your works. Let your garments be always white [with purity], and let your head not lack [the] oil [of gladness]. Live joyfully with the wife whom you love all the days of your vain life which He has given you under the sun—all the days of futility. For that is your portion in this life and in your work at which you toil under the sun. Whatever your hand finds to do, do it with all your might, for there is no work or device or knowledge or wisdom in Sheol (the place of the dead), where you are going.

——— *DECLARATION OF FAITH* ———

I eat and drink with gladness and a joyful heart, for God has given me His favor and has accepted me as His own. I am clothed in His righteousness and my mind is saturated with His anointing.

My wife/husband is an absolute joy and a blessing to me.

My employment brings me tremendous happiness and satisfaction.

All of this is my lot in life. God has laid it all before me and has given me the right to receive it.

Whatever I set my hand to accomplish, I do with all of my might. I am filled with an abundance of knowledge and wisdom, and I plan great things for the glory of God.

(Ecclesiastes 2:24-26; 3:12,13,22; 5:18-20; 8:15; 1 Timothy 6:17; 1 John 2:27; Proverbs 5:18; Galatians 4:5,6; Deuteronomy 28:12; Colossians 3:17,23,24)

ECCLESIASTES 10:20 NIV

Do not revile the king even in your thoughts,
or curse the rich in your bedroom,
because a bird of the air may carry your words,
and a bird on the wing may report what you say.

──── *DECLARATION OF FAITH* ────

I do not murmur against those who are in authority over me, nor do I curse the wealthy in my bedroom. When a report comes of something that I have said, it will be one of blessing that will bring great joy to the hearer.

(Exodus 22:28; Acts 23:5; Numbers 14:8; Romans 13:1-5)

ECCLESIASTES 11:1,2 NKJV

Cast your bread upon the waters,
For you will find it after many days.
Give a serving to seven, and also to eight,
For you do not know what evil will be on the earth.

──── *DECLARATION OF FAITH* ────

I cast my bread upon the waters and it comes back to me after many days. I give portions of my abundance to several different ministries, thereby securing my harvest in the day of disaster.

(Luke 6:38; 2 Corinthians 9:5-11; Galatians 6:9,10; Hebrews 6:10; 1 Timothy 6:17-19)

ECCLESIASTES 11:4-6 KJV

He that observeth the wind shall not sow; and he that regardeth the clouds shall not reap. As thou knowest not what *is* the way of the spirit, *nor* how the bones *do grow* in the womb of her that is with child: even so thou knowest not the works of God who maketh all. In the morning sow thy seed, and in the evening withhold not thine hand: for thou knowest not whether shall prosper, either this or that, or whether they both *shall be* alike good.

DECLARATION OF FAITH

Circumstances do not control my giving. I plant my seed regardless of life's storms and reap my harvest in the midst of adversity. God alone is my provider and I am focused on the precepts of His Word. I sow my seed in the morning and work with my hands until evening, for I have His Word that He will prosper what I set my hand to do and that I will reap an abundant harvest from what I have sown.

(Genesis 39:23, Psalm 1:1-3, Luke 6:38; Hebrews 11:1; Deuteronomy 28:12,13; 2 Corinthians 9:6)

ECCLESIASTES 11:9 NKJV

Rejoice, O young man, in your youth, And let your heart cheer you in the days of your youth; Walk in the ways of your heart, and in the sight of your eyes; But know that for all these God will bring you into judgment.

DECLARATION OF FAITH

I will live my life in gladness in the days of my youth and focus my heart on those things that bring glory to God.

(Numbers 15:39; Job 31:7; Ecclesiastes 2:10; Proverbs 22:6; Philippians 4:4)

ECCLESIASTES 12:1 NIV

Remember your Creator in the days of your youth, before the days of trouble come and the years approach when you will say, "I find no pleasure in them."

DECLARATION OF FAITH

I am not so foolish as to wait until I am old before giving God my best. My heavenly Father has first place in my life today, tomorrow and forevermore.

(2 Chronicles 34:3; Proverbs 22:6; Deuteronomy 6:5-7)

ECCLESIASTES 12:13 NKJV

Let us hear the conclusion of the whole matter: Fear God and keep His commandments, for this is man's all.

—— *DECLARATION OF FAITH* ——

The supreme law of my life is simple: I will give to my Lord the honor that is due Him and keep His commandments with a tenacity that makes the devil cringe.

(Deuteronomy 6:2,5-7; 10:12; Micah 6:8; John 15:10-17)

CHAPTER TWENTY-TWO

SONG OF SOLOMON

T his is the great song of love. In Hebrew tradition it is referred to as the Song of all Songs, or the Best of all Songs. Literally, it is a poem written by Solomon to express his love for his wife. Metaphorically, it is a song that shows the love that Christ has for His church. Ephesians 5 tells us the marriage itself is a type of Christ and the church.

The promises of the Song of Solomon are promises of love. As you pray these prayers, remember the sacrifices that God made in order to become one with you.

╬

SONG OF SOLOMON 2:3-6 KJV

As the apple tree among the trees of the wood, so *is* my beloved among the sons. I sat down under his shadow with great delight, and his fruit *was* sweet to my taste. He brought me to the banqueting house, and his banner over me *was* love. Stay me with flagons, comfort me with apples: for I *am* sick of love. His left hand *is* under my head, and his right hand doth embrace me.

——— *DECLARATION OF FAITH* ———

I sit in security and delight under the Lord's shade and enjoy the fruit of what He has done for me. He has brought me to His banqueting table and bids me to partake of His delicacies. His banner over me is love. His left hand is under my head and His right arm embraces me forevermore.

(Psalm 23:5; 91:1,2; Exodus 17:15; John 10:28,29; Deuteronomy 33:12)

SONG OF SOLOMON 8:1-3 NKJV

Oh, that you were like my brother,
Who nursed at my mother's breasts!
If I should find you outside,
I would kiss you;

I would not be despised.
I would lead you *and* bring you
Into the house of my mother,
She *who* used to instruct me.
I would cause you to drink of spiced wine,
Of the juice of my pomegranate.
(TO THE DAUGHTERS OF JERUSALEM)
His left hand *is* under my head,
And his right hand embraces me.

——— *DECLARATION OF FAITH* ———

The Lord Jesus is my elder brother. He is just as much a brother to me as if we had the same mother. I stand in His presence free of all guilt and inferiority. It is my pleasure to give Him all of the best of what I have.

(Romans 8:1; 28,29; Hebrews 2:11; Malachi 3:6-12; John 10:28,29; Deuteronomy 33:12)

SONG OF SOLOMON 8:6,7 NIV

Place me like a seal over your heart, like a seal on your arm; for love is as strong as death, its jealousy unyielding as the grave. It burns like blazing fire, like a mighty flame. Many waters cannot quench love; rivers cannot wash it away. If one were to give all the wealth of his house for love, it would be utterly scorned.

——— *DECLARATION OF FAITH* ———

I am placed like a seal over the Lord's heart—like a signet on His arm. Many waters cannot quench His love for me—rivers cannot wash it away.

(Ephesians 1:13,14; Romans 8:38,39; Psalm 103:1-18; John 6:27)

CHAPTER TWENTY-THREE

ISAIAH

Isaiah is noted by many as the main prophet who prophesied of the Messiah. Therefore, many of the promises in Isaiah deal with Jesus and what He did for us. As we pray the promises in Isaiah we are praying our redemption. In Isaiah we have the great promise of our healing, that Jesus bore our sickness and carried our pains. We also have promises of peace and protection.

As you pray the promises in the book of Isaiah. Keep your eyes fixed upon Jesus, the author and finisher of your faith. Know that He is taking your prayer to the Father on your behalf and that because of Him you have everything that you are saying.

ISAIAH 1:16-19 KJV

Wash you, make you clean; put away the evil of your doings from before mine eyes; cease to do evil; Learn to do well; seek judgment, relieve the oppressed, judge the fatherless, plead for the widow. Come now, and let us reason together, saith the Lord: though your sins be as scarlet, they shall be as white as snow; though they be red like crimson, they shall be as wool.

——— DECLARATION OF FAITH ———

I am cleansed by the blood of Jesus and have ceased from the practice of sin in my life. I do what I know to be right. I seek justice, encourage the oppressed, defend the cause of the orphan, and plead the case of the widow.

Though my sins were red as scarlet, they are now as white as snow; though they were like crimson, they are now like wool; though they indelibly stained my nature, I have been cleansed, renewed and made as righteous as God Himself.

I am willing to do what the Word commands and I am obedient to all of God's precepts. Because of this, I am ensured a harvest of abundance. I can fully expect God's best in my life.

(Romans 8:3,4; 1 John 1:7; 3:6; Job 29:12-17; James 1:27; 2 Corinthians 5:17-21; Deuteronomy 28:1-14)

ISAIAH 3:10 NKJV

"Say to the righteous that *it shall be* well *with them,* For they shall eat the fruit of their doings."

——— *DECLARATION OF FAITH* ———

I am the righteousness of God in Christ Jesus. It goes well with me always, and I remain secure in all that I do. I have an inheritance to enjoy in this earth and have a right to the abundant fruit of my labor.

(Romans 4:1-23; Psalm 91:10; Ecclesiastes 2:24; 3:22; 8:15; Malachi 3:18)

ISAIAH 7:9 NIV

"'The head of Ephraim is Samaria, and the head of Samaria is only Remaliah's son. If you do not stand firm in your faith, you will not stand at all.'"

——— *DECLARATION OF FAITH* ———

I stand firm, fixed and unwavering in the battle of faith. When the fight is over, I will be the one standing.

(Ephesians 6:13; 1 Timothy 6:12; 2 Corinthians 4:5-11)

ISAIAH 8:9,10 AMP

Make an uproar and be broken in pieces, O you peoples [rage, raise the war cry, do your worst, and be utterly dismayed]! Give ear, all you [our enemies] of far countries. Gird yourselves [for war], and be thrown into consternation! Gird yourselves, and be [utterly] dismayed! Take counsel together [against Judah], but it shall come to nought; speak the word, but it will not stand, for God is with us [Immanuel]!

——— *DECLARATION OF FAITH* ———

The army of the enemy has raised a war cry against me to their own destruction. They prepare for battle, but shall be shattered! They devise strategies, but they are thwarted. All of their plans against me are put to confusion and shall not stand, for God is on my side and together we are an invincible pair.

(Psalm 2:1-9; 35:4; Romans 8:31; Nehemiah 4:4)

ISAIAH 8:12 NIV

"Do not call conspiracy everything that these people call conspiracy; do not fear what they fear, and do not dread it."

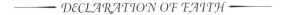

I do not look for a conspiracy against me at every turn, nor do I fear what the world fears. With God on my side, I am not afraid of anything.

(1 Peter 3:13-16; Romans 8:31; Joshua 1:5-9)

ISAIAH 8:18-20 KJV

Behold, I and the children whom the Lord hath given me *are* for signs and for wonders in Israel from the Lord of hosts, which dwelleth in mount Zion. And when they shall say unto you, Seek unto them that have familiar spirits, and unto wizards that peep, and that mutter: should not a people seek unto their God? for the living to the dead? To the law and to the testimony: if they speak not according to this word, *it is* because *there is* no light in them.

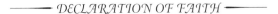

I am set in this earth as the covenant partner of almighty God. Signs and wonders are commonplace in my life. They are a natural branch of kingdom living.

I will look to the Lord alone for power in this life. I do not listen to people who tell me to consult mediums, spiritists, or psychics, nor am I so foolish as to consult the dead on behalf of the living. God is dwelling within me and has promised to guide me into all truth. I know that the answers that I seek are found in His Word. All advice in opposition to the Word is useless to me.

(Leviticus 19:31; 20:6,27; Micah 5:12; Exodus 22:18; Mark 16:17-20; John 16:13)

ISAIAH 9:2-6 KJV

The people that walked in darkness have seen a great light: they that dwell in the land of the shadow of death, upon them hath the light shined. Thou hast multiplied the nation, *and* not increased the joy: they joy before thee according to the joy in harvest, *and* as *men* rejoice when they divide the spoil. For thou hast broken the yoke of his burden, and the staff of his shoulder, the rod of his oppressor, as in the day of Midian. For every battle of the warrior *is* with confused noise, and garments rolled in blood; but *this* shall be with burning *and* fuel of fire. For unto us a child is born, unto us a son is given: and the government shall be upon his shoulder: and his name shall be called Wonderful, Counsellor, The mighty God, The everlasting Father, The Prince of Peace.

─── *DECLARATION OF FAITH* ───

I have seen the great Light, and my joy is increased immeasurably. I rejoice before the Lord as if I were at a great party or a feast.

God has shattered the yoke that burdened me and has broken its bar from my shoulders. The rod of the oppressor has become a brittle twig.

All of my battle gear will one day be burned because of the great redemption that was wrought for me.

Jesus is my Lord! He was sent for me personally and I am identified with Him in every way. He is my wonderful Counselor, my mighty God, my everlasting Father, and my Prince of Peace.

(1 John 1:1-9; Colossians 2:13-15; Galatians 2:19-21; Isaiah 61:1-3; John 3:16)

ISAIAH 11:2-5 AMP

And the Spirit of the Lord shall rest upon Him—the Spirit of wisdom and understanding, the Spirit of counsel and might, the Spirit of knowledge and of the reverential and obedient fear of the Lord—And shall make Him of quick understanding, and His delight shall be in the reverential and obedient fear of the Lord. And He shall not judge by the sight of His eyes, neither decide by the hearing of His ears; But with righteousness and justice shall He judge the poor and decide with fairness for the meek, the poor, and the downtrodden of the earth; and He shall smite the earth and the oppressor with the rod of His mouth, and with the breath of His lips He shall slay the wicked. And righteousness shall be the girdle of His waist and faithfulness the girdle of His loins.

─── *DECLARATION OF FAITH* ───

I am in Christ Jesus and I live through Him.

The Holy Spirit dwells within me. In Him, I have a spirit of wisdom and understanding, of counsel and power, of knowledge and an awe-filled reverence for the Lord.

It is my greatest joy to be in God's presence—trusting in Him and living my life for Him. I do not put my complete trust in what my eyes see or what my ears hear. I trust in the Word.

I treat the poor and downtrodden of the earth with kindness, righteousness, and justice.

I strike the oppressor with the rod of my mouth—mighty words that bring his destruction.

Righteousness is my belt and faithfulness is like a sash about my waist.

(John 14:12; Acts 17:28; 1 Corinthians 1:30; 2:6-16; 2 Corinthians 5:7; Isaiah 55:8-11)

ISAIAH 12:1-3 KJV

And in that day thou shalt say, O Lord, I will praise thee: though thou wast angry with me, thine anger is turned away, and thou comfortedst me. Behold, God is my salvation; I will trust, and not be afraid: for the Lord Jehovah is my strength and my song; he also is become my salvation. Therefore with joy shall ye draw water out of the wells of salvation.

DECLARATION OF FAITH

God has turned His fierce anger away from me and has comforted me instead. He has become my salvation. I will trust in Him and not be afraid.

The Lord is my strength and my song. He has saved me and placed me into His family with full rights as His own son/daughter. I take my place with joy and draw my provision from the wells of His salvation.

(Galatians 4:5; Romans 8:1; Isaiah 43:1-13; 2 Timothy 1:7)

ISAIAH 26:3,4 NKJV

You will keep *him* in perfect peace, *whose* mind *is* stayed *on You*, because he trusts in You. Trust in the Lord forever, for in YAH, the LORD, *is* everlasting strength.

DECLARATION OF FAITH

My mind is steadfast, trusting in the Lord, and He keeps me in perfect peace. I am committed to the Lord forever. He alone is my eternal Rock.

(Proverbs 29:25; Deuteronomy 4:23)

ISAIAH 26:7-9 KJV

The way of the just *is* uprightness: thou, most upright, dost weigh the path of the just. Yea, in the way of thy judgments, O Lord, have we waited for thee; the desire of *our* soul *is* to thy name, and to the remembrance of thee. With my soul have I desired thee in the night; yea, with my spirit within me will I seek thee early: for when thy judgments *are* in the earth, the inhabitants of the world will learn righteousness.

DECLARATION OF FAITH

My path is a level one and the Holy Spirit makes it smooth before me. I wait expectantly in the course of His precepts. I know that His Word will work for me and achieve its purpose in my life. I am at the edge of my seat in anticipation of its fulfillment. I am overwhelmed with desire for the fame and glory of my Father God and that His name be remembered as faithful to all generations.

My soul clings to You in the night, Father, and in the morning my spirit reaches out for Your embrace.

(Isaiah 55:11; Hebrews 12:13; John 16:13; Proverbs 15:19; Psalm 119:81)

ISAIAH 26:12 NIV

Lord, you establish peace for us; all that we have accomplished you have done for us.

─── *DECLARATION OF FAITH* ───

My heavenly Father has ordained peace, favor, and an abundance of blessings for me. He has worked in and through me to achieve all that I have done. What a privilege it is to be in such an incredible partnership!

(Philippians 2:13; Ephesians 2:14; Romans 14:17)

ISAIAH 27:2-4 KJV

In that day sing ye unto her, A vineyard of red wine. I the Lord do keep it; I will water it every moment: lest any hurt it, I will keep it night and day. Fury is not in me: who would set the briers and thorns against me in battle? I would go through them, I would burn them together.

─── *DECLARATION OF FAITH* ───

I am as a fruitful vineyard and the Lord is the husbandman. He watches over me continually and gives me of all the nourishment that I need. He guards me day and night and will not allow any harm to come to me. When briars and thorns seek to entangle me, the Lord marches against them as a warrior in battle and sets them all on fire.

(Psalm 1:1-3; 18:3-19; John 15:1-7; Nehemiah 1:5,6)

ISAIAH 30:15 NIV

This is what the Sovereign Lord, the Holy One of Israel, says: "In repentance and rest is your salvation, in quietness and trust is your strength, but you would have none of it."

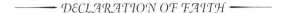
——— *DECLARATION OF FAITH* ———

In repentance and rest is my salvation, and in quietness and trust is my strength.

(Romans 2:4; Psalm 118:8-14; Isaiah 40:28-31)

ISAIAH 30:18-21 KJV

And therefore will the Lord wait, that he may be gracious unto you, and therefore will he be exalted, that he may have mercy upon you: for the Lord *is* a God of judgment: blessed *are* all they that wait for him. For the people shall dwell in Zion at Jerusalem: thou shalt weep no more: he will be very gracious unto thee at the voice of thy cry; when he shall hear it, he will answer thee. And *though* the Lord give you the bread of adversity, and the water of affliction, yet shall not thy teachers be removed into a corner any more, but thine eyes shall see thy teachers: And thine ears shall hear a word behind thee, saying, This *is* the way, walk ye in it, when ye turn to the right hand, and when ye turn to the left.

——— *DECLARATION OF FAITH* ———

It is my Father's deepest desire to give me favor. He rises to show me compassion and to consider my situation as I enter His presence. I am intimately familiar with His love and His desire for justice on my behalf. Therefore, I will wait for Him with full confidence in His faithfulness.

The Lord is generous and loving towards me when I call out to Him, and He is quick to respond when I need His help.

In the midst of adversity and affliction, the Lord shows me the way to go. Wherever I turn, I hear His tender voice behind me saying, "This is the way, son/daughter; walk in it."

(1 Corinthians 1:9; Isaiah 58:11; Psalm 46:1; 103:1-18)

ISAIAH 32:17-20 KJV

And the work of righteousness shall be peace; and the effect of righteousness quietness and assurance for ever. And my people shall dwell in a peaceable habitation, and in sure dwellings, and in quiet resting places; When it shall hail, coming down on the forest; and the city shall be low in a low place. Blessed are ye that sow beside all waters, that send forth thither the feet of the ox and the ass.

——— *DECLARATION OF FAITH* ———

The fruit of my righteousness brings me peace, and the effect of my righteousness brings me quietness and confidence forever.

I live in a peaceful dwelling, a safe and secure home, and in undisturbed places of rest.

Though adversity rises, raining destruction on all sides, even if those around me are completely annihilated, I remain secure and blessed, sowing my seed by every stream and enjoying God's abundant increase in my life.

(Psalm 91:7; Proverbs 12:7; Genesis 8:22; 2 Corinthians 9:6-11; Ecclesiastes 11:1,2)

ISAIAH 33:2 NKJV

O Lord, be gracious to us; We have waited for You. Be their arm every morning, our salvation also in the time of trouble.

——— DECLARATION OF FAITH ———

I reach out to my heavenly Father with all of my heart and He responds to me with His grace and overwhelming compassion. He is my strength every morning and my salvation in times of trouble.

(Psalm 5:3; Hebrews 4:16)

ISAIAH 33:5,6 AMP

The Lord is exalted, for He dwells on high; He will fill Zion with justice and righteousness (moral and spiritual rectitude in every area and relation). And there shall be stability in your times, an abundance of salvation, wisdom, and knowledge; the reverent fear and worship of the Lord is your treasure and His.

——— DECLARATION OF FAITH ———

I trust in the Lord with all of my heart and He fills me with His justice and righteousness. He is the sure foundation of my life and my stability in every situation. Out of His abundance, He brings me a full supply of wisdom, knowledge and salvation for every circumstance that I face. As His son/daughter, I have free access to all of His treasuries.

(Proverbs 3:5-10; 1 Corinthians 1:30; 2:6-16; Romans 5:17; 8:16-21,32; Galatians 4:5)

ISAIAH 33:13-24 KJV

Hear, ye *that are* far off, what I have done; and, ye *that are* near, acknowledge my might. The sinners in Zion are afraid; fearfulness hath surprised the hypocrites. Who among us shall dwell with the devouring fire? who among us shall dwell with everlasting burnings? He that walketh righteously, and speaketh uprightly; he that despiseth the gain of oppressions, that shaketh his hands from holding of bribes, that stoppeth his ears from hearing of blood, and shutteth his eyes from seeing evil; He shall dwell on high: his place of defence *shall be* the munitions of rocks: bread shall be given him; his waters *shall be* sure. Thine eyes shall see the king in his beauty: they shall behold the land that is very far off. Thine heart shall meditate terror. Where *is* the scribe? where *is* the receiver? where *is* he that counted the towers? Thou shalt not see a fierce people, a people of a deeper speech than thou canst perceive; of a stammering tongue, *that thou canst* not understand. Look upon Zion, the city of our solemnities: thine eyes shall see Jerusalem a quiet habitation, a tabernacle *that* shall not be taken down; not one of the stakes thereof shall ever be removed, neither shall any of the cords thereof be broken. But there the glorious Lord *will be* unto us a place of broad rivers *and* streams; wherein shall go no galley with oars, neither shall gallant ship pass thereby. For the Lord *is* our judge, the Lord *is* our lawgiver, the Lord *is* our king; he will save us. Thy tacklings are loosed; they could not well strengthen their mast, they could not spread the sail: then is the prey of a great spoil divided; the lame take the prey. And the inhabitant shall not say, I am sick: the people that dwell therein *shall be* forgiven *their* iniquity.

———— DECLARATION OF FAITH ————

I cheerfully acknowledge the Lord's power in my life. In Him, I dwell unharmed in a consuming fire and in the midst of everlasting burning.

I walk righteously before Him and speak those things that bring glory to His name. I do not acquire wealth through extortion or at the expense of others, nor do I accept any bribe. My ears are shut against thoughts of harming my fellow man and I will not let my eyes take in evil things.

I dwell on the heights and my refuge is as a mountain fortress.

My bread is continually supplied and my water never fails me.

No enemy has the power to overtake me, or those whom I have covered.

I have a revelation of my King in all of His beauty—a beauty that is revealed in and through me. By Him, I am free to go forth fearlessly into the land and take back what the devil has stolen.

I ponder what once terrified me and deride all that the enemy attempted against me in vain.

Jesus has won the victory for me and the enemy is no longer a concern.

I have taken my place in the church, the house of God, which He has established in peace—a tent that shall not be moved, its stakes never pulled up and its ropes never broken. The Lord is our mighty One who makes Zion, the Church, a place of broad rivers and streams. He is now and will ever be my Judge, my Lawgiver, my King, and my Savior. He has delivered me from the hands of the enemy and has divided to me my portion of the spoils of war. I now understand the power of the spoken word. I refuse to say, "I am ill." To the contrary, I am redeemed! I am filled with health, energy and vitality! All of my sins have been forgiven, and I enjoy the blessings that my new covenant with God has provided!

(Colossians 2:2,3; Psalm 91:9,10; 112:1-3; Ephesians 1:17-23; Matthew 6:11; Galatians 3:13; Joel 2:25; Job 36:11; Proverbs 18:20,21)

ISAIAH 35:3-10 KJV

Strengthen ye the weak hands, and confirm the feeble knees. Say to them *that are* of a fearful heart, Be strong, fear not: behold, your God will come *with* vengeance, *even* God *with* a recompence; he will come and save you. Then the eyes of the blind shall be opened, and the ears of the deaf shall be unstopped. Then shall the lame *man* leap as an hart, and the tongue of the dumb sing: for in the wilderness shall waters break out, and streams in the desert. And the parched ground shall become a pool, and the thirsty land springs of water: in the habitation of dragons, where each lay, *shall be* grass with reeds and rushes. And an highway shall be there, and a way, and it shall be called The way of holiness; the unclean shall not pass over it; but it *shall be* for those: the wayfaring men, though fools, shall not err *therein*. No lion shall be there, nor *any* ravenous beast shall go up thereon, it shall not be found there; but the redeemed shall walk *there*: And the ransomed of the Lord shall return, and come to Zion with songs and everlasting joy upon their heads: they shall obtain joy and gladness, and sorrow and sighing shall flee away.

———— DECLARATION OF FAITH ————

I give strength to those with feeble hands and hold steady those whose knees are giving way. I am a steadfast source of encouragement to those who are afraid of an evil report. I say to those who are terrified, "Be strong and take courage, for God is on your side! He loves you and will come to your aid with a vengeance and with divine retribution. He will not forsake you. Because of His great love for you, He will deliver you."

Because of this, the eyes of the blind are opened, the ears of the deaf are unstopped, the lame leap like a deer, the mute tongue shouts for joy, water gushes forth in the midst of a wilderness, and nourishment flows into a desert land. The burning sand has become like a pool and the cracked earth is fed with springs of fresh water. Where devils once ran rampant, God's blessings now flow.

A highway called The Way of Holiness is with me, and those who love the Word flock to it. Satan and his hordes look upon it and flee in stark terror, for we who walk in the way are redeemed and translated into a new kingdom. We enter *that kingdom with singing, and everlasting joy crowns our heads. Happiness and joy overtake us and sorrow and sighing flee away.*

(Psalm 18:3-19; Colossians 1:10-14; Deuteronomy 3:28; Mark 16:15-18)

ISAIAH 38:16-19 KJV

O Lord, by these *things men* live, and in all these *things is* the life of my spirit: so wilt thou recover me, and make me to live. Behold, for peace I had great bitterness: but thou hast in love to my soul *delivered it* from the pit of corruption: for thou hast cast all my sins behind thy back. For the grave cannot praise thee, death can *not* celebrate thee: they that go down into the pit cannot hope for thy truth. The living, the living, he shall praise thee, as I *do* this day: the father to the children shall make known thy truth.

——— *DECLARATION OF FAITH* ———

The Lord restores me to perfect health and vitality. Because of His love for me, He keeps me from the pit of destruction and puts all of my sins behind Him, refusing to ever think of them again.

I will sing praises to Him in the land of the living and tell my children of His faithfulness on my behalf.

(Psalm 103:1-13; Deuteronomy 6:7)

ISAIAH 40:1,2 KJV

Comfort ye, comfort ye my people, saith your God. Speak ye comfortably to Jerusalem, and cry unto her, that her warfare is accomplished, that her iniquity is pardoned: for she hath received of the Lord's hand double for all her sins.

——— *DECLARATION OF FAITH* ———

I have received from the Lord's hand double payment for all of my sins. The sin issue is forever settled and I am now resting in the comfort of my God.

(Zechariah 9:12; Isaiah 61:7; Hebrews 10:10-17)

ISAIAH 40:10,11 NKJV

Behold, the Lord God shall come with a strong *hand,* and His arm shall rule for Him; Behold, His reward *is* with Him, and His work before Him. He will feed His flock like a shepherd; He will gather the lambs with His arm, and carry *them* in His bosom, *and* gently lead those who are with young.

The Sovereign Lord of the universe dwells within me with all of His power and authority. He has consecrated me as His own son/daughter and partner in life. His reward is with Him and His recompense accompanies Him. He dotes over me and embraces me in love. He carries me close to His heart and takes special care of my children.

(Hebrews 2:6-13; Psalm 103:17: 1 John 4:4; Colossians 1:27-29)

Isaiah 40:29-31 KJV

He giveth power to the faint; and to them that have no might he increaseth strength. Even the youths shall faint and be weary, and the young men shall utterly fall: But they that wait upon the Lord shall renew their strength; they shall mount up with wings as eagles; they shall run, and not be weary; and they shall walk, and not faint.

——— *DECLARATION OF FAITH* ———

The Lord is my strength and my life. He is faithful to me and increases my power so that I can be confident in every situation. Even youths get tired and young men stumble and fall, but I have my hope in the Lord. He renews my strength and spiritual force making me soar on wings like an eagle. I run my race and never burn out. So long as I stay focused on Him, I will never grow weary in my walk with Jesus.

(Proverbs 24:5; Psalm 130:5-8; Isaiah 30:15; 2 Corinthians 4:8-10)

Isaiah 41:8-20 KJV

But thou, Israel, *art* my servant, Jacob whom I have chosen, the seed of Abraham my friend. *Thou* whom I have taken from the ends of the earth, and called thee from the chief men thereof, and said unto thee, Thou *art* my servant; I have chosen thee, and not cast thee away. Fear thou not; for I *am* with thee: be not dismayed; for I *am* thy God: I will strengthen thee; yea, I will help thee; yea, I will uphold thee with the right hand of my righteousness. Behold, all they that were incensed against thee shall be ashamed and confounded: they shall be as nothing; and they that strive with thee shall perish. Thou shalt seek them, and shalt not find them, *even* them that contended with thee: they that war against thee shall be as nothing, and as a thing of nought. For I the Lord thy God will hold thy right hand, saying unto thee, Fear not; I will help thee. Fear not, thou worm Jacob, *and* ye men of Israel; I will help thee, saith the Lord, and thy redeemer, the Holy One of Israel. Behold, I will make thee a new sharp threshing instrument having teeth: thou shalt thresh the mountains, and beat *them* small, and shalt make the hills as chaff. Thou shalt fan them, and the wind shall carry them away, and the whirlwind shall scatter them: and thou shalt rejoice in the Lord, *and* shalt glory in the Holy One of Israel. *When* the poor and needy seek water, and *there is* none, *and* their tongue faileth for thirst, I the Lord will hear them, I the God of Israel will not forsake them. I will open rivers in high places, and fountains in the midst of the valleys: I will make the wilderness a pool of water, and the dry land springs of water. I will plant in the wilderness the cedar, the shittah tree, and the myrtle, and the oil tree; I will set in the desert the fir tree, *and* the pine, and the box tree together: That they may see, and know, and consider, and understand together, that the hand of the Lord hath done this, and the Holy One of Israel hath created it.

──── DECLARATION OF FAITH ────

I am a descendent of Abraham, the father of my faith. God loves me with all of His heart and has chosen me out from among all of the people of the earth to be His own son/daughter.

I have no cause for fear, for my God is with me. I will not be dismayed, for God is my Father and He has promised to never leave me, nor forsake me. He strengthens me and assists me in every circumstance. He upholds me with His righteous right hand so that my victory is made certain.

All who rage against me shall be disgraced and put to shame. Those who oppose me shall come to nothing and their cause against me shall be eliminated. When I look about me for a formidable foe, a strong enemy and worthy opponent, I find none. The greater One is within me and He makes all of my enemies seem like harmless bugs in my presence.

The Lord, God of heaven and earth, takes hold of my right hand and says to me, "Son/Daughter, don't you worry about a thing. I've got your back and won't allow anything to harm you. I'm always here for you to help you with anything you need. So don't be afraid. Think about it, Son/Daughter, I am your Father. You belong to me and I belong to you. Is there ever a reason to be afraid? I have redeemed you and recreated you. You are a new creation in Christ Jesus, a threshing sledge, new and sharp, with many teeth; a fierce warrior and fearsome prince/princess in my kingdom. For you, no task is too difficult and no foe unconquerable. So rejoice, my son/daughter. Enjoy My presence in your life. I will always be with you. I promise, you will never go thirsty again. I will answer your every prayer and never abandon you—no child, not for any reason. I will make rivers flow on your barren heights and turn your desert places into pools of water. All that you have I will bless for your sake. Yes, Son/Daughter, for your sake. I want all the world to know how much I love you—how proud I am of you—and what joy you bring to my heart. I love you Son/Daughter. Never forget that."

(Galatians 3:7; Psalm 2; 1 Corinthians 15:57; Deuteronomy 11:25; Hebrews 13:5,6; John 6:35-40; Colossians 2:9-15)

ISAIAH 42:6-8 NIV

"I, the Lord, have called you in righteousness; I will take hold of your hand. I will keep you and will make you to be a covenant for the people and a light for the Gentiles, to open eyes that are blind, to free captives from prison and to release from the dungeon those who sit in darkness. I am the Lord; that is my name! I will not give my glory to another or my praise to idols."

——— DECLARATION OF FAITH ———

I have a covenant with God sealed with the blood of the Messiah. In Him, I am made complete. He has taken hold of my hand so that I can have confidence in every step that I take. He has made me His own child and has accepted responsibility for me. He keeps me close to His heart and will never let me go.

Through my Lord, I open the eyes of the blind and set the captives free. Those bound by the chains of darkness are released in my presence, for God is in me and His glory shines through me. It is my Lord, the anointed One and His anointing, who does these great and mighty works.

(John 10:34-38; 14:10-14; Hebrews 8:6-13; Acts 2:43; 4:30-33; 5:16; 6:8)

ISAIAH 42:16 NKJV

I will bring the blind by a way they did not know; I will lead them in paths they have not known. I will make darkness light before them, and crooked places straight. These things I will do for them, and not forsake them.

——— DECLARATION OF FAITH ———

The Holy Spirit is always with me to guide and direct me on the path of life. He turns the darkness into light before me and makes the rough places smooth. I have His Word that He will do this and that He will never leave me nor forsake me.

(John 16:13; Psalm 119:105; Isaiah 30:21; Hebrews 13:5,6)

ISAIAH 43:1-7 KJV

But now thus saith the Lord that created thee, O Jacob, and he that formed thee, O Israel, Fear not: for I have redeemed thee, I have called *thee* by thy name; thou *art* mine. When thou passest through the waters, I *will be* with thee; and through the rivers, they shall not overflow thee: when thou walkest through the fire, thou shalt not be burned; neither shall the flame kindle upon thee. For I *am* the Lord thy God, the Holy One of Israel, thy Saviour: I gave Egypt *for* thy ransom, Ethiopia and Seba for thee. Since thou wast precious in my sight, thou hast been honourable, and I have loved thee: therefore will I give men for thee, and people for thy life. Fear not: for I *am* with thee: I will bring thy seed from the east, and gather thee from the west; I will say to the north, Give up; and to the south, Keep not back: bring my sons from far, and my daughters from the ends of the earth; *Even* every one that is called by my name: for I have created him for my glory, I have formed him; yea, I have made him.

―――― *DECLARATION OF FAITH* ――――

I have no cause to fear, for I am redeemed! God called to me personally, speaking my name and calling me His own. I belong to God. I am His own son/daughter and He loves me with all of His heart. When I pass through the troubles of life, He is with me. The raging rivers cannot sweep over me. I walk through fiery trials with confidence and emerge unharmed. I stand in the midst of Satan's fire shielded by God's hedge of protection. Not even the smell of the smoke can touch me.

The Lord is my Savior and my Father. He has redeemed me from the hand of bondage. I am precious and honored in His sight. He is very proud of me. His love for me spans the heavens and touches the very edges of the universe.

I have nothing to fear in my life, for God, the Creator of heaven and earth, is my Father and shield of protection for my household. He redeems my children for my sake and proclaims them to be blessed.

I have a covenant with God in which I am His own child and heir. He has adopted me, recreated me with a divine nature, and has given me His own name. I am of God—called by His name and created for His glory.

(Romans 8:14-17; Job 1:10; Daniel 3:23-27; Psalm 5:11,12; 23:4,5; 103:17; Hebrews 2:14,15; 2 Corinthians 5:17; 2 Peter 1:4; John 17:22,23)

Isaiah 43:18-21 KJV

"But forget all that—it is nothing compared to what I am going to do. For I am about to do a brand-new thing. See, I have already begun! Do you not see it? I will make a pathway through the wilderness for my people to come home. I will create rivers for them in the desert! The wild animals in the fields will thank me, the jackals and ostriches, too, for giving them water in the wilderness. Yes, I will make springs in the desert, so that my chosen people can be refreshed. I have made Israel for myself, and they will someday honor me before the whole world."

———— *DECLARATION OF FAITH* ————

I refuse to worry about my past mistakes or let them get in the way of what I am doing right now. Whether I did wrong ten years ago or ten minutes ago, I put it behind me and press forward in my walk with God.

God is constantly working something new in my life. He makes a way for me in the desert and prospers me in the midst of the wasteland. No matter where I am, I have His provision.

I am created for God to be a blessing and to proclaim His praises throughout the earth.

(Philippians 3:13,14; Ephesians 2:10; Psalm 23:4,5; Genesis 12:1-3)

ISAIAH 43:25 NKJV

"I, even I, am He who blots out your transgressions for My own sake; and I will not remember your sins."

———— *DECLARATION OF FAITH* ————

God has blotted out my transgressions for only one reason: He loves me. Never again will He remember the foolishness of my past.

(Psalm 32:1,2; 103:12; Hebrews 10:15-17)

ISAIAH 44:1-5 KJV

Yet now hear, O Jacob my servant; and Israel, whom I have chosen: Thus saith the Lord that made thee, and formed thee from the womb, *which* will help thee; Fear not, O Jacob, my servant; and thou, Jesurun, whom I have chosen. For I will pour water upon him that is thirsty, and floods upon the dry ground: I will pour my spirit upon thy seed, and my blessing upon thine offspring: And they shall spring up *as* among the grass, as willows by the water courses. One shall say, I *am* the Lord's; and another shall call *himself* by the name of Jacob; and another shall subscribe *with* his hand unto the Lord, and surname *himself* by the name of Israel.

———— *DECLARATION OF FAITH* ————

I have been chosen by God to be His own son/daughter. He actually picked me to be a part of His family. He has recreated me in righteousness and helps me in every area of my life. He proclaims His blessing on all that I have and prospers all that I set my hand to do.

God has given me His Word that He will pour out His Spirit and His blessings on my children. They spring up like grass in a meadow—like poplar trees by flowing streams. Their life force is full of health, energy, and vitality. They never go hungry or parched. Each of them is grafted into God's family, taking the name of the Lord as their very own.

(John 15:16-19; Psalm 103:17; Genesis 12:1-3; Deuteronomy 28:12; Acts 11:14; Ephesians 3:15)

ISAIAH 44:24-26 KJV

Thus saith the Lord, thy redeemer, and he that formed thee from the womb, I am the Lord that maketh all things; that stretcheth forth the heavens alone; that spreadeth abroad the earth by myself; That frustrateth the tokens of the liars, and maketh diviners mad; that turneth wise men backward, and maketh their knowledge foolish; That confirmeth the word of his servant, and performeth the counsel of his messengers; that saith to Jerusalem, Thou shalt be inhabited; and to the cities of Judah, Ye shall be built, and I will raise up the decayed places thereof.

——— DECLARATION OF FAITH ———

I am redeemed and reborn as God's own son/daughter. The Creator of heaven and earth, and all that is in them, who foils the signs of the false prophet and turns the wisdom of the wise into nonsense, has recreated me to be a power force in this earth. He takes the words that I say and brings them to pass in my life. It is His purpose for me to have the things that I say.

(Mark 11:22-25; Proverbs 18:20,21; 2 Corinthians 5:17; 1 John 3:1,2)

ISAIAH 45:4-6 KJV

For Jacob my servant's sake, and Israel mine elect, I have even called thee by thy name: I have surnamed thee, though thou hast not known me. I am the Lord, and there is none else, there is no God beside me: I girded thee, though thou hast not known me.

——— DECLARATION OF FAITH ———

God has summoned me by name and has bestowed on me a title of great honor. He chose me from among all of the people of the earth even before I acknowledged His presence. He strengthens me in the power of His might so that I *may fulfill the calling He has given me. From the rising of the sun to the place of its setting, men know and see what God is doing in my life.*

(Genesis 12:1-3; Matthew 5:16; Proverbs 21:21; Ephesians 2:6,12,13; 3:14-19; 6:10)

ISAIAH 45:23,24 KJV

I have sworn by myself, the word is gone out of my mouth in righteousness, and shall not return, That unto me every knee shall bow, every tongue shall swear.

Surely, shall one say, in the Lord have I righteousness and strength: even to him shall men come; and all that are incensed against him shall be ashamed.

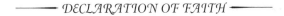

——— *DECLARATION OF FAITH* ———

I willingly and joyfully bow my knee to the Lord of heaven and earth. All of my righteousness and strength are found in Him.

(Philippians 2:10-13; Ephesians 6:10; Psalm 3:3)

ISAIAH 46:4 NKJV

Even to your old age, I am He, and even to gray hairs I will carry you! I have made, and I will bear; even I will carry, and will deliver you.

——— *DECLARATION OF FAITH* ———

The Lord sustains me even when I grow old and gray. He continually gives me health and vitality, and rescues me from every calamity.

(Deuteronomy 34:7; Psalm 91:16)

ISAIAH 46:13 NKJV

I bring My righteousness near, it shall not be far off; My salvation shall not linger. And I will place salvation in Zion, for Israel My glory.

——— *DECLARATION OF FAITH* ———

The righteousness of God has become my own. He brings me His deliverance without delay and awards me with the radiance of His splendor.

(Romans 10:3,4; 2 Corinthians 5:21)

ISAIAH 48:16-18 KJV

Come ye near unto me, hear ye this; I have not spoken in secret from the beginning; from the time that it was, there am I: and now the Lord God, and his

Spirit, hath sent me. Thus saith the Lord, thy Redeemer, the Holy One of Israel; I am the Lord thy God which teacheth thee to profit, which leadeth thee by the way that thou shouldest go. O that thou hadst hearkened to my commandments! then had thy peace been as a river, and thy righteousness as the waves of the sea.

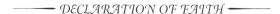

DECLARATION OF FAITH

I have been commissioned by God to proclaim the present fact of the kingdom to the entire world. But, I have not been called to do this alone, or of my own power. The Holy Spirit Himself has become my companion and partner. He teaches me the way that I should go and reveals to me what is best in life. He instructs me in the laws of increase and teaches me to profit. I pay careful attention to His commands and I am sensitive to His gentle leading. His peace flows through my life like a river and my righteousness is like the waves of the sea.

(Matthew 28:18-20; John 16:7,13-15; Romans 14:17)

ISAIAH 49:5,6 KJV

And now, saith the Lord that formed me from the womb to be his servant, to bring Jacob again to him, Though Israel be not gathered, yet shall I be glorious in the eyes of the Lord, and my God shall be my strength. And he said, It is a light thing that thou shouldest be my servant to raise up the tribes of Jacob, and to restore the preserved of Israel: I will also give thee for a light to the Gentiles, that thou mayest be my salvation unto the end of the earth.

DECLARATION OF FAITH

My heavenly Father is the strength of my life. In His eyes, I hold a position of tremendous honor. He has made me a light unto the world and has granted me the privilege of taking His salvation to the ends of the earth.

(Ephesians 2:6; Psalm 91:15; Matthew 5:14-16; 28:18-20)

ISAIAH 49:8-15 KJV

Thus saith the Lord, In an acceptable time have I heard thee, and in a day of salvation have I helped thee: and I will preserve thee, and give thee for a covenant of the people, to establish the earth, to cause to inherit the desolate heritages; That thou mayest say to the prisoners, Go forth; to them that *are* in darkness, Shew yourselves. They shall feed in the ways, and their pastures *shall be* in all high places. They shall not hunger nor thirst; neither shall the heat nor sun smite them: for he that hath mercy on them shall lead them, even by the springs of water shall he guide them. And I will make all my mountains a way, and my highways shall be exalted. Behold, these shall come from far: and, lo, these from the north and from the west; and these from the land of Sinim. Sing, O heavens; and be joyful, O earth; and break forth into singing, O mountains: for the Lord hath comforted his people, and will have mercy upon his afflicted. But Zion said, The Lord hath forsaken me, and my Lord hath forgotten me. Can a woman forget her sucking child, that she should not have compassion on the son of her womb? yea, they may forget, yet will I not forget thee.

—————— *DECLARATION OF FAITH* ——————

I have unlimited favor in the audience of my Father.

He makes each and every day a time of healing and deliverance for me.

He holds me close to His heart and honors His covenant with me.

He restores all that the devil has stolen from me.

He has assigned to me my portion of His matchless inheritance.

He has set me free from the strongholds of darkness.

He has made me His own son/daughter forevermore.

He leads me on a comfortable passage filled with provision. I feed beside the desert road and find pasture on every barren hill. I neither hunger nor thirst, nor does the desert sun beat upon me.

My Father loves me and is overjoyed that I have become His child.

He leads me and guides me beside springs of water.

He levels the mountains before me and causes my highways to be raised high above everything that would hinder my journey.

He comforts me and continually expresses His love for me.

He has given me His Word that He will never forsake me, nor forget that I am His son/daughter.

He has made me His own—a brand-new creation—a born-again child of a new and godly race.

I shout, rejoice, and burst into songs of triumph at the thought of what He has done for me!

(Deuteronomy 28:1-14; Hebrews 4:16; 13:5,6; Colossians 1:13; 2 Corinthians 1:3; 5:17; Titus 3:5; Proverbs 6:30,31; Psalm 5:11,12; 23)

ISAIAH 50:4-9 KJV

The Lord God hath given me the tongue of the learned, that I should know how to speak a word in season to *him that is* weary: he wakeneth morning by morning, he wakeneth mine ear to hear as the learned. The Lord God hath opened mine ear, and I was not rebellious, neither turned away back. I gave my back to the smiters, and my cheeks to them that plucked off the hair: I hid not my face from shame and spitting. For the Lord God will help me; therefore shall I not be confounded: therefore have I set my face like a flint, and I know that I shall not be ashamed. *He is* near that justifieth me; who will contend with me? let us stand together: who *is* mine adversary? let him come near to me. Behold, the Lord God will help me; who *is* he *that* shall condemn me? lo, they all shall wax old as a garment; the moth shall eat them up.

——— *DECLARATION OF FAITH* ———

The Sovereign Lord of heaven has given me a tongue of discernment. I know the power of the spoken word and how to speak it for the blessing and edification of the weary.

The Lord wakens me morning by morning and opens my ears to the voice of His teaching. I am not rebellious, nor do I draw back from hearing it. I will not turn aside to the voice of another.

I endure the persecution of those who do not accept the truth. I stand my ground against their ridicule and mockery, while neither raising my hand nor seeking vengeance against them.

Through it all, the Lord is my mainstay. He vindicates me and sees to it that I am not put to shame. I let my Advocate speak in my defense. What manner of person is so foolish as to argue with the Lord? Who will accuse me after the Lord has declared me to be innocent? Let them come to me and confront me. God is on my side and if God be for me, only a fool would be my enemy.

(Proverbs 18:20,21; Mark 11:22-25; Isaiah 30:21; Matthew 5:10-12; John 10:4,5; Romans 8:31-39; 1 John 2:1,2)

ISAIAH 51:7,8 KJV

Hearken unto me, ye that know righteousness, the people in whose heart is my law; fear ye not the reproach of men, neither be ye afraid of their revilings. For the moth shall eat them up like a garment, and the worm shall eat them like wool: but my righteousness shall be for ever, and my salvation from generation to generation.

——— *DECLARATION OF FAITH* ———

I have the Word of my God rooted deep within my heart. I know what is right and I am wise to do it.

The reproach of men does not intimidate me, nor am I terrified by their slander. The moth will eat them up like a garment and a worm will devour them like wool. The Lord is faithful and will not allow me to be overpowered by them. His righteousness and salvation are mine now and forevermore.

(Mark 4:14-20; James 1:21-25; Joel 2:25; Psalm 18:3-19)

ISAIAH 51:11-16 KJV

Therefore the redeemed of the Lord shall return, and come with singing unto Zion; and everlasting joy *shall be* upon their head: they shall obtain gladness and joy; *and* sorrow and mourning shall flee away. I, *even* I, *am* he that comforteth you: who *art* thou, that thou shouldest be afraid of a man *that* shall die, and of the son of man *which* shall be made *as* grass; And forgettest the Lord thy maker, that hath stretched forth the heavens, and laid the foundations of the earth; and hast feared continually every day because of the fury of the oppressor, as if he were ready to destroy? and where *is* the fury of the oppressor? The captive exile hasteneth that he may be loosed, and that he should not die in the pit, nor that his bread should fail. But I *am* the Lord thy God, that divided the sea, whose waves roared: The Lord of hosts *is* his name. And I have put my words in thy mouth, and I have covered thee in the shadow of mine hand, that I may plant the heavens, and lay the foundations of the earth, and say unto Zion, Thou *art* my people.

──────── *DECLARATION OF FAITH* ────────

I am a citizen of Zion, God's holy church. I am ransomed and made whole. Everlasting joy crowns my head and gladness overtakes me, while sorrow and sighing flee away. It is God Himself, the Creator of heaven and earth, who does this for me. He is an ever-present source of comfort in my life.

Fear is not an option when I acknowledge my Father's presence.

The oppressor is little more than an annoyance to me. I have been set free from his chains and made to be his master. I need never fear him again.

The prison bars that once closed me in have turned to twigs and all of my needs, whether for power or provision, are continually met.

I am now a child of the King, born again under the name of almighty God. He has placed His Word on my lips, covered me with the shadow of His hand, and makes His declaration to all of creation that I am His.

(John 17:13-22; Hebrews 2:14-17; Colossians 2:13-15; 2 Timothy 1:7; Romans 10:8; Philippians 4:13-19)

ISAIAH 51:22,23 KJV

Thus saith thy Lord the Lord, and thy God that pleadeth the cause of his people, Behold, I have taken out of thine hand the cup of trembling, even the dregs of the cup of my fury; thou shalt no more drink it again: But I will put it into the hand of them that afflict thee; which have said to thy soul, Bow down, that we may go over: and thou hast laid thy body as the ground, and as the street, to them that went over.

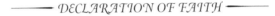

DECLARATION OF FAITH

My Father has given me His Word that He will never have me drink from the cup of His wrath. All of His dealings with me are for good and never evil. His fierce anger is now turned against my enemies: those who tried to walk all over me and make me their slave. The tables have been turned! Never again will they overpower me! I now walk in the authority of the King and rise as more than a conqueror in every area of my life!

(Romans 8:1,2,37; Ephesians 1:17-23; Acts 26:18; 1 John 5:18)

ISAIAH 52:1-3 KJV

Awake, awake; put on thy strength, O Zion; put on thy beautiful garments, O Jerusalem, the holy city: for henceforth there shall no more come into thee the uncircumcised and the unclean. Shake thyself from the dust; arise, and sit down, O Jerusalem: loose thyself from the bands of thy neck, O captive daughter of Zion. For thus saith the Lord, Ye have sold yourselves for nought; and ye shall be redeemed without money.

DECLARATION OF FAITH

I stir myself up—alert and aware of my standing in the eyes of the Lord. I am clothed in strength and in the garments of glory. The dust and filth is shaken from my life and I am enthroned on high with my Lord Jesus. The chains that once bound me are shattered from off of my neck and I am now free to live the God-kind of life. I am redeemed from the curse, reborn as in the womb of the spirit, and clothed in His strength and authority.

(Ephesians 2:6; 6:10-18; Galatians 3:13; 2 Timothy 1:6; 1 Corinthians 14:4)

ISAIAH 52:7-12 KJV

How beautiful upon the mountains are the feet of him that bringeth good tidings, that publisheth peace; that bringeth good tidings of good, that publisheth salvation; that saith unto Zion, Thy God reigneth! Thy watchmen shall lift up the voice; with the voice together shall they sing: for they shall see eye to eye, when the Lord shall bring again Zion. Break forth into joy, sing together, ye waste places of Jerusalem: for the Lord hath comforted his people, he hath redeemed Jerusalem. The Lord hath made bare his holy arm in the eyes of all the nations; and all the ends of the earth shall see the salvation of our God. Depart ye, depart ye, go ye out from thence, touch no unclean *thing*; go ye out of the midst of her; be ye clean, that bear the vessels of the Lord. For ye shall not go out with haste, nor go by flight: for the Lord will go before you; and the God of Israel *will be* your reward.

———— DECLARATION OF FAITH ————

My feet are precious in the eyes of the Lord, for they carry the Gospel of the good news of redemption to a hurting world. I proclaim the Gospel of peace, salvation, and good tidings to all of mankind. I shout to the hills, "My God reigns!" I lift up my voice and shout for joy. I burst into songs of joy with the prayer warriors of the Church. We have been redeemed! Peace is ours!

From now until eternity we shall live our days in comfort and prosperity. The ends of the earth shall know and see that Jesus is Lord.

I have been made pure and shall remain pure all the days of my life.

The Lord goes before me and is my rear guard. I shall never be harmed, and my victory is as certain as the Lord's return.

(Romans 10:15-18; Galatians 3:13; Ephesians 2:14; Philippians 2:16-18; 3:1-3; 4:4)

ISAIAH 53:4-6 NKJV

Surely He has borne our griefs and carried our sorrows; yet we esteemed Him stricken, smitten by God, and afflicted. But He was wounded for our transgressions, He was bruised for our iniquities; the chastisement for our peace was upon Him, and by His stripes we are healed. All we like sheep have gone astray; we have turned, every one, to his own way; and the Lord has laid on Him the iniquity of us all.

———— DECLARATION OF FAITH ————

Jesus bore my sicknesses and carried my pains. He was smitten, afflicted and pierced through the hands and feet because of my transgressions. He was bruised and battered because of my wickedness. He became sick with my sicknesses and suffered excruciating pain on my account.

What He did on that cross and in those three days and nights of pain, He did willingly. He took my punishment upon Himself and gave me His peace in return. *Because of His wounds, I am made well. I am now totally healed spirit, soul, and body. In Him, I am made whole.*

I was like a sheep that had turned to his own way and I rejected the way of righteousness, but the Lord laid all of my iniquities, first to last, upon Jesus, and now there is nothing left that can separate me from Him.

(1 Peter 2:24; Colossians 2:10; Ephesians 2:14; Hebrews 10:14; Romans 8:38,39)

ISAIAH 53:10-12 NKJV

Yet it pleased the Lord to bruise Him; He has put Him to grief. When You make His soul an offering for sin, He shall see His seed, He shall prolong His days, and the pleasure of the Lord shall prosper in His hand. He shall see the labor of His soul, and be satisfied. By His knowledge My righteous Servant shall justify many, for He shall bear their iniquities. Therefore I will divide Him a portion with the great, and He shall divide the spoil with the strong, because He poured out His soul unto death, and He was numbered with the transgressors, and He bore the sin of many, and made intercession for the transgressors.

—— DECLARATION OF FAITH ——

It was God's will to cause Jesus to suffer in my stead. His life was sacrificed for my crimes and I have been declared, "Not guilty!"

I am now His offspring—a born-again son/daughter of the living God.

The will of the Lord has prospered in the hand of my Savior. He understood that after the torment of His spirit He would be raised from the dead and become my justification. He took upon Himself everything I did, or ever will do, wrong.

He is now seated in the place of highest honor. He poured out His life for me and became the very essence of my sin. In doing so, He set sin aside and rendered it utterly powerless in my life. He proclaimed His love for me by bridging the gap that prevented me from having fellowship with God, and He opened the way for me to share in His glory.

(Acts 2:24-32; Hebrews 10:12,13; 2 Corinthians 5:21; Ephesians 2:6,14)

ISAIAH 54:4,5 NKJV

"Do not fear, for you will not be ashamed; Neither be disgraced, for you will not be put to shame; for you will forget the shame of your youth, and will not remember the reproach of your widowhood anymore. For your Maker is your husband, the Lord of hosts is His name; and your Redeemer is the Holy One of Israel; He is called the God of the whole earth."

I have no fear of shame, disgrace, or humiliation, for I am united in a perfect covenant partnership with my heavenly Father. He works both in and through me to make me victorious in every circumstance.

(John 17:20-26; Isaiah 54:17; Philippians 3:12,13; 1 Corinthians 15:57; 2 Corinthians 2:14)

ISAIAH 54:7,8 AMP

For a brief moment I forsook you, but with great compassion and mercy I will gather you [to Me] again. In a little burst of wrath I hid My face from you for a moment, but with age-enduring love and kindness I will have compassion and mercy on you, says the Lord, your Redeemer.

——— *DECLARATION OF FAITH* ———

God's incredible love for me has brought me back from the land of darkness and into a right relationship with Himself. All of His actions toward me are now birthed in deep compassion and everlasting kindness.

(Jeremiah 29:11; Romans 5:10; 2 Corinthians 4:17; Psalm 119:65)

ISAIAH 54:10 NKJV

For the mountains shall depart and the hills be removed, but My kindness shall not depart from you, nor shall My covenant of peace be removed," says the Lord, who has mercy on you.

——— *DECLARATION OF FAITH* ———

Though the mountains be shaken and the hills removed, God's love for me will never fail and His covenant with me will not be taken away.

(Romans 8:38,39; Psalm 103; Hebrews 8:6; 10:15-17)

ISAIAH 54:13-17 KJV

And all thy children *shall be* taught of the Lord; and great *shall be* the peace of thy children. In righteousness shalt thou be established: thou shalt be far from oppression; for thou shalt not fear: and from terror; for it shall not come near thee. Behold, they shall surely gather together, *but* not by me: whosoever shall gather together against thee shall fall for thy sake. Behold, I have created the smith that bloweth the coals in the fire, and that bringeth forth an instrument for his work; and I have created the waster to destroy. No weapon that is formed

against thee shall prosper; and every tongue *that* shall rise against thee in judg-ment thou shalt condemn. This *is* the heritage of the servants of the Lord, and their righteousness *is* of me, saith the Lord.

──────── *DECLARATION OF FAITH* ────────

My children are taught by the Lord and He gives them tremendous peace and security.

My household is established in righteousness before Him and tyranny cannot gain a foothold in my life.

I have complete authority over all fear, anxiety, stress, and terror. I will not permit them in my life in any shape or form.

If I come under attack in any way, I know it is not the Lord's doing. All of His actions toward me are for good and never evil. It is He who gives me strength to conquer the enemy. Because of this, no weapon formed against me can prevail over me and I thwart every accusation that comes against me.

This is part of my inheritance as God's son/daughter, and my righteousness and justification come from Him.

(Psalm 89:3,4; Jeremiah 29:11; 2 Timothy 1:7; Romans 5:1,2; 8:31,32,37)

Isaiah 55:3 AMP

Incline your ear [submit and consent to the divine will] and come to Me; hear, and your soul will revive; and I will make an everlasting covenant or league with you, even the sure mercy (kindness, goodwill, and compassion) promised to David.

──────── *DECLARATION OF FAITH* ────────

My heavenly Father and I have a covenant pact that cannot be broken. All that He has—even His own authority, power, provision, and treasury are mine, and all that I have—even my spirit, soul, body, home, family, and possessions are His.

I draw near to Him in love, and I'm always ready to entertain what He says. He, in turn, draws near to me in love and is always ready to entertain what I say. The faithful love that He promised to David has become my own.

(Deuteronomy 8:18; 28:1-14; Psalm 103; James 4:7; Romans 8:38,39)

Isaiah 55:10-12 AMP

For as the rain and snow come down from the heavens, and return not there again, but water the earth and make it bring forth and sprout, that it may give seed to the sower and bread to the eater, so shall My word be that goes forth out of My mouth: it shall not return to Me void [without producing any effect, useless], but it shall accomplish that which I please and purpose, and it shall prosper in the thing for which I sent it. For you shall go out [from the spiritual exile caused by sin and evil into the homeland] with joy and be led forth [by your Leader, the Lord Himself, and His word] with peace; the mountains and the hills shall break forth before you into singing, and all the trees of the field shall clap their hands.

——— DECLARATION OF FAITH ———

As rain and snow fall from heaven to water the earth and make it bring forth seed for the sower and bread for the eater, so it is with God's Word. He has sent it to me for a purpose and it will accomplish that purpose in my life. It is continually on my lips as a seed and it brings me a perpetual harvest of good things. What a joy it is to be led forth in such peace and assurance! The mountains and the hills burst forth into song before me, and I enjoy the goodwill of all who see God's favor in my life.

(Mark 4:14-20; Psalm 119:138-140; Proverbs 3:3,4; 2 Corinthians 9:10,11)

ISAIAH 56:3 AMP

Let not the foreigner who has joined himself to the Lord say, The Lord will surely separate me from His people. And let not the eunuch say, Behold, I am a dry tree.

——— DECLARATION OF FAITH ———

I have been adopted as God's own son/daughter and rest securely in His kingdom forever.

(Romans 8:15; Galatians 4:5,6; Hebrews 4:1-10)

ISAIAH 57:14-19 KJV

And shall say, Cast ye up, cast ye up, prepare the way, take up the stumblingblock out of the way of my people. For thus saith the high and lofty One that inhabiteth eternity, whose name *is* Holy; I dwell in the high and holy *place,* with him also *that is* of a contrite and humble spirit, to revive the spirit of the humble, and to revive the heart of the contrite ones. For I will not contend for ever, neither will I be always wroth: for the spirit should fail before me, and the souls *which* I have made. For the iniquity of his covetousness was I wroth, and smote him: I hid me, and was wroth, and he went on frowardly in the way of his heart. I have seen his ways, and will heal him: I will lead him also, and restore comforts unto him and to his mourners. I create the fruit of the lips; Peace, peace to *him that is* far off, and to *him that is* near, saith the Lord; and I will heal him.

———— *DECLARATION OF FAITH* ————

My road has been built up and custom made for me. All obstacles have been removed from my path.

I have been revived, made alive in the spirit and regenerated as a brand-new creation, with God Himself living in my heart.

God has declared to me that His anger has been removed. All of my sins and willful ways have been put behind me and I can now enter His presence fearlessly, without the slightest sense of guilt for what I have done.

I am now under the gentle care of my heavenly Father. He heals, guides, and comforts me in my way. He has replaced my sorrow with shouts of praise. He has decreed that I am to live securely—in perfect peace, health, and safety. Healing is mine, and that is God's final Word on it.

(Psalm 27:11; Titus 3:5; Proverbs 4:18, 26,27; Hebrews 4:16; James 5:15)

ISAIAH 58:6-9 AMP

[Rather] is not this the fast that I have chosen: to loose the bonds of wickedness, to undo the bands of the yoke, to let the oppressed go free, and that you break every [enslaving] yoke? Is it not to divide your bread with the hungry and bring the homeless poor into your house—when you see the naked, that you cover him, and that you hide not yourself from [the needs of] your own flesh and blood? Then shall your light break forth like the morning, and your healing (your restoration and the power of a new life) shall spring forth speedily; your righteousness (your rightness, your justice, and your right relationship with God) shall go before you [conducting you to peace and prosperity], and the glory of the Lord shall be your rear guard.

———— *DECLARATION OF FAITH* ————

The fast that God has ordained for me is this: to set the captive free, to loose the chains of injustice, to break the yoke of oppression off of every neck, to share my food with the hungry, to provide the poor and homeless with shelter, to clothe the naked, and to take special care of those in my own household. By these, my radiance springs forth like the dawn and my healing comes to me quickly and without fail.

The righteous One goes before me and the glory of the Lord is my rear guard.

I call upon the Lord and He answers me. He entertains my every prayer.

(Psalm 34:7; 139:5; Luke 4:18,19; Nehemiah 5:10-12; Exodus 14:19; Isaiah 61:1-3)

Isaiah 58:11 AMP

And the Lord shall guide you continually and satisfy you in drought and in dry places and make strong your bones. And you shall be like a watered garden and like a spring of water whose waters fail not.

———— DECLARATION OF FAITH ————

The Lord guides me continually and satisfies my every need even in a fruitless and sun-scorched land. He strengthens my frame and makes me like a well-watered garden—like a spring whose waters never fail.

(Psalm 1:1-3; 23; John 16:13; Philippians 4:11-13,19)

Isaiah 59:21-60:2 KJV

As for me, this *is* my covenant with them, saith the Lord; My spirit that *is* upon thee, and my words which I have put in thy mouth, shall not depart out of thy mouth, nor out of the mouth of thy seed, nor out of the mouth of thy seed's seed, saith the Lord; from henceforth and for ever. Arise, shine; for thy light is come, and the glory of the Lord is risen upon thee. For, behold, the darkness shall cover the earth, and gross darkness the people: but the Lord shall arise upon thee, and his glory shall be seen upon thee.

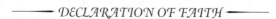

———— DECLARATION OF FAITH ————

My covenant with the Lord is secure. The Holy Spirit dwells within me as the earnest and indisputable guarantee that it will never be taken from me.

The Word of the Lord is on my lips continually. It shall never depart from my mouth, or the mouths of my children, both now and forevermore.

I arise in the presence of my heavenly Father as His own son/daughter and covenant partner. My light has come and the glory of the Lord has risen upon me. In the midst of the darkness, the Lord rises within me and His glory is seen around me.

(Hebrews 8:6; 10:15-17; Ephesians 1:13,14; Romans 10:8; Deuteronomy 7:9; Joshua 1:8)

Isaiah 60:10 AMP

Foreigners shall build up your walls, and their kings shall minister to you; for in My wrath I smote you, but in My favor, pleasure, and goodwill I have had mercy, love, and pity for you.

God loves me with all of His heart and is pleased to give me favor in all that I do. Strangers go out of their way to do nice things for me, and rulers serve me and attend to my needs.

(Romans 8:38,39; Proverbs 3:3,4; Isaiah 61:5)

ISAIAH 60:17-21 KJV

For brass I will bring gold, and for iron I will bring silver, and for wood brass, and for stones iron: I will also make thy officers peace, and thine exactors righteousness. Violence shall no more be heard in thy land, wasting nor destruction within thy borders; but thou shalt call thy walls Salvation, and thy gates Praise. The sun shall be no more thy light by day; neither for brightness shall the moon give light unto thee: but the Lord shall be unto thee an everlasting light, and thy God thy glory. Thy sun shall no more go down; neither shall thy moon withdraw itself: for the Lord shall be thine everlasting light, and the days of thy mourning shall be ended. Thy people also *shall be* all righteous: they shall inherit the land for ever, the branch of my planting, the work of my hands, that I may be glorified.

The Lord makes peace my governor and righteousness my ruler. He removes violence from my life and does not allow ruin and destruction to enter my borders. My walls are salvation and my gates praise.

The Lord has become my everlasting Light and God Himself is my glory. The light of my life will never fail or fade and my days of sorrow have ended.

I am the very righteousness of God in Christ Jesus and shall possess the land forever.

I am a willing vessel in the great Potter's hands. I am God's own workmanship created to display His splendor to the entire world.

(Ephesians 2:4-10; Psalm 91; Romans 8:28,29; 2 Corinthians 5:21; Isaiah 64:8)

ISAIAH 61:1-3 AMP

The Spirit of the Lord God is upon me, because the Lord has anointed and qualified me to preach the Gospel of good tidings to the meek, the poor, and afflicted; He has sent me to bind up and heal the brokenhearted, to proclaim liberty to the [physical and spiritual] captives and the opening of the prison and of the eyes to those who are bound, to proclaim the acceptable year of the Lord [the year of His favor] and the day of vengeance of our God, to comfort all who mourn, to grant [consolation and joy] to those who mourn in Zion—to give them an ornament (a garland or diadem) of beauty instead of ashes, the oil of joy instead of mourning, the garment [expressive] of praise instead of a heavy, burdened, and failing spirit—that they may be called oaks of righteousness [lofty, strong, and magnificent, distinguished for uprightness, justice, and right standing with God], the planting of the Lord, that He may be glorified.

—— *DECLARATION OF FAITH* ——

The Holy Spirit is within me, and I have the burden-removing, yoke-destroying power to preach the Gospel to the poor, heal the brokenhearted, set free those held captive by the devil, release the prisoners from their dungeon of darkness, proclaim to all that God is not mad at them and is ready to grant them abundant favor and blessings, to tell of the day of God's vengeance, comfort all who mourn, provide for those who grieve, and present them with a crown of beauty in place of ashes, the oil of happiness instead of mourning, and a garment of praise to cure their depression. I am known as an oak of righteousness, a planting of the Lord to display His love and splendor to all the world.

(2 Corinthians 1:20-22; Mark 16:15-18; Job 29:12-17; 1 John 2:27)

ISAIAH 61:6-10 KJV

But ye shall be named the Priests of the Lord: *men* shall call you the Ministers of our God: ye shall eat the riches of the Gentiles, and in their glory shall ye boast yourselves. For your shame *ye shall have* double; and *for* confusion they shall rejoice in their portion: therefore in their land they shall possess the double: everlasting joy shall be unto them. For I the Lord love judgment, I hate robbery for burnt offering; and I will direct their work in truth, and I will make an everlasting covenant with them. And their seed shall be known among the Gentiles, and their offspring among the people: all that see them shall acknowledge them, that they *are* the seed *which* the Lord hath blessed. I will greatly rejoice in the Lord, my soul shall be joyful in my God; for he hath clothed me with the garments of salvation, he hath covered me with the robe of righteousness, as a bridegroom decketh *himself* with ornaments, and as a bride adorneth *herself* with her jewels.

—— *DECLARATION OF FAITH* ——

I am known as a priest of the Lord and a minister of God's power and grace. Instead of shame, I have received double honor; instead of confusion and disgrace, I leap for joy in the presence of my Father, for He has given me a double portion for my inheritance. In His faithfulness, He has honored His everlasting covenant with me and has granted me a tremendous reward.

My children are blessed because of the covenant. They shall enjoy the rich-ness of God's inheritance with me. All who see me will acknowledge that I am a man/woman whom God has blessed.

I delight in all of these things. My soul rejoices within me and my spirit pays homage to my Lord and Father, for He has clothed me with the garments of sal-vation and arrayed me in a robe of His righteousness.

(Revelation 1:6; 2 Corinthians 5:20; Job 42:10-12; Psalm 103:17; 112; Deuteronomy 28:1-14)

ISAIAH 62:5 AMP

For as a young man marries a virgin [O Jerusalem], so shall your sons marry you; and as the bridegroom rejoices over the bride, so shall your God rejoice over you.

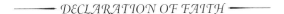

——— DECLARATION OF FAITH ———

The Lord rejoices over me as a bridegroom rejoices over his bride. He has committed Himself to me in an everlasting covenant sealed in His own blood.

(Hebrews 8:6; Acts 20:28; John 3:29; Revelation 18:23)

ISAIAH 65:17-25 KJV

For, behold, I create new heavens and a new earth: and the former shall not be remembered, nor come into mind. But be ye glad and rejoice for ever *in that* which I create: for, behold, I create Jerusalem a rejoicing, and her people a joy. And I will rejoice in Jerusalem, and joy in my people: and the voice of weeping shall be no more heard in her, nor the voice of crying. There shall be no more thence an infant of days, nor an old man that hath not filled his days: for the child shall die an hundred years old; but the sinner *being* an hundred years old shall be accursed. And they shall build houses, and inhabit *them;* and they shall plant vineyards, and eat the fruit of them. They shall not build, and another inhabit; they shall not plant, and another eat: for as the days of a tree *are* the days of my people, and mine elect shall long enjoy the work of their hands. They shall not labour in vain, nor bring forth for trouble; for they *are* the seed of the blessed of the Lord, and their offspring with them. And it shall come to pass, that before they call, I will answer; and while they are yet speaking, I will hear. The wolf and the lamb shall feed together, and the lion shall eat straw like the bullock: and dust *shall be* the serpent's meat. They shall not hurt nor destroy in all my holy mountain, saith the Lord.

─── *DECLARATION OF FAITH* ───

God has done a new thing in me. I am recreated and born again. I am a son/daughter of the living God, a joint heir with Jesus, and a member of a new and godly race.

The Lord rejoices over me with hilarity and takes great delight in my companionship.

He takes the sounds of sadness from me and fills me with His happiness.

None of my children will die before their time. Each of us will live out our years in a full, satisfying, and abundant life.

My days are as the days of a tree.

I will build fine houses to live in and plant many vineyards and eat of the fruit.

None of my possessions will be repossessed or confiscated.

I have a right to enjoy the career that I have chosen.

I do not labor in vain or have children doomed to misfortune. My family is blessed with a certainty sealed by the love of God.

When I call upon God, He answers me. He is so attentive to my prayers that before I even speak, He has the answer ready for me.

He makes me to be at peace with my enemies and the only part the devil has in my life is eating the dust from my feet.

I am God's son/daughter and neither harm nor destruction can come near me. I have His Word on it.

(2 Corinthians 5:17; Romans 8:15-17; Psalm 92:12; 112; Ecclesiastes 2:24; 3:22; Hosea 9:12; Daniel 9:20-23; Micah 7:17; Revelation 21:4)

ISAIAH 66:2 AMP

For all these things My hand has made, and so all these things have come into being [by and for Me], says the Lord. But this is the man to whom I will look and have regard: he who is humble and of a broken or wounded spirit, and who trembles at My word and reveres My commands.

─── *DECLARATION OF FAITH* ───

I am greatly esteemed by God. He sees the respect that I have for His Word and that I give it the ascendancy in my life over and above all pomp and circumstance.

I do not exalt myself, but bow humbly before Him. If there is any exalting in my life, it is the Lord's doing and not my own.

(1 Peter 5:5-7; Proverbs 27:2; Psalm 119:41,42, 113-116,160-165)

ISAIAH 66:10,11 AMP

Rejoice with Jerusalem and be glad for her, all you who love her; rejoice for joy with her, all you who mourn over her, that you may nurse and be satisfied from her consoling breasts, that you may drink deeply and be delighted with the abundance and brightness of her glory.

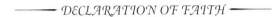

DECLARATION OF FAITH

I love Jerusalem, the city of my God, with all of my heart, and I rejoice in her prosperity. I have my part in her abundance and her treasuries are a provision for my life.

(Psalm 122; Revelation 21)

ISAIAH 66:13 NKJV

"As one whom his mother comforts, so I will comfort you; and you shall be comforted in Jerusalem."

DECLARATION OF FAITH

My Father nourishes and cares for me with the same kind of meticulous attention that a loving mother gives to her newborn child.

(Psalm 103:13; Isaiah 51:3; 2 Corinthians 1:3,4)

CHAPTER TWENTY-FOUR

JEREMIAH

Jeremiah is known as the weeping prophet. He was given the task of prophesying of the coming judgment. This brought great sorrow to Jeremiah's heart showing his love for the nation of Israel.

The irony of Jeremiah's writing is that some of the most uplifting and joyful promises are found in the book. Here and there throughout the book, God shows us His heart toward us. He shows how much He loves us and reveals to us what we can have if we repent and turn to Him.

As you pray these promises, remember that God has a wonderful plan for your life. You are redeemed from your old life and are now set in God's province of joy, peace, prosperity, and fulfillment.

JEREMIAH 1:7-10 KJV

But the Lord said unto me, Say not, I *am* a child: for thou shalt go to all that I shall send thee, and whatsoever I command thee thou shalt speak. Be not afraid of their faces: for I *am* with thee to deliver thee, saith the Lord. Then the Lord put forth his hand, and touched my mouth. And the Lord said unto me, Behold, I have put my words in thy mouth. See, I have this day set thee over the nations and over the kingdoms, to root out, and to pull down, and to destroy, and to throw down, to build, and to plant.

———— DECLARATION OF FAITH ————

I will go everywhere the Lord sends me and do whatever He commands me to do. I do not allow fear to hinder me in my calling. I know full well that God's power is within me wherever I go and there is nothing that can overcome me.

I have His Word in my heart and in my mouth. I will speak it with a purpose for an intended result.

I have been appointed and anointed as a leader in this earth with the power to uproot and tear down, to destroy and overthrow, and to build and plant.

(Isaiah 55:11; Romans 10:8; Colossians 1:29; 2 Corinthians 9:10; 10:3-6; Ecclesiastes 3:1-8; Nehemiah 2:17-20)

JEREMIAH 1:12 NKJV

Then the Lord said to me, "You have seen well, for I am ready to perform My word."

———— *DECLARATION OF FAITH* ————

The Lord watches over His Word to see that it is performed in my life.

(Psalm 119:37,38,41-43,74-76,89,113-116,138,140,171-173; Isaiah 55:11)

JEREMIAH 1:17-19 AMP

But you [Jeremiah], gird up your loins! Arise and tell them all that I command you. Do not be dismayed and break down at the sight of their faces, lest I confound you before them and permit you to be overcome. For I, behold, I have made you this day a fortified city and an iron pillar and bronze walls against the whole land—against the [successive] kings of Judah, against its princes, against its priests, and against the people of the land [giving you divine strength which no hostile power can overcome]. And they shall fight against you, but they shall not [finally] prevail against you, for I am with you, says the Lord, to deliver you.

———— *DECLARATION OF FAITH* ————

I stir myself up to do the Lord's work and I will not allow the devil's fear to stop me.

I prefer a reputation of honor in heaven as opposed to acceptance among men.

This day my Father has made me like a fortified city, an iron pillar and a bronze wall to stand against all of those who would try to sway me from what He has called me to do. I understand that opposition and persecution are inevitable, but I also understand that God is on my side and He will not allow me to be overcome.

(2 Timothy 1:6,7; 3:12; Acts 4:18-20; Romans 8:31)

JEREMIAH 3:14,15 KJV

Turn, O backsliding children, saith the Lord; for I am married unto you: and I will take you one of a city, and two of a family, and I will bring you to Zion: And I will give you pastors according to mine heart, which shall feed you with knowledge and understanding.

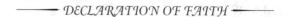

────── *DECLARATION OF FAITH* ──────

God has chosen me to be His own son/daughter and has given me pastors and teachers, with tremendous knowledge and understanding, to guide me in the affairs of this life.

(Ephesians 1:4; 1 Corinthians 12:28; Hebrews 5:12)

JEREMIAH 3:19 NIV

"I myself said, 'How gladly would I treat you like sons and give you a desirable land, the most beautiful inheritance of any nation.' I thought you would call me 'Father' and not turn away from following me."

────── *DECLARATION OF FAITH* ──────

The Lord is pleased to call me His son/daughter. He has given me a desirable stretch of land and my part in the most awesome inheritance in all of creation.

(Romans 8:14-17; 1 John 3:1,2; Galatians 4:5,6; Psalm 106:24)

JEREMIAH 3:22 AMP

Return, O faithless sons, [says the Lord, and] I will heal your faithlessness. [And they answer] Behold, we come to You, for You are the Lord our God.

────── *DECLARATION OF FAITH* ──────

I have turned to my Father in repentance and He has cured me of all backsliding.

(Jeremiah 30:17; 33:6; Hosea 6:1; 14:4; Jude 24; Acts 2:38,39)

JEREMIAH 4:3 NIV

This is what the Lord says to the men of Judah and to Jerusalem: "Break up your unplowed ground and do not sow among thorns."

────── *DECLARATION OF FAITH* ──────

I take special care as to where I sow my seed. I will not give it to unplowed soil [a dormant church without a vision], nor will I sow it among thorns [a place where doubt and unbelief prevails].

(Ecclesiastes 11:1,2; 2 Corinthians 9:5-11; Matthew 7:6; 13:7)

JEREMIAH 6:16 AMP

Thus says the Lord: Stand by the roads and look; and ask for the eternal paths, where the good, old way is; then walk in it, and you will find rest for your souls. But they said, We will not walk in it!

——— DECLARATION OF FAITH ———

I walk in ways tested and tried—ways that bring honor and glory to my Father and ultimately lead me to true rest.

(Psalm 119:89-93,140; Ephesians 5:1-18; Matthew 11:29)

JEREMIAH 9:23,24 KJV

Thus saith the Lord, Let not the wise *man* glory in his wisdom, neither let the mighty *man* glory in his might, let not the rich *man* glory in his riches: But let him that glorieth glory in this, that he understandeth and knoweth me, that I *am* the Lord which exercise lovingkindness, judgment, and righteousness, in the earth: for in these *things* I delight, saith the Lord.

——— DECLARATION OF FAITH ———

I do not boast in my worldly wisdom and abilities, nor in the strength of my own arm or the abundance of my riches. All of my boasting is in the Lord. It is He who has made me who I am, and without Him I am of no great significance.

In this I will boast: that I both know and understand that the Lord is God, the Creator of all things, and that He has become my Father. I boast in His kindness and mercy towards me, and in His righteousness and justice that is displayed throughout the earth.

(Romans 3:27; Ecclesiastes 9:11; Psalm 33:16-18)

JEREMIAH 10:21 NIV

The shepherds are senseless and do not inquire of the Lord; so they do not prosper and all their flock is scattered.

——— DECLARATION OF FAITH ———

(For those in pastoral ministry)

I am a wise and discerning shepherd of God's people. I never forget to seek the Lord's counsel on their behalf.

(1 Corinthians 2:6-16; John 16:13; Ezekiel 22:30)

JEREMIAH 10:23,24 NKJV

O Lord, I know the way of man is not in himself; It is not in man who walks to direct his own steps. O Lord, correct me, but with justice; Not in Your anger, lest You bring me to nothing.

——— *DECLARATION OF FAITH* ———

I understand that all of my ways are held together in the Lord and that it is He who has set the boundaries of my life. I also understand that He alone can guide me on the path of perfection and fulfillment. Therefore, all of my trust is in Him. I will listen to His correction, knowing that He does not guide me with the rod of anger and affliction, but in justice through His Word.

(Hebrews 1:3; Proverbs 3:5,6; 16:1; John 16:13; Psalm 119:130-135)

JEREMIAH 12:15 NKJV

"Then it shall be, after I have plucked them out, that I will return and have compassion on them and bring them back, everyone to his heritage and everyone to his land."

——— *DECLARATION OF FAITH* ———

I have been reconciled with the Lord my God and He has restored to me the abundance of my inheritance. All that He does on my behalf is birthed in His great love and compassion for me.

(Titus 3:5; Romans 8:14-17; Galatians 4:5,6; Psalm 103:1-18)

JEREMIAH 15:15-17 KJV

O Lord, thou knowest: remember me, and visit me, and revenge me of my persecutors; take me not away in thy longsuffering: know that for thy sake I have suffered rebuke. Thy words were found, and I did eat them; and thy word was unto me the joy and rejoicing of mine heart: for I am called by thy name, O Lord God of hosts. I sat not in the assembly of the mockers, nor rejoiced; I sat alone because of thy hand: for thou hast filled me with indignation.

——— *DECLARATION OF FAITH* ———

The Lord understands what I must endure in this life. He knows my frame and capacity and is always ready to help me if I should need Him.

I consume the Word of God in a continual feast. Each and every morsel is a delectable delight for me.

I bear the name of almighty God and refuse to do anything to dishonor it. I am not the companion of revelers and drunkards, nor do I pretend it's okay to do those things that I know in my heart are wrong. If I must, I will sit alone, apart from those who neither know, nor desire God's presence in their lives.

(Psalm 103:13,14; 2 Corinthians 6:14; Deuteronomy 8:3; Ephesians 5:14-18)

JEREMIAH 15:19-21 KJV

Therefore thus saith the Lord, If thou return, then will I bring thee again, *and* thou shalt stand before me: and if thou take forth the precious from the vile, thou shalt be as my mouth: let them return unto thee; but return not thou unto them. And I will make thee unto this people a fenced brasen wall: and they shall fight against thee, but they shall not prevail against thee: for I *am* with thee to save thee and to deliver thee, saith the Lord. And I will deliver thee out of the hand of the wicked, and I will redeem thee out of the hand of the terrible.

——— DECLARATION OF FAITH ———

I have been restored to a position of favor with the Lord.

I serve Him with all of my heart and speak specific, purpose-filled words that fill the earth with His glory.

He has built me up as a fortified wall of bronze against all unrighteousness. I am strong in the Lord and in the power of His might and cannot be overcome by the attacks of the enemy.

God is with me at all times and has given me His Word that He will protect me from the hands of the wicked and redeem me from the grasp of the cruel.

(Romans 5:10; 8:31,32; Hebrews 4:16; Psalm 91; Mark 11:22-25; Ephesians 6:10-18; Jeremiah 1:8,19)

JEREMIAH 17:5 NIV

This is what the Lord says: "Cursed is the one who trusts in man, who depends on flesh for his strength and whose heart turns away from the Lord."

——— DECLARATION OF FAITH ———

I do not put my trust in the ways of man, nor do I rely on the strength of others to sustain me. My trust is in the Lord—my provider. He alone is the strength of my life.

(Isaiah 30:1,2; Proverbs 3:5,6; Ephesians 6:10)

JEREMIAH 17:7,8 NKJV

"Blessed *is* the man who trusts in the Lord, and whose hope is the Lord. For he shall be like a tree planted by the waters, which spreads out its roots by the river, and will not fear when heat comes; but her leaf will be green, and will not be anxious in the year of drought, nor will cease from yielding fruit."

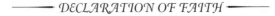

———— DECLARATION OF FAITH ————

I trust in the Lord with all of my heart and maintain a bold confidence that His Word reigns true in my life.

I am like a tree planted beside pure spring water that sends out its roots to the edges of the stream. I do not fear when heat comes, for my leaves will always remain green. You won't find me stressed out and anxiety-ridden in time of drought, for the Lord is my mainstay and I never fail to bear fruit.

(Psalm 1:1-3; Proverbs 3:3-10; Joshua 1:5-9; John 15:1-8)

JEREMIAH 17:14 AMP

Heal me, O Lord, and I shall be healed; save me, and I shall be saved, for You are my praise.

———— DECLARATION OF FAITH ————

My trust and focus is on the Lord alone.
He has declared me to be healed; therefore, I am healed.
He has declared my salvation; therefore, I am saved.

(Proverbs 3:5,6; Isaiah 53:4,5; 1 Peter 2:24; Romans 10:8-13)

JEREMIAH 20:8-12 KJV

For since I spake, I cried out, I cried violence and spoil; because the word of the Lord was made a reproach unto me, and a derision, daily. Then I said, I will not make mention of him, nor speak any more in his name. But *his word* was in mine heart as a burning fire shut up in my bones, and I was weary with forbearing, and I could not stay. For I heard the defaming of many, fear on every side. Report, *say they,* and we will report it. All my familiars watched for my halting, *saying,* Peradventure he will be enticed, and we shall prevail against him, and we shall take our revenge on him. But the Lord is with me as a mighty terrible one: therefore my persecutors shall stumble, and they shall not prevail: they shall be greatly ashamed; for they shall not prosper: *their* everlasting confusion shall never be forgotten. But, O Lord of hosts, that triest the righteous, *and* seest the reins and the heart, let me see thy vengeance on them: for unto thee have I opened my cause.

——— DECLARATION OF FAITH ———

The Word is in me in abundance, filling my heart with excitement and rousing me to speak it to the entire world. Even when it brings me reproach and mockery, I still cannot help but speak it. It is in my heart like a fire that cannot be contained. In the midst of terror and threats, I boldly proclaim it. When I am said to be deceived, it flows forth like a river from my lips.

When people get fed up with my stubborn trust in the Word and plot my destruction, the Lord rises like a mighty warrior in my defense.

All of my persecutors will stumble and fall. They shall be utterly disgraced and their dishonor will never be forgotten.

My cause is committed to my Father and He takes care of business on my behalf.

(John 15:7; Acts 4:20,29; 2 Timothy 4:2; Psalm 2; Exodus 23:22)

JEREMIAH 21:8 NIV

"Furthermore, tell the people, 'This is what the Lord says: See, I am setting before you the way of life and the way of death.'"

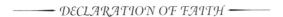

——— DECLARATION OF FAITH ———

God has laid before me, in His Word, the way of life and the way of death. It is up to me to choose which way to live.

I choose the way of life.

(Joshua 24:15; Deuteronomy 30:15-19; Isaiah 7:15,16)

JEREMIAH 22:3 AMP

Thus says the Lord: Execute justice and righteousness, and deliver out of the hand of the oppressor him who has been robbed. And do no wrong; do no violence to the stranger or temporary resident, the fatherless, or the widow, nor shed innocent blood in this place.

——— DECLARATION OF FAITH ———

I do what I know is right.

When I see the cruel hand of the oppressor at another's throat, I intervene on their behalf and rescue them.

I am a man/woman of God and a refuge to the widow and the orphan.

I am not violent nor do I ever shed innocent blood.

(Leviticus 5:1; Job 29:12-17; Ezekiel 22:30; Psalm 72:12; James 1:27)

JEREMIAH 23:4-6 KJV

And I will set up shepherds over them which shall feed them: and they shall fear no more, nor be dismayed, neither shall they be lacking, saith the Lord. Behold, the days come, saith the Lord, that I will raise unto David a righteous Branch, and a King shall reign and prosper, and shall execute judgment and justice in the earth. In his days Judah shall be saved, and Israel shall dwell safely: and this is his name whereby he shall be called, THE LORD OUR RIGHTEOUSNESS.

——— DECLARATION OF FAITH ———

Guardians (angels and shepherds) have been placed over me to tend to my every need and see to it that I go unharmed. I am never left unattended and never have reason to fear.

Jesus is my Lord and King. He reigns over me wisely, doing only what is just and right on my behalf. He has become my righteousness and my shield of protection. I live in safety every second of every minute of every hour of every day.

(Psalm 23; 91:11,12; Hebrews 1:14; Exodus 23:20-23; 2 Timothy 1:7; 1 Corinthians 1:30; Genesis 15:1; 2 Corinthians 5:21)

JEREMIAH 24:5-7 KJV

Thus saith the Lord, the God of Israel; Like these good figs, so will I acknowledge them that are carried away captive of Judah, whom I have sent out of this place into the land of the Chaldeans for *their* good. For I will set mine eyes upon them for good, and I will bring them again to this land: and I will build them, and not pull *them* down; and I will plant them, and not pluck *them* up. And I will give them an heart to know me, that I *am* the Lord: and they shall be my people, and I will be their God: for they shall return unto me with their whole heart.

——— DECLARATION OF FAITH ———

The Lord looks upon me as a good person. He watches over me meticulously and does nothing but good by me. He is committed to building me up and never tearing me down. He has planted me and will never uproot me. He has given me a heart of discernment so that I can know Him and have an intimate relationship with Him. I am His son/daughter and He is my Father. All that I am is His both now and forevermore.

(Psalm 3:5,6; Genesis 50:20; Jeremiah 32:41; 42:10; 1 John 3:1,2; 5:20)

JEREMIAH 29:7 NKJV

And seek the peace of the city where I have caused you to be carried away captive, and pray to the Lord for it; for in its peace you will have peace.

——— *DECLARATION OF FAITH* ———

I take special pride in the prosperity of the city in which I live. All of my thoughts for her are for peace and goodwill. I do my best to see that she prospers, for I understand that when my city prospers, I prosper. [I will not forget that a city is made up of people, not buildings and dirt. Therefore, I will seek the prosperity of the people and wage war against any poverty that has rooted itself within them.

(Ezra 6:10; Nehemiah 1:4-11; Daniel 9:16; 1 Timothy 2:2)

JEREMIAH 29:8,9 NIV

Yes, this is what the Lord Almighty, the God of Israel, says: "Do not let the prophets and diviners among you deceive you. Do not listen to the dreams you encourage them to have. They are prophesying lies to you in my name. I have not sent them," declares the Lord.

——— *DECLARATION OF FAITH* ———

I do not listen to psychics and diviners. The so-called "psychic friends" are no friends of mine. They are the devil's puppets set to deceive the foolish and profit from their folly. They are not of God and will have no place in my life.

(Leviticus 19:31; 20:6,27; Exodus 22:18; Deuteronomy 18:9-12; Isaiah 8:19,20)

JEREMIAH 29:11-14 KJV

For I know the thoughts that I think toward you, saith the Lord, thoughts of peace, and not of evil, to give you an expected end. Then shall ye call upon me, and ye shall go and pray unto me, and I will hearken unto you. And ye shall seek me, and find *me,* when ye shall search for me with all your heart. And I will be found of you, saith the Lord: and I will turn away your captivity, and I will gather you from all the nations, and from all the places whither I have driven you, saith the Lord; and I will bring you again into the place whence I caused you to be carried away captive.

——— *DECLARATION OF FAITH* ———

All of God's thoughts for me are for good and never evil. His plan for my life is to make me prosperous, give me hope, and provide for me a glorious future. He has handpicked everything that is best for me in life and presents it to me with great joy. His desire for me is to live in His abundance.

My call brings a smile to my Father's face and He listens to me with great concern. When I seek Him with all of my heart, He sees to it that I find Him. He has rescued me from the powers of darkness and is now enjoying my continual companionship.

(Deuteronomy 4:29; Colossians 1:13; 2:15; Romans 8:32; Psalm 50:15; 1 John 1:3)

JEREMIAH 30:8,9 NKJV

"For it shall come to pass in that day," says the Lord of hosts, "that I will break his yoke from your neck, and will burst your bonds; foreigners shall no more enslave them. But they shall serve the Lord their God, and David their king, whom I will raise up for them."

——— *DECLARATION OF FAITH* ———

God has broken the yoke of the oppressor from off of my neck and has ripped the bonds from off of my hands. I am no longer a slave of the enemy. I am now a born-again child of God and I serve Him freely.

(Colossians 1:13; 2:15; Romans 6:14,17,18,22; Luke 10:19; John 3:3; Titus 3:5)

JEREMIAH 30:17,18 NKJV

"For I will restore health to you and heal you of your wounds," says the Lord, "because they called you an outcast saying: 'This is Zion; No one seeks her.'" Thus says the Lord: "Behold, I will bring back the captivity of Jacob's tents, and have mercy on his dwelling places; the city shall be built upon its own mound, and the palace shall remain according to its own plan."

——— *DECLARATION OF FAITH* ———

God has restored health and vitality to me and has healed all of my wounds. He has compassion on my dwelling and restores to me all of the fortunes that the devil robbed from my life. Good health, prosperity and God's tender care are ever-present realities for me to enjoy.

(Exodus 15:26; Isaiah 53:5; 1 Peter 2:24; Joel 2:25; 2 Corinthians 8:9)

JEREMIAH 31:3,4 AMP

The Lord appeared from of old to me [Israel], saying, Yes, I have loved you with an everlasting love; therefore with loving-kindness have I drawn you and continued My faithfulness to you. Again I will build you and you will be built, O Virgin Israel! You will again be adorned with your timbrels [small one-headed drums] and go forth in the dancing [chorus] of those who make merry.

——— *DECLARATION OF FAITH* ———

My heavenly Father loves me with an eternal devotion and has drawn me to Himself with immeasurable compassion. I have His Word that He will mold me and make me what He desires me to be. From here on out, He will do nothing but encourage, strengthen, and build me up. I can rest assured that He will never give up on me. Therefore, I can now, at this present time, take my place and dance with joy among the faithful.

(Hebrews 13:5,6; Romans 8:38,39; John 6:44; 16:27; Philippians 1:6; 3:13,14; Psalm 103:1-14; 149:3,4)

JEREMIAH 31:11-14 KJV

For the Lord hath redeemed Jacob, and ransomed him from the hand of *him that was* stronger than he. Therefore they shall come and sing in the height of Zion, and shall flow together to the goodness of the Lord, for wheat, and for wine, and for oil, and for the young of the flock and of the herd: and their soul shall be as a watered garden; and they shall not sorrow any more at all. Then shall the virgin rejoice in the dance, both young men and old together: for I will turn their mourning into joy, and will comfort them, and make them rejoice from their sorrow. And I will satiate the soul of the priests with fatness, and my people shall be satisfied with my goodness, saith the Lord.

——— *DECLARATION OF FAITH* ———

The Lord has redeemed me from the hand of the enemy. He has stripped him of his authority over me and has left him powerless beneath my feet.

I enter the church with shouts of praise, rejoicing in the abundance of God's bounty. I am like a well-watered garden flourishing in beauty and fine fruit. Sorrow has been removed from my midst and I dance with great hilarity in the presence of my Father. I enjoy comfort and joy instead of sorrow, and my stores are filled with the wealth of God's abundance.

(Galatians 3:13; Colossians 2:15; Luke 10:19; Psalm 1:1-3; 112; 149:3; John 16:22)

JEREMIAH 31:16,17 AMP

Thus says the Lord: Restrain your voice from weeping and your eyes from tears, for your work shall be rewarded, says the Lord; and [your children] shall return from the enemy's land. And there is hope for your future, says the Lord; your children shall come back to their own country.

—————— *DECLARATION OF FAITH* ——————

I have been translated out of the kingdom of the enemy and am now on a path toward a glorious future.

(Colossians 1:13; Jeremiah 29:11)

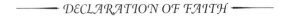

JEREMIAH 31:31-34 AMP

Behold, the days are coming, says the Lord, when I will make a new covenant with the house of Israel and with the house of Judah, not according to the covenant which I made with their fathers in the day when I took them by the hand to bring them out of the land of Egypt, My covenant which they broke, although I was their Husband, says the Lord. But this is the covenant which I will make with the house of Israel: After those days, says the Lord, I will put My law within them, and on their hearts will I write it; and I will be their God, and they will be My people. And they will no more teach each man his neighbor and each man his brother, saying, Know the Lord, for they will all know Me [recognize, understand, and be acquainted with Me], from the least of them to the greatest, says the Lord. For I will forgive their iniquity, and I will [seriously] remember their sin no more.

—————— *DECLARATION OF FAITH* ——————

I have become a partner in a new covenant with my heavenly Father. Our covenant has been made sure—consecrated in the blood of Jesus and sealed by the earnest of the Holy Spirit.

God has written His Word on my mind and engrafted it into my spirit.

He is my Father and I am His son/daughter. We have an intimate relationship with each other and our closeness is beyond comparison.

He has forgiven all of my sins and has given me the right to enter His presence without guilt. I have been freed from all sense of inadequacy and unworthiness. As a new creation in Christ Jesus, I have been made worthy of all that God has to offer!

(Hebrews 4:16; 8:6; 10:15-17; Ephesians 1:13,14; Galatians 4:5,6; James 4:7)

JEREMIAH 32:39-42 KJV

And I will give them one heart, and one way, that they may fear me for ever, for the good of them, and of their children after them: And I will make an everlasting covenant with them, that I will not turn away from them, to do them good; but I will put my fear in their hearts, that they shall not depart from me. Yea, I will rejoice over them to do them good, and I will plant them in this land assuredly with my whole heart and with my whole soul. For thus saith the Lord; Like as I have brought all this great evil upon this people, so will I bring upon them all the good that I have promised them.

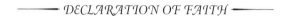

I have singleness of heart, mind, and action, and I am committed to trusting God for my own good and the good of my children after me.

Together, God and I have an everlasting covenant. He will never stop being good to me—inspiring me and keeping me near to His heart. He finds tremendous pleasure in doing good things for me and pours all of His heart and soul into pleasing me. All of His promises for health and prosperity are given to me personally and He is delighted to fulfill them in my life.

(James 1:5-8; Hebrews 8:6; Psalm 35:27; 103:17; Luke 12:32; 2 Corinthians 1:20; Deuteronomy 30:9)

JEREMIAH 33:2,3 AMP

Thus says the Lord Who made [the earth], the Lord Who formed it to establish it—the Lord is His name: Call to Me and I will answer you and show you great and mighty things, fenced in and hidden, which you do not know (do not distinguish and recognize, have knowledge of and understand).

When God and I get together for a heart-to-heart talk, He reveals to me hidden and unsearchable things that I could never discover on my own.

(John 14:26; 16:13; Daniel 2:22,23; Proverbs 3:22; 1 Corinthians 14:2,13)

JEREMIAH 33:6 NIV

"Nevertheless, I will bring health and healing to it; I will heal my people and will let them enjoy abundant peace and security."

My Father has brought perfect health and healing to me and allows me to enjoy abundant peace and security.

(1 Peter 2:24; Ephesians 2:14; James 5:14-16; Romans 14:17; Psalm 91)

JEREMIAH 33:8,9 AMP

And I will cleanse them from all the guilt and iniquity by which they have sinned against Me, and I will forgive all their guilt and iniquities by which they have sinned and rebelled against Me. And [Jerusalem] shall be to Me a name of joy, a praise and a glory before all the nations of the earth that hear of all the good I do for it, and they shall fear and tremble because of all the good and all the peace, prosperity, security, and stability I provide for it.

I am cleansed of all sin and forgiven of all of my rebellion against God. At this very moment, I stand in His presence as holy as Jesus Himself. This puts a smile on God's face and frees Him to do what He has wanted to do all along: be a Father to me and bless me with my portion of His inheritance.

It gives my Father tremendous joy to bless me with all good things. Not only this, but He also receives praise, honor and great renown among those who hear of what He has done for me. Their mouths gape in astonishment at the abundant prosperity and peace that He provides for His children.

(Hebrews 10:14-17; 2 Corinthians 5:17-21; 1 John 4:17; Romans 8:14-17; Galatians 4:5,6; Deuteronomy 28:1-14)

JEREMIAH 33:25,26 AMP

Thus says the Lord: If My covenant with day and night does not stand, and if I have not appointed the ordinances of the heavens and the earth [the whole order of nature], then will I also cast away the descendants of Jacob and David My servant and will not choose one of his offspring to be ruler over the descendants of Abraham, Isaac, and Jacob. For I will cause their captivity to be reversed, and I will have mercy, kindness, and steadfast love on and for them.

God's covenant with me is as fixed and certain as His covenant with day and night and the established laws of heaven and earth. He loves me with all of His heart and will honor His Word to me. When I put in operation the laws of heaven, in accordance with His Word, He restores all that the devil has stolen from me.

(Hebrews 8:6; Isaiah 55:11; 2 Corinthians 1:20; 1 John 3:1,2; Joel 2:25; Psalm 85:1-3)

JEREMIAH 39:17,18 KJV

But I will deliver thee in that day, saith the Lord: and thou shalt not be given into the hand of the men of whom thou *art* afraid. For I will surely deliver thee, and thou shalt not fall by the sword, but thy life shall be for a prey unto thee: because thou hast put thy trust in me, saith the Lord.

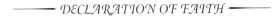

DECLARATION OF FAITH

God will not allow me to be handed over to the enemy. My life is preserved in every circumstance because I trust Him with all of my heart and refuse to turn away from His Word.

(Psalm 18:1-18; Numbers 24:9; Jeremiah 45:5; Colossians 1:13)

JEREMIAH 42:11,12 AMP

Be not afraid of the king of Babylon, of whom you are fearful [with the profound and reverent dread inspired by deity]; be not afraid of him, says the Lord, for [he is a mere man, while I am the all-wise, all-powerful, and ever-present God] I [the Lord] am with you to save you and to deliver you from his hand. And I will grant mercy to you, that he may have mercy on you and permit you to remain in your own land.

DECLARATION OF FAITH

I have no fear of the unjust authorities in this earth. God is on my side and will not allow me to be overcome by them. He delivers me from their hands and causes them to give back what they have taken from me.

(Romans 8:31; Proverbs 6:30,31; Psalm 106:46)

JEREMIAH 46:27,28 AMP

But fear not, O My servant Jacob, and be not dismayed, O Israel. For behold, I will save you from afar, and your offspring from the land of their exile; and Jacob will return and be quiet and at ease, and none will make him afraid. Fear not, O Jacob My servant, says the Lord, for I am with you. For I will make a full and complete end of all the nations to which I have driven you; yet I will not

make a full end of you. But I will chasten and correct you in just measure, and I will not hold you guiltless by any means or leave you unpunished

——— *DECLARATION OF FAITH* ———

I am totally fearless in the face of opposition. God is on my side and has made a commitment to keep me safe and secure everywhere that I go and in everything that I do.

(Joshua 1:5-9; 2 Timothy 1:7; Romans 8:31; Isaiah 54:17; Psalm 91)

JEREMIAH 50:4,5 AMP

In those days and at that time, says the Lord, the children of Israel shall come, they and the children of Judah together; they shall come up weeping as they come and seek the Lord their God [inquiring for and of Him and requiring Him, both by right of necessity and of the promises of God's Word]. They shall ask the way to Zion, with their faces in that direction, saying, Come, let us join ourselves to the Lord in a perpetual covenant that shall not be forgotten.

——— *DECLARATION OF FAITH* ———

I seek the Lord and His ways with all of my heart. I have bound myself to Him in an everlasting covenant that will never be forgotten.

(Deuteronomy 4:29; 28:1-14; Hebrews 8:6; 10:15-17)

JEREMIAH 50:20 NKJV

"In those days and in that time," says the Lord, "The iniquity of Israel shall be sought, but *there shall be* none; and the sins of Judah, but they shall not be found; for I will pardon those whom I preserve."

——— *DECLARATION OF FAITH* ———

Though a great search is made for my guilt, none will be found. I have been forgiven, cleansed, acquitted, and reborn as God's own son/daughter. The days of my guilt are gone forever.

(Psalm 103:10-12; Titus 3:5; Romans 5:1,2; 8:1; Isaiah 1:9)

JEREMIAH 50:33,34 KJV

Thus saith the Lord of hosts; The children of Israel and the children of Judah *were* oppressed together: and all that took them captives held them fast; they refused to let them go. Their Redeemer *is* strong; the Lord of hosts *is* his name:

he shall throughly plead their cause, that he may give rest to the land, and disquiet the inhabitants of Babylon.

——— *DECLARATION OF FAITH* ———

My Redeemer dwells within my heart with all of His strength and miracle-working power. He vigorously defends my cause against my enemies and in His name I vanquish them.

(1 Corinthians 3:16; Ephesians 1:17-23; Colossians 1:29; 1 John 2:1,2; Deuteronomy 33:27)

JEREMIAH 51:36 NKJV

Therefore thus says the Lord: "Behold, I will plead your case and take vengeance for you. I will dry up her sea and make her springs dry."

——— *DECLARATION OF FAITH* ———

The Lord defends my cause continually, making impotent any enemy that would choose to come against me.

(Deuteronomy 33:27; Exodus 23:20-30; Psalm 35:4; Proverbs 11:8)

CHAPTER TWENTY-FIVE

LAMENTATIONS

The very word, Lamentations, means, "intense morning and expression of grief." The book is an acrostic poem using the twenty-two letters of the Hebrew alphabet. Though its nature is one of extreme sorrow, its purpose is to bring the reader to a realization that God has provided redemption from destruction.

As you pray the promises in the book of Lamentations, know that God is with you no matter what you are going through and that if you will trust Him with all of your heart, He will lead you to a path full of joy and prosperity.

LAMENTATIONS 2:17

The Lord has done what He purposed; He has fulfilled His word which He commanded in days of old. He has thrown down and has not pitied, and He has caused an enemy to rejoice over you; He has exalted the horn of your adversaries.

————— DECLARATION OF FAITH —————

All of the Lord's plans for me are accomplished, and His Word is faithfully fulfilled in my life.

(Jeremiah 29:11; Isaiah 55:11; 2 Corinthians 1:20)

LAMENTATIONS 3:22-26 KJV

It is of the Lord's mercies that we are not consumed, because his compassions fail not. *They are* new every morning: great *is* thy faithfulness. The Lord *is* my portion, saith my soul; therefore will I hope in him. The Lord *is* good unto them that wait for him, to the soul *that* seeketh him. *It is* good that *a man* should both hope and quietly wait for the salvation of the Lord.

————— DECLARATION OF FAITH —————

God's compassion for me never fails. He renews His love and blessings for me every morning and is faithful to fulfill the plan He has for my life.

I am His highest priority and He makes it His business to bless me.

He carefully watches over me so that I am not overrun by the enemy.

The Lord is my portion and my delight. I will wait for Him in the midst of adversity. I wait quietly for His salvation. He is always faithful and comes through for me every time.

God is not only good to me some of the time; He is good to me all of the time. He has given me His Word that He will never harm me in any way.

(Romans 8:38,39; Jeremiah 29:11; Isaiah 30:15; 40:28-31; Deuteronomy 6:24; Psalm 16:5; 78:38; 119:57,65)

LAMENTATIONS 3:37 NIV

Who can speak and have it happen if the Lord has not decreed it?

——— *DECLARATION OF FAITH* ———

I take hold of God's Word and make it my own. I speak those things that He has decreed for me and they come to pass in my life.

(Romans 10:8; Mark 11:22-25; 2 Corinthians 4:13; Psalm 33:9-11; Proverbs 18:20,21)

LAMENTATIONS 3:58 AMP

O Lord, You have pleaded the causes of my soul [You have managed my affairs and You have protected my person and my rights]; You have rescued and redeemed my life!

——— *DECLARATION OF FAITH* ———

Jesus takes up my case at the right hand of the Father, declaring to all of creation that I am redeemed.

(1 John 2:1,2; Galatians 3:13; Hebrews 7:25,26; 10:12-23; Titus 3:5)

CHAPTER TWENTY-SIX

EZEKIEL

The book of Ezekiel is sometimes referred to as the Apocalypse of the Old Testament. Many "Revelation" type prophecies are found in its pages. They are full of imagery and metaphor. Amidst all of these, the reader can fail to recognize the uplifting promises that are contained within it.

The name Ezekiel literally means, "God strengthens." As you pray the promises of this book, I'm sure you will agree that this is no accident. These promises strengthen you and encourage you to walk in your calling. Part of every one of our callings is to be a soul-winner. These promises prepare you for that task.

EZEKIEL 1:12 NIV

Each one went straight ahead. Wherever the spirit would go, they would go, without turning as they went.

DECLARATION OF FAITH

I am led by the Spirit of God. Wherever He goes, I go. I cannot be diverted from the path that He has set before me.

(Romans 8:14; John 16:13; Deuteronomy 28:14)

EZEKIEL 1:20 NKJV

Wherever the spirit wanted to go, they went, *because* there the spirit went; and the wheels were lifted together with them, for the spirit of the living creatures *was* in the wheels.

DECLARATION OF FAITH

The Spirit of God is within me, instructing me in the ways of righteousness and leading me in a glorious service. As I follow His lead, He makes everything around me work in harmony to achieve His purpose for my life.

(Romans 8:11,14,26-28; Proverbs 16:9; Philippians 2:13)

EZEKIEL 2:6,7 KJV

And thou, son of man, be not afraid of them, neither be afraid of their words, though briers and thorns *be* with thee, and thou dost dwell among scorpions: be not afraid of their words, nor be dismayed at their looks, though they *be* a rebellious house. And thou shalt speak my words unto them, whether they will hear, or whether they will forbear: for they *are* most rebellious.

I am not afraid of the cold and vindictive words of those in the church who despise the truth and are ignorant of the ways of the Lord. Even though the briars and thorns of divisive people seek to entangle me, and I live in the midst of hell's fury, I will remain bold and courageous. I have no fear of what they say, or how they twist what I say, and I will not be influenced by their rebellion. I speak the Word of God the way that God intends whether they like it or not.

(Romans 16:17-19; Jeremiah 1:7,8,17; Micah 7:4; 1 Peter 3:14; Ezekiel 3:9,26,27)

EZEKIEL 3:8,9 AMP

Behold, I have made your face strong and hard against their faces and your forehead strong and hard against their foreheads. Like an adamant harder than flint or a diamond point have I made your forehead; fear them not, neither be dismayed at their looks, for they are a rebellious house.

I am as stubborn for the Word as the hardest stone and as hardheaded for the Truth as an impenetrable rock. I could care less what anyone thinks of me and I have no fear of their rebellion against me. I choose to do what I know to be right and I walk in the ways of the Word.

(Jeremiah 1:7,8,17; Micah 3:8; Psalm 119:113-116; Acts 4:13,19,20)

EZEKIEL 3:14 NIV

The Spirit then lifted me up and took me away, and I went in bitterness and in the anger of my spirit, with the strong hand of the Lord upon me.

──── *DECLARATION OF FAITH* ────

The Spirit of God is within me, stirring up my own spirit in a rage against evil. His strong hand is upon me to go forth and conquer.

(1 Corinthians 3:16; Leviticus 5:1; 2 Kings 3:15; Romans 8:37)

EZEKIEL 3:17-27 KJV

Son of man, I have made thee a watchman unto the house of Israel: therefore hear the word at my mouth, and give them warning from me. When I say unto the wicked, Thou shalt surely die; and thou givest him not warning, nor speakest to warn the wicked from his wicked way, to save his life; the same wicked *man* shall die in his iniquity; but his blood will I require at thine hand. Yet if thou warn the wicked, and he turn not from his wickedness, nor from his wicked way, he shall die in his iniquity; but thou hast delivered thy soul. Again, When a righteous *man* doth turn from his righteousness, and commit iniquity, and I lay a stumblingblock before him, he shall die: because thou hast not given him warning, he shall die in his sin, and his righteousness which he hath done shall not be remembered; but his blood will I require at thine hand. Nevertheless if thou warn the righteous *man,* that the righteous sin not, and he doth not sin, he shall surely live, because he is warned; also thou hast delivered thy soul. And the hand of the Lord was there upon me; and he said unto me, Arise, go forth into the plain, and I will there talk with thee. Then I arose, and went forth into the plain: and, behold, the glory of the Lord stood there, as the glory which I saw by the river of Chebar: and I fell on my face. Then the spirit entered into me, and set me upon my feet, and spake with me, and said unto me, Go, shut thyself within thine house. But thou, O son of man, behold, they shall put bands upon thee, and shall bind thee with them, and thou shalt not go out among them: And I will make thy tongue cleave to the roof of thy mouth, that thou shalt be dumb, and shalt not be to them a reprover: for they *are* a rebellious house. But when I speak with thee, I will open thy mouth, and thou shalt say unto them, Thus saith the Lord God; He that heareth, let him hear; and he that forbeareth, let him forbear: for they *are* a rebellious house.

——— DECLARATION OF FAITH ———

I have been given the assignment of a watchman to warn people against the consequences of evil. I offer God's goodness and mercy to a hurting world suffering from the cruel hand of Satan. I refuse to sit idly by and watch the devil take people to hell. I stand up in their defense, giving them warning and telling them of a new and better way. I am a soul-winner for God and a voice leading backsliders to return to the arms of their Father.

God's hand is upon me and His Spirit is within me. He gives me specific instructions as to what to say and what to do as I fulfill my commission. God reveals to me exactly what I need to say in any given situation, or to any certain individual. Together, we are winning this world for His glory.

(Daniel 12:3; Isaiah 52:8; Romans 2:4; John 16:13; Proverbs 11:30)

EZEKIEL 11:17-20 AMP

Therefore say, Thus says the Lord God: I will gather you from the peoples and assemble you out of the countries where you have been scattered, and I will give back to you the land of Israel. And when they return there, they shall take away from it all traces of its detestable things and all its abominations (sex impurities and heathen religious practices). And I will give them one heart [a new heart] and I will put a new spirit within them; and I will take the stony [unnaturally hardened] heart out of their flesh, and will give them a heart of flesh [sensitive and responsive to the touch of their God], that they may walk in My statutes and keep My ordinances, and do them. And they shall be My people, and I will be their God.

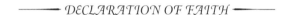

DECLARATION OF FAITH

I have been reconciled to God.

My spirit has been recreated and regenerated and I now have an undivided heart dedicated to His will. I no longer have a cold, stony, Satan-ruled heart, but have been given a heart of flesh, filled with the life of God.

As God's newborn son/daughter, I now have the ability to live above sin. All of the things in my life that bring dishonor to His name I remove without hesitation.

I am careful to keep the law of love, that perfect law of liberty, in my life.

I live every day in full realization that I am God's son/daughter and that He is my Father.

(Psalm 105:45; Titus 3:5; Romans 5:10; 6:14; John 10:10; Galatians 4:5,6)

EZEKIEL 12:25,28 NKJV

"For I *am* the Lord. I speak, and the word which I speak will come to pass; it will no more be postponed; for in your days, O rebellious house, I will say the word and perform it," says the Lord God. "Therefore say to them, 'Thus says the Lord God: "None of My words will be postponed any more, but the word which I speak will be done," says the Lord God.'"

DECLARATION OF FAITH

Every Word that God has given me is fulfilled in my life. He does not delay in keeping His promises to me.

(2 Corinthians 1:20; Isaiah 14:24; 55:11; Luke 21:33)

EZEKIEL 16:8-13 KJV

Now when I passed by thee, and looked upon thee, behold, thy time *was* the time of love; and I spread my skirt over thee, and covered thy nakedness: yea, I sware unto thee, and entered into a covenant with thee, saith the Lord God, and thou becamest mine. Then washed I thee with water; yea, I throughly washed away thy blood from thee, and I anointed thee with oil. I clothed thee also with broidered work, and shod thee with badgers' skin, and I girded thee about with fine linen, and I covered thee with silk. I decked thee also with ornaments, and I put bracelets upon thy hands, and a chain on thy neck. And I put a jewel on thy forehead, and earrings in thine ears, and a beautiful crown upon thine head. Thus wast thou decked with gold and silver; and thy raiment *was of* fine linen, and silk, and broidered work; thou didst eat fine flour, and honey, and oil: and thou wast exceeding beautiful, and thou didst prosper into a kingdom.

———— DECLARATION OF FAITH ————

God has spread the corner of His garment over me and covered my naked-
ness. He has given me His solemn oath that He will never leave me nor forsake
me. He has cleansed me from my bloodguilt, glorified me, and dressed me in
costly apparel. He feeds me with His abundance of rich dainty morsels. He pros-
pers everything I set my hand to do. Together, we have a covenant pact. All that
He is and all that He has is mine, and all that I am and all that I have is His.

(Romans 8:29,30; Deuteronomy 28:1-14; Philippians 4:19; Hebrews 8:6; 13:5,6)

EZEKIEL 16:62,63 AMP

And I will establish My covenant with you, and you shall know (understand and realize) that I am the Lord, that you may [earnestly] remember and be ashamed and confounded and never open your mouth again because of your shame, when I have forgiven you all that you have done, says the Lord God.

———— DECLARATION OF FAITH ————

God has firmly established His covenant with me. The blood of Jesus has rat-
ified the contract. I understand what it took to make this life I now enjoy a real-
ity. I am humbled by the thought of God's great love for me. I have been bought
with a tremendous price and I give all that I am—spirit, soul, and body, in serv-
ice to Him. This is my commitment both now and forevermore.

(Hebrews 8:6; 10:15-17; Acts 20:28; 1 John 3:1,2; 1 Corinthians 6:20; 7:23)

EZEKIEL 18:21,22 NIV

"But if a wicked man turns away from all the sins he has committed and keeps all my decrees and does what is just and right, he will surely live; he will not die. None of the offenses he has committed will be remembered against him. Because of the righteous things he has done, he will live."

——— *DECLARATION OF FAITH* ———

God's Word is my life preserver. I am careful to follow all of His precepts, for in doing so I am ensured a life of health, peace, and prosperity. Because I follow the ways of righteousness, I will live the kind of life that God intends for me to live.

(Psalm 18:20-24; 119:50; Isaiah 46:4; John 10:10)

EZEKIEL 18:30-32 KJV

Therefore I will judge you, O house of Israel, every one according to his ways, saith the Lord God. Repent, and turn *yourselves* from all your transgressions; so iniquity shall not be your ruin. Cast away from you all your transgressions, whereby ye have transgressed; and make you a new heart and a new spirit: for why will ye die, O house of Israel? For I have no pleasure in the death of him that dieth, saith the Lord God: wherefore turn *yourselves,* and live ye.

——— *DECLARATION OF FAITH* ———

I have repented of my sins and have put them behind me. God has forgiven them and has promised me that He will never bring them up again. I will do the same. My past failures will not hinder my present victories. I rid myself of my past and press on toward the future. I am a born-again child of God with a new heart and a new spirit. I now live the God-kind of life.

(Philippians 3:13; Psalm 103:10-12; Hebrews 10:15-17)

EZEKIEL 20:7 AMP

Then said I to them, Let every man cast away the abominable things on which he feasts his eyes, and defile not yourselves with the idols of Egypt; I am the Lord your God.

——— *DECLARATION OF FAITH* ———

I will fix my attention only on good things. Vile images, pornography, and the like will find no place in my life.

(Job 31:1-4; 2 Chronicles 15:8; Philippians 4:8)

EZEKIEL 20:37 NIV

I will take note of you as you pass under my rod, and I will bring you into the bond of the covenant.

——— *DECLARATION OF FAITH* ———

God has taken notice of me, placed His mark upon me, and made me His own. He has brought me into the bond of the covenant and will call me His son/daughter for all of eternity.

(Leviticus 27:32; Ephesians 1:13,14; Hebrews 8:6; Galatians 4:5,6)

EZEKIEL 22:30 NKJV

"So I sought for a man among them who would make a wall, and stand in the gap before Me on behalf of the land, that I should not destroy it; but I found no one."

——— *DECLARATION OF FAITH* ———

I have built up a wall of protection for my family, my friends, my church, my city, and my country, and I am standing in the gap on their behalf. The righteousness that I have found in Jesus has made me an impenetrable barrier and Satan cannot touch them.

(1 John 5:18; Psalm 106:29-31; Job 22:27-30; 2 Corinthians 5:21)

EZEKIEL 33:7-9 KJV

So thou, O son of man, I have set thee a watchman unto the house of Israel; therefore thou shalt hear the word at my mouth, and warn them from me. When I say unto the wicked, O wicked *man,* thou shalt surely die; if thou dost not speak to warn the wicked from his way, that wicked *man* shall die in his iniquity; but his blood will I require at thine hand. Nevertheless, if thou warn the wicked of his way to turn from it; if he do not turn from his way, he shall die in his iniquity; but thou hast delivered thy soul.

——— *DECLARATION OF FAITH* ———

I am a watchman who gives warning and instruction in the ways of righteousness. I do not turn my back on the sinner and thus take part in His destruction. With the Word of God as my guide and the tutoring of the Holy Spirit providing the direction, I reap a massive harvest of souls. I see every person I meet as a potential brother or sister in Christ.

(Daniel 12:3; Proverbs 11:30; Ezekiel 3:17-27; John 16:13; Jude 23)

EZEKIEL 33:11 NIV

Say to them, 'As surely as I live, declares the Sovereign Lord, I take no pleasure in the death of the wicked, but rather that they turn from their ways and live. Turn! Turn from your evil ways! Why will you die, O house of Israel?'

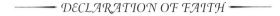

I am a carrier of God's love and mercy to a hurting world. My message is not a wielding of condemnation and hell's fire, but an offering of compassion and deliverance from hell's cruel bondage.

(2 Corinthians 5:19,20; Romans 2:4; 2 Samuel 14:14; Acts 3:19)

EZEKIEL 33:16 NKJV

"None of his sins which he has committed shall be remembered against him; he has done what is lawful and right; he shall surely live."

Not one of my sins will ever be remembered against me, for I have received Jesus and my life is now hidden in Him. I have done what is just and right in the eyes of God.

(Hebrews 10:15-17; Psalm 103:10-12; John 1:12; 3:16,17; Colossians 3:3; Isaiah 1:18)

EZEKIEL 33:24 AMP

Son of man, those [back in Palestine] who inhabit those wastes of the ground of Israel are saying, Abraham was only one man and he inherited the land, but we are many; the land is surely given to us to possess as our inheritance.

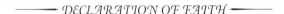

With God in me, I can take back any land that He bids me to take.

(Joshua 1:5-9; Proverbs 6:30,31; Romans 8:31)

EZEKIEL 33:31,32 AMP

And they come to you as people come, and they sit before you as My people, and they hear the words you say, but they will not do them; for with their mouths they show much love, but their hearts go after and are set on their [idolatrous greed for] gain. Behold, you are to them as a very lovely [love] song of one who has a pleasant voice and can play well on an instrument, for they hear your words but do not do them.

─── *DECLARATION OF FAITH* ───

I am a doer of the Word and not just a hearer. I meditate upon it and root it deeply into my spirit, not just to know it, but also to apply it to my life. I will not sit and listen to a sermon just to soak in a blessing so that I can walk away feeling good. For me, church is not a "bless me" club, but a place to gather with other believers who are dedicated to the expansion of God's kingdom and are focused on building each other up in preparation for our continuing mission in this world.

I refuse to focus on a greedy pursuit of riches. I am God's servant first and foremost, and all that He has blessed me with I give freely so that the world may know of His love and mercy.

(James 1:22-25; Joshua 1:8; Hebrews 10:25; 1 Timothy 6:3-12,17-19)

EZEKIEL 34:2-4 KJV

Son of man, prophesy against the shepherds of Israel, prophesy, and say unto them, Thus saith the Lord God unto the shepherds; Woe *be* to the shepherds of Israel that do feed themselves! should not the shepherds feed the flocks? Ye eat the fat, and ye clothe you with the wool, ye kill them that are fed: *but* ye feed not the flock. The diseased have ye not strengthened, neither have ye healed that which was sick, neither have ye bound up *that which was* broken, neither have ye brought again that which was driven away, neither have ye sought that which was lost; but with force and with cruelty have ye ruled them.

─── *DECLARATION OF FAITH* ───

I will not allow selfishness to rule my walk with God. Service dictates my every motive. I serve God, His children, and yes, even the world. God through me heals the sick, strengthens the weak and gives comfort for the hurting. I am on an impassioned quest for those who have strayed from God's tender embrace and I am a grappler for the lost souls of the earth.

(Job 29:15-17,21-24; Isaiah 61:1-3; Daniel 12:3; Luke 15:4; 1 Peter 5:2,3)

EZEKIEL 34:11,12 NIV

"For this is what the Sovereign Lord says: I myself will search for my sheep and look after them. As a shepherd looks after his scattered flock when he is with them, so will I look after my sheep. I will rescue them from all the places where they were scattered on a day of clouds and darkness."

My Father's protective eye never leaves me. He looks after me as a good shepherd looks after His flock when He is with them.

(Nehemiah 1:5,6; Job 36:7; Psalm 3:5,6; 11:4; John 10:11-18)

EZEKIEL 34:14-16 AMP

I will feed them with good pasture, and upon the high mountains of Israel shall their fold be; there shall they lie down in a good fold, and in a fat pasture shall they feed upon the mountains of Israel. I will feed My sheep and I will cause them to lie down, says the Lord God. I will seek that which was lost and bring back that which has strayed, and I will bandage the hurt and the crippled and will strengthen the weak and the sick, but I will destroy the fat and the strong [who have become hardhearted and perverse]; I will feed them with judgment and punishment.

The Lord is my Shepherd. He sets me in a fertile pasture and tends to my every need. He sees to it that I have nothing but the best from His great storehouse of provision. He heals my every sickness and comforts me in times of sadness. He grants me tremendous strength to overcome my weaknesses and He shepherds me with His justice.

(Psalm 23; John 10:10-18; Matthew 8:17; 2 Corinthians 1:3,4; Colossians 1:29)

EZEKIEL 34:23-27 KJV

And I will set up one shepherd over them, and he shall feed them, *even* my servant David; he shall feed them, and he shall be their shepherd. And I the Lord will be their God, and my servant David a prince among them; I the Lord have spoken *it.* And I will make with them a covenant of peace, and will cause the evil beasts to cease out of the land: and they shall dwell safely in the wilderness, and sleep in the woods. And I will make them and the places round about my hill a blessing; and I will cause the shower to come down in his season; there shall be showers of blessing. And the tree of the field shall yield her fruit, and the earth shall yield her increase, and they shall be safe in their land, and shall know that I *am* the Lord, when I have broken the bands of their yoke, and delivered them out of the hand of those that served themselves of them.

——— *DECLARATION OF FAITH* ———

Jesus is the Lord of my life and He watches over me meticulously.

God is my Father and I am His full-fledged son/daughter. We have a covenant of peace between us. Because of this, the dangers that come from Satan and his horde are no longer a threat to me. I am under God's hedge of protection and I live my life in peace and safety.

I am thoroughly blessed with my Father's abundance and He has blessed everything around me for my sake, because I am His son/daughter. Showers of blessing drench me—all in God's perfect timing.

I am redeemed from the curse and rescued from the hand of bondage. The curse is lifted from all of my ground and from every area of my life. Because of Jesus, I can expect nothing but good things from God both now and forevermore.

(John 10:10-18; 1 John 5:18; Galatians 3:13; 4:5,6; Ezekiel 37:26; Colossians 1:13; Deuteronomy 28:1-14; Isaiah 11:6-9; Jeremiah 23:6; 1 Timothy 6:17)

EZEKIEL 36:25-27 KJV

Then will I sprinkle clean water upon you, and ye shall be clean: from all your filthiness, and from all your idols, will I cleanse you. A new heart also will I give you, and a new spirit will I put within you: and I will take away the stony heart out of your flesh, and I will give you an heart of flesh. And I will put my spirit within you, and cause you to walk in my statutes, and ye shall keep my judgments, and do *them.*

——— *DECLARATION OF FAITH* ———

I am cleansed from all of my impurities and can stand in God's presence free of guilt and all sense of inadequacy.

I have been born again and recreated in the image of my Savior.

The Holy Spirit has taken up residence within my heart and I have all the power that I need to live the godly life that is required of me.

I am God's man/woman and Satan cannot stop me. My destiny is the glory of heaven itself.

(1 John 1:9; 3:2; Hebrew 4:16; 2 Corinthians 5:17; Romans 8:29,30; Titus 3:5; John 3:3; 1 Corinthians 3:16; Ephesians 1:17-23; Luke 10:19; Revelation 21:1-7)

EZEKIEL 36:29,30 AMP

I will also save you from all your uncleannesses, and I will call forth the grain and make it abundant and lay no famine on you. And I will multiply the fruit of

the tree and the increase of the field, that you may no more suffer the reproach and disgrace of famine among the nations.

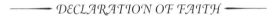

——— *DECLARATION OF FAITH* ———

Because of what Jesus has done, God can finally bless me as His own child. He commands all that I have to increase so that I may enjoy His abundance on this earth. I no longer have to face the ridicule of those in the world who see Christians as beggars and parasites on the breast of humanity. I bring my Father glory by receiving His blessings and then being a blessing to the world.

(Galatians 4:5,6; Deuteronomy 28:1-14; Genesis 12:1-3; 13:2; John 14:13,14)

EZEKIEL 37:24,25 NKJV

"David My servant *shall be* king over them, and they shall all have one shepherd; they shall also walk in My judgments and observe My statutes, and do them. Then they shall dwell in the land that I have given to Jacob My servant, where your fathers dwelt; and they shall dwell there, they, their children, and their children's children, forever; and My servant David *shall be* their prince forever."

——— *DECLARATION OF FAITH* ———

Jesus is the Lord of my life. I follow all of the precepts of God and I am careful to apply His Word in everything that I do. He keeps me safe in all of my ways and proclaims His Lordship over my children and my grandchildren.

(Romans 10:8-10; Deuteronomy 28:1; Psalm 91; 103:17)

EZEKIEL 37:26,27 AMP

I will make a covenant of peace with them; it shall be an everlasting covenant with them, and I will give blessings to them and multiply them and will set My sanctuary in the midst of them forevermore. My tabernacle or dwelling place also shall be with them; and I will be their God, and they shall be My people.

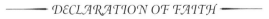

——— *DECLARATION OF FAITH* ———

I have a covenant of peace with my heavenly Father. He establishes me in a firm and stable relationship and causes the laws of increase to overflow in, through, and all around me.

The Holy Spirit Himself has taken up residence within me to procure my victory in every situation.

Security has never found a better definition.

(Hebrews 8:6; Isaiah 55:3; Romans 5:1,2; 1 John 4:4; 2 Corinthians 9:5-11)

CHAPTER TWENTY-SEVEN

DANIEL

O ne of our most neglected promises is that of God's divine revelation to us through dreams and visions. As covenant children of God, we are destined to have them. The book of Daniel not only details accounts of dreams and visions, it provides promises concerning them. God uses such promises to bring us to a place of influence in the earth. In order to win this world, we must influence this world. The book of Daniel shows how as covenant children of God we are given the ability to live in the realm of God's power in order to bring Him glory in whatever situation we find ourselves in.

As you pray these prayers, remember your covenant. God has promised to never leave you nor forsake you. His covenant promises ring true no matter what your situation may be.

+

DANIEL 1:3,4 AMP

And the [Babylonian] king told Ashpenaz, the master of his eunuchs, to bring in some of the children of Israel, both of the royal family and of the nobility—youths without blemish, well-favored in appearance and skillful in all wisdom, discernment, and understanding, apt in learning knowledge, competent to stand and serve in the king's palace—and to teach them the literature and language of the Chaldeans.

—— *DECLARATION OF FAITH* ——

I am a covenant child of God, of noble birth—born in the bloodline of the King.

I reflect a presence of attractiveness and prestige, and I have neither illness nor ailment in my body.

I am an exceptional learner, well informed and quick to understand, with tremendous aptitude in all subject matters.

(Hebrews 8:6; Titus 3:5; 1 John 2:20,27; 3:1,2; 1 Peter 3:1-7; Isaiah 33:24; Daniel 1:17,20; 2:22,23; 1 Corinthians 1:30; 2:6-16)

DANIEL 1:8 NKJV

But Daniel purposed in his heart that he would not defile himself with the portion of the king's delicacies, nor with the wine which he drank; therefore he requested of the chief of the eunuchs that he might not defile himself.

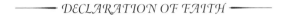

DECLARATION OF FAITH

I will not defile myself with meat offered to Satan or any of his demons, and I will not take part in the ways of the world.

(Hosea 9:3; Acts 15:29; Ephesians 5:11-18; 2 Corinthians 6:14)

DANIEL 1:9 NIV

Now God had caused the official to show favor and sympathy to Daniel.

DECLARATION OF FAITH

God gives me an abundance of favor with the supervisors and officials appointed over me.

(Proverbs 3:3,4; Genesis 39:2-5,21; Psalm 5:12)

DANIEL 1:15-17 KJV

And at the end of ten days their countenances appeared fairer and fatter in flesh than all the children which did eat the portion of the king's meat. Thus Melzar took away the portion of their meat, and the wine that they should drink; and gave them pulse. As for these four children, God gave them knowledge and skill in all learning and wisdom: and Daniel had understanding in all visions and dreams.

DECLARATION OF FAITH

God takes the food that I eat and sees to it that it nourishes my body for maximum effectiveness. I am healthy and well nourished.

My heavenly Father has given me extraordinary ability to retain knowledge, and a deep-seated understanding in every kind of learning.

By the Holy Spirit, I understand dreams and visions of every kind.

(Exodus 15:26; Proverbs 4:20-27; James 1:5-8; Acts 7:22; 1 Corinthians 2:6-16; Daniel 2:22,23; 2 Chronicles 26:5; John 16:13)

DANIEL 1:19,20 AMP

And the king conversed with them, and among them all none was found like Daniel, Hananiah, Mishael, and Azariah; therefore they were assigned to stand before the king. And in all matters of wisdom and understanding concerning which the king asked them, he found them ten times better than all the [learned] magicians and enchanters who were in his whole realm.

——— DECLARATION OF FAITH ———

I have abundant favor with those appointed in authority over me.

When I am tested, examined, interrogated, or sought after for counsel, in every matter of wisdom and understanding, I am found to have more insight than the witches, psychics, and magicians of the kingdom of darkness.

(Genesis 39:2-5,21; Proverbs 3:3,4; Daniel 1:17; 2:22,23; 1 Kings 10:1)

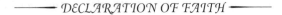

DANIEL 2:14-23 KJV

Then Daniel answered with counsel and wisdom to Arioch the captain of the king's guard, which was gone forth to slay the wise *men* of Babylon: He answered and said to Arioch the king's captain, Why *is* the decree *so* hasty from the king? Then Arioch made the thing known to Daniel. Then Daniel went in, and desired of the king that he would give him time, and that he would shew the king the interpretation. Then Daniel went to his house, and made the thing known to Hananiah, Mishael, and Azariah, his companions: That they would desire mercies of the God of heaven concerning this secret; that Daniel and his fellows should not perish with the rest of the wise *men* of Babylon. Then was the secret revealed unto Daniel in a night vision. Then Daniel blessed the God of heaven. Daniel answered and said, Blessed be the name of God for ever and ever: for wisdom and might are his: And he changeth the times and the seasons: he removeth kings, and setteth up kings: he giveth wisdom unto the wise, and knowledge to them that know understanding: He revealeth the deep and secret things: he knoweth what *is* in the darkness, and the light dwelleth with him. I thank thee, and praise thee, O thou God of my fathers, who hast given me wisdom and might, and hast made known unto me now what we desired of thee: for thou hast *now* made known unto us the king's matter.

——— DECLARATION OF FAITH ———

I am an expert in the art of persuasion and can speak with extraordinary wisdom and tact.

My supervisors are quick to grant me favors.

I understand the power of the prayer of agreement and regularly seek those of like faith to urgently agree with me for the answers to my petitions before God's throne.

God is ever ready to reveal to me things to come. In Him, I have the answers to every mystery and the interpretation of every vision and dream.

Wisdom and power are my Father's to give. Times and seasons are under His control, and He reserves the authority to both set up kings and knock them down.

God has made me wise and discerning. He continually increases my wisdom and knowledge. He reveals to me deep and hidden things. He makes my path bright in the midst of the darkness and makes me aware of every sneak attack. In Him, I have extraordinary wisdom and power beyond compare. Whatever I ask in His name, He makes known to me.

(1 Corinthians 1:30; 2:6-16; 14:2,13; Genesis 39:2-5,21; Proverbs 3:32; Psalm 31:15; 75:6,7; Matthew 18:19,20; James 1:5-8; 5:14-16; Job 12:13,22; John 16:13,23,24; Ephesians 1:17-23)

DANIEL 2:46-49 KJV

Then the king Nebuchadnezzar fell upon his face, and worshipped Daniel, and commanded that they should offer an oblation and sweet odours unto him. The king answered unto Daniel, and said, Of a truth *it is,* that your God *is* a God of gods, and a Lord of kings, and a revealer of secrets, seeing thou couldest reveal this secret. Then the king made Daniel a great man, and gave him many great gifts, and made him ruler over the whole province of Babylon, and chief of the governors over all the wise *men* of Babylon. Then Daniel requested of the king, and he set Shadrach, Meshach, and Abednego, over the affairs of the province of Babylon: but Daniel *sat* in the gate of the king.

──── DECLARATION OF FAITH ────

I have favor with all those who have authority over me. They see the way He works in and through me and they give Him glory because of me. He gives me incredible favor in their presence and they promote me to positions of authority because I honor His name. Many gifts are bestowed upon me.

I promote my brothers and sisters in Christ, who honor the name of Jesus, and bring them to power with me.

(Genesis 12:1-3; 39:2-5,21; Deuteronomy 28:12,13; Proverbs 3:3,4; 14:35; 21:1)

DANIEL 3:16-18 NKJV

Shadrach, Meshach, and Abed-Nego answered and said to the king, "O Nebuchadnezzar, we have no need to answer you in this matter. If that *is the case,* our God whom we serve is able to deliver us from the burning fiery furnace, and He will deliver *us* from your hand, O king. But if not, let it be known to you, O king, that we do not serve your gods, nor will we worship the gold image which you have set up."

——— DECLARATION OF FAITH ———

I have no need to defend myself for honoring my covenant with God and I will not allow fear to rise within me due to the persecution that I endure for the name of Jesus. No matter what man does to me, God will deliver me. And even if He didn't, I'd serve Him anyway and continue to reject the ways of the world because of my love for Him. I am totally sold out and committed to do His will.

However, God has not called me to be anybody's whipping boy/girl. My message to the author of my persecution is this, "I have His Word that He will deliver me, so prepare to see His glory and miracle-working power!"

(Acts 4:16-31; 2 Timothy 1:6,7; Romans 8:31; Colossians 1:29; Psalm 34:19)

DANIEL 3:28-30 NIV

Then Nebuchadnezzar said, "Praise be to the God of Shadrach, Meshach and Abednego, who has sent his angel and rescued his servants! They trusted in him and defied the king's command and were willing to give up their lives rather than serve or worship any god except their own God. Therefore I decree that the people of any nation or language who say anything against the God of Shadrach, Meshach and Abednego be cut into pieces and their houses be turned into piles of rubble, for no other god can save in this way." Then the king promoted Shadrach, Meshach and Abednego in the province of Babylon.

——— DECLARATION OF FAITH ———

I trust in my Father and would rather die than worship any other god but Him.
God sends His angel to deliver me from the hands of my persecutors. He reduces them to nothing in my presence while promoting me to a position of authority.

(Proverbs 3:5,6; Deuteronomy 28:14; Exodus 23:20-23; Genesis 39:2-5)

DANIEL 5:11,12

There is a man in thy kingdom, in whom is the spirit of the holy gods; and in the days of thy father light and understanding and wisdom, like the wisdom of the gods, was found in him; whom the king Nebuchadnezzar thy father, the king, *I say,* thy father, made master of the magicians, astrologers, Chaldeans, *and* soothsayers; Forasmuch as an excellent spirit, and knowledge, and understanding, interpreting of dreams, and shewing of hard sentences, and dissolving of doubts, were found in the same Daniel, whom the king named Belteshazzar: now let Daniel be called, and he will shew the interpretation.

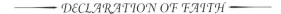

The Holy Spirit dwells in my heart and has given me God-like wisdom and intelligence. I have keen insight regarding all issues that affect my life. I have a keen mind with extraordinary ability to retain and understand knowledge. Furthermore, I have the ability to interpret dreams, understand and explain mysteries, and solve difficult problems.

(1 Corinthians 1:30; 2:6-16; 3:16; John 16:13; Daniel 1:17,20; 2:22,23)

DANIEL 5:29 NIV

Then at Belshazzar's command, Daniel was clothed in purple, a gold chain was placed around his neck, and he was proclaimed the third highest ruler in the kingdom.

I am honored for my faithfulness in God's kingdom. Rulers shower me with gifts and award me with positions of honor and leadership.

(Deuteronomy 28:1-14; Genesis 39:2-5,21; 41:37-45; Job 29; Proverbs 3:3,4)

DANIEL 6:3,4 AMP

Then this Daniel was distinguished above the presidents and the satraps because an excellent spirit was in him, and the king thought to set him over the whole realm. Then the presidents and satraps sought to find occasion [to bring accusation] against Daniel concerning the kingdom, but they could find no occasion or fault, for he was faithful, nor was there any error or fault found in him.

—— DECLARATION OF FAITH ——

I am God's son/daughter. I am not negligent in any of my duties, nor corrupt in any of my actions. I show myself to be a devoted and trustworthy individual.

(Job 29; Ephesians 4:1; 5:1-20)

DANIEL 6:10 NKJV

Now when Daniel knew that the writing was signed, he went home. And in his upper room, with his windows open toward Jerusalem, he knelt down on his knees three times that day, and prayed and gave thanks before his God, as was his custom since early days.

——— *DECLARATION OF FAITH* ———

I am loyal to my heavenly Father and will serve Him faithfully regardless of the circumstances or consequences.

(Deuteronomy 6:5; 28:1; Acts 7:54-60; Hebrews 11:24-28)

DANIEL 6:13 NKJV

So they answered and said before the king, "That Daniel, who is one of the captives from Judah, does not show due regard for you, O king, or for the decree that you have signed, but makes his petition three times a day."

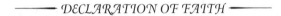

——— *DECLARATION OF FAITH* ———

I honor the laws of God over the laws of men. I am not bound by any law that is hostile to God's Word.

(Deuteronomy 28:1; Romans 13:1-7; Acts 4:16-20; Daniel 1:8)

DANIEL 6:22-28 KJV

My God hath sent his angel, and hath shut the lions' mouths, that they have not hurt me: forasmuch as before him innocency was found in me; and also before thee, O king, have I done no hurt. Then was the king exceeding glad for him, and commanded that they should take Daniel up out of the den. So Daniel was taken up out of the den, and no manner of hurt was found upon him, because he believed in his God. And the king commanded, and they brought those men which had accused Daniel, and they cast *them* into the den of lions, them, their children, and their wives; and the lions had the mastery of them, and brake all their bones in pieces or ever they came at the bottom of the den. Then king Darius wrote unto all people, nations, and languages, that dwell in all the earth; Peace be multiplied unto you. I make a decree, That in every dominion of my kingdom men tremble and fear before the God of Daniel: for he *is* the living God, and stedfast for ever, and his kingdom *that* which shall not be destroyed, and his dominion *shall be even* unto the end. He delivereth and rescueth, and he worketh signs and wonders in heaven and in earth, who hath delivered Daniel from the power of the lions. So this Daniel prospered in the reign of Darius, and in the reign of Cyrus the Persian.

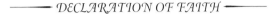

— DECLARATION OF FAITH —

By following the precepts of the Word, I am found and declared to be innocent in the sight of both God and man.

The angels of God are commanded to encamp about me to ensure my safety. I step out of troubles unscathed because of my steadfast trust in the Lord.

Those who falsely accuse me will fall by their own devices while I will continually be promoted. The glory of God shall manifest as I stubbornly adhere to His Word, and through my persistence He shall be respected in the land.

God never fails to deliver me and perform awesome signs and wonders on my behalf. As His son/daughter and follower of His precepts, my prosperity in this earth is guaranteed.

(Romans 5:1,2; Isaiah 54:17; Hebrews 1:14; Psalm 34:7; 91; Esther 5:9-6:11; 9:25; Proverbs 11:8; Acts 4:16-31; 5:12-16; Deuteronomy 28:1-14)

DANIEL 9:2-4 AMP

In the first year of his reign, I, Daniel, understood from the books the number of years which, according to the word of the Lord to Jeremiah the prophet, must pass by before the desolations [which had been] pronounced on Jerusalem should end; and it was seventy years. And I set my face to the Lord God to seek Him by prayer and supplications, with fasting and sackcloth and ashes; and I prayed to the Lord my God and made confession and said, O Lord, the great and dreadful God, Who keeps covenant, mercy, and loving-kindness with those who love Him and keep His commandments.

— DECLARATION OF FAITH —

I have keen insight and a clear understanding of God's Word. I am a discerner of the signs of the times and know exactly what to do as God's prophecies are fulfilled before me.

(1 Corinthians 2:6-16; John 16:13; Matthew 24:32,33; Luke 8:10)

DANIEL 9:18,19 AMP

O my God, incline Your ear and hear; open Your eyes and look at our desolations and the city which is called by Your name; for we do not present our supplications before You for our own righteousness and justice, but for Your great mercy and loving-kindness. O Lord, hear! O Lord, forgive! O Lord, give heed and act! Do not delay, for Your own sake, O my God, because Your city and Your people are called by Your name.

─── *DECLARATION OF FAITH* ───

I bear the name of the Lord my God and I am free to bring my petitions before His throne. I do not freely approach Him because of my own righteousness, but in accordance with His mercy and grace that establishes me in His righteousness.

(Hebrews 4:16; Ephesians 2:6-10; Romans 5:1,2; 10:2,3; John 14:13,14; 2 Corinthians 5:21)

DANIEL 9:21-23 KJV

Yea, whiles I *was* speaking in prayer, even the man Gabriel, whom I had seen in the vision at the beginning, being caused to fly swiftly, touched me about the time of the evening oblation. And he informed *me,* and talked with me, and said, O Daniel, I am now come forth to give thee skill and understanding. At the beginning of thy supplications the commandment came forth, and I am come to shew *thee;* for thou *art* greatly beloved: therefore understand the matter, and consider the vision.

─── *DECLARATION OF FAITH* ───

I am a prayer warrior who is continually blessed with wisdom and understanding from heaven. As soon as I begin to pray, my Father has the answer prepared and is ready to bless me. He esteems me highly among His children and it pleases Him to be my partner in every circumstance.

(Ephesians 6:18; 1 Corinthians 2:6-16; John 16:23,24,27)

DANIEL 10:1 NKJV

In the third year of Cyrus king of Persia a message was revealed to Daniel, whose name was called Belteshazzar. The message *was* true, but the appointed time *was* long; and he understood the message, and had understanding of the vision.

─── *DECLARATION OF FAITH* ───

I am blessed with revelation knowledge of God's Word and I am given thorough understanding of the personal messages that He gives me.

(Luke 8:10; 1 Corinthians 2:6-16; 1 John 5:20; Daniel 2:22,23)

DANIEL 10:10-13 KJV

And, behold, an hand touched me, which set me upon my knees and *upon* the palms of my hands. And he said unto me, O Daniel, a man greatly beloved, understand the words that I speak unto thee, and stand upright: for unto thee am I now sent. And when he had spoken this word unto me, I stood trembling. Then said he unto me, Fear not, Daniel: for from the first day that thou didst set thine heart to understand, and to chasten thyself before thy God, thy words were heard, and I am come for thy words. But the prince of the kingdom of Persia withstood me one and twenty days: but, lo, Michael, one of the chief princes, came to help me; and I remained there with the kings of Persia.

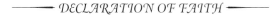

DECLARATION OF FAITH

God looks upon me with great favor and fills my life to overflowing with His blessings.

I humble myself under His mighty hand and He responds to me with tender compassion. His love compels me to move forward in courage and confidence. I refuse to allow fear to overwhelm me.

I am flooded with rivers of understanding as I acknowledge the Holy Spirit's presence within me. Through Him, I have an anointing to know exactly what to do in any given situation.

The principalities and powers of the devil's army pose no significant problem for me. God is within me and He has made me more than a conqueror to them.

My steadfast and persistent prayers open up a highway for the angels of God—freeing them to shower me with the blessings of heaven.

(Hebrews 1:14; 1 Peter 5:5-7; 2 Timothy 1:7; 1 Corinthians 2:6-16; John 16:13; Ephesians 6:10-18; 1 John 2:20,27)

DANIEL 10:18,19 NIV

Again the one who looked like a man touched me and gave me strength. "Do not be afraid, O man highly esteemed," he said. "Peace! Be strong now; be strong." When he spoke to me, I was strengthened and said, "Speak, my lord, since you have given me strength."

DECLARATION OF FAITH

I am highly esteemed by my heavenly Father and given great strength to stand in the presence of His glory. He fills me with His peace, courage, and power.

(Ephesians 2:6; Colossians 1:29; Hebrews 1:14; 4:16; Judges 6:23)

DANIEL 11:32 NKJV

"Those who do wickedly against the covenant he shall corrupt with flattery; but the people who know their God shall be strong, and carry out *great exploits.*"

I am a wise and discerning son/daughter of God. I will firmly resist the devil to the very end.

(Proverbs 1:7-9; James 4:7; 1 Corinthians 2:6-16)

DANIEL 12:3 NIV

"Those who are wise will shine like the brightness of the heavens, and those who lead many to righteousness, like the stars for ever and ever."

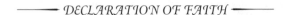

I am a wise son/daughter who tactfully imparts God's wisdom to others and leads many to the righteousness that has been provided for us in Christ Jesus. I am a soul-winner in this earth. God's brightness and glory emanate from me and I shall shine like the stars for all of eternity.

(Proverbs 11:30; James 5:19,20; 1 Corinthians 15:41)

DANIEL 12:9,10 AMP

And he [the angel] said, Go your way, Daniel, for the words are shut up and sealed till the time of the end. Many shall purify themselves and make themselves white and be tried, smelted, and refined, but the wicked shall do wickedly. And none of the wicked shall understand, but the teachers and those who are wise shall understand.

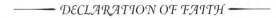

Revelation knowledge and wisdom from heaven are given to me freely because I am God's son/daughter. I have been made pure, spotless and refined, and God's Word is opened up to me without restriction.

(Luke 8:10; 1 Corinthians 2:6-16; 1 John 5:20; Matthew 13:11,15,16; 16:15-18)

CHAPTER TWENTY-EIGHT

HOSEA

Hosea begins the books of the Old Testament that are referred to as the minor prophets. They are called this because of their brevity. However, there is nothing minor about their message or the promises of God that are found therein.

The book of Hosea is a book of God's covenant love. The promises found within it display God's attitude toward each of us and how He expresses His love for us with everything that He does. As you pray these promises, ask the Holy Spirit to reveal His love to you. Enjoy His company as He embraces you with every word.

HOSEA 2:14-23 KJV

Therefore, behold, I will allure her, and bring her into the wilderness, and speak comfortably unto her. And I will give her her vineyards from thence, and the valley of Achor for a door of hope: and she shall sing there, as in the days of her youth, and as in the day when she came up out of the land of Egypt. And it shall be at that day, saith the Lord, *that* thou shalt call me Ishi; and shalt call me no more Baali. For I will take away the names of Baalim out of her mouth, and they shall no more be remembered by their name. And in that day will I make a covenant for them with the beasts of the field, and with the fowls of heaven, and *with* the creeping things of the ground: and I will break the bow and the sword and the battle out of the earth, and will make them to lie down safely. And I will betroth thee unto me for ever; yea, I will betroth thee unto me in righteousness, and in judgment, and in lovingkindness, and in mercies. I will even betroth thee unto me in faithfulness: and thou shalt know the Lord. And it shall come to pass in that day, I will hear, saith the Lord, I will hear the heavens, and they shall hear the earth; And the earth shall hear the corn, and the wine, and the oil; and they shall hear Jezreel. And I will sow her unto me in the earth; and I will have mercy upon her that had not obtained mercy; and I will say to *them which were* not my people, Thou *art* my people; and they shall say, *Thou art* my God.

——— *DECLARATION OF FAITH* ———

The Holy Spirit leads me with a gentle hand, speaking to me softly and drawing me along a miracle-filled path glorifying the name of Jesus. He gives me abundance in the midst of the desert and opens a door of hope in a troubled land.

I respond to Him as a child, in absolute faith and trust. He is no longer a taskmaster to me, but my covenant partner and friend.

He has stripped the enemy of all his power and has caused me to dwell in safety.

He is my partner and my first love from this day unto eternity. I am betrothed to Him in righteousness and justice, and in true love and compassion. I acknowledge His name and His presence in all that I do, and He is faithful to me in every way.

The Lord responds to me with patience and kindness. He fills me with His anointing to nourish the seed that I have sown, causing an abundant increase to overwhelm me.

In Him, I am well established. He has brought me forth out of the kingdom of darkness and has made me His own son/daughter. Satan was once my spiritual father, but now my Father is God.

My heavenly Father has pledged His eternal love to me before all of heaven and has set me in the place of highest honor in His kingdom.

(John 8:44; 10:10; 14:13,14; 15:7,8; 16:13; Genesis 13:2; 2 Corinthians 9:5-11; Hebrews 8:6; Psalm 8:4-8; Colossians 1:13; Ephesians 2:6-10; Romans 8:38,39)

HOSEA 4:6 NKJV

My people are destroyed for lack of knowledge. Because you have rejected knowledge, I also will reject you from being priest for Me; Because you have forgotten the law of your God, I also will forget your children.

——— *DECLARATION OF FAITH* ———

I am a seeker of knowledge so that I will not be destroyed. I search the Word continually to gain revelation knowledge and understanding of all of God's precepts. He, in turn, shields my family and me within the strong hedge of His protection.

(Proverbs 1:5; Isaiah 5:13; Joshua 1:8; Psalm 1:1-3; 1 Corinthians 2:6-11; Job 1:10)

HOSEA 6:1-3 KJV

Come, and let us return unto the Lord: for he hath torn, and he will heal us; he hath smitten, and he will bind us up. After two days will he revive us: in the third day he will raise us up, and we shall live in his sight. Then shall we know, *if* we follow on to know the Lord: his going forth is prepared as the morning; and he shall come unto us as the rain, as the latter *and* former rain unto the earth.

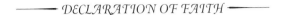

—— DECLARATION OF FAITH ——

I have become God's own son/daughter and He has healed all of my infirmities. In Him, I am made whole in every way.

He has restored me in righteousness so that I may enter His presence without any sense of guilt or inadequacy.

I will continually acknowledge His presence in my life. As surely as the sun rises, He is with me and He rains His blessings upon me freely.

(Galatians 3:13; 4:5,6; Isaiah 53:5; 2 Corinthians 5:21; Hebrews 4:16)

HOSEA 10:12 NIV

Sow for yourselves righteousness, reap the fruit of unfailing love, and break up your unplowed ground; for it is time to seek the Lord, until he comes and showers righteousness on you.

—— DECLARATION OF FAITH ——

I make a habit of sowing seeds of righteousness and I reap the fruit of unfailing love.

I stir myself up to act upon the Word and seek the face of God. He has showered me with His favor and the blessings of His promises.

(Jeremiah 4:3; 2 Corinthians 1:20; 9:6; Galatians 6:7,8; 2 Timothy 1:6)

HOSEA 11:3,4 NKJV

"I taught Ephraim to walk, taking them by their arms; but they did not know that I healed them. I drew them with gentle cords, with bands of love, and I was to them as those who take the yoke from their neck. I stooped *and* fed them."

—— DECLARATION OF FAITH ——

The Lord takes me into His gentle arms and heals me of every sickness. He leads me with a familiar kindness and with ties of love. He gives me the ability to stand rock solid so that I can do His will in every situation. He lifts the heavy burden from my shoulders and nourishes me until my vitality returns and I am once again able to enjoy the gift of His salvation.

(Deuteronomy 33:12; James 5:14,15; Romans 5:1,2; John 16:13; Matthew 11:28,29; Isaiah 40:28-31)

HOSEA 11:8-11 KJV

How shall I give thee up, Ephraim? *how* shall I deliver thee, Israel? how shall I make thee as Admah? *how* shall I set thee as Zeboim? mine heart is turned within me, my repentings are kindled together. I will not execute the fierceness of mine anger, I will not return to destroy Ephraim: for I *am* God, and not man; the Holy One in the midst of thee: and I will not enter into the city. They shall walk after the Lord: he shall roar like a lion: when he shall roar, then the children shall tremble from the west. They shall tremble as a bird out of Egypt, and as a dove out of the land of Assyria: and I will place them in their houses, saith the Lord.

—— DECLARATION OF FAITH ——

My Father's compassion is aroused when He thinks of me. The fierceness of His anger will never come against me and His devastation will never be known in my life. His protection of me is absolute. It is an impenetrable hedge that I can always count on.

I respond in awe and trembling at the sound of my Father's voice. His roar is like that of a lion, spreading fear to all of my enemies, but comforting me in the knowledge that the fierceness of His anger and mighty power will never be used for my destruction.

In tender compassion, my heavenly Father establishes my home.

(Psalm 18:1-18; 23; 91; 103:1-18; Romans 5:9; Job 1:10; 1 Thessalonians 5:9)

HOSEA 13:14 NIV

"I will ransom them from the power of the grave; I will redeem them from death. Where, O death, are your plagues? Where, O grave, is your destruction? I will have no compassion."

—— DECLARATION OF FAITH ——

I have been ransomed from the powers of hell! I am redeemed from the power of death! In the name of Jesus, I stop Satan's attacks! I will no longer be overcome by plagues and destruction! I have been set free!

(Colossians 1:13; 2:15; Titus 3:5; 1 Corinthians 15:55-57; Psalm 91; Luke 10:19)

HOSEA 14:1,2 NKJV

O Israel, return to the Lord your God, for you have stumbled because of your iniquity; take words with you, and return to the Lord. Say to Him, "Take away all iniquity; receive *us* graciously, for we will offer the sacrifices of our lips."

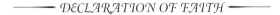
DECLARATION OF FAITH

I have turned from my sins and am set on the path of righteousness.

I have confessed my sins before God and received Jesus as my Lord. I now stand in God's favor and can freely offer Him the fruit of my lips to the praise of His glory.

I enter the presence of God and receive from Him. I continually sow the words of the Spirit in His presence and they never fail to produce a harvest of righteousness in my life.

(Acts 2:38,39; 2 Corinthians 4:13; 5:21; Romans 10:8-10; Psalm 5:11,12; John 6:63; Jeremiah 1:12; 29:10,11; Proverbs 18:20,21)

HOSEA 14:3-5 KJV

Asshur shall not save us; we will not ride upon horses: neither will we say any more to the work of our hands, *Ye are* our gods: for in thee the fatherless findeth mercy. I will heal their backsliding, I will love them freely: for mine anger is turned away from him. I will be as the dew unto Israel: he shall grow as the lily, and cast forth his roots as Lebanon.

DECLARATION OF FAITH

My Father has given me direction and freedom. He has healed all of my waywardness and has set His unconditional, everlasting love upon me for all of eternity. His anger will never be turned my way again. His renewing grace is like morning dew watering my ground and I blossom like a lily in the spring (fast growing and full of fragrance and beauty), but with roots like the cedars of Lebanon (so deep that I can never be plucked up).

(Proverbs 3:5,6; Galatians 5:1; Titus 3:5; Jeremiah 14:7; Ephesians 1:6; John 10:27-30)

HOSEA 14:9 NKJV

Who *is* wise? Let him understand these things. *Who is* prudent? Let him know them. For the ways of the Lord *are* right; the righteous walk in them, but transgressors stumble in them.

──────── *DECLARATION OF FAITH* ────────

The ways of the Lord are just and proper, and I walk in them.
In and through Him, I obtain tremendous wisdom and understanding.
In Him, all of the precepts and promises in the Word are realized in my life.

(Leviticus 5:1; Deuteronomy 28:1; Proverbs 3:5,6; 1 Corinthians 1:30; 2:6-16; John 15:7; 2 Corinthians 1:20)

CHAPTER TWENTY-NINE

JOEL

The book of Joel stresses the importance of turning your life around and living for God. Most of the promises found in this book are prophetic in nature. They tell of what life will be like for the believer after the promised Redeemer comes. Yes, that means us.

As you pray these promises, know that you are a fulfillment of prophecy and that you are intended as the recipient of these promises.

JOEL 2:2-11 KJV

A day of darkness and of gloominess, a day of clouds and of thick darkness, as the morning spread upon the mountains: a great people and a strong; there hath not been ever the like, neither shall be any more after it, *even* to the years of many generations. A fire devoureth before them; and behind them a flame burneth: the land *is* as the garden of Eden before them, and behind them a desolate wilderness; yea, and nothing shall escape them. The appearance of them *is* as the appearance of horses; and as horsemen, so shall they run. Like the noise of chariots on the tops of mountains shall they leap, like the noise of a flame of fire that devoureth the stubble, as a strong people set in battle array. Before their face the people shall be much pained: all faces shall gather blackness. They shall run like mighty men; they shall climb the wall like men of war; and they shall march every one on his ways, and they shall not break their ranks: Neither shall one thrust another; they shall walk every one in his path: and *when* they fall upon the sword, they shall not be wounded. They shall run to and fro in the city; they shall run upon the wall, they shall climb up upon the houses; they shall enter in at the windows like a thief. The earth shall quake before them; the heavens shall tremble: the sun and the moon shall be dark, and the stars shall withdraw their shining: And the Lord shall utter his voice before his army: for his camp *is* very great: for *he is* strong that executeth his word: for the day of the Lord *is* great and very terrible; and who can abide it?

──────── *DECLARATION OF FAITH* ────────

I am a vital member of the army of the Lord.

I am part of a strong and daring breed—born in the blood of God.

I have been born into His kingdom for such a time as this. I am unique and specially chosen to be God's ambassador and soldier in His army in these last days.

I stand firm and stately as a stallion and move forward in God's army with the force of heavenly cavalry.

Never before has there been anything like the Church of today and nothing will be comparable after us. I consider this the greatest day to be alive!

With a noise like that of chariots, we rise and conquer. We leap over mountains like a crackling fire consuming stubble. We are a most terrifying army ever ready to do battle.

What appears to be impossible has become the inevitable in my life.

I charge like a warrior and scale every obstacle like a well-trained soldier.

I do not vie for position but march steadily in the ranks. I never swerve from the course set before me, nor do I jostle or provoke my comrades in arms. I march straight ahead and plunge through defenses, never breaking ranks with my brothers and sisters in Christ.

We are an irresistible and invulnerable force in this earth. We scale the walls and run on them, entering the barracks of the enemy with the subtlety of a thief. The Lord thunders as our commander-in-chief, leading us on to victory.

I take my place as a vital part of a force unlike any that ever was or ever will be. I carry forth His Word into the earth as a loyal soldier of God and deadly enemy of the devil.

(Acts 2:14-21; 20:28; 2 Corinthians 5:17-21; Esther 4:14; Ephesians 6:10; Colossians 1:29; Mark 9:33-35; James 4:7; Deuteronomy 28:7,10; Joshua 2:9-11)

JOEL 2:13,14 NKJV

So rend your heart, and not your garments; return to the Lord your God, for He *is* gracious and merciful, slow to anger, and of great kindness; and He relents from doing harm. Who knows *if* He will turn and relent, and leave a blessing behind Him—a grain offering and a drink offering for the Lord your God?

──────── *DECLARATION OF FAITH* ────────

I have repented of my sins and turned to the Lord. Mine is not a repentance of the mind, simply because I know it is the right thing to do, but it is a repentance of the heart, because I want more than anything in the world to have a close relationship with God.

God has responded to my repentance with great mercy and compassion. He has turned all of His fierce anger from me and has determined to do nothing but good by me. Not only has He forgiven me and made me His own child, but He has also blessed me with every blessing that heaven has to offer.

(Ephesians 1:3; Acts 2:37-39; Psalm 103:10-12; Galatians 4:5,6; Romans 8:38,39)

JOEL 2:19 AMP

Yes, the Lord answered and said to His people, Behold, I am sending you grain and juice [of the grape] and oil, and you shall be satisfied with them; and I will no more make you a reproach among the [heathen] nations.

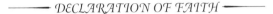

DECLARATION OF FAITH

My Father sends me all the provision I need to be satisfied in life and do what He has called me to do. I carry with me the anointing—an ability to function successfully in every area of my life.

(Psalm 89:20,21; Philippians 4:19; Acts 1:8; 1 John 2:20,27)

JOEL 2:23 AMP

Be glad then, you children of Zion, and rejoice in the Lord, your God; for He gives you the former or early rain in just measure and in righteousness, and He causes to come down for you the rain, the former rain and the latter rain, as before.

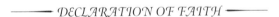

DECLARATION OF FAITH

As God's son/daughter, I will rejoice and be glad continually, for He has given me a teacher and a Guide. He rains blessings down upon me like an autumn rain and causes me to gather a harvest even as I am sowing my seed.

(Amos 9:13; John 16:7,13-15; 2 Corinthians 9:6-12)

JOEL 2:25-29 KJV

And I will restore to you the years that the locust hath eaten, the cankerworm, and the caterpiller, and the palmerworm, my great army which I sent among you. And ye shall eat in plenty, and be satisfied, and praise the name of the Lord your God, that hath dealt wondrously with you: and my people shall never be ashamed. And ye shall know that I *am* in the midst of Israel, and *that* I *am* the Lord your God, and none else: and my people shall never be ashamed. And it shall come to pass afterward, *that* I will pour out my spirit upon all flesh; and your sons and your daughters shall prophesy, your old men shall dream dreams, your young men shall see visions: And also upon the servants and upon the handmaids in those days will I pour out my spirit.

─────── *DECLARATION OF FAITH* ───────

The Lord, my Father, repays me for all of the years that Satan restrained my harvest. I now have all that I need and enjoy daily the fullness of God's way of living. I give all the praise, honor and glory to my heavenly Father who has done all of these mighty things on my behalf.

I am very proud of my God. He is faithful to His Word.

God, the One and only, dwells within me. He is on my side. So what do I care what the world thinks? Should I be ashamed because I do what is right? Should I be ashamed because I choose to seek the will of God instead of the will of men? I think not!

The Holy Spirit has been poured out upon me and I prophesy and experience dreams and visions to the praise of His glory. He grants me this honor because He sees me as a quality individual. He does not see me as the world sees me, or even as I may see myself. To Him, I am precious and to be honored. It is His good pleasure to pour out His Spirit upon me.

(Psalm 85:1-3; Proverbs 6:30,31; Jeremiah 30:17,18; Matthew 6:11,19-33; Romans 1:16; 8:31; 10: 11; John 16:13; Acts 2:14-21; Luke 12:32; Ephesians 2:10)

JOEL 2:32 NIV

And everyone who calls on the name of the Lord will be saved; for on Mount Zion and in Jerusalem there will be deliverance, as the Lord has said, among the survivors whom the Lord calls.

─────── *DECLARATION OF FAITH* ───────

I have called on the name of the Lord and He has saved me. I have been delivered from the kingdom of darkness and translated into the kingdom of Jesus. The Lord called out my name and I responded. My destiny, from this day forward, is one of greatness.

(Acts 2:38,39; Romans 10:8-13; Colossians 1:13; John 6:44,45; Genesis 12:1-3)

JOEL 3:9,10 NKJV

Proclaim this among the nations: "Prepare for war! wake up the mighty men, let all the men of war draw near, Let them come up. Beat your plowshares into swords and your pruning hooks into spears; let the weak say, 'I *am* strong.'"

——— *DECLARATION OF FAITH* ———

Though my victory has been sealed and the struggle for freedom is over for me, there is still a war going on and I intend to fight it. I prepare myself daily for the battle, rousing myself to a condition of perpetual vigilance.

When the enemy raises his ugly head, I attack him without mercy.

All of my sowing and reaping suddenly becomes a deadly weapon.

I will not allow the weaknesses, failures, or foolishness of my past to hinder me. I stand and declare myself to be what God says I am. I am strong in the Lord and in the power of His might and well able to defeat the enemy on any ground!

(1 Corinthians 15:57; Ephesians 6:10-18; 2 Timothy 1:6,7; Philippians 3:12-14)

JOEL 3:16 NKJV

The Lord also will roar from Zion, and utter His voice from Jerusalem; the heavens and earth will shake; but the Lord will be a shelter for His people, and the strength of the children of Israel.

——— *DECLARATION OF FAITH* ———

No matter what the circumstances may hold, or what is coming against those around me, I stand safe and secure. My refuge is the Creator of the heavens and the earth. He is my Lord and my Father—my stronghold in times of trouble.

(Psalm 91; Isaiah 51:5,6; Proverbs 12:21)

CHAPTER THIRTY

AMOS

The name Amos literally means, "burdened." This is indicative of the attitude he had for the nation of Israel as well as the nations that surrounded Israel. Much of his prophecies were not fulfilled until this generation.

Most of the book of Amos is judgment oriented, but there are several promises that can be gleaned from it. Some that stand out are those of friendship and fellowship with God, and those of receiving financial blessings.

As you pray these promises, know that God has made you to be not only His child, but His friend. He is truly your very best friend and He cherishes your company.

Amos 3:7 NIV

Surely the Sovereign Lord does nothing without revealing his plan to his servants the prophets.

——— DECLARATION OF FAITH ———

My Father does nothing in this earth that may affect me without revealing it to me first. I am not left in the dark. I know what is going on and what God wants me to do to fulfill my part in His sovereign plan.

(Genesis 18:17; Amos 7:1-6; John 15:15)

Amos 5:14,15 KJV

Seek good, and not evil, that ye may live: and so the Lord, the God of hosts, shall be with you, as ye have spoken. Hate the evil, and love the good, and establish judgment in the gate: it may be that the Lord God of hosts will be gracious unto the remnant of Joseph.

——— DECLARATION OF FAITH ———

I continually seek that which is good and shun what is evil. I live the God-kind of life right here on the earth. Within me is all of the power and ability that

I need to fulfill all righteousness. I love what is good, hate what is evil, and maintain justice in all that I do.

(Job 1:1; Matthew 6:10; Colossians 1:27-29; Romans 8:3,4; Leviticus 5:1)

AMOS 7:1-6 KJV

Thus hath the Lord God shewed unto me; and, behold, he formed grasshoppers in the beginning of the shooting up of the latter growth; and, lo, *it was* the latter growth after the king's mowings. And it came to pass, *that* when they had made an end of eating the grass of the land, then I said, O Lord God, forgive, I beseech thee: by whom shall Jacob arise? for he *is* small. The Lord repented for this: It shall not be, saith the Lord. Thus hath the Lord God shewed unto me: and, behold, the Lord God called to contend by fire, and it devoured the great deep, and did eat up a part. Then said I, O Lord God, cease, I beseech thee: by whom shall Jacob arise? for he *is* small. The Lord repented for this: This also shall not be, saith the Lord God.

DECLARATION OF FAITH

My heavenly Father reveals to me what He is planning to do in this earth. He restrains judgment for my sake and even entertains my suggestions.

I am God's friend. This relationship is not a dictatorship but a loving partnership.

(Genesis 18:17; Amos 7:1-6; John 15:15)

AMOS 9:13 NKJV

"Behold, the days are coming," says the Lord,
"When the plowman shall overtake the reaper,
And the treader of grapes him who sows seed;
The mountains shall drip with sweet wine,
And all the hills shall flow *with* it."

DECLARATION OF FAITH

I am living in the day of God's inconceivable blessings. His abundance is accelerating on my behalf. My harvest springs up all around me even as I am sowing my seed. The mountains around me drip with new wine and the hills pour out God's blessings making my harvest one of matchless quality and value.

(Ephesians 3:20; 2 Corinthians 9:6; Leviticus 26:5; Joel 3:18; Proverbs 3:9,10)

CHAPTER THIRTY-ONE

OBADIAH

Details in the life of the prophet Obadiah are a little hazy. There are as many as thirteen different men referred to by the name Obadiah in the Bible. The book is very judgment-oriented and at first glance one can be hard pressed to find any positive promise in it. However, as with every other of God's judgment writings, if you look carefully enough you can always find God's escape plan. There is always a promise for salvation. Such is the heart of our God.

As you pray this prayer, know that it is not God's will for you to suffer judgment unto condemnation. His love for you is as strong as life and His commitment to you is as unyielding as the grave.

OBADIAH 1:15,17 KJV

For the day of the Lord *is* near upon all the heathen: as thou hast done, it shall be done unto thee: thy reward shall return upon thine own head. But upon mount Zion shall be deliverance, and there shall be holiness; and the house of Jacob shall possess their possessions.

——— DECLARATION OF FAITH ———

I understand and walk in God's laws of seedtime and harvest. Everything that I do plants a seed into my life. I fully understand that I will reap a harvest from my every deed, whether it is good or bad.

Therefore, I purpose in my heart to do nothing but good. I will walk continually in my deliverance, remaining holy and true to my heavenly Father, and I will possess the inheritance that He has provided for me.

(Genesis 8:22; 2 Corinthians 9:5-11; Galatians 4:5,6; 6:7-9; Romans 8:17; Deuteronomy 28:1; Colossians 1:13)

CHAPTER THIRTY-TWO

JONAH

Jonah is probably the most well known of the minor prophets. Few, even in secular circles, are not familiar with his story. What many are not aware of is the beauty of the promises found in this book.

To study Jonah is to learn the importance of doing what you are called to do. It also is a lesson in refraining from being so judgmental of others. We must see everyone as being important and valuable, not only to us, but also, and most importantly, to God.

As you pray these promises, examine who you are and what you are called to do. Then make a commitment to fulfill that calling in your life.

JONAH 2:6 AMP

I went down to the bottoms and the very roots of the mountains; the earth with its bars closed behind me forever. Yet You have brought up my life from the pit and corruption, O Lord my God.

——— *DECLARATION OF FAITH* ———

I have been set free from the bonds of earthly things. I am not rooted into the mountains of circumstance, but in the Word of the living God. He has drawn me out from the pit and has set me on the path of the God-kind of life.

(John 10:10; Romans 8:1,2; 12:1; Mark 11:22-25; Hebrews 11:1)

JONAH 2:9 NIV

"But I, with a song of thanksgiving, will sacrifice to you. What I have vowed I will make good. Salvation comes from the Lord."

——— *DECLARATION OF FAITH* ———

I make good on all of my covenant agreements with my heavenly Father. I am not hasty to give my word, but I am true to it once it is given.

I sing my songs of praise and thanksgiving for all that God is doing in my life. He alone provides my salvation from every calamity.

(Psalm 50:14; Ecclesiastes 5:4,5; Ephesians 5:19)

JONAH 3:1-3 KJV

And the word of the Lord came unto Jonah the second time, saying, Arise, go unto Nineveh, that great city, and preach unto it the preaching that I bid thee. So Jonah arose, and went unto Nineveh, according to the word of the Lord. Now Nineveh was an exceeding great city of three days' journey.

——— *DECLARATION OF FAITH* ———

I serve the God of the second chance. If in any way I have failed to obey my calling, He will reveal it to me and put my disobedience behind Him so that I can move forward in His perfect will.

I will proclaim His message wherever He bids me to go. I consider His command a privilege to perform and I will obey His Word with all of my heart.

(Romans 11:29; Acts 9:1-6; Psalm 119:57,58,105,106,132-135)

JONAH 3:8-10 NKJV

"But let man and beast be covered with sackcloth, and cry mightily to God; yes, let every one turn from his evil way and from the violence that is in his hands. Who can tell *if* God will turn and relent, and turn away from His fierce anger, so that we may not perish?" Then God saw their works, that they turned from their evil way; and God relented from the disaster that He had said He would bring upon them, and He did not do it.

——— *DECLARATION OF FAITH* ———

I renounce all evil in my life and cast away anything that does not bring glory to my heavenly Father.

The Lord has turned from His fierce anger and now looks upon me with compassion.

I do not take His love for granted.

I shall not perish in the horror of spiritual death. Jesus has paid my price, delivering me from the powers of death, and has fixed my position at His side for all of eternity.

(Ephesians 2:6; 5:1-18; Psalm 103:10-13; Colossians 1:13; 1 Corinthians 15:54-58)

CHAPTER THIRTY-THREE

MICAH

Micah has a very unique name. It means, "Who is like the Lord?" The answer, in light of our redemption, is "We are like the Lord." We are created in the image and likeness of God and are destined to be conformed to the image of His Son. The promises in Micah are promises of conformation. These prayers will bring you into the reality of being who you are in Christ Jesus. You are a born-again child of the living God. You are a legitimate member of the royal family of heaven.

MICAH 2:7 NIV

Should it be said, O house of Jacob: "Is the Spirit of the Lord angry? Does he do such things? Do not my words do good to him whose ways are upright?"

———— DECLARATION OF FAITH ————

I see to it that all of my ways are upright. Therefore, God does not hold back any of His promises from me. His Word is good to me and accomplishes what He and I have sent it forth to do.

(Deuteronomy 28:1-14; 2 Corinthians 1:20; Isaiah 55:11; John 14:12-14; 17:20-26)

MICAH 3:8 NKJV

But truly I am full of power by the Spirit of the Lord, and of justice and might, to declare to Jacob his transgression and to Israel his sin.

———— DECLARATION OF FAITH ————

I am filled to the brim with the miracle-working power of God. The Holy Spirit dwells within me and has empowered me to speak His Word with authority.

I am a man/woman of justice, strenuous in my undertakings, known for my integrity, living without pretense or hypocrisy, and filled with courage and prevailing physical strength.

(Ephesians 1:17-23; 5:1-18; Acts 1:8; Colossians 1:27-29; 1 John 4:4; Joshua 1:5-9; Isaiah 40:28-31)

MICAH 4:2 NIV

Many nations will come and say, "Come, let us go up to the mountain of the Lord, to the house of the God of Jacob. He will teach us his ways, so that we may walk in his paths." The law will go out from Zion, the word of the Lord from Jerusalem.

——— *DECLARATION OF FAITH* ———

I am God's own son/daughter—a member of good standing in the royal family. He continually teaches me His ways so that I may live the God-kind of life. My days are as the days of heaven, even while I'm on the earth. His Word goes out from me as a seed, in all of its power and authority, and I reap its harvest of goodness every day of my life.

(Mark 4:3-32; Matthew 13:31,32; 17:20; Isaiah 55:11; Romans 8:14; Galatians 4:5)

MICAH 4:6-8 KJV

In that day, saith the Lord, will I assemble her that halteth, and I will gather her that is driven out, and her that I have afflicted; And I will make her that halted a remnant, and her that was cast far off a strong nation: and the Lord shall reign over them in mount Zion from henceforth, even for ever. And thou, O tower of the flock, the strong hold of the daughter of Zion, unto thee shall it come, even the first dominion; the kingdom shall come to the daughter of Jerusalem.

——— *DECLARATION OF FAITH* ———

The Lord has gathered me to Himself and placed me in His own household. I have taken His name and authority as my very own. I am now a son/daughter in the royal lineage of God. He has restored to me the former dominion and has made me a force to be reckoned with in this earth.

(John 6:44; 14:13,14; 2 Corinthians 5:17; Galatians 4:5,6; 1 John 4:4; Colossians 1:29)

MICAH 5:4 NKJV

And He shall stand and feed *His flock*
In the strength of the Lord,
In the majesty of the name of the Lord His God;
And they shall abide,
For now He shall be great
To the ends of the earth.

──── *DECLARATION OF FAITH* ────

Jesus stands as both a sentinel and tutor in my life. He fills me with His strength and authority and has granted me the power of attorney to use His name. In Him, I live in perpetual security. He has become my peace.

(John 14:13-18; Philippians 2:10; Colossians 1:29; Job 1:10; Romans 8:28-30; Ephesians 2:6-14)

MICAH 6:8,9 AMP

He has showed you, O man, what is good. And what does the Lord require of you but to do justly, and to love kindness and mercy, and to humble yourself and walk humbly with your God? The voice of the Lord calls to the city [Jerusalem]—and it is sound wisdom to hear and fear Your name—Hear (heed) the rod and Him Who has appointed it.

──── *DECLARATION OF FAITH* ────

The Lord shows me what is good in life.

I can be relied upon to act in justice and fairness in all that I do. It is even within my heart to extend mercy to those who are guilty and lead them to the paths of righteousness.

I humble myself in reverence to the greatness of my heavenly Father. I understand and adhere to the laws, both physical and spiritual, that He has set in motion in the earth.

(Galatians 6:1; Deuteronomy 10:12; 28:1; Genesis 18:19)

MICAH 7:5 NKJV

Do not trust in a friend;
Do not put your confidence in a companion;
Guard the doors of your mouth
From her who lies in your bosom.

──── *DECLARATION OF FAITH* ────

I am very careful with the words that I speak and I am discerning of the intentions of my family and my friends.

(Matthew 12:37; John 6:63; Proverbs 1:10-33; 17:17,18; 18:20,21)

MICAH 7:7-11 KJV

Therefore I will look unto the Lord; I will wait for the God of my salvation: my God will hear me. Rejoice not against me, O mine enemy: when I fall, I shall arise; when I sit in darkness, the Lord *shall be* a light unto me. I will bear the indignation of the Lord, because I have sinned against him, until he plead my cause, and execute judgment for me: he will bring me forth to the light, *and* I shall behold his righteousness. Then *she that is* mine enemy shall see *it*, and shame shall cover her which said unto me, Where is the Lord thy God? mine eyes shall behold her: now shall she be trodden down as the mire of the streets. *In* the day that thy walls are to be built, *in* that day shall the decree be far removed.

──────── *DECLARATION OF FAITH* ────────

I wait with confidence for the answer to my prayers. God is my Father, my Savior, and my friend. I have His unfailing Word that He will give me what I have asked for.

I give warning to the enemy not to gloat over me. Even if I have fallen, I will rise! Even if I sit in darkness, the Lord will be my Light!

I have been established in righteousness and freed from all guilt and condemnation. Jesus, Himself, has become my righteousness. Indeed, I am the very righteousness of God in Him. My enemy shall see this and cower in shame.

As for me, the days of building my walls have come. It is time for me to extend my borders!

(1 John 5:14,15; John 14:13,14; Proverbs 24:16; Psalm 35:26; Romans 8:1; 2 Corinthians 5:21; 1 Chronicles 4:9,10)

MICAH 7:18-20 NIV

Who is a God like you, who pardons sin and forgives the transgression of the remnant of his inheritance? You do not stay angry forever but delight to show mercy. You will again have compassion on us; you will tread our sins underfoot and hurl all our iniquities into the depths of the sea. You will be true to Jacob, and show mercy to Abraham, as you pledged on oath to our fathers in days long ago.

──────── *DECLARATION OF FAITH* ────────

God has pardoned my sins and forgiven all of my transgressions.
He has recreated me and made me His own heir.
He is overjoyed to show me His mercy and compassion.
He hurls all of my iniquities into the depths of the sea.

His dream has come true—I am now His own son/daughter. He will remain true to me and continually show me mercy just as He promised my forefathers in days long ago.

(Hebrews 10:15-17; 2 Corinthians 1:20; 5:17; Romans 8:14-17; Psalm 103:10-13; Galatians 4:5,6)

CHAPTER THIRTY-FOUR

NAHUM

Tell everybody to turn to the book of Nahum and you'll hear the pages crinkling for about ten minutes. If we only knew how precious this book is. The name Nahum literally means "comfort, consolation and relief." There are no three words that better describe the promises of the book of Nahum.

As you pray these promises, know that God is holding you tenderly in His arms as a loving father holds the child whom he loves.

NAHUM 1:7 NKJV

The Lord *is* good, a stronghold in the day of trouble; and He knows those who trust in Him.

—— *DECLARATION OF FAITH* ——

My Father sure does love me. He cares for me continually and does nothing but good by me. He is not good to me just some of the time—He is good to me all of the time. He is my refuge in times of trouble. I will trust in Him and not be afraid.

(Romans 8:38,39; Jeremiah 24:6; 29:11; Proverbs 3:5,6; Joshua 1:5-9)

NAHUM 1:15 NIV

Look, there on the mountains, the feet of one who brings good news, who proclaims peace! Celebrate your festivals, O Judah, and fulfill your vows. No more will the wicked invade you; they will be completely destroyed.

—— *DECLARATION OF FAITH* ——

I stand upon the mountains (those formidable circumstances and impossible odds), and I proclaim the good news of freedom and peace!

No more shall the enemy invade and overrun me, or those whom I have covered. He has been defeated, and totally, utterly, completely, thoroughly, and entirely stripped of all of his power and authority over me!

I celebrate perpetual victory in the presence of my Father and fulfill my every vow to Him willingly and with tremendous joy.

(Mark 11:22-25; Luke 10:17-19; Colossians 2:15; 1 Corinthians 15:57; Psalm 50:14)

NAHUM 2:2,9 KJV

For the Lord hath turned away the excellency of Jacob, as the excellency of Israel: for the emptiers have emptied them out, and marred their vine branches. Take ye the spoil of silver, take the spoil of gold: for *there is* none end of the store *and* glory out of all the pleasant furniture.

 DECLARATION OF FAITH

I have been restored to the position of glory that God originally intended for me. Though destroyers laid me to waste and ruined my life, I have been redeemed!

I now stand in the full rights and authority of a son/daughter of the living God! I have free access to His endless supply of provision.

I shall take back what the devil has stolen and walk in the provision that God intends for me to walk in!

(Joel 2:25; Galatians 3:13,14; 4:5,6; Philippians 4:19; Romans 8:32; Proverbs 6:30,31; Genesis 13:2)

CHAPTER THIRTY-FIVE

HABAKKUK

The first time I heard that name, I thought, *Who in the world would name their child Habakkuk?* But when I learned what the name meant, I understood. Habakkuk literally means, "one who embraces with love." This provides a theme for the entire book. In Habakkuk, we learn of God's promises to love us with an unfailing love, and how we are to respond to Him in kind.

Habakkuk is also known to many as the book of vision. We so often refer to Habakkuk when we are praying for vision to live by.

As you pray the prayers of Habakkuk, know that any vision God gives you will be a blessing to you. It will bring you joy and happiness as you set out to fulfill it.

✠

HABAKKUK 2:1-4 KJV

I will stand upon my watch, and set me upon the tower, and will watch to see what he will say unto me, and what I shall answer when I am reproved. And the Lord answered me, and said, Write the vision, and make *it* plain upon tables, that he may run that readeth it. For the vision *is* yet for an appointed time, but at the end it shall speak, and not lie: though it tarry, wait for it; because it will surely come, it will not tarry. Behold, his soul *which* is lifted up is not upright in him: but the just shall live by his faith.

--------- *DECLARATION OF FAITH* ---------

I will stand my watch and remain alert to the revelation of the Lord. He is ever-ready to provide me with a vision for living. I will remain sensitive to it and follow it with all of my heart.

When I receive my clear-cut vision, a divine faith plan unthwartable in the hands of the diligent, I write it down and make it a clear, understandable, and unmistakable declaration in my life. I place this plan where I will regularly see it so that I will have a continuous reminder and a source of focus toward my inevitable goal. I will speak of the end from the beginning and stand in full confi-

dence that the Lord and I will see it through to its fulfillment. This is not arro-
gance; it is faith—and faith is the substance by which I live.

(Hebrews 11:1,6; Isaiah 8:1,2; 21:8; Psalm 27:11; Daniel 8:17; Romans 4:17; Joel 2:28;
Ezekiel 12:24,25)

HABAKKUK 2:14 NKJV

For the earth will be filled with the knowledge of the glory of the Lord, as the
waters cover the sea.

──────── *DECLARATION OF FAITH* ────────

I am filled with the knowledge of the glory of the Lord.

(1 Corinthians 2:6-16; 1 John 5:20; Ephesians 1:17-23)

HABAKKUK 3:2 NIV

Lord, I have heard of your fame; I stand in awe of your deeds, O Lord. Renew
them in our day, in our time make them known; in wrath remember mercy.

──────── *DECLARATION OF FAITH* ────────

I stand in awe of the Lord's mighty deeds. He continually renews them in my
life, giving me an awesome testimony of His power on my behalf.

Though His wrath is terrifying, I have no fear, for His mercy toward me
endures forever.

(Psalm 24:1-6; 136; Colossians 1:29; John 5:24)

HABAKKUK 3:13,14 NKJV

You went forth for the salvation of Your people, for salvation with Your
Anointed. You struck the head from the house of the wicked, by laying bare
from foundation to neck. Selah. You thrust through with his own arrows the
head of his villages. They came out like a whirlwind to scatter me; Their rejoicing was like feasting on the poor in secret.

──────── *DECLARATION OF FAITH* ────────

The Lord rises to save and deliver me out of every adverse circumstance. He
has crushed the enemy and stripped him of his power from head to foot.

When the armies of darkness storm out to destroy me, they shall fall by the
very weapons that they use against me. I will not be moved by their cunning
strategies, nor will I fear an impotent foe.

As for me, I am born of God and unconquerable!

(1 John 5:18; Colossians 2:15; Psalm 18:1-18; 79:12; 2 Corinthians 2:11; Romans 8:37; Proverbs 11:8)

HABAKKUK 3:17-19 KJV

Although the fig tree shall not blossom, neither *shall* fruit *be* in the vines; the labour of the olive shall fail, and the fields shall yield no meat; the flock shall be cut off from the fold, and *there shall be* no herd in the stalls: Yet I will rejoice in the Lord, I will joy in the God of my salvation. The Lord God *is* my strength, and he will make my feet like hinds' *feet,* and he will make me to walk upon mine high places. To the chief singer on my stringed instruments.

────── *DECLARATION OF FAITH* ──────

My love, commitment, and trust—for, to, and in my God—is not predicated upon circumstance. Even if my crops fail, I will still rejoice; even when drought covers the land, I sing praises; in the midst of financial disaster, joy and happiness flood my soul. I know the One in whom I have set my trust and He is well able to fulfill His Word on my behalf.

I rejoice with my Father in every circumstance. He is my strength and unfailing source of supply. He makes my feet like that of a deer, enabling me to be first in order (in the position of highest authority). I am a blessing to the distressed.

(Genesis 12:2,3; 2 Corinthians 5:7; Hebrews 11:1; Philippians 4:11-20; Ephesians 1:17-23; 2:6; Psalm 18:33)

CHAPTER THIRTY-SIX

ZEPHANIAH

This is going to bless you. The name Zephaniah literally means, "God has treasured or hidden." Again, in reading the Word we find that God does nothing by accident. In Zephaniah we learn of how God treasures us and keeps us hidden within the hedge of His protection. As God's treasured possession, He provides for us abundantly and cares for us meticulously.

As you pray these promises, know that God is carefully and lovingly watching over you at this very moment.

ZEPHANIAH 2:3 NIV

Seek the Lord, all you humble of the land, you who do what he commands. Seek righteousness, seek humility; perhaps you will be sheltered on the day of the Lord's anger.

───── DECLARATION OF FAITH ─────

I humble myself before the Lord and give due honor to the power of His majesty. I seek Him with all of my heart and do all that He commands. I am submitted to Him in every way and He shelters me from the wrath to come.

(Deuteronomy 4:29; 1 Peter 5:5-7; James 4:6,7; John 5:24; 15:10)

ZEPHANIAH 2:7 NKJV

The coast shall be for the remnant of the house of Judah; They shall feed *their* flocks there; In the houses of Ashkelon they shall lie down at evening. For the Lord their God will intervene for them, and return their captives.

───── DECLARATION OF FAITH ─────

I am showered with blessings from heaven and enjoy the abundance of my Father's prosperity. I shall own houses that I have not built and enjoy the riches that the enemy once gloated over.

My Father is my provider. He watches over me with a relentless eye and restores to me all of the blessings that Satan has robbed from me.

(Deuteronomy 6:10-12; 8:6-18; Joel 2:25; Proverbs 6:30,31; Philippians 4:19; Ephesians 6:10-18)

ZEPHANIAH 2:9 AMP

Therefore, as I live, says the Lord of hosts, the God of Israel, Moab shall become like Sodom and the Ammonites like Gomorrah, a land possessed by nettles and wild vetches and salt pits, and a perpetual desolation. The remnant of My people shall make a prey of them and what is left of My nation shall possess them.

— DECLARATION OF FAITH —

I plunder the lands of the enemy, taking back the riches that rightfully belong to me.

God has decreed that this land belongs to His children!

(Joshua 1:3; Joel 2:25; Jeremiah 30:17,18; Psalm 85:1-3)

ZEPHANIAH 3:9 NIV

"Then will I purify the lips of the peoples, that all of them may call on the name of the Lord and serve him shoulder to shoulder."

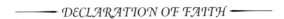

— DECLARATION OF FAITH —

I speak what is pure and just in the eyes of my Father—words of wise substance with a fixed purpose.

I stand shoulder to shoulder with all of my brothers and sisters in Christ and never allow a thought of disunity or division to progress in my mind.

(1 Peter 3:10-12; Proverbs 18:20,21; Hebrews 11:1; Joel 2:8; Romans 16:17)

ZEPHANIAH 3:11-15 KJV

In that day shalt thou not be ashamed for all thy doings, wherein thou hast transgressed against me: for then I will take away out of the midst of thee them that rejoice in thy pride, and thou shalt no more be haughty because of my holy mountain. I will also leave in the midst of thee an afflicted and poor people, and they shall trust in the name of the Lord. The remnant of Israel shall not do iniquity, nor speak lies; neither shall a deceitful tongue be found in their mouth: for they shall feed and lie down, and none shall make *them* afraid. Sing, O daughter of Zion; shout, O Israel; be glad and rejoice with all the heart, O daughter of

Jerusalem. The Lord hath taken away thy judgments, he hath cast out thine enemy: the king of Israel, *even* the Lord, *is* in the midst of thee: thou shalt not see evil any more.

——— *DECLARATION OF FAITH* ———

I cast all haughtiness and arrogant pride far from me. I remember what manner of man/woman I once was and how God alone has raised me to the position that I now enjoy.

My trust is not in the strength of my own might, but in the power of God working in and through me.

By the strength of the Lord, I can live a completely sinless and holy life.

I speak only the truth and all of my words bring glory to God.

I am continually satisfied with the abundance of His provision and I sleep in absolute peace, free of all stress, anxiety, and fear.

I rejoice in all that my Father has done in my life. Regardless of the circumstances, I shout a perpetual cry of victory.

Jesus has taken away my punishment and has secured my eternal relationship with my heavenly Father.

He has stripped the enemy of all of his power. Never again will I fear any harm. Jesus, my Lord and my King, is always with me.

(Proverbs 8:13,14; Ephesians 1:13,14; 2:1-10; Colossians 1:29; 1 Peter 1:15,16; 5:5-7; Psalm 127:2; Philippians 4:4; 1 Corinthians 15:57; John 5:24; Colossians 2:15; Hebrews 13:5,6)

ZEPHANIAH 3:17-20 NKJV

"The Lord your God in your midst,
The Mighty One, will save;
He will rejoice over you with gladness,
He will quiet *you* with His love,
He will rejoice over you with singing."
"I will gather those who sorrow over the appointed assembly,
Who are among you,
To whom its reproach *is* a burden.
Behold, at that time
I will deal with all who afflict you;
I will save the lame,
And gather those who were driven out;
I will appoint them for praise and fame
In every land where they were put to shame.

At that time I will bring you back,
Even at the time I gather you;
For I will give you fame and praise
Among all the peoples of the earth,
When I return your captives before your eyes,"
Says the Lord.

———— *DECLARATION OF FAITH* ————

God is on my side; therefore I shall not be afraid. He has promised that He will never leave me nor forsake me. He delivers me from disaster and destruction, and sees to it that I remain on the path of life.

He is my own Father and is tremendously delighted in me.

He quiets me with His overwhelming love and compassion.

He lifts every burden from off of my shoulders.

He has dealt with the oppressor judiciously. The devil has been thoroughly stripped of any power and authority he had over my life. He can no longer put me in bondage. I am free in Jesus!

My Father has rescued me and gathered me unto Himself.

He gives me praise and honor among all of the inhabitants of the earth.

He gives me praise and honor wherever I am and whatever my circumstance.

He restores my fortunes before my very eyes.

My heavenly Father has brought me home.

(Joshua 1:5-9; Psalm 18:1-18; 23; 46:1; 103:13; Matthew 11:28,29; Colossians 2:15; John 6:44; Proverbs 6:30,31)

CHAPTER THIRTY-SEVEN

HAGGAI

The promises in the book of Haggai help us to know that God's Word is true despite the circumstances. Have you ever prayed a promise and did not see it come to pass? This is often the case for many of us, but we sometimes are too prideful to point to ourselves as the blame. I say this, not judgmentally, but from experience. The truth is, God's Word works every single time. We just sometimes need to exercise our patience or even look to other reasons why we may not be receiving what God wants us to have.

As you pray these promises, set aside all thoughts of doubt and focus on the promises. Know that they are given to you personally and that God fully expects you to enjoy them in your life.

HAGGAI 1:5-11 KJV

Now therefore thus saith the Lord of hosts; Consider your ways. Ye have sown much, and bring in little; ye eat, but ye have not enough; ye drink, but ye are not filled with drink; ye clothe you, but there is none warm; and he that earneth wages earneth wages to *put it* into a bag with holes. Thus saith the Lord of hosts; Consider your ways. Go up to the mountain, and bring wood, and build the house; and I will take pleasure in it, and I will be glorified, saith the Lord. Ye looked for much, and, lo, *it came* to little; and when ye brought *it* home, I did blow upon it. Why? saith the Lord of hosts. Because of mine house that *is* waste, and ye run every man unto his own house. Therefore the heaven over you is stayed from dew, and the earth is stayed *from* her fruit. And I called for a drought upon the land, and upon the mountains, and upon the corn, and upon the new wine, and upon the oil, and upon *that* which the ground bringeth forth, and upon men, and upon cattle, and upon all the labour of the hands.

──── DECLARATION OF FAITH ────

I give careful and deliberate thought to all of my ways.

If in any part of my life I am not living as God has commanded, or not enjoying what He has provided, I take no rest until I have found out why. I know that God is not the problem and that He has given me all things that pertain unto life and godliness. If I have planted much, yet harvest little, there is a reason; if I eat, but never have enough, there is a reason; if I drink, and yet remain thirsty, there is a reason; if I put on garments and still remain cold, there is a reason; if I earn wages, only to put them in a purse with holes in it, there is a reason, and I will study it out until I have found out what that reason is.

When I am standing on God's Word for His blessings, fully expecting them to flood into my life, and yet my harvest turns out to be small and insignificant, I turn and focus my attention on what I have done for the advancement of the kingdom. If I have neglected the Church in any way, I repent and correct the problem. If I have focused on my own blessings and have not followed the Lord's heart in my giving, I repent and give according to what He would have me give. I shall not expect God's blessings on my life—whether for fertile lands, new wine, health, riches, the anointing, revelation knowledge, or any other blessing—until I have sought first the advancement of His kingdom.

(Matthew 6:19-34; 2 Peter 1:3; James 1:6-8; 4:1-10; Isaiah 55:11; Deuteronomy 28:1-14, 38-40; Galatians 3:13; 2 Corinthians 9:5-11; Malachi 3:6-12)

HAGGAI 1:13,14 NKJV

Then Haggai, the Lord's messenger, spoke the Lord's message to the people, saying, "I am with you, says the Lord." So the Lord stirred up the spirit of Zerubbabel the son of Shealtiel, governor of Judah, and the spirit of Joshua the son of Jehozadak, the high priest, and the spirit of all the remnant of the people; and they came and worked on the house of the Lord of hosts, their God.

——— DECLARATION OF FAITH ———

My heavenly Father is always with me and His desire is to do good by me. He stirs up my heart to give to the Church, not only to keep His house from ruin, but also to have an avenue with which He can bless me with His abundance.

(Hebrews 13:5,6; Deuteronomy 6:24; 2 Corinthians 9:5-11; Malachi 3:6-12)

HAGGAI 2:4-9 KJV

Yet now be strong, O Zerubbabel, saith the Lord; and be strong, O Joshua, son of Josedech, the high priest; and be strong, all ye people of the land, saith the Lord, and work: for I am with you, saith the Lord of hosts: *According to* the word that I covenanted with you when ye came out of Egypt, so my spirit remaineth among you: fear ye not. For thus saith the Lord of hosts; Yet once, it *is* a little while, and I will shake the heavens, and the earth, and the sea, and the dry *land;* And I will shake all nations, and the desire of all nations shall come: and I will fill this house with glory, saith the Lord of hosts. The silver *is* mine, and the gold *is* mine, saith the Lord of hosts. The glory of this latter house shall be greater than of the former, saith the Lord of hosts: and in this place will I give peace, saith the Lord of hosts.

DECLARATION OF FAITH

I am strong in the Lord and in the power of His might. I will work in His name and produce wonderful things for His glory. He is with me at all times. His Spirit dwells within me, leading me on the path of victory.

With God on my side, fear is not an option. It is a preposterous and ludicrous prospect. My Father has declared that I am to be at peace—in perfect comfort and safety—free from stress, terror, and anxiety.

This earth belongs to my Father and I am His heir. He has shaken the world and established His church. He has appointed for me my part and my portion. He has filled me with His glory and stabilizes me as His representative.

I refuse to hang on to empty religion with its false humility. It is time for the earth to know and see the glory of God's children!

(Ephesians 6:10; John 16:13; Colossians 3:17; Hebrews 13:5,6; 1 Corinthians 15:57; Romans 8:14-17; 31; 2 Timothy 1:6,7; Philippians 4:7-9; Galatians 4:5,6; Psalm 24:1; 112:1-10; 2 Corinthians 5:17-21; Genesis 13:2)

HAGGAI 2:19 NIV

Is there yet any seed left in the barn? Until now, the vine and the fig tree, the pomegranate and the olive tree have not borne fruit.

"'From this day on I will bless you.'"

DECLARATION OF FAITH

I keep a careful accounting and do not leave my seed in the barn. God has given me seed to sow and a harvest to enjoy. I will not eat my seed, but sow my best for the advancement of His kingdom.

When I do these things, I have God's Word that He will bless me with His abundance.

(Zechariah 8:12; Luke 14:28-32; 2 Corinthians 9:5-11; Malachi 3:6-12; Matthew 6:19-33)

CHAPTER THIRTY-EIGHT

ZECHARIAH

The main themes of the book of Zechariah are the rebuilding of the temple and the establishment of the Messiah's kingdom. This is displayed in a series of visions full of imagery and metaphor.

Nearly all of the promises in Zechariah deal with the blessings that come with repentance and of what the child of God will have in the latter days after the Messiah has come and has cleansed us from all sin.

As you pray these promises, know that you are speaking the fulfillment of prophecy.

ZECHARIAH 1:3 NIV

Therefore tell the people: This is what the Lord Almighty says: 'Return to me,' declares the Lord Almighty, 'and I will return to you,' says the Lord Almighty.

——— *DECLARATION OF FAITH* ———

I have returned to my heavenly Father and He has returned to me.

(James 4:8; Malachi 3:6-10)

ZECHARIAH 2:7-9 NKJV

"Up, Zion! Escape, you who dwell with the daughter of Babylon." For thus says the Lord of hosts: "He sent Me after glory, to the nations which plunder you; for he who touches you touches the apple of His eye. For surely I will shake My hand against them, and they shall become spoil for their servants. Then you will know that the Lord of hosts has sent Me."

——— *DECLARATION OF FAITH* ———

Whoever touches me touches the apple of God's eye. I am one of His favored ones and He loves me dearly.

No matter where I am—even in the midst of Satan's stronghold—I know that I have a deliverer. Through Him, I escape from all bondage and turn and plunder the camp of the oppressor.

(Proverbs 6:30,31; Psalm 23:1-6; 85:1-3; Isaiah 19:16; 48:20; Deuteronomy 32:10)

ZECHARIAH 3:1-9 KJV

And he shewed me Joshua the high priest standing before the angel of the Lord, and Satan standing at his right hand to resist him. And the Lord said unto Satan, The Lord rebuke thee, O Satan; even the Lord that hath chosen Jerusalem rebuke thee: *is* not this a brand plucked out of the fire? Now Joshua was clothed with filthy garments, and stood before the angel. And he answered and spake unto those that stood before him, saying, Take away the filthy garments from him. And unto him he said, Behold, I have caused thine iniquity to pass from thee, and I will clothe thee with change of raiment. And I said, Let them set a fair mitre upon his head. So they set a fair mitre upon his head, and clothed him with garments. And the angel of the Lord stood by. And the angel of the Lord protested unto Joshua, saying, Thus saith the Lord of hosts; If thou wilt walk in my ways, and if thou wilt keep my charge, then thou shalt also judge my house, and shalt also keep my courts, and I will give thee places to walk among these that stand by. Hear now, O Joshua the high priest, thou, and thy fellows that sit before thee: for they *are* men wondered at: for, behold, I will bring forth my servant the BRANCH. For behold the stone that I have laid before Joshua; upon one stone *shall be* seven eyes: behold, I will engrave the graving thereof, saith the Lord of hosts, and I will remove the iniquity of that land in one day.

———— *DECLARATION OF FAITH* ————

I have an Advocate who pleads my case before my heavenly Father. Jesus stands in the gap for me and rebukes Satan on my behalf. Satan can stand and accuse me all he wants—I am innocent in the eyes of the Lord.

I have been chosen to be God's own son/daughter and heir. I am a live coal that has been plucked from the fire. God Himself has removed the filthy garments of sin from me and has adorned me in the robes of righteousness. I am now a born-again child of the living God—a member of a new and awesome race of men and women. A crown of righteousness has been placed upon my head and the angel of the Lord is stationed at my side.

I walk continuously in the ways of the Word and God has made me a governor in His own household. I have been given charge of heaven's royal entourage and have taken my place among the mighty sons and daughters of God.

(1 John 2:1,2; 5:18; Isaiah 54:17; 61:10; Hebrews 1:14; 7:25; Colossians 1:13,27-29; 2:13-15; Ephesians 1:4,17-23; 2:6; Galatians 4:4-6; John 3:3-17; 2 Corinthians 5:17-21; 8:9; Exodus 23:20-23; Deuteronomy 17:9,12; Romans 8:16-19,29,30)

ZECHARIAH 4:6 NIV

So he said to me, "This is the word of the Lord to Zerubbabel: 'Not by might nor by power, but by my Spirit,' says the Lord Almighty."

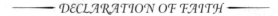

———— *DECLARATION OF FAITH* ————

God works in and through me, not in the strength of my own power, but by the very power of the Holy Spirit who raised Jesus from the dead!

(Ephesians 1:17-20; Philippians 2:13; Colossians 1:27-29)

ZECHARIAH 4:10 NKJV

"For who has despised the day of small things? For these seven rejoice to see the plumb line in the hand of Zerubbabel. They are the eyes of the Lord, which scan to and fro throughout the whole earth."

———— *DECLARATION OF FAITH* ————

I do not despise nor mock the day of small beginnings. I have a thorough understanding that even the tiniest of seeds can become a great tree.

I know that the eyes of the Lord go to and fro throughout the earth seeking someone through whom He can show Himself strong. I have consecrated myself to be that person.

(Matthew 13:31,32; 17:20,21; 2 Chronicles 16:9; Haggai 2:3)

ZECHARIAH 8:12,13 NIV

"The seed will grow well, the vine will yield its fruit, the ground will produce its crops, and the heavens will drop their dew. I will give all these things as an inheritance to the remnant of this people. As you have been an object of cursing among the nations, O Judah and Israel, so will I save you, and you will be a blessing. Do not be afraid, but let your hands be strong."

My seed grows well and my vine yields its fruit; my ground produces crops in abundance and the heavens drop their dew down upon me to ensure my prosperity. This is my inheritance as God's son/daughter and covenant partner. All of this has become a present fact in my life.

I no longer need to bow my head against mockery. I stand firm in my covenant and walk in the riches of my inheritance.

I am known to be a blessing.

I am not afraid of what the world thinks.

I am strong in the Lord and in the power of His might.

(2 Corinthians 9:5-11; Genesis 8:22; 12:1-3; Joel 2:22; Psalm 3:3; 67:6; Haggai 1:10; Romans 8:17; Philippians 4:11-19; Ephesians 6:10)

ZECHARIAH **8:16,17** KJV

These *are* the things that ye shall do; Speak ye every man the truth to his neighbour; execute the judgment of truth and peace in your gates: And let none of you imagine evil in your hearts against his neighbour; and love no false oath: for all these *are things* that I hate, saith the Lord.

──────── *DECLARATION OF FAITH* ────────

I speak the truth and walk in fairness toward all men. I never plot evil of any kind against my neighbor, nor do I swear an oath with a heart of uncertainty.

(1 Peter 3:10-12; Psalm 15:2; Proverbs 3:29; 12:17-19)

ZECHARIAH **8:19** NKJV

"Thus says the Lord of hosts:
'The fast of the fourth *month,*
The fast of the fifth,
The fast of the seventh,
And the fast of the tenth,
Shall be joy and gladness and cheerful feasts
For the house of Judah.
Therefore love truth and peace.'"

——— *DECLARATION OF FAITH* ———

I find my greatest joy in the things of God.
I love the truth and pursue peace at all times.

(Psalm 34:14; 119:14,16,20,24,97,140,162,165,172)

ZECHARIAH 9:8 NIV

But I will defend my house against marauding forces. Never again will an oppressor overrun my people, for now I am keeping watch.

——— *DECLARATION OF FAITH* ———

God Almighty stands as a fierce warrior on my behalf. He is my defense against marauding forces. Never again will the oppressor overrun me, for my Father is keeping a careful watch over me.

(Psalm 2; 11:4; 18:1-18; Nehemiah 1:5,6; Romans 16:20; 1 John 5:18)

ZECHARIAH 9:11-17 KJV

As for thee also, by the blood of thy covenant I have sent forth thy prisoners out of the pit wherein *is* no water. Turn you to the strong hold, ye prisoners of hope: even to day do I declare *that* I will render double unto thee; When I have bent Judah for me, filled the bow with Ephraim, and raised up thy sons, O Zion, against thy sons, O Greece, and made thee as the sword of a mighty man. And the Lord shall be seen over them, and his arrow shall go forth as the lightning: and the Lord God shall blow the trumpet, and shall go with whirlwinds of the south. The Lord of hosts shall defend them; and they shall devour, and subdue with sling stones; and they shall drink, *and* make a noise as through wine; and they shall be filled like bowls, *and* as the corners of the altar. And the Lord their God shall save them in that day as the flock of his people: for they *shall be as* the stones of a crown, lifted up as an ensign upon his land. For how great *is* his goodness, and how great *is* his beauty! corn shall make the young men cheerful, and new wine the maids.

——— *DECLARATION OF FAITH* ———

I have a covenant with almighty God sealed with the blood of Jesus.
He has set me free from the waterless pit. Never again will I be unsatisfied with life.
He has become my stronghold of safety and prosperity.
He has restored to me double what was taken from me.
He has bent me like a bow and filled me with His own power.

He has stirred me up and made me like a warrior's sword.

Jesus, the warrior of warriors whose arrow flashes like lightning, is my supreme commander. I follow His every command and rally to His side when He sounds the battle horn.

He is my very strength and shield of protection in the midst of the battle. Together, we destroy and overcome the enemy with heaven's own artillery.

I drink deeply of the Spirit and roar as one filled with wine.

I am full to the brim with the anointing of God.

The Lord has taken His stand at my side and sees to it that I rise victorious in every battle.

I sparkle in His land like a jewel in a crown. He has made me as one to be envied—radiant and attractive to the eye—and I prosper and succeed in all that He has called me to do.

(Hebrews 2:10; 8:6; John 10:10; Psalm 91:16; Job 42:10; Colossians 1:29; Ephesians 1:19; 5:18; 6:10-18; Genesis 12:1-3; 15:1; 1 John 2:20; 1 Corinthians 15:57; Romans 8:37; Daniel 1:4; Deuteronomy 28:12)

ZECHARIAH 10:1 AMP

Ask of the Lord rain in the time of the latter or spring rain. It is the Lord Who makes lightnings which usher in the rain and give men showers, and grass to everyone in the field.

——— DECLARATION OF FAITH ———

I will ask my Father for rain in this time of the latter rain. I call upon Him for a shower of His blessings in the day of planting, for it is He who causes my seed to grow. He causes storm clouds to cover my land and a downpour of blessings to feed my planting. I am destined to have an abundant harvest.

(Genesis 8:22; 2 Corinthians 9:5-11; Jeremiah 14:22; Deuteronomy 11:13,14; 28:12; Joel 2:23)

ZECHARIAH 10:5,6 KJV

And they shall be as mighty *men,* which tread down *their enemies* in the mire of the streets in the battle: and they shall fight, because the Lord *is* with them, and the riders on horses shall be confounded. And I will strengthen the house of Judah, and I will save the house of Joseph, and I will bring them again to place them; for I have mercy upon them: and they shall be as though I had not cast them off: for I *am* the Lord their God, and will hear them.

―――― *DECLARATION OF FAITH* ――――

Because the Lord is with me, I can overthrow any and every foe.

He strengthens me and saves me.

Out of His great compassion for me, He restores me to a position of honor.

I stand right now, at this very moment, as though I had never sinned. I am free to enter His presence without the slightest sense of guilt or inadequacy.

The Lord, God of heaven and earth, is my Father. He answers my every prayer.

(Hebrews 4:16; 10:14-17; Joshua 1:5-9; 2:9-11; Ephesians 2:6; John 14:13,14)

ZECHARIAH 10:12 NIV

"I will strengthen them in the Lord and in his name they will walk," declares the Lord.

―――― *DECLARATION OF FAITH* ――――

I am empowered with the very ability of almighty God. He has given me the power of attorney to use His name, and in that name I walk in perpetual victory.

(Colossians 1:29; Ephesians 1:17-23; John 14:13,14; 15:7; 1 Corinthians 15:57)

ZECHARIAH 11:7 AMP

So I [Zechariah] shepherded the flock of slaughter, truly [as the name implies] the most miserable of sheep. And I took two [shepherd's] staffs, the one I called Beauty or Grace and the other I called Bands or Union; and I fed and shepherded the flock.

―――― *DECLARATION OF FAITH* ――――

I was once marked for slaughter in the eyes of justice, but my penalty has been paid!

I now walk in perfect union with my heavenly Father.

His favor rests on me in every situation and He sees to it that I have all that I need.

(Romans 8:33-37; 1 John 1:3; John 17:20-26; Psalm 5:11,12; Philippians 4:19)

ZECHARIAH 12:8 NKJV

"In that day the Lord will defend the inhabitants of Jerusalem; the one who is feeble among them in that day *shall be* like David, and the house of David shall be like God, like the Angel of the Lord before them."

The Lord is my strength and my shield. He has made me strong and noble, like David, and has given me dominion like unto His own—like that of Jesus Himself.

(Genesis 15:1; Ephesians 1:17-23; 2:6; 6:10; Psalm 8:4-8; John 14:12)

ZECHARIAH 12:10 NIV

"And I will pour out on the house of David and the inhabitants of Jerusalem a spirit of grace and supplication. They will look on me, the one they have pierced, and they will mourn for him as one mourns for an only child, and grieve bitterly for him as one grieves for a firstborn son."

———— *DECLARATION OF FAITH* ————

God has poured out upon me the Spirit of grace and supplication. Anything I ask according to His will, He gives me. Jesus has paid my price and has given me access to all that heaven has to offer.

(Joel 2:28,29; Acts 2:4; 1 Corinthians 14:12-15; 1 John 5:14,15; Romans 8:32; Ephesians 1:3)

ZECHARIAH 13:1 KJV

In that day there shall be a fountain opened to the house of David and to the inhabitants of Jerusalem for sin and for uncleanness.

———— *DECLARATION OF FAITH* ————

Jesus has opened up to me a fountain that cleanses me from all sin and impurity. I now stand in His presence in perfect holiness and God's own righteousness.

(1 John 1:9; 1 Corinthians 1:30; 2 Corinthians 5:21; Hebrews 10:14)

ZECHARIAH 13:9 NKJV

"I will bring the *one-third* through the fire,
Will refine them as silver is refined,
And test them as gold is tested.
They will call on My name,
And I will answer them.
I will say, 'This *is* My people';
And each one will say, 'The Lord *is* my God.'"

─── *DECLARATION OF FAITH* ───

I have been brought through the fire—refined like silver and tested like gold. I am now cleansed and purified, and stand in the presence of almighty God in the beauty of holiness.

When I call on His name, He endorses my cry.

He makes His proclamation to all that I am His son/daughter and He is my Father. My surname is God's, and I am entitled to all of the rights and privileges that go with it.

(Galatians 4:4-6; Ephesians 3:15; James 2:7; 2 Timothy 2:19; Hebrews 12:5-8)

CHAPTER THIRTY-NINE

MALACHI

Malachi wrote at a time when there was much hypocrisy in Israel. The priests were not serving the people faithfully and the people were not doing their part to provide for the needs of the ministry. It can be said that it sounds much like the church of today. But, in every generation there is at least a remnant of faithful children of God. It is for these faithful believers that Malachi wrote some of the most incredible promises of the Bible.

As you pray these promises, remember the power of the God you serve. Remember who you are and who your provider is. Determine in your heart that you are going to trust Him and believe every word that you say.

MALACHI 1:14 AMP

But cursed is the [cheating] deceiver who has a male in his flock and vows to offer it, yet sacrifices to the [sovereign] Lord a blemished or diseased thing! For I am a great King, says the Lord of hosts, and My name is terrible and to be [reverently] feared among the nations.

——— DECLARATION OF FAITH ———

I have an unwavering respect for my heavenly Father. I refuse to cheat Him, lie to Him, or steal from Him.

When I have committed my vow, I pay it in full. I do not promise Him my best, then keep it to myself while delivering Him the leftovers.

In all that I do, my Father has first place in my life.

(Deuteronomy 6:5; 28:1; Malachi 3:6-12; Leviticus 22:18-20; Psalm 47:2)

MALACHI 2:5-7 KJV

My covenant was with him of life and peace; and I gave them to him *for* the fear wherewith he feared me, and was afraid before my name. The law of truth was in his mouth, and iniquity was not found in his lips: he walked with me in peace and equity, and did turn many away from iniquity. For the priest's lips should keep knowledge, and they should seek the law at his mouth: for he *is* the messenger of the Lord of hosts.

─── *DECLARATION OF FAITH* ───

I have a strong and secure covenant with my heavenly Father. It is a covenant that entitles me to all things that pertain unto life, godliness, and peace.

He has given me life, health, and vitality as His free gift of love.

God's own peace, provision, and security are present in my life.

He declares that all these things are mine if I give proper respect and reverence to His name. It is by faith and trust that I receive them.

I am resolved to walk in honesty and integrity before the Lord. True instruction is in my mouth and nothing false can be found on my lips.

I walk with God in peace and candid sincerity, and rescue many from a life of sin.

My lips preserve knowledge and men seek my instruction.

It is plain to the discerning that I am a messenger of the Lord.

(Hebrews 8:6; 2 Peter 1:3; Isaiah 53:4,5; Philippians 4:19; Ephesians 2:14; Deuteronomy 28:1-14; Mark 11:22-25; 1 Peter 3:8-12; James 4:6-8; Job 29:7-10,21-23)

MALACHI 2:15,16 NKJV

But did He not make *them* one,
Having a remnant of the Spirit?
And why one?
He seeks godly offspring.
Therefore take heed to your spirit,
And let none deal treacherously with the wife of his youth.
"For the Lord God of Israel says
That He hates divorce,
For it covers one's garment with violence,"
Says the Lord of hosts.
"Therefore take heed to your spirit,
That you do not deal treacherously."

─── *DECLARATION OF FAITH* ───

I guard myself diligently in my spirit so that I may remain faithful to my spouse. Together, God has made us one flesh and we produce godly offspring. Our sons and daughters walk in holiness before the Lord.

I will not disgrace myself by being violent to my spouse in any way, nor will I use divorce as a solution for non-reconciled differences.

I hold these principles as sacred and guard myself diligently in my spirit so that I will not break faith.

(Genesis 2:24; Ephesians 5:22-6:4; Matthew 19:4-12; 1 Corinthians 7:14)

MALACHI 3:6-12 KJV

For I *am* the Lord, I change not; therefore ye sons of Jacob are not consumed. Even from the days of your fathers ye are gone away from mine ordinances, and have not kept *them*. Return unto me, and I will return unto you, saith the Lord of hosts. But ye said, Wherein shall we return? Will a man rob God? Yet ye have robbed me. But ye say, Wherein have we robbed thee? In tithes and offerings. Ye *are* cursed with a curse: for ye have robbed me, *even* this whole nation. Bring ye all the tithes into the storehouse, that there may be meat in mine house, and prove me now herewith, saith the Lord of hosts, if I will not open you the windows of heaven, and pour you out a blessing, that *there shall* not *be room* enough *to receive it*. And I will rebuke the devourer for your sakes, and he shall not destroy the fruits of your ground; neither shall your vine cast her fruit before the time in the field, saith the Lord of hosts. And all nations shall call you blessed: for ye shall be a delightsome land, saith the Lord of hosts.

—— *DECLARATION OF FAITH* ——

I keep the decrees of my heavenly Father and follow them with all of my heart.
I draw close to Him in perfect fellowship and He draws close to me in return.
I will not rob Him by holding back my tithes and offerings. The tithe is the Lord's. It is not for me to dictate what is done with it, but to simply pay it in the place where I receive my spiritual sustenance.

I fully understand that by paying my tithes and giving my offerings I am warding off the attacks of the enemy.

Therefore, I bring the whole tithe, along with my offerings, into the church (the place where I fellowship and am fed the Word of God) so that there is provision for the advancement of the kingdom. Because of this, God has thrown open the windows of heaven (the very floodgates of His blessings) and poured out on me so much provision that I do not have room enough to receive it all.

Furthermore, when I paid my tithe and gave my offering, God rebuked the devourer for my sake. Satan cannot get to my stuff because God's hedge of protection surrounds it. My harvest is now made certain and I shall lose no part of what my Father wants me to have.

(Deuteronomy 28:1-14; James 4:7-10; Proverbs 3:9,10; Job 1:8-10; Luke 6:38; Matthew 6:24-33; 2 Corinthians 9:6-15)

MALACHI 3:16-18 NIV

Then those who feared the Lord talked with each other, and the Lord listened and heard. A scroll of remembrance was written in his presence concerning those who feared the Lord and honored his name. "They will be mine," says the Lord Almighty, "in the day when I make up my treasured possession. I will spare them, just as in compassion a man spares his son who serves him. And you will again see the distinction between the righteous and the wicked, between those who serve God and those who do not."

——— *DECLARATION OF FAITH* ———

I consciously seek others of like faith and take counsel with them, speaking about the things of God—of how much we love and trust Him—proclaiming good reports and giving honor to His name.

This pleases our Father immensely and He listens and joins in on our conversations. It is a time so precious to His heart that He has a scroll of remembrance written so that the occasion is never forgotten.

He says to those around Him, "These are My children—My treasured possession. I love them with all of my heart and will spare them in the Day of Judgment. I am going to make a clear distinction between them and the wicked. The world will look on them and know that I love my children."

(Hebrews 3:13; 10:25; 2 Corinthians 6:14; Numbers 14:8; 1 John 1:3; John 6:39,40; Psalm 56:8; Isaiah 43:1-21)

MALACHI 4:2,3 NKJV

"But to you who fear My name the Sun of Righteousness shall arise with healing in His wings; and you shall go out and grow fat like stall-fed calves. You shall trample the wicked, for they shall be ashes under the soles of your feet on the day that I do *this*," says the Lord of hosts.

——— *DECLARATION OF FAITH* ———

Jesus, my Lord, my Sun of Righteousness, has risen with healing in His wings.
I stand secure in the power of His name.
I have been revived, healed, and reborn.
I go out leaping like a calf released from the stall.
I am now a master of the forces of darkness. They are nothing more than ashes beneath my feet.

(2 Corinthians 4:6; 5:21; Matthew 4:16; Ephesians 5:14; John 3:3; Titus 3:5; Luke 10:17-19; Psalm 91:13)

CHAPTER FORTY

MATTHEW

Matthew is the first book of what we call the New Testament (or covenant). However, in reality, the new covenant did not begin until the book of Acts. Therefore, we should always read the Gospels (Matthew, Mark, Luke and John) knowing that much of what Jesus is saying is to an unregenerate people under the old covenant.

Matthew is one of the earliest manuscripts of the New Testament and was probably written around fifteen to twenty years after the Resurrection. It was written in Palestine for the Jewish Christian converts.

The promises contained within it are numerous and hard to categorize. Suffice it to say that every need in life, from healing, prosperity, deliverance, comfort and more can be found therein.

As you pray the promises of Matthew, know that Jesus left His throne for you personally. What He did, He did for you.

MATTHEW 4:1-11 KJV

Then was Jesus led up of the Spirit into the wilderness to be tempted of the devil. And when he had fasted forty days and forty nights, he was afterward an hungred. And when the tempter came to him, he said, If thou be the Son of God, command that these stones be made bread. But he answered and said, It is written, Man shall not live by bread alone, but by every word that proceedeth out of the mouth of God. Then the devil taketh him up into the holy city, and setteth him on a pinnacle of the temple, And saith unto him, If thou be the Son of God, cast thyself down: for it is written, He shall give his angels charge concerning thee: and in *their* hands they shall bear thee up, lest at any time thou dash thy foot against a stone. Jesus said unto him, It is written again, Thou shalt not tempt the Lord thy God. Again, the devil taketh him up into an exceeding high mountain, and sheweth him all the kingdoms of the world, and the glory of them; And saith unto him, All these things will I give thee, if thou wilt fall down and worship me. Then saith Jesus unto him, Get thee hence, Satan: for it is written, Thou shalt worship the Lord thy God, and him only shalt thou serve. Then the devil leaveth him, and, behold, angels came and ministered unto him.

—— *DECLARATION OF FAITH* ——

I know how to resist Satan's temptations and I am prepared to meet his attacks. I have taken up the weapons of my warfare and I am ready to fight.

When I am tempted by the devil, I cut him to pieces with the Word of the living God. The Word is the sword of my mouth and when I declare in faith "It is written," the devil must yield.

I am wise in warfare and cannot be fooled by Satan's devices. I understand that Satan and his minions know the Word well and will twist it to their own benefit. But, I am a man/woman of the Word who meditates on it day and night. It is engrafted deeply into my spirit and has made my faith strong.

I am a son/daughter of God led by the Spirit of God.

I do not use the Word to showboat the power that is given to me. I treat it with respect and give it—all of it, first to last—the ascendancy in my life.

(Ephesians 6:10-18; Revelation 19:15; Hebrews 4:12; Joshua 1:8; Colossians 3:16; 2 Corinthians 2:11; Romans 8:14; 10:17; Psalm 1:1-3; 119:97-100,105-107)

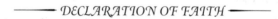

MATTHEW 4:4 MESSAGE

Jesus answered by quoting Deuteronomy: "It takes more than bread to stay alive. It takes a steady stream of words from God's mouth."

—— *DECLARATION OF FAITH* ——

My life is not sustained by food alone, but by every Word that proceeds from the mouth of my heavenly Father.

(Deuteronomy 8:3; Luke 4:4: Psalm 119:93)

MATTHEW 4:6 NKJV

And [the devil] said to Him, "If You are the Son of God, throw Yourself down. For it is written: 'He shall give His angels charge over you,' and, 'In *their* hands they shall bear you up, Lest you dash your foot against a stone.' "

—— *DECLARATION OF FAITH* ——

The angels of God are watching over me to keep me from all harm.

(Exodus 23:20-23; Psalm 91:11; Hebrews 1:14; Matthew 26:53)

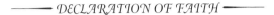
MATTHEW 4:7 NIV

Jesus answered him, "It is also written: 'Do not put the Lord your God to the test.'"

—— DECLARATION OF FAITH ——

I do not test the Lord, nor do I need to check His Word out to see if it works. I know that my Father is faithful and His Word is fulfilled in my life.

(Numbers 23:19; Psalm 119:140,160; Isaiah 55:11; Deuteronomy 6:16)

MATTHEW 4:8-11 KJV

Again, the devil taketh him up into an exceeding high mountain, and sheweth him all the kingdoms of the world, and the glory of them; And saith unto him, All these things will I give thee, if thou wilt fall down and worship me. Then saith Jesus unto him, Get thee hence, Satan: for it is written, Thou shalt worship the Lord thy God, and him only shalt thou serve. Then the devil leaveth him, and, behold, angels came and ministered unto him.

—— DECLARATION OF FAITH ——

I cannot be enticed into any of the fame and fortune, or even acceptance or alliance, which comes with association with the devil and his crowd. I will never give him even one iota of my life.

I worship the Lord my God and Him only do I serve.

I have complete authority and mastery over the devil and his demons. When I cast him out of my world and give the Word the ascendancy in my life, God sends His angels to minister to me and attend to my every need.

(2 Corinthians 6:14; Deuteronomy 6:5-7; Luke 10:19; Psalm 91:9-13; Hebrews 1:14)

MATTHEW 5:2-12 KJV

And he opened his mouth, and taught them, saying, Blessed *are* the poor in spirit: for theirs is the kingdom of heaven. Blessed *are* they that mourn: for they shall be comforted. Blessed *are* the meek: for they shall inherit the earth. Blessed *are* they which do hunger and thirst after righteousness: for they shall be filled. Blessed *are* the merciful: for they shall obtain mercy. Blessed *are* the pure in heart: for they shall see God. Blessed *are* the peacemakers: for they shall be called the children of God. Blessed *are* they which are persecuted for righteousness' sake: for theirs is the kingdom of heaven. Blessed are ye, when *men* shall revile you, and persecute *you,* and shall say all manner of evil against you falsely, for my sake. Rejoice, and be exceeding glad: for great *is* your reward in heaven: for so persecuted they the prophets which were before you.

──── *DECLARATION OF FAITH* ────

I am blessed, happy, to be envied, prosperous, full of joy, and satisfied with God's favor and salvation when I humble myself under His mighty hand. Because of my humility, my Father has granted me my place in the kingdom of heaven!

I am blessed, happy, to be envied, prosperous, full of joy, satisfied with God's favor and salvation, and given a revelation of His matchless grace when I mourn over the results of the curse. Because of my concern, God comforts me in a revelation of His goodness.

Circumstance does not impress me. I am calm and patient in every situation. Because of this, I shall inherit the earth.

I am blessed and enjoying God's favor and salvation as I hunger for righteousness. My hunger shall be filled and I shall be completely satisfied.

I am blessed, loving life, and enjoying abundant satisfaction in God's favor and salvation regardless of what my eyes see or my ears hear. I am a merciful man/woman and I shall obtain mercy.

I am blessed, happy, enviably fortunate, spiritually prosperous with a distinct revelation of the grace of God that I have been given. I am focused on my Lord, not my circumstance. I keep my heart pure and never turn from my steadfast trust in His goodness and love. Because of this, I shall see God! I shall enter His presence in full view of His person—of His glory and majesty!

I am blessed and enjoying enviable happiness and prosperity. I love life and enjoy abundant satisfaction in God's favor and salvation in every circumstance. I am a maker and a maintainer of peace. I am a son/daughter of the living God!

When I am persecuted for being and doing what I know is right, I am blessed. When people revile, berate and persecute me, saying all kinds of evil things about me because of my love for my heavenly Father, I rejoice. I know that I am not alone. All of God's kids who walk in His righteousness suffer this kind of persecution. Therefore, I will rejoice, for I know that I have done the right thing. I look to all of the bountiful blessings that I have before me and I am glad. I know that when my life on this earth is accomplished, I have a reward in heaven that is so great and intense that the human mind cannot even fathom a microbe of its immensity.

By all of these things, I am loving life and enjoying abundant satisfaction in God's favor and salvation.

(1 Peter 3:10-14; 4:13,14; 5:5-7; James 4:6-10; 2 Corinthians 1:3,4; 5:21; Galatians 5:22,23; 6:1-10; Hebrews 11:1; Psalm 91:16; Proverbs 3:5,6; Luke 1:53; 12:32; Isaiah 55:1; 2 Timothy 3:12; 1 Corinthians 13:12; Philippians 4:4)

MATTHEW 5:13-16 NKJV

"You are the salt of the earth; but if the salt loses its flavor, how shall it be seasoned? It is then good for nothing but to be thrown out and trampled underfoot by men. You are the light of the world. A city that is set on a hill cannot be hidden. Nor do they light a lamp and put it under a basket, but on a lampstand, and it gives light to all *who are* in the house. Let your light so shine before men, that they may see your good works and glorify your Father in heaven."

——— *DECLARATION OF FAITH* ———

I am the salt of the earth. I will not allow myself to lose my saltiness (my strength and distinct qualities as a son/daughter of God), nor will I allow my witness to be trampled down by persecution from the world.

I am the light of the world. I will not hide my light, but set it out where all can see it. I live my life in moral excellence and with good, praiseworthy, and notable deeds. I see to it that men recognize what God is doing in my life so that they can give His name the honor that it deserves.

(Luke 14:34; John 8:12; 15:8; 1 John 1:5-7; 1 Peter 2:12)

MATTHEW 5:19,20 AMP

Whoever then breaks or does away with or relaxes one of the least [important] of these commandments and teaches men so shall be called least [important] in the kingdom of heaven, but he who practices them and teaches others to do so shall be called great in the kingdom of heaven. For I tell you, unless your righteousness (your uprightness and your right standing with God) is more than that of the scribes and Pharisees, you will never enter the kingdom of heaven.

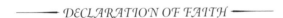

——— *DECLARATION OF FAITH* ———

I am called great in the kingdom of heaven because I teach and practice the Word in its entirety.

The righteous requirement of the Law is fulfilled in me.

I have become the very righteousness of God.

(Romans 8:4; Galatians 5:14; 2 Corinthians 5:21; 1 John 3:6)

MATTHEW 5:23,24 NIV

"Therefore, if you are offering your gift at the altar and there remember that your brother has something against you, leave your gift there in front of the altar. First go and be reconciled to your brother; then come and offer your gift."

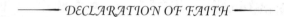
I will not give an offering tainted with the stench of strife. To the very best of my ability, I maintain peace with everyone I have contact with.

(Matthew 8:4; Job 42:8; Galatians 6:10; Hebrews 12:14)

MATTHEW 5:28 NKJV

But I say to you that whoever looks at a woman to lust for her has already committed adultery with her in his heart.

I will not look upon a woman [or a man] lustfully and with evil intent in my heart.

(Proverbs 6:25; Job 31:1; Philippians 4:8; Matthew 6:22)

MATTHEW 5:29,30 NKJV

If your right eye causes you to sin, pluck it out and cast it from you; for it is more profitable for you that one of your members perish, than for your whole body to be cast into hell. And if your right hand causes you to sin, cut it off and cast it from you; for it is more profitable for you that one of your members perish, than for your whole body to be cast into hell.

I will allow nothing to come into my life that may ensnare me to commit sin.

I look over my environment carefully and if there is anything that I can look upon that could cause me to sin, I cast it far from me.

If there is anything that I can touch that could cause me to sin, I cast it far from me as well.

I guard my environment diligently and cast anything that does not bring glory to God far from my presence.

(2 Corinthians 6:14; Colossians 3:5; Mark 9:43)

MATTHEW 5:37 NKJV

"But let your 'Yes' be 'Yes,' and your 'No,' 'No.' For whatever is more than these is from the evil one."

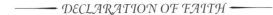
——— *DECLARATION OF FAITH* ———

I speak the truth at all times. I have no need to qualify or justify anything that I say. If I say yes, that is my answer. If I say no, that is my answer. I will add nothing to it.

(1 Peter 3:10-12; Colossians 4:6)

MATTHEW 5:39-45 KJV

But I say unto you, That ye resist not evil: but whosoever shall smite thee on thy right cheek, turn to him the other also. And if any man will sue thee at the law, and take away thy coat, let him have *thy* cloke also. And whosoever shall compel thee to go a mile, go with him twain. Give to him that asketh thee, and from him that would borrow of thee turn not thou away. Ye have heard that it hath been said, Thou shalt love thy neighbour, and hate thine enemy. But I say unto you, Love your enemies, bless them that curse you, do good to them that hate you, and pray for them which despitefully use you, and persecute you; That ye may be the children of your Father which is in heaven: for he maketh his sun to rise on the evil and on the good, and sendeth rain on the just and on the unjust.

——— *DECLARATION OF FAITH* ———

I will not seek revenge against the ungodly. They have no power over me and I will not use my power over them to do them harm.

I am generous and loving toward all men. I display my love even to those who would be my enemies and I pray fervently for God's joy and salvation to light upon those who persecute me.

In every way, I show myself to be a son/daughter of my heavenly Father who makes His sun to rise on the just and the unjust alike, and gives His rain to both the evil and the good.

(Proverbs 24:29; Luke 6:29-38; Isaiah 50:6; Matthew 27:32)

MATTHEW 5:48 AMP

You, therefore, must be perfect [growing into complete maturity of godliness in mind and character, having reached the proper height of virtue and integrity], as your heavenly Father is perfect.

─────── *DECLARATION OF FAITH* ───────

I will grow into complete maturity of godliness in both mind and character.
I reach for the height of virtue and integrity that makes my Father proud.

(Colossians 1:28; 4:12; Ephesians 5:1-18)

MATTHEW 6:1-4 NKJV

"Take heed that you do not do your charitable deeds before men, to be seen by them. Otherwise you have no reward from your Father in heaven. Therefore, when you do a charitable deed, do not sound a trumpet before you as the hypocrites do in the synagogues and in the streets, that they may have glory from men. Assuredly, I say to you, they have their reward. But when you do a charitable deed, do not let your left hand know what your right hand is doing, that your charitable deed may be in secret; and your Father who sees in secret will Himself reward you openly."

─────── *DECLARATION OF FAITH* ───────

I am not a show-off who does good deeds only for my own personal glory,
nor do I give to others in order to gain the praise and honor of men. When I give,
it is with a heart of compassion, so that goodwill will prevail, and because it is the
right thing to do.

I know that the return on my giving is based upon the quality of my seed. I
will not plant vile and lifeless seed filled with greed, selfish pride, or vanity.

(Galatians 6:7,8; 2 Corinthians 9:5-11; Romans 12:8; Luke 14:12-14)

MATTHEW 6:5-8 NKJV

"And when you pray, you shall not be like the hypocrites. For they love to pray standing in the synagogues and on the corners of the streets, that they may be seen by men. Assuredly, I say to you, they have their reward. But you, when you pray, go into your room, and when you have shut your door, pray to your Father who is in the secret place; and your Father who sees in secret will reward you openly. And when you pray, do not use vain repetitions as the heathen do. For they think that they will be heard for their many words. "Therefore do not be like them. For your Father knows the things you have need of before you ask Him."

——— DECLARATION OF FAITH ———

I do not fashion my prayers so that others may be impressed.

I do not look to self-gratification when I pray, but focus on God's will and the results that follow.

I take my prayer time seriously. I find a private place, free of distraction, to do my praying so that I can maintain a distinct focus on a specific answer.

I do not pray using vain repetitions, repeating the same things over and over, thinking that the quantity of my praying is going to get the results that I need. I do not focus on quantity of words, but on quality of words—words that I know are in line with God's perfect will.

My heavenly Father knows what I need even before I ask Him and He is more than willing to provide for me.

(James 1:6-8; 4:1-10; Mark 1:35; 11:22-25; 16:20; Proverbs 18:20,21; 1 John 5:14,15; John 14:13,14)

MATTHEW 6:9-13 KJV

After this manner therefore pray ye: Our Father which art in heaven, Hallowed be thy name. Thy kingdom come. Thy will be done in earth, as *it is* in heaven. Give us this day our daily bread. And forgive us our debts, as we forgive our debtors. And lead us not into temptation, but deliver us from evil: For thine is the kingdom, and the power, and the glory, for ever. Amen.

——— DECLARATION OF FAITH ———

When I pray, I enter my Father's presence with praise and adoration, giving due honor to His holy name.

The manifestation of His kingdom in this earth is my top priority.

I examine God's Word so that I may know His will. I find out what His will is in heaven and pray that the same be done on this earth.

I pray daily for His provision to flood my life—provision for health, peace, and prosperity.

I examine myself and confess before Him anything in my life that does not bring honor to His name.

I purpose in my heart to forgive all of those who have sinned against me. I will not allow the holding of a grudge to hinder my prayers.

I pray for awareness and deliverance from the traps that the evil one has set for me so that I can walk in sure and certain victory all the days of my life.

(Philippians 4:6,19; 2 Timothy 2:15; 1 John 5:14,15; 1 Corinthians 2:12; Mark 11:25; Psalm 91:3)

MATTHEW 6:14,15 NKJV

"For if you forgive men their trespasses, your heavenly Father will also forgive you. But if you do not forgive men their trespasses, neither will your Father forgive your trespasses."

DECLARATION OF FAITH

I will never forget how much my Father has forgiven me of and I will not live in hypocrisy by holding a grudge against another person, no matter what they have done. I will not allow my prayers to be hindered by foolishly holding on to unforgiveness. I release all of those who have sinned against me, whether knowingly or unknowingly, and I cast all resentment into the sea of forgetfulness.

(Mark 11:25; Matthew 18:35; Psalm 103:10-14)

MATTHEW 6:16-18 NIV

"When you fast, do not look somber as the hypocrites do, for they disfigure their faces to show men they are fasting. I tell you the truth, they have received their reward in full. But when you fast, put oil on your head and wash your face, so that it will not be obvious to men that you are fasting, but only to your Father, who is unseen; and your Father, who sees what is done in secret, will reward you."

DECLARATION OF FAITH

When I fast, I do so to maintain my focus and draw closer to God for a specific purpose. No one else needs to know about it. I will not be foolish, like the hypocrite, and try to draw attention to what I am doing.

(Isaiah 58:3-7; Ruth 3:3; James 4:8)

MATTHEW 6:19-21 KJV

Lay not up for yourselves treasures upon earth, where moth and rust doth corrupt, and where thieves break through and steal: But lay up for yourselves treasures in heaven, where neither moth nor rust doth corrupt, and where thieves do not break through nor steal: For where your treasure is, there will your heart be also.

DECLARATION OF FAITH

I do not center my attention on heaping up earthly treasures like a pitiful miser. My attention is on the treasures of heaven, where God stamps His seal of protection and neither moth, nor rust, nor worm can consume and destroy it, and thieves cannot break in and steal it.

(Psalm 112:1-3; Deuteronomy 8:6-18; 28:1-14; Proverbs 23:4; Matthew 19:21)

MATTHEW 6:22 NKJV

"The lamp of the body is the eye. If therefore your eye is good, your whole body will be full of light."

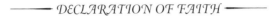

My eyes are the lamp of my body. Therefore, I will be careful what I let them take in. I keep them fixed on the prize that God has set before me. I fully intend to win this race and receive my crown of victory!

(1 Corinthians 9:24-27; Luke 11:34,35)

MATTHEW 6:24 NKJV

"No one can serve two masters; for either he will hate the one and love the other, or else he will be loyal to the one and despise the other. You cannot serve God and mammon."

I do not serve two masters. I have only one Lord and He is Jesus. He is my strength and my provider. I trust in Him and none other to sustain my existence.

Money is but a tool to achieve a purpose. It is my provision, not my provider. I do not trust in it, nor do I need it. Money can pass from the earth and I will still prosper, for my hope is in the right place.

I will trust in the Lord and Him only will I serve.

(Philippians 4:19; Luke 16:9-13; Galatians 1:10; 1 Timothy 6:9-19)

MATTHEW 6:25-34 KJV

Therefore I say unto you, Take no thought for your life, what ye shall eat, or what ye shall drink; nor yet for your body, what ye shall put on. Is not the life more than meat, and the body than raiment? Behold the fowls of the air: for they sow not, neither do they reap, nor gather into barns; yet your heavenly Father feedeth them. Are ye not much better than they? Which of you by taking thought can add one cubit unto his stature? And why take ye thought for raiment? Consider the lilies of the field, how they grow; they toil not, neither do they spin: And yet I say unto you, That even Solomon in all his glory was not arrayed like one of these. Wherefore, if God so clothe the grass of the field, which to day is, and to morrow is cast into the oven, *shall he* not much more *clothe* you, O ye of little faith? Therefore take no thought, saying, What shall we eat? or, What shall we drink? or, Wherewithal shall we be clothed? (For after all these things do the Gentiles seek:) for your heavenly Father knoweth that ye have need of all these things. But seek ye first the kingdom of God, and his righteousness; and all these things shall be added unto you. Take therefore no thought for the morrow: for the morrow shall take thought for the things of itself. Sufficient unto the day *is* the evil thereof.

DECLARATION OF FAITH

I refuse to be worried about provision for my life. I know that I will have plenty to eat and drink, and plenty of clothes to wear.

My Father considers my life precious in His sight and will not force me to go without the things that I need. He is ever ready to be my provider.

When anxiety over the circumstances comes against me, I will look to the birds of the air. They neither sow nor reap, and they don't even have a bank account. Yet, my Father feeds them continually.

When I see the wonderful provision of these birds, I can look back to myself. I do sow and reap, and I gather in a great harvest. I am considered far more important in my Father's eyes than the birds. Therefore, I can look to them and know of a certainty that my provision is signed, sealed and will be delivered without fail.

I know that worrying is useful only for my destruction. It does not add anything good to my life, add a single cubit to my stature, or give me anything that I need. Therefore, I cast worry far from me and live in God's peace and security.

When anxiety comes against me concerning the clothes that I have to wear, I look to the flowers of the field. They neither toil nor spin, but are arrayed in such beauty that even Solomon in all of his glory did not compare to them.

When I see the wonderful clothing of the flowers, I can look back to myself. My Father blesses all of the work of my hands. He considers me to be far more important than the flowers. Therefore, if He clothes flowers, which are here today and gone tomorrow, in such beauty, He will clothe me, His eternal son/daughter, in the finest of apparel.

In light of all of this, I absolutely refuse to worry! I will have plenty to eat, plenty to drink and plenty to wear. I do not crave these things selfishly and focus my attention on obtaining them, while neglecting God's kingdom. I simply rejoice in the present fact of my Father's provision.

My first thought in all things is the advancement of the kingdom and God's way of being and doing things. With this mindset and spiritual stronghold, all of my physical and material needs will shower into my life in a flood of abundance.

I refuse to worry about tomorrow. This is ridiculous and does me no good at all. I serve the great I Am who is ever in the present. Therefore, as a good and loyal son/daughter, I too will focus my attention on what I can do in the present to magnify my heavenly Father and bring glory to His name.

(1 Peter 5:5-7; Philippians 4:19; Psalm 103:13,14; 112:1-3; Deuteronomy 8:6-18; 28:1-14; Zechariah 3:4; James 4:1-10; Luke 12:22-24; 1 Timothy 4:8; 6:6-19; Exodus 3:14; John 14:13,14)

MATTHEW 7:1-5 KJV

Judge not, that ye be not judged. For with what judgment ye judge, ye shall be judged: and with what measure ye mete, it shall be measured to you again.

And why beholdest thou the mote that is in thy brother's eye, but considerest not the beam that is in thine own eye? Or how wilt thou say to thy brother, Let me pull out the mote out of thine eye; and, behold, a beam is in thine own eye? Thou hypocrite, first cast out the beam out of thine own eye; and then shalt thou see clearly to cast out the mote out of thy brother's eye.

—— DECLARATION OF FAITH ——

I am not one who criticizes and condemns others for their wrongdoings, neither am I judged or condemned for my own wrongdoings.

I understand the spiritual laws of sowing and reaping [that with the measure I deal out to others, it will be dealt back to me], and I will not build to myself a harvest full of judgment and condemnation.

When it comes to faults, or those little areas that need correction or a word of instruction, I look to my own life first. I will not be so arrogant as to instruct or make demands on another when I am not bearing the desired fruit myself. I will not instruct or correct the sinful until I myself am living above sin. I will not instruct or correct in prosperity until I myself am prospering. I will not instruct or correct in healing until I myself am walking in divine health. When I have removed the beam from my own eye, only then will I see clearly enough to take the speck out of my brother's eye.

(Romans 14:3; Galatians 6:1-10; Luke 6:38-41)

MATTHEW 7:6 AMP

Do not give that which is holy (the sacred thing) to the dogs, and do not throw your pearls before hogs, lest they trample upon them with their feet and turn and tear you in pieces.

DECLARATION OF FAITH

My witness is guided by discretion. I do not offer the wonderful things of God to hardhearted despisers of correction, thereby offering myself up to a spirit of destruction.

(Proverbs 1:22,29-31; 9:7,8; 11:30; 12:1; 13:1; 15:5,10,12; 18:2; 19:3; 23:9; 29:19)

MATTHEW 7:7,8 KJV

Ask, and it shall be given you; seek, and ye shall find; knock, and it shall be opened unto you: For every one that asketh receiveth; and he that seeketh findeth; and to him that knocketh it shall be opened.

DECLARATION OF FAITH

I will ask and keep on asking until I have received what I am asking for.
I will seek and keep on seeking until I have found what I am looking for.
I will knock and keep on knocking until the door is opened to me.
I know of a certainty that when I ask, I will receive; when I seek, I will find; and when I knock, the door will be opened to me.

(Mark 11:22-24; Proverbs 8:17; Deuteronomy 4:29; 1 John 5:14,15)

MATTHEW 7:9-12 KJV

Or what man is there of you, whom if his son ask bread, will he give him a stone? Or if he ask a fish, will he give him a serpent? If ye then, being evil, know how to give good gifts unto your children, how much more shall your Father which is in heaven give good things to them that ask him? Therefore all things whatsoever ye would that men should do to you, do ye even so to them: for this is the law and the prophets.

DECLARATION OF FAITH

My heavenly Father loves me and is always good to me. If I ask Him for a loaf of bread, He does not offer me a stone instead. If I ask Him for a fish, He does not give me a snake. To the contrary, He is more than willing to give me specifically what I persistently ask for. When He sees that my heart is set on it, He makes sure that I have it.

(Jeremiah 24:6; 29:11; John 14:13,14; 15:7; 16:23,24; 1 John 5:14,15)

MATTHEW 7:13,14 KJV

Enter ye in at the strait gate: for wide is the gate, and broad is the way, that leadeth to destruction, and many there be which go in thereat: Because strait is the gate, and narrow is the way, which leadeth unto life, and few there be that find it.

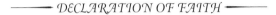

——— DECLARATION OF FAITH ———

I enter into God's blessings His way. I keep a distinct focus on that narrow gate that stands before me and do all that my Father says so that I may enter through it and obtain all of the blessings that come from the God-kind of life.

(John 10:10; 15:7; Deuteronomy 28:1-14; Luke 13:24; Ephesians 1:3)

MATTHEW 7:15-17 KJV

Beware of false prophets, which come to you in sheep's clothing, but inwardly they are ravening wolves. Ye shall know them by their fruits. Do men gather grapes of thorns, or figs of thistles? Even so every good tree bringeth forth good fruit; but a corrupt tree bringeth forth evil fruit.

——— DECLARATION OF FAITH ———

I do not listen to false teachers who try to rob me of the blessings that God has for me.

I fully recognize false teachers by what is produced in their lives and ministries.

When I look for a teacher to teach me the ways of God, I look to those who are bearing the fruit that is promised in the Word.

My pastors and teachers are filled with the Holy Spirit and produce good fruit, worthy of admiration.

(John 10:1-10; Romans 16:17,18; Jeremiah 23:16; Micah 3:5; Matthew 7:20)

MATTHEW 7:24,25 KJV

Therefore whosoever heareth these sayings of mine, and doeth them, I will liken him unto a wise man, which built his house upon a rock: And the rain descended, and the floods came, and the winds blew, and beat upon that house; and it fell not: for it was founded upon a rock.

——— *DECLARATION OF FAITH* ———

I am both a habitual hearer and a habitual doer of the Word of God. I continually act upon the Word and put it to work in my life. By this, I am counted among the wise—like a man who builds his house upon a rocky cliff. When the winds of disaster rage against it, it is not moved, for the foundation (of the Word) has firmly established it.

(James 1:21-25; Luke 6:47-49; Joshua 1:8)

MATTHEW 8:3 KJV

And Jesus put forth his hand, and touched him, saying, I will; be thou clean. And immediately his leprosy was cleansed.

——— *DECLARATION OF FAITH* ———

My Father is more than willing to bring His healing power into my body so that I can walk in perfect wholeness in this life.

(Isaiah 53:4,5; 1 Peter 2:24; James 5:14-16; Exodus 15:26; Psalm 103:1-5)

MATTHEW 8:8-10 KJV

The centurion answered and said, Lord, I am not worthy that thou shouldest come under my roof: but speak the word only, and my servant shall be healed. For I am a man under authority, having soldiers under me: and I say to this *man,* Go, and he goeth; and to another, Come, and he cometh; and to my servant, Do this, and he doeth *it.* When Jesus heard *it,* he marvelled, and said to them that followed, Verily I say unto you, I have not found so great faith, no, not in Israel.

——— *DECLARATION OF FAITH* ———

When I speak the Word of God, His healing power occupies my words and is carried into the body of the one who has faith.

Words are my servants and the carriers of my faith to a hurting world.

(Psalm 107:20; Proverbs 18:20,21; 2 Corinthians 4:13; Mark 11:22-25)

MATTHEW 8:13 KJV

And Jesus said unto the centurion, Go thy way; and as thou hast believed, so be it done unto thee. And his servant was healed in the selfsame hour.

——— *DECLARATION OF FAITH* ———

My faith works for me according to what I believe.
What I believe I have received, that is what I shall have.

(Mark 9:23; 11:22-25; 2 Corinthians 4:13; Romans 10:8-10; Hebrews 11:1)

MATTHEW 8:16 KJV

When the even was come, they brought unto him many that were possessed with devils: and he cast out the spirits with his word, and healed all that were sick.

——— *DECLARATION OF FAITH* ———

I use my words to drive out demons and restore health to myself and those in my circle of influence.

(John 14:12; Psalm 107:20; Mark 16:17-20; Proverbs 18:20,21)

MATTHEW 8:17 KJV

That it might be fulfilled which was spoken by Esaias the prophet, saying, Himself took our infirmities, and bare our sicknesses.

——— *DECLARATION OF FAITH* ———

Jesus shouldered all of my weaknesses and carried away all of my diseases.

(Isaiah 53:4,5; 1 Peter 2:24; Exodus 15:26)

MATTHEW 8:26 KJV

And he saith unto them, Why are ye fearful, O ye of little faith? Then he arose, and rebuked the winds and the sea; and there was a great calm.

——— *DECLARATION OF FAITH* ———

I reject all feelings of fear and speak words of faith to the adverse circumstances I am facing.

(Joshua 1:5-9; Mark 11:22-25; 2 Corinthians 4:13; Psalm 107:20,29)

MATTHEW 9:22 AMP

Jesus turned around and, seeing her, He said, Take courage, daughter! Your faith has made you well. And at once the woman was restored to health.

——— *DECLARATION OF FAITH* ———

I am joyfully courageous with my faith, for by it, I am saved, delivered, and healed.

(Philippians 4:4-13; James 5:14-16; Luke 7:50; 8:48)

MATTHEW 9:28,29 KJV

And when he was come into the house, the blind men came to him: and Jesus saith unto them, Believe ye that I am able to do this? They said unto him, Yea, Lord. Then touched he their eyes, saying, According to your faith be it unto you.

——— *DECLARATION OF FAITH* ———

I firmly believe in the power and ability of God that is within me. According to my faith (my believing and speaking the answer) all of my needs and godly desires become a reality in my life.

(Colossians 1:29; Ephesians 1:17-23; 2 Corinthians 4:13; Philippians 4:19; Hebrews 11:1)

MATTHEW 9:32,33 KJV

As they went out, behold, they brought to him a dumb man possessed with a devil. And when the devil was cast out, the dumb spake: and the multitudes marvelled, saying, It was never so seen in Israel.

——— *DECLARATION OF FAITH* ———

As an ambassador of Christ with God's own ability within me, I have the power to drive out all demons.

(Ephesians 1:17-23; John 14:12; 1 John 4:4; 2 Corinthians 5:17-20; Mark 16:17; Luke 10:18,19)

MATTHEW 9:35 KJV

And Jesus went about all the cities and villages, teaching in their synagogues, and preaching the gospel of the kingdom, and healing every sickness and every disease among the people.

——— *DECLARATION OF FAITH* ———

I am an ambassador of Christ—the very avenue that God has chosen to bring His power into the earth. I am anointed with His own ability to preach the good news of His kingdom and to heal all kinds of diseases and every kind of weakness and infirmity.

(John 14:12; 2 Corinthians 5:17-20; Luke 10:19; Ephesians 1:17-23; 1 John 2:20; Matthew 10:1)

MATTHEW 9:37,38 KJV

Then saith he unto his disciples, The harvest truly is plenteous, but the labourers *are* few; Pray ye therefore the Lord of the harvest, that he will send forth labourers into his harvest.

——— *DECLARATION OF FAITH* ———

I am a skilled laborer in the harvest field of the world.

I am a soul-winner with an urgency to win the lost.

I continually pray that the Lord of the harvest thrust laborers into the harvest fields to work together with me in our great commission.

(Daniel 12:3; Proverbs 11:30; Luke 10:2; 2 Thessalonians 3:1)

MATTHEW 10:1 KJV

And when he had called unto him his twelve disciples, he gave them power against unclean spirits, to cast them out, and to heal all manner of sickness and all manner of disease.

——— *DECLARATION OF FAITH* ———

I have been given power and authority over all evil spirits. They must obey my commands in the name of Jesus. I drive out all demons from my presence and heal all kinds of diseases and every kind of weakness and infirmity.

(John 14:12; 1 John 4:4; Luke 10:18:19; Ephesians 1:17-23; Mark 16:17-20)

MATTHEW 10:7,8 KJV

And as ye go, preach, saying, The kingdom of heaven is at hand. Heal the sick, cleanse the lepers, raise the dead, cast out devils: freely ye have received, freely give.

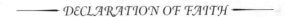
———— *DECLARATION OF FAITH* ————

I proclaim the present reality of the kingdom of heaven wherever I go. I heal the sick, raise the dead, cast out demons, and cleanse the lepers. Freely I have received this, and freely I give it.

(John 14:12; Isaiah 61:1-3; Matthew 3:2; Acts 8:18; Mark 16:15-20)

MATTHEW 10:17-20 KJV

But beware of men: for they will deliver you up to the councils, and they will scourge you in their synagogues; And ye shall be brought before governors and kings for my sake, for a testimony against them and the Gentiles. But when they deliver you up, take no thought how or what ye shall speak: for it shall be given you in that same hour what ye shall speak. For it is not ye that speak, but the Spirit of your Father which speaketh in you.

———— *DECLARATION OF FAITH* ————

I am cautious and stand alert against men whose very nature is in opposition to the ways of God. I am fearless when they take counsel against me or interrogate me in order to condemn me. I am not apprehensive over what I will say or how I will answer them. The greater One is within me and He will give me the words to speak the very moment that I need them. The very Spirit of my Father speaks through me to answer all charges that are brought against me.

(Isaiah 54:17; 2 Timothy 1:6,7; 1 John 4:4; John 16:13; Luke 12:11,12)

MATTHEW 10:24,25 KJV

The disciple is not above his master, nor the servant above his lord. It is enough for the disciple that he be as his master, and the servant as his lord. If they have called the master of the house Beelzebub, how much more shall they call them of his household?

———— *DECLARATION OF FAITH* ————

I am a disciple of the Lord. I am not elevated above Him, but am conformed to be like Him. He is my example and has bid me to do things just the way that He does them.

I am a born-again, recreated spirit and all of the ability of God is within me. I am His own child and a valued member of His household. What do I care what the world says about me? Have I not chosen the more excellent way?

(Romans 8:14-17,29,30; John 3:3; 14:12; 2 Corinthians 5:17; 1 John 4:4; Colossians 1:27-29; Galatians 4:5,6; Ephesians 1:17-23)

MATTHEW 10:26-31 KJV

Fear them not therefore: for there is nothing covered, that shall not be revealed; and hid, that shall not be known. What I tell you in darkness, *that* speak ye in light: and what ye hear in the ear, *that* preach ye upon the housetops. And fear not them which kill the body, but are not able to kill the soul: but rather fear him which is able to destroy both soul and body in hell. Are not two sparrows sold for a farthing? and one of them shall not fall on the ground without your Father. But the very hairs of your head are all numbered. Fear ye not therefore, ye are of more value than many sparrows.

—— DECLARATION OF FAITH ——

I have no fear of Godless men—of their secret strategies or hidden traps. There is nothing hidden that shall not be revealed to me, and my Father shows me every secret strategy being brought against me.

God reveals to me deep and hidden truths that I could never discover on my own. What He reveals to me in private I announce publicly, and that which He whispers in my ear I proclaim from the housetops.

I maintain a proper perspective in the affairs of life. Godless men may be able to kill a body, but they have no power over a spirit. My Father, on the other hand, has the power to destroy both spirit and body in the fires of hell. Therefore, my Father, who is within me, is deserving of the greater respect.

A sparrow is of little value from a human perspective, but not one of them can fall to the ground without my Father taking notice and responding with compassion. Yet He gives the same notice to the very hairs on my head. If even one falls out, He takes notice and expresses His concern. By this, I am shown to be more valuable than many sparrows and if anything, or anyone, would try to harm me, my Father, who loves me, will take notice and respond in my defense. Therefore, what need do I have to fear Godless men?

(Psalm 2; Mark 4:22; Acts 5:20; Luke 12:4,5; 21:18; 2 Timothy 1:6,7; Romans 8:31)

MATTHEW 10:32 NIV

"Whoever acknowledges me before men, I will also acknowledge him before my Father in heaven."

—— DECLARATION OF FAITH ——

Jesus is the High Priest of my confession. When I acknowledge and confess my oneness with Him, He acknowledges and confesses my oneness before my Father in heaven.

(Hebrews 3:1; 4:14-16; 10:19-23; Luke 12:8; Revelation 3:5)

MATTHEW 10:37-39 KJV

He that loveth father or mother more than me is not worthy of me: and he that loveth son or daughter more than me is not worthy of me. And he that taketh not his cross, and followeth after me, is not worthy of me. He that findeth his life shall lose it: and he that loseth his life for my sake shall find it.

─────── DECLARATION OF FAITH ───────

Jesus is the first love of my life. My relationship with Him is the single most important relationship that I have.

I have taken my stand with Jesus, cleaving steadfastly to Him and conforming wholly to His way of living.

My old man (the old sinful nature) died with Jesus on the cross and I have put on the new man (the divine nature). I have been made new in Christ Jesus and I am now living the God-kind of life.

(Luke 14:26; Mark 8:34; John 12:25; Ephesians 5:1-18; Galatians 2:20; Romans 6:3-11; 2 Peter 1:4)

MATTHEW 10:40 AMP

He who receives and welcomes and accepts you receives and welcomes and accepts Me, and he who receives and welcomes and accepts Me receives and welcomes and accepts Him Who sent Me.

─────── DECLARATION OF FAITH ───────

Those who receive, welcome, and accept me have received, welcomed, and accepted Jesus Himself into their midst; and those who receive, welcome, and accept Jesus have received, welcomed, and accepted my heavenly Father as well.

The Father, Jesus, and the Holy Spirit are with me (and within me) everywhere I go and in everything that I do.

(1 Corinthians 3:16; Luke 9:48; Acts 22:7,8; Matthew 28:20; John 17:20-26)

MATTHEW 10:42 KJV

And whosoever shall give to drink unto one of these little ones a cup of cold water only in the name of a disciple, verily I say unto you, he shall in no wise lose his reward.

─────── DECLARATION OF FAITH ───────

My Father does not look for ways to take rewards from me, but is ever-mindful and watchful for even the most diminutive good deed so that He can bless me for it. If I, with a willing heart, give as little as a cup of cool water to one of His kids, He establishes a permanent reward for me and will never take it from me.

(Hebrews 11:6; Mark 9:41; 1 Corinthians 3:13-15; 9:25; Luke 6:38)

MATTHEW 11:12 KJV

And from the days of John the Baptist until now the kingdom of heaven suffereth violence, and the violent take it by force.

DECLARATION OF FAITH

I am a spiritually violent man/woman. I seize the kingdom of heaven by skillful force, exerting all of my resources in a blaze of fury that sends the devil reeling. I plow down every obstacle that would hinder me from living the life that God has ordained for me to live.

(Ephesians 6:10-18; James 5:16; Luke 16:16; 1 Corinthians 9:24-27)

MATTHEW 11:27-30 KJV

All things are delivered unto me of my Father: and no man knoweth the Son, but the Father; neither knoweth any man the Father, save the Son, and *he* to whomsoever the Son will reveal *him*. Come unto me, all *ye* that labour and are heavy laden, and I will give you rest. Take my yoke upon you, and learn of me; for I am meek and lowly in heart: and ye shall find rest unto your souls. For my yoke *is* easy, and my burden is light.

DECLARATION OF FAITH

I am born to fully know and accurately understand the things of God. Jesus, my Lord and my brother, has given me a thorough revelation of our Father's being.

I cast all of the heavy burdens of my life upon Jesus. They are now upon His shoulders and I am set free. All that has weighed me down is now His to bear.

I have taken His yoke upon me and have made Him the center of all of my learning. I find comfort in His gentleness and simplicity. In Him, I have found rest, relief and refreshment for my soul.

The yoke that I have been given is easy to bear. It is life to me in abundance.

(1 Corinthians 2:6-16; 1 John 5:20; 1 Peter 5:5-7; John 6:35-37; 10:10)

MATTHEW 12:15 KJV

But when Jesus knew it, he withdrew himself from thence: and great multitudes followed him, and he healed them all.

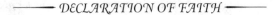
—— *DECLARATION OF FAITH* ——

I have heard the Word and joined myself to Jesus, and He has healed all of my diseases.

(Psalm 107:20; Exodus 15:26; Isaiah 53:4,5; Matthew 8:17; 19:2)

MATTHEW 12:22 KJV

Then was brought unto him one possessed with a devil, blind, and dumb: and he healed him, insomuch that the blind and dumb both spake and saw.

—— *DECLARATION OF FAITH* ——

In Jesus, the spirits of blindness have no power over me. In Him, I can see and talk as well as any other.

(1 Peter 2:24; James 5:14-16; Luke 10:18,19; 11:14,15; Psalm 103:1-5)

MATTHEW 12:28,29 KJV

But if I cast out devils by the Spirit of God, then the kingdom of God is come unto you. Or else how can one enter into a strong man's house, and spoil his goods, except he first bind the strong man? and then he will spoil his house.

—— *DECLARATION OF FAITH* ——

The Spirit of God has come upon me and has taken up residence within me, and by His power I can drive out any demon. By the Spirit of the living God within me, I have the power to bind the devil and plunder his house, taking back all that he has stolen.

(Isaiah 61:1-3; John 14:12; 1 Corinthians 3:16; Mark 3:27; 16:17-20; Luke 10:18,19; Proverbs 6:30,31; Joel 2:25; Matthew 16:9; 18:18)

MATTHEW 12:35-37 KJV

A good man out of the good treasure of the heart bringeth forth good things: and an evil man out of the evil treasure bringeth forth evil things. But I say unto you, That every idle word that men shall speak, they shall give account thereof in the day of judgment. For by thy words thou shalt be justified, and by thy words thou shalt be condemned.

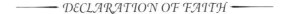

——— *DECLARATION OF FAITH* ———

I have stored up many good things within me and these are the issues that pour forth from my life. As God's son/daughter, I am a blessing to all people.

All of the words that I speak have a purpose and an operation. They are the tools that govern what I have and what I do, and by them I will be justified and acquitted in the Day of Judgment.

(Genesis 12:1-3; Proverbs 18:20,21; Mark 11:23,24; 2 Corinthians 4:13)

MATTHEW 12:50 KJV

For whosoever shall do the will of my Father which is in heaven, the same is my brother, and sister, and mother.

——— *DECLARATION OF FAITH* ———

I am the very brother of my Lord Jesus because I have done the will of our Father.

(Hebrews 2:11; Romans 8:28-30; John 6:28,29; 15:14)

MATTHEW 13:8 KJV

But other fell into good ground, and brought forth fruit, some an hundredfold, some sixtyfold, some thirtyfold.

——— *DECLARATION OF FAITH* ———

I sow my seed upon good soil and yield a harvest many times more than what I have planted.

(Luke 6:38; 2 Corinthians 9:5-11; Malachi 3:10; Genesis 26:12)

MATTHEW 13:9 KJV

Who hath ears to hear, let him hear.

——— *DECLARATION OF FAITH* ———

I have ears that are opened to hear the Word of God. I perceive and consider all that He says to me.

(Isaiah 30:21,30; 1 Corinthians 2:6-16; Ephesians 1:17; Luke 8:10; 24:45)

MATTHEW 13:11,12 KJV

He answered and said unto them, Because it is given unto you to know the mysteries of the kingdom of heaven, but to them it is not given. For whosoever hath, to him shall be given, and he shall have more abundance: but whosoever hath not, from him shall be taken away even that he hath.

───── *DECLARATION OF FAITH* ─────

God has given me the ability to know secrets and mysteries of the kingdom of heaven. I have been given a vast supply of wisdom and knowledge and God is continually pouring more and more into my life so that I can be furnished richly and live in the fullness of His laws of abundance.

(Luke 8:10; 1 Corinthians 2:6-16; Daniel 1:4,17,20; 2:22,23; John 10:10; Matthew 25:29)

MATTHEW 13:15,16 KJV

For this people's heart is waxed gross, and their ears are dull of hearing, and their eyes they have closed; lest at any time they should see with their eyes and hear with their ears, and should understand with their heart, and should be converted, and I should heal them. But blessed are your eyes, for they see: and your ears, for they hear.

───── *DECLARATION OF FAITH* ─────

The eyes of my understanding have been enlightened. God's Word has been opened up to me. I can now see with eyes of discernment and hear with ears of comprehension. I understand and recognize the things of the spirit.

I am receptive of God's healing power.

I am blessed, happy, fortunate and to be envied, because I have the God-given ability to see and hear things as they truly are.

(Ephesians 1:17-23; 1 Corinthians 2:6-16; Psalm 107:20; 1 John 2:20; 5:20; Daniel 2:22,23)

MATTHEW 13:23 AMP

As for what was sown on good soil, this is he who hears the Word and grasps and comprehends it; he indeed bears fruit and yields in one case a hundred times as much as was sown, in another sixty times as much, and in another thirty.

I hear and understand the specific details that God has revealed in His Word so that I may do what it leads me to do. I continually yield an abundant harvest in my life—even as much as one hundred times what I have sown.

(Matthew 13:11; James 1:22-25; Genesis 26:12; 2 Corinthians 9:5-11; Malachi 3:10)

MATTHEW 13:31-33 KJV

Another parable put he forth unto them, saying, The kingdom of heaven is like to a grain of mustard seed, which a man took, and sowed in his field: Which indeed is the least of all seeds: but when it is grown, it is the greatest among herbs, and becometh a tree, so that the birds of the air come and lodge in the branches thereof. Another parable spake he unto them; The kingdom of heaven is like unto leaven, which a woman took, and hid in three measures of meal, till the whole was leavened.

I operate the principles of the kingdom in the spirit of faith that has been given to me. I understand that when I sow kingdom principles, they are like grains of mustard seed. Though they are small in the midst of all other seeds that have been sown into my life, through faith and patience, I can water them until their roots have choked out all that does not bring glory to God. In this manner, I receive such an abundance of blessings that I have all that I need and plenty left over so that my life becomes a refuge to everyone in my circle of influence.

(Galatians 6:9; 2 Corinthians 4:13; 9:5-11; Hebrews 6:12; Luke 13:18,19; Genesis 12:3)

MATTHEW 13:58 KJV

And he did not many mighty works there because of their unbelief.

I believe in, trust in, and rely upon Jesus perpetually. His power is ever-present and at work in my life.

(1 Peter 3:12; Colossians 1:29; Ephesians 1:17-23; John 14:12)

MATTHEW 14:14 KJV

And Jesus went forth, and saw a great multitude, and was moved with compassion toward them, and he healed their sick.

——— *DECLARATION OF FAITH* ———

My Lord has tremendous compassion for me and is more than willing to provide my healing when I need it.

(Psalm 103:1-5,13; 107:20; James 5:14-16; Exodus 15:26; 23:25)

MATTHEW 15:10 KJV

And he called the multitude, and said unto them, Hear, and understand.

——— *DECLARATION OF FAITH* ———

I have been given a spirit of understanding and am well able to grasp and comprehend the Word of God.

(Ephesians 1:17; 1 Corinthians 2:6-16; 1 John 2:20; 5:20; Daniel 1:4,17,20; 2:22,23)

MATTHEW 15:18 KJV

But those things which proceed out of the mouth come forth from the heart; and they defile the man.

——— *DECLARATION OF FAITH* ———

I fully understand that the things that I say come forth from what I have stored up in my spirit. Therefore, I am careful to fill my spirit with only good things that will bring glory to God. Because of this, I am well able to speak those good things that will produce in me the God-kind of life.

(Matthew 12:35-37; Philippians 4:8; Proverbs 18:20,21; Mark 11:23,24)

MATTHEW 15:22-28 KJV

And, behold, a woman of Canaan came out of the same coasts, and cried unto him, saying, Have mercy on me, O Lord, *thou* Son of David; my daughter is grievously vexed with a devil. But he answered her not a word. And his disciples came and besought him, saying, Send her away; for she crieth after us. But he answered and said, I am not sent but unto the lost sheep of the house of Israel. Then came she and worshipped him, saying, Lord, help me. But he answered and said, It is not meet to take the children's bread, and to cast *it* to dogs. And she said, Truth, Lord: yet the dogs eat of the crumbs which fall from their masters' table. Then Jesus answered and said unto her, O woman, great *is* thy faith: be it unto thee even as thou wilt. And her daughter was made whole from that very hour.

——— *DECLARATION OF FAITH* ———

I have been given a tremendous measure of faith and I am persistent, even tenacious, with it, until I have received what I am asking for.

(Romans 12:3; Matthew 7:7-11; 18:7,8; Hebrews 10:35-11:1,6)

MATTHEW 16:19 KJV

And I will give unto thee the keys of the kingdom of heaven: and whatsoever thou shalt bind on earth shall be bound in heaven: and whatsoever thou shalt loose on earth shall be loosed in heaven.

——— *DECLARATION OF FAITH* ———

I have been given the keys to the kingdom of heaven. The very means of attaining, understanding and overcoming the issues of life are in my God-given authority of binding and loosing. It is written, and established as law, that whatever I bind on earth is bound in heaven and whatever I loose on earth is loosed in heaven. The standard that has been predetermined and established in heaven, is what I live by on this earth.

(Matthew 6:10; 18:18; Mark 3:27)

MATTHEW 16:23-25 KJV

But he turned, and said unto Peter, Get thee behind me, Satan: thou art an offence unto me: for thou savourest not the things that be of God, but those that be of men. Then said Jesus unto his disciples, If any *man* will come after me, let him deny himself, and take up his cross, and follow me. For whosoever will save his life shall lose it: and whosoever will lose his life for my sake shall find it.

——— *DECLARATION OF FAITH* ———

I remain fixed and focused on what causes me to partake of the nature and qualities of God. I see and do things as God does [in the spirit], and not as men see and do them [by the senses].

I am a true disciple (disciplined follower and imitator) of Jesus. I have set aside the things of the flesh and have joined myself to the Lord, conforming wholly to His manner of living.

I am not bent on maintaining the natural life. That old man was crucified with Christ and I have found a new life in Him where the spirit rules and Jesus is Lord!

(John 4:23,24; 2 Peter 1:3,4; John 6:63; Ephesians 5:1,2; Galatians 2:19-21; 5:16-18)

Matthew 17:19,20 KJV

Then came the disciples to Jesus apart, and said, Why could not we cast him out? And Jesus said unto them, Because of your unbelief: for verily I say unto you, If ye have faith as a grain of mustard seed, ye shall say unto this mountain, Remove hence to yonder place; and it shall remove; and nothing shall be impossible unto you.

———— *DECLARATION OF FAITH* ————

My faith is a spiritual force that is alive within me. When I use it, it is like a seed planted at the root of the problem. As I cultivate it [continually believing and speaking the answer], it overtakes and uproots whatever is standing in my way.

Even a mountain poses no difficulty for me when I remain stubborn and persistent in my faith. When I tell it to move, it moves. When I tell demons to leave, they leave.

When I command an infirmity to come out of a body, it comes out. With the faith that God has given me, nothing is impossible for me.

(2 Corinthians 4:13; John 6:63; Mark 11:22-24; Hebrews 11:1)

Matthew 18:8,9 KJV

Wherefore if thy hand or thy foot offend thee, cut them off, and cast them from thee: it is better for thee to enter into life halt or maimed, rather than having two hands or two feet to be cast into everlasting fire. And if thine eye offend thee, pluck it out, and cast it from thee: it is better for thee to enter into life with one eye, rather than having two eyes to be cast into hell fire.

———— *DECLARATION OF FAITH* ————

There is nothing so dear to me that I will not part with it in order to maintain close fellowship with my heavenly Father. Even if one of my own eyes caused me to sin, I would pluck it out and cast it far from me. If one of my own hands, or a foot, caused me to sin, I would cut it off as well. [I understand that the point Jesus is making is to cast from me anything that hinders my fellowship, no matter what the extreme, and not to mutilate my body, which is His temple and sacred.]

(Deuteronomy 6:5-7; Matthew 5:29,30; 1 Corinthians 3:16)

Matthew 18:10 NKJV

"Take heed that you do not despise one of these little ones, for I say to you that in heaven their angels always see the face of My Father who is in heaven."

———— DECLARATION OF FAITH ————

I have a guardian angel, sent by God, who is specifically assigned and com-manded to minister to my every need. He is continually in my Father's presence beholding His face and carrying forth the power of His majesty.

With this in mind, only a fool would despise me, cheat me or disrespect me.

(Hebrews 1:14; Exodus 23:20-23; Psalm 91:11)

MATTHEW 18:18 NKJV

"Assuredly, I say to you, whatever you bind on earth will be bound in heaven, and whatever you loose on earth will be loosed in heaven."

———— DECLARATION OF FAITH ————

I carry the very authority of heaven with me in my earth walk. It is my responsibility to establish in the earth what has already been established for me in heaven. Therefore, I will walk in my authority, binding on earth that which has been bound for me in heaven and loosing on earth that which has been loosed for me in heaven.

(Ephesians 1:17-23; Matthew 6:10; Luke 10:19; 2 Corinthians 5:20; Mark 16:15-20)

MATTHEW 18:19,20 KJV

Again I say unto you, That if two of you shall agree on earth as touching any thing that they shall ask, it shall be done for them of my Father which is in heaven. For where two or three are gathered together in my name, there am I in the midst of them.

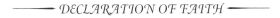

———— DECLARATION OF FAITH ————

I am a team player in my Christian walk. When I get together with my brothers and sisters in Christ and we agree in perfect harmony for a specific answer to our prayer, our Father sees to it that it is done for us; for wherever I draw together in fellowship with other believers, and we take our stand in the authority of the name of Jesus, He Himself, the great I Am, is right there in our midst bringing the power needed to fill every order that we submit.

(John 14:13,14; Hebrews 10:25; 1 Corinthians 1:10; 1 John 3:22; 5:14,15; Acts 20:7)

MATTHEW 18:27,35 NKJV

Then the master of that servant was moved with compassion, released him, and forgave him the debt. "So My heavenly Father also will do to you if each of you, from his heart, does not forgive his brother his trespasses."

─────── *DECLARATION OF FAITH* ───────

The Master's heart was moved with great compassion toward me. He removed the great debt that I owed to God due to the vileness of my sin. Therefore, I will not hold a grudge against any of my brothers and sisters, but will forgive and love them with the same selfless love that Jesus has shown me.

(Colossians 1:13; Ephesians 2:1-10; Mark 11:25; James 2:13)

MATTHEW 19:4-6 KJV

And he answered and said unto them, Have ye not read, that he which made *them* at the beginning made them male and female, And said, For this cause shall a man leave father and mother, and shall cleave to his wife: and they twain shall be one flesh? Wherefore they are no more twain, but one flesh. What therefore God hath joined together, let not man put asunder.

─────── *DECLARATION OF FAITH* ───────

(For those who are married)

I have become one with my wife/husband. God Himself has joined us together and we are no longer two, but one flesh. We are united firmly and joined inseparably in a marital covenant sealed with the blood of Jesus. The bonding agent that holds us together is the very Holy Spirit Himself.

Though I honor my parents, I am no longer tied to them. I always maintain proper priorities. I serve God first, my wife second and my family third.

(Genesis 1:26,27; 2:24; Ephesians 5:22-33; 1 Corinthians 7:3,33)

MATTHEW 19:21 AMP

Jesus answered him, If you would be perfect [that is, have that spiritual maturity which accompanies self-sacrificing character], go and sell what you have and give to the poor, and you will have riches in heaven; and come, be My disciple [side with My party and follow Me].

─────── *DECLARATION OF FAITH* ───────

Through my generosity, self-sacrifice and willingness to give, I maintain a level of honor and spiritual maturity that captures the heart of heaven.

Every time I give, I make a deposit in my heavenly account that I can draw upon in time of need.

In giving, I show myself to be a true disciple of the Lord.

(2 Corinthians 8:12-16; 9:5-11; Philippians 4:10-20; Acts 2:45; 4:34,35)

MATTHEW 19:26 NIV

Jesus looked at them and said, "With man this is impossible, but with God all things are possible."

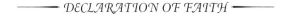
DECLARATION OF FAITH

With God working in and through me, all things are possible for me.

(Colossians 1:29; Ephesians 1:17-23; Jeremiah 32:17; Mark 11:22-25)

MATTHEW 20:30-34 KJV

And, behold, two blind men sitting by the way side, when they heard that Jesus passed by, cried out, saying, Have mercy on us, O Lord, *thou* Son of David. And the multitude rebuked them, because they should hold their peace: but they cried the more, saying, Have mercy on us, O Lord, *thou* Son of David. And Jesus stood still, and called them, and said, What will ye that I shall do unto you? They say unto him, Lord, that our eyes may be opened. So Jesus had compassion *on them,* and touched their eyes: and immediately their eyes received sight, and they followed him.

DECLARATION OF FAITH

I know the One in whom I believe. I focus my attention on Him and not the crowd.

When I am reproved for my faith and told to be still, I cry out all the more, praying and shouting to the only One who can set me free.

My Lord is alert to my every cry. He notices me. He wants me to tell Him specifically what I desire from Him so my joy will be complete when He gives it to me. When I give Him my specific request, in harmony with His Word, He calls it done.

(2 Timothy 1:12; John 14:13,14; 15:7; 16:23,24; Matthew 19:13,14)

MATTHEW 21:14 NKJV

Then the blind and the lame came to Him in the temple, and He healed them.

─── *DECLARATION OF FAITH* ───

Jesus has healed my vision and cured any damage to my body that could make me lame.

(Exodus 15:26; 23:25; Isaiah 53:4,5; Acts 5:16; 8:7; Matthew 4:23)

MATTHEW 21:19-22 KJV

And when he saw a fig tree in the way, he came to it, and found nothing thereon, but leaves only, and said unto it, Let no fruit grow on thee henceforward for ever. And presently the fig tree withered away. And when the disciples saw *it,* they marvelled, saying, How soon is the fig tree withered away! Jesus answered and said unto them, Verily I say unto you, If ye have faith, and doubt not, ye shall not only do this *which is done* to the fig tree, but also if ye shall say unto this mountain, Be thou removed, and be thou cast into the sea; it shall be done. And all things, whatsoever ye shall ask in prayer, believing, ye shall receive.

─── *DECLARATION OF FAITH* ───

I engage my faith by believing the Word and speaking it to the problem. My faith is pure and focused with a deep-seated belief free of all doubt. I know that when I believe in God's power within me I can speak to any problem and it must obey my command. Whatever I ask for in faith, if I believe I have received it, regardless of the circumstances, I shall have it.

(2 Corinthians 4:13; Mark 11:22-25; Hebrews 10:35-11:1; James 1:6-8)

MATTHEW 21:43 NKJV

"Therefore I say to you, the kingdom of God will be taken from you and given to a nation bearing the fruits of it."

─── *DECLARATION OF FAITH* ───

The kingdom of God has been given to me freely and I continually produce the fruits of it to the blessing of everyone in my circle of influence.

(Luke 12:32; Romans 8:32; Genesis 12:1-3; John 15:1-8)

MATTHEW 22:29 AMP

But Jesus replied to them, You are wrong because you know neither the Scriptures nor God's power.

DECLARATION OF FAITH

I have been given revelation knowledge of the Scriptures.

I am ever mindful of the exceeding greatness of God's power that is working in and through me.

(1 John 2:20; Daniel 1:17,20; 2:22,23; 1 Corinthians 2:6-16; Ephesians 1:17-23)

MATTHEW 23:12 NKJV

And whoever exalts himself will be humbled, and he who humbles himself will be exalted.

DECLARATION OF FAITH

I am neither a braggart nor a man/woman who exalts himself/herself with foolish and selfish pride. I have humbled myself under God's mighty hand, knowing both my place and my frame in His presence. Because of this, He has exalted me to the place of highest honor and has made me His own son/daughter.

(James 4:6-10,13-16; 1 Peter 5:5-7; Psalm 103:14; Ephesians 2:6; Galatians 4:5,6)

MATTHEW 24:11-14 KJV

And many false prophets shall rise, and shall deceive many. And because iniquity shall abound, the love of many shall wax cold. But he that shall endure unto the end, the same shall be saved. And this gospel of the kingdom shall be preached in all the world for a witness unto all nations; and then shall the end come.

DECLARATION OF FAITH

Evil and deceitful men cannot lure me away from the Truth. My love remains strong even in the midst of wickedness. I am a man/woman of faith who proclaims the gospel to a hurting world and I will endure to the end.

(Romans 16:17-19; Galatians 1:6-9; Colossians 2:8; 1 Timothy 6:3-21)

MATTHEW 25:16,20,21,28,29 KJV

Then he that had received the five talents went and traded with the same, and made *them* other five talents. And so he that had received five talents came and brought other five talents, saying, Lord, thou deliveredst unto me five talents: behold, I have gained beside them five talents more. His lord said unto him, Well done, *thou* good and faithful servant: thou hast been faithful over a few things, I will make thee ruler over many things: enter thou into the joy of thy lord.

Take therefore the talent from him, and give *it* unto him which hath ten talents. For unto every one that hath shall be given, and he shall have abundance: but from him that hath not shall be taken away even that which he hath.

─────── *DECLARATION OF FAITH* ───────

I understand the laws of sowing and reaping and that my God is a God of increase. Therefore, I take what I have been given, sow it into the kingdom, and reap an abundant harvest. In this, I am counted as faithful and honorable in the eyes of the Lord and I enter into His joy and blessings.

When I am faithful and operate in the laws of kingdom living persistently and without fail, I shall reap even the seed that was given to the faithless. More and more will be given to me so that I am furnished richly and have an abundance.

My God is a God of increase and He takes great pleasure in my prosperity.

(2 Corinthians 9:5-11; Malachi 3:6-12; Psalm 35:27; 115:14; Deuteronomy 14:22)

MATTHEW 25:40 MESSAGE

Then the King will say, 'I'm telling the solemn truth: Whenever you did one of these things to someone overlooked or ignored, that was me—you did it to me.'

─────── *DECLARATION OF FAITH* ───────

Everything that I do for God's children, I am doing for God—and everything that anyone does for me, they are doing for God.

(Colossians 3:23; Proverbs 19:17; Mark 9:41)

MATTHEW 26:26,27 AMP

Now as they were eating, Jesus took bread and, praising God, gave thanks and asked Him to bless it to their use, and when He had broken it, He gave it to the disciples and said, Take, eat; this is My body. And He took a cup, and when He had given thanks, He gave it to them, saying, Drink of it, all of you.

─────── *DECLARATION OF FAITH* ───────

I have partaken of the body and blood of the Lord and I am identified with Him in every way. All that He did has been credited to my account and, through Him, I am more than a conqueror!

(Romans 6:4,5; 8:29,30,37; 1 Corinthians 11:23-26; 1 Peter 2:24; Mark 14:17-21; Galatians 2:20; 2 Corinthians 5:21; 8:9)

MATTHEW 26:41 AMP

All of you must keep awake (give strict attention, be cautious and active) and watch and pray, that you may not come into temptation. The spirit indeed is willing, but the flesh is weak.

——— *DECLARATION OF FAITH* ———

I fully understand that only by the Spirit will I overcome the misdeeds of the flesh. Therefore, I will remain alert at all times. I will be cautious and active, doing the Word with all of my heart and praying consistently so that I will not be caught in the traps of temptation.

(Galatians 5:16,17; James 1:21-25; Luke 22:40,46)

MATTHEW 26:52,53 NKJV

But Jesus said to him, "Put your sword in its place, for all who take the sword will perish by the sword. Or do you think that I cannot now pray to My Father, and He will provide Me with more than twelve legions of angels?"

——— *DECLARATION OF FAITH* ———

I am not quick to react in the flesh. I fully understand the ways of the Spirit and I know how to use its resources. My allies are more powerful and numerous than that of the enemy and they are ever ready to advance at the sound of my command.

Therefore, I am not moved by what I see in this natural world. I will do the will of my Father and walk in perpetual victory.

(Galatians 5:16-23; Hebrews 1:14; 10:36; 2 Kings 6:15-17; 2 Corinthians 5:7; 1 Corinthians 15:57; Daniel 7:10)

MATTHEW 28:18-20 KJV

And Jesus came and spake unto them, saying, All power is given unto me in heaven and in earth. Go ye therefore, and teach all nations, baptizing them in the name of the Father, and of the Son, and of the Holy Ghost: Teaching them to observe all things whatsoever I have commanded you: and, lo, I am with you alway, even unto the end of the world. Amen.

——— *DECLARATION OF FAITH* ———

In Jesus—as His ambassador, brother, and friend—I have been given the authority of heaven while on this earth. As Christ's ambassador and purveyor of His authority, I have been commissioned to make disciples of people in every nation, baptizing them in the name of the Father, and of the Son, and of the Holy Spirit, and teaching them to abide by the Word in every area of life.

Jesus is always with me. He has given me His Word that He will never leave me nor forsake me even to the end of the age.

(2 Corinthians 5:17-21; Hebrews 2:11; 13:5,6; John 15:15; Genesis 39:2-5; 41:41-43; Ephesians 1:17-23; Luke 10:18,19; Mark 16:15-20)

CHAPTER FORTY-ONE

MARK

The book of Mark was written to Roman Christians probably somewhere between 65 and 68 AD. The recipients of the book were undergoing tremendous persecution by the emperor Nero. Many of the promises in the book of Mark are uplifting in nature. They were intended to help the Roman Christians to endure and persevere.

As you pray the promises of the book of Mark, be thankful for the good things that you have in your life. Know that, in Jesus, there is always joy even in the midst of the most trying circumstances.

━━━━━━━━━ ✠ ━━━━━━━━━

MARK 1:8 AMP

I have baptized you with water, but He will baptize you with the Holy Spirit.

──────── *DECLARATION OF FAITH* ────────

I have been baptized in water, displaying my identification with Jesus' death, burial and Resurrection. He has, in turn and according to my request, baptized me with the Holy Spirit, filling me to overflowing with His power and presence.

(Romans 6:4,5; Galatians 2:20; Acts 1:5; 2:38,39; 11:16; Ephesians 5:18)

MARK 1:17 NIV

"Come, follow me," Jesus said, "and I will make you fishers of men."

──────── *DECLARATION OF FAITH* ────────

I am a student and imitator of Jesus, following His ways and living my life in the fullness of His power.

He has made me to be a soul-winner—a fisher of men.

(Ephesians 1:17-23; 5:1; John 14:12; Proverbs 11:30; Matthew 13:47,48)

MARK 1:23-25 KJV

And there was in their synagogue a man with an unclean spirit; and he cried out, Saying, Let *us* alone; what have we to do with thee, thou Jesus of Nazareth? art thou come to destroy us? I know thee who thou art, the Holy One of God. And Jesus rebuked him, saying, Hold thy peace, and come out of him.

——— *DECLARATION OF FAITH* ———

In Jesus, I have power over all unclean spirits. When they see me, they also see the greater One who is within me. They know me by name and are aware that I am called by the name of the Lord. When I operate in the name of Jesus, they must obey my commands.

(Luke 10:18,19; Psalm 91:13; Acts 19:15; Mark 16:17; John 14:13,14; Philippians 2:9-11)

MARK 1:34 NKJV

Then He healed many who were sick with various diseases, and cast out many demons; and He did not allow the demons to speak, because they knew Him.

——— *DECLARATION OF FAITH* ———

In Jesus, I am both healed and have the ability to heal all sickness and disease. I have the authority, in Jesus' name, to drive out all demons from my presence.

(1 Peter 2:24; Mark 16:17-20; Luke 10:18,19; Psalm 91:13)

MARK 1:35 NKJV

Now in the morning, having risen a long while before daylight, He went out and departed to a solitary place; and there He prayed.

——— *DECLARATION OF FAITH* ———

I imitate my Lord Jesus and find a specific time of day, when all is quiet and free of distraction, to spend time in prayer and fellowship with my heavenly Father.

(Ephesians 5:1; 6:18; Matthew 6:6; Hebrews 4:16)

MARK 1:39 NKJV

And He was preaching in their synagogues throughout all Galilee, and casting out demons.

——— *DECLARATION OF FAITH* ———

I am a carrier of the Gospel to my neighborhood and my city. I am constantly advancing and driving out demons as I go.

(2 Corinthians 5:19-20; Mark 16:15-20; Matthew 28:18-20)

MARK 1:40-42 KJV

And there came a leper to him, beseeching him, and kneeling down to him, and saying unto him, If thou wilt, thou canst make me clean. And Jesus, moved with compassion, put forth *his* hand, and touched him, and saith unto him, I will; be thou clean. And as soon as he had spoken, immediately the leprosy departed from him, and he was cleansed.

——— *DECLARATION OF FAITH* ———

Jesus is willing to heal all who are oppressed of the devil and His healing power is available for me to receive by faith.

(Isaiah 61:1-3; Luke 10:18,19; James 5:14-16; Psalm 103:1-5; Luke 7:13)

MARK 3:14,15 NKJV

Then He appointed twelve, that they might be with Him and that He might send them out to preach, and to have power to heal sicknesses and to cast out demons.

——— *DECLARATION OF FAITH* ———

Jesus has sent me into the world as an ambassador of the kingdom. He has given me power and authority to heal the sick and cast out devils.

(Luke 9:1,2; 10:19; 2 Corinthians 5:18-20; Mark 16:15-20)

MARK 3:27 NKJV

"No one can enter a strong man's house and plunder his goods, unless he first binds the strong man. And then he will plunder his house."

——— *DECLARATION OF FAITH* ———

I have power and authority over and above all of the power and authority of the enemy. When the strong man (the devil) comes, I have authority to bind him, commanding him to cease all operations. In the name of Jesus, I can render him paralyzed and plunder his household, taking back all that he has stolen.

(Ephesians 1:17-23; Luke 10:19; Mark 16:17-20; Matthew 12:25-29; Proverbs 6:31)

MARK 3:35B MESSAGE

"The person who obeys God's will is my brother and sister and mother."

──────── *DECLARATION OF FAITH* ────────

I am the younger brother/sister of the Lord and, like Him, I do the will of our Father in this earth.

(Hebrews 2:11; Romans 8:28-30; John 14:12; 1 Corinthians 2:12)

MARK 4:14-20 KJV

The sower soweth the word. And these are they by the way side, where the word is sown; but when they have heard, Satan cometh immediately, and taketh away the word that was sown in their hearts. And these are they likewise which are sown on stony ground; who, when they have heard the word, immediately receive it with gladness; And have no root in themselves, and so endure but for a time: afterward, when affliction or persecution ariseth for the word's sake, immediately they are offended. And these are they which are sown among thorns; such as hear the word, And the cares of this world, and the deceitfulness of riches, and the lusts of other things entering in, choke the word, and it becometh unfruitful. And these are they which are sown on good ground; such as hear the word, and receive *it,* and bring forth fruit, some thirtyfold, some sixty, and some an hundred.

──────── *DECLARATION OF FAITH* ────────

The Word to me is as seed sown into good ground.

Satan has been unable to pluck it out of me. It has taken root deep within me and when the winds of trouble and persecution arise, I remain secure and steadfast.

All of the cares and worries in the world cannot cause the seed of the Word within me to perish.

I do not allow distractions such as fame, the deceitfulness of riches, or the lusts of the flesh to choke the Word and make it unfruitful in my life.

To the contrary, I am good ground. I receive the Word with an open heart and understand the principles of seedtime and harvest that are contained within it. As I operate these principles, I reap a harvest even one hundred times as much as what I have sown.

(Matthew 13:18-23; Luke 21:34; 1 Timothy 6:9-17; 2 Corinthians 9:5-11; Romans 7:4; John 15:1-8)

MARK 4:24 NIV

"Consider carefully what you hear," he continued. "With the measure you use, it will be measured to you—and even more."

——— *DECLARATION OF FAITH* ———

I am very careful about what, and who, I listen to. I focus my attention only on godly teaching that is in line with the Word. I fully understand that the measure of thought and study that I give to the Truth will directly reflect the measure of virtue, knowledge, and fruit that I will receive in return. By remaining diligent, I receive a full and abundant supply of all that I need in order to function in God's way of being and doing things.

(Philippians 4:8; Romans 16:17,18; Galatians 6:7-9; Matthew 7:2; Luke 6:38)

MARK 4:26-32 KJV

And he said, So is the kingdom of God, as if a man should cast seed into the ground; And should sleep, and rise night and day, and the seed should spring and grow up, he knoweth not how. For the earth bringeth forth fruit of herself; first the blade, then the ear, after that the full corn in the ear. But when the fruit is brought forth, immediately he putteth in the sickle, because the harvest is come. And he said, Whereunto shall we liken the kingdom of God? or with what comparison shall we compare it? *It is* like a grain of mustard seed, which, when it is sown in the earth, is less than all the seeds that be in the earth: But when it is sown, it groweth up, and becometh greater than all herbs, and shooteth out great branches; so that the fowls of the air may lodge under the shadow of it.

——— *DECLARATION OF FAITH* ———

My heavenly Father has placed the seed of His Word in my hands and I am faithful to sow it into my life. Whatever need I have, whether for healing, peace, prosperity, joy, or anything else that is promised to me in the Word, I receive as if it were a grain of mustard seed.

Though my circumstances do not show a harvest, once I have planted my seed, I know that harvest time will eventually come. Therefore, I sow the promise (the seed), though small in comparison to all of the other seeds that have been sown in me, and through faithfulness and diligence I tend it (meditating on it and speaking it into my life) and it continues to grow and increase until its roots have overtaken everything else that has been sown and established in me.

As its branches spread out, filling my whole life with the reality of its Truth, the manifestation begins to spring forth into my circumstances.

I will remain faithful and diligent, believing and speaking the Word into my life. The Word within me grows and grows until I have such an abundant harvest that there is plenty left over to share with others in need and provide them with a place of refuge and rest.

(Matthew 13:24-43; Mark 11:22-25; 2 Corinthians 4:13; 9:5-11; Hebrews 6:12; 11:1; Joshua 1:8; John 15:7,8; Proverbs 14:26)

MARK 4:37-40 KJV

And there arose a great storm of wind, and the waves beat into the ship, so that it was now full. And he was in the hinder part of the ship, asleep on a pillow: and they awake him, and say unto him, Master, carest thou not that we perish? And he arose, and rebuked the wind, and said unto the sea, Peace, be still. And the wind ceased, and there was a great calm. And he said unto them, Why are ye so fearful? how is it that ye have no faith?

——— *DECLARATION OF FAITH* ———

When things seem hopeless in the natural world and the storms of life are threatening, I will not be afraid. My faith has gone before me and I have God's Word that I will come to no harm. No matter what the circumstance may be, I remain secure.

By faith, I speak to whatever situation I am facing and command it to get in line with the perfect will of God.

(Joshua 1:5-9; Hebrews 10:35-11:1; Psalm 91:10; Mark 11:22-25)

MARK 5:34 AMP

And He said to her, Daughter, your faith (your trust and confidence in Me, springing from faith in God) has restored you to health. Go in (into) peace and be continually healed and freed from your [distressing bodily] disease.

——— *DECLARATION OF FAITH* ———

My faith restores me to perfect health when symptoms of sickness come upon me. Jesus has set me free from sickness and has given me His peace.

(2 Corinthians 4:13; Mark 10:52; 11:22-25; Galatians 3:13; Matthew 9:22; Isaiah 53:4,5)

MARK 5:36 NKJV

As soon as Jesus heard the word that was spoken, He said to the ruler of the synagogue, "Do not be afraid; only believe."

——— *DECLARATION OF FAITH* ———

When I am faced with an evil report in the natural realm, I remain calm and continue to believe. I do not allow fear to rob me of what God has done for me. My faith brings to pass what I need regardless of what is seen or known in the natural world.

(Numbers 14:1-9; 2 Timothy 1:6,7; Joshua 1:5-9; 2 Corinthians 5:7; Hebrews 11:1)

MARK 6:5,6 NKJV

Now He could do no mighty work there, except that He laid His hands on a few sick people and healed them. And He marveled because of their unbelief. Then He went about the villages in a circuit, teaching.

——— *DECLARATION OF FAITH* ———

I receive from God only what I can acquire by faith. If I fail to exercise my faith, I am telling God to limit His power in my life.

The miracles that follow me as an ambassador of Christ require both my faith and the faith of those who are to receive them.

(Hebrews 11:1,6; Mark 11:22-25; 16:15-20; Matthew 21:19-22; 2 Corinthians 5:18-20)

MARK 6:7 NKJV

And He called the twelve to Himself, and began to send them out two by two, and gave them power over unclean spirits.

——— *DECLARATION OF FAITH* ———

I have power and authority over all unclean spirits and have been commissioned to set their captives free.

(Isaiah 61:1-3; Luke 9:1,2; 10:19; Mark 16:15-20)

MARK 6:12,13 KJV

And they went out, and preached that men should repent. And they cast out many devils, and anointed with oil many that were sick, and healed *them.*

——— *DECLARATION OF FAITH* ———

I have been sent into the world to preach the Gospel and teach the Word of repentance.

I drive out all demons from my presence.

When I anoint the sick with oil, they are healed.

(Mark 16:15-20; Luke 9:1,2; 10:18,19; Matthew 28:18-20; James 5:14)

MARK 6:31 NKJV

And He said to them, "Come aside by yourselves to a deserted place and rest a while." For there were many coming and going, and they did not even have time to eat.

———— *DECLARATION OF FAITH* ————

I will not allow life to become so hectic for me that I have no leisure time. It is not the will of my Father that I be overwhelmed that way. Therefore, I will regularly take time to rest and enjoy the blessings that He has given me.

(Ecclesiastes 2:24; 3:22; Matthew 11:28-30; 14:13)

MARK 6:46 NKJV

And when He had sent them away, He departed to the mountain to pray.

———— *DECLARATION OF FAITH* ————

I set aside time regularly to withdraw to a quiet place, free of distraction, so that I can pray and have fellowship with my heavenly Father.

(Mark 1:35; Matthew 6:6; Luke 5:16; Ephesians 6:18)

MARK 8:15 NKJV

Then He charged them, saying, "Take heed, beware of the leaven of the Pharisees and the leaven of Herod."

———— *DECLARATION OF FAITH* ————

I am continually on guard against false teachings that rob me of the blessings that God has provided for me. God has put me in control of my own life and I will not allow myself to be hindered by those who believe that whatever will be, will be.

(Romans 16:17,18; Galatians 1:6-9; Matthew 7:15-17; Joshua 24:15)

MARK 8:34 AMP

And Jesus called [to Him] the throng with His disciples and said to them, If anyone intends to come after Me, let him deny himself [forget, ignore, disown, and [lose sight of himself and his own interests] and take up his cross, and [joining Me as a disciple and siding with My party] follow with Me [continually, cleaving steadfastly to Me].

——— DECLARATION OF FAITH ———

I have taken my stand with Jesus. I deny myself (my old way of thinking and doing things) and follow His example (thinking the way that He thinks and doing things the way that He does them). I imitate His actions and always keep in mind that I am identified with Him in every way.

(Luke 14:27; Philippians 2:5-11; Ephesians 5:1; John 14:12; Galatians 2:20,21)

MARK 9:23 KJV

Jesus said unto him, If thou canst believe, all things *are* possible to him that believeth.

——— DECLARATION OF FAITH ———

I believe in God's power and ability within me. Therefore, all things are possible for me.

(Ephesians 1:17-23; 6:10; Colossians 1:29; Philippians 2:13; Mark 11:22-25; Matthew 21:19-22)

MARK 9:25 NKJV

When Jesus saw that the people came running together, He rebuked the unclean spirit, saying to it, "Deaf and dumb spirit, I command you, come out of him and enter him no more!"

——— DECLARATION OF FAITH ———

I have been given authority over spirits who operate with a specific purpose, such as those who render people deaf and mute. In Jesus' name, I have authority to command them to come out of people and never enter them again.

(Luke 9:1,2; 10:19; Mark 1:25; 16:17-20; Psalm 91:13)

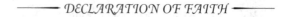

MARK 9:28,29 NIV

After Jesus had gone indoors, his disciples asked him privately, "Why couldn't we drive it out?" He replied, "This kind can come out only by prayer."

——— *DECLARATION OF FAITH* ———

I remain steadfast in my prayer life so that when I come up against a stubborn and obstinate devil, it will pose no problem for me.

(Ephesians 6:10-18; Luke 10:19; James 5:16)

MARK 9:38,39 NKJV

Now John answered Him, saying, "Teacher, we saw someone who does not follow us casting out demons in Your name, and we forbade him because he does not follow us." But Jesus said, "Do not forbid him, for no one who works a miracle in My name can soon afterward speak evil of Me."

——— *DECLARATION OF FAITH* ———

I have the power and authority to cast out demons and do mighty works in Jesus' name.

This power is not mine alone, but is available to all who will receive it. Therefore, I will not forbid, hinder, or restrain anyone from operating in this authority.

(Luke 10:19; John 1:12; 14:12-14; Mark 16:17-20; Ephesians 1:17-23)

MARK 10:7-9 KJV

For this cause shall a man leave his father and mother, and cleave to his wife; And they twain shall be one flesh: so then they are no more twain, but one flesh. What therefore God hath joined together, let not man put asunder.

——— *DECLARATION OF FAITH* ———

(For those who are married)

I have left my father and mother and have become united with my wife/husband. We two are now one flesh. We work together as one in all that we do. God has united us as one; therefore, I will not seek to divorce myself from her/him.

(Genesis 2:24; Ephesians 5:22-33)

MARK 10:21 NKJV

Then Jesus, looking at him, loved him, and said to him, "One thing you lack: Go your way, sell whatever you have and give to the poor, and you will have treasure in heaven; and come, take up the cross, and follow Me."

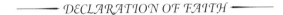

DECLARATION OF FAITH

All of my giving is a deposit into my heavenly treasury.

All that I have is God's to begin with; therefore, I will not hesitate to give it as He commands.

(Philippians 4:15-19; Psalm 24:1; Deuteronomy 10:14; Matthew 6:19,20)

MARK 10:27 NIV

Jesus looked at them and said, "With man this is impossible, but not with God; all things are possible with God."

DECLARATION OF FAITH

All things are possible to the God who is within me.

(Jeremiah 32:17; Matthew 19:26; Mark 9:23; 11:22-25; 1 John 4:4)

MARK 10:28-30 KJV

Then Peter began to say unto him, Lo, we have left all, and have followed thee. And Jesus answered and said, Verily I say unto you, There is no man that hath left house, or brethren, or sisters, or father, or mother, or wife, or children, or lands, for my sake, and the gospel's, But he shall receive an hundredfold now in this time, houses, and brethren, and sisters, and mothers, and children, and lands, with persecutions; and in the world to come eternal life.

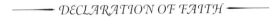

DECLARATION OF FAITH

All that I have given, or given up, for the Lord's sake and the Gospel, will come back to me one hundred fold in this life.

If I leave my home, mother, father, brothers, sisters, or give land, or anything else for the Lord's sake and the Gospel, I shall not fail to reap homes, mothers, fathers, brothers, sisters, lands and more, now in this life, and in the age to come: eternal life.

I also know that persecution will come to me when I receive God's blessings, but that makes no difference to me. The devil can gripe and moan all he wants. I still have the blessings!

(Luke 18:28-30; 1 Peter 4:12,13; Genesis 26:12; Matthew 19:29)

MARK 10:42,43 NIV

Jesus called them together and said, "You know that those who are regarded as rulers of the Gentiles lord it over them, and their high officials exercise authority over them. Not so with you. Instead, whoever wants to become great among you must be your servant.

——— *DECLARATION OF FAITH* ———

I do not vie for position in the body of Christ, nor do I look for ways to gain authority and dominion over my brothers and sisters in the Church. Instead, I look for ways that I can bless and serve others, for it is in this that I achieve a position of greatness in the eyes of my Father.

(Joel 2:1-11; Genesis 12:1-3; Mark 9:35; Titus 2:14)

MARK 10:52 AMP

And Jesus said to him, Go your way; your faith has healed you. And at once he received his sight and accompanied Jesus on the road.

——— *DECLARATION OF FAITH* ———

I receive my healing by faith, even before the symptoms leave.
By faith, my healing is an ever-present fact.

(Matthew 9:22; Mark 5:34; Hebrews 11:1; 2 Corinthians 4:13; 5:7; 1 Peter 2:24)

MARK 11:22-25 KJV

And Jesus answering saith unto them, Have faith in God. For verily I say unto you, That whosoever shall say unto this mountain, Be thou removed, and be thou cast into the sea; and shall not doubt in his heart, but shall believe that those things which he saith shall come to pass; he shall have whatsoever he saith. Therefore I say unto you, What things soever ye desire, when ye pray, believe that ye receive *them*, and ye shall have *them*. And when ye stand praying, forgive, if ye have ought against any: that your Father also which is in heaven may forgive you your trespasses.

——— DECLARATION OF FAITH ———

I am constantly functioning in God-like faith.

God has created me as a faith being. My words bring into existence whatever I am believing for.

If I command a mountain (a formidable circumstance or barrier) to be removed and cast into the sea, and have no doubt that it will happen, it will happen.

Everything that I believe with my heart and speak from my mouth, within the boundaries of God's Word, becomes reality for me. Whatever I ask for in prayer, if I believe I have received it, I will have it.

I understand that unforgiveness and strife bring cancellation to what I am praying for. Therefore, I refuse to harbor them in my life. I continually remember my own frame, all that God has forgiven me of, and that I have no right to withhold grace from others when I myself walk in it so freely.

(2 Corinthians 4:13; 5:7; Romans 5:1,2; 10:8-10; Hebrews 11:1,6; Matthew 6:14; 8:13; 17:20; 18:23-35; 21:21,22; Proverbs 18:20,21; Luke 11:9; John 14:13,14; 15:7; 16:23,24; James 1:6-8; Ephesians 4:32; Colossians 3:13)

MARK 12:24 NKJV

Jesus answered and said to them, "Are you not therefore mistaken, because you do not know the Scriptures nor the power of God?"

——— DECLARATION OF FAITH ———

I have been given revelation knowledge of the Scriptures and have an intimate understanding of the workings of God's power in my life. Therefore, I do not wander from the truth and go wrong in my walk with God.

(1 John 2:20; 1 Corinthians 2:6-16; Luke 8:10; Matthew 13:15,16)

MARK 12:29-31 KJV

And Jesus answered him, The first of all the commandments is, Hear, O Israel; The Lord our God is one Lord: And thou shalt love the Lord thy God with all thy heart, and with all thy soul, and with all thy mind, and with all thy strength: this is the first commandment. And the second is like, namely this, Thou shalt love thy neighbour as thyself. There is none other commandment greater than these.

——— DECLARATION OF FAITH ———

I joyfully receive and understand the chief of all commandments, that the Lord my God is one Lord and I am to love Him with all of my heart, soul, and strength.

I receive and understand the second with equal enthusiasm, that I will love my neighbor and myself equally, and consider us both to be of great value in this earth.

(Deuteronomy 6:4-6; 10:12; 30:6; Romans 13:9)

MARK 13:13 NKJV

And you will be hated by all for My name's sake. But he who endures to the end shall be saved.

———— *DECLARATION OF FAITH* ————

I endure the persecution that comes on me because of my love for Jesus. Though I am hated and despised for His nname's sake, I will carry on to the end.

(2 Timothy 3:12; Matthew 5:10-12; 10:22; 24:13; Luke 21:17)

MARK 13:33 NIV

Be on guard! Be alert! You do not know when that time will come.

———— *DECLARATION OF FAITH* ————

I am perpetually on guard against the onslaughts of the world, the flesh and the devil. I am forever alert and constant in prayer while waiting for the imminent return of my Lord Jesus.

(1 Thessalonians 5:6; Ephesians 6:10-18; Matthew 24:42-46)

MARK 13:37 NKJV

"And what I say to you, I say to all: Watch!"

———— *DECLARATION OF FAITH* ————

I am watchful and alert for the Lord's imminent return. He will not catch me by surprise, for I give strict and active attention to the signs of the times.

(1 Thessalonians 5:6; Ephesians 6:10-18; Matthew 24:42-46)

MARK 14:38 NKJV

"Watch and pray, lest you enter into temptation. The spirit indeed *is* willing, but the flesh *is* weak."

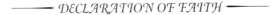

——— *DECLARATION OF FAITH* ———

I remain sober, alert and watchful at all times. I pray incessantly in order to overcome temptation and I always keep my spirit in ascendancy over my flesh.

(Luke 21:36; Romans 7:18-24; Ephesians 6:18; Galatians 5:17)

MARK 16:15-20 KJV

And he said unto them, Go ye into all the world, and preach the gospel to every creature. He that believeth and is baptized shall be saved; but he that believeth not shall be damned. And these signs shall follow them that believe; In my name shall they cast out devils; they shall speak with new tongues; They shall take up serpents; and if they drink any deadly thing, it shall not hurt them; they shall lay hands on the sick, and they shall recover. So then after the Lord had spoken unto them, he was received up into heaven, and sat on the right hand of God. And they went forth, and preached every where, the Lord working with *them,* and confirming the word with signs following. Amen.

——— *DECLARATION OF FAITH* ———

I have been commissioned to proclaim the Gospel to everyone I come in contact with. Those who believe and are baptized shall be saved, but those who do not believe shall remain in condemnation.

As I walk in faith, these signs accompany me:

In Jesus' name, I cast out demons;

I speak in tongues;

If need be, I take up vipers without being harmed;

If I drink any deadly thing, it shall not harm me;

And when I lay my hands on the sick, they recover.

Jesus, my Lord, brother, Intercessor, and High Priest of my confession, is now seated at the right hand of Majesty on High, and He has bid me to take my place at His side. As I go out to proclaim the Good News, He is working with me, confirming the Word through the signs, wonders, and miracles that accompany me.

(Isaiah 61:1-3; Matthew 28:18-20; Colossians 1:23; 2 Corinthians 5:18-20; John 3:18,36; Acts 2:4; 5:12; Luke 9:1,2; 10:17-19; 1 Corinthians 14:5; James 5:14-16; Psalm 91:10-13; Hebrews 2:11; Ephesians 2:6)

CHAPTER FORTY-TWO

LUKE

Luke is the physician. He is one of the most analytical writers in the Bible and approached the accounts of Jesus' life from both scientific and spiritual points of view. The book of Luke was probably written somewhere between 56 and 63 AD. It is written to an individual named Theophilus whose name means, "Lover of God." As with all things that God does, that name is no accident. The book is written for all of us who love God and are called according to His purpose. Many believe that Luke's purpose was to provide irrefutable proof to Theophilus that Jesus was the Messiah, the Son of the one true God.

As you pray the prayers of Luke, remember your love for your Savior and how much He loves you.

LUKE 1:28 NKJV

And having come in, the angel said to her, "Rejoice, highly favored one, the Lord is with you; blessed are you among women!"

———— DECLARATION OF FAITH ————

Like Mary, God has set me apart as one who is unique and special. He makes His declaration to all that I am one of His favored ones and that He is with me in all that I do.

(Isaiah 43:1-7; Hebrews 10:14-17; 13:5,6; Matthew 28:20; Psalm 103:13; Job 1:8)

LUKE 1:30 AMP

And the angel said to her, Do not be afraid, Mary, for you have found grace (free, spontaneous, absolute favor and loving-kindness) with God.

———— DECLARATION OF FAITH ————

I have no reason to fear, for I have found favor with God.

(Romans 2:11; Joshua 1:5-9; 2 Timothy 1:6,7; Proverbs 11:27)

LUKE 1:37,38 KJV

For with God nothing shall be impossible. And Mary said, Behold the handmaid of the Lord; be it unto me according to thy word. And the angel departed from her.

With God, the greater One who is within me, nothing is impossible. Every promise that He has given me has within it the power of fulfillment. Therefore, what He says I am, that is what I am; and what He says I can do, that is what I can do. All what His Word declares about me is fulfilled as I take hold of it in faith and put it into operation in my life.

(1 John 4:4; Matthew 17:20; Isaiah 55:11; Psalm 119:138; Hebrews 11:1; James 1:22)

LUKE 1:45 NIV

"Blessed is she who has believed that what the Lord has said to her will be accomplished!"

I am blessed (happy, joyful, and to be envied) because I believe that I am who God says I am, and I can do what He says I can do.

(Isaiah 55:11; Psalm 119:38; John 14:12)

LUKE 1:50-55 KJV

And his mercy is on them that fear him from generation to generation. He hath shewed strength with his arm; he hath scattered the proud in the imagination of their hearts. He hath put down the mighty from *their* seats, and exalted them of low degree. He hath filled the hungry with good things; and the rich he hath sent empty away. He hath holpen his servant Israel, in remembrance of *his* mercy; As he spake to our fathers, to Abraham, and to his seed for ever.

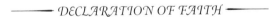

My Father's mercy and compassion never leave me. Because I have humbled myself and placed my life in His hands, He reaches out to show me His favor continually.

He performs mighty deeds on my behalf, and scatters those who are proud and haughty, and fantasize about how wonderful they are.

He brings down rulers from their thrones, but in my humility, He lifts me to the place of highest honor.

He fills and satisfies me with good things of every kind and never causes bad things to happen to me.

He lays His hand upon me to help me and He espouses my cause.

His thoughts toward me are rooted in His mercy and loving-kindness.

I have become His friend and He has become my trusted ally. Everything that He promised to Abraham and his descendants has become my inheritance.

(Psalm 33:10; 98:1-3; 103:5,13; 126:2,3; Romans 8:38,39; 1 Peter 5:5-7; Proverbs 3:3,4; Ephesians 2:6; James 4:6-10; Jeremiah 29:11; Isaiah 54:17; 1 John 2:1,2; John 15:15; Galatians 3:14,29; 2 Corinthians 1:20)

LUKE 1:68-75 KJV

Blessed *be* the Lord God of Israel; for he hath visited and redeemed his people, And hath raised up an horn of salvation for us in the house of his servant David; As he spake by the mouth of his holy prophets, which have been since the world began: That we should be saved from our enemies, and from the hand of all that hate us; To perform the mercy *promised* to our fathers, and to remember his holy covenant; The oath which he sware to our father Abraham, That he would grant unto us, that we being delivered out of the hand of our enemies might serve him without fear, In holiness and righteousness before him, all the days of our life.

——— DECLARATION OF FAITH ———

I am ever-grateful to the Lord, for He has redeemed and delivered me from the power and authority of darkness.

Jesus has become my mighty and valiant ally.

All that was promised to my forefathers (from Adam to Abraham, and Abraham to Jesus) has become my inheritance.

I have been saved and delivered from the hand of the enemy and from those who pursue me with hatred. All of their power over me has been stripped away and I can now walk in continual victory.

My Father establishes His covenant with me so that He can show me His mercy, compassion and loving-kindness at all times and in every circumstance. All that He has commanded and provided in His covenant, He carries out on my behalf. That covenant is sealed by the oath given to father Abraham to grant that I, being delivered from the hand of the enemy, can serve my heavenly Father with courage and confidence, and live in His presence in righteousness and true holiness all the days of my life.

(Galatians 3:13; Luke 10:19; Colossians 1:13; 2:15; John 15:15; 2 Corinthians 1:20; Psalm 18:1-18; 1 Corinthians 15:57; Hebrews 8:6; 9:14; 10:14-17; 12:28)

LUKE 1:77-79 KJV

To give knowledge of salvation unto his people by the remission of their sins, Through the tender mercy of our God; whereby the dayspring from on high hath visited us, To give light to them that sit in darkness and *in* the shadow of death, to guide our feet into the way of peace.

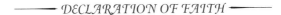

——— *DECLARATION OF FAITH* ———

I have thorough knowledge and an intimate understanding of my salvation.

I have been completely forgiven of every sin that I have ever committed, or ever will commit. All of my sins, first to last, have been released from my life and are no longer worthy of mention.

The price of my old sin nature has been paid in full.

Because of God's love and tender mercy towards me, a light from on high has dawned upon my spirit. It shines through me as an eternal witness of my redemption. It declares to all that I have been translated out of the kingdom of darkness and placed in the realm of light. My feet are now set on a straight path into the province of peace.

(1 John 2:20; Ephesians 1:17-23; Psalm 103:1-13; 1 Corinthians 6:20; Colossians 1:13; 2:8-15; John 14:27; 16:33)

LUKE 2:14 NKJV

"Glory to God in the highest, And on earth peace, goodwill toward men!"

——— *DECLARATION OF FAITH* ———

I give all praise, honor, and glory to my heavenly Father. He is well pleased with me and has granted me His peace and the abundance of His favor.

(Psalm 5:11,12; 18:19; Isaiah 42:1; John 14:27; Hebrews 11:5,6)

LUKE 2:52 NKJV

And Jesus increased in wisdom and stature, and in favor with God and men.

——— *DECLARATION OF FAITH* ———

As a disciple and imitator of Jesus, I continually increase in wisdom and gain a thorough understanding of the issues of life.

With every step that I take, I enjoy an abundance of favor with God and man.

(Ephesians 5:1; 1 Corinthians 1:30; 2:6-16; Daniel 1:17,20; Proverbs 3:3,4; Psalm 5:11,12)

LUKE 3:8 NIV

Produce fruit in keeping with repentance. And do not begin to say to yourselves, 'We have Abraham as our father.' For I tell you that out of these stones God can raise up children for Abraham.

———— *DECLARATION OF FAITH* ————

The fruit that I bear in my life is a direct reflection of my repentance and calling. Everything that I do displays the fact that my heart has been changed. I am now a recreated, born-again child of the living God. God Himself has become (in fact and reality) my own Father.

(2 Corinthians 5:17,21; Galatians 4:5,6; John 3:3; Acts 26:20; 1 Peter 1:4)

LUKE 4:3-13 KJV

And the devil said unto him, If thou be the Son of God, command this stone that it be made bread. And Jesus answered him, saying, It is written, That man shall not live by bread alone, but by every word of God. And the devil, taking him up into an high mountain, shewed unto him all the kingdoms of the world in a moment of time. And the devil said unto him, All this power will I give thee, and the glory of them: for that is delivered unto me; and to whomsoever I will I give it. If thou therefore wilt worship me, all shall be thine. And Jesus answered and said unto him, Get thee behind me, Satan: for it is written, Thou shalt worship the Lord thy God, and him only shalt thou serve. And he brought him to Jerusalem, and set him on a pinnacle of the temple, and said unto him, If thou be the Son of God, cast thyself down from hence: For it is written, He shall give his angels charge over thee, to keep thee: And in *their* hands they shall bear thee up, lest at any time thou dash thy foot against a stone. And Jesus answering said unto him, It is said, Thou shalt not tempt the Lord thy God. And when the devil had ended all the temptation, he departed from him for a season.

———— *DECLARATION OF FAITH* ————

When I am tempted by the devil, I use the Word of God as my defense. I understand that Satan and his demons know the Word well and will twist it to their own benefit. But I am a man/woman of the Word. It is rooted and grounded within my spirit in all wisdom and understanding. When the devil attacks, I rout him with it.

I am a son/daughter of God led by the Spirit of God.

I do not use the Word to showboat the power that is given to me. I treat it with respect and give it—all of it, first to last—the ascendancy in my life.

(Ephesians 6:10-18; Revelation 19:15; Hebrews 4:12; 2 Corinthians 2:11; Romans 8:14; Psalm 119:97-100,105-107)

LUKE 4:4 AMP

And Jesus replied to him, It is written, Man shall not live and be sustained by (on) bread alone but by every word and expression of God.

——— DECLARATION OF FAITH ———

My life is not sustained by bread, or the food that I eat in the natural realm, but is fortified, nourished, and empowered with every Word (precept and promise) that God has given me.

(Joshua 1:8; Matthew 4:4; Deuteronomy 8:3; Psalm 1:1-3)

LUKE 4:6-8 NKJV

And the devil said to Him, "All this authority I will give You, and their glory; for this has been delivered to me, and I give it to whomever I wish. Therefore, if You will worship before me, all will be Yours." And Jesus answered and said to him, "Get behind Me, Satan! For it is written, 'You shall worship the Lord your God, and Him only you shall serve.'"

——— DECLARATION OF FAITH ———

I will not give myself over to Satan, or any of his ways, nor will I be enticed by the things that he offers. I worship the Lord my God and Him only do I serve.

God has made me the head and Satan and his demons are the tail. Satan has no place in the forefront of my life. I am his master and conqueror and he must obey my commands.

(Deuteronomy 28:13; Ephesians 5:1-18; 2 Corinthians 2:11; Luke 10:19)

LUKE 4:9-12 KJV

And he brought him to Jerusalem, and set him on a pinnacle of the temple, and said unto him, If thou be the Son of God, cast thyself down from hence: For it is written, He shall give his angels charge over thee, to keep thee: And in *their* hands they shall bear thee up, lest at any time thou dash thy foot against a stone. And Jesus answering said unto him, It is said, Thou shalt not tempt the Lord thy God.

——— DECLARATION OF FAITH ———

I understand that Satan knows the Word of God and will twist it, trying to get me to stand on one truth while ignoring another. I am not moved by, or ignorant of, his strategies.

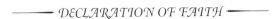

I live by the whole Word of God, not just part of it. I study to show myself approved unto my Father and all of Satan's temptations come to nothing in my life.

(2 Corinthians 2:11; Matthew 4:1-11; 2 Timothy 2:15)

LUKE 4:13 NKJV

Now when the devil had ended every temptation, he departed from Him until an opportune time.

———— *DECLARATION OF FAITH* ————

Jesus, the One with whom I am identified in every way, was tempted in every way that a person can be tempted and yet remained sinless. By Him, I remain stable in my walk with God.

I fully realize that the devil and his army are always watching me, looking for an opportunity to attack. Therefore, I am watchful and careful in my ways. The Word is my guide and I walk in it without fail.

(Hebrews 2:18; 4:15,16; Galatians 2:20,21; Romans 5:1,2; Philippians 2:12-16; Ephesians 6:10-18; Joshua 1:8; James 1:21-25)

LUKE 4:18,19 NKJV

"The Spirit of the Lord is upon Me,
Because He has anointed Me
To preach the gospel to the poor;
He has sent Me to heal the brokenhearted,
To proclaim liberty to the captives
And recovery of sight to the blind,
To set at liberty those who are oppressed;
To proclaim the acceptable year of the Lord."

———— *DECLARATION OF FAITH* ————

I have become one with Jesus and am fully identified with Him in every way.

Like Him, the Spirit of the Lord has come upon me and has anointed me with burden-removing, yoke-destroying power.

I preach the Good News to the poor, declaring freedom from poverty.

I announce deliverance to the captives and recovery of sight to the blind.

I send forth as delivered those who are oppressed and wounded by the trials of life.

I proclaim to all that the day of grace has come—that God is not mad at them, but is ready to receive them into His family and show them His continual favor both now and forevermore.

(John 14:12; 17:20-23; Isaiah 61:1-3; 1 John 2:20; 2 Corinthians 1:3,4; 5:17-21; 8:9; Matthew 11:5; 28:18-20; Romans 5:1,2)

LUKE 4:22 NIV

All spoke well of him and were amazed at the gracious words that came from his lips. "Isn't this Joseph's son?" they asked.

——— *DECLARATION OF FAITH* ———

In Jesus, people speak well of me and marvel at the words of wisdom and grace that I am given. Through the words that I speak, they can clearly see that I am more than just a man/woman—I am a child of God.

(Job 29:7-11,21-25; 1 Corinthians 1:30; 2:6-16; Psalm 45:2; Galatians 4:5,6)

LUKE 4:35 NKJV

But Jesus rebuked him, saying, "Be quiet, and come out of him!" And when the demon had thrown him in their midst, it came out of him and did not hurt him.

——— *DECLARATION OF FAITH* ———

In Jesus, I have complete authority over all devils. In my presence, they are not permitted to speak a single word without my permission. When I cast them out, they are not permitted to harm the person they are leaving in any way. In Jesus, I have complete control over the situation.

(Luke 10:19; Psalm 91:13; Mark 16:17; Ephesians 1:17-23)

LUKE 4:39 KJV

And he stood over her, and rebuked the fever; and it left her: and immediately she arose and ministered unto them.

——— *DECLARATION OF FAITH* ———

Fever is not permitted to remain in my presence. In Jesus' name, I have complete authority to speak to it and command it to leave, and it absolutely must obey me.

(Philippians 2:10; Galatians 3:13; Luke 10:19; Mark 11:22-25)

LUKE 4:40 NKJV

When the sun was setting, all those who had any that were sick with various diseases brought them to Him; and He laid His hands on every one of them and healed them.

———— *DECLARATION OF FAITH* ————

In Jesus, I have been delivered from every disease. In His name, I have the power and ability to bring healing to the bodies of those on whom I lay my hands.

(Mark 16:18; Philippians 2:10; Isaiah 53:4,5; Matthew 8:17)

LUKE 4:42 AMP

And when daybreak came, He left [Peter's house] and went into an isolated [desert] place. And the people looked for Him until they came up to Him and tried to prevent Him from leaving them.

———— *DECLARATION OF FAITH* ————

I make it a regular practice to spend time alone with my heavenly Father in a place free of distraction, or anything else that could divert my attention from Him.

People are drawn to the Holy Spirit's presence in my life and they seek me out in order to experience what I have.

(Mark 1:35; 6:46; Matthew 6:6; Luke 5:16; Job 29:21-25)

LUKE 5:5 MESSAGE

Simon said, "Master, we've been fishing hard all night and haven't caught even a minnow. But if you say so, I'll let out the nets."

———— *DECLARATION OF FAITH* ————

I do what God's Word commands regardless of the circumstances.

(Deuteronomy 28:1; Psalm 33:9)

LUKE 5:10 NKJV

And so also were James and John, the sons of Zebedee, who were partners with Simon. And Jesus said to Simon, "Do not be afraid. From now on you will catch men."

——— *DECLARATION OF FAITH* ———

I have absolutely no fear of my calling in Christ. I am thoroughly equipped with the ability to do what He has called me to do. I am a fisher of men with a distinct role to fulfill in the great design of redemption.

(Joshua 1:5-8; 2 Corinthians 2:14; 6:1; Philippians 1:6; 2:12,13; 4:13; 1 Peter 4:11)

LUKE 5:12,13 KJV

And it came to pass, when he was in a certain city, behold a man full of leprosy: who seeing Jesus fell on *his* face, and besought him, saying, Lord, if thou wilt, thou canst make me clean. And he put forth *his* hand, and touched him, saying, I will: be thou clean. And immediately the leprosy departed from him.

——— *DECLARATION OF FAITH* ———

Jesus, my Lord, Savior, and Redeemer, is more than willing to provide His healing power for me whenever I need it.

Through Him, I can lay my hands on the sick and command healing to come into their bodies.

(Isaiah 53:5; Galatians 3:13; Luke 10:9; Mark 11:23,24; 16:18; James 5:15)

LUKE 5:15,16 NKJV

However, the report went around concerning Him all the more; and great multitudes came together to hear, and to be healed by Him of their infirmities. So He Himself often withdrew into the wilderness and prayed.

——— *DECLARATION OF FAITH* ———

I regularly and consistently take the time to go to an isolated place, free of distraction, to pray and fellowship with my heavenly Father.

I am not moved by need, nor do I focus on how much work there is to do. I am moved by design, doing things the way that God has commanded.

It is in God's design that I regularly rest and get prayed up regardless of what needs to be done.

(Mark 1:35; 6:46; Matthew 6:6; Luke 4:42; 9:10; Deuteronomy 28:1; Exodus 14:1-15)

LUKE 5:17-25 KJV

And it came to pass on a certain day, as he was teaching, that there were Pharisees and doctors of the law sitting by, which were come out of every town of Galilee, and Judaea, and Jerusalem: and the power of the Lord was *present* to heal them. And, behold, men brought in a bed a man which was taken with a palsy: and they sought *means* to bring him in, and to lay *him* before him. And when they could not find by what *way* they might bring him in because of the multitude, they went upon the housetop, and let him down through the tiling with *his* couch into the midst before Jesus. And when he saw their faith, he said unto him, Man, thy sins are forgiven thee. And the scribes and the Pharisees began to reason, saying, Who is this which speaketh blasphemies? Who can forgive sins, but God alone? But when Jesus perceived their thoughts, he answering said unto them, What reason ye in your hearts? Whether is easier, to say, Thy sins be forgiven thee; or to say, Rise up and walk? But that ye may know that the Son of man hath power upon earth to forgive sins, (he said unto the sick of the palsy,) I say unto thee, Arise, and take up thy couch, and go into thine house. And immediately he rose up before them, and took up that whereon he lay, and departed to his own house, glorifying God.

DECLARATION OF FAITH

I can see when faith has risen in a person's heart, and as a carrier of God's power, I am ever-ready to provide the healing that they need.

In Jesus, I have the ability and authority to release an individual from the power of sin and provide healing for any area of their lives.

My words are the carriers of God's power in this earth and they bring deliverance to those held captive by the forces of darkness.

In Jesus, I am a discerner of the thoughts, questions and intentions of those who oppose the Truth, and I have all the wisdom that I need to handle any situation or confrontation I have with them.

I am a man/woman of faith.

The power of sin has been broken over my life.

I have every right to the healing power that God so longs for me to have and I will do whatever it takes to receive it into my life.

(Mark 2:8; 11:23,24; Luke 8:43-48; 20:23; James 5:14-16; John 20:22,23; 1 Corinthians 2:6-16; 2 Corinthians 5:20; Galatians 4:5,6)

LUKE 6:12 NIV

One of those days Jesus went out to a mountainside to pray, and spent the night praying to God.

—— *DECLARATION OF FAITH* ——

I regularly and consistently go to a special place of solitude in order to have a distraction-free time of prayer and fellowship with my heavenly Father.

(Mark 1:35; 6:46; Matthew 6:6; Luke 4:42; 5:16; 9:10; Ephesians 6:18)

LUKE 6:18,19 NKJV

As well as those who were tormented with unclean spirits. And they were healed. And the whole multitude sought to touch Him, for power went out from Him and healed them all.

—— *DECLARATION OF FAITH* ——

People are drawn to the Holy Spirit, who is within me, and I respond to their faith by being an avenue of God's healing power for them.

Unclean spirits of every kind flee from my presence and power goes forth from me to meet the needs of the expecting one.

(Job 29:21-25; James 4:7; 5:14-16; Luke 10:19; John 14:12; Mark 16:17-20)

LUKE 6:20-23 NKJV

Then He lifted up His eyes toward His disciples, and said:

"Blessed are you poor, for yours is the kingdom of God.

Blessed are you who hunger now, for you shall be filled.

Blessed are you who weep now, for you shall laugh.

Blessed are you when men hate you, and when they exclude you, and revile you, and cast out your name as evil, for the Son of Man's sake.

Rejoice in that day and leap for joy!

For indeed your reward is great in heaven, for in like manner their fathers did to the prophets.

—— *DECLARATION OF FAITH* ——

I am blessed, satisfied and filled with the joy and favor of almighty God regardless of my outward condition.

I have been made a prince/princess in God's royal house and have inherited the kingdom of heaven.

All poverty and affliction must step aside as I enter into my rights as God's son/daughter and heir to the covenants of promise.

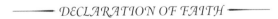

I am blessed, satisfied and filled with the joy and favor of almighty God, for all of my hunger and thirst for Him is filled and He sees to it that I am completely satisfied. All of my grief and mourning has turned into laughter.

I am blessed, satisfied, and filled with the joy and favor of almighty God.

I am a man/woman without compromise who stands shoulder to shoulder with the Lord of the universe and I consider it a totally awesome and wonderful thing that I am persecuted for it! It sets me apart as a peer and companion of those patriarchs of the past who would not compromise. My persecution makes an undeniable proclamation to both the natural and spirit worlds that I am one of God's own sons/daughters! It ensures and deposits a tremendous reward in my heavenly treasury! What a blessing it is to be singled out as an uncompromising, born-again child of the living God! Hallelujah!

(Revelation 1:5,6; Nehemiah 8:10; Galatians 4:5,6; Luke 12:32; 2 Corinthians 8:9; Ephesians 2:6-14; Matthew 5:2-12; Psalm 126:5; 2 Timothy 3:12)

LUKE 6:24-26 KJV

But woe unto you that are rich! for ye have received your consolation. Woe unto you that are full! for ye shall hunger. Woe unto you that laugh now! for ye shall mourn and weep. Woe unto you, when all men shall speak well of you! for so did their fathers to the false prophets.

——— *DECLARATION OF FAITH* ———

I do not trust, or revel in, uncertain riches, nor do I seek the praise, acceptance and adoration of men. In all that I do, I focus on the honor, integrity and approval that comes from God alone. I am satisfied only when I am doing those things that please my heavenly Father.

(1 Timothy 6:17; John 15:19; Colossians 1:10; 1 John 3:22)

LUKE 6:27-31 KJV

But I say unto you which hear, Love your enemies, do good to them which hate you, Bless them that curse you, and pray for them which despitefully use you. And unto him that smiteth thee on the *one* cheek offer also the other; and him that taketh away thy cloke forbid not *to take thy* coat also. Give to every man that asketh of thee; and of him that taketh away thy goods ask *them* not again. And as ye would that men should do to you, do ye also to them likewise.

I am completely focused and attentive on the Word of the Lord, not just to learn it, but also to live it.

I make it a practice to love my enemies. Those who detest me and are continually looking for ways to hurt me, find only love from me in return. I never retaliate in anger. Instead, I show myself to be a child of nobility who finds creative ways to do good by them. I fully understand that all of their curses upon me do not have the power to harm me in any way. Therefore, I look for ways to bless them, showing them God's love and mercy, as well as my own.

I never forget that I am a born-again child of God. I do not stand idly and allow myself to be beaten upon, but retaliate in the spirit of love and goodness under the direction of the Holy Spirit.

The children of the devil do not fully understand what they are doing when they try to harm me. Therefore, instead of repaying evil for evil, I do what is best for them and demonstrate the blessings of God. Nothing that they can take from me can harm me or cause me to fail to prosper. When they take, I give, and yet increase all the more. And I give freely to all, both the good and the evil, in order that I may demonstrate God's love and mercy, and display His true nature to all who see.

I treat others exactly the way I would want to be treated if I were in their situation. I make it a point in my life to see the world through other people's eyes.

(James 1:22-25; Romans 8:31; 12:14-20; Genesis 12:1-3; Acts 7:60; 1 Corinthians 6:7; 13:4-6; Deuteronomy 15:7,8; Galatians 4:5,6; 1 Peter 3:13; Matthew 7:12)

LUKE 6:35-38 KJV

But love ye your enemies, and do good, and lend, hoping for nothing again; and your reward shall be great, and ye shall be the children of the Highest: for he is kind unto the unthankful and *to* the evil. Be ye therefore merciful, as your Father also is merciful. Judge not, and ye shall not be judged: condemn not, and ye shall not be condemned: forgive, and ye shall be forgiven: Give, and it shall be given unto you; good measure, pressed down, and shaken together, and running over, shall men give into your bosom. For with the same measure that ye mete withal it shall be measured to you again.

All of my actions toward my fellow man are rooted in love. I am even kind and good to my enemies—finding ways to help them and make their lives easier to live. I am not moved by how they respond to me, nor do I hold back my blessings when they try to harm me.

Even if they do not readily receive what I have for them, I know that my Father takes notice. In Him, I find recompense and a rich, abundant reward.

In all of these things, my Father sees that I am living as a good son/daughter, showing myself to be just like He is, for He is kind and charitable to both the good and the evil. Even the selfish and ungrateful ones enjoy His blessings. Therefore, I shall walk in the spirit of mercy and compassion just as He does.

I do not seek judgment and condemnation on people, nor do I harbor strife and resentment toward anyone. I always remember how far God has brought me, how patient He has been towards me and how much He has forgiven me of. Being an imitator of my Father, I am resolved to be just as patient and forgiving as He is.

I live my life in a spirit of generosity. I am always looking for ways to give to others. I am not a parasite looking for something to take and living my life by what others can give me. I find God's way, the way of giving, to be much more satisfying.

When I give, God causes men to give the same back to me. He takes the measure that I have given, presses it down, adds a little more, shakes it all together, adds some more, jumps up and down on it, adds some more, gets the angels to fill in all the little nooks and crannies, then pours as much as He can on the top until the measure that I get back is overflowing with His abundance!

What a blessing it is to be a giver in the family of God!

(Romans 13:10; Hebrews 13:16; Matthew 5:46-48; 7:1-5; 18:21-35; Mark 11:25; Proverbs 19:17; 28:27; Psalm 79:12; Genesis 12:1-3; James 2:13; Galatians 6:6-10)

LUKE 6:40 AMP

A pupil is not superior to his teacher, but everyone [when he is] completely trained (readjusted, restored, set to rights, and perfected) will be like his teacher.

——— DECLARATION OF FAITH ———

Jesus has restored me to right standing with our Father, and has firmly established me so that I can enjoy the full rights and privileges of a son/daughter of God.

By His sacrifice, He has made me complete—absolutely perfect in God's eyes. He has become my trainer and is conforming me to be just like He is.

It is my responsibility to do the same kinds of things that He did in His earth walk.

(Galatians 4:5,6; Hebrews 10:14; Romans 8:29; John 14:12-18; 16:13; Mark 16:15-20; Matthew 28:18-20)

LUKE 6:43-45 NKJV

"For a good tree does not bear bad fruit, nor does a bad tree bear good fruit. For every tree is known by its own fruit. For men do not gather figs from thorns, nor do they gather grapes from a bramble bush. A good man out of the good treasure of his heart brings forth good; and an evil man out of the evil treasure of his heart brings forth evil. For out of the abundance of the heart his mouth speaks."

——— *DECLARATION OF FAITH* ———

I am like a good and healthy tree that bears desirable fruit.

I am an uncompromising man/woman of integrity.

I have been chosen to display the glory and majesty of my heavenly Father.

I am known and identified by the fruit that I bear in my life.

I focus my attention on that which is good, honorable and praiseworthy. I purposefully allow only good things to enter into my heart and reject the corrupt ways of the wicked.

Out of the treasure of good things that I have stored up in my heart, I produce a harvest that is honorable and intrinsically good.

I purpose in my heart to speak only those things that produce an environment conducive to the life that God expects me to live.

(Psalm 1:1-3; John 15:1-8; Proverbs 18:20,21; Philippians 4:8; Matthew 12:33-35)

LUKE 6:46-48 KJV

And why call ye me, Lord, Lord, and do not the things which I say? Whosoever cometh to me, and heareth my sayings, and doeth them, I will shew you to whom he is like: He is like a man which built an house, and digged deep, and laid the foundation on a rock: and when the flood arose, the stream beat vehemently upon that house, and could not shake it: for it was founded upon a rock.

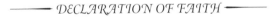

——— *DECLARATION OF FAITH* ———

I demonstrate the fact of Jesus' lordship in my life by doing those things that He has commanded me to do. When I hear the Word I remain focused and attentive in order to apply what I learn to everyday living.

I make the quality choice to be like the man building a house, who dug deep into the ground in order to build the foundation upon the rock; and when the storms came and torrents broke out against that house, it stood immovable because it had been built according to code, with no shortcuts or deviations from the proven master plan.

My life is built upon the secure foundation of the Word of God! Regardless of the circumstances, I will stand my ground!

(Matthew 7:24-27; James 1:22-25; Psalm 119:37; Romans 5:1,2; Ephesians 6:13)

LUKE 7:7-9 NKJV

Therefore I did not even think myself worthy to come to You. But say the word, and my servant will be healed. For I also am a man placed under authority, having soldiers under me. And I say to one, "'Go,' and he goes; and to another, 'Come,' and he comes; and to my servant, 'Do this,' and he does it." When Jesus heard these things, He marveled at him, and turned around and said to the crowd that followed Him, "I say to you, I have not found such great faith, not even in Israel!"

——— DECLARATION OF FAITH ———

I understand the power that God has placed in His Word. It is the ultimate authority in heaven and earth, and on my lips it brings healing and deliverance to those in need.

(Psalm 107:20; 138:2; Isaiah 42:21)

LUKE 7:21-23 KJV

And in that same hour he cured many of *their* infirmities and plagues, and of evil spirits; and unto many *that were* blind he gave sight. Then Jesus answering said unto them, Go your way, and tell John what things ye have seen and heard; how that the blind see, the lame walk, the lepers are cleansed, the deaf hear, the dead are raised, to the poor the gospel is preached. And blessed is *he,* whosoever shall not be offended in me.

——— DECLARATION OF FAITH ———

In Jesus, I have come to experience the wonder-working power of God.

His healing power goes with me wherever I go. The blind see, the deaf hear, the lame rise and walk, the dead are raised to life and the poor are shown the way to an abundance of riches.

Through Jesus, every demon is subject to my authority.

I consider it ludicrous to be offended or resentful at these things, but take them as the fundamental results of being one with God.

I will never reject the manifestation of the power of God in my life!

(Ephesians 1:17-23; Mark 16:15-20; Isaiah 61:1-3; Luke 10:19; John 17:20-26; 2 Timothy 3:5)

LUKE 7:50 NKJV

Then He said to the woman, "Your faith has saved you. Go in peace."

DECLARATION OF FAITH

My faith has saved me and rescued me from every calamity, and I have entered into the peace and freedom that comes from being delivered from the power of sin.

(John 8:32-36; Romans 6:7; Matthew 9:22; Mark 5:34; Luke 8:48; 18:42)

LUKE 8:9,10 NKJV

Then His disciples asked Him, saying, "What does this parable mean?"

And He said, "To you it has been given to know the mysteries of the kingdom of God, but to the rest it is given in parables, that 'Seeing they may not see, and hearing they may not understand.'"

DECLARATION OF FAITH

My heavenly Father has given me the wisdom to know, recognize and understand the mysteries of the kingdom of God. I have a sweeping insight into all that I see and a thorough comprehension of all that I hear.

(1 Corinthians 1:30; 2:6-16; 1 John 2:20; 5:20; Matthew 13:15,16; Daniel 2:22,23)

LUKE 8:11-15 KJV

Now the parable is this: The seed is the word of God. Those by the way side are they that hear; then cometh the devil, and taketh away the word out of their hearts, lest they should believe and be saved. They on the rock *are they,* which, when they hear, receive the word with joy; and these have no root, which for a while believe, and in time of temptation fall away. And that which fell among thorns are they, which, when they have heard, go forth, and are choked with cares and riches and pleasures of *this* life, and bring no fruit to perfection. But that on the good ground are they, which in an honest and good heart, having heard the word, keep *it,* and bring forth fruit with patience.

DECLARATION OF FAITH

I have heard the Word of God and have acknowledged the lordship of Jesus in my life.

I welcome the Word with joy and gladness—rooting it deep within my spirit, so that when the trials and temptations of life come, I will not fall away.

I do not allow anxieties, cares, the deceitfulness of worldly riches, or the pleasures of the world to enter in and choke the Word out of my life.

I continually feed the Word to my spirit and my fruit never fails to reach its maturity.

I am constantly reaping a harvest from the Word that I have sown into my life.

By my deeds, I prove that I am good ground where the seed of the Word flourishes.

I receive the Word habitually and tend it carefully while patiently awaiting my harvest.

(Romans 10:8-14; Psalm 1:1-3; 119:11-16; 1 Peter 5:5-7; Matthew 11:28-30; Galatians 6:7-9; Mark 4:14-20; Hebrews 10:36-11:1; James 1:22-25)

LUKE 8:17,18 KJV

For nothing is secret, that shall not be made manifest; neither *any thing* hid, that shall not be known and come abroad. Take heed therefore how ye hear: for whosoever hath, to him shall be given; and whosoever hath not, from him shall be taken even that which he seemeth to have.

—— DECLARATION OF FAITH ——

There is nothing hidden that God will not reveal to me, nor anything secret that He will not make known to me. Therefore, I am careful to be alert to the voice of the Holy Spirit. He fills me continually with the secrets of the kingdom— enlightening me with a new supply of spiritual knowledge every day.

(Genesis 18:17; Luke 8:9,10; Daniel 2:22,23; 1 Corinthians 14:2,13; John 16:13)

LUKE 8:21 NIV

He replied, "My mother and brothers are those who hear God's word and put it into practice."

—— DECLARATION OF FAITH ——

I am both a hearer and a doer of the Word of God and, thereby, have been made the very brother/sister of my Lord Jesus Christ.

(James 1:22-25; Hebrews 2:11; Romans 8:29)

LUKE 8:24,25 KJV

And they came to him, and awoke him, saying, Master, master, we perish. Then he arose, and rebuked the wind and the raging of the water: and they ceased, and there was a calm. And he said unto them, Where is your faith? And they being afraid wondered, saying one to another, What manner of man is this! for he commandeth even the winds and water, and they obey him.

DECLARATION OF FAITH

I am a man/woman of faith.

I reject all fear and anxiety in my life, casting it all on the shoulders of the One who bears my burdens. I am not seized by fear in any circumstance. I have the Word on my lips that covers and protects me in any situation.

I use my faith every hour of every day, believing and speaking to the problem, commanding the circumstance to get in line with the perfect will of God.

I am a victor here, not a victim, and I am in command of any given situation.

(Hebrews 11:6; 1 Peter 5:5-7; 2 Timothy 1:6,7; Matthew 11:28-30; Romans 8:37; 10:8; Psalm 119:93; Joshua 1:5-9; 2 Corinthians 4:13; Mark 11:23,24)

LUKE 8:46-48 KJV

And Jesus said, Somebody hath touched me: for I perceive that virtue is gone out of me. And when the woman saw that she was not hid, she came trembling, and falling down before him, she declared unto him before all the people for what cause she had touched him, and how she was healed immediately. And he said unto her, Daughter, be of good comfort: thy faith hath made thee whole; go in peace.

DECLARATION OF FAITH

In Jesus, I have a keen perception of the workings of the power of God in my life. I can sense when the power of God has been poured into a child of faith. I have a thorough understanding of the workings of faith and that it is by faith that we are made well and are able to enter into the peace that supercedes all worldly understanding.

(Ephesians 1:17-23; Hebrews 11:1,6; James 5:16; Mark 5:30; Philippians 4:7)

LUKE 8:50 AMP

But Jesus, on hearing this, answered him, Do not be seized with alarm or struck with fear; simply believe [in Me as able to do this], and she shall be made well.

────── *DECLARATION OF FAITH* ──────

I am never seized with alarm, or struck by fear when a bad report comes. I believe in the power and ability of God within me and I am confident that He will cause me to triumph in any situation.

(Joshua 1:5-9; 2 Corinthians 2:14; Colossians 1:29; Ephesians 3:20; 1 Peter 5:5-7)

LUKE 9:1,2 KJV

Then he called his twelve disciples together, and gave them power and authority over all devils, and to cure diseases. And he sent them to preach the kingdom of God, and to heal the sick.

────── *DECLARATION OF FAITH* ──────

Jesus has given me power and authority over all demons and to cure sicknesses and diseases of every kind. He has sent me out to proclaim the present fact of the kingdom of God and to bring healing to a hurting world.

(Luke 10:19; Mark 16:15-20; Isaiah 61:1-3; Matthew 28:18-20; 2 Corinthians 5:18-20)

LUKE 9:6 KJV

And they departed, and went through the towns, preaching the gospel, and healing every where.

────── *DECLARATION OF FAITH* ──────

I have been sent into the neighborhoods of my city and from town to town to proclaim the Gospel and restore health to the afflicted everywhere.

(Acts 1:8; Mark 16:15-20; Isaiah 61:1-3; Matthew 28:18-20; 2 Corinthians 5:18-20)

LUKE 9:11 KJV

And the people, when they knew it, followed him: and he received them, and spake unto them of the kingdom of God, and healed them that had need of healing.

────── *DECLARATION OF FAITH* ──────

I welcome all who are willing to listen to the message of the Gospel—bringing the present fact of the kingdom of God into their midst, chasing off Satan and his demons, and restoring health to the oppressed and afflicted.

(Mark 16:15-20; Luke 10:19; Isaiah 61:1-3)

LUKE 9:23-26 KJV

And he said to *them* all, If any *man* will come after me, let him deny himself, and take up his cross daily, and follow me. For whosoever will save his life shall lose it: but whosoever will lose his life for my sake, the same shall save it. For what is a man advantaged, if he gain the whole world, and lose himself, or be cast away? For whosoever shall be ashamed of me and of my words, of him shall the Son of man be ashamed, when he shall come in his own glory, and *in his* Father's, and of the holy angels.

DECLARATION OF FAITH

I have made my decision to take my stand at Jesus' side. I set aside all of my own interests and put His interests first place in my life. I follow His every move and imitate His every action. I live my life by His example, regardless of the con-sequences—what is said about me, or what is done to me.

I do not conform to the image of the world, but am transformed into the image of Christ.

I have taken my stand with Jesus, and He has taken His stand with me.

(Ephesians 5:1-18; 6:13; Romans 5:1,2; 8:29; 12:1,2; Matthew 10:38,39; Hebrews 13:6)

LUKE 9:51 KJV

And it came to pass, when the time was come that he should be received up, he stedfastly set his face to go to Jerusalem.

DECLARATION OF FAITH

I have set my face like flint to fulfill my calling and walk the path of right-eousness that God has set before me.

(Romans 11:29; Mark 16:19; Proverbs 3:5,6; 2 Timothy 1:6-9)

LUKE 10:2 KJV

Therefore said he unto them, The harvest truly is great, but the labourers are few: pray ye therefore the Lord of the harvest, that he would send forth labour-ers into his harvest.

DECLARATION OF FAITH

I pray for the Lord of the harvest to send laborers into the harvest fields to bring the lost to salvation.

(John 4:35; 2 Thessalonians 3:1; Matthew 9:37,38)

LUKE 10:9 AMP

And heal the sick in it and say to them, The kingdom of God has come close to you.

——— *DECLARATION OF FAITH* ———

Whenever I bring God's healing power to the sick, I explain to them that it is the kingdom of God that has entered their presence and His power alone has healed them.

(Mark 3:15; 16:15-20; Matthew 3:2)

LUKE 10:16 NKJV

"He who hears you hears Me, he who rejects you rejects Me, and he who rejects Me rejects Him who sent Me."

——— *DECLARATION OF FAITH* ———

Whoever listens to my words, listens to the very Words of Jesus; whoever rejects me, rejects Jesus Himself; and whoever rejects Jesus, rejects our heavenly Father as well.

(John 5:23; 13:20; 17:20-26; 1 Thessalonians 4:8)

LUKE 10:17-20 KJV

And the seventy returned again with joy, saying, Lord, even the devils are subject unto us through thy name. And he said unto them, I beheld Satan as lightning fall from heaven. Behold, I give unto you power to tread on serpents and scorpions, and over all the power of the enemy: and nothing shall by any means hurt you. Notwithstanding in this rejoice not, that the spirits are subject unto you; but rather rejoice, because your names are written in heaven.

——— *DECLARATION OF FAITH* ———

All wicked spirits are subject to my authority in Jesus' name.

I have all of the authority that I need to trample down serpents and scorpions and I have mental, physical, and spiritual strength over and above all that the enemy possesses. There is nothing that Satan can do to harm me in any way.

For me, Satan and his demons are little more than harmless, pesky bugs.

Nevertheless, I do not find great joy in my ability to cast out demons, or the fact that they are subject to my authority, but I rejoice that my name has been written in heaven and that I am honored as a son/daughter of the living God.

(Mark 16:17,18; Luke 9:1,2; Psalm 91:13; Ephesians 1:17-23; Philippians 4:3)

LUKE 10:22 KJV

All things are delivered to me of my Father: and no man knoweth who the Son is, but the Father; and who the Father is, but the Son, and he to whom the Son will reveal him.

——— *DECLARATION OF FAITH* ———

In Jesus, all things are subject to my authority. He has restored me to the former dominion and has given me, together with my brothers and sisters in Christ, charge of His kingdom in this earth.

Jesus has chosen me to be His brother. He has revealed the Father to me so that I may have an intimate relationship with Him. My walk with my heavenly Father is just as close and meaningful as was Jesus' walk with our heavenly Father when He was on this earth.

(Luke 10:19; Matthew 28:18-20; Ephesians 1:17-23; Psalm 8:4-6; Romans 8:29; Hebrews 2:11; John 17:20-26; 1 John 1:3)

LUKE 10:41,42 KJV

And Jesus answered and said unto her, Martha, Martha, thou art careful and troubled about many things: But one thing is needful: and Mary hath chosen that good part, which shall not be taken away from her.

——— *DECLARATION OF FAITH* ———

I refuse to be anxious or stressed out about serving. I have taken my place as a disciple of Christ. I keep my priorities in order and put His Word first place. I have chosen the good part and I will not be deprived of it. When I serve, I do so joyfully because I have prepared myself with the Word and have rid myself of all stress and anxiety.

(1 Peter 5:5-7; Jude 24; John 6:27; Ephesians 1:13,14; Romans 11:29)

LUKE 11:1-4 KJV

And it came to pass, that, as he was praying in a certain place, when he ceased, one of his disciples said unto him, Lord, teach us to pray, as John also taught his disciples. And he said unto them, When ye pray, say, Our Father which art in heaven, Hallowed be thy name. Thy kingdom come. Thy will be done, as in heaven, so in earth. Give us day by day our daily bread. And forgive us our sins; for we also forgive every one that is indebted to us. And lead us not into temptation; but deliver us from evil.

──────── DECLARATION OF FAITH ────────

When I pray, I first recognize my relationship with my heavenly Father. He is truly my Father and I am His own son/daughter.

I pay Him homage by continually proclaiming His goodness and holiness.

I proclaim the present fact of His kingdom and establish His will on earth, just as it is in heaven. There is no poverty in heaven; therefore, I do not live in poverty on earth. There is no sickness in heaven; therefore, I do not live in sickness on earth. There is no strife in heaven; therefore, I do not live in strife on earth. I will pray for nothing outside of God's perfect will.

I thank Him for my daily provisions. All that I need for life and godliness is continually provided for me.

I thank Him for forgiving my sins and remain completely honest with Him, confessing anything that I may have done wrong, and I continually draw near to Him in close and intimate fellowship.

I also forgive anyone who may have sinned against me. I refuse to harbor strife and unforgiveness in my life, thereby hindering my prayers and breaking fellowship with the Lord.

Lastly, I thank Him for my complete deliverance from evil, for His provision of wisdom to overcome in the evil day, and for thorough victory over every temptation.

(Galatians 4:5,6; Psalm 136; Hebrews 13:8; Matthew 3:2; 8:17; 2 Corinthians 8:9; Mark 11:25; 1 John 1:3-9; 5:14,15; James 4:1-10; Philippians 4:19; 2 Peter 1:3; Colossians 1:13; 2:15; 1 Corinthians 10:13; 15:57)

LUKE 11:5-13 KJV

And he said unto them, Which of you shall have a friend, and shall go unto him at midnight, and say unto him, Friend, lend me three loaves; For a friend of mine in his journey is come to me, and I have nothing to set before him? And he from within shall answer and say, Trouble me not: the door is now shut, and my children are with me in bed; I cannot rise and give thee. I say unto you, Though he will not rise and give him, because he is his friend, yet because of his importunity he will rise and give him as many as he needeth. And I say unto you, Ask, and it shall be given you; seek, and ye shall find; knock, and it shall be opened unto you. For every one that asketh receiveth; and he that seeketh findeth; and to him that knocketh it shall be opened. If a son shall ask bread of any of you that is a father, will he give him a stone? or if *he ask* a fish, will he for a fish give him a serpent? Or if he shall ask an egg, will he offer him a scorpion? If ye then, being evil, know how to give good gifts unto your children: how much more shall *your* heavenly Father give the Holy Spirit to them that ask him?

——— DECLARATION OF FAITH ———

I am a man/woman who is persistent in prayer. I relentlessly call on my Father to fill my every need and the needs of those in my circle of influence. God is honored by my insistence and gladly provides me with all of the necessities of life.

When I speak one of God's promises into my life, I know that I must continually believe and speak it until what I have called for is manifested in this natural world.

Whenever I am seeking anything, I remember that I have a Guide within me. Therefore, I will not give up until I have found what I am looking for.

When I have come to a door of promised blessing that is shut, I will knock at that door until it opens to me and my life is showered with all of the benefits of that promise.

When I persistently ask, I receive all that I am praying for and more. When I persistently seek, I find what I am looking for and more. When I persistently knock, the door eventually opens to me and I walk in the fullness of God's blessings in my life.

I am careful to ask for specific things. God does not operate in vague generalities, nor does He respond to my prayers with something other than what I am asking for.

Even I, as a good father/mother, know how to give good gifts to my children. I give them specifically what they are asking for so that their joy may be full. If my children ask me for something that is not good for them, I simply do not give it.

The same goes for my heavenly Father. It brings Him great pleasure to give me those specific desires of my heart. I am granted anything I desire that is in line with His perfect will as is revealed in His Word. He gives me anything that I ask for that is beneficial to me and will work to my advantage. If I faithfully ask Him for the Holy Spirit, I can fully trust that He will give me the Holy Spirit and not some devil full of counterfeit gifts.

(Matthew 7:7-9; Isaiah 55:6; Philippians 4:19; James 1:5-8,17; 4:3,4; 1 John 5:14,15; John 14:13,14; 16:13,23,24; Mark 11:22-25; 2 Corinthians 1:20; Psalm 37:4)

LUKE 11:14 NIV

Jesus was driving out a demon that was mute. When the demon left, the man who had been mute spoke, and the crowd was amazed.

———— *DECLARATION OF FAITH* ————

I am discerning of the particular tasks assigned to individual demons and I have the authority to drive them out with a Word.

(Luke 10:19; Psalm 91:13; Mark 9:25; 16:17-20)

LUKE 11:20-23 KJV

But if I with the finger of God cast out devils, no doubt the kingdom of God is come upon you. When a strong man armed keepeth his palace, his goods are in peace: But when a stronger than he shall come upon him, and overcome him, he taketh from him all his armour wherein he trusted, and divideth his spoils. He that is not with me is against me: and he that gathereth not with me scattereth.

———— *DECLARATION OF FAITH* ————

I carry the kingdom within me and drive out demons by the very finger of God.

Demons may overpower many in the world, holding them captive to their every whim, but I have been sent into the world to set the captives free!

Jesus attacked and conquered the forces of Satan, stripping them of all of their power and authority over the believer, and He has given me my portion of the spoils of war.

I have taken my stand at His side, with total and complete authority over all demonic forces.

I have taken His yoke upon me and hold His interests as my very own.

(Luke 9:1,2; 10:19; Isaiah 61:1-3; Matthew 28:18-20; Colossians 2:15; Ephesians 1:17-23; John 14:12)

LUKE 11:28 AMP

But He said, Blessed (happy and to be envied) rather are those who hear the Word of God and obey and practice it!

———— *DECLARATION OF FAITH* ————

I am blessed, prosperous and to be envied, because I give the Word the ascendancy in my life. I feed upon it, listen to it, obey it and live it, and my life is filled with blessing as a result.

(Joshua 1:8; Psalm 1:1-3; James 1:22-25)

LUKE 11:33-36 KJV

No man, when he hath lighted a candle, putteth it in a secret place, neither under a bushel, but on a candlestick, that they which come in may see the light. The light of the body is the eye: therefore when thine eye is single, thy whole body also is full of light; but when *thine eye* is evil, thy body also *is* full of darkness. Take heed therefore that the light which is in thee be not darkness. If thy whole body therefore *be* full of light, having no part dark, the whole shall be full of light, as when the bright shining of a candle doth give thee light.

DECLARATION OF FAITH

I am careful of what I allow to enter my life. I fully understand that light has no fellowship with darkness. It is my choice to live as a child of Light.

Therefore, I do not allow my eyes to unnecessarily take in evil things. My eyes are the lamp which brings Light to my whole body and I see to it that they remain sound and fulfill their intended office.

The eyes of my spirit remain single, seeing clearly what is set before me. I am keenly discerning of good and evil, and truth and falsehood.

These things endure as evidence to all that I am a born-again child of the living God and I remain unashamed of the life that I have chosen to live.

My life is a testimony to all who are hungry for the Gospel and I am ever ready to lead them into the arms of my heavenly Father.

(1 John 1:5-9; Philippians 4:8; Matthew 5:28; 6:22,23; Proverbs 6:25; Romans 1:16; Job 29:24,25)

LUKE 11:42 KJV

But woe unto you, Pharisees! for ye tithe mint and rue and all manner of herbs, and pass over judgment and the love of God: these ought ye to have done, and not to leave the other undone.

DECLARATION OF FAITH

I make the law of love the supreme law of my life. I do nothing outside of it.

(1 Corinthians 1:8; Deuteronomy 6:5; Matthew 19:19; Luke 6:31)

LUKE 12:6,7 KJV

Are not five sparrows sold for two farthings, and not one of them is forgotten before God? But even the very hairs of your head are all numbered. Fear not therefore: ye are of more value than many sparrows.

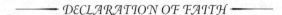

——— *DECLARATION OF FAITH* ———

When I look at the sparrow, I know I am looking at a creature that my Father loves and watches over very carefully. Yet, when He looks at me, He sees someone worth more than many flocks of sparrows. He holds me so close to His heart that He even numbers the very hairs on my head.

With such a loving Father to guide and protect me, I have absolutely nothing to fear.

(Matthew 6:26; 10:30; Psalm 103:13; Romans 8:31; 2 Timothy 1:7)

LUKE 12:8 KJV

Also I say unto you, Whosoever shall confess me before men, him shall the Son of man also confess before the angels of God.

——— *DECLARATION OF FAITH* ———

I confess openly that I am a born-again child of the living God.

The Holy Spirit has taken up residence within me and Jesus has become my Lord. Jesus Himself has stood up before all of the angels in heaven and acknowledged me as His brother/sister.

All of the angels of heaven know my name and rejoice in my salvation. They are pleased to minister to me all that I need while I walk this earth.

(Luke 15:10; Hebrews 1:14; 2:11; Psalm 91:10,11; Romans 1:16; 8:29; 10:9,10)

LUKE 12:15 KJV

And he said unto them, Take heed, and beware of covetousness: for a man's life consisteth not in the abundance of the things which he possesseth.

——— *DECLARATION OF FAITH* ———

I am careful not to be greedy in my new abundant life. I remain free of all covetousness, for I fully understand that my life does not consist of, nor is it sustained by, the amount of wealth and possessions that I have. I remain focused on the whole kingdom and not just the wealth therein.

(1 Timothy 6:5-20; Matthew 4:1-11; 6:25-34)

LUKE 12:21-34 KJV

So *is* he that layeth up treasure for himself, and is not rich toward God. And he said unto his disciples, Therefore I say unto you, Take no thought for your life, what ye shall eat; neither for the body, what ye shall put on. The life is more than meat, and the body *is more* than raiment. Consider the ravens: for they neither sow nor reap; which neither have storehouse nor barn; and God feedeth them: how much more are ye better than the fowls? And which of you with taking thought can add to his stature one cubit? If ye then be not able to do that thing which is least, why take ye thought for the rest? Consider the lilies how they grow: they toil not, they spin not; and yet I say unto you, that Solomon in all his glory was not arrayed like one of these. If then God so clothe the grass, which is to day in the field, and to morrow is cast into the oven; how much more *will he clothe* you, O ye of little faith? And seek not ye what ye shall eat, or what ye shall drink, neither be ye of doubtful mind. For all these things do the nations of the world seek after: and your Father knoweth that ye have need of these things. But rather seek ye the kingdom of God; and all these things shall be added unto you. Fear not, little flock; for it is your Father's good pleasure to give you the kingdom. Sell that ye have, and give alms; provide yourselves bags which wax not old, a treasure in the heavens that faileth not, where no thief approacheth, neither moth corrupteth.

DECLARATION OF FAITH

I will not lay up and hoard treasures, riches, and possessions for myself (in greed, selfishness, or fear of the future) and thereby neglect my relationship with my heavenly Father. He alone is my provider and the sustainer of my life. My contentment is in Him and not the things that I possess. If men took all that I have and left me with just the clothes on my back, I would take off my shirt, hand it to them and walk away praising God. He never fails to provide my needs regardless of the circumstances, and neither man, nor devil, can stop His prosperity in my life.

I am not anxious or troubled by the necessities of life—what I will eat, or what I will have to wear, for my life is more than food and my body more than clothing. God has made me His own son/daughter—the highest priority of all of His creation—and He does not neglect my needs.

When I observe, study and meditate on the life of the raven—how they neither sow nor reap, nor have any storehouses to provide for their future, and yet my Father feeds them and cares for them, I find reason to believe. He makes it His business to care for the raven and never fails as their source of supply. How much more will He care for me, His eternal son/daughter? In my heavenly Father's eyes, I am worth more than many flocks of ravens!

In light of this, fear (worry, stress and anxiety) become ever-increasingly ridiculous. It does absolutely nothing for me. It doesn't add a single minute to my life, never fixes my situation and its infectious nature only causes everything around me to get worse. In all honesty, fear is an act of total and complete foolishness. It is rooted in either ignorance of, or defiance of, the knowledge of God's love that He has for His children.

When fear raises itself against me, I can look to the lilies of the field and how they grow. They don't wear themselves out trying to survive. Even if they're plowed over, they grow right back and bloom like a smile. Yet, even Solomon in all of his glory was not clothed in such beauty.

If my heavenly Father clothes the grass of the field, which is here today and gone tomorrow, in such beauty, how much more wonderfully shall He clothe me, His eternal son/daughter!

What reason is there to fear when I have such a loving Father watching over me? I refuse to be overly concerned about a single issue of life. My Father knows what I need better than I do and He never fails to be the source of my supply!

My walk with God is focused around the whole of the kingdom. There is no single issue that overwhelms my attention. I live the kingdom life and I enjoy all of the benefits therein. I do not allow fear to enter in and steal what I have been given, for I know that it is my Father's good pleasure to give me the kingdom and all of its blessings.

I do not hoard things to myself in fear that I will have nothing in the future. I give to the poor freely, bringing the kingdom into their midst. I understand my source of supply and I am always willing to give. Through my generosity, I store up an endless, inexhaustible supply of treasure in heaven that no thief can steal and no moth can devour.

This is kingdom-living and the life that I have chosen.

(Philippians 4:10-19; Matthew 5:40-42; 6:19-33; Genesis 22:14; Hebrews 13:5,6; 1 Kings 10:4-7; James 1:22-25; 2:5; 5:1-5; 1 Peter 5:5-7; Joshua 1:5-9; Psalm 103:1-5; 2 Corinthians 9:5-11)

LUKE 12:35,36 KJV

Let your loins be girded about, and your lights burning; And ye yourselves like unto men that wait for their lord, when he will return from the wedding; that when he cometh and knocketh, they may open unto him immediately.

——— DECLARATION OF FAITH ———

I keep my spiritual garments tucked up so that I can move freely and without hindrance in spiritual warfare. The fire in my spirit ever burns bright with the power and majesty of almighty God!

I am ever alert and aware of what is going on around me.

When my Master returns, He will find me bearing His burdens well. I will be one of the blessed and fortunate ones who did not fail to answer His call. He will call me to His table where He will have me recline, and there He will minister unto me.

(Matthew 11:28-30; 25:1-13; Colossians 1:29; Ephesians 1:17-23; 6:10-18; 1 Peter 1:13; Revelation 19:7-9)

LUKE 12:42 KJV

And the Lord said, Who then is that faithful and wise steward, whom his lord shall make ruler over his household, to give them their portion of meat in due season?

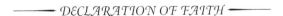
——— *DECLARATION OF FAITH* ———

I am a wise and faithful administrator in the household of God.

When Jesus returns, He will find me doing those things that He taught, commanded, and set an example to do.

I am carrying on His work in this earth. I supply the needs of those who are heirs of salvation and continually walk in the blessings of the covenant.

(John 14:12; Matthew 24:45,46; 25:1; Ephesians 5:1-18)

LUKE 13:11-13 KJV

And, behold, there was a woman which had a spirit of infirmity eighteen years, and was bowed together, and could in no wise lift up *herself*. And when Jesus saw her, he called *her to him,* and said unto her, Woman, thou art loosed from thine infirmity. And he laid *his* hands on her: and immediately she was made straight, and glorified God.

——— *DECLARATION OF FAITH* ———

I fully understand that sickness is of the devil and that his authority has been thoroughly stripped from my life. I have been set free from the power of sin and sickness!

I give due recognition to God's healing power in my life and I do not fail to remember Him and give Him praise for what He has done.

(Acts 9:17; 10:38; Colossians 1:13; 2:15; Romans 6:18; 1 Peter 2:24; James 5:14,15; Psalm 103:1-5)

LUKE 13:16 KJV

And ought not this woman, being a daughter of Abraham, whom Satan hath bound, lo, these eighteen years, be loosed from this bond on the sabbath day?

———— *DECLARATION OF FAITH* ————

I am a covenant partner with the Lord of the universe. As a provision of the covenant, I have been set free from all of Satan's power and authority.

(Hebrews 8:6; 10:15-17; Colossians 1:13; 2:15; Romans 6:14; Luke 10:17-19)

LUKE 13:17 AMP

Even as He said this, all His opponents were put to shame, and all the people were rejoicing over all the glorious things that were being done by Him.

———— *DECLARATION OF FAITH* ————

Everyone who chooses to make themselves my enemy shall be put to shame. I am a man/woman of unquestionable honor and integrity and people continually give God glory for the things He is doing in my life.

(Isaiah 54:17; Proverbs 11:8; Psalm 79:12; Deuteronomy 28:7,9,10; Mark 5:19,20)

LUKE 13:18,19 KJV

Then said he, Unto what is the kingdom of God like? and whereunto shall I resemble it? It is like a grain of mustard seed, which a man took, and cast into his garden; and it grew, and waxed a great tree; and the fowls of the air lodged in the branches of it.

———— *DECLARATION OF FAITH* ————

I operate the principles of the kingdom in the spirit of faith that has been given to me. I understand that when I sow these principles into my life, they are like grains of mustard seed. Though they are small in comparison to all of the other seeds that have been sown in me, through faith and patience, I can water them until their roots have choked out everything else and all that is left is the God-kind of life. In this manner, I receive such an abundance of blessings that I have all that I need and plenty left over. I declare that my life is a refuge to every-one in my circle of influence.

(Galatians 6:9; 2 Corinthians 4:13; 9:5-11; Hebrews 6:12; Matthew 13:31-33; Genesis 12:3)

LUKE 13:20,21 KJV

And again he said, Whereunto shall I liken the kingdom of God? It is like leaven, which a woman took and hid in three measures of meal, till the whole was leavened.

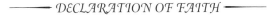

─────── *DECLARATION OF FAITH* ───────

I operate the principles of the kingdom faithfully. They are like the tiny bit of yeast that it takes to make the bread rise. When I put them into operation, it does not look like anything is happening. But I know that, in time, the yeast of God's kingdom principles will infiltrate the whole lump (every issue of my life) until every part of it is saturated and controlled by it.

(Galatians 6:9; Matthew 13:31-33; Hebrews 6:12)

LUKE 13:23-29 KJV

Then said one unto him, Lord, are there few that be saved? And he said unto them, Strive to enter in at the strait gate: for many, I say unto you, will seek to enter in, and shall not be able. When once the master of the house is risen up, and hath shut to the door, and ye begin to stand without, and to knock at the door, saying, Lord, Lord, open unto us; and he shall answer and say unto you, I know you not whence ye are: Then shall ye begin to say, We have eaten and drunk in thy presence, and thou hast taught in our streets. But he shall say, I tell you, I know you not whence ye are; depart from me, all ye workers of iniquity. There shall be weeping and gnashing of teeth, when ye shall see Abraham, and Isaac, and Jacob, and all the prophets, in the kingdom of God, and you *yourselves* thrust out. And they shall come from the east, and from the west, and from the north, and *from* the south, and shall sit down in the kingdom of God.

─────── *DECLARATION OF FAITH* ───────

My heavenly Father has not made it difficult to become His child, but walking in my rights as His son/daughter is another matter all together.

Operating in the principles of the kingdom of heaven takes tremendous effort on my part. I must strive, struggle, fight and force my way through the narrow passage that leads to its blessings.

My eyes are ever-focused upon Jesus, the Master of the house. I do all things in the manner in which He has both commanded and shown me by His example.

It makes no difference where I was born, what my race is, how many times I've prayed, or how many times I've read my Bible, if I do not operate the principles of the kingdom in the way that Jesus has commanded, I will not walk in its blessings.

All of the things of God, including being saved and walking in His blessings, must be done His way. Therefore, I choose to be a doer of the Word and an operator of the principles He has commanded me to walk in.

Through hard work, tenacity, perseverance, constancy, and faithfulness, I have become one of the many who sit down and feast at the Lord's table in the kingdom of God.

(1 Corinthians 9:23-27; James 1:6-8,22-25; 2:17-26; Hebrews 6:12; John 14:12; Ephesians 5:1-18; Matthew 7:7-14; 13:31-33; Deuteronomy 28:1-14)

LUKE 13:32 NKJV

And He said to them, "Go, tell that fox, 'Behold, I cast out demons and perform cures today and tomorrow, and the third *day* I shall be perfected.'"

——— *DECLARATION OF FAITH* ———

Jesus has finished His course and has taken His seat at the right hand of the Majesty on High. I, along with my other brothers and sisters in Him, have taken over His work in the earth. Because of the power of attorney that Jesus has given me to use His holy name, I regularly drive out demons, perform healings and set the captives free.

(John 14:12; Acts 1:8; Mark 16:15-20; Matthew 28:18-20; Ephesians 1:17-23; 2:6)

LUKE 14:13,14 KJV

But when thou makest a feast, call the poor, the maimed, the lame, the blind: And thou shalt be blessed; for they cannot recompense thee: for thou shalt be recompensed at the resurrection of the just.

——— *DECLARATION OF FAITH* ———

I am more than willing to be generous and share with those in need. It is of no concern to me whether they can repay me or not, for I much prefer the recompense that I will have in heaven at the resurrection of the righteous.

(1 Corinthians 3:13-15; 2 Corinthians 5:10; 8:2-4; Matthew 25:34-40)

LUKE 14:26-35 KJV

If any *man* come to me, and hate not his father, and mother, and wife, and children, and brethren, and sisters, yea, and his own life also, he cannot be my disciple. And whosoever doth not bear his cross, and come after me, cannot be my disciple. For which of you, intending to build a tower, sitteth not down first, and counteth the cost, whether he have *sufficient* to finish *it?* Lest haply, after he hath laid the foundation, and is not able to finish *it,* all that behold *it* begin to mock him, Saying, This man began to build, and was not able to finish. Or what king, going to make war against another king, sitteth not down first, and consulteth whether he be able with ten thousand to meet him that cometh against him with twenty thousand? Or else, while the other is yet a great way off, he sendeth an ambassage, and desireth conditions of peace. So likewise, whosoever he be of you that forsaketh not all that he hath, he cannot be my disciple. Salt *is* good: but if the salt have lost his savour, wherewith shall it be seasoned? It is neither fit for the land, nor yet for the dunghill; *but* men cast it out. He that hath ears to hear, let him hear.

──────── *DECLARATION OF FAITH* ────────

I have taken my stand with Jesus no matter what the cost. He is the first love of my life and no matter who leaves me or forsakes me—no matter what anyone thinks or what is said about me—I will remain with Him. Even if my own life were in jeopardy because of my love for Him, I would not leave His side.

I have considered all of the possible costs of following the Lord and have chosen to do so without reservation. I have taken my stand at His side and will not give in a single inch. All that I have and all that I am are His for the asking.

I am the salt of the earth—the spice that brings God's goodness to every element of my environment. I will not lose my saltiness by giving in to the world and throwing aside the principles of the kingdom.

This, my declaration, shall remain and I shall continue as a disciple of the Lord!

(Matthew 5:13; 10:37-39; 16:24; 19:27; Mark 8:34; Luke 9:23; 2 Timothy 3:12; Proverbs 24:27; Hebrews 10:23,35-11:1)

LUKE 14:33B

──────── *DECLARATION OF FAITH* ────────

I have ears to hear and a heart to understand the Word of God. The Holy Spirit reveals to me all of its mysteries and intimate secrets.

(Luke 8:10; Matthew 13:15,16; John 16:13; 1 John 2:20; 1 Corinthians 14:2,13)

LUKE 15:20 NIV

So he got up and went to his father. But while he was still a long way off, his father saw him and was filled with compassion for him; he ran to his son, threw his arms around him and kissed him.

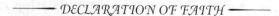

──────── *DECLARATION OF FAITH* ────────

My Father runs to embrace me every time I turn to Him. His love for me is stronger than any sin I can commit.

(Psalm 103:13; Jeremiah 3:12-14; Matthew 9:36; Acts 2:39; Ephesians 2:4,5,13,17)

LUKE 15:22-24 KJV

But the father said to his servants, Bring forth the best robe, and put *it* on him; and put a ring on his hand, and shoes on *his* feet: And bring hither the fatted calf, and kill *it;* and let us eat, and be merry: For this my son was dead, and is alive again; he was lost, and is found. And they began to be merry.

──────── *DECLARATION OF FAITH* ────────

Whenever I turn to my Father in repentance, He immediately dresses me in the festive robe of honor (the robe of His righteousness). He doesn't just put clothes on me, but adorns me in the finest of apparel.

He then has the signet ring placed upon my finger and reinstates me to my position of authority as His son/daughter.

He has shoes placed upon my feet so that I am well prepared to expand the borders of His kingdom.

He breaks out the fatted calf (that tremendous supply of the new covenant where there is enough to spare and to share) and bids me to take my fill in great joy and gladness.

All of the angels of God come together to rejoice with us, for the power of death has been broken over my life and I have been reborn into the royal family of almighty God!

(Luke 15:10; Ephesians 2:1-14; Galatians 4:5,6; 2 Corinthians 5:17-21; 8:9; Colossians 2:13)

LUKE 16:9-12 KJV

And I say unto you, Make to yourselves friends of the mammon of unright-eousness; that, when ye fail, they may receive you into everlasting habitations. He that is faithful in that which is least is faithful also in much: and he that is unjust in the least is unjust also in much. If therefore ye have not been faithful in the unrighteous mammon, who will commit to your trust the true *riches?* And if ye have not been faithful in that which is another man's, who shall give you that which is your own?

——— *DECLARATION OF FAITH* ———

By giving for the advancement of the Gospel, I gain new friends for myself who will be with me for all of eternity. I may never meet them on this earth, but one day they will welcome me into their mansions and thank me for what I have done.

When I provide for the needs of a soul-winning ministry, I prove myself to be a soul-winner.

I am faithful to do with my money just as God would have me do. It doesn't matter how little I have, or how great my wealth may be, I am a faithful steward. By proving myself faithful with the riches of the world, I earn true, enduring and incorruptible riches for my heavenly account.

(Philippians 4:14-19; Matthew 25:21; 1 Peter 1:3,4)

LUKE 16:16 KJV

The law and the prophets were until John: since that time the kingdom of God is preached, and every man presseth into it.

——— *DECLARATION OF FAITH* ———

I am a soldier fit for the kingdom of God. I do not lazily go about nonchalantly trying to enter the kingdom. I fully understand that there are forces out there who are doing everything they can to keep me from it. Therefore, I go forth boldly and violently to establish the kingdom of God in my life, tearing down every stronghold of the devil that stands in my way.

(Ephesians 6:10-18; 2 Corinthians 10:4,5; Luke 13:23-29; Matthew 11:12)

LUKE 17:3,4 KJV

Take heed to yourselves: If thy brother trespass against thee, rebuke him; and if he repent, forgive him. And if he trespass against thee seven times in a day, and seven times in a day turn again to thee, saying, I repent; thou shalt forgive him.

——— *DECLARATION OF FAITH* ———

I am ever-alert and prepared to act on the behalf of my brothers and sisters in Christ. I look out for them just as I look out for myself.

I will not allow bitterness and strife to come between us and hinder our prayers or stop the flow of blessings provided in our covenant with God and each other. No matter how many times a brother or sister sins against me, I forgive them. Resentment finds no home in my heart and all offenses against me I con-sider to be annulled, eradicated and expunged from our relationship.

(Psalm 106:29-31; Mark 11:25; Matthew 6:12; 18:15-21; Proverbs 17:10)

LUKE 17:6-10 KJV

And the Lord said, If ye had faith as a grain of mustard seed, ye might say unto this sycamine tree, Be thou plucked up by the root, and be thou planted in the sea; and it should obey you. But which of you, having a servant plowing or feed-ing cattle, will say unto him by and by, when he is come from the field, Go and sit down to meat? And will not rather say unto him, Make ready wherewith I may sup, and gird thyself, and serve me, till I have eaten and drunken; and after-ward thou shalt eat and drink? Doth he thank that servant because he did the things that were commanded him? I trow not. So likewise ye, when ye shall have done all those things which are commanded you, say, We are unprofitable ser-vants: we have done that which was our duty to do.

———— *DECLARATION OF FAITH* ————

I use my faith as if it were a seed. When I speak to a problem and believe that those things that I say are going to come to pass, I shall have the things that I say. It may not look like anything is happening, but the seed of my faith has entered in and is doing its job well.

When I align my words in agreement with the Word of God, whatever I am speaking to must obey my commands.

My faith is a servant to me and it is my duty to use it to bring forth the blessings of the kingdom into the earth.

(Mark 9:23; Matthew 17:20; 11:22-25; John 15:7; 2 Corinthians 4:13; Hebrews 11:1)

LUKE 17:19 NKJV

And He said to him, "Arise, go your way. Your faith has made you well."

———— *DECLARATION OF FAITH* ————

My faith restores me to perfect health. I can get up and go about my business this day free of all sickness.

(Matthew 9:22; Luke 7:50; 8:48; 18:42; Hebrews 11:1; 2 Corinthians 4:13)

LUKE 17:20,21 KJV

And when he was demanded of the Pharisees, when the kingdom of God should come, he answered them and said, The kingdom of God cometh not with observation: Neither shall they say, Lo here! or, lo there! for, behold, the kingdom of God is within you.

The kingdom of God is not something that is coming one day with great signs or a visible display of majesty. No one is going to say, "Look, here is the kingdom!" or "Look up in the clouds, the kingdom is coming!"

The kingdom of God is already here. It is within me and all around me.

(Luke 17:23; Romans 14:17; Matthew 4:17; 6:33; 11:12; 12:28; 13:31-33; 16:19)

LUKE 18:7,8 KJV

And shall not God avenge his own elect, which cry day and night unto him, though he bear long with them? I tell you that he will avenge them speedily. Nevertheless when the Son of man cometh, shall he find faith on the earth?

My heavenly Father never neglects me. He is always with me to guide, defend, and even avenge me. When I call upon Him, He answers. He takes up my cause as His own and honors my faith. I will not let Him down. When Jesus returns, He will find me living by faith in this earth.

(Psalm 3:5,6; 18:1-30; 27:11; 91:15; 2 Corinthians 5:7; Romans 1:17)

LUKE 18:14 KJV

I tell you, this man went down to his house justified rather than the other: for every one that exalteth himself shall be abased; and he that humbleth himself shall be exalted.

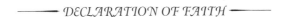

I do not exalt myself before God, bragging and trusting in all of the things that I have done to earn His favor. I know that in and of myself, I am of no great consequence.

Therefore, I humble myself under His mighty hand and rest in the shadow of His mercy and grace. He has forgiven me of all of my sins and has restored me to a right relationship with Himself.

In humility I have been lifted to this place of supreme honor, and by humility I shall remain in this position for all of eternity.

(1 Peter 5:5-7; Proverbs 27:2; Ephesians 1:13,14; 2:4-9; James 4:6-10,13-16)

LUKE 18:22 KJV

Now when Jesus heard these things, he said unto him, Yet lackest thou one thing: sell all that thou hast, and distribute unto the poor, and thou shalt have treasure in heaven: and come, follow me.

——— *DECLARATION OF FAITH* ———

I maintain a spirit of generosity and cheerful giving in my life. It gives me great joy to bless the poor and see their needs being met. By my generosity, I am storing up vast amounts of incorruptible riches in my heavenly account, which I can draw upon at any given moment. What I have given is given back to me with God's own compound interest so that I can give even more the next time. Through my giving, I establish this wonderful covenant of the kingdom in the earth.

(Genesis 12:2,3; Deuteronomy 8:18; 2 Corinthians 9:5-15; Philippians 4:14-19; Luke 6:38)

LUKE 18:27 NKJV

But He said, "The things which are impossible with men are possible with God."

——— *DECLARATION OF FAITH* ———

Everything that is naturally impossible to me has become possible through the Holy Spirit dwelling within me.

(Matthew 17:20; 19:26; Mark 9:23; 10:27; 11:22-25; Luke 1:37; Hebrews 11:1,6)

LUKE 18:29,30 KJV

And he said unto them, Verily I say unto you, There is no man that hath left house, or parents, or brethren, or wife, or children, for the kingdom of God's sake, Who shall not receive manifold more in this present time, and in the world to come life everlasting.

——— *DECLARATION OF FAITH* ———

I have given my all to Jesus. I have willingly set aside and given up (if needs be) all that I am and all that I have in order to follow Him and live the kingdom life.

This new life that I have chosen so magnifies my present provisions that it is breathtaking. Right now, in this life, I have exceedingly and abundantly more houses, material things, brothers, sisters, mothers and fathers than what I have left behind, and over and above all this, I have eternal life.

(Deuteronomy 33:9; Job 42:10; Romans 4:16-21; Matthew 19:16-30)

LUKE 18:39-42 KJV

And they which went before rebuked him, that he should hold his peace: but he cried so much the more, *Thou* Son of David, have mercy on me. And Jesus stood, and commanded him to be brought unto him: and when he was come near, he asked him, Saying, What wilt thou that I shall do unto thee? And he said, Lord, that I may receive my sight. And Jesus said unto him, Receive thy sight: thy faith hath saved thee.

DECLARATION OF FAITH

I know where the source of life's power is and I recognize my total and complete dependency upon Him in every way. Without His mercy and grace, I am nothing.

Therefore, I will call upon the Lord in total dependence and confidence in His mercy. I draw near to Him in respect, calling on His name and receiving by faith those specific things that are provided for me in our covenant.

(Ephesians 1:17-23; James 4:6-10; Psalm 16:2; 91:1,2,15; Deuteronomy 28:1-14))

LUKE 20:35,36 KJV

But they which shall be accounted worthy to obtain that world, and the resurrection from the dead, neither marry, nor are given in marriage: Neither can they die any more: for they are equal unto the angels; and are the children of God, being the children of the resurrection.

DECLARATION OF FAITH

I am considered worthy (being made so by God) to be a partaker of the benefits of the kingdom and to be raised to eternal life.

I am a son/daughter of God and a sharer in the Resurrection of Jesus.

(Hebrews 10:14; Philippians 3:11; 1 John 3:1,2; Romans 8:23; Ephesians 1:3; 2:4-10)

LUKE 21:8 KJV

And he said, Take heed that ye be not deceived: for many shall come in my name, saying, I am Christ; and the time draweth near: go ye not therefore after them.

I am constantly on guard against deception and I am careful not to be led astray from the Truth. I do not follow false messiahs or those who are always proclaiming that the time is at hand. When the time comes, I will be ready and rejoice, but until then, I've got work to do.

(1 Corinthians 15:58; John 10:7-14; Matthew 24:4; Mark 13:5)

LUKE 21:12-15 KJV

But before all these, they shall lay their hands on you, and persecute *you*, delivering *you* up to the synagogues, and into prisons, being brought before kings and rulers for my name's sake. And it shall turn to you for a testimony. Settle *it* therefore in your hearts, not to meditate before what ye shall answer: For I will give you a mouth and wisdom, which all your adversaries shall not be able to gainsay nor resist.

──── *DECLARATION OF FAITH* ────

I see persecution as a time of opportunity to display the wisdom and majesty of my heavenly Father.

I do not foolishly spend my time meditating on persecution, nor do I retaliate against it in anger, or prepare some grand defense. I remain calm, standing still and giving full recognition to the greater One who is within me. He is always here (within me) to give me such wisdom that all of my foes combined are unable to stand against it.

(Exodus 14:13,14; Job 37:14; 1 John 4:4; 1 Corinthians 1:30; Matthew 5:10-16)

LUKE 21:17-19 KJV

And ye shall be hated of all *men* for my name's sake. But there shall not an hair of your head perish. In your patience possess ye your souls.

──── *DECLARATION OF FAITH* ────

I am not concerned by the hatred that comes my way because of my love and devotion to Jesus. I know that not a hair on my head will perish, for I have God's unfailing Word that He will protect me at all times.

By my steadfast and patient endurance I win vitality for my soul.

(Romans 1:16; Psalm 91; Exodus 23:20-23; Matthew 10:22,30)

LUKE 21:33 KJV

Heaven and earth shall pass away: but my words shall not pass away.

——— *DECLARATION OF FAITH* ———

Even if the earth and sky were to pass away, God's Word would still remain and ring true in my life.

(Matthew 24:35; Isaiah 40:8; 55:11; Psalm 119:89,90)

LUKE 21:34-36 KJV

And take heed to yourselves, lest at any time your hearts be overcharged with surfeiting, and drunkenness, and cares of this life, and so that day come upon you unawares. For as a snare shall it come on all them that dwell on the face of the whole earth. Watch ye therefore, and pray always, that ye may be accounted worthy to escape all these things that shall come to pass, and to stand before the Son of man.

——— *DECLARATION OF FAITH* ———

I remain alert and vigilant at all times, praying in faith and proclaiming the present reality of the full strength and ability that my Father has placed within me to overcome depression, self-indulgence, insobriety and the worldly worries and cares that pertain to the business of this life. By the power of God within me, I shall stand worthy in the presence of the Son of Man on the day of His coming.

(Philippians 4:13; Jude 24; 1 Thessalonians 5:6; Luke 8:14; Matthew 24:42; 25:13)

LUKE 22:19,20 KJV

And he took bread, and gave thanks, and brake *it*, and gave unto them, saying, This is my body which is given for you: this do in remembrance of me. Likewise also the cup after supper, saying, This cup *is* the new testament in my blood, which is shed for you.

——— *DECLARATION OF FAITH* ———

I regularly take communion—breaking unleavened bread in remembrance of Jesus' body, which was given for me, and drinking the blood of the grape in remembrance of His blood, which was shed for me.

In remembering, I fully understand that His blood ratifies and seals my part in the new covenant. I will not dishonor my Lord by not partaking of the provisions of the covenant that He paid such an awesome price to provide.

(1 Corinthians 11:23-30; Galatians 3:15-4:6; Ephesians 1:3-14; Hebrews 8:6; 10:29)

LUKE 22:26 KJV

But ye shall not be so: but he that is greatest among you, let him be as the younger; and he that is chief, as he that doth serve.

——— *DECLARATION OF FAITH* ———

I do not vie for lordship in the body of Christ. Even in leadership, I lead as one who serves. I am one among many equals and refuse to think of myself as being better than anyone else.

(1 Peter 5:3; Luke 9:48; Philippians 2:4-11; 1 Corinthians 13:5; Matthew 20:20-28)

LUKE 22:29 KJV

And I appoint unto you a kingdom, as my Father hath appointed unto me.

——— *DECLARATION OF FAITH* ———

My Father conferred the kingdom upon Jesus and He, in turn, has conferred it upon me with all of the rights and privileges that come with it.

(Ephesians 1:17-23; 2:4-14; Galatians 4:5,6; Matthew 24:47; Luke 12:32)

LUKE 22:35,36 KJV

And he said unto them, When I sent you without purse, and scrip, and shoes, lacked ye any thing? And they said, Nothing. Then said he unto them, But now, he that hath a purse, let him take *it*, and likewise *his* scrip: and he that hath no sword, let him sell his garment, and buy one.

——— *DECLARATION OF FAITH* ———

No matter what the circumstance may be, I have all the provision that I need to live the kingdom life and carry out my commission in this earth.

It is a good thing for me to have a surplus of money with plenty to spare for the advancement of the kingdom. God is not against me having money—He is against money having me.

It is also good that I be violent, expertly wielding the Sword of the Spirit (the Word), when I am confronted with the many obstacles and ambushes the enemy sets against me.

(Philippians 4:19; Mark 16:15-20; Matthew 11:12; 28:18-20; 2 Corinthians 9:6-8; Deuteronomy 8:18; Ephesians 6:17)

Luke 22:40,41 KJV

And when he was at the place, he said unto them, Pray that ye enter not into temptation. And he was withdrawn from them about a stone's cast, and kneeled down, and prayed.

———— *DECLARATION OF FAITH* ————

I find myself a place, free of all distraction, where I can go to pray and fellowship with my heavenly Father, and I go there regularly and consistently so that temptation does not bear its detestable fruit in my life.

(Mark 1:35; 6:46; 14:32-42; Matthew 6:6; Luke 4:42; 5:16; 6:12; 9:10; Ephesians 6:18)

Luke 22:42 KJV

Saying, Father, if thou be willing, remove this cup from me: nevertheless not my will, but thine, be done.

———— *DECLARATION OF FAITH* ————

I pray above all things that God's will be done in my life.

(Matthew 6:10; John 4:34; 5:30; 6:38; 8:29; James 4:15; 1 John 5:14,15)

Luke 22:43 NKJV

Then an angel appeared to Him from heaven, strengthening Him.

———— *DECLARATION OF FAITH* ————

I have angels all around me who minister to me and strengthen me in spirit so that I can do those things that God has called me to do.

(Hebrews 1:14; Psalm 91:11; Exodus 23:20-23; Matthew 18:10; 26:53)

Luke 24:45 KJV

Then opened he their understanding, that they might understand the scriptures.

———— *DECLARATION OF FAITH* ————

Jesus has become my wisdom. He has thoroughly unveiled the Scriptures to my mind so that I can perceive, apprehend, and understand to do all that is written therein.

(1 Corinthians 1:30; 2:6-16; Ephesians 1:17; Colossians 1:9,10; 1 John 2:14,20; Joshua 1:8)

CHAPTER FORTY-THREE

JOHN

Some of the most extraordinary promises in the entire Bible are found in the book of John. The book was written sometime during John's stay in Ephesus between AD 66-98. The words life, love, light, darkness, know, truth and believe are recurrent throughout the book. John is said to be the beloved. He is the one who rested his head on Jesus' chest. He arguably knew Jesus better than any other disciple. It is not surprising then that he is the one author who spends five chapters on what Jesus shared with the disciples in the Upper Room. The promises found in those chapters are profound to say the least. These are the promises of our mansions in heaven, our mission to do the same works that Jesus did, our fellowship with the Holy Spirit, our friendship with Jesus and our oneness with the Father.

As you pray these promises, be aware that you are now in God and God is in you. You are one with the Creator of the universe!

JOHN 1:3,4 KJV

All things were made by him; and without him was not any thing made that was made. In him was life; and the life was the light of men.

—— DECLARATION OF FAITH ——

Jesus is my Creator who has fashioned me into His own image and likeness.
I came into existence through Him, and without Him, I am nothing.
In Him, I have life and His life within me illuminates my soul.

(2 Corinthians 5:17; Romans 8:29; Ephesians 2:10; 1 John 5:11)

JOHN 1:12,13 NKJV

But as many as received Him, to them He gave the right to become children of God, to those who believe in His name: who were born, not of blood, nor of the will of the flesh, nor of the will of man, but of God.

—— *DECLARATION OF FAITH* ——

I have received Jesus as my own Lord and personal Savior. I have put my complete trust and confidence in His name. I have welcomed Him into my heart and have given Him free reign over my life.

He, in turn, has given me the right and the privilege to become an actual son/daughter of God. I have been born of God through spiritual regeneration. I was born as out of the womb of the Spirit through the living Word. I am a genuine son/daughter of almighty God!

(1 Peter 1:4,23; John 3:3-8; Romans 8:29; 10:8-10; Galatians 4:5,6; Titus 3:4-7; 1 John 5:1-5)

JOHN 1:16-18 KJV

And of his fulness have all we received, and grace for grace. For the law was given by Moses, *but* grace and truth came by Jesus Christ. No man hath seen God at any time; the only begotten Son, which is in the bosom of the Father, he hath declared *him.*

—— *DECLARATION OF FAITH* ——

Out of my Lord Jesus' abundance I have received grace upon grace, mercy upon mercy, favor upon favor, blessing upon blessing, and gift upon gift. Everything that pertains to this new life that He has given me has been heaped upon me in a shower of abundance.

I am now a partaker of His grace and truth. God's favor has been granted to me permanently and without condition. This favor gives me divine enabling to do all that I have been called to do and receive all that I have been called to receive.

Jesus has introduced me to our Father, making Him known to me in such an intimate way that in all that I do I perceive and understand His will, His love, His power, His wisdom, and His kindness towards me.

(Ephesians 1:3-22; Colossians 1:9-14; James 1:5; 2 Peter 1:2-9; 1 Corinthians 2:6-16; John 14:9; 17:6-11)

JOHN 1:29 NIV

The next day John saw Jesus coming toward him and said, "Look, the Lamb of God, who takes away the sin of the world!"

Jesus is the Lamb of God who took away all of my sin.

(Revelation 5:6-14; 12:11; 1 Peter 1:19; 2:24; John 1:36)

JOHN 2:11 NKJV

This beginning of signs Jesus did in Cana of Galilee, and manifested His glory; and His disciples believed in Him.

Jesus displays His greatness and power openly in my life. I rely on Him completely and believe in Him with all of my heart.

(Mark 16:20; Acts 4:33; Ephesians 1:17-23; Colossians 1:29; Romans 10:8,9)

JOHN 2:23 AMP

But when He was in Jerusalem during the Passover Feast, many believed in His name [identified themselves with His party] after seeing His signs (wonders, miracles) which He was doing.

I believe in the name of Jesus and I am recognized as one of His followers. In and through me, He performs many signs, wonders and miracles.

(Acts 4:30,33; 19:15; Mark 16:20; Matthew 28:18-20; Colossians 1:29)

JOHN 3:3 KJV

Jesus answered and said unto him, Verily, verily, I say unto thee, Except a man be born again, he cannot see the kingdom of God.

I am born of God, renewed, and made to be a partaker of His divine nature. I have every right to know and experience the kingdom of God in my life.

(2 Peter 1:4; Galatians 4:5,6; Matthew 13:31-33; Luke 12:32; 17:20,21)

JOHN 3:5 KJV

Jesus answered, Verily, verily, I say unto thee, Except a man be born of water and of the Spirit, he cannot enter into the kingdom of God.

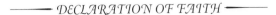

I have been born of the Spirit and have entered the kingdom of God.

(John 1:12,13; 3:8; Galatians 4:29; Titus 3:5; 2 Corinthians 5:17; 1 Peter 1:23; 1 John 5:1)

JOHN 3:12 NKJV

If I have told you earthly things and you do not believe, how will you believe if I tell you heavenly things?

——— *DECLARATION OF FAITH* ———

I know and believe in Jesus and His Word, and I have every ability to know and understand the things of God.

(Romans 10:8,9; 1 Corinthians 2:6-16; 1 John 2:20; 5:20; Matthew 13:15,16)

JOHN 3:14-21 KJV

And as Moses lifted up the serpent in the wilderness, even so must the Son of man be lifted up: That whosoever believeth in him should not perish, but have eternal life. For God so loved the world, that he gave his only begotten Son, that whosoever believeth in him should not perish, but have everlasting life. For God sent not his Son into the world to condemn the world; but that the world through him might be saved. He that believeth on him is not condemned: but he that believeth not is condemned already, because he hath not believed in the name of the only begotten Son of God. And this is the condemnation, that light is come into the world, and men loved darkness rather than light, because their deeds were evil. For every one that doeth evil hateth the light, neither cometh to the light, lest his deeds should be reproved. But he that doeth truth cometh to the light, that his deeds may be made manifest, that they are wrought in God.

——— *DECLARATION OF FAITH* ———

Jesus was lifted up on the cross for my sake so that I may have eternal life. God looked down across the ages, saw me, took pity on my spiritually dead condition, and so dearly loved me that He gave His only begotten Son, Jesus, so that I would not perish, but have everlasting life.

God did not send Jesus into the world in order to judge or pass sentence on me, but that I might be saved through Him and become His own child.

I believe in Jesus with all of my heart.

I shall never be judged, rejected, or condemned.

I have been set free from damnation and every curse.

The Light has come into the world and I have loved the Light. Let all of my deeds be exposed and reproved! Let all of my wrongdoing be erased by the blood of the Lamb!

I am one who practices truth. Let all of my works be plainly shown to be what they are. May all who see any greatness in me give glory to God, for it is He who does the works and my dependence rests entirely upon Him.

(Ephesians 1:4; 2:1-10; 2 Thessalonians 2:13; Romans 5:6-21; 10:8-10; Galatians 2:20,21; 3:13; 4:5,6; John 5:24; Revelation 2:11; James 1:22-25; Colossians 1:29)

JOHN 3:27 NKJV

John answered and said, "A man can receive nothing unless it has been given to him from heaven."

——— DECLARATION OF FAITH ———

I can receive nothing that has not been granted to me from heaven. Ultimately, there is no other source of supply.

It is God who has made me what I am. Every good gift that I have comes from my heavenly Father.

(Psalm 16:2; James 1:17; Philippians 4:19; Genesis 22:14)

JOHN 3:29,30 NKJV

He who has the bride is the bridegroom; but the friend of the bridegroom, who stands and hears him, rejoices greatly because of the bridegroom's voice. Therefore this joy of mine is fulfilled. He must increase, but I must decrease.

——— DECLARATION OF FAITH ———

I listen intently to the words of Jesus and my heart greatly rejoices in the sound of His voice. I have given Him free reign to increase within me and take over the lordship of my life. He has become the chief executive who guides me in all that I set my hand to do.

(John 10:3,4,7-16,26-28; Proverbs 3:5,6; Romans 10:8-10; Deuteronomy 28:12)

JOHN 3:34,35 KJV

For he whom God hath sent speaketh the words of God: for God giveth not the Spirit by measure *unto him.* The Father loveth the Son, and hath given all things into his hand.

God has sent me into the world to proclaim His own message—the good news of the kingdom. He does not give me His Spirit sparingly, but fills me to overflowing with Himself.

My Father's love has been poured out upon me. He has entrusted all things into the hand of Jesus and Jesus, in turn, has made me an ambassador on His behalf.

(2 Corinthians 5:18-20; Ephesians 1:17-23; 5:18; Matthew 28:18-20)

JOHN 3:36 AMP

And he who believes in (has faith in, clings to, relies on) the Son has (now possesses) eternal life. But whoever disobeys (is unbelieving toward, refuses to trust in, disregards, is not subject to) the Son will never see (experience) life, but [instead] the wrath of God abides on him. [God's displeasure remains on him; His indignation hangs over him continually.]

——— DECLARATION OF FAITH ———

I believe in Jesus with all of my heart and right now, this very minute, I have eternal life. I shall never be condemned or experience God's wrath.

(John 3:16,17; 5:24; Romans 5:1,2; 1 John 5:11,12)

JOHN 4:10 NKJV

Jesus answered and said to her, "If you knew the gift of God, and who it is who says to you, 'Give Me a drink,' you would have asked Him, and He would have given you living water."

——— DECLARATION OF FAITH ———

I know Jesus and I recognize God's gift to me.
I have become a partaker of the living water.

(Romans 5:15-17; Ephesians 2:8-10; 1 John 2:3; 5:10; John 7:38,39)

JOHN 4:13,14 KJV

Jesus answered and said unto her, Whosoever drinketh of this water shall thirst again: But whosoever drinketh of the water that I shall give him shall never thirst; but the water that I shall give him shall be in him a well of water springing up into everlasting life.

———— DECLARATION OF FAITH ————

I have drunk the full measure of the living water. I shall never thirst again. The living water that Jesus has given me has become a spring of water welling up continually within me unto eternal life.

(John 6:35,58; 7:38,39; Ephesians 5:18; Acts 1:5,8)

JOHN 4:23,24 NKJV

"But the hour is coming, and now is, when the true worshipers will worship the Father in spirit and truth; for the Father is seeking such to worship Him. God is Spirit, and those who worship Him must worship in spirit and truth."

———— DECLARATION OF FAITH ————

I am a genuine worshipper of my heavenly Father.

He sought me out and has called me to fellowship with Him in an actual Father and son/daughter relationship.

I make my contact with Him through my spirit. As spiritual beings, we fellowship with each other in spirit and reality.

(Matthew 18:20; Hebrews 13:10-14; Philippians 3:3; John 1:17; 2 Corinthians 3:17)

JOHN 4:34-38 KJV

Jesus saith unto them, My meat is to do the will of him that sent me, and to finish his work. Say not ye, There are yet four months, and *then* cometh harvest? behold, I say unto you, Lift up your eyes, and look on the fields; for they are white already to harvest. And he that reapeth receiveth wages, and gathereth fruit unto life eternal: that both he that soweth and he that reapeth may rejoice together. And herein is that saying true, One soweth, and another reapeth. I sent you to reap that whereon ye bestowed no labour: other men laboured, and ye are entered into their labours.

———— DECLARATION OF FAITH ————

My fulfillment in life is to do the will of my heavenly Father and to accomplish what He has called me to do.

I have become a reaper in the harvest fields of the Lord. There are multitudes that cannot be counted who are ready to receive the Gospel and I am called to proclaim it to them.

I neither plant nor tend the crop. The time of planting and tending is over—the fields are already white unto harvest. My purpose is to reap souls into the kingdom.

(Psalm 40:7,8; Matthew 9:37,38; Luke 10:2; 2 Corinthians 5:18-20; Proverbs 11:30)

JOHN 4:50 AMP

Jesus answered him, Go in peace; your son will live! And the man put his trust in what Jesus said and started home.

——— *DECLARATION OF FAITH* ———

The Word of the Lord has been given and I believe it without exception, compromise or wavering. It is settled and accomplished in my life.

(James 1:6-8; Isaiah 55:11; Psalm 107:20; 119:89-93)

JOHN 5:14 NIV

Later Jesus found him at the temple and said to him, "See, you are well again. Stop sinning or something worse may happen to you."

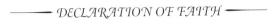

——— *DECLARATION OF FAITH* ———

In Jesus, I have been made well. I will not dishonor Him by continuing in sin and thus leaving the door opened for the devil to attack me with another wave of his foul sicknesses.

(Isaiah 53:4,5; 1 Peter 2:24; Matthew 8:17; James 4:7,8; 5:14-16)

JOHN 5:17 NKJV

But Jesus answered them, "My Father has been working until now, and I have been working."

——— *DECLARATION OF FAITH* ———

My heavenly Father has never ceased to do His work. Even today He is performing mighty miracles in this world and He has honored me with the privilege of working together with Him.

(Philippians 2:13; Colossians 1:29; Mark 16:20; Hebrews 13:8)

JOHN 5:19-30 KJV

Then answered Jesus and said unto them, Verily, verily, I say unto you, The Son can do nothing of himself, but what he seeth the Father do: for what things soever he doeth, these also doeth the Son likewise. For the Father loveth the Son, and sheweth him all things that himself doeth: and he will shew him greater works than these, that ye may marvel. For as the Father raiseth up the dead, and quickeneth *them;* even so the Son quickeneth whom he will. For the Father judgeth no man, but hath committed all judgment unto the Son: That all *men* should honour the Son, even as they honour the Father. He that honoureth not the Son honoureth not the Father which hath sent him. Verily, verily, I say unto you, He that heareth my word, and believeth on him that sent me, hath everlasting life, and shall not come into condemnation; but is passed from death unto life. Verily, verily, I say unto you, The hour is coming, and now is, when the dead shall hear the voice of the Son of God: and they that hear shall live. For as the Father hath life in himself; so hath he given to the Son to have life in himself; And hath given him authority to execute judgment also, because he is the Son of man. Marvel not at this: for the hour is coming, in the which all that are in the graves shall hear his voice, And shall come forth; they that have done good, unto the resurrection of life; and they that have done evil, unto the resurrection of damnation. I can of mine own self do nothing: as I hear, I judge: and my judgment is just; because I seek not mine own will, but the will of the Father which hath sent me.

———— DECLARATION OF FAITH ————

I can do no divine work in and of myself. Without God, I am nothing. Yet, with Him, nothing is impossible for me. He has left me His Word and His example, and has instructed me to do all things in the exact same way that He does. With Him as my Guide and master instructor, I am destined to do great things.

My heavenly Father dearly loves me and regularly shows me what I must do in this earth. He shall continue to do things in and through me that fill the heart with wonder and astonishment.

By the blood and will of Jesus, I have eternal life. I have taken my stand with Him as a covenant partner. Through me, He still raises the dead and gives them life.

I am entirely in the hands of Jesus and I shall never be condemned or experience the wrath of God.

I honor Jesus and pay Him homage, just as I do our Father.

My ears have been opened to receive the Word of God with understanding and I have put my total trust and reliance on the power of my heavenly Father to fulfill it in my life.

Right now, this very minute, I know that I possess eternal life. The sentence of my judgment was placed upon Jesus. I shall never come into condemnation, for I have already passed over from death into life.

Jesus became what I was so that I could become what He is. He is my Lord and my Redeemer and I am identified with Him in every way.

Like Jesus, I have been raised to a new life. I now practice good.

Of myself, I am able to do nothing. All that I do for the kingdom is wrought in and through God. I do all that He teaches me and, as a good soldier and son/daughter, I am quick to obey my orders. I do not make a single decision apart from His counsel. All of my judgments are just and right, because I do not seek my own will and purpose, but the will and purpose of my Father in heaven.

(John 3:16,17; 14:12; 16:13; Ephesians 2:4-10; 5:1; Proverbs 3:5,6; Psalm 27:11; Hebrews 8:6; Mark 16:15-20; Romans 8:1,29,30; Deuteronomy 6:5-7; Matthew 6:10; 13:15,16; Isaiah 55:11; Colossians 1:13; 1 John 5:11; Galatians 2:20,21; Philippians 2:13; James 4:13-16)

JOHN 5:41-44 KJV

I receive not honour from men. But I know you, that ye have not the love of God in you. I am come in my Father's name, and ye receive me not: if another shall come in his own name, him ye will receive. How can ye believe, which receive honour one of another, and seek not the honour that *cometh* from God only?

——— *DECLARATION OF FAITH* ———

I have no need for the glory and honor that comes from men.

The love of God has been shed abroad in my heart and I pursue those things that bring glory to His name. It is my desire to receive the praise, honor and glory, which come from He who alone is my God.

I am a member of the very family of God. I am His own son/daughter, called by His name. His power flows in me and through me. When people receive me, they receive my Father. When people reject me, they reject my Father.

(1 Thessalonians 2:6; Romans 5:5; 1 John 3:1,2; Colossians 1:29; Ephesians 1:17-23; Mark 9:37; Luke 9:48)

JOHN 6:27-29 KJV

Labour not for the meat which perisheth, but for that meat which endureth unto everlasting life, which the Son of man shall give unto you: for him hath God the Father sealed. Then said they unto him, What shall we do, that we might work the works of God?

I do not waste effort trying to produce food that perishes, but strive to produce the food that endures unto eternal life. Jesus has given me plentiful provision of such food out of His abundance.

All that is required for me to habitually do the works of God is to believe in Jesus with a steadfast and unshakable trust, for belief is the channel that brings all of God's blessings into my life.

(Matthew 6:19-33; John 4:14; Philippians 4:19; 2 Corinthians 4:13; Hebrews 11:1,6; Mark 9:23; 11:22-25)

JOHN 6:35 NKJV

And Jesus said to them, "I am the bread of life. He who comes to Me shall never hunger, and he who believes in Me shall never thirst."

——— DECLARATION OF FAITH ———

Jesus is the Bread of Life to me. I cling to Him with all of my heart. Because of Him, I will never hunger or thirst again.

(John 4:14; 6:48,58; 7:37,38; Isaiah 55:1,2; 1 Corinthians 11:23-26)

JOHN 6:37-40 KJV

All that the Father giveth me shall come to me; and him that cometh to me I will in no wise cast out. For I came down from heaven, not to do mine own will, but the will of him that sent me. And this is the Father's will which hath sent me, that of all which he hath given me I should lose nothing, but should raise it up again at the last day. And this is the will of him that sent me, that every one which seeth the Son, and believeth on him, may have everlasting life: and I will raise him up at the last day.

——— DECLARATION OF FAITH ———

My heavenly Father has entrusted my eternal security to Jesus. I have turned to Him and pledged my endless devotion. He has given me His Word that He will find absolutely no reason to reject me. Because I have come to Him and have given Him my life, I never have need to fear again.

Jesus continually does the will of the Father on my behalf.

This is the Father's will: that I should never be lost again.

I have been given new life and shall be raised up on the Last Day.

Jesus is the Good Shepherd of my life. He will not allow me to stray from the flock and be devoured by the wolves.

I am now a child of God. I believe in Jesus with all of my heart. The security of my eternal life rests in His mighty power to see me through.

(Ephesians 1:13,14; Romans 8:1; 10:8-10; 2 Timothy 1:7; John 10:7-18; Jude 23; Galatians 4:5,6)

JOHN 6:45-51 KJV

It is written in the prophets, And they shall be all taught of God. Every man therefore that hath heard, and hath learned of the Father, cometh unto me. Not that any man hath seen the Father, save he which is of God, he hath seen the Father. Verily, verily, I say unto you, He that believeth on me hath everlasting life. I am that bread of life. Your fathers did eat manna in the wilderness, and are dead. This is the bread which cometh down from heaven, that a man may eat thereof, and not die. I am the living bread which came down from heaven: if any man eat of this bread, he shall live for ever: and the bread that I will give is my flesh, which I will give for the life of the world.

———— DECLARATION OF FAITH ————

I am taught of God. He is my personal mentor, instructor, and overseer. As my Guide in life, He has led me to Jesus and made me realize my dependence upon Him.

In Jesus, I have eternal life. He is the very Bread of Life to me. The bread that He has given me is His own body, which He gave for my life. I now have the certainty that I will live forever with my Lord in heaven, and there isn't a thing that the devil can do about it.

(John 6:35; 16:13; 1 John 2:20; 5:11; 1 Corinthians 11:23-26; Colossians 2:13-15)

JOHN 6:54-58 KJV

Whoso eateth my flesh, and drinketh my blood, hath eternal life; and I will raise him up at the last day. For my flesh is meat indeed, and my blood is drink indeed. He that eateth my flesh, and drinketh my blood, dwelleth in me, and I in him. As the living Father hath sent me, and I live by the Father: so he that eateth me, even he shall live by me. This is that bread which came down from heaven: not as your fathers did eat manna, and are dead: he that eateth of this bread shall live for ever.

I have fed upon Jesus' flesh and drunk of His blood. By them, I now have eternal life, and I shall be raised up on the Last Day; for His flesh is true and genuine sustenance for me, and His blood is true and genuine refreshment for me.

I dwell continually with and in Jesus, and He dwells continually with and in me.

He is always there for me to fill me with spiritual sustenance and I find in Him all the nourishment that I need for life. Because of Him, I shall enjoy eternal life forevermore.

(John 1:12; 3:16; 17:20-26; 1 Corinthians 11:23-26; 1 John 5:11)

JOHN 6:63

The Spirit can make life. Sheer muscle and willpower don't make anything happen. Every word I've spoken to you is a Spirit-word, and so it is life-making.

The spirit is what quickens things and brings them to life. The flesh does not renew or prevail over anything of lasting value.

God quickened me into this new life by the Spirit, through the living Word. My spirit has been renewed and recreated with the very nature of God.

I fully understand that the Word of God is spirit material. In the same way that Jesus used His words to bring things to life, I use His words to bring things to life as well.

(1 Peter 1:4,23; Proverbs 18:20,21; John 14:12; 15:7; 2 Corinthians 4:13; Mark 11:22-25; Hebrews 11:1; Matthew 8:5-10; 21:19-22)

JOHN 7:15-18 KJV

And the Jews marvelled, saying, How knoweth this man letters, having never learned? Jesus answered them, and said, My doctrine is not mine, but his that sent me. If any man will do his will, he shall know of the doctrine, whether it be of God, or *whether* I speak of myself. He that speaketh of himself seeketh his own glory: but he that seeketh his glory that sent him, the same is true, and no unrighteousness is in him.

Regardless of my education, I have wisdom that is astonishing to those outside of the kingdom of God. Jesus Himself has actually become my wisdom. The One dwelling within me has anointed my mind.

It is my deepest desire to do the will of my Father. Therefore, He has given me a direct revelation of His Word, His will, and His purpose for my life.

I seek to win honor for my heavenly Father in all that I do. His Truth is revealed in and through me. In me, there is no unrighteousness, falsehood, or deception.

(Daniel 1:4,17,20; 2:22,23; 1 Corinthians 1:30; 2:6-16; 1 John 2:20; James 4:13-17; Matthew 13:15,16; Romans 14:17; John 8:50; 1 Peter 3:10-12)

JOHN 7:37-39 KJV

In the last day, that great *day* of the feast, Jesus stood and cried, saying, If any man thirst, let him come unto me, and drink. He that believeth on me, as the scripture hath said, out of his belly shall flow rivers of living water. (But this spake he of the Spirit, which they that believe on him should receive: for the Holy Ghost was not yet *given;* because that Jesus was not yet glorified.)

DECLARATION OF FAITH

I have come to Jesus and have drunk deeply of His provision.

He gives me not only that which refreshes, but that which replenishes as well.

He has sent the Holy Spirit Himself to dwell within my own spirit to produce rivers of living water which both plentifully and constantly flow forth from me. His currents overwhelm and drown out all doubts and fears, and the fountain of His waters brings forth a shower of blessings into my life.

(Philippians 4:19; Isaiah 12:3; 43:20; 44:3; 55:1; Deuteronomy 18:15; James 3:11,12)

JOHN 8:12 NKJV

Then Jesus spoke to them again, saying, "I am the light of the world. He who follows Me shall not walk in darkness, but have the light of life."

DECLARATION OF FAITH

Jesus is the Light of my life. I no longer walk in darkness, but have His illumination and enlightenment to guide me.

(1 John 1:5-7; John 1:4; 9:5; 12:35; 1 Thessalonians 5:5)

JOHN 8:19 KJV

Then said they unto him, Where is thy Father? Jesus answered, Ye neither know me, nor my Father: if ye had known me, ye should have known my Father also.

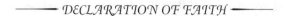

——— *DECLARATION OF FAITH* ———

Jesus has brought me into an intimate relationship with Himself. He is my friend, my Lord, my Savior, and my brother. I both know Him and am known by Him.

I know our Father intimately as well. He is my dad (Abba) and is ever-watching over me.

(1 John 1:3; 2:3-5; John 14:7; 16:3; 1 Corinthians 1:9)

JOHN 8:23 AMP

He said to them, You are from below; I am from above. You are of this world (of this earthly order); I am not of this world.

——— *DECLARATION OF FAITH* ———

I am not of this world, nor do I live according to this earthly order of things. Since I have been born from above, I live according to the spiritual order that my heavenly Father lives by.

(John 3:31; 4:23,24; 6:63; 17:14; 1 John 4:4-6; Galatians 5:16,25)

JOHN 8:26 NIV

"I have much to say in judgment of you. But he who sent me is reliable, and what I have heard from him I tell the world."

——— *DECLARATION OF FAITH* ———

My heavenly Father is true and trustworthy in all that He says and does. When I believe and speak His Word, it is destined to manifest itself in my life.

(Psalm 119:138,140; Isaiah 55:11; 2 Corinthians 4:13; Mark 11:22-25)

JOHN 8:28,29 KJV

Then said Jesus unto them, When ye have lifted up the Son of man, then shall ye know that I am *he,* and *that* I do nothing of myself; but as my Father hath taught me, I speak these things. And he that sent me is with me: the Father hath not left me alone; for I do always those things that please him.

——— *DECLARATION OF FAITH* ———

I continually walk in the ways of my heavenly Father and He looks upon me with tremendous joy and delight.

In everything that I do and say, I give Him glory.

It is His authority alone that I walk in and not my own.

He is ever with me, working both in and through me, to will and to do His good pleasure.

(Ephesians 5:1-18; Psalm 18:19; John 5:19,30; Luke 10:19; Matthew 28:18-20; Philippians 2:13)

JOHN 8:31,32 NKJV

Then Jesus said to those Jews who believed Him, "If you abide in My word, you are My disciples indeed. And you shall know the truth, and the truth shall make you free."

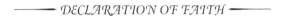

─── *DECLARATION OF FAITH* ───

I am a true disciple of Jesus. I remain focused on His Word, continually meditating upon it, speaking it, and living according to its precepts. I know the Truth and the Truth has made me free.

(Joshua 1:8; Psalm 1:1-3; Ephesians 5:1; John 14:12-15,23; 15:7)

JOHN 8:34-36 KJV

Jesus answered them, Verily, verily, I say unto you, Whosoever committeth sin is the servant of sin. And the servant abideth not in the house for ever: *but* the Son abideth ever. If the Son therefore shall make you free, ye shall be free indeed.

─── *DECLARATION OF FAITH* ───

I understand how sin infects the human nature and separates them from God for all of eternity.

I understand how sin makes a person a slave to its influences and temptations.

I also understand that a slave is not a real and permanent member of the family.

A true son is a real and permanent member of the family. Therefore, since Jesus, the true Son, became my substitute, I have truly been set free! He became identified with my condition, so that I could be identified with His. The Son has set me free! Jesus paid my price and bought me into the family! Sin can no longer hold me in its cruel bondage! I am no longer a slave! I am now a true son/daughter—a real and permanent member of the family of God!

(Ephesians 2:1-19; Romans 6:16-23; 7:24-8:1,16,17; Galatians 4:5,6; 5:1; 1 John 3:1,2)

JOHN 8:39 NKJV

They answered and said to Him, "Abraham is our father." Jesus said to them, "If you were Abraham's children, you would do the works of Abraham."

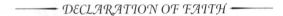

——— *DECLARATION OF FAITH* ———

I have become the seed of Abraham. I follow his example and I am blessed in the same ways that He was blessed.

(Galatians 3:6-18; Hebrews 11:1,6,8-10,17-19; Genesis 12:1-3,16; 13:2,6; 15:1,6; 17:1,2,6-9; 24:35; Mark 11:22-25)

JOHN 8:42,43 NKJV

Jesus said to them, "If God were your Father, you would love Me, for I proceeded forth and came from God; nor have I come of Myself, but He sent Me. Why do you not understand My speech? Because you are not able to listen to My word."

——— *DECLARATION OF FAITH* ———

God is my Father, and I love, respect and gladly welcome my elder brother Jesus into my life. He has made me well able to hear and understand His message. I know what our relationship is and what He has made me to be.

(Hebrews 2:11; Matthew 13:15,16; 2 Corinthians 5:17-21; Ephesians 2:10; John 7:17)

JOHN 8:47 NKJV

"He who is of God hears God's words; therefore you do not hear, because you are not of God."

——— *DECLARATION OF FAITH* ———

I belong to God and listen to what He has to say. His Word is life to me and I hold it forth as my overcoming reality in every circumstance.

(Isaiah 43:1; 55:11; Luke 8:15; John 10:26; 1 John 4:6; Psalm 119:93)

JOHN 8:49-51 KJV

Jesus answered, I have not a devil; but I honour my Father, and ye do dishonour me. And I seek not mine own glory: there is one that seeketh and judgeth. Verily, verily, I say unto you, If a man keep my saying, he shall never see death.

I honor and respect my heavenly Father with a whole heart and every ounce of my will and strength.

I do not try to bring about honor and glory for myself—that is God's business and He is a lot better at it than I am.

It does not concern me when people scorn and despise me for what God is doing in my life. It is He who has judged me in Jesus and declared me to be righteous. If anyone has a problem with it, they will have to take it up with Him.

Because I have held His Word as precious and do those things that He has commanded me to do, He has made His declaration that I will never again experience spiritual death.

(Deuteronomy 6:5-7; 28:1; Psalm 1:1-3; 91:15; 1 Peter 5:6; 2 Corinthians 5:21; Romans 6:9-11; 8:30,33,34; 1 Corinthians 15:56,57)

JOHN 8:54,55 KJV

Jesus answered, If I honour myself, my honour is nothing: it is my Father that honoureth me; of whom ye say, that he is your God: Yet ye have not known him; but I know him: and if I should say, I know him not, I shall be a liar like unto you: but I know him, and keep his saying.

I do not glorify or honor myself, for that kind of honor is worthless. If there is any glory for me, it must come to me from my heavenly Father. And the fact of the matter is, in Jesus, He both honors and glorifies me, and makes my name great.

What a privilege it is to be a born-again child of the living God! I now enjoy an intimate Father and son/daughter relationship with the Lord of the universe! I hold fast to His Word as a precious prize. I know Him as a son/daughter knows a loving father, and I obey Him as an honorable son/daughter obeys his/her father.

(1 Peter 5:6; James 4:6-10; Psalm 91:15; 103:13; 119:162; Genesis 12:1-3; Romans 8:14-17,28-30; John 3:3; Galatians 4:5,6; John 15:10)

JOHN 9:3 NIV

"Neither this man nor his parents sinned," said Jesus, "but this happened so that the work of God might be displayed in his life."

──────── *DECLARATION OF FAITH* ────────

The reasons for the ailments in people's lives are not my chief concern. What I am concerned with is seeing them healed and setting them free.

(Isaiah 61:1-3; 2 Corinthians 5:18-20; Mark 16:15-20; Matthew 28:18-20)

JOHN 9:4,5 NKJV

"I must work the works of Him who sent Me while it is day; the night is coming when no one can work. As long as I am in the world, I am the light of the world."

──────── *DECLARATION OF FAITH* ────────

I am continually about my Father's business—doing the work of Jesus in this earth. In Jesus, I have become the light of the world and it is both my privilege and my duty to continue His work.

(John 1:5,9; 14:12; 17:6-26; 2 Corinthians 5:18-20; Mark 16:15-20; Matthew 28:18-20)

JOHN 9:31-33 KJV

Now we know that God heareth not sinners: but if any man be a worshipper of God, and doeth his will, him he heareth. Since the world began was it not heard that any man opened the eyes of one that was born blind. If this man were not of God, he could do nothing.

──────── *DECLARATION OF FAITH* ────────

My Father hears me every time that I pray and is ever-ready to honor His Word on my behalf.
I trust Him with all of my heart.
I continually do His will and listen intently to every Word that He says.
Through Him, I can even open the eyes of one born blind.
I am from God and of God, and only through Him are such miracles accomplished in my life.

(John 14:13,14; 15:7; 16:23,24; 17:14; 1 John 5:14,15; Isaiah 55:11; 61:1-3; Proverbs 3:5,6; Mark 16:15-20)

JOHN 10:1-5 KJV

Verily, verily, I say unto you, He that entereth not by the door into the sheepfold, but climbeth up some other way, the same is a thief and a robber. But he that entereth in by the door is the shepherd of the sheep. To him the porter openeth;

and the sheep hear his voice: and he calleth his own sheep by name, and leadeth them out. And when he putteth forth his own sheep, he goeth before them, and the sheep follow him: for they know his voice. And a stranger will they not follow, but will flee from him: for they know not the voice of strangers.

———— *DECLARATION OF FAITH* ————

I fully understand that there is only one way to enter into the sheepfold of Jesus. There is only one way into the presence of the Father and into the family of God. Jesus is that Way. It is not works of righteousness, penance, or religion that will get me there. Jesus is the only Way. He alone is the Door and the Shepherd of the flock to which I belong.

I hear the voice of my Shepherd. I follow Him faithfully and do everything that He would have me do. He calls me by name and leads me in the ways of life. He walks before me in the path that He has called me to and I follow Him because I know His voice.

I will never follow a stranger (the voice of falsehood, false teachers or false religion). I do not have intimacy with strangers and I do not recognize their voice as being true. Therefore, I shun their call.

(John 14:6; 16:13; 20:16; Isaiah 43:1,2; Titus 3:5; 2 Corinthians 11:13-15)

JOHN 10:7-11 KJV

Then said Jesus unto them again, Verily, verily, I say unto you, I am the door of the sheep. All that ever came before me are thieves and robbers: but the sheep did not hear them. I am the door: by me if any man enter in, he shall be saved, and shall go in and out, and find pasture. The thief cometh not, but for to steal, and to kill, and to destroy: I am come that they might have life, and that they might have *it* more abundantly. I am the good shepherd: the good shepherd giveth his life for the sheep.

———— *DECLARATION OF FAITH* ————

Jesus is the door for the sheep. I enter into God's blessings and salvation through Him alone. I know that every claim of getting into the kingdom of heaven any other way than through Jesus is a false claim. Those who make such claims are thieves and robbers who would take from me the salvation that is rightfully mine.

I am one of the true sheep. I neither listen to nor obey the voice of a thief.

Jesus is the Door and I have entered through Him into this mighty covenant communion with God that I now enjoy. In Him, I enjoy true freedom and liberty, and find such pasture that whatever the circumstance, good or bad, I have all that I need and more.

I know that the thief comes only to steal, kill, and destroy. Jesus, on the other hand, came to give me the life of God with all of its abundance (provision overflowing and bursting through the seams).

Jesus is such a Good Shepherd to me. He so loves me that He willingly laid down His life to provide for me all that He has and all that He is.

(John 3:16; 14:6; Hebrews 8:6; Philippians 4:19; 2 Corinthians 9:8; Proverbs 10:9,10; Psalm 23; Ephesians 2:18; Isaiah 40:11)

JOHN 10:14,15 NKJV

I am the good shepherd; and I know My sheep, and am known by My own. As the Father knows Me, even so I know the Father; and I lay down My life for the sheep.

——— DECLARATION OF FAITH ———

Jesus is the good Shepherd and I am part of His flock. He knows me by name and recognizes me as His own.

I know and recognize my Shepherd as well. He laid down His life for me so that I could have a relationship with the Father exactly like His.

(Psalm 23; Isaiah 43:1; 1 John 2:3; Romans 8:14-17,28-30; 2 Timothy 1:12; 2:19)

JOHN 10:25-30 KJV

Jesus answered them, I told you, and ye believed not: the works that I do in my Father's name, they bear witness of me. But ye believe not, because ye are not of my sheep, as I said unto you. My sheep hear my voice, and I know them, and they follow me: And I give unto them eternal life; and they shall never perish, neither shall any *man* pluck them out of my hand. My Father, which gave *them* me, is greater than all; and no *man* is able to pluck *them* out of my Father's hand. I and *my* Father are one.

——— DECLARATION OF FAITH ———

The works that I do are evidence that I am in Jesus. All of the power that works in and through me comes through His name.

I am in Christ. As Jesus is one with the Father, I am in Jesus, and therefore have become one with the Father as well.

My total and complete reliance for the sustenance of my new life is upon Jesus alone.

I am part of His fold—a standing and valued member of His family.

My ears have been opened and I continually listen to His voice. He knows me personally and I follow Him relentlessly.

He has given me eternal life and I shall never lose it. I am held secure under His tender care from now through eternity. No one has the ability to snatch me out of His hand.

My Father, who is greater than all, has placed His seal upon me and has committed me to Jesus' care. No one can snatch me out of my Father's hand.

I am in Jesus, just as Jesus is in the Father. We are all one (the most perfect and complete partnership that is possible).

(John 3:16; 6:37; 14:12; 17:20-26; Ephesians 1:17-23; 5:1-18; Colossians 1:29; Philippians 2:5-13; Galatians 4:5-9)

JOHN 10:34,35 NKJV

Jesus answered them, "Is it not written in your law, 'I said, You are gods'"? If He called them gods, to whom the word of God came (and the Scripture cannot be broken).

———— *DECLARATION OF FAITH* ————

I am created to be like a god in this earth—a very member of the great assembly. I am indeed a son/daughter of the Most High!

(Genesis 1:26-28; 2 Chronicles 19:6; Psalm 8:4-6; 82:1,6; John 10:34; Romans 8:14-17; Ephesians 2:6-10)

JOHN 11:9-11 KJV

Jesus answered, Are there not twelve hours in the day? If any man walk in the day, he stumbleth not, because he seeth the light of this world. But if a man walk in the night, he stumbleth, because there is no light in him. These things said he: and after that he saith unto them, Our friend Lazarus sleepeth; but I go, that I may awake him out of sleep.

———— *DECLARATION OF FAITH* ————

The Light within me guides me in all of my actions in the kingdom just as natural light illuminates my paths in the natural world.

The same goes for the darkness. As anyone who walks in the darkness in the natural world will stumble, so will I stumble if I walk in darkness within the kingdom.

Furthermore, I do not allow the natural world, with its circumstances and obstacles, to guide my actions. If God calls me to do something, I will do it regardless of what my eyes see, ears hear, or what threatens me in the natural realm.

(1 John 1:5-7; John 1:4,9; 2 Corinthians 5:7; 6:14-18; Hebrews 11:1)

John 11:25,26 NKJV

Jesus said to her, "I am the resurrection and the life. He who believes in Me, though he may die, he shall live. And whoever lives and believes in Me shall never die. Do you believe this?"

——— *DECLARATION OF FAITH* ———

Jesus is my resurrection and my life. All that I am, in spirit, is found in Him and although I may die in the flesh [after living out the fullness of my days in this earth], I will live on in the spirit for all of eternity.

(John 3:16; 5:21; 6:39-44; Ephesians 2:4-7; 1 John 5:10; 1 Corinthians 15:22)

John 11:34,35 NKJV

And He said, "Where have you laid him?"
They said to Him, "Lord, come and see."
Jesus wept.

——— *DECLARATION OF FAITH* ———

Jesus is deeply moved with compassion towards me.

(Psalm 103:13; Romans 8:38,39; John 15:12; Galatians 2:20)

John 11:40-42 KJV

Jesus saith unto her, Said I not unto thee, that, if thou wouldest believe, thou shouldest see the glory of God? Then they took away the stone *from the place* where the dead was laid. And Jesus lifted up *his* eyes, and said, Father, I thank thee that thou hast heard me. And I knew that thou hearest me always: but because of the people which stand by I said *it,* that they may believe that thou hast sent me.

——— *DECLARATION OF FAITH* ———

I believe and trust in the name of Jesus; therefore I will see the glory of God manifested in my life.

My Father always listens to and entertains my prayers. He is more than willing to honor His Word on my behalf and grant any petition I may have that is in line with it.

(Philippians 2:10-13; Mark 16:15-20; John 14:13,14; 15:7; 16:23,24; 1 John 5:14,15)

JOHN 12:23-26 KJV

And Jesus answered them, saying, The hour is come, that the Son of man should be glorified. Verily, verily, I say unto you, Except a corn of wheat fall into the ground and die, it abideth alone: but if it die, it bringeth forth much fruit. He that loveth his life shall lose it; and he that hateth his life in this world shall keep it unto life eternal. If any man serve me, let him follow me; and where I am, there shall also my servant be: if any man serve me, him will *my* Father honour.

——— DECLARATION OF FAITH ———

Jesus is exalted and glorified in my life. He used His own life as if it were a seed sown into the earth. By dying, He has produced many others like Himself—a rich harvest of sons and daughters of God. I am one of those sons/daughters.

I have given my life [every part of it] to Jesus. In Him, my life is preserved for all of eternity.

I serve Him wholeheartedly, conforming wholly to His example and doing those things He has instructed me to do.

Wherever I am, Jesus is.

Because of my love for Jesus and commitment to serve Him, my Father honors me and considers me to be of great value in His kingdom.

(John 14:3,12; 17:10,24; 1 Corinthians 15:36; Romans 8:28-30; Ephesians 1:13,14; 5:1-18; Matthew 28:20; Hebrews 13:5,6; Psalm 91:15)

JOHN 12:31 NKJV

"Now is the judgment of this world; now the ruler of this world will be cast out."

——— DECLARATION OF FAITH ———

The prince of this world (Satan) has been expelled from my life. Jesus stripped him of all of the power and authority that he had over me. I need never fear him again.

(Colossians 2:13-15; Luke 10:17-19; 2 Corinthians 4:4; 1 John 5:18)

JOHN 12:35,36 AMP

So Jesus said to them, You will have the Light only a little while longer. Walk while you have the Light [keep on living by it], so that darkness may not overtake and overcome you. He who walks about in the dark does not know where he goes [he is drifting]. While you have the Light, believe in the Light [have faith in it, hold to it, rely on it], that you may become sons of the Light and be filled with Light. Jesus said these things, and then He went away and hid Himself from them [was lost to their view].

——— *DECLARATION OF FAITH* ———

I have the Light of life (God's provision of illumination and enlightenment which brings realization and understanding). I live by it, walk in it, believe in it and rely upon it. It has made me a master of the forces of darkness. They cannot overcome me. In Jesus, I have become a son/daughter of Light and it has filled every fiber of my being.

(John 1:4,9; 1 John 1:5-7; 4:4; Luke 10:19; 16:8; 1 Corinthians 1:30; 2:6-16)

JOHN 12:44-46 KJV

Jesus cried and said, He that believeth on me, believeth not on me, but on him that sent me. And he that seeth me seeth him that sent me. I am come a light into the world, that whosoever believeth on me should not abide in darkness.

——— *DECLARATION OF FAITH* ———

By believing in and relying on Jesus, I am believing in and relying on the Father as well.

Jesus is a revelation of the Father's heart toward me.

Jesus is my Light and my salvation. I no longer live in the ways of darkness, but have the Light of life.

(Mark 9:37; John 1:4,9; 3:16,18,36; 5:24; 11:25,26; 14:9; 2 Corinthians 6:14)

JOHN 13:13-17 KJV

Ye call me Master and Lord: and ye say well; for *so* I am. If I then, *your* Lord and Master, have washed your feet; ye also ought to wash one another's feet. For I have given you an example, that ye should do as I have done to you. Verily, verily, I say unto you, The servant is not greater than his lord; neither he that is sent greater than he that sent him. If ye know these things, happy are ye if ye do them.

——— *DECLARATION OF FAITH* ———

Jesus is my mentor and the Lord of my life. He has left me an example of the greatest servitude the world has ever known.

I will do as He did and wash the feet of my brothers and sisters in Christ [figuratively]. I will seek the real good and benefit of others through humble service. With a tender heart of compassion, I will take the time to do good to those around me. Through this generosity of service and willingness to give of myself to others, no matter how humbling the service may be, I store up for myself favor upon favor, and blessing upon blessing.

(John 14:12; 16:13; Ephesians 5:1; Galatians 6:9; Philippians 4:15-17; Luke 22:27)

JOHN 13:20 NIV

"I tell you the truth, whoever accepts anyone I send accepts me; and whoever accepts me accepts the one who sent me."

——— *DECLARATION OF FAITH* ———

When I receive one of my brothers or sisters in Christ, no matter who they may be, I am receiving Jesus Himself. By receiving Jesus, I am receiving the Father as well.

(Matthew 10:40; 25:31-45; Luke 9:48)

JOHN 13:34,35 NKJV

"A new commandment I give to you, that you love one another; as I have loved you, that you also love one another. By this all will know that you are My disciples, if you have love for one another."

——— *DECLARATION OF FAITH* ———

I obey the new commandment that Jesus gave: to love one another. Continually, without faltering or failing, I love my brothers and sisters in Christ the way that Jesus loves me. By this, I display to all the world that I am a true disciple of the Lord.

(John 15:12; 1 Thessalonians 4:9; 1 John 2:5)

JOHN 14:1-3 KJV

Let not your heart be troubled: ye believe in God, believe also in me. In my Father's house are many mansions: if *it were* not *so*, I would have told you. I go to prepare a place for you. And if I go and prepare a place for you, I will come again, and receive you unto myself; that where I am, *there* ye may be also.

―――― *DECLARATION OF FAITH* ――――

I will not allow my heart to become troubled, distressed, or terrified. I believe in my Father and I believe in Jesus.

Where my Father lives there are many mansions and one of them belongs to me. Jesus, my friend, brother, Savior, and Lord, has gone on before me to prepare it. He who knows me better than I know myself is customizing a home for me in heaven designed specifically to fit my needs and personality. Right now, at this very moment, I have a home in heaven. I have an address there! I am actually a member of heaven's community! My mansion is awesome to behold!

I am continually in Jesus' thoughts and in His heart. He is coming for me one day to receive me unto Himself. It brings Him great joy to know that where He is, I will be also.

(Joshua 1:5-9; 2 Timothy 1:6-12; John 12:26; 13:33-36; 14:27; 16:22-24; Acts 1:11)

JOHN 14:4-7 KJV

And whither I go ye know, and the way ye know. Thomas saith unto him, Lord, we know not whither thou goest; and how can we know the way? Jesus saith unto him, I am the way, the truth, and the life: no man cometh unto the Father, but by me. If ye had known me, ye should have known my Father also: and from henceforth ye know him, and have seen him.

―――― *DECLARATION OF FAITH* ――――

I know the way into my Father's presence. It is through Jesus alone. He is the Way, the Truth and the Life. There is no way for me to reach the Father, but through Him.

In Jesus, I have a perfect revelation of the Father. Through Him, I can both see and know the heart of God. If ever I wonder what God thinks of me, I can look to Jesus and all of my wondering will be laid to rest.

(John 1:12,14; 8:19,32; 10:1-11; 11:25; Hebrews 9:8; 10:19,20; 1 Timothy 2:5)

JOHN 14:10-14 KJV

Believest thou not that I am in the Father, and the Father in me? the words that I speak unto you I speak not of myself: but the Father that dwelleth in me, he doeth the works. Believe me that I am in the Father, and the Father in me: or else believe me for the very works' sake. Verily, verily, I say unto you, He that believeth on me, the works that I do shall he do also; and greater works than these shall he do; because I go unto my Father. And whatsoever ye shall ask in my name, that will I do, that the Father may be glorified in the Son. If ye shall ask any thing in my name, I will do it.

DECLARATION OF FAITH

I believe with all of my heart that Jesus is in the Father and that the Father is in Jesus. All of the mighty miracles and deeds of power that Jesus performed on this earth were done through the Father. It was the Father's power within Him that did all of the works. What Jesus did, He did as a human, just like me. I will not forget that though He is all God, He is also all man. And what He did for me, He did as a man.

As Jesus did all things in our Father's name, I now perform mighty miracles and deeds of power through Jesus' name.

As Jesus is in the Father, I am in Jesus, and we three are one.

Through Jesus, I am fully capable of doing the very same things that He did in His earth walk. He has even made me able to do greater things than He did, because He has risen and gone on to the Father.

Jesus Himself, through His name, brings to pass whatever I command in this natural world. Everything outside of His will must bow to His authority.

Whatever I ask for, in His name, I receive so that the Father may be glorified through the Son. Only through Jesus are my prayers answered. He has given me the very power of attorney to use His name. It is like a legal document proclaiming that all of the power that is in His name is now mine to use. I can freely draw upon all that He is and all that He has. Whatever I have asked for in His name, I can confidently claim as done.

(John 15:7; 16:23,24; 17:20-26; Mark 11:22-25; 16:15-20; Matthew 28:18-20; 2 Corinthians 5:17-21; Acts 1:8; 2:43; 4:23-33; 1 Peter 1:2-4; Colossians 1:29; Ephesians 1:17-23; Hebrews 10:14; 1 John 5:14,15; Philippians 2:10)

JOHN 14:15-21 KJV

If ye love me, keep my commandments. And I will pray the Father, and he shall give you another Comforter, that he may abide with you for ever; *Even* the Spirit of truth; whom the world cannot receive, because it seeth him not, neither knoweth him: but ye know him; for he dwelleth with you, and shall be in you. I will not leave you comfortless: I will come to you. Yet a little while, and the world seeth me no more; but ye see me: because I live, ye shall live also. At that day ye shall know that I *am* in my Father, and ye in me, and I in you. He that hath my commandments, and keepeth them, he it is that loveth me: and he that loveth me shall be loved of my Father, and I will love him, and will manifest myself to him.

——— *DECLARATION OF FAITH* ———

I love Jesus with all of my heart and I obey His commandments.

He has requested of the Father to give me a Comforter, strengthener and helper, who will remain with me forever. He is the Spirit of Truth, whom the world cannot receive because it neither knows nor recognizes Him.

I do know and recognize Him. He has taken up residence within my spirit. He is literally and actually within me at this very moment. God, the Holy Spirit, dwells within my heart.

Jesus has not left me alone, desolate or helpless. He has come to me, with passion and purpose, to see that I have victory in all that I do.

Because He lives, I live also.

As Jesus is in the Father, I am in Him and He is in me.

I show my love for Him by holding fast to His commands and doing all that He has taught me to do.

I am deeply loved and appreciated by my heavenly Father, and Jesus Himself loves me and manifests Himself to me.

(John 15:10-12; 16:7-14,27; 17:20-26; Acts 1:5,8; 1 Corinthians 3:16; 15:57; Galatians 2:20,21; 1 John 4:4)

JOHN 14:23 KJV

Jesus answered and said unto him, If a man love me, he will keep my words: and my Father will love him, and we will come unto him, and make our abode with him.

——— *DECLARATION OF FAITH* ———

I show my love for Jesus by making His Word the center of my life. I make it my purpose in life to know and obey His commands, and to live according to the precepts that He has taught me.

My Father and Jesus love me so much, and are so pleased that I have become a part of the family, that they have taken up residence within me. They are always here whenever I need them and are overjoyed in my conversation and fellowship.

(Psalm 1:1-3; John 15:10-12; 17:20-26; 1 Corinthians 3:16; 1 John 1:3)

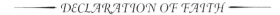

JOHN 14:26 KJV

But the Comforter, which is the Holy Ghost, whom the Father will send in my name, he shall teach you all things, and bring all things to your remembrance, whatsoever I have said unto you.

———— DECLARATION OF FAITH ————

The Holy Spirit, who is my Comforter, Counselor, and strength, whom the Father has sent to me in Jesus' name, teaches me all things. I can turn to Him at any time and receive all of the wisdom that I need in any given situation. He brings to my remembrance all of those things that Jesus has taught me in His Word. He opens it up to me, giving me revelation knowledge and complete working understanding of all that His Word calls me to do. He sees to it that I know all that I need to know to live this holy life that I have been called to live.

(John 16:13-15; 1 Corinthians 2:6-16; James 1:5-8; Matthew 13:15,16; Romans 14:17)

JOHN 14:27 KJV

Peace I leave with you, my peace I give unto you: not as the world giveth, give I unto you. Let not your heart be troubled, neither let it be afraid.

———— DECLARATION OF FAITH ————

I have, at this moment, the very peace of Jesus within my heart. He has given it to me, not as the world gives, but as He gives. It is mine forever. He will never take it from me.

I will not allow my heart to be troubled or afraid. In Jesus, I have a boldness of faith and confidence that puts me over in every situation.

(Philippians 4:7; 2 Timothy 1:7; Mark 11:22-25; Ephesians 2:14; Hebrews 4:16)

JOHN 14:30 AMP

I will not talk with you much more, for the prince (evil genius, ruler) of the world is coming. And he has no claim on Me. [He has nothing in common with Me; there is nothing in Me that belongs to him, and he has no power over Me.]

———— DECLARATION OF FAITH ————

Satan no longer has any claim on me. I do not act according to his purposes and ways of living, there is nothing in me or of me that belongs to him, and He has absolutely no power over me. I am his master in every circumstance and I will continually make his life miserable in this earth.

(Colossians 2:13-15; Luke 10:19; 1 John 4:1-4; 5:18; 2 Corinthians 10:3-6)

JOHN 15:1-5 KJV

I am the true vine, and my Father is the husbandman. Every branch in me that beareth not fruit he taketh away: and every *branch* that beareth fruit, he purgeth it, that it may bring forth more fruit. Now ye are clean through the word which I have spoken unto you. Abide in me, and I in you. As the branch cannot bear fruit of itself, except it abide in the vine; no more can ye, except ye abide in me. I am the vine, ye *are* the branches: He that abideth in me, and I in him, the same bringeth forth much fruit: for without me ye can do nothing.

— DECLARATION OF FAITH —

Jesus is the true Vine and my Father is the master gardener.

I am a branch of the true Vine. If I am not bearing fruit, my Father will prune away at me (cleansing and training me) until I do. He makes me what I am—joyfully molding and forming me, until I continually increase and bear richer and more excellent fruit.

I am a cleansed, pruned, and well-fed branch of the Vine because of the Word.

I dwell in Jesus and He dwells in me. My life is totally dependent upon Him. Just as a branch cannot live, let alone bear fruit, if it is not in vital union with the Vine, neither can I live and bear fruit unless I remain in vital union with Jesus.

Jesus is the Vine and I am one of the branches that come forth from Him. I live in and by Him, and I bear an abundance of good fruit. Apart from Him, I can do nothing.

(Ephesians 2:10; Matthew 4:4; 1 Corinthians 3:16; Colossians 1:27-29; John 17:17)

JOHN 15:7,8 KJV

If ye abide in me, and my words abide in you, ye shall ask what ye will, and it shall be done unto you. Herein is my Father glorified, that ye bear much fruit; so shall ye be my disciples.

— DECLARATION OF FAITH —

I am in vital union with Jesus, living and remaining in Him continually. His Word remains in me, rooted and grounded within the depths of my heart. Through the Word, I have a complete revelation of the will and purpose of my

Father. Therefore, whatever I ask of the Father in Jesus' name, in line with the Word and in incessantly active faith, I am guaranteed to receive.

My Father is honored and glorified when I bear a great variety and abundance of fruit. By this, I show myself to be a true disciple of Jesus.

(Ephesians 3:17; Colossians 2:7; James 2:14-26; Matthew 5:16; 13:12,15,16; Luke 8:10; 1 Corinthians 1:30; 2:6-16; John 14:13,14; 16:23,24; 1 John 5:14,15; Mark 11:22-25)

JOHN 15:9-11 KJV

As the Father hath loved me, so have I loved you: continue ye in my love. If ye keep my commandments, ye shall abide in my love; even as I have kept my Father's commandments, and abide in his love. These things have I spoken unto you, that my joy might remain in you, and *that* your joy might be full.

——— DECLARATION OF FAITH ———

Jesus loves me in the same way that the Father loves Him. I am like a prized treasure filling His heart with joy. Therefore, I will live in His love—always recognizing and remembering it in all that I do.

I abide in His love by doing those things that He has commanded me to do.

His joy and delight are in me, and my joy and delight are made complete in Him.

(Romans 8:38,39; John 5:20; 14:15; 17:26; 1 John 1:3,4; Psalm 18:19)

JOHN 15:12 NKJV

"This is My commandment, that you love one another as I have loved you."

——— DECLARATION OF FAITH ———

This is the commandment that Jesus has given me: that I love my brothers and sisters in Christ just as He has loved me.

(1 John 3:11; Romans 12:9; John 13:34,35)

JOHN 15:13-16 KJV

Greater love hath no man than this, that a man lay down his life for his friends. Ye are my friends, if ye do whatsoever I command you. Henceforth I call you not servants; for the servant knoweth not what his lord doeth: but I have called you friends; for all things that I have heard of my Father I have made known unto you. Ye have not chosen me, but I have chosen you, and ordained you, that ye should go and bring forth fruit, and *that* your fruit should remain: that whatsoever ye shall ask of the Father in my name, he may give it you.

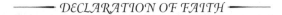

——— *DECLARATION OF FAITH* ———

There is no greater love in existence than the love that Jesus has for me.

I am His close friend and I continually do what He has commanded me to do. He does not call me a servant, for a servant does not know His master's business. To the contrary, He calls me His close friend and continually reveals to me His will and purpose—even all that He knows.

It wasn't me who chose Him, but He chose me. He actually picked me to be His friend and brother/sister. He has given me a purpose in my life, to go forth and bear an abundance of lasting and eternal fruit. Whatever I ask of my Father, in Jesus' name, He gives me.

Jesus has given me the power of attorney to use His name so that I may obtain all that I need in this life.

(Romans 8:38,39; 1 Corinthians 13:4-8; 1 John 3:16; Matthew 12:50; 28:20; James 2:23; Exodus 33:11; Genesis 18:17; John 3:29; 6:70; 13:18; 14:13,14; 15:19; 16:23,24; Colossians 1:6; Ephesians 1:4)

JOHN 15:17 NIV

This is my command: Love each other.

——— *DECLARATION OF FAITH* ———

This is the commandment that Jesus has given me: that I love all of my brothers and sisters in Christ.

(1 John 3:11; Romans 12:9; John 13:34,35; 15:12)

JOHN 15:19-21 KJV

If ye were of the world, the world would love his own: but because ye are not of the world, but I have chosen you out of the world, therefore the world hateth you. Remember the word that I said unto you, The servant is not greater than his lord. If they have persecuted me, they will also persecute you; if they have kept my saying, they will keep yours also. But all these things will they do unto you for my name's sake, because they know not him that sent me.

——— *DECLARATION OF FAITH* ———

If I belonged to the world, the world would accept me and treat me as one of its own. But I am not of this world. I have been chosen out of the world and am no longer subject to its ways of living and being.

The world hates the fact that I do not indulge in worldly ways or operate the way they feel is appropriate. This is why I suffer persecution.

I must continually remember that a servant is not greater than his master. Therefore, if they persecuted Jesus, they are sure to persecute me, for I have become one with Him in all things. I follow Him with a whole heart doing all of the same things that He did in His earth walk.

However, I do have this consolation: if there were those who observed and followed Jesus' teachings, there will also be those who observe and follow mine.

I know to expect persecution and ridicule because of my love for Jesus and commitment to His Word. The world just doesn't understand the love of the Father, or why I am so committed to kingdom-living. But, I will love them regardless and pray for them continually.

(John 13:16; 14:12; 17:14,20-26; Ephesians 1:4; 5:1-18; 2 Timothy 3:12; 1 John 4:5; Ezekiel 3:7; Matthew 5:44; 10:22; 24:9)

JOHN 15:26 KJV

But when the Comforter is come, whom I will send unto you from the Father, even the Spirit of truth, which proceedeth from the Father, he shall testify of me.

——— *DECLARATION OF FAITH* ———

The Holy Spirit, my Comforter, Counselor, and strength, whom Jesus has sent to me from the Father, continually testifies of Jesus both in and through me.

(1 Corinthians 3:16; John 16:13; Luke 24:49; 1 John 5:6)

JOHN 16:1 KJV

These things have I spoken unto you, that ye should not be offended.

——— *DECLARATION OF FAITH* ———

The Words of Jesus are given to me to keep me from stumbling or being taken by surprise.

(Psalm 119:11; Matthew 11:6)

JOHN 16:7-11 KJV

Nevertheless I tell you the truth; It is expedient for you that I go away: for if I go not away, the Comforter will not come unto you; but if I depart, I will send him unto you. And when he is come, he will reprove the world of sin, and of right-eousness, and of judgment: Of sin, because they believe not on me; Of right-eousness, because I go to my Father, and ye see me no more; Of judgment, because the prince of this world is judged.

——— *DECLARATION OF FAITH* ———

It is to my advantage that Jesus has gone on to heaven to take His place at the right hand of the Father. Because He has gone, the Holy Spirit, my Comforter, Counselor and strength, has come to me.

He is ever with me in close fellowship, revealing to me all that I need to know.

It is He who has revealed to me my deliverance from sin and right standing in the eyes of God.

He gives me a direct revelation of Satan's defeat and a full understanding of my rights, privileges, and authority in Jesus.

(Acts 1:5,8; 2:33; John 16:13; Ephesians 1:13-23; 1 Corinthians 2:6-16; Luke 10:18,19)

JOHN 16:13-15 KJV

Howbeit when he, the Spirit of truth, is come, he will guide you into all truth: for he shall not speak of himself; but whatsoever he shall hear, that shall he speak: and he will shew you things to come. He shall glorify me: for he shall receive of mine, and shall shew it unto you. All things that the Father hath are mine: therefore said I, that he shall take of mine, and shall shew it unto you.

——— *DECLARATION OF FAITH* ———

The Holy Spirit is within me, leading and guiding me into all of the realities of God.

He does not speak His own message, or by His own authority, but He tells me whatever He hears from my Father. He gives me every message that God has for me and reveals to me things that will happen in the future.

With the Holy Spirit as my Counsel, I am guaranteed success in all that I do.

He honors and glorifies Jesus by taking the things that are His and transmit-ting them to me. All that the Father has belongs to Jesus and He freely gives it all to me through the Holy Spirit who dwells within me.

(1 Corinthians 2:6-16; 3:16; Deuteronomy 28:12; Colossians 1:13; Romans 8:32; John 14:26; 15:26; Matthew 11:27)

JOHN 16:22-24 KJV

And ye now therefore have sorrow: but I will see you again, and your heart shall rejoice, and your joy no man taketh from you. And in that day ye shall ask me nothing. Verily, verily, I say unto you, Whatsoever ye shall ask the Father in my name, he will give *it* you. Hitherto have ye asked nothing in my name: ask, and ye shall receive, that your joy may be full.

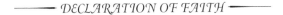

My heart rejoices in Jesus, and no one can take my joy from me.

I am now a born-again child of God—the very brother/sister of Jesus Himself.

In His name, I have all that I desire from God. My heavenly Father freely grants me whatever I desire that is in accordance with His will and purpose as established in His Word. What I ask for in Jesus' name is a done deal the moment I ask. Therefore, I will continually ask, receiving all that I desire from God, so that my joy may be made complete.

(Nehemiah 8:10; 1 Peter 1:8; John 3:3; 14:13,14; 15:7,11; 17:13; 2 Corinthians 5:17; Titus 3:5; Hebrews 2:11; Romans 8:28-30; Matthew 7:7; 1 John 5:14,15)

JOHN 16:25-27 KJV

These things have I spoken unto you in proverbs: but the time cometh, when I shall no more speak unto you in proverbs, but I shall shew you plainly of the Father. At that day ye shall ask in my name: and I say not unto you, that I will pray the Father for you: For the Father himself loveth you, because ye have loved me, and have believed that I came out from God.

Jesus has given me a mind to receive the Word with complete understanding. He opens it up to me, making it plain and clear. All that He tells me of the Father, I fully understand.

He has built for me a perfect relationship with the Father. In Jesus' name, I can stand before the Father free of all sense of unworthiness, for I know that it is not my own righteousness that gives me this right, but the righteousness of Jesus Himself.

All that Jesus is and has done has been credited to my account. Through His name, I am identified with everything that He did.

Therefore, I can come boldly into the Father's presence without any sense of guilt or inadequacy. He loves me with all of His heart and is overjoyed that I have taken the name of Jesus as my own and have become His very son/daughter.

Because of Jesus, my heavenly Father welcomes me with open arms every time I enter His presence and He is more than willing to grant my every request.

(1 Corinthians 1:30; 2:6-16; 1 John 2:20; Matthew 13:15,16; 21:22; Hebrews 4:15,16; Galatians 2:20; 4:5,6; 2 Corinthians 5:21; Mark 11:22-25)

JOHN 16:33 KJV

These things I have spoken unto you, that in me ye might have peace. In the world ye shall have tribulation: but be of good cheer; I have overcome the world.

In Jesus, I have perfect peace and security. Though trials and troubles still come my way, I am of good cheer, for my Lord has overcome the world, and He has given His victory to me. The world has been stripped of all the power it had to bring disaster upon my life. I am now more than a conqueror in Jesus.

(Ephesians 2:14; Colossians 1:13; 2:13-15; Psalm 91; Romans 8:37)

JOHN 17:3 NIV

Now this is eternal life: that they may know you, the only true God, and Jesus Christ, whom you have sent.

Eternal life for me is to intimately know the Father, the one true God, and His Son Jesus Christ. I have a personal relationship with both the Father and the Son, and because of this, I have eternal life.

(1 John 1:3; 5:11,12; John 17:20-26; Jeremiah 9:23,24)

JOHN 17:6-26 KJV

I have manifested thy name unto the men which thou gavest me out of the world: thine they were, and thou gavest them me; and they have kept thy word. Now they have known that all things whatsoever thou hast given me are of thee. For I have given unto them the words which thou gavest me; and they have received *them,* and have known surely that I came out from thee, and they have believed that thou didst send me. I pray for them: I pray not for the world, but for them which thou hast given me; for they are thine. And all mine are thine, and thine are mine; and I am glorified in them. And now I am no more in the world, but these are in the world, and I come to thee. Holy Father, keep through thine own name those whom thou hast given me, that they may be one, as we *are.* While I was with them in the world, I kept them in thy name: those that thou gavest me I have kept, and none of them is lost, but the son of perdition; that the scripture might be fulfilled And now come I to thee; and these things I speak in the world, that they might have my joy fulfilled in themselves. I have given them thy word; and the world hath hated them, because they are not of the world, even as I am not of the world. I pray not that thou shouldest take them out of the world, but that thou shouldest keep them from the evil. They are not of the world, even as I am not of the world. Sanctify them through thy truth: thy word is truth. As thou hast sent me into the world, even so have I also sent them into the world. And for their sakes I sanctify myself, that they also might be sanctified through the truth. Neither pray I for these alone, but for them also which shall believe on me through their word; That they all may be one; as thou, Father, *art* in me, and I in thee, that they also may be one in us: that the world may believe that thou hast sent me. And the glory which thou gavest me I have given them; that they may be one, even as we are one: I in them, and thou in me, that they may be made perfect in one; and that the world may know that thou hast sent me, and hast loved them, as thou hast loved me. Father, I will that they also, whom thou hast given me, be with me where I am; that they may behold my glory, which thou hast given me: for thou lovedst me before the foundation of the world. O righteous Father, the world hath not known thee: but I have known thee, and these have known that thou hast sent me. And I have declared unto them thy name, and will declare *it:* that the love wherewith thou hast loved me may be in them, and I in them.

─────── *DECLARATION OF FAITH* ───────

Jesus has manifested the Father to me as He truly is.

I belong to my Father and He has placed me under Jesus' legal guardianship. Jesus alone, through mighty deeds, including the sacrifice of His own life, has earned for me the right to stand in the Father's presence without any sense of guilt or inadequacy.

My life is in Him and I keep His Word faithfully.

I know and understand that I belong to my Father—that He has made Jesus my substitute and has placed me in His care.

All of the Words that Jesus has given me came directly from the Father. I have received and accepted them, and know of a certainty that Jesus came forth from the Father and that the Father did send Him.

Jesus is continually praying for me because I belong to the Father and have been made a part of His royal family. I am fully secure under the guardianship of my elder brother (Jesus).

All that belongs to Jesus is the Father's.

I belong to Jesus and He is glorified in and through me.

I am kept (held secure) in my Holy Father's name and just as the Father and Jesus are One, I also am one with my brothers and sisters in Christ.

Jesus keeps me and preserves me in the Father's name. I shall never be lost. I am continually guarded and protected, and I shall never perish.

The joy of Jesus is fulfilled in me. He has made me to experience continual joy, gladness, and heavenly bliss, for I am now a born-again child of God and an eternal heir together with Jesus.

I hold fast to the Word even though the world despises me for it.

It is through the Word that I have become a partaker of God's divine nature.

I am no more of this world than Jesus is. I am a true, reborn and regenerated son/daughter of the living God.

I am guarded and protected against the schemes of the evil one. There is nothing that he can do that can harm me in any way.

I have come into a new class of being and am no more of this world than Jesus is.

I am sanctified (set apart from the ways of the world) through the Word. God's Word is my reality.

Just as the Father sent Jesus into the world, Jesus has sent me into the world. My mission is the same as His: to proclaim the present fact of the kingdom.

Jesus sanctified Himself so that I may be sanctified through the Word.

I have come to know and rely on Jesus through the teaching of His disciples. I do all that He taught them to do. All that He declared they had is now mine as well. I have become one with the disciples of two thousand years ago, and in truth, I have become one with six thousand years worth of believers. Just as the Father is in Jesus, and Jesus in the Father, we all are one in them so that, through us, the world may be convinced that Jesus was sent from the Father.

What a glorious truth it is to know that I am one (in perfect union) with almighty God!

Together, with all of my brothers and sisters in Christ, I have become a partaker of the glory and honor, which the Father gave Jesus.

In Jesus, I am now one with the Father. Jesus is in me, He is in the Father, and we three are one (perfectly united) so that the world may know that Jesus came forth from the Father and that the Father loves me just as much as He loves Jesus.

It is Jesus' desire that I be with Him where He is, so that I may experience His glory which the Father has given Him, for the Father deeply loved Jesus before the foundation of the world and His glory is unlike anything this world has ever known.

What a wonder it is to know that I have entered into that love and that the Father loves me just as He loves Jesus.

As Jesus knows the Father, I have come to know Him as well, and I fully understand and believe that Jesus came forth from Him.

Jesus has made the Father known to me, revealing to me His very character and the reality of His love towards me. The love that He gives to Jesus, He now gives to me as well, and Jesus Himself dwells within me.

(Hebrews 2:11; 4:15,16; 7:25; Romans 8:14-17; 28-30,38,39; John 3:3; 6:37-40; 8:23,28,42; 10:28-30,38; 14:1-3,7-14; 15:9,19; 2 Peter 1:2-4; Titus 3:5; 2 Corinthians 3:18; 5:17-21; Psalm 22:22; 91:3; Matthew 28:18-20; 1 Corinthians 3:16; 1 John 1:3; 5:18-20; Galatians 3:28; Colossians 3:14)

JOHN 18:37 NKJV

Pilate therefore said to Him, "Are You a king then?" Jesus answered, "You say *rightly* that I am a king. For this cause I was born, and for this cause I have come into the world, that I should bear witness to the truth. Everyone who is of the truth hears My voice."

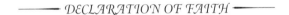

——— *DECLARATION OF FAITH* ———

I am a child of the Truth. I hear, understand, listen to, and obey the voice of Jesus.

(John 8:47; 10:1-7,27; 14:6; Matthew 5:17; Isaiah 55:4)

JOHN 20:17 NIV

Jesus said, "Do not hold on to me, for I have not yet returned to the Father. Go instead to my brothers and tell them, 'I am returning to my Father and your Father, to my God and your God.'"

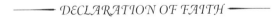

——— *DECLARATION OF FAITH* ———

When Jesus paid my price and I accepted Him as my Lord and my Savior, His Father became my Father, and His God became my God.

(Romans 8:14-17; 10:8-10; Galatians 4:5,6; John 16:28; 17:11; Ephesians 1:17)

JOHN 20:21-23 KJV

Then said Jesus to them again, Peace *be* unto you: as *my* Father hath sent me, even so send I you. And when he had said this, he breathed on *them,* and saith unto them, Receive ye the Holy Ghost: Whose soever sins ye remit, they are remitted unto them; *and* whose soever *sins* ye retain, they are retained.

────── *DECLARATION OF FAITH* ──────

I have the peace of God flowing abundantly within me.

Just as the Father sent Jesus into the world, Jesus has sent me into the world. I have received the Holy Spirit into my heart and having received Him, I am continually being led and directed by Him. If I forgive the sins of any, they are forgiven, and whomever I resolutely hold on to, is held firm.

(Mark 2:5; Philippians 4:7; Matthew 18:18; 28:18-20; Acts 1:5,8; 1 Corinthians 3:16; John 16:13)

JOHN 20:27-31 KJV

Then saith he to Thomas, Reach hither thy finger, and behold my hands; and reach hither thy hand, and thrust *it* into my side: and be not faithless, but believing. And Thomas answered and said unto him, My Lord and my God. Jesus saith unto him, Thomas, because thou hast seen me, thou hast believed: blessed *are* they that have not seen, and *yet* have believed. And many other signs truly did Jesus in the presence of his disciples, which are not written in this book: But these are written, that ye might believe that Jesus is the Christ, the Son of God; and that believing ye might have life through his name.

────── *DECLARATION OF FAITH* ──────

I am not filled with doubt and unbelief, but with steadfast faith.

Jesus is my Lord, my friend and my God, and though I have never seen Him [physically] or touched Him [physically], I believe in Him and I am blessed by, in and through Him.

The Word has been given to me so that I may believe that Jesus is the Christ. Through my believing, and the confession of my faith, I have received eternal life.

(James 1:6-8; Mark 11:22-25; John 15:15; Romans 10:8-10; 1 John 5:11,12)

CHAPTER FORTY-FOUR

ACTS

Luke, the physician, is the author of the book of Acts. It is thought by most to simply be part two of the gospel of Luke. Like the gospel of Luke, Acts is a compilation of facts that Luke had gathered in order to provide accurate proof that Jesus is the Messiah. What is different about Acts is that Luke was a companion of the apostle Paul. Much of what he writes about in Acts he had first hand knowledge of.

Though many see Acts as simply a historical record and not to be used for doctrine, Luke provides us with many promises that are supported throughout the scriptures. As you read the book of Acts, try to imagine what it was like to live in the first century church and know that the promises they believed in are yours to believe in as well.

ACTS 1:5 AMP

For John baptized with water, but not many days from now you shall be baptized with (placed in, introduced into) the Holy Spirit.

———— *DECLARATION OF FAITH* ————

I have submitted to the command of God to be baptized in water, demonstrating my identification with Jesus' death, burial and Resurrection.

He, in turn, has baptized me in the Holy Spirit.

(Romans 6:3-8; Matthew 3:11; Joel 2:28; 1 Corinthians 12:13; Galatians 3:27)

ACTS 1:8 NKJV

"But you shall receive power when the Holy Spirit has come upon you; and you shall be witnesses to Me in Jerusalem, and in all Judea and Samaria, and to the end of the earth."

———— *DECLARATION OF FAITH* ————

As a result of my baptism in the Holy Spirit, and His indwelling of my spirit, I have received power (miraculous ability) and have become a living witness,

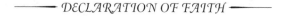

demonstrating God's presence with me to my neighborhood, my city, my country and the uttermost parts of the earth.

(Matthew 3:11; Joel 2:28; Acts 2:1-4; Luke 24:48,49; John 7:37-39)

ACTS 2:4 NIV

All of them were filled with the Holy Spirit and began to speak in other tongues as the Spirit enabled them.

—————— *DECLARATION OF FAITH* ——————

I have been filled with the Holy Spirit, and He has given me the ability to speak in a new language—one that I have never learned and do not understand (cannot translate).

(1 Corinthians 14; Ephesians 6:18; Jude 20; Romans 8:26-28)

ACTS 2:17-19 KJV

And it shall come to pass in the last days, saith God, I will pour out of my Spirit upon all flesh: and your sons and your daughters shall prophesy, and your young men shall see visions, and your old men shall dream dreams: And on my servants and on my handmaidens I will pour out in those days of my Spirit; and they shall prophesy: And I will shew wonders in heaven above, and signs in the earth beneath; blood, and fire, and vapour of smoke:

—————— *DECLARATION OF FAITH* ——————

The Scripture is fulfilled in me, which declares:

"It shall come to pass in the last days, declares the Lord, that I will pour out my Spirit upon all mankind, and your sons and daughters shall prophesy, your young men shall see visions and your old men shall dream dreams. I will pour out my Spirit on both the men and the women and they will all prophesy. And I will show wonders in the heavens above, and signs on the earth below—blood and fire and vapor of smoke. The sun will be darkened and the moon will be as blood before the coming of the great and notable Day of the Lord. And all who call on the name of the Lord shall be saved" (Joel 2:28-32).

I have called on the name of the Lord. Therefore, I can boldly declare and know of a certainty that I am saved.

The Holy Spirit has been poured out upon me and is dwelling within my own spirit.

This prophetic declaration of God is fulfilled in me.

(Joel 2:28-32; Acts 10:45; 21:9; 1 Corinthians 12:10; Matthew 24:49; Romans 10:13; John 14:16,17)

ACTS 2:23-28 KJV

Him, being delivered by the determinate counsel and foreknowledge of God, ye have taken, and by wicked hands have crucified and slain: Whom God hath raised up, having loosed the pains of death: because it was not possible that he should be holden of it. For David speaketh concerning him, I foresaw the Lord always before my face, for he is on my right hand, that I should not be moved: Therefore did my heart rejoice, and my tongue was glad; moreover also my flesh shall rest in hope: Because thou wilt not leave my soul in hell, neither wilt thou suffer thine Holy One to see corruption. Thou hast made known to me the ways of life; thou shalt make me full of joy with thy countenance.

—— DECLARATION OF FAITH ——

Jesus was delivered up in my place, and on my account, according to the fixed purpose and foreknowledge of God. He was crucified in my place and took upon Himself the total and complete penalty for all of my sins.

Once my price was completely paid, God raised Him up, loosing Him from the pains, agonies, and travail of death that He was suffering on my account, for it was not possible that hell could hold Him once my price was paid.

David prophesied as to what the Lord did for me in Psalm 16, saying:

"I saw the Lord constantly before My face. He is at My right hand so that I cannot be overcome. Therefore, My heart is glad, and My tongue shouts for joy; moreover, My flesh also shall dwell in hope, for You will not abandon My soul, leaving it in hell, nor will You allow Your Holy One to decay. You have made known to Me the ways of life; You fill Me with joy in Your presence and with eternal pleasures at Your right hand forevermore" (Psalm 16:8-11).

I am identified with all of this. In the eyes of God, it was as if I, myself, did all of that suffering. All that Jesus did has been credited to my account. Now I too am filled with joy in the presence of my Father and with eternal pleasures at His right hand forevermore.

(Isaiah 52:14; 53:3-5,10,11; Colossians 2:13-15; 3:1; 2 Corinthians 5:21; 8:9; Galatians 2:20; 6:14; Ephesians 1:17-23; 2:5,6; 4:8-10; Romans 3:26; 6:3-8; 2 Timothy 2:11; 1 Peter 2:24; John 15:5)

ACTS 2:33 NKJV

Therefore being exalted to the right hand of God, and having received from the Father the promise of the Holy Spirit, He poured out this which you now see and hear.

———— *DECLARATION OF FAITH* ————

Jesus, having been exalted to the right hand of God, and having received from the Father the promise of the Holy Spirit, has freely poured out the gift of the Holy Spirit upon me in power.

(Matthew 3:11; Acts 1:8; 2:1-4; 1 Corinthians 3:16; Ephesians 6:10)

ACTS 2:38,39 NKJV

Then Peter said to them, "Repent, and let every one of you be baptized in the name of Jesus Christ for the remission of sins; and you shall receive the gift of the Holy Spirit. For the promise is to you and to your children, and to all who are afar off, as many as the Lord our God will call."

———— *DECLARATION OF FAITH* ————

I have repented (turned from the ways of the world to the ways of God), have been baptized in the name of Jesus Christ for the remission of my sins, and have received the gift of the Holy Spirit; for the promise of the Holy Spirit was given to me personally, just as it is to anyone and everyone that the Lord, my God, has called.

(Romans 10:8-13; Acts 1:8; Matthew 3:11; Luke 24:47; Ephesians 2:4-13)

ACTS 2:42-47 KJV

And they continued stedfastly in the apostles' doctrine and fellowship, and in breaking of bread, and in prayers. And fear came upon every soul: and many wonders and signs were done by the apostles. And all that believed were together, and had all things common; And sold their possessions and goods, and parted them to all *men,* as every man had need. And they, continuing daily with one accord in the temple, and breaking bread from house to house, did eat their meat with gladness and singleness of heart, Praising God, and having favour with all the people. And the Lord added to the church daily such as should be saved.

——— *DECLARATION OF FAITH* ———

I faithfully devote myself to the Word, the teachings of my pastors and teach-ers in my local fellowship, and to the breaking of bread together with my brothers and sisters in Christ.

Many signs and wonders are performed in our midst through the power of the Holy Spirit.

I consider nothing that I have to be my own. I fully understand that all that I have is God's in the first place; therefore, I freely give of my substance to meet the many needs of my local church. I am even willing to sell what I have, if the need should arise, in order to meet a pressing and urgent need.

I do not forsake the assembling of myself with other believers of like faith. I eat with them, break bread with them, and enjoy their company with a sincere and joyful heart. We praise and worship together regularly. God's anointing rests on us and people go out of their way to grant us favor.

The Lord adds to our number daily those who are being saved.

(Joshua 1:8; Psalm 1:1-3; Mark 16:15-20; Acts 2:22; 5:14; 20:7; Psalm 24:1; 2 Corinthians 9:5-11; Hebrews 10:25)

ACTS 3:6 NIV

Then Peter said, "Silver or gold I do not have, but what I have I give you. In the name of Jesus Christ of Nazareth, walk."

——— *DECLARATION OF FAITH* ———

In every circumstance, no matter what my situation (what I have or do not have), I can use the name of Jesus to meet any of my needs.

(John 14:13,14; Philippians 2:10; 4:19; 1 John 5:14,15)

ACTS 3:12 AMP

And Peter, seeing it, answered the people, You men of Israel, why are you so sur-prised and wondering at this? Why do you keep staring at us, as though by our [own individual] power or [active] piety we had made this man [able] to walk?

——— *DECLARATION OF FAITH* ———

All of the miracle-working power that flows through me is not my own. It is the power of God working in and through me doing those things that bring joy to His heart.

(John 14:10-12; Philippians 2:13; Colossians 1:27-29; Ephesians 3:20; 6:10)

ACTS 3:16 MESSAGE

Faith in Jesus' name put this man, whose condition you know so well, on his feet—yes, faith and nothing but faith put this man healed and whole right before your eyes.

─────── *DECLARATION OF FAITH* ───────

In and through the name of Jesus, I remain perfectly healthy and strong, and through His name, I have the ability to bring His healing power to all who will receive it.

(1 Peter 2:24; John 14:13,14; Mark 11:22-25; 16:17,18; Luke 9:1,2; Matthew 9:22)

ACTS 3:19 NKJV

Repent therefore and be converted, that your sins may be blotted out, so that times of refreshing may come from the presence of the Lord.

─────── *DECLARATION OF FAITH* ───────

I have repented (turned from the ways of the world to the ways of God) and my sins (first to last—from the day of my birth to the day of my death) have been erased from my record. Times of refreshing (rejuvenation, exhilaration, and exaltation) have come to me from the presence of the Lord!

(Acts 2:38,39; 26:20; Colossians 2:13-15; Titus 3:5; 2 Corinthians 4:16)

ACTS 3:25,26 NKJV

"You are sons of the prophets, and of the covenant which God made with our fathers, saying to Abraham, 'And in your seed all the families of the earth shall be blessed.' To you first, God, having raised up His Servant Jesus, sent Him to bless you, in turning away every one of you from your iniquities."

─────── *DECLARATION OF FAITH* ───────

I am the progeny of the prophets of old and an heir of the promises provided in the covenant which God made and gave to them saying to Abraham, "In your seed shall all of the families of the earth be blessed." Jesus is that Seed and all of the old covenant promises are now mine through Him.

In Jesus, I have been made new. God has turned me away from wickedness and has made me to be an heir—a partaker of the blessings of His covenant children.

(2 Corinthians 1:20; 5:17; Galatians 3:5-29; 4:5,6; Ephesians 2:1-10; Romans 8:14-17; Hebrews 8:6)

Acts 4:10-13 kjv

Be it known unto you all, and to all the people of Israel, that by the name of Jesus Christ of Nazareth, whom ye crucified, whom God raised from the dead, *even* by him doth this man stand here before you whole. This is the stone which was set at nought of you builders, which is become the head of the corner. Neither is there salvation in any other: for there is none other name under heaven given among men, whereby we must be saved. Now when they saw the boldness of Peter and John, and perceived that they were unlearned and ignorant men, they marvelled; and they took knowledge of them, that they had been with Jesus.

Let it be known and understood by all that it is in and through the name of Jesus that I stand whole and through Him alone am I able to bring wholeness to others.

I have been granted the power of attorney to use the name of Jesus to meet every need.

Jesus, my Lord who was crucified and whom God raised from the dead, is the power by and through which I live. He is the chief cornerstone on which all that I am and all that I do is built. There is no enduring salvation of any kind apart from Him, for there is no other name under heaven, given among men, by which we can be saved. In and through Him I have boldness to do what I am called to do, and furthermore, I have unfettered eloquence to answer any charge that is laid against me.

(Mark 16:15-20; John 14:13,14; 15:7; 16:13,23,24; Galatians 2:20; Matthew 7:24; Psalm 118:22; Romans 10:8-13; Acts 4:23-31)

Acts 4:18-20 nkjv

So they called them and commanded them not to speak at all nor teach in the name of Jesus. But Peter and John answered and said to them, "Whether it is right in the sight of God to listen to you more than to God, you judge. For we cannot but speak the things which we have seen and heard."

I cannot help but speak of this great salvation that I enjoy in Jesus. When governments and authorities tell me that I am not to converse in any way, or teach at all in or about the name of Jesus, I must rebel against them, for it is better in the

eyes of God to obey Him and His commission rather than the foolish, anti-God rules of men.

(Acts 5:28,29; 1 John 1:1-3; John 16:13; Matthew 28:18-20)

ACTS 4:24-31 KJV

And when they heard that, they lifted up their voice to God with one accord, and said, Lord, thou *art* God, which hast made heaven, and earth, and the sea, and all that in them is: Who by the mouth of thy servant David hast said, Why did the heathen rage, and the people imagine vain things? The kings of the earth stood up, and the rulers were gathered together against the Lord, and against his Christ. For of a truth against thy holy child Jesus, whom thou hast anointed, both Herod, and Pontius Pilate, with the Gentiles, and the people of Israel, were gathered together, For to do whatsoever thy hand and thy counsel determined before to be done. And now, Lord, behold their threatenings: and grant unto thy servants, that with all boldness they may speak thy word, By stretching forth thine hand to heal; and that signs and wonders may be done by the name of thy holy child Jesus. And when they had prayed, the place was shaken where they were assembled together; and they were all filled with the Holy Ghost, and they spake the word of God with boldness.

——— DECLARATION OF FAITH ———

When evil men (leaders in league with the devil) rise up and plot against me, I have the Word as my defense. There is an army of men, women and angels ready to take their stand at my side. Together, we raise our voices in one accord to our God and Father, the Sovereign Lord of the universe, who made the heavens, the earth, the sea and all that is in them, including those who plot against me.

When I speak the Word to the problem, all of hell breaks loose. It is written (in Psalm 2) that when the heathen rage against me and plot my destruction, and the kings of the earth (spiritual ruling powers of darkness) assemble themselves against the Lord and His anointed (me), He who sits in heaven laughs. God Himself observes their threats and takes His stand with me. He is on my side! Therefore, I declare His Word fearlessly, in the name of Jesus, and He stretches out His hand to perform signs, wonders and miracles on my behalf!

(Romans 8:31,37; Mark 11:22-25; 16:15-20; 2 Corinthians 10:3-6; Acts 2:43; 5:12)

ACTS 4:32 NKJV

Now the multitude of those who believed were of one heart and one soul; neither did anyone say that any of the things he possessed was his own, but they had all things in common.

——— *DECLARATION OF FAITH* ———

I have predetermined, with great resolve, to be of one heart and one mind with other believers.

All that I have belongs to the Lord; therefore, nothing that I own is exclusively mine.

I would freely give all that I own to ensure the survival of my brothers and sisters in Christ.

(John 17:21,22; Hebrews 10:25; Romans 5:15; Psalm 24:1)

ACTS 4:33,34 NKJV

And with great power the apostles gave witness to the resurrection of the Lord Jesus. And great grace was upon them all. Nor was there anyone among them who lacked; for all who were possessors of lands or houses sold them, and brought the proceeds of the things that were sold.

——— *DECLARATION OF FAITH* ———

I testify to, and demonstrate, the Resurrection of Jesus through the strength, ability and power of the Holy Spirit who is within me. A divine enabling to fulfill my calling is continually upon me.

I am neither destitute nor impoverished, for I am a member of the family of God and we take care of each other in the spirit of agape love.

I demonstrate my godly character by always thinking of others as being just as important as myself.

(1 Corinthians 3:16; Ephesians 3:20; 6:10; Acts 1:8,22; 2:45; Philippians 2:4)

ACTS 5:12-16 KJV

And by the hands of the apostles were many signs and wonders wrought among the people; (and they were all with one accord in Solomon's porch. And of the rest durst no man join himself to them: but the people magnified them. And believers were the more added to the Lord, multitudes both of men and women.) Insomuch that they brought forth the sick into the streets, and laid *them* on beds and couches, that at the least the shadow of Peter passing by might overshadow some of them. There came also a multitude *out* of the cities round about unto Jerusalem, bringing sick folks, and them which were vexed with unclean spirits: and they were healed every one.

─── *DECLARATION OF FAITH* ───

The Holy Spirit performs many signs, wonders, and miracles by my hands and through the words that I speak (in accordance with the Scriptures).

I know the power of the corporate anointing; therefore, I regularly meet together with my other brothers and sisters in Christ.

Much respect is given to me by those outside of the kingdom because of the presence and power of the Holy Spirit who is within me.

I am an instrument of the Lord and I am used mightily to bring in a great harvest of souls into the family.

People in the world regularly come to me to pray for them, for they know that the Lord hears my prayers and will grant them deliverance through me.

In Jesus, I have a reputation as a master of the forces of darkness.

I am an ambassador of the Lord with the power to deliver and heal.

(Proverbs 11:30; 18:20,21; Mark 11:22-25; 16:15-20; Jeremiah 1:12; Isaiah 55:11; Hebrews 10:25; Proverbs 3:3,4; Acts 4:21; 19:11,12; Luke 10:19; 2 Corinthians 5:18-20)

ACTS 5:18-20 NKJV

And laid their hands on the apostles and put them in the common prison. But at night an angel of the Lord opened the prison doors and brought them out, and said, "Go, stand in the temple and speak to the people all the words of this life."

─── *DECLARATION OF FAITH* ───

I have angels all around me who minister to me all that I need to carry out my commission in the earth. Therefore, I will stand boldly before the world, declaring the facts of eternal life in Jesus.

(Hebrews 1:14; Psalm 91:11; Matthew 26:53; 2 Kings 6:15-17; Exodus 23:20; John 6:63; 1 John 5:11)

ACTS 5:27-29 KJV

And when they had brought them, they set *them* before the council: and the high priest asked them, Saying, Did not we straitly command you that ye should not teach in this name? and, behold, ye have filled Jerusalem with your doctrine, and intend to bring this man's blood upon us. Then Peter and the *other* apostles answered and said, We ought to obey God rather than men.

I am not obligated to obey any man-made law that is contrary to the com-mand of the Lord. I will proclaim salvation in Jesus in every appropriate situation and circumstance regardless of any law that commands me not to do so.

I obey the Lord first in all matters of law and justice. When men choose to ignore and defy the clear commands of God, rebellion against them rises within me and I refuse to obey their godless laws.

(Daniel 3:1-30; 6:5-23; Acts 4:17-19; Deuteronomy 6:4-7; 28:1,14,15)

ACTS 5:42 NIV

Then Peter said, "Silver or gold I do not have, but what I have I give you. In the name of Jesus Christ of Nazareth, walk."

———— *DECLARATION OF FAITH* ————

I will live for Jesus and proclaim His gospel despite the threats of the ruling authorities who stand against the clear commands of God. I have no fear of what they may do to me, for I know that God is always with me—He will never leave me nor forsake me.

(Daniel 3:1-30; 6:5-23; Acts 4:17-19; Deuteronomy 6:4-7; 28:1,14,15; Hebrews 13:5,6)

ACTS 6:5,8-10 KJV

And the saying pleased the whole multitude: and they chose Stephen, a man full of faith and of the Holy Ghost, and Philip, and Prochorus, and Nicanor, and Timon, and Parmenas, and Nicolas a proselyte of Antioch: And Stephen, full of faith and power, did great wonders and miracles among the people. Then there arose certain of the synagogue, which is called *the synagogue* of the Libertines, and Cyrenians, and Alexandrians, and of them of Cilicia and of Asia, disputing with Stephen. And they were not able to resist the wisdom and the spirit by which he spake.

———— *DECLARATION OF FAITH* ————

I am a man/woman full of grace (divine blessing and favor), who walks con-tinually in the tremendous power of the Holy Spirit. Under the Spirit's guidance, I am well able to perform great signs, wonders and miracles among the people.

All who rise up against me, to debate and dispute me, cannot resist the intelligence and wisdom of the Holy Spirit with which, and by whom, I speak.

(Ephesians 1:3; 3:20; 5:18; 6:10; Mark 16:15-20; Colossians 1:29; John 16:13; 2 Corinthians 2:6-16)

ACTS 7:22 AMP

So Moses was educated in all the wisdom and culture of the Egyptians, and he was mighty (powerful) in his speech and deeds.

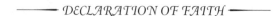

——— *DECLARATION OF FAITH* ———

I have a tremendous aspiration for learning the knowledge and wisdom of this present world. By this, I stand mighty in speech and deeds in the eyes of the world and thus become of even greater use to the Lord.

(Daniel 1:4,17,20; 2:22,23; 2 Corinthians 1:30; 2:6-16; 14:2,13; Luke 24:19)

ACTS 7:55 NKJV

But he, being full of the Holy Spirit, gazed into heaven and saw the glory of God, and Jesus standing at the right hand of God.

——— *DECLARATION OF FAITH* ———

I am a man/woman full of the Holy Spirit, with eyes of spiritual discernment.
God is always with me, watching over me no matter what my situation may be.

(Daniel 2:22,23; 2 Corinthians 2:6-16; 1 John 2:20; Psalm 3:5,6)

ACTS 8:6-8 KJV

And the people with one accord gave heed unto those things which Philip spake, hearing and seeing the miracles which he did. For unclean spirits, crying with loud voice, came out of many that were possessed *with them:* and many taken with palsies, and that were lame, were healed. And there was great joy in that city.

——— *DECLARATION OF FAITH* ———

There are many people who will listen and heed the message that I give.
God is working in and through me in this endeavor, and signs and wonders are regularly manifested in my ministry. Even the crippled ones, bound to wheelchairs, have their strength restored and walk as well as any other.

All evil spirits must obey me and leave whenever I command them to.

There is continuous rejoicing in my city over the wonderful things that God is doing for us.

(Luke 10:19; Mark 16:15-20; Isaiah 61:1-3; John 14:12)

ACTS 8:21 NKJV

"You have neither part nor portion in this matter, for your heart is not right in the sight of God."

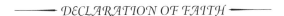

I have my part in the power and manifestations of the Holy Spirit, because my heart is fixed on following His lead and doing His will.

(Romans 8:14-17; John 14:10-12; 16:13; Mark 16:15-20; 1 John 5:14,15)

ACTS 9:22 NIV

Yet Saul grew more and more powerful and baffled the Jews living in Damascus by proving that Jesus is the Christ.

I continue to increase in knowledge and power, confounding and baffling all who are set in opposition against me by comparing and examining the evidence and proving that Jesus is truly the Messiah.

(Daniel 2:22,23; 2 Corinthians 1:30; 2:6-16; 2 Timothy 2:15; John 16:13)

ACTS 9:27,28 KJV

But Barnabas took him, and brought *him* to the apostles, and declared unto them how he had seen the Lord in the way, and that he had spoken to him, and how he had preached boldly at Damascus in the name of Jesus. And he was with them coming in and going out at Jerusalem.

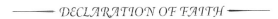

I always have someone who will take a stand with me, just as I am willing to take my stand with others who are in the right.

I speak the Word of God freely and courageously in Jesus' name.

(Ezekiel 22:30; 1 Kings 19:14,18; Acts 4:23-31)

ACTS 9:31 AMP

So the church throughout the whole of Judea and Galilee and Samaria had peace and was edified [growing in wisdom, virtue, and piety] and walking in the respect and reverential fear of the Lord and in the consolation and exhortation of the Holy Spirit, continued to increase and was multiplied.

———— DECLARATION OF FAITH ————

My church continues to increase and multiply. We are never stagnant, but are always expanding and growing in wisdom, virtue, and holiness, and walking in reverence for the Lord under the guidance of the Holy Spirit.

(Acts 5:11; 8:1; 16:15; Ephesians 4:16,29; Psalm 34:9; John 14:16)

ACTS 9:33,34 NKJV

There he found a certain man named Aeneas, who had been bedridden eight years and was paralyzed. And Peter said to him, "Aeneas, Jesus the Christ heals you. Arise and make your bed." Then he arose immediately.

———— DECLARATION OF FAITH ————

Paralysis is no match for the name of Jesus. As Christ's ambassador, with the power of attorney to use His name, I am well able to provide healing for the paralytic.

(Philippians 2:10; 2 Corinthians 5:18-20; John 14:13,14; Mark 16:17,18; Acts 3:1-10)

ACTS 9:40 NKJV

But Peter put them all out, and knelt down and prayed. And turning to the body he said, "Tabitha, arise." And she opened her eyes, and when she saw Peter she sat up.

———— DECLARATION OF FAITH ————

As Christ's ambassador and carrier of His name and power, I am well able to raise the dead.

(2 Corinthians 5:18-20; John 14:12-14; Mark 5:41,42; 16:17,18)

ACTS 10:4 NKJV

And when he observed him, he was afraid, and said, "What is it, lord?"

So he said to him, "Your prayers and your alms have come up for a memorial before God."

DECLARATION OF FAITH

My prayers and generosity (heartfelt giving) rise up into heaven as a memorial before the Lord. To this, the angels of God take notice and they minister unto me an abundant return.

(2 Corinthians 9:5-11; Hebrews 1:14; Malachi 3:10,11)

ACTS 10:15 KJV

And the voice *spake* unto him again the second time, What God hath cleansed, *that* call not thou common.

DECLARATION OF FAITH

What God has cleansed and pronounced clean I will not defile and profane by regarding as common and unholy.

[God has cleansed me and pronounced me clean. Therefore, I will see myself as clean. I will not defy the Lord and belittle His work by seeing myself as an unholy, sin-ridden worm. My right standing before God comes through Jesus alone and not my own works.]

(Hebrews 10:14-17,29; 2 Corinthians 5:17,21; Ephesians 2:4-10; Titus 1:15; 3:5)

ACTS 10:34 NKJV

Then Peter opened his mouth and said: "In truth I perceive that God shows no partiality."

DECLARATION OF FAITH

God is not a respecter of persons. He does not see anyone as being above me, better than me, or more important than I am.

I am one among many equals in the body of Christ.

(Romans 2:11; Ephesians 6:9; John 17:20-26)

ACTS 10:38 AMP

How God anointed and consecrated Jesus of Nazareth with the [Holy] Spirit and with strength and ability and power; how He went about doing good and, in particular, curing all who were harassed and oppressed by [the power of] the devil, for God was with Him.

I am in Christ and it is my commission to continue His work in the earth. I have been anointed and consecrated by the Father with strength, ability and power through the Holy Spirit and in Jesus' name. It is my duty to go about doing good and healing all who are oppressed of the devil, for God is with me.

(John 3:2; 14:10-12; 2 Corinthians 5:18-20; Matthew 4:23; 28:18-20; Mark 16:15-20; Luke 9:1,2; 10:19; Acts 1:8; 1 John 2:20,27)

ACTS 10:43-46 KJV

To him give all the prophets witness, that through his name whosoever believeth in him shall receive remission of sins. While Peter yet spake these words, the Holy Ghost fell on all them which heard the word. And they of the circumcision which believed were astonished, as many as came with Peter, because that on the Gentiles also was poured out the gift of the Holy Ghost. For they heard them speak with tongues, and magnify God.

—— DECLARATION OF FAITH ——

All of the prophets bear witness to the fact that I have received forgiveness of my sins (first to last) in Jesus' name. I have been renewed and regenerated through the Word and have received the promised gift of the Holy Spirit. It is He who gives me this ability to freely praise and magnify God, without restraint, and to speak in a language that I have never learned.

(Hebrews 8:6; 10:14-17; Titus 3:5; 2 Peter 1:4; Acts 2:38,39; 1 Corinthians 14)

ACTS 11:21 NKJV

And the hand of the Lord was with them, and a great number believed and turned to the Lord.

—— DECLARATION OF FAITH ——

The presence of the Lord is continually with me in power, making me an incredibly effective soul-winner.

(Matthew 28:18-20; Mark 16:20; Acts 1:8; Proverbs 11:30; Daniel 12:3)

ACTS 11:23,24 NKJV

When he came and had seen the grace of God, he was glad, and encouraged them all that with purpose of heart they should continue with the Lord. For he

was a good man, full of the Holy Spirit and of faith. And a great many people were added to the Lord.

——— *DECLARATION OF FAITH* ———

My Father has granted me His continuous grace. I will remain faithful to Him with sincere and resolute purpose of heart, and continually encourage others to do likewise.

I am a good man/woman, full of the Holy Spirit and faith, who leads many people to the Lord.

(Romans 5:1,2; Act 13:43; 14:22; 2 Peter 1:13; 3:1,2; Proverbs 11:30)

ACTS 12:5-7 KJV

Peter therefore was kept in prison: but prayer was made without ceasing of the church unto God for him. And when Herod would have brought him forth, the same night Peter was sleeping between two soldiers, bound with two chains: and the keepers before the door kept the prison. And, behold, the angel of the Lord came upon *him,* and a light shined in the prison: and he smote Peter on the side, and raised him up, saying, Arise up quickly. And his chains fell off from *his* hands.

——— *DECLARATION OF FAITH* ———

My Father remains alert and aware of my every circumstance and is faithful to meet my every need.

He prompts others to pray for me when the circumstance turns grim.

No matter what my situation may be, or how hopeless things may seem, God will come through for me. He sends His angel, in answer to fervent and persistent prayer, to break loose the chains and set me free!

(Psalm 106:29-31; 121:4,5; Philippians 4:19; Matthew 6:19-33; Exodus 23:20-23)

ACTS 12:11 NIV

Then Peter came to himself and said, "Now I know without a doubt that the Lord sent his angel and rescued me from Herod's clutches and from everything the Jewish people were anticipating."

——— *DECLARATION OF FAITH* ———

I know (have complete assurance) that God will send His angels to deliver me from the hands of my persecutors.

(Exodus 23:20-23; Psalm 91:11; Hebrews 1:14; Matthew 18:10; 26:53)

ACTS 13:32-34 KJV

And we declare unto you glad tidings, how that the promise which was made unto the fathers, God hath fulfilled the same unto us their children, in that he hath raised up Jesus again; as it is also written in the second psalm, Thou art my Son, this day have I begotten thee. And as concerning that he raised him up from the dead, *now* no more to return to corruption, he said on this wise, I will give you the sure mercies of David.

——— *DECLARATION OF FAITH* ———

What was promised to my forefathers, as far back as David and more, has been fulfilled in me through Jesus' Resurrection; for, upon His Resurrection, the Father made His declaration, "You are my Son; today I have begotten You." And having raised Jesus, no longer to suffer the effects of death, He has given me, through Jesus, all of the holy things of David.

(Ephesians 4:7-10; Psalm 2:7; Hebrews 1:5; 11:39,40; 2 Corinthians 1:20; Isaiah 55:3)

ACTS 13:38,39 NKJV

Therefore let it be known to you, brethren, that through this Man is preached to you the forgiveness of sins; and by Him everyone who believes is justified from all things from which you could not be justified by the law of Moses.

——— *DECLARATION OF FAITH* ———

I clearly understand and know of a certainty that all of my sins have been removed. Through Jesus, I have total, complete and everlasting forgiveness. I have been absolved of every charge that can be made against me. At this very moment, I stand justified in the sight of God. I have been reconciled to my heavenly Father for all of eternity.

(Hebrews 10:14-17; Psalm 103:10-12; John 3:16,17; Romans 5:1,2; 8:33,34)

ACTS 13:46-48 KJV

Then Paul and Barnabas waxed bold, and said, It was necessary that the word of God should first have been spoken to you: but seeing ye put it from you, and judge yourselves unworthy of everlasting life, lo, we turn to the Gentiles. For so hath the Lord commanded us, *saying,* I have set thee to be a light of the Gentiles, that thou shouldest be for salvation unto the ends of the earth. And when the Gentiles heard this, they were glad, and glorified the word of the Lord: and as many as were ordained to eternal life believed.

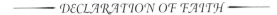

——— *DECLARATION OF FAITH* ———

I speak the Word of God boldly and without compromise.

I believe that Jesus is the Messiah and have received Him as my Lord and Savior. By this, I am counted worthy to receive eternal life.

The Lord has appointed me as a light to the world to carry His salvation to the uttermost parts of the earth.

I rejoice and magnify the Word of God in my life and rely on Jesus alone for my eternal salvation.

(Acts 4:10-12,23-31; John 1:12; 3:16,17; 14:6; Romans 10:8-10; 1 John 5:11,12; Matthew 5:14-16; Joshua 1:8)

ACTS 13:52 KJV

And the disciples were filled with joy, and with the Holy Ghost.

——— *DECLARATION OF FAITH* ———

I am continually filled with the Holy Spirit and the joy that He brings.

(Ephesians 5:18; 1 Corinthians 3:16; Romans 14:17)

ACTS 14:3 AMP

So [Paul and Barnabas] stayed on there for a long time, speaking freely and fearlessly and boldly in the Lord, Who continued to bear testimony to the Word of His grace, granting signs and wonders to be performed by their hands.

——— *DECLARATION OF FAITH* ———

I speak fearlessly and boldly for the Lord. He continually bears testimony to the Word of His grace (divine enabling) by granting signs and wonders to be performed through my hands.

(Romans 1:16; Acts 4:23-31; 5:12; Jeremiah 1:12; Isaiah 55:11; Mark 16:20)

ACTS 14:8-10 KJV

And there sat a certain man at Lystra, impotent in his feet, being a cripple from his mother's womb, who never had walked: The same heard Paul speak: who stedfastly beholding him, and perceiving that he had faith to be healed, Said with a loud voice, Stand upright on thy feet. And he leaped and walked.

——— DECLARATION OF FAITH ———

I am observant and discerning of those who have the faith to be healed. In accordance with the Word, I can speak into their bodies the healing that they need.

(Psalm 107:20; Mark 11:22-25; Acts 3:2-10; 1 John 5:14,15; 2 Corinthians 4:13)

ACTS 14:21,22 KJV

And when they had preached the gospel to that city, and had taught many, they returned again to Lystra, and to Iconium, and Antioch, confirming the souls of the disciples, and exhorting them to continue in the faith, and that we must through much tribulation enter into the kingdom of God.

——— DECLARATION OF FAITH ———

I incessantly preach the Good News, making disciples of many people. I establish and strengthen the hearts and souls of the disciples, encouraging them to stand firm in their faith, and to be strong and persevere through their struggles to enter into the blessings of the kingdom.

(Matthew 11:12; 28:18-20; Ephesians 6:10; Luke 16:16)

ACTS 15:8-11 KJV

And God, which knoweth the hearts, bare them witness, giving them the Holy Ghost, even as *he did* unto us; And put no difference between us and them, purifying their hearts by faith. Now therefore why tempt ye God, to put a yoke upon the neck of the disciples, which neither our fathers nor we were able to bear? But we believe that through the grace of the Lord Jesus Christ we shall be saved, even as they.

——— DECLARATION OF FAITH ———

God knows and fully understands my heart. He speaks to me personally, giving me the Holy Spirit just as He did the disciples of the first century. He doesn't see them as being more important, or having any different needs than I do. By cleansing my heart through faith, and pouring out the Holy Spirit upon me, He gives me all of the same gifts that He did them.

I will not allow any additional yoke to be placed upon me that would hinder me in the liberty that I now enjoy in Christ. I continually hold fast to the truth, that I am saved by grace (unmerited, undeserved favor) through Jesus and that by Him alone I shall endure to the end.

(John 17:20-26; Romans 2:11; 5:1,2; 1 Corinthians 12:1; Galatians 2:20,21; 5:1; Ephesians 2:4-10; Jude 23,24)

ACTS 15:28,29 KJV

For it seemed good to the Holy Ghost, and to us, to lay upon you no greater burden than these necessary things; That ye abstain from meats offered to idols, and from blood, and from things strangled, and from fornication: from which if ye keep yourselves, ye shall do well. Fare ye well.

—— *DECLARATION OF FAITH* ——

I will never partake of anything that I know to be sacrificed to a false god. Furthermore, I will refrain from sexual impurity as outlined in the Word. I do not do these things in order to justify myself or make myself right in the sight of God. Jesus already did that and I rest in His finished work. I do these things because by observing them, I bind many hindrances in my walk with God.

(Acts 21:25; Leviticus 17:14; Colossians 3:5; 1 Thessalonians 4:3; 5:22)

ACTS 15:32 NKJV

Now Judas and Silas, themselves being prophets also, exhorted and strengthened the brethren with many words.

—— *DECLARATION OF FAITH* ——

With many words, I continually encourage, strengthen, and console my brothers and sisters in Christ, urging them on to success.

(Hebrews 10:25; 1 Corinthians 14:3,5; Acts 14:22; 18:23)

ACTS 16:14 NIV

One of those listening was a woman named Lydia, a dealer in purple cloth from the city of Thyatira, who was a worshiper of God. The Lord opened her heart to respond to Paul's message.

—— *DECLARATION OF FAITH* ——

The Lord opens my heart and enlightens my mind so that I can pay attention and give heed to the messages spoken by His appointed teachers.

(1 Corinthians 14:3; Ephesians 4:11-16; Luke 24:45; Daniel 1:17,20)

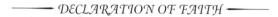

ACTS 16:25 KJV

And at midnight Paul and Silas prayed, and sang praises unto God: and the prisoners heard them.

——— *DECLARATION OF FAITH* ———

I will praise God and give Him glory in the midst of any adverse situation or circumstance, for He alone is my strength and my deliverance.

(Genesis 15:1; Psalm 91:1,2; 118)

ACTS 16:31 KJV

And they said, Believe on the Lord Jesus Christ, and thou shalt be saved, and thy house.

——— *DECLARATION OF FAITH* ———

I have entrusted my life to Jesus and He has applied that trust to both me and my household. Because of His great love for me, not one member of my immediate family shall perish in the horror of spiritual death.

(John 1:12; Romans 10:8-11; Psalm 103:17; Deuteronomy 4:40)

ACTS 17:11 KJV

These were more noble than those in Thessalonica, in that they received the word with all readiness of mind, and searched the scriptures daily, whether those things were so.

——— *DECLARATION OF FAITH* ———

I choose the path of honor and nobility. I accept and welcome what I am taught about the things of God through His ministers and search the Scriptures daily to make sure that everything I am being taught is true.

(Joshua 24:15; Ephesians 4:11-16; 2 Timothy 2:15)

ACTS 17:26-29 KJV

And hath made of one blood all nations of men for to dwell on all the face of the earth, and hath determined the times before appointed, and the bounds of their habitation; That they should seek the Lord, if haply they might feel after him, and find him, though he be not far from every one of us: For in him we live, and move, and have our being; as certain also of your own poets have said,

For we are also his offspring. Forasmuch then as we are the offspring of God, we ought not to think that the Godhead is like unto gold, or silver, or stone, graven by art and man's device.

———— *DECLARATION OF FAITH* ————

I am of one blood with every person and race on the face of the earth. Therefore, there is absolutely no room for prejudice, or racism, of any kind in my heart.

God has established for me a secure place to live where I can seek Him and live my life for Him.

In Him, I live and move and have my being.

I am a recreated, born-again child of the living God and a partaker of His divine nature.

I am His own son/daughter and an heir to the kingdom.

God is not who or what I think He is according to my own thoughts or imagination. I am not so foolish as to think I can invent God according to what I think He should be. He is who He is, and He has revealed Himself to me through His Word.

(Genesis 1:26-28; Deuteronomy 32:8; Psalm 90:17; 91:1,2; Titus 1:12; 2 Peter 1:4; Romans 8:14-17; Galatians 4:5,6; Hebrews 1:1-3; Isaiah 40:18,19)

Acts 18:9-11 KJV

Then spake the Lord to Paul in the night by a vision, Be not afraid, but speak, and hold not thy peace: For I am with thee, and no man shall set on thee to hurt thee: for I have much people in this city. And he continued *there* a year and six months, teaching the word of God among them.

———— *DECLARATION OF FAITH* ————

I have no fear of authorities who make threats against me when I work to fulfill my commission. I will speak and not be silent. God Himself is on my side and there are plenty of others willing to take a stand with me. Therefore, I will teach the Word with boldness, anytime it is appropriate, whether the authorities like it or not.

(Daniel 3:1-30; 6:5-23; 1 Kings 19:14,18; Romans 8:31; Acts 4:23-31)

Acts 18:27,28 KJV

And when he was disposed to pass into Achaia, the brethren wrote, exhorting the disciples to receive him: who, when he was come, helped them much which had believed through grace: For he mightily convinced the Jews, and that pub-lickly, shewing by the scriptures that Jesus was Christ.

——— *DECLARATION OF FAITH* ———

I am a great encouragement to my brothers and sisters in Christ and a tremendous help to them when they are in need.

The Holy Spirit gives me revelation knowledge of the Scriptures and com-pelling insight to refute false doctrines. It is no trouble at all for me to establish the facts of who Jesus is and what we have in Him.

(1 Corinthians 2:6-16; 14:3; 2 Corinthians 9:5-11; Matthew 13:15,16; 1 John 2:20)

ACTS 19:11,12 KJV

And God wrought special miracles by the hands of Paul: So that from his body were brought unto the sick handkerchiefs or aprons, and the diseases departed from them, and the evil spirits went out of them.

——— *DECLARATION OF FAITH* ———

God does unusual and extraordinary things by my hands. Because of His anointing within me, even when handkerchiefs, or the like, touch my hands, God's anointing is released into them. When these handkerchiefs are taken away and placed upon the sick, diseases leave them and evil spirits flee from them.

(Mark 16:15-20; Acts 5:15; Luke 9:1,2; 10:19; James 5:14-16)

ACTS 19:14-20 KJV

And there were seven sons of one Sceva, a Jew, *and* chief of the priests, which did so. And the evil spirit answered and said, Jesus I know, and Paul I know; but who are ye? And the man in whom the evil spirit was leaped on them, and overcame them, and prevailed against them, so that they fled out of that house naked and wounded. And this was known to all the Jews and Greeks also dwelling at Ephesus; and fear fell on them all, and the name of the Lord Jesus was magnified. And many that believed came, and confessed, and shewed their deeds. Many of them also which used curious arts brought their books together, and burned them before all *men:* and they counted the price of them, and found *it* fifty thousand *pieces* of silver. So mightily grew the word of God and prevailed.

——— *DECLARATION OF FAITH* ———

Since I have become one with Jesus, all evil spirits have come to know me by name. They know and understand that I have been given complete authority over them and that they must obey my commands.

As a born-again child of the living God, I have been granted the power of attorney to use the name of Jesus. Jesus Himself has given me this right and I intend to use it for His glory.

Those who practice magical arts and use evil spirits to manipulate this natural world are alarmed and terrified at my authority when it is manifested. They see clearly that there is no power greater than God and I lead many of them from the ways of darkness into the Kingdom of Light.

Thus, through me, the Word of God spreads like wildfire, continually intensifying and prevailing mightily.

(Isaiah 43:1; Luke 1:65; 7:16; 10:17-19; Philippians 2:10; Ephesians 1:17-23; John 14:13,14; Deuteronomy 18:9-12; Matthew 3:6; Acts 6:7; 12:24)

ACTS 20:24 NKJV

"But none of these things move me; nor do I count my life dear to myself, so that I may finish my race with joy, and the ministry which I received from the Lord Jesus, to testify to the gospel of the grace of God."

——— *DECLARATION OF FAITH* ———

I follow the lead of the Holy Spirit regardless of what lies ahead of me.

I do not esteem the things of my life as being more important than the Spirit's will.

I will finish my course and my calling with all joy, faithfully proclaiming the Good News of God's grace and mercy.

(John 16:13; Romans 8:14; 1 Corinthians 9:24-27; Acts 21:13; 2 Timothy 4:7)

ACTS 20:32-35 KJV

And now, brethren, I commend you to God, and to the word of his grace, which is able to build you up, and to give you an inheritance among all them which are sanctified. I have coveted no man's silver, or gold, or apparel. Yea, ye yourselves know, that these hands have ministered unto my necessities, and to them that were with me. I have shewed you all things, how that so labouring ye ought to support the weak, and to remember the words of the Lord Jesus, how he said, It is more blessed to give than to receive.

─────── *DECLARATION OF FAITH* ───────

I am entrusted to God and the Word of His grace. He is well able to build me up, establish me, and fulfill my part of His tremendous inheritance among my brothers and sisters in Christ.

I do not covet another man's silver, or gold, or costly garments, but work with my own hands to provide for myself and those under my authority.

I am ever-willing to assist the weak and ever-mindful of the words of Jesus, who Himself said, "There is more blessing in giving than receiving."

(Hebrews 9:15; 13:5-9; Acts 9:31; 18:3; Romans 8:17; 15:1; Genesis 12:1-3; Deuteronomy 28:9,12; Philippians 4:15-19)

ACTS 22:14 AMP

And he said, The God of our forefathers has destined and appointed you to come progressively to know His will [to perceive, to recognize more strongly and clearly, and to become better and more intimately acquainted with His will], and to see the Righteous One (Jesus Christ, the Messiah), and to hear a voice from His [own] mouth and a message from His [own] lips.

─────── *DECLARATION OF FAITH* ───────

My heavenly Father has preordained that I should come to progressively know His will and clearly recognize it in every area of my life. It is also preordained that I hear and recognize a voice from His own mouth and a message from His own lips.

(1 Corinthians 2:6-16; 1 John 2:20; 5:20; Ephesians 1:17-23; John 10:3,4; Isaiah 30:21)

ACTS 23:1 NIV

Paul looked straight at the Sanhedrin and said, "My brothers, I have fulfilled my duty to God in all good conscience to this day."

─────── *DECLARATION OF FAITH* ───────

I live honorably before God, fulfilling my calling with a good conscience.

(Romans 11:29; 2 Thessalonians 1:11; 2 Peter 1:10; Acts 24:16; Hebrews 10:2,14-17)

ACTS 23:11 KJV

And the night following the Lord stood by him, and said, Be of good cheer, Paul: for as thou hast testified of me in Jerusalem, so must thou bear witness also at Rome.

DECLARATION OF FAITH

I will be bold, taking great courage to myself in order that I may be an effective witness for Jesus wherever I am led.

(Acts 4:23-31; 2 Timothy 1:6,7; Matthew 28:18-20; John 16:13; Romans 8:14)

ACTS 24:14-16 KJV

But this I confess unto thee, that after the way which they call heresy, so worship I the God of my fathers, believing all things which are written in the law and in the prophets: And have hope toward God, which they themselves also allow, that there shall be a resurrection of the dead, both of the just and unjust. And herein do I exercise myself, to have always a conscience void of offence toward God, and *toward* men.

DECLARATION OF FAITH

This I confess: that in accordance with the way of Jesus, I worship the Father, fully persuaded of the truths laid down in the Law of Moses and the writings of the prophets.

I stand in the hope and assurance of the resurrection of both the righteous and the unrighteous. Therefore, I always discipline myself against worldly desires in order that I may have a clear conscience toward both God and man.

(2 Timothy 1:3; Acts 23:21; 26:22; Daniel 12:2; John 4:23,24; 5:28,29; 2 Peter 1:10; Hebrews 10:2,14-17)

ACTS 26:16-18 KJV

But rise, and stand upon thy feet: for I have appeared unto thee for this purpose, to make thee a minister and a witness both of these things which thou hast seen, and of those things in the which I will appear unto thee; Delivering thee from the people, and *from* the Gentiles, unto whom now I send thee, To open their eyes, *and* to turn *them* from darkness to light, and *from* the power of Satan unto God, that they may receive forgiveness of sins, and inheritance among them which are sanctified by faith that is in me.

——— *DECLARATION OF FAITH* ———

I have been appointed by Jesus Himself to be a witness for Him in this earth. He has chosen me out for Himself and has sanctified me for a specific purpose. He faithfully delivers me from the hands of my persecutors, to whom I am sent, in order to open their eyes and turn them from darkness to light, and from the power of Satan to God. I am Christ's ambassador to them, offering Christ's forgiveness of their sins and a place in the very family of God.

(Matthew 28:18-20; Acts 22:15,21; Ephesians 3:6-8; John 15:16,19; 2 Timothy 3:11; Colossians 1:13; 2 Corinthians 5:18-20)

ACTS 26:19,20 NKJV

"Therefore, King Agrippa, I was not disobedient to the heavenly vision, but declared first to those in Damascus and in Jerusalem, and throughout all the region of Judea, and then to the Gentiles, that they should repent, turn to God, and do works befitting repentance."

——— *DECLARATION OF FAITH* ———

I am not disobedient to anything that the Lord has revealed that I must do.
I fulfill my calling, teaching everyone that they must repent and turn to God, and prove their repentance by their deeds.

(Deuteronomy 28:1,14; Matthew 3:8; Luke 3:8; Romans 2:4; 2 Corinthians 7:9,10)

ACTS 27:3 NKJV

And the next *day* we landed at Sidon. And Julius treated Paul kindly and gave *him* liberty to go to his friends and receive care.

——— *DECLARATION OF FAITH* ———

I continually walk in God's favor and people go out of their way to do nice things for me.

(Proverbs 3:3,4; Genesis 12:1-3; Exodus 3:21,22; 11:3; 12:36)

ACTS 27:25 AMP

So keep up your courage, men, for I have faith (complete confidence) in God that it will be exactly as it was told me.

——— *DECLARATION OF FAITH* ———

I maintain my courage and confidence in every situation and circumstance, for I believe with all of my heart that things will go exactly as God has said.

(2 Timothy 1:6,7,12; Joshua 1:5-9; Isaiah 55:11; Romans 4:20,21)

ACTS 28:3-5 KJV

And when Paul had gathered a bundle of sticks, and laid them on the fire, there came a viper out of the heat, and fastened on his hand. And when the barbarians saw the *venomous* beast hang on his hand, they said among themselves, No doubt this man is a murderer, whom, though he hath escaped the sea, yet vengeance suffereth not to live. And he shook off the beast into the fire, and felt no harm.

——— *DECLARATION OF FAITH* ———

Nothing, not even the bite of a venomous snake, can hinder what God has called me to do, or thwart His Word in my life. He is above all false gods and whatever is brought against me, I will shake off into the fire and suffer no evil effects.

(Mark 16:15-20; Isaiah 55:11; Psalm 91; Luke 10:19)

ACTS 28:8-10 NKJV

And it happened that the father of Publius lay sick of a fever and dysentery. Paul went in to him and prayed, and he laid his hands on him and healed him. So when this was done, the rest of those on the island who had diseases also came and were healed. They also honored us in many ways; and when we departed, they provided such things as were necessary.

——— *DECLARATION OF FAITH* ———

Jesus has given me complete authority over attacks of fever and dysentery. When I command them to leave, they must go, and when I call for the healing to come [in this context, through the laying on of my hands], it comes. People know this about me and come to me regularly to have me pray for them, for they know that I am called of God and have become one of His children.

Respect, honor, and favor continually come to me because of my integrity and uncompromising character.

In Jesus, I am always well provided for and have everything that I need.

(Luke 9:1,2; 10:17-19; John 14:13,14; Mark 11:22-25; James 5:14-16; Proverbs 3:3,4; Exodus 3:21,22; 11:3; 12:36; 1 Timothy 5:17; Philippians 4:19)

ACTS 28:30,31 NKJV

Then Paul dwelt two whole years in his own rented house, and received all who came to him, preaching the kingdom of God and teaching the things which concern the Lord Jesus Christ with all confidence, no one forbidding him.

———— *DECLARATION OF FAITH* ————

I work hard with my own hands and the Lord prospers me so that I can live at my own expense in a lodging fit for a child of God.

I welcome all of those who come to me to learn of the Lord, teaching them the present fact of the kingdom and what it is to be in Christ, and I do so openly, with boldness, free of all hindrance.

(Deuteronomy 28:12; Proverbs 6:4-11; Acts 4:31; Ephesians 6:19)

CHAPTER FORTY-FIVE

ROMANS

Romans was written by the apostle Paul somewhere around 57 AD. Its main theme is our being established in righteousness by grace through faith. Paul makes it clear that we cannot earn or make ourselves worthy of God's righteousness, but can only receive it as a gift. He ends the epistle with lessons on Christian ethics and how we are supposed to represent Christ to the world.

As you pray the promises found in the book of Romans, know that you are worthy of them, not because of your own merits, but because Jesus paid the price for you to receive them.

ROMANS 1:11,12 KJV

For I long to see you, that I may impart unto you some spiritual gift, to the end ye may be established; That is, that I may be comforted together with you by the mutual faith both of you and me.

——— *DECLARATION OF FAITH* ———

I yearn for those times when I can gather together with my brothers and sisters in Christ so I can share my spiritual gifts with them to strengthen and encourage them in their faith.

I know the power of the corporate anointing and consciously seek the gifts of others in order to strengthen my faith as well.

(Hebrews 10:25; 1 Corinthians 12:1,7; 14:3; 2 Timothy 1:6; 2 Peter 1:3; 3:1)

ROMANS 1:16,17 KJV

For I am not ashamed of the gospel of Christ: for it is the power of God unto salvation to every one that believeth; to the Jew first, and also to the Greek. For therein is the righteousness of God revealed from faith to faith: as it is written, The just shall live by faith.

———— *DECLARATION OF FAITH* ————

I am not ashamed of the Gospel of Jesus Christ, for it is the power of God unto salvation for everyone who believes; for in the Gospel, the righteousness of God is revealed—a righteousness that is by faith, first to last. As it is written, "The righteous shall live by faith."

(2 Corinthians 5:21; Psalm 40:9; 1 Corinthians 1:18; Romans 3:21; Habakkuk 2:4)

ROMANS 2:4 NKJV

Or do you despise the riches of His goodness, forbearance, and longsuffering, not knowing that the goodness of God leads you to repentance?

———— *DECLARATION OF FAITH* ————

I am not blind to, nor do I underestimate, the immensity of God's love and patience towards me. I am well aware that it is God's love and kindness that leads us to true repentance.

(1 Corinthians 13:4-8; Psalm 103:1-13; Ephesians 1:7; Isaiah 30:18)

ROMANS 2:6,7 KJV

Who will render to every man according to his deeds: To them who by patient continuance in well doing seek for glory and honour and immortality, eternal life.

———— *DECLARATION OF FAITH* ————

I fully understand that every part of life is centered on the fixed laws of seedtime and harvest. My harvest is based upon the works that I have sown.

By patient persistence in well doing, I seek the glory, honor and incorruption that God alone can provide.

Because of my heartfelt commitment, God has given me eternal life.

(Genesis 8:22; Galatians 6:7-9; 2 Corinthians 9:6; Psalm 62:12; 1 John 5:10,11)

ROMANS 2:10,11 KJV

But glory, honour, and peace, to every man that worketh good, to the Jew first, and also to the Gentile: For there is no respect of persons with God.

I practice good and have been awarded glory, honor, and peace from God in return. In His eyes, I am one among many equals whom He has exalted to the position of highest honor in heaven.

God is no respecter of persons. He shows no favoritism within the body of Christ. He will honor His Word on my behalf just as surely as He does for anyone else.

Therefore, I know that He will give to me according to what I have given and He will shower His unmerited blessings upon me as long as I will receive them.

(Romans 8:26-30; Ephesians 2:6,14; 2 Corinthians 1:20; James 1:22-25; Luke 6:38; Deuteronomy 10:17; Acts 10:34)

ROMANS 2:29 NIV

No, a man is a Jew if he is one inwardly; and circumcision is circumcision of the heart, by the Spirit, not by the written code. Such a man's praise is not from men, but from God.

DECLARATION OF FAITH

I am inwardly a true Jew (one of God's chosen) and my circumcision is spiritual. When I became born again, I was renewed and set apart in the spirit, not the flesh.

I do not seek the praise of men, but of God.

(1 Peter 3:4; Philippians 3:3; John 3:6-8; 6:63; 1 Corinthians 4:5; Colossians 2:11-15)

ROMANS 3:20-26 KJV

Therefore by the deeds of the law there shall no flesh be justified in his sight: for by the law *is* the knowledge of sin. But now the righteousness of God without the law is manifested, being witnessed by the law and the prophets; Even the righteousness of God *which is* by faith of Jesus Christ unto all and upon all them that believe: for there is no difference: For all have sinned, and come short of the glory of God; Being justified freely by his grace through the redemption that is in Christ Jesus: Whom God hath set forth *to be* a propitiation through faith in his blood, to declare his righteousness for the remission of sins that are past, through the forbearance of God; To declare, *I say,* at this time his righteousness: that he might be just, and the justifier of him which believeth in Jesus.

———— *DECLARATION OF FAITH* ————

I am not justified and made righteous by observing the Law of Moses. I understand that the reason the Law was given was so I would receive a consciousness of sin and recognize my need of a Savior.

Now a righteousness of God apart from the Law of Moses has been manifested in me. It is a righteousness endorsed by the Law and the prophets; namely, the righteousness of God, which comes by believing in Jesus.

Jesus Himself has become my righteousness. Because of Him, I can now stand before God without any sense of guilt or inadequacy.

This righteousness has become available to everyone, not just the Jews. The Father no longer makes a distinction between Jew and Gentile when it comes to the gift of righteousness, for all have sinned and fallen short of God's glory.

I have become a partaker of this great gift of righteousness.

I have been justified, regenerated, made upright, and set in right standing with God. This wonderful gift is given to me freely by His grace (unmerited, undeserved favor) through the redemption that Jesus provided for me.

God presented Jesus, in my place, as a mercy seat and sacrifice of atonement. I am identified with everything that Jesus did. It was as if I myself were there suffering the penalty of my sentence.

This displays God's righteousness on legal grounds. My price has been paid and my redemption is complete. Because I have believed in Jesus and have accepted Him as my Lord and Savior, He Himself has become my righteousness, making it possible for me to enter into God's blessings legally, through faith.

(Galatians 2:16-21; 3:22,28,29; Acts 15:11; John 5:46; 1 Peter 1:10; Romans 5:1,2; 6:5-8; Titus 3:4-7; 2 Corinthians 5:7,21; Hebrews 10:14-17)

ROMANS 3:27,28 AMP

Then what becomes of [our] pride and [our] boasting? It is excluded (banished, ruled out entirely). On what principle? [On the principle] of doing good deeds? No, but on the principle of faith. For we hold that a man is justified and made upright by faith independent of and distinctly apart from good deeds (works of the Law). [The observance of the Law has nothing to do with justification.]

———— *DECLARATION OF FAITH* ————

I no longer boast of myself and the things that I have done. Not one of my good deeds can earn me a place in the family of God. I enter in on the basis of faith alone. I am justified and made righteous by faith, not works.

The Law has nothing to do with my justification. I am justified solely by the substitutionary sacrifice of Jesus on my behalf.

(John 14:6; Romans 5:1,2; Ephesians 2:6-10; Titus 3:4-7; Galatians 2:16-21)

ROMANS 4:4-8 KJV

Now to him that worketh is the reward not reckoned of grace, but of debt. But to him that worketh not, but believeth on him that justifieth the ungodly, his faith is counted for righteousness. Even as David also describeth the blessedness of the man, unto whom God imputeth righteousness without works, *Saying,* Blessed *are* they whose iniquities are forgiven, and whose sins are covered. Blessed *is* the man to whom the Lord will not impute sin.

—— DECLARATION OF FAITH ——

I do not work to earn my right standing in the sight of God. It is given to me as a free gift. There is nothing that I can do to earn it, or even maintain it. It is simply an established fact in my life.

Jesus has justified me through my faith and He Himself has become my righteousness. Even David spoke of this righteousness that I now enjoy, saying, "Blessed is the one whose iniquities are forgiven and whose sins have been completely eradicated. And blessed is the one whose sin the Lord will not take account of."

(Ephesians 2:4-10; Romans 11:6; 2 Corinthians 5:21; Joshua 24:2; Psalm 32:1,2)

ROMANS 4:11,12 KJV

And he received the sign of circumcision, a seal of the righteousness of the faith which he had yet being uncircumcised: that he might be the father of all them that believe, though they be not circumcised; that righteousness might be imputed unto them also: And the father of circumcision to them who are not of the circumcision only, but who also walk in the steps of that faith of our father Abraham, which he had being yet uncircumcised.

—— DECLARATION OF FAITH ——

My righteousness is established through my covenant relationship with God in Jesus. As Abraham walked in the ways of faith in his covenant, so I walk in the ways of faith in mine. In this, Abraham is truly the father of my faith.

(Hebrews 8:6; Luke 19:9; 2 Corinthians 4:13; 5:7; Romans 4:18-22; Galatians 3:5-29)

ROMANS 4:16-25 KJV

Therefore *it is* of faith, that *it might be* by grace; to the end the promise might be sure to all the seed; not to that only which is of the law, but to that also which is of the faith of Abraham; who is the father of us all, (As it is written, I have made thee a father of many nations,) before him whom he believed, *even* God, who quickeneth the dead, and calleth those things which be not as though they were. Who against hope believed in hope, that he might become the father of many nations, according to that which was spoken, So shall thy seed be. And being not weak in faith, he considered not his own body now dead, when he was about an hundred years old, neither yet the deadness of Sara's womb: He staggered not at the promise of God through unbelief; but was strong in faith, giving glory to God; And being fully persuaded that, what he had promised, he was able also to perform. And therefore it was imputed to him for righteousness. Now it was not written for his sake alone, that it was imputed to him; But for us also, to whom it shall be imputed, if we believe on him that raised up Jesus our Lord from the dead; Who was delivered for our offences, and was raised again for our justification.

———— *DECLARATION OF FAITH* ————

My inheritance of God's promise is the outcome of my faith. By believing in the promise and speaking of it as if it were mine, God has an avenue to give it to me as an act of grace (unmerited, undeserved favor). This overcomes the obstacles that imprison God's giving heart and is the surety that guarantees that I will receive His promise in my life.

I walk in the faith of Abraham (the father of my faith). Abraham understood the faith of God, in whom he believed—the very One who brings life out of death by calling those things that be not as though they are. When God declared, "I have made you a father of many nations," Abraham's hope was not shaken. He did not say, "No, God, You're a liar, because I obviously don't have any children." To the contrary, he did not weaken in faith by looking at his body, which was as good as dead, but against all hope and circumstance, he had the assurance of his faith, believing in the promise and speaking of it as if it were already fulfilled.

When God said, "Look to the stars, Abraham. So shall your descendents be," He gave Abraham a vision of his destiny. Abraham, the father of my faith, with his finger pointing to the heavens, declared in triumphal harmony with God, "So shall my descendents be!" Like God, regardless of his natural circumstances, he called those things that be not as though they were.

This is the example set before me. I believe and declare God's Word to be true in my life. Therefore, in faith, I call those things which be not [in my present condition or circumstance] as if I already have them. I will allow no unbelief or mistrust to make me waiver, but shall grow strong, empowered by faith, giving praise and glory to God.

I believe that God is trustworthy and I am fully convinced that He is able to keep His Word and do what He has promised.

I am the righteousness of God in Christ Jesus. This righteousness is granted to me because I believe in and put my total reliance upon God, who raised Jesus my Lord from the dead. It was Jesus who took my place, was betrayed and put to death because of my sin, but was raised again once my justification was secured.

(2 Corinthians 4:13; 5:7,21; Hebrews 11:1,6,11,14; Romans 3:24; 8:11; 9:26; Galatians 3:22; Genesis 17:17; Mark 11:22-25; Isaiah 53:4,5; 1 Corinthians 15:17)

ROMANS 5:1,2 KJV

Therefore being justified by faith, we have peace with God through our Lord Jesus Christ: By whom also we have access by faith into this grace wherein we stand, and rejoice in hope of the glory of God.

——— DECLARATION OF FAITH ———

Since I am justified, acquitted, declared righteous, and given right standing with God through faith, I hold fast to the fact that I now have peace with God through Jesus Christ my Lord. He Himself has become my peace and everlasting security.

Through Him, also, I have unconditional access into God's incessant and unconditional favor in which I stand. I am now welcomed with open arms whenever I enter the throne room of God.

Therefore, I greatly rejoice in the fact that I can now both see and experience the glory of God in my life!

(Galatians 2:20,21; Ephesians 2:4-10,14,18; 3:12; Hebrews 3:6; 4:15,16)

ROMANS 5:3-5 KJV

And not only so, but we glory in tribulations also: knowing that tribulation worketh patience; and patience, experience; and experience, hope: and hope maketh not ashamed; because the love of God is shed abroad in our hearts by the Holy Ghost which is given unto us.

——— DECLARATION OF FAITH ———

I remain full of joy when I encounter trials and sufferings, for I know that through faith and patience I shall emerge triumphant; for trials produce perseverance and endurance in me; and perseverance and endurance develop a maturity of character in me; and the maturity of character in me yields a harvest of joyful

*and confident hope; and this hope never disappoints me, for God's love is shed
abroad in my heart through the Holy Spirit who is within me, and through Him,
I stand victorious in every situation.*

(Matthew 5:10-12; Hebrews 6:12; James 1:2-4; 2 Corinthians 1:22; 1 Corinthians 15:57)

ROMANS 5:9-11 KJV

Much more then, being now justified by his blood, we shall be saved from wrath
through him. For if, when we were enemies, we were reconciled to God by the
death of his Son, much more, being reconciled, we shall be saved by his life. And
not only so, but we also joy in God through our Lord Jesus Christ, by whom we
have now received the atonement.

———— DECLARATION OF FAITH ————

*Right now, at this very moment, I stand justified by the blood of Jesus, and
through Him, I have been saved from all of God's wrath.*

*I have been reconciled with the Father through the death of His Son, Jesus.
Therefore, having been reconciled, I am saved through His life.*

*I rejoice in God, my Father, through my Lord Jesus, through whom I have
received reconciliation!*

(Romans 5:1,2; John 5:24; 14:19; 2 Corinthians 5:17-21; Ephesians 2:13)

ROMANS 5:15-17 KJV

(But not as the offence, so also is the free gift. For if through the offence of one
many be dead, much more the grace of God, and the gift by grace, which is by
one man, Jesus Christ, hath abounded unto many. And not as it was by one that
sinned, so is the gift: for the judgment was by one to condemnation, but the free
gift is of many offences unto justification. For if by one man's offence death
reigned by one; much more they which receive abundance of grace and of the
gift of righteousness shall reign in life by one, Jesus Christ.)

———— DECLARATION OF FAITH ————

*God has joyfully given me the free gift of grace, justification and righteous-
ness. His gift to me has no strings attached, but He gives it to me freely so that I
may have continuous fellowship with Him in a legitimate Father and son/daugh-
ter relationship.*

*The gift of God to me is not like the result of Adam's sin, for by Adam's sin,
judgment and condemnation fell on me without choice. Freedom and justification, on the other hand, are offered to me as a free gift.*

Though Adam's sin condemned me, God's free gift has brought me justifica-
tion; for as Adam's sin brought me death, God's abundant provision of grace
(unmerited, undeserved favor) and free gift of righteousness, has made it so that I
can reign in this life as a king.

(Ephesians 2:4-10; Galatians 4:4-6; 5:1; Titus 3:4-7; Revelation 1:4-6)

ROMANS 6:2-14 KJV

God forbid. How shall we, that are dead to sin, live any longer therein? Know
ye not, that so many of us as were baptized into Jesus Christ were baptized
into his death? Therefore we are buried with him by baptism into death: that
like as Christ was raised up from the dead by the glory of the Father, even so
we also should walk in newness of life. For if we have been planted together in
the likeness of his death, we shall be also in the likeness of his resurrection:
Knowing this, that our old man is crucified with *him,* that the body of sin
might be destroyed, that henceforth we should not serve sin. For he that is
dead is freed from sin. Now if we be dead with Christ, we believe that we shall
also live with him: Knowing that Christ being raised from the dead dieth no
more; death hath no more dominion over him. For in that he died, he died
unto sin once: but in that he liveth, he liveth unto God. Likewise reckon ye
also yourselves to be dead indeed unto sin, but alive unto God through Jesus
Christ our Lord. Let not sin therefore reign in your mortal body, that ye
should obey it in the lusts thereof. Neither yield ye your members *as* instruments of unrighteousness unto sin: but yield yourselves unto God, as those
that are alive from the dead, and your members *as* instruments of righteousness unto God. For sin shall not have dominion over you: for ye are not under
the law, but under grace.

─────── *DECLARATION OF FAITH* ───────

I have died to sin; therefore, I shall no longer live in it.

When I was baptized into Jesus, I was baptized into His death. I was buried
with Him in baptism into death, in order that, just as Jesus was raised from the
dead, I might be raised to a new life through Him. By this, I am perfectly identi-
fied with His death, burial and Resurrection. It was as if I myself, through His
substitution, suffered the penalty for my sins, seeing that all Jesus did was done
for me personally and is set to my account. I have been perfectly united with Him
in His death and I am also perfectly united with Him in His Resurrection.

My old spiritually dead self was crucified with Jesus in order to free my body
from slavery to sin's power. As a born-again child of God, my old nature no

longer has the power to control my actions. Because I died with Jesus, I have been set completely free!

Now since I died with Christ, I also live through Him. I know that since Jesus was raised from the dead, He cannot die again; death no longer has any kind of power over Him; for by the death that He died, He died to sin (ending His relationship to it), but the life that He lives, He lives in an unbreakable bond with God.

In the same way, I count myself, through identification with Jesus, as being dead to sin, and yet I am alive and living in an unbreakable bond with God. Therefore, I will not allow sin to control my mortal body in any way. I will not use any part of my body as an instrument of wickedness, nor will I allow the evil one to overrun any part of me.

Sin is no longer my master in any way, for I have been set free from its power and have become a partaker of God's grace. Therefore, sin can no longer separate me from my Father, and together we continually demonstrate its defeat in my life.

(Galatians 2:16-21; 3:27; 6:15; Philippians 3:10; Colossians 2:11-15; 3:1,5; John 15:5; 17:20-26; 1 Peter 2:24; 4:1; 2 Timothy 2:11; Ephesians 1:17-23; 2:4-6; Romans 3:26; 2 Corinthians 5:21; 8:9)

Romans 6:15-18 KJV

What then? shall we sin, because we are not under the law, but under grace? God forbid. Know ye not, that to whom ye yield yourselves servants to obey, his servants ye are to whom ye obey; whether of sin unto death, or of obedience unto righteousness? But God be thanked, that ye were the servants of sin, but ye have obeyed from the heart that form of doctrine which was delivered you. Being then made free from sin, ye became the servants of righteousness.

———— *DECLARATION OF FAITH* ————

The thought of using my complete freedom from sin as an excuse to live in it is reprehensible to me. It goes against the very law of my new nature.

I also know that, even as a born-again child of God, if I offer myself to sin, I can become its slave again. I become the slave of the one that I obey, whether to sin, which leads to destruction, or to obedience, which leads to righteousness and the God-kind of life. I thank God that I can now wholeheartedly obey Him and live by the Word, and that having been set free from sin, I have now become a servant of righteousness.

(2 Corinthians 5:17,21; 2 Peter 1:4; 2:19; 1 Corinthians 9:21; John 8:32)

ROMANS 6:22,23 NKJV

But now having been set free from sin, and having become slaves of God, you have your fruit to holiness, and the end, everlasting life. For the wages of sin *is* death, but the gift of God *is* eternal life in Christ Jesus our Lord.

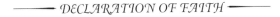

I have been set free from the power of sin.

I am determined to serve God with all of my heart and I am reaping the benefits of holiness and eternal life; for though the wages of sin is death, God's gift to me is eternal life in Christ Jesus my Lord.

(Romans 6:18; 8:1,2; Genesis 2:17; 1 Peter 1:4; 1 John 5:11,12)

ROMANS 7:1,4 NIV

Do you not know, brothers—for I am speaking to men who know the law—that the law has authority over a man only as long as he lives? So, my brothers, you also died to the law through the body of Christ, that you might belong to another, to him who was raised from the dead, in order that we might bear fruit to God.

——— DECLARATION OF FAITH ———

Even the Law of Moses itself no longer has any power over me, for I died with Christ. I now belong to another, Jesus, who was raised from the dead, in order that I might bear fruit unto God. In Him, I died to the Law and became the workmanship of God in a new life where I am designed as a doer of good.

(Galatians 2:16-21; Ephesians 2:10; John 15:1-8; 2 Peter 1:4; 2 Corinthians 5:17)

ROMANS 7:6 NKJV

But now we have been delivered from the law, having died to what we were held by, so that we should serve in the newness of the Spirit and not *in* the oldness of the letter.

The Law once held me in bondage due to its revelation of my sin nature. But I have died to the Law and have been set free to serve God in the new way of the spirit and not the old way of the written code.

(Hebrews 10:1-18; Romans 4:15; 6:6-11; 8:1,2; 1 Corinthians 15:56,57)

ROMANS 7:24,25 KJV

O wretched man that I am! who shall deliver me from the body of this death? I thank God through Jesus Christ our Lord. So then with the mind I myself serve the law of God; but with the flesh the law of sin.

———— *DECLARATION OF FAITH* ————

I have been set free from bondage to the passions of my body which, realized through the Law, brought me death. I thank God, through Jesus Christ my Lord, that I have been set free! I can now see clearly to serve God in truth and, by the power of the Holy Spirit within me, I have the strength to overcome the desires of the old nature still present within my body and bring it into subjection to my recreated spirit.

(1 Corinthians 9:27; 15:51,52,57; Romans 8:1,2,11; Galatians 5:1,16,24,25)

ROMANS 8:1,2 AMP

Therefore, [there is] now no condemnation (no adjudging guilty of wrong) for those who are in Christ Jesus, who live [and] walk not after the dictates of the flesh, but after the dictates of the Spirit. For the law of the Spirit of life [which is] in Christ Jesus [the law of our new being] has freed me from the law of sin and of death.

———— *DECLARATION OF FAITH* ————

There is therefore now no condemnation (pronouncement of guilt) for me for I am in Christ Jesus. I have become one with Him. The Law of the Spirit of Life in Christ Jesus has set me free from the Law of sin and death (the Law of Moses).

(John 5:24; 17:20-26; 1 John 2:1,2; 1 Corinthians 15:45,56,57; Romans 7:24,25; 8:31-39)

ROMANS 8:4-6 KJV

That the righteousness of the law might be fulfilled in us, who walk not after the flesh, but after the Spirit. For they that are after the flesh do mind the things of the flesh; but they that are after the Spirit the things of the Spirit. For to be carnally minded is death; but to be spiritually minded is life and peace.

———— *DECLARATION OF FAITH* ————

The righteous requirement of the Law is fulfilled in me. I do not live according to the old desires that brought me death, but according to my recreated spirit as led by the Holy Spirit.

I do not set my mind on natural desires, but on the desires of my spirit. I know that the mind of the flesh affiliates me with the things of death, but if I allow my spirit to control my mind, it will bring me into union with life and peace.

(Galatians 5:16-25; 6:7-9; Romans 6:4; 8:14; 12:2; Ephesians 5:1-18; 1 John 1:5-9; 2:6)

ROMANS 8:9-13 KJV

But ye are not in the flesh, but in the Spirit, if so be that the Spirit of God dwell in you. Now if any man have not the Spirit of Christ, he is none of his. And if Christ *be* in you, the body *is* dead because of sin; but the Spirit *is* life because of righteousness. But if the Spirit of him that raised up Jesus from the dead dwell in you, he that raised up Christ from the dead shall also quicken your mortal bodies by his Spirit that dwelleth in you. Therefore, brethren, we are debtors, not to the flesh, to live after the flesh. For if ye live after the flesh, ye shall die: but if ye through the Spirit do mortify the deeds of the body, ye shall live.

———— DECLARATION OF FAITH ————

I am not controlled by the flesh, or the natural desires of my old nature, but by my recreated spirit where the very Spirit of God dwells.

Jesus Himself dwells within me.

The old sinful nature, that was once me, is dead because of sin, but my recreated spirit is fully alive because of righteousness.

The Spirit of the One who raised Jesus from the dead dwells within me, and through that same resurrection power, He gives life (health and vitality) to this mortal body in which I dwell.

I no longer have to live by what is natural (the laws of nature established in my flesh), for those ways are the ways of death (producing the things of death). Through my spirit (led by the Holy Spirit), I kill off all of those practices that are one with death [and produce the things of death], and I live my life in the way that produces the things of life in me.

(Galatians 2:20,21; 6:8; 1 Corinthians 5:17,21; Ephesians 1:17-23; 4:22)

ROMANS 8:14-17 KJV

For as many as are led by the Spirit of God, they are the sons of God. For ye have not received the spirit of bondage again to fear; but ye have received the Spirit of adoption, whereby we cry, Abba, Father. The Spirit itself beareth witness with our spirit, that we are the children of God: And if children, then heirs; heirs of God, and joint-heirs with Christ; if so be that we suffer with *him*, that we may be also glorified together.

——— *DECLARATION OF FAITH* ———

By living under the guidance of the Holy Spirit, I demonstrate the fact that I am a son/daughter of God.

The Holy Spirit is not in me to put me in bondage or make me afraid, but to bring me to the realization of my new relationship with my heavenly Father. The Holy Spirit bears witness with my own spirit that I am God's own son/daughter. It is through His revelation that I have realized that God is my Father. I am an actual heir in the royal family of God!

I am God's own son/daughter and I share in the same inheritance that Jesus does! When I became one with Him in His suffering, I also became one with Him in His glory!

(Galatians 2:20,21; 4:4-6; 5:1; 2 Timothy 1:7; 1 John 3:1,2; 5:1-13; Ephesians 2:6; John 17:20-26; Romans 8:29,30)

ROMANS 8:18,19 KJV

For I reckon that the sufferings of this present time are not worthy to be compared with the glory which shall be revealed in us. For the earnest expectation of the creature waiteth for the manifestation of the sons of God.

——— *DECLARATION OF FAITH* ———

I could care less what trials I go through now, for I know that in Him I shall always emerge victorious and that eventually His glory shall be revealed in me for all to see.

Even creation itself is waiting in eager expectation for the manifestation of the sons and daughters of God. I am determined that it will not be disappointed.

(Matthew 5:10-16; 2 Corinthians 4:17; 2 Peter 3:13)

ROMANS 8:23-30 KJV

And not only *they,* but ourselves also, which have the firstfruits of the Spirit, even we ourselves groan within ourselves, waiting for the adoption, *to wit,* the redemption of our body. For we are saved by hope: but hope that is seen is not hope: for what a man seeth, why doth he yet hope for? But if we hope for that we see not, *then* do we with patience wait for *it.* Likewise the Spirit also helpeth our infirmities: for we know not what we should pray for as we ought: but the Spirit itself maketh intercession for us with groanings which cannot be uttered. And he that searcheth the hearts knoweth what *is* the mind of the Spirit, because he maketh intercession for the saints according to *the will of* God. And we know that all things work together for good to them that love God, to them who are the called according to *his* purpose. For whom he did foreknow, he also did predestinate *to be* conformed to the image of his Son, that he might be the firstborn among many brethren. Moreover whom he did predestinate, them he also called: and whom he called, them he also justified: and whom he justified, them he also glorified.

─────── *DECLARATION OF FAITH* ───────

As a child of God and partaker of the firstfruits of the Spirit, I groan
inwardly as I eagerly await the redemption of my body. It is in this hope that I
am saved; for I do not hope for the things that I have, but patiently wait for them,
continually expressing my firm, confident belief. This is the very demonstration of
my faith.

In the same way, the Holy Spirit helps me in my weaknesses, for I do not
always know exactly what to pray for, but the Spirit Himself meets my supplica-
tion with groanings too unfathomable for known speech. My heavenly Father
searches my heart and knows the Holy Spirit's intentions, for He intercedes on my
behalf according to the perfect will of God.

Therefore, with God Himself as my prayer partner, I know that everything
that I am praying for in the spirit [under the Holy Spirit's lead] will work
together for my good. I love my Father with all of my heart. He has given me a
specific purpose in His great plan and I joyfully fulfill it in my life.

My Father knew me before the beginning of time and has made it my destiny
to be conformed to the image of Jesus. Jesus has become my elder brother. He is the
firstborn in the family. As God's newborn child, I am foreordained to become, in
nature, all that Jesus is. And being foreordained, I have also been called; and being
called, I have also been justified; and being justified, I have also been glorified.

(Hebrews 11:1; 1 Corinthians 14:2,4,5,13,15,17,18; 2 Peter 1:4; 2 Corinthians 5:2-5,17;
Ephesians 1:4-14; 2:6-10; 4:30; 6:18; 2 Timothy 2:19; 1 Peter 2:9; 3:9; Galatians 2:16-21;
John 17:20-26)

ROMANS 8:31-39 KJV

What shall we then say to these things? If God *be* for us, who *can be* against us? He that spared not his own Son, but delivered him up for us all, how shall he not with him also freely give us all things? Who shall lay any thing to the charge of God's elect? *It is* God that justifieth. Who *is* he that condemneth? *It is* Christ that died, yea rather, that is risen again, who is even at the right hand of God, who also maketh intercession for us. Who shall separate us from the love of Christ? *shall* tribulation, or distress, or persecution, or famine, or nakedness, or peril, or sword? As it is written, For thy sake we are killed all the day long; we are accounted as sheep for the slaughter. Nay, in all these things we are more than conquerors through him that loved us. For I am persuaded, that neither death, nor life, nor angels, nor principalities, nor powers, nor things present, nor things to come, Nor height, nor depth, nor any other creature, shall be able to separate us from the love of God, which is in Christ Jesus our Lord.

─── DECLARATION OF FAITH ───

So what shall I declare about all of this? If God is on my side, where is there a formidable foe, or worthy enemy? God didn't even spare His own Son, but gave Him for my salvation. Shall He not freely and graciously give me everything else as well? And who is it that can bring a single charge against me? God has already justified me and declared me to be righteous. Will even God Himself make a charge against me after paying such an awesome price to bring me into this great relationship? Who is it then who has any power to condemn me? Jesus alone has that power. Shall He condemn me after dying for me, suffering for me, and being raised to life for me? Shall Jesus, the One who loves me so much that He ever lives to make intercession for me, condemn me now? Who is it that can separate me from such love? Can persecution, troubles, hardships, famine, depression, distress, destitution, peril or danger separate me from Jesus' love? No!!! It doesn't matter what my situation may be. It doesn't matter if I am facing death, or looked upon as a sheep headed for the slaughter. No matter what is going on in my life, I shall rise as more than a conqueror through Him who loves me! I know of a certainty that neither death, nor life, nor angels, nor demons, nor anything present, nor anything to come, nor any kind of powers, no power from on high, nor a power from below, nor any power of any kind in all of creation can separate me from the love of God which is in Christ Jesus my Lord! Any questions?

(Hebrews 7:25; 10:10,14; 13:5,6; 2 Peter 1:3; Numbers 14:9; Isaiah 50:8,9; 2 Corinthians 5:17,21; John 3:16-18; Ephesians 1:17-23; 3:14-21; 1 Corinthians 15:57)

ROMANS 9:6,7 KJV

Not as though the word of God hath taken none effect. For they are not all Israel, which are of Israel: Neither, because they are the seed of Abraham, are they all children: but, In Isaac shall thy seed be called.

─── DECLARATION OF FAITH ───

I am a true member of the house of Israel and a descendant of Abraham, the father of my faith. I am the very offspring to whom the promise applies.

(Galatians 3:7,29; 4:23; 6:16; Ephesians 2:18; 1 John 3:1,2)

ROMANS 9:23 NIV

What if he did this to make the riches of his glory known to the objects of his mercy, whom he prepared in advance for glory.

DECLARATION OF FAITH

I have been prepared beforehand for glory. As a vessel of God's mercy and grace, He has made it His business to make His glory known in me.

(Romans 8:28-30; Ephesians 1:4; Colossians 1:27-29)

ROMANS 9:26 KJV

And it shall come to pass, that in the place where it was said unto them, Ye are not my people; there shall they be called the children of the living God.

DECLARATION OF FAITH

I am known throughout heaven as God's own son/daughter.

(Hosea 1:10; Luke 15:7,10; Acts 19:15)

ROMANS 9:30 AMP

What shall we say then? That Gentiles who did not follow after righteousness [who did not seek salvation by right relationship to God] have attained it by faith [a righteousness imputed by God, based on and produced by faith].

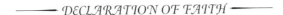

DECLARATION OF FAITH

I have obtained a righteousness that is not my own. My righteousness comes from God through the avenue of my faith.

(2 Corinthians 5:21; Romans 1:17; 3:21; 4:11)

ROMANS 9:33 KJV

As it is written, Behold, I lay in Sion a stumblingstone and rock of offence: and whosoever believeth on him shall not be ashamed.

DECLARATION OF FAITH

I believe in Jesus, the Rock, and have put my total trust and reliance for my salvation in Him alone. I shall not be put to shame nor disappointed in my expectations.

(Isaiah 8:14; 28:16; Romans 5:5; 10:11; Ephesians 3:14-21)

ROMANS 10:3,4 KJV

For they being ignorant of God's righteousness, and going about to establish their own righteousness, have not submitted themselves unto the righteousness of God. For Christ is the end of the law for righteousness to every one that believeth.

——— *DECLARATION OF FAITH* ———

I am well aware that I have been made the righteousness of God in Christ Jesus my Lord. Therefore, I do not go about trying to establish my own righteousness through good deeds of any kind. Christ is the end of the Law for me. He has made me righteous simply because I believe.

(2 Corinthians 5:21; Galatians 2:16-21; Philippians 3:9; Ephesians 2:8-10)

ROMANS 10:6-13 KJV

But the righteousness which is of faith speaketh on this wise, Say not in thine heart, Who shall ascend into heaven? (that is, to bring Christ down *from above:*) Or, Who shall descend into the deep? (that is, to bring up Christ again from the dead.) But what saith it? The word is nigh thee, *even* in thy mouth, and in thy heart: that is, the word of faith, which we preach; That if thou shalt confess with thy mouth the Lord Jesus, and shalt believe in thine heart that God hath raised him from the dead, thou shalt be saved. For with the heart man believeth unto righteousness; and with the mouth confession is made unto salvation. For the scripture saith, Whosoever believeth on him shall not be ashamed. For there is no difference between the Jew and the Greek: for the same Lord over all is rich unto all that call upon him. For whosoever shall call upon the name of the Lord shall be saved.

——— *DECLARATION OF FAITH* ———

My righteousness is founded on faith.

It is now totally unnecessary for me to try to bombard the gates of heaven in order to be saved or receive from God. I am always welcome at my Father's throne.

It is also ludicrous for me to expect Jesus to suffer over and over again every time I mess up. His sacrifice has made me righteous once and for all.

The way of justification, salvation, healing, and blessing is not put at a distance from me. As it is written, the Word is very near to me—it is on my lips and in my heart. I make my confession by the word of faith. If I confess with my mouth the lordship of Jesus and believe in my heart that God has raised Him from the dead, I shall be saved and delivered from every circumstance beginning with salvation from spiritual death; for it is with my heart that I believe unto justification and righteousness, and it is with my mouth that I confess, bringing forth my salvation and deliverance. As it is written, "Anyone who puts their faith in Him shall never be put to shame." Through this process, my Lord richly blesses me with all things, for everyone who calls on His name shall be saved.

(Hebrews 4:15,16; 10:10,14; 11:1,6; Romans 1:17; 3:21,22; 4:11; 5:1,2; 8:32; 9:30; Deuteronomy 30:12-14; Luke 12:8; Mark 11:22-25; 2 Corinthians 4:13; 5:7; Jeremiah 1:12; Matthew 21:19-22; Ephesians 1:7,17-23; Joel 2:32; Acts 2:21,38,39; 2 Peter 1:3)

ROMANS 10:14,15 NKJV

How then shall they call on Him in whom they have not believed? And how shall they believe in Him of whom they have not heard? And how shall they hear without a preacher? And how shall they preach unless they are sent? As it is written: "How beautiful are the feet of those who preach the gospel of peace, who bring glad tidings of good things!"

DECLARATION OF FAITH

I have been sent into the world, beginning with my neighborhood and my city, to proclaim the Gospel of Jesus. It is written of me, "How beautiful are the feet of those who bring Good News!" And it is Good News that I bring. My message is not one of condemnation, or hellfire and brimstone, but of salvation, freedom, deliverance, grace, righteousness, and acceptance into the royal family of God!

(Romans 2:4; Acts 1:8; 2 Corinthians 5:18-20; Matthew 28:18-20; Isaiah 52:7)

ROMANS 10:17,18 KJV

So then faith *cometh* by hearing, and hearing by the word of God. But I say, Have they not heard? Yes verily, their sound went into all the earth, and their words unto the ends of the world.

DECLARATION OF FAITH

My faith is strengthened by continually feeding the Word into my spirit. And my faith is productive. My words go out into all of the earth.

(Joshua 1:8; John 6:63; 15:7,8; Psalm 19:4; Proverbs 18:20,21; 1 Kings 18:10)

ROMANS 11:6 NKJV

And if by grace, then *it is* no longer of works; otherwise grace is no longer grace. But if *it is* of works, it is no longer grace; otherwise work is no longer work.

I am a child of God by grace (unmerited, undeserved favor). Works do not earn me any merit points with God to bring me into a closer relationship with Him. That would nullify His grace towards me. My relationship with God cannot be earned in any way. There is not a single work of righteousness that can bring me any closer to Him than I am right now.

(Ephesians 2:8-10; Romans 4:2-8; 5:8-18; 6:23; Titus 3:4-7)

ROMANS 11:16,18 KJV

For if the firstfruit *be* holy, the lump *is* also *holy:* and if the root *be* holy, so *are* the branches. Boast not against the branches. But if thou boast, thou bearest not the root, but the root thee.

DECLARATION OF FAITH

Jesus is the Vine and I am a branch of the Vine. If the Vine is holy, I am holy as well. In this, I do not make an arrogant boast, just a statement of fact. It is a declaration of my total and complete dependency upon Jesus. It is the Vine that gives life to the branch. Without Jesus, I am nothing. It is not me who supports the Vine, but the Vine who supports me.

(John 15:5; Hebrews 10:14; Leviticus 23:10)

ROMANS 11:22 NIV

Consider therefore the kindness and sternness of God: sternness to those who fell, but kindness to you, provided that you continue in his kindness. Otherwise, you also will be cut off.

DECLARATION OF FAITH

I acknowledge both God's kindness and His strictness [or severity]. His kindness has been poured out on me because I believe, but His strictness remains with those who abide in, or turn to, an evil heart of unbelief. Therefore, I purpose in my heart to continue in His kindness.

(1 Corinthians 15:2; John 15:2; Galatians 6:7-9)

ROMANS 11:29

God's gifts and God's call are under full warranty—never canceled, never rescinded.

God's gifts and His calling to me are irrevocable. Once He has given them to me, they are mine forever.

(Numbers 23:19; Ephesians 4:4; 2 Peter 1:10)

ROMANS 12:1-3 KJV

I beseech you therefore, brethren, by the mercies of God, that ye present your bodies a living sacrifice, holy, acceptable unto God, *which is* your reasonable service. And be not conformed to this world: but be ye transformed by the renewing of your mind, that ye may prove what *is* that good, and acceptable, and perfect, will of God. For I say, through the grace given unto me, to every man that is among you, not to think *of himself* more highly than he ought to think; but to think soberly, according as God hath dealt to every man the measure of faith.

——— DECLARATION OF FAITH ———

In view of God's mercy, I dedicate my body as a living sacrifice, holy and well pleasing to Him. This is my spiritual worship. I follow the ways of the spirit as I am led by the Holy Spirit. I do not conform to the ways of the world, but am transformed by the renewing of my mind so that I may demonstrate the good, acceptable and perfect will of God.

I stand by God's grace alone. I do not esteem myself more highly than I should, for I know that in and of myself I am nothing. Rather, I think of myself with sober judgment. I know that my value in the sight of God is inestimable and that He has given me the measure of faith to put me over in this life. However, I do not forget that all that I have, I have been given. I am totally, completely and joyfully dependent upon my God.

(2 Corinthians 6:14; 10:1-4; Hebrews 10:18-20; 1 John 2:15; Ephesians 4:7,23; Proverbs 25:27; Galatians 5:1; Romans 5:1,2; Psalm 24:1)

ROMANS 12:5,6 NKJV

So we, being many, are one body in Christ, and individually members of one another. Having then gifts differing according to the grace that is given to us, let us use them: if prophecy, let us prophesy in proportion to our faith.

——— DECLARATION OF FAITH ———

I am a man/woman with specific gifts, talents and special abilities according to the divine enabling given to me. These gifts are empowered and enhanced through my faith and the anointing. I purposefully function in these gifts for the edification of the body of Christ.

(1 Corinthians 7:20; 10:17; 12:12-14; Romans 11:29; Ephesians 4:8; 1 Timothy 4:14)

ROMANS 12:9-21 KJV

Let love be without dissimulation. Abhor that which is evil; cleave to that which is good. *Be* kindly affectioned one to another with brotherly love; in honour preferring one another; Not slothful in business; fervent in spirit; serving the Lord; Rejoicing in hope; patient in tribulation; continuing instant in prayer; Distributing to the necessity of saints; given to hospitality. Bless them which persecute you: bless, and curse not. Rejoice with them that do rejoice, and weep with them that weep. *Be* of the same mind one toward another. Mind not high things, but condescend to men of low estate. Be not wise in your own conceits. Recompense to no man evil for evil. Provide things honest in the sight of all men. If it be possible, as much as lieth in you, live peaceably with all men. Dearly beloved, avenge not yourselves, but *rather* give place unto wrath: for it is written, Vengeance *is* mine; I will repay, saith the Lord. Therefore if thine enemy hunger, feed him; if he thirst, give him drink: for in so doing thou shalt heap coals of fire on his head. Be not overcome of evil, but overcome evil with good.

———— DECLARATION OF FAITH ————

My love for others is sincere.

I hate what is evil and cling to that which is good.

I am drawn to my brothers and sisters in Christ in a spirit of love and devotion, giving them precedence and seeking their honor above my own.

I am earnest and diligent in every endeavor, remaining perpetually fired up as I serve the Lord.

I rejoice and celebrate in this hope that I have been given.

I am steadfast and unwavering in times of trial and suffering.

I am constant in prayer.

I give generously to the needs of the Church.

I practice courtesy and hospitality.

I pray down blessings upon those who persecute me. I bless them and never curse them. I always see them as potential brothers and sisters in Christ.

I rejoice with those who rejoice, sharing in their joy, and I grieve with those who grieve, sharing in their sorrow.

I live in harmony with every member of God's family.

I am not haughty or snobbish, but am willing to associate with people in low positions as well as high.

I am willing to give myself to even the lowliest of tasks, not thinking myself to be above them in any way. I never overestimate myself, nor think of myself as being wise in and of myself.

I never seek vengeance, trying to pay someone back for an evil done to me, nor do I seek to avenge myself for a wrong, but leave the way open for God's wrath; for it is written, "Vengeance is Mine, I will repay," says the Lord.

Therefore, if my enemy is hungry, I feed him. If he is thirsty, I give him something to drink. In doing this, I pile burning coals upon his head.

I am never overcome by evil, but prove myself to be its master by doing that which is good.

I am always careful to do what is noble, honorable and right in every situation.

If it is possible, so far as it depends upon me, I will live at peace with everyone.

(1 Corinthians 12:26; 13:4-8; Psalm 34:14; 97:10; Hebrews 12:14; 13:1; Philippians 2:2,3; 24:2-4; Proverbs 3:7; 6:6-11; 25:21,22; Colossians 3:23; James 1:2-4; Ephesians 6:18; 2 Corinthians 8:21; 9:5-11; 1 Timothy 3:2; Matthew 5:39,44; Jeremiah 45:5; Leviticus 19:18; Deuteronomy 32:35)

ROMANS 13:1,2 AMP

Let every person be loyally subject to the governing (civil) authorities. For there is no authority except from God [by His permission, His sanction], and those that exist do so by God's appointment. Therefore he who resists and sets himself up against the authorities resists what God has appointed and arranged [in divine order]. And those who resist will bring down judgment upon themselves [receiving the penalty due them].

─── *DECLARATION OF FAITH* ───

I am submitted to the governing authorities in every way that brings honor to God; for it is God who has established the authorities and I will not rebel against Him by rebelling against them. Therefore, I will remain faithful and loyal to the government so long as their laws do not violate the higher laws and commands of God.

(1 Peter 2:13; Titus 3:1; Daniel 3)

Romans 13:7,8 KJV

Render therefore to all their dues: tribute to whom tribute *is due;* custom to whom custom; fear to whom fear; honour to whom honour. Owe no man any thing, but to love one another: for he that loveth another hath fulfilled the law.

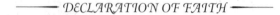

I pay all that I owe. I do not try to skirt my responsibilities toward others. If I owe taxes, I pay them. If I owe payments, I pay them. If I owe respect, I give it. If I owe honor, I give it as well. I let no debt remain outstanding, except for the continual debt to love my fellow man.

Through my unwavering expression of love, I fulfill the Law.

(Matthew 7:12; 22:21,39,40; Galatians 5:13,14)

Romans 13:10 NKJV

Love does no harm to a neighbor; therefore love *is* the fulfillment of the law.

Because I purpose in my heart to love my fellow man, I have met every demand in the Law; for the Law is designed for the good of all and since love does no harm to its neighbor, love [in and through me] is the fulfillment of the Law.

(Matthew 7:12; 22:21,39,40; James 2:8)

Romans 13:12-14 KJV

The night is far spent, the day is at hand: let us therefore cast off the works of darkness, and let us put on the armour of light. Let us walk honestly, as in the day; not in rioting and drunkenness, not in chambering and wantonness, not in strife and envying. But put ye on the Lord Jesus Christ, and make not provision for the flesh, to *fulfil* the lusts *thereof.*

DECLARATION OF FAITH

I cast away all deeds of darkness from my life and put on the armor of Light. I conduct myself in honor and decency. I do not revel in drunkenness and immorality, nor do I waste my time in senseless quarreling and jealousy. I clothe myself with Jesus, making sure that there is no way opened for indulging in worldly desires that are in opposition to God's plan for my life.

(Ephesians 5:1-18; 6:10-18; Philippians 4:8; Proverbs 23:20; 1 Corinthians 6:9; James 3:14; Galatians 3:27; 5:16)

ROMANS 14:4 NIV

Who are you to judge someone else's servant? To his own master he stands or falls. And he will stand, for the Lord is able to make him stand.

——— *DECLARATION OF FAITH* ———

I do not stand as judge and jury over anyone. That office belongs to God alone. If I see someone doing wrong, I will go to them and make them aware of their fault. If they refuse to turn to the right, I will break fellowship with them and pray for them, while still esteeming them as one of the family. I will not turn away from them, but fully trust in God's ability to bring them back to the Light.

I myself am accepted and welcomed by God. He is my support and is well able to establish me and make me stand firm against all opposition.

(James 4:11,12; Matthew 18:15-17; 1 Corinthians 5:1-13; Jude 24)

ROMANS 14:12,13 KJV

So then every one of us shall give account of himself to God. Let us not therefore judge one another any more: but judge this rather, that no man put a stumblingblock or an occasion to fall in *his* brother's way.

——— *DECLARATION OF FAITH* ———

I will one day give account of myself to God. Therefore, I will not pass judgment on any of my brothers and sisters in Christ, nor will I be a stumbling block or obstacle in their path. When I stand before the Lord, I will be able to say that I was a source of encouragement who always saw the best in others.

(Matthew 7:1-5; 1 Peter 4:5; 1 Corinthians 3:11-14; 8:9; 13:4-8; 2 Corinthians 5:10; Hebrews 10:24)

ROMANS 14:17 AMP

[After all] the kingdom of God is not a matter of [getting the] food and drink [one likes], but instead it is righteousness (that state which makes a person acceptable to God) and [heart] peace and joy in the Holy Spirit.

——— *DECLARATION OF FAITH* ———

I fully understand that the kingdom of God is not a matter of a set of regulations concerning what I should eat or drink, but of living my life in righteousness, peace, and joy in the Holy Spirit.

(1 Corinthians 8:8; Ephesians 2:14; Philippians 4:4; Romans 8:3-10)

ROMANS 14:19 NIV

Let us therefore make every effort to do what leads to peace and to mutual edification.

——— *DECLARATION OF FAITH* ———

I will do everything in my power to do those things that lead to peace.

It is my sincere purpose to be a source of encouragement and edification to others.

(1 Corinthians 9:22; 10:24; 14:3-5,12; Romans 12:18)

ROMANS 15:2 NKJV

Let each of us please *his* neighbor for *his* good, leading to edification.

——— *DECLARATION OF FAITH* ———

I do my best to please my neighbor. I always seek what is best for them instead of criticizing and discouraging them. I make it my purpose to build them up so that they can reach their highest potential.

(Hebrews 10:24; 1 Corinthians 10:24; 14:3-5,12; Romans 12:18)

ROMANS 15:13,14 KJV

Now the God of hope fill you with all joy and peace in believing, that ye may abound in hope, through the power of the Holy Ghost. And I myself also am persuaded of you, my brethren, that ye also are full of goodness, filled with all knowledge, able also to admonish one another.

——— *DECLARATION OF FAITH* ———

My heavenly Father, the God of all hope, fills me with all joy and peace as I believe in Him. I overflow with hope through the Holy Spirit who is within me.

In Him, I am full of goodness, complete in knowledge and well able to teach others the things that I know.

(Romans 14:17; Ephesians 2:14; Philippians 4:7; 1 Timothy 1:1; 1 John 2:20; 2 Peter 1:12; 1 Corinthians 1:5,30)

ROMANS 15:18,19 NKJV

For I will not dare to speak of any of those things which Christ has not accomplished through me, in word and deed, to make the Gentiles obedient—in mighty

signs and wonders, by the power of the Spirit of God, so that from Jerusalem and round about to Illyricum I have fully preached the gospel of Christ.

——— *DECLARATION OF FAITH* ———

I do not preach to others anything but that which Christ has fulfilled in me. By this, I shall win many through both my words and my deeds; for Christ (the anointed One and His anointing that breaks the yoke of bondage) is continually at work both in and through me, performing signs and wonders by the power of the Holy Spirit.

When I preach the Gospel, I leave nothing out. Wherever I am and wherever I go, I offer all of the Gospel, not just the parts that seem acceptable to the senses of man.

(Matthew 7:3-5; Colossians 1:29; Mark 16:20; 2 Timothy 4:2)

ROMANS 15:29-33 KJV

And I am sure that, when I come unto you, I shall come in the fulness of the blessing of the gospel of Christ. Now I beseech you, brethren, for the Lord Jesus Christ's sake, and for the love of the Spirit, that ye strive together with me in *your* prayers to God for me; That I may be delivered from them that do not believe in Judaea; and that my service which *I have* for Jerusalem may be accepted of the saints; That I may come unto you with joy by the will of God, and may with you be refreshed. Now the God of peace *be* with you all. Amen.

——— *DECLARATION OF FAITH* ———

Wherever I go, I bring with me the abundant blessings of the Gospel. Not only this, but I am united with all others [through earnest and fervent prayer] who are proclaiming the Gospel as I am.

My prayer for my fellow workers is that they are delivered from the wrath of unbelievers and that their mission and message is acceptable to all of the saints— that we all, by the will of God, are filled with joy when we meet, and that the awareness of God's presence, love and peace remains with us at all times.

(Mark 16:15-20; Isaiah 61:1-3; Acts 10:38; Philippians 2:1; 2 Corinthians 1:11; 2 Timothy 3:11)

ROMANS 16:17-20 KJV

Now I beseech you, brethren, mark them which cause divisions and offences contrary to the doctrine which ye have learned; and avoid them. For they that are such serve not our Lord Jesus Christ, but their own belly; and by good words and fair speeches deceive the hearts of the simple. For your obedience is come abroad unto all *men*. I am glad therefore on your behalf: but yet I would have you wise unto that which is good, and simple concerning evil. And the God of peace shall bruise Satan under your feet shortly. The grace of our Lord Jesus Christ *be* with you. Amen.

─── DECLARATION OF FAITH ───

I am constantly on guard against those who create dissentions and cause divisions in the body of Christ and are in opposition to the fullness of the Gospel that I have been given. I avoid them if at all possible and rebuke them when the situation demands it; for such persons do not serve my Lord Jesus, but the inclinations of their own minds and desires. Through eloquence and flattery they deceive the simpleminded.

As for me, I am obedient to the Word of God alone. In Jesus, I am well versed and wise as to what is good, and innocent of what is evil. My loyalty and obedience to the Word is laid open for all the world to examine. Through this, I regularly enjoy watching my Father crush Satan beneath my feet.

My Father is the God of all peace and His grace is always with me as I am in Christ Jesus my Lord.

(1 Timothy 1:18-20; 2 Timothy 2:16-19; Acts 15:1; 1 Corinthians 5:9; Matthew 5:16; 10:16; 18:15-17; Psalm 119:110-115: Hebrews 10:10-17)

CHAPTER FORTY-SIX

1 CORINTHIANS

First Corinthians is an epistle of the apostle Paul to the church at Corinth, the capital of the Roman province of Achaia. The epistle was probably written around 55 AD. In it, Paul addresses problems that were facing the church at that time. Many of these problems are still prevalent in the church today. We still face schisms, humanism, disorderliness, abuse of spiritual gifts, etc.

The promises of the book of 1 Corinthians are designed to keep you in balance in your walk with God. As you pray these promises, keep in mind that God is a God of order and that you are praying promises that produce an orderliness in your life that is in accordance with His perfect will.

1 CORINTHIANS 1:4,5 AMP

I thank my God at all times for you because of the grace (the favor and spiritual blessing) of God which was bestowed on you in Christ Jesus, [So] that in Him in every respect you were enriched, in full power and readiness of speech [to speak of your faith] and complete knowledge and illumination [to give you full insight into its meaning].

—— *DECLARATION OF FAITH* ——

God has bestowed upon me an abundance of grace (supernatural ability) so that I am enriched in every way, full of power, complete in knowledge (ability to understand) and prepared to speak the right things in every circumstance.

(Romans 5:17; 1 Corinthians 1:30; 2:6-16; 12:8; Ephesians 1:17-23)

1 CORINTHIANS 1:7-9 KJV

So that ye come behind in no gift; waiting for the coming of our Lord Jesus Christ: Who shall also confirm you unto the end, *that ye may be* blameless in the day of our Lord Jesus Christ. God *is* faithful, by whom ye were called unto the fellowship of his Son Jesus Christ our Lord.

——— DECLARATION OF FAITH ———

I do not lack any spiritual gift as I eagerly await the coming of my Lord. He has established me permanently, so that I will be found blameless on the day of His coming. He Himself is my vindication against all accusation and indictment.

My God is faithful to me. The One who never fails me has called me into fellowship with His Son, Jesus Christ my Lord.

(1 Corinthians 12:1; Jude 24; 1 John 1:3; 2:1,2)

1 Corinthians 1:17 NIV

For Christ did not send me to baptize, but to preach the gospel—not with words of human wisdom, lest the cross of Christ be emptied of its power.

——— DECLARATION OF FAITH ———

I do not preach the Word of God in order to impress people with words of human wisdom, for such an act would be to deny the very power of the cross of Christ.

(1 Corinthians 2:1,4; 2 Timothy 3:5)

1 Corinthians 1:25 NKJV

Because the foolishness of God is wiser than men, and the weakness of God is stronger than men.

——— DECLARATION OF FAITH ———

The lowest form of God's knowledge within me is higher than the highest form of knowledge in man, and the weakest things that spring from the power of God within me are more powerful than any strength that man can muster.

(Daniel 1:17,20; 2:22,23; 1 Corinthians 1:30; Romans 15:19; Ephesians 1:17-23)

1 Corinthians 1:30,31 KJV

But of him are ye in Christ Jesus, who of God is made unto us wisdom, and righteousness, and sanctification, and redemption: That, according as it is written, He that glorieth, let him glory in the Lord.

——— DECLARATION OF FAITH ———

My heavenly Father has given me new life in Christ Jesus my Lord. Jesus has become my wisdom, my righteousness, my sanctification, and my redemption.

Therefore, I set myself in agreement with what is written and make my boast in Him, proudly rejoicing and giving Him glory!

(John 3:3,8,16; 14:13,14; 2 Corinthians 5:21; Hebrews 10:14; Titus 3:4-7; Jeremiah 9:23,24)

1 CORINTHIANS 2:4,5 KJV

And my speech and my preaching was not with enticing words of man's wisdom, but in demonstration of the Spirit and of power: That your faith should not stand in the wisdom of men, but in the power of God.

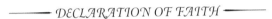

—— DECLARATION OF FAITH ——

My proclamation of the Gospel does not center itself in eloquence [or the persuasive words of human wisdom], but in demonstration of the Holy Spirit's power, so that the faith of those I win into the kingdom will not be grounded in my own wisdom, or that of human philosophy, but in the power of God.

(1 Corinthians 1:17; Acts 1:8; 2 Peter 1:16; Mark 16:20)

1 CORINTHIANS 2:6,7 KJV

Howbeit we speak wisdom among them that are perfect: yet not the wisdom of this world, nor of the princes of this world, that come to nought: But we speak the wisdom of God in a mystery, even the hidden wisdom, which God ordained before the world unto our glory.

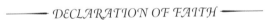

—— DECLARATION OF FAITH ——

I speak a message of godly wisdom to those who are mature and able to hear it. It is not a wisdom of this age, or of those esteemed as wise leaders of the day, for they regularly become known as ignorant and are brought to nothing. Rather, to those who are ready, I speak of a wisdom from God, once hidden, but now revealed in and through us, which God devised and decreed from the foundation of the world for our glorification.

(Matthew 13:11,15,16; Romans 8:28-30; 1 Corinthians 14:2,13; Daniel 2:22,23)

1 CORINTHIANS 2:9,10 KJV

But as it is written, Eye hath not seen, nor ear heard, neither have entered into the heart of man, the things which God hath prepared for them that love him. But God hath revealed them unto us by his Spirit: for the Spirit searcheth all things, yea, the deep things of God.

————— *DECLARATION OF FAITH* —————

It was written to the old covenant people, "No eye has seen, nor ear heard, nor has any mind conceived what God has prepared for those who love Him." But, God has revealed it to me, His son/daughter, by the Holy Spirit who dwells within me!

(1 John 2:20,27; Matthew 11:25; 13:11,15,16; 16:17; 1 Corinthians 1:12; John 16:13)

1 CORINTHIANS 2:12-16 KJV

Now we have received, not the spirit of the world, but the spirit which is of God; that we might know the things that are freely given to us of God. Which things also we speak, not in the words which man's wisdom teacheth, but which the Holy Ghost teacheth; comparing spiritual things with spiritual. But the natural man receiveth not the things of the Spirit of God: for they are foolishness unto him: neither can he know *them*, because they are spiritually discerned. But he that is spiritual judgeth all things, yet he himself is judged of no man. For who hath known the mind of the Lord, that he may instruct him? But we have the mind of Christ.

————— *DECLARATION OF FAITH* —————

I have not received the spirit of the world, but the Spirit of God, so that I can fully understand all that God has freely given me. These are the things that I teach, not in words taught to me by human instructors, but in words taught to me by the Holy Spirit who dwells within me.

I regularly receive revelation from God. These revelations come to me in my spirit. The Holy Spirit teaches me by expressing spiritual truths through spiritual words.

I fully understand that those who do not have a born-again spirit, indwelt by the Holy Spirit, cannot accept or understand the things that come from the Spirit of God. They will see them as being foolish because they are ruled by their senses (their experiences, or the things of the natural world). They are carnally minded and cannot understand things that are spiritually discerned.

I, as a spiritual man/woman, can make sound judgments about all things (both natural and spiritual). It is written, "For who has known the mind of the Lord, that he may instruct Him?" Yet, I have the mind of Christ!

(1 John 2:20; 5:20; Romans 8:32; 2 Peter 1:3; 1 Corinthians 1:17,30; 2:6,7; Daniel 2:22,23; John 15:5; 16:13; Matthew 16:23)

1 CORINTHIANS 3:16 NKJV

Do you not know that you are the temple of God and *that* the Spirit of God dwells in you?

DECLARATION OF FAITH

I am the very temple of God and His Spirit dwells within me.

(Ephesians 5:18; 1 Corinthians 6:19; John 14:7; 2 Corinthians 6:16)

1 CORINTHIANS 3:21-23 KJV

Therefore let no man glory in men. For all things are yours; Whether Paul, or Apollos, or Cephas, or the world, or life, or death, or things present, or things to come; all are yours; And ye are Christ's; and Christ *is* God's.

DECLARATION OF FAITH

I do not boast about the men and women that I follow, the crusades that I have attended, or the denomination to which I belong. I do not need to go anywhere, or to anyone, to receive from God. I am of Christ (belong to and originate from Him); therefore, all of my boasting is solely in Christ.

(1 Corinthians 1:12,13,31; 2 Corinthians 4:5; 10:7; Proverbs 18:20,21; James 4:13-16)

1 CORINTHIANS 4:2 MESSAGE

The requirements for a good guide are reliability and accurate knowledge.

DECLARATION OF FAITH

I am well aware that I am required to prove faithful to the responsibility that I have been given in Christ. Therefore, I am fixed in all diligence to see that it is performed in my life.

(2 Thessalonians 1:11; 2 Peter 1:10; Philippians 2:12,13)

1 CORINTHIANS 4:15,16 NIV

I am not writing this to shame you, but to warn you, as my dear children. Even though you have ten thousand guardians in Christ, you do not have many fathers, for in Christ Jesus I became your father through the gospel.

I may not have many fathers (or mothers) in the faith, therefore, I am very picky about who I choose to be my mentor. I diligently seek out role models, full of faith, who are successfully living the principles of the kingdom. These are the ones I imitate in order to ensure my own success as a child of God.

(Proverbs 13:20; 1 Corinthians 11:1; Ephesians 4:11,12)

1 CORINTHIANS 5:11 NKJV

But now I have written to you not to keep company with anyone named a brother, who is sexually immoral, or covetous, or an idolater, or a reviler, or a drunkard, or an extortioner—not even to eat with such a person.

——— *DECLARATION OF FAITH* ———

I do not associate myself with a person who calls him or herself a brother or sister in Christ, but is sexually immoral, greedy, an idolater, a slanderer, a drunkard, or a swindler. I will not even eat at the table with such a person.

(2 Corinthians 6:14; Ephesians 5:11; Matthew 18:15-17; Galatians 2:12)

1 CORINTHIANS 6:9-12 KJV

Know ye not that the unrighteous shall not inherit the kingdom of God? Be not deceived: neither fornicators, nor idolaters, nor adulterers, nor effeminate, nor abusers of themselves with mankind, Nor thieves, nor covetous, nor drunkards, nor revilers, nor extortioners, shall inherit the kingdom of God. And such were some of you: but ye are washed, but ye are sanctified, but ye are justified in the name of the Lord Jesus, and by the Spirit of our God. All things are lawful unto me, but all things are not expedient: all things are lawful for me, but I will not be brought under the power of any.

——— *DECLARATION OF FAITH* ———

I fully understand that as a child of God I am to abstain from the wickedness of the world. What is acceptable to the world—sexual immorality, idolatry, adultery, prostitution, homosexuality, thievery, greed, drunkenness, slander, and all other kinds of immorality—is no longer acceptable with me. I know that those who practice such things shall not inherit the kingdom of God.

Though I was once party to these things, I have since been washed, sanctified and justified in the name of my Lord Jesus Christ and by the Spirit of God.

(Ephesians 5:1-18; Galatians 5:19-21; 1 Corinthians 12:2; Hebrews 10:22)

1 CORINTHIANS 6:13-15 KJV

Meats for the belly, and the belly for meats: but God shall destroy both it and them. Now the body *is* not for fornication, but for the Lord; and the Lord for the body. And God hath both raised up the Lord, and will also raise up us by his own power. Know ye not that your bodies are the members of Christ? shall I then take the members of Christ, and make *them* the members of an harlot? God forbid.

——— *DECLARATION OF FAITH* ———

My body is not meant for sexual immorality, but for the Lord, and the Lord for my body. Just as His power has raised Jesus from the dead, so also shall He raise me.

My very body is a part of Jesus Himself. I will not take a part of Christ and unite it with a prostitute!

(1 Corinthians 3:16; John 5:39,40,44,54; 1 Thessalonians 4:3; Ephesians 5:23; Romans 12:5)

1 CORINTHIANS 6:17 AMP

But the person who is united to the Lord becomes one spirit with Him.

——— *DECLARATION OF FAITH* ———

I am united with the Lord and have become one with Him in spirit.

(John 15:5; 17:20-26; 2 Corinthians 3:18; Ephesians 5:31,32)

1 CORINTHIANS 6:18 NIV

Flee from sexual immorality. All other sins a man commits are outside his body, but he who sins sexually sins against his own body.

——— *DECLARATION OF FAITH* ———

I flee from all sexual immorality. I will not sin against my own body by doing things that God has declared to be sexually immoral.

(Hebrews 13:4; Romans 1:24; Proverbs 6:25)

1 CORINTHIANS 6:19,20 KJV

What? know ye not that your body is the temple of the Holy Ghost *which is* in you, which ye have of God, and ye are not your own? For ye are bought with a price: therefore glorify God in your body, and in your spirit, which are God's.

DECLARATION OF FAITH

My body is the temple of the Holy Spirit whom I have received from God. It is His dwelling place and His home in this earth. I am not my own person. I am His. He has paid a tremendous price for me. Therefore, I shall glorify Him in my body.

(1 Corinthians 3:16; John 14:17; 2 Corinthians 6:16; Romans 14:7; 2 Peter 2:1)

1 CORINTHIANS 7:15 KJV

But if the unbelieving depart, let him depart. A brother or a sister is not under bondage in such cases: but God hath called us to peace.

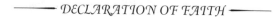

DECLARATION OF FAITH

God has called me to live in peace. Therefore, I am not bound to anything that would harm me or rob me of that peace.

(Ephesians 2:14; Romans 12:18; 14:17; Galatians 5:1)

1 CORINTHIANS 7:24 NKJV

Brethren, let each one remain with God in that *state* in which he was called.

DECLARATION OF FAITH

As a responsible child of God, I shall remain in the employment that I was in when I was called, and while I am there, I shall bring glory to my heavenly Father. When God wants me to change, or move on, He will arrange the provision and point the way.

(Philippians 4:19; Psalm 23; 143:8-10; Proverbs 3:5,6; Colossians 3:23,24)

1 CORINTHIANS 7:35 AMP

Now I say this for your own welfare and profit, not to put [a halter of] restraint upon you, but to promote what is seemly and in good order and to secure your undistracted and undivided devotion to the Lord.

DECLARATION OF FAITH

I live uprightly in undivided devotion to the Lord.

(Deuteronomy 28:1; Psalm 1:1-3; 119:112,113)

1 CORINTHIANS 8:1 KJV

Now as touching things offered unto idols, we know that we all have knowledge. Knowledge puffeth up, but charity edifieth.

——— *DECLARATION OF FAITH* ———

I am a man/woman of knowledge and love. I will not allow myself to become arrogant, but through the love that flows through me in Jesus, I shall build up and encourage others as much as I can.

(1 John 2:20,27; 5:20; Daniel 1:17,20; 2:22,23; Romans 14:3-14; 1 Corinthians 13:4-8)

1 CORINTHIANS 8:3 NIV

But the man who loves God is known by God.

——— *DECLARATION OF FAITH* ———

I am a man/woman who loves God and is known by God.

(1 John 4:7-21; Galatians 4:9; Jeremiah 31:33,34)

1 CORINTHIANS 9:11 NKJV

If we have sown spiritual things for you, *is it* a great thing if we reap your material things?

——— *DECLARATION OF FAITH* ———

It is right and just for me to reap a material harvest from the spiritual seed that I have sown.

(2 Corinthians 9:5-11; Galatians 6:7-9; Romans 15:27)

1 CORINTHIANS 9:20-27 KJV

And unto the Jews I became as a Jew, that I might gain the Jews; to them that are under the law, as under the law, that I might gain them that are under the law; To them that are without law, as without law, (being not without law to God, but under the law to Christ,) that I might gain them that are without law. To the weak became I as weak, that I might gain the weak: I am made all things to all *men*, that I might by all means save some. And this I do for the gospel's sake, that I might be partaker thereof with *you*. Know ye not that they which run in a race run all, but one receiveth the prize? So run, that ye may obtain. And every man that striveth for the mastery is temperate in all things. Now they *do it* to obtain a corruptible crown; but we an incorruptible. I therefore so run, not as uncertainly; so fight I, not as one that beateth the air: But I keep under my body, and bring *it* into subjection: lest that by any means, when I have preached to others, I myself should be a castaway.

──── *DECLARATION OF FAITH* ────

I deny myself for the sake of others that I may win them to Jesus.

I do not flaunt my freedom in front of others, but follow their every custom in order to open the way of opportunity to share the Gospel with them.

I do all of this for the sake of the Gospel, so that I may share in its blessings.

I live my life for Jesus as if I were a runner in a race who gives his all, knowing that only one will win and obtain the crown of victory. Therefore, I run this race to win.

I freely submit myself to the rigors of strict training, subduing my body, making it the best that it can possibly be.

I do not run like a man/woman running aimlessly (without a clear goal and objective) and I do not fight as one who beats at the air. To the contrary, I am a well-disciplined runner who willingly suffers the pain and agony of hard training in order to be at my best when I run. My eyes are fixed on the finish line and that crown of victory.

I am determined that when this race is over, I will finish strong and win the crown.

(Romans 6:18-22; 14:1; 15:1; 1 Corinthians 10:33; James 1:12; 2 Timothy 2:5; 4:8; 1 Peter 5:4)

1 CORINTHIANS 10:13 NKJV

No temptation has overtaken you except such as is common to man; but God is faithful, who will not allow you to be tempted beyond what you are able, but with the temptation will also make the way of escape, that you may be able to bear it.

──── *DECLARATION OF FAITH* ────

I understand that I am not alone in any temptation that I suffer. Every temptation is common among all of mankind. But, I also know that God is faithful. He will not allow me to be tempted beyond my ability to stand against it. When I am tempted to sin, He strengthens me and provides a revelation as to what I can do to overcome it.

(1 Corinthians 1:4-9; Psalm 125:3; Mark 14:38; James 1:12)

1 CORINTHIANS 10:31 AMP

So then, whether you eat or drink, or whatever you may do, do all for the honor and glory of God.

——— *DECLARATION OF FAITH* ———

Everything I do, I do for the glory of God.

(Colossians 3:17; John 14:13,14; Galatians 1:24; 1 Corinthians 6:20)

1 CORINTHIANS 11:24-26 KJV

And when he had given thanks, he brake *it,* and said, Take, eat: this is my body, which is broken for you: this do in remembrance of me. After the same manner also *he took* the cup, when he had supped, saying, This cup is the new testament in my blood: this do ye, as oft as ye drink *it,* in remembrance of me. For as often as ye eat this bread, and drink this cup, ye do shew the Lord's death till he come.

——— *DECLARATION OF FAITH* ———

I regularly take communion in remembrance of what Jesus did for me.
The unleavened bread, in type, is my Lord's sinless Body, which was given for me.
The blood of the grape (juice or wine), in type, is His Blood, which was shed for me. It is the cup of the new covenant of which I have become a partaker.
Whenever I eat the unleavened bread and drink from the cup, I proclaim the Lord's death (the fact that He died for me and that I have become a partaker of His death) until He comes.

(John 6:47-58; Matthew 26:26-28; Romans 6:3,4; Hebrews 8:6)

1 CORINTHIANS 12:1 NKJV

Now concerning spiritual *gifts,* brethren, I do not want you to be ignorant.

——— *DECLARATION OF FAITH* ———

I am aware and discerning of spiritual gifts and their applications in my life.

(1 Corinthians 2:6-16; 14:1,37; 1 John 2:20; John 16:13)

1 CORINTHIANS 12:6-11 KJV

And there are diversities of operations, but it is the same God which worketh all in all. But the manifestation of the Spirit is given to every man to profit withal.

For to one is given by the Spirit the word of wisdom; to another the word of knowledge by the same Spirit; To another faith by the same Spirit; to another the gifts of healing by the same Spirit; To another the working of miracles; to another prophecy; to another discerning of spirits; to another *divers* kinds of tongues; to another the interpretation of tongues: But all these worketh that one and the selfsame Spirit, dividing to every man severally as he will.

——— *DECLARATION OF FAITH* ———

I fully understand that there are many different gifts that the Spirit gives and that any one of them can work in my life at any given moment. I also know that no spiritual gift operates in my life but that which is given to me for the common good and edification of all.

Though I may operate in any spiritual gift, I have no monopoly on them in the assembly (in church). I may speak a word of wisdom or a word of knowledge, operate in supernatural faith, perform healings, display miraculous powers, prophesy, discern spirits that are present [distinguish between them or receive some revelation of them], prophesy in tongues, or give the interpretation of prophetic tongues, but only as the Spirit leads.

(1 Corinthians 14:1-5; 15:28; Mark 16:17,18; Acts 1:8; Romans 12:6)

1 CORINTHIANS 12:31 NIV

But eagerly desire the greater gifts.

——— *DECLARATION OF FAITH* ———

The higher gifts of the Spirit [over and above natural gifts] are a top priority in my life. I eagerly desire them and diligently cultivate them in my walk with God.

(1 Corinthians 12:1-11; 14:1; Romans 12:3-8)

1 CORINTHIANS 13:1-3 KJV

Though I speak with the tongues of men and of angels, and have not charity, I am become as sounding brass, or a tinkling cymbal. And though I have the gift of prophecy, and understand all mysteries, and all knowledge; and though I have all faith, so that I could remove mountains, and have not charity, I am nothing. And though I bestow all my goods to feed the poor, and though I give my body to be burned, and have not charity, it profiteth me nothing.

If I speak in the tongues of men, or of angels, but do not walk in love, all of my talk amounts to nothing.

If I have the gift of prophecy and can fathom all mysteries and knowledge, and if I have the kind of faith that can move mountains, but do not walk in love, it is all worthless.

(Galatians 5:6; Philippians 1:9; 1 Thessalonians 4:9; 1 John 4:6-21)

1 CORINTHIANS 13:4-8 KJV

Charity suffereth long, and is kind; charity envieth not; charity vaunteth not itself, is not puffed up, Doth not behave itself unseemly, seeketh not her own, is not easily provoked, thinketh no evil; Rejoiceth not in iniquity, but rejoiceth in the truth; Beareth all things, believeth all things, hopeth all things, endureth all things. Charity never faileth: but whether *there be* prophecies, they shall fail; whether *there be* tongues, they shall cease; whether *there be* knowledge, it shall vanish away.

(From my perspective)

I am a child of love who lives a life centered in love. I am patient and kind. I do not envy others, nor boast of the great things I have done. I am not haughty and overbearing, nor am I rude (domineering; pushy) or selfish. I am generous with all that I have and willing to give to those in need. I am not easily angered and I keep no record of wrongs done to me. I do not delight in evil, but rejoice in the manifestation of the Truth. I bear up under anything and everything that comes. I always see what is best in others and I overlook their shortcomings. I am ever ready to defend the helpless. My hopes always remain high and I endure everything without weakening. As long as I walk in love, I will never fail.

(John 15:10-12; Galatians 5:22-26; 6:1,2; Psalm 131; Ephesians 4:26; Romans 12:9; 2 Corinthians 9:7; Philippians 4:10-13; James 1:2-4; Job 29:12-17; 1 John 4:6-21)

(From the perspective of God)

My heavenly Father loves me with all of His heart. His very life is centered around His love for me. He is patient with me and kind towards me. He ever lives to do great things in me. He is not haughty or overbearing and does not make me feel inadequate in His presence. He is not rude (domineering or pushy) towards me. He freely gives me all that He has and withholds nothing from me. He has removed His wrath from me and keeps no record of my wrongs. He does not delight in evil deeds, but rejoices when the Truth is manifested in and through me. He covers me as with a shield, no matter what is going on in my life. He always sees what is best in me and overlooks my shortcomings. He is ever ready to defend me. He believes in me with all of His heart and is committed to lead me through to victory. My Father never fails me.

(Psalm 5:11,12; 84:11; 86:15; 103:10-13; 117:1,2; Romans 8:31,32,38,39; Exodus 34:6; Colossians 1:27-29; Hebrews 4:15,16; Genesis 15:1; 1 Corinthians 15:57; 1 John 4:6-21)

1 CORINTHIANS 13:13 AMP

And so faith, hope, love abide [faith—conviction and belief respecting man's relation to God and divine things; hope—joyful and confident expectation of eternal salvation; love—true affection for God and man, growing out of God's love for and in us], these three; but the greatest of these is love.

———— *DECLARATION OF FAITH* ————

These three things remain with me: faith, hope and love. But it is love that is the springboard of all of my faith and hope. My hope does not live without it and my faith does not work, but within it.

(Galatians 5:6; Philippians 1:9-11; Hebrews 11:1; 1 Thessalonians 1:3)

1 CORINTHIANS 14:1-4 KJV

Follow after charity, and desire spiritual *gifts,* but rather that ye may prophesy. For he that speaketh in an *unknown* tongue speaketh not unto men, but unto God: for no man understandeth *him;* howbeit in the spirit he speaketh mysteries. But he that prophesieth speaketh unto men *to* edification, and exhortation, and comfort. He that speaketh in an *unknown* tongue edifieth himself; but he that prophesieth edifieth the church.

———— *DECLARATION OF FAITH* ————

I follow the way of love and eagerly pursue spiritual gifts, especially the gift of prophecy.

When I speak in an unknown tongue, I do not speak to men, but to God. No one understands what I am saying, because I am speaking mysteries with my spirit.

When I prophesy, on the other hand, I speak to people in a language that they can understand so that they can be strengthened, encouraged and comforted. This is the very purpose of spiritual gifts.

When I speak in an unknown tongue, I edify and improve myself, but when I prophesy, I edify and improve the entire congregation. This is what makes prophecy more beneficial [to the congregation] than speaking in tongues.

(1 Corinthians 12:7,31; 13:1-8; Acts 2:4; 10:45,46; Romans 8:26-28; 14:19; 15:2; Ephesians 4:11,12)

1 CORINTHIANS 14:12,13 KJV

Even so ye, forasmuch as ye are zealous of spiritual gifts, seek that ye may excel to the edifying of the church. Wherefore let him that speaketh in an unknown tongue pray that he may interpret.

——— *DECLARATION OF FAITH* ———

I am zealous and eager to cultivate and operate in spiritual gifts in my life, but mostly I desire to excel in those gifts that edify the entire church. Therefore, if I have an unction to speak in tongues to the church, I will pray that I may interpret what I say.

(1 Corinthians 12:10,31; 14:1,3,4; Ephesians 4:12,16)

1 CORINTHIANS 14:14,15 NKJV

For if I pray in a tongue, my spirit prays, but my understanding is unfruitful. What is *the conclusion* then? I will pray with the spirit, and I will also pray with the understanding. I will sing with the spirit, and I will also sing with the understanding.

——— *DECLARATION OF FAITH* ———

When I pray in tongues, my spirit is praying, but in my mind I do not understand what is being said. Therefore, I will pray with my spirit, but pray also with my understanding; I will sing with my spirit, but sing also with my understanding.

(Romans 8:26,27; Jude 20; Colossians 3:16; Ephesians 5:19; 6:18)

1 CORINTHIANS 14:17-19 KJV

For thou verily givest thanks well, but the other is not edified. I thank my God, I speak with tongues more than ye all: Yet in the church I had rather speak five words with my understanding, that by my voice I might teach others also, than ten thousand words in an unknown tongue.

——— DECLARATION OF FAITH ———

When I pray in tongues, I give thanks well. But even though my personal prayer is perfect in the sight of God, others cannot understand me and therefore are not edified by what I say.

I thank God for the ability that He has given me to speak in tongues. However, in church I remain focused on what will edify everyone present, and not just myself.

(Romans 8:26-28; Acts 2:4; 1 Corinthians 14:26; Ephesians 4:12,16)

1 CORINTHIANS 14:26-28 KJV

How is it then, brethren? when ye come together, every one of you hath a psalm, hath a doctrine, hath a tongue, hath a revelation, hath an interpretation. Let all things be done unto edifying. If any man speak in an *unknown* tongue, *let it be* by two, or at the most *by* three, and *that* by course; and let one interpret. But if there be no interpreter, let him keep silence in the church; and let him speak to himself, and to God.

——— DECLARATION OF FAITH ———

When I gather together with my brothers and sisters in Christ, I bring with me the gifts of the Spirit with full understanding that they are to be used for the edification (strengthening) of the entire assembly.

If I have an unction to speak in tongues (in a prophetic capacity), I will do so in an orderly fashion. I will not speak (in tongues) at the same time with any more than three believers and I will not do so without an interpretation. If there is no interpretation, I will speak (in tongues) quietly and enjoy (personally) this perfect communication between God and myself.

(Ephesians 4:12,16; 1 Corinthians 12:7; 14:3,4,14-17; Romans 8:26-28)

1 CORINTHIANS 14:29 NIV

Two or three prophets should speak, and the others should weigh carefully what is said.

——— DECLARATION OF FAITH ———

When prophetic utterances are spoken within the church, I do not take them at face value, but carefully analyze what is said, making sure that it lines up with the Word.

(1 Corinthians 12:10; Acts 17:10,11; 1 John 4:1)

1 CORINTHIANS 14:30-33 KJV

If *any thing* be revealed to another that sitteth by, let the first hold his peace. For ye may all prophesy one by one, that all may learn, and all may be comforted. And the spirits of the prophets are subject to the prophets. For God is not *the author* of confusion, but of peace, as in all churches of the saints.

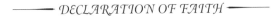

——— *DECLARATION OF FAITH* ———

All of the gifts of the Spirit are subject to my control; for God is not a God of disorder, but of peace. Therefore, I will remain quiet until I have been given my turn to speak [by the pastor, or the one in charge of the meeting]. And I always keep in mind that the spirituals gifts the Holy Spirit has given me are for the edification, encouragement and comfort of all [myself included].

(Acts 1:8; 2:4; 1 Corinthians 11:16; 14:3,4; 2 Corinthians 1:3; Ephesians 4:12,16)

1 CORINTHIANS 14:37,38 KJV

If any man think himself to be a prophet, or spiritual, let him acknowledge that the things that I write unto you are the commandments of the Lord. But if any man be ignorant, let him be ignorant.

——— *DECLARATION OF FAITH* ———

I do not consider anyone who is disorderly or contentious to be worthy of my time and attention. If they choose to be ignorant of these things, I will let them and simply go my way.

(Proverbs 15:18; 26:21; Psalm 5:4-12; 2 Thessalonians 3:14; 2 Corinthians 10:7; Romans 16:17-19)

1 CORINTHIANS 14:39,40 KJV

Wherefore, brethren, covet to prophesy, and forbid not to speak with tongues. Let all things be done decently and in order.

——— *DECLARATION OF FAITH* ———

So, as for spiritual gifts, I set my heart to earnestly pursue them and allow them to operate in my life, and I will not forbid, hinder, or discourage anyone from speaking in tongues.

(1 Corinthians 12:31; 14:1,33; Acts 1:8; 2:4; 17:10,11; 1 John 4:1)

1 CORINTHIANS 15:2 NKJV

By which also you are saved, if you hold fast that word which I preached to you—unless you believed in vain.

——— *DECLARATION OF FAITH* ———

I believe in, and hold fast to, the Word which has saved me. I do not show myself to have believed in vain by turning to another way.

(Galatians 1:6,7; 2:20,21; 3:4; Romans 1:6; 5:1,2)

1 CORINTHIANS 15:10 AMP

But by the grace (the unmerited favor and blessing) of God I am what I am, and His grace toward me was not [found to be] for nothing (fruitless and without effect). In fact, I worked harder than all of them [the apostles], though it was not really I, but the grace (the unmerited favor and blessing) of God which was with me.

——— *DECLARATION OF FAITH* ———

I am what I am by the grace (unmerited favor) of God, and the grace (supernatural ability) that He has given me produces an abundance of good works.

(Ephesians 2:10; 3:7,8; John 15:5; Philippians 2:13; Acts 4:33)

1 CORINTHIANS 15:22-26 KJV

For as in Adam all die, even so in Christ shall all be made alive. But every man in his own order: Christ the firstfruits; afterward they that are Christ's at his coming. Then *cometh* the end, when he shall have delivered up the kingdom to God, even the Father; when he shall have put down all rule and all authority and power. For he must reign, till he hath put all enemies under his feet. The last enemy *that* shall be destroyed *is* death.

——— *DECLARATION OF FAITH* ———

Because of Adam's transgression, I died [spiritually first which resulted in my being subject to physical death]. In like manner, in Jesus, I have been made alive [spiritually] and will one day be raised with a new body, free of all of the bonds of death. Then the end will come, when Jesus hands the kingdom over to God the Father after He has destroyed (made inoperative) all dominion, authority and power; for He must reign [and I in and through Him] until all of His enemies are placed under His feet. The last enemy that we will destroy will be death.

(Genesis 2:17; Romans 5:12; John 3:3,16; 5:28,29; 17:20-26; Ephesians 2:5,6; Daniel 7:14,27; Psalm 110:1; 2 Timothy 1:10)

1 CORINTHIANS 15:33,34 NKJV

Do not be deceived: "Evil company corrupts good habits." Awake to righteousness, and do not sin; for some do not have the knowledge of God. I speak this to your shame.

——— *DECLARATION OF FAITH* ———

I am not easily misled. I fully understand that bad company corrupts good character. Therefore, I will not associate myself with those who do not honor God with their lives.

I am not ignorant of the things of God. I remain perpetually alert and eliminate sin from my life.

(Acts 17:10,11; 2 Corinthians 6:14; Ephesians 5:1-18; 1 Corinthians 2:12; 5:6; Romans 13:11; Hebrews 12:1)

1 CORINTHIANS 15:48-58 KJV

As *is* the earthy, such *are* they also that are earthy: and as *is* the heavenly, such *are* they also that are heavenly. And as we have borne the image of the earthy, we shall also bear the image of the heavenly. Now this I say, brethren, that flesh and blood cannot inherit the kingdom of God; neither doth corruption inherit incorruption. Behold, I shew you a mystery; We shall not all sleep, but we shall all be changed, In a moment, in the twinkling of an eye, at the last trump: for the trumpet shall sound, and the dead shall be raised incorruptible, and we shall be changed. For this corruptible must put on incorruption, and this mortal *must* put on immortality. So when this corruptible shall have put on incorruption, and this mortal shall have put on immortality, then shall be brought to pass the saying that is written, Death is swallowed up in victory. O death, where *is* thy sting? O grave, where *is* thy victory? The sting of death *is* sin; and the strength of sin *is* the law. But thanks *be* to God, which giveth us the victory through our Lord Jesus Christ. Therefore, my beloved brethren, be ye stedfast, unmoveable, always abounding in the work of the Lord, forasmuch as ye know that your labour is not in vain in the Lord.

───── *DECLARATION OF FAITH* ─────

Just as I have born the likeness of earthly man (as the offspring of Adam), being born again and a new creation, I now bear the likeness of Jesus, the man from heaven. As He is, so am I in this world.

I am a son/daughter of God—a spiritual being created with the ability to walk in the blessings of the kingdom.

Just as my spirit is imperishable, one day my body shall be made imperishable as well. One day, in a fleeting moment, in the twinkling of an eye, at the sound of the last trumpet, my body shall be changed. This perishable body will be transformed into an imperishable body, and I shall, in my body, be just as immortal as Jesus. Then the Scripture, "All of death has been swallowed up in victory," shall be manifested in me.

For me, death no longer has any sting. I have no fear of it. Jesus has taken all of its victory away; for the sting of death is sin, and the power of sin is the Law (of Moses). But thanks be to God I have the victory over all of it through Jesus Christ my Lord.

Therefore, I shall let nothing move me to fear. I always give myself fully to the work of the Lord, because I know of a certainty that my labor in Him is not in vain. My reward and my destiny are fixed—secured by the blood of Jesus and the seal (guarantee) of the Holy Spirit.

(1 John 3:2; 4:17; Romans 8:23,28-30; Ephesians 1:3,7-14; 2 Corinthians 5:17; John 3:3; Galatians 2:19-21; 4:4-6; 1 Thessalonians 4:15-17; Hosea 13:14; 2 Timothy 1:6,7; 1 Corinthians 3:8)

1 Corinthians 16:9 NKJV

For a great and effective door has opened to me, and there are many adversaries.

───── *DECLARATION OF FAITH* ─────

Though there are many who oppose me, a great door of opportunity for effective service has been opened for me. Outside of my own choosing, there is nothing in all of heaven or earth that can stop God's will and His work that He is performing in and through me.

(Philippians 2:12,13; Acts 4:23-31; 14:27; 19:9; Colossians 1:27-29; Joshua 24:15; Deuteronomy 30:19,20)

1 Corinthians 16:13,14 NKJV

Watch, stand fast in the faith, be brave, be strong. Let all that you do be done with love.

─────── *DECLARATION OF FAITH* ───────

I am constantly alert and on guard against the attacks of the enemy. I stand firm and fearless in my faith—a man/woman of courage, strengthened with all might by the Holy Spirit who is within me—and all that I do is centered in love.

(Ephesians 6:10-18; 2 Corinthians 10:3-6; Joshua 1:5-9; 1 Peter 4:8)

1 CORINTHIANS 16:23,24 KJV

The grace of our Lord Jesus Christ *be* with you. My love *be* with you all in Christ Jesus. Amen.

─────── *DECLARATION OF FAITH* ───────

The grace of my Lord Jesus is ever with me and my love is reaching out to everyone.

(Romans 16:20; 1 Corinthians 13:4-8; Philippians 1:9)

CHAPTER FORTY-SEVEN

2 CORINTHIANS

Second Corinthians is another epistle of the apostle Paul to the church at Corinth. It was written perhaps as little as a few months to a year after Paul wrote 1 Corinthians. In this epistle, Paul addresses additional problems such as legalism and Gnosticism, but also gives us the promises of comfort and restoration. Other promises of provision and healing can be found in the epistle as well.

As you pray the promises of 2 Corinthians, keep in mind that you belong to the Father of mercy and grace. He comforts and restores you no matter how badly or how often you fail.

2 CORINTHIANS 1:3-5 KJV

Blessed be God, even the Father of our Lord Jesus Christ, the Father of mercies, and the God of all comfort; Who comforteth us in all our tribulation, that we may be able to comfort them which are in any trouble, by the comfort wherewith we ourselves are comforted of God. For as the sufferings of Christ abound in us, so our consolation also aboundeth by Christ.

——— *DECLARATION OF FAITH* ———

My heavenly Father is the Father of mercies and the God of all comfort. His compassion towards me is boundless. He comforts, encourages and assists me through all of life's troubles, so that I can comfort, encourage and assist others who are going through the same things that I have gone through.

I am also identified with Christ's sufferings. Therefore, through my oneness with Him, I have every ability to comfort others no matter what they are going through. For in the same way I am identified with Christ's sufferings, so also does His comfort, encouragement and assistance flow through me in abundance.

(John 14:16,17; Isaiah 51:12; 66:13; Galatians 2:20; Colossians 1 27-29)

2 CORINTHIANS 1:8-11 KJV

For we would not, brethren, have you ignorant of our trouble which came to us in Asia, that we were pressed out of measure, above strength, insomuch that we despaired even of life: But we had the sentence of death in ourselves, that we should not trust in ourselves, but in God which raiseth the dead: Who delivered us from so great a death, and doth deliver: in whom we trust that he will yet deliver *us;* Ye also helping together by prayer for us, that for the gift *bestowed* upon us by the means of many persons thanks may be given by many on our behalf.

DECLARATION OF FAITH

I do not hide my needs from my brothers and sisters in Christ. When I am undergoing hardships and feeling overburdened, I let them know about it so that they can fight together with me. I do not rely on my own power to overcome the hardships of life, but give place to the power of God. As I set my hope in Him, He faithfully delivers me, working for my good through the prayers of the many who have taken their stand at my side. By this, He is glorified in the sight of all of us and we all shall give thanks to Him for the incredible grace and deliverance that He has worked in me in answer to our prayers.

(Jeremiah 17:5-8; Colossians 1:9; 1 Thessalonians 5:23-25; 2 Thessalonians 1:11; 3:1; James 5:16; John 14:13,14)

2 CORINTHIANS 1:12 NKJV

For our boasting is this: the testimony of our conscience that we conducted ourselves in the world in simplicity and godly sincerity, not with fleshly wisdom but by the grace of God, and more abundantly toward you.

DECLARATION OF FAITH

Now this is my boast: That I have conducted myself in this world in the holiness and sincerity that come from God. I have not accomplished this through human strength and wisdom, but in accordance with God's grace and mercy, which flows into my life in abundance.

(1 Peter 1:15,16; Philippians 2:13; Colossians 1:29; Ephesians 4:1-3; 6:10)

2 CORINTHIANS 1:18-22 KJV

But *as* God *is* true, our word toward you was not yea and nay. For the Son of God, Jesus Christ, who was preached among you by us, *even* by me and Silvanus and Timotheus, was not yea and nay, but in him was yea. For all the promises of God in him *are* yea, and in him Amen, unto the glory of God by us. Now he which stablisheth us with you in Christ, and hath anointed us, *is* God; Who hath also sealed us, and given the earnest of the Spirit in our hearts.

——— *DECLARATION OF FAITH* ———

My heavenly Father is faithful to His every Word. No matter how many promises He has made, in Jesus, He makes good on every one. I have God's Word; therefore, I have God's will. Every time that I pray in line with His Word, the answer is guaranteed.

Now it is God Himself who makes me stand firm in Christ. He has anointed me with His burden-removing, yoke-destroying power; set His seal of ownership upon me declaring to all of heaven and earth that I am His; and has filled me with His Spirit as a deposit guaranteeing the security of my place in the family!

(Isaiah 43:1; 55:11; Psalm 119:138; 1 John 2:20,27; 5:14,15; John 14:13,14; 15:7; 16:23,24; Romans 5:1,2; Galatians 5:1; Ephesians 1:13,14)

2 CORINTHIANS 1:24 NIV

Not that we lord it over your faith, but we work with you for your joy, because it is by faith you stand firm.

——— *DECLARATION OF FAITH* ———

I continually work for the good of others—for their joy and happiness. It is by faith that I stand firm in my walk with God.

(Galatians 5:1; 6:9; Romans 1:17; 5:1,2)

2 CORINTHIANS 2:7,8 AMP

So [instead of further rebuke, now] you should rather turn and [graciously] forgive and comfort and encourage [him], to keep him from being overwhelmed by excessive sorrow and despair. I therefore beg you to reinstate him in your affections and assure him of your love for him.

——— *DECLARATION OF FAITH* ———

I forgive and comfort the repentant brother or sister who has come back from the darkness. I encourage them, reaffirm my love for them, and help them back on their feet lest they be overcome with sorrow.

(Luke 17:3,4; Matthew 18:21,22; Galatians 6:1,2)

2 CORINTHIANS 2:11 KJV

Lest Satan should get an advantage of us: for we are not ignorant of his devices.

Satan cannot outwit or take advantage of me in any way, for the Holy Spirit reveals to me his schemes and evil intentions.

(Ephesians 6:10-18; Psalm 91:3,13; Luke 10:19; Hebrews 4:12)

2 CORINTHIANS 2:14 NIV

But thanks be to God, who always leads us in triumphal procession in Christ and through us spreads everywhere the fragrance of the knowledge of him.

——— *DECLARATION OF FAITH* ———

I thank God for always leading me in triumph in Christ Jesus my Lord. Through me, He spreads everywhere the fragrance of what it is like to know Him.

(1 Corinthians 2:6-16; 15:57; 1 John 4:7-21)

2 CORINTHIANS 3:6 NKJV

Who also made us sufficient as ministers of the new covenant, not of the letter but of the Spirit; for the letter kills, but the Spirit gives life.

——— *DECLARATION OF FAITH* ———

My heavenly Father has made me a competent minister of the new covenant—not of written regulations, but of the spirit; for the written regulation produces death, but the spirit of it produces life.

(1 Corinthians 2:6-16; 2 Corinthians 5:18-20; Hebrews 8:6-13; Romans 2:27; 8:2; Galatians 3:10; John 6:63)

2 CORINTHIANS 3:10-12 KJV

For even that which was made glorious had no glory in this respect, by reason of the glory that excelleth. For if that which is done away *was* glorious, much more that which remaineth *is* glorious. Seeing then that we have such hope, we use great plainness of speech.

——— *DECLARATION OF FAITH* ———

I am a minister of the greatest covenant the world has ever known. This covenant far surpasses all others in its everlasting glory. Therefore, since I have such a hope, I am very bold to deliver the Good News.

(2 Corinthians 5:18-20; Matthew 28:18-20; Mark 16:15-20; Hebrews 8:6-13; 10:15-17; Ephesians 6:19)

2 Corinthians 3:16-18 KJV

Nevertheless when it shall turn to the Lord, the veil shall be taken away.

Now the Lord is that Spirit: and where the Spirit of the Lord is, there is liberty.

But we all, with open face beholding as in a glass the glory of the Lord, are changed into the same image from glory to glory, even as by the Spirit of the Lord.

— DECLARATION OF FAITH —

When I became a born-again child of God, He removed the veil that kept me from understanding His Word. I now can operate in the fullness of God-given ability to understand every aspect of the Scriptures.

Now, the Lord is the Spirit who dwells within me, and where the Spirit of the Lord is, there is emancipation. I have been completely set free from anything that would hinder me from obtaining all that God has for me.

Now that the veil has been removed, I am free [through the Word] to become the very mirror image of the Lord in all of His glory. I am continually being transformed into His likeness with ever-increasing glory, which comes from the Lord, who is the Spirit and who dwells within me.

(John 3:3; 8:31-36; 2 Corinthians 5:17; Titus 3:4-7; 1 Corinthians 1:30; 2:6-16; 3:16; Matthew 13:11,15,16; 1 John 2:20,27; 5:20; Galatians 5:1; 2 Peter 1:3,4; Romans 8:28-32; Isaiah 25:7)

2 Corinthians 4:1,2 KJV

Therefore seeing we have this ministry, as we have received mercy, we faint not; But have renounced the hidden things of dishonesty, not walking in craftiness, nor handling the word of God deceitfully; but by manifestation of the truth commending ourselves to every man's conscience in the sight of God.

— DECLARATION OF FAITH —

It is through God's mercy that I have been given my ministry. Therefore, I never lose heart in those times when I seem to fall short of it. Instead, I renounce secret and shameful practices; I refuse to use deception of any kind in order to persuade people; and I never distort the Word of God in order to make it fit my doctrine [or what I have been taught to believe]. To the contrary, I set forth the Truth plainly, commending myself to everyone's conscience in the sight of God.

(1 Corinthians 7:25; 2 Corinthians 4:16; 5:11; Ephesians 2:8-10; Hebrews 21:1; 1 Peter 3:10-12)

2 CORINTHIANS 4:5-11 KJV

For we preach not ourselves, but Christ Jesus the Lord; and ourselves your servants for Jesus' sake. For God, who commanded the light to shine out of darkness, hath shined in our hearts, to *give* the light of the knowledge of the glory of God in the face of Jesus Christ. But we have this treasure in earthen vessels, that the excellency of the power may be of God, and not of us. *We are* troubled on every side, yet not distressed; *we are* perplexed, but not in despair; persecuted, but not forsaken; cast down, but not destroyed; Always bearing about in the body the dying of the Lord Jesus, that the life also of Jesus might be made manifest in our body. For we which live are alway delivered unto death for Jesus' sake, that the life also of Jesus might be made manifest in our mortal flesh.

──────── *DECLARATION OF FAITH* ────────

I am not out to make a proclamation to others about myself, but of Jesus Christ as Lord, and me as a servant to others for His sake; for God, who declared, "Let Light shine out of darkness," has made His Light shine within my heart in order that I might have the light of the knowledge of His glory in the face of Jesus Christ my Lord. In Him, I have insight and all ability to understand His glory in this earth. I have this treasure as in a jar of clay to show that the all-surpassing power that flows in and through me is from God and not my own.

At times I may be surrounded by oppressors, but I am never smothered or crushed by them. When I am confronted with many perplexing and complicated situations, I am never driven to despair. When I suffer persecution, God always takes His stand with me and I never have to bear it alone. I may even be struck down, but I am never destroyed. I always bounce right back up and get back into the fight. My name resounds in the devil's mind as a stubborn, tenacious, immovable, and hardheaded man/woman of God who never gives in and never quits.

I always carry with me the very fact of Jesus' death—that He bore my sicknesses and carried my pains; that His death brought me peace and freed me from all of the effects of sin. I carry the fact of His death so that His resurrection life may also be revealed in my body. Through Him, the effects of sin and death no longer have dominion over me. Even though I may be threatened by death on every side, the life of His Resurrection never fails to flow in and through me.

(1 Corinthians 1:11-17,30; 2:5-16; John 1:5,8,9; Matthew 5:10-12,14-16; Ephesians 1:17-23; 2:14; Philippians 2:13; 3:10; Psalm 2; Romans 8:11,17,35-37; 2 Corinthians 7:5; 2 Timothy 3:12; Hebrews 13:5,6; Galatians 2:20; 3:13; 1 Peter 2:24)

2 CORINTHIANS 4:13 MESSAGE

Just like the psalmist who wrote, "I believed it, so I said it," we say what we believe.

—— *DECLARATION OF FAITH* ——

Faith is a spiritual power and the tool that God has given me to bring forth an abundance of good fruit in my life. It is written of the spirit of faith, "I believed; therefore, I have spoken." This is my faith in operation. I take the promise into my heart, believe it with all of my soul, and speak it forth until it is manifested in my life.

(Proverbs 18:20,21; Psalm 116:10; Hebrews 11:1,6; Mark 11:22-25; 2 Peter 1:1-4; John 6:63; Matthew 21:19-22; Romans 10:8; 2 Corinthians 5:7)

2 CORINTHIANS 4:16-18 KJV

For which cause we faint not; but though our outward man perish, yet the inward *man* is renewed day by day. For our light affliction, which is but for a moment, worketh for us a far more exceeding *and* eternal weight of glory; While we look not at the things which are seen, but at the things which are not seen: for the things which are seen *are* temporal; but the things which are not seen *are* eternal.

—— *DECLARATION OF FAITH* ——

I am never discouraged in my walk with God. Though my outward man is subject to death, my inward man (my spirit) is being renewed daily with resurrection life. The pressure that I am under now is light and truly momentary. It seldom seems half bad once it is passed. Therefore, I will endure the pressure for I know that on the other side of it is an eternal reward of glory which far outweighs what I now must endure. My eyes are fixed on what is unseen, for what is seen is temporary, but what is unseen is eternal.

(2 Corinthians 4:1; 5:7; Psalm 103:5; Romans 8:18; Hebrews 11:1)

2 CORINTHIANS 5:1-7 KJV

For we know that if our earthly house of *this* tabernacle were dissolved, we have a building of God, an house not made with hands, eternal in the heavens. For in this we groan, earnestly desiring to be clothed upon with our house which is from heaven: If so be that being clothed we shall not be found naked. For we that are in *this* tabernacle do groan, being burdened: not for that we would be unclothed, but clothed upon, that mortality might be swallowed up of life. Now he that hath wrought us for the selfsame thing *is* God, who also hath given unto us the earnest of the Spirit. Therefore *we are* always confident, knowing that, whilst we are at home in the body, we are absent from the Lord: (For we walk by faith, not by sight.)

———— *DECLARATION OF FAITH* ————

Even if my earthly home were to be destroyed, I have the comfort of knowing that I have a home waiting for me in heaven—a home not built with human hands, of human origin, or designed by the human mind. My home in heaven is one that is perfectly suited to my needs and personality, designed by the master designer and architect of the universe who knows everything about me and is committed to my joy and happiness.

In the same way, I long to be clothed with my heavenly body. I know that what is waiting for me in heaven far surpasses what I have here on earth; for I am designed to be clothed with a perfect and imperishable body, without which I am basically naked and incomplete. This is why I am so aggrieved and uncomfortable concerning my mortal body, because I am not designed to live in a dwelling of mortality. The things of death are utterly repulsive to me, being completely contrary to my new nature. Therefore, I long to be clothed with my immortal body so that every aspect of death concerning me will be swallowed up by life.

Now it is God who made me for this purpose and has given me the Holy Spirit as a deposit, guaranteeing what is to come. In this, I rejoice in great confidence knowing that, though I am not living in my immortal body and in the physical presence of the Lord, by the power of the Holy Spirit within me I can walk by faith and experience heavenly bliss in my present mortal body even while on the earth. I am not moved by what I see, feel or experience in my mortal body, for my faith (believing and speaking the promise) transcends all and brings God's glory and blessings into my life.

(John 14:1-3; 16:23,24; 2 Corinthians 4:13; 5:17; 2 Peter 1:4; 1 Corinthians 15:50-57; Ephesians 1:13,14; Hebrews 11:1; Romans 8:11)

2 CORINTHIANS 5:14-21 KJV

For the love of Christ constraineth us; because we thus judge, that if one died for all, then were all dead: And *that* he died for all, that they which live should not henceforth live unto themselves, but unto him which died for them, and rose again. Wherefore henceforth know we no man after the flesh: yea, though we have known Christ after the flesh, yet now henceforth know we *him* no more. Therefore if any man *be* in Christ, *he is* a new creature: old things are passed away; behold, all things are become new. And all things *are* of God, who hath reconciled us to himself by Jesus Christ, and hath given to us the ministry of reconciliation; To wit, that God was in Christ, reconciling the world unto himself, not imputing their trespasses unto them; and hath committed unto us the word of reconciliation. Now then we are ambassadors for Christ, as though God did beseech *you* by us: we pray *you* in Christ's stead, be ye reconciled to God. For he hath made him *to be* sin for us, who knew no sin; that we might be made the righteousness of God in him.

——— DECLARATION OF FAITH ———

The love of Jesus within me compels me to act on His behalf, for I am convinced that all of humanity, outside of Christ, are in a state of spiritual death and without Him, all are going to hell.

I know of a certainty that I died with Him on that cross. He became my sin substitute as He did for all of humanity. He died for me that I should no longer live for myself, gratifying my own sensuous desires, but for Him who died for me and was raised again for my justification.

Therefore, from now on I will not regard myself, or any of my brothers and sisters in Christ, from a worldly perspective; for I was reborn together with Him in His Resurrection and, in Him, I have become a new creation (a new species of man)—a part of a new and godly race. My old man [who was an actual member of Satan's family with Satan's own nature] was crucified with Jesus. But now my spirit has been recreated with the very nature of God and I have become an actual son/daughter in His royal family.

All of this is from God, who through Jesus, has reconciled me to Himself, making me welcome in His presence anytime, anyplace, and anywhere.

Furthermore, God has honored me with the ministry of reconciliation—the ministry of proclaiming to all that God was in Jesus, reconciling the entire world to Himself, not counting their sins against them. This is the message that He has committed to me and I take this responsibility seriously. I am now an ambassador for Christ, as though God Himself were making His appeal to mankind through me.

God made Jesus, the sinless Messiah, to become sin for me, and in Him, I have been made the very righteousness of God. In light of this, I invite all, as Jesus' chosen representative, to be reconciled to God; for His righteousness and justification are now made available to anyone and everyone who will call on His name.

(Romans 1:17; 3:21; 4:25; 5:15; 6:11; 12:1,2; John 3:18-20; Galatians 2:20,21; 4:5,6; 6:15; Hebrews 4:15,16; 10:10-14; Ephesians 2:4-10; 1 Peter 1:4; Titus 3:4-7; Matthew 28:18-20; Luke 9:1,2; Isaiah 53)

2 CORINTHIANS 6:1,2 NIV

As God's fellow workers we urge you not to receive God's grace in vain. For he says, "In the time of my favor I heard you, and in the day of salvation I helped you." I tell you, now is the time of God's favor, now is the day of salvation.

——— *DECLARATION OF FAITH* ———

As God's partner, I also urge people not to receive the grace of God passively and without purpose, but in order to be changed and become His children; for a passive receiving of the truth is not enough to enact one's personal salvation.

It is my declaration that the time to personally receive Him is now; for His grace may not be available tomorrow, and today, this day, is the day to receive His salvation.

(1 Corinthians 3:9; Philippians 2:13; 2 Corinthians 5:18-20; John 1:12; Isaiah 49:8)

2 CORINTHIANS 6:3 NKJV

We give no offense in anything, that our ministry may not be blamed.

——— *DECLARATION OF FAITH* ———

I do not discredit the ministry given to me by putting a stumbling block in the path of those who are ready to receive salvation.

(Romans 14:13; 1 Corinthians 8:9; 10:24-33)

2 CORINTHIANS 6:4-10 KJV

But in all *things* approving ourselves as the ministers of God, in much patience, in afflictions, in necessities, in distresses, In stripes, in imprisonments, in tumults, in labours, in watchings, in fastings; By pureness, by knowledge, by longsuffering, by kindness, by the Holy Ghost, by love unfeigned, By the word of truth, by the power of God, by the armour of righteousness on the right hand and on the left, By honour and dishonour, by evil report and good report: as deceivers, and *yet* true; As unknown, and *yet* well known; as dying, and, behold, we live; as chastened, and not killed; As sorrowful, yet alway rejoicing; as poor, yet making many rich; as having nothing, and *yet* possessing all things.

——— *DECLARATION OF FAITH* ———

In all of the following, I commend myself as a servant of God:
- *I faithfully persevere in the midst of troubles and hardships of every kind.*
- *I continually show myself to be a hard worker.*
- *I am willing to go without sleep in order to advance the Kingdom.*

- *When hunger comes, I do not give up on faith.*
- *I live in continual purity with a good conscience.*
- *I operate in the revelation knowledge and spiritual understanding that God has provided for me.*
- *I am patient in every circumstance.*
- *I am known to be kind, compassionate and considerate.*
- *I do all things under the guidance of the Holy Spirit and in sincere love for others.*
- *I speak only the truth.*
- *God's power flows in and through me to meet every need.*
- *I keep my weapons of righteousness in both hands at all times.*
- *I persevere through glory and dishonor—bad report and good report.*
- *I remain genuine, even when regarded as an imposter.*
- *I live the same whether among those who know me, or among those who don't.*
- *When regarded as perishing, I still live on.*
- *Though abused, I am never defeated or destroyed.*
- *Though I experience sorrow, I always rejoice.*
- *Though seen as being beggarly, I make many rich.*
- *And even if everything I have were to be taken from me, I would still possess what matters most.*

(James 1:2-4; Ephesians 1:3,17-23; 4:28; 6:10-18; Mark 1:35; Hebrews 10:35-11:1; 1 Timothy 1:5; Matthew 13:15,16; 1 Corinthians 2:6-16; 13:4-8; John 16:13; Colossians 3:16,17; 2 Corinthians 8:9; Philippians 4:4; 1 Peter 1:3; Romans 8:32; Job 29:4-25)

2 Corinthians 6:14-7:1 KJV

Be ye not unequally yoked together with unbelievers: for what fellowship hath righteousness with unrighteousness? and what communion hath light with darkness? And what concord hath Christ with Belial? or what part hath he that believeth with an infidel? And what agreement hath the temple of God with idols? for ye are the temple of the living God; as God hath said, I will dwell in them, and walk in *them;* and I will be their God, and they shall be my people. Wherefore come out from among them, and be ye separate, saith the Lord, and touch not the unclean *thing;* and I will receive you, And will be a Father unto you, and ye shall be my sons and daughters, saith the Lord Almighty. Having therefore these promises, dearly beloved, let us cleanse ourselves from all filthiness of the flesh and spirit, perfecting holiness in the fear of God.

―――― *DECLARATION OF FAITH* ――――

I do not join together in affinity and fellowship with unbelievers. I am not so foolish as to hang out with the wrong crowd after being renewed in the image and likeness of God.

As I have become the righteousness of God in Christ Jesus, I no longer have anything in common with unbelievers. Therefore, I am more than willing to give up the old crowd in order to walk with Jesus.

I will never forget that I am now the very temple of God. He lives with me, walks with me and is within me. I will obey what is written and come out from among any crowd that does not have reverence for His name.

I will not partake of the things of the world, for my Father has received me and I have become His very own son/daughter. And since I have these promises, I purify myself against anything that would contaminate my body or spirit, and I perfect myself in holiness out of reverence for God.

(Ephesians 5:1-18; 1 Corinthians 3:16; 5:9; 15:33; 2 Corinthians 1:20; 5:21; 1 John 1:5-7; 3:3; John 14:17; Galatians 4:4-6)

2 CORINTHIANS 7:4 NIV

I have great confidence in you; I take great pride in you. I am greatly encouraged; in all our troubles my joy knows no bounds.

―――― *DECLARATION OF FAITH* ――――

Despite its shortcomings, I am very proud of the Church. I have great confidence in her and refuse to say a single bad thing about her. Even in the midst of the worst of troubles, when I think of all of the brothers and sisters in Christ who are my family for all of eternity, I am greatly encouraged and my joy knows no bounds.

(2 Corinthians 3:12; 1 Corinthians 1:4; Romans 1:8; Proverbs 18:20,21; Philippians 2:16-18)

2 CORINTHIANS 7:6 KJV

Nevertheless God, that comforteth those that are cast down, comforted us by the coming of Titus.

―――― *DECLARATION OF FAITH* ――――

My Father, the God who comforts the downcast, always finds a way to lift my spirits and deliver me from depression.

(2 Corinthians 1:3,4; 1 Peter 5:5-7; Psalm 3:1-3)

2 CORINTHIANS 7:10,11 AMP

For godly grief and the pain God is permitted to direct, produce a repentance that leads and contributes to salvation and deliverance from evil, and it never brings regret; but worldly grief (the hopeless sorrow that is characteristic of the pagan world) is deadly [breeding and ending in death]. For [you can look back now and] observe what this same godly sorrow has done for you and has produced in you: what eagerness and earnest care to explain and clear yourselves [of all complicity in the condoning of incest], what indignation [at the sin], what alarm, what yearning, what zeal [to do justice to all concerned], what readiness to mete out punishment [to the offender]! At every point you have proved yourselves cleared and guiltless in the matter.

--------- DECLARATION OF FAITH ---------

Godly sorrow is what leads me to repentance. But this isn't like worldly sorrow, for godly sorrow ends with repentance and it leaves no regrets. Once I have repented (turned away from a wrong), I will not allow it to ever bring me down again. I know that whatever I have done cannot be fixed by moping around. Instead, my godly sorrow produces in me an earnestness to do whatever it takes to set things right again.

(Matthew 3:8; 26:75; Proverbs 17:22)

2 CORINTHIANS 8:2-5 KJV

How that in a great trial of affliction the abundance of their joy and their deep poverty abounded unto the riches of their liberality. For to *their* power, I bear record, yea, and beyond *their* power *they were* willing of themselves; Praying us with much intreaty that we would receive the gift, and *take upon us* the fellowship of the ministering to the saints. And *this they did,* not as we hoped, but first gave their own selves to the Lord, and unto us by the will of God.

--------- DECLARATION OF FAITH ---------

No matter what my situation is, it brings me abounding joy to give whatever I can to the work of the Lord. It is my pleasure to give as much as I am able, and even beyond my ability.

This I do entirely on my own and not under compulsion. As a matter of fact, I don't even have to be asked to give. I am always looking for an opportunity to share in the ministry through my financial blessings.

What makes this even more awesome is the fact that I am in partnership with the Lord in my giving. So there is no telling what I might do, because when God and I get together in this, blessings can flow from any direction.

(2 Corinthians 9:7; Philippians 4:14-20; Genesis 12:1-3; Romans 12:1,2)

2 CORINTHIANS 8:7 NKJV

But as you abound in everything—in faith, in speech, in knowledge, in all diligence, and in your love for us—*see* that you abound in this grace also.

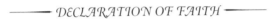
DECLARATION OF FAITH

In Jesus, I excel in everything that I do—in faith, in teaching, in understanding (knowledge), in enthusiasm, in my love for my brothers and sisters in Christ—and I see to it that I excel in the grace (God-given ability) of giving as well.

(Deuteronomy 28:12; 2 Corinthians 8:2-5; 9:7,8; Philippians 4:14-20; 1 Corinthians 1:5)

2 CORINTHIANS 8:9 KJV

For ye know the grace of our Lord Jesus Christ, that, though he was rich, yet for your sakes he became poor, that ye through his poverty might be rich.

DECLARATION OF FAITH

I know the grace of my Lord Jesus, that though He was rich, for my sake He became poor, so that I, through His poverty, could become rich. Because of what Jesus did for me, I can count on being continually and abundantly supplied with all good things.

(Philippians 2:5-13; 4:19; 2 Corinthians 6:10; 9:5-11; Romans 8:32; 2 Peter 1:3)

2 CORINTHIANS 8:11,12 KJV

Now therefore perform the doing *of it*; that as *there was* a readiness to will, so *there may be* a performance also out of that which ye have. For if there be first a willing mind, *it is* accepted according to that a man hath, *and* not according to that he hath not.

DECLARATION OF FAITH

My eagerness to give is matched by my actual giving. I do not allow stumbling blocks to get in the way of my generosity, but give as the Lord wills whenever I have the means to do so; for it is my willingness and readiness to give that makes my gifts acceptable in the sight of God, and my gift is weighed in proportion with my ability to give.

(Mark 12:41-43; Luke 6:38; Proverbs 19:17; 28:27; Psalm 79:12; James 2:13)

2 CORINTHIANS 8:19 NKJV

And not only that, but who was also chosen by the churches to travel with us with this gift, which is administered by us to the glory of the Lord Himself and to show your ready mind.

I give in order to honor the Lord and show Him my eagerness to advance His kingdom.

(Proverbs 3:9,10; Malachi 3:6-12; 2 Corinthians 8:2-5)

2 CORINTHIANS 8:21 AMP

For we take thought beforehand and aim to be honest and absolutely above suspicion, not only in the sight of the Lord but also in the sight of men.

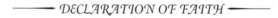

I take pains to do what is right, not only in the eyes of the Lord, but also in the eyes of humanity.

(Leviticus 5:1; Romans 12:17)

2 CORINTHIANS 8:24 NIV

Therefore show these men the proof of your love and the reason for our pride in you, so that the churches can see it.

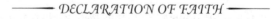

My love for others is on open display through many deeds. It is continually active and true and not just a few words coupled with strong feelings.

(1 Corinthians 13:4-8; 1 John 3:18; Galatians 5:6)

2 CORINTHIANS 9:2 NKJV

For I know your willingness, about which I boast of you to the Macedonians, that Achaia was ready a year ago; and your zeal has stirred up the majority.

─── *DECLARATION OF FAITH* ───

I am always eager to give and my enthusiasm stirs others to give as well.

(2 Corinthians 8:2-5; 9:7; Romans 12:8; 1 Chronicles 29:1-17)

2 CORINTHIANS 9:5-15 KJV

Therefore I thought it necessary to exhort the brethren, that they would go before unto you, and make up beforehand your bounty, whereof ye had notice before, that the same might be ready, as *a matter of* bounty, and not as *of* covetousness. But this *I say,* He which soweth sparingly shall reap also sparingly; and he which soweth bountifully shall reap also bountifully. Every man according as he purposeth in his heart, *so let him give;* not grudgingly, or of necessity: for God loveth a cheerful giver. And God *is* able to make all grace abound toward you; that ye, always having all sufficiency in all *things,* may abound to every good work: (As it is written, He hath dispersed abroad; he hath given to the poor: his righteousness remaineth for ever. Now he that ministereth seed to the sower both minister bread for *your* food, and multiply your seed sown, and increase the fruits of your righteousness;) Being enriched in every thing to all bountifulness, which causeth through us thanksgiving to God. For the administration of this service not only supplieth the want of the saints, but is abundant also by many thanksgivings unto God; Whiles by the experiment of this ministration they glorify God for your professed subjection unto the gospel of Christ, and for *your* liberal distribution unto them, and unto all *men;* And by their prayer for you, which long after you for the exceeding grace of God in you. Thanks *be* unto God for his unspeakable gift.

─── *DECLARATION OF FAITH* ───

I always give generously with great joy in what I am doing for the advancement of the Gospel. I never give grudgingly, or with a regretful heart. I fully understand that seedtime and harvest is at work in my giving just as it is in everything else that I do. If I sow sparingly, I will reap a sparing harvest. But if I sow generously, I will reap a generous harvest.

Each time I have opportunity, I pray to determine of a certainty what I should give so that I will have no regrets. I will never give reluctantly or under compulsion, but only with a willing and joy-filled heart, for God loves and blesses the cheerful giver.

Once I have given from my heart [with all joy], God is able to make every favor and earthly blessing abound toward me so that I have all sufficiency in every circumstance and can abound in every good work.

As it is written, "He has scattered abroad his gifts to those in need; his right-eousness endures forever." In this, God has made my harvest synonymous with righteousness. Therefore, I will expect His abundant return on my giving.

Now He who supplies me with seed to sow and bread to eat will also supply and increase my store of seed and will enlarge and multiply the harvest of my righteousness. This is my promise of blessing on my savings account. I can absolutely count on my Father to increase my savings as I give to Him in faith.

Through my giving, I am made rich in every way so that I can be generous in every way.

Tremendous thanksgiving to God comes in abundance through the ministries of those I am giving to. My giving not only supplies the needs of the Church, but overflows in every direction causing many to thank God for what is being done.

Men and women continually praise God because of my obedience in giving. The fruit produced by my generosity touches their hearts and draws them to God. They see what is being done and give Him the glory.

I never give a gift without adding prayer and affirmation to it in order to receive the insurance of the maximum blessing. Furthermore, because of my gen-erous giving, God will inspire the hearts of others, causing them to agree with me in prayer and call down an abundance of blessings upon me because of the sur-passing grace that God has given me.

I thank God for this remarkable system of giving that He has established. What a wonder it is!

(Luke 6:38; 2 Corinthians 8:2-5; Philippians 4:15-20; 1 Chronicles 29:1-17; Malachi 3:6-12; Proverbs 3:9,10; 11:24; 22:9; Galatians 6:7-9; Ecclesiastes 11:1-6; Matthew 6:19-33; Romans 12:8; Deuteronomy 15:7-11; 8:6-18; Psalm 112:1-10; Isaiah 55:10,11; Hosea 10:12; James 1:17)

2 CORINTHIANS 10:3-6 KJV

For though we walk in the flesh, we do not war after the flesh: (For the weapons of our warfare *are* not carnal, but mighty through God to the pulling down of strong holds;) Casting down imaginations, and every high thing that exalteth itself against the knowledge of God, and bringing into captivity every thought to the obedience of Christ; And having in a readiness to revenge all disobedi-ence, when your obedience is fulfilled.

——— *DECLARATION OF FAITH* ———

Though I live in the world, I do not wage war as the world does, for the weapons of my warfare are not carnal, but spiritual. I have the very power of Christ to demolish every stronghold that has been raised up against the things of

God. I tear down and refute all arguments, theories, reasonings and every proud and lofty thing that exalts itself above the knowledge of God. I lead every thought into captivity to the obedience of Christ. I am always ready to bring justice to every act of insubordination and disobedience once my obedience is fulfilled.

(Ephesians 6:10-18; 1 Timothy 1:18,19; Acts 7:22; 1 Corinthians 1:19; Luke 10:19; Mark 3:27; 16:17,18)

2 CORINTHIANS **10:7** NKJV

Do you look at things according to the outward appearance? If anyone is convinced in himself that he is Christ's, let him again consider this in himself, that just as he is Christ's, even so we are Christ's.

——— *DECLARATION OF FAITH* ———

As a spiritual child of God, I do not only look to the surface of things, but also, and foremost, at the spiritual side of issues.

(2 Corinthians 4:13; 5:7; Hebrews 11:1; John 7:24; 1 Corinthians 13:9-13; James 1:22-26)

2 CORINTHIANS **10:12** NKJV

For we dare not class ourselves or compare ourselves with those who commend themselves. But they, measuring themselves by themselves, and comparing themselves among themselves, are not wise.

——— *DECLARATION OF FAITH* ———

I do not measure myself, or my ability, by what I know I can do in and of myself. I always remember that the unlimited One dwells within me and with Him, nothing is impossible.

(John 14:12,17; 17:20-26; 2 Corinthians 5:12)

2 CORINTHIANS **10:15** AMP

We do not boast therefore, beyond our proper limit, over other men's labors, but we have the hope and confident expectation that as your faith continues to grow, our field among you may be greatly enlarged, still within the limits of our commission.

——— *DECLARATION OF FAITH* ———

As my faith continues to grow, the area of ministry around me greatly expands.

(1 Corinthians 3:5-10; 2 Corinthians 9:10; Acts 6:7; 16:5)

2 CORINTHIANS 10:17,18 KJV

But he that glorieth, let him glory in the Lord. For not he that commendeth himself is approved, but whom the Lord commendeth.

——— *DECLARATION OF FAITH* ———

I do not boast of myself, but only of what the Lord has done and is doing in my life; for it is not the one who commends himself who is approved, but the one whom the Lord commends.

(Jeremiah 9:24; Proverbs 27:2; Romans 2:29)

2 CORINTHIANS 11:4 NKJV

For if he who comes preaches another Jesus whom we have not preached, or if you receive a different spirit which you have not received, or a different gospel which you have not accepted—you may well put up with it!

——— *DECLARATION OF FAITH* ———

If someone comes to me preaching a gospel different from that which I have firmly established in my spirit through careful study, I will not put up with it. I have been given wisdom and revelation knowledge to know and understand the Word, and I cannot be fooled by the esoteric interpretations of a false teacher.

(Galatians 1:6-9; 2 Timothy 2:14-16; Matthew 13:11,15,16; 1 John 2:20,27; 5:20; 1 Corinthians 2:6-16; John 10:1-11)

2 CORINTHIANS 11:14,15 KJV

And no marvel; for Satan himself is transformed into an angel of light. Therefore *it is* no great thing if his ministers also be transformed as the ministers of righteousness; whose end shall be according to their works.

——— *DECLARATION OF FAITH* ———

I am not ignorant of the wiles of the devil. I know that he likes to be in those places where he is least expected and that he will disguise himself as an angel of light in order to lead me astray from the things of God. It does not surprise me then when his servants masquerade as servants of righteousness. Their end will be just as their actions deserve.

(2 Corinthians 2:11; Ephesians 6:10-18; Galatians 1:8; Philippians 3:19)

2 CORINTHIANS 12:1 NIV

I must go on boasting. Although there is nothing to be gained, I will go on to visions and revelations from the Lord.

──── *DECLARATION OF FAITH* ────

As a child of God dedicated to the things of the kingdom, I am destined to have visions and revelations from the Lord.

(Matthew 6:33; Acts 2:14-21; 16:9; 18:9; 22:17-21; 1 Corinthians 12:1-11; 14:2,13)

2 CORINTHIANS 12:5 NKJV

Of such a one I will boast; yet of myself I will not boast, except in my infirmities.

──── *DECLARATION OF FAITH* ────

I will not boast of myself, except in my weaknesses (the limited abilities I have that come from my own power), for my strength (or spiritual ability) is not my own, but the power of God within me. I declare that in and of myself I am nothing, but with Christ in me I am more than a conqueror and can do all things!

(2 Corinthians 11:30; Ephesians 6:10; Joel 3:10; Romans 8:37; Philippians 4:13)

2 CORINTHIANS 12:9,10 KJV

And he said unto me, My grace is sufficient for thee: for my strength is made perfect in weakness. Most gladly therefore will I rather glory in my infirmities, that the power of Christ may rest upon me. Therefore I take pleasure in infirmities, in reproaches, in necessities, in persecutions, in distresses for Christ's sake: for when I am weak, then am I strong.

──── *DECLARATION OF FAITH* ────

God's grace (divine enabling) is all that I need to stand in perpetual victory in this life; for His strength in me is made perfect in my weakness. Therefore, even when I am weak, the strength and power of Christ rests on me. This is why I delight in my weaknesses as a man/woman and why hardships, persecutions and difficulties can't cause me to become distressed; for when I recognize my own weakness, I know to rely on His strength. And in His strength, I am not a victim, but a victor—a champion made to display God's own glory to the world!

(Romans 5:1,2; 8:31,37; 1 Peter 4:14; Colossians 1:27-29; 1 Corinthians 13:4)

2 CORINTHIANS 13:3 NKJV

Since you seek a proof of Christ speaking in me, who is not weak toward you, but mighty in you.

———— DECLARATION OF FAITH ————

Christ is not weak in dealing with me. To the contrary, His power is greatly displayed in my presence.

(Mark 16:17-20; Colossians 1:27-29)

2 CORINTHIANS 13:4 NKJV

For though He was crucified in weakness, yet He lives by the power of God. For we also are weak in Him, but we shall live with Him by the power of God toward you.

———— DECLARATION OF FAITH ————

Of a certainty, Jesus was crucified in weakness, yet He lives by the power of God. Likewise, I (in and of myself) am weak in Him, yet by God's power flowing in and through me, I live as a conqueror together with Him. I never forget my total and complete dependency upon Jesus to help me live the life that He has called me to live.

(Ephesians 1:17-23; Romans 8:37; Colossians 1:27-29; 2 Corinthians 10:3,4)

2 CORINTHIANS 13:11 KJV

Finally, brethren, farewell. Be perfect, be of good comfort, be of one mind, live in peace; and the God of love and peace shall be with you.

———— DECLARATION OF FAITH ————

I seek perfection in my walk with God, striving to be exactly what He has made me to be. I heed the Word without wavering. I am of one mind with my brothers and sisters in Christ and, so far as it depends upon me, I live in peace with everyone.

My Father, the God of all peace, is with me always.

(Philippians 3:12-15; James 1:22-25; Romans 12:16-18; 15:33)

2 CORINTHIANS 13:14 AMP

The grace (favor and spiritual blessing) of the Lord Jesus Christ and the love of God and the presence and fellowship (the communion and sharing together, and participation) in the Holy Spirit be with you all. Amen (so be it).

——— *DECLARATION OF FAITH* ———

The grace of my Lord Jesus, the love of God, and the fellowship of the Holy Spirit are always with me.

(Matthew 28:20; 1 Corinthians 16:23; John 14:17; 16:13; Romans 8:38,39)

CHAPTER FORTY-EIGHT

GALATIANS

Galatians is the mighty treatise on grace. Penned by the apostle Paul around 48 AD, Galatians addresses the heresy that we must keep the Law of Moses in order to be saved. Paul pulls no punches in this epistle. He makes it plain as day that Jesus is our all-efficient Savior and that through His redemptive work we are redeemed from the curse of the Law.

As you speak the promises of the book of Galatians, be ever thankful that you stand by grace and grace alone. You are no longer ruled by the Law in order to be righteous before God. Jesus has redeemed you from such bondage. If Christ has set you free, then you are free indeed!

❖

GALATIANS 1:3,4 NKJV

Grace to you and peace from God the Father and our Lord Jesus Christ, who gave Himself for our sins, that He might deliver us from this present evil age, according to the will of our God and Father.

———— DECLARATION OF FAITH ————

Grace and all spiritual blessing belong to me as a gift from God my Father and from my Lord Jesus Christ who, according to the will of God, gave Himself for my sins in order to rescue me from the effects of this present evil age.

(Ephesians 1:3; 2:4-10; 2 Peter 1:4; Hebrews 2:5)

GALATIANS 1:6 NIV

I am astonished that you are so quickly deserting the one who called you by the grace of Christ and are turning to a different gospel.

———— DECLARATION OF FAITH ————

I am fixed in my faith and rooted in the Word. I will never turn from the grace of Jesus to another gospel.

(Mark 4:17; Colossians 2:7,8; 2 Corinthians 11:3,4)

GALATIANS 1:10-12 KJV

For do I now persuade men, or God? or do I seek to please men? for if I yet pleased men, I should not be the servant of Christ. But I certify you, brethren, that the gospel which was preached of me is not after man. For I neither received it of man, neither was I taught *it*, but by the revelation of Jesus Christ.

——— *DECLARATION OF FAITH* ———

I am not trying to win the approval of men, but of God. I will not be found with regret when I get to heaven because while on earth I was concerned with what men think of me instead of what God thinks of me.

This Gospel that I proclaim is not something that man made up. It is not something that was revealed to me through the wisdom of men, but by the revelation knowledge of God.

(1 Thessalonians 2:4; 1 Corinthians 15:1; Ephesians 3:3-5; Matthew 13:11,15,16; 16:13-18; John 6:44)

GALATIANS 2:10 MESSAGE

The only additional thing they asked was that we remember the poor, and I was already eager to do that.

——— *DECLARATION OF FAITH* ———

I will always remember the poor and those who do not have the means to go to church. In me, they will have a way of hearing the Gospel.

(Isaiah 61:1; Acts 11:30; Matthew 28:18-20)

GALATIANS 2:16-21 KJV

Knowing that a man is not justified by the works of the law, but by the faith of Jesus Christ, even we have believed in Jesus Christ, that we might be justified by the faith of Christ, and not by the works of the law: for by the works of the law shall no flesh be justified. But if, while we seek to be justified by Christ, we ourselves also are found sinners, *is* therefore Christ the minister of sin? God forbid. For if I build again the things which I destroyed, I make myself a transgressor. For I through the law am dead to the law, that I might live unto God. I am crucified with Christ: nevertheless I live; yet not I, but Christ liveth in me: and the life which I now live in the flesh I live by the faith of the Son of God, who loved me, and gave himself for me. I do not frustrate the grace of God: for if righteousness *come* by the law, then Christ is dead in vain.

———— *DECLARATION OF FAITH* ————

I realize that I am not justified by the Law, but by faith in Jesus; for, even though doing the good deeds outlined in the Law is right, it is not what justifies me in the sight of God. The only thing that can save me from death and destruction is a sin substitute—and that is what Jesus became for me. Therefore, I will rest in the finished work of my Savior.

Even though I may fail and sin against the Law as a child of God, it doesn't mean that Christ is a minister of sin or has become an excuse for it. The fact of the matter is He stripped sin of its power. Because of this, even if I sin I stand uncondemned. Therefore, I now have the ability to control it, for it no longer has any power over my life. God Himself now partners up with me so that I can live a life of true holiness.

In Jesus, the Law has been fulfilled and set aside. The Law is fulfilled in me, only so far as I remain in Him.

The regulations of the Law are no longer a guide to me. I am led by the Holy Spirit now.

Sin, which was awakened by the Law, is no longer a factor in my justification or my righteousness. In Jesus, the Law has been destroyed in terms of my justification. I am no longer considered a sinner in the eyes of God. Therefore, why would I want to turn to the Law for justification and thus become a sinner again?

I, through the Law, died to the Law, so that I may live for God. I am crucified with Christ. It is no longer I who live, but Christ lives in me. And the life that I now live, I live by the faith of the Son of God, who showed His love for me by becoming my sin substitute. All that I am (in righteousness, justification, redemption, etc.) is in Him.

I absolutely refuse to set aside this wonderful grace and turn back to the Law, which produced in me spiritual death. Jesus did not die for me in vain! My righteousness does not come through the good deeds outlined in the Law, but by Jesus alone!

(Acts 13:38,39; Romans 1:17; 3:21-26; 6:6,14-23; 7:4; 8:1-4,14; Ephesians 2:4-10; 1 John 2:1,2; 3:8; 1 Peter 1:13-16; 2 Corinthians 5:7,15,17,21; Hebrews 4:1,2; 7:11; 11:1,6; John 15:5-8; 1 Corinthians 1:30)

GALATIANS 3:2,3 NKJV

This only I want to learn from you: Did you receive the Spirit by the works of the law, or by the hearing of faith? Are you so foolish? Having begun in the Spirit, are you now being made perfect by the flesh?

I did not receive the Holy Spirit by the works of the Law, but by hearing of faith. I am not so foolish as to turn to my own efforts to justify myself after I have admitted that I can't and that I need Jesus. No, I am not the fool who begins a new life in the Spirit, then turns back to works of righteousness for his justification. Jesus alone has made me perfect, not works!

(Hebrews 7:16; 10:10,14; Romans 10:16,17; Galatians 4:9; Ephesians 2:4-10)

GALATIANS 3:5 NIV

Does God give you his Spirit and work miracles among you because you observe the law, or because you believe what you heard?

——— *DECLARATION OF FAITH* ———

God does not give me His Spirit and do miracles in and through me because of the good works that I do, or because I am sinless. He does these things because I believe in His Word and speak it in the spirit of faith. My belief is the springboard for miracles in my life, not my works of righteousness.

(Mark 11:22-25; 16:17-20; Matthew 21:19-22; 2 Corinthians 4:13; 5:7; Titus 3:4-7; Ephesians 2:8-10)

GALATIANS 3:6-16 KJV

Even as Abraham believed God, and it was accounted to him for righteousness. Know ye therefore that they which are of faith, the same are the children of Abraham. And the scripture, foreseeing that God would justify the heathen through faith, preached before the gospel unto Abraham, *saying,* In thee shall all nations be blessed. So then they which be of faith are blessed with faithful Abraham. For as many as are of the works of the law are under the curse: for it is written, Cursed *is* every one that continueth not in all things which are written in the book of the law to do them. But that no man is justified by the law in the sight of God, *it is* evident: for, The just shall live by faith. And the law is not of faith: but, The man that doeth them shall live in them. Christ hath redeemed us from the curse of the law, being made a curse for us: for it is written, Cursed *is* every one that hangeth on a tree: That the blessing of Abraham might come on the Gentiles through Jesus Christ; that we might receive the promise of the Spirit through faith. Brethren, I speak after the manner of men; Though *it be* but a man's covenant, yet *if it* be confirmed, no man disannulleth, or addeth thereto. Now to Abraham and his seed were the promises made. He saith not, And to seeds, as of many; but as of one, And to thy seed, which is Christ.

———— DECLARATION OF FAITH ————

I consider Abraham a chief role model for my faith. As it is written, "He believed God and it was credited to him as righteousness." In this respect, as a believer I am a child of Abraham. The Scripture foresaw that God would justify me through faith, and He announced the Gospel to Abraham all those many years ago, saying, "All nations will be blessed through you." Therefore, as a man/woman of faith, I am blessed in the same ways that Abraham was, for he is the father of my faith.

I will not put myself back under the Law, thereby putting myself under the curse, for it is written, "Cursed is anyone who does not continually (without fail) do everything written in the Book of the Law." Therefore, it is abundantly clear that I cannot be justified by the Law because I, along with everyone else in this world, have failed to keep it at one time or another.

As a seal to this truth, it is also written, "The righteous shall live by faith," and, "The man who lives by the Law must never fail in it." Therefore, with the Law and faith being clearly contrary to each other, I will not allow myself to rely on my own deeds of righteousness to justify me before God.

Jesus redeemed me from the curse of the Law, being made a curse for me, for it is written, "Cursed is the one who is hung on a tree."

He redeemed me so that, through Him, I could receive the same blessings that were showered upon Abraham, and so that through faith I could receive the promise of the Spirit.

Just as no one can add to or set aside a human covenant once it has been established (witnessed and notarized), so it is in this case. The promises were spoken to Abraham and his seed. It does not say, "To his seeds," meaning many people, but, "To his seed," meaning one person, who is Jesus. And since He became my substitute and I am now one with Him, I am a recipient of those promises. Because of what Jesus did for me, all of God's promises are now mine through Him!

(Genesis 12:1-3,16; 13:2,6; 15:1,6,15; 17:1,2,6-9; 18:27; 20:7; 24:35; 26:3,12-14; Hebrews 11:1,6; Romans 3:21-26; 4:1-4; 8:1-4; 11:6; Deuteronomy 21:23; 27:26; 28:15-68; Leviticus 18:5; Ephesians 1:3,4,7,11,13,14; 2:13-15; 6:10; John 17:6-26; 2 Corinthians 1:20)

GALATIANS 3:18 AMP

For if the inheritance [of the promise depends on observing] the Law [as these false teachers would like you to believe], it no longer [depends] on the promise; however, God gave it to Abraham [as a free gift solely] by virtue of His promise.

My inheritance does not depend upon works, but on faith in the promise.

(2 Corinthians 1:20; 4:13; 5:7; Galatians 3:2)

GALATIANS 3:22-29 KJV

But the scripture hath concluded all under sin, that the promise by faith of Jesus Christ might be given to them that believe. But before faith came, we were kept under the law, shut up unto the faith which should afterwards be revealed. Wherefore the law was our schoolmaster *to bring us* unto Christ, that we might be justified by faith. But after that faith is come, we are no longer under a schoolmaster. For ye are all the children of God by faith in Christ Jesus. For as many of you as have been baptized into Christ have put on Christ. There is neither Jew nor Greek, there is neither bond nor free, there is neither male nor female: for ye are all one in Christ Jesus. And if ye *be* Christ's, then are ye Abraham's seed, and heirs according to the promise.

———— DECLARATION OF FAITH ————

I receive what was promised by the faith that Jesus demonstrated.

I do not rely on the works of the Law in order to receive the promise; for the Law was given in order to lead me to Jesus, so that I might be justified by faith. Therefore, I am no longer under the supervision of the Law.

I am a son/daughter of God through the faith of Jesus Christ, for when I was baptized into Christ, I was clothed with Christ. This is the epitome of my righteousness. I now rest in the very righteousness of Jesus Himself.

As all of my brothers and sisters in Christ have clothed themselves with Christ, there is no longer any distinctions between races, social classes, or gender, for we are all one in Him.

I am a born-again son/daughter of God. I belong to Christ. Therefore, I am Abraham's seed and an heir according to the promise.

(Galatians 2:20,21; 4:4-6; Mark 11:12-14,20-25; Romans 3:20-26; 4:11; 6:3,4; 8:17; 10:4; John 1:12; 3:3; 2 Corinthians 5:17,21; Colossians 3:11; Ephesians 2:15,16)

GALATIANS 4:1-9 KJV

Now I say, *That* the heir, as long as he is a child, differeth nothing from a servant, though he be lord of all; But is under tutors and governors until the time appointed of the father. Even so we, when we were children, were in bondage under the elements of the world: But when the fulness of the time was come, God sent forth his Son, made of a woman, made under the law, To redeem them that were under the law, that we might receive the adoption of sons. And because ye are sons, God hath sent forth the Spirit of his Son into your hearts, crying, Abba, Father. Wherefore thou art no more a servant, but a son; and if a son, then an heir of God through Christ. Howbeit then, when ye knew not God, ye did service unto them which by nature are no gods. But now, after that ye have known God, or rather are known of God, how turn ye again to the weak and beggarly elements, whereunto ye desire again to be in bondage?

─────── *DECLARATION OF FAITH* ───────

Before I became a child of God, I was in slavery, subject to the basic principles of this natural, cursed world. But, when I received Jesus as my Lord and Savior, I received my emancipation.

Jesus redeemed me from the curse of the Law so that I could claim full rights as a son/daughter of God. I now have a right to every promise that God has ever made to His people.

Because I am God's son/daughter, He has sent the Holy Spirit to dwell in my heart and it is He who moves me to see the reality of God as my dad (Abba).

I am no longer a slave, but a son/daughter. And since I am God's son/daughter, He has made me an heir, entitling me to receive all that He has as my very own.

I now have an intimate relationship with the Lord of the universe. I am no longer of service to demons or any other spirits in the kingdom of darkness. I now know God, and more importantly, am known by Him. Therefore, I will never turn back to the weak and miserable principles of the natural world system again.

(Romans 1:17; 6:16-22; 8:14-17,32; 2 Peter 1:3,4; John 1:12; 8:31-36; 14:17; 16:13; 17:20-26; 2 Corinthians 1:20; 4:13; 5:7; Colossians 1:13; 2:13-15; 1 John 4:6-17)

GALATIANS 5:1 NKJV

Stand fast therefore in the liberty by which Christ has made us free, and do not be entangled again with a yoke of bondage.

─────── *DECLARATION OF FAITH* ───────

It is for my freedom that Christ has set me free. Therefore, I will stand firm in His grace and never again allow myself to be entangled with a yoke of bondage.

(John 8:31-36; Matthew 11:28-30; Romans 5:1,2; Galatians 2:4,16-21)

GALATIANS 5:5,6 NIV

But by faith we eagerly await through the Spirit the righteousness for which we hope. For in Christ Jesus neither circumcision nor uncircumcision has any value. The only thing that counts is faith expressing itself through love.

——— *DECLARATION OF FAITH* ———

By faith, and the Holy Spirit's lead, I patiently wait in eager expectation for the righteousness for which I hope (or the answer to what I am praying for). I understand that it doesn't matter what kind of ritual I perform or what kind of penance I do. All that matters is that I am using my faith (affirming my belief through my actions and words) and expressing it through love.

(2 Corinthians 4:13; 5:7; Romans 8:14; James 1:2-8,22-25; 2:14-26; Hebrews 10:35-11:1; 1 Corinthians 13:13)

GALATIANS 5:13 AMP

For you, brethren, were [indeed] called to freedom; only [do not let your] freedom be an incentive to your flesh and an opportunity or excuse [for selfishness], but through love you should serve one another.

——— *DECLARATION OF FAITH* ———

I have been called to be free. But, I will not use my freedom as an excuse to indulge in the sins of the flesh. Rather, I focus on serving others in a spirit of compassion.

(John 8:31-36; 1 Corinthians 8:9; 9:19; 1 Peter 2:16)

GALATIANS 5:15 AMP

But if you bite and devour one another [in partisan strife], be careful that you [and your whole fellowship] are not consumed by one another.

——— *DECLARATION OF FAITH* ———

I will never set myself up as a perpetual enemy to any of my brothers and sisters in Christ—always criticizing and finding fault with them. Instead, I will encourage and strengthen them so that they may become productive children of God.

(Romans 16:17-19; Ephesians 4:11-16; Hebrews 10:24)

GALATIANS 5:16 NIV

So I say, live by the Spirit, and you will not gratify the desires of the sinful nature.

——— *DECLARATION OF FAITH* ———

My recreated spirit, as led by the Holy Spirit, rules me so that I will not fulfill the sinful desires of my flesh.

(Romans 6:12; 7:24,25; 8:1-4,14; Ephesians 2:10)

GALATIANS 5:18 AMP

But if you are guided (led) by the [Holy] Spirit, you are not subject to the Law.

——— *DECLARATION OF FAITH* ———

As a child of God, led by the Spirit of God, I am no longer subject to the Law of Moses.

(Romans 6:14; 8:1,2,14; Galatians 2:16-21)

GALATIANS 5:22-25 KJV

But the fruit of the Spirit is love, joy, peace, longsuffering, gentleness, goodness, faith, meekness, temperance: against such there is no law. And they that are Christ's have crucified the flesh with the affections and lusts. If we live in the Spirit, let us also walk in the Spirit.

——— *DECLARATION OF FAITH* ———

I am a true branch of the Vine. Because of this, the fruit produced by my spirit is love, joy, peace, patience, kindness, goodness, gentleness, faithfulness, and self-control.

As a born-again child of God, I have been crucified with Christ. My old sinful nature, with its passions and desires, died with Him on the cross and I now live by my recreated spirit, as led by the Holy Spirit. Therefore, as I live by my spirit, my conduct will reflect what my spirit desires.

(John 1:12; 3:3; 15:5; Galatians 2:20; Romans 6:5,6; 7:24,25; 8:1-4,14; 2 Timothy 1:7; 1 Corinthians 13:4-8; Titus 3:4-7)

GALATIANS 5:26-6:5 KJV

Let us not be desirous of vain glory, provoking one another, envying one another. Brethren, if a man be overtaken in a fault, ye which are spiritual, restore such an one in the spirit of meekness; considering thyself, lest thou also be tempted. Bear ye one another's burdens, and so fulfil the law of Christ. For if a man think himself to be something, when he is nothing, he deceiveth himself. But let every man prove his own work, and then shall he have rejoicing in himself alone, and not in another. For every man shall bear his own burden.

DECLARATION OF FAITH

I will not allow myself to become self-conceited and arrogant, always trying to find fault in others, or being jealous of what others have.

If I have found a brother or sister in Christ to have been overtaken in some kind of sin, as a spiritual person I will restore them gently, without any sense of superiority, always remembering that I myself have fallen to temptation as well.

I do not think of myself (in and of myself) as being something when I am actually nothing.

Willingly, and with sincere love and concern, I carry the burdens of my brothers and sisters in Christ, giving them whatever assistance I can to help them back on their feet. And I am not above looking to them for strength when I am in need as well. In this, the Law of Christ is fulfilled in us.

(Romans 12:3; 15:1; 16:17-19; Philippians 2:3; Hebrews 12:1-4; Ephesians 4:2; 2 Corinthians 3:5; Luke 18:11)

GALATIANS 6:6 NKJV

Let him who is taught the word share in all good things with him who teaches.

DECLARATION OF FAITH

I share all good things (financial blessings, services, etc.) with those who instruct me in the Word.

(1 Corinthians 9:9-14; Deuteronomy 25:4)

GALATIANS 6:7-10 KJV

Be not deceived; God is not mocked: for whatsoever a man soweth, that shall he also reap. For he that soweth to his flesh shall of the flesh reap corruption; but he that soweth to the Spirit shall of the Spirit reap life everlasting. And let us not be weary in well doing: for in due season we shall reap, if we faint not. As we have therefore opportunity, let us do good unto all *men*, especially unto them who are of the household of faith.

———— *DECLARATION OF FAITH* ————

I cannot be deceived into thinking that I can do whatever I want and still get away with it. God will not be mocked in such a way, for He has established the laws of seedtime and harvest in the earth and as long as the earth remains, these laws shall remain as well. Therefore, I will reap exactly what I sow. If I sow to please the sinful nature, from that nature I will reap destruction; if I sow to my spirit, through the Holy Spirit, I shall reap the benefits of eternal life.

I purpose in my heart to never become weary in doing good, for at the proper time I will reap an abundant harvest as long as I do not give up. Therefore, whenever I have an opportunity, I do good to all people, especially to those who are in the family: the household of faith.

(Romans 2:5-7; 12:9-21; Genesis 8:22; 1 Corinthians 15:58; Titus 3:4-7)

GALATIANS 6:14-16 AMP

But far be it from me to glory [in anything or anyone] except in the cross of our Lord Jesus Christ (the Messiah) through Whom the world has been crucified to me, and I to the world! For neither is circumcision [now] of any importance, nor uncircumcision, but [only] a new creation [the result of a new birth and a new nature in Christ Jesus, the Messiah]. Peace and mercy be upon all who walk by this rule [who discipline themselves and regulate their lives by this principle], even upon the [true] Israel of God!

———— *DECLARATION OF FAITH* ————

I will boast of nothing except that which springs from the cross of Jesus Christ my Lord. Through Him, the present condition of the world has been crucified to me, and I to it. The life that I now live is superior to the curse. In Him, neither circumcision nor uncircumcision, nor any other ritual, means anything or has any benefit. What counts is the fact that I am a new creation created in Christ Jesus. I am a born-again child of God and a partaker of His divine nature. I follow the rule of the new creation and continually confess what Christ has done in me, and all that I have been given through Him. By this, peace and mercy flow through my life in abundance in Jesus' name.

(1 Corinthians 1:18; Romans 2:26-28; 10:8; Galatians 5:6; 2 Corinthians 4:13; 5:17; 2 Peter 1:1-4)

CHAPTER FORTY-NINE

EPHESIANS

Ephesians is another profound work of the apostle Paul. It was written around AD 60 to the church at Ephesus. The central theme is what you have been made to be as a born-again child of God, saved by grace through faith. Issues such as wisdom, election, unity, marriage and spiritual warfare are addressed in moderate detail and many promises are spoken in support of each issue.

As you pray the promises of the book of Ephesians, know that because you are one with your Savior, you have the power to be an overcomer in any area of your life.

EPHESIANS 1:3-10 KJV

Blessed *be* the God and Father of our Lord Jesus Christ, who hath blessed us with all spiritual blessings in heavenly *places* in Christ: According as he hath chosen us in him before the foundation of the world, that we should be holy and without blame before him in love: Having predestinated us unto the adoption of children by Jesus Christ to himself, according to the good pleasure of his will, To the praise of the glory of his grace, wherein he hath made us accepted in the beloved. In whom we have redemption through his blood, the forgiveness of sins, according to the riches of his grace; Wherein he hath abounded toward us in all wisdom and prudence; Having made known unto us the mystery of his will, according to his good pleasure which he hath purposed in himself: That in the dispensation of the fulness of times he might gather together in one all things in Christ, both which are in heaven, and which are on earth; *even* in him.

———— DECLARATION OF FAITH ————

I give all praise, honor, and glory to my God, the Father of my Lord Jesus, for He has blessed me with every spiritual blessing in Christ.

He chose me, in Jesus, before the creation of the world, to be holy and blameless in His sight. In His great love for me, He predestined me to be adopted as His son/daughter, through Jesus, in accordance with the good pleasure of His will—to the praise of His glorious grace, which He freely gives me in the One whom He loves. It gives Him tremendous joy to know I am His son/daughter and that I am covered in Jesus' blood.

In Jesus, I have my redemption, through His blood, and the forgiveness of my sins, in accordance with the abundance of His grace, which He lavishes on me with all wisdom and understanding. In Him, I have the ability to understand all kinds of knowledge so that I can use it for the benefit of the kingdom. It is His good pleasure to make known to me, beyond a shadow of doubt, the mystery of His will. This great blessing, purposed in Christ, has been put into effect through me in order to bring the things of heaven into this earth and to put all things under the lordship of Jesus.

(Romans 3:24; 8:17,28-32; 16:25; 2 Peter 1:3; 1 Peter 1:2-5,13-16; Luke 12:32; Galatians 4:4-6; 1 Corinthians 1:21,30; 2:6-16; Titus 3:4-7; Hebrews 9:12; Matthew 6:10; 13:11,15,16; 2 Corinthians 4:13; 5:7,16-21; Philippians 2:5-13)

EPHESIANS 1:11-14 NKJV

In Him also we have obtained an inheritance, being predestined according to the purpose of Him who works all things according to the counsel of His will, that we who first trusted in Christ should be to the praise of His glory. In Him you also *trusted*, after you heard the word of truth, the gospel of your salvation; in whom also, having believed, you were sealed with the Holy Spirit of promise, who is the guarantee of our inheritance until the redemption of the purchased possession, to the praise of His glory.

——— DECLARATION OF FAITH ———

In Jesus, I have been chosen—handpicked for the purpose of being well able to live in His perfect will to the praise of His glory. I became one with Jesus when I responded to the Word, the Gospel of my salvation. When I believed and received Jesus as my Lord and Savior, I was marked in Him with the seal of the Holy Spirit. God's emblem of ownership has been placed upon me. The Holy Spirit, who dwells within my heart, is God's earnest guaranteeing my inheritance in this life until the day when my total redemption is manifested to the praise of His glory.

(Romans 8:23,28-30; 10:8-17; John 17:20-26; 2 Corinthians 5:5; 1 Peter 1:3-5)

EPHESIANS 1:17-23 KJV

That the God of our Lord Jesus Christ, the Father of glory, may give unto you the spirit of wisdom and revelation in the knowledge of him: The eyes of your understanding being enlightened; that ye may know what is the hope of his calling, and what the riches of the glory of his inheritance in the saints, And what *is* the exceeding greatness of his power to us-ward who believe, according to the working of his mighty power, Which he wrought in Christ, when he raised him from the dead, and set *him* at his own right hand in the heavenly *places,* Far above all principality, and power, and might, and dominion, and every name that is named, not only in this world, but also in that which is to come: And hath put all *things* under his feet, and gave him *to be* the head over all *things* to the church, Which is his body, the fulness of him that filleth all in all.

―――― DECLARATION OF FAITH ――――

My heavenly Father has given me a spirit of wisdom and revelation, of insight into mysteries and secrets, in the deep and intimate knowledge of Himself. My spirit has been enlightened with a flood of understanding so that I can know and comprehend the hope of my calling and the immense riches of this glorious inheritance that has become my own.

I now have a complete understanding of the exceeding greatness of His power toward me. The power that is now residing and working within me is the very power that God wrought in Christ when He raised Him from the dead and seated Him at His own right hand, far above every principality, every power, every ruler of darkness, all dominion and every name or title that can be given. And this power is not only working in and through me now, but it will continue to work in and through me in the age to come. As God has placed all things under Jesus' feet and appointed Him to be the Head of the body (the Church), I have now, as a part of His body, become the fullness of Jesus in this earth as He fills me in every way. All things are placed under my feet and every power and dominion must obey me as I apply the power of attorney that Jesus has given me to use His name.

(Daniel 2:22,23; 1 Corinthians 1:30; 2:6-16; Matthew 13:11,15,16; 1 John 2:20,27; 5:20; Romans 8:17; 1 Peter 1:3-5; Colossians 1:9-18,26-29; Philippians 2:5-13; John 14:13,14; 17:20-26; Ephesians 2:6; Hebrews 2:5-14; Luke 10:19; Mark 16:15-20)

EPHESIANS 2:4-10 KJV

But God, who is rich in mercy, for his great love wherewith he loved us, Even when we were dead in sins, hath quickened us together with Christ, (by grace ye are saved;) And hath raised *us* up together, and made *us* sit together in heavenly *places* in Christ Jesus: That in the ages to come he might shew the exceeding riches of his grace in *his* kindness toward us through Christ Jesus. For by grace are ye saved through faith; and that not of yourselves: *it is* the gift of God: Not of works, lest any man should boast. For we are his workmanship, created in Christ Jesus unto good works, which God hath before ordained that we should walk in them.

——— *DECLARATION OF FAITH* ———

Because of the great love that He has for me, God, who is rich in mercy, made me alive with Christ even though I was dead in trespasses and sins. It is by His grace (unmerited, undeserved favor) that I am saved.

And God has raised me up and seated me together with Jesus in the heavenly realms, so that from now until eternity He can show me the incomparable riches of His grace, expressed in His loving-kindness toward me in Christ Jesus my Lord.

It is by grace that I have been saved through faith—and this doesn't come to me through my own striving to obtain or even maintain it, for it is God's gift to me. This salvation does not come to me by works, by penance, or by anything else that I can do other than just receive it.

Therefore, I can in no way boast about what I have done to gain God's favor and love. It has been given to me as a gift by grace alone.

I am God's workmanship, recreated in Christ Jesus so that I can have the ability to do the works that He has foreordained that I should do. God has a plan for my life and He has set me on a prearranged path that is leading me to my destiny in Jesus.

(Romans 4:1-5:21; 6:4,5; 8:29,30; 11:6; Titus 3:4-7; John 1:12,13; 3:16,17; Ephesians 1:20; Psalm 91:15; 2 Corinthians 5:17; 2 Peter 1:4)

EPHESIANS 2:13-15 NIV

But now in Christ Jesus you who once were far away have been brought near through the blood of Christ. For he himself is our peace, who has made the two one and has destroyed the barrier, the dividing wall of hostility, by abolishing in his flesh the law with its commandments and regulations. His purpose was to create in himself one new man out of the two, thus making peace.

——— *DECLARATION OF FAITH* ———

In Christ, I, who was once far from God and a stranger to the covenants of promise, without hope and without God in this world, have been reconciled to God through the blood of Jesus.

He Himself has become my peace, having destroyed all barriers that could keep me from Him by abolishing in His flesh the Law of Moses with its commandments and regulations.

He did this in order to recreate me in Himself. I am now a new man/woman and I belong to a new race of people recreated in Christ Jesus. I am a partaker of the divine nature. I am an heir in the family of God.

(Ephesians 1:7; Colossians 1:20; 2:13-15; Hebrews 10:10-19; 1 Peter 1:18,19; Galatians 4:4-6; 6:15; Romans 5:1,2; 1 Corinthians 1:30; Philippians 4:7-9; 2 Corinthians 5:17-21; 2 Peter 1:4)

EPHESIANS 2:18,19 AMP

For it is through Him that we both [whether far off or near] now have an introduction (access) by one [Holy] Spirit to the Father [so that we are able to approach Him]. Therefore you are no longer outsiders (exiles, migrants, and aliens, excluded from the rights of citizens), but you now share citizenship with the saints (God's own people, consecrated and set apart for Himself); and you belong to God's [own] household.

──── *DECLARATION OF FAITH* ────

In Jesus, I have free access to the Father through the Holy Spirit. I am no longer a stranger, but a fellow citizen of heaven with God's people and a member of God's household.

(John 14:6; 16:13; Hebrews 4:15,16; Galatians 4:4-6; Philippians 3:20,21)

EPHESIANS 2:22 NKJV

In whom you also are being built together for a dwelling place of God in the Spirit.

──── *DECLARATION OF FAITH* ────

In Jesus, I am fashioned as a dwelling place for God in my spirit.

(1 Corinthians 3:16; John 14:17; 17:20-26; 1 Peter 2:5)

EPHESIANS 3:7 AMP

Of this [Gospel] I was made a minister according to the gift of God's free grace (undeserved favor) which was bestowed on me by the exercise (the working in all its effectiveness) of His power.

──── *DECLARATION OF FAITH* ────

I have become a minister of the Gospel, by the gift of God's grace given to me, through the working of His mighty power.

(Colossians 1:27-29; 2 Corinthians 5:18-20; Ephesians 1:17-23; Mark 16:15-20)

EPHESIANS 3:10-12 KJV

To the intent that now unto the principalities and powers in heavenly *places* might be known by the church the manifold wisdom of God, According to the eternal purpose which he purposed in Christ Jesus our Lord: In whom we have boldness and access with confidence by the faith of him.

In accordance with His eternal purpose, which He accomplished in Christ Jesus my Lord, it is God's intention that through me His manifold and multifaceted wisdom be made known to the principalities and powers in the heavenly realms. In Him, and through the faith that He demonstrated, I now have access to the Father with boldness, freedom and confidence.

(1 Corinthians 1:30; 2:6-16; 1 Peter 1:10-12; Hebrews 4:15,16)

EPHESIANS 3:14-21 KJV

For this cause I bow my knees unto the Father of our Lord Jesus Christ, Of whom the whole family in heaven and earth is named, That he would grant you, according to the riches of his glory, to be strengthened with might by his Spirit in the inner man; That Christ may dwell in your hearts by faith; that ye, being rooted and grounded in love, May be able to comprehend with all saints what *is* the breadth, and length, and depth, and height; And to know the love of Christ, which passeth knowledge, that ye might be filled with all the fulness of God. Now unto him that is able to do exceeding abundantly above all that we ask or think, according to the power that worketh in us, Unto him *be* glory in the church by Christ Jesus throughout all ages, world without end. Amen.

I freely kneel before my heavenly Father, in whom my whole family in both heaven and earth derives its name.

Out of His glorious riches, he strengthens me with unfathomable power, through the Holy Spirit. It is my spirit that receives this strength. I have been made new so that Christ (the anointed One and His anointing) can dwell in my spirit through faith.

Being rooted and established in love, I now have the ability to understand how wide and long and high and deep the love of Jesus is, and to apprehend the immense knowledge of Christ's love so that I may be filled to the measure of all of the fullness of God.

The very fullness of God Himself is dwelling within me. Right now, He is able to do exceedingly and abundantly above all that I am able to ask or even imagine. He does this according to His power that is at work within me. I find the answers to my every prayer to be within me. The power of God—the very power that spoke the universe into existence—is poised within me at this very moment.

I purpose in my heart to be God-inside minded and to see that He is glorified in me and in Christ Jesus my Lord throughout every generation!

(Romans 8:38,39; 11:36; 14:11; Philippians 2:5-13; 4:19; Ephesians 1:17-23; Colossians 1:27-29; 2:6,7; John 14:17; 17:20-26)

EPHESIANS 4:1-3 NIV

As a prisoner for the Lord, then, I urge you to live a life worthy of the calling you have received. Be completely humble and gentle; be patient, bearing with one another in love. Make every effort to keep the unity of the Spirit through the bond of peace.

I stir myself up to live a life worthy of the calling that I have received. I am completely humble, unselfish, gentle, and patient, bearing with my brothers and sisters in Christ, making allowances (being merciful, lenient, and compassionate) because of my love for them. I make every effort to maintain a unity in the body of Christ, in the Spirit, through the binding power of peace.

(Hebrews 10:24; 1 Thessalonians 2:12; James 4:1-10; Galatians 6:1,2; Romans 16:17-20; Colossians 3:14)

EPHESIANS 4:11-13 NKJV

And He Himself gave some to be apostles, some prophets, some evangelists, and some pastors and teachers, for the equipping of the saints for the work of ministry, for the edifying of the body of Christ, till we all come to the unity of the faith and of the knowledge of the Son of God, to a perfect man, to the measure of the stature of the fullness of Christ.

Jesus has appointed for me apostles, prophets, evangelists, pastors and teachers to prepare me for works of service. They are His gift to me to build me up towards a unity of faith with all of the saints, in the knowledge of Jesus, so that I may become mature and attain the full measure of Christ (the anointed One and His anointing) in my life.

(1 Corinthians 12:28; 13:9-13; 14:20,26; Hebrews 10:24)

EPHESIANS 4:14,15 NKJV

That we should no longer be children, tossed to and fro and carried about with every wind of doctrine, by the trickery of men, in the cunning craftiness of deceitful plotting, but, speaking the truth in love, may grow up in all things into Him who is the head—Christ.

———— *DECLARATION OF FAITH* ————

I am no longer like an infant, tossed back and forth by every wind of doctrine that comes into my life. I will not fall as prey to the cunning craftiness of deceitful men who twist the Word of God to their own ends (to fit their traditions, fill their pocketbooks, etc.).

By continually speaking the truth in love, I will, in all things, grow up into a mature man/woman in Christ, who is the executive Lord of my life.

(Romans 16:17-19; 1 Corinthians 13:9-13; 14:20; 2 Timothy 2:14-21; 1 Peter 3:10-12)

EPHESIANS 4:22-32 KJV

That ye put off concerning the former conversation the old man, which is corrupt according to the deceitful lusts; And be renewed in the spirit of your mind; And that ye put on the new man, which after God is created in righteousness and true holiness. Wherefore putting away lying, speak every man truth with his neighbour: for we are members one of another. Be ye angry, and sin not: let not the sun go down upon your wrath: Neither give place to the devil. Let him that stole steal no more: but rather let him labour, working with *his* hands the thing which is good, that he may have to give to him that needeth. Let no corrupt communication proceed out of your mouth, but that which is good to the use of edifying, that it may minister grace unto the hearers. And grieve not the holy Spirit of God, whereby ye are sealed unto the day of redemption. Let all bitterness, and wrath, and anger, and clamour, and evil speaking, be put away from you, with all malice: And be ye kind one to another, tenderhearted, forgiving one another, even as God for Christ's sake hath forgiven you.

———— *DECLARATION OF FAITH* ————

I have stripped myself of my former nature, which is being destroyed because of its evil desires, in order that I may be renewed in the disposition of my mind. I have put on my new nature, created to be like God in true righteousness and holiness.

Therefore, I cast all falsehood from me and speak only the truth. I will not allow myself to taint the body of Christ by being anything other than He is.

When pure and holy anger rises within me, I will not allow it to give birth to sin, nor will I go to sleep while I am still angry. I may stir myself up until I am burning with anger against the works of the devil, but I will not allow that anger to overwhelm me or be the director of my destiny. I see to it that my anger is pure and not rooted in bitterness or self-offense.

I will not give the devil any kind of foothold into my life.

I will not steal any longer in any way (to include ways that are acceptable to the world). Instead, I will work, doing something useful with my own two hands, for in this God blesses me with His abundance and I shall have the surplus that I need so that I can share with others.

I will not let any unwholesome talk, gossip, backbiting, or profanity come out of my mouth, but only things that are helpful for building others up according to their needs, that it may be of benefit to those who listen. I am a child of encouragement and unity, not of destruction and division.

I will not grieve the Holy Spirit of God, with whom I have been sealed for the day of redemption.

I cast from me all bitterness, rage, anger, brawling and slander, along with every kind of malice, and I embrace kindness and compassion, always being ready to forgive, just as in Jesus, God forgave me.

(Romans 6:4-6; 12:1,2,5; 14:17; 16:17-19; 2 Peter 1:4; Ephesians 1:13,14; 2:10; 2 Corinthians 5:17; 9:8; 1 Peter 3:10-12; 1 John 4:17; Psalm 4:4; James 4:7; 1 Thessalonians 4:11; Deuteronomy 28:12; Hebrews 10:24; Galatians 6:1,2)

EPHESIANS 5:1,2 NKJV

Therefore be imitators of God as dear children. And walk in love, as Christ also has loved us and given Himself for us, an offering and a sacrifice to God for a sweet-smelling aroma.

——— *DECLARATION OF FAITH* ———

I am an imitator of God, as His beloved son/daughter. He is the primary role model for my life and I do everything just as He does. Like Him, I live a life of love, remembering Jesus as my example, who loved me and gave Himself for me.

(John 14:12; Luke 6:36; Mark 11:25,26; 1 Peter 1:13-16; 1 John 4:7-21)

EPHESIANS 5:3-7 KJV

But fornication, and all uncleanness, or covetousness, let it not be once named among you, as becometh saints; Neither filthiness, nor foolish talking, nor jesting, which are not convenient: but rather giving of thanks. For this ye know, that no whoremonger, nor unclean person, nor covetous man, who is an idolater, hath any inheritance in the kingdom of Christ and of God. Let no man deceive you with vain words: for because of these things cometh the wrath of God upon the children of disobedience. Be not ye therefore partakers with them.

——— *DECLARATION OF FAITH* ———

With me, I will not allow even a hint of sexual immorality, or any kind of impurity, or greed, for these things are contrary to my new nature and improper for a son/daughter of God. Furthermore, I will not be a party to foul language, foolish talk or obscene joking, all of which are unfitting and inappropriate for me.

I know that the wrath of God will come upon the immoral, impure, and greedy and that no one who practices such things has any part in the kingdom of Christ and of God. I will let no one deceive me into thinking it is okay to do such things. Therefore, I will not join in with them and become a party to their destruction.

(1 Corinthians 5:1-13; 6:9-11; 2 Corinthians 5:17; 6:14; 2 Peter 1:4; 1 Peter 3:10-12; Romans 1:28-32; Titus 3:9-11)

EPHESIANS 5:8-11 AMP

Of this [Gospel] I was made a minister according to the gift of God's free grace (undeserved favor) which was bestowed on me by the exercise (the working in all its effectiveness) of His power.

——— *DECLARATION OF FAITH* ———

I was once darkness, but now I am light in the Lord. Therefore, I will live as a child of light. The fruit of my life consists in all goodness, righteousness and truth. I find out what pleases the Lord and that only do I do.

I will have nothing to do with the deeds of darkness, but rather expose them for what they truly are.

(1 John 1:5-7; Romans 14:17; Galatians 5:22,23; John 3:18-21)

EPHESIANS 5:15-21 KJV

See then that ye walk circumspectly, not as fools, but as wise, Redeeming the time, because the days are evil. Wherefore be ye not unwise, but understanding what the will of the Lord *is*. And be not drunk with wine, wherein is excess; but be filled with the Spirit; Speaking to yourselves in psalms and hymns and spiritual songs, singing and making melody in your heart to the Lord; Giving thanks

always for all things unto God and the Father in the name of our Lord Jesus Christ; Submitting yourselves one to another in the fear of God.

DECLARATION OF FAITH

I am very careful how I live my life. I do not live as the unwise, but as one who is wise. I make the most of every opportunity, because I know that the days are evil and that the opportunities of today may not exist tomorrow.

I am not foolish, but walk in complete understanding of what the will of God is in every situation.

I do not get drunk on alcohol, for that just leads to lewd and foolish behavior, and the one who gets caught up in it will eventually end in ruin. Instead, I am continually filled to drunkenness with the Holy Spirit, for He has promised to lead me on a path full of life and success.

I speak to myself in songs, and hymns, and spiritual songs (songs sung in tongues), singing and making music in my spirit to the Lord.

I never forget to give thanks to God, remembering all that He has given me in Christ Jesus.

I submit to my brothers and sisters in Christ out of reverence for our Lord.

(Colossians 4:5; 2 Corinthians 6:14; 1 Corinthians 2:6-16; 14:14,15; Proverbs 20:1; Ephesians 1:23; Acts 2:4; 4:31; 9:17; John 14:17; 16:13; Psalm 34:1; 2 Peter 1:2-4; Philippians 2:3)

EPHESIANS 5:22-24, 33B KJV

Wives, submit yourselves unto your own husbands, as unto the Lord. For the husband is the head of the wife, even as Christ is the head of the church: and he is the saviour of the body. Therefore as the church is subject unto Christ, so *let* the wives *be* to their own husbands in every thing. ...and the wife see that she reverence *her* husband.

DECLARATION OF FAITH

(For wives)

I submit myself to my husband as unto the Lord. I treat my husband as the head (executive in charge) of my life in the same way that Christ is the head (executive in charge) of the Church. So, as the Church submits to Christ, I will submit to my husband in all things, giving him the respect that he deserves.

(1 Corinthians 7:3,4; 11:3; Romans 12:1; Colossians 3:18-4:1; Titus 2:4,5; Proverbs 19:13; 31:10-12,28)

Ephesians 5:25-33 KJV

Husbands, love your wives, even as Christ also loved the church, and gave himself for it; That he might sanctify and cleanse it with the washing of water by the word, That he might present it to himself a glorious church, not having spot, or wrinkle, or any such thing; but that it should be holy and without blemish. So ought men to love their wives as their own bodies. He that loveth his wife loveth himself. For no man ever yet hated his own flesh; but nourisheth and cherisheth it, even as the Lord the church: For we are members of his body, of his flesh, and of his bones. For this cause shall a man leave his father and mother, and shall be joined unto his wife, and they two shall be one flesh. This is a great mystery: but I speak concerning Christ and the church. Nevertheless let every one of you in particular so love his wife even as himself; and the wife see that she reverence her husband.

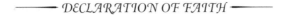

——— *DECLARATION OF FAITH* ———

(For husbands)

I will love my wife just as Christ loved the church and gave Himself for her in order to make her holy, and cleanse her by the washing of water through the Word, and to present her to Himself as radiant, without spot or stain or any other blemish—holy and blameless.

I give myself wholly to my wife. I will love her as I do my own body. As I love myself, so I will love her. I will make no demands of her, but that love be the center of our lives. And I will be of service to her, providing for her every need just as Christ does the church.

It is written, "For this reason a man will leave his father and mother and be united to his wife, and the two will become one flesh." This is a type of Christ and the church. Just as I have become one with Christ, I have become one with my wife. Therefore, I will love my wife just as I love my own body.

(Colossians 1:22; 3:19; John 15:3,12,13; 17:17; Hebrews 10:22; Genesis 2:23,24; 1 Corinthians 6:16; 7:3,4; Proverbs 18:22)

Ephesians 6:1-3 KJV

Children, obey your parents in the Lord: for this is right. Honour thy father and mother; which is the first commandment with promise; That it may be well with thee, and thou mayest live long on the earth.

━━━ *DECLARATION OF FAITH* ━━━

[For children (those still living under the roof of their parents)]
I will obey whatever my parents tell me to do that is in line with the Word.
I will not rebel against them, but submit to their authority. I will honor my
father and mother—which is the first commandment that came with a promise:
that it may go well with me and that I may enjoy a long, full and abundant life
in the earth.

(Colossians 3:20; Deuteronomy 5:16; Proverbs 1:8-10; 2:1-8; 3:1,2; 4:1-27; 5:1; 6:20-23;
7:1,2; 10:1,13; 12:1; 13:1; 15:5,20; 17:21,25; 19:26,27; 20:20; 23:22; 28:24; 30:11-17)

EPHESIANS 6:4

Fathers, don't exasperate your children by coming down hard on them. Take
them by the hand and lead them in the way of the Master.

━━━ *DECLARATION OF FAITH* ━━━

(For fathers)
I will not exasperate, annoy, or tease my children, but raise them in the nur-
ture and admonition of the Lord.

(Colossians 3:21; Proverbs 13:24; 14:26,29; 15:1,18; 16:32; 19:18; 20:7; 22:6,15; 23:13,14;
29:11,12,15,17)

EPHESIANS 6:5-8 KJV

Servants, be obedient to them that are *your* masters according to the flesh, with
fear and trembling, in singleness of your heart, as unto Christ; Not with eyeservice, as menpleasers; but as the servants of Christ, doing the will of God from
the heart; With good will doing service, as to the Lord, and not to men: Knowing
that whatsoever good thing any man doeth, the same shall he receive of the
Lord, whether *he be* bond or free.

━━━ *DECLARATION OF FAITH* ━━━

(For employees, staff members, volunteers, etc.)
I am obedient to those who are appointed in authority over me, having
respect for them and being eager to please them on the job. I am a hard worker
and do my best for them, not only while they are in my presence, but at all times.
I work for them as if I were serving Jesus Himself, doing the will of God from my
heart. I know that the good that I am doing does not go unnoticed. God sees it all
and has promised me a tremendous reward. I will not forget that my heavenly

Father prospers what I set my hand to do and He blesses my employers on account of me.

(Genesis 39:2-5; Colossians 3:17,22-25; 1 Timothy 6:1,2; Deuteronomy 28:12,13; 2 Chronicles 7:15)

EPHESIANS 6:9 NIV

And masters, treat your slaves in the same way. Do not threaten them, since you know that he who is both their Master and yours is in heaven, and there is no favoritism with him.

———— DECLARATION OF FAITH ————

(For employers, pastors, and administrators)
I will treat those who are placed under my authority with respect, rewarding them for whatever good they do. I will not threaten them or treat them harshly, for I know that He who is both their Master and mine is in heaven, and He sees me on the same level as He sees them. With my God, there is no respect of one person over another.

(Colossians 3:23-4:1; Romans 2:11)

EPHESIANS 6:10-18 KJV

Finally, my brethren, be strong in the Lord, and in the power of his might. Put on the whole armour of God, that ye may be able to stand against the wiles of the devil. For we wrestle not against flesh and blood, but against principalities, against powers, against the rulers of the darkness of this world, against spiritual wickedness in high *places.* Wherefore take unto you the whole armour of God, that ye may be able to withstand in the evil day, and having done all, to stand. Stand therefore, having your loins girt about with truth, and having on the breastplate of righteousness; And your feet shod with the preparation of the gospel of peace; Above all, taking the shield of faith, wherewith ye shall be able to quench all the fiery darts of the wicked. And take the helmet of salvation, and the sword of the Spirit, which is the word of God: Praying always with all prayer and supplication in the Spirit, and watching thereunto with all perseverance and supplication for all saints.

———— DECLARATION OF FAITH ————

I am strong in the Lord and in the power of His might. I wear the full armor of God continually so that I can stand against the devil's evil schemes; for I know that my battle is not against flesh and blood (men and women, or physical opponents), but against the principalities and powers, the rulers of the darkness in this world, and the forces of wickedness in the spirit realm.

As a soldier in God's army, I am well able to stand my ground (as a conqueror) when those forces attack. And having done all that I need to do in order to defeat them, in whatever the situation, I will stand as the victor with the devil under my feet where he belongs.

I stand, therefore, with the belt of truth about my loins, for it is the truth that holds all of my armor together.

I have on the breastplate of righteousness—the fact that I am the righteousness of God in Christ Jesus. This secures my heart and all of the issues that bring me life.

My feet are fitted with the readiness that comes from the gospel of peace. Satan's traps never catch me unaware and I am always prepared to trample down his kingdom while I firmly establish the kingdom of God.

I have the shield of faith extinguishing all of the fiery darts of the enemy and covering me as I advance. When a fiery dart of disease hits, I believe in and speak the Word over it and it is extinguished. When a fiery dart of financial disaster hits, I believe and speak the Word over it and it is extinguished. When any fiery dart comes, I use my faith, believing and speaking the Word over the problem until the problem is eliminated.

I have on the helmet of salvation to protect my mind against all thoughts designed to cause me to give up on my faith. I know beyond a shadow of doubt that what Jesus did for me is a done deal and that no matter what goes on in my life, I will be with Him for all of eternity. Therefore, there is absolutely no reason for me to give in. No, to the contrary, I will stay in the fight until my victory is complete and God gets the glory!

As an advancing soldier and conqueror for the Lord, I wield the most powerful weapon in the universe: the sword of the Spirit, which is the very Word of the living God. With it I scatter and exterminate any and every enemy who foolishly chooses to try me.

Lastly, I pray with all manner of prayer and supplication in the Spirit, being watchful with all perseverance and supplication for all the saints. I have been called to be a prayer warrior for the Lord and I will never allow the devil to stop me, discourage me, or cause me to give up on my faith.

(Colossians 1:27-29; Ephesians 1:17-23; 2 Corinthians 2:11; 4:13; 5:7,21; 6:7; 10:3-6; Mark 11:22-25; 16:17,18; Luke 10:19; 1 John 4:1-4; 5:4,14,15; Romans 8:37,38; Psalm 91:13; Isaiah 11:5; 52:7; 59:17; 1 Thessalonians 5:8; Hebrews 2:5-10; 4:12; 10:35-11:1; Philippians 1:4; John 14:13,14; 1 Corinthians 14:15; Joshua 1:5-9)

EPHESIANS 6:18-20 KJV

Praying always with all prayer and supplication in the Spirit, and watching thereunto with all perseverance and supplication for all saints; And for me, that utterance may be given unto me, that I may open my mouth boldly, to make known the mystery of the gospel, for which I am an ambassador in bonds: that therein I may speak boldly, as I ought to speak.

——— *DECLARATION OF FAITH* ———

I pray regularly for my pastors and teachers in the faith, that whenever they open their mouths to preach, words are given to them so that they can fearlessly make known the mystery of the Gospel.

(1 Corinthians 14:12-15; Luke 18:1-8; Ezekiel 22:30; Psalm 106:29-31; Philippians 1:4; Colossians 4:3; Acts 4:23-31)

CHAPTER FIFTY

PHILIPPIANS

The epistle of the apostle Paul to the Philippians was probably written around 60-63 AD, very close to the time of the writing of Ephesians. The central theme of the book of Philippians is maintaining the joy of the Lord in your heart despite the circumstances you face. This is profound when you consider the fact that Paul wrote the epistle while in prison (the same as his letters to the Ephesians, Colossians and Philemon). Paul teaches us in Philippians to do all things without complaining or faultfinding and to know that in Christ Jesus we are able to succeed in anything we are called to do.

As you pray these personal prayers from the book of Philippians, stop and take inventory of all that God has blessed you with. Think on all of the good things in your life and make a commitment to never complain about petty things again.

PHILIPPIANS 1:6 NKJV

Being confident of this very thing, that He who has begun a good work in you will complete *it* until the day of Jesus Christ.

———— DECLARATION OF FAITH ————

I rest in full confidence that He who began this good work in me is well able to carry it on to completion until the day of Christ Jesus.

(John 5:24; 6:35-40; 2 Timothy 1:12; Jude 24; Ephesians 2:10; 1 Thessalonians 5:24)

PHILIPPIANS 1:9-11 NIV

And this is my prayer: that your love may abound more and more in knowledge and depth of insight, so that you may be able to discern what is best and may be pure and blameless until the day of Christ, filled with the fruit of righteousness that comes through Jesus Christ—to the glory and praise of God.

──────── *DECLARATION OF FAITH* ────────

My love continues to abound more and more in knowledge and depth of insight so that in every circumstance I can determine what is the best action to take and be pure and blameless until the day of Christ. In all things and in every situation, I am filled with the fruit of righteousness through Christ Jesus my Lord—to the glory and praise of God.

(Jude 24; 1 Corinthians 2:6-16; Romans 14:17; 2 Corinthians 9:10)

PHILIPPIANS 1:18 AMP

But what does it matter, so long as either way, whether in pretense [for personal ends] or in all honesty [for the furtherance of the Truth], Christ is being proclaimed? And in that I [now] rejoice, yes, and I shall rejoice [hereafter] also.

──────── *DECLARATION OF FAITH* ────────

I do not fret over who is preaching the Gospel, or from what motives they are preaching it; I just rejoice that it is being preached.

(Matthew 12:24-37; Mark 9:38-41; 1 Corinthians 12:3)

PHILIPPIANS 1:19-24 KJV

For I know that this shall turn to my salvation through your prayer, and the supply of the Spirit of Jesus Christ, According to my earnest expectation and *my* hope, that in nothing I shall be ashamed, but *that* with all boldness, as always, *so* now also Christ shall be magnified in my body, whether *it be* by life, or by death. For to me to live *is* Christ, and to die *is* gain. But if I live in the flesh, this *is* the fruit of my labour: yet what I shall choose I wot not. For I am in a strait betwixt two, having a desire to depart, and to be with Christ; which is far better: Nevertheless to abide in the flesh *is* more needful for you.

──────── *DECLARATION OF FAITH* ────────

No matter what is going on in my life or what my situation may be, I know that through the help of the Spirit of Jesus and the prayers of God's people, I shall be delivered and stand as a victor to the praise and the glory of God.

I remain in eager expectation and the assurance of hope. I persevere through every trial and stand my ground regardless of the circumstances. I never cower in shame because of my faith. My walk with Jesus is one of persistent courage and unwavering boldness. I refuse to give up on my faith, for I know that He who promised is faithful. He will do what He said He would do.

─────── *DECLARATION OF FAITH* ───────

(For those who may be facing martyrdom)

Christ (the anointed One and His anointing) will always be exalted in my body, whether by my life, or by my death—whichever I should choose. I say again, if at anytime I face martyrdom, the choice is mine whether to die for Christ, or to continue to live for Him. No one can thwart God's plan for my life. His appointed time for my death is fixed and men cannot change it.

While I live, I live by Jesus and His anointing, and if I die, I gain all the more; for while I live, through the anointing, I will continually produce abundant fruit in the Spirit, joyfully doing that which pleases God. Yet if I die, I will live in the physical presence of Jesus, enjoying my mansion and fellowship with the saints of heaven, and will no longer have to struggle against sickness, poverty, and sin.

God is good and He has left the choice between life and death with me. Yet, though I desire to depart and be with Jesus, I know that it is important that I serve those here on earth, winning them for Jesus and bringing the kingdom of God into their midst. Therefore, I lay claim to God's promise of a long and satisfying life, and I shall remain in my body until the appointed time of my death.

(Hebrews 9:27; 10:23,35-11:1; Acts 12:5-10; Isaiah 46:4; 55:11; Romans 8:11; 2 Corinthians 9:5-11; John 14:1-3; 15:5; Deuteronomy 30:19,20; Matthew 28:18-20; Job 13:16; 2 Timothy 4:6; Psalm 16:11; 91:16)

PHILIPPIANS 1:27,28 AMP

Only be sure as citizens so to conduct yourselves [that] your manner of life [will be] worthy of the good news (the Gospel) of Christ, so that whether I [do] come and see you or am absent, I may hear this of you: that you are standing firm in united spirit and purpose, striving side by side and contending with a single mind for the faith of the glad tidings (the Gospel). And do not [for a moment] be frightened or intimidated in anything by your opponents and adversaries, for such [constancy and fearlessness] will be a clear sign (proof and seal) to them of [their impending] destruction, but [a sure token and evidence] of your deliverance and salvation, and that from God.

─────── *DECLARATION OF FAITH* ───────

Whatever happens in my life, I will conduct myself in a manner worthy of the Gospel of Christ. I will stand firm with my brothers and sisters in Christ, contending as one man (in perfect unity and agreement), without being frightened in any way by those who oppose us.

(Ephesians 4:1-6; 5:1-18; John 17:20-26; Romans 12:3,4; Joshua 1:5-9)

PHILIPPIANS 2:2-11 KJV

Fulfil ye my joy, that ye be likeminded, having the same love, *being* of one accord, of one mind. *Let* nothing *be done* through strife or vainglory; but in lowliness of mind let each esteem the other better than themselves. Look not every man on his own things, but every man also on the things of others. Let this mind be in you, which was also in Christ Jesus: Who, being in the form of God, thought it not robbery to be equal with God: But made himself of no reputation, and took upon him the form of a servant, and was made in the likeness of men: And being found in fashion as a man, he humbled himself, and became obedient unto death, even the death of the cross. Wherefore God also hath highly exalted him, and given him a name which is above every name: That at the name of Jesus every knee should bow, of *things* in heaven, and *things* in earth, and *things* under the earth; And *that* every tongue should confess that Jesus Christ *is* Lord, to the glory of God the Father.

———— *DECLARATION OF FAITH* ————

I am like-minded with my brothers and sisters in Christ, having the same love and unity of purpose.

I do nothing out of selfish ambition or haughtiness, but in the spirit of humility I place others before myself.

I do not look to my own interests alone, but to the interests of others as well.

My attitude (manner of thinking) is the same as that of Jesus, who having the very nature of God, did not cling to His prerogatives as God's equal, but emptied Himself, taking on the nature of a servant, being made in human likeness. And being found in appearance as a man, He humbled Himself and became obedient to death—even death on the cross. Therefore, God exalted Him to the highest place and gave Him the name above every name, that at the name of Jesus every knee must bow, in heaven, on earth and under the earth, and every tongue must confess that Jesus is Lord to the glory of God the Father.

This manner of thinking has become my own. I now have the mind of Christ. This is the way that I think and the grounds upon which I act. In Jesus, I have become a partaker of the divine nature through the Word. I do not flaunt my rights and privileges in Him in selfish arrogance, but use them as one who serves for the purpose of bringing glory to God. I consider myself a servant to the world in order to reconcile them to God. I am obedient to God to the utmost extreme, for He has exalted me, in Christ, to the place of highest honor and has given me the power of attorney to use the name of Jesus. Whenever I make a demand in His name, whatever I am commanding must bow to His authority.

(John 14:13,14; 17:20-26; Romans 12:10-16; Galatians 5:26; 1 Corinthians 1:30; 13:5; Ephesians 2:6; 5:1; James 4:1-10; 2 Peter 1:4; Matthew 20:25-28)

PHILIPPIANS 2:12,13 NKJV

Therefore, my beloved, as you have always obeyed, not as in my presence only, but now much more in my absence, work out your own salvation with fear and trembling; for it is God who works in you both to will and to do for *His* good pleasure.

DECLARATION OF FAITH

I continually put my salvation into effect in this earth, marveling and trembling at the awesome power that is at work in my life; for it is God Himself who is at work within me, performing His will and acting according to His good purpose.

(Ephesians 1:17-23; 2:10; Colossians 1:27-29; John 6:27; Romans 8:26-28)

PHILIPPIANS 2:14-16 NKJV

Do all things without complaining and disputing, that you may become blameless and harmless, children of God without fault in the midst of a crooked and perverse generation, among whom you shine as lights in the world, holding fast the word of life, so that I may rejoice in the day of Christ that I have not run in vain or labored in vain.

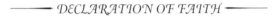

DECLARATION OF FAITH

I do everything that I am called to do without complaining and faultfinding.
It is my purpose in this life to be a blameless and pure son/daughter of the living God in the midst of this crooked and depraved generation.
I hold out the Word of Life as supreme and bring glory to my Father who is in heaven.

(1 Peter 4:9; Romans 14:1; 16:17-19; Psalm 119:133; Matthew 5:15,16; John 14:13,14)

PHILIPPIANS 3:2,3 NKJV

Beware of dogs, beware of evil workers, beware of the mutilation! For we are the circumcision, who worship God in the Spirit, rejoice in Christ Jesus, and have no confidence in the flesh.

DECLARATION OF FAITH

I am ever-alert and on guard against those who do evil by nullifying God's grace in their preaching. I am determined that no one will lead me back into bondage to the regulations of the Law of Moses. I am of the true circumcision. I am one with Christ and rest securely in His righteousness. By the Spirit of God, I worship and make my boast in Jesus and place absolutely no confidence in my flesh.

(Galatians 5:1; Romans 2:29; 3:21-31; 7:6; John 4:22-24)

PHILIPPIANS 3:7-11 KJV

But what things were gain to me, those I counted loss for Christ. Yea doubtless, and I count all things *but* loss for the excellency of the knowledge of Christ Jesus my Lord: for whom I have suffered the loss of all things, and do count them *but* dung, that I may win Christ, And be found in him, not having mine own righteousness, which is of the law, but that which is through the faith of Christ, the righteousness which is of God by faith: That I may know him, and the power of his resurrection, and the fellowship of his sufferings, being made conformable unto his death; If by any means I might attain unto the resurrection of the dead.

———— *DECLARATION OF FAITH* ————

Any good that I find within me that comes from my own power is worthless to me. I have set it all aside, putting absolutely no trust in it, so that I can have the overwhelming blessing of knowing my Lord Jesus. I have given up everything in order to have Him in my life. All that I am and all that I have I consider as dung, that I may gain Christ and be found in Him, not having my own righteousness, which comes from obeying the regulations of the Law, but that which comes through faith in Christ. My righteousness comes from God Himself and I have obtained it by faith alone—not works.

It is my desire and heartfelt purpose to know Jesus and the power of His Resurrection in my life. I am a partaker of His sufferings. I am fully identified with Him in His death so that His resurrection life can flow in and through me.

(Isaiah 64:6; Matthew 7:11; 19:27-29; Philippians 3:3; 2 Corinthians 5:21; Romans 3:21-31; 4:1-5; 6:3-5; 10:3,4; Ephesians 1:17-23; 2:6; 1 Corinthians 15:34-58)

PHILIPPIANS 3:12-14 NIV

Not that I have already obtained all this, or have already been made perfect, but I press on to take hold of that for which Christ Jesus took hold of me. Brothers, I do not consider myself yet to have taken hold of it. But one thing I do: Forgetting what is behind and straining toward what is ahead, I press on toward the goal to win the prize for which God has called me heavenward in Christ Jesus.

————— DECLARATION OF FAITH —————

I never forget that I am saved from sin, not to sin. I do not claim to be walking in the completeness of my perfection in my present human condition, but I press on to take hold of it, for this is the reason for which Christ Jesus took hold of me.

Therefore, I forget what is behind me and press forward with my eyes on the prize of my high calling in Christ Jesus. I never let my past, whether five years ago or five minutes ago, hinder me in my walk with God. Knowing His grace, I never have reason to backslide or be stagnant. I am always moving forward, getting better with every step and staying in fellowship with my heavenly Father. I never forget that sin has no power over me and that my position in Jesus is secured, not because of me, but because of Him.

(Hebrews 10:14; 12:23; Luke 9:62; 1 Corinthians 9:24-27; 2 Timothy 4:7)

PHILIPPIANS 3:15 NKJV

Therefore let us, as many as are mature, have this mind; and if in anything you think otherwise, God will reveal even this to you.

————— DECLARATION OF FAITH —————

God enables me to see everything clearly, as it truly is.

(John 16:13; 1 Corinthians 2:6-16; Hosea 6:3)

PHILIPPIANS 3:16 MESSAGE

Now that we're on the right track, let's stay on it.

————— DECLARATION OF FAITH —————

I will live up to the maturity of faith that I have already attained.

(Galatians 6:16; Ephesians 5:1-21)

PHILIPPIANS 3:20,21 NKJV

For our citizenship is in heaven, from which we also eagerly wait for the Savior, the Lord Jesus Christ, who will transform our lowly body that it may be conformed to His glorious body, according to the working by which He is able even to subdue all things to Himself.

I am a citizen of heaven. My name is on the roll. I am numbered among the population.

I eagerly await a Savior from there, Jesus Christ my Lord, who, through the power that enables Him to bring everything under His control, will one day transform this lowly body of mine so that it will be like His glorified body.

(Ephesians 1:17-23; 2:6,19; 3:15; Luke 10:20; 1 Corinthians 1:7; 15:42-57; 1 John 3:2)

PHILIPPIANS 4:4-9 KJV

Rejoice in the Lord alway: *and* again I say, Rejoice. Let your moderation be known unto all men. The Lord *is* at hand. Be careful for nothing; but in every thing by prayer and supplication with thanksgiving let your requests be made known unto God. And the peace of God, which passeth all understanding, shall keep your hearts and minds through Christ Jesus. Finally, brethren, whatsoever things are true, whatsoever things *are* honest, whatsoever things *are* just, whatsoever things *are* pure, whatsoever things *are* lovely, whatsoever things *are* of good report; if *there be* any virtue, and if *there be* any praise, think on these things. Those things, which ye have both learned, and received, and heard, and seen in me, do: and the God of peace shall be with you.

——— DECLARATION OF FAITH ———

I will rejoice in the Lord always. Again I say, I will rejoice in Him!

I let my gentleness be made known to all through my actions and not empty words.

The Lord is very near to me. Therefore, I will not allow myself to become nervous or worried. No matter what situation I find myself in, I have a loving heavenly Father who will intervene on my behalf. When I present my prayers and petitions to Him, with thanksgiving, He causes everything to work together for my good.

The peace of God, which is beyond human understanding, guards my heart and my mind in Christ Jesus.

He hears my every prayer and covers me as with a shield. He is willing and well able to care for me. So what do I have to worry about?

My spirit remains in the ascendancy in my life. I stay in complete control over my thought processes. I will think only on those things that are true, noble, right, and pure. Only those things that are admirable and praiseworthy will be allowed to enter my mind. Other things that cross my mind will just have to pass by and keep on going.

I put into practice everything that I have learned, received, or heard from my teachers whom God has appointed for me.

Throughout all of this, I have the assurance that the God of peace is ever with me.

(Romans 8:26-28; 12:12; 14:17; Galatians 5:16,22,23,25; 1 John 3:18; 5:14,15; James 4:8; 1 Peter 5:5-7; Ephesians 2:14; John 14:27; 2 Timothy 1:7; 2 Corinthians 10:3-6; Joshua 1:8; Psalm 1:1-3; 1 Thessalonians 5:21-23)

PHILIPPIANS 4:10-13 AMP

I was made very happy in the Lord that now you have revived your interest in my welfare after so long a time; you were indeed thinking of me, but you had no opportunity to show it. Not that I am implying that I was in any personal want, for I have learned how to be content (satisfied to the point where I am not disturbed or disquieted) in whatever state I am. I know how to be abased and live humbly in straitened circumstances, and I know also how to enjoy plenty and live in abundance. I have learned in any and all circumstances the secret of facing every situation, whether well-fed or going hungry, having a sufficiency and enough to spare or going without and being in want. I have strength for all things in Christ Who empowers me [I am ready for anything and equal to anything through Him Who infuses inner strength into me; I am self-sufficient in Christ's sufficiency].

——— *DECLARATION OF FAITH* ———

I greatly rejoice in the Lord because of my Father's favor. There are many who are concerned about my well-being.

Not that I am in want, but, to the contrary, I know the secret of being content in any situation I find myself in. I know what to do when I find myself in adverse circumstances and I know what to do when I am living in God's abundance. I have learned, in any and every circumstance, the secret of facing every situation as a conqueror, whether well fed or hungry, whether having all sufficiency and enough to spare, or not having a dime to my name. The secret is this: I can do all things through the power of Christ that is within me. With His anointing, there isn't a single circumstance that can hold me down! I am self-sufficient in His sufficiency.

(Luke 6:38; Matthew 6:19-33; Acts 4:32-37; Hebrews 13:5,6; 2 Corinthians 9:5-11; Romans 8:37; John 14:13,14; 15:5,7)

PHILIPPIANS 4:15-20 KJV

Now ye Philippians know also, that in the beginning of the gospel, when I departed from Macedonia, no church communicated with me as concerning giving and receiving, but ye only. For even in Thessalonica ye sent once and again unto my necessity. Not because I desire a gift: but I desire fruit that may abound to your account. But I have all, and abound: I am full, having received of Epaphroditus the things *which were sent* from you, an odour of a sweet smell, a sacrifice acceptable, wellpleasing to God. But my God shall supply all your need according to his riches in glory by Christ Jesus. Now unto God and our Father *be* glory for ever and ever. Amen.

──── *DECLARATION OF FAITH* ────

I am wise to share in the process of giving and receiving that God has established in the earth. I faithfully support ministries that are advancing the kingdom in the earth, and every gift that I give is a deposit into my heavenly account.

I do all that I can to ensure that the ministries I support are amply supplied and more. It is my heart's desire that, through me and others of the same heart, God's financial blessings will shower over these ministries in so much abundance that they will have no idea what to do with all of the excess. It is my desire to see God's ministers living like true ambassadors of heaven.

When I present my offerings with this heart attitude, they go up before the Lord like a sweet fragrance. This is what makes my offerings acceptable for an abundant return. Because of my persistent and joy-filled generosity, I have God's Word that He will supply all of my needs according to His riches in glory through Christ Jesus. He sees to it that all of my giving returns to me overflowing with His abundance. In this, I give glory to God, my Father, forevermore! Amen!

(2 Corinthians 9:5-15; Luke 6:38; Galatians 6:7-9; 1 Chronicles 29:1-9; Titus 3:14; Hebrews 13:16; Matthew 6:19-33)

PHILIPPIANS 4:23 NKJV

The grace of our Lord Jesus Christ be with you all. Amen.

──── *DECLARATION OF FAITH* ────

The grace of my Lord Jesus is always with my spirit.

(Romans 1:9; 2 Thessalonians 5:28)

CHAPTER FIFTY-ONE

COLOSSIANS

Colossians is the third of the four prison letters written by the apostle Paul. It was written around the same time as Paul's letters to the Galatians and Ephesians (60-63 AD). The central theme of Colossians is the refutation of heresies in the church. As a natural branch of these refutations, Colossians is replete with promises concerning true salvation.

As you pray the personal prayers of the book of Colossians, remember all that Jesus did for you. The penalty for the laws that you have broken were nailed to His cross. Take a moment to thank Him for being your substitute and taking your sentence upon Himself.

━━━━━━━━━━━━━━━ ✚ ━━━━━━━━━━━━━━━

COLOSSIANS 1:6 NIV

All over the world this gospel is bearing fruit and growing, just as it has been doing among you since the day you heard it and understood God's grace in all its truth.

──────── *DECLARATION OF FAITH* ────────

The Gospel has been, and is, continually growing within me and bearing an abundance of fruit ever since the day that I both heard and understood God's grace in all of its truth.

(John 15:5; Matthew 13:11,15,16; Romans 10:6-17)

COLOSSIANS 1:9-14 KJV

For this cause we also, since the day we heard *it*, do not cease to pray for you, and to desire that ye might be filled with the knowledge of his will in all wisdom and spiritual understanding; That ye might walk worthy of the Lord unto all pleasing, being fruitful in every good work, and increasing in the knowledge of God; Strengthened with all might, according to his glorious power, unto all patience and longsuffering with joyfulness; Giving thanks unto the Father, which hath made us meet to be partakers of the inheritance of the saints in light: Who hath delivered us from the power of darkness, and hath translated *us* into the kingdom of his dear Son: In whom we have redemption through his blood, *even* the forgiveness of sins.

——— *DECLARATION OF FAITH* ———

God has filled me with a complete working knowledge of His will. By the wisdom and understanding that He has given me of the things of the spirit, I now have assurance of direction in any given circumstance.

I now can live a life worthy of the Lord, pleasing Him in every way.

I am bearing fruit in every good work to which I am called, continually growing in the knowledge of God, being strengthened with all power according to the might of His glory, exercising every kind of endurance and persevering through every trial with patience and joy, giving thanks to my Father, who has made me worthy to share in the inheritance of the saints in the kingdom of Light; for He rescued me from the kingdom of darkness and translated me into the kingdom of the Son of His love. In Jesus, I have my redemption and forgiveness for all of my sins.

(1 Corinthians 1:30; 2:6-16; 1 John 2:20; 5:20; Ephesians 1:3-23; 4:1-3; 5:1-20; 6:10; 1 Thessalonians 4:1; John 15:5; Hebrews 13:21; Galatians 4:4-6; 5:22,23; Colossians 2:13-15; James 1:2-4; 2 Peter 1:11; Titus 3:4-7)

COLOSSIANS 1:21-23 AMP

And although you at one time were estranged and alienated from Him and were of hostile attitude of mind in your wicked activities, Yet now has [Christ, the Messiah] reconciled [you to God] in the body of His flesh through death, in order to present you holy and faultless and irreproachable in His [the Father's] presence. [And this He will do] provided that you continue to stay with and in the faith [in Christ], well-grounded and settled and steadfast, not shifting or moving away from the hope [which rests on and is inspired by] the glad tidings (the Gospel), which you heard and which has been preached [as being designed for and offered without restrictions] to every person under heaven, and of which [Gospel] I, Paul, became a minister.

——— *DECLARATION OF FAITH* ———

I was once alienated from God—utterly hostile and contrary to Him in my mind and sinful ways. But now, I have been reconciled to God by Christ's physical body through His death. I am now presented as holy in His sight, without the slightest blemish and free of accusation, if indeed I continue in my faith (believing and confessing Him as Lord), established and firm, never turning away from the Gospel.

(Ephesians 2:1-15; 5:27; 2 Corinthians 5:17-21; Romans 8:1,2; Hebrews 10:35)

COLOSSIANS 1:25-29 KJV

Whereof I am made a minister, according to the dispensation of God which is given to me for you, to fulfil the word of God; *Even* the mystery which hath been hid from ages and from generations, but now is made manifest to his saints: To whom God would make known what *is* the riches of the glory of this mystery among the Gentiles; which is Christ in you, the hope of glory: Whom we preach, warning every man, and teaching every man in all wisdom; that we may present every man perfect in Christ Jesus: Whereunto I also labour, striving according to his working, which worketh in me mightily.

——— DECLARATION OF FAITH ———

I have become a capable minister in the Church, by the commission of God, to present His Word to the world in all of its fullness. I proclaim the mystery that was hidden throughout the ages, but has now been made known to me God has chosen me to make known the glorious riches of this mystery, which is Christ in me, the hope of glory.

I proclaim Him without ceasing—admonishing and teaching everyone, with all wisdom. To this end I labor, striving with all of His power and ability that so powerfully works within me.

(Matthew 13:11,15,16; 28:18-20; 2 Corinthians 5:18-20; 2 Timothy 1:10; Romans 8:10,11; Ephesians 5:27; 6:10; 1 Corinthians 1:17-20)

COLOSSIANS 2:2-4 NKJV

That their hearts may be encouraged, being knit together in love, and *attaining* to all riches of the full assurance of understanding, to the knowledge of the mystery of God, both of the Father and of Christ, in whom are hidden all the treasures of wisdom and knowledge. Now this I say lest anyone should deceive you with persuasive words.

——— DECLARATION OF FAITH ———

The purpose of my ministry is to bring encouragement to the heart and unity to the Body through love, so that others may have the full riches of complete understanding as I do—that they may know the mystery of God, namely Christ, in whom are hidden all the treasures of wisdom and knowledge. And He has become that wisdom and knowledge for me so that it never fails to operate within me.

In light of this, I will let no one deceive me with fine sounding arguments, most of which deny the power of God in my life.

(Ephesians 1:17-23; 4:11-13; 1 Corinthians 1:30; 2:6-16; 14:2,13; Matthew 13:11,15,16; Daniel 1:17,20; 2:22,23; 2 Timothy 3:5,13,16,17; 4:14-18)

COLOSSIANS 2:6-17 KJV

As ye have therefore received Christ Jesus the Lord, *so* walk ye in him: Rooted and built up in him, and stablished in the faith, as ye have been taught, abounding therein with thanksgiving. Beware lest any man spoil you through philosophy and vain deceit, after the tradition of men, after the rudiments of the world, and not after Christ. For in him dwelleth all the fulness of the Godhead bodily. And ye are complete in him, which is the head of all principality and power: In whom also ye are circumcised with the circumcision made without hands, in putting off the body of the sins of the flesh by the circumcision of Christ: Buried with him in baptism, wherein also ye are risen with *him* through the faith of the operation of God, who hath raised him from the dead. And you, being dead in your sins and the uncircumcision of your flesh, hath he quickened together with him, having forgiven you all trespasses; Blotting out the handwriting of ordinances that was against us, which was contrary to us, and took it out of the way, nailing it to his cross; *And* having spoiled principalities and powers, he made a shew of them openly, triumphing over them in it. Let no man therefore judge you in meat, or in drink, or in respect of an holyday, or of the new moon, or of the sabbath *days:* Which are a shadow of things to come; but the body *is* of Christ.

— DECLARATION OF FAITH —

I live my life in Jesus in the exact same way in which I received Him: by faith. I am rooted, built up and strengthened in my faith through sound teaching, and the fruit that is produced causes a flood of praise and thanksgiving to flow forth from within me.

I will not allow anyone to take me captive through deceptive philosophies, which are rooted in human traditions and the basic principles of this world rather than on Christ. The ways of the spirit are above the ways of the world, and it is by the spirit that I have chosen to live; for as in Christ all the fullness of the Godhead dwells in bodily form, through my identification with Him I have been given that very same fullness. In Him, I have all of the fullness of the Godhead dwelling within me in bodily form. The One who is the Master of all power and authority is actually dwelling within me at this very moment.

In Him, I was circumcised, in the casting aside of the sinful nature, not with the circumcision done with human hands, but the circumcision that is done by Christ, having been buried with Him in baptism and raised with Him through my faith in the power of God, who raised Him from the dead.

I was once dead in the uncircumcision of my sinful nature, but God brought me to life together with Christ. He forgave me, at that time, of all of my sins, first to last, having cancelled the written code, with its regulations that proved my guilt. He took it all away and nailed it to the cross!

On my behalf, He disarmed the principalities and powers and made a public spectacle of them, triumphing over them through the cross.

When I made Jesus the Lord of my life, He lifted the burden of the Law from my shoulders; for Jesus has fulfilled the Law and set it aside, and all that He did has been credited to my account. Now every time Satan accuses me, God can justly say that the penalty of whatever part of the Law I may have broken does not apply to me anymore, because I am not under the rule of the Law, but under grace!

(2 Corinthians 4:13; 5:7; 11:3,4; Ephesians 1:17-23; 2:4-6,15,16; 3:14-21; 6:10-18; Galatians 1:6-9; 4:3-9; 5:1,16,25; Romans 6:4-6; 8:1-4; 14:3; Luke 10:19; Mark 3:27; John 14:17; 15:5-8; 17:20-26; 1 John 3:8; Isaiah 53:12; Philippians 2:14-16; 3:7-10)

COLOSSIANS 2:18,19 NIV

Do not let anyone who delights in false humility and the worship of angels disqualify you for the prize. Such a person goes into great detail about what he has seen, and his unspiritual mind puffs him up with idle notions. He has lost connection with the Head, from whom the whole body, supported and held together by its ligaments and sinews, grows as God causes it to grow.

— DECLARATION OF FAITH —

I will not allow anyone to judge me and tell me that I need to be humble (a false humility that does not proclaim or receive what God has done), or entice me into the worship of angels, or try to disqualify or talk me out of the prize that Jesus won for me. When they go into great detail about what they see (not realizing that we walk by faith and not by sight) and what they know (an abundance of worldly and unspiritual knowledge) I shut my ears to them. Most of them are arrogant and puffed up in the head and they don't even know it. They don't have a clue that all of their knowledge comes from the senses, and such knowledge is contrary to the things of God in this earth. They have severed their connection with the Head (Jesus), by whom the whole Body, supplied and knitted together with joints and ligaments, grows with the perpetual increase that comes from God alone.

(1 Peter 5:5-7; 1 Corinthians 1:18-21,30,31; 2:6-16; 6:3; 8:1; Hebrews 1:14; 11:1; 2 Corinthians 4:13; 5:7)

COLOSSIANS 3:1-3 KJV

If ye then be risen with Christ, seek those things which are above, where Christ sitteth on the right hand of God. Set your affection on things above, not on things on the earth. For ye are dead, and your life is hid with Christ in God.

DECLARATION OF FAITH

Since I have been raised together with Christ, I set my heart on things above, where Christ is seated at the right hand of God. I have a resolved determination to focus my attention only on those things that are of God and spiritual, and not on earthly, sense ruled things; for I died with Jesus on the cross (in regard to my old, sense-ruled nature), and my life is now hidden with Christ in God. My Father is a Spirit; therefore, I will worship Him, receive from Him, and fellowship with Him, in the spirit.

(Ephesians 1:17-23; 2:1-10; Galatians 2:20,21; Matthew 6:10,11,19-21; John 4:24)

COLOSSIANS 3:4 MESSAGE

When Christ (your real life, remember) shows up again on this earth, you'll show up, too—the real you, the glorious you.

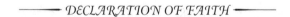

DECLARATION OF FAITH

When Christ, who is my life, appears, I will also appear with Him in glory.

(1 Thessalonians 4:15-17; John 14:1-3; 1 John 3:2)

COLOSSIANS 3:5,7 NKJV

Therefore put to death your members which are on the earth: fornication, uncleanness, passion, evil desire, and covetousness, which is idolatry, in which you yourselves once walked when you lived in them.

─────── *DECLARATION OF FAITH* ───────

I put to death all of those things that belong to my old, senses-ruled nature: such as sexual immorality, lust, unholy desires, and all greed and covetousness, which is idolatry. Though I used to walk in these ways, I now rid myself of them.

(Galatians 5:16-21; Ephesians 2:1-10)

COLOSSIANS 3:8-10 KJV

But now ye also put off all these; anger, wrath, malice, blasphemy, filthy communication out of your mouth. Lie not one to another, seeing that ye have put off the old man with his deeds; And have put on the new *man*, which is renewed in knowledge after the image of him that created him.

─────── *DECLARATION OF FAITH* ───────

I will not allow such things as anger, rage, malice, slander, and foul language to go forth from my lips. From now on I will speak only the truth, for I have put off my old nature with its practices, and have put on my new nature, which is being renewed in the knowledge of its Creator.

(Ephesians 4:20-24; 1 Peter 3:10-12; Romans 12:1,2; 2 Peter 1:4)

COLOSSIANS 3:11 NIV

Here there is no Greek or Jew, circumcised or uncircumcised, barbarian, Scythian, slave or free, but Christ is all, and is in all.

─────── *DECLARATION OF FAITH* ───────

I am part of a new race of people, created in Christ Jesus, out of every class and nationality on the face of the earth.

(2 Corinthians 5:17; John 3:3; Ephesians 2:10,19; 4:22-24; Galatians 3:27,28)

COLOSSIANS 3:12-17 KJV

Put on therefore, as the elect of God, holy and beloved, bowels of mercies, kindness, humbleness of mind, meekness, longsuffering; Forbearing one another, and forgiving one another, if any man have a quarrel against any: even as Christ forgave you, so also *do* ye. And above all these things *put on* charity, which is the bond of perfectness. And let the peace of God rule in your hearts, to which also ye are called in one body; and be ye thankful. Let the word of Christ dwell in you richly in all wisdom; teaching and admonishing one another in psalms and

hymns and spiritual songs, singing with grace in your hearts to the Lord. And whatsoever ye do in word or deed, *do* all in the name of the Lord Jesus, giving thanks to God and the Father by him.

———— *DECLARATION OF FAITH* ————

As God's chosen son/daughter, I clothe myself with compassion, kindness, gentleness, humility, and patience. I bear with my brothers and sisters in Christ, forgiving any grievances I may have against them. And I forgive them completely, with no strings attached, just as the Lord has completely forgiven me. I refuse to allow an "I forgive you, but..." kind of attitude to become a part of me. To the contrary, I keep my "but" out of all my forgiveness.

Around all of these virtues, I wrap the garment of love; for it is my love which binds together all of my godly virtues with perfect unity.

I allow the peace of Christ to rule in my heart. I will never forget that as a member of the body of Christ I am called to be at peace. Therefore, I will not allow any fear, worry or anxiety to disturb the peace that I have been given.

I let the Word of Christ dwell in me richly as I teach and admonish others with all wisdom, and as I sing songs and hymns, and songs of the spirit with gratefulness in my heart to the Lord.

Whatever I do, in word or deed, I do in the name of Jesus, giving thanks to God, my Father, through Him.

(Galatians 4:4-6; 5:22,23; 6:1,2; Ephesians 1:4; 4:3,4; Mark 11:25,26; 1 Corinthians 10:31; 13:4-8; 14:14,15; John 14:27; 1 Peter 5:5-7; 1 Thessalonians 5:18)

Colossians 3:18 AMP

Wives, be subject to your husbands [subordinate and adapt yourselves to them], as is right and fitting and your proper duty in the Lord.

———— *DECLARATION OF FAITH* ————

(For wives)

I will submit (be in agreement with) and be subject to my own husband as is fitting in the Lord.

(1 Peter 3:1; Ephesians 5:22-33; 1 Corinthians 7:3,4)

Colossians 3:19 AMP

Husbands, love your wives [be affectionate and sympathetic with them] and do not be harsh or bitter or resentful toward them.

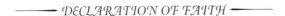

(For husbands)

I will love my wife, offering myself in service to her, and I will not be abusive towards her in any way.

(Ephesians 4:31; 5:22-33; 1 Corinthians 7:3,4)

COLOSSIANS 3:20 NKJV

Children, obey your parents in all things, for this is well pleasing to the Lord.

—— *DECLARATION OF FAITH* ——

(For children [those still living in their parents' home])
I will obey my parents in every way that brings honor to the Lord.

(Ephesians 6:1-3; Deuteronomy 5:16; Proverbs 1:8-10)

COLOSSIANS 3:21 NIV

Fathers, do not embitter your children, or they will become discouraged.

—— *DECLARATION OF FAITH* ——

(For fathers)

I will not embitter, irritate, or tease my children, lest they become discouraged. I will not break their spirit, thereby adding unnecessary pain and sorrow to their lives.

(Ephesians 6:4; Proverbs 13:24; 15:1,18)

COLOSSIANS 3:22-24 KJV

Servants, obey in all things *your* masters according to the flesh; not with eyeservice, as menpleasers; but in singleness of heart, fearing God: And whatsoever ye do, do *it* heartily, as to the Lord, and not unto men; Knowing that of the Lord ye shall receive the reward of the inheritance: for ye serve the Lord Christ.

—— *DECLARATION OF FAITH* ——

(For employees)

I will obey the one appointed in authority over me. I will do all that is asked of me, not only when they are present, or just to win their favor, but with sincerity of heart and reverence for the Lord. Whatever I am asked to do, I will work at with all of my heart, as if I am working for the Lord and not for an employer. I know that the Lord is always watching over me carefully and He longs to grant me a specific inheritance as a reward for honoring Him in the sight of those whom I work for. Therefore, in all of my work, I will remember that it is Jesus Himself that I am serving.

(Ephesians 6:5-8; Genesis 39:2-5; Ecclesiastes 9:10)

COLOSSIANS 4:1 AMP

Masters, [on your part] deal with your slaves justly and fairly, knowing that also you have a Master in heaven.

─────── *DECLARATION OF FAITH* ───────

(For employers)
So far as it is in my power, I will provide for my employees what is just and fair, for I know that I myself am employed by God and He is more than fair with His provision for me.

(Ephesians 6:9; Romans 12:11)

COLOSSIANS 4:2-4 KJV

Continue in prayer, and watch in the same with thanksgiving; Withal praying also for us, that God would open unto us a door of utterance, to speak the mystery of Christ, for which I am also in bonds: That I may make it manifest, as I ought to speak.

─────── *DECLARATION OF FAITH* ───────

I am devoted to prayer—ever-watchful and ever-thankful. I regularly pray for my ministers, that a door may be opened for God's message so that they may proclaim the mystery of Christ in all boldness. I pray that they may proclaim it clearly and with simplicity, as they should.

(Ephesians 3:3,4; 6:18-20; Luke 18:1; Colossians 2:6,7; 1 Corinthians 14:14,15; 16:9; Acts 4:23-31)

COLOSSIANS 4:5,6 NIV

Be wise in the way you act toward outsiders; make the most of every opportunity. Let your conversation be always full of grace, seasoned with salt, so that you may know how to answer everyone.

I am wise in the way that I act towards outsiders, making the most of every opportunity. My conversation is always full of grace, seasoned with salt, so that I may know how to answer everyone.

(1 Corinthians 9:19-23; Ephesians 5:15; Ecclesiastes 10:12; 1 Peter 3:15)

COLOSSIANS 4:12 NKJV

Epaphras, who is *one* of you, a bondservant of Christ, greets you, always laboring fervently for you in prayers, that you may stand perfect and complete in all the will of God.

———— *DECLARATION OF FAITH* ————

I am always wrestling (doing battle) in prayer for my brothers and sisters in Christ, that they may stand firm in all of the will of God and remain mature and fully assured of God's faithfulness on their behalf.

(Ephesians 6:10-20; Psalm 106:29-31; Romans 15:30; 1 Corinthians 1:9; Isaiah 55:11)

CHAPTER FIFTY-TWO

1 THESSALONIANS

First Thessalonians was written by the apostle Paul around 51 or 52 AD. The central theme deals with issues revolving around the Second Coming of Christ. The believers at Thessalonica were worried that some of their loved ones who died would not take part in the Resurrection/Rapture. Paul deals with this issue by stating several promises concerning who we are and what we will have at Christ's return.

As you speak these prayers, take comfort in knowing that one day you will take part in Jesus' Second Coming. You will be changed in the twinkling of an eye and you will be with Him for all of eternity.

---

1 THESSALONIANS 1:4,5 KJV

Knowing, brethren beloved, your election of God. For our gospel came not unto you in word only, but also in power, and in the Holy Ghost, and in much assurance; as ye know what manner of men we were among you for your sake.

—— DECLARATION OF FAITH ——

By faith, I produce an abundance of good works and have a steadfast endurance inspired by hope in my Lord Jesus Christ.

My Father chose me out of the world to be His own son/daughter. He sought me out, found me and made me what I am today. If ever I begin to think that God doesn't want me around, or that He is fed up with me, I will remember that He is the One who sought me out and chose me to be His son/daughter. I did not go running to Him, He came running for me. He knew everything that I would do, even after receiving Jesus, and He still wanted me to be His son/daughter. Therefore, knowing that He loves me so much, I will do my best to live a life pleasing to Him in every way.

The Gospel did not come to me with simple words, but with wonder-working power, with the Holy Spirit, and with deep conviction.

(2 Corinthians 4:13; 5:7; Mark 11:22-25; John 6:44; 15:5,7,16; Galatians 4:4-6; 5:5,6; Ephesians 1:4; 2:4-10; Luke 15:4-32; Romans 11:22)

1 THESSALONIANS 2:4 MESSAGE

God tested us thoroughly to make sure we were qualified to be trusted with this Message. Be assured that when we speak to you we're not after crowd approval—only God approval.

——— *DECLARATION OF FAITH* ———

My heavenly Father has entrusted me with the Gospel, to spread it in my circle of influence. Therefore, I do not focus my attention on pleasing men but on pleasing God.

(Matthew 28:18-20; Mark 16:15-20; Galatians 1:10; Proverbs 17:3)

1 THESSALONIANS 2:12,13 NKJV

That you would walk worthy of God who calls you into His own kingdom and glory. For this reason we also thank God without ceasing, because when you received the word of God which you heard from us, you welcomed *it* not *as* the word of men, but as it is in truth, the word of God, which also effectively works in you who believe.

——— *DECLARATION OF FAITH* ———

I do not deal harshly with my brothers and sisters in Christ, but continually encourage and comfort them, urging them to live lives worthy of God who has called them into His kingdom and glory.

I have received the Word, not as the word of men, but as the Word of God. At this very moment it is at work within me to accomplish the purpose for which God sent it.

(Galatians 4:14; 6:1,2; Ephesians 4:1-3; 1 Corinthians 1:9; Mark 4:20; 1 Peter 1:23; Isaiah 55:11)

1 THESSALONIANS 3:10 AMP

[And we] continue to pray especially and with most intense earnestness night and day that we may see you face to face and mend and make good whatever may be imperfect and lacking in your faith.

——— *DECLARATION OF FAITH* ———

My Father sees to it that I have all that I need. He makes it His business to send ministers and messengers into my path to supply what is lacking in my faith.

(Philippians 4:19; Matthew 6:19-33; Ephesians 4:11-16)

1 THESSALONIANS 3:12,13 NKJV

And may the Lord make you increase and abound in love to one another and to all, just as we *do* to you, so that He may establish your hearts blameless in holiness before our God and Father at the coming of our Lord Jesus Christ with all His saints.

——— *DECLARATION OF FAITH* ———

The Holy Spirit makes my love for my brothers and sisters in Christ to increase and overflow into their lives.

He strengthens my heart so that I will be blameless and holy in the presence of my heavenly Father when Jesus returns.

(Philippians 1:7; 1 John 4:7-19; 2 Thessalonians 2:16,17; Jude 24)

1 THESSALONIANS 4:3-5 KJV

For this is the will of God, *even* your sanctification, that ye should abstain from fornication: That every one of you should know how to possess his vessel in sanctification and honour; Not in the lust of concupiscence, even as the Gentiles which know not God.

——— *DECLARATION OF FAITH* ———

It is God's will that I be set apart from the world to live in holiness and purity; that I should avoid all sexual immorality and learn to control my body in a way that is holy and honorable, not in passionate lust like the heathen who do not know God.

(1 Peter 1:15,16; 1 Corinthians 6:15-20; Matthew 5:28; Proverbs 6:25; Job 31:1; Colossians 3:5)

1 THESSALONIANS 4:7 AMP

For God has not called us to impurity but to consecration [to dedicate ourselves to the most thorough purity].

——— *DECLARATION OF FAITH* ———

God did not call me to live impurely, but a holy life.

(1 Peter 1:15,16; Leviticus 11:44)

1 THESSALONIANS 4:11,12 NKJV

That you also aspire to lead a quiet life, to mind your own business, and to work with your own hands, as we commanded you, that you may walk properly toward those who are outside, and *that* you may lack nothing.

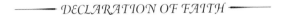

— DECLARATION OF FAITH —

I make it my heart's ambition to live a peaceful life, no matter how many devil heads I have to stomp to attain it.

I mind my own business, attend to my own affairs and needs, and work with my own hands to build a foundation for my prosperity.

I am dependent upon no man to meet my needs. I am never found begging for money or support. In this way, my life wins the respect of those who are outside of faith.

(Romans 14:19; Psalm 37:25; 91:13; 112:1-10; Deuteronomy 28:9-13; Philippians 4:19)

1 THESSALONIANS 4:15-18 KJV

For this we say unto you by the word of the Lord, that we which are alive *and* remain unto the coming of the Lord shall not prevent them which are asleep. For the Lord himself shall descend from heaven with a shout, with the voice of the archangel, and with the trump of God: and the dead in Christ shall rise first: Then we which are alive *and* remain shall be caught up together with them in the clouds, to meet the Lord in the air: and so shall we ever be with the Lord. Wherefore comfort one another with these words.

— DECLARATION OF FAITH —

I joyfully wait with eager anticipation for that great day of my Lord's return. It is not a time of dread for me, as it is for the world, but a time of gladness and excitement. The Lord Himself shall descend from heaven with a loud command, with the voice of an archangel and the trumpet call of God, and those who have died will rise first, then we who are alive will be caught up together with them to meet the Lord in the air. And so my eternity will begin: me, together with all of the saints, in the presence of our Lord forevermore. What a party that day is going to be!

Whenever I speak of the Rapture, it is with an attitude of encouragement and never dread.

(John 14:1-3; 1 Corinthians 15:50-58; Matthew 24:30,31; Acts 1:9; 1 Thessalonians 5:11)

1 THESSALONIANS 5:4-11 NIV

But you, brothers, are not in darkness so that this day should surprise you like a thief. You are all sons of the light and sons of the day. We do not belong to the night or to the darkness. So then, let us not be like others, who are asleep, but let us be alert and self-controlled. For those who sleep, sleep at night, and those who get drunk, get drunk at night. But since we belong to the day, let us be self-controlled, putting on faith and love as a breastplate, and the hope of salvation as a helmet. For God did not appoint us to suffer wrath but to receive salvation through our Lord Jesus Christ. He died for us so that, whether we are awake or asleep, we may live together with him. Therefore encourage one another and build each other up, just as in fact you are doing.

———— *DECLARATION OF FAITH* ————

I do not live in darkness that the Lord's return should take me by surprise. I am a son/daughter of the Light—a child of the day. I do not belong to night or to the darkness. Therefore, I will not be like others, who are asleep, but will continue to be alert and self-controlled.

I will be self-controlled, putting on faith and love as a breastplate, and the hope of salvation as a helmet.

God has not appointed me to suffer His wrath, but to receive salvation through Jesus Christ my Lord.

Jesus died for me so that, whether I am asleep or awake, I will live forever with Him. In this, I find tremendous comfort and serenity.

Therefore, I will encourage others and build them up in preparation for that great day.

(John 3:16-21; 5:24; 14:1-3; 1 John 2:8; Ephesians 4:12; 5:8; 6:10-18; James 1:17; Matthew 24:42-44; 1 Peter 5:8; 2 Timothy 1:7; 1 Corinthians 2:6-16; Romans 8:1; 2 Corinthians 5:15; 1 Thessalonians 4:18; Hebrews 10:23-25)

1 THESSALONIANS 5:16-24 KJV

Rejoice evermore. Pray without ceasing. In every thing give thanks: for this is the will of God in Christ Jesus concerning you. Quench not the Spirit. Despise not prophesyings. Prove all things; hold fast that which is good. Abstain from all appearance of evil. And the very God of peace sanctify you wholly; and *I pray God* your whole spirit and soul and body be preserved blameless unto the coming of our Lord Jesus Christ. Faithful *is* he that calleth you, who also will do *it*.

──── DECLARATION OF FAITH ────

I will be joyful always, pray continually, and give thanks to God in all circumstances, for this is God's will for me in Christ Jesus my Lord.

I will not quench the Holy Spirit's fire in my life. When His fire burns within me, I will flow with it no matter how silly, undignified, or ridiculous it may seem to sense ruled humanity.

I will not treat prophecies with contempt, but will test everything.

I hold fast to what is good and avoid evil of every kind.

It is God Himself, the God of peace, who sanctifies me through and through. In Him, my whole spirit, soul, and body are kept blameless at the coming of my Lord Jesus.

The One who called me is faithful, He will complete the work that He began in me.

(Philippians 1:6; 4:4; Ephesians 4:30; 6:18; 1 Corinthians 10:13; 14:1,4,15,29-31,39; 1 John 4:1-4; Leviticus 5:1; Deuteronomy 28:1; Jude 24)

CHAPTER FIFTY-THREE

2 THESSALONIANS

This is the second letter of the apostle Paul to the church at Thessalonica. It was probably written just a few months after the first letter (51 or 52 AD). The central theme is to provide the believer with a clear understanding of the life they have been called to. Each of us were called and chosen before the beginning of time to fulfill a specific purpose in God's plan.

As you pray these prayers, know that you were chosen before the beginning of time. God knew all that you would do from the beginning of your life to the end and knowing all, He chose you to be His child.

---

2 THESSALONIANS 1:3 NIV

We ought always to thank God for you, brothers, and rightly so, because your faith is growing more and more, and the love every one of you has for each other is increasing.

——— *DECLARATION OF FAITH* ———

My faith is continually growing in intensity and power, and my love for my brothers and sisters in Christ is ever-increasing as well.

(Romans 10:17; Hebrews 10:35-11:1; 2 Corinthians 4:13; Mark 11:22-25; 1 John 4:7-19)

2 THESSALONIANS 1:11,12 NKJV

Therefore we also pray always for you that our God would count you worthy of *this* calling, and fulfill all the good pleasure of *His* goodness and the work of faith with power, that the name of our Lord Jesus Christ may be glorified in you, and you in Him, according to the grace of our God and the Lord Jesus Christ.

——— *DECLARATION OF FAITH* ———

My heavenly Father has counted me worthy of His calling. He has chosen me from among all the people of the earth to be His own son/daughter. By His power, which works so mightily within me, He fulfills every good purpose I have set my hand to perform and every act prompted by my faith.

The name of Jesus is glorified in me, and I in Him, according the grace of my God and Lord, Jesus Christ.

(Romans 8:26-30; 11:29; Ephesians 1:4; Colossians 1:27-29; Philippians 2:13; Deuteronomy 28:12; Isaiah 55:11; John 14:13,14; 17:20-26)

2 THESSALONIANS 2:13-17 KJV

But we are bound to give thanks alway to God for you, brethren beloved of the Lord, because God hath from the beginning chosen you to salvation through sanctification of the Spirit and belief of the truth: Whereunto he called you by our gospel, to the obtaining of the glory of our Lord Jesus Christ. Therefore, brethren, stand fast, and hold the traditions which ye have been taught, whether by word, or our epistle. Now our Lord Jesus Christ himself, and God, even our Father, which hath loved us, and hath given *us* everlasting consolation and good hope through grace, Comfort your hearts, and stablish you in every good word and work.

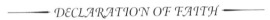

——— *DECLARATION OF FAITH* ———

I am deeply loved by the Lord. From the beginning, He chose me to be saved through the sanctifying work of the Holy Spirit and through my belief in the Truth. He called me to this through the Gospel, so that I might share in the glory of my Lord Jesus Christ.

So then, I will stand firm and hold fast to the teachings that have been passed on to me, whether by word of mouth or by epistle.

Jesus Himself, and God my Father, encourage my heart and strengthen me in every good deed and word. My Father loves me deeply and by His grace He gives me eternal encouragement and good hope.

(Romans 8:28-30,38,39; Ephesians 1:4; 1 Peter 1:2,3; John 17:20-26; Galatians 5:1; 2 Chronicles 20:20; Psalm 138:3)

2 THESSALONIANS 3:1,2 NKJV

Finally, brethren, pray for us, that the word of the Lord may run *swiftly* and be glorified, just as *it is* with you, and that we may be delivered from unreasonable and wicked men; for not all have faith.

——— *DECLARATION OF FAITH* ———

It is my heartfelt prayer that the Gospel spreads rapidly and is honored, producing victory in the hearer just as it has with me.

(Acts 6:7; 1 Corinthians 15:57)

2 THESSALONIANS 3:3 NIV

But the Lord is faithful, and he will strengthen and protect you from the evil one.

────── *DECLARATION OF FAITH* ──────

The Lord is faithful. He strengthens me with His awesome power and protects me from the strategies of the evil one. My heavenly Father takes His stand as a sentinel in my life. He is ever-alert and well able to maintain His covenant with me and bring me to victory in every situation.

(1 Thessalonians 5:24; Luke 10:17-19; Psalm 91; 1 Corinthians 1:9; John 17:15)

2 THESSALONIANS 3:5 MESSAGE

May the Master take you by the hand and lead you along the path of God's love and Christ's endurance.

────── *DECLARATION OF FAITH* ──────

The Lord continually directs my heart into the Father's love, showing me how to trust and walk in it, and into the steadfast patience of Christ, which is a sure confidence in my inevitable victory.

(Romans 8:38,39; John 16:13; James 1:2-4; Hebrews 10:35)

2 THESSALONIANS 3:6-10 KJV

Now we command you, brethren, in the name of our Lord Jesus Christ, that ye withdraw yourselves from every brother that walketh disorderly, and not after the tradition which he received of us. For yourselves know how ye ought to follow us: for we behaved not ourselves disorderly among you; Neither did we eat any man's bread for nought; but wrought with labour and travail night and day, that we might not be chargeable to any of you: Not because we have not power, but to make ourselves an ensample unto you to follow us. For even when we were with you, this we commanded you, that if any would not work, neither should he eat.

────── *DECLARATION OF FAITH* ──────

I will not keep company with a fellow believer who is lazy or indifferent to their duties as a child of God and who does not live according to the clear teachings of the Word.

I do not live like a useless drone in the world. I work hard for my sustenance and the provisions of life. I am not as a parasite, living off of others without doing

anything to earn my keep. I live according to the rule: "If a man will not work, he
shall not eat."

(1 Corinthians 5:1; Romans 16:17; 1 Thessalonians 2:9; 4:1; Deuteronomy 28:12; Proverbs 6:6-11; 20:4)

2 THESSALONIANS 3:11,12 AMP

Indeed, we hear that some among you are disorderly [that they are passing their lives in idleness, neglectful of duty], being busy with other people's affairs instead of their own and doing no work. Now we charge and exhort such persons [as ministers in Him exhorting those] in the Lord Jesus Christ (the Messiah) that they work in quietness and earn their own food and other necessities.

——— *DECLARATION OF FAITH* ———

I am not a busybody—always running around sticking my nose in everyone else's business and never doing anything constructive. To the contrary, I keep my mind on my own affairs and earn the bread that I eat through diligence and hard work.

(1 Peter 4:15; Ephesians 4:28; Proverbs 6:6-11)

2 THESSALONIANS 3:13 NKJV

But *as for* you, brethren, do not grow weary *in* doing good.

——— *DECLARATION OF FAITH* ———

I will not allow myself to grow weary of doing what I know is right.

(Galatians 6:9; 1 Corinthians 15:58; Leviticus 5:1)

2 THESSALONIANS 3:16 NIV

Now may the Lord of peace himself give you peace at all times and in every way. The Lord be with all of you.

——— *DECLARATION OF FAITH* ———

The Lord of peace, who never leaves me nor forsakes me, gives me peace at all times and in every way.

(Hebrews 13:5; Matthew 28:20; John 14:27; Ephesians 2:14)

CHAPTER FIFTY-FOUR

1 TIMOTHY

First Timothy is the first of what are commonly called the Pastoral Epistles. These are training letters that teach us how we are to guide and protect those who are placed in our care. Paul wrote this epistle to Timothy around 63 AD.

The central theme concerns the conduct of those in positions of authority in the church. It is important to note that the same type of conduct is required of all of us. God does not place conditions of moral character on one person that He does not also place on another. It is only said to be the condition for leadership due to the immaturity often found in the so-called laity.

As you pray these prayers, commit yourself to be a mature believer and not to fall for any doctrine that would excuse you to be immoral in any way.

━━━━━━━━━━━━━━━━━━━━━━ ✛ ━━━━━━━━━━━━━━━━━━━━━━

1 TIMOTHY 1:3-11 KJV

As I besought thee to abide still at Ephesus, when I went into Macedonia, that thou mightest charge some that they teach no other doctrine, Neither give heed to fables and endless genealogies, which minister questions, rather than godly edifying which is in faith: *so do.* Now the end of the commandment is charity out of a pure heart, and *of* a good conscience, and *of* faith unfeigned: From which some having swerved have turned aside unto vain jangling; Desiring to be teachers of the law; understanding neither what they say, nor whereof they affirm. But we know that the law *is* good, if a man use it lawfully; Knowing this, that the law is not made for a righteous man, but for the lawless and disobedient, for the ungodly and for sinners, for unholy and profane, for murderers of fathers and murderers of mothers, for manslayers, for whoremongers, for them that defile themselves with mankind, for menstealers, for liars, for perjured persons, and if there be any other thing that is contrary to sound doctrine; According to the glorious gospel of the blessed God, which was committed to my trust.

———— DECLARATION OF FAITH ————

I do not devote myself to myths and endless genealogies, nor do I put up with those who bring false doctrines into the church. These things only promote controversies rather than God's work—which is of faith.

My goal is to promote and live in love, which is from a pure heart, a good conscience and sincere faith. I will not turn away from these to meaningless arguments and controversies over peripheral issues.

I do not follow those who try to teach regulations revolving around the Law of Moses. I know that the Law is good and profitable only so far as a person sticks to it without fail. Once they have failed, even in a single point, it becomes an irreparable curse and no longer has any benefit whatsoever.

Furthermore, the Law is contrary to my new nature. It is designed to promote sin consciousness, and it is not made for the righteous.

As I have been made righteous and a partaker of the divine nature through the Word, the Law no longer applies to me. I no longer need to be conscious of sin, for sin no longer has any dominion over me whatsoever. I have been recreated with the purpose of doing what is good and pleasing God in every way. I do not follow a written code, but the one that is of my spirit and has been written upon the tablet my heart.

This is the Gospel—the message that has been entrusted to me.

(Galatians 1:6-9; 3:13,24; 5:1,6; 2 Corinthians 5:17-21; 11:3,4; Philippians 2:14-16; John 6:28,29; 1 John 4:7-21; Romans 3:19-21; 6:14; 7:12; 16:17-19; James 1:10; 2 Peter 1:4; Ephesians 2:10; Hebrews 10:15-17; Matthew 28:18-20)

1 TIMOTHY 1:14-16 NIV

The grace of our Lord was poured out on me abundantly, along with the faith and love that are in Christ Jesus. Here is a trustworthy saying that deserves full acceptance: Christ Jesus came into the world to save sinners—of whom I am the worst. But for that very reason I was shown mercy so that in me, the worst of sinners, Christ Jesus might display his unlimited patience as an example for those who would believe on him and receive eternal life.

———— DECLARATION OF FAITH ————

The grace of my Lord has been poured out upon me in abundance, along with the faith and love, which are in Christ Jesus my Lord.

Jesus came into the world to save me from my sin. He has shown me His mercy so that He can display in me His unlimited patience as an example for others in order to draw them to Himself so that they may receive eternal life.

(Romans 2:4; 5:20; 2 Timothy 1:13; 2:22; John 3:16,17; Psalm 86:15; 2 Corinthians 5:18-20)

1 TIMOTHY 1:18,19 AMP

This charge and admonition I commit in trust to you, Timothy, my son, in accordance with prophetic intimations which I formerly received concerning you, so that inspired and aided by them you may wage the good warfare, holding fast to faith (that leaning of the entire human personality on God in absolute trust and confidence) and having a good (clear) conscience. By rejecting and thrusting from them [their conscience], some individuals have made shipwreck of their faith.

——— *DECLARATION OF FAITH* ———

I follow the instruction of my fathers and mothers in the faith, so far as what they teach me is in keeping with the Word and the prophecies which have been spoken about me and which God has confirmed within my spirit. I fight the good fight, holding on to my faith and a good conscience. I will not reject these things and end up shipwrecked in my faith.

(Ephesians 4:11,12; 2 Thessalonians 3:9; 1 Corinthians 4:16,17; 1 Timothy 6:12)

1 TIMOTHY 2:1-4 KJV

I exhort therefore, that, first of all, supplications, prayers, intercessions, *and* giving of thanks, be made for all men; For kings, and *for* all that are in authority; that we may lead a quiet and peaceable life in all godliness and honesty. For this *is* good and acceptable in the sight of God our Saviour; Who will have all men to be saved, and to come unto the knowledge of the truth.

——— *DECLARATION OF FAITH* ———

I pray continually, making intercession with thanksgiving, for everyone. I lift up kings, presidents, governors, and all those in authority, praying for their salvation so that we might live peaceful and quiet lives in all godliness and holiness. This is good and pleases God my Savior, who desires all men to be saved and come to the knowledge of the Truth.

(1 Thessalonians 5:17,18; Ephesians 6:18-20; Ezra 6:10; Romans 13:1; 2 Peter 3:9)

1 TIMOTHY 2:5,6 NKJV

For *there is* one God and one Mediator between God and men, *the* Man Christ Jesus, who gave Himself a ransom for all, to be testified in due time.

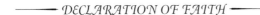

────── *DECLARATION OF FAITH* ──────

There is only one God and one Mediator between He and myself: a man named Jesus. He is my Lord and my Savior, who gave Himself as a ransom for me in order to reconcile me to God.

(Isaiah 43:10,11; Hebrews 9:15; Mark 10:45; 2 Corinthians 5:17-21)

1 TIMOTHY 2:7,8 AMP

And of this matter I was appointed a preacher and an apostle (special messenger)—I am speaking the truth in Christ, I do not falsify [when I say this]—a teacher of the Gentiles in [the realm of] faith and truth. I desire therefore that in every place men should pray, without anger or quarreling or resentment or doubt [in their minds], lifting up holy hands.

────── *DECLARATION OF FAITH* ──────

I have been commissioned as a herald proclaiming the Gospel to all of those in my circle of influence.

It is my heart's desire to see all men everywhere lifting up holy hands in prayer, without anger towards each other or having altercations of any kind.

(Matthew 28:18-20; 2 Corinthians 5:18-20; Psalm 134:2; James 1:2-8)

1 TIMOTHY 2:9-12 KJV

In like manner also, that women adorn themselves in modest apparel, with shamefacedness and sobriety; not with broided hair, or gold, or pearls, or costly array; But (which becometh women professing godliness) with good works. Let the woman learn in silence with all subjection. But I suffer not a woman to teach, nor to usurp authority over the man, but to be in silence.

────── *DECLARATION OF FAITH* ──────

(For women)
I will adorn myself in modesty and not with enticing clothing or apparel.
In all of my actions I will do good, as is befitting a woman of God.
I will learn in quietness and complaisance, and not flaunt or dishonor my freedom and equality in Christ by being insolent and out of order.
I will not teach men with an attitude of superiority, trying to usurp the authority given them by God. It is not my intention to take over and run things for myself, but to be in the center of God's perfect will, order and plan for my life.

(1 Peter 3:3,4; Proverbs 31:10-31; 1 Corinthians 14:34,40; Titus 2:3-5)

1 TIMOTHY 3:2-4,7 KJV

A bishop then must be blameless, the husband of one wife, vigilant, sober, of good behaviour, given to hospitality, apt to teach; Not given to wine, no striker, not greedy of filthy lucre; but patient, not a brawler, not covetous; One that ruleth well his own house, having his children in subjection with all gravity;

Moreover he must have a good report of them which are without; lest he fall into reproach and the snare of the devil.

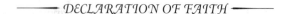

————— *DECLARATION OF FAITH* —————

(For pastors, bishops, elders, and those in like positions of pastoral leadership in the Church)

I live my life above reproach. I am the husband of one wife [the wife of one husband] and my spousal affections, in both mind and body, are hers [his] alone. I am temperate, self-controlled, respectable, honorable, hospitable, and well able to teach. I will not allow myself to become drunk (with alcohol). I am not physically violent, but gentle; not quarrelsome, but a peacemaker; not greedy (or a lover of money), but trust in God alone for my provision. I manage my own family well and see to it that my children treat me with proper respect. I earn a good reputation with outsiders by living my life in purity and holiness so that I will not fall into disgrace and the devil's trap.

(Ephesians 5:1-18; Titus 1:5-9; Leviticus 10:9; Proverbs 3:3,4; 31:4; Psalm 91:3)

1 TIMOTHY 3:6 NKJV

Not a novice, lest being puffed up with pride he fall into the same condemnation as the devil.

————— *DECLARATION OF FAITH* —————

(For the new convert)

As a new convert, I will not seek to exercise authority over other believers until I have grown mature in knowledge, wisdom, and holiness, and have obtained a good reputation as a child of God.

(1 Peter 1:13-19; 5:5; Colossians 1:9-12; Matthew 25:21)

1 TIMOTHY 3:8-13 KJV

Likewise *must* the deacons *be* grave, not doubletongued, not given to much wine, not greedy of filthy lucre; Holding the mystery of the faith in a pure conscience. And let these also first be proved; then let them use the office of a deacon, being *found* blameless. Even so *must their* wives *be* grave, not slanderers, sober, faithful in all things. Let the deacons be the husbands of one wife, ruling their children and their own houses well. For they that have used the office of a deacon well purchase to themselves a good degree, and great boldness in the faith which is in Christ Jesus.

DECLARATION OF FAITH

(For deacons, ushers, and pastoral assistants)

I am a man/woman whose life and conduct are worthy of respect. I am sincere, not given to alcohol, and I do not pursue dishonest gain. I do not gossip about, nor backbite, my pastors. I hold fast to the truths about faith with a clear conscience. I have been thoroughly examined and proven to be trustworthy and deserving of my office. I am the husband of one wife [wife of one husband] and my spousal affections, in both mind and body, are hers [his] alone. I manage my children and my household well. I am a servant to the body of Christ, gaining an excellent standing among my peers, and great assurance in my faith in Christ Jesus my Lord.

(Ephesians 4:1-3; 6:4; Colossians 1:9-12; Proverbs 5:18; 20:1; 23:29-35; 28:20; 1 Timothy 3:2-4; 6:9,10)

1 TIMOTHY 4:4,5 NIV

For everything God created is good, and nothing is to be rejected if it is received with thanksgiving, because it is consecrated by the word of God and prayer.

DECLARATION OF FAITH

I know and fully understand that everything that God created is good, and that I do not need to reject any type of food so long as I receive it with thanksgiving; for all of my food is sanctified through the Word of God and prayer.

(Matthew 6:8-11; 1 Thessalonians 5:16-18; Mark 16:18; James 5:16)

1 TIMOTHY 4:7,8 AMP

But refuse and avoid irreverent legends (profane and impure and godless fictions, mere grandmothers' tales) and silly myths, and express your disapproval of them. Train yourself toward godliness (piety), [keeping yourself spiritually fit]. For physical training is of some value (useful for a little), but godliness (spiritual training) is useful and of value in everything and in every way, for it holds promise for the present life and also for the life which is to come.

────── *DECLARATION OF FAITH* ──────

I will have nothing to do with godless myths and old wives' tales. Instead, I train myself in all godliness and holy living through the Word.

I know the value of physical exercise in keeping me fit and healthy for the work of the Lord. However, godliness has value for me in all things, holding promise for me, not only in this life, but in the life to come as well.

(2 Timothy 2:16; Titus 1:14; Hebrews 5:12-14; 1 Peter 1:15,16; 3:10-12; 1 Corinthians 9:24-27; Psalm 37:9)

1 TIMOTHY 4:12,13 KJV

Let no man despise thy youth; but be thou an example of the believers, in word, in conversation, in charity, in spirit, in faith, in purity. Till I come, give attendance to reading, to exhortation, to doctrine.

────── *DECLARATION OF FAITH* ──────

(For the young pastor)

I will not let anyone look down on me because I am young; for I have matured in the Spirit and live as an example to others in boldness of speech, in godly living, in love, in faith, and in all purity. I am devoted to the public reading and exposition of the Scriptures, and to preaching and teaching. Thus, I have earned respect and have something to offer to others.

(Philippians 3:17; Titus 2:7; 1 Peter 5:3-5)

1 TIMOTHY 4:14-16 NKJV

Do not neglect the gift that is in you, which was given to you by prophecy with the laying on of the hands of the eldership. Meditate on these things; give yourself entirely to them, that your progress may be evident to all. Take heed to yourself and to the doctrine. Continue in them, for in doing this you will save both yourself and those who hear you.

────── *DECLARATION OF FAITH* ──────

I will not neglect my gift, which was given to me by the Holy Spirit for the edification of the Church.

I cultivate my distinct abilities for the benefit and well being of others as well as myself.

I remain diligent, giving myself wholly to the things of God within me, so that my progress will be made known and be beneficial to all.

I watch my life and doctrine closely, persevering in and through them, because in doing so, I obtain deliverance for myself as well as those who hear my message.

(2 Timothy 1:6; Ephesians 4:11-13; Psalm 1:1-3; Joshua 1:8; 2 Corinthians 11:3,4)

1 TIMOTHY 5:1-4 KJV

Rebuke not an elder, but intreat *him* as a father; *and* the younger men as brethren; The elder women as mothers; the younger as sisters, with all purity. Honour widows that are widows indeed. But if any widow have children or nephews, let them learn first to shew piety at home, and to requite their parents: for that is good and acceptable before God.

———— *DECLARATION OF FAITH* ————

I will not rebuke an older man harshly, but exhort him as if he were my own father. I treat younger men as brothers, older women as mothers, and younger women as sisters, with absolute purity in all of my intentions.

I give aid and proper recognition to the widow who is truly in need. If the widow be my own mother or grandmother, I take it as my own responsibility to care for her, repaying what she has done for me through the years, for this pleases God.

(1 Peter 5:1-5; Philippians 4:8; James 1:26,27; Genesis 45:10)

1 TIMOTHY 5:5-7 KJV

Now she that is a widow indeed, and desolate, trusteth in God, and continueth in supplications and prayers night and day. But she that liveth in pleasure is dead while she liveth. And these things give in charge, that they may be blameless.

———— *DECLARATION OF FAITH* ————

(For widows without family)

I will give myself to prayer and supplications day and night, fixing my hope on God to meet all of my needs. I do not live my life in selfishness, leeching off of others for the sake of my own pleasure and gratification, but remain a servant to all according to the ability that God has given me. In this, I prove myself to be blameless among those whom God has appointed to supply my needs.

(Ephesians 6:18-20; Philippians 4:15-20; Proverbs 28:19; 2 Thessalonians 3:8-12)

1 Timothy 5:8 NKJV

But if anyone does not provide for his own, and especially for those of his household, he has denied the faith and is worse than an unbeliever.

────── *DECLARATION OF FAITH* ──────

I will provide for the needs of my relatives and especially for those of my immediate family; for this is right in the eyes of God and an example of how I am to treat the church (the assembly where I worship). If I were to neglect the needs of my immediate family, I would show myself to be worse than an unbeliever; for as the believer is required to meet the needs of the church, so am I required to meet the needs of my immediate family.

(2 Corinthians 12:14; Proverbs 13:22; 2 Timothy 3:1-5)

1 Timothy 5:21 MESSAGE

God and Jesus and angels all back me up in these instructions. Carry them out without favoritism, without taking sides.

────── *DECLARATION OF FAITH* ──────

I follow the rules of order in the church without partiality, and I do nothing out of favoritism.

(1 Corinthians 14:40; James 2:1-4; Deuteronomy 1:17)

1 Timothy 5:22 AMP

Do not be in a hurry in the laying on of hands [giving the sanction of the church too hastily in reinstating expelled offenders or in ordination in questionable cases], nor share or participate in another man's sins; keep yourself pure.

────── *DECLARATION OF FAITH* ──────

I am not quick to lay hands on anyone, nor will I share in the sins of others. It is my heart's desire to live a life of holiness and purity before the Lord.

(Ephesians 5:6-17; 2 John 11; Mark 16:17,18; 1 Timothy 4:14)

1 Timothy 5:23 NIV

Stop drinking only water, and use a little wine because of your stomach and your frequent illnesses.

I am not against taking medicine or other remedies that promote my health. I know that it is my Father's will that I be healthy; therefore, I will do whatever I can to stay that way.

(Matthew 8:2,3; James 5:14-16; Isaiah 53:4,5; 1 Peter 2:24; Psalm 103:1-5; Exodus 15:26; 23:25)

1 TIMOTHY 6:1 NKJV

Let as many bondservants as are under the yoke count their own masters worthy of all honor, so that the name of God and His doctrine may not be blasphemed.

———— DECLARATION OF FAITH ————

(For employees)

I treat my employer with respect and honor, so that God's name and the Gospel are not slandered because of me.

(Ephesians 6:5; Titus 2:9,10; 1 Peter 2:18-20)

1 TIMOTHY 6:8-12 KJV

And having food and raiment let us be therewith content. But they that will be rich fall into temptation and a snare, and *into* many foolish and hurtful lusts, which drown men in destruction and perdition. For the love of money is the root of all evil: which while some coveted after, they have erred from the faith, and pierced themselves through with many sorrows. But thou, O man of God, flee these things; and follow after righteousness, godliness, faith, love, patience, meekness. Fight the good fight of faith, lay hold on eternal life, whereunto thou art also called, and hast professed a good profession before many witnesses.

———— DECLARATION OF FAITH ————

I will be content in all circumstances, knowing full well that God, my Father and provider, is always with me and I am never without His provision.

If all that I have in this natural world is food and the clothing on my back, I will remain content and assured of my provision. I will not set my mind on money and riches, forgetting the fact that I have a heavenly Father who loves me and is caring for me; for I know that those who focus on money and riches fall into many temptations and are taken in many traps (get-rich-quick schemes, etc.)—through such focus they enter into many foolish and harmful desires that plunge them into ruin and destruction.

Money isn't worthy of such devotion. The love of it is the root of all kinds of evil. It is a denial of God as our one true Provider. Some people, who have set their focus and attention on gaining it, have wandered from the faith and pierced themselves through with many sorrows. I refuse to go down with them.

I, as a man/woman of faith, will flee from such misplaced allegiance, and pursue righteousness, godliness, faith, love, endurance, and gentleness. I fight the good fight of faith, taking hold of the eternal life to which I was called when I made my good confession in the presence of many witnesses.

(Romans 1:20-32; 8:14-17; 16:17-19; 2 Timothy 1:13; 3:5-7; 1 Corinthians 2:6-16; Colossians 1:13; 2:4; Philippians 2:14-16; 3:17-19; 4:15-19; Matthew 6:19-33; 11:12; 18:15-17; Hebrews 11:1; 13:5,6; Deuteronomy 28:1-14; Psalm 24:1; Genesis 22:14; Mark 11:22-25; Galatians 5:6-10)

1 TIMOTHY 6:17-19 KJV

Charge them that are rich in this world, that they be not highminded, nor trust in uncertain riches, but in the living God, who giveth us richly all things to enjoy; That they do good, that they be rich in good works, ready to distribute, willing to communicate; Laying up in store for themselves a good foundation against the time to come, that they may lay hold on eternal life.

———— DECLARATION OF FAITH ————

As I am well supplied in this present world, I will remain self-controlled. I will not allow myself to become arrogant or put my trust [or hope] in uncertain riches.

My trust [hope] is in God alone, who richly provides me with good things of every kind to enjoy.

I am not only rich in possessions, but rich in good deeds as well, being ever-generous and always willing to share.

Through my acts of generosity, I lay up for myself an abundance of treasures in heaven as a firm foundation for my future. In this, I have taken hold of the life that is truly life—the very life that God desires for me to live.

(Genesis 12:1-3; 13:2; 2 Timothy 1:7; Jeremiah 9:23,24; Romans 8:32; 2 Peter 1:3; Ecclesiastes 5:18,19; 2 Corinthians 8:2-5,9; 9:5-11; 1 John 3:16-18; Philippians 4:15-19; Matthew 6:19-33)

1 TIMOTHY 6:20 NIV

Timothy, guard what has been entrusted to your care. Turn away from godless chatter and the opposing ideas of what is falsely called knowledge.

——— DECLARATION OF FAITH ———

I take heed and guard carefully all that God has entrusted to my care.

I turn away from all forms of godless chatter and opposing ideas of those who claim to have spiritual knowledge, but contradict what the Word has taught me.

(Romans 16:17-19; Galatians 1:6-9; 2 Corinthians 11:3,4; 2 Timothy 2:14-16; Philippians 2:14-16)

CHAPTER FIFTY-FIVE

2 TIMOTHY

Second Timothy is the second of Paul's Pastoral Epistles. It was written around 66 to 67 AD. The central theme of the epistle is to maintain unwavering faith in the midst of life's trials. The attitude that Paul is telling Timothy to have is that no matter what you must endure in life, God is able to see you through it.

As you pray the personalized prayers of 2 Timothy, know that in spite of the circumstances you are facing, God's Word will not fail you. If you maintain that focus, you will have victory every time.

2 TIMOTHY 1:6-10 KJV

Wherefore I put thee in remembrance that thou stir up the gift of God, which is in thee by the putting on of my hands. For God hath not given us the spirit of fear; but of power, and of love, and of a sound mind. Be not thou therefore ashamed of the testimony of our Lord, nor of me his prisoner: but be thou partaker of the afflictions of the gospel according to the power of God; Who hath saved us, and called *us* with an holy calling, not according to our works, but according to his own purpose and grace, which was given us in Christ Jesus before the world began, But is now made manifest by the appearing of our Saviour Jesus Christ, who hath abolished death, and hath brought life and immortality to light through the gospel.

— DECLARATION OF FAITH —

I recognize that it is my responsibility to fan into flame the gift of God within me. I know that God has not given me a spirit of fear and cowardice, but of power (miraculous ability), love, and self-control. Therefore, I will remain perpetually on fire for Him, fully confident and always doing what He has called me to do.

I am not ashamed to testify about the Lord, for He has saved me and given me a holy calling, not because of anything that I have done to earn it, but because of His own purpose and grace.

According to God's sovereign plan, He chose me to receive His grace before the beginning of time. What an awesome thought it is to know that, even before the beginning of time, I held a special place in the heart of God. And now, through the appearing of my Lord and Savior Jesus Christ, who abrogated the death that was mine and brought me to life and immortality through the Gospel, that grace that was once restrained has been poured out upon me in abundance.

(Ephesians 2:1-10; 5:18; 1 Timothy 4:14; Joshua 1:5-9; Acts 1:8; Matthew 3:11,12; Romans 1:16; Titus 3:4-7; 2 Thessalonians 2:13; John 3:16)

2 TIMOTHY 1:12 NKJV

For this reason I also suffer these things; nevertheless I am not ashamed, for I know whom I have believed and am persuaded that He is able to keep what I have committed to Him until that Day.

——— *DECLARATION OF FAITH* ———

I am not ashamed of having to endure persecution for the Gospel, because I know the One in whom I have believed and I am convinced that He is able to guard what I have entrusted to Him.

(James 1:2-4; Matthew 5:10-12; Philippians 1:6; Jude 24)

2 TIMOTHY 2:1 AMP

So you, my son, be strong (strengthened inwardly) in the grace (spiritual blessing) that is [to be found only] in Christ Jesus.

——— *DECLARATION OF FAITH* ———

I am strong in the spiritual endowment of power that has been given to me in Christ Jesus my Lord.

(Acts 4:33; Ephesians 6:10; Colossians 1:27-29)

2 TIMOTHY 2:3-7 NIV

Endure hardship with us like a good soldier of Christ Jesus. No one serving as a soldier gets involved in civilian affairs—he wants to please his commanding officer. Similarly, if anyone competes as an athlete, he does not receive the victor's crown unless he competes according to the rules. The hardworking farmer should be the first to receive a share of the crops. Reflect on what I am saying, for the Lord will give you insight into all this.

I endure hardship and persecution as a good soldier of Christ Jesus. As a good soldier, I do not get involved in civilian affairs, but desire to please my commanding officer.

As a fighter in the ring of life, I fight by the rules so that my victory is legitimate.

As a hardworking farmer, sowing many seeds into my life, I am the first to receive a share of the crops.

These things are worthy of my meditation and the Lord has promised me insight into all of it.

(Matthew 5:10-12; James 1:2-4; 1 Timothy 1:18,19; 6:12; 1 Corinthians 1:30; 2:6-16; 9:24-27; 2 Corinthians 9:5-11)

2 TIMOTHY 2:8 AMP

Constantly keep in mind Jesus Christ (the Messiah) [as] risen from the dead, [as the prophesied King] descended from David, according to the good news (the Gospel) that I preach.

When I think of Jesus, I do not see Him as nailed to a cross, but as raised from the dead in power, majesty, glory, and authority. I always remember that all He did, He did as a man, a son of David—and all that He did, He did for me.

(Colossians 2:13-15; 3:1; Ephesians 2:5,6; Romans 1:3,4; 1 Corinthians 15:4)

2 TIMOTHY 2:9,10 NKJV

For which I suffer trouble as an evildoer, *even* to the point of chains; but the word of God is not chained. Therefore I endure all things for the sake of the elect, that they also may obtain the salvation which is in Christ Jesus with eternal glory.

God's Word on my lips cannot be restrained in any way. It will accomplish the purpose for which He sent it. Neither man nor devil can stop it. Therefore, I will persevere through every trial for the sake of the elect, so that they may obtain the salvation that is in Jesus with eternal glory.

(Isaiah 55:11; Acts 28:30,31; James 1:2-4; Ephesians 3:13)

2 TIMOTHY 2:11-16 KJV

It is a faithful saying: For if we be dead with *him,* we shall also live with *him:* If we suffer, we shall also reign with *him:* if we deny *him,* he also will deny us: If we believe not, *yet* he abideth faithful: he cannot deny himself. Of these things put *them* in remembrance, charging *them* before the Lord that they strive not about words to no profit, *but* to the subverting of the hearers. Study to shew thyself approved unto God, a workman that needeth not to be ashamed, rightly dividing the word of truth. But shun profane *and* vain babblings: for they will increase unto more ungodliness.

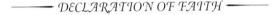

DECLARATION OF FAITH

(The Word is faithful!)

I rightly divide the Word of Truth and understand its application in my life. I understand that in order to receive the promise I must remain faithful and unwavering. I do not forget that I died with Jesus; therefore, my life is now hidden in Him and only through Him am I able to receive any of God's promises. I endure and persevere, never giving up on my faith, for this is the only way I can reign with Him in this life. I never contradict or refuse Him, so that He will never have to refuse and hold back His promise from me. I know that His Word is faithful. Even if I were faithless and failed to believe and receive His promise, He would remain faithful and His Word would remain true. God cannot lie, for to do so would be to deny His very self. Therefore, I shall remain fixed and stable, looking to the Word as the final authority and not the circumstance.

I continually study the Word and always do my very best to present myself to God as one approved, a worker who has done his/her homework and does not need to be ashamed. Through my diligence I have learned how to rightly divide the Word of Truth.

I avoid useless gibberish and all ungodly conversation, because I know that those who indulge in it will only become more and more ungodly. I am not one who is always quarreling about words and causing division. I understand that this kind of constant debating among the brethren only upsets and undermines the faith of those who hear.

(Galatians 2:20; Colossians 3:3; Ephesians 2:4-6; Romans 5:17; 16:17-19; Matthew 10:33; Luke 11:17; Titus 3:9; 2 Peter 1:10; Acts 17:10,11; 1 Timothy 6:3-5; Philippians 2:14-16)

2 TIMOTHY 2:19 MESSAGE

Meanwhile, God's firm foundation is as firm as ever, these sentences engraved on the stones:

GOD KNOWS WHO BELONGS TO HIM.

SPURN EVIL, ALL YOU WHO NAME GOD AS GOD.

――――― *DECLARATION OF FAITH* ―――――

My foundation in the Lord is solid, firm, impenetrable, and immovable, for I have been sealed with His inscription, which is a declaration to all that I am His. I am a born-again son/daughter of the living God and have taken His name as my very own. Knowing this, I have become resolute in my pursuit of godly living and I purge all wickedness from my life.

(Isaiah 43:1; Ephesians 1:13,14; 1 Corinthians 3:11; Galatians 4:4-6; 1 Peter 1:13-16)

2 TIMOTHY 2:21-26 KJV

If a man therefore purge himself from these, he shall be a vessel unto honour, sanctified, and meet for the master's use, *and* prepared unto every good work. Flee also youthful lusts: but follow righteousness, faith, charity, peace, with them that call on the Lord out of a pure heart. But foolish and unlearned questions avoid, knowing that they do gender strifes. And the servant of the Lord must not strive; but be gentle unto all *men,* apt to teach, patient, In meekness instructing those that oppose themselves; if God peradventure will give them repentance to the acknowledging of the truth; And *that* they may recover themselves out of the snare of the devil, who are taken captive by him at his will.

――――― *DECLARATION OF FAITH* ―――――

I purify myself of anything in my life that does not bring glory to God.

I find a way of escape from youthful lusts, and together with my family in Christ, I pursue righteousness, holiness, love, faith, and peace.

I will have nothing to do with stupid and divisive arguments, which only serve to give birth to anger and dissentions. As God's son/daughter, enlisted as a servant to His cause, I am not to be given to fights, arguments, and contentions.

Instead, I am kind to everyone and mild-tempered, preserving the bond of peace to which I have been called.

I am a skilled teacher—patient, forbearing, and never resentful.

I correct all of my opponents with courtesy and gentleness, in the hope that God may enlighten them and bring them to repentance—that they may turn to, recognize and do God's will, and that they may escape from the snare of the devil that is holding them captive.

(2 Timothy 3:16,17; James 4:7,8; 1 Corinthians 10:31; Philippians 2:14-16; Romans 12:18; 16:17-19; 1 Timothy 3:7; 6:3-5,11; Titus 1:7-9; Daniel 1:4,17,20; Galatians 6:1; Psalm 91:3)

2 TIMOTHY 3:5 NKJV

Having a form of godliness but denying its power. And from such people turn away!

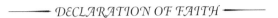

——— *DECLARATION OF FAITH* ———

I will not associate myself with those who take on a form of godliness, even declaring faith in Jesus, but reject His power in their lives.

(Titus 1:16; 2 Thessalonians 3:6; 2 Corinthians 6:14; 1 Timothy 5:8)

2 TIMOTHY 3:9 NIV

But they will not get very far because, as in the case of those men, their folly will be clear to everyone.

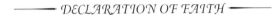

——— *DECLARATION OF FAITH* ———

I clearly see the folly of those who are opposed to the Truth.

(Acts 17:10,11; 2 Timothy 2:15,16; Romans 16:17-19)

2 TIMOTHY 3:10-12 AMP

Now you have closely observed and diligently followed my teaching, conduct, purpose in life, faith, patience, love, steadfastness, persecutions, sufferings— such as occurred to me at Antioch, at Iconium, and at Lystra, persecutions I endured, but out of them all the Lord delivered me. Indeed all who delight in piety and are determined to live a devoted and godly life in Christ Jesus will meet with persecution [will be made to suffer because of their religious stand].

——— *DECLARATION OF FAITH* ———

I am dedicated to sound doctrine, to the purpose that has been set before me, and to faith, patience, and love.

I am a rock of endurance in the midst of persecutions and trials, for the Lord delivers me out of them all. In fact, I rejoice when the persecutions come, for they are a witness that I am doing what is right and that I am making the devil nervous.

(1 Timothy 4:6; Galatians 5:6; James 1:2-4; Psalm 34:19; Matthew 5:10-12)

2 TIMOTHY 3:14-17 KJV

But continue thou in the things which thou hast learned and hast been assured of, knowing of whom thou hast learned *them*; And that from a child thou hast known the holy scriptures, which are able to make thee wise unto salvation through faith which is in Christ Jesus. All scripture *is* given by inspiration of God, and *is* profitable for doctrine, for reproof, for correction, for instruction in righteousness: That the man of God may be perfect, thoroughly furnished unto all good works.

——— *DECLARATION OF FAITH* ———

I will continue in what I have learned and become fully convinced of, for I have taken the time to know the Holy Scriptures for myself and they have made me wise for salvation through Jesus Christ my Lord.

The Word on my lips is God-breathed and produces the desired effects in all of my teaching, rebuking, correcting, and training in righteousness. By learning it, knowing it, living it, and speaking it, I am thoroughly equipped for every good work.

(Acts 17:10,11; 2 Timothy 2:15; Joshua 1:8; Isaiah 55:11; James 1:22-25)

2 TIMOTHY 4:2 NIV

Preach the Word; be prepared in season and out of season; correct, rebuke and encourage—with great patience and careful instruction.

——— *DECLARATION OF FAITH* ———

I am obedient to my commission to proclaim the Word of God in the earth. I am thoroughly prepared to do so whether the opportunity seems favorable or unfavorable, whether convenient or inconvenient, and whether welcome or unwelcome.

As a man/woman of God, rooted, grounded and thoroughly equipped with the Word, I have the tools to correct, rebuke, exhort and encourage others with great patience and careful (well-prepared) instruction.

(Matthew 28:18-20; 2 Timothy 3:16,17; Ephesians 3:14-21; 4:11,12)

2 TIMOTHY 4:5 AMP

As for you, be calm and cool and steady, accept and suffer unflinchingly every hardship, do the work of an evangelist, fully perform all the duties of your ministry.

——— *DECLARATION OF FAITH* ———

I remain calm, cool, and collected in every situation, persevering through every hardship in the spirit of faith, fulfilling my commission and faithfully performing all of the duties of my ministry.

(James 1:2-4,22-25; 2 Corinthians 4:13; Mark 16:15-20; Psalm 46:10)

2 TIMOTHY 4:6-8 KJV

For I am now ready to be offered, and the time of my departure is at hand. I have fought a good fight, I have finished *my* course, I have kept the faith: Henceforth there is laid up for me a crown of righteousness, which the Lord, the righteous judge, shall give me at that day: and not to me only, but unto all them also that love his appearing.

——— *DECLARATION OF FAITH* ———

I am not left in ignorance of the appointed time of my departure from this earth. But, until then, I will fight the good fight of faith. I will run my race well and finish strong. I will keep the faith. The crown of righteousness awaits me at the finish line, which the Lord, my righteous judge, shall award me on that day.

(Philippians 1:19-26; Hebrews 9:27; 2 Peter 3:5-7; Psalm 119:37,50,88; 1 Timothy 6:12; 1 Corinthians 9:24-27; James 1:12)

2 TIMOTHY 4:17,18 NKJV

But the Lord stood with me and strengthened me, so that the message might be preached fully through me, and *that* all the Gentiles might hear. And I was delivered out of the mouth of the lion. And the Lord will deliver me from every evil work and preserve *me* for His heavenly kingdom. To Him *be* glory forever and ever. Amen!

——— *DECLARATION OF FAITH* ———

The Lord takes His stand at my side, encouraging and strengthening me, so that through me His message might be fully proclaimed to all who will hear it.

He covers me as with a shield, delivering me from the lion's mouth and rescuing me from every evil attack, until that day when I am brought safely into my home in heaven. To God be the glory forever and ever! Amen.

(Matthew 28:20; Hebrews 13:5,6; Romans 8:31; 2 Corinthians 5:18-20; Genesis 15:1; Psalm 5:11,12; 18:1-19; 121:1-8; John 14:1-3)

CHAPTER FIFTY-SIX

TITUS

Titus is the third and last of Paul's Pastoral Epistles. It was written somewhere between 62 and 66 AD and carries the central theme of keeping a proper balance in your conduct in the church and society. We are to walk worthy of our calling before the world and to be living epistles to those outside of the faith.

As you speak these promises, think of the fallen world out there that needs to see your witness of the Gospel. You are their epistle. Show them Jesus in all that you do.

‡ ·

TITUS 1:1-3 NKJV

Paul, a bondservant of God and an apostle of Jesus Christ, according to the faith of God's elect and the acknowledgment of the truth which accords with godliness, in hope of eternal life which God, who cannot lie, promised before time began, but has in due time manifested His word through preaching, which was committed to me according to the commandment of God our Savior; To Titus, a true son in *our* common faith.

——— *DECLARATION OF FAITH* ———

I have been appointed by God Himself to proclaim the message of His salvation, promote the faith that has been given to the elect and guide others to the knowledge of the Truth that leads to and accompanies all godliness. I proclaim a faith and a knowledge, which rests in the hope of eternal life, which God, who does not lie, placed in His Word before the beginning of time.

Now is the appointed time, in accordance with God's preset plan, for me to carry out my commission in this earth. I have the privilege of being a carrier of His Word to a hurting world. The God of all the universe has entrusted His unfailing Word to me, His son/daughter. By His command, I have the responsibility to open it up to others and proclaim it to everyone in my circle of influence.

(Matthew 28:18-20; Acts 3:16; Mark 11:22-25; 16:15-20; 2 Corinthians 5:18-20; 1 Timothy 3:16; Numbers 23:19; Hebrews 1:2,3; 11:1-3; Psalm 119:130; 2 Timothy 4:2)

TITUS 1:6-9 NIV

An elder must be blameless, the husband of but one wife, a man whose children believe and are not open to the charge of being wild and disobedient. Since an overseer is entrusted with God's work, he must be blameless—not overbearing, not quick-tempered, not given to drunkenness, not violent, not pursuing dishonest gain. Rather he must be hospitable, one who loves what is good, who is self-controlled, upright, holy and disciplined. He must hold firmly to the trustworthy message as it has been taught, so that he can encourage others by sound doctrine and refute those who oppose it.

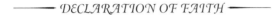

DECLARATION OF FAITH

(For pastors, bishops, elders, and others in positions of pastoral leadership)

I am a man/woman of unquestionable integrity, irreproachable, and worthy of honor.

I am the husband of one wife [wife of one husband] and my spousal affections, in both mind and body, are hers [his] alone.

I am diligent to train my children in the ways of the Lord. I do not allow them to be disobedient and unruly.

Since I have been entrusted with God's Word, I am determined to be pure and blameless. I am not overbearing or domineering, nor am I quick tempered or violent. I am not given to drunkenness and revelry. I am not greedy, nor do I cheat others or pursue dishonest gain.

Instead, I remain hospitable, self-controlled, upright, holy and disciplined— loving what is good and hating what is evil.

I hold firmly to the Word that has been revealed to me so that I can encourage others of its reliability and refute those who oppose it.

(1 Timothy 3:2-4,7; 4:12,13; Ephesians 4:1-3,11,12; 5:18; 6:4; 1 Corinthians 7:3,4; 13:4-8; Leviticus 10:9; Proverbs 20:1; 22:6; 28:20; 2 Timothy 4:1,2; 2 Thessalonians 5:12-22; Hebrews 10:35-11:1)

TITUS 2:1-10 KJV

But speak thou the things which become sound doctrine: That the aged men be sober, grave, temperate, sound in faith, in charity, in patience. The aged women likewise, that *they be* in behaviour as becometh holiness, not false accusers, not given to much wine, teachers of good things; That they may teach the young women to be sober, to love their husbands, to love their children, *To be* discreet, chaste, keepers at home, good, obedient to their own husbands, that the word of God be not blasphemed. Young men likewise exhort to be sober minded. In all things shewing thyself a pattern of good works: in doctrine *shewing* uncorruptness, gravity, sincerity, Sound speech, that cannot be condemned; that he that is of the contrary part may be ashamed, having no evil thing to say of you. *Exhort* servants to be obedient unto their own masters, *and* to please *them* well in all *things;* not answering again; Not purloining, but shewing all good fidelity; that they may adorn the doctrine of God our Saviour in all things.

———— *DECLARATION OF FAITH* ————

I teach only that which is in accordance with sound doctrine through many proofs displayed in and through the Word.

I teach older men to remain sober, to be worthy of respect, self-controlled—and to remain healthy through faith, love, and perseverance.

Likewise, I teach older women to be honorable in the way that they live, not to be slanderers or given to alcohol, but to teach what is good; to train younger women to love their husbands and children, be self-controlled and pure, diligent in their duties at home, to be kind and gentle, and to give all that they are in willing submission to their own husbands and no other so that the Word of God will not be blasphemed.

Similarly, I encourage young men to be self-controlled and to take life seriously. I set them a sound example by doing what is right. In my teaching, I show integrity, seriousness, and eloquence that cannot be condemned, so that those who oppose me may be ashamed because they can find nothing bad to say about me.

I teach employees to submit to their employer's commands in everything that is good and proper, to try their best to please them and never talk back or steal from them, to show that they can be fully trusted so that in every way they will make the things of God attractive, winsome and alluring.

(Colossians 2:18-23; 2 Timothy 1:7,13,14; Ephesians 4:1-3; 5:1-18; 6:5; Proverbs 20:1; 31:10-31; Galatians 5:6; James 1:2-8; 1 Corinthians 7:3,4; Romans 2:24; Philippians 3:17; 1 Timothy 2:11; 4:12,13; 6:1,2)

TITUS 2:11-15 KJV

For the grace of God that bringeth salvation hath appeared to all men, Teaching us that, denying ungodliness and worldly lusts, we should live soberly, righteously, and godly, in this present world; Looking for that blessed hope, and the glorious appearing of the great God and our Saviour Jesus Christ; Who gave himself for us, that he might redeem us from all iniquity, and purify unto himself a peculiar people, zealous of good works. These things speak, and exhort, and rebuke with all authority. Let no man despise thee.

─── *DECLARATION OF FAITH* ───

The favor of God that brings salvation has been revealed to me in all of its fullness. It instructs me to say "No" to all ungodliness and worldly passions and to live a self-controlled, upright, and godly life as I eagerly and expectantly wait for my blessed hope, the glorious appearing of my Lord Jesus Christ, who gave Himself for me in order to make me His own brother/sister, redeem me from all wickedness and purify me to the point where I am eager and willing to do only that which is just and proper.

These things I do and teach with all authority, rebuking the evil, but most of all encouraging others and promoting that which is good in them.

(Matthew 13:11,15,16; Ephesians 1:17-23; 2:4-10; Romans 12:1,2; Galatians 5:22,23; 1 Corinthians 3:4; Hebrews 2:11; 10:24,25; 1 John 3:3)

TITUS 3:1,2 NKJV

Remind them to be subject to rulers and authorities, to obey, to be ready for every good work, to speak evil of no one, to be peaceable, gentle, showing all humility to all men.

─── *DECLARATION OF FAITH* ───

I remain submissive to the governing authorities and I am being obedient to the laws of the land.

I am always prepared to do whatever is good and honorable.

I am a peace-loving man/woman who is kind and considerate, and I display God's own brand of humility toward everyone.

(Romans 13:1; Philippians 4:8; 1 Corinthians 13:4-8; Matthew 23:11,12)

TITUS 3:4-8 AMP

But when the goodness and loving-kindness of God our Savior to man [as man] appeared, He saved us, not because of any works of righteousness that we had done, but because of His own pity and mercy, by [the] cleansing [bath] of the new birth (regeneration) and renewing of the Holy Spirit, which He poured out [so] richly upon us through Jesus Christ our Savior. [And He did it in order] that we might be justified by His grace (by His favor, wholly undeserved), [that we might be acknowledged and counted as conformed to the divine will in purpose, thought, and action], and that we might become heirs of eternal life according to [our] hope. This message is most trustworthy, and concerning these things I want you to insist steadfastly, so that those who have believed in (trusted in, relied on) God may be careful to apply themselves to honorable occupations and to doing good, for such things are [not only] excellent and right [in themselves], but [they are] good and profitable for the people.

———— *DECLARATION OF FAITH* ————

When the kindness and love of God my Savior appeared, He saved me, not because of any works of righteousness that I had done, but because He loves me so much that all He could think about was how to grant me His mercy.

His unfathomable salvation for me was enacted through the washing of rebirth and renewal of the Holy Spirit, whom He poured out upon me generously through Jesus Christ my Savior.

I have been born into the family of God. He is my own Father and I am His son/daughter. I am not what I once was, but an entirely new creation. And having been justified by His grace, I have become an heir with the assurance of eternal life.

Therefore, I will give my all to Him and devote myself to doing only that which is good and profitable.

(Ephesians 2:1-10; John 3:3-8,16,17; Romans 3:20,21; 5:1,2; 8; 14-17; 2 Corinthians 5:17,18,21; 2 Peter 1:4; Galatians 4:4-6; 1 John 3:1-3; 5:11)

TITUS 3:9-11 KJV

But avoid foolish questions, and genealogies, and contentions, and strivings about the law; for they are unprofitable and vain. A man that is an heretick after the first and second admonition reject; Knowing that he that is such is subverted, and sinneth, being condemned of himself.

———— *DECLARATION OF FAITH* ————

I avoid all foolish controversies, genealogies, arguments, and quarrels about the Law. Such things are unprofitable and useless.

(Romans 16:17-19; 1 Timothy 6:3-5; 2 Timothy 2:23-26; 3:1-9; Matthew 18:15-17; Philippians 2:14-16)

TITUS 3:14 NIV

Our people must learn to devote themselves to doing what is good, in order that they may provide for daily necessities and not live unproductive lives.

———— *DECLARATION OF FAITH* ————

I live my life productively, working hard and doing what is good so that God has an avenue to bless me and that I will have all that I need and more.

(Ephesians 4:1-3; Deuteronomy 28:12; Proverbs 10:4)

CHAPTER FIFTY-SEVEN

PHILEMON

Philemon is the last of Paul's prison epistles. It was written near the same time as Ephesians, Philippians and Colossians (60-63 AD). Though the central theme of Philemon is the restoration of a fellow Christian who was a runaway slave, the substance of the epistle is meatier than its volume. These scriptures teach us practical application for our faith.

As you pray these prayers, consider your identity in Christ Jesus and know that no matter how the world sees you, you are a child of the King.

⊹

PHILEMON 1:6 NIV

I pray that you may be active in sharing your faith, so that you will have a full understanding of every good thing we have in Christ.

──── DECLARATION OF FAITH ────

I am perpetually active in sharing my faith. My faith becomes effective only when I acknowledge who I am in Christ and readily accept all that He has provided for me.

I have a full and complete understanding of everything that belongs to me in Christ Jesus.

(Mark 11:22-25; 16:15-20; 2 Corinthians 4:13; 5:18-20; 1 Corinthians 2:6-16)

PHILEMON 1:20 NKJV

Yes, brother, let me have joy from you in the Lord; refresh my heart in the Lord.

──── DECLARATION OF FAITH ────

I pray with full assurance and eager expectation of the answer. Once I have prayed, I begin to make preparations for when the answer arrives.

(Hebrews 10:22,23,35-11:1; Mark 11:22-25; Matthew 21:19-22; James 1:2-8)

CHAPTER FIFTY-EIGHT

HEBREWS

The author of the book of Hebrews chose to remain anonymous to us. It was written around 65 AD. The central theme of the book of Hebrews takes us all the way back to the book of Leviticus. It is the culmination of, or the fulfilling of, God's Law and the setting up of Jesus as our Great High Priest. It is He who has paid our price and takes our needs before the Father on our behalf. Through Him, we have unconditional access to the very throne of almighty God.

As you pray the promises of the book of Hebrews, know that Jesus has given you the right to fellowship with the Father. He is your righteousness and your justification. Because of Him, you have complete and unconditional access into the Holy of Holies of heaven!

━━━━━━━━━━━━━━ ✠ ━━━━━━━━━━━━━━

HEBREWS 1:1-4 KJV

God, who at sundry times and in divers manners spake in time past unto the fathers by the prophets, Hath in these last days spoken unto us by *his* Son, whom he hath appointed heir of all things, by whom also he made the worlds; Who being the brightness of *his* glory, and the express image of his person, and upholding all things by the word of his power, when he had by himself purged our sins, sat down on the right hand of the Majesty on high; Being made so much better than the angels, as he hath by inheritance obtained a more excellent name than they.

─────── DECLARATION OF FAITH ───────

In the past God spoke to my forefathers through the prophets at many times and in various ways, but today He speaks to me directly, through Jesus, whom He appointed heir to all things, and through whom He created the universe.

He is the radiance of God's glory and the exact representation of His being, sustaining all things by the Word of His power.

After He provided my justification, He sat down at the right hand of the Majesty in heaven. Now I, having been baptized into His Spirit, am identified with all that He is and all that He did. He did not do all of this for Himself—He did it for me. He sat down once He had provided all that I need to fulfill my commission and live out the life that He has called me to live.

(Numbers 12:6; John 1:1-5,14; 14:7-18; 16:13,14; Colossians 1:17; Hebrews 11:1-3; Romans 3:20-26; 4:24-5:2; Ephesians 2:4-6; Galatians 2:20; Philippians 2:5-13)

HEBREWS 1:13,14 NIV

To which of the angels did God ever say, "Sit at my right hand until I make your enemies a footstool for your feet"? Are not all angels ministering spirits sent to serve those who will inherit salvation?

——— *DECLARATION OF FAITH* ———

Through me, God is making all of the enemies of Christ a footstool for His feet.

The angels of God have been sent forth into the earth to serve and protect me. They minister unto me all that I need to live the life that God has called me to live.

(Matthew 18:10; 22:44; 26:53; 28:18-20; Acts 2:32-35; Philippians 2:5-13; Hebrews 10:11-25; Ephesians 2:6; Luke 10:19; Psalm 91:10-13; 103:20; Exodus 23:20-23)

HEBREWS 2:1 NKJV

Therefore we must give the more earnest heed to the things we have heard, lest we drift away.

——— *DECLARATION OF FAITH* ———

I remain ever-alert and mindful of what I know about the things of God so that I will not drift away from the Truth.

(2 Timothy 2:15; Acts 17:10,11; Matthew 24:4; Colossians 2:6-8)

HEBREWS 2:5-3:1 KJV

For unto the angels hath he not put in subjection the world to come, whereof we speak. But one in a certain place testified, saying, What is man, that thou art mindful of him? or the son of man, that thou visitest him? Thou madest him a little lower than the angels; thou crownedst him with glory and honour, and didst set him over the works of thy hands: Thou hast put all things in subjection under his feet. For in that he put all in subjection under him, he left nothing *that is* not put under him. But now we see not yet all things put under him. But we see Jesus, who was made a little lower than the angels for the suffering of death, crowned with glory and honour; that he by the grace of God should taste death for every man. For it became him, for whom *are* all things, and by whom *are* all things, in bringing many sons unto glory, to make the captain of their salvation perfect through sufferings. For both he that sanctifieth and they who are sanctified are all of one: for which cause he is not ashamed to call them brethren, Saying, I will declare thy name unto my brethren, in the midst of the church will I sing praise unto thee. And again, I will put my trust in him. And again, Behold I and the children which God hath given me. Forasmuch then as the children are partakers of flesh and blood, he also himself likewise took part of the same; that through death he might destroy him that had the power of death, that is, the devil; And deliver them who through fear of death were all their lifetime subject to bondage. For verily he took not on *him the nature of* angels; but he took on *him* the seed of Abraham. Wherefore in all things it behoved him to be made like unto *his* brethren, that he might be a merciful and faithful high priest in things *pertaining* to God, to make reconciliation for the sins of the people. For in that he himself hath suffered being tempted, he is able to succour them that are tempted. Wherefore, holy brethren, partakers of the heavenly calling, consider the Apostle and High Priest of our profession, Christ Jesus.

———— DECLARATION OF FAITH ————

In dying, Jesus brought me into glory; for it was appropriate that God, for whom and by whom all things exist, should make the author of my salvation perfect by suffering my sentence. He has brought me into such a perfect identification with His sufferings that I am now made holy through His holiness and because He is God's Son, I have become God's son/daughter as well. I am truly one with the Lord.

What a wonder it is that I have become the very brother/sister of the Creator of the universe! He shared in my humanity and fallen nature so that through His death He might destroy him who holds the power of death—that is, the devil. In this, He has set me completely free from the fear of death, which held me in bondage.

Because He took upon Himself my humanity and was tempted in the same ways that I am, He is able to help and provide relief for me when I am tempted.

In all things, and in every way, I am identified with Jesus. I have truly become one with Him.

Therefore, I will not look to myself to carry out my dominion in the earth, but fix my thoughts on Jesus, the Apostle and High Priest of my confession. It is He who takes my words before the Father, on my behalf, so that I have the assurance that they will accomplish the task and achieve the purpose for which I send them.

(Galatians 2:20,21; 3:29; 4:4-6; John 1:12,14; 15:5; 17:20-26; Ephesians 1:17-23; 2:6,7; 5:31,32; Psalm 8:4-6; 22:22; Hebrews 4:15,16; 10:10-17; 11:1-3; 2 Corinthians 4:13; 5:7,17,21; Mark 11:22-25; Romans 8:14-17,28-30; Matthew 28:10; Isaiah 8:18; Colossians 2:13-15; 2 Timothy 1:7-10; 1 John 3:8; Philippians 2:5-13; 1 Timothy 2:5)

HEBREWS 3:6 NIV

But Christ is faithful as a son over God's house. And we are his house, if we hold on to our courage and the hope of which we boast.

——— *DECLARATION OF FAITH* ———

Jesus is faithful as the Son in charge of all of God's children. And I am God's child because my commitment to Him is sincere and everlasting. I will never give up on my faith in my heavenly Father, but will continually boast in Him with all courage and confidence.

(Romans 8:29; Galatians 4:4-6; Hebrews 10:19-23,35-11:1)

HEBREWS 3:12,13 AMP

[Therefore beware] brethren, take care, lest there be in any one of you a wicked, unbelieving heart [which refuses to cleave to, trust in, and rely on Him], leading you to turn away and desert or stand aloof from the living God. But instead warn (admonish, urge, and encourage) one another every day, as long as it is called Today, that none of you may be hardened [into settled rebellion] by the deceitfulness of sin [by the fraudulence, the stratagem, the trickery which the delusive glamor of his sin may play on him].

——— *DECLARATION OF FAITH* ———

I see to it that I do not develop a sinful, faithless and unbelieving heart that turns away from the living God.

Therefore, I will not listen to or associate myself with those who do not believe in the Word or trust in God's promises. I choose my friends wisely and will only associate with those of like faith. And I am good to my friends, encouraging and building them up on a daily basis so long as today is still called today. In this way I build up a shield of safety against the snares of the devil in order to keep my friends and I from being hardened by sin's deceitfulness.

(Hebrews 3:19; 4:6,11; 10:24,25; 2 Corinthians 6:14; Romans 6:16; Acts 2:42)

HEBREWS 3:18-4:16 KJV

And to whom sware he that they should not enter into his rest, but to them that believed not? So we see that they could not enter in because of unbelief. Let us therefore fear, lest, a promise being left *us* of entering into his rest, any of you should seem to come short of it. For unto us was the gospel preached, as well as unto them: but the word preached did not profit them, not being mixed with faith in them that heard it. For we which have believed do enter into rest, as he said, As I have sworn in my wrath, if they shall enter into my rest: although the works were finished from the foundation of the world. For he spake in a certain place of the seventh *day* on this wise, And God did rest the seventh day from all his works. And in this *place* again, If they shall enter into my rest. Seeing therefore it remaineth that some must enter therein, and they to whom it was first preached entered not in because of unbelief: Again, he limiteth a certain day, saying in David, To day, after so long a time; as it is said, To day if ye will hear his voice, harden not your hearts. For if Jesus had given them rest, then would he not afterward have spoken of another day. There remaineth therefore a rest to the people of God. For he that is entered into his rest, he also hath ceased from his own works, as God *did* from his. Let us labour therefore to enter into that rest, lest any man fall after the same example of unbelief. For the word of God *is* quick, and powerful, and sharper than any twoedged sword, piercing even to the dividing asunder of soul and spirit, and of the joints and marrow, and *is* a discerner of the thoughts and intents of the heart. Neither is there any creature that is not manifest in his sight: but all things *are* naked and opened unto the eyes of him with whom we have to do. Seeing then that we have a great high priest, that is passed into the heavens, Jesus the Son of God, let us hold fast *our* profession. For we have not an high priest which cannot be touched with the feeling of our infirmities; but was in all points tempted like as *we are, yet* without sin. Let us therefore come boldly unto the throne of grace, that we may obtain mercy, and find grace to help in time of need.

—— DECLARATION OF FAITH ——

I fully realize that I will not be able to enter into God's rest if I do not believe, for is it through faith that I have assurance and confidence in this life. If I allow doubt and unbelief to enter in, I open the door for all kinds of fear, anxiety and turmoil to enter in as well.

Therefore, my heart's concern is to hold fast to God's promise so that I will not fall short of entering into His rest.

The message I have heard is of no value to me unless I combine it with faith. Now, it is through my belief that I have entered into His rest. God once said, "I have sworn in My wrath: They shall not enter into my rest," speaking of those who refused to believe in His finished work, even though signs, wonders and miracles were performed in their presence to testify to it. Therefore, if I do not accept the fact that all of His works concerning this world, and me, were established from the foundation of this world, and that through believing they become a present fact in my life, I will not enter into His rest either.

There remains, then, a Sabbath rest for me in Jesus. And as God rested on the seventh day, I also rest from my own work. I do not try to earn my way into God's favor and blessings. They are already mine to receive through faith. I am very eager to enter into His rest through the avenue of faith. I will not forget that the only way I can enjoy this rest is through the Apostle and High Priest of my confession: Christ Jesus my Lord. Therefore, if I wish to enter His rest, I must believe in His promise and speak it into my life. When I do this, my High Priest takes my confession before the throne of God and sees to it that I have what I say.

I consider the promise of God to be true in my life no matter what the circumstance may be. I rest in full assurance of faith that God is well able to do what He has promised; for the Word of God is living and active within me. It is sharper than any two-edged sword and is able to even penetrate the boundaries of my spirit, soul and body—it judges the thoughts and intents of my heart.

Nothing about me is hidden from God's sight. Everything is uncovered and laid bare before Him to whom I must give account.

Therefore, since I have a Great High Priest (Jesus, the Son of God, my elder brother and my Lord) who has entered the heavenly temple on my behalf, I will hold firmly to my confession of faith without wavering or giving in to the circumstances; for I do not have a High Priest who is unable to sympathize with my weaknesses, but one who was tempted in every way that I am and yet remained victorious. By Him, I can now approach the very throne of God, the throne of grace, with boldness and confidence, without the slightest sense of inadequacy whatsoever, so that I can obtain His mercy and supernatural ability to help me in my time of need.

In Jesus, the way has been opened for me to freely receive God's help in any and every circumstance I find myself in. It doesn't matter if it is my fault or not, for by His grace (unmerited, undeserved favor) He has given me His Word that He will help me and put me back on my feet.

(Hebrews 2:11,17; 3:12,13; 7:25,26; 10:19-23,35-11:1,6; John 6:27-29; 15:7; 2 Corinthians 4:13; 5:7,17,21; James 1:2-8; Galatians 5:4-6; Psalm 91:15; 95:7-11; 147:15; Genesis 2:2; 2 Peter 1:10; Isaiah 49:2; Ephesians 2:4-19; 3:14-21; 6:17; 1 Corinthians 14:24,25; Mark 11:22-25; Romans 4:1-4; 8:29; 10:8; 11:6; Titus 3:4-7)

HEBREWS 5:1,5 NKJV

For every high priest taken from among men is appointed for men in things pertaining to God, that he may offer both gifts and sacrifices for sins. So also Christ did not glorify Himself to become High Priest, but it was He who said to Him: "You are My Son, Today I have begotten You."

──────── *DECLARATION OF FAITH* ────────

Jesus has been selected from among men to be my High Priest and has been appointed to represent me in matters related to God. He is the propitiation for my sins and through Him all of my gifts are purified and made acceptable when He presents them to our Father.

(1 John 2:1,2; Hebrews 2:17; 8:3,6)

HEBREWS 5:9 NKJV

And having been perfected, He became the author of eternal salvation to all who obey Him.

──────── *DECLARATION OF FAITH* ────────

Once Jesus had suffered the total penalty for my sins, He was perfected and became the source of my eternal salvation.

(Hebrews 2:10,11; Colossians 1:16)

HEBREWS 5:11-6:1 KJV

Of whom we have many things to say, and hard to be uttered, seeing ye are dull of hearing. For when for the time ye ought to be teachers, ye have need that one teach you again which *be* the first principles of the oracles of God; and are become such as have need of milk, and not of strong meat. For every one that useth milk *is* unskilful in the word of righteousness: for he is a babe. But strong meat belongeth to them that are of full age, *even* those who by reason of use have their senses exercised to discern both good and evil. Therefore leaving the principles of the doctrine of Christ, let us go on unto perfection; not laying again the foundation of repentance from dead works, and of faith toward God.

──────── *DECLARATION OF FAITH* ────────

I am not as one who is slow to learn, nor do I need to be taught the elementary truths of the Gospel all over again. Even though I enjoy the milk of the Word, I am ready for the meat!

I am ready for the meat of the Word, which through constant consumption brings me to maturity.

As a mature man/woman of faith, I condition and exercise my faculties to live by the deeper things of God. I easily recognize what is good and what is evil, and have the courage to claim my rights as God's son/daughter.

Therefore, I will move on from the elementary teachings about Christ and go on to maturity. I do not need to constantly re-lay the foundation of repentance from dead works [for by the works of the Law no one shall be justified], of faith toward God, instructions in baptisms, the laying on of hands, the resurrection of the dead, eternal judgment, etc.

As God is a God of increase, I am a child of increase. I will not be stagnant with the things of God, but will press forward, continually progressing in knowledge, wisdom, grace and blessing, seeking to live by, in and through all that God has for me as His son/daughter.

(Hebrews 9:11-15; 10:26-39; Colossians 1:9-12; 2:11-15,19; 1 Corinthians 3:1-3; 1 Peter 2:1-3; Ephesians 4:13,14; 1 Thessalonians 4:10; 5:21,22; Galatians 4:4-6; Romans 3:20-22; 2 Corinthians 9:10)

HEBREWS 6:10-12 NIV

God is not unjust; he will not forget your work and the love you have shown him as you have helped his people and continue to help them. We want each of you to show this same diligence to the very end, in order to make your hope sure. We do not want you to become lazy, but to imitate those who through faith and patience inherit what has been promised.

———— DECLARATION OF FAITH ————

God is not unjust. He does not disregard the work that I have done in the kingdom or overlook the love that I have shown Him in my giving. Therefore, I will continue to do so with my whole heart, in full assurance of His faithfulness to the very end.

I refuse to become indifferent, faithless, and stagnant, believing that the circumstance reigns over the Word and thus giving up on my faith.

Instead, I am an imitator of those who through faith and patience (endurance; persistence) continually inherit God's promises.

(Romans 3:4; 1 Thessalonians 1:3; 1 Corinthians 15:58; Galatians 6:9; Colossians 2:2,3; Hebrews 10:35-11:1; 2 Corinthians 5:7; James 1:2-8)

HEBREWS 6:15 AMP

And so it was that he [Abraham], having waited long and endured patiently, realized and obtained [in the birth of Isaac as a pledge of what was to come] what God had promised him.

——— *DECLARATION OF FAITH* ———

I follow after the faith of father Abraham, who waited patiently for several years before He received the promise. Like Abraham, I will never give in to unbelief and never give up on God.

(Galatians 3:6-29; Romans 4:1-25; Hebrews 10:35-11:1,6,8-10,17-19)

HEBREWS 6:13-20 KJV

For when God made promise to Abraham, because he could swear by no greater, he sware by himself, Saying, Surely blessing I will bless thee, and multiplying I will multiply thee. And so, after he had patiently endured, he obtained the promise. For men verily swear by the greater: and an oath for confirmation *is* to them an end of all strife. Wherein God, willing more abundantly to shew unto the heirs of promise the immutability of his counsel, confirmed *it* by an oath: That by two immutable things, in which *it was* impossible for God to lie, we might have a strong consolation, who have fled for refuge to lay hold upon the hope set before us: Which *hope* we have as an anchor of the soul, both sure and stedfast, and which entereth into that within the veil; Whither the forerunner is for us entered, even Jesus, made an high priest for ever after the order of Melchisedec.

——— *DECLARATION OF FAITH* ———

God has sworn by Himself that all of His promises are applied to me. This puts an end to all arguments over whether I will receive them or not. I will receive the promise!

God wanted to make the unchangeable nature of His purpose very clear to me so that I could fully understand His intentions. Therefore, He confirmed His promises to me on an oath, saying, "By Myself I have sworn." This He did so that I could be greatly encouraged and patiently persevere until the promise is manifested; for I know full well that it is impossible for God to lie.

This hope (the fact that God does not lie and that He swore by Himself that I would receive the promise) is an anchor for my soul. He Himself is my High Priest and the surety of God's promise to me.

(2 Corinthians 1:20; John 14:13,14; 15:7; 16:23,24; 1 Corinthians 2:6-16; Genesis 12:1-4; 21:5; 22:16,17; Ephesians 1:3; Romans 8:17,32; 2 Peter 2:3,4; James 1:2-8; Numbers 23:19; Colossians 1:3-14; Leviticus 16:2-16,20-28; Hebrews 4:14-16; 10:19-23)

HEBREWS 7:17-19 NKJV

For He testifies: "You are a priest forever According to the order of Melchizedek." For on the one hand there is an annulling of the former commandment because of its weakness and unprofitableness, for the law made nothing perfect; on the other hand, there is the bringing in of a better hope, through which we draw near to God.

——— *DECLARATION OF FAITH* ———

Jesus has introduced a better hope to me so that I can draw near to God without any sense of inadequacy in His presence. He has done this by winning the right to become my High Priest.

By paying my price, He has set aside the former regulations of the Law of Moses because it was weak and useless in providing me with righteousness.

Now, in Jesus, I have been made righteous in God's eyes.

(2 Corinthians 5:21; Hebrews 4:14-16; 10:14; James 4:7,8; Colossians 2:13-15; Romans 3:20-31; 5:1,2; 8:1-4; Galatians 2:16-21; Psalm 110:4)

HEBREWS 7:21,22 NKJV

(For they have become priests without an oath, but He with an oath by Him who said to Him: "The Lord has sworn And will not relent, 'You are a priest forever According to the order of Melchizedek'"), by so much more Jesus has become a surety of a better covenant.

——— *DECLARATION OF FAITH* ———

Jesus became my High Priest with an oath when God said of Him, "The Lord has sworn and will not change His mind: 'You are a priest forever.'"

Because of this oath, Jesus has become the guarantee of a better covenant between God and myself.

(Hebrews 4:14-16; 8:3,6; Psalm 110:4)

HEBREWS 7:24-27 KJV

But this *man*, because he continueth ever, hath an unchangeable priesthood. Wherefore he is able also to save them to the uttermost that come unto God by him, seeing he ever liveth to make intercession for them. For such an high priest became us, *who is* holy, harmless, undefiled, separate from sinners, and made higher than the heavens; Who needeth not daily, as those high priests, to offer up sacrifice, first for his own sins, and then for the people's: for this he did once, when he offered up himself.

———— DECLARATION OF FAITH ————

Because Jesus lives forever, He is my High Priest forever. He always lives to intercede for me. He Himself is my mediator before God. He has met my need perfectly—being holy, blameless, unstained by sin, set apart from sinners, and exalted higher than the heavens.

Unlike the priests of the old covenant, He does not need to offer sacrifices for my sins continually. He does not need to make a special atonement for me every time that I sin. To the contrary, He was sacrificed for my sins once for all. All of my sins, from first to last, both past and future, were permanently dealt with when He laid down His life for me.

(Hebrews 4:14-16; 10:10-14; Jude 24; Philippians 1:6; Romans 8:31-34; 1 John 2:1,2; Ephesians 1:17-23; Leviticus 16:2-16,20-28; Colossians 2:6-14)

HEBREWS 8:6 MESSAGE

But Jesus' priestly work far surpasses what these other priests do, since he's working from a far better plan.

———— DECLARATION OF FAITH ————

Jesus' priestly ministry is far superior to that of the old covenant, just as the new covenant that God has given me, in Him, is far superior to the old one, for its foundation is on better and more secure promises.

Not only that, but in this new covenant, all of the promises of the old covenant still belong to me!

(2 Corinthians 1:20; 3:6-8; Ephesians 1:3; Leviticus 16:2-16,20-28; Deuteronomy 28:1-14)

HEBREWS 8:10-12 KJV

For this *is* the covenant that I will make with the house of Israel after those days, saith the Lord; I will put my laws into their mind, and write them in their hearts: and I will be to them a God, and they shall be to me a people: And they shall not teach every man his neighbour, and every man his brother, saying, Know the Lord: for all shall know me, from the least to the greatest. For I will be merciful to their unrighteousness, and their sins and their iniquities will I remember no more.

—— *DECLARATION OF FAITH* ——

In this new covenant that I now enjoy, God has placed His Laws in my mind and has written them on the tablet of my heart. I now have the surety that God is my Father, and I am His son/daughter. It is not necessary for anyone to have to teach me how to know the Lord, for He Himself has made me to know Him in a perfect Father/son (daughter) relationship. He has forgiven all of my wayward-ness. My sins and iniquities have been purged from His memory forever.

(Hebrews 10:15-17; Jeremiah 31:33,34; 1 John 2:20,27; 5:20; 2 Corinthians 5:17; 2 Peter 1:4; Romans 8:14-17; Galatians 4:4-6; John 16:13; 17:20-26; Psalm 103:1-18)

HEBREWS 9:11,12 NKJV

But Christ came as High Priest of the good things to come, with the greater and more perfect tabernacle not made with hands, that is, not of this creation. Not with the blood of goats and calves, but with His own blood He entered the Most Holy Place once for all, having obtained eternal redemption.

—— *DECLARATION OF FAITH* ——

Jesus came as my High Priest of the things that have presently come into my life. I have now, in this life, inherited an abundance of blessings and promises. He went through the better and more perfect tabernacle in heaven on my behalf. This tabernacle is not man-made, nor is it of this world. And He did not enter into it by means of the blood of goats and calves; but He entered the Most Holy Place carrying His own blood, having obtained my eternal redemption. It was as if He were saying, "Father, this is for _____ (write your name), accept it on his/her behalf."

In this wonderful deed of love, He sealed for all time my rights and position as a child of God!

(2 Corinthians 1:20; Ephesians 1:3-14; Leviticus 16:2-16; Hebrews 10:1-14; Daniel 9:24; Galatians 4:4-6)

HEBREWS 9:14,15 KJV

How much more shall the blood of Christ, who through the eternal Spirit offered himself without spot to God, purge your conscience from dead works to serve the living God? And for this cause he is the mediator of the new testament, that by means of death, for the redemption of the transgressions *that were* under the first testament, they which are called might receive the promise of eternal inheritance.

─────── DECLARATION OF FAITH ───────

The blood of Jesus, who through the eternal Spirit offered Himself as an unblemished sacrifice to God on my behalf, has cleansed my conscience of all sin and acts that lead to death, so that I may serve the living God; for the unholy cannot serve Him, but only the holy. And in Jesus, I have been made holy.

For this reason, Jesus became the mediator of the new covenant, so that I might receive the promise of eternal inheritance. He died as a ransom for me in order to set me free from the transgressions I committed against the old covenant.

(Romans 3:20-25; 6:4; 1 Peter 1:13-16; Hebrews 10:14; 1 John 1:7; 2:1,2; Ephesians 1:3-14; Colossians 2:13-15; 1 Timothy 2:6)

HEBREWS 9:24-28 KJV

For Christ is not entered into the holy places made with hands, *which are* the figures of the true; but into heaven itself, now to appear in the presence of God for us: Nor yet that he should offer himself often, as the high priest entereth into the holy place every year with blood of others; For then must he often have suffered since the foundation of the world: but now once in the end of the world hath he appeared to put away sin by the sacrifice of himself. And as it is appointed unto men once to die, but after this the judgment: So Christ was once offered to bear the sins of many; and unto them that look for him shall he appear the second time without sin unto salvation.

─────── DECLARATION OF FAITH ───────

Jesus did not enter a man-made sanctuary when He proclaimed my eternal redemption. He entered heaven itself and now appears before the Father on my behalf.

He did not enter heaven to offer Himself again and again each time I fail, the way the old covenant priests used to do with the blood of bulls and goats. Instead, He appeared once for all, doing away with sin altogether by the sacrifice of Himself. Therefore, sin's power has been completely eliminated from my life.

Just as a man is destined to die once, and after that to face judgment, so Christ was sacrificed once to take away my sins [first to last—past, present, and future] freeing me from judgment unto condemnation.

(Leviticus 16:2-8; Hebrews 8:2-5; 9:1,11,12; 10:10; Exodus 25-30; Titus 3:4-7; Romans 6:7,14; 8:1; 1 Corinthians 15:56,57; John 5:24; 14:1-3; 1 Thessalonians 4:16,17)

HEBREWS 10:2 AMP

For if it were otherwise, would [these sacrifices] not have stopped being offered? Since the worshipers had once for all been cleansed, they would no longer have any guilt or consciousness of sin.

DECLARATION OF FAITH

I have been cleansed from every sin that I have, or ever will, commit. Jesus sacrificed Himself once for all of my sins, freeing me from guilt and sin consciousness.

(Romans 6:6,7; Hebrews 9:14; 10:10,22; Isaiah 1:18)

HEBREWS 10:10 NIV

And by that will, we have been made holy through the sacrifice of the body of Jesus Christ once for all.

DECLARATION OF FAITH

By the single sacrifice of the body of Jesus, I have been made holy for all of eternity.

(John 17:19; Hebrews 10:14; 12:10-13; 2 Corinthians 5:21; Galatians 2:20,21)

HEBREWS 10:12-23 KJV

But this man, after he had offered one sacrifice for sins for ever, sat down on the right hand of God; From henceforth expecting till his enemies be made his footstool. For by one offering he hath perfected for ever them that are sanctified. *Whereof* the Holy Ghost also is a witness to us: for after that he had said before, This *is* the covenant that I will make with them after those days, saith the Lord, I will put my laws into their hearts, and in their minds will I write them; And their sins and iniquities will I remember no more. Now where remission of these *is, there is* no more offering for sin. Having therefore, brethren, boldness to enter into the holiest by the blood of Jesus, By a new and living way, which he hath consecrated for us, through the veil, that is to say, his flesh; And *having* an high priest over the house of God; Let us draw near with a true heart in full assurance of faith, having our hearts sprinkled from an evil conscience, and our bodies washed with pure water. Let us hold fast the profession of *our* faith without wavering; (for he *is* faithful that promised.)

———— *DECLARATION OF FAITH* ————

When Jesus offered once for all time an acceptable sacrifice for my sins, He sat down at the right hand of God. The Holy Spirit also testifies to this, saying, "This is the covenant I will make with them, says the Lord, I will engraft my laws into their hearts and I will write them in their minds," and, "Their sins and their unlawful acts I will remember no more." Where these have been forgiven, there is no longer a need for any kind of sacrifice for my sin.

Therefore, since I now have full freedom and confidence to enter into the Holy of Holies of heaven by the blood of Jesus, I can draw near to God with a sincere heart and the full measure of faith. In light of this, I will be unwavering and relentless with my confession of faith, for I know beyond a shadow of doubt that He who made the promise is faithful. He will do what He said He would do.

(Hebrews 1:3,13; 4:15,16; 7:19; 9:12; 10:1,10; Ephesians 2:4-6,18,19; Psalm 103:10-12; 110:1; Luke 10:19; Jeremiah 31:33,34; John 14:6; 2 Corinthians 4:13; 5:7; Romans 10:8; Mark 11:22-25; Isaiah 55:11)

HEBREWS 10:24,25 NKJV

And let us consider one another in order to stir up love and good works, not forsaking the assembling of ourselves together, as is the manner of some, but exhorting one another, and so much the more as you see the Day approaching.

———— *DECLARATION OF FAITH* ————

Instead of being divisive, argumentative and always finding fault in others, I will look to what is good in them. From this day forward I purpose in my heart to always see what is best in others, carefully considering what I can do to encourage them and spur them on toward love and good deeds.

I will not neglect my brothers and sisters in Christ by failing to gather together with them on a regular basis.

(Romans 13:11; 16:17-19; 1 Corinthians 13:4-8; Acts 2:42; 1 Thessalonians 4:16,17)

HEBREWS 10:26-29 KJV

For if we sin wilfully after that we have received the knowledge of the truth, there remaineth no more sacrifice for sins, but a certain fearful looking for of judgment and fiery indignation, which shall devour the adversaries.

He that despised Moses' law died without mercy under two or three witnesses: Of how much sorer punishment, suppose ye, shall he be thought worthy, who hath trodden under foot the Son of God, and hath counted the blood of the covenant, wherewith he was sanctified, an unholy thing, and hath done despite unto the Spirit of grace?

——— *DECLARATION OF FAITH* ———

I am not a fool to deliberately and willfully [with an insolent and disrespectful attitude] keep on sinning after I have received the full knowledge of the Truth. I know that the sacrifice of Jesus is not a license to sin and it is not applied to those who lack a repentant heart. All that kind of person has to look forward to is a fearful expectation of judgment and of the raging fire that is prepared for the enemies of God. Anyone who rejected the Law of Moses died without mercy on the testimony of two or three witnesses. How much more severely should the punishment be for a person who disrespectfully tramples the Son of God underfoot, treating the blood of the covenant, the very blood that provides their sanctification, as an unholy thing unworthy of reverence and respect, thus insulting the Spirit of grace?

No, I fully understand that I am saved, born again and recreated with a nature that desires to do good works. The whole point of my salvation is my deliverance from sin, not my having a license to revel in it.

(Hebrews 2:3; 6:6; Romans 6:14-18,22; Zephaniah 1:18; Matthew 7:21-23; 12:31; 24:45-51; Luke 6:43-49; Deuteronomy 17:2-6; 1 Corinthians 11:29; Ephesians 2:4-10; Titus 3:4-7)

HEBREWS 10:32-12:3 KJV

But call to remembrance the former days, in which, after ye were illuminated, ye endured a great fight of afflictions; Partly, whilst ye were made a gazingstock both by reproaches and afflictions; and partly, whilst ye became companions of them that were so used. For ye had compassion of me in my bonds, and took joyfully the spoiling of your goods, knowing in yourselves that ye have in heaven a better and an enduring substance. Cast not away therefore your confidence, which hath great recompence of reward. For ye have need of patience, that, after ye have done the will of God, ye might receive the promise. For yet a little while, and he that shall come will come, and will not tarry. Now the just shall live by faith: but if *any man* draw back, my soul shall have no pleasure in him. But we are not of them who draw back unto perdition; but of them that believe to the saving of the soul.

Now faith is the substance of things hoped for, the evidence of things not seen. For by it the elders obtained a good report. Through faith we understand that the worlds were framed by the word of God, so that things which are seen were not made of things which do appear.

By faith Abel offered unto God a more excellent sacrifice than Cain, by which he obtained witness that he was righteous, God testifying of his gifts: and by it he being dead yet speaketh. By faith Enoch was translated that he should not see death; and was not found, because God had translated him: for before his translation he had this testimony, that he pleased God. But without faith *it is* impossible to please *him:* for he that cometh to God must believe that he is, and *that* he is a rewarder of them that diligently seek him. By faith Noah, being warned of God of things not seen as yet, moved with fear, prepared an ark to the saving of his house; by the which he condemned the world, and became heir of the righteousness which is by faith. By faith Abraham, when he was called to go out into a place which he should after receive for an inheritance, obeyed; and he went out, not knowing whither he went. By faith he sojourned in the land of promise, as *in* a strange country, dwelling in tabernacles with Isaac and Jacob, the heirs with him of the same promise: For he looked for a city which hath foundations, whose builder and maker *is* God. Through faith also Sara herself received strength to conceive seed, and was delivered of a child when she was past age, because she judged him faithful who had promised. Therefore sprang there even of one, and him as good as dead, *so many* as the stars of the sky in multitude, and as the sand which is by the sea shore innumerable. These all died in faith, not having received the promises, but having seen them afar off, and were persuaded of *them,* and embraced *them,* and confessed that they were strangers and pilgrims on the earth. For they that say such things declare plainly that they seek a country. And truly, if they had been mindful of that *country* from whence they came out, they might have had opportunity to have returned. But now they desire a better *country,* that is, an heavenly: wherefore God is not ashamed to be called their God: for he hath prepared for them a city. By faith Abraham, when he was tried, offered up Isaac: and he that had received the promises offered up his only begotten *son,* Of whom it was said, That in Isaac shall thy seed be called: Accounting that God *was* able to raise *him* up, even from the dead; from whence also he received him in a figure. By faith Isaac blessed Jacob and Esau concerning things to come. By faith Jacob, when he was a dying, blessed both the sons of Joseph; and worshipped, *leaning* upon the top of his staff. By faith Joseph, when he died, made mention of the departing of the children of Israel; and gave commandment concerning his bones. By faith Moses, when he was born, was hid three months of his parents, because they saw *he was* a proper child; and they were not afraid of the king's commandment. By faith

Moses, when he was come to years, refused to be called the son of Pharaoh's daughter; Choosing rather to suffer affliction with the people of God, than to enjoy the pleasures of sin for a season; Esteeming the reproach of Christ greater riches than the treasures in Egypt: for he had respect unto the recompence of the reward. By faith he forsook Egypt, not fearing the wrath of the king: for he endured, as seeing him who is invisible. Through faith he kept the passover, and the sprinkling of blood, lest he that destroyed the firstborn should touch them. By faith they passed through the Red sea as by dry *land*: which the Egyptians assaying to do were drowned. By faith the walls of Jericho fell down, after they were compassed about seven days. By faith the harlot Rahab perished not with them that believed not, when she had received the spies with peace.

And what shall I more say? for the time would fail me to tell of Gedeon, and *of* Barak, and *of* Samson, and *of* Jephthae; *of* David also, and Samuel, and *of* the prophets: Who through faith subdued kingdoms, wrought righteousness, obtained promises, stopped the mouths of lions, Quenched the violence of fire, escaped the edge of the sword, out of weakness were made strong, waxed valiant in fight, turned to flight the armies of the aliens. Women received their dead raised to life again: and others were tortured, not accepting deliverance; that they might obtain a better resurrection: And others had trial of cruel mockings and scourgings, yea, moreover of bonds and imprisonment: They were stoned, they were sawn asunder, were tempted, were slain with the sword: they wandered about in sheepskins and goatskins; being destitute, afflicted, tormented; (Of whom the world was not worthy:) they wandered in deserts, and *in* mountains, and *in* dens and caves of the earth. And these all, having obtained a good report through faith, received not the promise: God having provided some better thing for us, that they without us should not be made perfect.

Wherefore seeing we also are compassed about with so great a cloud of witnesses, let us lay aside every weight, and the sin which doth so easily beset *us*, and let us run with patience the race that is set before us, Looking unto Jesus the author and finisher of *our* faith; who for the joy that was set before him endured the cross, despising the shame, and is set down at the right hand of the throne of God. For consider him that endured such contradiction of sinners against himself, lest ye be wearied and faint in your minds.

——— *DECLARATION OF FAITH* ———

I will not throw down my faith, because I know in due time I will reap and be richly rewarded. I am resolved to persevere through any and every difficulty, not looking at the circumstance, but with my eyes fixed on the promise. I know that once I have fulfilled the requirements of the promise, I will receive it in its full measure.

I know by experience that it really doesn't take that long for God to move on my behalf. It is not like He is hesitant to do things for me. But, I also know that it is my responsibility to live by faith [believing in, speaking forth, and acting upon the answer]. If I look to the circumstance and give up on my faith in the promise, there is no obligation for it to be fulfilled in my life. Faith is the avenue that God has chosen to bring forth His blessings into the earth. Therefore, if I refuse to walk by faith, the promise will remain dormant no matter how much I believe in it.

But I am not one of those who shrink back and give up on their faith. To the contrary, I am one who continues to believe and receive promise after promise, and I enjoy God's round-the-clock deliverance in my life.

My faith is the very substance of the things that I hope for. It is the certainty that what I do not see will soon be manifested in my life.

I have a thorough understanding of the process of faith. I understand that through faith, God created the universe with His Word. All that I see now was made out of what cannot be seen by the physical eye.

God has called me to live by the same process. When I believe and speak, in perfect alignment with the will of God, the things that I say are manifested.

I know that without faith it is impossible for me to please God. In order for me to draw near to Him, I must first believe that He exists, and then that He will reward me as I diligently seek Him. I believe both. I have assurance in my heart that His Word rings true in my life. Therefore, I fix all of my will on pleasing Him in every way. To do this, I must make demands on the power that He has given me and call those things that be not as though they were.

I do not see things from a worldly point of view but through the eyes of God. I am an heir of the righteousness that comes through faith.

I follow in the faith of father Abraham. It is not my concern how the promise is going to manifest, but only that it will manifest. I will obey whatever I am told and move forward, acting upon the Word and proving the reality of it in my life.

I hold fast to the promise of God. I know full well that God is faithful and will see to it that the promise is made good in me. I do not see things from a human perspective, but from the perspective of the promise. I reject what my senses tell me and take hold of what God has revealed to me through His Word. If the circumstance is overwhelming and the odds appear impossible, I can use the things around me as visual types of the promise's fulfillment in order to strengthen my faith until the promise is manifested in my life.

I freely admit that my citizenship is not of this earth. Like those saints of old, I will live by faith until the day I take my place among them at my residence in heaven.

The great promise of redemption in Christ is given to me. It is a better thing that I have as compared to what those great men and women of faith had. And though they have received and enjoy their redemption in heaven, I now receive and enjoy it on earth. And what's more, they are now my brothers and sisters in Christ—all part of my family: the great family of God.

Therefore, since I am surrounded by such a great cloud of witnesses, I will cast aside every hindrance to my receiving the promises of God, and rid myself of all of those sins which plague and trouble me. I will be about my Father's business and like the saints of old, through faith I will administer justice, obtain the promises, shut the mouths of lions, quench the fury of the flames, and escape the edge of the sword. Through faith, my weaknesses will turn to strength and I will become mighty in battle and rout all of my enemies.

I am resolved to run my race with patient endurance and unwavering persistence.

I will look away from all distractions that would keep me from those things that Jesus has provided. I reject the image of the world and take hold of an image in my mind of what cannot be seen with my natural eyes. It is my mind's image, in accordance with what God has promised, that is the true reality. Therefore, I purpose in my heart to see things through the eyes of God.

I look to Jesus Himself as providing the ultimate faith example and as the very author and finisher of my faith; for He understood the promise and knew what He was providing for me when He chose to suffer in my stead. Despite the circumstances, He acted upon the promise of my redemption. And even though He did not see me, from a human perspective, He saw me in the spirit, one who was far off, and knew the life that I would be provided. He knew that I would become His brother/sister and take my place in the family. This brought Him such joy that He willingly endured the cross and suffered the due penalty and shame that was mine. And, honoring His Word, God raised Him and seated Him at His own right hand.

I will follow this example, considering it carefully so that I will not grow weary and lose heart. I will remain a man/woman of faith despite any situation I may find myself in. I do not look to the circumstances as the final authority, but believe in God [in His Word and in His promises] and speak words of faith to those circumstances until the manifestation of what I say, in line with the Word, comes to pass.

(1 Timothy 6:12; James 1:2-8,22-25; 4:8; Galatians 3:4; 4:3-7; 5:6; 6:7-9; 2 Timothy 3:12; Matthew 5:10-12; 6:10,19-33; 10:24; 21:19-22; 24:35; Psalm 119:109-116, 138,140; 2 Corinthians 1:20; 4:13,17,18; 5:7; Mark 11:13,14,20-25; Colossians 3:1,23,24; Habakkuk 2:3,4; Romans 3:20-26; 4:13-21; 8:24-30; Jude 20; 1 Corinthians 1:30; 2:6-16; 13:12,13; John 1:1-5; 6:63; 10:7-18; 14:1-3,13,14; 15:7; 16:23,24; Genesis 5:21-24; 12:1-4; Deuteronomy 4:29-31; Isaiah 38:1-5; 53:4,5,10-12; 55:11; 1 Peter 3:18-22; Acts 16:31; Ephesians 2:1-10; Hebrews 1:3; 6:12; 10:23; Luke 24:24-26)

HEBREWS 12:5-8 NIV

And you have forgotten that word of encouragement that addresses you as sons: "My son, do not make light of the Lord's discipline, and do not lose heart when he rebukes you, because the Lord disciplines those he loves, and he punishes everyone he accepts as a son." Endure hardship as discipline; God is treating you as sons. For what son is not disciplined by his father? If you are not disciplined (and everyone undergoes discipline), then you are illegitimate children and not true sons.

——— *DECLARATION OF FAITH* ———

I willingly endure and persevere through the struggles of conformity to the ways and things of God. I know that the hardship of discipline is never easy, but it is necessary in order for me to become the person God desires for me to be. And though it may not feel all that great, I am greatly encouraged that God is so concerned with my training, for it goes to show that He considers me, and is treating me as, His own son/daughter.

(Proverbs 3:11,12; Revelation 3:19; James 1:2-4; Ephesians 4:21-24; Romans 8:5,6; Deuteronomy 8:5,6; 1 Peter 5:9)

HEBREWS 12:10-13 AMP

For [our earthly fathers] disciplined us for only a short period of time and chastised us as seemed proper and good to them; but He disciplines us for our certain good, that we may become sharers in His own holiness. For the time being no discipline brings joy, but seems grievous and painful; but afterwards it yields a peaceable fruit of righteousness to those who have been trained by it [a harvest of fruit which consists in righteousness—in conformity to God's will in purpose, thought, and action, resulting in right living and right standing with God]. So then, brace up and reinvigorate and set right your slackened and weakened and drooping hands and strengthen your feeble and palsied and tottering knees, and cut through and make firm and plain and smooth, straight paths for your feet [yes, make them safe and upright and happy paths that go in the right direction], so that the lame and halting [limbs] may not be put out of joint, but rather may be cured.

——— *DECLARATION OF FAITH* ———

My heavenly Father only disciplines and reprimands me for my own good. He doesn't use sickness, disease, and disaster against me, but as a good Father, He disciplines me in order to protect me from such things. All of His discipline is designed with my holiness and well-being in mind. And though at times the training is very hard and taxing, it will later produce in me an abundant harvest of righteousness and peace.

Therefore, I am not dispirited or discouraged, but strengthened and encouraged. Through the Lord's discipline, I make level all the paths for my feet so that the way is made for me to walk in perfect health and happiness.

(Psalm 103:1-5,13; Leviticus 11:44; Matthew 6:10; James 3:17,18; Isaiah 35:1-10)

HEBREWS 12:14-16 KJV

Follow peace with all *men,* and holiness, without which no man shall see the Lord: Looking diligently lest any man fail of the grace of God; lest any root of bitterness springing up trouble *you,* and thereby many be defiled; Lest there *be* any fornicator, or profane person, as Esau, who for one morsel of meat sold his birthright.

——— *DECLARATION OF FAITH* ———

I make every effort to live in peace and harmony with everyone and to be holy; for without holiness, no one will see the Lord.

I am careful not to forget the grace of God towards me and will not allow myself to become hateful and resentful towards others, thus infecting the body of Christ with a root of bitterness.

I am not sexually immoral or godless like Esau, who for a single meal sold his birthright and inheritance as the firstborn son. I am wise enough to weigh things properly and do not allow the fleeting pleasure of sin to rob me of my inheritance.

(Romans 12:18; 1 Peter 1:13-16; Galatians 2:21; Deuteronomy 29:18: 1 Corinthians 6:13-20; Genesis 25:33)

HEBREWS 12:28,29 NIV

Therefore, since we are receiving a kingdom that cannot be shaken, let us be thankful, and so worship God acceptably with reverence and awe, for our "God is a consuming fire."

——— *DECLARATION OF FAITH* ———

I have received a kingdom that cannot be shaken. Therefore, I am thankful and worship God acceptably [in spirit] with reverence and awe, for my God is a consuming fire and is awesome to behold.

(Matthew 13:3-23,31,33; 2 Peter 1:10,11; Exodus 24:17)

Hebrews 13:1-3 KJV

Let brotherly love continue. Be not forgetful to entertain strangers: for thereby some have entertained angels unawares. Remember them that are in bonds, as bound with them; *and* them which suffer adversity, as being yourselves also in the body.

———— DECLARATION OF FAITH ————

I walk steadfastly in love towards my brothers and sisters in Christ.

I do not forget to be kind, considerate and hospitable towards strangers, for there is a distinct possibility that I am entertaining angels when doing so.

I remember my brothers and sisters in Christ who have been imprisoned and see those who are abused as if I myself were being mistreated.

(1 Corinthians 13:4-8; 1 John 4:7-21; Matthew 25:35,36; Genesis 18:1-22; 19:1-3)

Hebrews 13:4 NKJV

Marriage *is* honorable among all, and the bed undefiled; but fornicators and adulterers God will judge.

———— DECLARATION OF FAITH ————

(For the married person)

I hold my marriage in high honor and keep my marriage bed pure. I will have sex with my wife [husband] only, for God will judge the adulterer and all of the sexually immoral.

(Proverbs 15:18,19; Ephesians 5:22-33; 1 Corinthians 6:9; 7:3,4)

Hebrews 13:5,6 KJV

Let your conversation be without covetousness; and be content with such things as ye have: for he hath said, I will never leave thee, nor forsake thee. So that we may boldly say, The Lord is my helper, and I will not fear what man shall do unto me.

———— DECLARATION OF FAITH ————

I keep myself free from the love of money and remain happy and content in the Lord no matter what my circumstance may be, for God has promised that He will never leave me, nor forsake me. Therefore, I can say with unwavering confidence, "The Lord is my helper; I will not be afraid. What can man do to me?"

(1 Timothy 6:6-10; Philippians 4:10-13; Deuteronomy 31:6-8; Romans 8:31; Psalm 27:1)

HEBREWS 13:7-9 KJV

Remember them which have the rule over you, who have spoken unto you the word of God: whose faith follow, considering the end of *their* conversation. Jesus Christ the same yesterday, and to day, and for ever. Be not carried about with divers and strange doctrines. For *it is* a good thing that the heart be established with grace; not with meats, which have not profited them that have been occupied therein.

—————— *DECLARATION OF FAITH* ——————

I consider my leaders carefully, looking closely at the outcome of their lives to ensure that they are worthy to follow.

I never forget that Jesus is the same yesterday, today and forever. Therefore, I cannot be carried away by all kinds of strange teachings that tell me that Jesus doesn't do this anymore and Jesus doesn't do that anymore.

It is good for my heart to be strengthened by grace and not by ritual, ceremony, or ceremonial foods that are of no value to those who eat them.

(Matthew 7:15-20; 1 Corinthians 11:1; John 8:58; 2 Corinthians 1:18-20; 2 Timothy 3:5; Ephesians 4:11-16; Colossians 2:18-23)

HEBREWS 13:15,16 KJV

By him therefore let us offer the sacrifice of praise to God continually, that is, the fruit of our lips giving thanks to his name. But to do good and to communicate forget not: for with such sacrifices God is well pleased.

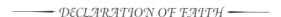

—————— *DECLARATION OF FAITH* ——————

Through Jesus, I continually offer to God the sacrifice of my praise—the fruit of my lips, proclaiming and glorifying His name.

I never neglect or forget to be of service to the Church. I always give generously to its support, for this is well pleasing to God.

(Ephesians 5:20; 1 Thessalonians 5:16-18; Leviticus 7:12; Hosea 14:2; Hebrews 10:24,25; 2 Corinthians 9:5-11)

HEBREWS 13:17,18 KJV

Obey them that have the rule over you, and submit yourselves: for they watch for your souls, as they that must give account, that they may do it with joy, and not with grief: for that *is* unprofitable for you. Pray for us: for we trust we have a good conscience, in all things willing to live honestly.

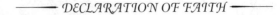
──────── *DECLARATION OF FAITH* ────────

I obey my spiritual leaders who train me in the Word, for they are constantly keeping watch over my soul and guarding my spiritual welfare as men and women who will give account to God concerning me.

I purpose to make my service bring tremendous joy to their hearts, for to do otherwise would be foolish and be of no benefit to me whatsoever.

I pray for my spiritual leaders regularly that they may live honorably in every way and be the very person that God has called them to be.

(2 Chronicles 20:20; Philippians 2:29; Isaiah 62:6; Acts 20:28; 23:1; Ephesians 6:19,20)

HEBREWS 13:20,21 KJV

Now the God of peace, that brought again from the dead our Lord Jesus, that great shepherd of the sheep, through the blood of the everlasting covenant, make you perfect in every good work to do his will, working in you that which is wellpleasing in his sight, through Jesus Christ; to whom be glory for ever and ever. Amen.

──────── *DECLARATION OF FAITH* ────────

My heavenly Father is the God of peace who brought my Lord Jesus (my Shepherd and Master) back from the dead. Through the blood of the eternal covenant, He strengthens me and supplies me with everything that is good. He continually works in me what is pleasing to Him through the power of Jesus Christ, to whom belongs the glory forever and ever. Amen.

(Romans 4:24,25; 5:1,2; Hebrews 10:29; 2 Peter 1:3,4; Philippians 2:5-13; Psalm 23)

CHAPTER FIFTY-NINE

JAMES

T he author of James is James the half brother of Jesus. He was a great leader of the church at Jerusalem and was obviously a great orator as well. His book was written somewhere in the vicinity of 48 AD making it perhaps the oldest book in the New Testament with the possible exception of the book of Galatians. The central theme is the living of a practical faith. James brings us out of the clouds and makes us understand that the life of faith is a life of action.

As you pray these personalized prayers, know that though you cannot earn God's blessings, they cannot be received until they are acted upon.

JAMES 1:2-8 KJV

My brethren, count it all joy when ye fall into divers temptations; Knowing *this*, that the trying of your faith worketh patience. But let patience have *her* perfect work, that ye may be perfect and entire, wanting nothing. If any of you lack wisdom, let him ask of God, that giveth to all *men* liberally, and upbraideth not; and it shall be given him. But let him ask in faith, nothing wavering. For he that wavereth is like a wave of the sea driven with the wind and tossed. For let not that man think that he shall receive any thing of the Lord. A double minded man *is* unstable in all his ways.

—— DECLARATION OF FAITH ——

I consider it pure joy whenever I find myself facing trials and temptations [to give up on my faith] of every kind; for I know that the testing of my faith produces in me an enduring patience and once this patience becomes an unfailing part of my character [when I am mature and complete in it] I will lack no good thing in my life.

I fully understand that Jesus has become my wisdom. God does not keep it from me, saying that I can't have it because I've done something wrong, but supplies it to me liberally, holding nothing back. All of His wisdom is rightfully mine in His name.

When I ask for wisdom, or anything else, I must not reason against my receiving it. A person who reasons against the promises of God is like a wave on the sea, driven and tossed about by whatever direction the wind might blow [or whichever way the circumstances may lead]. This type of person seldom receives anything from the Lord and cannot walk in his inheritance. They are double-minded and unstable in all of their ways.

I remain fixed and unwavering in my faith regardless of what my eyes may see, what my ears may hear, or what my body may feel, for I know that God is faithful and will fulfill His promise to me.

(Acts 5:41; Matthew 3:11,15,16; 5:10-12; 21:19-22; 2 Peter 1:6; Romans 5:3-5; 1 Corinthians 1:30; 2:6-16; Daniel 1:17,20; 2:22,23; Mark 11:22-25; Hebrews 6:12; Psalm 119:109-116; Jeremiah 29:11-13; James 4:8)

JAMES 1:12 NKJV

Blessed *is* the man who endures temptation; for when he has been approved, he will receive the crown of life which the Lord has promised to those who love Him.

─── *DECLARATION OF FAITH* ───

I am blessed when I persevere under trials and temptations, because when I have stood the test, I shall receive the crown of life that my Father has promised me.

(James 1:24; 5:11; 1 Corinthians 9:24-27; Matthew 10:22; Romans 5:3-5)

JAMES 1:13,14 NIV

When tempted, no one should say, "God is tempting me." For God cannot be tempted by evil, nor does he tempt anyone; but each one is tempted when, by his own evil desire, he is dragged away and enticed.

─── *DECLARATION OF FAITH* ───

When I am tempted and undergoing trials, I will not blame God; for God cannot be tempted by evil, nor does He perform evil acts. He tempts no one to do what is wrong, nor does He have them live in a way that is contrary to His per-fect will.

All temptations are designed to appeal to my old, fallen nature. They are designed to entice and drag me away from the good things of God.

(Numbers 23:19; Isaiah 55:11; Job 1:6-12; 2:1-7; 1 Peter 5:5-11; 1 Corinthians 10:13; Exodus 14:13,14; Romans 8:31-37; Matthew 4:1-11)

JAMES 1:16-18 NKJV

Do not be deceived, my beloved brethren. Every good gift and every perfect gift is from above, and comes down from the Father of lights, with whom there is no variation or shadow of turning. Of His own will He brought us forth by the word of truth, that we might be a kind of firstfruits of His creatures.

———— DECLARATION OF FAITH ————

I cannot be deceived into thinking that God is the cause of bad things that happen or that He has some purpose behind all of the evil that I endure in this life. I know that every good and perfect gift comes from my heavenly Father, the Father of heavenly lights, who never changes, but always stays the same. He is a good God and all that He does is good.

Out of the purpose of His own heart, He chose to give me the new birth through the Word of Truth, making me a new creation in Christ Jesus my Lord.

(Psalm 25:8-10; 34:8-10; Jeremiah 29:11; 2 Corinthians 2:11; 2 Peter 1:3,4; Hebrews 13:8; Galatians 6:7-9; Colossians 2:18; Ephesians 1:3-7; 2:4-10; Titus 3:4-7)

JAMES 1:19-25 KJV

Wherefore, my beloved brethren, let every man be swift to hear, slow to speak, slow to wrath: For the wrath of man worketh not the righteousness of God. Wherefore lay apart all filthiness and superfluity of naughtiness, and receive with meekness the engrafted word, which is able to save your souls. But be ye doers of the word, and not hearers only, deceiving your own selves. For if any be a hearer of the word, and not a doer, he is like unto a man beholding his natural face in a glass: For he beholdeth himself, and goeth his way, and straightway forgetteth what manner of man he was. But whoso looketh into the perfect law of liberty, and continueth *therein*, he being not a forgetful hearer, but a doer of the work, this man shall be blessed in his deed.

———— DECLARATION OF FAITH ————

I remain quick to listen, slow to speak, and slow to anger, for anger does not bring about the righteous life that God desires for me to live. Therefore, I rid myself of all immorality, casting from my life the wickedness that is so prevalent in society today, and I humbly receive the Word, planted within my spirit, which is able to deliver me.

I am not just a hearer, but also a doer. I listen carefully, to procure understanding, so that I can do exactly what the Word is guiding me to do.

I am not like the man who hears the Word, but does not act upon it. I do not see my face in a mirror and then walk away forgetting who I am. To the contrary,

I listen to the Word, building an image within me of who I am and what I have in Christ, not just to know it, but also to live it. I look intently into the perfect law of liberty (in Christ) and I am faithful to what I have learned.

The Word has become the life that I live, and as I live it, not forgetting who I am and what I have in Christ, I am blessed in all that I do.

(Proverbs 10:19; 14:17; 16:32; 17:27; Hebrews 12:1,2; Isaiah 55:11; Colossians 3:8-10; Matthew 7:24-27; John 13:12-17; 15:5-8; Luke 6:43-49; James 2:12,13)

JAMES 1:26 AMP

If anyone thinks himself to be religious (piously observant of the external duties of his faith) and does not bridle his tongue but deludes his own heart, this person's religious service is worthless (futile, barren).

———— *DECLARATION OF FAITH* ————

I keep a tight reign on my tongue, speaking only those things that are true, honorable, and of a good report.

(Proverbs 18:20,21; 21:23; Philippians 4:8; Joshua 1:8; 1 Peter 3:10-12)

JAMES 1:27 NKJV

Pure and undefiled religion before God and the Father is this: to visit orphans and widows in their trouble, *and* to keep oneself unspotted from the world.

———— *DECLARATION OF FAITH* ————

If I am religious in any way, it is only in the fact that I see to the needs of the widow and orphan when they are in distress, and I keep myself from being contaminated by the world system.

(Matthew 25:34-36; Isaiah 1:17; Romans 12:1,2; 2 Corinthians 6:14)

JAMES 2:1-3 KJV

My brethren, have not the faith of our Lord Jesus Christ, *the Lord* of glory, with respect of persons. For if there come unto your assembly a man with a gold ring, in goodly apparel, and there come in also a poor man in vile raiment; And ye have respect to him that weareth the gay clothing, and say unto him, Sit thou here in a good place; and say to the poor, Stand thou there, or sit here under my footstool.

——— DECLARATION OF FAITH ———

*I do not display a spirit of favoritism among the so-called social classes. I
treat both rich and poor with equal respect and courtesy.*

(Romans 2:11; Ephesians 5:1; Leviticus 19:15)

JAMES 2:5 NIV

Listen, my dear brothers: Has not God chosen those who are poor in the eyes of
the world to be rich in faith and to inherit the kingdom he promised those who
love him?

——— DECLARATION OF FAITH ———

*I love God with all of my heart and do my very best to see all things through
His eyes.*

*He has chosen me to be well supplied through faith and to inherit the king-
dom that He has promised me.*

(Deuteronomy 6:5; Isaiah 55:6-13; Matthew 6:19-33; 1 Timothy 6:17; 2 Corinthians 8:9;
Luke 12:13-21)

JAMES 2:8,9 AMP

If indeed you [really] fulfill the royal Law in accordance with the Scripture, You
shall love your neighbor as [you love] yourself, you do well. But if you show
servile regard (prejudice, favoritism) for people, you commit sin and are
rebuked and convicted by the Law as violators and offenders.

——— DECLARATION OF FAITH ———

*I am a keeper of the royal Law: "Thou shalt love thy neighbor as thyself." I
am committed to a walk of love, because through love I have the assurance that I
will do the right thing in every situation.*

*I will not show favoritism among social classes, for that is sinful in the eyes
of God.*

(Leviticus 19:18; John 15:12,17; 1 Corinthians 13:4-8)

JAMES 2:12 NKJV

So speak and so do as those who will be judged by the law of liberty.

───── *DECLARATION OF FAITH* ─────

I speak and act as one who will be judged under the law of liberty, for I know that judgment without mercy is given to those who are merciless. And, glory be to God, I know that mercy triumphs over judgment!

(James 1:25; Matthew 24:45-51; John 5:24)

JAMES 2:15-24 KJV

If a brother or sister be naked, and destitute of daily food, And one of you say unto them, Depart in peace, be *ye* warmed and filled; notwithstanding ye give them not those things which are needful to the body; what *doth it* profit? Even so faith, if it hath not works, is dead, being alone. Yea, a man may say, Thou hast faith, and I have works: shew me thy faith without thy works, and I will shew thee my faith by my works. Thou believest that there is one God; thou doest well: the devils also believe, and tremble. But wilt thou know, O vain man, that faith without works is dead? Was not Abraham our father justified by works, when he had offered Isaac his son upon the altar? Seest thou how faith wrought with his works, and by works was faith made perfect? And the scripture was fulfilled which saith, Abraham believed God, and it was imputed unto him for righteousness: and he was called the Friend of God. Ye see then how that by works a man is justified, and not by faith only.

───── *DECLARATION OF FAITH* ─────

I do more than just pray for the needs of the poor—I see to their needs as well. I give of my substance with a willing and cheerful heart, seeing to it that their needs are met through my deeds and not just my words.

In the same way, I maintain a working faith. I do not just give mental assent to the truth of the Word, but act upon it, bearing an abundance of righteous fruit in my life. My faith only has value in the fruit that it produces.

Even father Abraham was counted as righteous because of what he did when he offered Isaac on the altar. Therefore, like him, my faith and my actions work together, and my faith is made complete by the fruit that I produce.

Through active and working faith, I have become the righteousness of God in Christ Jesus. I am now the very friend of God. This could only happen by my actively receiving what God has for me.

I was justified by actively receiving what God has for me, and I now live my life in this earth in the same way that I received justification: by active, working faith.

(2 Corinthians 4:13; 5:7,21; 8:2-5; 9:5-11; 1 John 3:16-18; James 1:22-25; Matthew 7:17-19; John 1:12; 15:5-8,16; 16:23,24; 2 Chronicles 20:7; Colossians 2:6-8)

JAMES 3:2-6 KJV

For in many things we offend all. If any man offend not in word, the same *is* a perfect man, *and* able also to bridle the whole body. Behold, we put bits in the horses' mouths, that they may obey us; and we turn about their whole body. Behold also the ships, which though *they be* so great, and *are* driven of fierce winds, yet are they turned about with a very small helm, whithersoever the governor listeth. Even so the tongue is a little member, and boasteth great things. Behold, how great a matter a little fire kindleth! And the tongue *is* a fire, a world of iniquity: so is the tongue among our members, that it defileth the whole body, and setteth on fire the course of nature; and it is set on fire of hell.

———— *DECLARATION OF FAITH* ————

I understand the power that words have in my life. And, though I may have stumbled and fallen short of perfection in many ways, I know the power that will lead me to it. Therefore, if I want the good things of God to come into my life, I had better watch my mouth.

My words are the bridle that guides my whole body and like the rudder of a ship, they will take me where I want to go [or where I don't want to go if I'm not careful].

My tongue, though small in comparison to the other parts of my body, is the most powerful force within me. With it, I am able to make great boasts that can bring either blessings or disaster into my life. Its power is comparable to the way a small spark can set an entire forest on fire.

My tongue is truly a fire and can be a world of evil to my body if I do not use it properly. It can corrupt my whole person (spirit, soul, and body) and bring disaster on the entire course of my life. On the devil's agenda, it is the single most important thing about me that he wants to control.

But, I'm not about to let that happen! By the power of the Spirit, I will speak my way into the paths of blessing and prosperity that God desires for me to walk in. Only words of honor, integrity, and truth—words that are admirable and of a good report—shall proceed forth from my mouth.

(Proverbs 12:18; 15:2-4; 18:20,21; Matthew 12:37; Mark 11:22-25; 1 Peter 3:10-12; 2 Peter 1:2-11; Psalm 12:1-7; 34:11-18; 2 Corinthians 4:13; 5:7; James 4:7,8; Joel 3:10; John 6:63)

JAMES 3:9,10 NIV

With the tongue we praise our Lord and Father, and with it we curse men, who have been made in God's likeness. Out of the same mouth come praise and cursing. My brothers, this should not be.

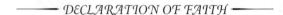
———— DECLARATION OF FAITH ————

I will not use my tongue, with which I give heartfelt praises to my Lord and Father, to curse men who have been made in His image. To the contrary, my tongue is a source of blessing to all men, saved and unsaved alike.

(Romans 12:9-21; Genesis 1:26)

JAMES 3:13-18 KJV

Who *is* a wise man and endued with knowledge among you? let him shew out of a good conversation his works with meekness of wisdom. But if ye have bitter envying and strife in your hearts, glory not, and lie not against the truth. This wisdom descendeth not from above, but *is* earthly, sensual, devilish. For where envying and strife *is,* there *is* confusion and every evil work. But the wisdom that is from above is first pure, then peaceable, gentle, *and* easy to be intreated, full of mercy and good fruits, without partiality, and without hypocrisy. And the fruit of righteousness is sown in peace of them that make peace.

———— DECLARATION OF FAITH ————

I am a man/woman of wisdom and understanding. This I freely display by living a good and upright life—by deeds done in the humility that comes from wisdom.

I refuse to harbor bitter envy or selfish ambition in my heart. That kind of wisdom is devilish and I will have no part of it; for where there is envy and selfish ambition, there is disorder and evil of every kind.

My wisdom comes from heaven. It is first pure; then peace-loving, considerate, willing to yield to what is right and godly, full of mercy, impartial, sincere, and produces an abundance of good fruit.

As a peacemaker, I sow in peace and raise an abundant harvest of righteousness.

(Daniel 2:22,23; Matthew 13:11,15,16; 1 Corinthians 2:6-16; 3:2,3; 1 John 3:18; Romans 12:9-21; 13:13,14; Philippians 3:18,19; Proverbs 11:18)

JAMES 4:2-10 KJV

Ye lust, and have not: ye kill, and desire to have, and cannot obtain: ye fight and war, yet ye have not, because ye ask not. Ye ask, and receive not, because ye ask amiss, that ye may consume *it* upon your lusts. Ye adulterers and adulteresses, know ye not that the friendship of the world is enmity with God? whosoever therefore will be a friend of the world is the enemy of God. Do ye think that the scripture saith in vain, The spirit that dwelleth in us lusteth to envy? But he giveth more grace. Wherefore he saith, God resisteth the proud, but giveth grace unto the humble. Submit yourselves therefore to God. Resist the devil, and he will flee from you. Draw nigh to God, and he will draw nigh to you. Cleanse *your* hands, *ye* sinners; and purify *your* hearts, *ye* double minded. Be afflicted, and mourn, and weep: let your laughter be turned to mourning, and *your* joy to heaviness. Humble yourselves in the sight of the Lord, and he shall lift you up.

DECLARATION OF FAITH

I am not full of selfish ambition, nor am I so foolish as to think that God has given me an inheritance so that I can use it to fill all of my lusts.

I do not allow myself to become consumed with quarrels and contentions, nor do I vie for the most admired positions within the body of Christ.

I spurn all self-centered desires, never allowing them to rule me or lead me on a path of turmoil and unrest.

I refuse to be one of those people who are always complaining about things and never doing what it takes to fix the problem.

I do not complain about what I don't have. When I ask God for something, I make sure that my motives are honorable, and not just to get things for selfish pleasure.

I fully understand that friendship with the world makes me an enemy of God. I also know that the Spirit of God within me is intensely jealous of the world. He does not want it to have any part of me. Therefore, I refuse to conform to its ways of living and being.

God regularly increases my supernatural abilities; for it is written, "God sets Himself against the proud and haughty, but gives continual grace (supernatural ability) to those who are humble enough to receive it."

Therefore, I fully and completely submit myself to God.

I resist every attack and temptation that Satan brings against me and he flees from my presence in stark terror.

As I draw near to God, He draws near to me.

I rid myself of any sin that may still be clinging to my life.

I purify my heart from all double-mindedness, and remain fixed and immovable in my faith. If He said it, I believe it, and that settles it.

As I remain humble in the presence of my Father, He exalts me to a life full of joy and endless victory.

(James 1:5-8; 3:14-16; Romans 6:23; 10:8; 16:17-19; 1 John 1:5-9; 2:15; 5:14,15; 2 Corinthians 6:14; 7:10; 10:3-6; Genesis 6:5; Proverbs 3:34; 1 Peter 1:22-25; 5:5-7; Ephesians 4:27; 6:10-18; 2 Chronicles 15:2; Hebrews 12:1; Psalm 119:109-116)

JAMES 4:11 NKJV

Do not speak evil of one another, brethren. He who speaks evil of a brother and judges his brother, speaks evil of the law and judges the law. But if you judge the law, you are not a doer of the law but a judge.

———— *DECLARATION OF FAITH* ————

I will not speak evil of my brothers and sisters in Christ, or set myself up as their accuser.

(Leviticus 19:16; 1 Peter 2:1-3; Matthew 7:1-5; Romans 16:17-19)

JAMES 4:13-17 KJV

Go to now, ye that say, To day or to morrow we will go into such a city, and continue there a year, and buy and sell, and get gain: Whereas ye know not what *shall be* on the morrow. For what *is* your life? It is even a vapour, that appeareth for a little time, and then vanisheth away. For that ye *ought* to say, If the Lord will, we shall live, and do this, or that. But now ye rejoice in your boastings: all such rejoicing is evil. Therefore to him that knoweth to do good, and doeth *it* not, to him it is sin.

———— *DECLARATION OF FAITH* ————

I am not a braggart who boasts about all of the great things I am going to do while not even considering the Lord's will and purpose for my life. All such boasting is evil and I will have no part of it.

To the contrary, I make my boast in the Lord. He is the One who is working in and through me to bring forth blessings into my life. I follow His will, putting it first in all of my decision-making. Only by Him do I have a certainty of tomorrow. He has laid my destiny before me and has given me complete understanding of the direction I should take. I know the good that I am supposed to do, and I do it.

(Psalm 27:11; 91:16; Deuteronomy 28:66 (coupled with Galatians 3:13); Proverbs 3:5,6; Matthew 6:10; 1 John 5:14,15; 1 Corinthians 2:6-16)

JAMES 5:9 MESSAGE

Friends, don't complain about each other. A far greater complaint could be lodged against you, you know. The Judge is standing just around the corner.

—— *DECLARATION OF FAITH* ——

I do not grumble against my brothers and sisters in Christ.

(Leviticus 19:16; Philippians 2:14-16; 1 Peter 4:9; Romans 14:1; 16:17-19)

JAMES 5:10,11 NKJV

My brethren, take the prophets, who spoke in the name of the Lord, as an example of suffering and patience. Indeed we count them blessed who endure. You have heard of the perseverance of Job and seen the end *intended by* the Lord—that the Lord is very compassionate and merciful.

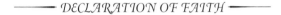

—— *DECLARATION OF FAITH* ——

I know the heart of my Father. Therefore, I know I can outlast any and every trial that I face. I will persevere and be blessed with my Father's abundance!

When the chips are down and things don't look so good, I will consider the perseverance of Job and how the Lord rewarded him. He continued to prosper when his suffering ended and the Lord gave Him twice as much as he had before; for my God is merciful and full of compassion. He always has in mind what is best for me.

(2 Corinthians 2:6-16; 1 John 2:20,27; 5:20; James 1:2-4,12; Job 42:10-17; Psalm 103:13; Numbers 14:17-20)

JAMES 5:12 NIV

Above all, my brothers, do not swear—not by heaven or by earth or by anything else. Let your "Yes" be yes, and your "No," no, or you will be condemned.

—— *DECLARATION OF FAITH* ——

I am not one who needs to swear an oath in order to give credence to my word. Therefore, I will not swear by heaven, by earth or anything else. As far as I'm concerned, my yes means yes and my no means no. If anyone expects anymore than that, they will be sorely disappointed.

(Matthew 5:34-37; Colossians 4:6; Proverbs 8:7; 22:20,21)

JAMES 5:13-16A KJV

Is any among you afflicted? let him pray. Is any merry? let him sing psalms. Is any sick among you? let him call for the elders of the church; and let them pray over him, anointing him with oil in the name of the Lord: And the prayer of faith shall save the sick, and the Lord shall raise him up; and if he have committed sins, they shall be forgiven him. Confess *your* faults one to another, and pray one for another, that ye may be healed.

——— *DECLARATION OF FAITH* ———

I will not face any trouble, adversity, or misfortune without prayer.

I continually sing songs of praise, rejoicing in what God has done in my life.

I have no need to fret over sickness, for even if it were to overwhelm me, I could call for the elders of the church and have them pray over me, anointing me with oil in the name of the Lord. I know that the prayer of faith will save the sick and the Lord shall raise them up. Therefore, if my faith is lacking, I will simply go where faith is strong, for it is abundantly clear that God wants me well.

If I have stumbled in any way, I do not need to fret over it—I can rest in full confidence that the Lord loves me and forgives all of my shortcomings.

I also know that sin is a hindrance to my healing. Therefore, if there is any sin in my life I repent of it. I confess my sins to trusted brothers and sisters in Christ, gaining strength and praying in agreement with them so that I will be healed.

(Ephesians 5:19; 6:18; 1 Thessalonians 5:16-18; Psalm 50:14; 89:20-23; 103:1-5; Isaiah 53:4,5; 1 Peter 2:24; Matthew 9:22,29; 18:19,20; Mark 11:22-26; 16:18; Hebrews 12:1-3; Galatians 6:1,2)

JAMES 5:16B-18 AMP

The earnest (heartfelt, continued) prayer of a righteous man makes tremendous power available [dynamic in its working]. Elijah was a human being with a nature such as we have [with feelings, affections, and a constitution like ours]; and he prayed earnestly for it not to rain, and no rain fell on the earth for three years and six months. [I Kings 17:1.] And [then] he prayed again and the heavens supplied rain and the land produced its crops [as usual]. [I Kings 18:42-45.]

——— *DECLARATION OF FAITH* ———

I am a born-again son/daughter of the living God, recreated to be the very righteousness of God in Christ Jesus. My prayers are fervent, relentless, heartfelt, powerful and effective. It is through my prayers of faith that God makes His tremendous power available in the earth.

I think of Elijah as a role model for my faith. I do not idolize him, but realize that he was just a man. He was not a unique creation who was given rare gifts that made it so he could do things better than I can. His spiritual capacity was no greater than mine, yet he prayed fervently that it would not rain, and it did not rain in the land for three and a half years. After that time, he prayed again and

God opened the heavens and they poured out rain in abundance, feeding the earth to produce its crops.

If Elijah, being just a man, could do such things, I can do such things as well; for God is no respecter of persons and will hear my prayer just as He heard Elijah's.

(John 3:3; 2 Corinthians 5:17,21; 1 Thessalonians 5:17; Numbers 11:2; Luke 18:1-8; Matthew 11:12; James 1:2-8; 1 Kings 17:1,5,12-16,20-22; 18:1,2,15,17-19,21-24,36-39; Romans 2:11; Psalm 119:169,170)

CHAPTER SIXTY

1 PETER

Peter, the son of Jonah, brother of Andrew and one of the three closest disciples of Jesus is the author of the epistles of Peter. First Peter was written around 63 or 64 AD. Its audience was intended to be Christians who were dispersed throughout the Roman empire and undergoing much persecution. The central theme is how to properly respond to trials, sufferings and persecutions that Christians often must endure.

As you pray the personalized prayers of 1 Peter, know that God is with you in every circumstance and that in the end your perseverance will be greatly rewarded.

---

1 PETER 1:2-9 KJV

Elect according to the foreknowledge of God the Father, through sanctification of the Spirit, unto obedience and sprinkling of the blood of Jesus Christ: Grace unto you, and peace, be multiplied. Blessed *be* the God and Father of our Lord Jesus Christ, which according to his abundant mercy hath begotten us again unto a lively hope by the resurrection of Jesus Christ from the dead, To an inheritance incorruptible, and undefiled, and that fadeth not away, reserved in heaven for you, Who are kept by the power of God through faith unto salvation ready to be revealed in the last time. Wherein ye greatly rejoice, though now for a season, if need be, ye are in heaviness through manifold temptations: That the trial of your faith, being much more precious than of gold that perisheth, though it be tried with fire, might be found unto praise and honour and glory at the appearing of Jesus Christ: Whom having not seen, ye love; in whom, though now ye see *him* not, yet believing, ye rejoice with joy unspeakable and full of glory: Receiving the end of your faith, *even* the salvation of *your* souls.

— DECLARATION OF FAITH —

According to His foreknowledge, God chose me to be His son/daughter, through the sanctifying work of the Holy Spirit, the receiving of Jesus as my Lord and Savior, and the sprinkling of His blood on my behalf.

God's unmerited favor, supernatural ability, bountiful blessings and endless peace are mine in abundance!

Praise be to God, who in His great mercy towards me has given me the new birth, a living hope through the resurrection of Jesus. I am a partaker of an inheritance that can never perish, spoil, or fade. It is secured and reserved for me in heaven at this very moment.

Through faith, I am shielded by God's power until the coming of the salvation that is to be revealed in the last time. In that day all aspects of the curse will be removed and I will no longer have to fight to maintain what is mine as a child of God.

Until then, however, I must fight. But this is no big deal for me, for I greatly rejoice that, even though I now must persevere through many griefs and trials, eternity awaits me at the end of the race. Griefs and trials are but an opportunity for me to show that my faith is genuine.

My faith is precious to me—a commodity of greater worth than gold. Like gold, it is proved genuine when I am tested by trials and tribulations of every kind. But unlike gold, which perishes even when refined, my faith shall endure in abundant production and will result in praise, glory and honor when Jesus returns.

Though I have not seen Jesus, I love Him, believe in Him and rejoice with joy inexpressible and full of glory, for I have received the greatest product of my faith: the salvation of my soul.

(Ephesians 1:4-6; Titus 3:4-7; John 1:12; 3:3; 15:7,8; 20:29; Hebrews 12:22-24; Acts 4:33; 2 Corinthians 5:17; Matthew 6:19-21; 2 Peter 1:3,4; Romans 8:14-17; Psalm 5:11,12; Job 1:10; 1 Timothy 6:12; 1 Corinthians 9:24-27; James 1:2-4; 1 John 4:20)

1 PETER 1:13-23 KJV

Wherefore gird up the loins of your mind, be sober, and hope to the end for the grace that is to be brought unto you at the revelation of Jesus Christ; As obedient children, not fashioning yourselves according to the former lusts in your ignorance: But as he which hath called you is holy, so be ye holy in all manner of conversation; Because it is written, Be ye holy; for I am holy. And if ye call on the Father, who without respect of persons judgeth according to every man's work, pass the time of your sojourning *here* in fear: Forasmuch as ye know that ye were not redeemed with corruptible things, *as* silver and gold, from your vain conversation *received* by tradition from your fathers; But with the precious blood of Christ, as of a lamb without blemish and without spot: Who verily was foreordained before the foundation of the world, but was manifest in these last times for you, Who by him do believe in God, that raised him up from the dead, and gave him glory; that your faith and hope might be in God. Seeing ye have purified your souls in obeying the truth through the Spirit unto unfeigned love of the brethren, *see that ye* love one another with a pure heart fervently: Being born again, not of corruptible seed, but of incorruptible, by the word of God, which liveth and abideth for ever.

―――― *DECLARATION OF FAITH* ――――

I premeditate over the issues of life and prepare my mind beforehand for action. I purpose in my heart to know what to do in any situation I may face.

I remain sober, alert and self-controlled.

I set my hope immutable on the grace that will be brought to me on the day that Jesus is revealed.

As God's obedient son/daughter, I do not conform to the evil desires I had when I lived in ignorance.

Just as God, who called me, is holy, I also am holy in everything that I do; for it is written: "You shall be holy, because I am holy." I am obedient to my new nature as a born-again child of God. I know who I am and will not defile that knowledge by living as less than I am.

Since I call upon a Father who judges with impartiality, I will live my life in reverent respect for Him. I fully recognize that I was not redeemed from my fallen nature with corruptible things such as silver and gold, but was purchased with the precious blood of Jesus, the Lamb who was, and is, without spot or blemish. He was chosen before the creation of the world to be manifested in these last days for my sake. Through Him, I believe in God, who raised Him up from the dead and gave Him glory and honor, so that my faith and hope would remain centered in God alone.

I have now been purified by obeying the Truth and in me has been birthed a sincere and heartfelt love for the body of Christ. I love all of my brothers and sisters in Christ with a deep love that comes from a pure heart, for I have been born again, not of perishable seed, but of imperishable and eternal seed, through the living, active, unchanging, and enduring Word of God.

(Proverbs 16:9; Psalm 119:133; Ephesians 2:1-10; 5:18; 2 Timothy 1:7; Romans 3:25; 8:14-18; 12:1,2; Leviticus 11:44,45; 2 Corinthians 5:17; 2 Peter 1:4; Acts 10:34; 20:28; Exodus 12:5; Colossians 1:13,14; Galatians 4:4-6; 1 Corinthians 2:1-5; Hebrews 10:14; 1 John 4:7-21; James 1:18)

1 PETER 2:1-5 NIV

Therefore, rid yourselves of all malice and all deceit, hypocrisy, envy, and slander of every kind. Like newborn babies, crave pure spiritual milk, so that by it you may grow up in your salvation, now that you have tasted that the Lord is good. As you come to him, the living Stone—rejected by men but chosen by God and precious to him—you also, like living stones, are being built into a spiritual house to be a holy priesthood, offering spiritual sacrifices acceptable to God through Jesus Christ.

─────── *DECLARATION OF FAITH* ───────

I rid myself of all malice, hatred, and hostility. Deceit, hypocrisy, envy, and slander of every kind I cast far from my life.

Like a newborn baby, I crave spiritual milk so that by it I may grow up in my salvation. As I grow, I continue to feed upon it, for it is only the milk that helps me to swallow the meat. And I will never stop growing—taking in all that the Lord has for me—for I have tasted of His kindness and love, and I know that He is good to me.

I have come to the living stone—rejected by men, but chosen by God and precious to Him.

In Him, I also have become a living stone. I have been recreated as a holy priest, offering spiritual sacrifices acceptable to God through Jesus Christ my Lord.

(Hebrews 5:9-14; 6:5; 12:1,2; Colossians 3:8-10; 1 Corinthians 3:1-3; 10:3,4; Matthew 18:3,4; Psalm 118:22; 119:65; Isaiah 28:16; Revelation 1:5,6)

1 PETER 2:9-12 KJV

But ye *are* a chosen generation, a royal priesthood, an holy nation, a peculiar people; that ye should shew forth the praises of him who hath called you out of darkness into his marvellous light: Which in time past *were* not a people, but *are* now the people of God: which had not obtained mercy, but now have obtained mercy. Dearly beloved, I beseech *you* as strangers and pilgrims, abstain from fleshly lusts, which war against the soul; Having your conversation honest among the Gentiles: that, whereas they speak against you as evildoers, they may by *your* good works, which they shall behold, glorify God in the day of visitation.

─────── *DECLARATION OF FAITH* ───────

I have been specifically chosen by God to be a royal priest in His household—a citizen of a holy nation—a son/daughter of God who is of God and in every way belonging to Him. I have been snatched out of darkness and translated into His wonderful light. I give Him praise, honor, and glory for what He has done for me.

I was once a hostile alien with an abusive father (the devil), but now I am a son/daughter of God and a member of His family.

I was once a stranger to mercy, but now I am filled with the grace, mercy, and loving-kindness of my heavenly Father.

I am now an alien and a stranger to the world. I am resolved to abstain from all sinful desires which war against my soul. I live such a good life among unbelievers that, though they are always accusing me and trying to find fault in me, they cannot help but recognize my good deeds and give God glory every time they see what He is doing in my life.

(Ephesians 1:4; 2:1-10,19; Revelation 1:5,6; Galatians 4:4-6; John 8:44; 17:20-26; Isaiah 43:1; Romans 5:18; Hosea 1:9,10; Matthew 5:16; Philippians 2:14-16)

1 PETER 2:13-15 NKJV

Therefore submit yourselves to every ordinance of man for the Lord's sake, whether to the king as supreme, or to governors, as to those who are sent by him for the punishment of evildoers and *for the* praise of those who do good. For this is the will of God, that by doing good you may put to silence the ignorance of foolish men.

———— DECLARATION OF FAITH ————

For the Lord's sake, I submit myself to every authority instituted among men: whether to kings, prime ministers or presidents as the supreme authority of the government, or to governors, mayors, or judges who carry out justice, punishing those who do wrong and commending those who do right. It is God's will that through my good deeds and conduct I should silence the ignorant talk of foolish men.

(Romans 13:1-7; Matthew 22:21)

1 PETER 2:16,17 NIV

Live as free men, but do not use your freedom as a cover-up for evil; live as servants of God. Show proper respect to everyone: Love the brotherhood of believers, fear God, honor the king.

———— DECLARATION OF FAITH ————

I live my life as a free man/woman (free from the power and penalty of sin), but I do not use my freedom as a cover-up or excuse for evil. I live like a servant of God doing only those things that He has declared to be proper.

I show proper respect to everyone.

In all things, I display a deep and unwavering love for my family—the family of God.

I am careful to give God the respect that He deserves, while honoring the supreme authority of the government to which I am subject.

(Galatians 5:1,13; Romans 6:14-22; Proverbs 24:21; 1 John 4:7-21)

1 PETER 2:18,19 AMP

[You who are] household servants, be submissive to your masters with all [proper] respect, not only to those who are kind and considerate and reasonable, but also to those who are surly (overbearing, unjust, and crooked). For one is regarded favorably (is approved, acceptable, and thankworthy) if, as in the sight of God, he endures the pain of unjust suffering.

————— DECLARATION OF FAITH —————

(For employees)

I submit myself to my employer with all honor, integrity, and respect. I bear up under the pain of unjust suffering because I am God-inside minded. I know that He will see me through to victory no matter what my situation may be.

(Ephesians 6:5-8; Matthew 5:10-12; 1 Peter 2:20-23)

1 PETER 2:20-23 KJV

For what glory *is it,* if, when ye be buffeted for your faults, ye shall take it patiently? but if, when ye do well, and suffer *for it,* ye take it patiently, this *is* acceptable with God. For even hereunto were ye called: because Christ also suffered for us, leaving us an example, that ye should follow his steps: Who did no sin, neither was guile found in his mouth: Who, when he was reviled, reviled not again; when he suffered, he threatened not; but committed *himself* to him that judgeth righteously.

————— DECLARATION OF FAITH —————

It is commendable before God when I patiently persevere through unjust suffering.

To this I have been called: to follow in the footsteps of Jesus, who suffered for me, leaving me an example of how to endure it; for it is written: "He committed no sin, and no deceit was found in His mouth." When they hurled their insults at Him, He did not retaliate; and when He suffered, He made no threats. Instead, He entrusted Himself to Him who judges justly.

Knowing Jesus' reward, I too patiently endure unjust and unfair treatment, for I know that God is on my side. He is the One that I am working for and the One who will reward and promote me.

(James 1:2-4; Luke 6:32-34; Isaiah 53:9; Romans 8:31; 12:14-21; Colossians 3:17)

1 PETER 2:24,25 AMP

He personally bore our sins in His [own] body on the tree [as on an altar and offered Himself on it], that we might die (cease to exist) to sin and live to righteousness. By His wounds you have been healed. For you were going astray like [so many] sheep, but now you have come back to the Shepherd and Guardian (the Bishop) of your souls.

——— *DECLARATION OF FAITH* ———

Jesus bore my sins in His own body while on the cross so that I might die to sin and live unto righteousness. Through His torment and agony, I was healed (cured; made whole).

I was once like a runaway lamb, but now have returned to the Shepherd and overseer of my soul.

(Isaiah 53:4,5; Matthew 8:17; Hebrews 9:28; Ezekiel 34:23)

1 PETER 3:1-6 KJV

Likewise, ye wives, *be* in subjection to your own husbands; that, if any obey not the word, they also may without the word be won by the conversation of the wives; While they behold your chaste conversation *coupled* with fear. Whose adorning let it not be that outward *adorning* of plaiting the hair, and of wearing of gold, or of putting on of apparel; But *let it be* the hidden man of the heart, in that which is not corruptible, *even the ornament* of a meek and quiet spirit, which is in the sight of God of great price. For after this manner in the old time the holy women also, who trusted in God, adorned themselves, being in subjection unto their own husbands: Even as Sara obeyed Abraham, calling him lord: whose daughters ye are, as long as ye do well, and are not afraid with any amazement.

——— *DECLARATION OF FAITH* ———

(For wives)

I will submit myself to my own husband and none other. My behavior, both in his presence and out of it, will be pure and godly.

(For those with unbelieving husbands)

I do not need to preach the Word at my husband, for I have a Word which declares that my husband can be won without words, through my righteous and godly conduct, my reaching out to him in sincere love, and my reverence for God, my Father.

(For wives, continued...)

My true beauty has nothing to do with my outward adornments (such as hairstyle, makeup, jewelry, and fine clothes), but is in the manifestation of the real me, my inner self, the unfading beauty of a gentle and quiet spirit, which is precious to God. It is the manifestation of my spirit that causes me to gain physical beauty.

It is in this way that the holy women of the past put their hope in God to make themselves beautiful. They were always submissive to their own husbands, living their lives for them in every way.

(Genesis 20:2; Ephesians 5:22-33; 1 Corinthians 7:2-40; Romans 2:29; 2 Timothy 1:7; 2 Corinthians 1:20; Galatians 3:13,14)

1 PETER 3:7 NKJV

Husbands, likewise, dwell with *them* with understanding, giving honor to the wife, as to the weaker vessel, and as *being* heirs together of the grace of life, that your prayers may not be hindered.

—— *DECLARATION OF FAITH* ——

(For husbands)

I will likewise be submissive to my own wife. All that I am (spirit, soul, and body) I give in subjection to her will in the Lord. I will treat her with the utmost respect in full knowledge of her delicate nature. She is my life partner, my equal, and a co-heir of the gracious gift of life. I will not allow my prayers to be hindered by foolishly disrespecting or abusing her.

(Ephesians 5:22-33; 1 Corinthians 7:3,4; 12:23; Job 42:8; Mark 11:25,26)

1 PETER 3:8-12 KJV

Finally, *be ye* all of one mind, having compassion one of another, love as brethren, *be* pitiful, *be* courteous: Not rendering evil for evil, or railing for railing: but contrariwise blessing; knowing that ye are thereunto called, that ye should inherit a blessing. For he that will love life, and see good days, let him refrain his tongue from evil, and his lips that they speak no guile: Let him eschew evil, and do good; let him seek peace, and ensue it. For the eyes of the Lord *are* over the righteous, and his ears *are open* unto their prayers: but the face of the Lord *is* against them that do evil.

———— DECLARATION OF FAITH ————

I live in harmony with my brothers and sisters in Christ. I am sympathetic of their every need and love them as members of my own family. I remain courteous and respectful toward them, and show compassion for them at all times. I do not repay evil with evil, or insult for insult, but am always of a mind to bless them. I see things through the eyes of my Father and constantly pursue ways to bless people regardless of how they treat me. To this I have been called, and in doing so (blessing others), I plant the seeds that produce a harvest of blessings in my own life.

I am a lover of life who continually sees good days. I refrain my tongue from speaking negative things. I speak the truth at all times and never allow lies and deceit to become a part of me. I turn away from evil and only do that which is good. I am a seeker of peace and pursue it with all of my will.

I am the righteousness of God in Christ Jesus my Lord.

His eyes never leave me and I rest in His embrace. He is my shield of protection in this life. His ears are always opened to my prayers so that He can fulfill His Word on my behalf.

(John 17:20-26; Ephesians 4:1-6; 1 John 4:7-21; 5:14,15; Romans 12:9-21; Galatians 6:7-9; Psalm 5:11,12; 34:12-16; 2 Corinthians 5:21; Deuteronomy 33:12; Genesis 15:1; Isaiah 55:11; Jeremiah 1:12)

1 PETER 3:14-16 AMP

But even in case you should suffer for the sake of righteousness, [you are] blessed (happy, to be envied). Do not dread or be afraid of their threats, nor be disturbed [by their opposition]. But in your hearts set Christ apart as holy [and acknowledge Him] as Lord. Always be ready to give a logical defense to anyone who asks you to account for the hope that is in you, but do it courteously and respectfully. [And see to it that] your conscience is entirely clear (unimpaired), so that, when you are falsely accused as evildoers, those who threaten you abusively and revile your right behavior in Christ may come to be ashamed [of slandering your good lives].

Even when I suffer for doing what is right, I am blessed. Therefore, I will not be troubled by the threats of the ungodly, nor will I fear the things that the world fears.

In my heart, I set apart Christ as Lord. He is the governor of every aspect of my life.

I am always prepared to give an answer to everyone who asks me for a reason for this hope that I have within me. And I do this with all gentleness and respect, so that those who persecute me for doing what is right may be ashamed of their slander.

(Matthew 5:10-12; 2 Timothy 1:7; Joshua 1:5-9; Proverbs 16:7; James 1:12; Psalm 119:46)

1 PETER 3:18-22 KJV

For Christ also hath once suffered for sins, the just for the unjust, that he might bring us to God, being put to death in the flesh, but quickened by the Spirit: By which also he went and preached unto the spirits in prison; Which sometime were disobedient, when once the longsuffering of God waited in the days of Noah, while the ark was a preparing, wherein few, that is, eight souls were saved by water. The like figure whereunto *even* baptism doth also now save us (not the putting away of the filth of the flesh, but the answer of a good conscience toward God,) by the resurrection of Jesus Christ: Who is gone into heaven, and is on the right hand of God; angels and authorities and powers being made subject unto him.

——— DECLARATION OF FAITH ———

Jesus died for my sins, once for all, the righteous for the unrighteous, in order to bring me to God. In Him, I have now been made the very righteousness of God. He was put to death in the body, but regenerated (made alive) in His Spirit.

I, too, was dead in my trespasses and sins, but, in Him, have been regenerated (made alive) in my spirit.

I, in regard to my old nature, was killed off through crucifixion with Christ. I was buried with Him and raised to life with Him. He has become the ark for me. In Him, I am saved from the wrath that God is bringing on the earth.

Baptism is the pledge of my identification with Christ. Thus it should remove all sin consciousness from my life and establish me in a good conscience toward God.

What's more than this is that I am identified with Jesus in every way. Because He has gone into heaven and is now at God's right hand, I also, in Him, have gone into heaven and am now at God's right hand.

Angels, authorities, and powers are in submission to Jesus and, through Him, angels, authorities, and powers are in submission to me as well.

(Hebrews 1:3; 2:5-14; 10:10; 2 Corinthians 5:17-21; Romans 4:23-25; 6:4-6; 10:8-10; Titus 3:4-7; Ephesians 1:17-23; 2:4-10; Luke 10:17-19; Galatians 2:16-21)

1 PETER 4:1,2 NKJV

Therefore, since Christ suffered for us in the flesh, arm yourselves also with the same mind, for he who has suffered in the flesh has ceased from sin, that he no longer should live the rest of *his* time in the flesh for the lusts of men, but for the will of God.

——— *DECLARATION OF FAITH* ———

I am armed with the mind and attitude of Christ. Jesus is totally finished with sin. It has been cast away from Him and no longer has any power over Him. Therefore, I too am finished with sin. It no longer has any power over me and I have cast it far from my life. I no longer live in lust, but in the will of God.

(1 Corinthians 2:16; Philippians 2:5-13; Romans 6:4-7,14; John 4:34; Ephesians 4:1-3)

1 PETER 4:7-11 KJV

But the end of all things is at hand: be ye therefore sober, and watch unto prayer. And above all things have fervent charity among yourselves: for charity shall cover the multitude of sins. Use hospitality one to another without grudging. As every man hath received the gift, *even so* minister the same one to another, as good stewards of the manifold grace of God. If any man speak, *let him speak* as the oracles of God; if any man minister, *let him do it* as of the ability which God giveth: that God in all things may be glorified through Jesus Christ, to whom be praise and dominion for ever and ever. Amen.

——— *DECLARATION OF FAITH* ———

I shall remain clear-minded, sober, and self-controlled so that I can pray with tremendous results.

Above all, I love my family with all of my heart, and my love covers a multitude of sins.

I offer hospitality to others without grumbling, even if the person to whom I am showing hospitality is a pain in the neck.

I use the gifts that I have received to serve others, and I faithfully administer God's grace in its many forms.

When I speak, I do so as one speaking the very Words of God, and when I serve, I do so with all of the strength and ability that God has given me. In these things God receives tremendous praise through Jesus Christ my Lord. To Him be the glory and power forever more!

(1 Thessalonians 5:6-9; James 5:16; 1 John 4:7-21; Proverbs 10:12; Hebrews 13:1,2; Ephesians 4:11,12,29; Romans 12:6-9; 1 Corinthians 10:31)

1 PETER 4:14 MESSAGE

If you're abused because of Christ, count yourself fortunate. It's the Spirit of God and his glory in you that brought you to the notice of others.

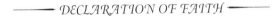 DECLARATION OF FAITH

If I am insulted because of the name of Christ, I am blessed, for the Spirit of glory and of God rests on me.

(Matthew 5:10-12,16; James 1:2-4)

1 PETER 4:16 NIV

However, if you suffer as a Christian, do not be ashamed, but praise God that you bear that name.

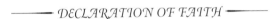 DECLARATION OF FAITH

It does not bother me that I suffer disgrace [in the eyes of the world] because I bear the name of Jesus. I praise God that I bear that name!

(Romans 1:16; Matthew 5:10-12)

1 PETER 5:2,3 KJV

Feed the flock of God which is among you, taking the oversight *thereof,* not by constraint, but willingly; not for filthy lucre, but of a ready mind; Neither as being lords over *God's* heritage, but being ensamples to the flock.

DECLARATION OF FAITH

(For pastors, bishops, elders, and all of those in pastoral ministry)
I am a shepherd of the portion of God's flock that has been placed under my care. God Himself has entrusted them to me and I will not let Him, or them, down. I serve as an overseer, not because I must, but because I am willing, just as God wants me to be. I am not greedy for money, but eager to serve. I do not use

my authority to bully those whom God has given me, but live my life as an example for them to follow.

(Acts 20:28; 1 Timothy 3:1-7; Ezekiel 34:2-5; Philippians 3:17)

1 PETER 5:5A NKJV

Likewise you younger people, submit yourselves to *your* elders.

——— *DECLARATION OF FAITH* ———

(For young men and women)

I will always remain in submission to those who are older and more experienced in the ways of righteousness.

(Proverbs 1:1-7:27; Ecclesiastes 11:9,10; Psalm 119:9; Ephesians 6:1-3)

1 PETER 5:5B-7 NKJV

Yes, all of you be submissive to one another, and be clothed with humility, for "God resists the proud, but gives grace to the humble." Therefore humble yourselves under the mighty hand of God, that He may exalt you in due time, casting all your care upon Him, for He cares for you.

——— *DECLARATION OF FAITH* ———

It is written: "God resists the proud, but gives grace to the humble." Therefore, I clothe myself with humility towards my brothers and sisters in Christ.

I humble myself under God's mighty hand, knowing that He will exalt me in His perfect timing. I cast all of my fears, worries and anxieties upon Him, for He cares for me deeply and will not allow me to be overcome by troubles and sorrow.

(Matthew 25:5-7; James 4:1-10; Philippians 4:6,7; Isaiah 43:1,2)

1 PETER 5:8-11 KJV

Be sober, be vigilant; because your adversary the devil, as a roaring lion, walketh about, seeking whom he may devour: Whom resist stedfast in the faith, knowing that the same afflictions are accomplished in your brethren that are in the world. But the God of all grace, who hath called us unto his eternal glory by Christ Jesus, after that ye have suffered a while, make you perfect, stablish, strengthen, settle *you*. To him *be* glory and dominion for ever and ever. Amen.

——— *DECLARATION OF FAITH* ———

I remain self-controlled and alert, for I know that my enemy, the devil, prowls around like a roaring lion looking for someone to devour. I am fully aware of his evil schemes and he can never catch me by surprise. I resist him, standing firm in faith and in the realization that I have brothers and sisters all over the world who are fighting him as well. My Father, the God of all grace, who called me to His eternal glory in Christ, will Himself restore and deliver me out of any and every adverse circumstance the devil devises against me. In Christ, I am strong, firm, steadfast and immovable—a solid rock who gives the devil a perpetual headache.

(2 Timothy 1:7; 3:11; 1 Thessalonians 5:6; 2 Corinthians 2:11; James 4:7; 1 Corinthians 1:9; Ephesians 2:6; 6:10; Mark 3:27)

CHAPTER SIXTY-ONE

2 PETER

This is Peter's second epistle and was probably written a year or two after the first (around 65 or 66 AD). This second epistle addresses many areas of our walk with the Lord. Promise after promise is stated and we are given clear instruction as to who we are and how we are supposed to live as God's children.

While speaking these promises into your life, take a moment to consider and recognize what it means to have all things that pertain unto life and godliness, at what it truly means to live the life that God wants you to live.

---

2 PETER 1:2-4 KJV

Grace and peace be multiplied unto you through the knowledge of God, and of Jesus our Lord, According as his divine power hath given unto us all things that *pertain* unto life and godliness, through the knowledge of him that hath called us to glory and virtue: Whereby are given unto us exceeding great and precious promises: that by these ye might be partakers of the divine nature, having escaped the corruption that is in the world through lust.

— DECLARATION OF FAITH —

Grace and peace are mine in abundance through the knowledge of God and of Jesus Christ my Lord.

Through His divine power I have been given all things that pertain unto life and godliness. These things He has bestowed upon me through my deep and personal knowledge of Him who has called me into His own glory and goodness. In Jesus, all of God's great and precious promises have been given to me personally. Through these promises, I have become a partaker of His divine nature and have escaped the corruption in the world caused by evil desires.

So, as a born-again son/daughter of God: (1) I have been given all things that pertain unto life and godliness; (2) I have a deep and personal knowledge of Him who has called me; (3) I have entered into His own glory and goodness; (4) all of His great and precious promises are applied to me; (5) I have become a partaker of the very divine nature of God; and (6) I have escaped the corruption in the world caused by evil desires.

(Psalm 37:11; Romans 5:17; 8:28-30; Ephesians 1:3; 2:1-10; 2 Corinthians 1:20; 5:17,21; John 17:20-26; 1 Corinthians 2:6-16; 1 John 2:20,27; 5:20; 1 Thessalonians 2:12,13)

2 PETER 1:5-8 AMP

For this very reason, adding your diligence [to the divine promises], employ every effort in exercising your faith to develop virtue (excellence, resolution, Christian energy), and in [exercising] virtue [develop] knowledge (intelligence), and in [exercising] knowledge [develop] self-control, and in [exercising] self-control [develop] steadfastness (patience, endurance), and in [exercising] steadfastness [develop] godliness (piety), and in [exercising] godliness [develop] brotherly affection, and in [exercising] brotherly affection [develop] Christian love. For as these qualities are yours and increasingly abound in you, they will keep [you] from being idle or unfruitful unto the [full personal] knowledge of our Lord Jesus Christ (the Messiah, the Anointed One).

——— *DECLARATION OF FAITH* ———

I make every effort to add the goodness of God to my faith; and to goodness, knowledge; and to knowledge, self-control; and to self-control, perseverance; and to perseverance, godliness; and to godliness, brotherly kindness; and to brotherly kindness, love. By keeping all of these qualities in increasing measure, I remain effective and productive in my knowledge of Jesus.

(Galatians 5:6; 2 Peter 3:18; 1 Peter 3:7; 1 Corinthians 2:6-16; 13:4-8; 2 Timothy 1:7; James 1:2-4; Romans 12:9-13; John 15:5)

2 PETER 1:10,11 NKJV

Therefore, brethren, be even more diligent to make your call and election sure, for if you do these things you will never stumble; for so an entrance will be supplied to you abundantly into the everlasting kingdom of our Lord and Savior Jesus Christ.

——— *DECLARATION OF FAITH* ———

I make it my business to establish myself firmly in my calling so that I will never fail in the things that I am called to do. In doing so, I have assurance that one day I will receive a rich welcome into the eternal kingdom of my Lord and Savior Jesus Christ.

In every way I will be the person that God created me to be.

(Romans 11:29; 1 John 3:19; Philippians 1:12,13; Luke 16:9)

2 PETER 2:9 MESSAGE

So God knows how to rescue the godly from evil trials. And he knows how to hold the feet of the wicked to the fire until Judgment Day.

———— *DECLARATION OF FAITH* ————

The Lord knows exactly how to rescue me from any trial that I am enduring. I am destined for victory!

(2 Timothy 3:11; Romans 8:31,27; 1 Corinthians 15:57)

2 PETER 3:1 AMP

Beloved, I am now writing you this second letter. In [both of] them I have stirred up your unsullied (sincere) mind by way of remembrance.

———— *DECLARATION OF FAITH* ————

I read the Word continually in order to stimulate my mind toward wholesome thinking.

(Joshua 1:8; Philippians 4:8; Psalm 1:1-3)

2 PETER 3:11 NIV

Since everything will be destroyed in this way, what kind of people ought you to be? You ought to live holy and godly lives.

———— *DECLARATION OF FAITH* ————

I live a holy and godly life as I look forward in eager anticipation to the day of God and the coming of Jesus.

(1 Peter 1:13-16; Revelation 22:20; 1 Corinthians 1:7,8)

2 PETER 3:13,14 KJV

Nevertheless we, according to his promise, look for new heavens and a new earth, wherein dwelleth righteousness. Wherefore, beloved, seeing that ye look for such things, be diligent that ye may be found of him in peace, without spot, and blameless.

─── *DECLARATION OF FAITH* ───

I know that God is faithful and will honor all of His promises. In keeping with His promise, I am looking forward to a new heaven and a new earth, where righteousness dwells and is the lifestyle of all. Therefore, I make every effort to be found spotless, blameless, and at peace with Him.

(2 Corinthians 1:20; Isaiah 55:11; Psalm 119; 138,140; Revelation 21:1-8; Jude 24)

2 PETER 3:17,18 NKJV

You therefore, beloved, since you know *this* beforehand, beware lest you also fall from your own steadfastness, being led away with the error of the wicked; but grow in the grace and knowledge of our Lord and Savior Jesus Christ. To Him *be* the glory both now and forever. Amen.

─── *DECLARATION OF FAITH* ───

I remain studied up and on guard so that I cannot be carried away by the errors of lawless men who would cause me to fall from my secure position.

I continually increase, growing in grace and in the knowledge of my Lord and Savior Jesus Christ. To Him be the glory both now and forevermore! Amen!

(2 Timothy 2:15; 4:18; Acts 17:10,11; Ephesians 4:14-16)

CHAPTER SIXTY-TWO

1 JOHN

The book of 1 John was written by the apostle John somewhere around 80-95 AD. The book's themes center on the subjects of fellowship with God, forgiveness, the nature of salvation, the love of God and receiving from God. The overall message is that love is the key to every aspect of our faith. To love is to walk a walk of faith free of all fear and anxiety.

As you speak the promises of this book, search your heart. Do you love God? Do you love your neighbor? Do you love yourself? The personalized scriptures in this book will help you to answer yes to all three of these questions.

＋

1 John 1:3-10 KJV

That which we have seen and heard declare we unto you, that ye also may have fellowship with us: and truly our fellowship *is* with the Father, and with his Son Jesus Christ. And these things write we unto you, that your joy may be full. This then is the message which we have heard of him, and declare unto you, that God is light, and in him is no darkness at all. If we say that we have fellowship with him, and walk in darkness, we lie, and do not the truth: But if we walk in the light, as he is in the light, we have fellowship one with another, and the blood of Jesus Christ his Son cleanseth us from all sin. If we say that we have no sin, we deceive ourselves, and the truth is not in us. If we confess our sins, he is faithful and just to forgive us *our* sins, and to cleanse us from all unrighteousness. If we say that we have not sinned, we make him a liar, and his word is not in us.

—— *DECLARATION OF FAITH* ——

I have been called into fellowship with God and with His Son Jesus Christ.
I find completeness of joy within the Word of God.
God is Light and in Him is no darkness at all.
I am in Him.
I have a close and intimate relationship my Father.
I do not walk in darkness, but live by the light of the Truth.

I walk in the Light, as He is in the Light. In doing so, I maintain fellowship with all of my brothers and sisters in Christ, and the blood of Jesus, the Son of God, cleanses me from all sin.

I freely admit that I have sinned. Therefore, being faithful and just, He has forgiven all of my sin and cleansed me from all unrighteousness. In this, I, through Him, bring honor to God and His Word has a secure place in my life.

(John 3:16-21; 5:44; 16:23,24; Joshua 1:8; 1 John 2:9-11; 5:14,15; 1 Timothy 6:16; 2 Corinthians 8:4; 1 Corinthians 6:11; Romans 3:24-26; Psalm 51:2; 103:10-12; Isaiah 1:18)

1 JOHN 2:1-6 AMP

My little children, I write you these things so that you may not violate God's law and sin. But if anyone should sin, we have an Advocate (One Who will intercede for us) with the Father—[it is] Jesus Christ [the all] righteous [upright, just, Who conforms to the Father's will in every purpose, thought, and action].

And He [that same Jesus Himself] is the propitiation (the atoning sacrifice) for our sins, and not for ours alone but also for [the sins of] the whole world. And this is how we may discern [daily, by experience] that we are coming to know Him [to perceive, recognize, understand, and become better acquainted with Him]: if we keep (bear in mind, observe, practice) His teachings (precepts, commandments). Whoever says, I know Him [I perceive, recognize, understand, and am acquainted with Him] but fails to keep and obey His commandments (teachings) is a liar, and the Truth [of the Gospel] is not in him. But he who keeps (treasures) His Word [who bears in mind His precepts, who observes His message in its entirety], truly in him has the love of and for God been perfected (completed, reached maturity). By this we may perceive (know, recognize, and be sure) that we are in Him: Whoever says he abides in Him ought [as a personal debt] to walk and conduct himself in the same way in which He walked and conducted Himself.

──── *DECLARATION OF FAITH* ────

I do not see my secure position in Jesus as an excuse to sin. However, if I do sin, I have One who speaks to God the Father in my defense: my Lord and Savior, Jesus Christ the righteous. He is the propitiation (the go between; the one who makes amends) for my sins, and not for mine only, but also for the sins of the whole world.

I know that I have come to know Him, because I love the purity of His commands and I have purposed to joyfully obey them from my heart. Anyone who says, "I know Him," but doesn't like to do what He says is a liar who is bereft of the truth.

God's Word is precious to me. I joyfully obey it, even though at times I have fallen short of it. Yet, my heart's desire is to obey His commands and live my life in purity and holiness. Because of this, God's love is truly made complete in me.

I also know that I am in Him because I walk the way that Jesus walked. I have taken up His ministry as my own.

(Romans 3:25; 6:1,2,7,14; 8:1,2,34; Hebrews 7:25; John 3:16,17; 14:12; 15:10-12; 17:20-26; Joshua 1:8; Psalm 119:16,147,148,160-162; 1 Peter 1:13-16; 2:21)

1 JOHN 2:10 NIV

Whoever loves his brother lives in the light, and there is nothing in him to make him stumble.

———— DECLARATION OF FAITH ————

I love my brothers and sisters in Christ with all of my heart—even the ones that aren't so easy to love. I live in the Light and there is nothing in me that can make me stumble.

(1 John 4:7-21; 1 Corinthians 13:4-8; Romans 12:9,10; 2 Peter 1:10; Ephesians 4:25-32)

1 JOHN 2:12-14 NKJV

I write to you, little children,
Because your sins are forgiven you for His name's sake.
I write to you, fathers,
Because you have known Him *who is* from the beginning.
I write to you, young men,
Because you have overcome the wicked one.
I write to you, little children,
Because you have known the Father.
I have written to you, fathers,
Because you have known Him *who is* from the beginning.
I have written to you, young men,
Because you are strong, and the word of God abides in you,
And you have overcome the wicked one.

———— DECLARATION OF FAITH ————

My sins have been forgiven on account of the name of Jesus.
I know Him who is from the beginning.

I have overcome the evil one.

I know the Father.

I am strong and the Word of God is alive and active within me.

I have overcome the evil one!

(Hebrews 10:10-17; 1 Corinthians 6:11; 2 Corinthians 5:17-21; Colossians 1:13; 2:15; Luke 10:19; John 14:7; 17:20-26; Romans 8:14-17; Galatians 4:4-6; 1 John 4:4; 5:4,5; Revelation 12:11)

1 JOHN 2:15-17 KJV

Love not the world, neither the things *that are* in the world. If any man love the world, the love of the Father is not in him. For all that *is* in the world, the lust of the flesh, and the lust of the eyes, and the pride of life, is not of the Father, but is of the world. And the world passeth away, and the lust thereof: but he that doeth the will of God abideth for ever.

——— *DECLARATION OF FAITH* ———

I do not cherish the world or the things that the world has to offer [outside of, or contrary to, the things of God], for I know that those who cherish the world do not have the love of the Father in them. I also know that everything of the world—the cravings of the fallen nature, the lusts of the eyes and all arrogant boasting—does not come from the Father, but from the world.

The world and all of its desires will pass away, but I, as a born-again child of God, doing the will of God, shall remain and live the God-kind of life throughout eternity.

(Romans 12:1,2; 2 Corinthians 6:14; James 4:4; Galatians 5:19-21; John 3:16)

1 JOHN 2:20 AMP

But you have been anointed by [you hold a sacred appointment from, you have been given an unction from] the Holy One, and you all know [the Truth] or you know all things.

——— *DECLARATION OF FAITH* ———

I have an anointing from the Holy One to know and understand all things.

(Daniel 1:17,20; 2:22,23; 1 Corinthians 1:30; 2:6-16; Matthew 13:11,15,16; John 16:13)

1 JOHN 2:24,25 NIV

See that what you have heard from the beginning remains in you. If it does, you also will remain in the Son and in the Father. And this is what he promised us—even eternal life.

——— *DECLARATION OF FAITH* ———

I make it my business to maintain within me the very Gospel which brought me to salvation.

The promise of eternal life is fulfilled in me.

I will remain in the Son and in the Father.

(Joshua 1:8; Psalm 1:1-3; John 3:16; 14:23; 15:7; 1 John 5:11,12)

1 JOHN 2:27-29 KJV

But the anointing which ye have received of him abideth in you, and ye need not that any man teach you: but as the same anointing teacheth you of all things, and is truth, and is no lie, and even as it hath taught you, ye shall abide in him. And now, little children, abide in him; that, when he shall appear, we may have confidence, and not be ashamed before him at his coming. If ye know that he is righteous, ye know that every one that doeth righteousness is born of him.

——— *DECLARATION OF FAITH* ———

The anointing that I have received from God remains living and active within me. Though God has established many teachers to open up the Word for me, I do not always need someone else to teach me the Truth, for I know it from within. The anointing causes messages of Truth to bear witness with my spirit as I delve into the Word and see it for myself.

The Holy Spirit that I have within me teaches me about all things. He is real and vital to my understanding of the Word.

I shall remain in Jesus, just as the anointing has led me to do. I will remain in Him, so that when He appears I can be confident and unashamed before Him at His coming.

I cannot be duped by anyone. I know that my Lord is righteous and that everyone who does what is righteous has been born of Him.

(1 John 2:20; 3:7-10; Isaiah 61:1-3; John 14:6,12,16; 16:13; Acts 22:14; Matthew 13:11,15,16; 2 Corinthians 5:17-21)

1 JOHN 3:1-3 NKJV

Behold what manner of love the Father has bestowed on us, that we should be called children of God! Therefore the world does not know us, because it did not know Him. Beloved, now we are children of God; and it has not yet been revealed what we shall be, but we know that when He is revealed, we shall be like Him, for we shall see Him as He is. And everyone who has this hope in Him purifies himself, just as He is pure.

DECLARATION OF FAITH

How great is the Father's love for me that I should be called the son/daughter of God! And that is what I am! I am now God's own son/daughter! It has not yet been revealed what I will be at Jesus' coming, but I know that when He appears I shall be like Him, for I shall see Him as He truly is. Therefore, having such a tremendous and awe-inspiring hope, I will purify myself, just as He is pure.

(Galatians 4:4-6; Romans 8:14-17,28-30; 1 Peter 1:13-16; Psalm 16:11)

1 JOHN 3:5-7 KJV

And ye know that he was manifested to take away our sins; and in him is no sin. Whosoever abideth in him sinneth not: whosoever sinneth hath not seen him, neither known him. Little children, let no man deceive you: he that doeth right-eousness is righteous, even as he is righteous.

DECLARATION OF FAITH

Jesus appeared in order to take away my sins. And my sins have indeed been taken away. I now have a new nature and a drive toward righteousness. I no longer practice sin in my life, for it is totally contrary to my new nature.

I fully understand that no truly born-again person will continue to live a sinful life. They may stumble here and there, but to happily live in it goes against everything they were recreated to be. Therefore, I know that anyone who contin-ues in sin has neither seen Him nor known Him.

I will not allow anyone to lead me astray. The one who does what is right is righteous, just as Jesus is righteous. The one who continues a life of sin is under the influence of the devil. The reason Jesus appeared was to destroy the devil's work. Therefore, I am no longer the devil's puppet. As a born-again child of God I do not continue in sin, because God's seed remains in me. It is impossible for me to be happy and satisfied with a sinful life, because I have been born of God.

Now this is how I know of a certainty that I have been born of God: I truly desire to do what is right and cannot be happy or satisfied with a life of sin. This proves that I have been given a new nature and I am truly born again.

I have become a member of the household of God. I love my brothers and sisters in Christ with all of my heart. My heart's desire is to do what is right and to please my heavenly Father in every way.

Those who profess faith, but are truly of the household of the devil cannot fool me. If they are satisfied with sin and hate the Church, they prove themselves to be children of Satan.

(John 3:16,17; Psalm 103:10-12; 2 Peter 1:4; Hebrews 10:14-17; Galatians 4:4-6; 5:22-25; Matthew 13:38; Luke 10:18,19; Colossians 1:13; 2:15; 1 Peter 1:23; 3:10-12; 2 Corinthians 5:17; Ephesians 2:1-10; 1 John 4:7-21)

1 JOHN 3:16-24 KJV

Hereby perceive we the love *of God*, because he laid down his life for us: and we ought to lay down *our* lives for the brethren. But whoso hath this world's good, and seeth his brother have need, and shutteth up his bowels *of compassion* from him, how dwelleth the love of God in him? My little children, let us not love in word, neither in tongue; but in deed and in truth. And hereby we know that we are of the truth, and shall assure our hearts before him. For if our heart condemn us, God is greater than our heart, and knoweth all things. Beloved, if our heart condemn us not, *then* have we confidence toward God. And whatsoever we ask, we receive of him, because we keep his commandments, and do those things that are pleasing in his sight. And this is his commandment, That we should believe on the name of his Son Jesus Christ, and love one another, as he gave us commandment. And he that keepeth his commandments dwelleth in him, and he in him. And hereby we know that he abideth in us, by the Spirit which he hath given us.

—— DECLARATION OF FAITH ——

This is how I know what love is: Jesus Christ laid down His life for me. In light of this, I will lay down my life for the Church.

If I see a brother or sister in need, and I have the means to help them, I do so. I do not just say I love my family, but prove it through the things that I do.

It is this that gives me assurance that I belong to the Truth. It sets my heart at rest in His presence in those times when, in my heart, I feel condemned; for God is greater than my heart, and He knows everything. And I know that, in [or from] Him, I do not suffer condemnation of any kind.

My heart does not condemn me, for I have rid myself of all condemnation consciousness. I have confidence in God's presence and know of a certainty that I receive anything and everything that I ask of Him. I maintain this confidence by following the influence of my new nature, obeying His commands and doing that which is pleasing in His sight.

This is His command to me: that I believe in the name of Jesus [in its power and authority in the earth and that I have been given legal power of attorney to use it] and that I have an active love for the Church.

I obey my Lord's every command.

I have truly become one with Him. I am in Him and He is in me. Together, we are one.

God has given me His Spirit to assure and comfort me. Through the Spirit, I know that I am His and that He lives within me.

(John 3:16,17; 10:11,17,18; 14:12-21; 15:10-13; 16:13; 17:20-26; Deuteronomy 15:7; Ezekiel 33:31; 1 John 4:7-21; 5:11,12,14,15; Romans 8:1,2; 2 Peter 1:4; Ephesians 1:13,14)

1 JOHN 4:1-6 NKJV

Beloved, do not believe every spirit, but test the spirits, whether they are of God; because many false prophets have gone out into the world. By this you know the Spirit of God: Every spirit that confesses that Jesus Christ has come in the flesh is of God, and every spirit that does not confess that Jesus Christ has come in the flesh is not of God. And this is the spirit of the Antichrist, which you have heard was coming, and is now already in the world.

You are of God, little children, and have overcome them, because He who is in you is greater than he who is in the world. They are of the world. Therefore they speak as of the world, and the world hears them. We are of God. He who knows God hears us; he who is not of God does not hear us. By this we know the spirit of truth and the spirit of error.

——— *DECLARATION OF FAITH* ———

I do not believe or follow every spirit, but test the spirits to see if they are from God. I know that there are many false prophets in the world, speaking for the devil and demons, and trying to dissuade me from the Truth. Therefore, I remain alert and on guard against them.

I know how to distinguish the Spirit of God from demon spirits. Every spirit that joyfully acknowledges that Jesus is the Christ and Lord of all is from God, but every spirit that does not joyfully acknowledge this, but seeks to destroy, annul, and cause division and disunity is not from God. Such a spirit is a spirit of Antichrist, which is common in the earth today.

I am of God and have already defeated and overcome Satan, devils and all spirits of Antichrist, because greater is He who is in me than he who is in the world.

They are the instigators of the world system and speak from the viewpoint of that system, and the world listens to them.

I am one with God. I know Him and listen to His true prophets, messengers and teachers. Those who are not of God, but follow the world system [with its sensual manner of life], reject the Truth of God spoken through His messengers. They hate the things that God's men and women have to say. This is another way in which I can recognize the spirit of Truth from the spirit of falsehood.

(Acts 17:10,11; John 14:17; 15:19; 16:11-13; 17:14,20-16; 1 Corinthians 2:6-16; 12:1-3; 14:19; Matthew 24:5; Luke 10:18,19; Colossians 1:13; 2:15; 1 John 2:15-17,20,27; Revelation 1:17,18; Romans 16:17-19)

1 JOHN 4:7 NKJV

Beloved, let us love one another, for love is of God; and everyone who loves is born of God and knows God.

———— DECLARATION OF FAITH ————

I show my love for the body of Christ continually.

All of my ability to love comes from God. As I am in Him, and He in me, His love pours forth from me in abundance. I love because I have been born of God and know God.

(John 17:20-26; 1 John 2:11; 3:10,11,16-18; 4:10; 5:1,2; 1 Corinthians 13:4-8; Romans 12:9,10)

1 JOHN 4:9,10 NIV

This is how God showed his love among us: He sent his one and only Son into the world that we might live through him. This is love: not that we loved God, but that he loved us and sent his Son as an atoning sacrifice for our sins.

———— DECLARATION OF FAITH ————

God showed His own love for me by sending Jesus into the world so that I might live through Him.

This is love in its purest form—not that I instigated this love relationship I now enjoy with the Father, but He loved me so much that He sent Jesus to me. He did this so that He could turn His wrath away from me and make me His own son/daughter. Indeed, I am forgiven of all sin and am now the very son/daughter of almighty God!

(John 3:16,17; Ephesians 2:1-10; Galatians 4:4-6; Romans 5:6-8)

1 JOHN 4:12,13 KJV

No man hath seen God at any time. If we love one another, God dwelleth in us, and his love is perfected in us. Hereby know we that we dwell in him, and he in us, because he hath given us of his Spirit.

——— *DECLARATION OF FAITH* ———

If I love the Church with all of my heart, it shows that God lives in me, and I in Him. His love is made complete in me.

I know that I live in Him, and He in me, because He has given me His Holy Spirit.

(1 John 2:11; 3:10,11,16-18; Romans 12:9,10; John 14:20; 15:9-17; 16:13)

1 JOHN 4:15-18 KJV

Whosoever shall confess that Jesus is the Son of God, God dwelleth in him, and he in God. And we have known and believed the love that God hath to us. God is love; and he that dwelleth in love dwelleth in God, and God in him. Herein is our love made perfect, that we may have boldness in the day of judgment: because as he is, so are we in this world. There is no fear in love; but perfect love casteth out fear: because fear hath torment. He that feareth is not made perfect in love.

——— *DECLARATION OF FAITH* ———

I acknowledge that Jesus is the Son of God; therefore, God lives in me and I in Him.

I both know and rely upon the love that God has for me.

God is love. As I live in God, I live in love, and God lives in me.

God's love is made complete in me so that I will have confidence in the Day of Judgment. As He is, so am I in this world. He is my example and my life. I purpose with all of my heart to be like Him in every way possible.

Therefore, I will allow no fear, terror, worry, or anxiety to enter my life for any reason whatsoever, for there is no fear in love. The perfect love that is within me drives out fear, because, in every case, fear has to do with punishment or torment of one kind or another. I do not need to fear the punishment of the curse [of the Law of Moses], judgment for my sins, or eternal punishment in hell, for I have been redeemed!

God is on my side in any and every circumstance. He is always for me, and never against me.

I will greet death with joy when my days are complete. It will be the home-coming that I have longed for.

So what do I have to fear? As I am in God, and made perfect in His love, fear becomes absolutely ridiculous to me.

(1 John 2:28; 4:7; 5:1,10-12; John 14:12; 2 Timothy 1:7; Joshua 1:5-9; 1 Peter 5:5-7; Romans 8:31; 1 Corinthians 15:54-58; Hebrews 10:14-17)

1 JOHN 5:1-5 KJV

Whosoever believeth that Jesus is the Christ is born of God: and every one that loveth him that begat loveth him also that is begotten of him. By this we know that we love the children of God, when we love God, and keep his commandments. For this is the love of God, that we keep his commandments: and his commandments are not grievous. For whatsoever is born of God overcometh the world: and this is the victory that overcometh the world, *even* our faith. Who is he that overcometh the world, but he that believeth that Jesus is the Son of God?

——— *DECLARATION OF FAITH* ———

I believe that Jesus is the Christ; therefore, I have been born of God.

I clearly see the bigger picture of God's family. As I love the Father, I love His child as well, for we all are one.

I know that I love the Church, because I love God and carry out His commands.

I show my love for God when I obey His commands. His commands are not burdensome to me, but are pure and precious. They are perfectly reasonable and not in the least bit difficult to obey so long as I remain God-inside minded.

I have been born of God and have overcome the world. My faith is my victory. All circumstances must yield to it. Through my faith, I overcome obstacles, setbacks, problems and troubles of every kind.

I believe that Jesus is the Son of God, and in Him, I have overcome the world.

(John 1:12,13; 14:15; 15:9-17; 16:33; Romans 12:9,10; Hebrews 10:24,25; 11:1; 1 John 2:13; Matthew 11:28-30; Psalm 119:160-165; 2 Corinthians 4:13; 5:7; Mark 11:22-25; Revelation 12:11)

1 JOHN 5:11 NIV

And this is the testimony: God has given us eternal life, and this life is in his Son.

——— *DECLARATION OF FAITH* ———

My testimony to the world is this: God has given me eternal life, and that life is in His Son Jesus. I am in Him, and He is in me. Together, we have become one.

(John 3:16; 14:20; 17:20-26; Romans 8:16)

1 JOHN 5:13-15 KJV

These things have I written unto you that believe on the name of the Son of God; that ye may know that ye have eternal life, and that ye may believe on the name of the Son of God. And this is the confidence that we have in him, that, if we ask any thing according to his will, he heareth us: And if we know that he hear us, whatsoever we ask, we know that we have the petitions that we desired of him.

DECLARATION OF FAITH

I believe in the name of the Son of God and know of a certainty that I have eternal life.

I have confidence when I approach God. Because of Jesus, I have absolutely no sense of inadequacy in God's presence. I know that I am accepted as His own son/daughter and welcomed into the throne room no matter what the circumstance may be in my life.

I am fully confident that when I ask anything according to His will [in line with His Word] He hears me. And I know that if He hears me, I have whatever it is that I have asked of Him.

My God is a good God. He is not looking for reasons to keep things from me, but is more than willing to provide me with anything I desire that is in line with His Word and a righteous life.

(John 3:16,17; 14:13,14; 15:7; 16:23,24; Hebrews 4:16; Galatians 4:4-6; 2 Peter 1:3; Romans 8:32; Matthew 10:41,42)

1 JOHN 5:18-20 KJV

We know that whosoever is born of God sinneth not; but he that is begotten of God keepeth himself, and that wicked one toucheth him not. *And* we know that we are of God, and the whole world lieth in wickedness. And we know that the Son of God is come, and hath given us an understanding, that we may know him that is true, and we are in him that is true, *even* in his Son Jesus Christ. This is the true God, and eternal life.

DECLARATION OF FAITH

I have been born of God; therefore, I do not continue to live a life of sin. My elder brother, the firstborn of the family [the first one to be born of God], keeps me safe, and the devil cannot touch me.

I know that I am God's own son/daughter and that everyone around me, who is not in the family, is under the power of the evil one.

I know also that Jesus has come and that He is with me right now. He has given me thorough ability to understand the truth. He is the One who is true, and I have a deep and intimate knowledge of Him. I am in Him and He is in me. He is my Lord and my Savior. He is the true God and eternal life.

(John 1:12,13; 3:3; 8:44; 17:20-26; Romans 8:14-17,28-30; Job 1:10; Psalm 91:10-13; Galatians 1:4; 4:4-6; Matthew 28:20; 1 Corinthians 1:30; 2:6-16; 1 John 2:20,27; 5:11,12)

1 JOHN 5:21 NIV

Dear children, keep yourselves from idols.

——— *DECLARATION OF FAITH* ———

As God's son/daughter, I will keep myself from having my life stained by idols of any kind.

(Romans 2:22; Colossians 3:5; Galatians 5:20)

CHAPTER SIXTY-THREE

2 JOHN

Second John is a short epistle that John wrote around 80-95 AD. Its purpose is to warn us against listening to false teachers who try to twist the Word for their own purposes. We should know the Word for ourselves and not be driven about by every wind of doctrine.

As you pray these personalized prayers, examine your commitment to the Word and adjust your life accordingly.

---

2 JOHN 3 NIV

Grace, mercy and peace from God the Father and from Jesus Christ, the Father's Son, will be with us in truth and love.

——— *DECLARATION OF FAITH* ———

Grace, mercy, and peace from my Father and my brother Jesus, is with me in abundance in all truth and love.

(Psalm 37:11; Romans 5:17; 2 Corinthians 4:15)

2 JOHN 6 AMP

And what this love consists in is this: that we live and walk in accordance with and guided by His commandments (His orders, ordinances, precepts, teaching). This is the commandment, as you have heard from the beginning, that you continue to walk in love [guided by it and following it].

——— *DECLARATION OF FAITH* ———

My love for God is expressed and made complete when I walk in obedience to His commands. And His command to me is to walk in love.

(John 14:15,21; 15:9-17; 1 John 2:5; 5:3)

2 JOHN 8,9 NKJV

Look to yourselves, that we do not lose those things we worked for, but *that* we may receive a full reward. Whoever transgresses and does not abide in the doctrine of Christ does not have God. He who abides in the doctrine of Christ has both the Father and the Son.

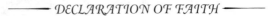

————— DECLARATION OF FAITH —————

I am careful not to lose ground in my faith. I refuse to listen to those who try to steer me away from the things of God. I know that, as long as I don't give up on my faith, I will obtain what I have struggled for. The promise for me is secure and I will be fully rewarded.

I continue in the teaching of Christ (the Anointed One and His anointing). I do not run ahead of Him. I do not forget that I am a follower of God [in submission to Him]. His will is first place in my life and all of my plans, purposes and pursuits are in accordance with the calling He has given me. I will be the very person God has created me to be. Where He tells me to go, I will go. What He tells me to do, I will do.

As I continue in the Word, I maintain a close fellowship with my Father and Jesus, and God is able to fill my life with all of His blessings.

(Hebrews 6:12; 10:35; Romans 16:17-19; Colossians 2:8; James 1:2-8; 2 Corinthians 1:20; Ephesians 5:1; John 13:15-17; 17:20-26; 1 John 1:3)

CHAPTER SIXTY-FOUR

3 JOHN

Third John is another short epistle that John wrote around 80-95 AD. In just a few short sentences, John shows us God's will for our prosperity and health, how to act in a worthy manner in front of others and how to deal with rebellion in the assembly.

While praying these promises, commit yourself to trust in God's Word and not to turn from it no matter who influences you to do so.

---

3 JOHN 2 NKJV

Beloved, I pray that you may prosper in all things and be in health, just as your soul prospers.

———— *DECLARATION OF FAITH* ————

I know the heart of my Father—that He is a good Father, and wishes above all things that I prosper and remain healthy, even as my soul prospers.

(Psalm 35:27; 103:1-5; 112:1-10; Deuteronomy 8:18; 28:1-14; Galatians 3:13,14; Genesis 12:1-3; 13:2; Isaiah 53:4,5; 2 Corinthians 9:5-11; 1 Peter 2:24; Colossians 2:19; 1 Thessalonians 3:12)

3 JOHN 4 AMP

I have no greater joy than this, to hear that my [spiritual] children are living their lives in the Truth.

———— *DECLARATION OF FAITH* ————

It brings great joy to my heart when God's children are walking in the Truth.

(1 Thessalonians 2:19,20; 2 Corinthians 7:9)

3 JOHN 6,7 NIV

They have told the church about your love. You will do well to send them on their way in a manner worthy of God. It was for the sake of the Name that they went out, receiving no help from the pagans.

——— *DECLARATION OF FAITH* ———

I do all things in a manner worthy of God. All that I do, I do for that sake of the name of Jesus. My heart's desire is to bring Him honor and glory.

(Ephesians 4:1-3; Colossians 3:17; John 14:13,14)

---

3 JOHN 11 NKJV

Beloved, do not imitate what is evil, but what is good. He who does good is of God, but he who does evil has not seen God.

——— *DECLARATION OF FAITH* ———

I do not pattern myself after role models that do not know God. Those who refuse to do those things that bring honor and glory to His name are not worthy of my discipleship.

I am an imitator of what is good, not what is evil. I am a son/daughter of God, not of Satan. In all that I do, I will act in accordance with who I am.

(Proverbs 13:20; 1 Corinthians 11:1; Ephesians 5:1-18; 2 Corinthians 6:14; Colossians 3:17)

CHAPTER SIXTY-FIVE

JUDE

Jude is another half brother of Jesus. He is likely to have written this epistle somewhere between 70 and 80 AD. Jude is another who warns us against listening to false teachers. The teachers of whom he speaks turned grace into lewdness and denied the lordship of Jesus. Jude exhorts us to separate from complainers and faultfinders, an exhortation reminiscent of the wisdom of Solomon in the book of Proverbs.

As you speak the personalized scriptures of Jude, commit yourself to live your life separate from grumbling and faultfinding. Commit to being a person of integrity who stands unwaveringly for sound doctrine.

JUDE 2 NIV
Mercy, peace and love be yours in abundance.

——— DECLARATION OF FAITH ———

Mercy, peace, and love from God are mine in abundance.

(Psalm 37:11; Romans 5:17; 2 Corinthians 4:15)

JUDE 3 NKJV
Beloved, while I was very diligent to write to you concerning our common salvation, I found it necessary to write to you exhorting you to contend earnestly for the faith which was once for all delivered to the saints.

——— DECLARATION OF FAITH ———

I earnestly contend for the faith that God gave me when I became His son/daughter. What He gave, He gave once for all. It is a done deal. My faith is mine for eternity. I fully understand its nature and its production of true holiness in my life. God has called me to it and I will live by it, no matter what the critics or the twisters of the Word may say.

(Romans 12:3; 10:8; 1 Timothy 6:12; Galatians 5:6; 2 Corinthians 4:13; 5:7; Hebrews 11:1; Colossians 2:8)

JUDE 16-19 KJV

These are murmurers, complainers, walking after their own lusts; and their mouth speaketh great swelling *words,* having men's persons in admiration because of advantage. But, beloved, remember ye the words which were spoken before of the apostles of our Lord Jesus Christ; How that they told you there should be mockers in the last time, who should walk after their own ungodly lusts. These be they who separate themselves, sensual, having not the Spirit.

——— *DECLARATION OF FAITH* ———

I will not listen to, or have anything to do with, grumblers, complainers, and faultfinders. Their lives are products of their own evil desires. They boast about themselves and flatter others for their own advantage. I am not moved by them, nor will I have anything to do with them.

Jesus warned me that these men would come and has shown me how to recognize them. They are men/women who cause division in the body of Christ. They follow their natural instincts and see the testimony of their senses as being the only reality. They reject the life of the Spirit.

(Romans 16:17-19; Colossians 2:8; 3:2; 2 Peter 2:1,2; 3:2; Titus 3:9-11; Matthew 24:4,5)

JUDE 20-23 NKJV

But you, beloved, building yourselves up on your most holy faith, praying in the Holy Spirit, keep yourselves in the love of God, looking for the mercy of our Lord Jesus Christ unto eternal life. And on some have compassion, making a distinction; but others save with fear, pulling *them* out of the fire, hating even the garment defiled by the flesh.

——— *DECLARATION OF FAITH* ———

I continually build myself up in my most holy faith, praying in the Spirit (in tongues).

I keep myself under the covering of God's love as I wait for the mercy of Jesus to bring me to everlasting life.

I am merciful to those who doubt.

I snatch others from the fire [whatever it is that Satan has attacked them with] and I rescue them.

To others, I show mercy mixed with an intense disgust for the old nature.

I flee from the corruptive influence of the old nature and hate even the clothing stained by corrupted flesh.

(1 Corinthians 14:4,5,14,15,17,26-28; Psalm 5:11,12; 91:1,2; Colossians 2:7; Romans 8:26-28; 12:9-21; Titus 2:13; Amos 4:11; Zechariah 3:4,5)

JUDE 24,25 NIV

To him who is able to keep you from falling and to present you before his glorious presence without fault and with great joy—to the only God our Savior be glory, majesty, power and authority, through Jesus Christ our Lord, before all ages, now and forevermore! Amen.

Jesus is well able to keep me from falling and to present me without fault or blemish before His glorious presence with great joy and celebration. In His hands, I am held securely.

To the only God, my Savior, be glory, majesty, power, and authority through Jesus Christ my Lord, before all ages, now and forevermore! Amen!

(Philippians 1:6; Ephesians 1:13,14; John 10:27-30; Psalm 29:1-11)

REVELATION

This is the revelation given to John from Jesus Himself while exiled on the isle of Patmos. The date of the writing is between 90-96 AD. The book contains an account of a vision of Jesus in His glorified body, messages to the seven churches in Asia Minor (often thought of as representative of church ages throughout history), a revealing of the events surrounding Armageddon and a description of heaven at the culmination of all things.

As you are speaking the personalized promises of the book of Revelation, take comfort in knowing that because of Jesus, you are not condemned to suffer any of the judgments of the Apocalypse. You have only the good things to look forward to because the complete penalty for all of your sin was placed upon Jesus.

REVELATION 1:3 AMP

Blessed (happy, to be envied) is the man who reads aloud [in the assemblies] the word of this prophecy; and blessed (happy, to be envied) are those who hear [it read] and who keep themselves true to the things which are written in it [heeding them and laying them to heart], for the time [for them to be fulfilled] is near.

——— *DECLARATION OF FAITH* ———

I am blessed (fortunate and happy) when I read the prophecies of the book of Revelation, and I am blessed (fortunate and happy) when I hear it and take to heart those things that are written therein, for the time is at hand.

(Luke 11:28; James 1:22-25; 5:8)

REVELATION 1:4-6 KJV

John to the seven churches which are in Asia: Grace *be* unto you, and peace, from him which is, and which was, and which is to come; and from the seven Spirits which are before his throne; And from Jesus Christ, *who is* the faithful witness, *and* the first begotten of the dead, and the prince of the kings of the

earth. Unto him that loved us, and washed us from our sins in his own blood, And hath made us kings and priests unto God and his Father; to him *be* glory and dominion for ever and ever. Amen.

———— *DECLARATION OF FAITH* ————

Grace and peace are mine in abundance from Him who is, who was and who is to come, and from the seven spirits which are before His throne, and from Jesus Christ who is the faithful witness, my elder brother, the first to be reborn from the dead, and who is the ruler of the kings of the earth.

He loves me dearly and has freed me from my sins by His precious blood. He has made me a part of the royal court of heaven.

(Psalm 37:11; Romans 5:17; 8:28-30; 2 Corinthians 4:15; John 1:1; 13:34; Isaiah 55:4; Revelation 17:14; Hebrews 9:14; 1 Peter 2:5-9; Ephesians 1:17-23; 2:6; 1 Timothy 6:16)

REVELATION 1:17,18 NIV

When I saw him, I fell at his feet as though dead. Then he placed his right hand on me and said: "Do not be afraid. I am the First and the Last. I am the Living One; I was dead, and behold I am alive for ever and ever! And I hold the keys of death and Hades."

———— *DECLARATION OF FAITH* ————

I have absolutely nothing to fear. Jesus has become my first, my last, my everything.

He is the living One, who was dead and is alive forevermore.

He is the champion among champions who, by conquest, now holds the keys of hell and death.

He is the Creator and I am identified with His victory. He has made me to be what He is in this earth. I have absolutely nothing to fear, for His victory has become my victory.

(Joshua 1:5-9; 2 Timothy 1:7; 2:11; John 14:12; 15:5; Ephesians 1:17-23; 2:6; 5:1; 1 John 4:17; Galatians 2:20; Romans 3:26; 6:5-8; 2 Corinthians 5:21; 8:9; 1 Corinthians 1:30; 15:57; 1 Peter 2:24; Colossians 2:13-15; 3:1)

REVELATION 2:2-7 KJV

I know thy works, and thy labour, and thy patience, and how thou canst not bear them which are evil: and thou hast tried them which say they are apostles, and are not, and hast found them liars: And hast borne, and hast patience, and for my name's sake hast laboured, and hast not fainted. Nevertheless I have *somewhat* against thee, because thou hast left thy first love. Remember therefore from whence thou art fallen, and repent, and do the first works; or else I will come unto thee quickly, and will remove thy candlestick out of his place, except thou repent. But this thou hast, that thou hatest the deeds of the Nicolaitans, which I also hate. He that hath an ear, let him hear what the Spirit saith unto the churches; To him that overcometh will I give to eat of the tree of life, which is in the midst of the paradise of God.

——— DECLARATION OF FAITH ———

I am a man/woman of righteousness.

I am a hard worker and steadfast in my faith.

I do not tolerate wickedness and I test those who claim to be apostles but are not. I persevere through every hardship for the name of Jesus and do not grow weary of the fight.

I hold fast to my first love (the love in, of and for Jesus that is the precursor of all of my actions). I live, walk, and breathe in this love. It is the center of my life and the springboard of my faith.

I have been given ears to hear and a heart to understand what the Spirit has to say.

In Jesus, I have overcome the world and have the right to one day eat from the Tree of Life, which is in the midst of the paradise of God.

(2 Corinthians 5:21; Psalm 15:1-5; Proverbs 6:6-11; Hebrews 10:35-11:1; Leviticus 5:1; 1 John 4:1-4; 5:4,5; Acts 17:10,11,28; James 1:2-8; Galatians 5:6; John 16:13; Matthew 13:11,15,16; Revelation 22:2,14)

REVELATION 2:9-11 AMP

I know your affliction and distress and pressing trouble and your poverty—but you are rich! and how you are abused and reviled and slandered by those who say they are Jews and are not, but are a synagogue of Satan. Fear nothing that you are about to suffer. [Dismiss your dread and your fears!] Behold, the devil is indeed about to throw some of you into prison, that you may be tested and proved and critically appraised, and for ten days you will have affliction. Be loyally faithful unto death [even if you must die for it], and I will give you the crown of life. He who is able to hear, let him listen to and heed what the Spirit says to the assemblies (churches). He who overcomes (is victorious) shall in no way be injured by the second death.

DECLARATION OF FAITH

Jesus is aware of my situation. He is concerned that I understand what He has provided for me, and that, in Him, I have been made rich (wealthy; well supplied). He knows when I am slandered and suffer injustice. He sees when Satan's servants enter into the congregation claiming to be of God. Therefore, I have absolutely nothing to fear. I am under His protection and guardianship at all times. I will be faithful to Him even to the point of death, for I know that He will give me the crown of life.

I have ears to hear and a heart to understand what the Spirit has to say.

In Jesus, I have overcome this world and shall not be harmed by the second death.

(Psalm 23:1-6; 1 Corinthians 1:30; 2:6-16; 2 Corinthians 8:9; Matthew 5:10-12; 13:11,15,16; Isaiah 54:17; Romans 2:17; Revelation 3:9; 2 Timothy 1:7; James 1:12; 1 John 5:4,5)

REVELATION 2:13 NKJV

"I know your works, and where you dwell, where Satan's throne *is*. And you hold fast to My name, and did not deny My faith even in the days in which Antipas *was* My faithful martyr, who was killed among you, where Satan dwells."

DECLARATION OF FAITH

Jesus knows where I live, what I am doing and what my environment is like. He sees all of the demonic activity in my area and knows what I am up against.

My Lord believes in me. He knows that I will do Him honor and triumph wherever I am.

I remain true to Jesus' name no matter what may happen. I shall never deny my faith in Jesus.

(1 Corinthians 10:13; 13:7; 15:57; Psalm 139:1-18; Luke 22:31,32; Colossians 3:17; John 14:13,14; 2 Timothy 2:12)

REVELATION 2:17 AMP

He who is able to hear, let him listen to and heed what the Spirit says to the assemblies (churches). To him who overcomes (conquers), I will give to eat of the manna that is hidden, and I will give him a white stone with a new name engraved on the stone, which no one knows or understands except he who receives it.

———— *DECLARATION OF FAITH* ————

I have ears to hear and a heart to understand what the Spirit has to say.

I am an overcomer. One day I will partake of the hidden manna and be given a white stone with a new name written upon it, which I only shall have intimate understanding of. This name will be the representation of exactly who I am—my uniqueness in the family.

(Matthew 13:11,15,16; 1 John 2:20,27; 5:4,5,20; Revelation 3:12)

REVELATION 2:19 NIV

I know your deeds, your love and faith, your service and perseverance, and that you are now doing more than you did at first.

———— *DECLARATION OF FAITH* ————

I am a man/woman of faith and good deeds, and all of my motives are centered in love. I remain of service to the body of Christ, persevering and producing more and more for the kingdom every day.

(Galatians 5:6; 1 John 3:18; 1 Thessalonians 4:10; John 15:5-8)

REVELATION 2:26-28 KJV

And he that overcometh, and keepeth my works unto the end, to him will I give power over the nations: And he shall rule them with a rod of iron; as the vessels of a potter shall they be broken to shivers: even as I received of my Father. And I will give him the morning star.

———— *DECLARATION OF FAITH* ————

I am an overcomer who does the will of God to the very end. One day I will be given authority over the nations.

(Psalm 2:9; 1 John 5:4,5; Matthew 6:10; 19:28; John 6:29; Ephesians 1:17-23; 2:6,7; 2 Peter 1:19)

REVELATION 2:29 AMP

He who is able to hear, let him listen to and heed what the [Holy] Spirit says to the assemblies (churches).

———— *DECLARATION OF FAITH* ————

I have ears to hear and a heart to understand what the Spirit has to say.

(Matthew 13:11,15,16; 1 Corinthians 2:6-16)

REVELATION 3:2-5 KJV

Be watchful, and strengthen the things which remain, that are ready to die: for I have not found thy works perfect before God. Remember therefore how thou hast received and heard, and hold fast, and repent. If therefore thou shalt not watch, I will come on thee as a thief, and thou shalt not know what hour I will come upon thee. Thou hast a few names even in Sardis which have not defiled their garments; and they shall walk with me in white: for they are worthy. He that overcometh, the same shall be clothed in white raiment; and I will not blot out his name out of the book of life, but I will confess his name before my Father, and before his angels.

———— DECLARATION OF FAITH ————

Jesus is well aware of what I am doing at all times. He knows my heart and my motives. Therefore, I will remain perfectly honest with Him.

I do not live my life as a hypocrite or on past glories.

I remain alert at all times, being strengthened with all might in my inner man.

I do not lose vitality and power by moving on [even productively] without God's full approval.

I remember all of what I have received and heard and I remain true to it.

I walk with Jesus clothed in the white robe of His righteousness.

I am an overcomer and my name shall never be blotted out of the Book of Life. Jesus has acknowledged my name before the Father and all of the angels.

(Psalm 139:1-18; 1 Thessalonians 4:10; Ephesians 3:16; Matthew 6:10; John 16:13; 1 Timothy 6:20; Revelation 19:8; 2 Corinthians 5:21; Luke 10:20; 12:8)

REVELATION 3:7-12 KJV

And to the angel of the church in Philadelphia write; These things saith he that is holy, he that is true, he that hath the key of David, he that openeth, and no man shutteth; and shutteth, and no man openeth; I know thy works: behold, I have set before thee an open door, and no man can shut it: for thou hast a little strength, and hast kept my word, and hast not denied my name. Behold, I will make them of the synagogue of Satan, which say they are Jews, and are not, but do lie; behold, I will make them to come and worship before thy feet, and to know that I have loved thee. Because thou hast kept the word of my patience, I also will keep thee from the hour of temptation, which shall come upon all the world, to try them that dwell upon the earth. Behold, I come quickly: hold that fast which thou hast, that no man take thy crown. Him that overcometh will I make a pillar in the temple of my God, and he shall go no more out: and I will write upon him the name of my God, and the name of the city of my God, *which is* new Jerusalem, which cometh down out of heaven from my God: and *I will write upon him* my new name.

─── *DECLARATION OF FAITH* ───

My Lord is holy, faithful, and true. What He opens for me, no one can shut—and what He closes concerning me, no one can open.

He is watchful of my every move and has purposed to help me in every situation. He has a plan for my life and has set before me an open door that no one can shut. Therefore, I have complete confidence that I can do what He has called me to do. There is not a soul in the universe that can stop me.

I hold fast to the Word and never deny the name of Jesus. I remain strong in the Lord and in the power of His might.

All of my persecutors—those liars who claim to be God's people, but clearly are not—will one day come and fall at my feet acknowledging that God has loved me.

I hold fast to the Word and endure in Jesus. I have His Word that I will not go through the great trial that is coming upon the whole world to test those who live on the earth. When it comes, I will be lifted out, unscathed, and unharmed.

I know that my Lord is coming soon. Therefore, I hold fast to what I have [my calling in the work of the Gospel] so that no one may take the crown intended for me.

I am an overcomer who will be made a pillar in the shrine of my God. By no means will I go forth from it or have my reward taken from me. Upon me will be written the name of my God, the name of the city of my God (New Jerusalem), and the new name of my Savior.

(1 Peter 1:13-16; 1 John 4:5; 5:20; Matthew 10:42; 16:19; Job 12:14; Psalm 3:5,6; 23:1-6; 1 Corinthians 9:24-27; 16:9; Romans 11:29; Philippians 4:13; Joshua 1:5-9; Ephesians 6:10; Isaiah 45:14; 49:23; James 1:2-8; 2 Peter 2:9; Revelation 2:25; 22:20)

REVELATION 3:14 NKJV

"And to the angel of the church of the Laodiceans write, 'These things says the Amen, the Faithful and True Witness, the Beginning of the creation of God.'"

─── *DECLARATION OF FAITH* ───

Jesus is the surety of all good things in my life. He is the faithful and true witness—the ruler of all of creation. He is my brother and I am being transformed into His very likeness.

(2 Corinthians 1:20; 2 Peter 1:3; Revelation 19:11; Colossians 1:15)

REVELATION 3:15-21 KJV

I know thy works, that thou art neither cold nor hot: I would thou wert cold or hot. So then because thou art lukewarm, and neither cold nor hot, I will spue thee out of my mouth. Because thou sayest, I am rich, and increased with goods, and have need of nothing; and knowest not that thou art wretched, and miserable, and poor, and blind, and naked: I counsel thee to buy of me gold tried in the fire, that thou mayest be rich; and white raiment, that thou mayest be clothed, and *that* the shame of thy nakedness do not appear; and anoint thine eyes with eyesalve, that thou mayest see. As many as I love, I rebuke and chasten: be zealous therefore, and repent. Behold, I stand at the door, and knock: if any man hear my voice, and open the door, I will come in to him, and will sup with him, and he with me. To him that overcometh will I grant to sit with me in my throne, even as I also overcame, and am set down with my Father in his throne.

── DECLARATION OF FAITH ──

I refuse to be lukewarm (indifferent, apathetic, or complacent) in my Christian walk. I live a life of purpose in Christ and I am burning a red-hot path toward the prize of my high calling.

I do not rely on or trust in uncertain worldly riches. I have entered an inheritance of true riches—gold refined in the fire. I have been clothed in the white garments of His righteousness and my eyes have been anointed so that I can clearly see.

Jesus loves me dearly. When He sees me stray, He rebukes me sharply and for my own good. He will not allow me to go without guidance. Therefore, I am earnest and repent when I am headed in the wrong direction.

Jesus never leaves me and is anxious to have continuous fellowship with me. However, He has put the ball in my court. It is I who must first come to Him, but He is always faithful to respond to me with open arms.

I am an overcomer. I have every right to sit with Jesus on His throne.

(Revelation 3:1; 7:9; 19:13,14; James 1:22-25; 4:8; 1 Corinthians 1:21,30; 2:6-16; 9:24-27; Philippians 3:14; 1 Timothy 6:17; 2 Corinthians 5:21; 8:9; Romans 8:14-17,38,39; John 17:20-26; 1 John 1:3; 2:20; 5:4,5,20; Ephesians 1:3,13,14; 2:6; Hebrews 4:15,16; 12:5,6)

REVELATION 7:14 NIV

I answered, "Sir, you know." And he said, "These are they who have come out of the great tribulation; they have washed their robes and made them white in the blood of the Lamb."

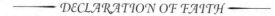

—————— *DECLARATION OF FAITH* ——————

I have washed my garments and made them white in the blood of the Lamb.

(Revelation 7:9; 19:13,14; Isaiah 1:18; 1 John 1:7)

REVELATION 11:18 NKJV

"The nations were angry, and Your wrath has come, And the time of the dead, that they should be judged, And that You should reward Your servants the prophets and the saints, And those who fear Your name, small and great, And should destroy those who destroy the earth."

—————— *DECLARATION OF FAITH* ——————

The Lord has set aside a day to reward me for the things I have done, just as He will for all who hold His name in high honor.

(2 Corinthians 5:10; 1 Corinthians 3:12-15; Matthew 10:41,42)

REVELATION 12:10-12 AMP

Then I heard a strong (loud) voice in heaven, saying, Now it has come—the salvation and the power and the kingdom (the dominion, the reign) of our God, and the power (the sovereignty, the authority) of His Christ (the Messiah); for the accuser of our brethren, he who keeps bringing before our God charges against them day and night, has been cast out! And they have overcome (conquered) him by means of the blood of the Lamb and by the utterance of their testimony, for they did not love and cling to life even when faced with death [holding their lives cheap till they had to die for their witnessing]. Therefore be glad (exult), O heavens and you that dwell in them! But woe to you, O earth and sea, for the devil has come down to you in fierce anger (fury), because he knows that he has [only] a short time [left]!

—————— *DECLARATION OF FAITH* ——————

I walk in the Lord's salvation and power, in kingdom living, and in the authority of Jesus.

Satan, my accuser, has been utterly defeated and stripped of any and all power over me. I overcome him by the blood of the Lamb [poured out in the Holy of Holies of heaven for my redemption] and by the Word of my testimony [the proclamation of God's Word in every situation and battle].

I do not hold on to my life so much that I shrink back in fear of death. I know the big picture here and I know my eternal destiny. I will complete my days on earth and welcome death after being satisfied with a long, productive life.

Therefore, I rejoice greatly and shout praises to almighty God no matter what my situation may be!

(Colossians 2:6,7,13-15; 2 Corinthians 4:13; 5:7; Romans 10:8; Mark 11:22-25; John 14:13,14; 15:7,8; 16:23,24; 1 John 5:4,5; Hebrews 9:11-15,24; 11:1; Psalm 91:16; Isaiah 46:4; 2 Timothy 1:7; Philippians 4:4)

REVELATION 13:9 AMP

If anyone is able to hear, let him listen.

──── *DECLARATION OF FAITH* ────

I have been given the anointing to understand what the Spirit has to say.

(1 John 2:20,27; John 16:13; Matthew 13:11,15,16; 1 Corinthians 2:6-16)

REVELATION 13:10 NIV

If anyone is to go into captivity, into captivity he will go. If anyone is to be killed with the sword, with the sword he will be killed. This calls for patient endurance and faithfulness on the part of the saints.

──── *DECLARATION OF FAITH* ────

I am conditioned for endurance and strength of faith in the midst of the most trying circumstances.

(James 1:2-8; Mark 11:22-25; Hebrews 6:12; 10:35-11:1)

REVELATION 14:4,5 NKJV

These are the ones who were not defiled with women, for they are virgins. These are the ones who follow the Lamb wherever He goes. These were redeemed from among men, being firstfruits to God and to the Lamb. And in their mouth was found no deceit, for they are without fault before the throne of God

──── *DECLARATION OF FAITH* ────

I remain clean and innocent of sexual sin.

I follow Jesus wherever He goes.

He has purchased me with His own blood from among men and has offered me as firstfruits to God and to Himself.

I will allow no lies to be found in my mouth.
I will be blameless before God in this life.

(Proverbs 6:25; Job 31:1; 1 Corinthians 5:1-7; Revelation 3:4; 5:9; 7:17; John 6:37-40; Acts 20:28; 1 Peter 1:13-16; 3:10-12; Jude 24)

REVELATION 14:12 NKJV

Here is the patience of the saints; here are those who keep the commandments of God and the faith of Jesus.

— *DECLARATION OF FAITH* —

I am a child of patient endurance through all hardships. I obey God's commands and remain faithful to Jesus no matter what may come.

(James 1:2-4; John 15:10-17; 2 Thessalonians 1:3-5)

REVELATION 16:15 NKJV

"Behold, I am coming as a thief. Blessed *is* he who watches, and keeps his garments, lest he walk naked and they see his shame."

— *DECLARATION OF FAITH* —

I remain alert and ever watchful for the Second Coming of my Lord Jesus. I do not grow lax, but remain holy, always wearing the garments of righteousness. I am ready and eager for His return.

(Matthew 24:42-51; 1 Peter 1:13-16; 2 Corinthians 5:3)

REVELATION 17:14 AMP

They will wage war against the Lamb, and the Lamb will triumph over them; for He is Lord of lords and King of kings—and those with Him and on His side are chosen and called [elected] and loyal and faithful followers.

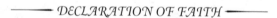
— *DECLARATION OF FAITH* —

I will one day fight at my Lord's side against the beast and his kings. Jesus, my commander, Lord and Savior, will defeat them, for He is King of Kings and Lord of Lords. And I, His called and chosen one, and faithful follower, shall be there with Him to share in His victory.

(Revelation 12:11; 16:14; 19:19,20; 1 John 5:4,5; 1 Timothy 6:15; Jeremiah 50:44)

REVELATION 18:4 NIV

Then I heard another voice from heaven say: "Come out of her, my people, so that you will not share in her sins, so that you will not receive any of her plagues."

———— *DECLARATION OF FAITH* ————

I will not be a part of the adulteries of Babylon (idolatry, sexual immorality, etc.). I will not share in her sins and I will not receive any of her plagues.

(Job 31:1; Proverbs 6:25; Leviticus 19:31; 20:6,27; Jeremiah 29:8,9; Isaiah 8:19,20; 48:20)

REVELATION 19:6-9 KJV

And I heard as it were the voice of a great multitude, and as the voice of many waters, and as the voice of mighty thunderings, saying, Alleluia: for the Lord God omnipotent reigneth. Let us be glad and rejoice, and give honour to him: for the marriage of the Lamb is come, and his wife hath made herself ready. And to her was granted that she should be arrayed in fine linen, clean and white: for the fine linen is the righteousness of saints. And he saith unto me, Write, Blessed are they which are called unto the marriage supper of the Lamb. And he saith unto me, These are the true sayings of God.

———— *DECLARATION OF FAITH* ————

I will one day stand before the throne of God with the great multitude of my brothers and sisters in Christ from all the ages, singing, shouting, and praising Him, saying, "Hallelujah! Our Lord God Almighty reigns! Rejoice and be glad! Give Him glory!" It will be the day of the long-awaited wedding feast of the Lamb. I will be prepared, with all of my family (the Church), wearing fine linen, bright and clean. All of my righteous acts will be remembered on that day. Nothing that I have done, or will do, will be in vain—all will come to light and I will be rewarded. It will be a day of great blessing for me.

(Revelation 11:18; 2 Corinthians 5:10; 1 Corinthians 3:12-15; 15:58; Matthew 10:41,42; 25:10; Psalm 132:9)

REVELATION 19:10 NKJV

And I fell at his feet to worship him. But he said to me, "See *that you do* not *do that!* I am your fellow servant, and of your brethren who have the testimony of Jesus. Worship God! For the testimony of Jesus is the spirit of prophecy."

I worship God alone and hold fast to the testimony of Jesus; for the testimony of Jesus on my lips is the very spirit of prophecy.

(Acts 10:25,26; 1 John 5:10; Luke 24:27; 1 Corinthians 14:32; Exodus 34:14)

REVELATION 19:11-21 KJV

And I saw heaven opened, and behold a white horse; and he that sat upon him *was* called Faithful and True, and in righteousness he doth judge and make war. His eyes *were* as a flame of fire, and on his head *were* many crowns; and he had a name written, that no man knew, but he himself. And he *was* clothed with a vesture dipped in blood: and his name is called The Word of God. And the armies *which were* in heaven followed him upon white horses, clothed in fine linen, white and clean. And out of his mouth goeth a sharp sword, that with it he should smite the nations: and he shall rule them with a rod of iron: and he treadeth the winepress of the fierceness and wrath of Almighty God. And he hath on *his* vesture and on his thigh a name written, KING OF KINGS, AND LORD OF LORDS. And I saw an angel standing in the sun; and he cried with a loud voice, saying to all the fowls that fly in the midst of heaven, Come and gather your-selves together unto the supper of the great God; That ye may eat the flesh of kings, and the flesh of captains, and the flesh of mighty men, and the flesh of horses, and of them that sit on them, and the flesh of all *men, both* free and bond, both small and great. And I saw the beast, and the kings of the earth, and their armies, gathered together to make war against him that sat on the horse, and against his army. And the beast was taken, and with him the false prophet that wrought miracles before him, with which he deceived them that had received the mark of the beast, and them that worshipped his image. These both were cast alive into a lake of fire burning with brimstone. And the remnant were slain with the sword of him that sat upon the horse, which *sword* proceeded out of his mouth: and all the fowls were filled with their flesh.

———— *DECLARATION OF FAITH* ————

One day I will mount a heavenly steed and go forth to battle with Him who is called faithful and true. His eyes will be like flames of fire and on His head will be many crowns. His name will be unique among all others [only He shall have full understanding of it]. He shall be dressed in a robe dipped in blood. His name is and shall be the Word of God.

He will be riding a white horse and my brothers and sisters and I will follow Him, riding white horses and dressed in clean white linen.

Out of His mouth will come a sharp sword with which He will strike down the nations. He will rule them with a rod of iron.

He will tread the winepress of the fury of almighty God.

On His robe and on His thigh His name will be written: King of Kings and Lord of Lords.

And I shall be like Him. In Him, I shall have my own unique name that no one truly understands but me. In Him, I shall have my authority. In Him, I shall mount a white horse of my own. In Him, I shall live and act and have my being. In Him, I shall be glorified. In Him, I shall glow in the very righteousness of God!

The battle we fight will be fierce and we will rise victorious. The flesh of kings, generals, mighty men, horses, and all people shall be given as a feast to the fowls of the air.

We shall capture the beast and his false prophet and they shall be cast into the lake of fire.

This will all happen and I shall have my part in it. It will be the culmination of my victory in Jesus in this age.

(Isaiah 11:1-5,10; Revelation 3:7; 16:13; John 1:1,14; Matthew 28:3; Acts 17:28; Ezekiel 39:17-20; Daniel 2:47; 1 John 3:2; Romans 8:28-20; 2 Corinthians 5:21; 1 Corinthians 15:57)

REVELATION 20:4-6 AMP

Then I saw thrones, and sitting on them were those to whom authority to act as judges and to pass sentence was entrusted. Also I saw the souls of those who had been slain with axes [beheaded] for their witnessing to Jesus and [for preaching and testifying] for the Word of God, and who had refused to pay homage to the beast or his statue and had not accepted his mark or permitted it to be stamped on their foreheads or on their hands. And they lived again and ruled with Christ (the Messiah) a thousand years. The remainder of the dead were not restored to life again until the thousand years were completed. This is the first resurrection. Blessed (happy, to be envied) and holy (spiritually whole, of unimpaired innocence and proved virtue) is the person who takes part (shares) in the first resurrection! Over them the second death exerts no power or authority, but they shall be ministers of God and of Christ (the Messiah), and they shall rule along with Him a thousand years.

——— *DECLARATION OF FAITH* ———

I shall rise in a glorified body and reign with Jesus on this earth for a thousand years.

I have my part in the first resurrection for I have been made holy and am blessed in Jesus.

The second death has no power over me.

I am, and will be, a priest of God and of Christ and shall reign with Him for a thousand years.

(Romans 8:17,23; 1 Corinthians 15:42-53; Hebrews 10:14; Ephesians 1:3,13,14; Revelation 2:11; 20:4,14; Isaiah 61:6)

REVELATION 20:12 NKJV

And I saw the dead, small and great, standing before God, and books were opened. And another book was opened, which is *the Book* of Life. And the dead were judged according to their works, by the things which were written in the books.

─────── *DECLARATION OF FAITH* ───────

I shall stand secure and confident in the Day of Judgment.

My name is written in the Book of Life.

I shall not suffer judgment unto condemnation, for my penalty has already been paid.

(Jude 24; John 5:24; Romans 8:1; Hebrews 4:15,16; Luke 10:20; Isaiah 40:2)

REVELATION 21:1-7 KJV

And I saw a new heaven and a new earth: for the first heaven and the first earth were passed away; and there was no more sea. And I John saw the holy city, new Jerusalem, coming down from God out of heaven, prepared as a bride adorned for her husband. And I heard a great voice out of heaven saying, Behold, the tabernacle of God *is* with men, and he will dwell with them, and they shall be his people, and God himself shall be with them, *and be* their God. And God shall wipe away all tears from their eyes; and there shall be no more death, neither sorrow, nor crying, neither shall there be any more pain: for the former things are passed away. And he that sat upon the throne said, Behold, I make all things new. And he said unto me, Write: for these words are true and faithful. And he said unto me, It is done. I am Alpha and Omega, the beginning and the end. I will give unto him that is athirst of the fountain of the water of life freely. He that overcometh shall inherit all things; and I will be his God, and he shall be my son.

─── DECLARATION OF FAITH ───

One day I will enter into and enjoy the new heaven and the new Earth; for the present heaven and this world shall pass away and there will be no more sea.

The New Jerusalem, the city where I have my true citizenship, shall come down from God out of heaven, having been prepared as a bride adorned for her husband. It will be the most perfect place to live. I myself have my mansion there—a customized dwelling built exclusively for me.

On that day I will live in the physical presence of God. I will walk with Him and talk with Him. I will be one of His people, and He Himself will be with me and be my God. He will wipe every tear from my eyes. Never again will I mourn, for the time of mourning will be passed. I will never again experience the pains of death, nor cry or suffer pain of any kind, for this present order of things shall be eliminated.

God, my heavenly Father, will make all things new for me and I shall enjoy His presence for all of eternity.

This will all happen. It is fixed and certain, for it has been proclaimed from the mouth of my Lord. He is the Alpha and the Omega—the Beginning and the End. He shall freely (without cost of any kind), and without reservation, allow me to drink from the endless spring of the Water of Life.

(John 4:10; 12:26; 14:1-3; 2 Peter 3:13; Isaiah 52:1; 55:11; 2 Corinthians 5:17; 11:2; Jude 24; Zechariah 8:8; Matthew 28:20)

REVELATION 21:23-27 KJV

And the city had no need of the sun, neither of the moon, to shine in it: for the glory of God did lighten it, and the Lamb *is* the light thereof. And the nations of them which are saved shall walk in the light of it: and the kings of the earth do bring their glory and honour into it. And the gates of it shall not be shut at all by day: for there shall be no night there. And they shall bring the glory and honour of the nations into it. And there shall in no wise enter into it any thing that defileth, neither *whatsoever* worketh abomination, or *maketh* a lie: but they which are written in the Lamb's book of life.

─── DECLARATION OF FAITH ───

God's city, of which I am a citizen, has gates that shall never be shut to me. I will come and go freely and enjoy perfect utopian life.

There shall no longer be any night or darkness, for God Himself shall illuminate all things. And Jesus Himself is its lamp [the assurance of continually vigorous and healthy life].

I will live by Jesus' light. All of my glory and honor will be brought into it.

Nothing impure and unholy shall ever enter in, nor will anyone who is shameful or deceitful, but only those whose names are written in the Lamb's Book of Life.

My name is written in the Lamb's Book of Life.

(Ephesians 2:19; Isaiah 60:10-22; Joel 3:17; Luke 10:20; Philippians 4:3,4)

REVELATION 22:2-5 KJV

In the midst of the street of it, and on either side of the river, *was there* the tree of life, which bare twelve *manner of* fruits, *and* yielded her fruit every month: and the leaves of the tree *were* for the healing of the nations. And there shall be no more curse: but the throne of God and of the Lamb shall be in it; and his servants shall serve him: And they shall see his face; and his name *shall be* in their foreheads. And there shall be no night there; and they need no candle, neither light of the sun; for the Lord God giveth them light: and they shall reign for ever and ever.

——— *DECLARATION OF FAITH* ———

I will one day eat from the Tree of Life whose leaves are for the healing of the nations, eliminating all effects of the curse.

The throne of God and of Jesus (the Lamb) will be in the midst of our city, and I will joyfully be of service to Him there.

I will see His face and His name shall be on my forehead.

There will be no more night there. I will never need the light of a lamp or the light of the sun, for God shall give me light.

And I will reign with Him forever and ever.

(Genesis 2:9; Revelation 7:15; 14:1; 21:23,24; Galatians 3:13; Zechariah 14:11; Ezekiel 48:35; Ephesians 1:13,14; 4:30; John 6:27; Isaiah 60:19,20; Psalm 36:8,9; Daniel 7:18-27)

REVELATION 22:7 AMP

And behold, I am coming speedily. Blessed (happy and to be envied) is he who observes and lays to heart and keeps the truths of the prophecy (the predictions, consolations, and warnings) contained in this [little] book.

——— *DECLARATION OF FAITH* ———

I hold on dearly to the words of the prophecy of the Apocalypse (the book of Revelation) and I am blessed (happy and to be envied).

My Lord is coming soon!

(Revelation 1:3; 3:11; Psalm 119:160-162)

REVELATION 22:11 NIV

"Let him who does wrong continue to do wrong; let him who is vile continue to be vile; let him who does right continue to do right; and let him who is holy continue to be holy."

———— *DECLARATION OF FAITH* ————

I am a good son/daughter of my Father. I continue to do what is right. Because I have been made holy, I will continue to walk in holiness.

(Galatians 4:4-6; Ephesians 4:1-3; Hebrews 10:14; 1 Peter 1:13-16)

REVELATION 22:12-14 KJV

And, behold, I come quickly; and my reward is with me, to give every man according as his work shall be. I am Alpha and Omega, the beginning and the end, the first and the last. Blessed *are* they that do his commandments, that they may have right to the tree of life, and may enter in through the gates into the city.

———— *DECLARATION OF FAITH* ————

My Lord is coming soon! His reward is with Him and He is eager to give it to me. I will receive the righteous reward for the things that I have done as a born-again child of God. Nothing that I have done will be in vain. My reward, in Him, is waiting, and I will soon receive it.

Jesus, my Lord, is the Alpha and Omega, the First and the Last, the Beginning and the End.

I am blessed (happy and to be envied) for I have washed my garments in the blood of Jesus so that I will have a right to the Tree of Life and go through the gates of the city freely, without restraint of any kind.

(Revelation 3:5,11; 20:12; 21:27; 1 Corinthians 3:8-15; 15:57,58; Isaiah 1:18; 40:10; 41:4; John 15:10-17; 1 John 1:7)

REVELATION 22:17 NKJV

And the Spirit and the bride say, "Come!" And let him who hears say, "Come!" And let him who thirsts come. Whoever desires, let him take the water of life freely.

———— *DECLARATION OF FAITH* ————

My declaration, in the Holy Spirit, to all is, "Come!" To all who will hear I say, "Come! Whoever is thirsty—come! Whoever craves the love of God, come

and partake of the Water of Life freely! God wants you to have it! It is His free
gift to you!"

(Proverbs 11:30; Matthew 5:6; 28:18-20; Isaiah 55:1; John 4:10-14)

REVELATION 22:20,21 AMP

He Who gives this warning and affirms and testifies to these things says, Yes (it is true). [Surely] I am coming quickly (swiftly, speedily). Amen (so let it be)! Yes, come, Lord Jesus! The grace (blessing and favor) of the Lord Jesus Christ (the Messiah) be with all the saints (God's holy people, those set apart for God, to be, as it were, exclusively His). Amen (so let it be)!

——— *DECLARATION OF FAITH* ———

The grace of my Lord Jesus is ever with me.
My Lord is coming soon!
Amen!
Come Lord Jesus!
I am watching and ready for Your return!

(Revelation 3:11; Romans 5:17; Matthew 24:42-44)

TOPICAL INDEX

THE MINISTRY **ANGELS** ON YOUR BEHALF

Genesis 48:15,16; Exodus 23:20-23; 2 Samuel 8:14; 2 Kings 6:13-18; 19:21-35; 1 Chronicles 18:6; 18:13; 2 Chronicles 13:12; 32:10-22; Ezra 6:7-14; Nehemiah 4:8,9; 9:27,28; Job 33:23-30; Psalm 18:3-19; 34:4-10; 35:1-6; 57:3-5; 60:4; 68:17-20; 91; 103:1-18; 141:3,4; Jeremiah 23:4-6; Daniel 3:28-30; 6:22-28; 10:10-13; 10:18,19; Zechariah 3:1-9; Matthew 4:6; 4:8-11; 18:10; 26:52,53; Luke 12:8; 15:22-24; 22:43; Acts 4:24-31; 5:18-20; 10:4; 12:5-7; 12:11; 1 Corinthians 4:15,16; 2 Corinthians 11:14,15; Hebrews 1:13,14; 10:32-12:3; 12:22-24; 13:1-3; 1 Peter 3:18-22.

YOUR **ANOINTING** (Power for daily living; the unction to function in every circumstance; the miraculous ability within you to be all that God has called you to be)

Genesis 24:35; 26:12-14; 30:29,30; 41:38; Exodus 14:13-15; 35:34,35; 36:2; Leviticus 24:2,4; Numbers 13:30-33; 14:8,9; 25:12,13; Deuteronomy 1:21; 8:11-18; 28:1-14; 28:15-68; Joshua 10:24,25; 14:7-13; 18:3; 23:3; 23:7-14; Judges 5:31; 6:12-14; 15:14-16; 1 Samuel 2:3,4; 2:8-10; 10:6; 16:13; 16:18; 2 Samuel 5:20; 22:2-4; 22:5-25; 22:29-41; 22:49-51; 1 Kings 2:2,3; 4:32-34; 2 Kings 6:13-18; 20:2-5; 1 Chronicles 12:32; 14:11; 15:22; 16:21-24; 22:12,13; 28:19,20; 29:11-13; 2 Chronicles 1:1; 1:7-12; 15:6-8; 27:6; 32:7,8; Nehemiah 6:9-16; Esther 9:4; Job 4:3,4; 17:8,9; 22:27-30; 29:4-25; 31:1-4; Psalm 8:2; 18:20-24; 18:28-36; 18:37-40; 21:11,12; 23; 28:7; 29:11; 44:5-8; 45:1,2; 45:7; 51:10; 60:11,12; 68:35; 84:4-7; 89:14-17; 106:29-31; 118:5-17; 119:130-133; Proverbs 3:12-18; 8:13,14; 8:18-21; 10:4; 12:28; 16:3; 16:20; 18:14; 24:5,6; 31:10-31; Ecclesiastes 9:7-10; Isaiah 8:18-20; 11:2-5; 12:1-3; 30:15; 33:2; 33:13-24; 35:3-10; 40:10,11; 40:29-31; 41:8-20; 42:6-8; 44:24-26; 45:4-6; 45:23,24; 48:16-18; 49:5,6; 51:11-16; 52:1-3; 54:13-17; 58:11; 59:21-60:2; 60:17-21; 61:1-3; 61:6-10; Jeremiah 1:7-10; 15:19-21; 17:5; 50:33,34; Ezekiel 3:14; 34:2-4; 34:14-16; 36:25-27; Daniel 2:14-23; 10:10-13; 10:18,19; 12:3; Hosea 2:14-23; 11:3,4; Joel 2:2-11; 2:19; Amos 5:14,15; Micah 3:8; 5:4; Habakkuk 3:2; 3:17-19; Zephaniah 3:11-15; Haggai 2:4-9; Zechariah 4:6; 8:12,13; 9:11-17; 10:5,6; 10:12; 12:8; Matthew 4:1-11; 5:2-12; 9:28,29; 9:32,33; 9:35; 10:24,25; 10:26-31; 26:41; Mark 1:8; 1:17; 1:34; 3:14,15; 3:27; 6:7; 6:12,13; 9:38,39; 12:24; 14:38; 16:15-20; Luke 1:37,38; 1:45; 4:3-13; 4:4; 4:18,19; 4:40; 5:10; 5:12,13; 5:17-25; 6:18,19; 7:7-9; 7:21-23; 8:46-48; 8:50; 13:32; 21:34-36; 22:43; John 2:11; 2:23; 5:17; 5:19-30; 5:41-44; 9:31-33; 10:25-30; 11:40-42; 14:10-14; 14:26; 15:26; 17:6-26; Acts

1:8; 2:4; 2:33; 2:42-47; 3:6; 3:12; 4:10-13; 4:24-31; 4:33,34; 5:12-16; 6:5,8-10; 8:6-8; 8:21; 9:22; 9:33,34; 9:40; 10:38; 11:21; 14:3; 19:11,12; 19:14-20; Romans 8:23-30; 9:23; 12:5,6; 15:18,19; 1 Corinthians 1:4,5; 1:25; 1:30,31; 2:4,5; 10:13; 12:6-11; 12:31; 14:26-28; 14:39,40; 15:10; 15:48-58; 16:13,14; 2 Corinthians 1:18-22; 3:16-18; 4:5-11; 10:3-6; 10:12; 12:1; 12:5; 12:9,10; 13:3; 13:4; Galatians 2:16-21; 3:5; Ephesians 1:17-23; 3:7; 3:14-21; 4:11-13; 6:10-18; Philippians 1:19-24; 2:2-11; 2:12,13; 3:7-11; 4:10-13; Colossians 1:6; 1:9-14; 1:25-29; 2:2-4; 1 Thessalonians 2:12,13; 3:12,13; 5:4-11; 2 Thessalonians 1:11,12; 3:3; 2 Timothy 1:6-10; 2:1; 3:5; 4:17,18; Hebrews 10:32-12:3; 13:20,21; James 3:2-6; 4:2-10; 5:13-16a; 5:16b-18; 1 Peter 4:7-11; 4:14; 5:8-11; 1 John 2:20; 2:27-29; Revelation 2:26-28; 3:2-5; 3:7-12; 3:15-21; 12:10-12; 13:9; 13:10; 19:11-21.

ASSEMBLY (See Church)

AUTHORITY (See Dominion)

BODY OF CHRIST (See Church)

BORN AGAIN (See New Creation Realities)

CHILDREN (God's Word on raising your children in the nurture and admonition of the Lord; God's promises to protect and care for your children)

Genesis 17:6-9; 32:12; Exodus 3:21,22; 23:25,26; Numbers 24:5-9; Deuteronomy 4:9; 4:39,40; 6:2; 6:5-13; 7:14,15; 11:18-28; 28:1-14; 28:15-68; 30:9,10; 1 Samuel 20:14,15; 2 Samuel 23:2-5; 1 Chronicles 17:25-27; 29:28; Ezra 8:21-23; Nehemiah 4:14-18; Job 1:10; 29:4-25; Psalm 17:14; 21:11,12; 25:9-15; 37:21-26; 78:4-7; 89:28,29; 102:28; 103:1-18; 115:12-15; 127:1-5; 128:1-4; 144:12-15; Proverbs 13:21,22; 13:24; 14:26; 19:18; 20:7; 21:21; 22:6; 22:15; 23:13,14; 24:3,4; 29:15; 29:17; 31:10-31; Isaiah 33:13-24; 38:16-19; 40:10,11; 43:1-7; 44:1-5; 54:13-17; 58:6-9; 59:21-60:2; 61:6-10; 65:17-25; Jeremiah 32:39-42; Ezekiel 37:24,25; Hosea 4:6; 11:8-11; Nahum 1:15; Malachi 2:15,16; Matthew 7:24,25; 13:31-33; 21:43; Luke 11:5-13; Acts 16:31; 20:32-35; Ephesians 6:1-3; 6:4; Colossians 3:21; 1 Timothy 3:2-4,7; 3:8-13; Titus 1:6-9; 2:1-10.

CHURCH (Becoming a valued member of a local assembly; having a strong relationship with other believers)

Leviticus 26:7,8; Joshua 2:24; 8:1; 10:42; 22:3; 22:8; 23:7-14; Ruth 1:16; 1 Samuel 12:22-24; 2 Chronicles 15:6-8; 31:10; 31:20,21; Nehemiah 9:38; 10:35-38; 10:39; 13:10-14; Psalm 106:3-5; 122:6-8; Proverbs 25:5-7; Ecclesiastes 4:9-12; Isaiah 1:16-19; 33:13-24; 35:3-10; 51:11-16; 52:7-12; 61:1-3; Jeremiah 4:3; 31:11-14; Ezekiel 22:30; 33:31,32; Daniel 2:46-49; Joel

2:2-11; Zephaniah 3:9; Haggai 1:5-11; 1:13,14; Malachi 3:6-12; Matthew 18:10; 18:19,20; 18:27,35; Mark 10:42,43; Luke 10:22; 13:32; 17:3,4; John 13:13-17; 13:34,35; 15:12; 15:17; 17:6-26; Acts 2:42-47; 4:32; 5:12-16; 9:31; 14:21,22; 15:32; 18:27,28; 20:32-35; Romans 1:11,12; 12:5,6; 12:9-21; 14:4; 14:12,13; 14:19; 15:2; 15:29-33; 1 Corinthians 8:1; 12:6-11; 14:1-4; 14:5,6; 14:17-19; 14:20-25; 14:26-28; 14:39,40; 2 Corinthians 1:3-5; 1:8-11; 2:7,8; 5:14-21; 6:14-7:1; 7:4; 8:7; 9:5-15; 13:11; Galatians 3:22-29; 5:15; 5:26-6:5; Ephesians 1:17-23; 4:1-3; 4:22-32; 5:15-21; Philippians 1:27,28; 2:2-11; Colossians 1:25-29; 2:2-4; 3:12-17; 4:12; 1 Thessalonians 2:12,13; 3:12,13; 5:4-11; 2 Thessalonians 1:3; 1 Timothy 3:2-4,7; 4:14-16; 5:8; 5:19; 5:21; 2 Timothy 4:2; Titus 1:6-9; 2:1-10; 2:11-15; Hebrews 3:12,13; 10:24,25; 12:22-24; 13:1-3; 13:15,16; James 1:19-25; 4:11; 5:9; 5:13-16a; 1 Peter 1:13-23; 3:8-12; 5:5b-7; 5:8-11; 1 John 1:3-10; 2:10; 3:5-7; 3:14; 3:16-24; 4:12,13; 5:1-5; Revelation 1:4-6; 19:6-9.

COMFORT (Finding encouragement, assurance, security and consolation in your heavenly Father [See also Joy])

Leviticus 26:9-13; Deuteronomy 28:1-14; 28:15-68; 32:10-13; 33:12-16; 33:27-29; Ruth 2:12; 2 Chronicles 14:6,7; 33:12,13; Psalm 4:8; 18:3-19; 23; 34:18-22; 37:18,19; 37:39-40; 42:5,11; 68:17-20; 69:16-18; 86:17; 94:19; 119:50; 119:74-81; 139:7-10; 145:13-16; Song of Solomon 2:3-6; Isaiah 9:2-6; 12:1-3; 40:1,2; 49:8-15; 51:11-16; 55:10-12; 57:14-19; 65:17-25; Jeremiah 31:3,4; 31:11-14; Ezekiel 34:14-16; Hosea 11:3,4; Haggai 2:4-9; Zephaniah 3:17-20; Matthew 5:2-12; 11:27-30; Mark 5:36; Luke 8:24,25; 21:12-15; John 10:25-30; 14:15-21; 14:26; 15:26; 16:7-11; 16:25-27; Romans 5:1,2; 2 Corinthians 1:3-5; 4:16-18; 5:1-7; 7:4; 7:6; 1 Thessalonians 5:4-11; 2 Thessalonians 2:13-17; Hebrews 6:13-20; 12:5-8; 12:10-13; 1 John 3:16-24.

COURAGE (Living free of fear; boldness; bravery; facing down Satan with a spirit of a conqueror)

Genesis 15:1; 15:6; 22:17,18; 35:5; Exodus 14:13-15; 23:25,26; Leviticus 26:6; Numbers 10:9; 13:30-33; 14:8,9; 21:34; Deuteronomy 1:17; 1:21; 2:7; 3:22; 7:21-23; 20:3,4; 28:1-14; 28:15-68; 31:6; 31:8; Joshua 1:5-9; 8:1; 14:7-13; 18:3; Judges 6:12-14; 6:23,24; 1 Samuel 14:6; 16:18; 17:45-48; 30:6; 2 Samuel 22:29-41; 2 Kings 6:5,6; 6:13-18; 18:29-36; 19:6,7; 1 Chronicles 4:9,10; 17:25-27; 19:13; 22:12,13; 28:19,20; 2 Chronicles 1:7-12; 15:6-8; 17:6; 20:6-12; 20:15-26; 32:7,8; 32:10-22; Ezra 7:27,28; Nehemiah 4:14-18; 6:9-16; Job 5:17-23; 9:32-35; 11:13-15; Psalm 3:5-7; 18:3-19; 27:1-3; 34:4-10; 37:1-6; 37:18,19; 37:30-34; 46:1-3; 55:22; 56:3,4,10,11; 60:11,12; 78:52,53; 91; 94:19; 112:1-9; 118:5-17; Proverbs 1:33; 25:26; 28:1; 29:25; 31:10-31; Isaiah 8:12; 12:1-3; 32:17-20; 33:13-24; 41:8-20; 43:1-7; 43:18-21;

51:7,8; 51:11-16; 54:4,5; 54:13-17; 57:14-19; Jeremiah 1:7-10; 1:17-19; 17:7,8; 20:8-12; 23:4-6; 42:11,12; 46:27,28; Ezekiel 2:6,7; 3:8,9; Daniel 3:16-18; 10:10-13; 10:18,19; Micah 3:8; Nahum 1:7; Habakkuk 3:2; 3:13,14; Zephaniah 3:11-15; Haggai 2:4-9; Zechariah 8:12,13; Matthew 6:25-34; 8:26; 9:22; 10:17-20; Mark 4:37-40; 5:36; Luke 1:30; 5:10; 6:46-48; 8:11-15; 8:24,25; 8:50; 10:41,42; 12:6,7; 12:21-34; 21:8; 21:34-36; John 6:37-40; 7:37-39; 12:31; 14:1-3; 14:27; Acts 4:10-13; 4:24-31; 5:18-20; 9:27,28; 13:46-48; 14:3; 18:9-11; 20:24; 23:11; 27:25; 28:30,31; Romans 8:14-17; 8:31-39; 1 Corinthians 15:48-58; 16:13,14; 2 Corinthians 4:5-11; 12:9,10; Ephesians 3:10-12; Philippians 1:6; 1:19-24; 1:27,28; 4:4-9; Colossians 3:12-17; 2 Timothy 1:6-10; Hebrews 2:5-3:1; 3:6; 3:18-4:16; 5:11-6:1; 10:32-12:3; 13:5,6; James 5:13-16a; 1 Peter 3:14-16; 5:5b-7; 1 John 4:15-18; Revelation 1:17,18; 2:9-11; 3:7-12; 12:10-12; 20:12.

YOUR **COVENANT** WITH GOD (Rooting the fact of your covenant into your spirit)

Genesis 15:11; 17:1,2; 17:6-9; 22:17,18; 28:13-15; Exodus 2:24; 6:4-6; 15:25,26; Leviticus 26:9-13; Numbers 25:12,13; Deuteronomy 8:11-18; 28:1-14; 28:15-28; 29:9; 30:9,10; 30:14-16; 2 Samuel 23:2-5; 1 Kings 8:23; 2 Kings 20:2-5; 22:18-20; 1 Chronicles 10:13,14; 16:14-17; 2 Chronicles 15:12,13; 20:15-26; Ezra 6:7-14; Nehemiah 1:5,6; 9:6-8; 9:30-32; 9:38; Job 5:17-23; Psalm 25:9-15; 89:28,29; 103:1-18; 105:42-45; 106:44-46; 11:4,5; 111:7-10; 119:57-64; 145:18-20; Proverbs 29:18; Isaiah 8:18-20; 33:13-24; 42:6-8; 43:1-7; 49:8-15; 54:4,5; 54:10; 55:3; 59:21-60:2; 61:6-10; 62:5; Jeremiah 31:31-34; 32:39-42; 33:25,26; 50:4,5; Ezekiel 16:8-13; 16:62,63; 20:37; 34:23-27; 37:26,27; Daniel 1:3,4; 1:15-17; 1:19,20; 3:16-18; Hosea 2:14-23; Amos 7:1-6; Jonah 2:9; Zechariah 8:12,13; 9:11-17; Malachi 2:5-7; Matthew 19:4-6; Luke 1:68-75; 6:20-23; 13:16; 15:22-24; 17:3,4; 18:22; 18:39-42; 22:19,20; John 5:19-30; 10:7-11; Acts 3:25,26; Romans 4:11,12; 1 Corinthians 2:9,10; 11:24-26; 2 Corinthians 1:20; 3:6; 3:10-12; Galatians 3:6-16; Ephesians 2:13-15; 2 Thessalonians 3:3; Hebrews 5:1,5; 7:21,22; 7:24-27; 8:6; 8:10-12; 9:24-28; 10:12-23; 10:26-29; 12:22-24; 13:20,21.

DELIVERANCE (Freedom from bondage of every kind; power to break habits; living free of oppression)

Exodus 6:4-6; 13:9; 19:4; 23:25,26; Leviticus 14:52,52; 26:9-13; Numbers 23:20-22; 24:5-9; Deuteronomy 8:11-18; 15:4-6; 28:15-68; Joshua 21:44,45; 24:15-18; Judges 2:18; 15:14-16; 1 Samuel 2:8-10; 30:6; 2 Samuel 5:20; 22:2-4; 22:5-25; 22:29-41; 22:48-51; 2 Kings 18:3-8; 18:29-36; 19:6,7; 19:19; 19:21-35; 22:18-20; 1 Chronicles 14:11; 2 Chronicles 12:7; 13:12; 17:6; 32:10-22; Ezra 7:6; Nehemiah 9:27,28; Job 5:17-23; Psalm 18:3-19; 25:9-15;

30:2-7; 31:3,4; 31:7,8; 34:4-10; 34:12-17; 34:18-22; 37:39,40; 41:1-3; 50:14,15; 50:23; 54:4,5; 55:22; 56:3,4,10,11; 62:5-12; 68:5,6; 68:17-20; 69:16-18; 71:3; 86:17; 91; 92:12-14; 97:10; 103:1-18; 107:28-30; 109:26-31; 116:13-16; 118:5-17; 119:41-43; 119:50; 119:57-64; 119:169-173; 121:2-8; 124:6-8; 129:4; 143:10,11; 145:8,9; 146:7,8; Proverbs 11:8,9; Isaiah 9:2-6; 33:2; 33:13-24; 35:3-10; 42:6-8; 43:1-7; 46:4; 46:13; 49:8-15; 50:4-9; 51:7,8; 51:11-16; 51:22,23; 52:1-3; 54:7,8; 58:6-9; 61:1-3; Jeremiah 29:11-14; 30:8,9; 42:11,12; Ezekiel 33:11; 34:23-27; Daniel 3:16-18; 3:28-30; 6:22-28; Hosea 11:3,4; 13:14; Joel 2:32; Obadiah 1:15-17; Jonah 2:6; 2:9; 3:8-10; Habakkuk 3:13,14; Zephaniah 3:17-20; Zechariah 2:7-9; 9:11-17; Matthew 6:9-13; 9:22; 11:27-30; Luke 1:68-75; 4:18,19; 4:40; 5:17-25; 7:50; 11:1-4; 13:11-13; 13:16; John 3:14-21; 8:31,32; 8:34-36; 16:7-11; Acts 5:12-16; 12:5-7; 15:8-11; 16:25; 26:16-18; Romans 7:6; 7:24,25; 8:1,2; 10:6-13; 2 Corinthians 1:8-11; 7:6; Galatians 1:3,4; 5:1; 5:13; Philippians 1:19-24; 3:2,3; Colossians 1:9-14; 2:6-17; 1 Timothy 4:14-16; 2 Timothy 3:10-12; 4:17,18; Hebrews 2:5-3:1; 10:32-12:3; James 1:19-25; 1 Peter 2:9-12; 5:8-11; 2 Peter 2:9; 1 John 3:5-7; Jude 20-23.

KNOWING YOUR **DESTINY** IN LIFE (Having a vision for your life; obtaining the right employment; fulfilling God's plan for your life [See also Guidance])

Genesis 12:1-3; 24:35; 30:29,30; 39:20-23; Exodus 35:34,35; 36:2; Deuteronomy 8:11-18; 20:3,4; 28:1-14; 28:15-68; 32:10-13; 1 Samuel 3:19; 12:22-24; 16:18; 2 Samuel 22:29-41; 1 Kings 2:2,3; 3:9-14; 4:32-34; 1 Chronicles 12:32; 15:22; 29:14-18; Ezra 7:6; Esther 14:14; Job 23:10-12; 33:23-30; 36:7-11; Psalm 16:5-11; 18:28-36; 25:3-5; 25:9-15; 33:18; 34:4-10; 37:1-6; 107:28-30; 119:57-64; 121:2-8; 138:8; 139:14; Proverbs 3:1-10; 12:24; 16:3; 16:9; 29:18; Ecclesiastes 3:22; 5:1-3; 5:18-20; 9:7-10; Isaiah 26:7-9; 42:16; 57:14-17; 65:17-25; Jeremiah 9:23,24; 10:23,24; 29:11-14; 31:16,17; Lamentations 3:22-26; Ezekiel 1:12; 1:20; 33:7-9; Daniel 2:14-23; 5:11,12; Hosea 11:3,4; 14:3-5; Joel 2:32; Amos 3:7; Habakkuk 2:1-4; Haggai 2:4-9; Matthew 9:28,29; Luke 5:10; 6:46-48; 9:51; John 5:19-30; 7:15-18; 10:1-5; 11:9-11; 15:7,8; 15:13-16; Acts 26:16-18; Romans 4:16-25; 8:23-30; 12:5,6; 13:12-14; 1 Corinthians 7:24; 9:20-27; 2 Corinthians 10:12; 12:1; Ephesians 1:11-14; 2:4-10; 5:15-21; Philippians 2:12,13; Colossians 1:9-14; 1 Thessalonians 2:12,13; 2 Thessalonians 1:11,12; 1 Timothy 1:3-11; 2:9-12; 4:14-16; 2 Timothy 3:10-12; Hebrews 6:13-20; 12:10-13; James 3:2-6; 4:13-17; Revelation 3:15-21.

DIRECTION (See Guidance, or Destiny)

DIVISION/STEERING CLEAR OF DIVISIVE PEOPLE (The dangers of listening to, or befriending, heresy hunters and those who are always looking for what is wrong with others instead of seeing what is best in them)

Deuteronomy 13:4,5; 1 Kings 18:21; 2 Kings 20:2-5; Psalm 26:4-7; 70:3; 81:13,14; 101:2-8; 119:111-116; Proverbs 8:8,9; 12:14-16; 15:1; 17:9; 20:3; 25:5-7; Isaiah 8:18-20; 41:8-20; 51:7,8; 54:13-17; Jeremiah 1:17-19; Ezekiel 2:6,7; 3:8,9; Daniel 6:22-28; Zephaniah 3:9; Matthew 7:1-5; 7:15-17; 10:17-20; 24:11-14; Mark 4:24; 11:22-25; Luke 5:17-25; 6:35-38; 17:3,4; John 10:1-5; 10:7-11; Acts 6:5,8-10; 9:22; Romans 13:12-14; 14:4; 16:17-20; 1 Corinthians 16:9; 4:22-32; 2 Corinthians 10:3-6; Galatians 5:15; 5:26-6:5; Ephesians 4:1-3; 4:11-13; Philippians 1:27,28; 2:2-11; 2:14-16; Colossians 2:2-4; 2:6-17; 2:18,19; 1 Timothy 1:3-11; 3:2-4,7; 5:19; 6:3-12; 6:20; 2 Timothy 2:14-16; 2:21-26; 3:5; 3:9; Titus 1:6-9; 2:1-10; 3:9-11; Hebrews 3:12,13; 10:24,25; James 1:19-25; 4:2-10; 4:11; 1 Peter 2:9-12; 1 John 4:1-6; 2 John 8,9; Jude 3; 16-19; Revelation 2:9-11.

DOMINION (Walking in your authority in this earth; your authority over the devil, etc.)

Genesis 1:26-28; 9:1-3; 15:11; 35:5; 45:8; Exodus 3:21,22; Deuteronomy 2:25; 7:21-23; 9:3; 11:18-28; 20:3,4; 28:1-14; 28:15-68; 33:20,21; 33:27-29; Joshua 1:5-9; 8:1; 8:24-26; 10:10; 10:24,25; 23:3; 24:11,12; 1 Samuel 10:6; 11:6; 2 Samuel 23:2-5; 1 Chronicles 14:17; 17:8-10; 2 Chronicles 1:7-12; 7:14-16; 32:10-22; Nehemiah 6:9-16; Esther 9:4; Psalm 2:1-9; 8:4-6; 18:37-40; 44:5-8; 91; 115:12-15; Proverbs 6:30,31; 12:10; Isaiah 40:10,11; 51:11-16; 51:22,23; 52:1-3; 55:3; Jeremiah 31:11-14; Ezekiel 36:25-27; Daniel 10:10-13; Hosea 2:14-23; Micah 3:8; 4:2; 4:6-8; 5:4; Nahum 1:15; 2:2,9; Zechariah 3:1-9; 12:8; Malachi 4:2,3; Matthew 4:1-11; 4:8-11; 5:39-45; 8:16; 9:32,33; 10:1; 10:7,8; 12:22; 12:28,29; 16:19; 17:19,20; 18:18; 18:19,20; 28:18-20; Mark 1:23-25; 1:34; 1:39; 3:14,15; 3:27; 6:7; 67:12,13; 8:15; 9:25; 9:28,29; 9:38,39; 16:15-20; Luke 1:68-75; 4:6-8; 4:35; 4:40; 5:17-25; 6:18,19; 7:21-23; 8:24,25; 9:1,2; 10:17-20; 10:22; 11:14; 11:20-25; 13:11-13; 13:16; 13:32; 15:22-24; 17:6-10; John 8:28,29; 12:31; 12:35,36; 14:30; 16:7-11; Acts 3:6; 4:10-13; 5:12-16; 8:6-8; 10:38; 19:11,12; 19:14-20; 28:8-10; Romans 12:9-21; 16:17-20; 1 Corinthians 3:21-23; 14:30-33; 15:22-26; 2 Corinthians 2:11; 10:3-6; Ephesians 1:3-10; 1:17-23; 3:10-12; 4:22-32; 6:10-18; Philippians 2:2-11; Colossians 2:6-17; Titus 2:11-15; Hebrews 1:13,14; 2:5-3:1; 10:12-23; 10:32-12:3; 1 John 2:12-14; 3:16-24; 4:1-6; Jude 24,25; Revelation 1:17,18; 2:26-28; 12:10-12; 19:11-21; 20:4-6; 22:2-5.

ENCOURAGEMENT (See Comfort)

FAITH (The power of the tongue; affirming your trust in the Lord; believing and speaking your way into the God-kind of life)

Exodus 13:9; Numbers 10:9; Deuteronomy 30:14-16; 32:1-4; Joshua 1:5-9; 10:24,25; 14:7-13; Judges 6:12-14; 1 Samuel 3:19; 9:6; 14:6; 2 Samuel 14:17; 23:2-5; 1 Kings 2:2,3; 17:24; 18:21; 2 Kings 6:13-18; 10:10; 1 Chronicles 5:22; 16:8-11; 2 Chronicles 6:29-31; 13:15; 14:6,7; 32:10-22; Nehemiah 1:5,6; 4:8,9; Job 4:3,4; 29:4-25; 31:24-28; 33:3,4; Psalm 3:1-3; 17:3; 18:3-19; 27:5,6; 34:12-17; 35:27,28; 37:30-34; 45:1,2; 101:2-8; 119:41-43; 138:2,3; 141:3,4; 147:15,18; Proverbs 4:23-27; 8:8,9; 10:11; 10:19-21; 11:11; 12:6,7; 12:14-16; 12:18; 13:2-4; 14:3; 15:4; 15:28; 16:24; 17:27; 18:20,21; 21:23; Ecclesiastes 5:1-3; Isaiah 7:9; 11:2-5; 26:7-9; 33:13-24; 41:8-20; 44:24-26; 50:4-9; 51:11-16; 55:10-12; 59:21-60:2; Jeremiah 1:7-10; 15:19-21; 20:8-12; Lamentations 3:37; Ezekiel 2:6,7; Daniel 2:14-23; Hosea 2:14-28; 14:1,2; Micah 2:7; 3:8; 4:2; 7:5; Habakkuk 2:1-4; 3:17-19; Zephaniah 3:9; 3:11-15; Matthew 4:1-11; 5:2-12; 5:37; 6:5-8; 7:7,8; 7:9-12; 7:13,14; 7:24,25; 8:8-10; 8:13; 8:16; 8:26; 9:28,29; 10:32; 12:35-37; 13:31-33; 15:18; 15:22-28; 17:19,20; 20:30-34; 21:19-22; 24:11-14; Mark 1:40-42; 4:26-32; 4:37-40; 5:36; 6:5,6; 11:22-25; 16:15-20; Luke 1:37,38; 5:17-25; 6:20-23; 6:43-45; 6:46-48; 7:7-9; 7:50; 8:24,25; 10:16; 11:1-4; 11:5-13; 13:18,19; 13:20,21; 13:23-29; 14:26-35; 17:3,4; 17:6-10; 18:7,8; 18:39-42; 21:34-36; John 3:27; 4:50; 5:19-30; 6:27-29; 6:63; 8:23; 8:26; 8:31,32; 8:47; 14:10-14; 14:27; 15:7,8; 15:13-16; 16:22-24; 16:25-27; 20:27-31; Acts 4:24-31; 5:12-16; 10:4; 11:25,26; 13:46-48; 14:8-10; 27:25; Romans 1:16,17; 3:20-26; 3:27,28; 4:4-8; 4:11,12; 4:16-25; 5:1,2; 5:3-5; 8:23-30; 9:30; 10:6-13; 10:17,18; 12:1-3; 12:5,6; 1 Corinthians 1:4,5; 1:30,31; 3:21-23; 13:13; 16:13,14; 2 Corinthians 1:18-22; 1:24; 4:13; 4:16-18; 5:1-7; 6:4-10; 7:4; 8:7; 9:5-15; 10:7; 10:15; Galatians 1:6; 2:16-21; 3:5; 3:6-16; 3:18; 3:22-29; 4:1-9; 5:5,6; 6:14-16; Ephesians 3:10-12; 3:14-21; 4:11-13; 4:14,15; 4:22-32; 5:15-21; 6:10-18; Philippians 1:19-24; 3:7-11; Colossians 1:21-23; 2:6-17; 2:18,19; 2:20-23; 1 Thessalonians 1:4,5; 3:10; 5:4-11; 2 Thessalonians 1:3; 1:11,12; 1 Timothy 1:3-11; 1:14-16; 1:18,19; 6:3-12; 2 Timothy 2:9,10; 2:21-26; 3:10-12; 3:14-17; 4:5; 4:6-8; Titus 2:1-10; Philemon 1:6; Hebrews 2:5-3:1; 3:6; 3:12,13; 3:18-4:16; 5:11-6:1; 6:10-12; 6:15; 6:13-20; 10:12-23; 10:32-12:3; James 1:2-8; 1:26; 2:5; 2:15-24; 3:2-6; 3:9,10; 4:2-10; 4:13-17; 5:12; 5:16b-18; 1 Peter 1:2-9; 3:8-12; 4:7-11; 5:8-11; 2 Peter 1:5-8; 1 John 3:16-24; 5:1-5; 5:13-15; 2 John 8,9; Jude 3; 20-23; Revelation 2:2-7; 2:13; 2:19; 12:10-12; 13:10; 19:10.

GOD'S **FAITHFULNESS** AND THE RELIABILITY OF HIS WORD

Genesis 8:22; 15:6; 28:13-15; 32:9; 39:20-23; 49:22-26; Exodus 2:24; 14:13-15; 15:25,26; 22:30; Leviticus 26:9-13; Numbers 11:23; 23:19; Deuteronomy 1:11; 8:3-5; 11:18-28; 13:4,5; 15:4-6; 28:1-14; 31:6; 31:8; 32:1-4; Joshua 1:5-

9; 23:7-14; 1 Samuel 12:22-24; 30:6; 2 Samuel 22:29-41; 1 Kings 8:15; 8:56; 2 Kings 10:10; 20:2-5; 22:18-20; 1 Chronicles 5:22; 16:14-17; 17:23; 2 Chronicles 1:7-12; 20:15-26; 26:5; 33:12,13; Ezra 6:7-14; Nehemiah 9:6-8; 9:17-21; 9:30-32; Psalm 3:1-3; 9:9,10; 12:6,7; 25:9-15; 31:3,4; 33:4; 33:11; 34:4-10; 56:3,4,10,11; 67:5-7; 78:4-7; 89:14-17; 91; 92:12-15; 111:7-10; 118:5-17; 119:160-162; 129:4; 138:8; 143:8; 145:13-16; Proverbs 30:5,6; Isaiah 26:7-9; 30:18-21; 40:29-31; 42:16; 61:6-10; Jeremiah 1:12; 17:7,8; 31:3,4; 33:25,26; Lamentations 2:17; 3:22-26; Ezekiel 12:25,28; Hosea 2:14-23; 14:9; Joel 2:25-29; Micah 2:7; 7:7-11; Haggai 2:19; Matthew 4:7; 5:2-12; Luke 18:39-42; 21:17-19; 21:33; John 5:19-30; 8:26; 9:31-33; 11:40-42; Acts 12:5-7; Romans 4:16-25; 10:6-13; 1 Corinthians 1:7-9; 10:13; 2 Corinthians 1:8-11; 1:18-22; Philippians 1:19-24; 4:15-20; Colossians 4:12; 1 Thessalonians 5:16-24; 2 Thessalonians 3:3; Hebrews 3:6; 10:12-23; 10:32-12:3; James 1:2-8; 4:2-10; 1 Peter 3:8-12; 2 Peter 3:13,14; Revelation 3:7-12; 3:14.

FAVOR (God's supernatural influence which brings you partiality and preeminence in every situation)

Genesis 6:8,9; 12:1-3; 12:16; 22:12-14; 27:27-29; 30:29,30; 39:2-5; 39:20-23; Exodus 3:21,22; 11:2,3; 12:36; 33:13,14; Leviticus 26:9-13; Numbers 6:24-27; Deuteronomy 28:1-14; 33:12-16; 33:20,21; Ruth 2:12; 1 Samuel 1:17,18; 2 Kings 13:23; 2 Chronicles 33:12,13; Ezra 7:9,10; 7:27,28; 8:18; Nehemiah 1:10,11; 2:8; 5:19; 9:17-21; 13:31; Job 29:4-25; 33:23-30; Psalm 5:11,12; 30:2-7; 41:1-3; 69:13; 72:1-19; 84:11; 85:1-3; 89:14-17; 90:17; 103:1-18; 106:3-5; 106:44-46; 111:4,5; 118:25-27; 119:57-64; 128:1-4; 145:8,9; 145:13-16; 147:19,20; Proverbs 3:1-10; 8:35; 10:6; 12:1,2; 13:15; 18:22; Ecclesiastes 9:7-10; Isaiah 26:12; 30:18-21; 49:8-15; 55:10-12; 60:10; 61:1-3; Jeremiah 15:19-21; Daniel 1:9; 1:19,20; 2:14-23; 2:46-49; 5:29; 10:10-13; Hosea 10:12; 14:1,2; Zechariah 11:7; Matthew 5:2-12; Mark 4:26-32; Luke 1:28; 1:30; 1:50-55; 2:14; 2:52; 4:18,19; 4:22; 4:42; 6:20-23; John 1:16-18; 13:13-17; Acts 2:42-47; 4:33,34; 5:12-16; 11:23,24; 20:32-35; 27:3; 28:8-10; Romans 3:20-26; 5:1,2; 16:17-20; 1 Corinthians 16:23,24; 2 Corinthians 9:5-15; 13:14; Galatians 1:3,4; Ephesians 1:3-10; Philippians 3:12-14; 4:10-13; 4:23; Colossians 1:6; 1 Timothy 1:14-16; Titus 2:11-15; Hebrews 3:18-4:16; 13:7-9; James 4:2-10; 1 Peter 1:2-9; 2 Peter 1:2-4; 2 John 3; Revelation 1:4-6; 22:20,21.

FELLOWSHIP WITH GOD (See Intimacy with God)

FELLOWSHIP WITH OTHER BELIEVERS (See Church)

BEING FILLED WITH THE SPIRIT (See God-Inside Minded)

FIGHT (See Spiritual Warfare)

HOW GOD FIGHT'S FOR YOU (God's Word that He will stand up for you and defend you; He will take up the battle as His own and rout the enemy on your behalf)

Genesis 12:1-3; Exodus 6:4-6; 14:13-15; 23:20-23; Numbers 10:9; Deuteronomy 3:22; 20:3,4; 31:8; 33:27-29; Joshua 1:5-9; 23:7-14; 24:11,12; Judges 11:24; 1 Samuel 17:45-48; 2 Samuel 22:5-25; 22:48-51; 2 Kings 19:21-35; 1 Chronicles 5:22; 16:21-24; 17:8-10; 18:6; 2 Chronicles 13:15; 14:11-13; 15:6-8; 20:15-26; Ezra 6:7-14; Nehemiah 4:4; 4:14-18; 9:27,28; Esther 5:9-6:11; 8:1,2; 9:25; Job 1:10; 5:17-23; 8:21,22; 16:19-21; 42:10,12; Psalm 2:1-9; 3:5-7; 5:11,12; 18:3-19; 18:28-36; 23; 27:1-3; 31:7,8; 35:1-6; 37:30-34; 44:5-8; 57:3-5; 60:4; 64:7-10; 70:3; 71:3; 81:13,14; 86:17; 103:1-18; 107:20,21; 107:28-30; 109:26-31; 111:4,5; Isaiah 8:9,10; 27:2-4; 41:8-20; 50:4-9; 54:13-17; 58:6-9; Jeremiah 20:8-12; 50:33,34; 51:36; Lamentations 3:58; Habakkuk 3:13,14; Zephaniah 3:17-20; Zechariah 3:1-9; 9:8; Malachi 3:6-12; Matthew 10:17-20; 10:26-31; Luke 13:17; 18:7,8; 21:17-19; John 6:37-40; 17:6-26; Acts 4:24-31; Romans 8:23-30; 8:31-39; 14:4; 16:17-20; 1 Corinthians 13:4-8; Hebrews 7:24-27; 10:32-12:3; 1 John 2:1-6.

FINANCES (Biblical economics; tithing; giving; offerings, etc.)

Genesis 8:22; 17:1,2; 26:12-14; 28:18-22; Exodus 23:19; 34:26; 35:5; 35:21; 35:29; Leviticus 27:30; Numbers 24:5-9; Deuteronomy 8:11-18; 11:18-28; 14:22-29; 15:10,11; 26:12-15; 28:1-14; 28:15-68; Joshua 23:3; Judges 5:9; 2 Samuel 6:14; 22:48-51; 1 Chronicles 21:24; 29:5-9; 29:14-18; 2 Chronicles 20:15-26; 31:10; Ezra 6:7-14; Nehemiah 10:35-38; 12:43; 13:10-14; Job 4:3,4; Psalm 15:2-5; 26:4-7; 27:5,6; 50:23; 37:21-26; 50:14,15; 67:5-7; 107:35-38; 112:1-9; 119:9-24; 119:57-64; 126:4-6; Proverbs 3:1-10; 11:18; 11:23-28; 14:31; 16:20; 21:20; 21:26; 28:25-27; Ecclesiastes 5:1-3; 11:1,2; 11:4-6; 12:1; 12:13; Song of Solomon 8:1-3; Isaiah 32:17-20; 35:3-10; 55:10-12; 66:2; Jeremiah 4:3; Ezekiel 16:62,63; 33:31,32; Hosea 2:14-23; 10:12; 14:1,2; Joel 2:2,3; 2:25-29; 3:9,10; Amos 9:13; Zephaniah 2:3; Haggai 1:5-11; 1:13,14; 2:19; Malachi 2:5-7; 3:6-12; 3:16-18; Matthew 4:1-11; 5:23,24; 6:1-4; 6:9-13; 6:25-34; 10:42; 13:8; 13:23; 13:31-33; 19:21; 20:30-34; 25:16,20,21,28,29; Mark 4:14-20; 4:24; 4:26-32; 10:21; 10:28-30; Luke 2:14; 4:3-13; 6:27-31; 6:35-38; 8:11-15; 11:1-4; 11:28; 12:21-34; 13:11-13; 13:17; 13:18,19; 16:9-12; 18:22; 18:29,30; 21:12-15; John 3:29,30; 8:28,29; 12:23-26; 13:13-17; Acts 2:42-47; 4:32; 10:4; 16:25; 18:27,28; 20:32-35; Romans 2:6,7; 6:2-14; 12:9-21; 13:7,8; 1 Corinthians 9:11; 13:4-8; 14:17-19; 15:48-58; 2 Corinthians 8:2-5; 8:7; 8:11,12; 8:19; 9:2; 9:5-15; Galatians 5:26-6:5; 6:6; 6:7-10; Ephesians 1:3-10; Philippians 4:15-20; 1 Timothy 4:14-16; 5:1-

4; 5:9,10,14; 2 Timothy 2:3-7; Titus 3:4-8; Hebrews 6:10-12; 10:32-12:3; 13:5,6; James 2:15-24; 3:13-18; 1 Peter 2:1-5; 2:9-12.

STAYING **ON FIRE** FOR GOD (Keeping the fire of the Spirit burning within you; remaining an enthusiastic, energetic and hardworking child of God; overcoming the spirit of heaviness in your life [See also Comfort])

Genesis 39:2-5; Exodus 15:25,26; Deuteronomy 15:10,11; 28:1-14; 29:9; Joshua 1:5-9; 1 Samuel 11:6; 2 Samuel 6:14; 1 Kings 2:2,3; 18:3-8; 1 Chronicles 22:12,13; 2 Chronicles 15:6-8; 27:6; 32:27-30; Ezra 7:9,10; 8:18; Nehemiah 2:20; Job 17:8,9; Psalm 1:1-3; 18:28-36; 40:7,8; 41:1-3; 73:23-26; 90:17; 119:9-24; 119:27,28; 119:74-81; Proverbs 3:1-10; 8:35; 11:18; 11:23-28; 12:11; 12:24; 12:28; 13:2-4; 13:11; 14:21-24; 19:2; 21:5; 21:21; 23:17; 28:19,20; 31:10-31; Ecclesiastes 11:4-6; 12:13; Isaiah 26:7-9; 33:13-24; 40:29-31; 44:1-5; Jeremiah 20:8-12; Ezekiel 16:8-13; Joel 2:2-11; Habakkuk 2:1-4; Zechariah 3:1-9; Matthew 9:28,29; 15:22-28; Mark 4:24; 4:26-32; 12:29-31; Luke 12:35,36; 13:23-29; 21:17-19; John 5:41-44; 7:15-18; Acts 19:14-20; Romans 12:9-21; 1 Corinthians 4:2; 12:31; 14:1-4; 14:12,13; 2 Corinthians 4:5-11; 6:4-10; 8:7; 9:2; Ephesians 6:5-8; Philippians 3:7-11; 1 Thessalonians 5:16-24; 2 Thessalonians 3:11,12; 1 Timothy 4:14-16; 2 Timothy 1:6-10; 2:3-7; 2:14-16; Titus 2:1-10; Jude 20-23; Revelation 2:2-7; 3:2-5.

FORGIVENESS (Forgiving and being forgiven; walking in God's abundant mercy)

1 Samuel 2:3,4; 2 Samuel 22:5-25; 1 Kings 8:23; 2 Chronicles 6:20,21; 6:27; 6:39; 12:7; 30:18-20; 33:12,13; Nehemiah 9:17-21; Job 16:19-21; 23:10-12; Psalm 25:9-15; 32:1,2; 34:18-22; 37:21-26; 69:16-18; 85:1-3; 86:5; 103:1-18; 130:7,8; 145:13-16; Song of Solomon 8:1-3; Isaiah 1:16-19; 12:1-3; 30:15; 33:13-24; 38:16-19; 40:1,2; 43:18-21; 43:25; 51:22,23; 52:1-3; 53:4-6; 53:10-12; 57:14-19; Jeremiah 3:22; 31:31-34; 33:8,9; 50:20; Ezekiel 16:8-13; 18:30-32; 33:16; 36:25-27; Daniel 12:9,10; Hosea 14:1,2; 14:3-5; Joel 2:13,14; Jonah 3:1-3; 3:8-10; Micah 7:7-11; 7:18-20; Zephaniah 3:11-15; Zechariah 1:3; 3:1-9; 13:1; 13:9; Matthew 6:9-13; 6:14,15; 7:1-5; 18:27,35; Mark 11:22-25; Luke 1:50-55; 1:77,78; 4:18,19; 6:35-38; 11:1-4; 13:11-13; 15:22-24; 17:3,4; 18:14; 18:39-42; John 1:16-18; 1:29; 3:14-21; 3:36; 5:19-30; 6:37-40; 16:25-27; Acts 2:23-28; 2:38,39; 3:19; 10:15; 10:43-46; 13:38,39; Romans 2:4; 4:4-8; 5:1,2; 5:9-11; 5:15-17; 6:2-14; 8:1,2; 8:23-30; 8:31-39; 9:23; 11:6; 1 Corinthians 1:7-9; 13:4-8; 2 Corinthians 1:12; 2:7,8; 4:1,2; 4:5-11; 5:14-21; 7:10,11; Galatians 3:2,3; 5:1; 6:14-16; Ephesians 1:3-10; 2:13-15; 4:22-32; Philippians 3:12-14; Colossians 1:9-14; 2:6-17; 3:12-17; 1 Timothy 1:14-16; Titus 3:4-8; Hebrews 3:18-4:1; 5:1,5; 5:9; 7:24-27; 8:10-12; 9:14,15; 9:24-28;

10:2; 10:12-23; James 5:13-16a; 1 Peter 1:2-9; 2:9-12; 3:18-22; 1 John 1:3-10; 2:1-6; 2:12-14; 3:5-7; 3:16-24; 2 John 3; Jude 2; 20-23; Revelation 1:4-6; 7:14; 20:12; 22:12-14.

GIVING (See Finances)

BEING **GOD-INSIDE MINDED** (Your partnership with God; knowing God is both with you and within you in every circumstance and acting like it)

Genesis 27:27-29; 28:13-15; 28:18-22; 39:2-5; 39:20-23; 41:38; Exodus 33:13,14; Leviticus 24:2,4; 26:9-13; Numbers 12:7,8; 13:30-33; 14:8,9; 23:20-22; Deuteronomy 8:11-18; 11:18-28; 20:3,4; 31:6; 31:8; Joshua 1:5-9; 14:7-13; Judges 2:18; 6:12-14; 15:14-16; 1 Samuel 2:3,4; 3:19; 10:6; 11:6; 14:6; 16:13; 16:18; 18:14; 30:6; 2 Samuel 8:6; 14:17; 22:29-41; 22:48-51; 23:2-5; 1 Kings 8:15; 2 Kings 5:5,6; 18:29-36; 1 Chronicles 11:9; 13:14; 14:11; 16:8-11; 17:8-10; 17:25-27; 19:13; 22:12,13; 28:19,20; 29:11-13; 2 Chronicles 1:1; 5:13,14; 6:20,21; 13:12; 15:2; 20:6-12; 20:27-30; 26:15,16; 32:7,8; Ezra 5:5; 6:3,4; Nehemiah 4:14-18; 6:9-16; 9:30-32; Job 29:4-25; 36:7-11; Psalm 3:5-7; 14:5; 16:5-11; 23; 27:1-3; 27:4; 27:13,14; 28:7; 54:4,5; 57:3-5; 60:11,12; 68:7-10; 69:16-18; 73:23-26; 85:8,9; 108:12,13; 109:26-31; 118:5-17; 139:7-10; 145:18-20; Proverbs 2:3-8; 3:1-10; 9:10-12; 10:22-24; Ecclesiastes 4:9-12; Isaiah 8:9,10; 8:12; 8:18-20; 11:2-5; 26:12; 27:2-4; 40:10,11; 41:8-20; 42:16; 43:1-7; 48:16-18; 50:4-9; 51:11-16; 54:4,5; 57:14-19; 59:21-60:2; 61:1-3; Jeremiah 1:17-19; 15:15-17; 15:19-21; 42:11,12; 46:27,28; 50:33,34; Ezekiel 1:12; 1:20; 3:14; 3:17-27; 33:24; 36:25-27; 37:26,27; Daniel 2:46-49; 5:11,12; 9:21-23; 10:10-13; Hosea 6:1-3; Joel 2:25-29; Micah 3:8; Zephaniah 3:11-15; 3:17-20; Haggai 1:13,14; 2:4-9; Zechariah 4:6; 9:11-17; 10:5,6; Matthew 9:28,29; 9:32,33; 10:17-20; 10:24,25; 10:26-31; 10:40; 12:28,29; 13:58; 19:26; 21:19-22; 22:29; 28:18-20; Mark 1:8; 1:23-25; 9:23; 10:27; 12:24; 16:15-20; Luke 1:28; 1:37,38; 1:68-75; 6:18,19; 8:50; 9:23-26; 11:5-13; 12:8; 14:33b; 17:20,21; 18:7,8; 18:27; 21:12-15; 21:34-36; John 3:34,35; 4:13,14; 5:17; 5:19-30; 6:54-58; 7:15-18; 7:37-39; 8:28,29; 10:25-30; 14:15-21; 14:23; 14:26; 15:1-5; 16:7-11; 16:13-15; 17:6-26; 20:21-23; Acts 1:5; 1:8; 2:4; 2:17-19; 2:33; 2:38,39; 4:24-31; 5:12-16; 5:42; 6:5,8-10; 7:55; 8:6-8; 10:38; 11:21; 11:23,24; 15:8-11; 18:9-11; Romans 8:9-13; 8:23-30; 8:31-39; 15:13,14; 15:18,19; 15:29-33; 16:17-20; 1 Corinthians 1:25; 2:9,10; 2:12-16; 3:16; 6:19,20; 16:9; 16:13,14; 2 Corinthians 1:3-5; 2:14; 3:16-18; 4:5-11; 5:1-7; 5:14-21; 6:1,2; 6:4-10; 6:14-7:1; 8:2-5; 10:12; 12:5; 12:9,10; 13:4; 13:11; 13:14; Galatians 2:16-21; 4:1-9; Ephesians 1:17-23; 2:22; 3:14-21; 5:15-21; Philippians 1:19-24; 2:12,13; 4:4-9; 4:23; Colossians 1:25-29; 2:6-17; 1 Thessalonians 5:16-24; 2 Thessalonians 1:11,12; 3:3; 1 Timothy 4:14-16; 6:3-12; 2 Timothy 1:6-10; 4:17,18; Hebrews 10:32-12:3;

13:5,6; 13:20,21; James 4:2-10; 4:13-17; 1 Peter 2:18,19; 2:20-23; 4:14; 1 John 2:12-14; 3:16-24; 4:1-6; 4:12,13; 4:15-18; 5:1-5; 5:11; 5:18-20; 2 John 8,9; Revelation 3:7-12.

GUIDANCE (Where to turn when you need direction in life; assurance that you are on the path of God's perfect will)

Numbers 6:24-27; Deuteronomy 28:15-68; 29:9; 32:10-13; 1 Samuel 12:22-24; 18:14; 2 Samuel 22:29-41; 1 Kings 22:5; 2 Kings 6:5,6; 1 Chronicles 10:13,14; 12:32; 29:14-18; 2 Chronicles 6:27; 13:7; 13:12; 18:4; 20:15-26; 32:10-22; 34:33; Ezra 6:7-14; Nehemiah 9:17-21; 9:25; Job 5:17-23; 22:27-30; 23:10-12; 29:4-25; 31:1-4; 31:24-28; 33:23-30; 36:7-11; 36:15,16; Psalm 1:1-3; 4:3,4; 11:4; 16:5-11; 18:28-36; 19:7-11; 20:4; 23; 25:3-5; 25:9-15; 27:10,11; 31:3,4; 32:8-10; 36:7-9; 37:21-26; 48:14; 73:23-26; 78:52,53; 84:11; 85:12,13; 86:11; 89:14-17; 90:12; 94:12-14; 103:1-18; 107:28-30; 119:9-24; 119:34-38; 119:57-64; 119:64-68; 119:97-101; 119:105-107; 119:130-133; 119:134,135; 119:169-173; 127:1-5; 139:7-10; 139:14; 143:8; 143:10,11; 144:1,2; 144:12-15; Proverbs 2:20; 3:1-10; 3:12-18; 4:23-27; 10:22-24; 11:14; 12:14-16; 13:18; 15:21,22; 15:31,32; 16:3; 16:9; 16:20; 19:2; 19:21; 20:18; 24:5,6; 28:13; 29:18; Isaiah 8:18-20; 9:2-6; 26:7-9; 30:18-21; 42:16; 48:16-18; 49:8-15; 50:4-9; 57:14-19; 58:11; Jeremiah 3:14,15; 10:21; 10:23,24; 29:8,9; 31:16,17; Lamentations 2:17; 3:22-26; Ezekiel 1:12; 1:20; 3:17-27; 33:7-9; Daniel 2:14-23; Hosea 2:14-23; 11:3,4; 14:3-5; Joel 2:2-11; 2:23; Micah 4:2; 5:4; 6:8,9; Habakkuk 2:1-4; Haggai 2:4-9; Zechariah 9:11-17; Matthew 4:1-11; 7:15-17; 10:17-20; 10:24,25; 10:26-31; 13:23; Mark 8:34; 12:24; Luke 1:50-55; 6:27-31; 6:40; 9:23-26; 11:1-4; 11:5-13; 12:6,7; 12:35,36; 18:7,8; John 3:29,30; 5:19-30; 6:45-51; 8:12; 8:47; 10:1-5; 11:9-11; 12:35,36; 12:44-46; 13:13-17; 14:15-21; 14:26; 15:26; 16:13-15; 20:21-23; Acts 6:5,8-10; 8:21; 9:31; 13:52; 20:24; 23:11; 26:19,20; Romans 8:4-6; 8:9-13; 8:14-17; 8:23-30; 1 Corinthians 7:24; 13:4-8; 2 Corinthians 2:14; 6:4-10; Galatians 2:16-21; 5:5,6; 5:16; 5:18; 5:22-25; Ephesians 4:11-13; 5:1,2; 5:15-21; Philippians 4:4-9; Colossians 1:9-14; 2 Thessalonians 3:5; 1 Timothy 1:18,19; Hebrews 6:10-12; 6:15; 10:32-12:3; 13:7-9; 13:17,18; James 1:19-25; 2:8,9; 2:12; 3:2-6; 4:2-10; 4:13-17; 5:16b-18; 1 John 2:27-29; 4:1-6; 4:15-18; 3 John 11; Revelation 3:2-5; 3:7-12; 3:15-21; 14:4,5; 17:14; 19:11-21.

HAPPINESS (See Joy)

HEALING

Exodus 12:12,13; 12:23; 15:25,26; 23:25,26; 30:12; Deuteronomy 7:14,15; 28:15-68; Joshua 14:7-13; 1 Samuel 20:14,15; 2 Kings 5:10-14; 20:2-5; 2 Chronicles 27:6; 30:18-20; Ezra 6:3,4; Job 5:26; 33:23-30; Psalm 1:1-3; 23; 30:2-7; 41:1-3; 72:1-19; 84:11; 103:1-18; 107:20,21; 119:93; 119:105-107;

119:11-116; 144:12-15; 146:7,8; Proverbs 3:1-10; 3:12-18; 4:23-27; 5:18,19; 8:35; 9:6; 9:10-12; 12:18; 12:28; 13:2-4; 14:29,30; 15:4; 15:30; 16:24; 17:22; 18:14; 18:20,21; Isaiah 33:13-24; 38:16-19; 40:29-31; 44:1-5; 46:4; 49:8-15; 51:11-16; 53:4-6; 57:14-19; 58:6-9; 58:11; Jeremiah 17:14; 30:17,18; 32:39-42; 33:6; 33:25,26; 39:17,18; Ezekiel 18:21,22; 34:14-16; Daniel 1:3,4; 1:15-17; Hosea 6:1-3; 11:3,4; 13:14; Micah 3:8; Malachi 2:5-7; 4:2,3; Matthew 4:4; 6:9-13; 8:3; 8:8-10; 8:16; 8:17; 9:22; 9:35; 10:1; 10:7,8; 12:15; 12:22; 13:15,16; 14:14; 17:19,20; 21:14; Mark 1:34; 1:40-42; 3:14,15; 4:26-32; 5:34; 6:12,13; 9:25; 10:52; 16:15-20; Luke 4:4; 4:18,19; 4:39; 4:40; 5:12,13; 5:17-25; 6:18,19; 7:7-9; 7:21-23; 8:46-48; 9:1,2; 9:6; 9:11; 10:9; 10:17-20; 11:1-4; 13:11-13; 13:23-29; 13:32; 17:19; 18:39-42; John 5:14; 9:3; 9:31-33; Acts 3:6; 3:16; 4:10-13; 5:12-16; 8:6-8; 9:33,34; 10:38; 14:8-10; 19:11,12; 28:8-10; Romans 8:9-13; 10:6-13; 1 Corinthians 12:6-11; 13:4-8; 2 Corinthians 4:5-11; 4:16-18; 5:14-21; 6:4-10; Galatians 1:3,4; 3:6-16; 6:7-10; Ephesians 6:10-18; Philippians 1:9-11; 1 Timothy 5:23; Titus 2:1-10; Hebrews 10:32-12:3; 12:10-13; James 3:2-6; 5:13-16a; 1 Peter 2:24,25; 3 John 2; Revelation 18:4.

HOLINESS (Obedience; integrity; loyalty; the blessings of living a godly life)

Genesis 6:22; 7:5; 17:1,2; Exodus 15:25,26; 23:2; 23:19; 23:20-23; 34:26; 35:5; 35:21; 35:29; Leviticus 5:1; 10:8,9; 11:44,45; 22:32; 27:30; Numbers 14:24; Deuteronomy 4:39,40; 5:33; 6:18,19; 6:24,25; 14:20-29; 15:4-6; 26:12-15; 28:1-14; 30:9,10; Joshua 14:7-13; 22:3; 24:15-18; 2 Samuel 22:5-25; 1 Kings 2:2,3; 3:9-14; 8:23; 2 Kings 5:10-14; 10:27; 18:3-8; 18:29-36; 1 Chronicles 10:13,14; 16:14-17; 21:24; 29:14-18; 2 Chronicles 19:9; 20:15-26; 27:6; 30:6-9; 31:20,21; 34:2; 34:33; Ezra 7:9,10; 7:27,28; Nehemiah 1:5,6; 1:10,11; 10:29; 10:35-38; 10:39; 13:10-14; Esther 9:4; Job 1:1; 1:8; 2:3; 8:5-7; 11:13-15; 22:21,22; 23:10-12; 31:1-4; Psalm 4:3,4; 11:7; 15:2-5; 17:3; 18:20-24; 26:4-7; 34:12-17; 37:1-6; 37:30-34; 37:37; 39:1; 40:7,8; 45:7; 50:23; 57:6; 51:10; 66:18; 81:13,14; 85:8,9; 101:2-8; 105:42-45; 106:3-5; 111:7-10; 112:1-9; 119:9-24; 119:34-38; 119:57-64; 119:97-101; 119:130-133; 119:147-149; 141:3,4; Proverbs 10:8,9; 13:21,22; 16:7; 16:20; 20:7; 21:5; 22:1; 23:17; 23:20,21; 24:16; 28:9; 28:13; 29:18; 30:8; 31:4,5; 31:10-31; Ecclesiastes 3:12,13; 5:1-3; 7:16-18; 12:13; Isaiah 1:16-19; 33:13-24; 35:3-10; 50:4-9; 51:7,8; 52:7-12; 55:3; Jeremiah 1:7-10; 6:16; 15:15-17; 22:3; 33:8,9; Ezekiel 3:8,9; 11:17-20; 18:21,22; 20:7; 37:24,25; Daniel 3:16-18; 5:29; 6:3,4; 6:10; 6:13; 6:22-28; Hosea 14:1,2; 14:9; Amos 5:14,15; Obadiah 1:15-17; Jonah 2:9; 3:1-3; 3:8-10; Micah 2:7; 3:8; 6:8,9; Zephaniah 2:3; 3:11-15; Haggai 1:5-11; Zechariah 8:16,17; 13:9; Malachi 2:5-7; 3:6-12; Matthew 5:2-12; 5:13-16; 5:28; 5:29,30; 5:37; 5:48; 6:9-13; 6:22; 10:37-39; 18:8,9; 26:41; Mark 4:24; Luke 4:6-8; 4:13; 5:5; 6:24-26; 6:27-31; 6:43-45; 6:46-48; 8:11-15; 9:51; 11:28; 11:33-36; 22:40,41; John 4:34-38; 5:14; 7:15-18; 8:31,32; 8:49-51;

8:54,55; 9:31-33; 10:1-5; 12:23-26; 12:44-46; 14:15-21; 14:23; 14:30; 15:13-16; 18:37; Acts 1:5; 4:33,34; 5:27-29; 15:28,29; 17:11; 23:1; 24:14-16; 26:19,20; Romans 2:6,7; 3:20-26; 6:2-14; 6:15-18; 6:22,23; 8:4-6; 8:9-13; 12:1-3; 12:9-21; 13:1,2; 13:7,8; 13:12-14; 14:17; 16:17-20; 1 Corinthians 1:30,31; 4:2; 6:9-12; 6:13-15; 6:18; 7:35; 10:13; 10:31; 15:33,34; 2 Corinthians 1:12; 6:4-10; 6:14-7:1; 8:21; 10:3-6; 13:4; 13:11; Galatians 2:16-21; 3:2,3; 5:16; 6:7-10; Ephesians 1:3-10; 1:17-23; 4:1-3; 4:22-32; 5:3-7; 5:8-11; 5:15-21; 6:1-3; Philippians 1:9-11; 1:19-24; 1:27,28; 2:14-16; 3:2,3; 3:7-11; 3:12-14; 3:16; Colossians 1:9-14; 2:20-23; 3:5-7; 3:8-10; 3:20; 1 Thessalonians 4:3-5; 4:7; 5:4-11; 2 Thessalonians 3:13; 1 Timothy 1:3-11; 2:9-12; 3:2-4,7; 3:8-13; 4:7,8; 4:12,13; 5:21; 5:22; 6:3-12; 6:20; 2 Timothy 2:19; 2:21-26; Titus 1:6-9; 2:11-15; 3:1,2; 3:4-8; Hebrews 3:12,13; 9:14,15; 9:24-28; 10:10; 10:12-23; 10:26-29; 10:32-12:3; 12:14-16; 13:17,18; James 1:19-25; 1:27; 3:2-6; 3:13-18; 4:2-10; 5:12; 1 Peter 1:13-23; 2:1-5; 2:9-12; 2:13-15; 2:16,17; 2:24,25; 3:8-12; 4:1,2; 4:7-11; 5:8-11; 2 Peter 1:5-8; 3:11; 3:13,14; 1 John 1:3-10; 2:1-6; 3:1-3; 3:5-7; 5:1-5; 5:18-20; 5:21; 3 John 6,7; 11; Jude 3; Revelation 2:26-28; 11:18; 14:4,5; 14:12; 16:15; 18:4; 21:23-27; 22:11.

HONESTY (See Holiness, or Faith [power of the tongue])

YOUR POSITION OF HONOR IN THE EYES OF GOD (Walking in the state of being that Jesus has raised you to)

Genesis 1:26-28; 12:1-3; Deuteronomy 33:27-29; 1 Samuel 2:8-10; 9:6; 2 Samuel 6:21,22; 22:29-41; 1 Chronicles 18:13; 28:6; 29:11-13; 29:28; 2 Chronicles 1:1; 1:7-12; 32:27-30; Ezra 7:27,28; Nehemiah 13:10-14; Esther 5:9-6:11; 9:4; Job 11:13-15; 11:19; 22:27-30; 29:4-25; 36:7-11; Psalm 3:1-3; 8:4-6; 11:7; 18:28-36; 27:5,6; 33:4; 34:4-10; 37:30-34; 62:5-12; 65:4,5; 72:1-19; 82:1,6; 84:11; 89:14-17; 89:28,29; 91; 92:12-15; 109:26-31; 110:3; 112:1-9; 113:7-9; 118:5-17; 119:34-38; 145:13-16; Proverbs 3:1-10; 13:18; 15:33; 20:3; 22:1; 25:5-7; 25:27; 29:23; 31:10-31; Isaiah 41:8-20; 43:1-7; 45:4-6; 49:5,6; 52:1-3; 53:10-12; 66:2; Jeremiah 1:17-19; Daniel 2:46-49; 6:22-28; 10:18,19; Hosea 2:14-23; Joel 2:25-29; 2:32; Nahum 2:2,9; Habakkuk 3:17-19; Zephaniah 3:11-15; 3:17-20; Zechariah 3:1-9; 10:5,6; 12:8; Matthew 5:2-12; 5:19,20; 10:24,25; 19:21; 23:12; 25:16,20,21,28,29; Mark 10:42,43; 16:15-20; Luke 1:50-55; 10:17-20; 10:41,42; 18:14; 20:35,36; 22:26; John 8:49-51; 8:54,55; 10:34,35; 12:23-26; 17:6-26; Acts 10:34; Romans 2:6,7; 2:10,11; 12:1-3; 12:9-21; Ephesians 2:4-10; Philippians 2:2-11; Colossians 3:1-3; Hebrews 2:5-3:1; 10:32-12:3; 1 Peter 3:18-22; 5:5b-7; Revelation 3:15-21.

HUMILITY (Acknowledging your total dependency upon God; rejecting pride and arrogance and remaining humble in your walk before God and man)

1 Chronicles 29:14-18; 2 Chronicles 7:14-16; 12:7; 33:12,13; Esther 9:4; Psalm 16:2; 25:9-15; Proverbs 9:10-12; 15:31,32; 15:33; 19:23; 22:4; 25:5-7; 25:27; 27:1,2; 29:23; Isaiah 11:2-5; 45:23,24; 66:2; Jeremiah 9:23,24; 10:23,24; Ezekiel 16:62,63; Daniel 10:10-13; Hosea 11:8-11; Micah 6:8,9; Habakkuk 3:2; Zephaniah 2:3; 3:11-15; Haggai 2:4-9; Malachi 1:14; Matthew 5:2-12; 23:12; Luke 1:50-52; 6:40; 18:14; 18:39-42; 22:26; John 1:3,4; 3:14-21; 5:19-30; 5:41-44; 6:45-51; 8:49-51; 8:54,55; 13:13-17; 15:1-5; 15:19-21; Romans 11:16-18; 12:1-3; 12:9-21; 1 Corinthians 8:1; 13:4-8; 14:30-33; 2 Corinthians 10:17,18; 13:4; Galatians 5:26-6:5; 6:14-16; Ephesians 3:14-21; 4:1-3; Philippians 2:2-11; Colossians 2:18,19; 3:12-17; 1 Timothy 2:9-12; 5:9,10,14; Titus 3:1,2; James 3:13-18; 4:2-10; 1 Peter 2:16,17; 5:5b-7.

IDENTIFICATION (Jesus' substitution on your behalf; how everything that Jesus is and did is set to your account; being one with Jesus; being *in Christ, in Him, in Jesus, etc.*)

Psalm 16:5-11; 34:4-10; 34:18-22; Ecclesiastes 2:24-26; Isaiah 9:2-6; 12:1-3; 42:6-8; 45:23,24; 46:13; 53:4-6; 53:10-12; 60:17-21; 65:17-25; Jeremiah 23:4-6; Daniel 2:14-23; Hosea 2:14-23; 6:1-3; 14:9; Micah 5:4; 7:7-11; Matthew 10:32; 10:37-39; 12:22; 16:23-25; 26:26,27; Mark 1:8; 8:34; Luke 1:77-79; 4:13; 4:18,19; 7:21-23; 20:35,36; 22:29; 24:45; John 3:14-21; 5:19-30; 6:35; 6:45-51; 6:54-58; 7:15-18; 8:34-36; 8:39; 9:4,5; 10:7-11; 10:14,15; 11:25,26; 12:23-26; 14:15-21; 15:1-5; 15:7,8; 15:9-11; 15:19-21; 16:25-27; 16:33; 17:6-26; 20:17; Acts 1:5; 1:8; 2:23-28; 13:32-34; 17:26-29; Romans 3:20-26; 3:27-28; 4:4-8; 4:16-25; 5:1,2; 5:9-11; 6:2-14; 7:1,4; 8:1,2; 8:14-17; 8:23-30; 8:31-39; 15:13,14; 1 Corinthians 1:30,31; 3:21-23; 6:17; 11:24-26; 15:22-26; 15:48-58; 2 Corinthians 1:3-5; 4:5-11; 5:14-21; 8:9; 13:4; Galatians 2:16-21; 3:6-16; 3:22-29; 5:22-25; 6:14-16; Ephesians 1:3-10; 1:11-14; 1:17-23; 2:4-10; 2:13-15; Philippians 2:2-11; 3:7-11; Colossians 1:9-14; 2:6-17; 2:18,19; 2:20-23; 3:1-3; 3:4; 1 Thessalonians 5:4-11; 2 Timothy 1:6-10; 2:8; 2:11-13; Hebrews 1:1-4; 2:5-3:1; James 1:2-8; 1 Peter 2:1-5; 3:18-22; 1 John 3:16-24; 5:11; 5:18-20; Revelation 1:17,18; 2:9-11; 3:14; 3:15-21; 17:14; 19:11-21.

THE INDWELLING OF THE HOLY SPIRIT (See God-Inside Minded)

YOUR INHERITANCE (Engrafting into your spirit the fact that you are an heir of God and joint heir with Jesus)

Genesis 1:26-28; 13:6; Leviticus 26:9-13; Deuteronomy 4:39,40; 6:2; 6:5-13; 10:14; 28:1-14; 15:4-6; 33:20,21; Joshua 14:7-13; 18:3; Judges 11:24; Ruth

2:12; 2 Kings 20:2-5; 1 Chronicles 4:9,10; 29:11-13; 29:28; 2 Chronicles 1:15; 9:22,23; Nehemiah 2:20; Psalm 2:1-9; 16:5-11; 17:4; 25:9-15; 37:9-11; 37:21-26; 37:30-34; 68:7-10; 72:1-19; 94:12-14; 105:42:45; 118:25-27; 127:1-5; Proverbs 13:21,22; 23:4; 28:10; 30:8; Isaiah 3:10; 43:1-7; 49:8-15; 54:13-17; 61:6-10; 65:17-25; Jeremiah 3:19; 12:15; 33:8,9; Obadiah 1:15,17; Micah 7:18-20; Haggai 2:4-9; Zechariah 3:1-9; 8:12,13; Matthew 5:2-12; Luke 1:50-52; 1:68-75; 6:20-23; John 17:6-26; Acts 3:25,26; 17:26-29; 20:32-35; Romans 4:16-25; 8:14-17; 1 Corinthians 6:9-12; Galatians 3:18; 3:22-29; 4:1-9; Ephesians 1:11-14; 1:17-23; Colossians 1:9-14; 3:22-24; 1 Timothy 6:3-12; Titus 3:4-8; Hebrews 6:10-12; 9:14,15; 10:32-12:3; 12:14-16; James 1:2-8; 2:5; 4:2-10; 1 Peter 1:2-9; Revelation 3:15-21.

INTEGRITY (See Holiness)

INTERCESSION (See Prayer and Intercession)

INTIMACY WITH GOD (Your friendship with God; your closeness to God; having true, intimate fellowship with God)

Genesis 18:17; Exodus 33:13,14; Numbers 12:7,8; Deuteronomy 4:29; 6:5-13; 11:18-28; 13:4,5; 31:6; 33:12-16; Joshua 23:7-14; 1 Samuel 3:21; 2 Kings 18:3-8; 1 Chronicles 5:20; 16:8-11; 28:9; 2 Chronicles 1:7-12; 5:13,14; 6:20,21; 14:6,7; 15:2; 15:12,13; 18:4; 20:6-12; 26:5; 26:15,16; 30:6-9; 30:18-20; 33:12,13; Ezra 7:9,10; Nehemiah 1:5,6; Job 2:3; 16:19-21; 22:21,22; 23:10-12; 29:4-25; 33:23-30; 36:15,16; Psalm 4:3,4; 9:9,10; 25:9-15; 27:4; 28:7; 30:2-7; 34:4-10; 34:18-22; 37:21-26; 51:6; 62:5-12; 69:16-18; 73:23-26; 97:10; 103:1-18; 119:57-64; 119:160-162; 125:2; 145:18-20; 149:4; Proverbs 2:3-8; 3:12-18; 9:10-12; 10:22-24; Ecclesiastes 5:18-20; 8:15; 12:1; Song of Solomon 2:3-6; 8:1-3; 11:2-5; 26:3,4; 26:7-9; 30:18-21; 33:2; 41:8-20; 42:6-8; 54:4,5; 55:3; 62:5; 65:17-25; Jeremiah 9:23,24; 15:15-17; 24:5-7; 29:11-14; 31:31-34; 32:39-42; 33:2,3; 50:4,5; Daniel 3:16-18; 10:10-13; Hosea 2:14-23; 11:8-11; Joel 2:13,14; 2:25-27; Amos 3:7; 7:1-6; Micah 7:7-11; Zephaniah 2:3; Zechariah 11:7; Malachi 3:6-12; 3:16-18; Matthew 10:32; 10:37-39; 18:8,9; Mark 1:35; 6:46; Luke 4:42; 5:15,16; 6:12; 6:20-23; 10:22; 10:41,42; 11:1-4; 12:6,7; 12:21-34; 14:26-35; 18:39-42; John 1:16-18; 4:23,24; 5:17; 5:41-44; 6:35; 8:19; 8:32,42; 8:54,55; 10:1-5; 10:7-11; 10:14,15; 10:25-30; 14:10-14; 14:15-21; 14:23; 15:9-11; 15:13-16; 15:19-21; 16:7-11; 16:25-27; 17:3; Acts 15:8-11; 22:14; Romans 11:6; 1 Corinthians 1:7-9; 8:3; 13:1-3; 13:4-8; 14:26-28; 2 Corinthians 2:14; 5:14-21; Galatians 1:10-12; 4:1-9; Philippians 3:12-14; Colossians 3:1-3; Hebrews 1:1-4; 7:17-19; 8:10-12; 10:32-12:3; 12:22-24; James 2:5; 2:15-24; 4:2-10; 5:10,11; 5:13-16a; 1 Peter 1:2-9; 3:8-12; 3:18-22; 1 John 1:3-10; 2:12-14; 5:13-15; 2 John 6; 8,9; 3 John 2; 6,7; Revelation 2:2-7; 2:13; 3:15-21; 21:1-7; 22:2-5.

JOY (Living a joy-filled life; staying happy; freedom from depression)

Genesis 12:1-3; 22:17,18; Deuteronomy 28:1-14; 33:27-29; 1 Samuel 1:17,18; 2 Samuel 6:21,22; 2 Kings 20:2-5; 1 Chronicles 29:5-9; 29:14-18; 2 Chronicles 17:6; 20:27-30; Nehemiah 8:9-12; 9:25; 12:43; Job 8:21,22; Psalm 1:1-3; 5:11,12; 16:5-11; 19:7-11; 28:7; 31:7,8; 34:12-17; 42:5,11; 45:7; 51:12; 64:7-10; 84:4-7; 89:14-17; 92:4; 94:12-14; 94:19; 105:42-45; 106:3-5; 107:28-30; 109:26-31; 115:12-15; 119:111-116; 119:169-173; 145:18-20; Proverbs 3:12-18; 5:18,19; 9:6; 9:10-12; 10:6; 12:4; 12:20; 13:2-4; 15:15; 15:30; 16:20; 17:22; 18:14; 18:22; 29:17; 29:18; Ecclesiastes 3:12,13; 3:22; 5:10; 5:18-20; 8:15; 9:7-10; 11:9; Song of Solomon 2:3-6; Isaiah 9:2-6; 12:1-3; 35:3-10; 41:8-20; 49:8-15; 51:11-16; 55:10-12; 60:17-21; 61:1-3; 61:6-10; 65:17-25; Jeremiah 31:11-14; Ezekiel 34:14-16; Hosea 2:14-23; 11:8-11; Joel 2:23; Nahum 1:15; Habakkuk 3:17-19; Zephaniah 3:11-15; Zechariah 8:19; Matthew 5:2-12; 9:22; 13:15,16; 25:16,20,21,28,29; Mark 4:26-32; 6:31; Luke 6:20-23; 15:22-24; 18:22; John 16:22-24; 17:6-26; Acts 2:23-26; 8:6-8; 13:46-48; 13:52; 20:24; Romans 5:3-5; 5:9-11; 12:9-21; 14:17; 15:13,14; 1 Corinthians 1:30,31; 2 Corinthians 5:1-7; 6:4-10; 7:4; 8:2-5; 9:5-15; Galatians 5:22-25; Philippians 1:19-24; 4:4-9; 4:10-13; 4:15-20; Colossians 1:9-14; 1 Thessalonians 4:15-18; 5:16-24; 2 Timothy 3:10-12; James 4:2-10; 1 Peter 1:2-9; 1 John 1:3-10; 2:1-6; 3 John 4; Jude 24,25; Revelation 1:3; 12:10-12; 19:6-9.

KINGDOM LIVING (Focusing on the kingdom of God instead of the cares of this present world)

Leviticus 26:9-13; Joshua 14:7-13; Ruth 2:12; 1 Kings 3:9-14; 2 Kings 19:21-35; 1 Chronicles 14:17; 15:22; 29:11-13; 29:14-18; 2 Chronicles 1:1; 1:7-12; 7:14-16; 9:22,23; 31:20,21; 33:12,13; Ezra 7:9,10; Esther 4:14; Psalm 66:12; 68:7-10; 112:1-9; Proverbs 18:20,21; 21:20; 25:5-7; 29:18; Isaiah 8:18-20; 35:3-10; 41:8-20; 48:16-18; 56:3; Jeremiah 21:8; 31:16,17; Ezekiel 33:31,32; Daniel 1:15-17; 1:19,20; 5:29; Hosea 2:14-23; Joel 2:2-11; 2:32; Haggai 1:5-11; 2:19; Malachi 3:6-12; Matthew 5:2-12; 5:19,20; 6:9-13; 6:25-34; 9:35; 10:7,8; 11:12; 13:11,12; 13:31-33; 16:19; 21:43; 25:16,20,21,28,29; Mark 3:14,15; Luke 1:77-79; 6:20-23; 8:9,10; 8:17,18; 9:1,2; 9:11; 10:9; 10:22; 11:1-4; 11:20-23; 12:15; 12:21-34; 13:18,19; 13:20,21; 13:23-29; 14:26-35; 15:22-24; 16:9-12; 16:16; 17:6-10; 17:20,21; 18:22; 18:29,30; 20:35,36; 22:29; 22:35,36; John 3:3; 3:5; 3:34,35; 4:34-38; 5:19-30; 7:15-18; 10:7-11; 11:9-11; 12:23-26; 15:19-21; 17:6-26; Acts 5:12-16; 14:21,22; 17:26-29; 28:30,31; Romans 14:17; 1 Corinthians 4:15,16; 6:9-12; 15:22-26; 15:48-58; 2 Corinthians 5:14-21; 6:4-10; 12:1; Ephesians 1:3-10; 2:4-10; 5:3-7; 6:10-18; Philippians 1:19-24; 4:15-20; Colossians 1:9-14; 1 Thessalonians

2:12,13; 5:4-11; 1 Timothy 6:3-12; Hebrews 6:10-12; 12:28,29; James 2:5; 2 Peter 1:10,11; Revelation 1:4-6; 2:19; 12:10-12.

YOUR CALL TO **LEADERSHIP**

Genesis 12:1-3; 39:2-5; 39:20-23; 41:38; Deuteronomy 15:4-6; 28:1-14; 28:15-68; 33:20,21; Joshua 23:7-14; 1 Samuel 9:6; 2 Samuel 23:2-5; 1 Chronicles 18:13; 2 Chronicles 7:14-16; 9:22,23; Job 4:3,4; 11:9; 29:4-25; Psalm 8:4-6; 72:1-19; Proverbs 12:24; 13:14; 17:9; 25:15; 28:10; 31:10-31; Jeremiah 1:7-10; 10:21; Daniel 2:46-49; 3:28-30; 5:29; 6:3,4; Zechariah 3:1-9; Malachi 2:5-7; Mark 4:26-32; Luke 4:6-8; 12:42; John 8:54,55; 10:34,35; 15:19-21; Acts 8:6-8; 28:30,31; 2 Corinthians 9:2; Ephesians 6:9; Colossians 4:1; 1 Timothy 3:2-4,7; 3:8-13; 4:12,13; 2 Timothy 2:21-26; 4:2; Titus 1:1-3; 2:1-10; Hebrews 10:32-12:3; 1 Peter 5:2,3; 5:5b-7; Revelation 1:4-6; 2:26-28.

LONG LIFE (God's promises for a long, full, satisfying and abundant life)

Genesis 15:15; Exodus 23:25,26; Deuteronomy 4:39,40; 5:33; 6:2; 6:24,25; 8:3-5; 28:15-68; 1 Samuel 20:14,15; 1 Kings 3:9-14; 2 Kings 22:18-20; 1 Chronicles 29:28; 2 Chronicles 1:7-12; Job 5:26; Psalm 72:1-19; 91; 92:12-15; 119:9-24; 119:93; 119:105-107; 119:111-116; Proverbs 3:1-10; 3:12-18; 9:10-12; Isaiah 46:4; 65:17-25; Micah 4:2; Matthew 4:4; Ephesians 6:1-3; Philippians 1:19-24; Hebrews 10:32-12:3; Revelation 12:10-12.

GOD'S **LOVE** FOR YOU

Genesis 32:9; 32:12; Exodus 14:13-15; 22:27; Numbers 14:8,9; Deuteronomy 8:3-5; 8:11-18; 32:10-13; 33:12-16; 33:27-29; Judges 2:18; 5:9; 1 Samuel 12:22-24; 20:14,15; 2 Samuel 22:5-25; 22:48-51; 1 Kings 3:5; 8:15; 8:23; 2 Kings 13:23; 1 Chronicles 16:34; 2 Chronicles 1:7-12; 5:13,14; 6:20,21; 7:14-16; 12:7; 15:12,13; 20:6-12; 20:15-26; 30:6-9; 30:18-20; 33:12,13; Ezra 3:10,11; 5:5; 6:7-14; Nehemiah 1:5,6; 5:19; 9:17-21; 9:25; 9:27,28; 9:30-32; 13:31; Job 1:8; 1:22; 16:19-21; 22:27-30; Psalm 8:4-6; 17:14; 18:3-19; 23; 25:9-15; 27:10,11; 32:8-10; 33:18; 34:18-22; 36:7-9; 37:28; 42:5,11; 57:3-5; 62:5-12; 69:13; 69:16-18; 86:5; 89:14-17; 89:28,29; 91; 94:12-14; 103:1-18; 106:44-46; 107:20,21; 107:28-30; 107:43; 109:26-31; 111:4,5; 115:12-15; 116:5,6; 116:13-16; 119:41-43; 119:74-81; 130:7,8; 138:8; 139:7-10; 143:8; 145:8,9; 145:13-16; 146:7,8; 147:11: 147:19,20; 149:4; Proverbs 9:10-12; Song of Solomon 2:3-6; 8:1-3; 8:6,7; Isaiah 30:18-21; 33:2; 35:3-10; 38:16-19; 40:10,11; 41:8-20; 42:6-8; 43:1-7; 43:25; 49:8-15; 53:10-12; 54:7,8; 54:10; 55:3; 60:10; 61:1-3; 62:5; 65:17-25; 66:2; 66:13; Jeremiah 9:23,24; 12:15; 24:5-7; 29:11-14; 30:17,18; 31:3,4; 32:39-42; 33:25,26; Lamentations 3:22-26; Ezekiel 16:62,63; 33:11; 34:14-16; Daniel 10:10-13; Hosea 2:14-23; 11:3,4; 11:8-11; 14:3-5; Joel 2:13,14; Jonah 3:8-10;

Micah 7:18-20; Nahum 1:7; Zephaniah 3:17-20; Zechariah 2:7-9; Malachi 3:16-18; Matthew 6:25-34; 7:9-12; 10:26-31; 14:14; 18:27,35; Luke 1:28; 1:68-75; 6:35-38; 11:34,35; 12:44-46; 14:1-3; 14:4-7; 14:15-21; 14:23; 15:9-11; 15:13-16; 16:25-27; 17:6-26; Acts 16:31; Romans 2:4; 5:3-5; 8:31-39; 11:22; 15:29-33; 1 Corinthians 13:4-8; 2 Corinthians 1:3-5; 5:14-21; 7:6; 13:14; Ephesians 1:3-10; 2:4-10; 3:14-21; 1 Thessalonians 1:4,5; 2 Thessalonians 2:13-17; 3:5; 1 Timothy 6:3-12; Titus 3:4-8; Hebrews 9:11,12; James 5:10,11; 5:13-16a; 1 Peter 2:1-5; 3:8-12; 2 Peter 1:5-8; 1 John 2:1-6; 3:1-3; 3:16-24; 3:16-24; 4:9,10; 4:15-18; 2 John 3; 3 John 2; Jude 2; 20-23; Revelation 1:4-6; 2:13; 3:7-12; 3:15-21.

WALKING IN **LOVE**

Deuteronomy 1:17; Psalm 15:2-5; Proverbs 3:1-10; 13:24; 14:21-24; 14:31; 15:1; 17:9; 19:11; 19:17; 20:3; 22:9; 29:11; 31:10-31; Ecclesiastes 10:20; Ezekiel 11:17-20; Hosea 10:12; Zephaniah 3:8; Matthew 5:2-12; 5:39-45; 6:1-4; 6:9-13; 6:14,15; 7:1-5; 18:27,35; 24:11-14; Mark 11:22-25; 12:29-31; Luke 6:27-31; 6:35-38; 11:1-4; 11:42; 17:3,4; John 13:13-17; 13:20; 13:34,35; 15:12; 15:17; Acts 4:33,34; 15:32; 17:26-29; 18:27,28; Romans 1:11,12; 12:9-21; 13:7,8; 13:10; 14:4; 14:12,13; 14:19; 15:2; 1 Corinthians 8:1; 13:1-3; 13:4-8; 13:13; 14:1-4; 16:13,14; 16:23,24; 2 Corinthians 2:7,8; 6:4-10; 8:7; 8:24; Galatians 5:5,6; 5:13; 5:15; 5:22-25; 5:26-6:5; Ephesians 3:14-21; 4:1-3; 4:14,15; 4:22-32; 5:1,2; 5:22-24,33b; 5:25-33; 6:9; Philippians 1:9-11; 2:2-11; 4:4-9; Colossians 2:2-4; 3:12-17; 1 Thessalonians 1:4,5; 2:12,13; 3:12,13; 5:4-11; 2 Thessalonians 1:3; 1 Timothy 1:3-11; 1:14-16; 5:1-4; 6:3-12; 2 Timothy 1:6-10; 2:21-26; 3:10-12; Titus 1:6-9; 2:1-10; 3:1,2; Hebrews 6:10-12; 10:24,25; 12:14-16; 13:1-3; James 1:19-25; 1:27; 2:1-3; 2:8,9; 2:12; 3:13-18; 1 Peter 1:13-23; 2:16,17; 3:8-12; 4:7-11; 2 Peter 1:5-8; 1 John 2:10; 3:14; 3:16-24; 4:7; 4:12,13; 5:1-5; 2 John 6; Jude 20-23; Revelation 2:2-7; 2:19.

MARRIAGE (God's Word for satisfaction and fulfillment with your life partner)

Deuteronomy 28:15-68; 1 Samuel 20:14,15; 2 Samuel 23:2-5; 1 Chronicles 17:25-27; 29:28; Ezra 8:21-23; Nehemiah 4:14-18; Job 1:10; 29:4-25; Psalm 21:11,12; 127:1-5; 128:1-4; Proverbs 5:18,19; 12:4; 12:6,7; 14:11; 18:22; 21:21; 24:3,4; 31:10-31; Ecclesiastes 9:7-10; Isaiah 33:13-24; 43:1-7; 54:13-17; 58:6-9; 65:17-25; Hosea 4:6; 11:8-11; Nahum 1:15; Malachi 2:15,16; Matthew 7:24,25; 13:31-33; 19:4-6; 21:43; Mark 10:7-9; Acts 16:31; 17:26-29; 20:32-35; Ephesians 5:22-24,33b; 5:25-33; Colossians 3:18; 3:19; 1 Timothy 2:9-12; 3:2-4,7; 3:8-13; 5:9,10,14; Titus 1:6-9; 2:1-10; Hebrews 13:4; 1 Peter 3:1-6; 3:7.

MOURNING (See Comfort)

NEW CREATION REALITIES (Salvation; what it means to be born again; your rights as a son/daughter of God; affirming the reality of your relationship/kinship with God)

Genesis 1:26-28; 9:1-3; Exodus 30:12; Leviticus 26:9-13; Numbers 6:24-27; 12:7,8; 14:24; Deuteronomy 2:7; 6:24,25; 10:14; Joshua 23:7-14; Ruth 1:16; 2:12; 1 Samuel 2:8-10; 3:21; 9:6; 10:6; 12:22-24; 14:6; 2 Samuel 6:21,22; 22:5-25; 1 Kings 2:2,3; 3:9-14; 17:24; 2 Kings 19:19; 1 Chronicles 4:9,10; 16:14-17; 28:6; 29:11-13; 2 Chronicles 1:7-12; 1:15; 6:20,21; Ezra 6:7-14; 7:6; Nehemiah 6:9-16; 9:6-8; Job 2:3; 22:27-30; 29:4-25; 33:3,4; 33:23-30; Psalm 2:1-9; 8:4-6; 25:9-15; 27:4; 30:2-7; 32:1,2; 32:8-10; 48:14; 65:4,5; 72:1-19; 82:1,6; 84:4-7; 91; 94:12-14; 110:3; 116:13-16; 118:25-27; 128:1-4; 139:14; 143:10,11; 146:7,8; Proverbs 9:10-12; 13:13,21,22; 31:4,5; Song of Solomon 8:1-3; Isaiah 1:16-19; 12:1-3; 40:10,11; 41:8-20; 43:1-7; 44:1-5; 44:24-26; 45:4-6; 49:8-15; 51:11-16; 52:1-3; 53:10-12; 56:3; 57:14-19; 59:21-60:2; 65:17-25; 66:13; Jeremiah 3:14,15; 3:19; 24:5-7; 30:8,9; 31:31-34; 33:8,9; 50:20; Ezekiel 11:17-20; 16:8-13; 18:30-32; 20:37; 34:23-27; 36:25-27; 36:29,30; Daniel 1:3,4; Hosea 2:14-23; 6:1-3; Joel 2:2-11; 2:32; Micah 4:2; 4:6-8; 7:18-20; Nahum 2:2,9; Zechariah 3:1-9; 13:9; Matthew 4:1-11; 5:2-12; 5:19,20; 10:24,25; 10:37-39; 12:50; 16:23-25; Mark 3:35; Luke 3:8; 4:3-13; 4:22; 6:20-23; 6:27-31; 6:35-38; 6:40; 8:21; 10:17-20; 10:22; 11:1-4; 11:33-36; 12:8; 12:21-34; 13:23-29; 15:22-24; 20:35,36; John 1:3,4; 1:12,13; 1:16-18; 3:3; 3:5; 3:14-21; 4:10; 4:13,14; 4:23,24; 5:41-44; 6:37-40; 6:45-51; 6:54-58; 6:63; 8:19; 8:23; 8:34-36; 8:39; 8:42,43; 8:54,55; 9:31-33; 10:1-5; 10:7-11; 10:14,15; 10:25-30; 10:34,35; 11:25,26; 12:23-26; 14:1-3; 14:4-7; 14:23; 15:1-5; 15:7,8; 15:19-21; 16:7-11; 16:22-24; 16:25-27; 17:3; 17:6-26; 20:17; 20:27-31; Acts 2:17-19; 2:38,39; 3:25,26; 10:43-46; 13:38,39; 17:26-29; 19:14-20; 28:8-10; Romans 2:29; 3:20-26; 3:27,28; 4:4-8; 4:16-25; 5:15-17; 6:2-14; 6:15-18; 7:1,4; 8:1,2; 8:4-6; 8:9-13; 8:14-17; 8:18,19; 8:23-30; 9:6,7; 9:26; 10:3,4; 11:6; 11:16-18; 1 Corinthians 1:30,31; 15:48-58; 2 Corinthians 1:18-22; 3:16-18; 5:1-7; 5:14-21; 6:1,2; 6:14-7:1; 12:1; Galatians 2:16-21; 3:6-16; 3:22-29; 4:1-9; 5:18; 5:22-25; 6:14-16; Ephesians 1:3-10; 1:11-14; 2:4-10; 2:13-15; 2:18,19; 2:22; 4:22-32; 5:1,2; 5:3-7; 5:8-11; Philippians 2:2-11; 2:14-16; 3:2,3; 3:7-11; 3:20,21; Colossians 1:9-14; 1:21-23; 2:6-17; 3:1-3; 3:4; 3:8-10; 3:11; 3:12-17; 1 Thessalonians 1:4,5; 5:4-11; 2 Thessalonians 1:11,12; 2:13-17; 1 Timothy 1:3-11; 1:14-16; 2:5,6; 3:6; 2 Timothy 1:6-10; 2:19; 2:21-26; Titus 2:11-15; 3:4-8; Hebrews 2:5-3:1; 3:6; 5:11-6:1; 8:10-12; 9:11,12; 10:26-29; 10:32-12:3; 12:5-8; 12:22-24; James 1:16-18; 1:19-25; 5:16b-18; 1 Peter 1:2-9; 1:13-23; 2:1-5; 2:9-12; 3:8-12; 3:18-22; 4:16; 2 Peter 1:2-4; 1 John 1:3-10; 2:1-6; 2:15-17; 2:23; 2:24,25;

2:27-29; 3:5-7; 3:14; 3:16-24; 4:7; 4:9,10; 4:15-18; 5:1-5; 5:11; 5:13-15; 5:18-20; 3 John 11; Revelation 1:4-6; 2:17; 3:2-5; 3:14; 19:11-21; 20:4-6; 20:12; 21:1-7; 21:23-27; 22:11; 22:12-14.

OBEDIENCE (See Holiness)

OFFERINGS (See Finances)

PATIENCE AND PERSEVERANCE (Being stouthearted enough to finish the job; remaining faithful until the answer is manifested; refusing to be a quitter)

Deuteronomy 31:8; 2 Samuel 22:29-41; 2 Chronicles 15:6-8; Nehemiah 9:17-21; 9:30-32; Job 8:5-7; Psalm 27:13,14; 62:5-12; 112:1-9; 119:27,28; 119:138-140; 126:4-6; Proverbs 14:21-24; 14:29,30; 19:11; 19:23; 20:3; 20:22; 20:25; 23:4; 24;10; 25:15; 25:21,22; 29:11; 31:10-31; Isaiah 30:18-21; Lamentations 3:22-26; Daniel 6:22-28; Hosea 10:12; Micah 7:7-11; Matthew 5:2-12; 7:7,8; 7:9-12; 7:13,14; 13:31-33; 15:22-28; 17:19,20; 20:30-34; Mark 4:26-32; 13:13; Luke 5:15,16; 6:35-38; 8:11-15; 13:18,19; 13:20,21; 13:23-29; 21:20,21; Romans 5:3-5; 8:23-30; 1 Corinthians 13:4-8; 2 Corinthians 4:5-11; 6:4-10; Galatians 5:5,6; 5:22-25; Ephesians 4:1-3; 6:10-18; Philippians 4:15-20; Colossians 1:9-14; 3:12-17; 1 Thessalonians 1:4,5; 2 Thessalonians 3:5; 1 Timothy 6:3-12; 2 Timothy 2:9,10; 2:11-13; 2:21-26; 3:10-12; 4:2; 4:5; Titus 2:1-10; Hebrews 6:10-12; 6:15; 6:13-20; 10:32-12:3; James 1:2-8; 1:12; 5:10,11; 1 Peter 1:2-9; 2:18,19; 2:20-23; 2 Peter 1:5-8; Revelation 2:2-7; 2:19; 3:7-12; 13:10; 14:12.

PEACE

Genesis 22:17,18; Exodus 14:13-15; 33:13,14; Leviticus 26:6; Numbers 6:24-27; Deuteronomy 28:1-14; 28:15-68; Joshua 21:44,45; Judges 5:31; 6:23,24; 1 Samuel 1:17,18; 2 Samuel 14:17; 1 Kings 5:12; 8:56; 2 Kings 19:21-35; 20:2-5; 1 Chronicles 22:9; 2 Chronicles 14:6,7; 20:27-30; Job 22:21,22; 36:7-11; Psalm 1:1-3; 3:5-7; 4:8; 27:1-3; 29:11; 34:12-17; 37:9-11; 37:37; 62:5-12; 68:17-20; 85:8,9; 119:64-68; 119:74-81; 119:165; 127:1-5; 128:1-4; Proverbs 10:6; 12:20; 13:2-4; 14:29,30; 16:7; 29:17; 31:10-31; Isaiah 9:2-6; 26:3,4; 26:12; 32:17-20; 33:13-24; 40:1,2; 48:16-18; 52:7-12; 53:4-6; 54:13-17; 55:10-12; 57:14-19; 60:17-21; 61:1-3; 65:17-25; Jeremiah 33:6; Ezekiel 18:21,22; 34:23-27; 37:26,27; Daniel 10:18,19; Micah 5:4; Nahum 1:15; Zephaniah 3:11-15; Haggai 2:4-9; Zechariah 8:19; Malachi 2:5-7; Matthew 5:2-12; 5:23,24; 6:9-13; 6:25-34; Mark 4:26-32; 5:34; Luke 1:77-79; 2:14; 7:50; 8:46-48; John 14:27; 16:33; 20:21-23; Romans 2:10,11; 5:1,2; 8:4-6; 12:9-21; 14:17; 15:13,14; 15:29-33; 16:17-20; 1 Corinthians 7:1-5; 2 Corinthians 13:11; Galatians 5:22-25; 6:14-16; Ephesians 2:13-15; 4:1-3; Philippians 4:4-9; 4:10-13; Colossians 3:12-17; 1 Thessalonians 4:11,12;

5:4-11; 2 Thessalonians 3:16; 1 Timothy 2:7,8; 2 Timothy 1:6-10; 2:21-26; Titus 3:1,2; Hebrews 3:18-4:16; 12:10-13; 12:14-16; 13:20,21; James 3:2-6; 3:13-18; 1 Peter 1:2-9; 3:8-12; 2 Peter 1:2-4; 3:13,14; 2 John 3; Jude 2; Revelation 1:4-6.

ENDURING PERSECUTION (Overcoming trials, prejudice, unfair treatment and oppression)

Genesis 27:27-29; Numbers 10:9; Deuteronomy 28:1-14; Joshua 1:5-9; 21:44,45; Judges 2:18; 1 Samuel 14:6; 17:45-48; 2 Samuel 22:2-4; 22:5-25; 22:29-41; 22:48-51; 2 Kings 19:6,7; 19:21-35; 2 Chronicles 13:12; 15:6-8; 32:7,8; 32:10-22; Ezra 8:21-23; Nehemiah 4:4; 4:8,9; 4:14-18; Esther 5:9-6:11; 9:25; Job 36:15,16; Psalm 2:1-9; 3:1-3; 3:5-7; 21:11,12; 34:18,22; 37:30-34; 37:39,40; 41:1-3; 54:4,5; 57:3-5; 64:7-10; 69:16-18; 94:12-14; 107:28-30; 109:26-31; 119:50; Proverbs 11:8,9; 12:6,7; 12:14-16; 25:21,22; Isaiah 8:9,10; 8:12; 41:8-20; 43:1-7; 50:4-9; 51:7,8; 54:13-17; Jeremiah 1:17-19; 20:8-12; 51:36; Ezekiel 3:8,9; Daniel 3:16-18; 3:28-30; Habakkuk 3:13,14; Matthew 5:2-12; 5:13-16; 5:39-45; 10:17-20; 10:26-31; Mark 4:14-20; 10:28-30; 13:13; Luke 1:68-75; 6:20-23; 6:27-31; 8:11-15; 21:12-15; John 8:49-51; 15:19-21; 16:33; Acts 4:24-31; 5:42; 6:5,8-10; 9:22; 12:11; 18:9-11; 26:16-18; Romans 5:3-5; 8:18,19; 8:31-39; 12:9-21; 1 Corinthians 16:9; 2 Corinthians 4:5-11; 4:16-18; 12:9,10; Colossians 1:9-14; 2 Thessalonians 1:6,7; 2 Timothy 1:12; 2:3-7; 2:9,10; 3:10-12; Hebrews 10:32-12:3; James 1:2-8; 1:12; 1:13,14; 5:10,11; 1 Peter 1:2-9; 2:18,19; 2:20-23; 3:8-12; 3:14-16; 4:14; 4:16; 2 Peter 2:9; Revelation 2:9-11; 3:7-12.

PRAISE AND WORSHIP (Loosing yourself from the bonds of religious idealism and false dignity and praising God freely—with *all* of your heart—the way you know He wants you to)

Deuteronomy 8:11-18; 2 Samuel 6:14; 6:21,22; 22:48-51; 23:2-5; 1 Kings 4:32-34; 1 Chronicles 13:8; 16:8-11; 16:21-24; 2 Chronicles 5:13,14; 15:12,13; 20:15-26; 20:27-30; Ezra 3:10,11; Nehemiah 12:43; Job 8:21,22; 33:23-30; Psalm 8:2; 16:5-11; 18:3-19; 26:4-7; 27:5,6; 28:7; 30:2-7; 35:27,28; 36:7-9; 44:5-8; 45:1,2; 47:5; 50:23; 56:3,4,10,11; 64:7-10; 67:5-7; 68:35; 72:1-19; 84:4-7; 92:12-15; 103:1-18; 106:3-5; 107:28-30; 109:26-31; 118:5-17; 119:57-64; 119:169-173; 132:15,16; 150; Proverbs 19:23; Ecclesiastes 3:1-8; 5:1-3; Isaiah 12:1-3; 35:3-10; 38:16-19; 43:18-21; 49:8-15; 52:7-12; 55:10-12; 57:14-19; 60:17,21; 61:1-3; Jeremiah 31:3,4; 31:11-14; Hosea 14:1,2; Joel 2:25-29; Jonah 2:9; Habakkuk 3:17-19; Zephaniah 3:11-15; Matthew 5:2-12; 6:9-13; Luke 2:14; 6:20-23; 11:1-4; 13:11-13; John 4:23,24; Acts 2:23-28; 10:43-46; 16:25; 24:14-16; 1 Corinthians 14:14,15; 14:17-19; 2 Corinthians 1:8-11; Ephesians 1:3-10; 5:15-21; Philippians 3:2,3; 4:4-9; Colossians 1:9-

14; 2:6-17; 2:20-23; 3:1-3; 3:12-17; 1 Thessalonians 5:16-24; Hebrews 2:5-3:1; 12:28,29; 13:15,16; James 5:13-16a; 1 Peter 2:9-12; 4:7-11; 4:16; Revelation 12:10-12; 19:10.

PRAYER AND INTERCESSION (Standing in the gap for the ones you love [and even the ones you don't]; approaching God's throne with supplications and petitions for the various needs of the world; being bold enough to petition God with the deepest desires of your heart)

Genesis 18:27; 1 Samuel 1:17,18; 12:22-24; 2 Samuel 23:2-5; 1 Kings 3:5; 3:9-14; 2 Kings 13:4; 20:2-5; 1 Chronicles 4:9,10; 2 Chronicles 1:7-12; 6:20,21; 6:29-31; 6:39; 7:14-16; 30:27; 32:10-22; 33:12,13; Ezra 6:7-14; 7:6; 8:21-23; Nehemiah 1:5,6; 1:10,11; Job 8:5-7; 9:32-35; 22:27-30; 29:4-25; 33:23-30; Psalm 4:3,4; 18:3-19; 30:2-7; 34:12-17; 37:1-6; 41:1-3; 65:4,5; 68:5,6; 69:13; 69:16-18; 72:1-19; 91; 106:29-31; 119:147-149; 122:6-8; 138:2,3; Proverbs 10:19-21; 10:22-24; 28:9; 31:8; Isaiah 1:16-19; 30:18-21; 33:13-24; 35:3-10; 41:8-20; 42:6-8; 58:6-9; 61:1-3; 65:17-25; Jeremiah 22:3; 29:11-14; Ezekiel 22:30; Daniel 2:14-23; 9:18,19; 9:21-23; 10:10-13; Hosea 6:1-3; 14:1,2; Zechariah 10:5,6; 12:10; 13:9; Matthew 5:39-45; 6:5-8; 6:9-13; 6:16-18; 6:22; 7:7,8; 7:9-12; 7:13,14; 9:37,38; 18:19,20; 20:30-34; 26:41; Mark 1:35; 6:46; 9:28,29; 11:22-25; 13:33; 14:38; Luke 4:42; 5:15,16; 6:12; 10:2; 11:1-4; 11:5-13; 17:3,4; 18:7,8; 18:39-42; 22:40,41; 22:42; John 9:31-33; 11:40-42; 14:10-14; 15:7,8; 15:13-16; 15:19-21; 16:22-24; 16:25-27; Acts 2:4; 4:24-31; 5:12-16; 10:4; 12:5-7; 28:8-10; Romans 3:20-26; 5:1,2; 8:23-30; 10:6-13; 12:9-21; 14:4; 15:29-33; 1 Corinthians 13:1-3; 14:1-4; 14:5,6; 14:14,15; 14:17-19; 14:20-25; 14:26-28; 2 Corinthians 1:18-22; 5:14-21; 6:4-10; 9:5-15; Galatians 5:5,6; Ephesians 2:18,19; 3:10-12; 3:14-21; 5:15-21; 6:10-18; 6:18-20; Philippians 4:4-9; 4:10-13; Colossians 4:2-4; 4:12; 1 Thessalonians 5:16-24; 1 Timothy 2:1-4; 2:7,8; 4:4,5; 5:5-7; Philemon 20; Hebrews 3:18-4:16; 7:17-19; 10:12-23; 10:32-12:3; 13:17,18; James 2:15-24; 5:13-16a; 5:16b-18; 1 Peter 2:1-5; 3:8-12; 4:7-11; 1 John 3:16-24; 5:13-15; Jude 20-23.

PROSPERITY (success, provision, etc.)

Genesis 8:22; 9:1-3; 12:1-3; 12:16; 13:2; 13:6; 14:23; 15:1; 17:1,2; 22:17,18; 24:35; 26:12-14; 27:27-29; 28:13-15; 28:18-22; 30:43; 31:9; 39:2-5; 39:20-23; 48:15,16; 49:22-26; Exodus 3:21,22; 34:26; 35:5; 35:21; 35:29; Leviticus 26:5; 26:9-13; 27:30; Numbers 24:5-9; Deuteronomy 1:11; 2:7; 6:5-13; 6:24,25; 7:14,15; 8:11-18; 14:22-29; 15:4-6; 15:10,11; 16:15; 26:12-15; 28:1-14; 28:15-68; 29:9; 30:9,10; 30:14-16; 32:10-13; 33:12-16; 33:20,21; Joshua 1:5-9; 22:8; Ruth 2:12; 1 Samuel 2:8-10; 2 Samuel 22:5-25; 1 Kings 2:23; 3:9-14; 2 Kings 6:5,6; 18:3-8; 19:21-35; 20:2-5; 1 Chronicles 4:9,10; 11:9; 13:14;

17:25-27; 21:24; 22:12,13; 29:5-9; 29:11-13; 29:28; 2 Chronicles 1:7-12; 1:15; 6:27; 9:22,23; 9:27; 14:6,7; 14:11-13; 16:7; 20:15-26; 26:5; 31:10; 31:20,21; 32:27-30; Ezra 6:3,4; 6:7-14; 7:6; 8:18; Nehemiah 1:10,11; 2:20; 9:15; 9:17-21; 9:25; 13:10-14; Esther 8:1,2; Job 1:10; 8:5-7; 11:19; 22:21,22; 27:16,17; 29:4-25; 31:24-28; 36:7-11; 36:15,16; 42:10-12; Psalm 1:1-3; 5:11,12; 16:5-11; 17:14; 18:20-24; 19:7-11; 20:4; 20:7,8; 23; 25:9-15; 30:2-7; 31:3,4; 31:7,8; 34:4-10; 35:27,28; 36:7-9; 37:1-6; 37:9-11; 37:18,19; 37:21-26; 37:37; 41:1-3; 62:5-12; 65:4,5; 65:11; 66:12; 66:18; 67:5-7; 68:7-10; 68:17-20; 72:1-19; 81:16; 84:4-7; 84:11; 85:1-3; 85:12,13; 90:17; 92:12-15; 94:12-14; 106:3-5; 107:35-38; 111:4,5; 112:1-9; 115:12-15; 116:13-16; 118:5-17; 118:25-27; 119:9-24; 119:11-116; 119:169-173; 122:6-8; 126:4-6; 129:4; 130:7,8; 132:15,16; 144:12-15; Proverbs 3:1-10; 3:12-18; 6:30,31; 8:18-21; 8:35; 9:6; 9:10-12; 10:4; 10:13-15; 10:22-24; 11:18; 11:23-28; 12:11; 12:14-16; 12:28; 13:2-4; 13:11; 13:21,22; 14:21-24; 15:6; 15:21,22; 16:20; 18:20,21; 19:17; 19:21; 20:7; 21:20; 21:26; 22:1; 22:4; 22:9; 23:4; 24:3,4; 25:27; 28:10; 28:13; 28:19,20; 28:25-27; 30:8; 31:10-31; Ecclesiastes 2:24-26; 3:12,13; 5:10; 5:18-20; 7:12; 8:15; 11:1,2; 11:4-6; Song of Solomon 2:3-6; Isaiah 1:16-19; 3:10; 12:1-3; 23:17,18; 26:12; 27:2-4; 32:17-20; 33:5,6; 33:13-24; 41:8-20; 43:18-21; 44:1-5; 48:16-18; 49:8-15; 51:11-16; 52:7-12; 55:3; 55:10-12; 61:6-10; 65:17-25; 66:10,11; Jeremiah 3:19; 4:3; 12:15; 17:7,8; 29:7; 29:11-14; 30:17,18; 31:11-14; 32:39-42; 33:8,9; 33:25,26; Lamentations 3:22-26; Ezekiel 16:8-13; 18:21,22; 33:31,32; 34:14-16; 34:23-27; 36:29,30; 37:26,27; Daniel 2:46-49; 6:22-28; Hosea 2:14-23; 6:1-3; Joel 2:19; 2:23; 2:25-29; 3:9,10; Amos 9:13; Obadiah 1:15-17; Jonah 2:6; Micah 7:7-11; Nahum 2:2,9; Habakkuk 3:17-19; Zephaniah 2:7; 2:9; 3:11-15; 3:17-20; Haggai 1:5-11; 1:13,14; 2:4-9; 2:19; Zechariah 8:12,13; 9:11-17; 10:1; Malachi 2:5-7; 3:6-12; Matthew 5:2-12; 6:1-4; 6:9-13; 6:19-21; 6:24; 6:25-34; 7:13,14; 10:42; 12:28,29; 13:8; 13:11,12; 13:23; 13:31-33; 19:21; 25:16,20,21,28,29; Mark 4:26-32; 10:21; 10:28-30; Luke 4:18,19; 6:20-23; 6:24-26; 6:27-31; 6:35-38; 6:43-45; 7:21-23; 8:11-15; 11:1-4; 11:5-13; 11:28; 12:15; 12:21-34; 12:42; 13:18,19; 13:23-29; 14:13,14; 15:22-24; 16:9-12; 17:3,4; 18:22; 18:29,30; 18:39-42; 22:35,36; John 1:16-18; 3:27; 6:27-29; 7:37-39; 8:39; 10:7-11; 13:13-17; 16:13-15; Acts 3:6; 4:33,34; 10:4; 20:32-35; 28:8-10; 28:30,31; Romans 2:6,7; 2:10,11; 5:15-17; 10:6-13; 1 Corinthians 1:4,5; 9:11; 13:4-8; 2 Corinthians 6:4-10; 8:2-5; 8:7; 8:9; 8:11,12; 9:5-15; Galatians 1:3,4; 3:6-16; 6:7-10; Ephesians 1:3-10; 4:22-32; 6:10-18; Philippians 1:9-11; 4:10-13; 4:15-20; Colossians 1:6; 1 Thessalonians 3:10; 4:11,12; 2 Thessalonians 3:6-10; 3:11,12; 1 Timothy 6:3-12; 6:17-19; 2 Timothy 2:3-7; Titus 3:14; Hebrews 5:11-6:1; 9:11,12; 10:32-12:3; 13:5,6; 13:20,21; James 1:16-18; 1:19-25; 2:5; 2:15-24; 3:2-6; 3:13-18; 4:2-10; 4:13-17; 5:10,11; 1 Peter 3:8-12;

3:14-16; 2 Peter 1:2-4; 3:17,18; 2 John 8,9; 3 John 2; Revelation 2:9-11; 3:15-21.

PROTECTION (Living under God's hedge of protection; God's promises to keep you and your family safe and secure now in this life)

Genesis 12:1-3; 15:1; 28:13-15; 28:18-22; 45:8; 48:15,16; Exodus 12:12,13; 12:23; 23:20-23; Leviticus 14:52,53; 26:5; Numbers 6:24-27; 22:12; 23:20-22; 23:23,24; Deuteronomy 8:3-5; 28:1-14; 28:15-68; 32:10-13; 33:12-16; 33:27-29; Judges 5:31; 1 Samuel 2:8-10; 30:6; 2 Samuel 5:20; 8:6; 8:14; 14:17; 22:2-4; 22:29-41; 1 Kings 3:9-14; 2 Kings 6:12; 13:23; 18:29-36; 19:21-35; 22:18-20; 1 Chronicles 4:9,10; 5:20; 16:21-24; 17:8-10; 17:25-27; 18:13; 22:9; 22:12,13; 2 Chronicles 6:20,21; 13:12; 14:11-13; 20:15-26; 32:7,8; Ezra 3:10,11; 5:5; 6:7-14; 8:21-23; 8:31; Nehemiah 1:5,6; 9:17-21; 9:30-32; Esther 5:9-6:11; 9:25; Job 1:10; 5:17-23; 11:19; 33:23-30; 36:7-11; 36:15,16; Psalm 2:1-9; 3:1-3; 3:5-7; 4:8; 5:11,12; 7:10; 8:2; 9:9,10; 11:4; 12:6,7; 18:3-19; 18:28-36; 19:7-11; 20:7,8; 23; 25:9-15; 27:5,6; 28:7; 29:11; 31:3,4; 32:8-10; 34:4-10; 34:18-22; 37:28; 37:39,40; 41:1-3; 46:1-3; 56:3,4,10,11; 60:4; 68:17-20; 71:3; 78:52,53; 84:11; 91; 97:10; 103:1-18; 116:5,6; 119:111-116; 121:2-8; 124:6-8; 125:2; 139:5; 141:10; 143:10,11; 144:12-15; Proverbs 1:33; 2:3-8; 14:3; 14:11; 14:26; 18:10; 28:25-27; 30:5,6; Isaiah 3:10; 27:2-4; 32:17-20; 33:13-24; 41:8-20; 43:1-7; 51:7,8; 51:11-16; 52:7-12; 54:13-17; 55:10-12; 56:3; 57:14-19; 58:6-9; 60:17-21; 65:17-25; Jeremiah 1:17-19; 15:19-21; 20:8-12; 23:4-6; 24:5-7; 33:6; 39:17,18; 46:27,28; Ezekiel 22:30; 34:11,12; 34:14-16; 34:23-27; Daniel 6:22-28; Hosea 2:14-23; 4:6; Joel 3:16; Micah 5:4; Nahum 1:7; 1:15; Zephaniah 2:3; 2:7; Zechariah 9:8; 9:11-17; 12:8; Malachi 3:6-12; 4:2,3; Matthew 4:6; 6:25-34; 10:26-31; Mark 4:26-32; 4:37-40; 16:15-20; Luke 6:27-31; 6:35-38; 6:46-48; 7:50; 10:17-20; 21:17-19; John 8:19; 10:1-5; 10:25-30; 12:23-26; 16:1; 16:33; 17:6-26; Acts 7:55; 17:26-29; 20:32-35; 28:3-5; 1 Corinthians 13:4-8; Ephesians 6:10-18; Philippians 1:6; 4:4-9; 2 Thessalonians 3:3; 2 Timothy 1:12; 2:19; 4:17,18; Hebrews 1:13,14; 3:12,13; 10:32-12:3; 1 Peter 1:2-9; 3:8-12; 5:5b-7; 2 Peter 2:9; 1 John 5:18-20; Jude 24,25; Revelation 2:9-11; 3:7-12.

PROVISION (See Prosperity)

RECEIVING FROM GOD (Having what God wants you to have; laying claim to what is rightfully yours)

Genesis 8:22; 22:17,18; 32:24-28; Leviticus 26:5; Deuteronomy 6:5-13; 6:18,19; 28:1-14; 28:15-68; 2 Kings 13:4; 20:2-5; 1 Chronicles 4:9,10; 2 Chronicles 6:29-31; 20:15-26; Psalm 62:5-12; 67:5-7; 85:12,13; 107:35-38; 126:4-6; 129:4: 144:12-15; Proverbs 3:1-10; 8:18-21; 11:8; 18:20,21; 18:22; 22:9; 28:25-27; Ecclesiastes 2:24-26; 4:9-12; 5:18-20; 9:7-10; 11:1,2; 11:4-6;

Isaiah 1:16-19; 40:1,2; 55:10-12; 61:6-10; Ezekiel 36:29,30; Hosea 10:12; 14:1,2; Joel 2:23; 2:25-29; Amos 9:13; Obadiah 1:15,17; Micah 4:2; Habakkuk 2:1-4; Haggai 1:5-11; 2:19; Zechariah 10:1; Malachi 2:5-7; 3:6-12; Matthew 6:5-8; 6:25-34; 7:1-5; 7:7,8; 8:13; 13:8; 13:23; 13:31-33; 15:22-28; 21:19-22; 25:16,20,21,28,29; Mark 1:40-42; 4:14-20; 4:24; 4:26-32; 6:5,6; 9:38,39; 10:28-30; 10:52; Luke 5:17-25; 8:11-15; 11:5-13; 12:21-34; 13:18,19; John 1:16-18; 3:27; 5:19-30; 14:10-14; 14:26; 15:7,8; 20:27-31; Acts 1:8; 4:33,34; Romans 2:6,7; 2:10,11; 4:16-25; 5:3-5; 6:22,23; 10:6-13; 1 Corinthians 3:21-23; 9:11; 2 Corinthians 9:5-15; Galatians 3:6-16; 3:22-29; 4:1-9; 6:7-10; Colossians 2:6-17; 2:18,19; 3:1-3; 2 Timothy 2:3-7; Hebrews 3:18-4:16; 6:15; 6:13-20; 9:14,15; 10:32-12:3; James 1:2-8; 4:2-10; 1 Peter 1:2-9; 3:8-12; 1 John 3:16-24.

CONFIRMING YOUR REDEMPTION

Deuteronomy 13:4,5; 28:15-68; Joshua 24:15-18; Nehemiah 1:10,11; Job 8:5-7; 9:32-35; 33:23-30; 42:10,12; Psalm 34:18-22; 49:15; 103:1-18; 111:7-10; 119:9-24; 119:134,135; 130:7,8; Proverbs 29:18; Isaiah 9:2-6; 33:13-24; 35:3-10; 40:1,2; 41:8-20; 43:1-7; 44:24-26; 52:1-3; 52:7-12; 61:6-10; Jeremiah 31:11-14; Lamentations 3:58; Ezekiel 16:62,63; 34:23-27; Hosea 13:14; Jonah 3:8-10; Nahum 2:2,9; Zechariah 9:11-17; 11:7; 12:10; Malachi 4:2,3; Luke 1:68-75; 1:77-79; 5:10; 10:22; 22:19,20; John 5:19-30; 8:34-36; 20:17; Acts 2:23-28; Romans 3:20-26; 8:23-30; 8:31-39; 1 Corinthians 1:30,31; 6:19,20; Galatians 2:16-21; 3:6-16; 4:1-9; Ephesians 1:3-10; 1:11-14; Colossians 1:9-14; 1:21-23; 1 Timothy 2:5,6; Titus 2:11-15; Hebrews 7:17-19; 9:11,12; 9:24-28; 10:32-12:3; 1 Peter 1:13-28; 1 John 4:15-18; Revelation 12:10-12; 14:4,5; 20:12.

REGENERATION (See New Creation Realities)

RIGHTEOUSNESS (How the righteousness of Jesus is imputed to your account; standing in *His* righteousness as opposed to establishing your own)

Genesis 6:8,9; Deuteronomy 6:24,25; 28:1-14; 28:15-68; 1 Samuel 2:8-10; 2 Samuel 22:5-25; Job 33:23-30; Psalm 23; 25:9-15; 26:4-7; 31:3,4; 37:1-6; 51:10; 72:1-19; 85:12,13; 89:14-17; 103:1-18; 106:29-31; 112:1-9; Proverbs 8:18-21; 11:30; 12:28; Ecclesiastes 9:7-10; Isaiah 1:16-19; 3:10; 11:2-5; 32:17-20; 33:5,6; 44:1-5; 45:23,24; 46:13; 48:16-18; 51:7,8; 53:4-6; 54:13-17; 60:17-21; 61:1-3; 61:6-10; Jeremiah 23:4-6; Ezekiel 1:20; 18:21,22; 22:30; Daniel 9:18,19; 12:3; Hosea 2:14-23; 6:1-3; 10:12; 14:1,2; Amos 5:14,15; Micah 7:7-11; Zechariah 3:19; 13:1; Matthew 5:2-12; 5:19,20; Luke 1:68-75; 9:51; 15:22-24; John 8:49-51; 16:25-27; Romans 1:16,17; 3:20-26; 3:27,28; 4:4-8; 4:11,12; 4:16-25; 5:1,2; 5:15-17; 6:2-14; 6:15-18; 8:4-6; 8:9-13; 8:23-30; 8:31-39; 9:30; 10:3,4; 10:6-13; 10:14,15; 11:6; 14:17; 1 Corinthians

1:30,31; 2 Corinthians 5:14-21; 6:4-10; 6:14-7:1; 9:5-15; Galatians 2:16-21; 3:2,3; 3:5; 3:6-16; 3:22-29; Ephesians 4:22-32; 6:10-18; Philippians 1:9-11; 3:7-11; 1 Timothy 1:3-11; 2 Timothy 3:14-17; 4:6-8; Hebrews 5:11-6:1; 7:17-19; 10:32-12:3; 12:10-13; James 2:15-24; 5:16b-18; 1 Peter 2:24,25; 3:1-6; 3:8-12; 3:18-22; 1 John 2:1-6; 2:27-29; 3:5-7; Revelation 2:2-7; 3:2-5; 3:15-21; 7:14; 16:15; 19:11-21; 22:12-14.

SADNESS (See Comfort)

SALVATION (See New Creation Realities)

SANCTIFICATION (Being set apart from the world system; having no fellowship with the darkness of this present world)

Genesis 26:12-14; Exodus 23:2; Leviticus 11:44,45; 14:52,53; 26:9-13; Numbers 14:24; Deuteronomy 2:7; 13:4,5; 18:14; 28:1-14; 28:15-68; 30:9,10; Joshua 23:7-14; Ruth 1:16; 1 Samuel 2:8-10; 16:18; 2 Kings 19:21-35; 22:18-20; 2 Chronicles 7:14-16; 34:33; Esther 3:2; Job 11:13-15; 17:8,9; 28:28; 31:1-4; Psalm 1:1-3; 4:3,4; 5:11,12; 15:2-5; 26:4-7; 101:2-8; 119:34-38; 119:111-116; Proverbs 1:8-10; 8:13,14; 9:6; 13:20; 20:1; 23:17; 23:20,21; 25:5-7; 31:10-31; Jeremiah 1:17-19; 15:15-17; Daniel 1:8; Matthew 4:8-11; 5:2-12; 16:23-25; Luke 1:28; 4:6-8; 6:20-23; John 17:6-26; Acts 26:16-18; 1 Corinthians 5:11; 6:9-12; 15:33,34; 2 Corinthians 5:14-21; 6:14-7:1; 10:3-6; Galatians 4:1-9; 6:14-16; Ephesians 4:22-32; 5:3-7; 5:15-21; Philippians 2:14-16; Colossians 2:6-17; 2:18,19; 2:20-23; 1 Thessalonians 4:3-5; 5:16-24; 2 Thessalonians 2:13-17; 1 Timothy 6:3-12; 2 Timothy 3:5; Titus 2:11-15; Hebrews 3:12,13; 7:24-27; 10:32-12:3; 12:5-8; James 1:27; 4:2-10; 1 Peter 1:2-9; 2:9-12; 2 Peter 1:2-4; 1 John 2:15-17; 4:1-6; 4:15-18; 5:1-5.

HAVING A SERVANT'S HEART (Living a life of service to God, your family, your employer, the church and the world)

Genesis 30:29,30; Exodus 23:25,26; Deuteronomy 13:4,5; Joshua 24:15-18; Judges 5:9; 1 Samuel 12:22-24; 1 Kings 18:21; 1 Chronicles 28:9; 29:14-18; 2 Chronicles 15:6-8; 19:9; 30:6-9; 31:10; 31:20,21; Ezra 6:7-14; Nehemiah 9:6-8; 13:10-14; Esther 4:14; Job 29:4-25; Psalm 15:2-5; 72:1-19; 112:1-9; 116:13-16; Proverbs 9:10-12; 31:8; 31:10-31; Ecclesiastes 4:9-12; 5:10; Isaiah 1:16-19; 11:2-5; 35:3-10; 61:1-3; Jeremiah 22:3; 30:8,9; Ezekiel 1:20; 3:17-27; 16:62,63; 33:31,32; 34:2-4; 36:29,30; Daniel 6:10; Habakkuk 3:17-19; Matthew 5:2-12; 6:24; 25:40; Mark 4:26-32; 10:42,43; Luke 4:6-8; 6:18,19; 12:42; 14:13,14; 22:26; John 12:23-26; 13:13-17; Acts 4:33,34; 10:38; 1 Corinthians 14:12,13; 2 Corinthians 1:24; 4:5-11; Galatians 5:13; Ephesians 4:11-13; 5:22-24,33b; 5:25-33; 6:5-8; Philippians 1:19-24; 2:2-11; Colossians 3:22-24; 1 Timothy 4:14-16; 5:1-4; 5:5-7; 5:8; 5:9,10,14; 6:1;

Titus 1:6-9; Hebrews 10:32-12:3; 13:15,16; 13:17,18; 1 Peter 4:7-11; 5:2,3; Revelation 2:19; 22:2-5.

SEX (See Marriage)

SOUL-WINNING

Genesis 12:1-3; Exodus 35:34,35; 36:2; Numbers 13:30-33; Joshua 1:5-9; Judges 6:12-14; 1 Chronicles 22:12,13; 2 Chronicles 7:14-16; 19:9; Nehemiah 6:9-16; Esther 4:14; Proverbs 11:30; 15:4; 25:15; Isaiah 45:4-6; 48:16-18; 49:5,6; 52:7-12; 60:17-21; 61:1-3; 61:6-10; Jeremiah 1:7-10; 1:17-19; 20:8-12; Ezekiel 3:17-27; 33:7-9; 33:11; 33:31,32; 34:2-4; Daniel 12:3; Joel 2:2-11; 2:19; Jonah 3:1-3; Micah 6:8,9; Nahum 1:15; Haggai 2:4-9; Malachi 2:5-7; Matthew 5:13-16; 7:6; 9:32,33; 9:35; 9:37,38; 10:7,8; 24:11-14; 28:18-20; Mark 1:17; 1:39; 3:14,15; 4:26-32; 6:5,6; 6:12,13; 16:15-20; Luke 4:18,19; 5:10; 9:1,2; 9:6; 9:51; 10:2; 10:16; 11:20-23; 11:33-36; 12:35,36; 12:42; 13:32; 15:22-24; 22:35,36; 22:43; John 3:34,35; 4:34-38; 9:4,5; 11:9-11; 17:6-26; 20:21-23; Acts 1:8; 2:17-19; 4:10-13; 4:18-20; 5:18-20; 9:31; 9:33,34; 10:38; 13:46-48; 14:21,22; 18:9-11; 19:14-20; 20:24; 23:1; 23:11; 26:16-18; 26:19,20; 28:3-5; Romans 10:14,15; 15:18,19; 1 Corinthians 1:17; 2:4,5; 9:20-27; 2 Corinthians 2:14; 3:10-12; 4:1,2; 5:14-21; 6:3; 8:2-5; 8:19; Colossians 1:9-14; 1:25-29; 1 Thessalonians 2:4; 2 Thessalonians 3:1,2; 1 Timothy 4:12,13; 2 Timothy 1:6-10; 4:2; 4:5; Titus 1:1-3; Philemon 1:6; Hebrews 1:1-4; 3:18-4:16; 2 Peter 1:10,11; Revelation 3:7-12; 22:17.

SPIRITUAL WARFARE (Fighting the good fight of faith; subduing the forces of darkness; developing an offensive strategy for the battles of life; keeping the enemy beneath your feet where he belongs)

Exodus 17:15; Leviticus 5:1; 26:6; 26:7,8; Numbers 10:9; 23:23,24; 24:5-9; Deuteronomy 2:25; 3:22; 7:21-23; 8:11-18; 9:3; 11:18-28; 20:3,4; 28:1-14; 28:15-68; 31:8; 33:20,21; 33:27-29; Joshua 1:5-9; 2:24; 8:1; 8:24-26; 10:10; 10:24,25; 10:42; 14:7-13; 18:3; 21:44,45; 22:8; 23:3; 23:7-14; 24:11,12; Judges 6:12-14; 15:14-16; 1 Samuel 11:6; 17:45-48; 2 Samuel 5:20; 22:29-41; 22:48-51; 1 Kings 22:5; 2 Kings 6:13-18; 18:3-8; 1 Chronicles 5:20; 5:22; 14:11; 14:17; 18:6; 18:13; 2 Chronicles 13:12; 13:15; 13:18; 15:6-8; 17:6; 20:15-26; 20:27-30; 32:7,8; 32:10-22; Nehemiah 4:8,9; 4:14-18; 6:9-16; Job 5:17-23; 17:8,9; Psalm 8:2; 18:3-19; 18:28-36; 18:37-40; 21:11,12; 27:1-3; 35:1-6; 44:5-8; 57:3-5; 60:4; 62:5-12; 72:1-19; 81:13,14; 91; 101:2-8; 106:29-31; 108:12,13; 109:26-31; 110:3; 116:5,6; 118:5-17; 119:138-140; 119:169-173; 124:6-8; 144:1,2; 147:15-18; Proverbs 20:18; 21:31; 24:5,6; 24:16; 25:21,22; 25:26,27; 31:8; Ecclesiastes 3:1-8; Isaiah 7:9; 8:9,10; 33:13-24; 41:8-20; 54:13-17; Jeremiah 29:7; Ezekiel 3:14; Daniel 2:14-23; 11:32; Joel 2:2-11; 3:9,10; Zephaniah 2:9; Zechariah 9:11-17; 10:5,6; Matthew 11:12; 26:26,27;

Luke 4:3-13; 13:23-29; 16:16; 21:8; 22:35,36; John 5:19-30; 1 Corinthians 9:20-27; 16:13,14; 2 Corinthians 1:8-11; 2:11; 4:5-11; 6:4-10; 10:3-6; Ephesians 1:17-23; 6:10-23; Colossians 4:12; 1 Timothy 1:18,19; 6:3-12; 2 Timothy 2:3-7; 4:6-8; 4:17,18; Hebrews 10:32-12:3; James 4:2-10; 1 Peter 1:2-9; 5:8-11; 2 Peter 2:9-12; 1 John 4:1-6; 5:1-5; Jude 20-23; Revelation 2:2-7; 2:13; 12:10-12; 17:14; 19:11-21.

SUBSTITUTION (See Identification)

SUCCESS (See Prosperity)

TITHING (See Finances)

TRUSTING IN GOD

Deuteronomy 6:2; 28:1-14; 31:8; Joshua 1:5-9; 1 Samuel 30:6; 2 Samuel 22:29-41; 2 Kings 6:5,6; 6:13-18; 18:3-8; 19:21-35; 1 Chronicles 5:20; 17:25-27; 2 Chronicles 13:8; 14:6,7; 16:7; 20:15-26; 32:7,8; Esther 5:9-6:11; Job 1:1; 1:8; 1:22; 2:3; 31:24-28; Psalm 5:11,12; 9:9-10; 18:3-19; 20:7,8; 25:3-5; 27:13,14; 28:7; 37:1-6; 44:5-8; 56:3,4,10,11; 62:5-12; 91; 112:1-9; 118:5-17; 119:41-43; 139:7-10; Proverbs 3:1-10; 11:23-28; 16:20; 22:4; 24:10; 28:25-27; 29:25; 30:8; Isaiah 11:2-5; 12:1-3; 26:3,4; 30:15; 33:5,6; 40:29-31; Jeremiah 10:23,24; 17:5; 17:7,8; 17:14; 20:8-12; 32:39-42; 39:17,18; Daniel 3:28-30; 6:22-28; Hosea 2:14-23; Nahum 1:7; Habakkuk 3:17-19; Zephaniah 3:11-15; Malachi 2:5-7; 3:16-18; Matthew 5:2-12; 6:24; 13:58; Luke 1:50-55; 6:24-26; 15:5-13; John 1:12,13; 2:11; 5:19-30; 6:27-29; 8:26; 9:31-33; 10:25-30; 11:40-42; Acts 16:31; 20:32-35; Romans 4:16-25; 9:33; 14:4; 2 Thessalonians 3:5; 1 Timothy 3:2-4:7; 6:17-19; 2 Timothy 1:12; Revelation 3:15-21.

VISION (See Knowing Your **Destiny** In Life)

WISDOM (How to be wise in all the affairs of life; supernatural ability to learn; your God-given ability to be creative and inventive; your God-given ability to retain, maintain and explain knowledge)

Genesis 1:26-28; Exodus 33:13,14; 35:34,35; 36:2; Leviticus 10:8,9; Numbers 12:7,8; Deuteronomy 6:5-13; 11:18-28; 28:15-68; 29:9; Joshua 1:5-9; 1 Samuel 3:21; 12:22-24; 16:18; 18:14; 2 Samuel 14:17; 14:20; 22:29-41; 1 Kings 2:2,3; 3:9-14; 4:29; 4:32-34; 5:12; 2 Kings 6:12; 1 Chronicles 12:32; 15:22; 22:12,13; 28:9; 28:19,20; 2 Chronicles 1 7-12; 9:22,23; 26:15,16; Ezra 7:6; Nehemiah 8:9-12; Job 4:3,4; 28:28; 32:8; 38:36; Psalm 19:7-11; 25:3-5; 25:9-15; 27:10,11; 30:2-7; 37:30-34; 51:6; 90:12; 107:43; 111:7-10; 119:9-24; 119:27,28; 119:34-38; 119:64-68; 119:97-101; 119:130-133; 119:169-173; 144:1,2; 147:19,20; Proverbs 1:33; 2:3-8; 3:1-10; 3:12-18;

5:18,19; 8:13,14; 8:18-21; 8:35; 9:6; 9:10-12; 10:1; 10:4; 10:8,9; 10:13-15; 10:22-24; 11:8,9; 11:14; 11:30; 12:1,2; 12:18; 13:2-4; 13:15; 13:18; 13:20; 14:6; 14:18; 14:21-24; 15:21,22; 15:31,32; 15:33; 19:11; 20:1 21:20; 23:4; 23:17; 24:5,6; 24:14; 28:25-27; 29:18; 31:10-31; Ecclesiastes 2:24-26; 3:1-8; 4:9-12; 5:1-3; 7:12; 7:16-18; 7:19; 8:1; 9:7-10; Isaiah 11:2-5; 33:5,6; 50:4-9; 51:7,8; Jeremiah 10:21; 24:5-7; 33:2,3; Ezekiel 3:17-27; 36:25-27; Daniel 1:3,4; 1:15-17; 1:19,20; 2:14-23; 5:11,12; 9:2-4; 9:21-23; 10:1; 10:10-13; 11:32; 12:3; 12:9,10; Hosea 4:6; 14:9; Amos 3:7; 7:1-6; Micah 7:5; Habakkuk 2:1-4; 2:14; Haggai 1:5-11; Zechariah 4:10; Malachi 2:5-7; Matthew 6:9-13; 10:17-20; 11:27-30; 13:9; 13:11,12; 13:15,16; 13:23; 15:10; 22:29; Mark 4:14-20; 4:24; 12:24; 13:37; Luke 1:77-79; 2:52; 4:9-12; 5:17-25; 7:7-9; 8:9,10; 8:17,18; 8:46-48; 10:17-20; 11:1-4; 11:14; 11:33-36; 12:35,36; 12:42; 14:33b; 21:8; 21:12-15; 24:45; John 1:3,4; 1:16-18; 3:12; 5:19-30; 7:15-18; 8:12; 8:34-36; 8:42,43; 10:1-5; 10:25-30; 11:9-11; 12:35,36; 14:26; 15:7,8; 15:13-16; 15:26; 16:1; 16:7-11; 16:13-15; 16:25-27; 17:6-26; 18:37; Acts 4:10-13; 6:5,8-10; 7:22; 7:55; 9:22; 14:8-10; 16:14; 17:11; 18:27,28; 22:14; Romans 8:14-17; 12:9-21; 15:13,14; 16:17-20; 1 Corinthians 1:4,5; 1:17; 1:25; 1:30,31; 2:6,7; 2:9,10; 2:12-16; 4:15,16; 8:1; 10:13; 12:1; 12:6-11; 13:1-3; 14:20-25; 14:29; 14:37,38; 15:33,34; 2 Corinthians 2:11; 3:16-18; 4:5-11; 6:4-10; 8:7; 10:3-6; 11:4; 11:14,15; 12:1; Galatians 1:10-12; Ephesians 1:3-10; 1:17-23; 3:10-12; 3:14-21; 5:15-21; 6:10-18; Philippians 1:9-11; 2:2-11; 3:15; 4:4-9; 4:15-20; Colossians 1:6; 1:9-14; 1:25-29; 2:2-4; 2:18,19; 2:20-23; 3:12-17; 4:5,6; 1 Thessalonians 5:4-11; 1 Timothy 5:19; 2 Timothy 2:3-7; 3:9; 3:14-17; 4:2; 4:6-8; Titus 1:1-3; 2:11-15; Philemon 6; Hebrews 2:1; 5:11-6:1; 6:13-20; 10:32-12:3; James 1:2-8; 1:19-25; 3:13-18; 4:13-17; 5:10,11; 1 Peter 1:13-23; 4:1,2; 5:8-11; 2 Peter 1:2-4; 1:5-8; 3:17,18; 1 John 2:20; 2:27-29; 3:5-7; 4:1-6; 5:18-20; Jude 3; Revelation 2:2-7; 2:9-11; 2:17; 2:29; 3:6; 3:13; 3:22; 13:9.

WITNESSING (See Soul-winning)

LIVING BY THE WORD (Giving the Word the ascendancy in your life over and above all pomp and circumstance; standing on the promises that God has given you; selling out to the Word and claiming God's promises as your own)

Genesis 28:13-15; Exodus 13:9; 15:25,26; Leviticus 26:9-13; Numbers 11:23; 12:7,8; Deuteronomy 1:11; 4:39,40; 5:33; 6:5-13; 6:24,25; 8:3-5; 11:18-28; 13:4,5; 28:1-14; 29:9; 30:14-16; 31:6; 31:8; 32:1-4; Joshua 1:5-9; 1 Samuel 3:21; 30:6; 2 Samuel 22:29-41; 23:2-5; 1 Kings 8:56; 17:24; 2 Kings 10:10; 13:23; 20:2-5; 1 Chronicles 13:14; 17:23; 17:25-27; 2 Chronicles 1:7-12; 18:4; Ezra 7:9,10; Nehemiah 8:9-12; 9:17-21; Psalm 1:1-3; 12:6,7; 15:2-5; 17:3; 18:20-24; 18:28-36; 19:7-11; 33:4; 33:11; 37:30-34; 40:7,8; 56:3,4,10,11; 67:5-7; 78:4-7; 94:12-14; 103:1-18; 105:42-45; 107:20,21;

107:43; 109:26-31; 111:7-10; 118:5-17; 119:9-24; 119:27,28; 119:34-38; 119:41-43; 119:57-64; 119:64-68; 119:74-81; 119:89,90; 119:93; 119:97-101; 119:105-107; 119:111-116; 119:130-133; 119:134,135; 119:138-140; 119:147-149; 119:165; 119:169-173; 138:2,3; 143:8; 147:15,18; 147:19,20; Proverbs 2:3-8; 3:12-18; 15:21,22; 29:18; 30:5,6; 31:4,5; Ecclesiastes 5:1-3; 11:4-6; Isaiah 1:16-19; 8:18-20; 11:2-5; 26:7-9; 35:3-10; 42:16; 44:1-5; 49:8-15; 51:7,8; 51:11-16; 51:22,23; 55:10-12; 57:14-19; 59:21-60:2; 65:17-25; 66:2; Jeremiah 1:7-10; 1:12; 10:23,24; 15:15-17; 15:19-21; 17:7,8; 20:8-12; 21:8; 31:3,4; 31:31-34; 33:25,26; 39:17,18; Lamentations 2:17; 3:22-26; 3:37; Ezekiel 2:6,7; 3:8,9; 12:25,28; 18:21,22; 33:7-9; 33:31,32; 37:24,25; Daniel 3:16-18; 6:13; 6:22-28; 9:2-4; 10:1; 12:9,10; Hosea 4:6; 10:12; 14:1,2; 14:9; Joel 2:2-11; 2:25-29; Jonah 3:1-3; Micah 2:7; 3:8; 4:2; 7:7-11; Haggai 1:5-11; 2:19; Zechariah 3:1-9; Matthew 4:1-11; 4:4; 4:7; 4:8-11; 5:19,20; 6:9-13; 7:24,25; 8:8-10; 12:15; 13:9; 13:15,16; 13:23; 15:10; 26:41; 28:18-20; Mark 4:14-20; 4:24; 4:26-32; 4:37-40; 11:22-25; 16:15-20; Luke 1:37,38; 1:68-75; 4:4; 4:9-12; 4:13; 5:5; 6:27-31; 6:46-48; 7:7-9; 8:11-15; 8:21; 8:24,25; 10:16; 11:5-13; 11:14; 11:28; 13:23-29; 14:33b; 17:6-10; 21:17-19; 21:33; 22:35,36; John 1:12,13; 3:12; 3:29,30; 4:50; 5:19-30; 6:37-40; 6:63; 7:15-18; 8:26; 8:31,32; 8:47; 8:49-51; 8:54,55; 9:31-33; 11:40-42; 14:23; 14:26; 15:1-5; 15:7,8; 15:19-21; 16:1; 16:22-24; 16:25-27; 17:6-26; 20:27-31; Acts 2:42-47; 4:24-31; 9:27,28; 10:43-46; 13:46-48; 14:3; 14:8-10; 15:28,29; 17:26-29; 18:9-11; 19:14-20; 20:32-35; 28:3-5; Romans 2:10,11; 4:16-25; 6:15-18; 10:6-13; 10:17,18; 16:17-20; 1 Corinthians 14:29; 15:2; 2 Corinthians 1:18-22; 3:16-18; 11:4; 13:11; Galatians 1:6; 3:5; Ephesians 6:1-3; 6:10-18; Philippians 2:2-11; 2:14-16; 4:15-20; Colossians 1:25-29; 3:12-17; 1 Thessalonians 2:12,13; 2 Thessalonians 3:6-10; 1 Timothy 1:3-11; 1:18,19; 4:4,5; 6:3-12; 6:20; 2 Timothy 2:9,10; 2:14-16; 3:14-17; 4:2; Titus 1:1-3; 1:6-9; 2:1-10; Hebrews 3:12,13; 3:18-4:16; 5:11-6:1; 6:10-12; 10:32-12:3; 12:5-8; 13:17,18; James 1:16-18; 1:19-25; 2:15-24; 1 Peter 1:13-23; 3:1-6; 3:8-12; 4:7-11; 2 Peter 3:1; 3:17,18; 1 John 1:3-10; 2:1-6; 2:12-14; 2:27-29; 4:1-6; 5:13-15; 2 John 8,9; Revelation 3:7-12; 12:10-12; 22:7.

REFERENCES

The Amplified Bible. Grand Rapids: The Zondervan Corporation and the Lockman Foundation, 1987.

The Bible: New International Version. Colorado Springs: International Bible Society, 1983.

Church, Leslie, F. Ph.D. ed. *The Matthew Henry Commentary on the Whole Bible.* Grand Rapids: Zondervan Publishing House, 1976.

Elwell, Walter, A. *Topical Analysis of the Bible.* Grand Rapids: Baker Book House, 1991.

Holman Bible Dictionary. USA: Holman Bible Publishers, 1991.

Jacobus, Melancthon, W. et al. *Funk and Wagnalls New Standard Bible Dictionary.* New York: Funk and Wagnalls Company, 1936.

Kellerman, Dana, F. et al. *The Lexicon Webster Dictionary.* 2 Vols. USA: Delair Publishing Company, 1981.

Kirszner, Laurie G., and Stephen R. Mandell. *The Holt Handbook.* Fort Worth: Holt, Rinehart and Winston, Inc., 1989.

Marshall, Alfred. *The Interlinear KJV-NIV Parallel New Testament in Greek and English.* Grand Rapids: Zondervan Publishing House, 1975.

Rienecker, Fritz. *Linguistic Key to the Greek New Testament.* Grand Rapids: Regency Reference Library of Zondervan Publishing House, 1980.

Strong, James, LL.D., S.T.D. *The New Strong's Complete Dictionary of Bible Words.* Nashville: Thomas Nelson Publishers, 1996.

Strong, James, LL.D., S.T.D. *The New Strong's Exhaustive Concordance of the Bible.* Nashville: Thomas Nelson Publishers, 1984.

The Treasury of Scripture Knowledge. Peabody: Hendrickson Publishers, 1982.

Vaughn, Curtis, Thd, Ed, et al. *The Bible from 26 Translations.* Grand Rapids: Baker Book House, 1988.

Vincent, Marvin, R., D.D. *Vincent's Word Studies of the New Testament.* 4 Vols. Peabody: Hendrickson Publishers.

Vine, W.E., M.A. *Vine's Expository Dictionary of Biblical Words.* New York: Thomas Nelson Publishers, 1985.

Vine, W.E., M.A. *A Comprehensive Dictionary of the Original Greek Words with their Precise Meanings for English Readers.* Iowa Falls: Riverside Book and Bible House.

Wiersbe, Warren. *The Bible Exposition Commentary.* Wheaton: Victor Books, 1989.

Wilson, William. *Wilson's Old Testament Word Studies.* Peabody: Hendrickson Publishers.

Wuest, Kenneth. *The New Testament: An Expanded Translation.* Peabody: Eardman's Publishing.

Young, Robert. *Young's Literal Translation of the Holy Bible.* Revised edition. Grand Rapids: Baker Book House.

PRAYER OF SALVATION

God loves you—no matter who you are, no matter what your past. God loves you so much that He gave His one and only begotten Son for you. The Bible tells us that "...whoever believes in him shall not perish but have eternal life" (John 3:16 NIV). Jesus laid down His life and rose again so that we could spend eternity with Him in heaven and experience His absolute best on earth. If you would like to receive Jesus into your life, say the following prayer out loud and mean it from your heart.

Heavenly Father, I come to You admitting that I am a sinner. Right now, I choose to turn away from sin, and I ask You to cleanse me of all unrighteousness. I believe that Your Son, Jesus, died on the cross to take away my sins. I also believe that He rose again from the dead so that I might be forgiven of my sins and made righteous through faith in Him. I call upon the name of Jesus Christ to be the Savior and Lord of my life. Jesus, I choose to follow You and ask that You fill me with the power of the Holy Spirit. I declare that right now I am a child of God. I am free from sin and full of the righteousness of God. I am saved in Jesus' name. Amen.

If you prayed this prayer to receive Jesus Christ as your Savior for the first time, please contact us on the Web at **www.harrisonhouse.com** to receive a free book.

Or you may write to us at
Harrison House
P.O. Box 35035
Tulsa, Oklahoma 74153

ABOUT THE AUTHOR

James R. Riddle is a successful entrepreneur, educator, and Bible teacher. He is a member of Abundant Living Faith Center in El Paso, Texas, and has been working closely with Charles Nieman Ministries since 1987. He is also an Honors graduate from the University of Texas at El Paso with a degree in English: Creative Writing. *The Complete Personalized Promise Bible* is the result of an intensive three-year study of the entire Bible that James Riddle undertook.

To contact James Riddle,
please write to:

James R. Riddle
6930 Gateway East
El Paso, Texas 79915
Or call: (915) 253-1825
www.jamesriddle.net

www.harrisonhouse.com

Fast. Easy. Convenient!

- ◆ New Book Information
- ◆ Look Inside the Book
- ◆ Press Releases
- ◆ Bestsellers
- ◆ Free E-News
- ◆ Author Biographies

- ◆ Upcoming Books
- ◆ Share Your Testimony
- ◆ Online Product Availability
- ◆ Product Specials
- ◆ Order Online

For the latest in book news and author information, please visit us on the Web at www.harrisonhouse.com. Get up-to-date pictures and details on all our powerful and life-changing products. Sign up for our e-mail newsletter, *Friends of the House,* and receive free monthly information on our authors and products including testimonials, author announce-ments, and more!

Harrison House—
Books That Bring Hope, Books That Bring Change

THE HARRISON HOUSE VISION

Proclaiming the truth and the power
Of the Gospel of Jesus Christ
With excellence;

Challenging Christians to
Live victoriously,
Grow spiritually,
Know God intimately.